Of the People

Of the People

SECOND EDITION

A HISTORY of the UNITED STATES

VOLUME 1 • TO 1877

James Oakes
City University of New York Graduate Center

Michael McGerr
Indiana University–Bloomington

Jan Ellen Lewis
Rutgers University, Newark

Nick Cullather
Indiana University–Bloomington

Jeanne Boydston
University of Wisconsin–Madison

Mark Summers
University of Kentucky–Lexington

Camilla Townsend
Rutgers University, New Brunswick

New York   Oxford
Oxford University Press

Oxford University Press is a department of the University of Oxford. It furthers the University's
objective of excellence in research, scholarship, and education by publishing worldwide.

Oxford   New York
Auckland   Cape Town   Dar es Salaam   Hong Kong   Karachi
Kuala Lumpur   Madrid   Melbourne   Mexico City   Nairobi
New Delhi   Shanghai   Taipei   Toronto

With offices in
Argentina   Austria   Brazil   Chile   Czech Republic   France   Greece
Guatemala   Hungary   Italy   Japan   Poland   Portugal   Singapore
South Korea   Switzerland   Thailand   Turkey   Ukraine   Vietnam

For titles covered by Section 112 of the US Higher Education Opportunity Act,
please visit www.oup.com/us/he for the latest information about pricing and
alternate formats.

Published by Oxford University Press.
198 Madison Avenue, New York, NY 10016
www.oup.com

Library of Congress Cataloging-in-Publication Data
Of the people: a history of the United States / by James Oakes . . . [et al.].—2nd ed.
    p. cm.
 Includes bibliographical references and index.
  ISBN 978-0-19-992467-7 (v. 1 : alk. paper)—ISBN 978-0-19-992468-4 (v. 2 : alk. paper)—
ISBN 978-0-19-992473-8 (instructors edition: alk. paper) 1. United States—History.
2. Democracy—United States—History. I. Oakes, James.
 E178.O34 2013
 973—dc23
                                                                2012032583

Printing number: 9 8 7 6 5 4 3 2 1

Printed in the United States of America
on acid-free paper

JEANNE BOYDSTON

1944–2008

Historian, Teacher, Friend

Brief Contents

Maps   xxi
Features   xxiii
Preface   xxv
About the Authors   xxxix

Chapter 1   Worlds in Motion, 1450–1550   2
Chapter 2   Colonial Outposts, 1550–1650   36
Chapter 3   The English Come to Stay, 1600–1660   68
Chapter 4   Continental Empires, 1660–1720   102
Chapter 5   The Eighteenth-Century World, 1700–1775   142
Chapter 6   Conflict in the Empire, 1713–1774   180
Chapter 7   Creating a New Nation, 1775–1788   218
Chapter 8   Contested Republic, 1789–1800   260
Chapter 9   A Republic in Transition, 1800–1819   298
Chapter 10   Jacksonian Democracy, 1820–1840   336
Chapter 11   Reform and Conflict, 1820–1848   372
Chapter 12   Slavery and the Nation, 1790–1860   402
Chapter 13   Manifest Destiny, 1836–1848   438
Chapter 14   The Politics of Slavery, 1848–1860   472
Chapter 15   A War for Union and Emancipation, 1861–1865   506
Chapter 16   Reconstructing a Nation, 1865–1877   550

Appendix A   Historical Documents   A-1
Appendix B   Historical Facts and Data   B-1
Glossary   G-1
Photo Credits   C-1
Index   I-1

Contents

Maps   xxi
Features   xxiii
Preface   xxv
 Supplements   xxxi
 Acknowledgments   xxxv
About the Authors   xxxix

CHAPTER **1** **Worlds in Motion, 1450–1550** **2**

AMERICAN PORTRAIT: **Malinche, Cultural Translator** **3**

The Worlds of Indian Peoples **4**

 Great Migrations 4
 The Emergence of Farming 5
 The Cradle of the Americas 6
 The Northern World Takes Shape 6

The Worlds of Christopher Columbus **8**

 The *Reconquista* 8
 The Age of Exploration 9

PRIMARY SOURCE: **Mapping the World** **11**

 New Ideas Take Root 12

Collision in the Caribbean **13**

 Columbus's First Voyage 14
 The Origins of a New World Political and Economic Order 15
 The Division of the World 16

Onto the Mainland **17**

AMERICA AND THE WORLD: **Debating the Morality of Conquest** **18**

 The First Florida Ventures 19
 The Conquest of Mexico 20

AMERICAN LANDSCAPE: **Tenochtitlan** **22**

 The Establishment of a Spanish Empire 23
 The Return to North America 24

The Consequences of Conquest **25**

 Demographic Disaster 25

DEBATING HISTORY: **Population of the Americas Precontact** **26**

 The Columbian Exchange 28
 Men's and Women's Lives 29

Conclusion **30**

CHAPTER **2** Colonial Outposts, 1550–1650   **36**

AMERICAN PORTRAIT: Don Luis de Velasco Finds His Way Home   37

Pursuing Wealth and Glory Along the North American Shore   38

European Objectives   38
The Huge Geographical Barrier   39
Spanish Outposts   42

New France: An Outpost in Global Politics and Economics   42

The Five Nations of Iroquois and the Political Landscape   43
Champlain Encounters the Hurons   44

AMERICAN LANDSCAPE: Huronia   46

Creating a Middle Ground in New France   47
An Outpost in a Global Political Economy   48

New Netherland: The Empire of a Trading Nation   49

Colonization by a Private Company   49
Slavery and Freedom in New Netherland   50
The Dutch-Indian Trading Partnership   51
The Beaver Wars   53

England Attempts an Empire   53

Competition with Spain   53
Rehearsal in Ireland   54
The Roanoke Venture   55

AMERICA AND THE WORLD: Indians on the Thames   56

PRIMARY SOURCE: Thomas Hariot, *A Brief and True Report of the New Found Land of Virginia* (1588)   58

The Abandoned Colony   61

DEBATING HISTORY: Encounters or Conflict?   62

Conclusion   63

CHAPTER **3** The English Come to Stay, 1600–1660   **68**

AMERICAN PORTRAIT: The Adventures of John Smith   69

The First Chesapeake Colonies   70

Founding Virginia   70
Starving Times   71

PRIMARY SOURCE: The Charter of Virginia, 1606   72

Troubled Relations with the Powhatans   74
Toward a New Economic Order and the Rise of Democracy   75

TECHNOLOGY AND IDEAS: Tobacco Cultivation in Virginia   77

Toward the Destruction of the Powhatans   78
A New Colony in Maryland   79

The Political Economy of Slavery Emerges   79

The Problem of a Labor Supply   80
The Origins of African Slavery in the Chesapeake   80
Gender and the Social Order in the Chesapeake   82

A Bible Commonwealth in the New England Wilderness   82

The English Origins of the Puritan Movement   83
What Did the Puritans Believe?   83
The Pilgrim Colony at Plymouth   84
The Puritan Colony at Massachusetts Bay   85

AMERICA AND THE WORLD: The English Enter the Slave Trade   86

The New England Way   87
Changing the Landscape to Fit the Political Economy   90
The Puritan Family   91

AMERICAN LANDSCAPE: New England Settlements   92

Dissension in the Puritan Ranks   93

Roger Williams and Toleration   94
Anne Hutchinson and the Equality of Believers   94
Puritan Indian Policy and the Pequot War   96

Conclusion   98

CHAPTER 4   Continental Empires, 1660–1720   **102**

AMERICAN PORTRAIT: Tituba Shapes Her World and Saves Herself   103

The Plan of Empire   104

Turmoil in England   104
The Political Economy of Mercantilism   106

New Colonies, New Patterns   106

New Netherland Becomes New York   106

PRIMARY SOURCE: The Navigation Act of 1651   107

Diversity and Prosperity in Pennsylvania   109

AMERICAN LANDSCAPE: New Amsterdam/New York   110

Indians and Africans in the Political Economy of Carolina   112
The Barbados Connection   115

The Transformation of Virginia   116

Social Change in Virginia   116
Bacon's Rebellion and the Abandonment of the Middle Ground   116
Virginia Becomes a Slave Society   117

DEBATING HISTORY: Origins of Slavery   120

New England Under Assault   121

Social Prosperity and the Fear of Religious Decline   121
King Philip's War   122
Indians and the Empire   123

The Empire Strikes   124

The Dominion of New England   124
The Glorious Revolution in Britain and America   124
The Rights of Englishmen   126
Conflict in the Empire   126

Massachusetts in Crisis   127

The Social and Cultural Contexts of Witchcraft   127
Witchcraft at Salem   128
The End of Witchcraft   128

AMERICA AND THE WORLD: Witchcraft in Global Perspective   129

Empires in Collision   130

France Attempts an Empire   130
The Spanish Outpost in Florida   133
Conquest, Revolt, and Reconquest in New Mexico   133
Native Americans and the Country Between   136

Conclusion   137

CHAPTER 5   The Eighteenth-Century World, 1700–1775   142

AMERICAN PORTRAIT: George Whitefield: Evangelist for a Consumer Society   143

The Population Explosion of the Eighteenth Century   144

The Dimensions of Population Growth   144
Bound for America: European Immigrants   145
Bound for America: African Slaves   147

AMERICAN LANDSCAPE: The Slave Ship   149

The Great Increase of Offspring   150

The Transatlantic Economy: Producing and Consuming   151

The Nature of Colonial Economic Growth   151
The Transformation of the Family Economy   152
Sources of Regional Prosperity   153
Merchants and Dependent Laborers in the Transatlantic Economy   155
Consumer Choices and the Creation of Gentility   156

AMERICA AND THE WORLD: Consumer Tastes in Global Perspective   159

The Varieties of Colonial Experience   160

Creating an Urban Public Sphere   160
The Diversity of Urban Life   162
The Maturing of Rural Society   163
The World That Slavery Made   164
Georgia: From Frontier Outpost to Plantation Society   165

The Head and the Heart in America: The Enlightenment and Religious Awakening   166

The Ideas of the Enlightenment   167

TECHNOLOGY AND IDEAS: Inoculation   168

The Economic and Social Foundations of Democracy   169

**PRIMARY SOURCE: *The Autobiography of
Benjamin Franklin*   170**

Enlightened Institutions   172
Origins of the Great Awakening   172
The Grand Itinerant   172
Cultural Conflict and Challenges to Authority   174
What the Awakening Wrought   175

Conclusion   175

CHAPTER 6 Conflict in the Empire, 1713–1774   **180**

AMERICAN PORTRAIT: Susannah Willard Johnson Experiences the Empire   181

The Victory of the British Empire   182

New War, Old Pattern   182
The Local Impact of Global War   183
The French Empire Crumbles from Within   184
The Virginians Ignite a War   187
From Local to Imperial War   187

PRIMARY SOURCE: George Washington on Braddock's Defeat   189

Problems with British-Colonial Cooperation   192
The British Gain the Advantage   193

Enforcing the Empire   196

Pontiac's Rebellion and Its Aftermath   196
Paying for the Empire: Sugar and Stamps   198

AMERICA AND THE WORLD: Paying for War   199

The British Empire in Crisis   200

An Argument About Rights and Obligations   201
The Imperial Crisis in Local Context   201

TECHNOLOGY AND IDEAS: The Role of Newspapers in the Imperial Crisis   202

Contesting the Townshend Duties   204

A Revolution in the Empire   207

"Massacre" in Boston   207

AMERICAN LANDSCAPE: Occupied Boston   209

The Empire Comes Apart   210
The First Continental Congress   212

Conclusion   214

CHAPTER 7 Creating a New Nation, 1775–1788   **218**

AMERICAN PORTRAIT: James Madison Helps Make a Nation   219

The War Begins   220

The First Battles   220
Congress Takes the Lead   222

Military Ardor   222

DEBATING HISTORY: Causes of the American Revolution   223

Declaring Independence   224
Creating a National Government   225
Creating State Governments   226

Winning the Revolution   227

Competing Strategies   227
The British on the Offensive: 1776   228

AMERICA AND THE WORLD: Mercenaries in Global Perspective   230

A Slow War: 1777–1781   231
Securing a Place in the World   233

AMERICAN LANDSCAPE: The South Carolina Backcountry   234

The Challenge of the Revolution   238

The Departure of the Loyalists   238
The Challenge of the Economy   238
Contesting the New Economy   241
Can Women Be Citizens?   242

PRIMARY SOURCE: Abigail to John Adams, "Remember the Ladies"   244

The Challenge of Slavery   246

A New Policy in the West   246

The Indians' Revolution   247
The End of the Middle Ground   248
Settling the West   248

Creating a New National Government   249

A Crippled Congress   251
Writing a New Constitution   251
Ratifying the Constitution: Politics   253
Ratifying the Constitution: Ideas   254

Conclusion   256

CHAPTER 8 Contested Republic, 1789–1800   **260**

AMERICAN PORTRAIT: Ona Judge Finds Her Freedom   261

The Struggle to Form a Government   263

Creating a National Government   263
The States and the Bill of Rights   264
Debating the Economy   265

A Society in Transition   267

A People on the Move   267

AMERICAN LANDSCAPE: Philadelphia   269

The First Emancipation Movements   271
Conflicting Visions of Republican Society   273

**PRIMARY SOURCE: Petition from the Pennsylvania Society for Promoting
the Abolition of Slavery   274**

The Culture of the Republic   277

Securing the Nation   280

Borders and Boundaries   280
Controlling the Borderlands   281
The Whiskey Rebellion   284
Other Revolutions   284
Between France and England   285

AMERICA AND THE WORLD: Citizenship in an Age of Revolution   286

To the Brink of War   288
The Administration of John Adams   288
Tensions at Home   291

DEBATING HISTORY: The Politics of the 1790s and Democracy   292

Conclusion   294

CHAPTER 9   A Republic in Transition, 1800–1819   **298**

AMERICAN PORTRAIT: Andrew Jackson's America   299

A Politics of Transition   300

A Contested Election, an Anxious Nation   301
Democratic Republicans in Office   301
The Louisiana Purchase   302
Embargo   305

The War of 1812   307

Madison and the War   307
Federalist Response   308

An Economy in Transition   311

International Markets   311

AMERICA AND THE WORLD: The United States in China   312

Crossing the Appalachian Mountains   314
Invention and Exploration   315

TECHNOLOGY AND IDEAS: The Steamboat   317

Early Industrial Society in New England   318
The Rule of Law and Lawyers   321

Ways of Life in Flux   322

Indian Resistance to American Expansion   322

PRIMARY SOURCE: Gibbons v. Ogden: Freedom of Interstate Commerce   323

Winners and Losers in the New Economy   327
Religion   328

AMERICAN LANDSCAPE: Religion in the Backcountry: Cane Ridge, Kentucky   329

The Problem of Trust in a Changing Society   330
The Panic of 1819   331

Conclusion   332

CHAPTER 10 Jacksonian Democracy, 1820–1840 **336**

AMERICAN PORTRAIT: **Harriet Noble   337**

A New National Politics   338

Changes in the Democratic Republican Party   338
James Monroe and National Republicanism   340
The Missouri Compromise   341

AMERICA AND THE WORLD: **The Monroe Doctrine   342**

The Election of 1824 and the "Corrupt Bargain"   344
The Adams Presidency and the Gathering Forces of Democracy   345

The Social and Political Bases of Jacksonian Democracy   346

Settlers   346
Free Labor   347
Suffrage Reform   348
Opposition to Special Privilege and Secret Societies   349

Jacksonian Democracy in Action   351

The Election of 1828   351
The Bank War   353
Dismembering the Bank   353

PRIMARY SOURCE: **Jackson's Bank Veto Message   354**

The Specie Act   357

A Policy of Removing Indigenous People   357

Jackson and Native Peoples   357
The Removal Act   359
History, Destiny, and the Remaking of Indian Societies   360

AMERICAN LANDSCAPE: **Liberty and the Land: Cherokee Removal   362**

The Growth of Sectional Tension   364

The Sources of Southern Discontent   364
South Carolina's Protest   364
The Nullification Crisis   365

DEBATING HISTORY: **The Nature of Jacksonian Democracy   367**

Conclusion   368

CHAPTER 11 Reform and Conflict, 1820–1848 **372**

AMERICAN PORTRAIT: **Charles Grandison Finney   373**

Perfectionism and the Theology of Human Striving   374

Millennialism and Communitarians   374
The Benevolent Empire   377

AMERICA AND THE WORLD: **The American Board of Commissioners for Foreign Missions   379**

Reform and the Urban Classes   381

Wage Dependency and Labor Protest   381

PRIMARY SOURCE: **Charles Dickens Describes Five Points, NYC   382**

A New Urban Middle Class   384

TECHNOLOGY AND IDEAS: Textile Mills   385

AMERICAN LANDSCAPE: Freedom and Wage Labor   386

Immigration and Nativism   387
Internal Migration   388

Self-Reform and Social Regulation   389

A Culture of Self-Improvement   389
Temperance   391
The Common School Movement and Democracy   393
Penal Reform   394
Electoral Politics and Moral Reform   394

Women's Rights   396

Women and Reform Movements   396
The Seneca Falls Convention   397

Conclusion   398

CHAPTER **12** Slavery and the Nation, 1790–1860   402

AMERICAN PORTRAIT: Joseph Cinqué and the *Amistad* Rebellion   403

Southern Slavery   404

"Property in Man"   404
The Domestic Slave Trade   405

TECHNOLOGY AND IDEAS: The Cotton Gin   406

Plantation Slavery   408

**AMERICAN LANDSCAPE: Gowrie: The Story of Profit and Loss on an
American Plantation   410**

Other Varieties of Slavery   411
Resistance and Creation Among Southern Slaves   413

**PRIMARY SOURCE: John Pendleton Kennedy's *Swallow Barn:* A Traveler's Account
of Antebellum Virginia   414**

Slavery and National Development   419

Slavery and Industrialization in the Northeast   419

AMERICA AND THE WORLD: The Demand for Raw Cotton   420

Slavery and the Laws of the Nation   422
Free Black People in a Republic of Slavery   423

The Politics of Slavery   425

The Antislavery Movement   426
Black Abolitionists   426
Immediatism   429
Antiabolition Violence   430
The Emergence of Political Abolitionism   432
Freedom National, Slavery Local   433

Conclusion   434

CHAPTER **13** Manifest Destiny, 1836–1848 **438**

AMERICAN PORTRAIT: **Mah-i-ti-wo-nee-ni Remembers Life on the Great Plains 439**

The Decline of Jacksonianism **440**
Political Parties in Crisis **440**
Van Buren and the Legacy of Jackson **442**

The Political Economy of the Trans-Mississippi West **445**
Manifest Destiny in Antebellum Culture **445**

PRIMARY SOURCE: **John O'Sullivan Proclaims a "Nation of Futurity" 446**
Texas **449**

AMERICAN LANDSCAPE: **Culture and Politics in Manifest Destiny: Tejanos in Texas 450**
Pacific Bound **452**
Nations of the Trans-Mississippi West **455**

Slavery and the Political Economy of Expansion **458**
Log Cabins and Hard Cider: The Election of 1840 **458**
And Tyler, Too **459**
Occupy Oregon, Annex Texas **460**

DEBATING HISTORY: **Manifest Destiny and Race 462**
War with Mexico **463**

AMERICA AND THE WORLD: **Lt. Rankin Dilworth in the War with Mexico 465**

Conclusion **468**

CHAPTER **14** The Politics of Slavery, 1848–1860 **472**

AMERICAN PORTRAIT: **Frederick Douglass 473**

The Political Economy of Freedom and Slavery **474**
A Changing Economy in the North **474**

TECHNOLOGY AND IDEAS: **The Telegraph 476**
The Slave Economy **477**
The Importance of the West **477**

Slavery Becomes a Political Issue **480**
Wilmot Introduces His Proviso **480**
A Compromise Without Compromises **482**
The Fugitive Slave Act Provokes a Crisis **483**
The Election of 1852 and the Decline of the Whig Party **484**

Nativism and the Origins of the Republican Party **485**
The Nativist Attack on Immigration **485**
The Kansas-Nebraska Act Revives the Slavery Issue **486**
Kansas Begins to Bleed **488**

AMERICA AND THE WORLD: **Slavery as a Foreign Policy 489**

AMERICAN LANDSCAPE: **Lawrence, Kansas 490**

A New Political Party Takes Shape **491**

PRIMARY SOURCE: **Sumner's "Crime Against Kansas" Speech**   492

The First Sectional Election   494
The Labor Problem and the Politics of Slavery   494
The Dred Scott Decision   496
The Lecompton Constitution Splits the Democratic Party   497
The "Irrepressible" Conflict   497

The Retreat from Union   499

John Brown's War Against Slavery   499
Northerners Elect a President   500

Conclusion   502

CHAPTER **15**   **A War for Union and Emancipation, 1861–1865**   **506**

AMERICAN PORTRAIT: **Edmund Ruffin**   507

Liberty and Union   508

The South Secedes   509
Civilians Demand a Total War   511
Slaves Take Advantage of the War   513
Military Strategy and the Shift in War Aims   513

PRIMARY SOURCE: **"The Battle Hymn of the Republic" and "Dixie"**   514

Mobilizing for War   518

The Confederate States of America   518
Union Naval Supremacy   520
Southern Military Advantages   520
The Slave Economy in Wartime   521
What Were Soldiers Fighting For?   523

The Civil War as Social Revolution   524

Union Victories in the West   524
Southern Military Strength in the East   526
Universal Emancipation   527

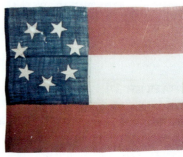

AMERICA AND THE WORLD: **The Diplomacy of Emancipation**   530

Emancipation in Practice   530

AMERICAN LANDSCAPE: **Freedman's Village, Arlington, Virginia**   531

The War at Home   533

The Care of Casualties   533

TECHNOLOGY AND IDEAS: **The Repeating Rifle**   534

Northern Reverses and Antiwar Sentiment   536
Gettysburg and the Justification of the War   537

Discontent in the Confederacy   539

The War Comes to a Bloody End   539

Grant Takes Command   539
The Theory and Practice of Hard War   540
Sherman Marches and Lee Surrenders   541
From Emancipation to Abolition   543
The Meaning of the Civil War   545

Conclusion   545

CHAPTER 16   Reconstructing a Nation, 1865–1877   **550**

AMERICAN PORTRAIT: **John Dennett Visits a Freedmen's Bureau Court   551**

Wartime Reconstruction   553

Experiments with Free Labor in the Lower Mississippi Valley   553
Lincoln's Ten-Percent Plan Versus the Wade-Davis Bill   554
The Freed People's Dream of Owning Land   555

Presidential Reconstruction, 1865–1867   557

The Political Economy of Contract Labor   557
Resistance to Presidential Reconstruction   558
Congress Clashes with the President   559

PRIMARY SOURCE: **How Free Is Free? A Sharecropping Contract   560**

Origins of the Fourteenth Amendment   562

AMERICAN LANDSCAPE: **Race Riots in Memphis and New Orleans   563**

Congressional Reconstruction   564

Origins of the Black Vote   564
Radical Reconstruction in the South   565
Achievements and Failures of Radical Government   566
The Political Economy of Sharecropping   567

The Retreat from Republican Radicalism   570

The Impeachment and Trial of Andrew Johnson   570
Republicans Become the Party of Moderation   571

AMERICA AND THE WORLD: **Reconstructing America's Foreign Policy   572**

Reconstructing the North   573

The Fifteenth Amendment and Nationwide African American Suffrage   573
Women and Suffrage   574
The Rise and Fall of the National Labor Union   574

The End of Reconstruction   575

Corruption as a National Problem   575
Liberal Republicans Revolt   576
A Depression and a Deal "Redeem" the South   577

DEBATING HISTORY: **The Nature of Reconstruction   579**

Conclusion   580

Appendixes

Appendix A Historical Documents   A-1

  The Declaration of Independence   A-1
  The Constitution of the United States of America   A-3
  Lincoln's Gettysburg Address   A-21

Appendix B Historical Facts and Data   B-1

  US Presidents and Vice Presidents   B-1
  Admission of States into the Union   B-3

Glossary   G-1
Photo Credits   C-1
Index   I-1

Maps

1–1   World Trade on the Eve of Discovery   *9*
1–2   Africa in the Age of Discovery   *13*
1–3   The Spanish Exploration   *19*
1–4   The Columbian Exchange   *28*
1–5   A New Global Economy   *31*
2–1   North Atlantic Trade Routes at the End of the 16th Century   *40*
2–2   Voyages of Exploration   *41*
2–3   European Colonization of the Southeast   *43*
2–4   The Iroquois Region in the Middle of the 17th Century   *44*
2–5   French Exploration and Settlement, 1603–1616   *45*
2–6   The Wampum Trade   *52*
3–1   English Encroachments on Indian Land, 1613–1652   *78*
3–2   The English Colonies, 1660   *88*
3–3   New England in the 1640s   *96*
4–1   Trade Routes in the Southeast   *114*
4–2   Frontier Warfare During King William's and Queen Anne's Wars   *126*
4–3   Colonial North America, East of the Mississippi, 1720   *131*
4–4   Region of Spanish Reconquest of New Mexico, 1692–1696   *135*
5–1   Expansion of Settlement, 1720–1760   *146*
5–2   Exports of the Thirteen Colonies, ca. 1770   *153*
5–3   Commerce and Culture in Philadelphia, ca. 1760   *161*
5–4   Printing Presses and Newspapers, 1760–1775   *162*
5–5   George Whitefield's Itinerary   *173*
6–1   The Ohio River Valley, 1747–1758   *186*
6–2   The Second Phase of the French and Indian War, 1758–1763   *194*
6–3   The North American Colonies Before and After the French and Indian War   *195*
6–4   Pontiac's Rebellion, 1763   *197*
7–1   Battles of Lexington, Concord, and Breed's Hill   *221*
7–2   New York and New Jersey Campaigns, 1776–1777   *229*
7–3   The Battles for New York   *232*
7–4   The War in the South, 1779–1781   *235*
7–5   The Treaty of Paris   *237*
7–6   Sites of Revolutionary War Battles Involving Indians   *247*
7–7   Western Land Cessions   *250*
8–1   Distribution of Black Population, 1775   *272*
8–2   Western Expansion, 1785–1805   *281*
8–3   Major Indian Villages and Indian–US Battle Sites, 1789–1800   *283*
8–4   Extension of US National Territories, 1783, and Extension of US National Territories, 1795   *289*
9–1   Louisiana Purchase   *303*
9–2   Battles and Campaigns of the War of 1812   *310*
9–3   The Development of Regions and of Roads and Canals   *319*
9–4   Mounting Land Pressure, 1784–1812, and the Rise of Tecumseh's Confederation   *326*

10–1   The Election of 1824   *344*

10–2   Toward Universal White Male Suffrage   *349*

10–3   The Election of 1828   *352*

10–4   Indian Removals   *360*

11–1   Revival and Reform   *375*

12–1   Westward Expansion and Slavery, 1820   *427*

13–1   Republic of Texas   *452*

13–2   Major Overland Trails   *454*

13–3   Major Trans-Mississippi Indian Communities, ca. 1850   *456*

13–4   Mexican War   *467*

14–1   Slavery's Expansion   *478*

14–2   Railroad Expansion   *479*

14–3   The Kansas-Nebraska Act of 1854   *487*

14–4   The Election of 1856   *496*

14–5   The Election of 1860   *502*

15–1   The Secession of the Southern States   *510*

15–2   The Virginia Campaigns of 1861–1862   *517*

15–3   The War in the West in 1862   *524*

15–4   The Battle of Antietam   *527*

15–5   The Battle of Gettysburg, July 1–3, 1863   *537*

15–6   The Siege of Vicksburg, 1862–1863   *538*

15–7   The Virginia Theater, 1864–1865   *540*

15–8   The Atlanta Campaign and Sherman's March, 1863–1865   *543*

16–1   Reconstruction and Redemption   *565*

16–2   Sharecropping   *568*

16–3   The Effect of Sharecropping on Southern Plantations: The Barrow Plantation in Oglethorpe County, Georgia   *569*

16–4   The Presidential Election, 1876   *578*

Features

AMERICAN PORTRAITS

Malinche, Cultural Translator (Chapter 1)   3
Don Luis de Velasco Finds His Way Home (Chapter 2)   37
The Adventures of John Smith (Chapter 3)   69
Tituba Shapes Her World and Saves Herself (Chapter 4)   103
George Whitefield: Evangelist for a Consumer Society (Chapter 5)   143
Susannah Willard Johnson Experiences the Empire (Chapter 6)   181
James Madison Helps Make a Nation (Chapter 7)   219
Ona Judge Finds Her Freedom (Chapter 8)   261
Andrew Jackson's America (Chapter 9)   299
Harriet Noble (Chapter 10)   337
Charles Grandison Finney (Chapter 11)   373
Joseph Cinqué and the *Amistad* Rebellion (Chapter 12)   403
Mah-i-ti-wo-nee-ni Remembers Life on the Great Plains (Chapter 13)   439
Frederick Douglass (Chapter 14)   473
Edmund Ruffin (Chapter 15)   507
John Dennett Visits a Freedmen's Bureau Court (Chapter 16)   551

AMERICAN LANDSCAPES

Tenochtitlan (Chapter 1)   22
Huronia (Chapter 2)   46
New England Settlements (Chapter 3)   92
New Amsterdam/New York (Chapter 4)   110
The Slave Ship (Chapter 5)   149
Occupied Boston (Chapter 6)   209
The South Carolina Backcountry (Chapter 7)   234
Philadelphia (Chapter 8)   269
Religion in the Backcountry: Cane Ridge, Kentucky (Chapter 9)   329
Liberty and the Land: Cherokee Removal (Chapter 10)   362
Freedom and Wage Labor (Chapter 11)   386
Gowrie: The Story of Profit and Loss on an American Plantation (Chapter 12)   410
Culture and Politics in Manifest Destiny: Tejanos in Texas (Chapter 13)   450
Lawrence, Kansas (Chapter 14)   490
Freedman's Village, Arlington, Virginia (Chapter 15)   531
Race Riots in Memphis and New Orleans (Chapter 16)   563

AMERICA AND THE WORLD

Debating the Morality of Conquest (Chapter 1)   18
Indians on the Thames (Chapter 2)   56
The English Enter the Slave Trade (Chapter 3)   86
Witchcraft in Global Perspective (Chapter 4)   129
Consumer Tastes in Global Perspective (Chapter 5)   159
Paying for War (Chapter 6)   199

Mercenaries in Global Perspective (Chapter 7)   *230*

Citizenship in an Age of Revolution (Chapter 8)   *286*

The United States in China (Chapter 9)   *312*

The Monroe Doctrine (Chapter 10)   *342*

The American Board of Commissioners for Foreign Missions (Chapter 11)   *379*

The Demand for Raw Cotton (Chapter 12)   *420*

Lt. Rankin Dilworth in the War with Mexico (Chapter 13)   *465*

Slavery as a Foreign Policy (Chapter 14)   *489*

The Diplomacy of Emancipation (Chapter 15)   *530*

Reconstructing America's Foreign Policy (Chapter 16)   *572*

PRIMARY SOURCES

Mapping the World (Maps) (Chapter 1)   *11*

Thomas Hariot, *A Brief and True Report of the New Found Land
    of Virginia* (1588) (Chapter 2)   *58*

The Charter of Virginia, 1606 (Chapter 3)   *72*

The Navigation Act of 1651 (Chapter 4)   *107*

The Autobiography of Benjamin Franklin (Chapter 5)   *170*

George Washington on Braddock's Defeat (Chapter 6)   *189*

Abigail to John Adams, "Remember the Ladies" (Chapter 7)   *244*

Petition from the Pennsylvania Society for Promoting the Abolition of Slavery (Chapter 8)   *274*

Gibbons v. Ogden: Freedom of Interstate Commerce (Chapter 9)   *323*

Jackson's Bank Veto Message (Chapter 10)   *354*

Charles Dickens Describes Five Points, NYC (Chapter 11)   *382*

John Pendleton Kennedy's *Swallow Barn:* A Traveler's Account
    of Antebellum Virginia (Chapter 12)   *414*

John O'Sullivan Proclaims a "Nation of Futurity" (Chapter 13)   *446*

Sumner's "Crime Against Kansas" Speech (Chapter 14)   *492*

"The Battle Hymn of the Republic" and "Dixie" (Chapter 15)   *514*

How Free Is Free? A Sharecropping Contract (Chapter 16)   *560*

DEBATING HISTORY

Population of the Americas Precontact (Chapter 1)   *26*

Encounters or Conflict? (Chapter 2)   *62*

Origins of Slavery (Chapter 4)   *120*

Causes of the American Revolution (Chapter 7)   *223*

The Politics of the 1790s and Democracy (Chapter 8)   *292*

The Nature of Jacksonian Democracy (Chapter 10)   *367*

Manifest Destiny and Race (Chapter 13)   *462*

The Nature of Reconstruction (Chapter 16)   *579*

TECHNOLOGY AND IDEAS

Tobacco Cultivation in Virginia (Chapter 3)   *77*

Inoculation (Chapter 5)   *168*

The Role of Newspapers in the Imperial Crisis (Chapter 6)   *202*

The Steamboat (Chapter 9)   *317*

Textile Mills (Chapter 11)   *385*

The Cotton Gin (Chapter 12)   *406*

The Telegraph (Chapter 14)   *476*

The Repeating Rifle (Chapter 15)   *534*

Preface

We are grateful that the first edition of *Of the People* has been welcomed by instructors and students as a useful instructional aid. Enhanced with even greater emphasis on American democracy and diversity, the second edition includes new features and innovative learning tools that help students draw connections among topics and think critically. In preparing the second edition, our primary goal has been to maintain the text's overarching focus on the evolution of American democracy, people, and power; its strong portrayal of political and social history; and its clear, compelling narrative voice. To that end, we have broadened the representation of Native Americans, African Americans, and other minority groups to better show the full diversity of the American people. Recognizing the increasingly visual orientation of our students and society, we have included new diagrams to help students see the connections among events in each chapter. And we have strengthened the text's critical-thinking pedagogy because the study of history entails careful analysis, not mere memorization of names and dates. In response to feedback from instructors, we have also added three new boxed features: **Primary Source** teaches students to analyze written and visual historical documents, **Debating History** presents two historians arguing different sides of a historical controversy, and **Technology and Ideas** presents innovations that played a key role in US history.

History continues, and the writing of history is never finished. The newest members of our author team, Camilla Townsend and Mark Summers, have substantially revised and expanded our coverage of Native American societies and the Gilded Age, respectively. For the second edition, we have updated the following elements based on the most recent scholarship:

>> **Chapters 1 through 3** have updated and expanded coverage of pre-Columbian America, including a fuller description of Native Americans and precontact civilizations of Latin America as well as native societies through the seventeenth century.

>> **Chapters 8 through 10** include updated scholarship on the New Republic as well as integrated content on slavery in the Americas and additional material on Native Americans.

>> **Chapters 11 and 12 (previously 12 and 10)** on slavery and reform movements in the early nineteenth century have been reordered and substantially revised to present a clearer picture of events that would ultimately erupt into violence. Coverage of the abolition movement appears in the chapter on slavery.

>> **Chapters 17 through 19** include updated scholarship on the Gilded Age, with more details about technological innovations of the period.

>> **Chapter 28** has a new title, **The Table of Democracy, 1960–1968.** This emphasizes a stronger focus on issues of power and democracy also seen in Chapters 23 and 27.

>> **Chapter 31** now includes an account of the Obama administration through 2012, the death of Osama bin Laden, and the nation's continuing response to challenging economic circumstances. The Tea Party and Occupy movements receive coverage as well.

At Gettysburg, Pennsylvania, on November 19, 1863, President Abraham Lincoln dedicated a memorial to the more than 3,000 Union soldiers who had died turning back a Confederate invasion in the first days of July. There were at least a few ways that the president could have justified the sad loss of life in the third year of a brutal war dividing North and South. He could have said it was necessary to destroy the Confederacy's cherished institution of slavery, to punish Southerners for seceding from the United States, or to preserve the nation intact. Instead, at this crucial moment in American history, Lincoln gave a short, stunning speech about democracy. The president did not use the word, but he offered its essence. To honor the dead of Gettysburg, he called on Northerners to ensure "that government of the people, by the people, for the people, shall not perish from the earth."

With these words, Lincoln put democracy at the center of the Civil War and at the center of American history. The authors of this book share his belief in the centrality of democracy; his words, "of the people," give our book its title and its main theme. We see American history as a story "of the people," of their struggles to shape their lives and their land.

Our choice of theme does not mean we believe that America has always been a democracy. Clearly, it has not. As Lincoln gave the Gettysburg Address, most African Americans still lived in slavery. American women, North and South, lacked rights that many men enjoyed; for all their disagreements, white Southerners and Northerners viewed Native Americans as enemies. Neither do we believe that there is only a single definition of democracy, either in the narrow sense of a particular form of government or in the larger one of a society whose members participate equally in its creation. Although Lincoln defined the Northern cause as a struggle for democracy, Southerners believed it was anything but democratic to force them to remain in the Union at gunpoint. As bloody draft riots in New York City in July 1863 made clear, many Northern men thought it was anything but democratic to force them to fight in Lincoln's armies. Such disagreements have been typical of American history. For more than 500 years, people have struggled over whose vision of life in the New World would prevail.

It is precisely such struggles that offer the best angle of vision for seeing and understanding the most important developments in the nation's history. In particular, the democratic theme concentrates attention on the most fundamental concerns of history: people and power.

Lincoln's words serve as a reminder of the basic truth that history is about people. Across the 31 chapters of this book, we write extensively about complex events, such as the five-year savagery of the Civil War, and long-term transformations, such as the slow, halting evolution of democratic political institutions. But we write in the awareness that these developments are only abstractions unless they are grounded in the lives of people. The test of a historical narrative, we believe, is whether its characters are fully-rounded, believable human beings.

The choice of Lincoln's words also reflects our belief that history is about power. To ask whether America was democratic at some point in the past is to ask whether all people had equal power to make their lives and their nation. Such questions of power necessarily take us to political processes, to the ways in which people work separately and collectively to enforce their will. We define politics quite broadly in this book. With the feminists of the 1960s, we believe that "the personal is the political," that power relations shape people's lives in private as well as in public. *Of the People* looks for democracy in the living room as well as the legislature, and in the bedroom as well as the business office.

Focusing on democracy, on people and power, we have necessarily written as wide-ranging a history as possible. In the features and in the main text, *Of the People* conveys both the unity and the great diversity of the American people across time and place. We chronicle the racial and ethnic groups who have shaped America, differences of religious and regional identity, the changing nature of social classes, and the different ways that gender identities have been constructed over the centuries.

While treating different groups in their distinctiveness, we have integrated them into the broader narrative as much as possible. A true history "of the people" means not only acknowledging their individuality and diversity but also showing their inter-relationships and their roles in the larger narrative. More integrated coverage of Native Americans and African Americans appears throughout the second edition.

Of the People also offers comprehensive coverage of the different spheres of human life—cultural as well as governmental, social as well as economic, environmental as well as military. This commitment to comprehensiveness is a reflection of our belief that all aspects of human existence are the stuff of history. It is also an expression of the fundamental theme of the book: the focus on democracy leads naturally to the study of people's struggles for power in every dimension of their lives. Moreover, the democratic approach emphasizes the interconnections between the different aspects of Americans' lives; we cannot understand politics and government without tracing their connection to economics, religion, culture, art, sexuality, and so on.

The economic connection is especially important. *Of the People* devotes much attention to economic life, to the ways in which Americans have worked and saved and spent. Economic power, the authors believe, is basic to democracy. Americans' power to shape their lives and their country has been greatly affected by whether they were farmers or hunters, plantation owners or slaves, wage workers or capitalists, domestic servants or bureaucrats. The authors do not see economics as an impersonal, all-conquering force: instead, we try to show how the values and actions of ordinary people, as well as the laws and regulations of government, have made economic life.

We have also tried especially to place America in global context. The history of America, or any nation, cannot be adequately explained without understanding its relationship to transnational events and global developments. That is true for the first chapter of the book, which shows how America began to emerge from the collision of Native Americans, West Africans, and Europeans in the fifteenth and sixteenth centuries. It is just as true for the last chapter of the book, which demonstrates how globalization and the war on terror transformed the United States at the turn of the twenty-first century. In the chapters in between these two, we detail how the world has changed America and how America has changed the world. Reflecting the concerns of the rest of the book, we focus particularly on the movement of people, the evolution of power, and the attempt to spread democracy abroad. Chapter 20 shows how Singer, a pioneering American multinational company, began to export an economic vision of a consumer democracy along with its sewing machines in the nineteenth and early twentieth centuries.

While Singer wanted to sell sewing machines, Abraham Lincoln wanted to sell a war. But both believed their audience would see democracy as quintessentially American. Whether they were right is the burden of this book.

New to the Second Edition

>> New "Primary Source" feature in each chapter

This feature prompts the student to analyze a written or visual historical document such as a sharecropping contract or photographs of the Kent State shootings.

>> New "Debating History" feature

In this feature, two historians argue different sides of an issue, from the origin of slavery to the causes of the Great Depression. Critical-thinking questions follow. This unique feature teaches students to interpret and synthesize secondary sources.

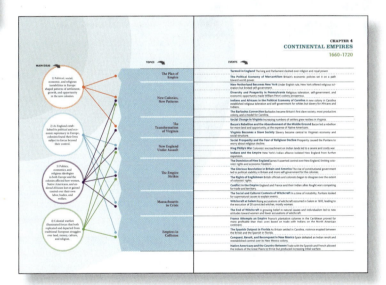

>> "Technology and Ideas" feature

These boxes present an innovation that played an important role in American history. Subjects include the cotton gin, the mail-order catalog, the atomic bomb, and video games.

>> New visual reviews with connections

Chapters now end with a diagram that lays out the important topics (based on headings and subheadings) and presents a brief summary of each as well as the ways they interrelate. Visual learners and all students will benefit from seeing the relationships among the topics illustrated.

>> Enhanced critical-thinking pedagogy

All chapters now end with both Review Questions, which test students' memory and understanding of chapter content, and Critical-Thinking Questions, which ask students to analyze and interpret chapter content.

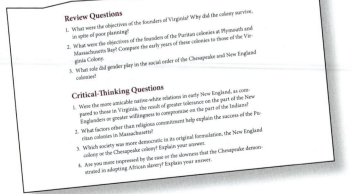

>> New additions to "American Portrait," "American Landscape," and "America and the World" features

These popular boxed features from the first edition have been updated with 10 new "American Portraits," 4 new "American Landscapes," and 5 new "America and the World" features.

Hallmark Features

>> Each chapter opens with an **"American Portrait"** feature, a story of someone whose life in one way or another embodies the basic theme of the pages to follow.

>> Each chapter presents an **"American Landscape"** feature, a particular place in time where issues of power appeared in especially sharp relief.

>> To underscore the fundamental importance of global relationships, each chapter includes a feature on **"America and the World."**

>> Focus questions at chapter openings

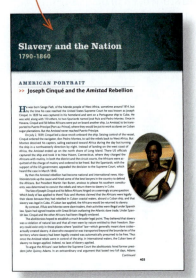

>> Time Lines in every chapter

>> "Who, What"

This list of chapter-ending key terms helps students recall the important people and events of that chapter.

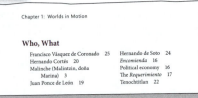

Supplements

For Students

Oxford University Press is proud to offer a complete and authoritative supplements package for students—including print and new media resources designed for chapter review, for primary source reading, for essay writing, for test preparation and for further research.

Student Companion Website at **www.oup.com/us/ofthepeople**

The open-access Online Study Center designed for *Of the People: A History of the United States* (comprehensive and concise editions) helps students to review what they have learned from the textbook as well as explore other resources online. Note-taking guides help students focus their attention in class, while interactive practice quizzes allow them to assess their knowledge of a topic before a test.

- **Online Study Guide,** including
  - Note-taking outlines
  - Multiple-choice and identification quizzes, (two quizzes per chapter, 30 question quizzes—*different* from those found in the Instructor's Manual/Testbank)
- **Primary Source Companion and Research Guide,** a brief online research primer, with a library of annotated links to primary and secondary sources in US history.
- **Interactive Flashcards,** using key terms and people listed at the end of each chapter, help students remember who's who and what's what.

Writing History: A Guide for Students, Fourth Edition by William Kelleher Storey, Professor of History at Millsaps College

Bringing together practical methods from both history and composition, *Writing History* provides a wealth of tips and advice to help students research and write essays for history classes. The book covers all aspects of writing about history, including **finding topics and researching** them, **interpreting source materials, drawing inferences from sources, and constructing arguments.** It concludes with three chapters that discuss writing effective sentences, using precise wording, and revising. Using numerous examples from the works of cultural, political, and social historians, *Writing History* serves as an ideal supplement to history courses that require students to conduct research. The third edition includes expanded sections on peer editing and topic selection, as well as new sections on searching and using the Internet. *Writing History* can be **packaged for free** with Oakes's *Of the People: A History of the United States.* Contact your Oxford University Press sales representative for more information.

The Information-Literate Historian: A Guide to Research for History Students, Second Edition by Jenny Presnell, Information Services Library and History, American Studies, and Women's Studies Bibliographer, Miami University of Ohio

This is the only book specifically designed to teach today's history student how to most successfully select and use sources—primary, secondary, and electronic—to carry out and present their research. Written by a college librarian, *The Information-Literate Historian* is an indispensable reference for historians, students, and other readers doing history research. *The Information-Literate Historian* can be **packaged for free** with Oakes's *Of the People: A History of the United States*, Second Edition. Contact your Oxford University Press sales representative for more information.

Primary Source Documents

Our Documents: 100 Milestone Documents from the National Archives brings documents to life, including facsimiles side-by-side with transcripts for students to explore, explanations, and a foreword provided by Michael Beschloss. This primary source book can be **packaged for free** with Oakes's *Of the People: A History of the United States*, Second Edition. Among the documents it contains are the following: Declaration of Independence; US Constitution; Bill of Rights; Louisiana Purchase Treaty; Missouri Compromise; *Dred Scott* decision; Emancipation Proclamation; Gettysburg Address; Fourteenth Amendment to the US Constitution; Thomas Edison's light bulb patent; Sherman Anti-Trust Act; executive order for the Japanese relocation during wartime; Manhattan Project notebook; press release announcing US recognition of Israel; President John F. Kennedy's inaugural address, as well as many more.

Other primary source books that can be packaged with Oakes's *Of the People: A History of the United States*, Second Edition, include Chafe's ***History of Our Time*** and Bloom's ***Takin' It to the Streets***, as well as ***The Boisterous Sea of Liberty: A Documentary History of America from Discovery Through the Civil War;*** and ***Documenting American Violence: A Sourcebook.***

For Professors

For decades American History professors have turned to Oxford University Press as the leading source for high quality readings and reference materials. Now, when you adopt Oakes's *Of the People: A History of the United States*, Second Edition, the Press will partner with you and make available its best supplemental materials and resources for your classroom. Listed here are several series of high interest, but you will want to talk with your sales representative to learn more about what can be made available, and about what would suit your course best.

Instructor's Manual and Testbank. This useful guide contains helpful teaching tools for experienced and first-time teachers alike. It can be made available to adopters upon request, and is also available electronically on the Instructor's Resource CD. This extensive manual and testbank contains the following:

- **Sample Syllabi**
- **Chapter Outlines**
- **In-Class Discussion Questions**
- **Lecture Ideas**
- **Oxford's Further Reading List**
- **Quizzes** (two per chapter, one per half of the chapter, content divided somewhat evenly down the middle of the chapter: 30 multiple-choice questions each)
- **Tests** (two per chapter, each covering the entire chapter contents: each offering 10 identification/matching; 10 multiple-choice; 5 short-answer, 2 essay)

Instructor's Resource CD. This handy CD-ROM contains everything you need in an electronic format—the Instructor's Manual (PDF), PowerPoint-based slides (fully customizable), Image Library with PDF versions of *all* maps from the textbook, and a Computerized Testbank, which was made specifically for this edition.

A complete **Course Management cartridge** is also available to qualified adopters. Instructor's resources are also available for download directly to your computer through a secure connection via the instructor's side of the companion website. Contact your Oxford University Press sales representative for more information.

Other Oxford Titles of Interest for the US History Classroom

Oxford University Press publishes a vast array of titles in American history. The following list is just a small selection of books that pair particularly well with Oakes's *Of the People: A History of the United States*, Second Edition. Any of the books in these series can be packaged with Oakes at a significant discount to students. Please contact your Oxford University Press sales representative for specific pricing information, or for additional packaging suggestions. Please visit www.oup.com/us for a full listing of Oxford titles.

NEW NARRATIVES IN AMERICAN HISTORY

At Oxford University Press, we believe that good history begins with a good story. Each volume in this series features a compelling tale that draws on a sustained narrative to illuminate a greater historical theme or controversy. Then, in a thoughtful Afterword, the authors place their narratives within larger historical contexts, discuss their sources and narrative strategies, and describe their personal involvement with the work. Intensely personal and highly relevant, these succinct texts are innovative teaching tools that provide a springboard for incisive class discussion as they immerse students in a particular historical moment.

Escaping Salem: The Other Witch Hunt of 1692 (Richard Godbeer)
Sleuthing the Alamo: Davy Crockett's Last Stand and Other Mysteries of the Texas Revolution (James E. Crisp)
In Search of the Promised Land: A Slave Family in the Old South (John Hope Franklin and Loren Schweninger)
The Making of a Confederate: Walter Lenoir's Civil War (William L. Barney)
"They Say": Ida B. Wells and the Reconstruction of Race (James West Davidson)
Wild Men: Ishi and Kroeber in the Wilderness of Modern America (Douglas Cazaux Sackman)
The Gentle Subversive: Rachel Carson, Silent Spring, *and the Rise of the Environmental Movement* (Mark Hamilton Lytle)
"To Everything There Is a Season": Pete Seeger and the Power of Song (Allan Winkler)

PAGES FROM HISTORY

Textbooks may interpret and recall history, but these books **are** history. Each title, compiled and edited by a prominent historian, is a collection of primary sources relating to a particular topic of historical significance. Documentary evidence includes news articles, government documents, memoirs, letters, diaries, fiction, photographs, advertisements, posters, and political cartoons. Headnotes, extended captions, sidebars, and introductory essays provide the essential context that frames the documents. All the books are amply illustrated, and each includes a documentary picture essay, chronology, further reading, source notes, and index.

Encounters in the New World (Jill Lepore)
Colonial America (Edward G. Gray)
The American Revolution (Stephen C. Bullock)
The Bill of Rights (John J. Patrick)

The Struggle Against Slavery (David Waldstreicher)

The Civil War (Rachel Filene Seidman)

The Gilded Age (Janette Thomas Greenwood)

The Industrial Revolution (Laura Levine Frader)

Imperialism (Bonnie G. Smith)

World War I (Frans Coetzee and Marilyn Shevin-Coetzee)

The Depression and the New Deal (Robert McElvaine)

World War II (James H. Madison)

The Cold War (Allan M. Winkler)

The Vietnam War (Marilyn B. Young)

PIVOTAL MOMENTS IN AMERICAN HISTORY

Oxford's *Pivotal Moments in American History Series* explores the turning points that forever changed the course of American history. Each book is written by an expert on the subject and provides a fascinating narrative on a significant instance that stands out in our nation's past. For anyone interested in discovering which important junctures in US history shaped our thoughts, actions, and ideals, these books are the definitive resources.

The Scratch of a Pen: 1763 and the Transformation of North America (Colin Calloway)

As if an Enemy's Country: The British Occupation of Boston and the Origins of the Revolution (Richard Archer)

Washington's Crossing (David Hackett Fischer)

James Madison and the Struggle for the Bill of Rights (Richard Labunski)

Adams vs. Jefferson: The Tumultuous Election of 1800 (John Ferling)

The Birth of Modern Politics: Andrew Jackson, John Quincy Adams, and the Election of 1828 (Lynn Parsons)

Storm over Texas: The Annexation Controversy and the Road to Civil War (Joel H. Silbey)

Crossroads of Freedom: Antietam (James M. McPherson)

The Last Indian War: The Nez Perce Story (Elliot West)

Seneca Falls and the Origins of the Women's Rights Movement (Sally McMillen)

Rainbow's End: The Crash of 1929 (Maury Klein)

Brown v. Board of Education *and the Civil Rights Movement* (Michael J. Klarman)

The Bay of Pigs (Howard Jones)

Freedom Riders: 1961 and the Struggle for Racial Justice (Raymond Arsenault)

VIEWPOINTS ON AMERICAN CULTURE

Oxford's Viewpoints on American Culture Series offers timely reflections for twenty-first-century readers. The series targets topics where debates have flourished and brings together the voices of established and emerging writers to share their own points of view in compact and compelling format.

Votes for Women: The Struggle for Suffrage Revisited (Jean H. Baker)

Long Time Gone: Sixties America Then and Now (Alexander Bloom)

Living in the Eighties (Edited by Gil Troy and Vincent J. Cannato)

Race on Trial: Law and Justice in American History (Annette Gordon-Reed)

Sifters: Native American Women's Lives (Theda Perdue)

Latina Legacies: Identity, Biography, and Community (Vicki L. Ruiz)

OXFORD WORLD'S CLASSICS

For over 100 years, Oxford World's Classics has made available a broad spectrum of literature from around the globe. With well over 600 titles available and a continuously growing list, this is the finest and most comprehensive classics series in print. Any volume in the series can be **packaged for free** with Oakes's *Of the People: A History of the United States*, Second Edition. Relevant titles include Benjamin Franklin's *Autobiography and Other Writings*, J. Hector St. John de Crèvecœur's *Letters from an American Farmer*, Booker T. Washington's *Up from Slavery*, and many others. **For a complete listing of Oxford World's Classics, please visit www.oup.com/us/owc.**

Acknowledgments

We are grateful to our families, friends, and colleagues who encouraged us during the planning and writing of this book.

Nick Cullather: To Isabel and Joey for (occasionally) allowing me to work, and to Melanie for the 16 best years.

Jan Lewis: I want to express special thanks to Andy Achenbaum, James Grimmelmann, Warren F. Kimball, Ken Lockridge, and Peter Onuf, who either read portions of the manuscript or discussed it with me, as well as Elizabeth M. Aaron, who helped me with the visual review. And I am grateful to Barry Bienstock for his enormous library, his vast knowledge, and his endless patience.

We would like once again to thank Bruce Nichols for helping launch this book years ago. We are grateful to the editors and staff at Oxford University Press, especially our acquisitions editor, Brian Wheel, and our development editors, Angela Kao, Frederick Speers, and Anne Kemper. Brian's commitment made this text possible; Fred's vision helped us shape the book's direction; and Anne guided the development of the second edition. Thanks also to our talented production team, Barbara Mathieu, senior production editor, and Michele Laseau, art director, who helped to fulfill the book's vision. And special thanks go to Linda Sykes, who managed the photo research; to Mary Anne Shahidi, our copyeditor; to Mike Powers and Martha Bostwick, cartographers, and Deane Plaister, editor, at Maps.com, who created the maps; and to the many other people behind the scenes at Oxford for helping this complex project happen.

The authors and editors would also like to thank the following people, whose time and insights have contributed to the first and second editions.

FEATURE AUTHORS

Lawrence Cappello
City University of New York Graduate Center

Joseph Murphy
City University of New York Graduate Center

Williamjames Hull Hoffer
Seton Hall University

SUPPLEMENT AUTHORS

Laura Graves
South Plains College
Instructor's Manual

Jim Jeffries
Clemson University
PowerPoint Slides

Andrew McMichael
Western Kentucky University
Student Companion Website

Archie McDonald
Stephen D. Austin State University
Test Bank

EXPERT REVIEWERS OF THE SECOND EDITION

Marjorie Berman
*Red Rocks Community
College–Lakewood*

Will Carter
*South Texas Community
College*

Jonathan Chu
*University of Massachusetts,
Boston*

Sara Combs
*Virginia Highlands
Community College*

Mark Elliott
*University of North
Carolina–Greensboro*

David Hamilton
University of Kentucky

James Harvey
Houston Community College

Courtney Joiner
East Georgia College

Timothy Mahoney
*University of
Nebraska–Lincoln*

Abigail Markwyn
Carroll University

Brian Maxson
*Eastern Tennessee State
University*

Matthew Oyos
Radford University

John Pinheiro
Aquinas College

James Pula
*Purdue University–North
Central*

John Rosinbum
Arizona State University

Christopher Thrasher
Texas Tech University

Jeffrey Trask
*University of
Massachusetts–Amherst*

Michael Ward
*California State
University–Northridge*

Bridgette Williams-Searle
The College of Saint Rose

EXPERT REVIEWERS OF THE FIRST EDITION

Thomas L. Altherr
*Metropolitan State College
of Denver*

Luis Alvarez
*University of California–San
Diego*

Adam Arenson
*University of Texas–
El Paso*

Melissa Estes Blair
University of Georgia

Lawrence Bowdish
Ohio State University

Susan Roth Breitzer
Fayetteville State University

Margaret Lynn Brown
Brevard College

W. Fitzhugh Brundage
*University of North
Carolina–Chapel Hill*

Gregory Bush
University of Miami

Brian Casserly
University of Washington

Ann Chirhart
Indiana State University

Bradley R. Clampitt
East Central University

William W. Cobb Jr.
Utah Valley University

Cheryll Ann Cody
Houston Community College

Sondra Cosgrove
College of Southern Nevada

Thomas H. Cox
*Sam Houston State
University*

Carl Creasman
Valencia Community College

Christine Daniels
Michigan State University

Brian J. Daugherity
*Virginia Commonwealth
University*

Mark Elliott
*University of North
Carolina–Greensboro*

Katherine Carté Enge
Texas A&M University

Michael Faubion
*University of Texas–Pan
American*

John Fea
Messiah College

Anne L. Foster
Indiana State University

Matthew Garrett
Arizona State University

Tim Garvin
*California State University–
Long Beach*

Suzanne Cooper Guasco
*Queens University of
Charlotte*

Lloyd Ray Gunn
University of Utah

Richard Hall
*Columbus State
    University*

Marsha Hamilton
*University of South
    Alabama*

Mark Hanna
*University of California–San
    Diego*

Joseph M. Hawes
University of Memphis

Melissa Hovsepian
*University of
    Houston–Downtown*

Jorge Iber
Texas Tech University

David K. Johnson
University of South Florida

Lloyd Johnson
Campbell University

Catherine O'Donnell
Kaplan
Arizona State University

Rebecca M. Kluchin
*California State
    University–Sacramento*

Michael Kramer
Northwestern University

Louis M. Kyriakoudes
*University of Southern
    Mississippi*

Jason S. Lantzer
Butler University

Shelly Lemons
St. Louis Community College

Charlie Levine
Mesa Community College

Denise Lynn
*University of Southern
    Indiana*

Lillian Marrujo-Duck
City College of San Francisco

Michael McCoy
*Orange County Community
    College*

Noeleen McIlvenna
Wright State University

Elizabeth Brand Monroe
*Indiana University–Purdue
    University Indianapolis*

Kevin C. Motl
Ouachita Baptist University

Todd Moye
University of North Texas

Charlotte Negrete
Mt. San Antonio College

Julie Nicoletta
*University of
    Washington–Tacoma*

David M. Parker
*California State
    University–Northridge*

Jason Parker
Texas A&M University

Burton W. Peretti
*Western Connecticut State
    University*

Jim Piecuch
Kennesaw State University

John Putman
San Diego State University

R. J. Rockefeller
Loyola College of Maryland

Herbert Sloan
*Barnard College, Columbia
    University*

Vincent L. Toscano
Nova Southeastern University

William E. Weeks
San Diego State University

Timothy L. Wood
Southwest Baptist University

Jason Young
SUNY–Buffalo

EXPERT REVIEWERS OF THE CONCISE SECOND EDITION

Hedrick Alixopulos
Santa Rosa Junior College

Guy Alain Aronoff
Humboldt State University

Melissa Estes Blair
Warren Wilson College

Amanda Bruce
Nassau Community College

Jonathan Chu
*University of
    Massachusetts–Boston*

Paul G. E. Clemens
Rutgers University

Martha Anne Fielder
Cedar Valley College

Tim Hacsi
*University of
    Massachusetts–Boston*

Matthew Isham
Pennsylvania State

Ross A. Kennedy
Illinois State University

Eve Kornfeld
San Diego State University

Peggy Lambert
Lone Star College-Kingwood

Shelly L. Lemons
St. Louis Community College

Carolyn Herbst Lewis
Louisiana State University

Catherine M. Lewis
Kennesaw State University

Daniel K. Lewis
California State Polytechnic University

Scott P. Marler
University of Memphis

Laura McCall
Metropolitan State College of Denver

Stephen P. McGrath
Central Connecticut State University

Vincent P. Mikkelsen
Florida State University

Julie Nicoletta
University of Washington Tacoma

Caitlin Stewart
Eastern Connecticut State University

Thomas Summerhill
Michigan State University

David Tegeder
Santa Fe College

Eric H. Walther
University of Houston

William E. Weeks
University of San Diego

Kenneth B. White
Modesto Junior College

Julie Winch
University of Massachusetts–Boston

Mary Montgomery Wolf
University of Georgia

Kyle F. Zelner
University of Southern Mississippi

EXPERT REVIEWERS OF THE CONCISE FIRST EDITION

Hedrick Alixopulos
Santa Rosa Junior College

Guy Alain Aronoff
Humboldt State University

Melissa Estes Blair
Warren Wilson College

Amanda Bruce
Nassau Community College

Jonathan Chu
University of Massachusetts–Boston

Paul G. E. Clemens
Rutgers University

Martha Anne Fielder
Cedar Valley College

Tim Hacsi
University of Massachusetts–Boston

Matthew Isham
Pennsylvania State

Ross A. Kennedy
Illinois State University

Eve Kornfeld
San Diego State University

Peggy Lambert
Lone Star College-Kingwood

Shelly L. Lemons
St. Louis Community College

Carolyn Herbst Lewis
Louisiana State University

Catherine M. Lewis
Kennesaw State University

Daniel K. Lewis
California State Polytechnic University

Scott P. Marler
University of Memphis

Laura McCall
Metropolitan State College of Denver

Stephen P. McGrath
Central Connecticut State University

Vincent P. Mikkelsen
Florida State University

Julie Nicoletta
University of Washington Tacoma

Caitlin Stewart
Eastern Connecticut State University

Thomas Summerhill
Michigan State University

David Tegeder
Santa Fe College

Eric H. Walther
University of Houston

William E. Weeks
University of San Diego

Kenneth B. White
Modesto Junior College

Julie Winch
University of Massachusetts–Boston

Mary Montgomery Wolf
University of Georgia

Kyle F. Zelner
University of Southern Mississippi

About the Authors

JAMES OAKES has published several books and numerous articles on slavery and antislavery in the nineteenth century, including *The Radical and the Republican: Frederick Douglass, Abraham Lincoln, and the Triumph of Antislavery Politics* (2007), winner of the Lincoln Prize in 2008. Professor Oakes is Distinguished Professor of History and Graduate School Humanities Professor at the City University of New York Graduate Center. In 2008 he was a fellow at the Cullman Center at the New York Public Library. His new book is *Freedom National: The Destruction of Slavery in the United States* (February 2013).

MICHAEL McGERR is the Paul V. McNutt Professor of History in the College of Arts and Sciences at Indiana University–Bloomington. He is the author of *The Decline of Popular Politics: The American North, 1865–1928* (1986) and *A Fierce Discontent: The Rise and Fall of the Progressive Movement, 1870–1920* (2003), both from Oxford University Press. He is writing *"The Public Be Damned": The Vanderbilts and the Unmaking of the Ruling Class*. The recipient of a fellowship from the National Endowment for the Humanities, Professor McGerr has won numerous teaching awards at Indiana, where his courses include the US Survey; War in Modern American History; Rock, Hip Hop, and Revolution; The Sixties; and American Pleasure. He has previously taught at Yale University and the Massachusetts Institute of Technology. He received his BA, MA, and PhD from Yale.

JAN ELLEN LEWIS is Professor of History and Acting Dean of the Faculty of Arts and Sciences, Rutgers University, Newark. She also teaches in the history PhD program at Rutgers, New Brunswick, and was a visiting professor of history at Princeton. A specialist in colonial and early national history, she is the author of *The Pursuit of Happiness: Family and Values in Jefferson's Virginia* (1983) as well as numerous articles and reviews. She has coedited *An Emotional History of the United States* (1998), *Sally Hemings and Thomas Jefferson: History, Memory, and Civic Culture* (1999), and *The Revolution of 1800: Democracy, Race, and the New Republic* (2002). She has served on the editorial board of the *American Historical Review* and as chair of the New Jersey Historical Commission. She is an elected member of the Society of American Historians and the American Antiquarian Society. She received her AB from Bryn Mawr College and MAs and PhD from the University of Michigan.

NICK CULLATHER is a historian of US foreign relations at Indiana University–Bloomington. He is author of three books on nation building: *The Hungry World* (2010), a story of foreign aid, development, and science; *Illusions of Influence* (1994), on US-Philippines relations; and *Secret History* (1999 and 2006), a history of the CIA's overthrow of the Guatemalan government in 1954. He received his PhD from the University of Virginia.

JEANNE BOYDSTON was Robinson-Edwards Professor of American History at the University of Wisconsin–Madison. A specialist in the histories of gender and labor, she was the author of *Home and Work: Housework, Wages, and the Ideology of Labor in the Early American Republic* (1990); coauthor of *The Limits of Sisterhood: The Beecher Sisters on Women's Rights and Woman's Sphere* (1988), and coeditor of *Root of Bitterness: Documents in the Social History of American Women,* second edition (1996). Her most recent article is "Gender as a Category of Historical Analysis," *Gender History* (2008). She taught courses in women's and gender history, the histories of the early republic and the antebellum United States, and global and comparative history, and she was the recipient of numerous awards for teaching and mentoring. Her BA and MA were from the University of Tennessee, and her PhD was from Yale University.

MARK SUMMERS is the Thomas D. Clark Professor of History at the University of Kentucky–Lexington. In addition to various articles, he has written *Railroads, Reconstruction, and the Gospel of Prosperity* (1984), *The Plundering Generation* (1988), *The Era of Good Stealings* (1993), *The Press Gang* (1994), *The Gilded Age; or, The Hazard of New Functions* (1997), *Rum, Romanism and Rebellion* (2000), *Party Games* (2004), and *A Dangerous Stir* (2009). At present, he has just completed a book about a Tammany politician, *Big Tim and the Tiger.* He is now writing a survey of Reconstruction and a book about 1868. He teaches the American history survey (both halves), the Gilded Age, the Progressive Era, the Age of Jackson, Civil War and Reconstruction, the British Empire (both halves), the Old West (both halves), a history of political cartooning, and various graduate courses. He earned his BA from Yale and his PhD from the University of California–Berkeley.

CAMILLA TOWNSEND is Professor of History at Rutgers University–New Brunswick. She is the author of four books, among them *Malintzin's Choices: An Indian Woman in the Conquest of Mexico* (2006) and *Pocahontas and the Powhatan Dilemma* (2004), and is the editor of *American Indian History: A Documentary Reader* (2010). The recipient of fellowships from the National Endowment for the Humanities and the John Simon Guggenheim Memorial Foundation, she has also won awards at Rutgers and at Colgate, where she used to teach. Her courses cover the colonial history of the Americas, as well as Native American history, early and modern. She received her BA from Bryn Mawr and her PhD from Rutgers.

Of the People

COMMON THREADS

>> In which ways might Native American societies before the arrival of Europeans be considered democratic? What forces shaped their societies?

>> How did Europeans' prior experiences affect their actions in the New World? In which ways did they adapt to new circumstances?

>> What made conquest possible? What different forms did it take? What role did gender play in conquest?

>> What were the intended and unintended consequences of conquest?

Worlds in Motion
1450–1550

>> **Malinche, Cultural Translator**

When the Native American woman who would later be known as La Malinche was a little girl, she listened to the poems and histories of her people on starlit evenings. Her father was a nobleman from Coatzacoalcos, on the Gulf of Mexico; his people had lived there for generations in adobe houses built around communal courtyards. Her mother, though, was lowborn, maybe even a captive concubine, and this made the child vulnerable. Trouble came when she was still young. The powerful Aztecs from the Central Valley of Mexico were expanding their dominion, and she was either taken in battle or, more likely, given away as a preemptive peace offering to the invaders. Then the Aztecs sold her to the Mayas, and she lived with them for years as a slave.

When strangers from across the sea came on huge canoes with cloth sails, the Mayas attacked them—and lost the battle. Once again the girl was given away as a peace offering. This time, she found herself among the newly arrived Spaniards, who baptized her "Marina." The Indians heard the name as "Malina" (as they had no "r") and called her "Malintzin" to convey respect. The Spaniards heard "Malinchi" or "Malinche" (as they had no "tz" sound), and so we still call her today. We will never know what her mother had once named her. She had become someone different, and she soon discovered her potential importance to her new captors. Her native language was Nahuatl, the same tongue spoken by the Aztecs, and by now she also spoke the coastal Mayan dialect. The Spaniards had with them one Jerónimo de Aguilar, who had lived for years among the Mayas as a shipwreck victim and also spoke their language. In a perfect translation chain, Hernando Cortés spoke to Aguilar, who spoke to Malinche, who in turn spoke to the Aztecs. She was a gifted young woman and learned Spanish quickly, soon becoming the only translator needed.

Malinche told the Spaniards about the Aztec capital where Moctezuma ruled, and helped to guide them there. She had no reason to protect the Aztec people; after all, they had threatened her own family and caused her enslavement. And she had every reason to work cooperatively with the newcomers: If she did, they would treat her well. If not, they would use her as a sexual slave. She also soon saw that the Spanish were brutal on the battlefield and learned that there were many thousands more of them ready to come. Often she advised indigenous villages that they passed to make peace with the strangers rather than fight them. She said, quite rightly, that they could be useful friends but would make dangerous enemies. When they reached the Aztec capital, she translated adroitly between Cortés and Moctezuma, refusing to be intimidated, and helped Cortés determine what to do at each stage.

Hernando Cortés probably would not have been able to bring down the Aztecs without the help of Malinche. And yet if he had failed, some other Spaniard almost certainly would eventually have found some other captive woman to act as translator and mediator, for the domineering Aztecs had many enemies.

Continued

>> AMERICAN PORTRAIT
Continued

Like many people who have been forced to become cultural mediators, Malinche survived as best she could. She bore a son by Cortés, and when, after the conquest, she demanded a Spanish husband for her own protection, he saw her married to one of his lieutenants. She later bore her husband a daughter. Malinche died when she was about 30 of one of the diseases brought by the Europeans, but not before she had helped her children enter the Spanish world on a firm footing, with wealth and position. She knew by then that the New World she had helped to create was proving dangerous to indigenous people, even those who befriended the Spaniards. She may have had fears for the future, but she could not have had any real regrets about the past, for at the time, she had had very few options. She had done the best she could in an extraordinarily difficult situation.

The Worlds of Indian Peoples

For most of human history, there were no people in the Americas. Archaeologists have found that modern humankind (*Homo sapiens*) originated in Africa about 400,000 years ago. In a sense, all people alive today are ultimately African, as we are all descended from those early humans. Some of them migrated northward and eventually populated Europe and Asia. Mutations occurred along the way, yielding populations who looked different but still had almost all of their genetic material—and their natures and abilities—in common.

Great Migrations

In the last Ice Age, arctic glaciers expanded so extensively that the world's sea level dropped, perhaps by as much as 350 feet. This phenomenon created a land bridge (called "Beringia") between Siberia in Asia and Alaska in America. Humans hunting mammoths and other big game traveled along the new corridor into America. Linguistic evidence indicates that there were three great waves of migration. Archaeologists argue fiercely about when the first one occurred. Most agree it was about 12,000 BCE, but there are a few sites that may suggest otherwise. The Monte Verde site in Chile—where a child's footprint next to a hearth has been forever preserved—seems to have been inhabited a thousand years earlier, for example. Eventually, about 9000 BCE, the ice melted, sea level rose, and the land bridge disappeared, closing off the Old World from what would later be called the New. The people living in the Americas, known now as Paleo-Indians, at first remained what they had been—hunter-gatherers who moved in small groups of no more than about 25, generally choosing their spouses from other bands whom they met in passing.

OUTLINE

The Worlds of Indian Peoples
  Great Migrations
  The Emergence of Farming
  The Cradle of the Americas
  The Northern World Takes Shape

The Worlds of Christopher Columbus
  The *Reconquista*
  The Age of Exploration

PRIMARY SOURCE:
  Mapping the World
  New Ideas Take Root

Collision in the Caribbean
  Columbus's First Voyage
  The Origins of a New World Political and Economic Order
  The Division of the World

Onto the Mainland

Because of the end of the Ice Age, the climate began to shift, yielding distinct changes in lifestyle. At the start of the Archaic period (approximately 8000 BCE), most of the large mammals that were hunted for food went extinct. Overhunting may have contributed to their disappearance, but climactic shifts probably explain the demise of species like the woolly mammoth. The men learned to hunt and trap smaller species, and the women foraged more determinedly for edible and useful plants. They moved through their environment in seasonal cycles, making satisfying and productive lives for themselves for many generations. By the time of Columbus's voyage, there were hundreds of indigenous groups in the Americas.

The Emergence of Farming

As temperatures rose and more species of plants appeared, people around the world began to experiment with planting the seeds of their favorite types. They continued to follow the game as they always had, but then returned to the same place months later to harvest what they had planted. In some places, the available plants proved so rich in protein—containing the amino acids necessary to support life—that human populations gradually ceased to be nomadic hunter-gatherers and became full-time farmers instead. In other places, the available plants were not nutritious enough to enable a major change in lifestyle. In Southwest Asia, for example, in the area traditionally known as "the Fertile Crescent," located between the Tigris and the Euphrates Rivers, wheat, barley, and peas were all native to the region, and all protein-rich. Not surprisingly, humans' early efforts to domesticate plants in this part of the world led relatively rapidly to the adoption of farming as a full-time occupation by about 8000 BCE. In New Guinea, to take a contrary example, the native plants included bananas and sugarcane, both delicious but not rich in protein. People planted them occasionally, but they continued their hunting-and-gathering lifestyle.

In the Americas, there were also very few plant species rich in the amino acids needed to synthesize protein. The ancestor of today's corn, which first appeared in what is today Mexico, was an exception to some extent, but the kernels at that time were extremely tiny, and they were missing some key amino acids. During the Archaic period (8000 BCE–2000 BCE), a number of groups did experiment with growing it (as well as squash and other plants). However, it took many generations of selective planting to create the ears of corn we know today. It took people even longer to discover that if they ate corn together with beans, they were left as well nourished as if they had eaten meat. (The beans provided the amino acids missing from corn: together, they form a complete protein.) Once these breakthroughs had occurred, more societies adopted full-time agriculture.

AMERICA AND THE WORLD:
   Debating the Morality of Conquest
The First Florida Ventures
The Conquest of Mexico

AMERICAN LANDSCAPE:
   Tenochtitlan
The Establishment of a Spanish Empire
The Return to North America

The Consequences of Conquest
   Demographic Disaster

DEBATING HISTORY:
   Population of the Americas Precontact
   The Columbian Exchange
   Men's and Women's Lives

Conclusion

The Cradle of the Americas

Mesoamerica, the area stretching from the Rio Grande to today's Panama, has been called "the Cradle of the Americas" because it was here that the hemisphere's first technologically advanced civilizations emerged. They appeared wherever corn became the centerpiece of a farming culture, beginning in about 2000 BCE. In every part of the ancient world, numerous technological innovations followed the advent of full-time farming. A sedentary lifestyle in which only a portion of the population was engaged in full-time food production enabled the emergence of such things as complex architecture, large ceramics, forges, irrigation techniques, and detailed recordkeeping. Mesoamerica was no exception.

By about 200 CE, two distinct zones of Mesoamerican culture had emerged. In the Yucatan Peninsula, the Classic Maya civilizations flourished. The central basin of Mexico saw a succession of prominent states, beginning with the city of Teotihuacan—the breathtaking ruins of which still stand—and ending with the Aztec Empire, dominant when the Europeans arrived. We know a great deal about the Mayas and Aztecs because they had their own pictoglyphic writing traditions, and they wrote down more about their culture when they learned the Roman alphabet from Spanish priests in the sixteenth century. In reading these individuals' writing, sometimes we stumble eerily into a moment from the past. One day in about the year 800, for example, a skilled Maya artisan crafted a cup for drinking hot chocolate as a gift for a young prince. In the midst of the complicated paintings on the cup, which had religious and astronomical significance, he composed a poem in glyphic writing. He ended it by connecting the earthly world to the divine world, honoring both a powerful prince and a creator god: "He who gave the open space its place / who gave Jaguar Night his place / was the Black-Faced Lord, the Star-Faced Lord."

Scholars studying the writings and other remains of ancient Mesoamerican peoples have helped dispel some of the myths about them. Like people everywhere, they could be gentle and had senses of humor, but they were also competitive and often fought for dominance. They sometimes sacrificed prisoners of war to the gods, but they were not inherently more violent than other humans; they did *not* routinely sacrifice thousands of people at a time, as was once believed. In general, victors in political power struggles preferred that outsiders choose to ally with them rather than be destroyed. The more scholars learn about individual ethnic groups in the pre-Columbian period, the clearer it becomes that they were nearly all based on alliances formed between disparate groups in a more remote past. As bands grew to become chiefdoms—and in some cases, actual states—they governed themselves successfully by allowing the different subunits to have a voice in the increasingly complex polity. Constituent groups negotiated with each other and rotated between them the duties of going to war, for example, or working on a temple. In some regards Mesoamerican native cultures thus constituted the hemisphere's first democracies although they were ruled by chiefs.

The Northern World Takes Shape

In the pre-Columbian period, North America was peripheral to Mesoamerica. Due to the centrality of farming in Mesoamerica, the population there was many millions strong (scholars debate the exact number), while the population of all of North America was about 1 million. Because a desert covered northern Mexico, the culture centered on corn did not travel northward as easily as comparable crops had once traveled from the Fertile Crescent throughout Europe and Asia. But ancient Mesoamerican migrants and traders did eventually spread their valuable commodities, largely through canoe travel along the coasts and eventually even across the Gulf of Mexico.

Beginning as early as 100 CE, small villages began to be established in what we call the American Southwest following the Mexican model. The Anasazi, the Mogollon, and the Hohokam cultures all experimented with agriculture and built houses around courtyards. Later, the climate and their nomadic enemies caused most of them to return to hunting and gathering for a time. The Anasazi, however, persistently circled back to planting corn and eventually built their remarkable cliff dwellings and the towns of Chaco Canyon, among them the 800-room complex at Pueblo Bonito.

Meanwhile, the Mississippi River had long functioned as a great highway for the exchange of goods and ideas. Once corn reached the mouth of the river, it was not long before it spread northward. We call the style of culture that traveled up the artery of the river "Mississippian." Mississippian sites, ranging from about 800 CE to 1500 CE, included the region's more ancient funerary mounds, as well as Mexican-style ball courts next to grand pyramids, central courtyards, and, of course, corn farming. Cahokia, a city-state located near the point where the Missouri River runs into the Mississippi, rose to become the greatest power in the region for a time, exacting tribute from surrounding villages. In the eleventh century, the town boasted about 10,000 people.

After that, its power declined and its people abandoned the site; perhaps the powerful lords had made too many enemies, or perhaps a terrible drought struck, or both.

Even as Cahokia saw its demise, however, Mississippian culture spread into the American Southeast, and corn also traveled up the Ohio River to the Great Lakes, to

> Oh our Mother the Earth, oh our Father the Sky,
>
> Your children are we, and with tired backs we bring you the gifts you love.
>
> Then weave for us a garment of brightness;
>
> May the warp be the white light of morning,
>
> May the weft be the red light of evening,
>
> May the fringes be the falling rain,
>
> May the border be the standing rainbow.
>
> Thus weave for us this bright garment,
>
> That we may walk where birds sing, where grass is green,
>
> Oh our Mother the Earth, oh our Father the Sky!
>
> A PUEBLO SONG OF THE
> SKY LOOM, n.d.

Image of Community of Cahokia The community at Cahokia, at eye level, as envisioned by a modern-day graphic artist. The town was surrounded by a stockade, which enclosed the mounds, plazas, temples, and homes.

the ancestors of the Iroquoian peoples. By the time the Europeans met the cultures of the Eastern Woodlands, many of them had been part-time farmers for a few hundred years, although they also continued to rely on hunting deer and gathering wild plants. Those groups who farmed most successfully saw their populations rise relative to their neighbors. The Iroquoian peoples in particular translated this into political power by resolving their internal differences through democratic discussion and presenting a united face to the world. At least a century before the Europeans arrived, the leader Deganawidah helped them found the entity later known as the League of Five Nations. Women, whose work in agriculture was deemed highly important, had a voice in the selection of chiefs.

Pacific Northwest Indian Mask

Some parts of North America were not subject to the influence of Mexican culture and corn. The peoples of the far north, relatively few in number, survived through expert hunting. The Great Plains were largely uninhabited, for in a world without horses, their vastness and aridity seemed impenetrable. However, corn farmers nestled around the edges of the prairies, and sometimes enterprising men drove roaming herds of buffalo over cliffs to harvest the meat. Farther west, along the coast of California and in the Pacific Northwest, large numbers of people lived by fishing and processing acorns. On the Columbia Plateau, a great annual trade fair centered on the buying and selling of dried salmon. Even here, although the people had not become farmers, some Mexican influence was felt. Travelers brought luxury goods to trade, like turquoise jewelry, which had come from the lands to the south.

These northwestern fisher peoples would be among the last to come face-to-face with Europeans. The newcomers were approaching from the south and east.

The Worlds of Christopher Columbus

In the world into which Christopher Columbus was born, Europe was peripheral. Great overland trade caravans and the sea routes of the Indian Ocean connected the known world. The Middle Eastern merchants at the center formed the hub (see Map 1–1). The goods of China were in greatest demand. Europeans constituted the least powerful element of the world's trade system. Princes and merchants there longed to be able to compete with other players on the world stage, and some desperately sought ways of doing so.

The *Reconquista*

Middle Eastern economic power had spurred the spread of the Islamic faith after its inception in the seventh century. By the year 711, most of the Iberian Peninsula (today's Spain and Portugal) had fallen to Muslim conquerors of Arab and Berber descent (called "Moors" by Christians). The new authorities were generally tolerant of those they had vanquished and allowed Christian and Jewish subjects to coexist peacefully alongside Muslims. Toward the end of the eleventh century, however, dissatisfied descendants of the ousted ruling families began a concerted effort toward reconquest, or *reconquista*. In 1085, Alfonso VI of Castile retook Toledo. "Inspired by God's grace," he wrote triumphantly, "I moved an army against this city, where my ancestors once reigned in power and wealth, deeming it acceptable in the sight of the Lord." Over the course of the next four centuries, other Christian princes followed Alfonso's lead. In these years, warfare shaped all aspects of Iberian society. The priests who proclaimed the *reconquista* a holy struggle against the Moorish infidel and the soldiers who waged

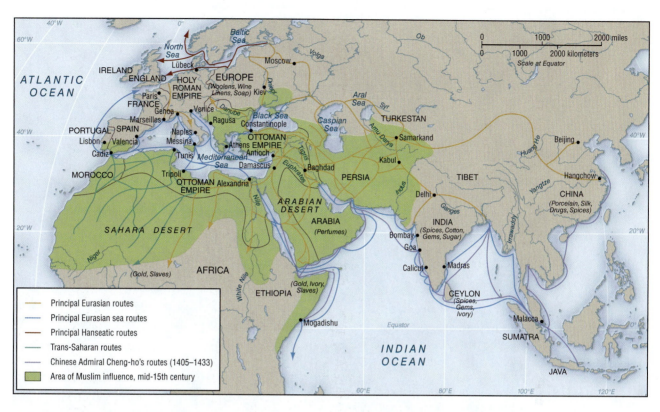

Map 1-1 World Trade on the Eve of Discovery For a thousand years, world trade centered on the Mediterranean. European, Arab, and Asian traders crisscrossed much of the Eastern Hemisphere, carrying spices, silks, and cottons from Asia; linens, woolens, and wine from Europe; and gold and slaves from Africa.

such wars were elevated to positions of prestige. The surest path to wealth and honor lay in plunder and conquest.

By the time the Italian-born Christopher Columbus arrived in Spain in 1485, the Muslim rulers had been ejected from the entire peninsula, except Granada. The 1469 marriage of Isabel, princess of Castile, and her cousin Ferdinand, prince of Aragon, had unified the heart of what would soon be the nation of Spain. Although Isabel was only 18 when she married (and her husband a year younger), she had already shown herself to be a woman of boldness and determination, and because Castile was more powerful than Aragon, she was able to dictate the terms of the marriage contract. Together, she and Ferdinand launched a final campaign against the Moors. In 1492, Isabel and Ferdinand defeated the Muslim ruler at Granada. Muslims who chose to remain in Spain had to convert to Christianity. The noblemen surrounding Ferdinand and Isabel then insisted that the monarchs banish the roughly 150,000 Jews living in Spain. Jews could depart, convert, or face public execution.

The Age of Exploration

The same energy that fueled the *reconquista* animated many Europeans in this era to attempt to expand their power. Some organized the Crusades; some expanded militarily into Ireland and others into the region around the Baltic Sea. Merchants and ambitious princes dreamed of finding a way to circumvent the Muslim traders who were the middlemen in a thriving trade with the Far East.

> This has been a marvelous thing and the most honorable in the world. . . . The dead weigh on me heavily, but they could not have gone better employed.
>
> **ISABEL**
> in a letter to Fernando, who was with the army, fighting in the *reconquista*, May 30, 1486

Mosque-Cathedral of Córdoba, Spain This building was begun as a mosque in the 8th century and turned into a cathedral in the 16th century. Note the statues above the arches added by Christian artisans.

Europe's nobility and prosperous urban peoples desired the East's sugar, spices, fabrics, jewels, and precious metals. They were dazzled by the Italian Marco Polo's accounts of his journeys between 1275 and 1292 to the cities of China. So it was that European explorers set off in search of new routes to Asia.

In the fifteenth century, for the first time, Europeans had the necessary technology to be able to travel far from home in numbers. While Norsemen had briefly established a settlement in Newfoundland in about the year 1000, it had remained an isolated event. Now times had changed. The printing press, invented by Johannes Gutenberg in the middle of the century, allowed the rapid spread of information—like Marco Polo's text, as well as valuable maps. Through the traditional international trade routes, Europeans had gleaned gunpowder (originally from China) and navigational tools such as the compass (from the Arabs). They took the cannons they had originally learned of in the East, and mounted them on ships so that they might make demands of people they encountered. The seafaring Portuguese absorbed all they had seen of other people's boats and designed the caravel, a ship that could sail faster than any previous vessel, making it possible to go farther with limited food and water.

Indeed, throughout the fifteenth century, having expelled the Muslims from their territory more rapidly than the Spaniards, the Portuguese had been gradually exploring the hitherto unknown coast of Africa. Prince Henry the Navigator encouraged many of these expeditions. By the 1470s, the Portuguese had discovered the kingdom

>> Mapping the World

Maps reflect not simply the world as it is, but also the world view of the map-makers. Like other primary sources such as diaries, letters, and literature, maps offer historians evidence of the past. Look closely at the maps reproduced here and answer the questions that follow.

World map with Mecca at the center by Moroccan cartographer al-Idrisi for King Roger of Sicily, 1154.

Medieval map of the world with Jerusalem at the center.

World Map by Francis Drake, 1628.

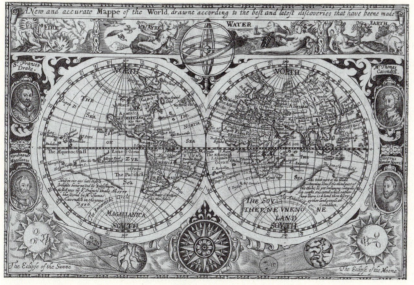

Questions

1. These maps all contain representations of Europe and the Mediterranean. What are the differences among the maps? What are their similarities?

2. What might the fact that these maps have different orientations tell us about the people who made the maps, and the societies they lived in?

3. If you were to draw a map of your world from your perspective, what would it look like? Would it be more like the first two maps or the third? Why? What would you place at the center?

of Benin (where Nigeria now is), and by the 1480s, they had rounded the southern tip of Africa at a point they named the Cape of Good Hope. This left them prepared to sail on to Asia and establish trading posts.

New Ideas Take Root

Because of the existence of the Sahara Desert, Europeans had previously known very little about Africa. Myths and stories had abounded, coming to Europe through the trade networks. Muslim merchants had established caravan routes across the desert and influenced the establishment of such states as the Mali and then the Songhay Empires (home of the fabled Timbuktu). But educated Europeans had learned from the works of the ancient Greeks that people could not live below the "burnt" zone and thus imagined that cities like Timbuktu were literally at the edge of the habitable world. It was therefore quite surprising to them to learn of such places as the densely populated, agricultural Benin as the Portuguese traveled farther down the African coast. And they were impressed to find that craftsmen in the neighboring Yoruba city-states produced stunningly beautiful items of bronze and ivory, including weapons (see Map 1–2).

However, even these kingdoms were no match, technologically speaking, for the Europeans. It would not have been possible, for example, for them to have come to explore Portugal. Because of a lack of protein-rich plants and domesticable animals, sub-Saharan Africans had turned to full-time farming significantly later than Eurasians and North Africans. When the Europeans found them in the fifteenth century, their technological power was roughly on a par with that of the ancient Sumerians of the Fertile Crescent, when they, too, had been relatively new to farming. The Portuguese thus found that the Africans were eager to trade desirable natural resources like gold, ivory, and also human slaves in exchange for textiles, metal goods like guns, and other items from the workshops of the North.

In these early years, the Portuguese sailors brought back only a few hundred Africans annually from their exploratory voyages and sold them in Mediterranean markets as household servants. They did not immediately imagine that the trade would grow, not associating slavery with Africans in particular. (The Latin root of the word "slave" referred to Slavic peoples taken in war.) In Africa, as almost everywhere on earth, there existed an ancient practice of selling prisoners of war into slavery. These slaves were mostly women and children who worked as domestics in other people's households. Theirs was not an enviable fate, but they generally were not treated cruelly, and their children were not usually considered slaves.

However, after Portugal gained control of the island of Madeira, off the coast of Africa, in the 1420s, and Spain seized the Canary Islands at the end of the century, businessmen conceived the idea of large-scale sugar cultivation based on slave labor. Enslaved Africans on the islands did not live in their captors' households or become enmeshed in ties of affection; and if they had any children, they became slaves, too. The new concept of chattel slavery was emerging. In the coming centuries, plantation slavery would strip the African continent of much of its population and bring new suffering to the Americas.

In the late fifteenth century, the findings of the Portuguese explorers led Christopher Columbus to think that if the experts had been wrong in their assumption that no people lived south of the Sahara, they might have been wrong about other things. Perhaps the globe was much smaller than they believed. It might be possible for a ship to travel west and arrive in the East before its food and water supplies ran out. And if

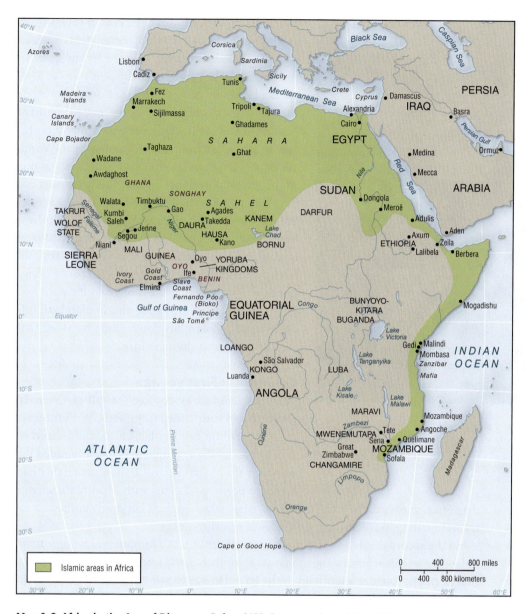

Map 1–2 Africa in the Age of Discovery Before 1450, Europeans knew little of Africa. Until that time, trade between Africa and Europe was controlled by Islamic traders whose empire extended across North Africa. In the middle of the 15th century, the Portuguese reached the western coast of Africa and began importing both trade goods and a small number of slaves. *Mark Kishlansky et al., Societies and Culture in World History (New York: Harper Collins, 1995), p. 414.*

the continent to the south of Europe was full of seemingly conquerable peoples, perhaps there was similar territory to the south of Asia. Such lands could be taken and used as a foothold in seeking the riches of the East. Columbus set about attempting to convince others of his theories.

Collision in the Caribbean

Exactly which part of the Old World would encounter the New, and when, was largely a matter of chance. In the early fifteenth century, the Chinese emperor had sent ships to explore beyond their usual routes in the Indian Ocean, but had eventually

Painting of Christopher Columbus No one knows exactly what Christopher Columbus looked like. Some thought he had prematurely white hair and a long face; others thought he had a broad face without a beard. Here is one artist's way of imagining him.

concluded it was not worth the cost of investing in expensive fleets, as the world's merchants seemed so bent on coming to his country in any case. In the late fifteenth century, Europeans were experiencing heady successes in their efforts to navigate the globe and compete with the once-dominant Muslim states. Still, there remained many obstacles to their reaching the unknown New World. We have often been taught that Columbus was one of the few who understood that the world was not flat. That is myth, however. All educated Europeans in his era knew the world was round. They also knew it was too big for their small ships to circumnavigate. Columbus was simply wrong in his hopeful calculations, which were based on ignorance. So it was that the monarchs of Spain and Portugal, and then of France and England, all initially turned Columbus down when he asked that they back his proposed venture.

Columbus's First Voyage

Then suddenly in 1492, after the fall of Granada, Queen Isabel summoned Columbus. With the wars over, she had money available and had decided to take a chance. The Portuguese had just rounded the southern tip of Africa, and Italian merchants had far more positive relations with Muslim merchants than Spanish ones did at present. She was desperate to prevent her newly unified country from falling into economic dependence on others.

In the accord that both sides signed, it is evident that Columbus was being sent on more than a trade mission. The monarchs were also clearly interested in the possibility that he might conquer a foothold in the East. He was to sail not due west, but southwest, toward Asian lands they hoped would be weaker than China. Columbus was also granted the position of governor-general of all the lands that he might conquer. Needless to say, he was also to conduct trade with China, and after deducting for expenses, he could keep one-tenth of the income from the enterprise, with the monarchy retaining the rest. The amount spent on the voyages, though larger than any individual merchant could afford, was relatively small in the context of Spain's budget; it would prove to be one of the shrewdest investments in the history of nations.

By his calculations, Columbus was sure his tiny fleet would be at sea no more than a few weeks. After nearly six weeks, with supplies dwindling, the men grew dangerously restless. They occasionally saw seagulls and tufts of grass in the water, but no land. Then, at two hours after midnight on October 12, 1492, a lookout spotted land. It was an island, and they named it San Salvador, after Jesus Christ the savior.

Columbus believed they were off the coast of China, Japan, or India. Not understanding that he had found an unknown continent, he called the people they met "Indians." He conducted a ceremony to take possession of the island in the name of Ferdinand and Isabel. When the Indians came to see the newly arrived strangers, he presented gifts to initiate trade. The people responded with alacrity, bringing cotton and parrots to exchange for what the Spaniards offered. Columbus wrote in his journal, "They should be good and intelligent servants, for I see that they say very quickly everything that is said to them; and I believe that they would become Christians very easily, for it seemed to me that they had no religion. Our Lord pleasing, at the time of my departure, I will take six of them from here to Your Highnesses in order that they may learn to speak." Modern readers often stop at this point, chagrined but not surprised by Columbus's evident condescension and the Native Americans' apparent innocence. Reading further in the journal, however, the picture becomes more complicated. The Indians did of course have a religion, a language, and a set of diplomatic understandings of their own, and they did not respond positively to everything the newcomers did. In frustration, Columbus seized a number of them with brutal violence.

Columbus and his men visited the islands in the area over the next three months. The Arawak (or Taino) people who lived there had been farmers for a few hundred years. They grew corn and beans, lived in settled villages, and had begun to weave cotton into cloth. They had no metal weapons of any kind, and their towns could not withstand concerted attacks by the Spaniards. Other Indians, relative newcomers coming up from today's Venezuela, were in the process of conquering some of the smaller islands for themselves. These were the Caribs who later gave the Caribbean its name. They were much vilified by the Spaniards due to the effectiveness of their guerilla warfare tactics. After a futile search for China, hampered not only by geographic realities but also by an absolute inability to communicate, Columbus decided to return to Spain. He traded for as much gold jewelry and wild cotton, and as many exotic birds as he could. Then he set sail for home, bearing the cargo, the kidnapped Indians, and his exciting news to an eager Spanish court.

> . . . it seemed to me that they were a people very poor in everything. All of them go around as naked as their mothers bore them; and the women also, . . . They are very well formed, with handsome bodies and good faces.
>
> CHRISTOPHER COLUMBUS'S first impression of the Taino he encountered on October 12, 1492

The Origins of a New World Political and Economic Order

Columbus was treated like a hero upon his return. Large investments were readily forthcoming, and within a year he embarked again. (He would sail two more times before he died.) Over a thousand people accompanied him this time. They were to settle the islands and from there continue to seek the fabulous wealth of China and Japan. This time, they would even be able to gather information from the indigenous people, as some of those they had brought back to Europe had learned to speak Spanish.

It soon became clear that the vast treasures Columbus had anticipated were not actually at hand. The people who had accompanied him, however, expected to be rewarded, and the queen and king who had financed his expedition awaited profits. Therefore, Columbus packed off more than 500 Indians to be sold as slaves in Europe and distributed another 600 or so among the Spanish settlers

Taino Throne This ceremonial seat, called a *duho*, would have been used by a Taino chief or priest to emphasize his authority. This one has the eyes and teeth inlaid with gold. It was found in Hispaniola (today's Dominican Republic).

of Hispaniola for them to use to establish plantations and gold mines. The level of violence increased considerably. One man wrote home with relish about a young Indian woman whom he had brought on board a ship and brutally raped.

Yet as the monarch who had driven the Muslims and then the Jews out of Spain, Isabel took seriously her responsibilities to evangelize and care for her Indian subjects. Isabel and her successors also had political and economic goals, all of which they attempted to reconcile by insisting that the Indians who inhabited the islands seized by the Spanish were her vassals, subjects of the Spanish crown. Like other vassals in Spain and its growing empire, the Indians were to be technically free, although they could be required to both work and pay tribute to the crown. Isabel instructed the governor to impose European-style civilization and Christianity on them. They were to be "made to serve us through work, and be paid a just salary," and in order to assure their salvation, "they must live in villages, each in a house with a wife, family and possessions, as do the people of our kingdoms, and dress and behave like reasonable beings." Humane treatment and freedom from slavery would thus depend on the Indians' willingness to abandon their religion and customs and adopt those of the Spanish. It is easy to be cynical about Isabel's motives, but her approach was in fact considerably more benevolent than that of some colonizers.

With the Spanish monarchy refusing to sanction the enslavement of friendly Indians, settlers had to devise an alternate means of getting labor from them. Out of this struggle a New World political economy emerged. For the first several years, the Spanish simply demanded a certain amount of tribute from the Tainos as a whole. Individual Spaniards found this arrangement insufficiently lucrative, and across the island of Hispaniola, they began subduing individual *caciques* (chiefs) and demanding that they compel their people to work for whomever the governor named. The settlers received neither land—which had to be obtained from Spanish royal officials through grant or purchase—nor actual ownership of the Indians. They possessed only the right to compel the Indians they held in *encomienda* (as the system was called) to work for them. In exchange, each *encomendero*, or holder of an *encomienda*, was to ensure that the Indians received Christian instruction and lived in godly villages. Theoretically, the colonists thus complied with Isabel's insistence that friendly Indians be made vassals of the crown rather than slaves. But although the system appeared to give due regard to the rights and spiritual requirements of the native people, they were in fact subjected to overwork and abuse even if they could not legally be bought and sold as slaves. This form of exploitation, though akin to European serfdom, was unique to the New World.

The Division of the World

Meanwhile, in Europe, the report of Christopher Columbus had touched off a veritable frenzy of international competition. In 1493, at the request of the Spanish monarchs, Pope Alexander VI confirmed Spanish dominion over all the lands that Columbus had explored and commanded the Spanish "to lead the peoples dwelling in those islands and countries to embrace the Christian religion." The Portuguese feared that they might lose control of Madeira and the nearby Azores and other current or future settlements on islands off the coast of Africa, so they complained to the pope. In 1494, the office of the pope arranged for both parties to sign the Treaty of Tordesillas, giving Spain all lands to be discovered to the west of an imaginary line 270 leagues west of the Azores, and Portugal all lands east of it. The treaty later formed the basis for Portugal's claim to Brazil, which her explorers accidentally reached in 1500. In the same period, in 1497, Henry VII of England, who deeply regretted having rejected Columbus's overture, sent off John Cabot to sail past Greenland and seek a "Northwest Passage" to the East. Cabot came to Newfoundland, concluded it must be part of Asia, and claimed it for England.

An Italian merchant named Amerigo Vespucci joined some of the expeditions sailing off to explore these new lands. In 1499, he saw the northeast coast of what we now know is South America. He still believed he was seeing some part of the Asian world, but he and his companions were increasingly convinced that these were significant southern territories—either an extensive peninsula or even a severed southern landmass—not previously heard of, as Columbus had predicted. A few years later, an embellished version of his letters was published. At the time, many intellectuals questioned whether the newly discovered lands actually fell within the Asian world or constituted an entire, previously unknown continent separating the great ocean into two. In 1507, a German cartographer concluded that the latter must be true. He published a map that circulated widely because it was the first to assert the geographic truth so unmistakably. He named the new landmass after Amerigo Vespucci, whom he wrongly believed to have been the first European to see it, and the unlikely label stuck.

Onto the Mainland

Even after the Europeans had become convinced that they were nowhere near the mainland of Asia, they continued their exploratory missions with zeal. In a little more than a quarter of a century, the population of the Caribbean islands had collapsed. The Spaniards who had arrived first divided its arable lands among themselves. Therefore, newly arriving European settlers, seeking both land and slaves, continued to sail beyond charted territories. In 1513, the crown issued the *Requerimiento*, or "Requirement," a document drafted by legal scholars and theologians. It promised all Indians that if they accepted Christianity, including the authority of the pope and the Spanish monarch, the conquerors would leave them in peace; but if they resisted, the conquerors would have the right to make war on them and capture and enslave prisoners. Some evidence suggests that explorers read the document in Latin to uncomprehending Indians, then proceeded to wage what could now be defined as a "just war" against them. The Indians learned to tantalize the Spaniards with accounts of glittering empires a little farther west, just far enough away to get the dangerous strangers out of their territory. It was not long before the Spaniards were convinced that there was a large continent to be found. Eventually, they discovered the Aztec Empire in Mexico and the Inca Empire in Peru, each of which rivaled the most fantastic images from literature and legend.

> If you do . . . that which you are obliged to do to their Highnesses . . . we . . . shall receive you in all love and charity, and shall leave you, your wives, and your children, and your lands, free without servitude . . . and they shall not compel you to turn Christians, unless you yourselves, when informed of the truth, should wish to be converted to our Holy Catholic Faith, as almost all the inhabitants of the rest of the islands have done. . . .
>
> But, if you do not do this . . . we shall powerfully enter into your country, and shall make war against you in all ways and manners that we can, and shall subject you to the yoke and obedience of the Church and of their Highnesses; we shall take you and your wives and your children, and shall make slaves of them . . . and we shall take away your goods, and shall do you all the mischief and damage that we can, as to vassals who do not obey, and refuse to receive their lord, and resist and contradict him.
>
> THE *REQUERIMIENTO*

AMERICA AND THE WORLD

>> Debating the Morality of Conquest

In 1550, Carlos V, the king of Spain, summoned two of the most important Catholic clerics in the nation, Bartolomé de Las Casas and Juan Ginés de Sepúlveda, to debate the morality of conquest before the Council of the Indies. These two priests advocated two sharply different points of view. Las Casas, whose father sailed with Columbus on his second voyage and who himself later became an *encomendero*, was convinced by personal experience that "everything which has been done to the Indians is unjust and tyrannical." Sepúlveda was an eminent scholar and a nationalist whose defense of conquest had already won him the thanks of the municipal council of Mexico City.

The two adversaries did not meet face-to-face. Sepúlveda appeared first, resting his case on the innate barbarism of the Indians. Some people, he said, were born to be masters and others, slaves. He ridiculed the argument that the Aztecs were "civilized" because they built cities and engaged in commerce. So what if they built houses? This "merely proves that they are neither bears nor monkeys and that they are not totally irrational." War against such people could be justified "not only on the basis of their paganism but even more so because of their abominable licentiousness, their prodigious sacrifice of human victims . . . their horrible banquets of human flesh." Subjecting them to Spanish rule would be the most "beneficial" thing that could be done for them.

Then Las Casas was summoned for his rebuttal. He spoke for five days—in Latin—until the exhausted council said they had heard enough. Warfare against the Indians was not justified, Las Casas argued. Instead, they could be won over by peaceful means, for they were "prudent and rational beings, of as good ability and judgment as other men and more able, discreet, and of better understanding than the people of many other nations." Las Casas denounced Sepúlveda's "deadly poison" and the greed of the Spanish, which "has led to such crimes . . . as have ever been committed by any other nation, no matter how fierce it may have been." He feared that Sepúlveda's course would, in the end, provoke God to "pour forth the fury of his anger and lay hold of all of Spain sooner than he had decreed." The Spanish must convert the Indians, not conquer them.

Although the judges left without rendering a verdict, Las Casas's ideas prevailed to some extent. Las Casas had already helped shape the Laws of Burgos (1513) and the New Laws of 1542, which attempted to regulate the working conditions of the Indians and forbade any further enslavement of the native population. His influence can be seen in the next set of regulations, issued in 1573, written to govern Spain's future colonial ventures, which were to be called "pacifications" rather than "conquests." Henceforth, Indians were to be treated gently "so as not to scandalize them or prejudice them against Christianity." But because by that time Spain's New World empire was essentially complete, there were relatively few Indians left to conquer or to pacify.

Sepúlveda argued for unlimited governmental power, but Las Casas's views were most useful to the monarchy. When Spain launched its overseas ventures, it was not even a nation itself. The century of Spanish expansion into most of Central and South America also saw the growth of national power in Spain. Las Casas's efforts on behalf of the Indians meshed nicely with the political plans of the Spanish monarchy for centralized state power. The conquistadors were attempting to set themselves up as feudal lords, with almost unlimited control over the land and inhabitants in their possession, but with only limited obligations to the monarch. In insisting on humane treatment of the Indians, the Spanish monarchs were undercutting the authority of these local *encomenderos*. In this way, as well as by forbidding the establishment of local representative governments, the monarchy prevented the development not only of a New World feudal aristocracy, which might challenge its power, but also democratic habits of self-government and local autonomy—all in the name of humanity.

The First Florida Ventures

Ambitious Spaniards set off on their exploratory missions in all directions (see Map 1–3). They crossed Central America at one point and saw the Pacific, and they touched on the northern coasts of South America. Juan Ponce de León was the first European explorer to reach the mainland that would later be called the United States. In March 1513 he reached the Atlantic shore of the land he named Florida, which he mistakenly thought was another island. He and his men sailed around Florida to the Gulf Coast, encountering hostile Indians who probably had already heard about the Spanish slave traders. On the west coast of Florida, he met the Calusas, the most

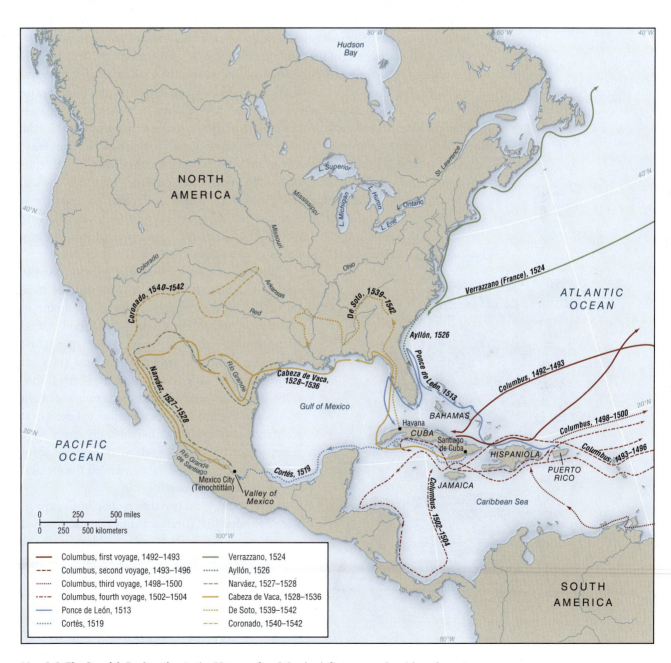

Map 1-3 The Spanish Exploration In the 50 years after Columbus's first voyage, Spanish explorers traveled across most of the southern half of the United States.

powerful ethnic group in the region. When Ponce de León returned with another expedition in 1521, they were ready for him. The Calusas attacked. Ponce de León was wounded by an arrow and returned to Cuba to die.

In Florida, the diseases the Spaniards brought with them struck the densely settled agricultural population particularly hard, and explorers routinely pillaged local villages and enslaved those whom they captured. Of the hundreds of small tribes, each with its own history, politics, economy, and culture, all that remains today are the names that the Spaniards recorded.

The Conquest of Mexico

For almost 30 years, the fabled cities of gold sought by the Spaniards proved elusive. However, the capital of a great empire really was nearby, and its ruler, through his network of spies, soon learned of the coming of the strangers. His name was Moctezuma II (later renamed "Montezuma" by the English), and he was the sixth in a line of powerful Aztec kings. The Maya states in the Yucatan had long ago declined from their former glory and now existed as relatively small, separate chiefdoms. But the star of the central basin of Mexico had risen. Waves of nomadic invaders from the north (that is, the southwestern part of the future United States) had regularly brought new blood and new ideas to the famed farming regions of central Mexico, and there they had been incorporated (as Europe sometimes incorporated the Vikings, or China the Mongolian hordes). Moctezuma's people, the Mexica (pronounced Me-SHEE-ka), arriving 200 years previously, had constituted the last wave of invaders. After several generations of jockeying for power with other local chiefs, through strategic alliances and extraordinary military bravado, they had launched the most powerful state yet known in the Americas.

Aztecs Performing Human Sacrifice Aztecs perform a human sacrifice atop a pyramid at Tenochtitlan. It was envisioned this way after the conquest. Before it had been understood as a much more complex and spiritual act.

Moctezuma's power was still growing. At the start of his reign, he had led the invasion of areas including the Coatzacoalcos region, the home of Malinche. Other ethnic groups were always offered the prospect of joining the empire voluntarily at first by paying an annual tribute. They were then left alone as largely self-governing entities. Only if they resisted did the Aztec lord bring his military might and that of his subject states and allies to bear. Great resistance was punished harshly: prisoners were taken as sacrifices for the gods, who in exchange for all they did for humankind demanded the greatest gift of all, that of human life.

In 1517 and 1518, two different Spanish expeditions rounded the Yucatan Peninsula and touched on the coast of central Mexico in Maya territory. Aztec merchants lived in the area, and through them, Moctezuma would have heard of the events. In 1519, Hernando Cortés followed the paths they had charted. He was both luckier and bolder than his predecessors. After a skirmish with the Mayas, he was given 20 women as a peace offering, and among them was the young woman, Malintzin. With her at his side translating, explaining, and bargaining for food, Cortés was able to learn the whereabouts of the

Aztec capital and begin to make his way upward into the mountains along the paths that led to the city. Messengers from the outskirts of his territories brought Moctezuma the news.

As Cortés and his entourage of about 500 made their way toward the city of Tenochtitlan (on the site of present-day Mexico City), they worked to form alliances with Moctezuma's avowed enemies, or with people recently conquered by him and still smarting from their defeat. When the Spaniards were occasionally attacked, they attacked back, sending mounted and armored men galloping through villages with long spears and torches, wreaking destruction, until the people sued for peace and declared themselves willing to join the Spanish.

Moctezuma himself probably ordered some of the attacks as he tested the strangers' military capabilities. He then sent messengers offering to pay the Spaniards an annual tribute if they would stay away (essentially what those whom he could defeat offered him). This, however, was not what the Spaniards wanted. They pressed forward, and Moctezuma decided to let them and their new indigenous allies enter the city. Politically, he could not afford a battle with major casualties close to home, and if he let them enter, he might be able to work out an arrangement satisfactory to both parties. In November 1519, Hernando Cortés and Moctezuma II met formally and exchanged ostentatious greetings on a grand causeway leading over the lake that surrounded the beautiful island city of Tenochtitlan.

For the next few months, the Spaniards were the unwelcome yet honored guests of Moctezuma. They visited all parts of the city and asked for and were given large quantities of gold. Both sides schemed to learn more of each other and gain control of the situation. Eventually, Cortés had his men seize Moctezuma and hold him prisoner. He then proceeded to issue orders to the populace through his new hostage. Not long after, some jumpy Spaniards panicked at the sight of a religious dance put on by warriors in full regalia and slaughtered all the performers. This was enough for the Mexica people. They decided to disregard the words of their king. Surrounding the building where their hated guests were staying, they moved in to kill. The terrified Spaniards broke out, but only about a third escaped. An unknown number of the Spaniards' indigenous allies were also killed, as well as Moctezuma himself.

Cortés gathered his shattered forces in Tlaxcala, home of the Aztecs' greatest enemies. While the Tlaxcalans publicly debated whether or not to continue the alliance—eventually deciding that they should—Cortés penned a letter to the king of Spain. He made little of his present plight and also made the claim that Moctezuma had voluntarily turned his kingdom over to him on the day they met and had been in Cortés's custody ever since. If that were true, then the warriors who had just driven him out could be defined as rebels, and he would be justified in bringing them to heel, which he fully intended to do. Interestingly, he made no claim at all that the Aztecs had taken him for a god. That was a flattering story invented by Spaniards many years later, a fiction that certainly took hold of the European imagination, but for which there was never any real evidence.

Cortés waited for more men, horses, and supplies from Europe and the Caribbean, and he worked actively to persuade other indigenous groups to join him. Many of these

> When we saw all those cities and villages built in the water, and the other great towns on dry land, and that straight and level causeway leading to Mexico, we were astounded. These great towns and cues [pyramid temples] and buildings rising from the water, all made of stone, seemed like an enchanted vision. . . . Indeed, some of our soldiers asked if it were not all a dream.
>
> BERNAL DÍAZ DEL CASTILLO,
> on first seeing Tenochtitlan

AMERICAN LANDSCAPE

>> Tenochtitlan

When the Spanish reached Tenochtitlan, they found a city so beautiful that it "seemed like an enchanted vision." Built on an island in a lake, and linked to the shore by extraordinary causeways, it was nevertheless larger than any city in Europe at that time. In the center were Moctezuma's palaces (including a zoo and a library), the public buildings, and huge pyramid temples sitting atop high platforms. All of these buildings were painted glistening white, then decorated in bright colors and surrounded by magnificent gardens, and all kept immaculately clean.

The society was arranged hierarchically, and the higher the status of the family, the better the housing. Nobles and the families of especially successful warriors lived in well-decorated two-story stucco homes, whereas ordinary people inhabited more modest dwellings, with those of the poorest built of wood and straw. Such houses were without any furnishings beyond reed mats for sleeping, straw baskets and chests, a few cooking pots, and the stones on which the women in the family ground maize. Each home had several rooms opening onto a courtyard, where family activities took place. Most people lived in extended family groupings—one or two nuclear families together—of 10 to 15 people. Married children, for example, often lived with the parents of either the bride or groom, or a wealthy man might have several wives, each with her own room in the complex.

Work was assigned by gender. Every woman, whatever her age or class, spent much of the day weaving. Girls were taught by their mothers how to spin and weave and how to grind corn and prepare meals. Fathers taught their sons an artisanal craft, but all young men also stood ready to go to war when needed. The heart of Tenochtitlan's economic life was the market at Tlatelolco, on the north side of town. It served 25,000 people daily, selling not only food, clothing, and household goods, but also luxuries such as craftwork made of feathers, gold, and precious stones. People sold their services, too, as barbers, fortune-tellers, scribes, and even prostitutes. Each kind of good and service was assigned its own section of the market, making it easier for customers to compare quality and price. The state regulated the market, setting an upper limit on prices and taxing each transaction. Stretching away from the market, the people of well-organized neighborhoods pursued their daily pastimes, and across the lake in the surrounding countryside, farmers tilled the soil and grew the life-sustaining corn and beans. Along the roads winding toward the city came the people of conquered city-states, either to pay their tribute or buy goods in the thriving marketplace.

groups did so when they saw additional European ships arrive. One of the newly arrived boats also brought the smallpox virus to Mexico for the first time. Most of the Spaniards were immune, but the disease decimated the Tlaxcalans as well as the Mexica.

Eventually, in April 1521, Cortés was ready to launch a great assault on Tenochtitlan. For over two months, the Aztecs and their allies fought him street by street. He kept the city surrounded as much as possible at all times to prevent its people from collecting food supplies, and he used his cannons to level the city block by block, leaving open areas in which mounted and armored Spaniards with long lances could fight with impunity against their adversaries. "Bit by bit they came pressing us back against the [city] wall," an Aztec warrior later remembered. When there were almost no warriors left to fight, and the starving women and children in the city were reduced to eating insects, Moctezuma's successor sought peace. The mighty Aztec state had been defeated.

The Establishment of a Spanish Empire

In many ways, the Aztecs' experiences were similar to those of most Native Americans in their early dealings with Europeans. An early period of tentative, even fumbling European exploration was followed by a formal, ceremonial exchange. Then came a brief time of mutual curiosity and trade, before European intentions became fully clear to the indigenous and a crisis erupted in which they violently rejected the outsiders. After a setback of greater or lesser extent, however, the Europeans always collected themselves and ultimately asserted their authority. The Indians strategized creatively and fought bravely, but they could not compete with European technology. The problem was that people who had only recently become farmers (or in some cases were still hunter-gatherers) were pitted against people who were the cultural heirs of 10,000 years of sedentary living. One side had such things as horses, protective metal armor, far-shooting crossbows, and ships constantly bringing new men and supplies, while the other side did not. The people of the central basin of Mexico had been farming longer than anyone else in the Americas, and not surprisingly, they were able to put up the most dramatic fight against the Europeans. However, even they could win only a battle, not a long, drawn-out war.

After defeating the Aztecs, the Spaniards continued to wage war against other ethnic groups, but it did not take many years to subdue most of Mexico, leaving only the most remote areas still independent and unconquered. Meanwhile, the Europeans built ships on the Pacific coast and began to make their way down the side of the continent. In the 1530s, they discovered and conquered the astounding Inca Empire (centered in today's Peru), another farming kingdom, whose network of roads had covered much of the Andes. Now the Spaniards had at least nominal control of the lands stretching from the tip of South America to halfway up what is now the United States, excepting only the Portuguese colony of Brazil.

Both Mexico and Peru were found to contain vast deposits of silver, and Colombia contained a significant amount of gold. This yielded extraordinary profits for both Spanish investors and the crown (as collector of the tax called the King's fifth). The Indians everywhere were given out in *encomienda* to work on the plantations of the Spaniards.

The plantations produced widely varying crops, but the most profitable one was sugar. As its cultivation spread, so did the demand for labor, as producing sugar was extremely labor intensive at certain seasons. The *encomienda* system could not meet the demand. By the second half of the sixteenth century, Indian laborers in sugar had been replaced by enslaved Africans. Brazil and some of the Caribbean colonies were largely dedicated to its cultivation. For the first time, Africans became yet another commodity to be transported across the seas, robbing Africa of its population and adding to the wealth of the Old World.

The Return to North America

After the conquest of Mexico, the Spaniards resumed their exploration of Florida with heightened expectations. There were several ventures, the most significant ones led by Lucas Vázquez de Ayllón, Pánfilo de Narváez, and Hernando de Soto. In 1526, Ayllón explored the South Carolina coast and established a short-lived town on the coast of Georgia. Two years later, Narváez landed near modern-day Tampa with 400 men. Battles and shipwrecks, however, destroyed the expedition. Ultimately, only four men survived: three Spaniards and an enslaved North African. They washed up on the shores of Texas. By good luck, they came to be accepted as healers and, eight years later, walked down into Spanish Mexico from the north.

The Spaniard who left the greatest mark on the southeastern part of the future United States was Hernando de Soto. He had participated in the assault on the Inca Empire in Peru, which provided him with a small fortune and the belief that more wealth could be found in exploring unknown territories. He and his forces landed near Tampa in 1539. His party of about 600 soldiers spent the next four years exploring the area, which was densely populated by Mississippian tribes, and eventually reached the Mississippi River.

De Soto took whatever food, treasure, and people he wanted in his journey. Some communities fought back fiercely, whereas others attempted to placate the invaders. The region never really recovered from the expedition's depredations: deaths from disease, the destruction of many chieftains, and losses incurred in battles made it impossible for ruling families to continue to command tribal members to produce food surpluses and build great towns. On the other hand, the resistance on the part of the Indians took its toll on the Spaniards as well. Only about 300 of them made it back to Mexico, and de Soto himself died en route in 1542.

In the Southeast, the Spanish never found the great sought-after cities of gold resembling the Aztec and Inca capitals. And because much of the land did not seem suitable for large-scale agriculture, and most of the peoples were still nomadic hunter-gatherers for part of each year—who therefore could not be given out in *encomienda*—Spain never colonized most of the territory de Soto saw. Instead, military outposts, such as St. Augustine, were established to protect the more valuable lands to the south.

Timucua Indians, 1591 Here they celebrate the defeat of the enemy.

To prevent rival nations from claiming the northern reaches of its empire, Spain did not disclose the geographic information it had secured from expeditions like de Soto's. This secrecy ultimately weakened Spain's claim to the region, however, because such claims traditionally depended on the right of prior exploration.

In the meantime, another group of Spaniards was setting out northward from Mexico City, toward the southwestern part of the future United States. They had heard tales of the Seven Cities of Cíbola, supposedly filled with gold and gems. In May 1539, a party guided by Esteban the Moor—one of the four survivors of the Narváez expedition, who had survived because they had attained the status of healers—reached the Zuni Pueblo in today's New Mexico. The inhabitants of the town no longer interpreted Esteban to be a healer; they killed him when he approached. A year later, another aspiring conquistador, Francisco Vásquez de Coronado, arrived at Zuni with about 300 Spaniards, 1,000 Indian allies, and 1,500 horses and pack animals. They took the pueblo and several others by force and later traveled west to the Grand Canyon and east as far as Wichita, Kansas, coming within 300 miles of de Soto's expedition.

Unprepared for the cold winter of 1540–1541, Coronado's party depleted the food and supplies of the Indians near their camp at Bernalillo. When a Spaniard raped an Indian woman, the Pueblos rebelled. By the time they were put down, at least 100 Indians had been burned at the stake and about 13 villages destroyed. To the relief of the local people, silver was shortly thereafter discovered in Mexico and became the focus of the settlers' attention for many years. The Southwest had proved disappointing to them; they left and did not return in numbers until the 1590s. A warning of the struggles to come, however, had been given to both sides.

The Consequences of Conquest

Some of the most important changes produced by contact between Europeans and Native Americans were wholly unintentional. Most indigenous communities needed the effort of all members to provide a food supply. Even those who demanded tribute from others were well aware of this. European demands often tipped a delicate social balance, though the newcomers did not realize it. The Europeans also unintentionally introduced new diseases that spread rapidly. If the biological effects of human contact were felt immediately, however, the consequences of plant and animal exchange took much longer. New breeds of animals were introduced into the Americas, and plants were exchanged between the Americas and Europe. The American landscape was forever changed, as domestic animals trampled grasslands and increasing acreage was turned over to the cultivation of Old World crops.

Demographic Disaster

The violent warfare that made conquest possible turned out to be only a small part of the problem faced by indigenous peoples. Although the *encomienda* system at first satisfied the Spanish settlers, it proved disastrous for the Indians. They could not produce the surplus necessary to support the Europeans in addition to feeding their own families. Besides facing the direct effects of malnutrition, the dislocation of their normal way of life was deeply disturbing, and the birthrate began to fall.

Within a few years after the appearance of Europeans, the Native American population began to decline, and the introduction of the smallpox virus to Hispaniola in 1518 hastened the process. Soon, no more than a thousand of the island's original half million inhabitants survived. Disease worked the same terrible destruction on the nearby islands of Cuba, Puerto Rico, and Jamaica. Sickness followed the Spanish and other Europeans wherever they went in the Americas, making conquest that much easier for them. Epidemics also spread to and decimated native populations that had not yet encountered Europeans.

Europeans did not set out to kill off the Native Americans, but the diseases they brought with them did just that. Isolation had protected the native peoples from the diseases of the Old World, whereas centuries of trade had caused Europeans,

DEBATING HISTORY

>> Population of the Americas Precontact

The European explorers who arrived in the Americas in the late fifteenth and six-teenth centuries encountered indigenous populations with a long and complex history stretching back thousands of years. Until very recently, scholars studying these societies approached them with Western European assumptions about society and productivity, assumptions whose roots went back to the era of conquest. Recent historians have pushed back against the long tradition of using Eurocentric assumptions to gauge precontact American societies. Anthropologist Alfred Louis Kroeber's 1939 description of precontact Eastern North America is representative of the older perspective, while historian Alvin Josephy Jr. represents the relatively recent criticism of that approach:

ALFRED LOUIS KROEBER, *Cultural and Natural Areas of Native North America*, (Berkeley: University of California Press, 1939).

We must think, then, of the East [pre-Columbian East-ern North America] as agricultural indeed, but as inhab-ited by agricultural hunters, not by farmers, peasants, or peons. There were no economic classes, no peasantry to exploit nor rulers to profit from a peasantry. Every man, or his wife, grew food for his household. The popula-tion remaining stationary, excess planting was not prac-ticed, nor would it have led to anything in the way of economic or social benefit nor of increase of numbers.

Ninety-nine per cent or more of what might have been developed remained virgin, and was tolerated, or appre-ciated, [by the Indians] as hunting ground, as waste in-tervening to the nearest enemy, or merely as something natural and inevitable.

ALVIN JOSEPHY JR., ed., *America in 1492: The World of the Indian Peoples Before the Arrival of Columbus* (New York: Alfred A. Knopf, 1992).

History still teaches falsely that pre-Columbian Amer-ica was a wilderness, a virgin land, virtually unten-anted, unknown, and unused, waiting for the white explorers and pioneers, with their superior brains, brawn, and cour-age, to conquer and "develop" it. . . . That image, leaving out the almost 75 million Indians who demographers now estimate may have been living in the Ameri-cas in 1492 (almost 6 million of them, perhaps, in the area of the present-day contiguous United States), perpetuates the myth of Euroamerican superiority. It says nothing of the challenges met and overcome by the Indians as the original pioneers, the first occupiers of a truly uninhabited hemisphere, of the thousands of years of their tenancy, of the many marvelous innovations, inven-tions, and adaptations of their societies and civilizations that enabled the Indians to live and govern themselves in America's different environments, of the distinctiveness, diversity, and complexity of their numerous cultures, developed without benefit of Western European advice and assistance, and of such Indian attainments and institutions as intricate calendrical systems, land and sea trade networks extending for hundreds and even thousands of miles, cities larger at the time than any in Europe, and political and social systems that, long before the Age of Enlightenment in Europe, recognized the dignity, worth, and liberty of the individual.

Questions

1. Kroeber's claim was published in 1939, while Josephy's appeared in 1992. How might this distance in time explain their different conclusions?

2. These two scholars have very different understandings of the population size of precontact America. Kroeber estimated that there were approximately 8.4 million people in the Americas in 1492, half of them in North America and half in the Caribbean and South America. In contrast, Josephy based his figures on modern findings. How might this have affected their arguments?

Africans, and Asians to become exposed to the microbes present in one another's environments and thus acquire some biological defenses. Without such immunities, Indians were overcome by wave after wave of European diseases, including smallpox, typhus, and influenza. Scholars debate the exact number of deaths, but it is clear that over the course of the first century, the indigenous population dropped by about 90 percent—in some places more, in some less. The psychological trauma

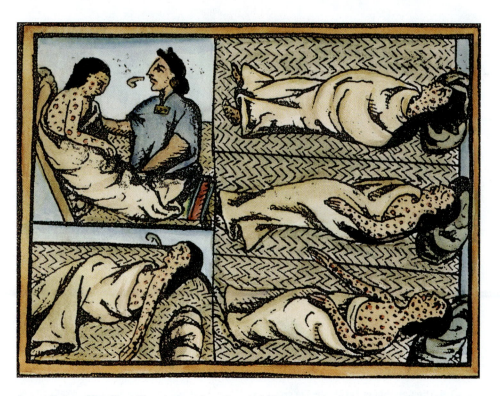

Aztecs Dying of Smallpox These images, from the mid-16th century, clearly depict the ravages of smallpox.

inflicted by such events is almost impossible for those who have not experienced them to imagine. A Cakchiquel Indian remembered the spread of a plague in his native Guatemala in 1521 that killed a substantial proportion of his community. "After our fathers and grandfathers succumbed, half of the people fled to the fields. The dogs and the vultures devoured the bodies. . . . Your grandfathers died, and with them died the son of the king and his brothers and kinsmen. So it was that we became orphans, oh my sons! . . . We were born to die."

The Columbian Exchange

In what historians have called the Columbian Exchange, plants and animals, as well as human beings and their diseases, were shared between the two worlds connected in 1492, eventually transforming them both. Along with the 1,500 Spaniards who joined

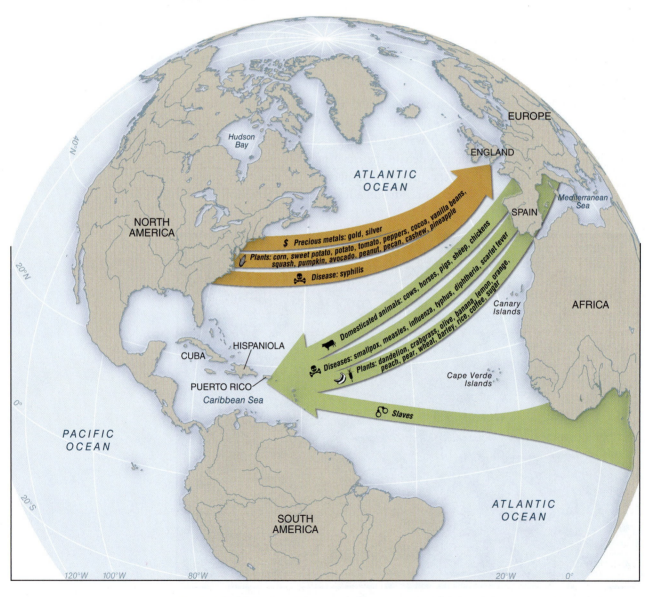

Map 1-4 The Columbian Exchange The exchanges of plants, animals, and diseases dramatically altered both the Old World and the New.

him on his second voyage, Columbus brought horses, pigs, cattle, sheep, and goats, as well as wheat, sugarcane, and seeds for fruits and vegetables (see Map 1–4). And he returned to Europe with a variety of plants hitherto unknown there.

The introduction of the new plants and animals had the negative effect of sometimes overrunning native farm fields and other ecosystems, but the new species also had some positive effects. Indians often adopted Old World life forms to their own purposes. American Southwestern and Plains Indians took to the horse, for example, which changed their way of life, making them more productive hunters and more dangerous enemies. Mounted Indians could easily kill more buffalo than they needed for their own subsistence, creating a surplus they could trade for European goods.

The Old World was also profoundly transformed by plants introduced from the Americas. Some plants that we associate with Europe came from the Americas. We might identify potatoes with Ireland, tomatoes with Italy, and fine chocolate with France, but none of these foods was produced in Europe before the sixteenth century. Moreover, the cultivation of American foods (particularly potatoes and corn) in the Old World, as well as of Old World foods (such as wheat) in the New, is often thought to have made possible the dramatic growth in world population that occurred in the ensuing centuries (see Figure 1–1).

Men's and Women's Lives

Every society has its own notion of the proper relationship between the sexes; this is one of the ways it establishes order. When one society conquers another, not only do different notions of gender come into conflict, but gender itself becomes one of the instruments of conquest. Conquerors often demonstrate dominance through rape, and the conquistadors wrote without self-consciousness of the ways in which they used native women whom they seized as commodities.

Yet not all encounters between European men and native women were violent. In many indigenous societies as well as in Europe, people were accustomed to using sexual relationships and marriage to cement alliances between prominent families—sometimes at great personal cost to the young women involved. Thus, for example, after Cortés defeated the Tlaxcalans, whose kingdom stood on the path to the Aztec capital, the Tlaxcalans presented a number of young women as part of the peace agreement. A page from a Tlaxcalan codex (a pictorial account painted on bark or paper) illustrates the ceremony. In the picture, Cortés sits on a chair, his officers behind him. In front of him is the Tlaxcalan leader, also backed up by his nobles. Malintzin stands addressing the Tlaxcalan women, who include elegantly dressed nobles, intended to be accepted as wives for Spanish leaders. The group also includes the daughters of lesser nobles, as well as some commoners intended as slaves.

Several decades later, the names and fates of some of the elite women were still remembered by

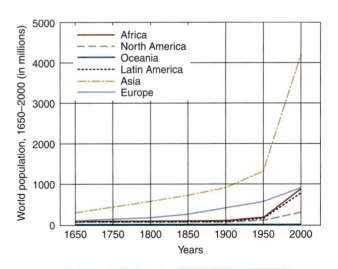

Figure 1-1 World Population, 1650–2000 These rough estimates of world population suggest the way that the colonization of the New World affected world population. The introduction of Old World disease led to population decline in the Americas, while the enslavement of millions of Africans led to population decline in Africa. At the same time, foods from the New World made possible the population increase of Europe and Asia. *Based on Alfred W. Crosby Jr.,* The Columbian Exchange: Biological and Cultural Consequences of 1492 *(Westport, CT: Greenwood Pub. Co., 1972), p. 166.*

Defeat of the Tlaxcalans Here, Malinche stands next to Cortés, receiving the Tlaxcalan women who have been presented to them as gifts from a defeated people.

both sides. Tlecuiluatzin, a daughter of Xicotencatl, an important Tlaxcalan chief, was renamed doña Luisa and became the mistress of Pedro de Alvarado, second in command after Cortés. She accompanied him to Guatemala, and although they were not married, their children entered the higher ranks of Spanish society in the New World. Many of the first generation of elite *mestizo* (or mixed) sons, including Malinche's son by Cortés, were brought up in their fathers' households and even sent to Spain for their education, while the daughters generally found prominent husbands.

This state of affairs did not last, however. Indigenous women continued to bear children by European men, but once there were more Spanish women in the colonies, fewer such women ended up married, and fewer of the children received places of honor when they reached adulthood. Nevertheless, many of the relationships between the Spaniards and Native American women were consensual. The women had few options, given the devastation in their communities, and their cultures had instilled the idea that true strength lay in survival, rather than choosing death over compromise. The mestizo population grew larger every year.

Conclusion

Within a half century after Columbus's arrival in the New World, both the world he had come from and the one he had reached had been transformed into a new, global political economy (see Map 1–5). Thanks to the decision made by Queen Isabel, Spain dominated exploration, colonization, and exploitation of the New World. The wealth that Spain extracted from her colonies encouraged rival nations to enter into overseas ventures. Eventually France, England, the Netherlands, Sweden, and Russia all established New World colonies. Because Spain (along with Portugal, which claimed

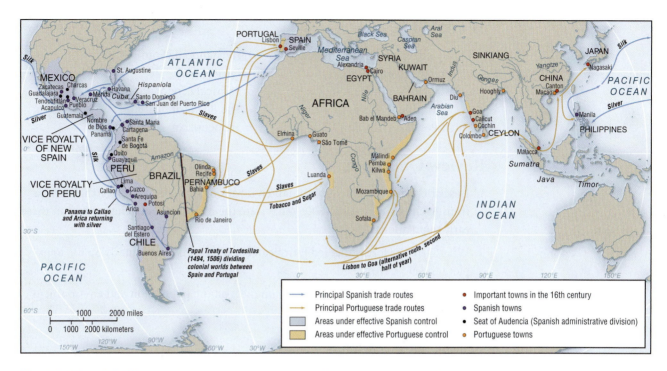

Map 1-5 A New Global Economy By 1600, both Spain and Portugal had established empires that reached from one end of the globe to the other.

Brazil) had such a head start, rival nations would have to settle for the lands Spain left unclaimed.

In the wake of the unprecedented wealth gained in the Americas, a new global economy was established, linking the Old and New Worlds. Gold and silver extracted from its empire sustained Spain's rise to power, and the plantation crops of the New World made many Europeans wealthy. Thus the divergence in the power of the two hemispheres grew wider, and Europe's power also grew relative to Asia's.

Native Americans faced enslavement or were given out in *encomienda*. As the native population was depleted and the morality of enslaving native populations was questioned, Europeans turned to the African slave trade. Suffering in the Americas was therefore intense, and yet at the same time, the people who survived learned to carry on with their lives. Ways of life stemming from multiple traditions unfolded, and cultures evolved in creative ways. The young girl named Malintzin, it turned out, had been pointing the way.

Who, What

Francisco Vásquez de Coronado   25   Hernando de Soto   24

Hernando Cortés   3   *Encomienda*   16

Malinche (Malintzin, doña   Political economy   16

    Marina)   3   The *Requerimiento*   17

Juan Ponce de León   19   Tenochtitlan   21

Review Questions

1. Describe the development of Indian civilizations in Central and North America from Archaic times until 1500. What were the major forces of change within these early populations?

2. What were the forces that led European countries, and particularly Spain, to explore the New World?

3. What was the impact of European conquest on the population and environment of the New World?

>> TIME LINE

▼c. 12,000 BCE
Indian peoples arrive in North America

▼711 CE
Moors invade Iberian Peninsula

▼1275–1292
Marco Polo travels in Asia

▼1347
Black Death (bubonic plague) arrives in Europe

▼1434
Portuguese arrive at West Coast of Africa

▼1488
Bartolomeo Dias rounds Cape Horn

▼1492
Spanish complete the *reconquista*, evicting Moors from Spain
Jews expelled from Spain
Columbus's first voyage to America

▼1493
Columbus's second voyage

▼1494
Treaty of Tordesillas divides New World between Spain and Portugal

▼1496
Spanish complete conquest of Canary Islands

▼1497
John Cabot arrives in North America

▼1498
Vasco da Gama reaches India
Columbus's third voyage to America, reaches South American coast

▼1500
Portuguese arrive in Brazil

▼1504
Columbus's fourth voyage to America ends

▼1508
Spanish conquer Puerto Rico

▼1513
Spanish *Requerimiento* promises freedom to all Indians who accept Spanish authority
Spanish conquer Cuba
Ponce de León reaches Florida
The Laws of Burgos attempt to regulate working conditions of Indians

Critical-Thinking Questions

1. Compare older ways of explaining the conquest (such as Moctezuma's supposed belief that Hernando Cortés was a god) with scholars' more recent explanations. What beliefs about Native Americans does each set of explanations reflect?

2. How would Native American men and women have experienced conquest differently?

3. Compare Spain's treatment of Muslims and Jews in Spain following the *reconquista* with the country's later treatment of conquered Native Americans in the New World. Do you think these groups received similar or different treatment? Why?

For further review materials and resource information, please visit www.oup.com/us/ofthepeople

▼**1518**
Spanish introduce smallpox to New World

▼**1519**
Cortés lands on Yucatan coast

▼**1519–1522**
Ferdinand Magellan's crew sails around the world

▼**1521**
Tenochtitlan falls to the Spanish
Ponce de León returns to Florida

▼**1526**
Ayllón explores South Carolina coast and establishes fort in Georgia

▼**1528**
Narváez explores Florida

▼**1534–42**
Jacques Cartier makes three trips to Canada for France

▼**1539**
Estevanico arrives at Zuni

▼**1539–1543**
De Soto and his party explore Southeast, arriving at Mississippi, devastating the Indians and their land

▼**1540–1542**
Coronado explores Southwest

▼**1542**
The New Laws ban further enslavement of Indians

▼**1565**
Spanish establish settlement at St. Augustine
Spanish destroy French settlement at Fort Caroline

▼**1565–1580**
The English conquer Ireland

TOPICS

MAIN IDEAS

1) Native American peoples and Europeans had distinct historical backgrounds that together explain what happened in 1492 and the ensuing years.

2) What the "Collision in the Caribbean" yielded can be understood in two ways—as a series of wars and political events that took place on the mainland of America, or as a set of changing circumstances that created a "New World" in a figurative sense.

The Worlds of Indian Peoples

The Worlds of Christopher Columbus

Collision in the Caribbean

Onto the Mainland

The Consequences of Conquest

WORLDS IN MOTION

1450–1550

EVENTS

Great Migrations Large numbers of humans migrated from Asia to the Americas via a land bridge.

The Emergence of Farming After much experimentation, some populations became full-time farmers.

The Cradle of the Americas The Mayas and people of the Central Valley of Mexico developed advanced civilizations.

The Northern World Takes Shape Ethnic identities formed in response to the arrival of corn-based agriculture in North America.

The *Reconquista* Isabel and Ferdinand forged a unified Spain in their campaign against the Moors.

The Age of Exploration European nations attempted to expand their power.

New Ideas Take Root The Portuguese established trade on the coast of sub-Saharan Africa.

Columbus's First Voyage Columbus made contact with the New World.

The Origins of a New World Political and Economic Order The Spanish created a labor system in the New World.

The Division of the World Columbus's voyage sparked an international competition for empire in the New World.

The First Florida Ventures The Spanish conducted exploratory missions on the North American mainland.

The Conquest of Mexico A Spanish expedition conquered the Aztec Empire.

The Establishment of a Spanish Empire The Spanish expanded their control beyond Mexico.

The Return to North America The Spanish attempted to conquer the Southeast and Southwest of North America.

Demographic Disaster Disease and malnutrition killed large numbers of indigenous people.

The Columbian Exchange The exchange of plants, animals, and peoples transformed both the Old and New Worlds.

Men's and Women's Lives Conquest led to many types of interactions between the European and native populations.

SECOTAN

2

Dasamonquepeuc

WE

Roanoac

Trinety harbor

Hatorasck

COMMON THREADS

>> Why did each colonizing European nation have a somewhat different relationship with Native Americans? How did this phenomenon cause the empires of Spain, France, Holland, and England to develop in different ways?

>> What did it mean for the English in North America that they came late to the business of establishing an overseas empire?

>> How might you chart the paths that each nation took toward offering greater self-determination for some groups and less for others?

>> **Don Luis de Velasco Finds His Way Home**

The Spanish gave him the name of don Luis de Velasco. His own people, the Powhatan Indians of the Virginia coast, knew him as Paquiquineo. The son of a chieftain, he was a young man, perhaps still a teenager, when the Spanish picked him up in 1561 on one of their exploratory expeditions. The Europeans often abducted young Indians and took them back to their own nations so that they could serve as translators and guides. Sometimes the process worked the other way around, and Europeans who were members of expeditions were accidentally left behind. To survive, they learned the Native Americans' language and customs. If and when they were ever reunited with their countrymen, they were valuable as interpreters. In the early years of colonization, those who had learned the ways of another culture gained influence far out of proportion to their numbers.

Don Luis did not see his own people again for 10 years. First the Spanish took him to Spain, where King Philip II asked him to convert to Christianity. He refused and asked only that he be taken home. The king, recognizing him as a fellow prince, agreed and sent him off in the next convoy to Mexico with orders that he be returned to his homeland on the expedition's return to Spain, following the winds. In Mexico, while he was staying with the Dominican Order, Paquiquineo became dangerously ill and decided to accept baptism. He was renamed don Luis de Velasco after the viceroy, who became his godfather. Unfortunately for him, the head of the order decided that such an astute young man would be invaluable as an intermediary in conversion efforts in North America, and would not let him leave. Finally don Luis managed to travel to Havana, from there back to Spain, and then back to Havana, where he persuaded some Jesuits that he would help them establish a Christian mission among his own people on the North American mainland.

In 1570, less than a week after the Jesuits and their Indian convert had settled in Virginia, don Luis returned to his own people and customs. He scandalized the Jesuits by taking several wives, a privilege of Indian men of high rank. The Jesuits had expected don Luis to act as an intermediary with his people, securing them supplies and favorable treatment, so they threatened to bring the wrath of Spain down upon him. But don Luis was being pressured by his own people to prove his loyalty. They were suspicious of someone who had been away so long and returned with arrogant foreigners who demanded food during a drought.

Don Luis had to make a choice, and he chose his native people. Powhatans killed eight of the nine people at the mission. According to Indian custom, a young boy named Alonso was spared, although don Luis apparently argued for his death also. Knowing that the Spanish would someday return, he wanted no witnesses. As don Luis predicted, the Spanish did come back. They retrieved Alonso, through him ordered don Luis to appear for an inquest, and began executing other Indians when he failed to appear. Don Luis never returned to the Spanish, and in frustration, they sailed home.

Continued

>> **AMERICAN PORTRAIT**
Continued

In 1607 the English planted their first permanent colony on the mainland at Jamestown among people who were kin to don Luis's people. Throughout the seventeenth century, the English heard rumors about a Powhatan Indian who had spent time in the Spanish colonies.

During this period of American history, no sharp geographic or cultural line separated the Indians and Europeans. Indians such as don Luis lived among the Europeans, and Europeans such as Alonso spent time with the Indians. Even before permanent colonies were established, each group thus knew the other moderately well. Although the customs and practices of the other group often seemed odd and even ungodly, they were never completely alien. By the time actual settlements were established, there were usually already people who could act as go-betweens.

Pursuing Wealth and Glory Along the North American Shore

The search for wealth and prestige soon propelled other European nations to cross the Atlantic. In the minds of European leaders, riches, glory, and power were almost inseparable. As the English explorer Sir Walter Raleigh explained, "Whosoever commands the sea commands the trade; whosoever commands the trade of the world commands the riches of the world, and consequently the world itself." Most of the North American colonies established by European nations in the first half of the seventeenth century were outposts in the global economy. Despite significant differences, these colonies all shared certain elements: First, they were intended to bring in the greatest amount of revenue to the mother country at the lowest cost. Second, success depended on harmonious relations with—or elimination of—local Indians. Third, colonial societies slowly developed their own distinctive patterns, depending on which route they followed to prosperity.

European Objectives

At first Europeans believed that Columbus had reached Asia by an Atlantic route. By the time they understood that he had discovered a new land, the Spanish were well on their way to conquering native peoples and stripping them of their wealth. Their success inspired other European nations to search for new sources of gold and silver in the regions Spain had not yet claimed. They also continued to seek a path through the Americas to Asia. For northern Europeans, colonization was not a goal for almost a century, and even then their colonies were designed primarily to provide a quick return on investment, not to transplant Europeans onto foreign soil.

The nations of northern Europe were unwilling to invest in permanent settlements for good reason. A foreign colony was costly. It involved procuring and provisioning

OUTLINE

Pursuing Wealth and Glory Along the North American Shore
European Objectives
The Huge Geographical Barrier
Spanish Outposts

New France: An Outpost in Global Politics and Economics
The Five Nations of Iroquois and the Political Landscape

Champlain Encounters the Hurons

AMERICAN LANDSCAPE:
  Huronia
Creating a Middle Ground in New France
An Outpost in a Global Political Economy

New Netherland: The Empire of a Trading Nation
Colonization by a Private Company
Slavery and Freedom in New Netherland

a ship, providing a settlement with food and equipment, and resupplying it until it could turn a profit. Spain had been lucky: Isabel and Ferdinand's risk paid off relatively quickly because they found a hospitable climate, deposits of precious metals, and, most important, sedentary farming peoples who were already accustomed to a political hierarchy and to paying tribute to others. The northern European nations could not afford expeditions comparable to that of Columbus when it became clear that the North American world was very different from New Spain in these key regards.

Northern European nations learned what they knew of the North American world by sponsoring small, economical expeditions designed to establish trade and seek a sea route to Asia. Would-be explorers sold their services to the highest bidder. John Cabot, who sailed for England, was, like Columbus, born in Genoa, Italy. (His real name was Giovanni Caboto.) Before coming to England, he had spent time in Muslim Arabia, Spain, and Portugal, apparently looking for sponsors for a voyage to Asia. He found them in the English port city of Bristol, from whence he sailed in 1497. He landed in Newfoundland and claimed the territory for England.

Soon both England and France sent fishing expeditions to the waters off Newfoundland (see Map 2–1). The population of northwestern Europe exploded in the sixteenth and seventeenth centuries, creating an increased demand for fish, and fishing expeditions to Newfoundland were relatively inexpensive to sustain.

The French colony of New France, planted in the St. Lawrence River region of Canada, grew out of the French fishing ventures off Newfoundland. Although early French explorers discovered neither gold nor a Northwest Passage to Asia, French fishermen found that the Indians were willing to trade beaver pelts at prices so low that a man could make a fortune in a few months' time.

> **It is of no value, and if the French take it, necessity will require them to abandon it.**
>
> SPANISH EMPEROR
> CHARLES V,
> 1541, speaking of France's
> expedition up the St. Lawrence

The Huge Geographical Barrier

At first, North America seemed little more than an obstacle on the way to Asia. In 1522 Ferdinand Magellan's expedition had completed the first round-the-world voyage for Spain, proving finally that one could get to the East by heading west. Other nations then became interested in finding a way through, rather than around, North America. Two years after Magellan's voyage, the Italian Giovanni da Verrazano sailed on behalf of France. He explored the coast from South Carolina to Maine and was the first European to see New York Harbor. To Europeans, however, all that Verrazano had discovered was a huge barrier between Europe and Asia (see Map 2–2).

On that "huge barrier" of North America lived Indians, some wary and some friendly. Unfamiliar with Indian customs, Europeans often could not distinguish

The Dutch-Indian Trading Partnership
The Beaver Wars

England Attempts an Empire
Competition with Spain
Rehearsal in Ireland
The Roanoke Venture

AMERICA AND THE WORLD:
Indians on the Thames

PRIMARY SOURCE:
Thomas Hariot, *A Brief and True Report of the New Found Land of Virginia* (1588)
The Abandoned Colony

DEBATING HISTORY:
Encounters or Conflict?

Conclusion

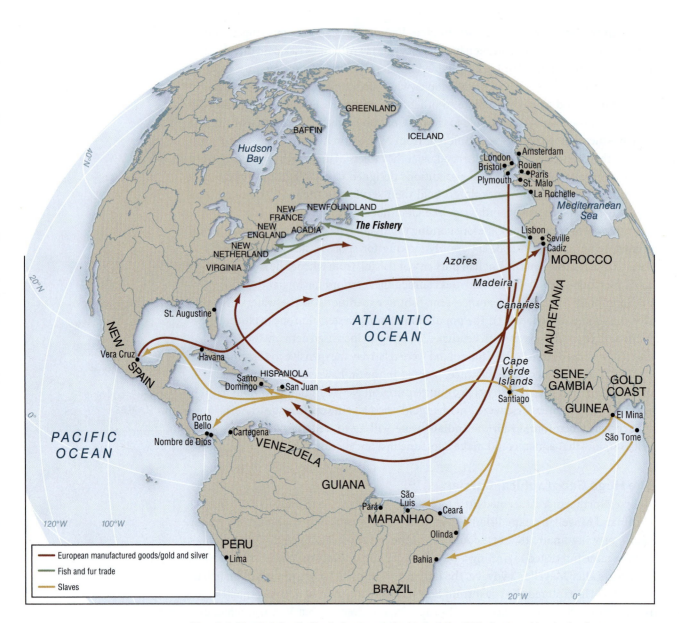

Map 2-1 North Atlantic Trade Routes at the End of the 16th Century Hundreds of entrepreneurs from England, France, and Portugal sent ships to fish off the coast of Newfoundland to feed the growing population of Europe. The fur trade grew out of the Newfoundland fishing enterprise when fishermen who built winter shelters on the shore began trading with local Algonquian Indians (green lines). At the same time, European cities sent foods, cloth, and manufactured goods to New Spain, in return for gold and silver (red lines). After 1580, the Portuguese began transporting slaves from Africa to sell in Brazil and New Spain (yellow lines). *D. W. Meinig, The Shaping of America (New Haven, CT: Yale University Press, 1986), vol. 1, p. 56.*

hospitality from malice. When Algonquian Indians attempted to dry out one of Verrazano's sailors, who had almost drowned, by setting him near a campfire, Verrazano feared that they "wanted to roast him for food." In the early years of exploration, survival often depended on local Indians, yet because the Europeans were looking either for treasure or for a Northwest Passage and were not necessarily thoughtful students of human nature, they tended to see cultural differences rather than similarities.

Between 1534 and 1542, King François I of France financed Jacques Cartier to make three expeditions to seek a route through North America and to look out for any riches along the way. All three came to naught. On their second trip, the French sailed up the St. Lawrence River as far as the town of Hochelaga (near present-day Montréal). The Iroquoian speakers there told of a wealthy land to the west. Although the Indians may have been trying to deceive the French, it is possible that the shiny metal they spoke of was the copper that the Hurons to the west mined and traded. The winter was brutal. Even with food and care from the Indians, at the end of the winter almost a quarter of the party was dead. The French found that their survival depended on the native peoples.

Later expeditions fared as badly. The region was cold and remote. The French quarreled with their Indian hosts and fought among themselves. Because their early attempts at finding easy riches failed, the French were in effect demonstrating that European profits in North America would have to rest on exploration, conquest of the

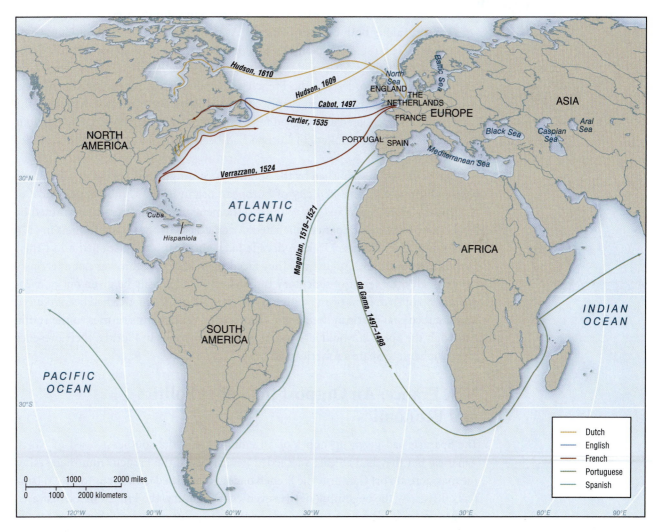

Map 2-2 Voyages of Exploration In a little over a century after Columbus's first voyage, European explorers had circled the world and charted most of the North American coastline.

natives, and colonization. Needless to say, this principle of European colonialism was gradually established without the consent of the Indians who inhabited the land.

Spanish Outposts

Throughout the sixteenth century, European nations jockeyed for power on their own continent. Because most of these nations were at war with each other, North America was often a low priority. But when the fighting in Europe abated, the Europeans looked across the Atlantic in hopes of gaining an advantage over a rival nation or finding a new source of wealth.

Soon the French and English, who found no gold or jewels along the coast, discovered an easier source of wealth—stealing from the Spanish. Every season, Spanish ships laden with treasure from Mexico and South America moved out of the Caribbean into the Atlantic and north along the coast until they caught the trade winds home. By the middle of the sixteenth century, French ships were lying in wait off Florida or the Carolinas. Because it was cheaper than exploration, preying on Spanish ships became a national policy.

To prevent these costly acts of piracy, King Philip II established a series of forts along both coasts of Florida. At the same time, a group of Huguenots (French Protestants) established a colony, Fort Caroline, near present-day Georgia. For the new commander of the Spanish forts, Pedro Menéndez de Avilés, the task was to destroy the French settlement. On a September morning in 1565, 500 Spanish soldiers surprised the French at Fort Caroline. Although the French surrendered and begged for mercy, they were slaughtered. The religious and nationalist conflicts of Europe had been transplanted to North America (see Map 2–3).

> *It seemed to me that to chastise them in this way would serve God Our Lord, as well as Your Majesty, and that we should thus be left more free from this wicked sect.*
>
> PEDRO MENÉNDEZ DE AVILÉS
> reporting to his king on the killing of the French Protestants at Fort Caroline

One of the forts established by the Spaniards, St. Augustine, settled in 1565, is the oldest continuously inhabited city of European origin in the United States. Most of Menéndez's ambitious plans for Spanish settlements, however, were undermined by local Indians whom the Spanish alienated. After attacks by the Orista Indians in 1576 and by England's Francis Drake a decade later, the Spanish abandoned all of their Florida forts except St. Augustine. They faced the reality that this was not a territory either of silver mines or of sedentary Indians who could easily be given out in *encomienda*. Spanish dreams of an empire in this part of North America had been reduced to a small coastal garrison designed to protect the far richer territories to the south. Although the Spanish would later establish other missions in Florida, their presence was peripheral to Spain's American empire.

New France: An Outpost in Global Politics and Economics

The Spanish had given up hopes of an empire along the southeast coast of North America, but they had at least succeeded in scaring off the French from there. After the massacre at Fort Caroline, the French once again turned their focus to the St. Lawrence River. By the beginning of the seventeenth century, the French had discovered the beaver trade. The pelts found a ready market in Europe, where they were turned into felt hats. A trade that began almost as an accident on fishing expeditions soon became the basis for the French empire in modern Canada. The French were drawing

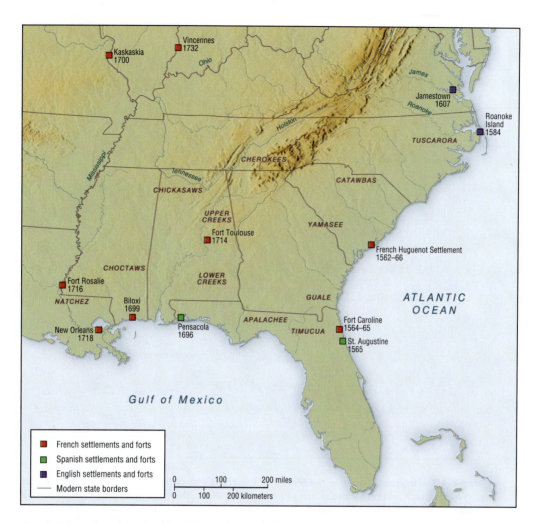

Map 2-3 European Colonization of the Southeast Beginning in the second half of the 16th century, the French, Spanish, and English established settlements in the Southeast. *Charles Hudson,* The Southeastern Indians *(Knoxville: University of Tennessee Press, 1976), pp. 430–431.*

the Indians into a global economy, a process that dramatically changed not only the world of the North Americans but that of the Europeans as well.

The Five Nations of Iroquois and the Political Landscape

The French intruded on a region where warfare among Indian tribes had recently been widespread. At least a century previously, five Iroquoian-speaking tribes living in today's New York State (see Map 2–4) had ended a period of feuding among themselves by establishing a league called the Five Nations. The members of this alliance were bound to keep peace among themselves and to coordinate a common defense against outsiders. Their new policy, combined with a relatively dense population due to their practicing agriculture for part of the year, easily rendered them the dominant political entity in the region. They made war against the Algonquian-speaking tribes living primarily to the north of the St. Lawrence, but they also attacked other Iroquoian-speaking groups and may even have annihilated some, such as the Hochelegans. The Hurons, for example, although speakers of an

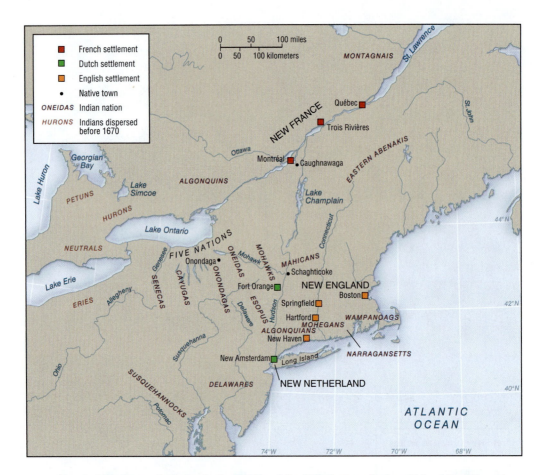

Map 2–4 The Iroquois Region in the Middle of the 17th Century By the middle of the 17th century, the French, Dutch, and English had all established trading posts on the fringe of the Iroquois homeland. In the Beaver Wars (ca. 1648–1660), discussed later in the chapter, the Iroquois lashed out at their neighbors, dispersing several Huron tribes. *Matthew Dennis,* Cultivating a Landscape of Peace *(Ithaca, NY: Cornell University Press, 1993), p. 16.*

Iroquoian language, were the avowed enemies of the Five Nations when the French arrived. Such schisms would have serious consequences indeed when the Europeans became a factor in the political landscape.

However, despite the endemic warfare, we must not imagine a world of unending violence. Casualties tended to be light, which was not the case in European wars. Most often, the goal was not to kill as many of the enemy as possible, but to take young women and children captive so that they might be adopted to replace deceased clan members. Furthermore, these wars focused violence outward. The cruelty that Indians practiced on their enemies shocked Europeans, but unlike in European society, violence or even crime within a clan or extended family was virtually unknown.

Champlain Encounters the Hurons

After Cartier's last voyage in 1541, the French waited more than half a century before again attempting to plant a settlement in Canada. They were preoccupied with a brutal civil war. In 1594, Henry of Navarre, a Huguenot, emerged the victor, converted to Catholicism, and in 1598 issued the Edict of Nantes, which granted limited religious toleration to the Huguenots. The French could once again look to North America.

The French had continued to fish off Newfoundland, sending ships to the mainland to trade for beaver pelts. The French crown now realized that extending commerce with the Indians could increase its power and wealth. Several early efforts to establish a permanent trading settlement failed, but in 1608, Samuel de Champlain and a small band retraced Cartier's route up the St. Lawrence River and established a post at Québec (see Map 2–5). Champlain, after several attempts, finally established the first French foothold in Canada, created a trading network along the St. Lawrence River, and learned how to live among people with a culture different from his own.

As the French government provided them with little support, Champlain's party depended on the aid of their Montagnais Indian hosts (an Algonquian-speaking tribe). To survive in New France they had to adapt to Indian customs and assist their Indian benefactors in wars against their enemy. Killing the enemy in warfare was relatively easy for an experienced soldier such as Champlain. Indian forms of torture, however, seemed barbaric, not because Europeans did not engage in torture—it was even a part of courtroom protocol to accept evidence elicited under torture—but because Europeans usually did not practice it against other soldiers.

Over the next several years, Champlain established a widespread fur trade in the region, linking the French and the Indians in a transformed transatlantic economy. Peasants were brought to New France in 1614 to raise food for the traders; Jesuits were sent to convert the Native Americans. The missionaries were more successful than the peasants. The persistence and adaptability of the missionaries and their ability to make Catholicism meaningful to Native Americans, as well as their encouragement of trading relationships, eventually gained them many converts.

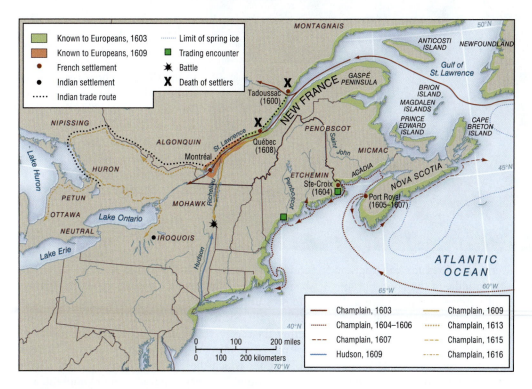

Map 2–5 French Exploration and Settlement, 1603–1616 Between 1603 and 1616, Samuel de Champlain and other French explorers made numerous trips up the St. Lawrence River and along the New England coast as far south as Cape Cod. They established several settlements, and they traded with local Indians and fought with them as well.

AMERICAN LANDSCAPE
>> Huronia

In the middle of the sixteenth century, over 20,000 Huron Indians lived in Huronia, a huge region bounded by Georgian Bay and Lakes Huron, Erie, Ontario, and Simcoe. Most Hurons inhabited triple-palisaded villages of 2,000 or so people. The palisades were sometimes 20 feet high in order to protect the Hurons from their Iroquois enemies.

The Hurons, like most of the Northern Woodlands tribes, lived in longhouses constructed out of bent tree branches covered with bark. These houses, sometimes as large as 25 by 100 feet, housed several families, all of the same clan. Inside the longhouse, two sets of racks extended along each side, on which members of the clan slept at night: children slept in the upper "bunks"

and adults in the lower ones. Fires for cooking and warmth were built in the middle of the floor. Europeans found the thick smoke oppressive, but it drove the insects away. There was no privacy inside, but people could find peace and commune with their gods in the nearby woods.

There were other village structures: sweat houses, where one went in the hope of sweating out an illness; small huts in which meat and fish were dried; and elevated racks on which the dead were placed prior to

burial. The grounds included piles of garbage, including the carcasses of dead animals. The stench must have been familiar to Europeans who came from crowded cities, where offal and human waste were also tossed onto the streets. Edging each village were the fields where the women raised vegetables, primarily corn, squash, and beans.

The Hurons, like numerous other Eastern Woodlands tribes, were matrilineal and matrilocal. Shortly after puberty, Huron men and women entered into sexual relations, which either party might initiate. The relationship might lead to marriage, or either party might move on to another partner. When a couple married, the man moved in with his wife's clan in her family's longhouse. When the marriage dissolved, which was common, he would return to the longhouse of his mother and sisters, while his wife's brothers assumed the role of male teachers of the children. Each longhouse was supervised by a clan matron, who saw to the domestic and economic needs of her group; she also chose two men to lead the clan. Because the men of the clan spent much of their time hunting, trading, or engaging in warfare, most of the day-to-day responsibilities, including raising crops, making clothing, and rearing the children, were performed by women.

Huron parents trained their children for "autonomous responsibility," to be independent men and women who were nevertheless loyal to their clan. Babies were indulged by their parents, breastfed by their mothers until the age of three or four, and allowed to "toilet train" themselves. Parents did not believe in punishing their very young children when their behavior got out of hand. One Frenchman observed, "There is nothing for which these peoples have a greater horror than restraint. The very children cannot endure it, and live as they please in the houses of their parents, without fear of reprimand or chastisement." Another observed,

"The mothers love their children with an extreme passion." Indian children prized their liberty and felt great loyalty to the group that had nurtured them.

Parents taught their children skills that they would need as adults. The girls stayed close to their mothers, performing the easier household tasks, while the boys formed gangs that played competitive games and learned to hunt and make war, sometimes leaving the village for days at a time. In this way, the boys learned to be independent of their parents and loyal to their group. Huronia taught its children to love both liberty and the collective.

After Champlain's original trade monopoly expired, his group competed with other Frenchmen in the fur trade. The French government was too busy with conflicts at home and abroad to support any of these outposts. To maintain a competitive edge, each summer Champlain pushed farther up the St. Lawrence River from his base at Québec to intercept the Indian tribes who were bringing pelts to the east. Each winter he also sent some of his men to live among the western Hurons and Algonquians to learn their languages and customs. These Indians already traded widely in corn, fish, nets, wampum, and other items. As French traders and Huron and Algonquian hunters created a trade network, each group became dependent on the others.

Creating a Middle Ground in New France

Indians and French traders accommodated each other's cultural practices. Together they created a middle ground neither fully European nor fully Indian, but rather a new world built from two different traditions. A middle ground came into being in other places in America as well, whenever Europeans and Indians needed each other and, at least for the present, could not achieve what they wanted through the use of force.

As the French drew the Native Americans into a global trade network, the Indians began to hunt more beaver than they needed for themselves, depleting the beaver population. Some historians believe that the introduction of European goods and commerce destroyed Native American cultures from within by making them dependent on those goods and inducing them to abandon their own crafts. Others have pointed out that the trade had different meanings for the French and for the Indians. For the French, trade was important for its cash value; for the Indians, trade goods were important both for the practical uses to which they could be put and for their symbolic value in religious ceremonies.

A métis (or mixed) culture soon emerged. Traders and priests learned to sleep on the cold ground without complaint and to eat Indian foods such as sagamité, a sort of cornmeal mush in which a small bird or animal was often boiled whole. Many French traders found Indian wives. Most Native Americans accepted the taking of more than one wife, so they were not troubled if the French also had wives at home. Moreover, the Hurons were accustomed to adopting members of different ethnic groups, and the French were not averse to racial mixing. Both the Indians and the French believed mixed marriages strengthened trading and military alliances.

The French were drawn into their Huron and Algonquian allies' political world as well. To keep the furs flowing east, they had to join war parties (usually against the Iroquois), finance their allies' battles, and purchase their loyalty with annual payments the Indians considered "presents" and the French thought of as the price of diplomacy.

The French and their Indian allies manipulated each other for their own benefit, and there were costs and benefits on both sides.

The arrival of the French stimulated competition among regional tribes for the positions of brokers between the French and the other Indians with furs to trade. The pace and nature of Indian warfare changed dramatically, for a new motive: control of the lucrative fur trade. Through diplomacy and the liberal dispensing of presents, French officials were usually able to quell the infighting among their allies, but not between their allies and the Five Nations. After the Dutch and English established colonies to the south and made alliances with the Iroquois, maintaining the loyalty of Huron and Algonquian allies became the major French objective in North America in the seventeenth and eighteenth centuries. Because they were receptive to Indian customs, the French were the best diplomats in North America, and their Indian allies the most loyal, but the latter paid dearly in lives lost to warfare and disease.

An Outpost in a Global Political Economy

New France began as a tiny outpost. By the end of the seventeenth century, it had increased in both size and importance. Its French population reached 2,000 in 1650 and 19,000 in 1714. In the same years, the Huron population decreased dramatically, cut in half by epidemics and warfare. The death of many of Huronia's leaders resulted in internal conflict and political instability that left the Hurons vulnerable to their Indian enemies and increasingly dependent on their French allies. At the same time, the French depended on the Hurons and Algonquians to keep bringing them furs. The Hurons operated solely as middlemen, acquiring beaver pelts from other tribes rather than hunting for them.

By the middle of the seventeenth century, the local beaver supply began to diminish. Before the arrival of the French, the Indians had trapped only enough for their own use. The huge European demand, however, led Indians to kill more beaver than could be replaced by natural reproduction. As a result, Europeans (or their Indian middlemen) extended trade routes north and west, drawing larger numbers of Indians into the emerging global economy.

The European demand for beaver coats and hats was insatiable. To increase trade, the French expanded domestic manufacturing of cloth, metal implements, guns, and other goods attractive to the Indians. This pattern, in which the mother country produced goods to be sold or traded in foreign colonies for raw materials, was replicated by England and Holland. None of these nations found either the treasures or the settled Indian populations that Spain did in Mexico and Peru. Instead, they found new products, such as beaver pelts, for which there was a growing demand in Europe.

A new economic theory called mercantilism guided the growth of European nation-states and their colonies: its objective was to strengthen the nation-state by making the economy serve its interests. According to the theory, the world's wealth, measured in gold and silver, could never be increased. As a result, each nation's economic objective must be to secure as much of the world's wealth as possible. One nation's gain was necessarily another's loss. Colonies were to provide raw materials and markets for manufactured goods for the mother country. National competition for colonies and markets was not only about economics but also about politics and diplomacy. The nation's strength would depend on its ability to dominate international trade.

New Netherland: The Empire of a Trading Nation

In many ways, the Dutch venture into North America resembled that of France. It began with an intrepid explorer in quest of a Northwest Passage and a government unwilling to invest heavily in a North American colony. Unlike the French, however, the Dutch government assigned the task of establishing a trading settlement almost entirely to a private company. And because Holland was a Protestant nation, there were no activist Catholic missionaries to spread their religion and oppose the excesses of a commercial economy. Even more than the French and Spanish colonies, New Netherland was shaped by the forces of commerce.

Colonization by a Private Company

The Netherlands had an unusual history in the context of Europe. The seven provinces hugged the coast, and the economy was dominated by merchants whose sailing ventures made them quite cosmopolitan. It had neither a powerful landed aristocracy nor an oppressed peasantry. It was thus no accident that it was home to such Renaissance thinkers as Erasmus and later Descartes. Jews expelled from Spain found a home there, as did zealous Protestants fleeing England. However, being a small, coastal territory also had its disadvantages: the Netherlands was subject to frequent invasion. Most recently, the powerful Spanish had annexed the country, and in the early 1600s the Dutch were in the midst of fighting for their political independence (which they would win in 1648). If anything, their political struggles made them even more ambitious to participate actively in international trade.

It was by chance that the Dutch and not the British claimed the Hudson River valley. Henry Hudson, an English explorer, sailed several times for the English, attempting to find the Northwest Passage by sailing over the North Pole. In 1609 Hudson persuaded a group of Dutch merchants who traded in Asia, the Dutch East India Company, to finance a venture. Sailing on the *Halve Maen* (Half Moon, in English), Hudson headed toward the Chesapeake Bay, which he believed offered a passage to the Pacific. He sailed along the coast, anchoring in New York Harbor and trading with local Algonquian Indians. He pushed up the river as far as Albany, where he discovered that the river narrowed, apparently disproving his theory about a water passage through North America.

The opportunity to profit from the fur trade soon drew investors and traders to New Netherland. Within two years of Hudson's "discovery" of the river that bears his name, Dutch merchants returned to the region, and in 1614 a group called the New Netherland Company secured from their government a temporary monopoly of trade between the Delaware and Connecticut Rivers. The profits drew other Dutch merchants to the region. In 1621 the Dutch West India Company obtained a monopoly of trade with the Americas. Within a few years, the Company established settlements at Fort Orange (present-day Albany) and New Amsterdam (present-day New York City) and purchased the island of Manhattan from local Algonquian Indians for 60 florins' worth of merchandise. The first 30 families arrived in 1624 to serve the fur trade, either by trading with Indians (the Iroquois and the Delaware) or by providing support for the traders. All profits went to the Company, with the settlers given small salaries.

> The Dutch say we are brothers and that we are joined together with chains, but that lasts only as long as we have beavers. After that we are no longer thought of.
>
> IROQUOIS SPOKESMAN, 1659

Until the Company was willing to offer better terms to settlers, the colony grew very slowly. There were 270 inhabitants in 1628 and 500 in 1640. In 1629, the Company began to offer huge plots of land (18 miles along the Hudson River) and extensive governing powers to *patroons*, men who would bring 50 settlers to the new colony. It also offered smaller grants of land to individuals who would farm the land and return to the Company one-tenth of what they produced. Both approaches placed restrictions on land ownership and self-government, and neither was successful. So in 1640, the Company offered greater rights of self-government and 200 acres to anyone who brought over five adult immigrants. This policy worked better. With its tolerant social attitudes, New Netherland soon became a magnet for peoples from many cultures and nations. As the colony grew, it expanded up the Hudson from the island of Manhattan into New Jersey and Long Island and south to the Delaware River.

The ethnic diversity of the colony increased even further when in 1655 it absorbed the small colony of New Sweden, a privately financed trading outpost on the Delaware that failed when it could not return a quick profit. The varied population of New Netherland was united by no single religion or culture that could have established social order. In most European nations at the time, social order was maintained by a combination of state authority and cohesive religious structures and values. In New Netherland, however, both of these were relatively weak. The governors were caught between the Company, which expected to earn a profit, and the settlers, who wanted to prosper themselves. Peter Stuyvesant, governor from 1647 until the English took over in 1664, was the most successful of the governors, but even he could not fully control New Netherland's people.

In one year alone, when the population numbered less than 1,000, there were 50 civil suits and almost as many criminal prosecutions. The rate of alcohol consumption seems to have been the highest of any North American colony. In 1645, there were only between 150 and 200 houses in New Amsterdam—but 35 taverns! Stuyvesant was unsuccessful in regulating either social life or the economy. He attempted to set prices on such commodities as beer and bread, but he was overruled by the Company, which feared that economic controls would thwart further immigration. In a pattern that would prevail in all of the Dutch and English North American colonies, commerce triumphed.

Slavery and Freedom in New Netherland

The settlers, the Company, and the government of the Netherlands all wanted to make themselves wealthy through commerce. This desire led to the introduction of African slavery into New Netherland. The fur trade did not prove as lucrative as investors had hoped, and the Company found that colonists tended to abandon agriculture for trade. The Company decided that the primary function of New Netherland should be to provide food for its more lucrative plantation colonies in Brazil and the Caribbean. Earlier in the century, the Dutch had seized a portion of northern Brazil from Portugal

A man of strong character, Peter Stuyvesant did his best to govern the Dutch colony of New Amsterdam effectively.

and developed a sugar-plantation slave economy, which it transplanted to islands in the Caribbean. By that time they had also entered the transatlantic slave trade. In fact, a Dutch warship dropped off the first 20 Africans at the English colony of Jamestown in 1619 in return for food. With its own plantation colonies needing slave labor, the Netherlands became a major player in the slave trade, transporting Africans to the colonies of other nations as well.

In the context of the lucrative Dutch trade in sugar and slaves, New Netherland was only a sideshow. Hoping to make the colony profitable, the Company turned to enslaved Africans. By 1664, there were perhaps 700 slaves in the colony, a considerable portion (about 8 percent) of New Netherland's population.

The Netherlands was perhaps the most tolerant nation of its day, and the Dutch Reformed Church accepted Africans, as well as Indians, as converts, provided they could demonstrate their knowledge of the Dutch religion. The Church did not oppose the institution of slavery, however. Moreover, the strict nature of Dutch Calvinism placed limits on the Church's tolerance. It insisted that its followers be able to read and understand the Bible and the doctrines of the Church.

The primary force for religious tolerance in New Netherland was, in fact, the Dutch West India Company, which saw it as necessary to commercial prosperity. When the head of the Dutch Reformed Church in New Netherland and Governor Stuyvesant attempted to prevent the entry of 23 Dutch Jews expelled from Portuguese Brazil, they were reversed by the Company.

After some early mistakes, the Company also came to advocate a policy of fairness to the local Indian tribes, with the ultimate goal of maintaining peace. They insisted that land must be purchased from its original owners before Europeans could settle on it. Because some settlers were coercing Indians to sell their land cheaply, in 1652 Stuyvesant forbade purchases of land without government approval.

It might appear puzzling that the Dutch, who encouraged toleration of religious minorities and justice toward Native Americans, would also introduce and encourage slavery in North America. The Dutch were not motivated, however, by abstract ideals. Their primary goal was profit through trade: religious and cultural toleration, amicable relations with local Indians, and African slavery all served that end.

The Dutch-Indian Trading Partnership

In the 40 years of New Netherland's existence, its most profitable activity was the fur trade. As the French had done, the Dutch disrupted the balance among regional Indian tribes. The arrival of the Europeans heightened long-standing local animosities. Tribes came to rely on their European allies not only for goods but also for weapons and even soldiers to fight their enemies.

The Indians and the Europeans were playing a dangerous game, one that required a constant low level of violence to prevent outsiders from encroaching on an established trade. Yet if the violence escalated into full-fledged warfare, it disrupted the very trade it was designed to protect. As a result, the trade frontier between Indians and Europeans was always filled with peril.

The Dutch began trading near Albany around 1614 and built Fort Orange there a decade later. This small outpost was in a region inhabited by the Mahican tribe, an Algonquian-speaking people who gave the Dutch access to the furs trapped by other Algonquian tribes to the north. The Dutch were assisting the Mahicans in their trade rivalry with the Mohawks (one of the Five Nations of Iroquois) when they were attacked—and defeated—by the Mohawks. The Mohawks, however, asked for peace: their objective was not to eliminate the Dutch but to secure them as trade partners.

By 1628 the Mohawks had defeated the Mahicans and forced them to move into Connecticut, establishing the Mohawks as the most powerful force in the region. The Dutch and the Mohawks abandoned their former hostility for a generally peaceful trading partnership.

By the 1660s, however, New Netherland was in serious economic trouble. The underlying problem was an oversupply of wampum, beads made from the shells of clams (see Map 2–6). Indians had placed a high value on wampum well before the arrival of Europeans, and the Dutch provided the tools to mass-produce it. They also helped the Indians establish a trade in wampum itself, in which wampum was traded to the Dutch for European goods. The Dutch then exchanged the wampum for furs from the Mohawks and other Indians, shipping the furs to the Netherlands for more European goods. By the middle of the seventeenth century, perhaps as many as 3 million pieces of wampum were in circulation in the area.

By the 1640s English traders in New England had cornered the market in wampum, just when New Englanders were ceasing to use the beads as money. The traders then dumped them into the Dutch market by buying up huge quantities of European goods with them. Almost immediately, the price of manufactured trade goods skyrocketed (due to their relative scarcity) and the value of wampum fell (due to its plentiful supply), leaving the Dutch with too few of the former and too much of the latter. Competition among Dutch traders increased, pressure on Iroquois trade partners mounted, and profits fell. The economic crisis tipped the delicate balance of violence on the frontier and precipitated a major war.

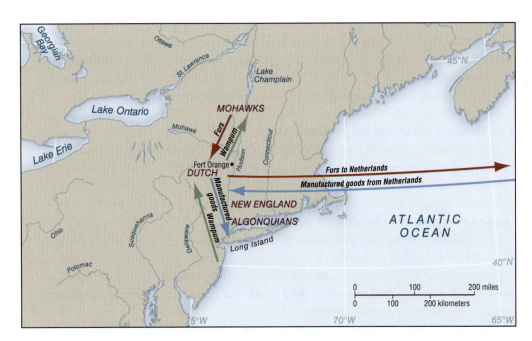

Map 2-6 The Wampum Trade In the wampum trade, southern New England Algonquians manufactured wampum, which they traded to the Dutch for European goods. The Dutch then exchanged the wampum for furs from the Mohawks and other Indian trade partners near Fort Orange. The Dutch conveyed the furs to the Netherlands for more European goods, which they traded to New England Algonquians for more wampum.

The Beaver Wars

As the Dutch economic position faltered, the balance of power among many north-eastern tribes collapsed. The Iroquois, dependent on the failing Dutch merchants for guns, were now vulnerable. Western Iroquois tribes came under assault from the Susquehannocks, a tribe to the south, while the Mohawks in the east faced renewed pressure from the Mahicans. Simultaneously, the Hurons had cut the Iroquois off from trade with the French to the north. Pressured, the Iroquois lashed out in desperate hostilities, known as the Beaver Wars, which raged between 1648 and the 1660s. They attacked almost all of their Indian neighbors and pushed the last French-allied Hurons to the west.

This warfare was horrendous for all sides. As Indian fought Indian, Europeans ultimately gained the upper hand. The Five Nations won the Beaver Wars, but their victory was hollow. Although the Hurons had been dispersed west, the Iroquois could not secure the French as trade partners. Once the Hurons were gone, the French began trading with other Algonquian tribes to the east. Although the Iroquois remained a powerful force until almost the end of the eighteenth century, the Beaver Wars marked an important turning point. The Indians were never able to replace population lost to warfare, even by raiding other tribes. By the middle of the seventeenth century, the pace of European colonization was increasing, filling the land once hunted by Indians.

Even before the English conquered New Netherland in 1664, the Iroquois were looking for new trade partners. They found them in the English. The transition in New Netherland from Dutch to English rule was relatively quiet. The Dutch had established the colony hoping to make money through trade. Having failed, they had little incentive to fight for its control.

England Attempts an Empire

England came late to empire building. The English did not achieve the necessary political unity until the second half of the sixteenth century. Between 1455 and 1485, England was torn by a dynastic struggle, the Wars of the Roses. King Henry VII and his son, Henry VIII, consolidated the power of the state by crushing resistant nobles. When the pope refused to let Henry VIII terminate his sonless marriage to Catherine of Aragon (a daughter of Ferdinand and Isabel), the king made Protestantism the official religion of the nation, banned Catholicism, and confiscated the land and wealth of the Catholic Church. Henry's daughter Mary, who reigned from 1553 through 1558, reinstated Catholicism, burning Protestants at the stake and throwing the nation into turmoil. Order was finally established under the rule of Henry's other daughter, Elizabeth I (reigning from 1558 to 1603), who reestablished Protestantism and strengthened the state. She, too, did not hesitate to use violence to subdue internal dissent, but in her case, she had the majority of the people behind her rather than against her. She succeeded in stabilizing a political entity worthy of being called a nation, but because the English came late to colonization, they found that the most profitable territories in the Americas were already claimed by others.

Competition with Spain

Queen Elizabeth, although an ardent nationalist, was unwilling to risk her treasury on North American adventures. Others, however, were convinced that a New World empire, even in the inhospitable north, could bring England wealth and glory. By the end of the sixteenth century, nationalists, such as two cousins both named Richard Hakluyt, were making the case for an overseas empire. The Hakluyts united nationalism, mercantilism, and militant Protestantism. They argued that if England had colonies for raw materials and as markets for manufactured goods, it could free itself from economic dependency on Spain and other nations. Moreover, colonies could drain off the growing numbers of the unemployed. The Hakluyts also believed that North American Indians could be relatively easily converted to English trade and religion, assuming they would prefer these to Spanish "pride and tyranie." The English could simultaneously strike a blow against Catholic Spain and advance "the glory of God." Although the Hakluyts' dream was never realized, their plans for an English mercantile empire became a blueprint for colonization.

England's first move was not to establish colonies but to try stealing from the Spanish. The English Crown did not have the money to found a colonial empire that would not immediately deliver profits, and Elizabeth I was unconvinced by colonial propagandists. Most concerned about international power politics in Europe, she was willing to let individual Englishmen try to poach on the Spanish. Her goal was to weaken Spain more than to establish a North American empire.

> **Wee found the people most gentle, loving, and faithfull, void of all guile, and treason, and such as lived after the manner of the golden age.**
>
> ARTHUR BARLOWE,
> reporting from the first English
> voyage to Roanoke

As early as the 1560s, John Hawkins tried to break into the slave trade, but the Spanish forced him out. The English moved on to privateering, that is, state-sanctioned piracy. In 1570 Sir Francis Drake set off for the Isthmus of Panama on a raiding expedition. Drake was motivated by dreams of glory and a conviction that his Protestant religion was superior to all others. Working in one of Hawkins's slaving expeditions, he had learned to hate the Spanish.

In years to come, Drake led the second expedition to sail around the world, crossed the Atlantic many times, helped defeat the huge Spanish naval fleet, the Armada, and became an architect of England's colonial strategies. He was the English version of the conquistador. His venture into Panama failed to produce any treasure, but it inspired a group of professional seamen, aggressive Protestants, and members of Elizabeth's court to plan for an English colonial empire. This group won the cautious queen's support. The success of Drake's round-the-world expedition (1577–1580) spurred further privateering ventures. He brought back to England enough treasure to pay for the voyage and proof that the Spanish empire was vulnerable. From 1585 to 1604, the English government issued licenses to privateers, sometimes as many as 100 per year. Each venture was financed by a joint-stock company, a relatively new form of business organization that was the forerunner to the modern corporation. These companies brought together merchants who saw privateering as a way to broaden their trade and gentlemen who saw it as a way to increase their incomes.

Rehearsal in Ireland

At the end of the sixteenth century, England embarked on a campaign to bring Ireland, which its people had first invaded in the twelfth century, under its full control. The conquest of Ireland between 1565 and 1576 became the model for England's colonial ventures. Ireland presented the monarchy with the same political problem that all early-modern rulers faced, that is, a set of powerful nobles who put their own interests ahead of those of the nation. Building the nation meant bringing the nobles into line.

England not only subdued the Irish leaders and their people but also forcibly removed some of them to make way for loyal Englishmen, who were given land as a reward for their service to the queen. By paying her followers with someone else's land and financing military expeditions from joint-stock companies, England made the conquest of Ireland relatively cheap. It showed a skeptical queen that establishing colonies was in England's interest, provided that the venture was paid for privately— by privateering, by charters to individuals, or by joint-stock companies.

The English conquest of Ireland provided not only practical experience in how to organize and finance a colonial venture but also a view of cultural difference that was later applied to the Indians. Although the Irish were Catholics and hence fellow Christians, the English thought that people who behaved as the Irish did must be barbarians. According to the English, the Irish "blaspheme, they murder, commit whoredome, hold no wedlocke, ravish, steal, and commit all abomination without scruple of conscience." Without a shred of evidence, the English even accused the Irish of cannibalism.

These attitudes were used to justify an official policy of terrorism. In two grisly massacres, one in the middle of a Christmas feast, hundreds of men, women, and children were slaughtered. The English governor, Sir Humphrey Gilbert, ordered that the heads of all those killed resisting the conquest be chopped off and placed along the path leading to his tent so that anyone coming to see him "must pass through a lane of heads." The English justified such acts by referring to the supposed barbarism of the Irish people. These ideas, similar to early Spanish depictions of the Indians of the Americas, were carried to the New World, England's next stop in its expanding empire.

The Roanoke Venture

Roanoke, England's first colony in what became the United States, was a military venture, intended as a resupply base for privateers raiding in the Caribbean. In 1584 Walter Raleigh received a charter to establish a colony in North America. Only 30 years old at the time, Raleigh was the half-brother of the late Sir Humphrey Gilbert. Elizabeth agreed to let Raleigh establish a combination colony and privateering base north of Spain's settlement at St. Augustine. Raleigh's scouts had found a potential site at Roanoke Island on the Outer Banks of today's North Carolina and had brought back to England two Indians, Manteo and Wanchese. Elizabeth gave the enterprise some support. She knighted Raleigh but refused to let the hotheaded young soldier lead the expedition himself.

The Roanoke expedition left Plymouth in April 1585 under

The arrival of the English at Roanoke, from a 1585 sketch by the artist John White.

AMERICA AND THE WORLD

>> Indians on the Thames

When we think about the cultural encounter between the Old World and the New, we tend to imagine European men coming ashore in a wilderness and meeting Native American people. Often, however, the encounter consisted of Indians docking at European cities for the first time. Over the course of the first century after contact, the colonizers brought hundreds of Native Americans back to Europe with them. Some of these Native Americans went on to take leading roles in the unfolding dramas.

The phenomenon began with Columbus and the Spaniards, but English colonizers also regularly kidnapped Indians. In 1530, an English captain explored the coast of Brazil (not yet firmly under Portuguese control) and reported that "one of the savage kings of the country was contented to take ship with him and to be transported into England." The indigenous man was brought to the court of Henry VIII. "The King and all the Nobilitie did not a little marvaile." The English spent a year teaching him their language, but when they tried to take him home, so that he might aid them in their efforts to profit in Brazil, "the said Savage king died at sea."

Other English explorers followed suit. Sir Walter Raleigh, for example, in the course of the explorations leading to the founding of Roanoke, ordered that two indigenous boys be taken from the Carolina coast. They were known as Manteo and Wanchese. Now we know that the latter was hiding his true name from those who had kidnapped him: the word he gave them simply meant "boy" in his own language. The two lived in Raleigh's home for two years until the expedition sailed.

Sometimes indigenous people coming to London from the Spanish world did not disclose their Indian origins. Martín Cortés, Malinche's son by the conqueror, was given to Philip II as a page when he was a young man, and in 1554, he accompanied Philip to London for his marriage to Queen Mary. He lived at court, where no one would have guessed that his mother had grown up in an indigenous chieftainship on the coast of Mexico.

This medallion was produced in England in the seventeenth century as an advertisement to the English interested in colonizing the New World. It shows an Indian who was actually staying in London at the time.

At the start of the seventeenth century, when the English became more active in colonization, interest in Native Americans spiked. In 1603 Bartholomew Gosnold seized some Indians from the Rappahannock River and had them perform daring feats on canoes on the Thames for riveted audiences. (They died of the plague shortly after, and their people were still asking angrily about them when John Smith arrived in their country.) In *The Tempest*, Shakespeare has one character complain of others' selfishness: "When they will not give a doit [a coin] to a lame beggar, they will lay out ten to see a dead Indian." And in *Henry VIII* (1613), a man responds to the sight of a gathering mob by saying, "Have we some Indian with the great tool come to court, the women so besiege us?" When Pocahontas came to London in 1616, she was the talk of the town, and the Virginia Company used her presence to secure investments.

In 1614, an English explorer of the Massachusetts coast seized about 14 Indians to sell in Spain. One of them was later taken to London, working for a shipbuilder. He traveled to Newfoundland with some fishermen, back to London, and then in 1619 sailed with a captain planning to go farther south, to New England. This was Tisquantum, known as "Squanto." No wonder the Pilgrims were greeted by an Indian saying very distinctly, in English, "Welcome."

It is easy to imagine the agonizing loneliness of these Indians and to be angry at the ways in which they were being used. (If only they had left us diaries and letters!) But we must remember that they also took action and made choices that sometimes had significant consequences. Some of the indigenous in Spain came to know religious men who later advocated for them, and the behavior of don Luis helped convince Spanish authorities that it was worthless to attempt to colonize North America. Wanchese harbored rage against the English and, once home, was instrumental in leading his people away from an alliance, thereby contributing to the destruction of the colony at Roanoke. Pocahontas died in England, but one of her father's advisers accompanied her on the trip. He returned home to warn his countrymen of the danger they faced and to encourage a great rebellion against Jamestown that later followed. Squanto offered his services to the Pilgrims in order to benefit his own clan, but in doing so, he also ensured the colony's survival.

These people were undoubtedly impressed by what they saw in Europe, but they were far from overwhelmed by it. Instead, they used their knowledge to strategize about how best to react to the Europeans.

the command of Sir Richard Grenville, an aristocrat who had fought in Ireland. Half of the crew of 600 were probably recruited or impressed (i.e., forcibly seized) from the unemployed poor of Britain. Little value was attached to their lives. When one of the ships separated from the fleet and found its supplies running low, 20 men were dropped off at Jamaica—only 2 of whom were ever heard from again—and another 32 were later left on an island in the Outer Banks.

Roanoke was a poor port, dangerous for small ships and inadequate for larger ones. When the primary ship was almost wrecked and a major portion of the food supply lost, Grenville's fleet departed for England. Colonel Ralph Lane, another veteran of war in Ireland, was left in charge as governor. He was supposed to look for a better port, build a fort, and find food for the 100 men left under his command.

Roanoke was established to gain an advantage over the treasure-filled Spanish ships traveling back to Spain. The men left on the island prepared for an attack by Spain and pointed the fort's guns out to sea. Raleigh intended to send another supply ship that summer, but the queen insisted he sail instead to Newfoundland to warn the English there about a probable sea war with Spain. The first settlers of Roanoke were ill equipped to build a self-sustaining

Watercolor of an Algonquian Village by John White Much of what we know about Algonquian life at the time of the Roanoke expedition comes from the paintings of John White, who was a member of the expedition. Here we see a small village, surrounded by a tall stockade.

>> Thomas Hariot, *A Brief and True Report of the New Found Land of Virginia* (1588)

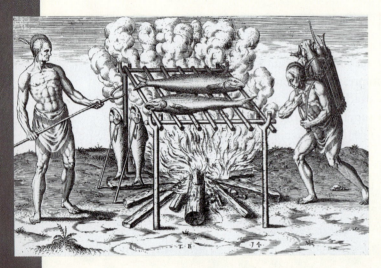

Thomas Hariot (1560–1621) was one of England's most versatile scientists and linguists. When still a young man, he was selected by Sir Walter Raleigh to join the first Virginia Company settlers in 1585. They traveled to Roanoke Island and built a fort and trading post to stake England's claim to the area. Raleigh also hoped that the settlement would trade profitably with the Indians. Because Hariot had taken the time to begin to learn some of the local language, his Report was the first largely accurate account of Indian life in the region. He wrote for the company's investors, but also with the intent to publish. Indeed, the European public was so keen to hear news of the New World that the book became a best seller by sixteenth-century standards.

* Editor's Note: The editor of this source has left it in the original language so that you can see for yourself the ways in which the use of English has and has not changed.

Wiróans or chiefe Lorde—Here we see Hariot struggling to explain a style of government that did not involve "kings," and yet sometimes included high chiefs who ruled over multiple villages.

This is the kind of observation that only a person taking down linguistic evidence very carefully could make. As readers, we can begin to trust Hariot.

In some places of the countrey one onely towne belongeth to the gouernment of a *Wiróans* or chiefe Lorde; in other some two or three, in some sixe, eight, & more; the greatest *Wiróans* that yet we had dealing with had but eighteene townes in his gouernment, and able to make not aboue seuen or eight hundred fighting men at the most: The language of euery gouernment is different from any other, and the farther they are distant the greater is the difference.

Their maner of warres amongst themselues is either by sudden surprising one an other most cõmonly about the dawning of the day, or moone light; or els by ambushes, or some suttle deuises: Set battels are very rare, except it fall out where there are many trees, where eyther part may haue some hope of defence, after the deliuerie of euery arrow, in leaping behind some or other.

Hariot seems eager to demonstrate the limits of the people's ability to resist conquest. It seems likely that this was one of Raleigh's largest concerns.

In Europe, pitched battles had become widespread and deadly for entire regions of countries because they were waged to destroy the enemy. Indian warfare was far more limited.

In other places, Europeans had learned that the Indians had no choice but to flee in the face of guns. Still, do you think Hariot may be overly optimistic here in speaking of the ease of conquest?

The English hoped to trade European tools, clothing, and ornaments in return for food, animal pelts, and, hopefully, gold.

What might Hariot mean by "means of good government"? Is he hoping for benevolence on the part of the English toward dependents? Or does he envision a full democracy?

If there fall out any warres between vs & them, what their fight is likely to bee, we hauing aduantages against them so many maner of waies, as by our discipline, our strange weapons and deuises els; especially by ordinance great and small, it may be easily imagined; by the experience we haue had in some places, the turning vp of their heeles against vs in running away was their best defence.

In respect of vs they are a people poore, and for want of skill and iudgement in the knowledge and vse of our things, doe esteeme our trifles before thinges of greater value: Notwithstanding in their proper manner considering the want of such meanes as we haue, they seeme very ingenious; For although they haue no such tooles, nor any such craftes, sciences and artes as wee; yet in those thinges they doe, they shewe excellencie of wit. And by howe much they vpon due consideration shall finde our manner of knowledges and craftes to exceede theirs in perfection, and speed for doing or execution, by so much the more is it probable that they shoulde desire our friendships & loue, and haue the greater respect for pleasing and obeying vs. Whereby may bee hoped if meanes of good gouernment bee vsed, that they may in short time be brought to ciuilitie, and the imbracing of true religion.

Some religion they haue already, which although it be farre from the truth, yet beyng as it is, there is hope it may bee the easier and sooner reformed. They beleeue that there are many Gods which they call *Montóac*, but of different sortes and degrees; one onely chiefe and great God, which hath bene from all eternitie. . . .

How do you think Hariot defines poverty? After all, the Indians were not hungry.

Hariot distinguishes between the possession of technology and intelligence. He has recognized keen minds among the people he has met and hopes they will accept English ways.

After briefly mentioning the Indians' belief in many gods, Hariot focuses on the aspects of Indian religion that resemble Christianity. Why might he do so?

Questions

1. What words does Hariot use to describe the Indians, and what impression do these words create for Hariot's readers?

2. What issues concern Hariot in this excerpt? Why do you think they matter to him? How do you think the reasons for Hariot's report influenced its content? Do you think this report would make the queen and other potential investors more or less likely to sponsor this colonial venture?

3. Having put the report in the context of Hariot's own perspective, what can you nevertheless learn from this passage about Native American life in the Roanoke area?

*A cheife Heroroans wyfe of Pomeoc.
and her daughter of the age of. 8. or.
10. yeares.*

Portrait of an Algonquian Mother and Child by John White This beautiful picture illustrates the indulgence of Algonquian mothers and the sensitivity of the English artist who painted this one.

colony. Half soldiers and gentlemen and half undisciplined and impoverished young men, no one knew how to build or support a town. Unable to find gold or provide for themselves, the colonists turned to the local Roanoke Indians (an Algonquian-speaking tribe), whom they soon alienated.

The Roanokes were familiar with Europeans through their contacts with the Spanish and through the stories of Wanchese, who had run away from the English and returned home. They were ready to trade with them. However, the English need for more food than the natives could easily supply led to tensions. Thinking that an Indian had stolen a silver cup, the English retaliated by burning an empty village and the surrounding cornfields, which fed both Indians and English. The Indians had to balance the benefits of trade against the costs of English aggression. After a failed ambush attempt, the Roanokes decided to withdraw from Roanoke Island, leaving the English to starve. When Lane learned of this plan, he attacked the Indians, beheading their chieftain Wingina. Indian-English relations deteriorated further, and Wanchese became an avowed enemy.

Not all the colonists, however, treated the Roanokes as an enemy to be conquered. Much of what we know about the Roanoke Colony and its Indian neighbors is due to the work of two sympathetic colonists. John White, a painter, and Thomas Hariot, who later became a great mathematician, were sent to survey the region and describe its inhabitants and natural features. Their illustrations, maps, and descriptions provide the most accurate information that we have about the people of this region before the arrival of large numbers of Europeans.

By June 1585, it was clear that Roanoke had failed in its mission. When Drake and his fleet appeared on their way back from a looting expedition in the Caribbean, the colonists decided to return to England, leaving behind only 15 men.

Yet the English advocates of colonization were not ready to give up. The original plan for a military-style base had failed, but a new vision of colonization would now be tried. Raleigh's commitment was lukewarm, for Roanoke had already cost £30,000 without returning a cent. John White, the painter, remained enthusiastic and assembled a group of settlers. It included 110 people—men, women, and children—who were prepared to raise their own crops, and also one loyal Roanoke Indian, Manteo. In exchange for their investment, Raleigh granted each man 500 acres of land. The new expedition arrived in July 1587. The second attempt to establish a colony at Roanoke was probably doomed by the poisoned relations with the Indians. White soon found that the 15 men who had remained had been attacked by Roanokes. As the survival of the colony now depended on support from England, the colonists, who included White's daughter and granddaughter, sent White back to act as their agent in England. No European ever saw any of the colonists again.

The Abandoned Colony

No one had planned to abandon the little colony. Raleigh assembled a supply fleet the next spring, but a sea war looming with the Spanish Armada prevented it from leaving. Finally, in August 1590, after the Armada had been defeated, White arrived in Roanoke only to find everyone gone. There were signs of an orderly departure, and the word CROATOAN, Manteo's home island, was carved in a post. White assumed that was where the group had gone. Short of water and with a storm brewing, the fleet decided to put out to sea and return the next year. They never got there.

The colony of Roanoke was not "lost," as legend usually puts it; it was abandoned. Serving no useful economic or military purpose, the people of Roanoke were entirely expendable. John White could not obtain the help of backers and seems to have died shortly thereafter. Raleigh and Queen Elizabeth soon after had a falling out, and he was placed under arrest. After he was released, he did send at least one search party, but no one was ever found. In 1603, Queen Elizabeth died, and her successor, James I, had Raleigh arrested as a traitor in his efforts to make peace with Spain.

What happened to the abandoned colonists? In 1607, the English returned to the region, establishing a permanent colony at Jamestown, on the Chesapeake. In 1608, Englishmen heard that many Roanoke colonists had made their way up to Virginia and settled among the friendly Chesapeake Indians before being attacked by the Powhatans. In fact, over the next two generations, there were numerous reports of sightings of people with "perfect yellow hair" or "white skin" at various places. One scholar has mapped these purported appearances and finds that a good number fall along a well-known trading path. This makes perfect sense. The seminomadic Algonquian-speaking people who either attacked the colonists or absorbed them peacefully would never have been able to keep such a large group together. The vulnerable newcomers would have been immediately dispersed, just like any other large group of prisoners or starving migrants, and traded along well-worn routes. Theories abound about the fate of the colonists, but this is the only one that has common sense and the realities of Native American life on its side.

The English were beginning to learn that they could not rely on the Indians for food. Unlike the Spanish, they had not found densely settled farming communities who were accustomed to paying tribute. As a result, the English colonies would have to grow their own food. Consequently, the history of the English in North America would by and large be that of the growth of the English population (augmented by Africans and other European immigrants) and the steady decline of the original inhabitants.

DEBATING HISTORY

>> Encounters or Conflict?

As European powers established North American colonies in the seventeenth and eighteenth centuries and integrated them into their growing empires, they brought Native American societies more fully into the European market economy and the broader global economy. This long-term, impersonal process broke up the traditional balance among Indian tribes in North America and created diverse relationships between Indians and Europeans. The terms of these relationships were never clear and varied from region to region. While violence flared up often between Europeans and Indians, both sides generally worked to minimize conflict in the hopes of accelerating commercial trade. The French explorers in the Great Lakes region, for example, often quarreled with the Hurons, yet worked with them to dominate the local fur trade. Farther south in New Netherland, the Dutch entered into the wampum exchange in an effort to facilitate the fur trade there. Historians have disagreed about the nature of European-Indian interaction in the era of colonial expansion. Francis Jennings argued that the indigenous people were victimized by hypocritical Europeans who used violence whenever it was expedient, whereas Richard White has envisioned indigenous people as having far more room for negotiation.

FRANCIS JENNINGS, *The Invasion of America: Indians, Colonialism, and the Cant of Conquest* (Chapel Hill: University of North Carolina Press, 1975), pp. 32, 105.

[The Europeans'] common purpose was to exploit rather than to settle. . . . Regularly the Europeans were welcomed by natives with gifts of food and tokens of honor until the moment came when the gifts were demanded as tribute and the honors were commanded as homage—a moment that sometimes came very rapidly. At the outset native hostility was never directed against European settlement as such; what made trouble was the European purpose of settling on top. . . . Europeans used a great variety of means to attain mastery [over Indians], of which armed combat was only one. Alternative means were adjusted to definable, attainable, and gainful goals. In sum and in time these goals, along with their unplanned accomplishments, added to conquest by Europeans generally over Indians generally, but along the way to the epochal climax specific situations required particular Europeans to cooperate with particular Indians. . . . [Still,] the Europeans pressed to turn alliance into clientage and clientage into subjection, with variable success. . . . Sooner or later the "natural" subjection of the Indians was to be translated into formal subjection. For Europeans the issue was not whether they should rule, but which of them should do it.

RICHARD WHITE, *The Middle Ground: Indians, Empires, and Republics in the Great Lakes Region, 1650–1815* (New York: Cambridge University Press, 1991), pp. ix–x.

Contact was not a battle of primal forces in which only one could survive. Something new could appear . . . [Indians and Europeans sought] accommodation and common meaning. . . . Europeans and Indians met and regarded each other as alien, as other, as virtually nonhuman . . . , [but] over the next two centuries, they constructed a common, mutually comprehensible world [and] created new systems of meaning and of exchange. . . . The process of accommodation [took place] on what I call the middle ground. The middle ground is the place in between: in between cultures, peoples, and in between empires and the nonstate world of villages. It is a place where many of the North American subjects and allies of empire lived. It is the area between the historical foreground of European invasion and occupation and the background of Indian defeat and retreat. . . . On the middle ground diverse peoples adjust their differences through what amounts to a process of creative, and often expedient, misunderstandings. People try to persuade others who are different from themselves by appealing to what they perceive to be the values and practices of those others. They often misinterpret and distort both the values and the practices of those they deal with, but from these misunderstandings arise new meanings and through them new practices—the shared meanings and practices of the middle ground. . . . This accommodation took place because for long periods of time in large parts of the colonial world whites could neither dictate to Indians nor ignore them. Whites needed Indians as allies, as partners in exchange, as sexual partners, as friendly neighbors.

Questions

1. Both historians recognize that a degree of cooperation between Indians and Europeans took place in this period. What role does cooperation play in each historian's argument, and how are they different?

2. Richard White focused primarily on the Indian-French relations of the Great Lakes region. How might this have affected his argument and his differences with Francis Jennings, who focused on early interactions along the coast?

Conclusion

European nations established colonies to achieve a political or economic advantage over their rivals. Most of these nations had only recently been unified by force, an experience that gave them the energy to establish colonies and a military model they could use for colonization. The distinctive domestic history of each nation, however, shaped its relations with the Indians it encountered, just as the distinctive societies of the Indian nations shaped their interactions with Europeans. The Spanish came prepared for a new *reconquista*, and the crown helped sponsor well-armed forces in the New World. There they found large, highly organized groups of native peoples, who had amassed treasure and were accustomed to working for others. The French found no such peoples, but they learned that the Indians there were expert providers of beaver pelts. Rather than uselessly attempting to conquer the nomadic and semi-nomadic hunters, they worked on establishing alliances to guarantee the trade and became entangled in the Indians' own conflicts. The Dutch, experienced as merchants, also recognized that the goodwill of the Indians was vital for a flourishing trade, and their businessmen worked to make New Amsterdam a crossroads in the international beaver economy. The English, like the Dutch, arrived on the scene late, but rather than joining the northern beaver economy as merchant traders, they still dreamed of competing with Spain in the warmer climes. They did so largely by preying on Spanish

ships. The English thought it would be relatively easy to convince the Indians to grow food for them, as the Spanish had done, but they had misunderstood the nature of the societies they were dealing with.

Out of these different interactions between natives and newcomers, a North Atlantic political economy began to emerge, shaped by the forces of trade and the quest for power. Europeans, Indians, and eventually Africans were drawn into a global economy in which the nations of the world competed for advantage. The early years of American colonial history were shaped by impersonal forces that built empires and subjugated peoples. But they were also shaped by individuals. Some set out to find new worlds, whereas others were forced into them. Captives such as don Luis de Velasco, Wanchese, and Manteo; explorers such as Jacques Cartier and Henry Hudson; soldiers such as Sir Francis Drake and Samuel de Champlain; the poor dragooned into sailing for Roanoke and left there to die; and Huron women who married French traders: all of them left their mark on the New World, even before the English planted their first permanent colonies in North America.

Who, What

Jacques Cartier   41

Samuel de Champlain   45

Sir Francis Drake   54

Walter Raleigh   38

Joint-stock company   54

Mercantilism   48

Privateering   54

Wampum   52

>> TIME LINE

▼1275–1292
Marco Polo travels in Asia

▼1400–1600
Five Iroquois nations create the Great League of Peace

▼1455–1485
War of the Roses in England

▼1497
John Cabot arrives in North America

▼1519–1522
Magellan expedition sails around the world for Spain

▼1522
Giovanni da Verrazano explores North American coast for France

▼1534–1542
Jacques Cartier makes three trips to Canada for France

▼1561
Spanish abduct don Luis de Velasco

▼1562
John Hawkins tries to break into the slave trade

▼1565
Spanish establish settlement at St. Augustine
Spanish destroy French settlement at Fort Caroline

▼1565–1576
The English conquer Ireland

▼1570
Don Luis de Velasco returns home to Virginia

▼1577–1580
Francis Drake sails around the world for England

▼1584
Walter Raleigh receives charter to establish colony at Roanoke

▼1585
First settlement at Roanoke established

Review Questions

1. What were the key European objectives in exploring North America in this period? To what extent did England, France, and the Netherlands achieve their objectives?

2. What do we know about the precontact history of the Five Nations of Iroquois? How did this history affect the world of colonial America? How did the European colonial ventures affect the Iroquois?

3. What was the "middle ground," and how was it created?

Critical-Thinking Questions

1. What were the ramifications of the northern Europeans failing to find cities equivalent to Tenochtitlan anywhere in North America?

2. Did the English, French, and Dutch have profoundly different attitudes toward the Indians at the outset? If the English had been the ones to spearhead the beaver trade, do you think that English traders and trappers might have married Huron women?

3. Early on, the Dutch faced the need to democratize their colony to some extent. Did other colonies of the era face a similar need? Why or why not?

> **For further review materials and resource information, please visit www.oup.com/us/ofthepeople**

▼**1587**
Second attempt to found colony at Roanoke

▼**1590**
English settlers at Roanoke have disappeared

▼**1607**
English establish permanent colony at Jamestown

▼**1608**
Samuel de Champlain establishes a fort at Quebec

▼**1609**
Henry Hudson arrives at New York, sailing for the Netherlands

▼**1614**
Dutch begin trading in Albany region
French settlers arrive in New France

▼**1621**
Dutch West India Company established

▼**1624**
First Dutch families arrive at Manhattan

▼**1648–1660s**
Beaver Wars fought

▼**1664**
English take over New Amsterdam

MAIN IDEAS

1) France was the first nation to demonstrate what the northern Europeans could and could not accomplish in America. The active Indian trade in New France inspired the Dutch to found a colony dependent on that trade.

2) While the English persisted longer in efforts to compete with or prey upon the Spanish, eventually they, too, joined the Indian trade. They started by taking over the Dutch colony and share of the trade.

TOPICS

Pursuing Wealth and Glory Along the North American Shore

New France: An Outpost in Global Politics and Economics

New Netherland: The Empire of a Trading Nation

England Attempts an Empire

EVENTS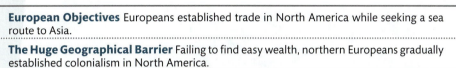

European Objectives Europeans established trade in North America while seeking a sea route to Asia.

The Huge Geographical Barrier Failing to find easy wealth, northern Europeans gradually established colonialism in North America.

Spanish Outposts Spain's efforts to establish North American colonies were hampered by the Indians and other Europeans.

The Five Nations of Iroquois and the Political Landscape Five Indian tribes formed an alliance before the French arrived in North America.

Champlain Encounters the Hurons France established small settlements in Canada and began trading with the Indians.

Creating a Middle Ground in New France A mixed culture emerged as the French and Indians interacted.

An Outpost in a Global Political Economy European nations competed to dominate international trade, and Indians joined the global economy.

Colonization by a Private Company The Dutch established an ethnically diverse colony in North America.

Slavery and Freedom in New Netherland The desire for wealth led to the introduction of African slavery into New Netherland.

The Dutch-Indian Trading Partnership The lucrative Dutch fur trade caused competition and violence among Indian tribes.

The Beaver Wars Indian tribes' warfare over access to Dutch trade made them vulnerable to intruding Europeans and decimated their populations.

Competition with Spain Lacking money to start their own colonies, the British entered the New World by stealing from the Spanish.

Rehearsal in Ireland The conquest of Ireland became the model for England's colonial ventures.

The Roanoke Venture The English made two ill-fated attempts to establish a colony in North America.

The Abandoned Colony The English returned to Roanoke to find it abandoned. The fate of the colonists remains unknown.

CHAPTER

3

...gure of the Indians fort or Palizado in
...W ENGLAND
...e maner of the deftroying
...Captayne Vnde...
...aptayne M...

Hear enttera Captayne Vnderhill

Their Streets

The Indians houses

Hear Enttera Captayne Majon

COMMON THREADS

>> After the failure at Roanoke, how were the English finally able to plant successful colonies?

>> Why did the Jamestown Colony almost fail, and why did the New England ones succeed almost immediately? Can the Chesapeake or the New England experience be considered more "typical" of what would become the United States?

>> What were the similarities and differences in each region's relations with Native Americans?

>> How and why did slavery become more prominent in the Chesapeake?

>> What role did religion play in shaping the Puritan colonies?

>> What elements of democracy existed in the New England and Chesapeake colonies?

AMERICAN PORTRAIT

>> The Adventures of John Smith

John Smith has attained almost mythical stature, but he was once a real person. In the 1590s, he was a rebellious adolescent in the English countryside. His yeoman father apprenticed him to a merchant in the nearby seaport town of King's Lynn. Then his father died, and young John seized the opportunity to leave his master. He made his way to the Netherlands and joined the rebel army there engaged in fighting for independence from Spain. Later, he hired himself out to Archduke Ferdinand of Austria to fight Ottoman Turks in Hungary. He was taken prisoner on the battlefield, sold as a slave, and sent to work on a farm in Tartary. He escaped on a stolen horse and got to Christian Russia, and from there he was able to return home.

Back in London by 1606, John Smith found everyone talking about plans for a colony in "Virginia." He wanted to go. His experiences in faraway countries apparently convinced officers of the Virginia Company to name him as one of the council members who were to direct the colony at Jamestown. Later, he would even briefly become president of the council.

The expedition touched land in April 1607. Because the colony starved and struggled, the daring Smith decided to make his way up the Chickahominy River in the dead of winter to try to persuade the Indians to give the settlers corn. He was captured by a party of Powhatans and taken to Werowocomoco, the seat of the paramount chief, named "Powhatan" for his people. Through signs and pantomime, he and the high chief tried to glean information about each other's purposes. Over the course of several weeks, Smith was encouraged to spend time with one of Powhatan's less important daughters, born to him by an ordinary woman, not a noblewoman. This was Pocahontas, then aged 10 or so. She quickly picked up the English phrases he taught her. In early January 1608, the Indians returned their prisoner to the fort at Jamestown, satisfied to have made inroads in forging an alliance with the newcomers.

Smith wrote a report almost immediately and sent it back to London. He said nothing about the purported events that have since become so famous—that Powhatan intended to bash his brains out, but his lovely daughter threw herself over him to save him. In fact, Smith said nothing about this in any of the several works he published in the ensuing decade. He told the illogical story 17 years later, when Pocahontas and everyone else involved were dead. He made the claim in the wake of an Indian rebellion, when Powhatan's kindred were viewed as the devil incarnate, and Pocahontas, who by then had been to London and was a celebrity, was seen as exceptional among all her people.

Furthermore, it is notable that in Smith's accounts of his exploits around the world, he never failed to mention that at each critical juncture, a beautiful young woman had fallen in love with him and interceded on his behalf. He claimed it happened in Turkey, in Russia, and in France. He always said that these beautiful girls had been willing to die for him—a sign of a woman's love in old medieval tales.

Continued

>> AMERICAN PORTRAIT
Continued

What Smith *did* talk about earlier on—and which was probably true—was that Powhatan had involved him in a special ceremony, which scholars now interpret as a ceremony of political adoption. Powhatan, in short, was willing to draw the English into his world and use them in any way he saw fit. The 10-year-old Pocahontas may even have been present as the only possible partial translator.

Smith was injured in a gunpowder accident not long after, and he seized the moment to leave the floundering colony and return to England. He became involved in the burgeoning efforts to colonize New England, but he did not settle there. He ended up making his living by writing about his travels and about the Americas, dying in 1631.

Smith was a man of his age. He was no friend to the Indians and often advocated violence. In fact, when Pocahontas saw him years later while she was visiting London, she accused him of having lied about his own and other Englishmen's intentions. On the other hand, he was unusual in that he did know the Indians as real people and respected them as adversaries. Smith never made the mistake of believing that the Indians of Virginia would be happy to do whatever the English wanted or of seeing them as subhuman. His detailed 1608 report, written before he allowed his fantasies to run away with him and before he was trying to sell books, remains one of the best sources of information we have about the important cultural encounter at Jamestown.

The First Chesapeake Colonies

When Queen Elizabeth died in 1603, she was succeeded by her Scottish cousin, King James I, who immediately signed a treaty with Spain ending decades of warfare. With peace established, all those who had lived off privateering and warfare had to look for another source of income. They joined with old advocates of colonization to establish new colonies in North America. In 1606, James granted charters to two groups of English merchants and military men, one in London and the other in Plymouth. The Plymouth group would colonize the northern coast, and the Londoners the Chesapeake region. Each operation was chartered as a private company, which would raise money from shareholders and finance, populate, and regulate its colonies.

Founding Virginia

In 1606, the Plymouth-based company deposited some settlers at the mouth of the Kennebec River in today's Maine, but the climate defeated them within a season. The Virginia Company (named in honor of the recently deceased, never-married queen) had wealthy London backers and met with greater success. Just before Christmas in 1606, it sent out three ships under Captain Christopher Newport, a one-legged veteran

OUTLINE

The First Chesapeake Colonies
Founding Virginia
Starving Times

PRIMARY SOURCE:
  The Charter of Virginia, 1606
Troubled Relations with the Powhatans
Toward a New Economic Order and the Rise of
  Democracy

TECHNOLOGY AND IDEAS:
  Tobacco Cultivation in Virginia
Toward the Destruction of the Powhatans
A New Colony in Maryland

The Political Economy of Slavery Emerges
The Problem of a Labor Supply
The Origins of African Slavery in the Chesapeake
Gender and the Social Order in the Chesapeake

**A Bible Commonwealth in the New England
  Wilderness**

Atlantic explorer. When the ships arrived at Virginia on April 26, 1607, the colonists learned that they were to be governed by a council of seven men. Unfortunately, two of them, Edward Maria Wingfield, an arrogant gentleman and investor in the company, and Captain John Smith, the equally arrogant but considerably more capable soldier of fortune, despised each other. By the end of the summer, another council member had been executed because he was supposedly a double agent for the Spanish. The early history of Jamestown was marked by internal wrangling. External conflict soon developed as well, as the colonists antagonized their Indian hosts. Almost everything that could go wrong did.

The experience of Roanoke notwithstanding, the English still hoped to find a land like Mexico, filled with gold and other less glamorous raw materials. Whatever limited manufacturing was needed could be performed either by English criminals, sent over to work as their punishment, or by indentured servants, English men and women from the lowest ranks of society who agreed to work for a set period to pay their transportation expenses. The colonists expected to trade with the local Indians, who would be the primary suppliers of food.

The Company planned to get the colony up and running within seven years. During that period, all colonists would work for the Company, which would give them food and shelter. At the end of that time, they would receive grants of land. The Company evidently thought the colony would need a great deal of direction, for about one-third of the original settlers were gentlemen, that is, members of the elite, a proportion of the colony's population that was six times higher than it was in England.

The Company also sent skilled laborers, many with skills of little use in the colony, such as tailors, goldsmiths, and a perfumer. Some were thought necessary to support the gentlemen. Others were to work the gold and precious gems colonists hoped to find. Farmers and ordinary laborers, on the other hand, were in short supply, for it was assumed that the Indians would fill these roles.

Starving Times

Poor planning and bad luck placed the colonists on swampy ground with bad water. The salty water of the James River could be poisonous, and in summer it became a breeding ground for typhoid and dysentery. Some historians have argued that these diseases left the survivors too weak to plant food, whereas others note that many of the healthy seemed to prefer prospecting for gold. The colonists depended on the resentful Powhatan Indians for food, and the resulting malnutrition made the effects of disease worse. These factors, along with skirmishes with the Powhatans, led to appallingly high

The English Origins of the Puritan Movement
What Did the Puritans Believe?
The Pilgrim Colony at Plymouth
The Puritan Colony at Massachusetts Bay

AMERICA AND THE WORLD:
   The English Enter the Slave Trade
The New England Way
Changing the Landscape to Fit the Political
   Economy

The Puritan Family

AMERICAN LANDSCAPE:
   New England Settlements

Dissension in the Puritan Ranks
   Roger Williams and Toleration
   Anne Hutchinson and the Equality of Believers
   Puritan Indian Policy and the Pequot War

Conclusion

>> The Charter of Virginia, 1606

The charter that James I's lawyers prepared for the Virginia Company of London combined medieval military concepts, newer commercial ideas, missionary zeal, and relatively modern socioeconomic concerns. The company was to act as border guard, engage in trade with and convert the Indians, and set up the colony as a repository for England's excess population. To this end, the company was granted a limited form of self-government, subject to crown supervision. The year, 1606, was a time of trouble in the home country, with riots in the countryside over poor economic conditions and crime in the cities filled with poor young people.

We would vouchsafe unto them our License, to make Habitation, Plantation, and to deduce a colony of sundry of our people into that part of America commonly called VIRGINIA, and other parts and Territories in America, either appertaining unto us, or which are not now actually possessed by any Christian Prince or People, situate, lies, and being all along the Sea Coasts, between four and thirty Degrees of Northerly Latitude from the Equinoctial Line, and five and forty Degrees of the same Latitude, and in the main Land between the same four and thirty and five and forty Degrees, and the Islands thereunto adjacent, or within one hundred Miles of the Coast thereof;

And to that End, and for the more speedy Accomplishment of their said intended Plantation and Habitation there, . . . consisting of certain Knights, Gentlemen, Merchants, and other Adventurers, of our City of London and elsewhere, which are, and from time to time shall be, joined unto them, which do desire to begin their Plantation and Habitation in some fit and convenient Place. . . .

We, greatly commending, and graciously accepting of, their Desires for the Furtherance of so noble a Work, which may, by the Providence of Almighty God, hereafter tend to the Glory of his Divine Majesty, in propagating of Christian Religion to such People, as yet live

The fort at Jamestown, as it may have appeared in 1607.

in Darkness and miserable Ignorance of the true Knowledge and Worship of God, and may in time bring the Infidels and Savages, living in those parts, to human Civility, and to a settled and quiet Government: DO, by these our Letters Patents, graciously accept of, and agree to, their humble and well-intended Desires. . . .

And shall and may inhabit and remain there; and shall and may also build and fortify within any the same, for their better Safeguard and Defence, according to their best Discretion, and the Discretion of the Council of that Colony; And that no other of our Subjects shall be permitted, or suffered, to plant or inhabit behind, or on the Backside of them, towards the main Land, without the Express License or Consent of the Council of that Colony, thereunto in Writing first had and obtained. . . .

And we do also ordain . . . that each of the said Colonies shall have a Council, which shall govern and order all Matters and Causes, which shall arise, grow, or happen, to or within the same several Colonies, according to such Laws, Ordinances, and Instructions, as shall be, in that behalf, given and signed with Our Hand. . . .

"The First Charter of Virginia, April, 10th through the 20th, 1606," in *Documentary Source Book of American History, 1606–1913*, ed. William Macdonald (New York: Macmillan Company, 1920), pp. 1–4.

Questions

1. How does this document demonstrate that England is becoming more interested in *settlement*, as opposed to simply establishing trading posts, as in the past?

2. What is the extent of the authority that this document grants to the settlers? Why do you think that the document grants the settlers authority over these matters and not others? What are the settlers *not* authorized to do?

3. What impact do you think this charter may have had on the social order of the Virginia colony, and why do you think so?

> This was that time, which still to this day we called the starving time; it were too vile to say, and scarce to be beleeved, what we endured: but the occasion was our owne, for want of providence, industrie and government, and not the barrennesse and defect of the Countrie, . . .
>
> CAPTAIN JOHN SMITH

mortality rates. By September 1607, half of the more than one hundred original colonists were dead, and by the following spring only 38 were still alive. Although the Company sent over more colonists, they continued to die off at extraordinary rates. As late as 1616, the English population was only 350, although more than five times that number had emigrated from England (see Table 3–1).

Troubled Relations with the Powhatans

In Virginia, the English encountered the powerful paramount chieftaincy of the Powhatan Indians. Originally a small tribe of Algonquian-speaking Indians like many others in the region, the Powhatans had attained great power when, through a series of politically motivated marriages, a young chief of theirs had inherited the rulerships of several other tribes, some through his mother and some through his father. This man, called Powhatan in honor of his people, took his larger-than-usual force of warriors and made a series of strategic attacks, then followed up by taking a wife from each of numerous chiefly families in the area. At the time of the arrival of the English, Powhatan's chieftaincy included about 20,000 Indians, divided into about three dozen tribes.

Powhatan hoped to use the English to buttress his power by trading for metal goods and textiles, but he recognized that the strangers might constitute a threat. In his negotiations first with Smith and then with others, he attempted to tie the English into his world as his vassals. But of course, the English hoped for the inverse. At one point, the English put a fake crown on the kneeling Powhatan's head, imitating the ceremonies in which feudal princes pledged allegiance to a king. The Indians, however, remained unmoved by the ceremony.

With his large force, Lord De La Warr immediately set out to subjugate the Indians. He ordered Powhatan to return all English captives taken in prior skirmishes. When Powhatan refused, De La Warr ordered an attack on an Indian village. The English killed about 75 inhabitants, burned the town and its cornfields, and captured the wife of a chieftain and her children. As the English sailed back to Jamestown, they threw the children overboard and shot them as they swam in the water. So opened the First Anglo-Powhatan War, the first of three conflicts between 1610 and 1646.

During this war, an English captain kidnapped the daughter of Powhatan named Pocahontas and brought her back to Jamestown. The English knew her because she and Smith had taught each other some of their languages when he was briefly held captive during the colony's first year, and she later had visited the fort. She had been a child then and now was a young woman. The English placed her in the care of a minister, hoping to convert her and render her "a perfect Interpreter." However, she remained unconverted. In the summer of 1614, the English took their hostage upriver to Powhatan's town and threatened to harm her if he did not do as they asked and agree to pay tribute in corn. The two sides were at an impasse. Suddenly John Rolfe, a young widower who had apparently tutored Pocahontas in English, asked for her hand in marriage. Messengers were sent to Powhatan, and he agreed. In permitting his daughter to marry an Englishman, Powhatan was adopting a means he had used to establish his powerful chieftaincy. Young Algonquian women frequently

Native American Tobacco Pipe Stone and clay pipes were of ceremonial and recreational importance and constituted a major trade good among Indian peoples of the East Coast.

Table 3-1 English Population of Virginia, 1607–1640

Population in Virginia Colony	Immigration to Virginia Colony
104 (April 1607)	104 (April 1607)
38 (Jan. 1608)	
	120 (Jan. 1608, 1st supply)
130 (Sept. 1608)	
	70 (Sept. 1608, 2nd supply)
200 (late Sept. 1608)	
100 (spring 1609)	
	300 (Fall 1609, 3rd supply)
	540 (1610)
450 (April 1611)	
	660 (1611)
682 (Jan. 1612)	
350 (Jan. 1613)	
	45 (1613–1616)
351 (1616)	
600 (Dec. 1618)	
	900 (1618–1620)
887 (Mar. 1620)	
	1051 (1620–1621)
943 (Mar. 1621)	
	1580 (1621–1622)
1240 (Mar. 1622)	
	1935 (1622–1623)
1241 (April 1623)	
	1646 (1623–1624)
1275 (Feb. 1624)	
1210 (1625)	
	9000 (1625–1634)
4914 (1634)	
	6000 (1635–1640)
8100 (1640)	total: 23,951

Source: Data from Carville Earle, Geographical Inquiry and American Historical Problems *(Stanford, CA: Stanford University Press, 1992), and Virginia Bernhard, "Men, Women, and Children at Jamestown: Population and Gender in Early Virginia, 1607–1610,"* Journal of Southern History, 58 *(1992).*

Note: Although about 24,000 men and women immigrated to Virginia between 1607 and 1640, in 1640 the population stood at only 8,100. Most of the inhabitants fell victim to disease, although the Indian uprising of 1622 took 347 lives.

married with the enemy for their people's sake. Pocahontas agreed, and three days later announced she had converted to Christianity. The marriage of John Rolfe and Pocahontas ushered in a brief period of peace, but it could not last.

Toward a New Economic Order and the Rise of Democracy

The tide finally turned against the Powhatans, not because of a failure in diplomacy or the politics of marriage, but because the English finally found a way to make money in Virginia. Pocahontas's husband, John Rolfe, developed a strain of tobacco

Powhatan and English Dwellings These are reconstructions of typical Powhatan Indian and English homes, ca. 1607. Both are dark and small.

that found a ready market in England. It transformed the colony almost overnight. Within three years, Virginia was shipping 50,000 pounds of tobacco to England per year. Suddenly Virginia experienced an economic boom. By 1619, a man working by himself was making £200 in one crop, and a man with six indentured servants could make £1,000, money only the nobility was accustomed to. Once fortunes this large could be made, the race to Virginia was on.

All that was needed to make money in Virginia was land and people to work it. In 1616 the Virginia Company, which had land but no money, offered land as dividends to its stockholders. Those already living in Virginia were given land, and anyone who came over (or brought another person over) was to be granted 50 acres a head (called a headright). The Company was moving toward private enterprise, away from the corporate, company-directed economy of the early years. The leadership of the colony also gave itself grants, laying the basis for its own wealth and power. It was far easier to obtain land in Virginia than in England.

To attract settlers, the Company replaced martial law with common law, guaranteeing colonists all the rights of the English people. The colonists were also granted greater rights to self-government than were enjoyed by those who lived in England. The first elected representative government in the New World, the Virginia House of Burgesses (renamed the General Assembly after the American Revolution), met in Jamestown on July 30, 1619.

These inducements attracted 3,500 settlers to Virginia in three years, three times as many as had come in the preceding ten years. By accident more than planning, Virginia had found the formula for a successful English colony. It was one that all other colonies generally followed: offering colonists greater opportunities to make money and greater rights of self-government than they had at home. These changes came too late, however, to rescue the Virginia Company, which went bankrupt in 1624. King James I dissolved the Company and turned Virginia into a royal colony under his control.

TECHNOLOGY AND IDEAS

>> Tobacco Cultivation in Virginia

Tobacco was the first successful staple crop in British North America. Shortly after its introduction in the Virginia colony, tobacco came to dominate commerce between Britain and the Chesapeake. Tobacco cultivation also led to increased inequality in seventeenth-century Virginia and Maryland. A marked rise in slave labor and the rise of a powerful planter class backed by English military and naval force were two of the most important consequences of tobacco production in Virginia.

Along with beaver furs and sugar, tobacco drove transatlantic trade in the early modern era. Its strong, drug-like appeal captivated a growing number of European consumers, who enjoyed the effects of nicotine and the social practice of tobacco smoking. When the first English settlers arrived in Jamestown, Spain held a monopoly on the tobacco trade; the warm and fertile Spanish colonies of the Caribbean produced the sweetest and most prized tobacco for the European market. In contrast, the Virginia variety of tobacco was too harsh for European tastes, and most settlers ignored tobacco production in favor of searching for precious metals. But when the dream of instant riches faded, innovative colonial leaders looked for new sources of wealth.

John Rolfe, a native of Norfolk, England, had acquired rare Spanish tobacco seeds from the Spanish West Indies. In 1611, Rolfe harvested the first commercially viable tobacco plants in North America. The acquisition and cultivation of these seeds—Rolfe named them "Orinoco" after the river in South America that Sir Walter Raleigh had explored in the search for El Dorado—was a true economic breakthrough, as it allowed English settlers to cultivate sweeter tobacco for European markets. By 1617, Rolfe and others, likely with the help and advice of Pocahontas and her family, who had extensive agricultural experience in the region, began to grow enough tobacco to export it to England. Though many Europeans still considered it inferior to the Spanish variety, Virginian tobacco was abundant and cheap. These conditions sparked a boom in tobacco production throughout the 1620s, making the Virginia colony profitable.

With the steady rise of European demand between 1620 and the 1660s, tobacco became central to the political economy of the Chesapeake. At first the boom created a relatively balanced economy: wealthy planters carved out new tobacco plantations along the James River, while former indentured workers grew tobacco on small farms. But by mid-century a social and economic gap yawned between wealthy plantations and smaller, family-run farms. Market demand for a labor-intensive crop like tobacco produced two key transitions in Chesapeake society. First, wealthy planters came to rely on African slaves, who could work large plantations at a cheaper cost than white indentured servants. Second, a powerful planter elite came to dominate Chesapeake political life. Slave labor increased the profitability of large plantations to the point at which smaller farms could not compete. A small group of planters attained nearly unchallenged power throughout the region. With tobacco's increased profitability, the English state arrived to solidify the dominance of the new planter elite. English naval might protected the lucrative tobacco trade against pirates and Dutch raiders, and the military pushed Indians from western lands, extending the Atlantic economy farther into North America. In less than 90 years, John Rolfe's "Orinoco" seeds had borne the fruits of empire.

By the eighteenth century, the tobacco trade had become a huge international business. Here is a typical product label used for sales in England.

Questions

1. John Rolfe did not cultivate tobacco in isolation. Identify some of the forces that shaped his efforts to grow a sweeter strain of tobacco in Virginia.

2. Do you think that John Rolfe was an exceptional figure? Or do you think that, sooner or later, someone else would have cultivated tobacco in Virginia?

Toward the Destruction of the Powhatans

As the new colonists spread out, establishing private plantations, English settlers claimed all the Indians' prime farmland on both sides of the James River and began to move up its tributaries (see Map 3–1). At the same time, the Powhatans became increasingly dependent on English goods such as metal tools. Moreover, as the English population began to grow its own food, it had less need of Indian food, the only significant commodity the Indians had to trade. The Indians slowly accumulated a debt to the English and lost their economic independence.

After Powhatan died, his more militant brother, Opechancanough, decided to get rid of the English. He wanted to convince them to go home or at least to limit their spreading. On the morning of March 22, 1622, in an extraordinarily well-planned attack, the Indians struck at most of the plantations along the James River, killing about one-quarter of the colonists. The Second Anglo-Powhatan War, which continued for another 10 years, had begun. This war marked a turning point in English policy. Although some of the English recognized that the Indian attack had been caused by their "own perfidiouse dealing," most decided that the Indians were untrustworthy and incapable of being converted to the English way of life. Therefore, a policy of extermination was justified. Some were almost happy that the Indians had attacked; John Smith concluded that the massacre "will be good for the Plantation, because now we have just cause to destroy them by all meanes possible." Until this point, the English had claimed only land that the Indians were not currently farming. Now they seized territory the Indians had just cleared and planted. In only 15 years' time, the English and Indians in Virginia had become implacable enemies.

Indian resistance only made the English more determined to stay, and with the tobacco economy booming, settlers poured into Virginia. They spread across the Chesapeake to the Eastern Shore and north to the Potomac River. The aged Opechancanough, determined to make one final push, struck again on April 18, 1644, killing about 400 and taking many prisoners.

The Third Anglo-Powhatan War ended, however, in the Indians' total defeat two years later. Opechancanough was killed. The English took complete possession of the land between the James and York Rivers. Henceforth, no Indian was allowed to enter this territory unless he was bringing

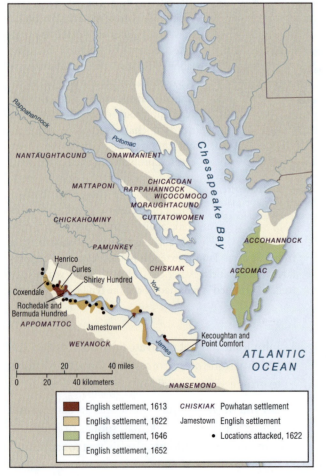

Map 3–1 English Encroachments on Indian Land, 1613–1652 After John Rolfe's development of a marketable strain of tobacco, the English spread out through the Chesapeake region, encroaching steadily on Indian land. Tobacco planters preferred land along the rivers, for casks filled with tobacco bound for England were more easily transported by ship. *Frederic Gleach,* Powhatan's World and Colonial Virginia *(Lincoln: University of Nebraska Press, 1997), and James Horn,* Adapting to a New World: English Society in the Seventeenth-Century Chesapeake *(Chapel Hill: University of North Carolina Press, 1994).*

a message from a chief. Any English person who sheltered an Indian without permission was to be put to death. The land north of the York River was set aside for the Indians, making it the first American Indian reservation. Soon, English settlers moved into that region, too. It was not the last time that the English settlers would break a treaty with the Indians.

A New Colony in Maryland

Virginia's original plan to make money from trading with the local Indians was not entirely forgotten. When tobacco prices dipped in the 1620s, trade became attractive once again. By the late 1620s, an outpost had been established at the northern end of Chesapeake Bay to obtain beaver furs from the Susquehannocks. Sir George Calvert, the first Lord Baltimore and a Catholic, saw the commercial potential of this region and in 1632 persuaded King Charles I, a Catholic sympathizer, to grant him the land north of the Potomac and south of the Delaware that was "not yet cultivated and planted." This territory became Maryland, the first proprietary colony, that is, a colony owned literally by an individual and his heirs. (Virginia was originally a charter colony, held by a group of private shareholders. Unlike royal colonies, in charter and proprietary colonies the English Crown turned over both financing and management to the shareholders or proprietors.) Maryland, named after the Catholic queen of England, remained the hereditary possession of the Calvert family until the American Revolution.

As the first proprietary colony, Maryland established a pattern for subsequent proprietorships. The proprietor had extensive powers to grant land and make laws by himself, but perhaps because Calvert knew he would have to compete for settlers with Virginia, which had a representative government, he agreed to a representative assembly. In 1649 that assembly passed the Act of Toleration, which said that no one would be "compelled to the beliefe or exercise of any other Religion against his or her consent." Even though religious toleration was extended only to Christians, Maryland was among the most tolerant places in the world. Moreover, this right was extended to women as well as men. (This experiment in religious toleration faced a crisis, however, in 1689, when Coode's Rebellion overthrew the proprietor, making Maryland temporarily a royal colony and, in 1702, establishing the Anglican Church. In 1715 the Calvert family was restored to power. See Chapter 4 for more on the effects of England's "Glorious Revolution" in America.)

Although Maryland's population increased slowly, the familiar political economy emerged quickly. As in Virginia, attracting colonists required greater opportunities and freedoms—of self-government and of religion—than they enjoyed in England. Even during the conflict with the Powhatan Confederacy, the booming tobacco economy drew settlers to Virginia and, after about 1650, to Maryland as well. Although they had separate governments, Virginia and Maryland had similar political economies, based on tobacco. The defeat of the Indians made more land available for cultivation; the colonies needed only people to work it.

The Political Economy of Slavery Emerges

Chesapeake society in the first half of the seventeenth century was shaped by four forces: weak government, the market for tobacco, the availability of land, and the need for labor. Because government was weak, the forces of plantation agriculture were unchecked, and the profit motive operated without restraint. Those who could take advantage of these opportunities—male and female both—profited wildly, whereas the poor, both white and African, were without defense. In this environment the political economy of slavery took root.

The Problem of a Labor Supply

Once the crises of the early years had passed, the Chesapeake's greatest problem was securing laborers to produce tobacco. As soon as John Rolfe brought in his first successful crop, the Virginia governor began pressing England to send him its poor. The Virginia Company also encouraged the emigration of women, for the young colony was primarily male. No matter how many colonists came, however, the demand for labor always outstripped the supply. By 1660, 50,000 Britons, mostly single men in their 20s, had migrated to the Chesapeake, but the population was still only a little over 35,000. Because of disease and malnutrition, the death rate remained extraordinarily high. It did not help that most of the colonists came from impoverished backgrounds and arrived alone and friendless to face a harsh new situation.

> And I have nothing to comfort me, nor is there nothing to be gotten here but sickness and death. . . . I have nothing at all—no, not a shirt to my back but two rags, nor clothes but one poor suit, nor but one pair of shoes, but one pair of stockings, but one cap. . . .
>
> RICHARD FRETHORNE,
> letter to his parents in England, 1623

The profits from tobacco were so great and the risk of death so high that landowners squeezed out every penny of profit as quickly as they could. Those with land and servants to work it could become rich overnight. Colonial officials, including members of the legislature, discovered a variety of ways to make themselves wealthy. Great wealth, however, could be achieved only by the labor of others, and the demand for labor was almost insatiable. Perhaps 90 percent of those who migrated to the Chesapeake in the seventeenth century came as servants, and half died before completing their term of service. In England, servants had some basic protections, but in Virginia, working conditions were deadly brutal. In 1623, Richard Frethorne, a young Virginia servant, "with weeping tears" wrote to his parents in England, "We must work early and late for a mess of water gruel and a mouthful of bread and beef."

Servants might be beaten so severely that they died, or they might find their indentures (the contract that bound them to service for a period of usually seven years) sold from one master to another. They found little protection from the courts. They were not, in fact, slaves. They would become free if they outlived their period of indenture; they retained all of the rights of English people, and their servitude was not hereditary. But they were far worse off than servants in England.

Some colonists tried to resolve the problem of the labor shortage by purchasing Indian slaves who had been captured by other Indians in wars farther west, but there were not nearly enough of these to meet the demand (see Chapter 4).

The Origins of African Slavery in the Chesapeake

Other New World plantation societies in which labor was in short supply had already turned to African slavery, so it was probably only a matter of time until the Chesapeake did as well. Historians do not know precisely when slavery was first practiced on a widespread basis in the Chesapeake, but Africans first arrived in Virginia in 1619, when a Dutch ship sailing off course sold its cargo of "twenty Negars" to the Virginians. As long as life expectancy was low, it was generally more profitable for a planter to purchase an indentured servant for a period of seven years than a slave for life. Not until life expectancy improved toward the end of the seventeenth century were significant numbers of African slaves imported into the Chesapeake.

All the English plantation colonies followed the same pattern in making the transition from white servitude to African slavery. The transition was quick in some places and slow in others; in Virginia, it took about three-quarters of a century. The primary factors dictating how readily English colonists adopted African slavery were the need for plantation laborers and the availability of African slaves at a good price. If there was any discussion about the justice of slavery, the English claimed that slavery was an appropriate punishment for certain crimes and for prisoners taken in just wars. No white people were ever enslaved in the English colonies, however. It was a practice reserved for "strangers," primarily foreigners of a non-Christian religion. At first, some of the Africans who ended up in the colonies were those who came as the domestic servants of well-to-do colonists, not as chattel slaves. In addition, some buyers in the early years allowed Africans to earn their freedom as did English indentured servants. Still, all the British colonies eventually practiced permanent chattel slavery, and it became critical to plantation economies. African slaves were even brought back to the British Islands, and by the middle of the eighteenth century, 2 percent of London's population was African.

Even before they had substantial contact with African people, the English and other northern Europeans probably harbored prejudice against dark-skinned people. By the second half of the sixteenth century, the English were depicting Africans in derogatory terms, saying that Africans were unattractive, with "dispositions most savage and brutish," a "people of beastly living" who "contract no matrimonie, neither have respect to chastity." Northern Europeans considered African women particularly monstrous, sexually promiscuous, and neglectful of their children. Although these views were not explicitly used to justify slavery, they formed the basis for the racism that would develop along with the slave system.

During the first half of the seventeenth century, African slavery and white and African servitude existed side by side. The Chesapeake was a society with slaves, but it was still not a slave society. The first clear evidence of permanent and generalized enslavement of Africans in the Chesapeake dates to 1639, when the Maryland Assembly passed a law guaranteeing "all the Inhabitants of this Province being Christians (Slaves excepted)" all the rights and liberties of "any natural born subject of England." The first Virginia law recognizing slavery, passed in 1661, said that any English servant who ran away with an African would have to serve additional time not only for himself but for the African as well. Such Africans were clearly already understood to be slaves for life and hence were incapable of serving any additional time.

Such laws reveal the great familiarity that existed between white and black servants. Slaves and white servants worked together, enjoyed leisure together, had sexual relations with each other, and ran away together. As late as 1680, most of the plantation laborers were still white indentured servants. There is no evidence that they were kept separate from Africans by law or inclination.

As long as the black population remained small, the color line was blurry. Not until late in the seventeenth century were laws passed that restricted free African Americans. In fact, in 1660, Anthony Johnson, an African who had arrived in Virginia as a servant in 1621, owned both land and African slaves. In the 40 years that he had been in Virginia, slavery had become institutionalized and recognized by the law, but laws separating the races had yet to be enacted.

Gender and the Social Order in the Chesapeake

The founders of England's colonies hoped to replicate the social order they had known at home. As early as 1619, the Virginia Company began to bring single women to the colony to become brides of the unmarried planters. As in England, it was expected that men would perform all the "outside" labor, including planting, farming, and tending large farm animals. Women would do all the "inside" work, including preserving and preparing food, spinning and weaving, making and repairing clothing, and gardening. In English society, a farmer's wife was not simply a man's sexual partner and companion; she was also the mistress of a successful household economy. Both men and women were vital to the society the English wanted to create in the Chesapeake.

However, the powerful tobacco economy transformed both the economy and society of the New World. With profits from tobacco so high, women went directly into the tobacco fields instead of the kitchen. Children were in the fields as soon as they could work. Only when a man became wealthy did he hire a servant—often a woman—to replace his wife in the fields. As a result, for many years, Virginia society lacked the "comforts of home" that women produced, such as prepared food, homemade clothing, and even soap. Tobacco was everything.

Colonial society also weakened patriarchal controls. Chesapeake governments tried—but failed—to control immigrant women, insisting, for example, that a woman receive government permission before marrying and prosecuting for slander women who spoke out against the government or their neighbors. But colonial government was relatively weak, and women, far from their own fathers, found themselves unexpectedly free from traditional restrictions.

Although women without the protection of fathers were vulnerable in seventeenth-century plantation societies, in a world where men outnumbered women three or four to one, women were often in a position of relative power. Local governments struggled to impose order by prosecuting women for adultery, fornication, and giving birth to illegitimate children. The public, however, was more tolerant of sexual misconduct than government officials were. The first generation of women to immigrate to the Chesapeake region married relatively late—in their mid-20s or later. As a result, they had relatively few children, and it was many decades before Chesapeake society reproduced itself naturally. Perhaps half of all children born in the colony died in infancy, and one marriage partner was also likely to die within seven years of marriage. At least until 1680 or so, to be a widow, widower, or orphan was the normal state of affairs. Widows who inherited their husband's possessions were powerful and in demand on the marriage market. Children, however, often lost their inheritances to a stepparent.

A Bible Commonwealth in the New England Wilderness

In 1620, 13 years after the founding of the Virginia Colony, England planted another permanent colony at Plymouth; 9 years after that, it planted one at Massachusetts Bay. In many ways the Virginia and Massachusetts colonies could not have been more different. The primary impetus behind the Massachusetts settlement was religious. Both the Pilgrims at Plymouth and the much more numerous Puritans at Massachusetts Bay sought to escape persecution and to establish new communities based on God's law as they understood it. The Puritans and Pilgrims were middle class, and their ventures were well financed and capably planned for the benefit of the settlers. The environment was much more healthful than that of the Chesapeake, and the population reproduced itself rapidly. Relations with the Indians were better than in the Chesapeake. Nonetheless, despite the colonies' differences, the Puritan movement was in fact originally a product of the same growth of national states in Europe and the expansion of commerce that led to the European exploration of the New World and the foundation of Jamestown. Furthermore, the Puritans themselves often demonstrated the same tendencies as other Englishmen.

The English Origins of the Puritan Movement

In Europe during the sixteenth century, ordinary people and powerful monarchs had vastly different reasons for abandoning the Roman Catholic Church in favor of one of the new Protestant churches. In England, these differing motives led to 130 years of conflict, including a revolution and massive religious persecution. In the 1530s, Henry VIII established his own state religion, the Church of England, for political rather than for pious reasons. After many years of marriage to Catherine of Aragon, Henry still did not have a male heir. With one of Catherine's ladies-in-waiting, Anne Boleyn, already pregnant, Henry pressed the pope for an annulment of his marriage. In 1533, the pope refused the annulment, and Henry removed the Catholic Church as the established religion of England, replacing it with his own Church of England. He confiscated Catholic Church lands, which he redistributed to members of the English nobility in return for their loyalty. In one move, Henry eliminated a powerful political rival, the Roman Catholic Church, and consolidated his rule over his nobility.

Replacing the Catholic Church did not bring stability, however. Henry's successors alternated between Protestantism and Catholicism. Under the reign of Catherine's daughter Mary, hundreds of Protestants left the country to avoid persecution. When Mary's Protestant sister, Elizabeth, ascended the throne, these exiles returned, having picked up the Calvinist doctrine of predestination on the Continent. John Calvin, the Swiss Protestant reformer, insisted that even before people were born, God foreordained "to some eternal life and to some eternal damnation." Although the Church of England adopted Calvin's doctrine of predestination, it never held to it thoroughly enough or followed through on other reforms well enough to please those who called themselves Puritans. And because the monarch viewed challenges to the state religion as challenges to the state itself, religious dissenters were frequently persecuted.

What Did the Puritans Believe?

Like all Christians, Puritans believed that humanity was guilty of the original sin committed by Adam and Eve when they disobeyed God in the Garden of Eden. They believed that God's son, Jesus Christ, had given his life to pay (or atone) for the original sin and that as a consequence, all truly faithful Christians would be forgiven their sins and admitted to heaven after they died. Unlike other Christians, Calvinists insisted there was nothing that people could do to guarantee that God, by an act of "grace," would grant them the faith that would save them from hell.

Protestants rejected the hierarchy of the Catholic Church, maintaining that the relationship between God and humanity should be direct and unmediated. Because every person had direct access to the word of God through the Bible, Protestants promoted literacy and translated the Bible into modern languages.

As Calvinists, Puritans wanted to "purify" the Church of England of all remnants of Catholicism, including rituals and priestly hierarchy. Furthermore, Anglicans (members of the established Church of England) had come to think that Catholics were partly right—that believing Christians *could* earn their way to heaven by good works, a doctrine the Puritans labeled Arminianism. Puritans, in contrast, continued to insist that salvation was the free gift of God and that human beings could not force God's hand. Individuals could only prepare for grace by reading and studying the Bible, so that they understood God's plan, and by attempting to live the best lives they could. Because they could never be certain of salvation, Puritans always lived with anxiety.

Puritanism contained a powerful tension between intellect and emotion. On the one hand, Puritanism was a highly rational religion, requiring all of its followers to study the Bible and listen to long sermons on fine points of theology. As a result, Puritans, male and female, were highly literate. On the other hand, Puritans believed that no amount of book learning could get a person into heaven, and that grace was as much a matter of the heart as of the mind. The Puritan movement always struggled to contain this tension, as some of its believers embraced a more fully rational religion and others abandoned book learning for emotion.

Puritans believed that church membership was only for those who could demonstrate that they were saved. As they were persecuted for their faith, they came to believe that, like the Israelites of old, they were God's chosen people—that they had a covenant or agreement with God, and that if they did his will, he would make them prosper.

The Puritans first attempted to reform the Church of England. Once they saw that the Church would resist more reformation and was moving further from the Calvinist principle of predestination, some Puritans began to make other plans.

The Pilgrim Colony at Plymouth

The first Puritan colony in North America was established in 1620 at Plymouth, by a group of Puritans known as the Pilgrims, "Separatists" who had given up hope of reforming the Church of England. The Pilgrims had already moved to Holland, thinking its Calvinism would offer a better home. It was hard for the Pilgrims to fit themselves into Holland's economy, however, and they found their children seduced by "the manifold temptations of the place."

By 1620 the Pilgrims were ready to accept the Virginia Company of London's offer of land in America for any English people who would pay their own way. With the colony at Jamestown foundering and the Company looking for other opportunities, it filled two ships, the *Mayflower* and the *Speedwell*, with the Pilgrims from Holland, other interested Puritans, and a large number of non-Puritans also willing to pay their own way.

The leaking *Speedwell* had to turn back, but the *Mayflower* arrived at Plymouth, Massachusetts, in November 1620, far north of its destination and outside the jurisdiction of the Virginia Company. Because the Pilgrims had landed in territory that had no legal claim and no lawful government, 41 of the adult men on board signed a document known as the Mayflower Compact. The men bound themselves into a "Civil Body Politic" to make laws and govern the colony and also to recognize the authority of the governor. Although the Compact provided a legal basis for joint government and to a large extent allowed for self-determination on the part of the people, it was by no means a wholly democratic document. By design, it excluded those who were not "Saints," or Puritans, from the body politic. Some of the non-Puritans (called "Strangers") had been talking about mutiny, so the Pilgrims wanted to make their power secure.

Only one of the 102 passengers had died en route, but only half of the party survived the harsh first winter. Years later the second governor, William Bradford, remembered the Pilgrims' ordeals. The Indians, he complained, were "savage barbarians . . . readier to fill their sides full of arrows than otherwise." And their new home was "a hideous and desolate wilderness, full of wild beasts and wild men."

In fact, the Plymouth Colony would never have survived had it not been for the assistance of friendly Indians. Like the French in New France and unlike the English at Jamestown, the Pilgrims established diplomatic relations both because they were good diplomats and because the local Indians desperately needed foreign allies. Before the Pilgrims' arrival, Plymouth Bay had been inhabited by as many as 2,000 people. Then European fishermen and traders introduced some fatal disease—possibly viral hepatitis—which was carried along the trading

> I shall . . . begin with a combination made by them before they came ashore; being the first foundation of their government in this place. Occasioned partly by the discontented and mutinous speeches that some of the strangers amongst them had let fall from them in the ship: That when they came ashore they would use their own liberty, for none had power to command them, the patent they had being for Virginia and not for New England, which belonged to another government, with which the Virginia Company had nothing to do. And partly that such an act by them done, this their condition considered, might be as firm as any patent and in some respects more sure.
>
> WILLIAM BRADFORD,
> writing about the origins of the Mayflower Compact in *Of Plymouth Plantation*

network and killed 90 percent of the local population. Indians "died in heaps as they lay in their houses," their villages filled with the bones of the unburied dead. So recently had Patuxet and Pokanoket Indians inhabited the region that the Pilgrims were able to supplement their meager supplies by rummaging Indian graves, homes, and stores of grain.

The world was vastly changed for Native Americans who survived. Tisquantum, or "Squanto," a Patuxet, had spent the plague years in Europe, having been kidnapped by an exploring Englishman (see Chapter 2). He had only recently made his way back and found that his tribe had almost entirely disappeared. The once-powerful Pokanokets, led by Massasoit, were now paying tribute to the Narragansetts, who had escaped the deadly disease. Squanto persuaded Massasoit that the English might be allies against the Narragansetts. Thus in the spring of 1621, Squanto offered his assistance to the Pilgrims and showed them how to grow corn.

From the Indian perspective, this assistance was a diplomatic initiative, enabling a treaty between the Pokanokets and the Pilgrims. It worked for the English, too, however. By the time Squanto died in 1622, he had helped secure the future of the Pilgrims' Plymouth Colony. Plymouth remained a separate colony until 1691, when it was absorbed into the larger, more influential Massachusetts Bay Colony. Plymouth demonstrated that New England could be inhabited by Europeans and that effective diplomatic relations with local Indians were critical for a colony's survival.

The Puritan Colony at Massachusetts Bay

In England, increasing numbers of people considered themselves Puritans and yet were not Separatists, like the Pilgrims. Many dreamed of founding colonies, but they wanted to serve as models to other Englishmen, not sever themselves from them. In February 1630, an English Puritan noted in his diary that the faithful had recently sent off ships to New England as well as to a place near Mexico. He was referring to Providence Island, off the coast of Nicaragua. Many Puritans were wealthy landowners and merchants who could not endure to think that the great wealth of the Americas should go mostly to Spain. They wanted an English colony in the tropics and so found an

AMERICA AND THE WORLD

>> The English Enter the Slave Trade

By the sixteenth century, slavery did not exist in England, and its people prided themselves on their "free air." History books in the Anglo-American world have tended to blame the Portuguese and the Spanish for initiating the African slave trade and the Dutch merchants for developing it. Yet by the eighteenth century, British shipping dominated the trade, and English merchants made immense profits from it. Slavery eventually took root everywhere in the Americas, including the English colonies. English traders entered the business as soon as it was feasible to do so, and their actions sped the rise of slavery in the Americas, which in turn encouraged the trade.

In the early years of the Atlantic slave trade, almost no one preserved images of the people who were taken. In later generations, the abolitionist movement encouraged the publication of engravings, such as this picture of emaciated survivors of the Middle Passage, almost all of them teenagers who had been taken from the Congo River.

In 1562, John Hawkins, from a wealthy seafaring family in Plymouth, decided to break into the Portuguese slave trade. He seized hundreds of Africans, as well as valuable trade goods, from Portuguese ships along the Guinea coast of West Africa and took them to Santo Domingo on Hispaniola to sell. Even after paying the necessary bribes to Spanish officials—as trade with England was illegal—the profits were enormous. Queen Elizabeth I, who had been against the slave trade, began to pay attention, and she later invested Crown resources. On his second voyage, Hawkins experimented with attacking African villages himself, but he found the costs to be high: in one incident, he seized 10 Africans but lost 7 crew members. Hawkins eventually learned that Africans could be his allies in the trade. An emissary from an African king approached him with a proposition: help the king defeat his enemies and share in the slaves taken as booty. Hawkins agreed and ended up with hundreds of captives. It was the beginning of a hideous guns-for-slaves cycle that would eventually cripple Africa. For Hawkins, ironically, the voyage ended badly. The Spaniards in the Caribbean, having been punished for their prior illegal dealings with him, refused his merchandise. Then they attacked his fleet off the coast of Veracruz, Mexico, and killed and imprisoned nearly all his men. Hawkins himself barely made it home to England.

It was the lack of a ready legal market in the New World that made the business impossible for the time being. In the first half of the seventeenth century, however, that situation changed as the English established colonies on the mainland of North America and on certain Caribbean islands. In 1630, wealthy Puritans established the colony they hoped would make England rich on Providence Island, off the coast of Nicaragua. The investors had in mind the widespread production of cash crops that grew readily in tropical climates. After only four years, the investors abandoned the importation of indentured English servants and filled the land with Africans—whom enthusiastic captains found they could buy along the Central American coast. After the Pequots lost a war with the New Englanders, Pequot prisoners were also sold on Providence Island. One man wrote with abhorrence of the turn of events; his Puritan brethren were unmoved. Only the constant rebellions frightened them, so they took steps to curb the total number relative to the number of English. Yet by the time the Spanish navy destroyed the colony in 1641, there were more than 380 African slaves and fewer than 350 English settlers.

From 1640 on, the numbers of African slaves grew in Barbados and other English island colonies, and after the 1660s in the Chesapeake as well. As soon as they were available cheaply enough, slaves became widespread wherever cash crops could grow—even in a Puritan colony. The English slave trade had blossomed.

uninhabited island upon which to establish a plantation economy. They first envisioned a labor force of indentured servants, as in the Chesapeake, but rapidly moved to African slavery. In 1641, however, the Spanish navy destroyed the fledgling colony.

In the meantime, friends and relatives of these same Puritans had remained focused on New England and the transport of Puritan settler families. In 1629, the Massachusetts Bay Company, a group of London merchants, had received a charter from King Charles I to establish a colony. The investors in the joint-stock company would have full rights to a swath of land reaching from Massachusetts Bay west across the entire continent. Along with Puritans looking for a new home where they could govern themselves, the company included some who hoped to turn a profit from trade. By the end of the year 1630, Boston and 10 other towns had been founded. By the early 1640s, between 20,000 and 25,000 Britons had migrated to the Puritan colonies of Plymouth, Massachusetts Bay, Connecticut, Rhode Island, and New Hampshire. Although fewer than half as many migrated to New England as to the Chesapeake region, by 1660 both had populations of a similar size—around 35,000 (see Map 3–2).

New England was able to catch up and keep pace with the Chesapeake for three reasons. First, New England was a much more healthful region. Long, cold winters killed the mosquitoes that carried fatal diseases, and the water supply was good. Second, Puritans migrated as families. Ninety percent came as part of a family group, a pattern almost exactly the reverse of that in the Chesapeake. In such circumstances, the population soon reproduced itself. Third, most of the settlers were not desperate; they had resources to help them make the transition. Most were prosperous members of the middle range of society. Many of the men were professionals—craftsmen, doctors, lawyers, and ministers—people who profited from the changing English economy of the late sixteenth and early seventeenth centuries. Again, the contrast with the Chesapeake was dramatic. There, the vast majority of migrants were people with few skills and dim prospects.

Elizabeth Paddy Wensley Far from the grim Massachusetts settler we imagine, Elizabeth Paddy Wensley dressed stylishly by the standards of the 1670s. A mother of five, she was married to the wealthy Boston merchant John Wensley.

The New England Way

The Puritans of Massachusetts Bay Colony were men and women with a mission. Their first governor, John Winthrop, set out the vision of a Bible commonwealth in a

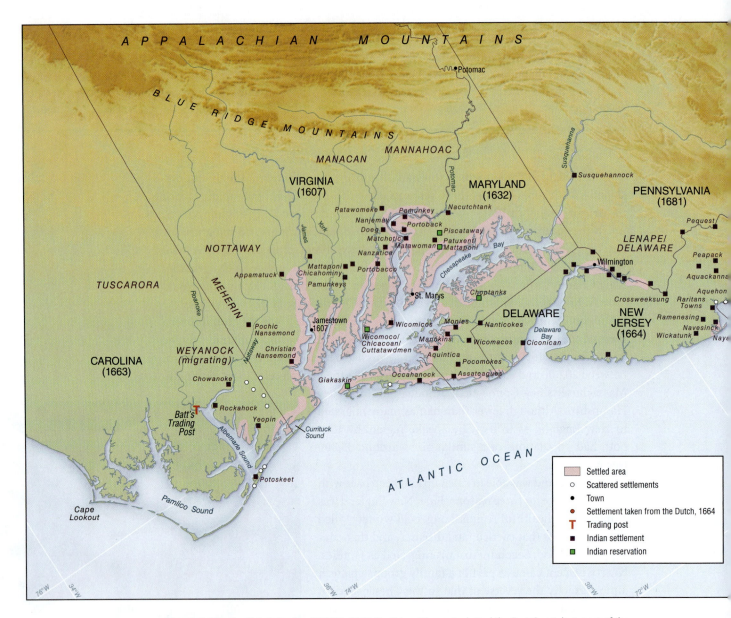

Map 3-2 The English Colonies, 1660 By 1660, English settlements dotted the East Coast, but most of the population was concentrated in two regions: New England and the Chesapeake. *Helen Hombeck Tanner, ed., Settling North America (New York: Macmillan, 1995), pp. 46–47.*

sermon he preached aboard the *Arbella* in the spring of 1630, even before the ship docked at Boston. God, Winthrop said, had entered into a covenant with the Puritans, just as they had entered into a covenant with one another. Together they had taken enormous risks and begun an extraordinary experiment to see whether they could establish a society based on the word of God: "We shall be as a city upon a hill, the eyes of all people are upon us. So that if we shall deal falsely with our God in this work we have undertaken, and so cause Him to withdraw his present help from us, we shall be made a story and a by-word through the world." This broad vision shaped the development of New England's society.

This communal vision made early New Englanders relatively cohesive. Each town was created by a grant of land by the Massachusetts General Court (the name given to

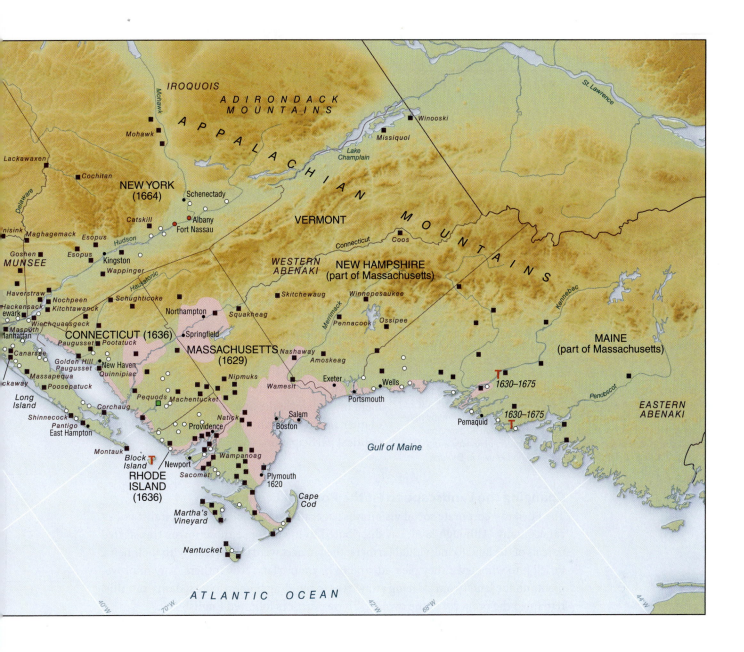

the legislature) to a group of citizens. The settlers in turn entered into a covenant with one another to establish a government and distribute the land they held collectively. This was not a modern democracy, for Puritans believed in hierarchy, and their vision was more communal than individualist. Nonetheless, there was considerably more economic equality and cohesion than in most parts of the world.

At first, the new towns divided up only a portion of the land that they held, reserving the rest for newcomers and the children of the original founders. The land was distributed unequally, according to social status and family size (see Table 3–2). Although New England society was relatively egalitarian, with only a small gap between the richest and poorest, the Puritans set out to create a social hierarchy. The rich and powerful were supposed to take care of the poor, and Puritan towns did assist all those who

Table 3-2 Distribution of Land in Rowley, Massachusetts, 1639–ca. 1642

Acres	No. of Grants
over 400	
351–400	
301–350	
251–300	
201–250	1
151–200	1
101–150	
51–100	7
21–50	22
20 or less	63
no record	1
Total	95

Source: David Grayson Allen, In English Ways: The Movement of Societies and the Transferal of English Local Law and Custom to Massachusetts Bay in the Seventeenth Century (Chapel Hill: University of North Carolina Press, 1981), p. 32.

Note: Between 1639 and 1642, the town of Rowley, Massachusetts, distributed a little over 2,000 acres to 95 families—an average of just 23 acres per family—even though the grant to the town was for many thousand acres. Although most grants were for fewer than 20 acres, some families received considerably more. The founders of Rowley wanted to re-create the hierarchical social order they had known in England.

could not care for themselves. Each town administered itself through a town meeting, a periodic gathering of the adult male property owners to attend to the town's business. In the past, historians pointed to the democratic elements in the town meeting as the source of American democracy. More recently, historians have emphasized undemocratic elements. Participation was restricted to adult male property holders, who were only 35 percent of the adult residents, once women are considered. In addition, the habit of deference to the powerful, prosperous, and educated was so strong that a small group of influential men tended to govern each town. Moreover, Puritans abhorred conflict, so great social pressure was used to ensure harmony and limit dissent. If democracy means the right to disagree and majority rule in open elections, then the New England town meeting was not fully democratic. However, even with all these restrictions, the New England town meeting was far more democratic than any form of government in England at the time, where the vast majority of men, not to mention women, were excluded from political participation.

Changing the Landscape to Fit the Political Economy

The Puritans' corporate social vision was generally compatible with a capitalist political economy. Although land was distributed to towns, once those towns transferred parcels of the land to individual farmers, the farmers were free to leave it to their heirs, to sell it to whomever they pleased, and to buy more land from others. Any improvements on the land (from clearing away trees to building homes, fences, dams, or mills) remained the property of the owners. These practices followed English law.

The contrast with Indian patterns of land use was dramatic. Indians held their land communally, not individually. The entire group had to consent to its sale. At first, when Indians "sold" land to the Puritans, they thought that they were giving them the right to use the land only and to share the land with them. They might allow the Puritans to build a village, plant, and hunt, while they retained similar rights over the same parcel of land, including the right to allow it to be used by several groups of Europeans at once.

The Puritans' notion of exclusive land rights was a cornerstone of their political economy. Because a man could profit from the improvements made on his land and pass those improvements on to his heirs, he had incentives to make them. Moreover, not only the land but its products became commodities to be sold. Thus, like other European colonists, the Puritans turned their Indian neighbors into commercial hunters. For centuries, the Indians had taken only as many beaver as they needed, but now that they found themselves fenced out of their former lands, they could no longer live part of the year by farming and became more committed to hunting. Overhunting led to the disappearance of beaver in the region.

The Puritans themselves cleared the forests of trees. They found a ready market for timber in England, as New England's trees were much taller and straighter than any known in Europe. The English navy came to depend on New England for its masts. Although the bounty of the land had seemed limitless, by 1800 much of southern New England had been stripped of its forests and native wildlife (see Figure 3–1).

Prosperity did not come to Massachusetts immediately. For the first decade, the colony maintained a favorable balance of trade with England only by sending back the money that new immigrants brought with them in return for goods from the mother country. New England's cold climate made it impossible to develop a cash crop such as tobacco. In the 1640s and 1650s, the government encouraged local manufacturing (to cut down on imports) and export of raw materials. Through government policy and individual initiative, New Englanders eventually made great profits from selling timber, wood products, and fish and by acting as merchants. In the meantime, successful family farms were the mainstay of the local economy.

The Puritan Family

Like most early-modern western Europeans, Puritans thought of the family as the society in microcosm, or "a little Church, and a little commonwealth." There was no sharp distinction between home and the wider world. Although Harvard College was founded in 1636 (to train ministers) and the Massachusetts General Court established

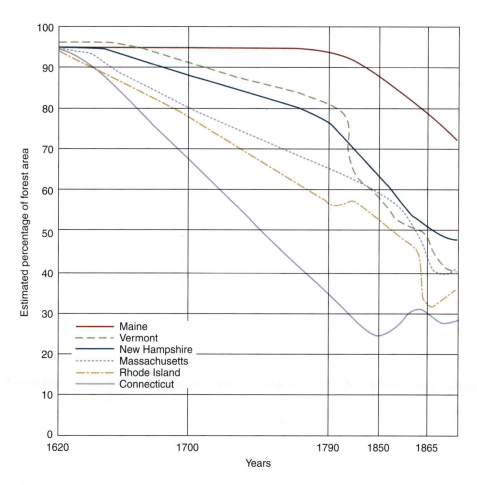

Figure 3-1 Disappearance of New England's Forests As the rate of settlement increased, the percentage of the land that was forested decreased. *Carolyn Merchant,* Ecological Revolutions: Nature, Gender, and Science in New England *(Chapel Hill: University of North Carolina Press, 1989), p. 225.*

AMERICAN LANDSCAPE

>> New England Settlements

When we picture a New England town, we think of a cluster of two-story, white-clapboard colonial homes with black shutters, arrayed around the town green, at one end of which sits a little church, its steeple rising above the village. Many such villages dot the New England countryside, but they date not from the colonial period but from the early nineteenth century.

When the Pilgrims and the Puritans after them moved to New England, they had to adapt to a new environment. Many of their preachers hoped that they would settle in small villages in which the houses were close to each other. In 1635, the Massachusetts General Court instructed that "noe dwelling howse shal be builte above half a myle from the meeting howse." This law, however, was an after-the-fact attempt to keep the population from dispersing. From the earliest years of Plymouth, the settlers spread out, seeking pastures for their cattle. It was by now too late to pull New Englanders back into clustered villages.

The only places in New England where settlers built their houses close to each other and to the church were more prosperous market and commercial towns. Many of the first New England settlers had lived in market towns in England, and they would have practiced their crafts and trades in the New World if they could have earned a living in that way. In New England, most of them turned to farming, and in particular raising cattle, which required large expanses of pastureland. Fortunately, New Englanders could spread themselves and their cattle out along the coast's many marshes and meadows. Even in Boston, the largest settlement, the farming population soon spread out. Boston's site was chosen because of its harbor, its water supply, and its defensive capacity rather than its farmlands. The original settlers sent their sons and servants to outlying areas to farm for them, and they eventually created new towns. The environment and the drive to earn a living were more powerful forces than religion or community.

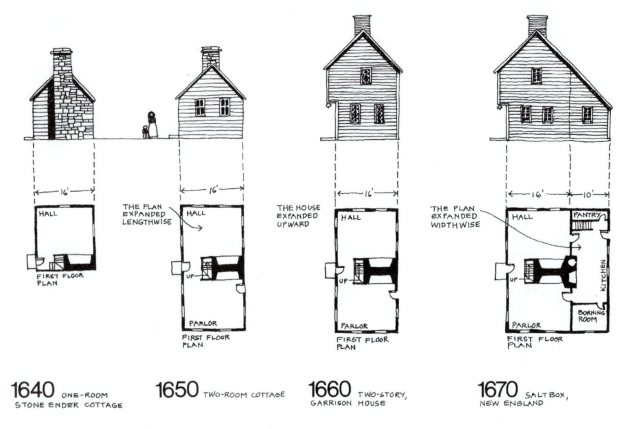

1640 ONE-ROOM STONE ENDER COTTAGE

1650 TWO-ROOM COTTAGE

1660 TWO-STORY, GARRISON HOUSE

1670 SALT BOX, NEW ENGLAND

Over time, this impulse toward economic independence would undermine the forces of cohesion.

The first houses the settlers built were little more than huts, small one-room windowless cottages with chimneys made out of clay-covered logs. But even later homes were modest one-and-a-half-story, unpainted houses with low ceilings and very few windows. Although affluent people such as Governor John Winthrop began to build larger and more elegant homes as late as the end of the eighteenth century, most New England homes were still very small by modern standards. The typical house was just over 800 square feet, perhaps 40 feet long by 20 feet wide, with many only half that size, or even smaller. Considering that eight or nine people typically lived in such homes, living conditions could be quite crowded.

Only when the scale of economic development changed, so that town centers could sustain a variety of stores and shops, did New Englanders build homes around the village green and begin painting them white. The classic New England village is in fact the creation of the nineteenth century. Until then, most New Englanders lived in small dark homes scattered across the countryside, closer to their farmlands than to their neighbors.

a system of public education in 1647, most early instruction and virtually all vocational teaching took place at home. Parents were required to teach their children to read the Bible.

The family was also the center of the Puritans' economy. Farmers, of course, worked at home, as did almost all craftsmen. Women also performed tasks critical to the survival of the family. Although tasks were assigned by gender, in the absence of her husband a woman could assume his responsibilities, selling the products he had made or even fighting off Indians. The family, like society, was a hierarchy, with the husband at the top and his wife as his "deputy."

Puritans lived in fear of lawlessness, and they used the family as an instrument of order. Puritans considered excessive affection and particularly excessive maternal love a danger. Children were subjected to strict discipline not out of cruelty but from deep religious convictions. Considering that Puritan women bore on average eight or nine children and that families were confined in small houses over long New England winters, this harmony was probably necessary for survival.

Despite the importance of control, Puritan households were hardly prisons. If Puritans believed that men were the natural heads of the household and that women bore particular responsibility for Eve's original sin, they also believed that both were equally capable of God's grace. Puritans distrusted the passion of love, which could lead to impulsiveness and disorder. They had great respect, however, for the natural affection that grew over the course of marriage, and encouraged playfulness when it helped rather than impeded social harmony.

So successful were the early Puritans in establishing tight-knit communities that only two years after their great migration to America had begun, the Reverend Thomas Welde could write proudly back to England, "[H]ere I find three great blessings, peace, plenty, and health. . . . I profess if I might have my wish in what part of the world to dwell I know no other place on the whole globe of the earth where I would be rather than here."

Dissension in the Puritan Ranks

Yet not everyone lived in such bliss. The Puritan movement embodied tensions that created individual and social turmoil. Puritans had difficulty balancing emotion and intellect, the individual and the community, spiritual equality and social hierarchy, and anxiety over salvation and the satisfaction of thinking oneself a member of a chosen people. The Puritans also had no mechanisms for handling dissent, which they interpreted as a replay of original sin. The migration to a strange land, populated by people they thought of as savages, as well as the pressure of thinking that the whole world was watching them, only increased the Puritans' desire to maintain a strict order.

Roger Williams and Toleration

The Massachusetts Bay Colony was only a year old when trouble appeared in the person of Roger Williams, a brilliant and obstinate young minister. No sooner had he landed than he announced that he was really a Separatist and would not accept appointment at a church unless it repudiated its ties to the Church of England. Massachusetts Bay was already walking a fine line between outward obedience to the laws of England and inner rejection of the English way of life, and an explicit repudiation of the established church was thought to be an act of political suicide.

Without a church of his own, Williams began preaching to those who would listen. Saying that the king had no right to grant land owned by the Indians, he questioned the validity of the Massachusetts charter and argued for strict separation of church and state, as well as strict separation of the converted and the unconverted. Williams went so far as to advocate religious toleration, with each congregation or sect governing itself completely free from state interference.

These doctrines were heresy to both Puritan church and state. In 1635, when Williams violated an order to stop preaching his unorthodox views, the magistrates decided to ship him immediately to England, where he might be imprisoned or even executed. John Winthrop warned Williams of his fate, giving him time to sneak away to Narragansett Bay, outside the jurisdiction of Massachusetts Bay. Williams and some followers established the new colony of Rhode Island, which was chartered in 1644. The colony, which became a refuge for dissenters of all sorts, was referred to by Massachusetts Puritans as "the sewer of New England."

Anne Hutchinson and the Equality of Believers

One of Puritanism's many tensions concerned the position of women. By insisting on the equality of all true believers before God and the importance of marriage, Protestantism and especially its Puritan branch undermined the starkly negative image of women that prevailed in sixteenth-century Europe. When Puritan ministers preached that women and men were both "joynt Heirs of salvation" and that women, rather than being a "necessary evil," were in fact "a necessary good," they were directly criticizing both the Catholic legacy and common folk belief.

Puritanism extended women respect, but it also insisted they be subordinate to men. In their hierarchical society, woman's position was clearly beneath that of man. Puritanism struggled to find the balance between women's spiritual equality and their earthly subordination: although most Puritan women deferred to male authority, others seized the opportunity that Puritanism seemed to offer. Without exception, the Puritan authorities put them back in their place.

Anne Hutchinson was just over 40 when she, her husband, and their 12 children followed the Reverend John Cotton to Massachusetts Bay. Cotton was a popular preacher who placed particular emphasis on the doctrine of predestination. Hutchinson pushed that doctrine to its logical, if unsettling, conclusion. She claimed that she

Anne Hutchinson on Trial Although Anne Hutchinson (1591–1643) alienated the Puritan authorities of her own day, many Americans remembered her intellectual courage with pride, as this nineteenth-century engraving of her trial demonstrates.

had experienced several direct revelations, one telling her to follow Cotton to Boston. At informal Bible discussion meetings at her Boston home, which even the new governor attended, Hutchinson challenged the Puritan doctrine of "preparation": if God had truly chosen those whom he would save, it was unnecessary for Puritans to prepare themselves for saving grace by leading sin-free lives. Nor was good behavior a reliable sign of salvation. Hutchinson did not favor sin; she simply believed her neighbors were wrong in thinking that good works would save them. She accused them of the heresy of Arminianism. By claiming that the Holy Spirit spoke directly to her, Hutchinson opened herself to charges of another heresy, antinomianism.

Hutchinson's views were so popular that many residents—possibly a majority—became her followers. Once she accused certain ministers of being unconverted, the colony leaders mounted a campaign against her and her allies. In 1637 they moved the site of the election for governor outside Boston, where her strength was greatest, so that John Winthrop could win. Then, after her most prominent ally among the ministers had been banished, Hutchinson was put on trial for slandering the ministry, convicted, and ordered to leave the colony. Followed by 80 other families, she and her family found temporary refuge in Roger Williams's Rhode Island. (She later moved to New Netherland, where she was killed in an Indian war.) The fact that Hutchinson's ideas came from a woman made them even more dangerous to the Massachusetts leadership. John Winthrop suggested that she might be a witch. Without any evidence at all of sexual misconduct, ministers asserted that Hutchinson and her female followers were driven by

Gov. John Winthrop:

Mrs. Hutchinson, you are called here as one of those that have troubled the peace of the commonwealth and the churches here: you are known to be a woman that hath had a great share in the promoting . . . those opinions that are the cause of this trouble, and to be nearly joined not only in affinity and affection with some of those the court had taken notice of and passed censure upon, but you have spoken divers thing . . . very prejudicial to the honour of the churches and ministers thereof, and you have maintained a meeting and an assembly in your house that hath been condemned by the general assembly as a thing not tolerable nor comely in the sight of God nor fitting for your sex, and notwithstanding that was cried down you have continued the same. Therefore we have thought good to send for you to understand how things are, that if you be in an erroneous way we may reduce you that so you may become a profitable member here among us. Otherwise if you be obstinate in your course that then the court may take such course that you may trouble us no further. Therefore I would intreat you to express whether you do assent and hold in practice to those opinions and factions that have been handled in court already, that is to say, whether you do not justify Mr. Wheelwright's sermon and the petition.

Mrs. Anne Hutchinson:

I am called here to answer before you but I hear no things laid to my charge.

From the transcript of the trial of Anne Hutchinson

lust and that unless they were punished, it would lead to communal living, open sex, and the repudiation of marriage.

It is sometimes asserted that Puritans came to New England in search of religious freedom, but they never would have made that claim. They wanted the liberty to follow their own religion but actively denied that opportunity to others. Puritans insisted on their right to keep out nonbelievers. "No man hath right to come into us," John Winthrop wrote, "without our consent."

Puritan Indian Policy and the Pequot War

The Puritan dissidents were all critical of the Puritans' Indian policy. Roger Williams insisted on purchasing land from the Indians instead of simply seizing it, and the men in the Hutchinson family refused to fight in the Pequot War of 1637. The Puritans had been fortunate in settling in a region in which the Indian population had recently been decimated and in having the English-speaking Squanto's diplomatic services. The Puritan communities expanded so rapidly, however, that they soon intruded on land populated by Indians who had no intention of giving them exclusive rights to it.

Within a few years of the founding of the Massachusetts Bay Colony, small groups of Puritans were spreading out in all directions (see Map 3–3). The Reverend John Wheelwright, Anne Hutchinson's brother-in-law and most ardent supporter, took a party into what is now New Hampshire. Others settled in Maine. In 1638, New Haven, Connecticut, was founded by the Reverend John Davenport and a London merchant, Theophilus Eaton, who purchased land from local Indians. Four years earlier, the first Puritan settlers had reached the Connecticut River in western Massachusetts. In 1636 the Reverend Thomas Hooker led his followers to the site of Hartford, Connecticut.

The Pequot War grew out of conflicts among Europeans about who would govern the fertile Connecticut River valley and among Native Americans about who would trade with the Europeans. Until the arrival of the English, the Dutch had controlled trade along the Connecticut River. They had granted trading privileges to the Pequots, which frustrated other tribes, who could trade only through these middlemen. When the English arrived, the Pequots' enemies attempted to attract them to the valley as trading rivals to the Dutch. The Pequots, afraid of losing their monopoly, made the mistake of inviting Massachusetts Bay to establish a trading post in the region. They were counting on their ability to control not only their Indian enemies but also the Dutch and English. As hundreds of settlers poured in, the Pequots became alarmed. They appealed to their one-time enemies, the Narragansetts, to join with them to get rid of the English. The Narragansetts, however, had already been approached by the Puritans to

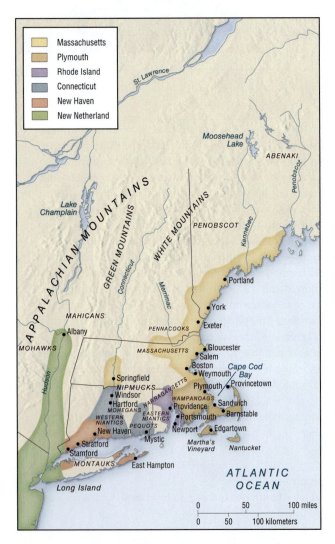

Map 3–3 New England in the 1640s This map shows the land settled by each of the New England colonies, the regions inhabited by Indian tribes, and the region of Dutch settlement. *John Murrin et al.,* Liberty, Equality, Power *(Orlando, FL: Harcourt College Publishers, 1995), p. 73.*

join them in fighting the Pequots. That is where the Narragansetts calculated that their long-term advantage lay. They themselves were in desperate need of land, having been squeezed beyond endurance by the English settlements. Their leaders recognized the greater power of the English as allies than the Pequots.

The Pequots were caught in a rivalry for their lands between the parent colony in Massachusetts and the new offshoot in Connecticut. The Connecticut group struck first, avenging an attack by the Pequots, which in itself was in revenge for an attack on their allies. At dawn on May 26, 1637, 90 Connecticut men accompanied by 500 Narragansett allies attacked a Pequot village at Mystic filled with women, children, and old men. The raiders knew most of the warriors were away from home. As his men encircled the village, the commander, Captain John Mason, set a torch to the wigwams, shouting, "We must burn them." Those Pequots who escaped the fire ran into the ring of Mason's party, who killed between 300 and 700 Indians, while losing only two of their own men. The Narragansetts' Indian allies were so horrified by the brutal attack that they refused to participate in it.

Deeply demoralized, the remainder of the Pequot tribe was easily defeated. Prisoners were sold into slavery in the sister Puritan colony of Providence Island. By 1638, the Puritans declared the Pequot tribe dissolved, and in 1639 Connecticut established its dominance over the Pequots' land. In that year Connecticut established its own government, modeled after that of Massachusetts. In 1662 it became a royal colony. The Puritans had demonstrated that where ecological changes were insufficient to destroy the Indians, they were more than willing to use violence.

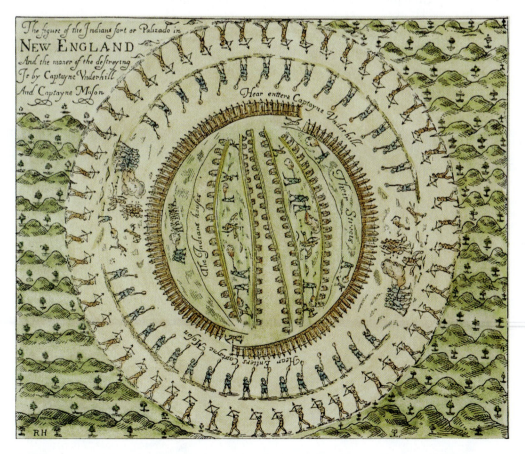

The Attack on Mystic Fort On the inner ring are the New Englanders, attacking the palisaded Indian village.

Conclusion

At the middle of the seventeenth century, the New England and Chesapeake colonies could hardly have appeared more different. Although the forces of capitalism shaped each region, other factors—disease, demographic patterns, relations with the Indians, and the objectives of the founders—left their distinctive imprints. The early history and relatively quick settlement of New England was shaped by the extraordinary cohesiveness and relatively high social standing of the Puritan settlers, which made them uniquely successful. By contrast, New France and New Netherland were rough frontier societies for many decades, and the Chesapeake colonies were still raw outposts long after New England had achieved a secure order.

All of the North American colonies except those of New England were outposts in the transatlantic political and economic order, created to enrich their mother countries and enhance those countries' power. Had the Virginia Company known that the Puritans wanted to create a religious refuge rather than a moneymaking venture, it might not have given them a charter. So successful was New England in achieving a stable society that we sometimes forget that it was the exception and not the rule.

Who, What

Anne Hutchinson   94
Pocahontas   69
Powhatan   69
Captain John Smith   71
Squanto   85
Roger Williams   94
John Winthrop   87
Anglo-Powhatan Wars   74
Antinomianism   95

Arminianism   84
Calvinism   84
Charter colony   79
Headright   76
Indentured servants   71
Pequot War   96
Proprietary colony   79
Royal colony   76

>> TIME LINE

▼**1533**
Henry VIII breaks with Roman Catholic Church, establishes Church of England

▼**1603**
Queen Elizabeth I dies, succeeded by King James I

▼**1606**
James I grants two charters for North American settlement to Virginia Company

▼**1607**
English found Jamestown

▼**1608**
John Smith named president of Virginia's council

▼**1609**
John Smith returns to England

▼**1610–1614**
First Anglo-Powhatan War

▼**1612–1617**
John Rolfe develops a marketable strain of tobacco

▼**1614**
John Rolfe and Pocahontas marry

▼**1616**
Virginia Company offers a 50-acre headright to each immigrant

▼**1619**
First meeting of Virginia General Assembly
First Africans arrive in Virginia
Virginia Company pays for transportation of women to Virginia

▼**1620**
Pilgrims found colony at Plymouth; Mayflower Compact signed

▼**1622–1632**
Second Anglo-Powhatan War

Review Questions

1. What were the objectives of the founders of Virginia? Why did the colony survive, in spite of poor planning?

2. What were the objectives of the founders of the Puritan colonies at Plymouth and Massachusetts Bay? Compare the early years of these colonies to those of the Virginia Colony.

3. What role did gender play in the social order of the Chesapeake and New England colonies?

Critical-Thinking Questions

1. Were the more amicable native-white relations in early New England, as compared to those in Virginia, the result of greater tolerance on the part of the New Englanders or greater willingness to compromise on the part of the Indians?

2. What factors other than religious commitment help explain the success of the Puritan colonies in Massachusetts?

3. Which society was more democratic in its original formulation, the New England colony or the Chesapeake colony? Explain your answer.

4. Are you more impressed by the ease or the slowness that the Chesapeake demonstrated in adopting African slavery? Explain your answer.

For further review materials and resource information, please visit www.oup.com/us/ofthepeople

▼1624
Virginia Company dissolved; Virginia becomes a royal colony

▼1625
James I dies, succeeded by King Charles I

▼1629
Massachusetts Bay Company receives charter to establish colony in North America

▼1630
Massachusetts Bay Colony founded

▼1632
George Calvert receives charter for Maryland

▼1636
Harvard College founded
Roger Williams exiled from Massachusetts

▼1637
Anne Hutchinson and her followers exiled
Pequot War

▼1638
New Haven founded

▼1639
First law mentioning slavery, in Maryland
Connecticut establishes its government

▼1644
Rhode Island receives charter

▼1644–1646
Third Anglo-Powhatan War

▼1647
Massachusetts establishes system of public education

▼1649
Act of Toleration passed in Maryland

▼1661
First Virginia law mentioning slavery

▼1691
Plymouth Colony absorbed into Massachusetts

1) The nature of the first Chesapeake colonies (profitable cash crops and a shortage of indentured servants) yielded a political and economic system based on African slavery.

2) The nature of the colonies in New England (largely middle-class families settling together, with a rigid social structure plus a reliance on the Indian trade) caused dissension and warfare, which ultimately decimated the Indians.

3) While notable, the contrast between the two sets of colonies should not be overemphasized. Puritans who settled in southern climes and relied on coerced labor created colonies (such places as Providence Island) similar to those of the Chesapeake.

The First Chesapeake Colonies

The Political Economy of Slavery Emerges

A Bible Commonwealth in the New England Wilderness

Dissension in the Puritan Ranks

CHAPTER 3

THE ENGLISH COME TO STAY

1600–1660

EVENTS

Founding Virginia The English established a new colony in Jamestown.

Starving Times The Jamestown colonists died in large numbers due to malnutrition and disease.

Troubled Relations with the Powhatans The Powhatans and the English clashed, each seeking power over the other.

Toward a New Economic Order and the Rise of Democracy Virginia expanded with the cultivation of tobacco, attracting settlers by offering economic opportunity and self-determination.

Toward the Destruction of the Powhatans After a series of wars, the English took nearly complete control of the Powhatans' land.

A New Colony in Maryland The English established the first proprietary colony in Maryland, extending broader rights to draw settlers.

The Problem of a Labor Supply Colonial officials' biggest problem was the lack of laborers.

The Origins of African Slavery in the Chesapeake African slavery was introduced to provide a cheap source of labor in the Chesapeake.

Gender and the Social Order in the Chesapeake The tobacco economy altered the gender roles found in England.

The English Origins of the Puritan Movement Religious dissension and persecution increased as England's monarchs alternated religious views.

What Did the Puritans Believe? Puritans wanted to remove all remnants of Catholicism from the English church.

The Pilgrim Colony at Plymouth The Pilgrims settled at Plymouth and survived only because of Indian assistance.

The Puritan Colony at Massachusetts Bay The English established a thriving colony in the Massachusetts Bay region.

The New England Way The Puritans established a relatively egalitarian social structure that created a stable society.

Changing the Landscape to Fit the Political Economy The colonists' development of the land and idea of land rights stood in sharp contrast to those of their Indian neighbors.

The Puritan Family A rigid family structure was central to Puritan society and economy.

Roger Williams and Toleration Religious dissenter Roger Williams established a separate colony in Rhode Island.

Anne Hutchinson and the Equality of Believers Anne Hutchinson was exiled for challenging Puritan religious doctrine.

Puritan Indian Policy and the Pequot War Conflicts over European control of the Connecticut River valley and trading partnerships with Indians led to war.

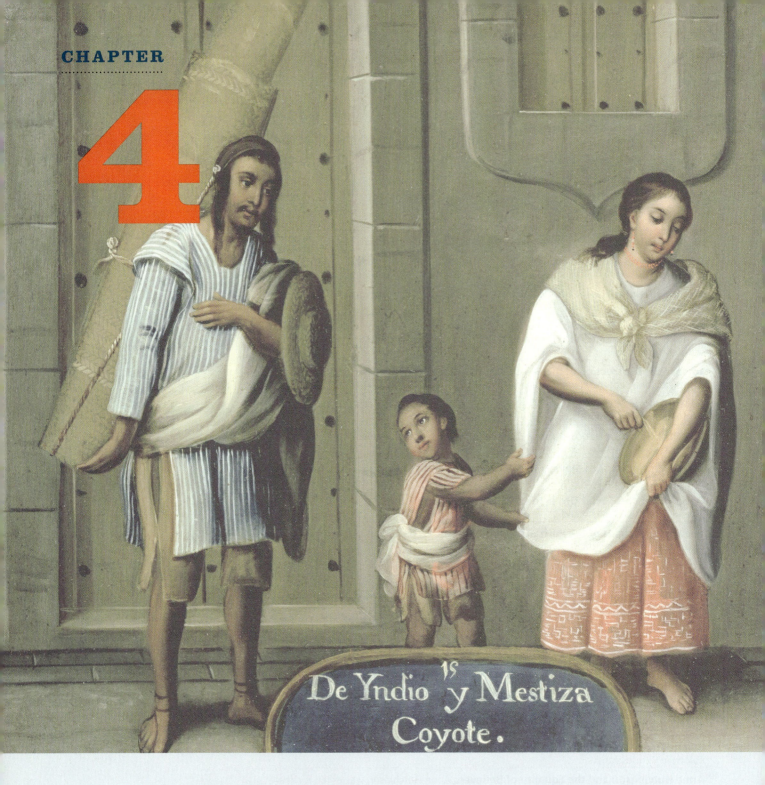

De Yndio, y Mestiza Coyote.

COMMON THREADS

>> What forces—political, economic, military, social, and cultural—gave shape to the English empire in the New World? Which of these forces figured in the conscious plan of empire, and which shaped the empire nonetheless?

>> How did imperial politics—in particular the contest between England and France, and England's larger geopolitical objectives—affect the lives of ordinary men and women in the colonies?

>> What is a slave society, and how did Virginia become one?

>> Which European institutions transplanted easily to North America, and which did not?

Continental Empires
1660–1720

AMERICAN PORTRAIT

>> **Tituba Shapes Her World and Saves Herself**

Her name was Tituba. Some say she was African, a Yoruba, others that she was an Arawak Indian from Guyana. Had she not been accused of practicing witchcraft in Salem, Massachusetts, in 1692, she surely would have been forgotten by history. Whether she came from South America or Africa, she had been torn away from her home and sent to work on a sugar plantation on the Caribbean island of Barbados, which the English had colonized almost 50 years before. Whatever her origins, Tituba lived in an African-majority society and absorbed African customs.

Tituba was probably a teenager when she was taken, again as a slave, to Massachusetts in 1680. She had been purchased by a young, Harvard-educated Barbadian, Samuel Parris. Parris's father had failed as a planter, and now he himself had failed as a merchant. In 1689 Parris moved his wife, their three children, Tituba, and her slave husband John Indian to Salem Village, where he had taken up a new profession, the ministry.

Three years later, all of their lives changed forever when one of Parris's daughters, Betty, and her cousin Abigail followed the folk custom of trying to see their futures in the white of an egg dropped into a glass of water. Soon several girls and young women were playing with magic. Then Betty began to experience strange and seemingly inexplicable pains, which spread to other young women. When neither doctors nor ministers could cure them, a neighbor asked Tituba to bake a "witchcake" out of rye flour and the girls' urine. This was "white magic," intended to uncover the identity of the witch who was thought to be bewitching Betty and the others. Their suffering, however, only got worse. Parris now questioned the girls: Who was bewitching them? This time the girls had an answer: two older, rather marginal white women—and Tituba.

The three women were charged with the capital offense of witchcraft. Under duress, the first woman, Sarah Good, implicated the second, Sarah Osborne. Osborne steadfastly denied her guilt and was returned to jail. Finally, Tituba was summoned. As a slave, she was particularly vulnerable. Perhaps calculating the odds carefully, Tituba slowly began to embroider a story. She named only two names—Sarah Good and Sarah Osborne. She talked about a tall, white-haired man in Boston who made her sign a mysterious book and about conspiring with other, unnamed witches.

Responding to the hints of her Puritan interrogators, Tituba confirmed that she had made a covenant with the devil, the tall man in Boston. But she also added elements that came from African and Indian cultures, such as a "thing all over hairy, all the face harye & a long nose. . . ." Tituba's tales of witches' meetings, flying to Boston on a broomstick, and wolves and birds and hairy imps persuaded her interrogators that their colony was beset by witches. A children's game spiraled into panic, but Tituba escaped with her life. Having spent her life as a prisoner in other people's lands, she had combined their cultures with her own, crafting them into a strategy for survival.

Colonial America in the second half of the seventeenth century was remarkably unstable. Without secure colonial governments, colonial societies were torn by conflicting cultural and

Continued

>> AMERICAN PORTRAIT
Continued

economic forces. In some ways, Tituba was a victim of these crosscurrents. She was in Salem because Samuel Parris failed as a merchant, unable to succeed in the world's economy. Tituba's freedom was sacrificed so that other, more powerful people could become prosperous. Instability, however, creates opportunity as it creates danger. By melding her own culture and that of her captors, Tituba became a cultural shape-shifter, and she was able to save herself when she faced accusations of witchcraft. Though more dramatic, Tituba's story is like that of many Americans of the late seventeenth century. Caught in the crosscurrents of cultural and economic transformation, they adapted their cultural inheritances to new circumstances.

The Plan of Empire

Trying to make sense of the haphazard development of Britain's American colonies, the English political theorist Edmund Burke explained in 1757, "The settlement of our colonies was never pursued upon any regular plan; but they were formed, grew, and flourished, as accidents, the nature of the climate, or the dispositions of private men happened to operate." In comparison, the Spanish and French governments more actively directed their colonies, but even then, the portions of their empires that would one day become the United States were so marginal that they, too, received relatively little attention. The British colonies were all private ventures, chartered by the government but little supervised or supported. So long as mainland colonies contributed little to the national wealth and cost the government less, they received the loosest of controls and were permitted to develop each in its own way.

The result was a period of significant instability at the end of the seventeenth century, as local colonial governments struggled to control their inhabitants, police their borders, and establish successful economies. In many of the colonies, elites vied for control, whereas in others poor people rose up against insecure leadership. As expanding populations and aggressive traders pushed against native populations, violence exploded. Elsewhere, the British, French, and Dutch—and their Indian allies—collided. In the midst of these struggles, colonists such as Tituba found themselves caught in—and taking advantage of—the crosscurrents.

Turmoil in England

In the middle of the seventeenth century, the British government was thrown into turmoil as Parliament and the king struggled over the future direction of the nation. Two

OUTLINE

The Plan of Empire
  Turmoil in England
  The Political Economy of Mercantilism

New Colonies, New Patterns
  New Netherland Becomes New York

PRIMARY SOURCE:
  The Navigation Act of 1651
  Diversity and Prosperity in Pennsylvania

AMERICAN LANDSCAPE:
  New Amsterdam/New York

Indians and Africans in the Political Economy of
  Carolina
  The Barbados Connection

The Transformation of Virginia
  Social Change in Virginia
  Bacon's Rebellion and the Abandonment of the
    Middle Ground
  Virginia Becomes a Slave Society

DEBATING HISTORY:
  Origins of Slavery

New England Under Assault

issues were at stake: religion and royal power. The uneasy balance that Elizabeth I had established between Puritans and the Church of England collapsed under her successors James I (1603–1625) and Charles I (1625–1649). Archbishop of Canterbury William Laud moved the Church of England away from the Calvinist belief in predestination, brought back worship that smacked of Catholicism, and persecuted Puritans, prompting Presbyterian Scotland to revolt.

Parliament refused to appropriate the funds that King Charles requested to quash the revolt. Instead, in 1628, Parliament passed the Petition of Right, which reasserted such basic freedoms as no taxation except by act of Parliament, no arbitrary arrest or imprisonment, and no quartering of soldiers in private homes. After years of stalemate, in 1642 Charles raised an army and moved against the Parliament, beginning the English Civil War, which concluded in 1647 with Parliament's victory. Two years later, Charles was beheaded. Oliver Cromwell, a Puritan, ruled as Lord Protector until his death in 1658. When Cromwell's son and successor proved an inept leader, Charles II was invited to reclaim the crown in 1660.

Execution of King Charles I This eyewitness picture was painted by John Weesop, a visiting Flemish artist.

Social Prosperity and the Fear of Religious Decline
King Philip's War
Indians and the Empire

The Empire Strikes
  The Dominion of New England
  The Glorious Revolution in Britain and America
  The Rights of Englishmen
  Conflict in the Empire

Massachusetts in Crisis
  The Social and Cultural Contexts of Witchcraft
  Witchcraft at Salem

The End of Witchcraft

AMERICA AND THE WORLD:
  Witchcraft in Global Perspective

Empires in Collision
  France Attempts an Empire
  The Spanish Outpost in Florida
  Conquest, Revolt, and Reconquest in New Mexico
  Native Americans and the Country Between

Conclusion

Although the monarchy had been restored, its authority had been diminished. Britain had been transformed into a constitutional monarchy in which the power of the Crown was balanced by that of Parliament. Britain also found a middle way between Calvinist Protestantism and Catholicism. When the Catholic King James II (1685–1688) tried to fill the government with Catholics and to rule without the consent of Parliament, he was removed in a bloodless revolution, known as the Glorious Revolution (1688). It brought Mary, James's Protestant daughter, and her Protestant husband, William of Orange (Holland), to the throne.

The Political Economy of Mercantilism

After the reassertion of Parliament's authority in 1688, the British state became increasingly strong and centralized. Britain then embarked on a course that would make it the world's most powerful nation by the early nineteenth century.

Throughout the political turmoil of the seventeenth century, Britain's economic policies were guided by a theory called mercantilism, which held that the chief object of a nation's economic policies was to serve the state. Mercantilism was developed to facilitate the consolidation of the new European nation-states, which required vast amounts of money to support their growing military and bureaucracies. Mercantilists considered the economy and politics as zero-sum games; one side's gain was another's loss. Wealth was defined exclusively as hard money, that is, gold and silver. With only a finite amount of gold and silver in the world, a nation could best improve its position by capturing a share of other nations' money. Mercantilism thus led to rivalry between nations. Between 1651 and 1696, the mercantilist British government passed a series of trade regulations, the Navigation Acts, requiring that all goods shipped to England and its colonies be carried in ships owned and manned by the English (including colonists). All foreign goods going to the colonies had to be shipped via Britain, where they could be taxed, and some colonial products (tobacco, sugar, indigo, and cotton, to start) had to be sent first to England before being shipped elsewhere. In mercantilist doctrine, the mother country was to produce finished products, and the colonies, raw materials. Hence, when the colonies began to manufacture items such as woolen cloth and hats, Parliament restricted those industries.

New Colonies, New Patterns

Lacking tight English control, each colony developed differently. In the second half of the seventeenth century, two important new English colonies, Pennsylvania and South Carolina, were established, and New Netherland was seized from the Dutch. As a rule, the most successful colonies offered the most opportunity to free white people and the greatest amount of religious toleration.

New Netherland Becomes New York

By the middle of the seventeenth century, the British were ready to challenge their chief trade rival, the Dutch, whom they defeated in three wars between 1652 and 1674. The Navigation Acts cut the Dutch out of international trade, and Britain began to challenge Dutch dominance of the slave trade. In 1663 King Charles II chartered the Royal Africa Company to carry slaves out of Africa to the British West Indies. Britain also made a move for New Netherland.

James, the Duke of York and King Charles II's younger brother, persuaded Charles to grant him the territory between the Connecticut and Delaware Rivers (present-day

>> The Navigation Act of 1651

The Navigation Act of 1651 was the first in a series that would number nearly 200 and end with the American revolutionary crisis. The act laid out a system later called mercantilism. *This system ensured a favorable balance of trade for the home country by forcing the colonies to ship certain raw materials to the mother country and pay for manufactured goods of greater value in exchange. This maximized the inflow of specie— gold and silver—for the mother country.*

For the increase of the shipping and the encouragement of the navigation of this nation, which under the good providence and protection of God is so great a means of the welfare and safety of this Commonwealth: be it enacted by this present Parliament, and the authority thereof, that from and after the first day of December, one thousand six hundred fifty and one, and from thence forwards, no goods or commodities whatsoever of the growth, production or manufacture of Asia, Africa or America, or of any part thereof; or of any islands belonging to them, or which are described or laid down in the usual maps or cards of those places, as well of the English plantations as others, shall be imported or brought into this Commonwealth of England, or into Ireland, or any other lands, islands, plantations, or territories to this Commonwealth belonging, or in their possession, in any other ship or ships, vessel or vessels whatsoever, but only in such as do truly and without fraud belong only to the people of this Commonwealth, or the plantations thereof, as the proprietors or right owners thereof; and whereof the master and mariners are also for the most part of them of the people of this Commonwealth, under the penalty of the forfeiture and loss of all the goods that shall be imported contrary to this act; as also of the ship (with all her tackle, guns and apparel) in which the said goods or commodities shall be so brought in and imported; the one moiety to the use of the Commonwealth, and the other moiety to the use and behoof of any person or persons who shall seize the goods or commodities, and shall prosecute the same in any court of record within this Commonwealth.

Continued

And it is further enacted by the authority aforesaid, that no goods or commodities of the growth, production, or manufacture of Europe, or of any part thereof, shall after the first day of December, one thousand six hundred fifty and one, be imported or brought into this Commonwealth of England, or into Ireland, or any other lands, islands, plantations or territories to this Commonwealth belonging, or in their possession, in any ship or ships, vessel or vessels whatsoever, but in such as do truly and without fraud belong only to the people of this Commonwealth, as the true owners and proprietors thereof, and in no other, except only such foreign ships and vessels as do truly and properly belong to the people of that country or place, of which the said goods are the growth, production or manufacture; or to such ports where the said goods can only be, or most usually are first shipped for transportation; and that under the same penalty of forfeiture and loss expressed in the former branch of this Act, the said forfeitures to be recovered and employed as is therein expressed.

And it is further enacted by the authority aforesaid, that no goods or commodities that are of foreign growth, production or manufacture, and which are to be brought into this Commonwealth in shipping belonging to the people thereof, shall be by them shipped or brought from any other place or places, country or countries, but only from those of their said growth, production, or manufacture, or from those ports where the said goods and commodities can only, or are, or usually have been first shipped for transportation; and from none other places or countries, under the same penalty of forfeiture and loss expressed in the first branch of this Act, the said forfeitures to be recovered and employed as is therein expressed.

"The Navigation Act, Ordinance of 1651, October 9th, 1651," in *American History Leaflets: Colonial and Constitutional. Number 19, Extracts from the Navigation Acts 1645–1696,* ed. Albert Bushnell Hart and Edward Channing (New York: A. Lovell and Company, 1895), pp. 6–7.

Questions

1. What are the targets of the law? What goods does it cover?

2. In this act, the word "Commonwealth" is used to describe England. What does the use of this word signify? Why might the authors of the act have chosen to use this word rather than another, such as "nation," for example?

3. What do you think were Parliament's goals in passing this law at this time? What benefits did Parliament hope to achieve for England?

Pennsylvania, New Jersey, New York, and part of Connecticut), which was occupied by the Netherlands. In 1664 James sent a governor, 400 troops, and several warships that easily conquered the small colony of New Amsterdam. In 1665 James gave away what is now New Jersey to two of his royal cronies, Lords John Berkeley and George Carteret, and in 1667 New York's governor gave the territory on the western side of the Connecticut River to Connecticut. New Netherland had become New York.

The new colony was part Dutch (in New York City and along the Hudson) and part English (on Long Island, where New England Puritans had migrated). The first governors attempted to satisfy both groups. The governors confirmed Dutch land-holdings, including huge estates along the Hudson, and guaranteed the Dutch religious freedom. The governors also distributed 2 million more acres of land, most of it in enormous chunks called manors. The owners of these manors, like feudal lords, rented land to tenants and set up courts on their estates.

If religious toleration attracted diverse peoples to the region, feudal land policies and England's failure to restore self-government kept others away. Without an elective legislature to raise taxes, the governors, following English mercantilist policy, used customs duties to raise the revenue necessary to run the colony and send a profit to James. These attempts to regulate trade and direct the economy angered local merchants and harmed the economy. Eventually, James gave in to popular discontent and, in 1683, allowed New York to have an elective assembly.

At its first meeting, this group of English and Dutch men passed a "Charter of Libertyes and Priviledges," which, had the king approved it, would have guaranteed New Yorkers a number of civil liberties and the continuing right to self-government by their elected assembly. The charter expressed the principles of liberalism starting to spread through both Britain and the Netherlands. (Liberalism places an emphasis on individual liberty and holds that all human beings are equally entitled to enjoy the freedom and fulfillment to be found in their social lives—their work, families, and churches.) The charter would have guaranteed all freemen the right to vote and to be taxed only by their elective representatives. It also provided for trial by jury, due process, freedom of conscience for Christians, and certain property rights for women, the latter two items reflecting Dutch practices. However, the king refused to approve the charter on two grounds: it would give New Yorkers more rights than any other colonists, and the New York Assembly might undermine the power of Parliament. Without secure self-government, New Yorkers fell to fighting among themselves, and political instability in combination with feudal land holdings slowed New York's population growth.

Diversity and Prosperity in Pennsylvania

Pennsylvania demonstrated the potential of a colony that offered both religious toleration and economic opportunity. Its founder, William Penn, was a Quaker and the son of one of King Charles II's leading supporters. After his restoration to the throne, Charles had a number of political

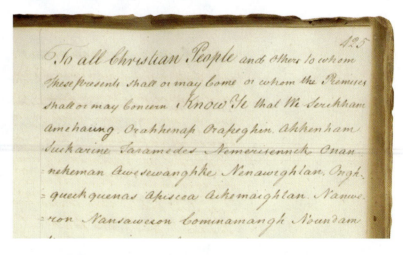

Deed Blandina Kierstede Bayard's purchase of land from Lenape Indians in 1700.

AMERICAN LANDSCAPE

>> New Amsterdam/New York

Today it is called Wall Street, and it represents the center of world finance, but in 1660, it was literally a wall that marked the northernmost edge of settlement on the island of Manhattan. Although some of the street grid remains—and today's Broad Street was once a huge canal—most of the other traces of the Dutch settlement of New Amsterdam have disappeared.

Lower Manhattan did not become a business and commercial center until the nineteenth century, however. Until then, it was a little urban village, first Dutch and then English. Even after the English takeover in 1664, the town retained its Dutch character and distinctive Dutch architectural styles. The original New Amsterdam was home to a variety of crafts- and tradespeople: not only the merchants, brokers, lawyers, and shipmasters one would expect in a commercial port but also druggists, painters, printers, tailors, and boardinghouse keepers. The homes and workshops were built in the Dutch style, out of red and yellow brick, with leaded-glass casement windows and terracotta tiles on the roofs. The comfortable feel of such homes was not unlike a middle-class home in Amsterdam.

Because buildings often functioned as both homes and workshops, they might contain not only the nuclear family but also the employees of the family business and slaves, both Indian and African. (In 1703, 40 percent of New York's households contained African slaves.) If New Amsterdam and its successor, New York, looked and felt like a European town, the presence of large numbers of Africans and Indians gave the little settlement a distinctive New World character.

Afbeeldinge van de Stadt Amsterdam in Nieuw Neederlandt.

From its earliest years, New Amsterdam was an urban village in a global economy, home to immigrants and natives, all buying and selling in a global market. The Kierstede family built its house at the corner of what today are Pearl and Whitehall Streets, looking out on the East River. Hans Kierstede, a German religious refugee, came to New Amsterdam and served as its first surgeon. His wife, Sara Roelofs, had been born in Amsterdam and lived as a child near present-day Albany, where she played with the local Indians and learned their languages. In New Amsterdam, she built a backyard shed where Indian women crafted goods to sell in the market across the street from the Kierstedes' home. In 1664, Sara Roelofs Kierstede served as a translator when Peter Stuyvesant negotiated a treaty with the local Indians. The Lenape Indian Sachem Oratam was so pleased with her translating abilities that he gave her some 2,000 acres of land on the Hackensack River, in present-day Bergen County, New Jersey.

When archeologists excavated the family home late in the twentieth century, they found bits and pieces of the cultures that mixed on the island of Manhattan: pipes made in Holland and imported even after the English takeover; a German wineglass; a piece of a sword; hair curlers for curling wigs; whistles carved from clay pipes and traded to the Indians for furs; and ceramic gambling tokens, similar to ones found at plantations in the South and the West Indies.

New Amsterdam was a crossroads of empire. There people—and goods—from both sides of the Atlantic, Europeans, Indians, and Africans, met and traded with each other, creating a new world made out of bits and pieces from each of their cultures.

---

debts to repay, and giving away vast chunks of North America was a cheap way of doing it. As a Quaker, Penn was eager to get out of England. In 1661 alone, 4,000 English Quakers were jailed, and Penn was imprisoned four times. The Quakers were a radical sect of Protestants who believed that God offered salvation to all and placed an "inner light" inside everyone. Hardworking, serious, and moral, Quakers rejected violence and refused to serve in the military or pay taxes for its support.

Penn received his charter in 1681. To raise money, he sold land to a group of wealthy Quaker merchants, who received government positions and economic concessions in return. To attract ordinary settlers, Penn promised self-government (although stacked in favor of the merchant elite), freedom of religion, and reasonably priced land.

In 1682, when Penn arrived at Philadelphia (Greek for "city of brotherly love"), the colony already had 4,000 inhabitants. Penn had clear ideas about how he wanted his colony to develop. He expected the orderly growth of farming villages, neatly laid out along rivers and creeks, and mapped the settlement of the city along a grid, with each house set far enough from its neighbors to prevent the spread of fires. He created harmonious relations with local Indians.

Penn's policies attracted a wide variety of Europeans. Soon Pennsylvania was populated by self-contained communities, each speaking a different language or practicing a different religion. Pennsylvania's early history was characterized by rapid growth and prosperity. However, this progress undermined Penn's plans for a cohesive, hierarchical society. People lived where and how they wanted, pursuing the economic activities they found most profitable.

> Now you might perhaps ask whether I with a pure and undisturbed conscience could advise one and another of you to come over to this place. . . . I would be heartily glad of your dear presence; yet unless you (1) find yourselves freedom of conscience to go, (2) can submit to the difficulties and dangers of a long journey, and (3) can resolve to go without most of the comforts to which you have been accustomed in Germany, such as stone houses, luxurious food and drink, for a year or two, then . . . stay where you are for some time yet.
>
> N. N.,
> German immigrant, writing home from Philadelphia,
> March 7, 1684

William Penn Concluding a Treaty with the Delaware Indians, as Depicted by Benjamin West In this exchange, Penn presents the Indians with cloth, one of the European trade goods most in demand by Indians.

While moving away from the inequalities of the Old World, Pennsylvania replicated those of the New World. Many of its European immigrants were indentured servants or redemptioners, people who worked for a brief period to pay back the ship's captain for the cost of transportation to the colony. And by 1700, the Pennsylvania Assembly had passed laws recognizing slavery, although not unanimously. That slavery could take root in a colony where some questioned its morality suggests both the force of its power in shaping early America and the weakness of the opposition.

Indians and Africans in the Political Economy of Carolina

Like Pennsylvania and Maryland, South Carolina was a proprietary colony. One of the proprietors, Anthony Ashley Cooper, the Earl of Shaftesbury, and his secretary John Locke drafted the Fundamental Constitutions for the new colony. Locke later became a leading political philosopher, and the Constitutions reflect the liberal, rights-guaranteeing principles that he later developed more fully.

The Constitutions provided for a representative government and widespread religious toleration. At the same time, they embodied the traditional assumption that liberty could be guaranteed only in a hierarchical society. Shaftesbury and Locke tried to set up a complex hierarchy of nobles at the top and hereditary serfs at the bottom. The Constitutions also recognized African slavery, and Carolina was the first colony that introduced slavery at the outset. The Constitutions never went into full effect, for the first Carolina representative assembly rejected many of its provisions. Predictably, the attempt to transplant a British-style nobility failed. The only aristocracy that the Carolinas developed was one of wealth, supported by the labor of slaves.

The first settlers arrived at Charles Town (later moved and renamed Charleston) in 1670. The area had a semitropical climate, wonderfully fertile soil, and a growing season of up to 295 days a year. The region had once been explored by the Spanish, who still claimed it. It was inhabited by mission Indians, that is, Indians who had converted to Catholicism.

As happened so often when Europeans arrived, Indian tribes competed to trade with them, and rival groups of Europeans struggled to dominate the trade. In the colonial period, Indian wars usually pitted one group of Europeans and their Indian allies against another group of Europeans and their native allies, with the Indians doing most of the fighting. Such wars were an extension of Europe's market economy: Indians fought for European goods, and Europeans fought for a monopoly over Indian products. The English were particularly successful in achieving dominance because of their sophisticated market economy. London's banks had perfected the mechanisms of credit, which financed a fur trade in the forests half a world away.

The Westos elbowed their way ahead of other tribes by offering the Carolina traders a commodity more valuable even than deerskins: Indian slaves. In fact, until about 1690, slaves were the most valuable commodity produced by the Carolina colony.

Carolina Indian traders quickly established control over the entire Southeast (see Map 4–1), pushing out the Spanish, the French, and even the Virginians. At the same

Trial of John Lawson In 1711, while exploring present-day western North Carolina for South Carolina, John Lawson and his party were captured by Tuscarora Indians. Lawson was put on trial and then executed. Notice his African slave, also bound and facing the Tuscarora tribunal.

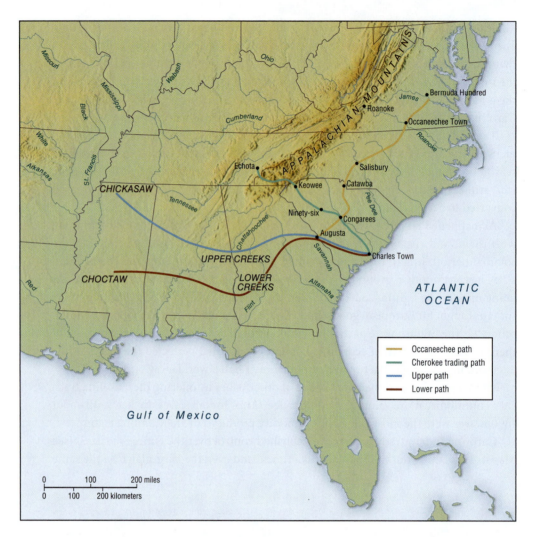

Map 4-1 Trade Routes in the Southeast Beginning in the 17th century, English traders from Virginia and later Carolina followed several paths to trade with Southeastern Indians as far west as the Mississippi. *Adapted from W. Stitt Robinson,* The Southern Colonial Frontier *(Albuquerque: University of New Mexico Press, 1979), p. 103.*

time, Indian tribes fought to become the chief slave supplier. In 1680, in the Westo War, the Carolina traders sent their allies, the Savannah Indians, out to destroy the Westos, who were the Virginians' link to the Native American trade of the Southeast. The Carolinians vanquished the Spanish by sending in other Indian allies to destroy the mission towns. In this way, the Carolina traders eliminated their European rivals. At the same time, the Chickasaws emerged to replace the Westos and, like them, obliterated less powerful tribes in order to obtain a steady supply of slaves. Between 1670 and 1715, perhaps 25,000 Indians were enslaved, with many more killed in the slaving raids. The slave trade increased dramatically the level of violence among Native Americans.

This violence was turned against the Carolinians in the Yamasee War (1715–1716). Although the Yamasees had been reliable trading partners for 40 years and had fought with the British in Queen Anne's War (see later in the chapter), South Carolina traders cheated them out of their land and enslaved their women and children. In retaliation, the Yamasees and their allies attacked, pushing the settlers almost back to Charleston before they were stopped. The war killed 400 white South Carolinians (7 percent of the population, more than in King Philip's War in New England), crippled the Indian slave trade, forced the colony to abandon frontier settlements, and revealed the fragility of the entire South Carolina venture. When international war began again in 1739, the frontier regions were, as they had been a quarter of a century earlier, dangerous and unstable for settlers, traders, and Indians alike.

The Barbados Connection

Carolina was part of a far-flung Atlantic political economy based on trade, plantation agriculture, and slavery. Many of the early Carolina settlers had substantial experience with African slavery in Barbados, a small Caribbean island settled in 1627 that within a decade became a major source of the world's sugar. By then, it had an African majority and was Britain's first slave society. By the end of the seventeenth century, Barbados was the most productive of all Britain's colonies, its per-person income much higher than in England.

This income was not shared equally, however. Owners of the largest plantations became fabulously wealthy, and even lesser planters enjoyed a high standard of living. Conditions for African slaves, however, were brutal. As in their other slave societies, the British magnified differences between Europeans and Africans to enhance the distinction between landowners and slaves. Barbadians were the first to portray Africans as beasts, and the racism of Caribbean planters was intense. Slave codes were the harshest of any in the Atlantic world, prescribing that male slaves convicted of crimes could be burned at the stake, beheaded, starved, or castrated. When Caribbean slavery was imported into Carolina, these attitudes came with it. The Carolina slave code was the harshest in North America. Laws and attitudes separated whites from blacks, but differences among Europeans were minimized, as some restrictions against Irish Catholics and Jews were lifted after Barbados became a slave society. In 1650, Barbados allowed the immigration of Jews and other religious minorities, six years before England did. As in the Chesapeake, increasing freedom for Europeans developed alongside the enslavement of Africans.

The sugar plantations of Barbados and Britain's other Caribbean islands made their extraordinary profits from the labor of African slaves. British planters worked Africans harder than European indentured servants. Profits came from keeping labor costs down, as well as from the growing demand for sugar. It is important to remember that the New World slave system would not have grown as it did without European demand for plantation crops. African slaves were imported into Carolina from the outset, but only after 1690 did the colony develop a staple crop—rice—that increased the demand for slave labor. After rice became the region's major cash crop, African slaves became more valuable. By 1720, Africans composed more than 70 percent of Carolina's population. With a black majority, a lethal environment, and wealth concentrated in an elite, Carolina resembled the Caribbean islands more than it did the other English colonies on the mainland. In only a few decades, Carolina had become a slave society, not simply a society with slaves: slavery stood at the center of everything.

The Transformation of Virginia

At the same time that a newly vigorous England was planting new colonies, those established earlier were reshaped. In the final quarter of the seventeenth century, the older colonies experienced political and sometimes social instability, followed by the establishment of a lasting order. In Virginia, the transition was marked by a violent insurrection known as Bacon's Rebellion. Significantly, the rebels sought not to overthrow the social and political order but to secure a legitimate government that could protect economic opportunity. In its aftermath, Virginia became a slave society.

Social Change in Virginia

As Virginia entered its second half-century, the health of its population finally began to improve. Apple orchards had matured, so Virginians could drink cider instead of impure water. Ships bringing new servants arrived in the fall, a healthy time of year. Increasingly, they lived to serve out their periods of indenture and set out on their own to plant tobacco. However, most of the best land in eastern Virginia had already been claimed, and the land to the west was occupied by Indian tribes with peace treaties with the English. In addition, the government was controlled by a small clique of men using it as a means of getting rich. Taxes, assessed in tobacco, were extraordinarily high, and as taxes rose, the price of tobacco began to fall. Caught in a squeeze, many ordinary planters went to work for others as tenants or overseers.

Still, servants kept coming to the colony, most from the lower ranks of society. Restless and unhappy, they joined in a series of disturbances beginning in the middle of the century. The elite responded by lengthening the time of service and stiffening the penalties for running away.

Bacon's Rebellion and the Abandonment of the Middle Ground

When the revolt came, it was led not by one of the poor or landless but by a member of the elite. Nathaniel Bacon was young, well educated, wealthy, and a member of a prominent family. Bacon made an immediate impression on Virginia's ruling clique, and Governor Berkeley invited him to join the colony's Council of State. For unknown reasons, Bacon cast his lot with Berkeley's enemies among the elite. The instability of elites created political factions in a number of colonies. When ruling elites, such as Berkeley's in Virginia, levied exorbitant taxes and ignored their constituents, they left themselves open to challenge.

The contest between Bacon and Berkeley might have remained minor had not Bacon capitalized on the discontent of the colony's freedmen (men who had served out their indentures). In 1676, Bacon's Rebellion was triggered by a routine episode of violence on the middle ground inhabited by Indians and Europeans. Seeking payment for goods they had delivered to a planter, a band of Doeg Indians killed the planter's overseer and tried to steal his hogs. Over the years, Europeans and Indians who shared the middle ground had adapted the Indian custom of providing restitution for crimes committed by one side or the other. Although this practice resulted in sporadic violence, it also helped maintain order. But this time, the conflict escalated, as Virginians sought revenge, prompting further Indian retaliation.

Soon an isolated incident escalated into a militia expedition of 1,000 men, an extraordinarily large force at the time. For six weeks the war party laid siege to the reservation of the Susquehannocks, a tribe drawn unwillingly into the conflict, who in turn avenged themselves on settlers on the frontier.

When Berkeley refused to fight the Susquehannocks, the frontier planters were infuriated. They complained that their taxes went to Berkeley's clique instead of being used to police the frontier. Planter women used their gossip networks to tell "hundreds" that Berkeley was "a greater friend to the Indians than to the English."

With his wife's encouragement, Nathaniel Bacon agreed to lead a wholesale war on "all Indians whatsoever." After his rebels massacred some formerly friendly Occoneechees, Bacon marched on the government at Jamestown with 400 armed men, demanding to fight "all Indians in general, for that they were all Enemies." Berkeley agreed, then changed his mind, but it was too late. Bacon was in control, and Berkeley fled to the eastern shore.

By the time a royal commission and 1,000 soldiers arrived in January 1677 to put down the disorder, Bacon had died, and Berkeley had regained control. Twenty-three rebel leaders were executed, and the king removed Berkeley from office. After Bacon's death, support for the rebellion quickly dissipated.

After Bacon's Rebellion, the government remained in the hands of the planter elite, but the rebels had achieved their primary objective. The frontier Indians had been dispersed, and their land was now free for settlement. Those in power became more responsive to white members of society. Other factors also improved economic conditions: tobacco prices began to climb, and planters replaced servants with slaves.

Virginia Becomes a Slave Society

No one had planned for Virginia to become a slave society. With new colonies such as New York and Pennsylvania offering greater opportunity to poor whites, the supply of European indentured servants to the Chesapeake dried up just when more Africans were becoming available. Britain entered the slave trade at the end of the seventeenth century, authorizing private merchants to carry slaves from Africa to North America in 1698. Planters could not get enough slaves to meet their needs. In 1680, only 7 percent of Virginia's population was African in origin, but by 1700 the proportion had increased to 28 percent, and half the labor force was enslaved (see Table 4–1). Within two decades, Virginia had become a slave society in which slavery was central to the political economy and the social structure. With the bottom tier of the social order enslaved and hence unable to compete for land or wealth, opportunity for all whites necessarily improved.

As the composition of Virginia's labor force changed, so did the laws to control it. Although all slave societies had certain features in common, each colony enacted its own slave code to maintain and define the institution. By 1705, Virginia had a thorough slave code in place.

All forms of slavery have certain elements in common: perpetuity, kinlessness, violence, and the master's access to the slave's sexuality. First, slavery is a lifelong condition. Second, a slave has no legally recognized family relationships. Because kinship is the basis of most social and political relationships in society, a slave is socially "dead," outside the bounds of the larger society. Third, slavery rests on violence or its threat, including the master's sexual access to the slave.

Table 4–1 Population of British Colonies in America, 1660 and 1710

Colony	White	1660 Black	Total	White	1710 Black	Total
Virginia	26,070	950	27,020	55,163	23,118	78,281
Maryland	7,668	758	8,426	34,796	7,945	42,741
Chesapeake	33,738	1,708	35,446	89,959	31,063	121,022
Massachusetts	22,062	422	22,484	61,080	1,310	62,390
Connecticut	7,955	25	7,980	38,700	750	39,450
Rhode Island	1,474	65	1,539	7,198	375	7,573
New Hampshire	1,515	50	1,565	5,531	150	5,681
New England	33,006	562	33,568	112,509	2,585	115,094
Bermuda	3,500	200	3,700	4,268	2,845	7,113
Barbados	26,200	27,100	53,300	13,000	52,300	65,300
Antigua	1,539	1,448	2,987	2,892	12,960	15,852
Montserrat	1,788	661	2,449	1,545	3,570	5,115
Nevis	2,347	2,566	4,913	1,104	3,676	4,780
St. Kitts	1,265	957	2,222	1,670	3,294	4,964
Jamaica				7,250	58,000	65,250
Caribbean	36,639	32,932	69,571	31,729	136,645	168,374
New York	4,336	600	4,936	18,814	2,811	21,625
New Jersey				18,540	1,332	19,872
Pennsylvania				22,875	1,575	24,450
Delaware	510	30	540	3,145	500	3,645
Middle Colonies	4,846	630	5,476	63,374	6,218	69,592
North Carolina	980	20	1,000	14,220	900	15,120
South Carolina				6,783	4,100	10,883
Lower South	980	20	1,000	21,003	5,000	26,003
Totals	109,209	35,852	145,061	318,574	181,511	500,085

Source: Jack P. Greene, Pursuits of Happiness *(Chapel Hill: University of North Carolina, 1988), pp. 178–179.*

> A white woman is rarely or never put to work in the ground, if she be good for anything else . . . whereas it is a common thing for to work a woman slave out of doors.
>
> VIRGINIA PLANTER ROBERT BEVERLEY

American slavery added other elements. First, slavery in all the Americas was hereditary, passed on from a mother to her children. Second, compared with other slave systems, including that of Latin America, manumissions—the freeing of slaves—in the American South were quite rare. Finally, slavery in the South was racial. Slavery was reserved for Africans, some Indians, and their children, even if the father was white. The line between slavery and freedom was defined as one of color.

Slave codes also defined gender roles. Two early pieces of legislation denied African women the privileges of European women. A 1643 statute made all adult men and African women taxable, assuming that they (and not white women) were performing productive labor in the fields. In 1652, another law said that children were to inherit the status of their mother.

The same laws that created and sustained racial slavery also increased the freedom of whites. New World plantation slavery was developed in a world in which the freedom of most Europeans also was limited in various ways. In fact, two-thirds of the Europeans who migrated to British America before the American Revolution were unfree—servants or redemptioners. (When Africans are added, virtually all of whom were enslaved, the total increases to 90 percent.) The increase in freedom for whites was the product of several sorts of policies. First, it depended on the widespread availability of cheap land, which whites could obtain only by dispossessing the Indians who inhabited it. Second, it depended on British government policies, such as permitting self-government in the colonies, which were designed to attract immigrants. Third, it depended on specific laws that improved the conditions of whites, often at the same time limiting the freedom of blacks. For example, in 1705 Virginia made it illegal for white servants to be whipped without an order from a justice of the peace (see Table 4–2).

Table 4-2 Codifying Race and Slavery

1640—Masters are required to arm everyone in their households except Africans (Virginia)

1643—All adult men and African women are taxable, on the assumption that they were working in the fields (Virginia)

1662—Children follow the condition of their mother (Virginia)

1662—Double fine charged for any Christian who commits fornication with an African (Virginia)

1664—All slaves serve for life; that is, slavery is defined as a lifelong condition (Maryland)

1664—Interracial marriage banned; any free woman who marries a slave will serve that slave's master until her husband dies, and their children will be enslaved (Maryland)

1667—Baptism as a Christian does not make a slave free (Virginia)

1669—No punishment is given if punished slave dies (Virginia)

1670—Free Blacks and Indians are not allowed to purchase Christian indentured servants (Virginia)

1670—Indians captured elsewhere and sold as slaves to Virginia are to serve for life; those captured in Virginia, until the age of 30, if children, or for 12 years, if grown (Virginia)

1680—In order to prevent "Negroes Insurrections": no slave may carry arms or weapons; no slave may leave his or her master without written permission; any slave who "lifts up his hand" against a Christian will receive 30 lashes; any slave who runs away and resists arrest may be killed lawfully (Virginia)

1682—Slaves may not gather for more than 4 hours at other than owner's plantation (Virginia)

1682—All servants who were "Negroes, Moors, Mollattoes or Indians" were to be considered slaves at the time of their purchase if neither their parents nor country were Christian (Virginia)

1691—Owners are to be compensated if "negroes, mulattoes or other slaves" are killed while resisting arrest (Virginia)

1691—Forbidden is all miscegenation as "that abominable mixture"; any English or "other white man or woman" who marries a "negroe, mulatto, or Indian" is to be banished; any free English woman who bears a "bastard child by any negro or mulatto" will be fined, and if she can't pay the fine, she will be indentured for five years and the child will be indentured until the age of 30 (Virginia)

1691—All slaves who are freed by their masters must be transported out of the state (Virginia)

1692—Special courts of "over and terminer" are established for trying slaves accused of crimes, creating a separate system of justice (Virginia)

1705—Mulatto is defined as "the child of an Indian, the child, grandchild, or great grandchild of a negro" (Virginia)

1705—Africans, mulattoes, and Indians are prohibited from holding office or giving grand jury testimony (Virginia)

1705—Slaves are forbidden to own livestock (Virginia)

1705—"Christian white" servants cannot be whipped naked (Virginia)

1723—Free Blacks explicitly excluded from militia (Virginia)

1723—Free Blacks explicitly denied the right to vote (Virginia)

Note: Slavery is a creation of law, which defines what it means to be a slave and protects the master's rights in his slave property. Slave codes developed piecemeal in the Chesapeake, over the course of the 17th century. Legislators in the Chesapeake colonies defined slavery as a racial institution, appropriate only for Africans, and protected it with a series of laws, which, in the process, also created a privileged position for whites.

DEBATING HISTORY

>> Origins of Slavery

Slavery in North America began when the first slaves arrived in Virginia in 1619. From 1619 until the middle of the seventeenth century, the number of slaves in the Chesapeake remained relatively small. Black slaves and white servants often lived in the same vicinity and worked side by side. As conditions in the colonies improved and life expectancy rose, white servants increasingly won their freedom or went elsewhere for work, leaving the plantation colonies with a high land-to-labor ratio. Between the 1660s and 1680s, most of the plantation colonies in English North America passed slave codes defining slave status and expanding white freedom, in effect creating slave societies. Historians have disagreed about the role of racism in this process. Winthrop Jordan believed that racism was inherent in Englishmen's first meetings with Africans, whereas Edmund Morgan argued that racism did not really exist until it became economically expedient to see blacks as inferior (that is, when the number of African slaves in the colonies rose dramatically).

WINTHROP JORDAN, *White Over Black: American Attitudes Toward the Negro, 1550–1812* (Chapel Hill: University of North Carolina Press, 1968), pp. 91, 97.

[W]hat was it about Indians and Negroes that set them apart, which rendered them different from Englishmen, which made them special candidates for degradation? . . . it seems likely that the colonists' initial sense of difference from the Negro was founded not on a single characteristic but on a congeries [i.e., collection] of qualities which, taken as a whole, seemed to set the Negro apart. Virtually every quality in the Negro invited pejorative feelings. What may have been his two most striking characteristics, his heathenism and his appearance, were probably prerequisite to his complete debasement. . . . [Yet] blackness itself did not urge the complete debasement of slavery. Other qualities—the utter strangeness of his language, gestures, eating habits, and so on—certainly must have contributed to the colonists' sense that he was very different, perhaps disturbingly so. In Africa these qualities had for Englishmen added up to savagery; they were major components in that sense of difference which provided the mental margin absolutely requisite for placing the European on the deck of the slave ship and the Negro in the hold.

EDMUND MORGAN, *American Slavery, American Freedom: The Ordeal of Colonial Virginia* (New York: Norton, 1975), pp. 327–328.

In Virginia . . . before 1660, it might have been difficult to distinguish race prejudice from class prejudice. And as long as slaves formed only a significant minority of the labor force, the

community of interest between blacks and lower-class whites posed no social problem. But Virginians had always felt threatened by the danger of a servile insurrection, and their fears increased as the labor force grew larger and the proportion of blacks in it rose. Although the replacement of servants by slaves reduced the annual increment of poor freemen, the numbers already on hand were still sufficient to keep the threat of another Bacon in everyone's mind. If freemen with disappointed hopes should make common cause with slaves of desperate hope, the results might be worse than anything Bacon had done. . . . The answer to the problem, obvious if unspoken and only gradually recognized, was racism, to separate dangerous free whites from dangerous slave blacks by a screen of racial contempt.

Questions

1. Inferring from these two brief statements, how might each of these two historians define *racism*? What are the differences between those definitions?

2. Each historian makes a distinct claim concerning the degree to which Englishmen were conscious of their decisions regarding slavery. What is the difference between the historians on this point, and how do their differing views affect their arguments?

New England Under Assault

New England's prosperity led to problems, both internal and external. How would a religion born in adversity cope with good fortune? A combination of internal colonial conflicts and a growing population encroaching on Indian lands led to the region's deadliest Indian war in 1675.

Social Prosperity and the Fear of Religious Decline

In many ways, the Puritan founders of the New England colonies saw their dreams come true. Although immigration virtually halted as the English Revolution broke out, natural increase kept the population growing, from about 23,000 in 1650 to more than 93,000 in 1700. Life expectancy was higher than in England, and families were larger.

Most New Englanders enjoyed a comfortable, if modest, standard of living. By the end of the century, the simple shacks of the first settlers had been replaced by two-story frame homes. By our standards, these homes would still have been almost unbearably cold in the winter, when indoor temperatures routinely dropped into the 40s. Still, New Englanders were beginning to enjoy the prosperous village life their ancestors had once known in England.

For Puritans, such good fortune presented a problem. Prosperity became a cause for worry, as people turned their minds away from God to more worldly things. In the 1660s and 1670s, New England's ministers preached a series of jeremiads, lamentations about spiritual decline. They criticized problems ranging from public drunkenness and sexual license to land speculation and excessively high prices and wages. If New Englanders did not change their ways, the ministers predicted, "Ruine upon Ruine, Destruction upon Destruction would come, until one stone were not left upon another."

Most of the churches were embroiled in controversy in the 1660s concerning who could be members. The founders had assumed that most people, sooner or later, would have the conversion experience that entitled them to full church membership. By the third generation, however, many children and grandchildren of full members had not had the experience of spiritual rebirth. In 1662 a group of ministers adopted the

Half-Way Covenant, which set out terms for church membership and participation. Full church membership was reserved for those who could demonstrate a conversion experience. Their offspring could still be "half-way" members of the church, receiving its discipline and having their children baptized. Those who wished to maintain the purity and exclusivity of the church resisted. Rather than settle this question, the Half-Way Covenant aggravated tensions always present in the Puritan religion.

Turmoil broke out as well in the persecution of Quakers, despite Charles II's having issued a protection order. In 1660, Massachusetts had executed the Quaker Mary Dyer, who had returned to Boston after her banishment. The Quakers had been brazen in their defiance of authority, not only returning to the colony when they knew it meant certain death but also even running naked through the streets or in church.

King Philip's War

Although New England's colonies developed along a common path, conflicts among them were intense and led to the region's deadliest Indian war. As in Bacon's Rebellion, the underlying cause of the war was the steady encroachment of English settlers on Native American lands. In the 1660s, Rhode Island, Massachusetts, and Plymouth all claimed the land occupied by the Wampanoags, Massasoit's tribe, now ruled by his son Metacom, known by the colonists as King Philip. By 1671, the colonies had resolved their dispute and ordered King Philip and his people to submit to the rule of Plymouth. No longer able to play one colony against another, King Philip prepared for war, as did the colonists of all the colonies except Rhode Island, which attempted to mediate. In June 1675 King Philip's men attacked the Plymouth village of Swansea.

During the next year, New Englanders attacked entire villages of noncombatants, and the Indians retaliated in kind. At the beginning of the war, New Englanders looked down on the Indians' traditional methods as evidence of depravity, saying they fought "more like wolves than men." By the end of the war, however, both sides committed brutalities, including scalpings and putting their victims' heads on stakes. That was the fate of King Philip. His wife and nine-year-old son were sold into slavery, along with hundreds of captives.

The New Englanders won King Philip's War, but the cost was enormous. The casualty rate was one of the highest for any American war ever. About 4,000 Indians died, many of starvation after the New Englanders destroyed their cornfields. The war eliminated any significant Native American presence in southeastern New England and killed 2,000 English settlers (1 out of every 25). The Indians pushed to within 20 miles of Boston, attacked more than half of New England's towns, and burned 1,200 homes. It took the region decades to rebuild.

The Puritans owed their victory to the Anglican colony of New York, its governor Edmund Andros, and his Mohawk allies. Andros worked effectively with local Indians, believing that the British Empire would be best served by maintaining peace among

King Philip's (Metacom's) Map, 1668 A map of the lands that Metacom (known by New Englanders as King Philip) sold in 1668. Note that Metacom's understanding of what it meant to "sell" land differed from English conceptions of property ownership. He insisted that the Indians who were living on the land could continue to do so.

its colonies and the Indians, strengthening the British position against their true enemies, the French and the Dutch. Over the protest of New England, Andros encouraged the Mohawks to attack King Philip's forces. Once the Mohawks entered the war, the tide was turned.

Indians and the Empire

New England's relations with Indian tribes were not simply a local concern. They were of deep interest to the British Empire, as Andros's participation demonstrated. The British government had to balance the desires of its colonists against the empire's larger objectives. As the French expanded their presence in North America, using friendly Indians to check their advance became one of those objectives. In 1673 the French explorers Jacques Marquette and Louis Joliet had traveled down the Mississippi River as far south as the Arkansas River, and nine years later René-Robert Cavelier, Sieur de La Salle, reached the mouth of the river and named the surrounding territory Louisiana, in honor of King Louis XIV. Biloxi was founded in 1699, New Orleans in 1718, and the forts at Cahokia and Kaskaskia several years later. The French and their Indian allies controlled the Great Lakes region and the eastern shore of the Mississippi all the way to its mouth, while the British were confined to the East Coast.

This geopolitical reality dictated Britain's Indian policy. Andros saw a role for Native Americans as trade partners and allies in Britain's conflict with the French. He welcomed the Indian survivors of King Philip's War into New York and refused to send them back to New England for execution and enslavement, thus becoming the "father" who offered protection to his Indian "children." The British and the Iroquois, who dominated all the other tribes in the region, joined in a strong alliance known as the Covenant Chain, which enhanced the positions of both New York and the Iroquois. The Iroquois became the middlemen between other tribes and the merchants at Albany and were allowed to push as far north and west against French-allied tribes as they could.

With New York dominating the British-Indian alliance, the New England colonies were effectively hemmed in. New York used the Mohawks to make a claim to Maine and blocked New England's movement to the west. Albany became the undisputed center of the Indian trade. In every way, King Philip's War proved exceedingly costly for the New England colonies.

> Thou English man hath provoked us to anger & wrath & we care not though we have war with you this 21 years for there are many of us 300 of which hath fought with you at this town. We hauve nothing but our lives to loose but thou hast many fair houses cattell & much good things.
>
> A NIPMUCK INDIAN,
> in a note attached to a tree near Medfield, Massachusetts, February 1676

Sir Edmund Andros Andros, Royal Governor of New York, was named by James II as "Governor of the Dominion of New England."

The Empire Strikes

As Britain regained political stability at the end of the seventeenth century, it tried to bring more order to its "accidental empire" by making the colonies play a larger role in its governance. As the Glorious Revolution that removed King James II from the British throne secured constitutional government for Britain's subjects on both sides of the Atlantic, it also made Britain strong and stable enough to challenge France for world supremacy. Between 1689 and 1763, the Anglo-French rivalry drew the colonies into four international wars that shaped them in important ways.

The Dominion of New England

When James II ascended the throne, he decided to punish New England for its disloyalty to the Crown during the Puritan Revolution. There were also reports that New Englanders were defying the Navigation Acts by smuggling. In France, Louis XIV had centralized his administration and brought both his nation and his empire under firm control, and James decided to try similar tactics. In North America, he began unilaterally to revoke the charters of the colonies. By 1688, Massachusetts, Plymouth, Connecticut, New York, New Jersey, New Hampshire, and Rhode Island had been joined together into the Dominion of New England, and Edmund Andros was named its governor.

Before James II and Andros were deposed by the Glorious Revolution of 1688, they wreaked considerable havoc in New England. Massachusetts, New York, and Maryland all suffered revolts. James's attempt to strengthen rule over the colonies failed, but it marked a turning point: the colonies' last period of significant political instability before the eve of the American Revolution.

James's attempt to tighten control affected Massachusetts most seriously. He ordered it to tolerate religious dissenters; some feared he would impose Catholicism on the colony. He took away liberties that residents had enjoyed for over half a century: Juries were now to be appointed by sheriffs, town meetings were limited to once a year, and town selectmen could serve no more than two two-year terms. All titles to land had to be reconfirmed, with the holder paying Andros a small fee. Andros claimed the right to levy taxes on his own and began seizing all common lands. Some Boston merchants allied themselves with Andros, hoping to win his favor. This alliance revealed a growing rift in the region between those who welcomed commerce and a more secular way of life and those who wished to preserve the old ways. Most people in Massachusetts, however, despised Andros and feared the road he was leading them down.

The Glorious Revolution in Britain and America

The Glorious Revolution made it clear that Parliament, not an autocratic monarch, would henceforth play the leading role in government. It also determined, after almost a century and a half of conflict, that the Anglican religion would prevail. The Glorious Revolution ushered in a period of remarkable political stability that enabled Britain to become the world's most powerful nation.

In the next century Britain's North American colonies looked to this moment in British history as a model of constitutional government. Their understanding of events in Britain was shaped by political philosopher John Locke's *Two Treatises of Government* (1690). Since the time that he and Shaftesbury had written Carolina's Fundamental Constitutions more than 20 years earlier, Locke had become increasingly radical. The *Treatises* boldly asserted fundamental human equality and universal rights and provided the political theories that would justify a revolution.

The *Treatises* have become the founding documents of political liberalism and its theory of human rights. Locke argued that governments were created by people, not by God. Man was born "with a Title to perfect Freedom," or "natural rights." When people created governments, they gave up some of that freedom in exchange for the rights that they enjoyed in society. The purpose of government was to protect the "Lives, Liberties," and "Fortunes" of the people who created it, not to achieve glory or power for the nation or to serve God. Moreover, should a government take away the civil rights of its citizens, they had a "right to resume their original Liberty." This right of revolution was Locke's boldest and most radical assertion. Once news of the Glorious Revolution reached Massachusetts, its inhabitants poured into the streets, seized the government, and threw the despised Andros in jail. They proclaimed loyalty to the new king and lobbied for the return of their charter. Rhode Island and Connecticut soon got their charters back, but Massachusetts, which was perceived as too independent, was made a royal colony in 1691, with a royal governor. Although Massachusetts lost some of its autonomy and was forced to tolerate dissenters, the town meeting was restored. At the same time, New Hampshire became a royal colony.

The citizens of Maryland and New York also took the opportunity presented by the Glorious Revolution to evict their royal governors. In Maryland, tensions between the tobacco planters and the increasingly dictatorial proprietor, Charles Calvert, Lord Baltimore, had been building for several decades. Four-fifths of the population was Protestant, but the colony's government was dominated by Catholics, who allocated to themselves the best land. When Protestant planters protested, Baltimore imposed a property qualification for voting and appointed increasingly dictatorial governors. When news of the Glorious Revolution reached Maryland in 1689, a group led by John Coode, a militia officer, took over the government in a bloodless coup (known as Coode's Rebellion), proclaimed loyalty to William and Mary, and got the new government in Britain to take away Baltimore's proprietorship. In 1691, Maryland became a royal colony, and in 1702, the Anglican Church was made the state church, ending Maryland's experiment with religious toleration.

New York's rebels were less successful. A group of prosperous Dutch traders led by Jacob Leisler took over the government. Unlike Coode in Maryland, Leisler was not willing to cede power to the new king's appointees. As a result, the new governor put the rebel leaders on trial, and Leisler and his son-in-law were executed, their bodies decapitated and quartered.

> The Province of Maryland is in a deplorable condition, for want of an established ministry. Here are ten or twelve counties, and in them at least twenty thousand souls, and but three Protestant ministers of the Church of England. The priests are provided for; the Quakers take care of those that are speakers; but no care is taken to build up churches in the Protestant religion. The Lord's day is profaned; religion is despised and all notorious vices are committed; so that it is become a Sodom of uncleanness and a pest-house of iniquity.
>
> THE REVEREND JOHN YEO,
> writing the Archbishop of Canterbury in support of Coode's Rebellion

This brutal conclusion to a bloodless revolt did not bring political stability to New York, however. Ethnic and regional divisions ran too deep. In the other colonies, by the end of the seventeenth century the elite had consolidated their position by both accepting British authority and providing opportunity and self-government for their fellow colonists. In New York, however, the top tier of the English elite competed with the second, Dutch, tier, creating political turmoil.

The Rights of Englishmen

Although the Glorious Revolution restored self-government to the North American colonies, the colonists and their British governors interpreted that event somewhat differently. Colonists felt it gave them all the rights of Englishmen. These rights were of two sorts: civil rights, from trial by jury to freedom from unreasonable searches, and the rights of self-government, including taxation only by their own elected representatives, self-rule, and civilian, not military, rule. The colonists believed that their legislatures were the local equivalent of Parliament and that, just as the citizens of Britain were governed by Parliament, so they should be governed by their own elective legislatures.

The British government held differently. First, it believed that the colonies were dependents of the mother country that needed a parent's protection and that owed that parent obedience. Second, the good of the empire as a whole was more important than that of any one of its parts. A colony was valued, as one British official put it, by what it contributed to "the gain or loss of *this* Kingdom." Third, colonial governments were subordinate to the British government. Finally, the British government had complete jurisdiction over every aspect of colonial life. The views of Britain and its colonists of how the empire should function radically diverged.

Conflict in the Empire

Between 1689 and 1713, Britain fought two wars against France and her allies, King William's War (1689–1697) and Queen Anne's War (1702–1713). At the same time, competition for the Indian alliances and the colonies' struggle over trade and territory made the European-Indian borderline uncertain and dangerous.

King William's War and Queen Anne's War followed a similar pattern in North America. Each was produced by a European struggle for power, and each resulted in a stalemate. The North American phase of each war began with a Canadian-Indian assault on isolated British settlements on the northern frontier (see Map 4–2). King William's War started with the capture of the British fort at Pemaquid, Maine, and the burning of Schenectady, New York, and Falmouth, Maine. Queen Anne's War began in North America in 1704 with a horrific raid on Deerfield, Massachusetts, in which half the town was torched and half the population was killed or captured.

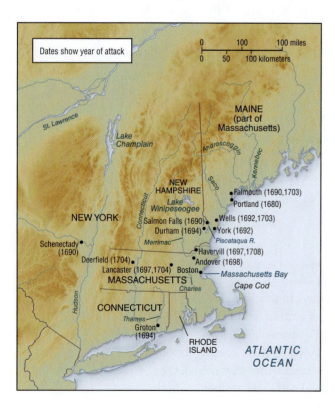

Map 4-2 Frontier Warfare During King William's and Queen Anne's Wars During these international conflicts, the New England frontier was exposed to attack by French Canadians and their Indian allies. *Adapted from Alan Gallay, ed.,* Colonial Wars of North America, 1512-1763 *(New York: Garland, 1996), p. 247.*

The British colonies responded with massive retaliation, sending raiding parties into ambitious but ultimately unsuccessful attacks on Québec. In 1690 Massachusetts governor Sir William Phips set out to seize Québec in an attack by land and sea. The failed expedition cost 1,000 lives and £40,000 and drove American colonists away from the northern frontier.

Queen Anne's War followed much the same course. Canadian-Indian attacks on frontier villages were met with raids on Indian villages. Again, New England attempted a two-pronged attack on Québec. When 900 troops (and 35 female camp followers) were killed as their ships sank in the St. Lawrence River, the commander canceled the expedition. Like King William's War, Queen Anne's War ended badly for New Englanders who had been eager to remove the twin threats of Catholicism and French-backed Indians to the north.

The imperial wars merged with and were survived by long-standing conflicts with Indian tribes. In North America, European rivals almost never confronted each other directly but instead mobilized their Indian allies and made war on those of their adversaries. These tactics, in addition to an expanding colonial population and the Native American attempt to monopolize trade, made conflict on the frontiers endemic.

Massachusetts in Crisis

If the imperial wars provide a window onto international tensions, the Salem witchcraft trials reveal a society in crisis, one coping with economic development, the conflict between old and new ways of understanding the world, and the threats presented by political instability, imperial war, and conflict with the Indians. In 1692 Massachusetts executed 20 people who had been convicted of witchcraft in Salem. Even in a society that believed in witchcraft, the execution of so many people at once was an aberration that revealed deep tensions.

The Social and Cultural Contexts of Witchcraft

Although the majority of New England's colonists were Puritan, many probably believed in magic. They subscribed to such tenets of Puritanism as predestination, but they also believed that they could use supernatural powers to predict the future, protect themselves from harm, and hurt their enemies. Although the ministry identified the use of magic with the devil, Tituba's folk religion and that of New Englanders were not incompatible. Before the development of scientific modes of explanation for such catastrophes as epidemics, droughts, and sudden death, people looked for supernatural causes.

In 1692, the inhabitants of Massachusetts were unusually anxious. They were without an effective government because they had not yet received their new charter. King William's War had just begun, with the French Catholics of Canada and their Algonquian Indian allies raiding the northern and eastern frontiers. Slaves reported that the French were planning to recruit New England's Africans as soldiers. These sources of stress increased underlying tensions, many of which concerned gender. Although men and women both attempted to use magic, the vast majority of those accused of witchcraft were women. Almost

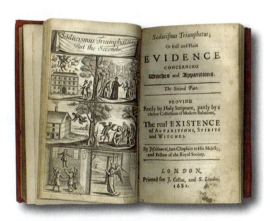

Frontispiece to Joseph Glanvill, *Saducismus Triumphatus; or, Full and Plain Evidence Concerning Witches* (1689) Books such as this combined folklore and Christian theology, providing graphic representations of Satan and witches alongside standard religious doctrine.

80 percent of the 355 persons officially accused of practicing witchcraft were women, as were an even higher proportion of the 103 persons actually put on trial. Because most of these women had neither sons nor other male heirs, they could control property, which made them an anomaly in Puritan society. By the end of the seventeenth century, local land was an increasingly scarce commodity, and any woman who controlled it could be seen as threatening to the men who wanted it.

In addition, declining opportunity also disrupted the tight Puritan social order. Because land was scarce, it became difficult for young couples to start out. Consequently, the age of marriage increased, and the number of women who were pregnant on their wedding days began to climb, as did the number of women who gave birth without marrying at all. Courts increasingly shifted the burden of child support from fathers to mothers. By the end of the seventeenth century, New Englanders were more inclined than ever to hold women responsible for sin.

Witchcraft at Salem

In this context of strain and anxiety, on February 29, 1692, magistrates John Hathorne and Jonathan Corwin went to Salem to investigate accusations of witchcraft. By the time the investigation and trials ended, 156 people had been jailed and 20 executed. As in previous witchcraft scares, most of the accused were women past the age of 40, and most of the accusers were women in their late teens and 20s.

> I desire to be humbled before God. It was a great delusion of Satan that deceived me in that sad time. I did not do it out of anger, malice, or ill-will.
>
> ANN PUTNAM JR.,
> in 1706, making public apology for the accusations of witchcraft she had made in Salem when she was 12

Most of the accused fell into categories that revealed the stresses in Puritan society. Many, like Sarah Good, were the sort of disagreeable women who had always attracted accusations of witchcraft. Others had ties to Quakers or Baptists. Several were suspiciously friendly with the Indians, whereas many of the accusers had been orphaned or displaced by the recent Indian wars, and they described the devil as "a Tawney, or an Indian color." As a dark-skinned woman from an alien culture, Tituba was also vulnerable. In addition, most of the accusers lived in Salem Village, an economic backwater, whereas most of the accused lived in or had ties to the more prosperous merchant community of Salem Town. The pattern of accusations suggested resentment, perhaps unconscious, about the increasing commercialization of New England's economy.

By late September, accusations were falling on wealthy and well-connected men and women, such as the wife of the governor. Accusers were paraded from town to town to root out local witchcraft, and other people were drawn to Salem like medieval pilgrims. Finally, the leading ministers of Boston, most of whom believed in witchcraft but had been skeptical of the trials, stepped in, and the governor adjourned the court. No one was ever convicted of witchcraft in New England again.

The End of Witchcraft

Although they continued to believe in witchcraft, magic, and the occult, by the end of the seventeenth century most colonists believed that the universe was orderly and that events were caused by natural, and knowable, forces. By the eighteenth century, educated people took pride in their rational understanding of nature and disdained a belief in the occult as mere superstition. This change in thinking reflected a new faith not only in human reason but also in the capacity of ordinary people to shape their lives. More and more people, especially those who were well educated, prosperous,

AMERICA AND THE WORLD

>> Witchcraft in Global Perspective

Set against the witchcraft panic that swept Europe in the sixteenth and seventeenth centuries, the trials at Salem appear relatively insignificant. In Europe, approximately 110,000 people were put on trial; more than half were convicted and executed, typically by hanging or burning at the stake. In comparison, fewer than 2 percent of those tried by the notorious Spanish Inquisition were put to death.

Yet even these numbers do not convey a full sense of the hysteria. Thousands more fell under suspicion, and entire communities were often paralyzed—900 people were executed in Würzberg during one seven-year period, 133 in one day in 1589 in Quedlinberg.

Witchcraft trials took place in every country in Europe during the period but were much more common in some places than in others. About half the prosecutions took place in the German states, and many of the others took place in regions, such as Poland, Switzerland, and France, that were facing religious and political instability during the Reformation and Counter-Reformation.

This was also the period in which modern nation-states emerged. As kings tried to consolidate their rule, they inspired witch hunts in order to impose conformity. Witchcraft trials were also common where the local prince was relatively weak. In such places, local magistrates could freely drum up a fear of witchcraft and conduct prosecutions. Moreover, an agitated populace might search for more witches, widening the scope of the original hunt. Such unchecked hysteria threatened to continue without end. In 1685, officials in the German town of Rottenburg worried that every local woman ultimately would be executed. In the same year, two other German villages had been reduced to one woman apiece.

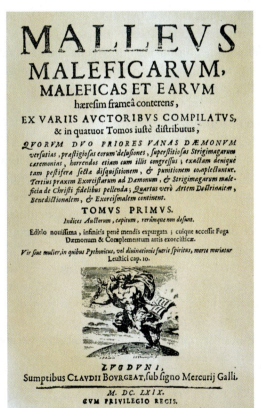

Almost everywhere in Europe, women constituted the majority of accused—and executed—witches. To be sure, the disproportionate number of women accused—as high as 90 percent in some regions—reflects an underlying misogyny in western European culture at the time. The *Malleus Maleficarum (The Witch Hammer)*, the guidebook for witch hunting, first published in 1486 but reprinted many times over the next several decades, claimed that the passionate and gullible nature of women made them vulnerable to the devil's wiles. Female witches were thought to engage in "carnal copulation" with Satan and to procure him children to eat. "Blessed be the most high who has so far preserved the male sex from such crime," the book concluded.

Such views found a ready audience. Some historians suggest that the witchcraft trials strengthened controls over women. The typical accused witch was unmarried and hence not under the direct control of a husband or father. Warfare and the plague had left an increasing number of women without husbands, and in some areas, by the seventeenth century, as many as 20 percent of women never married.

Early-modern Europe suffered from many forms of dislocation: warfare, religious upheaval, economic depression, epidemic disease. Witchcraft prosecutions sought to restore order by rooting out subversion that seemed to come from within. In societies organized by gender—rather than other forms of hierarchy—women became the focus. The witch hunts in New England, though much less sweeping than those of Europe, reveal the same pattern: a period of political instability that made people anxious to establish control, particularly of vulnerable women.

and lived in cities, believed that they could control their destinies and were not at the mercy of invisible evil forces. The seed of individualism had been planted in New England's rocky soil.

As individualism slowly spread and communities became larger, the cohesion of Puritan communities waned. In the eighteenth century new attitudes toward women freed them of their symbolic power to do harm.

The witchcraft trials also ended New England's belief in itself as a covenanted society with a collective future. Because Puritans had believed that God had chosen them for a mission, they read special meaning into every event, from a sudden snowstorm to an Indian attack. By the eighteenth century, however, they began to evaluate events separately, rather than as part of God's master plan.

Empires in Collision

As late as the middle of the eighteenth century, Native Americans still outnumbered Europeans on the North American continent. At the end of the seventeenth century in the territory that became the United States, Britain was the only European power with a substantial presence (see Map 4–3). The French and Spanish both had mainland outposts north of the Rio Grande, but these nations concentrated their resources on more valuable colonies: for the Spanish, Mexico and Latin America, and for the French, the West Indies. Nonetheless, imperial ambitions brought European powers into conflict in North America, where they jostled against each other and the Native Americans.

France Attempts an Empire

After its civil wars of religion ended early in the seventeenth century, France was free to establish foreign colonies. After 1664, France's minister Jean-Baptiste Colbert tried to formulate a coherent imperial policy, directed from Paris. He envisioned a series of settlements, each contributing to the wealth of the nation through the fur trade and fishing in North America and plantation agriculture in the West Indies. France tried to direct the development of its New World empire, but it could not control small settlements so far away.

Colbert attempted to control every aspect of life in Québec. He subsidized emigration and had female migrants investigated to make sure that they were healthy and morally sound. To encourage reproduction, dowries were offered to all men who married by the age of 20. Agriculture developed and the population grew, more from natural increase than immigration. Colbert's attempt to make Québec a hierarchical society on the Old World model failed, however. First, very few French men and women were willing to settle in the New World. Between 1670 and 1730, perhaps fewer than 3,000 moved to mainland North America (and only a few thousand more to the West Indies). Second, those who did move resisted being controlled from Paris.

Eventually, Native Americans were more successful than Colbert in shaping the fur trade, the mainstay of the Québec economy. The French depended on their Indian trading partners to supply them with furs and serve as military allies. When Indians tried to trade their furs to the British, the French built forts—at considerable cost—to intercept them. French traders smuggled furs to the British in return for British fabrics that the Indians preferred. Moreover, to maintain the allegiance of their Algonquian allies, the French gave them gifts of ammunition, knives, cloth, tobacco, and brandy. When the declining revenues from the fur trade are balanced against all these costs, it

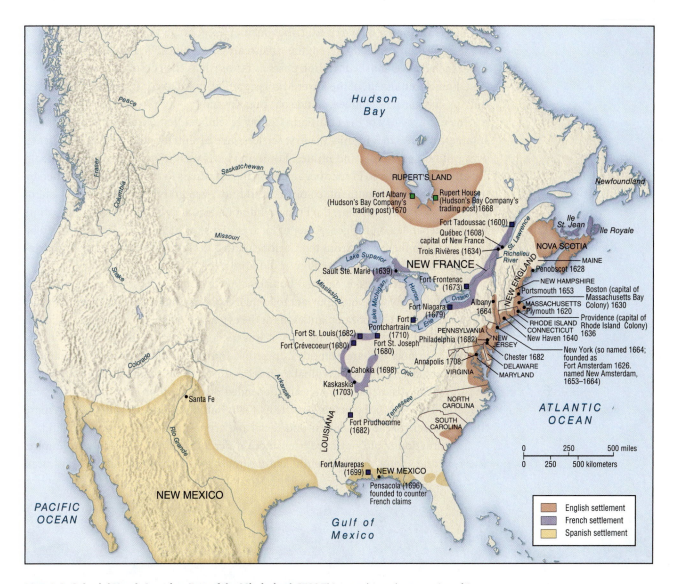

Map 4-3 Colonial North America, East of the Mississippi, 1720 This map shows the expansion of European settlement. English settlement was concentrated in a strip down the East Coast from Maine to North Carolina, with pockets of settlement in Canada and Carolina. French settlements formed a ring along the St. Lawrence River, from the Great Lakes south along the Mississippi, and along the Gulf Coast. The Spanish had outposts along the Gulf and in Florida. *Adapted from Geoffrey Barraclough, ed.,* The Times Concise Atlas of World History *(Maplewood, NJ: Hammond, 1994), p. 67.*

is questionable whether Canada was of any economic benefit to France, which maintained the fur trade more for political than for economic reasons.

It was for political reasons that France established outposts in present-day Louisiana and Mississippi, including Fort Biloxi (1699), Fort Toulouse (1717), and New Orleans (1718), all in the territory named Louisiana. (At the same time France built a number of forts in the north—such as Fort Niagara [1720] and Fort St. Frédéric [1731]—to guard against English encroachments.) When the French explorer La Salle reached the mouth of the Mississippi River in 1682 and claimed it for France, the Spanish mainland empire was cut in two, and the British faced a western rival. British traders had pushed into the lower Mississippi region looking for deerskins and Indian slaves. When the French arrived, tribes such as the Choctaws and Mobilians looked to the French for protection from the British and their allies. Within several decades, the French had established trading posts as far north as the Illinois Territory. Farther west, French settlement of the lower Mississippi Valley led to conflict with the Natchez Indians, whom they conquered and sold into slavery.

The early history of the Louisiana Colony resembled that of the British settlement at Jamestown. As in Virginia, the first settlers were ill suited to the venture, top-heavy with military personnel and pirates. Louisiana itself was so unattractive that it could not attract colonists, so France began deporting criminals to the colony. Debilitated by the unhealthful environment, colonists could not even grow their own food. Caught up in wars on the continent, the French did not adequately support the colony, so its survival depended on the generosity of local Indians. After African slaves began to be smuggled into the colony from the Caribbean, in 1719 France permitted the importation of African slaves, but the colony still foundered.

Unlike the Chesapeake, colonial Louisiana never developed a significant cash crop. Because the colony was not important to French economic interests, French mercantilist policies protected Caribbean plantations at the expense of those in Louisiana. Although Louisiana had a slave majority by 1727, it was not a slave society. Louisiana's economy was one of frontier exchange among Europeans, Indians, and Africans, rather than one of commercial agriculture. Marginal to France's empire, Louisiana was largely ignored, and Europeans, Indians, and Africans depended on each other for survival. They intermarried and worked together. As late as 1730, Native Americans still made up more than 90 percent of the population, and social and economic relations remained fluid.

The situation could not have been more different in France's Caribbean empire. There, by the end of the eighteenth century, most of the native population had been

The French Settlement at Biloxi The French outpost at Biloxi was moved to higher ground in 1720. Here we see both temporary dwellings, thrown up in haste, and a more permanent storehouse to the left, with the entire settlement a hive of activity.

killed by disease or war. It was soon replaced by African slaves. By 1670, the islands of Martinique and Guadeloupe were producing significant amounts of sugar with African slave labor. Between 1680 and 1730, 380,000 Africans were imported into those islands and the French colony of Saint-Domingue on the island of Santo Domingo, where they outnumbered Europeans by an astonishing ratio of 7.6 to 1. By the middle of the eighteenth century, Saint-Domingue was producing more sugar than any colony in America and would become the world's greatest producer of coffee. In a few decades, the French West Indies had been transformed into slave societies, in which slavery shaped every aspect of life. They were by far the most valuable part of France's New World empire.

The Spanish Outpost in Florida

Like France's colony at Louisiana, Spain's settlement at St. Augustine, Florida, was intended to be a self-supporting military outpost. Unable to attract settlers and costly to maintain, Florida grew so slowly and unsteadily that the Spanish considered abandoning it and moving the population to the West Indies.

When the British established their colony at Carolina, however, Florida again became important to Spain—and it gained a new source of settlers in runaway slaves. The British and Spanish began fighting, usually using Indian and African surrogates. Spanish raiders seized slaves from Carolina plantations, paid them wages, and introduced them to Catholicism. Soon, as Carolina's governor complained, slaves were "running dayly" to Florida. In 1693, Spain's king offered liberty to all British slaves who escaped to Florida.

The border between the two colonies was violent—and, for Africans, a place of opportunity. Africans gained valuable military experience and, in 1738, about 100 former slaves established the free black town of Gracia Real de Santa Teresa de Mose near St. Augustine. Mose's leader was the Mandinga captain of the free black militia, Francisco Menéndez. A former slave who had been reenslaved, he persisted in petitioning for his freedom. Spain freed Menéndez and other Africans like him and reiterated the policy that British slaves who escaped to Florida should be free. The persistence of Menéndez and the other escaped slaves established the first free black community on the North American continent.

Conquest, Revolt, and Reconquest in New Mexico

In the West, New Mexico developed into a colonial outpost on the far edge of a world empire, irrelevant to Spain's economy or political power. Early in the seventeenth century, the Spanish considered abandoning the settlement, but Franciscan missionaries persuaded Spain to stay so the priests could minister to the Native Americans. In the eastern half of the continent, Indians could play the European powers against each other, but in the West, only Spain was a presence, reducing the Pueblo Indians' leverage. When the Pueblo Indians rose up against the Spanish at the end of the seventeenth century, the survival of New Mexico was in doubt.

Spain had established its colony in New Mexico by conquest. Although Coronado's party had explored the region from Arizona to Kansas (1541–1542), it had not planted a permanent settlement. In 1598, Juan de Oñate was appointed governor and authorized to establish a colony. Like his great-grandfather Cortés, Oñate persuaded some local Pueblos to accept him as their ruler, and others he overcame by force. His harsh means proved effective, and the Spanish soon dominated the entire Southwest. In 1610 they established their capital at Santa Fe, and the colony, called New Mexico, began to grow slowly. The New Mexico Colony was to serve as an outpost against the French, just as St. Augustine was to defend against the English. The most important "business" in the colony was to convert the Pueblo Indians to Catholicism.

Franciscan priests established a series of missions in New Mexico. Although there were never more than 50 or so Franciscans at any time, they claimed to have converted about 80,000 Indians in less than a century. Most of these conversions, however, were in name only. The Indians deeply resented the priests' attempts to change their customs and beliefs. By forcing the Indians to adopt European sex roles and sexual mores, the Franciscans undermined not only Pueblo religion but also their society.

Spanish rule fell harshly on the Pueblos. Although Spanish law forbade enslavement of conquered Indians, some Spanish settlers openly defied it. More common was the *encomienda* system. Oñate rewarded his lieutenants by naming them *encomenderos*, which entitled them to tribute from the Indians living on the land they had been awarded. Some *encomenderos* instead demanded labor or personal service.

The Pueblo at Acoma The Acoma Pueblo sits atop a mesa that rises 400 feet aboveground. In January 1699, Spanish soldiers destroyed the pueblo and killed 800 of its inhabitants, in retaliation for the killing of a dozen soldiers. All the male survivors over the age of 12 and all female survivors were sentenced to 20 years of servitude to the Spanish, and the men over the age of 25 each had a foot cut off as well. The pueblo was rebuilt after its destruction.

Women working in Spanish households were vulnerable to sexual abuse by their masters. Facing such burdens, the Indian population declined from about 40,000 in 1638 to only 17,000 in 1670.

A combination of Spanish demands for labor and tribute and a long period of drought left the Pueblos without the food surpluses that they had been selling to the nomadic Apaches and Navajos. Those tribes began to raid the Pueblos, taking by force what they could no longer get by trade. Under siege, Pueblos turned once again to their tribal gods and religious leaders.

When the Spanish punished the Indians who returned to their traditional religion, they pushed the Pueblos into revolt. A medicine man named Popé united the leaders of most of the Pueblos, promising that if the Indians threw out the Spanish and prayed again to their ancient gods, food would be plentiful. Indians would never have to work for the Spanish again, he said, and Indian customs would be restored.

Popé's revolt began on August 10, 1680, when the Spanish were low on supplies. First, the Indians seized all horses and mules, immobilizing the Spanish. Next, they blocked the roads to Santa Fe. Then they destroyed all the Spanish settlements, one at a time. At day's end, more than 400 Spanish had been killed. The Pueblos laid siege to Santa Fe, forcing Spanish survivors to retreat to El Paso. In the most successful Indian revolt ever in North America, the Spanish had been driven from New Mexico.

The Pueblos held off the Spanish for 13 years, until 1696, but the struggles took a heavy toll. Contrary to Popé's promise, the drought continued. Warfare took more lives, and the population continued to drop.

The revolt taught the Spanish lessons. The new Franciscan missionaries were far less zealous than their predecessors. The *encomienda* was not reestablished, and exploitation was less common. Slowly the Spanish colony began rebuilding (see Map 4–4).

The population was divided into four groupings, from a small nobility at the top to enslaved Indians at the bottom. The nobility, a hereditary aristocracy of 20 or so families, included government officials. They developed codes of honor to distinguish themselves from lower orders. This nobility prided itself on its racial purity, considering white skin a clear sign of superiority. It scorned those of mixed blood, many of whom, of course, were the illegitimate children of elite Spanish men and the Indian women they raped or seduced. Aristocratic men placed a high value on the personal qualities of courage, honesty, loyalty, and sexual virility. Female honor consisted of extreme modesty and sexual purity.

The second group was landed peasants, most of them *mestizos*, half-Spanish and half-Indian. In this highly color-conscious colonial society,

> **Who shall kill a Spaniard will get an Indian woman for a wife, and who kills four will get four women.**
>
> POPÉ

Map 4-4 Region of Spanish Reconquest of New Mexico, 1692-1696
This map includes the pueblos reconquered by the Spanish, as well as Spanish settlements. *Adapted from Oakah L. Jones Jr.,* Pueblo Warriors and Spanish Conquest *(Norman: University of Oklahoma Press, 1966), p. 37.*

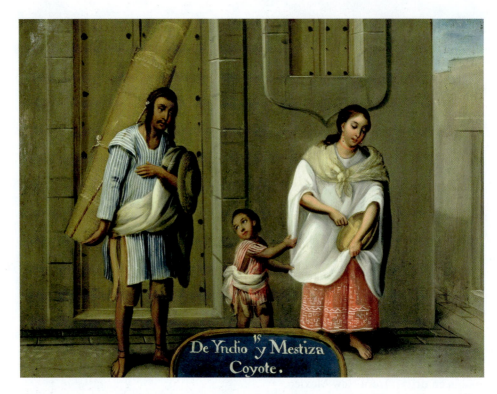

Eighteenth-century Spanish Illustrations of New World Racial Mixture In this case, the union of an Indian ("Yndio") and a "Mestiza" produces a "Coyote" child. The Spanish were much more attentive to color distinction than were the English, and they developed a large vocabulary so that they could make these distinctions with great precision.

the *mestizos* prized the Spanish part of their heritage and scorned the Indian. Next came the Pueblo Indians, living in their own communities. At the bottom were the *genízaros*, conquered Indians who had been enslaved. They were joined by Indians who left their tribes and moved to Spanish settlements. Often these immigrants were outcasts, such as women who had been raped by Spanish men. A century after their first conquest, the Pueblo Indians had begun to adopt the values of their conquerors.

Native Americans and the Country Between

Spain paid little attention to its impoverished outposts in New Mexico, leaving them vulnerable to the Indians to the east. When the French in Louisiana started arming their Comanche, Wichita, and Pawnee trading partners, New Mexicans—Spanish and Pueblos alike—were challenged.

The Indians of the Great Plains, however, profited from the conflict, obtaining guns from the French and horses from the Spanish. After the Pueblo revolt, the Spanish left behind hundreds of horses that Pueblo and Apache Indians passed on to the Plains Indians. By the middle of the eighteenth century, all the Plains Indians were on horseback, which transformed their lives dramatically. They became more effective buffalo hunters, thus making them better fed, clothed, and housed. Their new mobility gave them an increasing sense of freedom, too. But the horses—and the better living conditions they helped make possible—attracted other Indians to the Great Plains. In fact, most of the Indians we now associate with the Great Plains—Sioux, Arapaho, Cheyenne, Blackfoot, Cree—did not arrive there until the eighteenth century.

The result was increased warfare among the Plains Indians, and those with the best access to horses fared the best. For example, the Comanches came to dominate the southern plains, from western Kansas to New Mexico, where they intruded on both the Apaches and the Spanish. The Comanches raided the Apaches, taking not only their horses but also their women and children as captives, some of whom they sold as slaves—*genízaros*—to the Spanish. The Comanches cut the Apaches off from French traders to the east. The Apaches in turn moved west and south, bringing them into conflict with the Pueblos and the Spanish. In defense, the Spanish built a string of armed settlements in current-day Texas, but they could not withstand the Comanches, and even the New Mexican settlements were endangered.

Eventually, the new horse-centered way of life took its toll. Although some tribes grew stronger at the expense of others, all suffered from the increasing violence. European diseases proved deadly, as well. Under such pressures, gender roles changed. Men sought distinction as warriors, demonstrating success by the number of scalps or captives they seized. Yet so many fell in battle that they were soon outnumbered by women, which led to polygamy, as surviving warriors took multiple wives. As men's status as warriors and hunters rose, that of women—the agriculturalists—fell. Men also increased their status by seizing and selling female captives. In a warrior society, women were important markers of male prestige.

Conclusion

After a period of considerable instability, by the beginning of the eighteenth century, almost all of the British North American colonies had developed the societies that they would maintain until the American Revolution. For the most part, the colonies were prosperous, with a large white middle class. The efforts to replicate a European hierarchical order had largely failed. Each region had found a secure economic base: farming and shipping in New England, mixed farming in the middle colonies, and single-crop planting in the southern ones. The southern colonies had become slave societies, although slavery was practiced in every colony. For the most part, the colonies had figured out how to control their own populations, whether by affording them increased opportunity and political rights, in the case of Europeans, or by exercising tighter control, in the case of enslaved Africans. These strong economic foundations, when combined with political stability, were the preconditions for the rapid population growth of the eighteenth century, when the British population on the mainland would far surpass that of the French and Spanish colonies. The French and Spanish colonies on the mainland were still little more than frontier outposts, although both nations maintained imperial visions for North America. Native Americans remained a strong presence, but the competition among the European powers— and even the individual colonies—for the loyalty of the Indian tribes, their trade, and their land remained a source of conflict.

Who, What

Nathaniel Bacon   116
William Berkeley   116
John Locke   112
William Penn   109
Popé   135
Half-Way Covenant   122
King Philip's (Metacom's) War   115

Liberalism   109
Mercantilism   106
Navigation Acts   106
Quakers   111
Redemptioners   112
Glorious Revolution   106

Review Questions

1. What was Britain's plan of empire? What role were the American colonies supposed to play in it?

2. What effect did political turmoil and the change of leadership in Britain have on the American colonies in the second half of the seventeenth century?

3. Describe Indian-white relations in the American colonies in the second half of the seventeenth century. What was the Covenant Chain, and how did Edmund Andros's vision of Indian-white relations differ from that of settlers in New England?

>> TIME LINE

▼**1598**
Juan de Oñate colonizes New Mexico for Spain

▼**1610**
Santa Fe established

▼**1627**
Barbados settled

▼**1628**
Parliament passes Petition of Right

▼**1642-1647**
English Revolution

▼**1649**
King Charles I beheaded

▼**1651-1696**
Navigation Acts passed to regulate trade

▼**1652-1674**
Three Anglo-Dutch Wars

▼**1656**
Britain seizes Jamaica from Spain

▼**1660**
British monarchy restored, Charles II crowned king

▼**1662**
Half-Way Covenant

▼**1664**
British seize New Netherland, renaming it New York

▼**1665**
New Jersey established

▼**1669**
Fundamental Constitutions written for South Carolina

▼**1670**
Carolina settled

▼**1673**
Marquette and Joliet explore Mississippi for France

▼**1675-1676**
King Philip's War

▼**1676-1677**
Bacon's Rebellion

▼**1680**
Pueblo Revolt in New Mexico reestablishes Indian rule
Westo War, Carolina defeats the Westos

▼**1681**
William Penn granted charter for Pennsylvania

Critical-Thinking Questions

1. Many of the American colonies experienced a period of political instability in the last quarter of the seventeenth century. In many cases, ranging from the Salem witch trials to Popé's Rebellion of 1680, the sources of the instability appear specific and local, yet they may also reveal a pattern. To what extent were these instances of instability local, and to what extent may they reveal larger processes at work in the colonies of European imperial powers?

2. In this period, a number of colonies became slave societies. What forces propelled these changes? Were different outcomes possible?

3. What patterns, if any, do you see in Native Americans' accommodation and resistance to European expansion in North America in this period?

For further review materials and resource information, please visit www.oup.com/us/ofthepeople

▼**1683**
New York's assembly meets for first time

▼**1685**
King Charles II dies and James, Duke of York, becomes King James II

▼**1686**
Massachusetts, Plymouth, Connecticut, Rhode Island, and New Hampshire combined in Dominion of New England; New York and New Jersey added two years later

▼**1688**
Glorious Revolution

▼**1689**
Leisler's Rebellion in New York, Coode's Rebellion in Maryland

William and Mary become King and Queen of Britain; Dominion of New England overthrown

▼**1689–1697**
King William's War

▼**1690**
Publication of John Locke's *Two Treatises of Government*

▼**1691**
Massachusetts made a royal colony
Maryland made a royal colony
New Hampshire made a royal colony

▼**1692**
Salem witchcraft trials

▼**1696**
Reconquest of New Mexico

▼**1702–1713**
Queen Anne's War

▼**1706**
Spanish establish settlement at Albuquerque

▼**1715–1716**
Yamasee War

▼**1718**
French establish settlement at New Orleans

MAIN IDEAS

TOPICS

1) Political, social, economic, and religious instabilities in Europe shaped patterns of settlement, growth, and opportunity in the new colonies.

2) As England established its political and economic supremacy in Europe, colonists found their lives subject to forces beyond their control.

3) Politics, economics, and religious ideologies in both Europe and the colonies affected how women, Native Americans, and enslaved Africans lost or gained control over their own labor, bodies, and welfare.

4) Colonial warfare illuminated forces that both replicated and departed from traditional European struggles over land, money, culture, and religion.

The Plan of Empire

New Colonies, New Patterns

The Transformation of Virginia

New England Under Assault

The Empire Strikes

Massachusetts in Crisis

Empires in Collision

CHAPTER 4
CONTINENTAL EMPIRES
1660–1720

EVENTS

Turmoil in England The king and Parliament clashed over religion and royal power.

The Political Economy of Mercantilism Britain's economic policies set it on a path toward world power.

New Netherland Becomes New York Under English rule, New York offered religious toleration but limited self-government.

Diversity and Prosperity in Pennsylvania Religious toleration, self-government, and economic opportunity made William Penn's colony prosperous.

Indians and Africans in the Political Economy of Carolina A new colony in Carolina established religious toleration and self-government for whites but slavery for Africans and Indians.

The Barbados Connection Barbados became Britain's first slave society, most productive colony, and a model for Carolina.

Social Change in Virginia Increasing numbers of settlers grew restless in Virginia.

Bacon's Rebellion and the Abandonment of the Middle Ground Bacon led a rebellion for more land and opportunity, at the expense of Native Americans.

Virginia Becomes a Slave Society Slavery became central to Virginia's economy and social structure.

Social Prosperity and the Fear of Religious Decline Prosperity caused the Puritans to worry about religious decline.

King Philip's War Colonists' encroachment on Indian lands led to a severe and costly war.

Indians and the Empire New York's Indian alliance isolated New England from further expansion.

The Dominion of New England James II asserted control over New England, limiting colonists' rights and economic freedom.

The Glorious Revolution in Britain and America The rise of constitutional government led to political stability in Britain and more self-government for the colonies.

The Rights of Englishmen British officials and colonists began to disagree over the extent of colonists' rights.

Conflict in the Empire England and France and their Indian allies fought wars competing for trade and territory.

The Social and Cultural Contexts of Witchcraft In a time of instability, Puritans looked for supernatural causes to explain events.

Witchcraft at Salem Rising accusations of witchcraft occurred in Salem in 1692, leading to the execution of 20 convicted witches, mostly women.

The End of Witchcraft A growing belief in natural causes and individualism led to new attitudes toward women and fewer accusations of witchcraft.

France Attempts an Empire France's plantation colonies in the Caribbean proved far more profitable than their ones based on trade with Indians on the North American continent.

The Spanish Outpost in Florida As Britain settled in Carolina, violence erupted between the British and the Spanish in Florida.

Conquest, Revolt, and Reconquest in New Mexico Spain defeated an Indian revolt and reestablished control over its New Mexico colony.

Native Americans and the Country Between Trade with the Spanish and French allowed the Indians of the Great Plains to thrive but produced increasing tribal warfare.

The South East Prospect of The City of Philadelphia By Peter Cooper *Painter*

1 The Draw Bridge	7 John Witpain	13 Jo. Carpenter Store	19 Abr. Bickly
2 Buds Building	8 Capt Anthony	14 Sam Carpenter Store	20 Thomas Masters
3 Edw. Shipen	9 George Painter	15 S. Carpenter Dwelling Ho	21 Sam. Perry
4 Ant. Morris Brew Ho	10 Jos. Shipen	16 Saml Bunkley	22 Bank Meeting Hou
5 Capt. Vineing	11 Wm Fisbourn Store	17 Quak. Meeting Hou	23 Tho. Chalkey
6 Jonathan Dickinson	12 The Scales	18 The Court House	24 Penny Pott House

COMMON THREADS

>> What were some of the choices that individual men and women made in the eighteenth century—for example, about where to live, how to work, what to purchase, what to believe—and how did those choices affect their society?

>> How did such choices make everyday life more democratic? What were the forces that worked against such democratization?

>> How were free Americans able to become wealthier even without significant technological innovations?

>> How did the consumer revolution affect American society and culture?

>> As the colonial population became more diverse and complex, with separate regional cultures and an increasing variety of beliefs and religious practices, were there other experiences that colonial Americans had in common? Was it possible yet, on the eve of the American Revolution, to talk about a common American experience or culture?

The Eighteenth-Century World
1700–1775

AMERICAN PORTRAIT

>> George Whitefield: Evangelist for a Consumer Society

In 1740 there were no more than 16,000 people living in Boston, but on October 12, some 20,000 people filled the Common to hear an English minister preach. Everywhere he went, the crowds were unprecedented—8,000 in Philadelphia, 3,000 in the little Pennsylvania village of Neshaminy. Those who could not see the evangelist in person read about him in the newspapers. If there was one binding experience for the American people in the decades before the Revolution, it was George Whitefield's ministry.

Born in Bristol, England, in 1714, George Whitefield would become not only a leading preacher of the Great Awakening of religion in the American colonies but also one of the most influential preachers in the history of Christianity. Because of the growth of the market economy, men and women on both sides of the Atlantic could now participate in a consumer culture that offered many ways to spend money and leisure time. To those schooled in a traditional Calvinist religion, the consumer society was both attractive and frightening. Could one serve God and oneself at the same time?

At 17, when Whitefield discovered he had no aptitude for trade, the career he had chosen, the boy from a poor family faced a personal crisis. One morning, he blurted out, "God intends something for me which we know not of." Whitefield then prepared for the ministry. He enrolled at Oxford University, paying his way by working as a servant to wealthy students. He became friendly with the Methodists, a group of religious young men planning a mission to the new colony of Georgia. Under their influence, Whitefield turned his back on consumer culture. "Whatsoever I did," Whitefield explained, "I endeavoured to do all to the glory of God." Whitefield was determined to share what he had learned with all who would hear.

Whitefield helped create a mass public that broke down the boundaries of small communities in which each minister or priest had typically addressed only his own congregation. The crowds Whitefield drew were often so large that he preached outdoors, with a voice so loud that Benjamin Franklin calculated that it could be heard by 25,000 people at a time. Although Whitefield spoke directly to the heart of each individual, he also drew together entire communities in a way no one had ever done before.

Whitefield embodied the great contradictions of his age without threatening the political or economic order that sustained them. He appealed to men as well as women, to the poor as well as the rich, to slaves as well as their masters, and to those who were suffering from capitalism as well as those who were benefiting from it. Whitefield's strategy was to criticize the individual without attacking the system. In Philadelphia, he preached, "Do not say, you are miserable, and poor, and blind and naked, and therefore ashamed to come, for it is to such that this Invitation is now sent. The Polite, the Rich, the Busy, Self-Righteous Pharisees of this Generation have been

Continued

>> AMERICAN PORTRAIT
Continued

bidden already, but they . . . are too deeply engaged in going one to his Country House, another to his Merchandize."

He censured the religious leadership, but not the church itself. Cruel slave masters were condemned, but not the institution of slavery. He showed people how to acquire the self-discipline that would enable them either to succeed in a competitive market or to bear failures with Christian resignation. He helped them experience religion as an intense personal feeling and find meaning in a time of rapid economic transformation.

A world traveler who called Georgia his home, Whitefield died in Newburyport, Massachusetts, in 1770, preaching to the end. Five years later, a band of Continental army officers dug up his corpse. The body had decayed, but his clothing was still intact. The soldiers snipped pieces of it to take with them as protection.

The Population Explosion of the Eighteenth Century

George Whitefield could speak to the hearts of the American colonists because he understood their world. As the colonies matured, they were tied in to the North Atlantic world and brought dramatic changes. One of the most important changes was the increase in population, from both immigration and natural increase. This population produced products for the world economy and provided a market for them, as well, and its boom was both the product of American prosperity and the precondition for its further growth.

The Dimensions of Population Growth

The population in the American colonies grew at a rate unprecedented in human history, from just over 250,000 people in 1700 to more than 1 million by 1750. The rate of growth was highest in the free population in prosperous farming regions, but it was rapid everywhere, even among slaves.

Much of the colonies' population growth was caused by their unquenchable thirst for labor. They attracted an extraordinary number of immigrants, and when free labor did not meet the demand, unfree labor (slaves, indentured servants, and redemptioners) filled the gap. In fact, when the number of Africans who came in chains is added to the Europeans who came as indentured servants and redemptioners, 90 percent of the immigrants to the colonies between 1580 and 1775 were unfree when they arrived.

OUTLINE

The Population Explosion of the Eighteenth Century
The Dimensions of Population Growth
Bound for America: European Immigrants
Bound for America: African Slaves

AMERICAN LANDSCAPE:
The Slave Ship
The Great Increase of Offspring

The Transatlantic Economy: Producing and Consuming

The Nature of Colonial Economic Growth
The Transformation of the Family Economy
Sources of Regional Prosperity
Merchants and Dependent Laborers in the Transatlantic Economy
Consumer Choices and the Creation of Gentility

AMERICA AND THE WORLD:
Consumer Tastes in Global Perspective

The Varieties of Colonial Experience
Creating an Urban Public Sphere

Increasingly, these immigrants reflected the broad reach of the North Atlantic political world. At the beginning of the eighteenth century, the population of the American colonies was primarily English in origin. By the beginning of the American Revolution, the population had changed significantly. There were small numbers of people with Finnish, Swedish, French, Swiss, and Jewish heritage, and large numbers of Welsh, Scotch-Irish, Germans, Dutch, and Africans. The foundation for American diversity had been laid.

Bound for America: European Immigrants

Much of the population increase came from immigration. In the eighteenth century, about 425,000 Europeans migrated to the colonies, with large numbers from Scotland, Northern Ireland, Wales, and Germany.

The largest number of European immigrants were Scotch-Irish, that is, Scottish people who had moved to Northern Ireland to escape famine in their own country. As many as 250,000 came to seek a better life and to escape the religious persecution they experienced as Presbyterians in an Anglican society. At first, Massachusetts invited the Scotch-Irish to settle on its borders, as a buffer between the colony and the Indians. Once the impoverished Scotch-Irish began to arrive in large numbers, however, the English inhabitants worried that they would have to provide for them. In 1729 a Boston mob turned away a shipload of Scotch-Irish immigrants, and in 1738 the Puritans of Worcester burned down a Presbyterian church. Thereafter, the vast majority of Scotch-Irish immigrants headed for the more welcoming middle colonies and the South.

Going where land was the cheapest, the Scotch-Irish settled between the English seaboard settlements and the Indian communities to the west, from Pennsylvania to Georgia (see Map 5–1). As their numbers increased, the Scotch-Irish pressed against the Indians, seizing their lands. Like the Scotch-Irish, most German migrants settled in the backcountry from Pennsylvania to the Carolinas. Between 1700 and the start of the Revolution, more than 100,000 Germans arrived, and by 1775, a third of Pennsylvania's population was German. Including not only Lutherans and Catholics but also Quakers, Amish, and Mennonites, Germans established prosperous farming communities wherever they settled. Indeed, colonies such as Pennsylvania that welcomed the widest variety of immigrants became not only the most prosperous but also the ones in which that prosperity was most widely shared. Unlike most seventeenth-century

The Diversity of Urban Life
The Maturing of Rural Society
The World That Slavery Made
Georgia: From Frontier Outpost to Plantation
 Society

The Head and the Heart in America: The
 Enlightenment and Religious Awakening
The Ideas of the Enlightenment

TECHNOLOGY AND IDEAS:
 Inoculation

The Economic and Social Foundations of
 Democracy

PRIMARY SOURCE:
 The Autobiography of Benjamin Franklin
Enlightened Institutions
Origins of the Great Awakening
The Grand Itinerant
Cultural Conflict and Challenges to Authority
What the Awakening Wrought

Conclusion

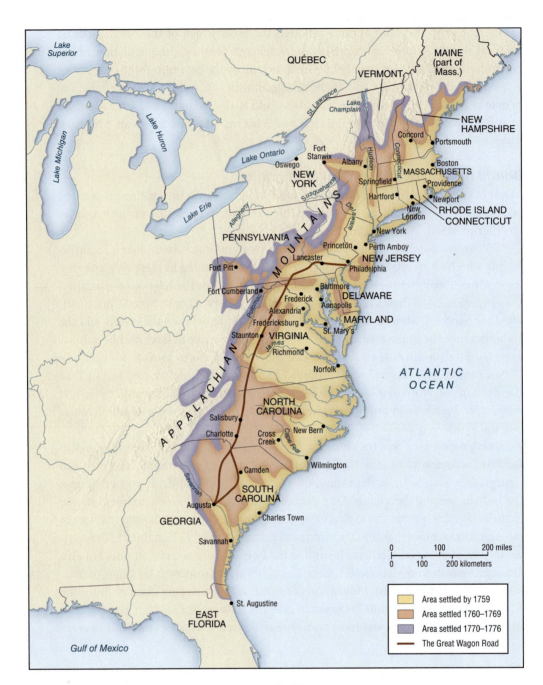

Map 5-1 Expansion of Settlement, 1720–1760 By 1760, the colonial population made up an almost continuous line of settlement from Maine to Florida and was pushing west over the Appalachian Mountains.

migrants, a large proportion of eighteenth-century migrants were artisans drawn to America by the demand for their labor. As African slaves became agricultural workers, especially in the South, the colonies needed skilled workers.

The majority of European migrants to the colonies were unfree, not only indentured servants and redemptioners but also the 50,000 British convicts whose sentences were commuted to a term of service in the colonies. Most English and Welsh migrants were single men between the ages of 19 and 23 who came as indentured servants. The Scotch-Irish migration included a larger number of families, and three-fourths of the

Germans came in family groups. For all, the passage to America, which could take three months or more, was grueling and profoundly unhealthful. Once the migrants arrived, servants and convicts were sold for terms of service in auctions that resembled those held for African slaves (see Figure 5–1).

Bound for America: African Slaves

The increase in the African population was even more dramatic than that of Europeans. In 1660 there were only 2,920 African or African-descended inhabitants of the mainland colonies. A century later there were more than 300,000. The proportion of Africans grew most rapidly in the southern colonies, to almost 40 percent on the eve of the Revolution. By 1720 South Carolina had an African majority. Most of the increase in the African population came from the slave trade. By 1808, when Congress closed off the importation of slaves to the United States, about 523,000 African slaves had been imported into the nation (see Figure 5–2).

The African slave trade was a profitable and well-organized segment of the world economy. Until the eighteenth century, when demand from the New World increased, the transatlantic slave trade was controlled by Africans. Generally, Europeans were not allowed into the interior of Africa, so slaves were brought to the coast for sale. Many African nations taxed the sale of slaves and regulated the trade. Some nations supplied a steady stream of slaves, whereas others offered them intermittently, suggesting that participation in the trade was a matter of conscious policy.

> I must own, to the shame of my own countrymen, that I was first kidnapped and betrayed by some of my own complexion, who were the first cause of my exile and slavery; but if there were no buyers there would be no sellers.
>
> OTTOBAH CUGOANO, describing his enslavement at the age of 13

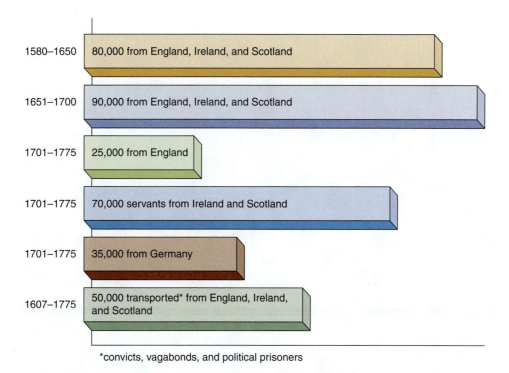

Period	Amount
1580–1650	80,000 from England, Ireland, and Scotland
1651–1700	90,000 from England, Ireland, and Scotland
1701–1775	25,000 from England
1701–1775	70,000 servants from Ireland and Scotland
1701–1775	35,000 from Germany
1607–1775	50,000 transported* from England, Ireland, and Scotland

*convicts, vagabonds, and political prisoners

Figure 5-1 The Importation of Servants from Europe into British America, 1580-1775 By the time of the American Revolution, 350,000 servants had been imported into the colonies, most of whom came from the British Isles. *Richard S. Dunn, "Servants and Slaves," in Jack P. Greene and J. R. Pole,* Colonial British America *(Baltimore: Johns Hopkins, 1984), p. 159.*

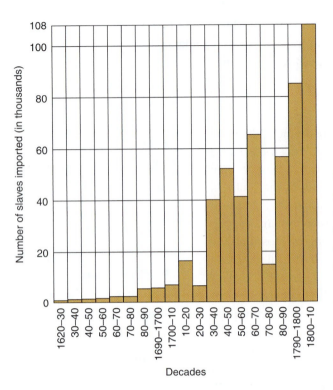

Figure 5-2 The Importation of Slaves into the Colonies, 1620–1810 The number of Africans imported into the colonies increased dramatically in the eighteenth century, and, except for an interruption during the American Revolution, continued until the African slave trade was made illegal in 1808. *Helen Hornbeck Tanner,* The Settling of North America *(New York: Macmillan, 1995), p. 51.*

Because African slaves were unwilling and sometimes rebellious passengers on the ships that transported them across the Atlantic, European slave ships needed larger crews and heavier weapons than usual. This resistance by slaves increased the cost of transporting them so much that the higher prices may have spared half a million Africans enslavement.

Most slaves were captives of war, and as the demand for slaves increased, the tempo of warfare in Africa intensified in response. In times of famine and epidemic, sometimes caused by the slave trade, desperate families might even sell their own children to a trader. The New World preferred male slaves, leaving most of the female captives to the African slave market, where they became domestic slaves or plural wives to wealthier Africans.

As bad as the voyage to America was for indentured servants, the trip for enslaved Africans was worse. Perhaps 10 percent died before reaching the African coast. Many had never seen an ocean or a white man, and both sights terrified them. They were confined in pens or forts for as long as half a year while waiting for a ship.

Enslaved Africans Bound for the New World This group is being force marched by an African slave trader from the interior of Africa to a European trading post on the coast.

AMERICAN LANDSCAPE

>> The Slave Ship

We do not usually think of a ship as part of a landscape, but the slave ship was one of the most important places in the eighteenth century. It was at once a floating factory, prison, and fortress. It was there that Africans were transformed into slaves.

Any ship, small or large, could be made into a slave ship. Because the cost of transporting slaves across the Atlantic was so high, accounting for three-quarters of the price of a slave, slave merchants tried to crowd as many Africans as possible into each ship—300, 400, or even 600. The English were particularly efficient, carrying twice as many slaves as crew members and half again as many slaves per ship as the other nations, thereby increasing the profits.

Continued

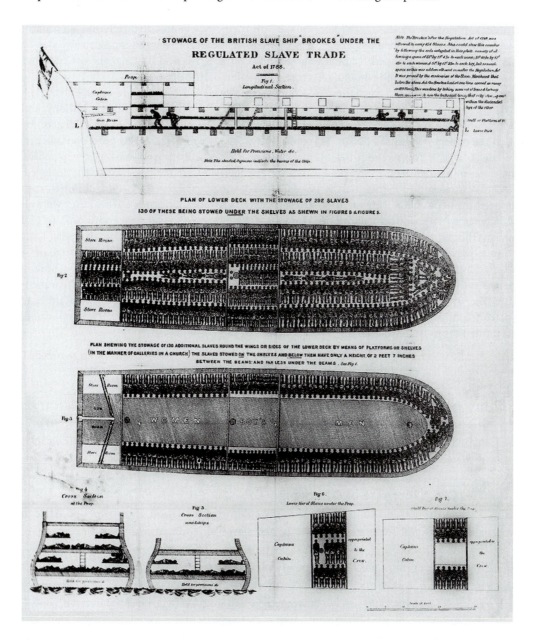

In order to maximize the number of Africans on each ship, platforms were built between decks, thus doubling the surface area upon which the slaves could be placed. With perhaps only four and a half feet between the platform and the ceiling, the Africans could not stand up. They were packed so tightly that they could not move from side to side. Even the smallest spaces were filled with children.

Packing so many human beings into such tight quarters created the risk of suffocation. But if the hatches were kept open, the Africans might escape confinement and overpower the crew. Hence, grates were placed over the hatches, and small air openings were cut into the sides of the ship. Later, some ships used large funnel tubes to carry air below decks.

Men and women were kept separate, divided by partitions. Male slaves were shackled and confined below deck for most of each day. Chained together and without enough room to stand up, many were unable to reach the large buckets that served as latrines. Some captains let the slaves lie in their own filth until the voyage's end. Heat and disease compounded the misery. One ship's doctor reported that the slaves' deck "was so covered with the blood and mucus which had proceeded from them in consequence of the flux, that it resembled a slaughterhouse." The women were left unshackled but were often prey to the sailors' lust. When slaves were brought above deck, some would jump overboard. Captains stretched netting around their ships to prevent such suicides.

In order to protect the crew in case of insurrection, slave ships often had thick, 10-foot-high walls—barricados—to separate the crew from the human cargo. Armed sailors patrolled atop the barricado. Ship captains gathered their human cargo from different regions, each with its own language, to make sure that the captives could not communicate with each other and foment rebellion. At the same time, the captains had to be careful not to bring together groups who might fight each other. With resistance from the enslaved the norm, ship captains used terror to maintain order. Flogging—a punishment for sailors, as well—was common. Some captains used instruments of torture, such as the thumbscrew, "a dreadful engine, which, if the screw be turned by an unrelenting hand, can give intolerable anguish." The object was not only to punish the disobedient but also to frighten their shipmates. That was surely the result after some of the Africans aboard the *Brownlow* rebelled. The captain dismembered the rebels with an axe "till their bodies remained only like a trunk of a tree when all the branches are lopped away," and he threw the severed heads and limbs at the other slaves, chained together on the deck.

Such terror hardened captain and crew. Few sailors signed on to a slave ship if they had better options, and one captain described his crew as the "very dregs of the community." The life of a sailor was hard enough; service on a slave ship—a floating prison—was even harder. Yet even the lowest sailor was superior to the enslaved. Even though many sailors were dark-skinned men from Asia, the Caribbean, or India, at sea, they were all known as "white people." Over time, both captain and crew became practiced in the ways of cruelty. Silas Todd was apprenticed to a slave ship captain at the age of 14 and hoped to become a captain himself. Then, ashore in Boston in 1734, he was "saved" in the Great Awakening. Had he not been, he later reflected, he might have become "as eminent a savage" as the captains under whom he had served.

The voyage, or "middle passage," proved lethal to many more. As the slave trade became more efficient in the eighteenth century, the mortality rate dropped, from perhaps 20 percent to half that amount. Those who survived were ready to begin their lives as New World slaves.

The Great Increase of Offspring

Most of the extraordinary increase in the colonies' population, European and African alike, came not from immigration or the slave trade but from natural increase (see Figure 5-3).

For European Americans, population increase was mainly due to the lower age of marriage for women and the higher proportion of women who married. In England, for example, as many as 20 percent of women did not marry by age 45, compared with only 5 percent in the colonies. The age of marriage for women in the colonies was also considerably lower, with women marrying in their late teens or early 20s, compared to the late 20s in England. Because more women married, and married earlier, they bore more babies, on average seven or eight each, with six or seven surviving to adulthood. As a rule, the more economic opportunity, the earlier the age of marriage for women and men, and the more children. In the better climate, more children survived to adulthood, but child mortality rates were high. Thanks to rapid population growth, the American population was exceptionally young.

In many ways, the African American population resembled the European American population. Slaves born in the colonies married young and established families as stable as slavery permitted. By the time they were 18, most slave women usually had had their first child. As in Africa, they might not form a lasting union with the father, but within a few years many settled into long-lasting relationships with the men who would father the rest of their children. Slave women bore between six and eight children, on average. With child mortality even higher for African Americans than for European Americans, between 25 and 50 percent of slave children died before reaching adulthood. Even so, the slave population more than reproduced itself, and by the middle of the eighteenth century it was growing more from natural increase than from the importation of slaves. Only a tiny fraction of the Africans sold into slavery ended up in mainland British colonies. Nonetheless, when slavery was abolished after the Civil War, the United States had the largest population of African descent in the New World.

> It seems indelicate, at least new, to strip, surrounded by different Ages & Sexes, & Rise in the Morning, in the Blaze of Day, with the Eyes of, at least, one blinking Irish Female searching out Subjects for Remark.
>
> PHILIP VICKERS FITHIAN,
> a young Presbyterian minister, who was lodged one night with an entire family in a single room in their small cabin on the Pennsylvania frontier

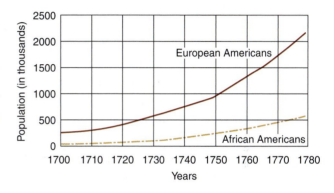

Figure 5-3 Population of the Thirteen Colonies, 1610–1780 Because of natural increase and immigration, the European population in the colonies grew even more rapidly than the African one. *Jacob Cooke, ed.,* Encyclopedia of North American Colonies *(New York: Scribner's, 1993), pp. 1, 470.*

The Transatlantic Economy: Producing and Consuming

In the eighteenth century, as the colonies matured, they became capitalist societies in an Atlantic trade network. More and more, people produced for the market, so that they could buy the goods the market had to offer. Throughout the Atlantic world, ordinary people reshaped their lives so they could buy more goods. Historians talk about two economic revolutions in this period: a consumer revolution—a steady increase in the demand for and purchase of consumer goods—and an industrious revolution (not *industrial* but *industrious* revolution), in which people worked harder and organized their households (their families, servants, and slaves) to produce goods for sale so that they would have money to pay for items they wanted. Income went up only slightly in the eighteenth century, yet people were buying more. In the process, they created a consumer society, in which most people eagerly purchased consumer goods.

The Nature of Colonial Economic Growth

Throughout human history, population growth has usually led to a decline in the standard of living as more people compete for fewer resources. In the American colonies, however, population growth led to an expansion of the economy, as more of the continent's abundant natural resources were brought under human control. The standard of living for most free Americans probably improved, although not dramatically. As the economy matured, a small segment—urban merchants and owners of large plantations—became wealthy. At the same time, the urban poor and tenant farmers began to slip toward poverty.

All of these changes took place, however, without any significant changes in technology (such as the power looms that would be invented later in the century). Most wealth was made from shipping and agriculture. Eighty percent of the colonies' population worked on farms or plantations, areas with no major technological innovations. Virtually all gains in productivity came instead from labor: more people were working, and they were working more efficiently.

The economy of colonial America was shaped by three factors: abundance of land and shortages of labor and of capital. The plantation regions of the South and the West Indies were best situated to take advantage of these circumstances, and the small-farm areas of New England were the least suitable. Tobacco planters in the Chesapeake and rice and indigo planters in South Carolina sold their products on a huge world market. Their large profits enabled them to purchase more land and more slaves to work it.

Because northern farmers raised crops and animals that were also produced in Europe, profits from agriculture alone were too low to permit them to acquire large tracts of land or additional labor (see Table 5–1). Northerners had to look to other opportunities for wealth. They found them in trade, exchanging their raw goods for European manufactured ones and selling them to American consumers.

The Transformation of the Family Economy

In colonial America, the family was the basic economic unit, and all family members contributed to it. Work was organized by gender. On farms, women were responsible for the preparation of food and clothing, child care, and care of the home. Women

Table 5-1 How Wealthy Were Colonial Americans?

Property-owning Class	New England	Mid-Atlantic Colonies	Southern Colonies	Thirteen Colonies
Men	169	194	410	260
Women	42	103	215	132
Adults 45 and older	252	274	595	361
Adults 44 and younger	129	185	399	237
Urban	191	287	641	233
Rural	151	173	392	255
Esquires, gentlemen	313	1,223	1,281	572
Merchants	563	858	314	497
Professions, sea captains	271	241	512	341
Farmers only, planters	155	180	396	263
Farmer-artisans, shipowners, fishermen	144	257	801	410
Shop and tavern keepers	219	222	195	204
Artisans, chandlers	114	144	138	122
Miners, laborers	52	67	383	62

Source: Alice Hanson Jones, Wealth of a Nation to Be: The American Colonies on the Eve of the Revolution (New York: Columbia University Press, 1980), p. 224.

Note: Numbers given are in pounds sterling.

grew vegetables and herbs, provided dairy products, and transformed flax and wool into clothing. Daughters worked under their mother's supervision, perhaps spinning extra yarn to be sold for a profit.

Men worked the rest of the farm. They raised grain and maintained the pastures. They cleared the land, chopped wood for fuel, and built and maintained the house, barn, and other structures. They took crops to market. Men's and women's work were complementary and necessary for survival. For example, men planted apple trees, children picked apples, and women pressed the apples into cider. When a husband was disabled, ill, or away from home, his wife could perform virtually all of his tasks as a sort of "deputy husband." Men almost never performed women's work, however, and men whose wives died remarried quickly to have someone to care for the household and children.

The eighteenth century's industrious revolution transformed the family economy: when people decided to produce goods to sell, they changed their family economies. Historians believe that increased production in this period came primarily from the labor of women and children, who worked harder and longer than they had before.

Sources of Regional Prosperity

The South, the most productive region, accounted for more than 60 percent of colonial exports (see Map 5–2). Tobacco was its chief cash crop. Next came cereals such as rice, wheat, corn, and flour, and then indigo, a plant used to dye fabric.

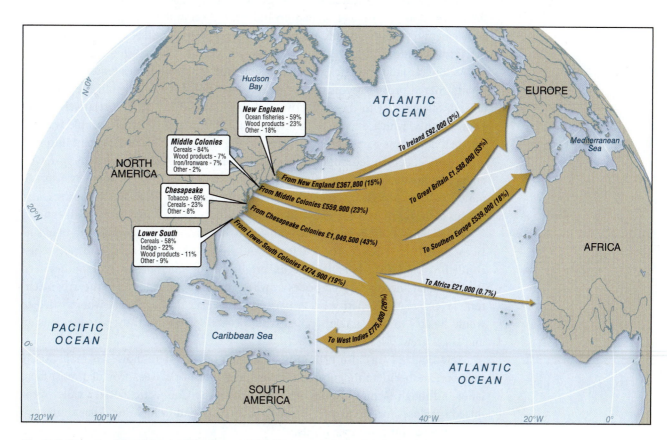

Map 5-2 Exports of the Thirteen Colonies, ca. 1770 Almost two-thirds of the exports from the colonies came from the South, and more than one-half went to Great Britain alone. Tobacco and grains were the most important exports of all. *Jacob Cooke, ed.,* Encyclopedia of North American Colonies *(New York: Scribner's, 1993), pp. 1, 514.*

Slave labor accounted for most of the southern agricultural output and was organized to produce for the market. When tobacco profits began to slip because of falling prices and the depletion of the soil, planters worked their slaves harder and, in the Chesapeake, began to plant corn and wheat. By diversifying their crops, planters were able to make maximum use of their slave labor force by keeping slaves busy throughout the year.

The work routine of slaves depended on the crops they tended. On tobacco plantations, where careful attention to the plants was necessary to ensure high quality, planters or white overseers worked the slaves in small gangs carefully selected and arranged to maximize productivity.

In the rice-growing lower South, however, slaves were usually assigned specific tasks, which they would work at until the job was completed. Rice growing required far less supervision than did tobacco planting. Because many Africans had grown rice in Africa and had likely taught Europeans how to grow it in America, rice planters let the slaves set their own pace. Once finished for the day, the slaves could use their time as they pleased. Many planted gardens to supplement their own diets or to earn a small income. Slaves trafficked in a wide range of products, from rice, corn, chickens, hogs, and catfish to canoes, baskets, and wax.

The inhabitants of the middle colonies grew prosperous by raising and selling wheat and other grains. The ports of Baltimore, Philadelphia, Wilmington, and New York became thriving commercial centers that collected grain from regional farms, milled it into flour, and shipped it to the West Indies, southern Europe, and other American colonies. Farmers relied on indentured servants, cottagers, and slaves to supplement the labor of family members. Cottagers were families who rented out part of a farmer's land, which they worked for wages.

As long as land was cheap and accessible, the middle colonies enjoyed the most evenly shared prosperity on the continent. Most inhabitants fell into the comfortable middle class, with the gap between the richest and the poorest relatively small. Pennsylvania, which offered both religious toleration and relatively simple ways to purchase land, was particularly prosperous. The energy that elsewhere went into religious conflict here fueled work and material accumulation. Gottlieb Mittelberger, who endured a horrendous journey to Pennsylvania, described his new home as a sort of paradise: "Our Americans live more quietly and peacefully than the Europeans; and all this is the result of the liberty which they enjoy and which makes them all equal."

When land became expensive or difficult to obtain, however, conflict might ensue. In the 1740s and 1750s, both New Jersey and New York experienced land riots when conflicting claims made land titles uncertain. In the Chesapeake and southeastern Pennsylvania, increasing land prices drove the poor into tenancy or to the urban centers. Widespread prosperity led Americans to expect that everyone who wished to would be able to own a farm. When land ownership was not fully possible, tension and anger grew.

New England was also primarily a farming region. Here, however, male family members, rather than indentured servants, cottagers, or slaves, provided most farm labor. Although farms in some regions, such as the Connecticut River valley, produced surpluses for the market, most farm families had to look for other sources of income to pay for consumer goods.

Town governments in New England encouraged enterprise, sometimes providing gristmills, sawmills, and fields on which cattle could graze. The region prospered, and

New Englanders came to expect their governments to enhance the economy. Agricultural exports were relatively slight, although both grain and livestock were sold to the slave plantations of the West Indies, which received more than 25 percent of the American colonies' exports (and more than 70 percent of New England's).

The other major colonial exports in the eighteenth century were fur and hides. By the eve of the Revolution, 95 percent of the furs imported into England came from North America—most of them provided by Indians, who traded them to European middlemen.

Merchants and Dependent Laborers in the Transatlantic Economy

Almost all colonies participated in a transatlantic economy. In each region, those most involved in the market were those with the most resources: large planters in the southern colonies, owners of the biggest farms in the middle colonies, and urban merchants in the northern colonies. The wealthiest never made their fortunes from farming or planting alone but always added income from activities such as speculating in land, practicing law, or lending money.

If some economic development was spurred from above, by enterprising individuals or by governments, much was also created by ambitious ordinary men and women. New England's mixed economy of grain, grazing, fishing, and lumbering required substantial capital improvements such as gristmills, sawmills, and tanneries to be profitable. By the beginning of the eighteenth century, shipbuilding was a major activity, and by 1775, one-third of the English merchant fleet had been built in the colonies.

The shipbuilding industry, in turn, spurred further economic development. In a process called linked economic development (because it ties together a variety of enterprises), shipbuilding stimulated other activities, such as lumbering, and the availability of ships enabled a flourishing trade. The profits generated by shipbuilding and trade were reinvested in sawmills to produce more lumber, in gristmills to grind grain into flour, and, of course, in more trading voyages. The growth of shipping in port cities such as Boston, Newport, New York, Philadelphia, and Charleston created an affluent merchant class, but trading was a risky business, and few who tried it rose to the top. One ship lost to a storm could ruin a merchant, as could a sudden turn in the market.

With an average of 10 times the capital of colonial merchants, English merchants could weather such reverses. Because capital was scarce in the colonies, merchants took great risks, seeking to turn a quick profit during wartime (see Chapter 6) or gambling on a sudden spurt in the price of wheat. Bad choices or bad luck could ruin any merchant.

The seafaring trades led capitalist development. A wealthy, risk-taking merchant class emerged, as well as that other distinguishing mark of a capitalist economy, a wage-earning class. As long as there was a labor shortage in the colonies, workers had an advantage. By the beginning of the eighteenth century, however, rapid population increase led to a growing supply of labor. Although they were free to shop around for the best wages, workers became part of a

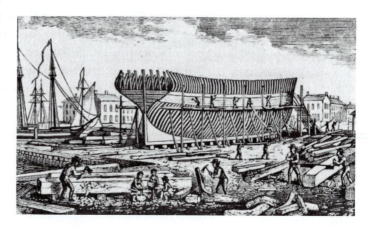

A Ship Being Built in New York Carpenters put together a ship for the growing trade out of colonial port cities.

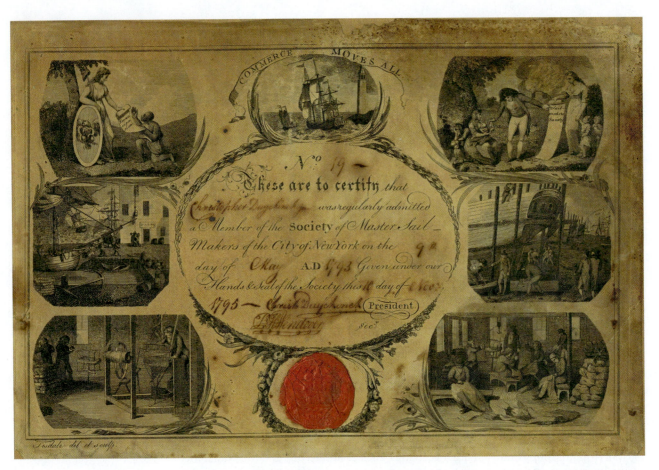

"Commerce Moves All," According to This Certificate of Membership in a Sailmakers' Society Here we see not only linked economic activities such as sailmaking (lower right-hand corner) and trade but also the moral benefits that were imagined to flow from commerce—charity (upper right-hand corner) and abolition of slavery (upper left-hand corner).

wage-earning class, dependent on others for employment and income. Only a small portion of Americans were wage-earners on the eve of the Revolution, but they were a sign of things to come.

Consumer Choices and the Creation of Gentility

Under the British mercantilist system (see Chapter 4), the colonies were supposed to export raw materials to the empire and import finished products back, sending West Indian sugar, tobacco, wheat, lumber, fish, and animal pelts to Britain in exchange for cloth and iron. Yet within this general pattern, individual men and women made choices about what to buy.

On both sides of the Atlantic, demand for plantation products and consumer goods was insatiable. At first only the wealthy could afford such luxuries as sugar and tobacco. But as more and more labor was organized to produce for the market, ordinary people had the added income needed to purchase luxury products. Tea, imported into both Britain and the colonies from Asia, became, like tobacco and sugar, a mass-consumed luxury. By the time of the Revolution, annual sugar consumption in England had skyrocketed to 23 pounds per person, and tobacco consumption was about 2 pounds per person. Demand for these plantation products led directly to the traffic in African slaves.

As plantation products flowed to England, so manufactured goods came back to the colonies. Consumer behavior on both sides of the Atlantic was similar: people smoked tobacco; sweetened their tea with sugar; and bought more clothing, household items, books, and every sort of manufactured goods.

This consumer revolution was not due to higher wages. Instead, people chose to work harder and chose work that brought in money. They decided what they would do with that money—they chose to buy particular items. Increasingly, people bought items that their friends and neighbors could see and that they could use in entertaining them. In seventeenth-century America, extra income was spent on items of lasting value, such as tablecloths and bed linens kept folded away in a chest, to pass on to one's children. In the eighteenth century, men and women bought more clothing made out of cheaper, less durable fabrics. Until this time, most people had only a few outfits. The wealthy, of course, always had large wardrobes made from fine fabrics. In the eighteenth century, however, fabric prices fell, and clothing made from cheaper fabrics satisfied growing consumer demand. Then people needed new pieces of furniture in which to store their new garments. Chests of drawers, or dressers, first available to the wealthy in the 1630s and 1640s, had, by 1760, become a standard item for the middle class.

People became increasingly interested in how they appeared to others. Ordinary people began to pay attention to the latest fashions, once a concern only of the wealthy. By 1700, two new items made it easier for those with the time and money to attend

James Balfour and His Wife Jemima James Balfour, the representative of an English mercantile firm, and his wife Jemima moved to Virginia, where they assumed the roles of proper members of the merchant elite. James is depicted with his business papers and his son, illustrating the two aspects of a gentleman's character: his acumen for business and his affection for his family. His wife is pictured holding a book, demonstrating that she is a woman of education, with the leisure to pursue it.

to their appearance: the dressing table and the full-length mirror. For the first time, people could see how they looked, head to toe. Washing oneself and styling one's hair or periwig became standard rituals for all who hoped to appear "genteel."

In the eighteenth century, the prosperous on both sides of the Atlantic created and tried to follow the standards of a new style of life, gentility. Gentility represented all that was polite, civilized, refined, and fashionable. It was everything that vulgarity, its opposite, was not. Gentility meant not only certain sorts of objects, such as a dressing table or a bone china teapot, but also the manners needed to use such objects properly. Standards of gentility established boundaries between the genteel and the vulgar. Those who considered themselves genteel looked down on those whose style of living seemed unrefined, and became uncomfortable when required to associate with social inferiors.

Yet if gentility erected a barrier between people, it also showed the vulgar how to become genteel. All they needed to do was acquire the right goods and learn how to use them. Throughout the colonies, ordinary people began to purchase goods that established their gentility. Even relatively poor people often owned a mirror, a few pieces of china, or a teapot. The slaves executed in New York City in 1741 (discussed subsequently) were probably conspiring not to burn the city down but to steal clothing and other fancy goods they could resell to poor people in the underground economy. This mass consumption and widespread distribution of consumer goods created and sustained the consumer revolution.

The consumer revolution had another egalitarian effect: it encouraged sociability. Throughout the Atlantic world, men and women, particularly those with a little leisure and money (perhaps half the white population), began to cultivate social life. Many believed that the purpose of life was the sort of society they created during an evening shared with friends and family in their parlors.

Coffee pot by Paul Revere.

To put all of their guests on an equal footing, people began to purchase matching sets of dinner plates, silverware, glasses, and chairs. Until the eighteenth century, the most important people at the table—the man of the house, his wife, and high-ranking men—got the best chairs. Children, servants, and those of lower social standing sat on stools, benches, or boxes, or they stood. Dishes, utensils, and mugs rarely matched. Matched sets of tableware and chairs underscored the symbolic equality of all guests.

The newest and most popular consumer goods made their way quickly to America— forks, drinking glasses, and teapots, each with its own etiquette. Such rules were daunting for the uneducated, but once they were mastered,

The New Gentility In 1750 in Charleston, South Carolina, Mr. Peter Manigault and his friends toasted each other, demonstrating their civility and their knowledge of the rules of polite behavior, including how to drink punch from a stem glass.

AMERICA AND THE WORLD

>> Consumer Tastes in Global Perspective

It is no surprise that Europeans got hooked on the products of colonial plantations: many of them were at least mildly addictive. The addictive properties of tobacco are well known today, but many of the other products of colonial plantations also were habit forming: coffee, cocoa, tea, and sugar (and its by-product rum). As consumer demand for such products grew in Europe, colonial plantation agriculture expanded.

Consider coffee. It originated in Ethiopia but was introduced into the Middle East by Arab traders around 1000 CE. The drink had made its way to the Ottoman Empire by the middle of the sixteenth century, and although some Muslim theologians disapproved of the drink, it soon became popular. European travelers to the major Muslim cities—Constantinople, Cairo, Alexandria, Aleppo—picked up a taste for coffee and began importing it into Europe. The first coffeehouse in London was built in 1652; 60 years later, there were at least 500. Coffeehouses in Europe quickly became what they were in the Middle East: places of male sociability.

By 1700, the prime coffee-growing region of Yemen could no longer meet the growing demand, so Muslim traders introduced coffee cultivation to India. Then Europeans expanded cultivation to their colonies in Jamaica, Barbados, and Indonesia, where the Dutch East India Company introduced both coffee planting and slavery. The French brought coffee cultivation to Martinique in the West Indies, and the Portuguese took it to Brazil.

The history of tea drinking in Europe is similar; tea was introduced to Britain in the seventeenth century and eventually became more popular than coffee. By the middle of the eighteenth century, tea was an item of mass consumption. Most of it was imported—legally and illegally—from China or India.

Europeans liked their coffee and tea very sweet, so sugar consumption skyrocketed, too. The plantations of the New World, particularly the French West Indies, supplied this demand. The demand for sugar also created a demand for people to grow it: slaves imported from Africa. In fact, New World slavery came into being to satisfy Europeans' craving for tobacco and sugar, which were luxuries, rather than the necessities of life.

The history of opium, the highly addictive drug that also became popular in the eighteenth century, is somewhat different. Here, the British East India Company—the firm that sold tea to the American colonies—pushed the drug into China, in order to help rectify an imbalance in trade. As British imports of tea from China increased, the British needed products to sell to China, ones that would be as popular as tea. The Chinese were not terribly interested in the British goods, but they developed a taste for Indian fabrics and Indian opium. The East India Company secured a monopoly over Indian opium in 1773 and exported it to China, even though the Chinese had officially banned the drug.

The trade in addictive substances tied the continents together in the eighteenth century. A global trade network, organized by state-supported companies and sustained in many cases by slave labor, supplied the world's consumers with the addictive substances they craved.

The port of Mocha in Yemen, here depicted in 1692, was the center of the global trade in coffee.

a person could enter polite society anywhere in the Atlantic world and be accepted. The eighteenth-century capitalist economy created a trade not only in goods and raw materials but in styles of life as well.

Historians debate the effects of the consumer revolution, but on balance it was a democratic force. Ordinary men and women and even slaves came to think it was their right to spend their money as they pleased. As one Bostonian put it in 1754, the poor should be allowed to buy "the Conveniencies, and Comforts, as well as Necessaries of Life . . . as freely as the Rich." After all, "I am sure we Work as hard as they do . . . ; therefore, I cannot see why we have not as good a natural Right to them as they have."

The consumer revolution rested on new systems of production that eventually led to the Industrial Revolution and the creation of a working class. Even as men and women worked harder so they could buy the new goods, some worked harder voluntarily, but many did not. In the southern colonies, slavery expanded in order to produce the luxury goods that new consumers wanted to buy.

The Varieties of Colonial Experience

Although the eighteenth-century industrious and consumer revolutions tied the peoples of the North Atlantic world together, climate, geography, immigration, patterns of economic development, and population density made for considerable variety. Although the vast majority of Americans lived in small communities or on farms, an increasing number lived in cities that played a critical role in shaping colonial life. At the same time, farming regions were maturing, changing the character of rural life, and the growing population continued to push at the frontiers, leading to the founding of Georgia.

Creating an Urban Public Sphere

At the end of the seventeenth century, Boston, with 7,000 people, was the only town that was much more than a rural village. By 1720, Boston's population had grown to 12,000, Philadelphia had 10,000 inhabitants, New York had 7,000, and Newport and Charleston almost 4,000 each. Forty years later, other urban centers had sprung up, each with populations around 3,000—Salem, Marblehead, and Newburyport in Massachusetts; Portsmouth, New Hampshire; Providence, Rhode Island; New Haven and Hartford, Connecticut; Albany, New York; Lancaster, Pennsylvania; Baltimore, Maryland; Norfolk, Virginia; and Savannah, Georgia. By the eve of the Revolution, Philadelphia had 30,000 residents, New York had 25,000, and Boston had 16,000 (see Map 5–3). All of these cities were either ports or centers for the fur trade. Colonial cities were centers of commerce; that was their reason for being.

Social life in colonial cities was characterized by two somewhat contradictory trends. On the one hand, nowhere in the colonies was social stratification among free people more pronounced. By the eve of the American Revolution, each city had an affluent elite, made up of merchants, professionals, and government officials, and each city also had a class of indigent poor. On the other hand, cities brought all classes of society together at theaters, in taverns, and at religious revivals such as the one led by George Whitefield. This civic life became one of the seedbeds of the Revolution because it provided a forum for the exchange of ideas.

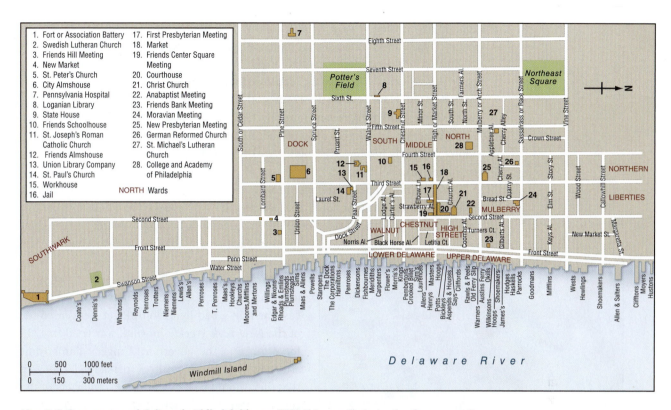

Map 5–3 Commerce and Culture in Philadelphia, ca. 1760 This map illustrates the close connection between commerce—note how many docks there are along the Delaware River—and culture. By 1760, Philadelphia was home to churches of many different denominations, as well as an array of enlightened institutions—a hospital, a college, and two libraries. *Lester Cappon, ed.,* The Atlas of Early American History *(Princeton, NJ: Princeton University Press, 1976), p. 10.*

Philadelphia seen from the southeast, looking across the harbor.

Affluent city dwellers created a life as much like that of London as they could. They imported European finery and established English-style institutions, founding social clubs, dancing assemblies, and fishing and hunting clubs. Although many of these associations were for men only, some brought men and women together. Such organizations helped the elite function as a class.

Urban associations reflected the ideals of the Enlightenment (see "The Ideas of the Enlightenment," p. 167). Some, such as the Masons, a European fraternal order with branches in all the major colonial cities, espoused the ideal of universalism, that all people were by their nature fundamentally the same. Other institutions advocated self-improvement. Whereas some urban institutions separated out the elite and others challenged the ruling hierarchy, still others brought together all members of society in a "public sphere." City dwellers could see stage plays in Williamsburg by 1716, in Charleston and New York by the 1730s, and in Philadelphia and Boston by the 1740s. Taverns brought all ranks even closer. By 1737, Boston had 177 taverns, one for every 99 inhabitants. (Between 30 percent and 40 percent were owned by women, usually widows.) Taverns became true public institutions in which people could meet and discuss the issues of the day.

Newspapers also played a critical role in creating a public sphere and extending it beyond the cities. The first newspaper was the *Boston News-Letter,* which appeared in 1704. By the time of the Revolution, 39 newspapers were being published, and the chief town in each colony except Delaware had at least one newspaper (see Map 5–4).

Strict libel laws prohibited the printing of opinions critical of public officials, or even the truth if it cast them in a bad light. John Peter Zenger, editor of the *New-York Weekly Journal,* was tried in 1735 for criticizing the governor. Zenger's flamboyant attorney, Andrew Hamilton, persuaded the jury that they should rule not simply on the facts of the case (Zenger had criticized the governor) but on whether the law itself was just. When the jury ruled in Zenger's favor, cheers went up in the courtroom. Although it would be many years before freedom of the press would be guaranteed by law, the Zenger case was a milestone in the developing relationship between the public and government officials. The verdict expressed the belief that in the contest between the two, the press spoke for the people, and hence it was the people themselves, not government, that would hold the press accountable.

City dwellers came to think of themselves as a "public" that had certain rights or liberties, such as making their views known and enjoying a fair price for their goods. At times, working people, acting as a public, and sometimes with support from the elite, used mob action to assert their political views. Mobs in both New York and Boston reacted violently to press gangs that scoured the waterfront for additional hands for the Royal Navy. By the time of the Revolution, city dwellers had a long history of asserting their rights in public.

Map 5-4 Printing Presses and Newspapers, 1760-1775 Between 1760 and 1775, the number of printing presses and newspapers in the colonies grew dramatically, as new cities acquired presses, and major cities such as Boston, New York, and Philadelphia gained additional ones. *Lester Cappon, ed.,* The Atlas of Early American History *(Princeton, NJ: Princeton University Press, 1976).*

The Diversity of Urban Life

Periodic downturns in the urban economy, especially after the middle of the century, led to increased activism by workers and the urban poor.

Colonial politics had been premised on the deference of the less powerful to their social and economic "betters," but by the middle of the eighteenth century, the increasing wealth of those at the top and the appearance of a small class of permanently poor at the bottom of the economic hierarchy began to undermine the assumption of a common interest and that the wealthy and well educated could be trusted to govern for the benefit of everyone.

Although by today's standards the colonial population, even in the cities, was remarkably equal economically, in the eighteenth century it became more stratified. At the beginning of the eighteenth century, none of the cities had a substantial number of poor people. In New York, in 1700, there were only 35 paupers, almost all of whom were aged or disabled. Over the course of the century, however, colonial wars sent men home disabled and left many women widowed and children orphaned. Each city responded to the growth in poverty by building almshouses for the poor who could not support themselves and workhouses for those, including women and children, who could. In Philadelphia and New York about 25 percent of the population was at or below the poverty level, and in Boston perhaps as much as 40 percent of the population was living at or near subsistence. Many colonists feared that colonial cities were coming to resemble London, with its mass of impoverished and desperate poor.

All the major cities had slaves, and in some cities the black population was considerable. By 1746, 30 percent of New York City's working class consisted of slaves. After a serious slave revolt in 1712 and a rumored revolt in 1741, the white population responded with harsh punishments (but without halting the slave trade). In the wake of the 1712 revolt, which had left 9 white men dead, city officials executed eighteen convicted rebels, burned 3 at the stake, let 1 starve to death in chains, and broke 1 on the wheel, a medieval instrument of torture. Six more committed suicide. The response to a rumored slave insurrection in 1741 resembled Salem's witchcraft trials: 18 slaves and 4 whites were hanged, and 13 slaves were burned at the stake.

New York enacted a stringent slave code after the 1712 revolt, and Boston and Pennsylvania imposed significant import duties on slaves. Nonetheless, the importation of slaves continued into all the port cities, where they were in demand as house servants and artisans. Almost all of Boston's elite owned at least one slave, as did many members of the middle class. Wealthy white artisans often purchased slaves instead of enlisting free whites as apprentices.

In Charleston, where more than half the population was enslaved, many masters let their slaves hire themselves out in return for a portion of their earnings. Such slaves set their own hours, chose their own recreational and religious activities, and participated in the consumer economy by selling their products and making purchases with the profits. Some whites complained about the fancy dresses of the black women at biracial dances attended by "many of the first gentlemen" of Charleston. Interracial sex in Charleston seems to have been common. Although white city dwellers were troubled by the impudence and relative freedom of urban slaves, urban slavery flourished.

The Maturing of Rural Society

Population increases had a different impact in rural areas than in cities. During the eighteenth century, some long-settled regions became relatively overcrowded. Land that once seemed abundant had been carelessly farmed and had lost some of its fertility. This relative overcrowding, which historians call land pressure, led to a

> Concord plains are sandy, Concord soil is poor; you have miserable farms there, and no fruit. There is little hope you will ever do better than your father. . . . Lucy had better marry her cousin John. His father will give him one of the best farms in the town, and Lucy shall match his land acre for acre. You must marry a Concord girl, who cannot tell good land from poor. As for Lucy, you must forget her.
>
> JONATHAN BARNES,
> refusing to let Joseph Hosmer marry his daughter Lucy. Then, Lucy became pregnant, and Barnes consented to their marriage.

number of changes in colonial society, felt most acutely in New England. Population density increased, and with no additional farmland available, migration from farms to newly settled areas and cities increased. Both the concentration of wealth and social differentiation intensified, dividing the farm community into rich and poor.

Such broad economic changes had a direct impact on individual men and women. Families with numerous children were hard pressed if the original plot of land could not be divided into homesteads large enough for each son. (Daughters were given movable property such as farm animals, household equipment, and slaves.) Some sons migrated to cities, looking for employment. Others worked on other men's farms for wages or, in the South in particular, became tenant farmers. Daughters became servants in other women's households. In such older regions, the average age of marriage crept upward.

As young men and women in long-settled regions had to defer marriage, increasing numbers had sexual relations before marriage. In some towns, by the middle of the eighteenth century, between 30 percent and 50 percent of brides bore their first child within eight months of their wedding day. The growing belief that marriage should be based primarily on love probably encouraged some couples to become intimate before they married, especially if poverty required them to postpone marriage. Young women who engaged in sexual relations before marriage took a huge risk, however. If their lovers declined to marry them, they would be disgraced, and their futures would be bleak.

The World That Slavery Made

The rural economy of the South depended on slave labor. Whites and their black slaves formed two distinctive cultures, one in the black-majority lower South and the other in the Chesapeake region. In both regions, the most affluent slave masters sold their crops on the international market and used the profits to buy elegant furniture and the latest London fashions.

Chesapeake planters modeled themselves after English country gentlemen, whereas low-country planters imitated the elite of London. Chesapeake planters designed their plantations to be self-sufficient villages, like English country estates. Because slaves produced most of the goods and services the plantation needed, planters such as William Byrd II imagined themselves living "in a kind of independence on everyone but Providence." But unlike English country gentlemen, southern slave owners were wholly dependent on both slave labor and the vagaries of the market for their fortunes. South Carolina planters used their wealth to build elegant homes in Charleston and other coastal cities, where they spent much time and established a flourishing urban culture. By the eve of the Revolution, the area around Charleston was the most affluent in the mainland colonies. In spite of their affluence, the southern planter elite never achieved the secure political power enjoyed by their English counterparts. In England the social elite dominated the government: not only the hereditary positions but also the appointive and elective ones. With noble rank inherited and voting rights limited to male property owners, the English government was remarkably stable. The colonial elite, however (in the North as well as the South), were cut off from the top levels of political power, which remained in England. The colonists were at the mercy of whichever officials the Crown happened to appoint.

Unable to count on support from above, the colonial elite needed to guarantee the loyalty of those below them. In Virginia, the elite acted as middlemen for lesser planters, advancing them credit and marketing their tobacco. In general, they wielded their authority with a light hand, and punishments for crimes committed by whites were light.

Although members of the Virginia gentry tried to distance themselves from their slaves, whom they considered "vulgar," some whites crossed the color line in a dramatic way, despite eighteenth-century racial views. Some historians believe that sexual relations between whites and blacks were common. Several prominent Virginians acknowledged and supported their mixed-race children. Some interracial relationships were affectionate; others were coerced. All the resulting offspring were in a vulnerable position; like all slaves they were dependent on the will of whites.

In the low country, the absenteeism of the planters combined with the task system to give plantation slaves an unusual degree of autonomy. As a majority, slaves in the low country were better able to retain their own religions, languages, and customs than were those in the Chesapeake. For example, the Gullah language, still spoken today on the Sea Islands off the coast of South Carolina and Georgia, combined English, Spanish, Portuguese, and African languages.

The mainland colonies' bloodiest slave revolt, the Stono Rebellion, took place in 1739, only a year after the founding of the Spanish free black outpost of Mose in Florida. The uprising was led by about 20 slaves born in Kongo (present-day Angola). The rebels were probably Catholics, for the king of Kongo, converted by the Portuguese, made Catholicism his nation's religion. Early in the morning of September 9, the rebels broke into a store near the Stono Bridge, taking weapons and ammunition and killing the storekeepers. The rebels moved south toward St. Augustine, killing whites and gathering blacks into their fold. Although the main body of the rebels was dispersed that evening and many were executed on the spot, skirmishes took place for another week, and the last of the ringleaders was not captured for three years.

The authorities reacted with predictable severity, putting dozens of slave rebels "to the most cruel Death" and revoking many liberties the slaves had enjoyed. A prohibitive duty was placed on the importation of slaves, and the immigration of white Europeans was encouraged. Although slave imports dropped significantly in the 1740s, by 1750 they rose to pre-Stono levels because slave owners had neither the heart nor the inclination for the sort of systematic policing of their slaves that would have kept them completely under their control.

Georgia: From Frontier Outpost to Plantation Society

Nowhere was the white determination to create and maintain a slave society stronger than in the colony of Georgia. It is sometimes said that the introduction of slavery in North America was an unthinking decision, that the colonies became slave societies slowly, as individual planters purchased Africans already enslaved, and without society as a whole ever committing itself to slavery. Although there is some truth to this analysis, it is not accurate for Georgia, where the introduction of slavery was a purposeful decision.

The establishment of the English colony at South Carolina had, of course, made the Spanish nervous because of its proximity to their settlement at St. Augustine, Florida. With the French founding of New Orleans (1718) and Fort Toulouse (1717), Carolinians felt increasingly threatened. They were therefore eager for the English to establish a colony to the south, which would both serve as a buffer between Florida and South Carolina and, if extended far enough west, cut the French colonial empire in two.

The British Crown issued a 21-year charter to a group of trustees led by James Oglethorpe, who had achieved prominence by bringing about reforms in England's debtors' prisons. The colony, Georgia, was designed as a combination philanthropic venture and military-commercial outpost. Its colonists, who were to be drawn from Britain's "deserving poor," were supposed to protect South Carolina's borders and to make the new colony a sort of Italy-on-the-Atlantic, producing wine, olives, and silk.

Unfortunately, Oglethorpe's humanitarianism was not matched by an understanding of the world economy. Because it was well known that excessive indulgence in alcohol was undermining the cohesion of many Indian tribes, Oglethorpe had banned liquor from the colony. However, without a product to sell, the colony could not prosper. South Carolina's wharves, merchants, and willingness to sell rum enabled it to dominate the trade with local Indians. Oglethorpe had also banned slavery for humanitarian reasons (making it the only colony expressly to prohibit slavery). As a result, Georgia farmers looked enviously across the Savannah River at South Carolinians growing rich off slave labor. The settlers were also angry that, contrary to colonial practice, women were not allowed to inherit property and that Georgia's trustees had made no provision for self-government. Georgia, despite its founders' noble intentions, lacked everything that the thriving colonies enjoyed: a cash crop or product, large plots of land, slaves to work the land, and laws of its own devising.

Never able to realize their dream of a colony of small and contented farmers, the trustees surrendered Georgia back to the Crown in 1752. With Oglethorpe's laws repealed and slavery introduced, the colony soon resembled the plantation society of South Carolina. Savannah became a little Charleston, with its robust civic and cultural life and its slave markets.

The Head and the Heart in America: The Enlightenment and Religious Awakening

American life in the eighteenth century was shaped by two movements, the Enlightenment and a series of religious revivals known as the Great Awakening. In many ways, these movements were separate, even opposite, appealing to different groups of people. The Enlightenment was a transatlantic intellectual movement that held that the universe could be understood and improved by the human mind. The Great Awakening was a transatlantic religious movement that held that all people were born sinners, that all could feel their own depravity without the assistance of ministers, and that all were equal in the eyes of God. Although the movements might seem fundamentally opposite, with one emphasizing the power of the human mind and the other disparaging it, both criticized established authority and valued the experience of the individual. Both contributed to the humanitarianism that emerged at the end of the century, and both were products of capitalism.

The Ideas of the Enlightenment

The roots of the Enlightenment can be traced to the Renaissance and its spirit of inquiry and faith in science that led explorers like Columbus halfway around the globe. Men and women of the Enlightenment, on both sides of the Atlantic, contrasted the ignorance, oppression, and suffering of the Middle or "Dark" Ages, as they called them, and their own enlightened time. Thomas Jefferson described the earlier period as "the times of Vandalism, when ignorance put everything in the hands of power and priestcraft." Enlightened thinkers believed fervently in the power of rational thinking and scoffed at superstition.

People of the Enlightenment believed that God and his world were knowable. Rejecting revelation as a guide, the Enlightenment looked instead to reason. Jefferson's "trinity of the three greatest men the world had ever produced" included not Jesus Christ but Isaac Newton, the scientist responsible for modern mathematics and physics; Francis Bacon, the philosopher who outlined the scientific method; and John Locke, the political philosopher of democracy. The Enlightenment was interested in knowledge not for its own sake but for the improvements it could make in human happiness.

Enlightenment thinkers were more interested in what all people had in common than in what differentiated them. No passage in the Bible was more important to them than Genesis 1:27: "So God created man in his own image." It was the basis not only for overcoming Calvinism's belief in humanity's innate depravity but also for asserting the principle of human equality. The Enlightenment encouraged a broad toleration of religion. Benjamin Franklin said that "if the Mufti of Constantinople were to send a missionary to preach Mahometanism to us, he would find a pulpit at his service."

Humanity's duties were clear and simple. Chief among them, according to Benjamin Franklin, was "doing good to [God's] other children." In fact, people served God best not by praying, which, as Thomas Paine put it, "can add nothing to eternity," but "by endeavouring to make his creatures happy." Scientific inquiry and experiments such as Franklin's with electricity all had as their object the improvement of human life.

Although there had been some improvements in the quality of life, life in the eighteenth century was still violent and filled with pain. The Enlightenment responded to the pain and violence of the world in two ways. First, it attempted to alleviate and curtail them. Scientists eagerly sought cures for diseases. The Reverend Cotton Mather of Boston learned about the procedure of inoculating against smallpox (using a small amount of the deadly virus) from a scientific article and from his African slave Onesimus, who knew of its practice in Africa. An epidemic gave him an opportunity to try out the technique. The revulsion against pain and suffering also encouraged

> The rapid Progress **true** Science now makes, occasions my regretting sometimes that I was born so soon. It is impossible to imagine the Height to which may be carried, in a thousand years, the Power of Man over Matter. . . . [A]ll Diseases may by sure means be prevented or cured. . . . O that moral Science were in as fair a way of Improvement, that Men would cease to be Wolves to one another, and that human Beings would at length learn what they now improperly call Humanity!
>
> BENJAMIN FRANKLIN

TECHNOLOGY AND IDEAS

>> Inoculation

Medicine at the start of the eighteenth century was closer in its ideas to ancient Greek concepts of the humors (people had green, red, black, and yellow bile) and medieval remedies (giving patients herbs that caused vomiting and diarrhea, bleeding patients with leeches, and dosing patients with poisonous heavy metals like mercury) than modern medical science. Keeping someone's humors in balance was the physician's goal, with the resulting cures often being worse than the disease. An oft-repeated saying captured the essence of medicine at this time: "English doctors kill you. The French ones let you die." One had to have a strong constitution to survive the doctor's visit. No one had the concept of the value of antisepsis, understood that mosquitoes and other vectors carried parasites and germs, or comprehended that tainted water sources caused illness, blaming instead effluvia in the air. Thus, when epidemics of smallpox, diphtheria, malaria, and measles struck, as they periodically did, doctors and their patients were all but helpless.

Of all the epidemic diseases that the colonists faced, smallpox was the most virulent, the most disfiguring, and the most prevalent. Technically a hemorrhaging disease of the skin, it could strike at any time of the year, in any climate, and it was no respecter of age, wealth, or ethnicity. This "spotted" virus was highly contagious and may have been the culprit in reducing Native American populations by 80 percent during the contact period. The vicious rash was the first symptom and lasting scars the reminder of a disease that had a mortality rate of about 30–35 percent.

All of this began to change when, in 1716, English doctors gradually adopted the Chinese and Indian practice of injecting pus (containing the live virus) into a scratch in the patient's skin, and found that patients inoculated with the live virus survived exposure to the disease. The patient was contagious, and had to be quarantined during the incubation period, but the results were astounding. Instead of getting the more serious version of the disease, the inoculated patient recovered quickly and without great discomfort.

American doctors watched the English experiment with great interest. Cotton Mather, one of Boston's most prestigious ministers and a member of the Royal Society of scientists, championed the introduction of inoculation, known today as vaccination, and the practice slowly spread. Doctors who performed inoculation gained status in society. While smallpox would periodically return, especially during wartime, the inoculation of children removed one of the major causes of childhood death, and would over time change parents' views of childrearing. It can be said that inoculation was one cause of the child-centered, affectionate family style of the nineteenth century as well as the declining birth rate that accompanied the new style, for parents expected that inoculated children would live to adulthood.

When Catherine the Great, empress of Russia, had herself inoculated in 1768, she was making a political statement as well as instituting a health-care policy for her poor,

In the eighteenth century, inoculation against smallpox was performed by puncturing the skin with a device like this and introducing smallpox fluid. This particular instrument is British.

medicine-starved country. Inoculations in the American colonies took on a similar tone as medicine became more effective, more research driven, and, as part of the so-called Enlightenment movement, challenged prevailing views of nature, human society, and concomitantly religious views. Inoculation programs rapidly became politically sensitive issues for the colonies, and they remain so in the United States to this day.

Questions

1. What does the spread of medical techniques such as inoculation (vaccines) tell us about the societies in which it occurs?

2. Why do you think public health programs in the colonies, such as requiring inoculation, were controversial? Mandatory vaccinations continue to be controversial in America today. Do you think the reasons that people question vaccines are the same now as they were during the colonial period? Why or why not?

---

humanitarian reform, such as James Oglethorpe's reform of English debtors' prisons and, eventually, the antislavery movement.

Men and women of the Enlightenment also cultivated a stoic resignation to the evils they could not change and a personal ideal of moderation, so that they would neither give nor receive pain. The gentility and politeness of the urban elite was an expression of this ideal of moderation. Both gentility and the Enlightenment were espoused by the same set of people, the urban elite: professionals, merchants, and prosperous planters tied in to the global economy.

The Economic and Social Foundations of Democracy

Enlightenment thinkers began to study the connections among society, politics, and the economy. John Locke, the English philosopher, was the first to link these in a theory. He argued that there was a systematic connection between social institutions (such as the family), political institutions, and property rights. He began with the claim that each person has the right to life and the right to preserve that life. To sustain their lives, people form families, and to support themselves and their families, they labor. The basic right to life thus gives people the right to the product of their labor—property. To protect their lives and their property, people create governments. They give up some of their liberty but receive protection of their lives and property in return.

Locke also developed a new economic theory. His idea that money has no intrinsic value was a departure from mercantilism, which said that the value of money was fixed. In the second half of the eighteenth century, Scottish philosophers such as Francis Hutcheson and Adam Smith carried Locke's ideas even further, arguing that human beings should be free to value the things that made them happy.

Using happiness as their standard for human life, the Scots argued that people should be free to produce. Adam Smith's influential *The Wealth of Nations* (1776) was both a critique of mercantilism and a defense of free markets and free labor. For Smith and other Enlightenment theorists, the best incentive to hard work was the

>> The Autobiography of Benjamin Franklin

*B*enjamin Franklin began writing his autobiography in 1771, while he was in England. He would return to the task periodically until he died in 1790, and no entirely correct version was published until the twentieth century. In this selection from the first pages, he describes how he came to read and write with the flair that made him one of the eighteenth century's leading men of letters. The excerpt provides some insight into life in the first half of the eighteenth century in Boston, Massachusetts, despite the fact that it was written at a substantially later date.

From a child I was fond of reading, and all the little money that came into my hands was ever laid out in books. Pleased with the *Pilgrim's Progress*, my first collection was of John Bunyan's works in separate little volumes. I afterward sold them to enable me to buy R. Burton's Historical Collections; they were small chapmen's books, and cheap, 40 or 50 in all. My father's little library consisted chiefly of books in polemic 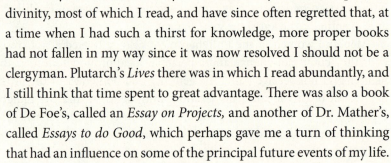 divinity, most of which I read, and have since often regretted that, at a time when I had such a thirst for knowledge, more proper books had not fallen in my way since it was now resolved I should not be a clergyman. Plutarch's *Lives* there was in which I read abundantly, and I still think that time spent to great advantage. There was also a book of De Foe's, called an *Essay on Projects,* and another of Dr. Mather's, called *Essays to do Good*, which perhaps gave me a turn of thinking that had an influence on some of the principal future events of my life.

This bookish inclination at length determined my father to make me a printer, though he had already one son (James) of that profession. In 1717 my brother James returned from England with a press and letters to set up his business in Boston. I liked it much better than that of my father, but still had a hankering for the sea. To prevent the apprehended effect of such an inclination, my father was impatient to have me bound to my brother. I stood out some time, but at last was persuaded, and signed the indentures when I was yet but twelve years old. I was to serve as an apprentice till I was twenty-one years of age, only I was to be allowed journeyman's wages during the last year. In a little time I made great proficiency in the business, and became a useful hand to my brother. I now had access to better books. An acquaintance with the apprentices of booksellers enabled me sometimes to borrow a small one, which I was careful to return soon and clean. Often I sat up in my room reading the greatest part of the night, when the book was borrowed in the evening and to be returned early in the morning, lest it should be missed or wanted. . . .

There was another bookish lad in the town, John Collins by name, with whom I was intimately acquainted. We sometimes disputed, and very fond we were of argument, and very desirous of confuting one another, which disputatious turn, by the way, is apt to become a very bad habit, making people often extremely disagreeable in company by the contradiction that is necessary to bring it into practice; and thence, besides souring and spoiling the conversation, is productive of disgusts and, perhaps enmities where you may have occasion for friendship. I had caught it by reading my father's books of dispute about religion. Persons of good sense, I have since observed, seldom fall into it, except lawyers, university men, and men of all sorts that have been bred at Edinborough.

A question was once, somehow or other, started between Collins and me, of the propriety of educating the female sex in learning, and their abilities for study. He was of opinion that it was improper, and that they were naturally unequal to it. I took the contrary side, perhaps a little for dispute's sake. He was naturally more eloquent, had a ready plenty of words; and sometimes, as I thought, bore me down more by his fluency than by the strength of his reasons. As we parted without settling the point, and were not to see one another again for some time, I sat down to put my arguments in writing, which I copied fair and sent to him. He answered, and I replied. Three or four letters of a side had passed, when my father happened to find my papers and read them. Without entering into the discussion, he took occasion to talk to me about the manner of my writing; observed that, though I had the advantage of my antagonist in correct spelling and pointing (which I ow'd to the printing-house), I fell far short in elegance of expression, in method and in perspicuity, of which he convinced me by several instances. I saw the justice of his remark, and thence grew more attentive to the manner in writing, and determined to endeavor at improvement.

About this time I met with an odd volume of the *Spectator* [Editor's note: a popular daily newspaper published in London from 1711–1712.] It was the third. I had never before seen any of them. I bought it, read it over and over, and was much delighted with it. I thought the writing excellent, and wished, if possible, to imitate it. With this view I took some of the papers, and, making short hints of the sentiment in each sentence, laid them by a few days, and then, without looking at the book, try'd to compleat the papers again, by expressing each hinted sentiment at length, and as fully as it had been expressed before, in any suitable words that should come to hand. Then I compared my *Spectator* with the original, discovered some of my faults, and corrected them.

Benjamin Franklin, *The Autobiography of Benjamin Franklin* (Rockville, MD: Arc Manor, 2008), pp. 15–17.

Questions

1. Make a list of the kinds of texts that Franklin read. What does your list tell you about the availability of reading materials in early eighteenth-century Boston?

2. How did Franklin respond to the reading material he encountered, particularly the volume of the *Spectator* that he discusses in the last paragraph of the excerpt? What did he gain from responding as he did?

3. What does this excerpt from Franklin's autobiography tell us about the Boston of Franklin's youth? For example, what does this passage show us about how young men in early eighteenth-century Boston learned a trade? (Remember that Franklin's reminiscences may not be perfectly accurate, given that they were written when he was living in England, many years after the events occurred.)

increased wealth and comforts it would bring. Human beings were happiest, they said, when they lived under free governments, which protected private property but left the market largely unregulated. These ideas became increasingly popular around the time of the Revolution.

Enlightened Institutions

The Enlightenment spurred the creation of institutions that embodied its principles. Humanitarianism led to the building of the Pennsylvania Hospital in 1751 and the Eastern State Mental Hospital at Williamsburg in 1773. In 1743 Benjamin Franklin proposed a society of learned men, modeled after the Royal Society of London, to study and share information about science and technology. He also helped establish the Library Company of Philadelphia in 1731, the first lending library in the colonies. Philadelphia acquired a second library in 1751 when the Quaker James Logan bequeathed his library, books and building both, to the city. By the time of the Revolution, Newport, New York, Charleston, and Savannah all had libraries.

The Enlightenment had a significant effect on organized religion as well. The Anglicans, in particular, were receptive to its ideals of moderation and rationalism. In England, John Tillotson, the Archbishop of Canterbury, preached a comforting and simple Christianity: God was "good and just" and required nothing "that is either unsuitable to our reason or prejudicial to our interest . . . nothing but what is easy to be understood, and is as easy to be practiced by an honest and willing mind."

This message became popular in the colonies, even among Congregationalist ministers, who abandoned the Calvinism of their forefathers. John Wise, the minister of Ipswich, Massachusetts, insisted that "to follow God and to obey Reason is the same thing." Arminianism, the belief that salvation was partly a matter of individual effort rather than entirely God's will, enjoyed a new popularity. Harvard University became a hotbed of liberal theology, and, in response, religious conservatives founded Yale University in 1701 to guarantee ministers a proper Calvinist education.

Origins of the Great Awakening

The problem with rational religion was that it was not emotionally fulfilling. In addition, rapid population growth had left the colonies without enough churches and ministers. Popular demand for more and better religion led to a series of revivals, known as the Great Awakening, that swept through the colonies between 1734 and 1745. At first, church leaders looked with pleasure on the stirrings of spiritual renewal. In the winter of 1734–1735, some of the rowdiest young people in Northampton, Massachusetts, who carried on parties for "the greater part of the night," began seeking religion at the church of a brilliant young minister, Jonathan Edwards. Everyone rejoiced at such signs of spiritual awakening.

The Grand Itinerant

When George Whitefield arrived in Philadelphia in 1739, the local ministers, including those of his own Anglican church, welcomed him. Whitefield drew audiences in the thousands everywhere he spoke. In the 15 months of his grand tour, he visited every colony from Maine to Georgia, met all the important ministers, and was heard at least once by most of the people of Massachusetts and Connecticut (see Map 5–5). He spoke to the entire community—rich, poor, slave, free, old, young, male, and

Map 5-5 George Whitefield's Itinerary In the 15 months between October 30, 1739, and January 18, 1741, Whitefield covered thousands of miles, visiting every colony from New Hampshire to Georgia, and stopping in some states such as Pennsylvania, South Carolina, and Georgia several times.

female—acting out simple scripts based on biblical stories. The message was always the same: the sinfulness of man and the mercy of God.

In a calculated move, perhaps to increase his audiences, Whitefield began speaking out against some in the ministry, accusing them of being unconverted. He started with the deceased Archbishop of Canterbury, John Tillotson. Following his lead, Gilbert Tennent, on a preaching tour of New England, warned about "The Danger of an Unconverted Ministry." Tennent implied that some ministers were in it for the money and that true Christians should leave their churches for those of honest preachers.

Even sympathetic ministers were shocked by these accusations, which turned their congregations against them and split their churches. Some leading ministers, who already had reservations about the revivalists because of their emotional style, now condemned the revival. That only made the revivalists more popular and attracted larger crowds.

Cultural Conflict and Challenges to Authority

The Great Awakening walked a fine line between challenging authority and supporting it, which may well explain its widespread appeal. It antagonized the most powerful and arrogant but did not challenge the fundamental structures of society. By attacking ministers but not government officials, the revivalists criticized authority without suffering any real consequences.

The Great Awakening appealed to all classes of people. Its greatest impact, however, was in areas facing the greatest change—in particular, cities (especially among the lower orders), the frontier, and older towns beginning to suffer from overcrowding. Here lived the people most disrupted by economic changes. Disturbed by an increasingly competitive society, men and women were attracted to the democratic fellowship of the revivalist congregation.

While criticizing the materialism and competitiveness of eighteenth-century society, the revival told people to look inside themselves for change, not to the structures of society. For example, a woman named Sarah Osborn blamed herself for her woes, which she saw as punishment for her sinful singing and dancing. After her spiritual rebirth, she trusted in God and accepted her poverty. Spiritual rebirth provided such people the joy and fulfillment that their world had been unable to supply.

The revival also walked a fine line in its treatment of slavery. Early in his travels, Whitefield spoke out against the cruelties of slavery and harangued slaveholders. At the same time, however, he maintained a slave plantation in South Carolina and pestered the trustees to permit slavery in Georgia. Like many slave owners after him, Whitefield argued that it was immoral to enslave Africans, but not to own them, provided that one treated them well and Christianized them. By linking humanitarianism, Christianity, and slavery, the Great Awakening anchored slavery in the South, at least for the time being.

Although it is hard to say whether slaves were treated more humanely on the plantations of evangelicals, beginning in the 1740s large numbers of slaves were converted to Christianity, and by some point in the nineteenth century virtually all slaves had become Christians. Although some may have converted to please their masters and to get Sundays off, blacks were attracted to evangelical religion for the same reason that whites were. It offered them a way to order and find meaning in their lives.

To a great extent, poor whites and slaves, especially in the South, had been left out of the society that more prosperous people had created. Evangelical religion placed the individual in a community of believers. It offered slaves the opportunity for church discipline and personal responsibility on almost the same terms as whites and gave some blacks the possibility of leadership in a biracial community. Africans grafted some of their religious practices, such as shouting and ecstatic visions, onto the revival, so that worship in southern Baptist and Methodist churches became a truly African American phenomenon.

What the Awakening Wrought

The opponents of the Great Awakening feared that it would turn the world upside down, but the leaders of the revival disciplined their own wildest members, such as New London's James Davenport. Davenport had led his flock through the streets late at night, singing at the tops of their lungs. They also made a bonfire to rid themselves of heresy, by burning the books of their opponents, and idolatry, by burning the clothes they were wearing. The stripping party was stopped by evangelicals in the crowd, and Davenport was brought back to his senses by his fellow ministers. In general, the Great Awakening took colonial society in the direction in which it was already heading: toward individualism. Church after church split into evangelical and traditional factions, and new denominations appeared. Choosing a religion became a personal matter, and colonies with established churches tolerated dissenters. Religion, as a general force, was strengthened, making the colonies simultaneously the most Protestant and the most religiously diverse culture in the world.

The Great Awakening also spurred the establishment of educational institutions. Princeton, chartered in 1748 as the College of New Jersey, grew out of an evangelical seminary. Next came Dartmouth, Brown, and Rutgers, chartered in 1766, to advance "true religion and useful knowledge." Columbia College, chartered in 1754, represented the Anglicans' response. The focus of higher education was slowly shifting from preparation for the ministry to the training of leaders more generally. The Great Awakening diminished the power of ministers while increasing the influence of personal religion.

At the height of the Awakening, religious enthusiasm was both attacked and defended. Yet the conflict was hardly a battle of the pious against the godless or the well educated against the uninformed. Jonathan Edwards, one of the greatest minds of his age, drew from the Enlightenment, as well as from Calvinist ideas. For Edwards, however, reason and good habits were not enough, and reason had to be supplemented by emotion, in particular the emotion of God's grace. By insisting that religious salvation and virtue were more matters of the heart than of the head, Edwards opened the way for a popular religion that was democratic, intensely personal, and humanitarian.

Conclusion

Eighteenth-century America was part of an expanding world market and a capitalist political economy. A growing population sustained a vigorous economy, one that produced for and purchased from the world market. As participants in an "industrious revolution," white Americans worked themselves and their slaves harder to purchase consumer goods. These new goods enabled people to live more genteelly and to cultivate a social life. Especially in the cities, this new emphasis on social life spawned an array of institutions in which people could acquire and display learning and gentility. The benefits of the economy were not shared equally, however. Slaves produced for the market economy but were denied its rewards. The increasing stratification of urban society and land pressures in rural regions meant many were too poor to profit from the expanding economy.

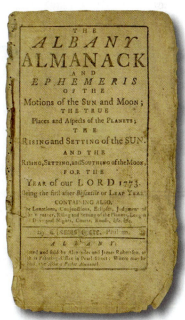

The eighteenth-century world spawned two different but related intellectual responses, the Enlightenment and the Great Awakening. Both were critical in shaping the eighteenth-century colonial world, and both paved the way for the Revolution. The Enlightenment led some to believe that rational thought and the scientific method would conquer human ills. At the same time, the Great Awakening reminded men and women that life was short and ultimately beyond their control. In different ways, then, the Enlightenment and the Great Awakening both encouraged the individualism that would characterize American life.

Who, What

Cottagers   154
Jonathan Edwards   172
James Oglethorpe   166
George Whitefield   143
Consumer revolution   151

The Enlightenment   161
The Great Awakening   166
Industrious revolution   151
Linked economic development   155
The Wealth of Nations   169

Review Questions

1. What were the primary sources of population increase in the eighteenth century? Compare the patterns of population growth of Europeans and Africans in the colonies.

>> TIME LINE

▼**1693**
College of William and Mary founded

▼**1701**
Yale founded

▼**1704**
First newspaper, *Boston News-Letter*, published in colonies

▼**1712**
Slave revolt in New York City

▼**1717**
French build Fort Toulouse

▼**1718**
French found New Orleans

▼**1731**
Library Company, first lending library in colonies, erected in Philadelphia

▼**1733**
Georgia founded
King of Spain guarantees freedom to English slaves who escape to Spanish territory

▼**1734**
Great Awakening begins

▼**1735**
John Peter Zenger acquitted of libeling New York's governor

2. What was the "industrious revolution"? How did it shape the development of the colonial economy? What were the other key factors shaping the development of the colonial economy? What effect did this development have on the lives of ordinary men and women?

3. What were the primary changes in urban and rural life in the eighteenth century?

Critical-Thinking Questions

1. Was the development of the eighteenth-century consumer culture a democratizing force—or the opposite?

2. Why were some eighteenth-century men and women drawn to the ideas of the Enlightenment while others were drawn to the Great Awakening?

3. Analyze the relationship between humanitarianism and slavery, which developed at the same time.

For further review materials and resource information, please visit www.oup.com/us/ofthepeople

▼**1739**
Stono Rebellion
George Whitefield begins his American
    tour

▼**1741**
Thirty-five people executed in New York
    City after slave-revolt scare

▼**1748**
College of New Jersey (Princeton) founded

▼**1751**
Pennsylvania Hospital built in Philadelphia

▼**1752**
Georgia becomes a Crown colony

▼**1754**
Columbia College founded

▼**1755**
Philadelphia College (University of
    Pennsylvania) founded

▼**1766**
Queens College
    (Rutgers) founded

▼**1773**
Eastern State Mental
    Hospital built in
    Williamsburg

1) Population growth in the seventeenth and eighteenth centuries had both short- and long-term consequences for colonial economies, culture, and society.

2) The demands that growing market economies placed on the colonies' institutions and inhabitants united and divided their populations.

3) Colonial society and culture provided opportunities for conversation and expression that laid the foundations for the expansion of democratic ideas and systems by the late eighteenth century.

4) The Great Awakening reflected changing ideas about identity, consumerism, religion, and government in the eighteenth century.

The Population Explosion of the Eighteenth Century

The Transatlantic Economy: Producing and Consuming

The Varieties of Colonial Experience

The Head and the Heart in America: The Enlightenment and Religious Awakening

EVENTS

The Dimensions of Population Growth The colonies' need for labor caused a massive increase in population, immigration, and ethnic diversity.

Bound for America: European Immigrants Large groups of free and unfree western Europeans immigrated.

Bound for America: African Slaves The African slave trade dramatically increased the number of African slaves in the colonies.

The Great Increase of Offspring Both free and slave women married earlier, increasing the number of children they bore.

The Nature of Colonial Economic Growth Population growth improved the standard of living for free colonists because of an abundance of land and shortages of labor and capital.

The Transformation of the Family Economy Producing goods for sale required more labor from women and children.

Sources of Regional Prosperity The economies of the southern, middle, and New England colonies varied, with slave labor making the South the most productive region.

Merchants and Dependent Laborers in the Transatlantic Economy The transatlantic economy created a wealthy, risk-taking merchant class and a wage-earning class.

Consumer Choices and the Creation of Gentility A growing economy led to a consumer revolution, with all colonists working harder to buy goods but also democratizing luxury.

Creating an Urban Public Sphere Urban centers grew, and public life developed with the help of associations and newspapers.

The Diversity of Urban Life Urban centers became more economically stratified with an increasing number of slaves.

The Maturing of Rural Society Relative overcrowding led to migration and economic uncertainty for larger families.

The World That Slavery Made Southern slavery created two distinct cultures and societies: the Chesapeake and the lower South.

Georgia: From Frontier Outpost to Plantation Society The colony in Georgia was initially unsuccessful until it allowed slavery and developed a cash crop.

The Ideas of the Enlightenment Enlightenment thinkers believed that God and the world were knowable and that life could be improved.

The Economic and Social Foundations of Democracy New ideas of political and economic liberalism emerged from the Enlightenment.

Enlightened Institutions The Enlightenment produced hospitals and libraries as well as influencing organized religion.

Origins of the Great Awakening Popular demand for increased and more fulfilling religion led to a series of revivals.

The Grand Itinerant George Whitefield became a leading preacher of the Great Awakening and attacked some established ministers.

Cultural Conflict and Challenges to Authority Appealing to all classes of people, the Great Awakening antagonized the powerful without challenging the fundamental structures of society.

What the Awakening Wrought The Great Awakening encouraged individualism, created new denominations, and established educational institutions.

COMMON THREADS

>> What role did the colonies play in imperial conflict? That is, how did they shape that conflict, and how were they shaped by it?

>> How were Native Americans drawn into imperial conflict? To what extent were they able to shape it for their own purposes?

>> What did it mean for the American colonies to be peripheral—literally—to the British Empire?

>> How did the colonists adapt the available political theories to their purposes? What in the American experience made those theories attractive to the colonists?

Conflict in the Empire
1713–1774

AMERICAN PORTRAIT

>> Susannah Willard Johnson Experiences the Empire

Today the town is Charlestown, New Hampshire, but then it was "No. 4," a small farming village on the northern frontier of Massachusetts. In 1754 Susannah Willard Johnson and her husband James lived there, having moved to the frontier during a break in the struggle between Britain and France for North America. At 24, Susannah had been married for seven years and had three children, with another due any day. James, a native of Ireland, had started his life in America as a servant indentured to Susannah's uncle. After working for him for 10 years, James purchased the remainder of his time, married Susannah, and made his way by farming and shopkeeping. He also became a lieutenant in the militia.

The region's Abenaki Indians—Algonquians who were allied with the French and had their own grievances against the encroaching settlers—presented both danger and opportunity. At first the settlers at No. 4 were so frightened that they stayed in the fort. However, Susannah later reported that "hostility at length vanished—the Indians expressed a wish to traffic, the inhabitants laid by their fears. . . ." James Johnson was part of the consumer revolution, selling goods to his fellow settlers and to the Abenakis, who gave him furs in return.

Susannah Johnson described her family's life as "harmony and safety" and "boasted with exultation that I should, with husband, friends, and luxuries, live happy in spite of the fear of savages." By the summer of 1754, however, the rumors of impending warfare with France would make the frontier village a target of France's Abenaki allies.

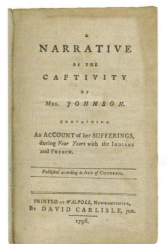

On August 30, 1754, just before daybreak, a neighbor coming to work for the Johnsons appeared at the door. As the Johnsons opened the door, the neighbor rushed in, followed by 11 Abenaki men. Soon, Susannah said, they were "all over the house, some upstairs, some hauling my sister out of bed, another had hold of me, and one was approaching Mr. Johnson, who stood in the middle of the floor to deliver himself up."

The Abenakis tied up the men, gathered the women and children, and marched the party to the north. On the second day of her captivity, Susannah went into labor. Attended by her sister and husband, she gave birth to a daughter, whom she named Captive. Before they returned home five years later, Susannah and her family were held captive in Canada and sent to England as part of a prisoner exchange.

Continued

>> **AMERICAN PORTRAIT** *Continued*

The French and Indian War had begun on the northern frontier, and the Indians were manipulating it to their advantage. In peacetime they traded furs for manufactured goods, but in wartime they seized British settlers, took them to Canada, and sold them to the French, who either ransomed them back to the British or traded them for prisoners of war. What to others might seem an imperial struggle was to Susannah Johnson a terrifying assault that took her from her home and family. The consumer revolution that gave settlers such as the Johnsons the opportunity to live a good life on the frontier was rooted in a struggle between France and England, two empires competing over both the markets the consumer revolution was creating and the lands it was populating. As families such as the Johnsons pushed at the frontiers, they became actors on a global stage.

The Victory of the British Empire

From 1689 to 1763, Britain and France were at war more than half of the time. These wars gave shape to the eighteenth century and created the international context for the American Revolution in several ways. First, the Revolution grew out of Britain's ineffective efforts to govern the enlarged empire it won from France in 1763. Second, France's support for the colonies in their war against Britain helped secure the colonies' victory. Third, once the colonies secured their independence, they entered a world still torn by conflict between Britain and France.

All of these wars were rooted in a struggle for world dominance between two powerful empires. To a great extent, colonial and imperial objectives coincided. Both Britain and the colonies would benefit from securing the empire's borders and from expanding British markets. Yet the imperial wars also exposed the growing divergence between the political economy of the colonies and that of the mother country. When the growing empire and its wars threatened to increase Britain's power over the colonists, raise their taxes to pay for the empire, and station among them a permanent army, the colonists resisted and finally rebelled.

New War, Old Pattern

England and France were at peace from the end of Queen Anne's War in 1713 (see Chapter 4) until 1739. It was an uneasy peace in the British North American colonies, however. In what is now Maine, New Englanders continued to fight the Abenakis, forcing them into a closer alliance with the French, who were attempting to stabilize relations with the Algonquians. The most common method was by providing "gifts" of trade goods.

France and Spain had also arrived at an uneasy peace in North America. Each had come to an arrangement with the increasingly powerful Comanche empire in the South-

OUTLINE

The Victory of the British Empire
  New War, Old Pattern
  The Local Impact of Global War
  The French Empire Crumbles from Within
  The Virginians Ignite a War
  From Local to Imperial War

PRIMARY SOURCE:
  George Washington on Braddock's Defeat

Problems with British-Colonial Cooperation
  The British Gain the Advantage

Enforcing the Empire
  Pontiac's Rebellion and Its Aftermath
  Paying for the Empire: Sugar and Stamps

AMERICA AND THE WORLD:
  Paying for War

west. When France built its forts along the lower Mississippi valley (see Chapter 4), Spain responded, in 1716, with an outpost in Texas. Both had hoped to expand their empires across the plains but were thwarted by the Comanches, who, like the Iroquois to the east, played the European powers off against each other. By the 1740s, the Comanches had forced both France and Spain to trade with them on advantageous terms, while blocking both from further expansion.

Another round of international warfare broke out in 1739 and lasted nine years. In the War of Jenkins's Ear (1739–1744), Britain attempted to expand into Spanish territories and markets in the Americas. Urged on by merchants, and with the approval of colonists who wanted to eliminate Spain as a rival, Britain found an excuse for declaring war: a ship's captain, Robert Jenkins, turned up in Parliament in 1738 holding in his hand what he claimed was his ear, severed by the Spanish seven years earlier in the Caribbean. Once again, colonists joined in what they hoped would be a glorious international endeavor, only to be disillusioned. In 1741, 3,600 colonists, mostly poor young men lured by the promise of Spanish plunder, joined 5,000 Britons in a failed attack on Cartagena, Colombia. More than half the colonial contingent died.

Another ambitious move against the Spanish Empire failed in 1740. James Oglethorpe and settlers hired by South Carolina, accompanied by Cherokee and Creek allies, failed to seize the Spanish outpost at St. Augustine and left the southern border vulnerable. When Oglethorpe's troops repulsed a Spanish attack in 1742, however, Spain's plan to demolish Georgia and South Carolina and arm their slaves was thwarted.

Just as the War of Jenkins's Ear ended in stalemate, so did King George's War (1744–1748), a conflict between Britain and Austria on one side and France and Prussia on the other over succession to the Austrian throne. A French raid on a fishing village in Nova Scotia met with a huge retaliation by the British. Troops from Massachusetts, supported by the British navy, captured the French fort at Louisbourg. Finally, a joint British-colonial venture had succeeded. But a planned attack on Québec was called off when the British fleet failed to arrive. At war's end, Britain returned Louisbourg to France and warned the colonists that they had to maintain the peace. The British blockade of French ports cut off trade to Canada, including the all-important presents to Indian allies and trade partners. Without these gifts, the French-Indian empire began to crumble.

The Local Impact of Global War

Successive rounds of warfare had a significant impact on politics and society in British North America. Although the colonists identified strongly with the British cause, decades of warfare were a constant drain on the colonial treasury and population.

The British Empire in Crisis
    An Argument About Rights and Obligations
    The Imperial Crisis in Local Context

TECHNOLOGY AND IDEAS:
    The Role of Newspapers in the Imperial Crisis
    Contesting the Townshend Duties

A Revolution in the Empire

"Massacre" in Boston

AMERICAN LANDSCAPE:
    Occupied Boston
    The Empire Comes Apart
    The First Continental Congress

Conclusion

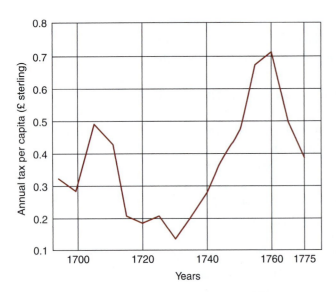

Figure 6–1 Tax Rates in Boston, 1645–1774 The per capita tax rate in Boston followed the course of imperial war in 1713, increasing during the War of Jenkins's Ear (1739–1744) and rising to unprecedented heights to support the French and Indian War (1754–1763). *Data from Gary B. Nash,* The Urban Crucible *(Cambridge, MA: Harvard University Press, 1974), p. 403.*

Wars are expensive. Generally, rates of taxation in colonial America were low, except when wars had to be financed (see Figure 6–1). In a rehearsal for the conflicts that would lead to the American Revolution, the British government complained that the colonists were unwilling to contribute their fair share to the imperial wars. As a rule, colonial legislatures were willing to go only so far in raising taxes to pay for imperial wars or expeditions against Indians. Then they simply issued paper money. Inevitably, the currency depreciated, making even worse the boom-and-bust cycles that war economies always produce.

No colony did more to support the imperial war efforts than Massachusetts, but the result was heightened political conflict at home. Royal governors, eager to please officials in London, pushed the colony to contribute to the imperial wars. As many as one-fifth of the colony's men may have served in the military in the middle of the eighteenth century. In 1747 Boston mobs rioted for three days to resist the Royal Navy's attempt to "impress" (force) men into service, and the local militia refused to restore order. For the first time, Bostonians began to speak about a right to resist tyranny.

Much more than in Europe, civilians in America became victims of war. By the eighteenth century, conventions of "civilized" warfare that held that civilians should be spared broke down in America for two reasons. First, without a transportation system to supply the army, troops often relied on plunder. Second, frontier Indians, adapting their traditional practices of war, routinely attacked villages, seizing captives to replenish their populations and to ransom to the French. Between 1675 and 1763, when frontier settlers such as Susannah Johnson were at risk, Indians took more than 1,600 New England settlers as captives, more than 90 percent during times of war (see Figure 6–2).

Almost half the colonists seized eventually returned home, but, as with Susannah Johnson's son Sylvanus, who had forgotten English entirely, Indian customs "wore off" only "by degree." Other captives died during the arduous march to Canada, sometimes killed by Indians who thought them too weak to survive the journey. Many died of disease, and a few, typically girls between 7 and 15, remained with their captors voluntarily. Historians debate why this was so. Perhaps it was because Puritan culture trained girls to respond without question to those in authority. Or perhaps it was because, after the rigors of a Puritan upbringing, the relative freedom of Indian culture was inviting.

> ## Jaghte oghte.
>
> EUNICE WILLIAMS, responding in Mohawk ("Maybe not") to an offer to be ransomed back to her family in Massachusetts 8 years after she had been captured at the age of seven. By this time, she had been adopted by the Mohawks, converted to Catholicism, taken a new name—Marguerite—and married a Mohawk man named Arosen, with whom she would live until his death 50 years later.

The French Empire Crumbles from Within

In the years after King George's War, a change in French policy offered a small band of Miami Indians the chance to gain an advantage over rivals. In the process, they started a chain of events that led to the French and Indian War.

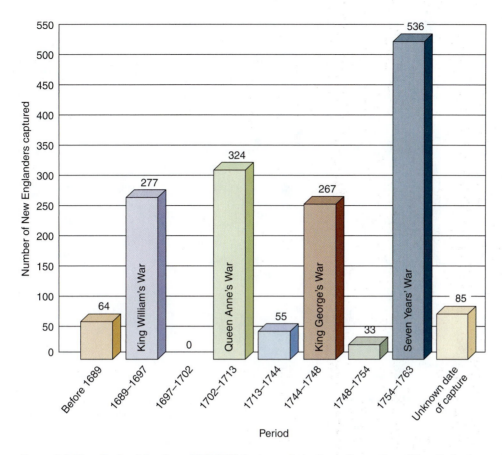

Figure 6-2 New England Captives, 1675-1763 During periods of war, the number of New Englanders taken captive by northern Indians and the French increased dramatically, with more than 90 percent of the captives being taken during times of war. *Alden Vaughan*, Roots of American Racism *(New York: Oxford University Press, 1990), p. 31.*

Although King George's War had ended in a stalemate, it weakened the French position in North America. The costs of war had forced the French to cut back on their presents to allied Algonquian tribes, especially in the Ohio River valley. To raise revenue, the French sharply increased their charges for the lease of trading posts; in turn, traders raised the prices that they charged the Indians for trade goods. These changes significantly weakened the French hold over their Indian allies, creating political instability that was the underlying North American cause of the French and Indian War.

The Ohio River valley was home to small, refugee tribes (see Map 6-1). As long as the French provided liberal presents and cheap trade goods, they maintained a loose control. Once that control ended, however, each tribe sought to increase its advantage over the others, at a time when the British recognized the strategic and economic importance of the region.

The temporary power vacuum afforded a small group of Miamis, led by a chieftain called Memeskia, an opportunity to play one group of colonists off another. The chain of events that led to the French and Indian War began in 1748 when Memeskia's group established a new village, Pickawillany, near the head of the Miami River. Memeskia welcomed English traders from Pennsylvania, because their goods were better and

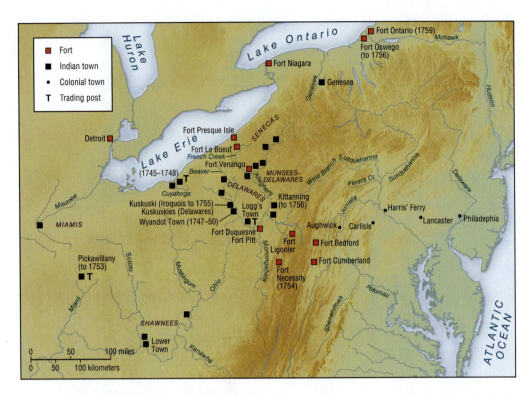

Map 6-1 The Ohio River Valley, 1747–1758 This territory, inhabited by a number of small bands of Indians, was coveted by both the French and the British, not to mention several competing groups of colonial land speculators. The rivalries between the imperial powers, among the Indian bands, and between rival groups of speculators made this region a powder keg. *Adapted from Michael McConnell,* A Country Between *(Lincoln: University of Nebraska, 1992), pp. 116–117.*

cheaper than those of the French. He hoped to trade with the British free of political or military obligations.

Memeskia's move threatened not only the balance of power between Britain and France but also that between Pennsylvania and Virginia. The Pennsylvanians welcomed trade with the Miamis, for it gave them a claim to the western lands that Virginians sought. At the same time, Memeskia used his access to British traders to attract many small bands of followers to his village. Alarmed, the French shifted away from trade to force. In 1749, they sent a small expedition to cow their former Indian allies back into submission. When it failed, they began to raid dissident Indian encampments and planned to establish a fort in the Ohio River valley. With this change in French policy, Indians faced two options: to gather Indian allies (Memeskia's tactic) or to make alliances with the British (the strategy of an Iroquois chieftain named Tanacharison). Neither route promised real security, but the chaos these bids for advantage created drew the French and British into war.

In 1752, Tanacharison agreed to give Virginia not only the 200,000 acres claimed by the Ohio Company, a group of Virginia speculators, but also all the land between the Susquehanna and Allegheny Rivers (today's Kentucky, West Virginia, and western Pennsylvania). In return, Virginia promised Tanacharison's people trade and protection from their enemies. Memeskia was isolated. With no European or Indian power dominant in the region, conflicts broke out, and the French pried off some of Memeskia's allies and conquered the rest. In a raid on Pickawillany, 250 pro-French

Ottawas and Chippewas killed Memeskia. Their village destroyed, the demoralized Miamis returned to the French for protection. For the moment, the French regained power, but by shifting their policy from trade to force, they set a course that would lead to the loss of their North American empire.

The Virginians Ignite a War

Both France and Virginia now claimed the Ohio River valley, and they raced to establish forts to secure their claims. Virginia entrusted the job to a well-connected 21-year-old with almost no qualifications for the post: George Washington. Washington was tied to the powerful Fairfax clan, a British family that owned 5 million acres in Virginia and held a share in the Ohio Company. In the Anglo-American world, advancement came through such linked ties of family and patronage.

In the spring of 1754, the French and Virginians scrambled to see who could build a fort first at the Forks of the Ohio (present-day Pittsburgh). The force that Virginia sent to the region, with Washington second in command, was pathetically small. Although the French army—numbering 1,000—was only 50 miles away, a combined Virginia-Indian band led by Washington attacked and defeated a small French reconnaissance party. The French and Indian War (known in Europe as the Seven Years' War) had begun.

The Virginians had bitten off more than they could chew. Washington's small fort was reinforced by British regulars but was quickly deserted by Indian allies, who recognized it as indefensible. The French overwhelmed the fort, driving Washington and his troops back to Virginia. Although war was not officially declared in Europe until May 1756, fighting soon spread throughout the frontier.

From Local to Imperial War

At the beginning of the war, the advantage was with the French. Although the population in the British colonies greatly outnumbered that of New France, France's population was three times larger than Britain's and its army 10 times the size. More important, the more centralized French state was better prepared to coordinate the massive effort an international war required. The British government, aware that lack of coordination among its colonies could cripple the war effort, in summer 1754 instructed all the colonies north of Virginia to plan for a collective defense and to shore up the alliance with the Six (Iroquois) Nations. Pennsylvania's Benjamin Franklin offered the delegates, who met in Albany, a plan, known as the Albany Plan of Union, which every colony rejected.

The localism of the American colonies made cooperation difficult if not impossible. A deeply ingrained value, localism was suspicious of the centralized European state and its army of professionals.

Britain was now in its fourth war with France in less than a century. It had authorized Virginia's foray into the Ohio River valley and sent two regiments, under the command of General Edward Braddock, to Virginia in late 1754, hoping that the

Edward Braddock General Edward Braddock was killed when the French ambushed the British and colonial troops he was leading toward Fort Duquesne.

DEFEAT and DEATH of GENERAL BRADDOCK in North America.

Braddock's Defeat This detail depicting Braddock's defeat is from a drawing by an engineer with the British army.

colonists could fight with only a little British assistance. But the disarray continued: colonial soldiers were reluctant to obey an officer from another colony, let alone one from the British army.

With four times as many troops as the British had in North America, superior leadership, and no intercolonial rivalries, the French dominated the first phase of the war, from 1754 through 1757. The British and colonial armies planned to besiege four French forts: Fort Duquesne (Pittsburgh), Fort Niagara (Niagara Falls), Fort St. Frédéric (Crown Point, at the southern end of Lake Champlain), and Fort Beauséjour (Nova Scotia).

Braddock was to attack Fort Duquesne with a combined force of British regulars and colonial troops, but without Indians. He had alienated the regional Indians, who rejoined the French alliance. After a grueling two-month march, on July 9, 1755, Braddock's forces were surprised close to their objective by a French and Indian force. Almost 1,000 British and colonial troops were killed or wounded; Braddock himself died from wounds suffered in the ambush. One of the survivors was George Washington, who had been serving as an unsalaried adjutant to Braddock to learn the art of war.

Two of the other three planned assaults ended in disappointment as well. William Shirley, who became the British commander in chief, led the attack on Fort Niagara himself and assigned Fort St. Frédéric to William Johnson, a Mohawk Valley Indian trader who was soon made superintendent of Indian affairs for the northern colonies. Well suited for leading Iroquois forays against the French, Johnson led a force of about 3,500, including 300 Iroquois. Their advance was stopped by the

>> George Washington on Braddock's Defeat

In 1755, an exhausted and ill George Washington wrote a letter to his mother describing General Edward Braddock's disastrous attempt to take the French fort at the Forks of the Ohio (the site of modern-day Pittsburgh). The letter, dated July 18, 1755, outlined Washington's defense of the conduct of the Virginia militia, blamed by the British for the battle's loss. Though the British ultimately prevailed over the French, the war's conduct led both the British and their colonists to reassess their relationship, the British officers expressing their distrust of the colonial troops and the colonists coming to regard the "lobsterbacks" as immoral and cruel.

This painting is from 1772, but depicts George Washington in his uniform from the French and Indian War.

HONORED MADAM: As I doubt not but you have heard of our defeat, and, perhaps, had it represented in a worse light, if possible, than it deserves, I have taken this earliest opportunity to give you some account of the engagement as it happened, within ten miles of the French fort, on Wednesday the 9th instant.

We marched to that place, without any considerable loss, having only now and then a straggler picked up by the French and scouting Indians. When we came there, we were attacked by a party of French and Indians, whose number, I am persuaded, did not exceed three hundred men; while ours consisted of about one thousand three hundred well-armed troops, chiefly regular soldiers [Editor's note: the "regulars" were British soldiers fighting under the command of General Braddock], who were struck with such a panic that they behaved with more cowardice than it is possible to conceive. The officers behaved gallantly, in order to encourage their men, for which they suffered greatly, there being near sixty killed and wounded; a large proportion of the number we had.

The Virginia troops showed a good deal of bravery, and were nearly all killed; for I believe, out of three companies that were there, scarcely thirty men are left alive. Captain Peyrouny, and all his officers down to a corporal, were killed. Captain Polson had nearly as hard a fate, for only one of his was left. In short, the dastardly behavior of those they call regulars exposed all others, that were inclined to do their duty, to almost certain death; and, at last, in despite of all the efforts of the officers to the contrary, they ran, as sheep pursued by dogs, and it was impossible to rally them.

Continued

The General was wounded, of which he died three days after. Sir Peter Halket was killed in the field, where died many other brave officers. I luckily escaped without a wound, though I had four bullets through my coat, and two horses shot under me. Captains Orme and Morris, two of the aids-de-camp, were wounded early in the engagement, which rendered the duty harder upon me, as I was the only person then left to distribute the General's orders, which I was scarcely able to do, as I was not half recovered from a violent illness, that had confined me to my bed and a wagon for above ten days. I am still in a weak and feeble condition, which induces me to halt here two or three days in the hope of recovering a little strength, to enable me to proceed homewards; from whence, I fear, I shall not be able to stir till toward September; so that I shall not have the pleasure of seeing you till then, unless it be in Fairfax. . . . I am, honored Madam, your most dutiful son.

George Washington, "Letter to Mary Washington, Fort Cumberland, July 18th, 1755," in *The Writings of George Washington; Being His Correspondence, Addresses, Messages, and Other Papers, Official and Private, Selected and Published from the Original Manuscripts; with a Life of the Author, Notes, and Illustrations, Vol. II*, ed. Jared Sparks (Boston: Ferdinand Andrews, 1840), pp. 86–88.

Questions

1. On whom does Washington place the blame for the defeat and why?

2. What is his assessment of the fighting abilities of the different parties involved in the battle?

3. What can you tell about Washington from this letter?

French and their Native American allies, but with equal casualties on both sides and the capture of the French commander, the British declared victory and elevated Johnson to the nobility. In the winter of 1755–1756 the British built Fort William Henry, and the French, Fort Carillon (which the British renamed Ticonderoga).

Hampered by rough terrain and intercolonial wrangling, Shirley's force never made it to Fort Niagara. The only outright success was at Fort Beauséjour, near the British colony at Nova Scotia. A British-financed expedition of New England volunteers easily seized the fort, and the British evicted 10,000 Acadians (French residents of Nova Scotia) who would not take an oath of loyalty. About 300 ended up in French Louisiana, where their name was abbreviated into "Cajuns."

Both the British and the French expected their colonists to carry most of the load of the war. Their defeats and continued intercolonial rivalries left the British vulnerable and the frontier exposed. The French began a cautious but successful offensive. First, they encouraged Indian raids along the frontier from Maine to South Carolina. Indians swung back to the French because the French appeared less dangerous than the land-hungry British. The price for French friendship, however, was participation in the war against the British. By the fall of 1756, some 3,000 settlers had been killed, and the line of settlement had been pushed back 150 miles in some places.

The French and their Indian allies seized Fort Bull in March 1756 and Fort Oswego several months later. A little over a year later, a massive French force attacked Fort William Henry. This loosely organized army of 8,000 included 1,000 Indian warriors and another 800 converted Algonquians accompanied by their Catholic priests.

Johnson's Home Iroquois Indians were frequent guests at the home of trader and British official William Johnson. He took an Iroquois woman, Molly Brant, as his common-law wife. Johnson's Iroquois allies followed him into battle in the French and Indian War.

Louis-Joseph de Montcalm Americans blamed the French commander for the massacre at Fort William Henry.

After a seven-day siege and heavy bombardment, the British commander surrendered on August 9, 1757. Louis-Joseph de Montcalm, the French commander, offered European-style terms: the British were to return their French and Indian prisoners, keep their personal weapons, and march back to Fort Edward, on the lower Hudson River, promising not to fight the French for 18 months. Historians still debate whether Montcalm knew what was about to take place. The Indians had expected, as was their custom, to be allowed to take plunder and captives. Denied this opportunity, they fell on the British, including the sick, women, and children, as they were evacuating the fort the next morning.

The massacre at Fort William Henry had significant repercussions. Still angry at being denied the spoils of war, Montcalm's Indian allies returned home, taking smallpox with them. The French would never again have the assistance of such a significant number of Indian allies. The British were outraged. The new British commander, Lord Jeffrey Amherst, declared the surrender terms null and void. Later, under his order, Delaware Indians who had been invited to a peace talk were given, ostensibly as presents, blankets that had been infected with smallpox. Historians are not certain whether these blankets were responsible for the outbreak of the disease among local Indians, but that was certainly Amherst's intent.

> I make war for plunder, scalps, and prisoners. You are satisfied with a fort, and you let your enemy and mine live. I do not want to keep such bad meat for tomorrow. When I kill it, it can no longer attack me.
>
> ANONYMOUS WESTERN INDIAN,
> explaining why he refused the French governor's offer of two gallons of rum instead of being allowed to attack the British prisoners

Problems with British-Colonial Cooperation

The British and the colonists blamed each other for their defeats. There was some truth in their accusations: unwillingness to sacrifice and disastrous infighting among the colonists, and arrogance among the British. These recriminations, more than any side's failing, created problems. The colonists and the British had different expectations about their roles in the war. The colonists were not prepared for the high taxes or sacrifice of liberty that waging an international war required.

The British were dismayed by what they perceived as the colonists' selfishness, as they engaged in profiteering and trading with the enemy. Colonial governments were no more generous. Braddock's expedition to Fort Duquesne was delayed by the colonies' unwillingness to provision his army.

After Braddock's defeat, colonials deserted in droves. The British began recruiting servants and apprentices, angering their masters. Another serious problem was that of quartering soldiers over the winter. Under English law, which did not extend specifically to the colonies, troops in England could be lodged in public buildings rather than private homes. In the colonies, however, there weren't enough buildings in which to house soldiers without resorting to private homes. The residents of Albany took in soldiers only under threat of force. Philadelphians were rescued by the ever-resourceful Franklin, who opened a newly built hospital to the troops. In Charleston, soldiers had to camp outdoors, where they fell victim to disease.

Other problems arose from joint operations. The British army was a disciplined professional fighting force, led by members of the upper classes; service in it was a career. In contrast, colonial soldiers were primarily civilian amateurs, led by members of the middle class from their hometowns. Colonial soldiers believed that they were fighting by contract for a set period of time, for a specific objective, for a set rate of pay, and under a particular officer. If any of the terms were violated, the soldier considered himself free to go home.

The British, however, expected the same discipline from the colonists as they did from their own army. All colonial soldiers operating with regular forces were subject to British martial law, which was cruel and uncompromising. One regular soldier, for example, was sentenced to 1,000 lashes for stealing a keg of beer, which a merciful officer reduced to a mere 900! The British officers were almost unanimous in their condemnation of colonial soldiers. According to Brigadier General James Wolfe, "The Americans are in general the dirtiest most contemptible cowardly dogs that you can conceive."

Yet the colonists certainly believed that they were doing their share. Tax rates were raised sharply, tripling in Virginia in three years, for example. The human contribution was even more impressive. At the height of the war, Massachusetts was raising 7,000 soldiers a year, from a colony of only 50,000 men. Perhaps as many as 3 out of 10 adult men served in the military during the war, and only the Civil War and the Revolution had higher casualty rates.

The British Gain the Advantage

Montcalm's victory at Fort William Henry marked the French high-water mark. After a change of government in 1757, Britain resolved to win the war, as William Pitt became head of the cabinet. His rise to power represented the triumph of the commercial classes and their vision of the empire. Pitt was the first British leader who was as committed to a victory in the Americas as in Europe, believing that the future of the British Empire lay in the extended empire and its trade. Britain's aim in North America now shifted from simply regaining territory to seizing New France itself. Pitt sent 2,000 additional troops, promised 6,000 more, and asked the colonies to raise 20,000 of their own. To support so large an army, Pitt raised taxes on the already heavily taxed British and borrowed heavily, doubling the size of the British debt. He won the cooperation of the colonies by promising that Britain would pay up to half of their costs for fighting the war. As all of this money poured into the colonies, it improved their economies dramatically.

Now the British could take the offensive (see Map 6–2). In a series of great victories, they won Louisbourg on Cape Breton Island in July 1758; then Fort Frontenac in August; and finally, in November, Fort Duquesne, which the British renamed Fort Pitt. The only defeat was at Fort Carillon (called Ticonderoga by the British). There, Susannah Johnson's husband James was one of the casualties. The British seized Fort Frontenac, disrupting the supply lines from the French to the Ohio valley Indians,

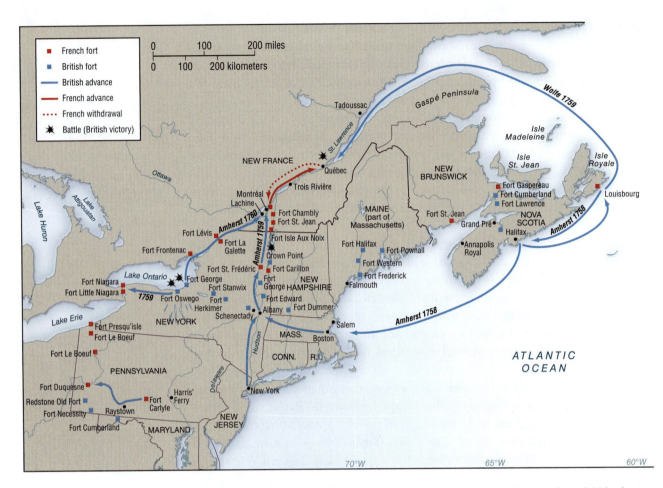

Map 6-2 The Second Phase of the French and Indian War, 1758–1763 This map shows British advances in Pennsylvania, New York, and Canada.

who shifted their allegiance. The British also moved from a policy of confrontation to one of accommodation. In the Treaty of Easton (1758), 13 Ohio valley tribes agreed to remain neutral in return for a promise to keep the territory west of the Alleghenies free of settlers. Also, gifts to the Iroquois brought them back into the fold.

The British were now ready for the final offensive. Historians always argue about when and why a war is "lost": unless an army has been annihilated and the population entirely subjugated, which is rare, when to surrender is always a subjective decision. Political and military leaders must decide when the loss in lives and resources can no longer be justified, and the population must agree that further fighting is pointless. By 1759, some of the French believed that the war was essentially over. Casualties were extremely high, food was in short supply, and inflation was rampant. Most of the Indian allies had deserted the cause, and the French government was unable to match Pitt's spending on the war. It would take two more years of fighting and the loss of thousands more lives before the French surrendered, however.

In the summer of 1759, General James Wolfe took the struggle for North America into the heart of Canada, laying siege to Québec. Québec's position on a bluff high above the St. Lawrence made it almost impregnable, so for months Wolfe bombarded the city and tried to wear down its citizens, terrorizing those who lived on its outskirts by burning crops and houses. In mid-September, Wolfe ordered an assault up the 175-foot cliff below the city. In a battle that lasted only half an hour, his soldiers claimed victory on the Plains of Abraham. Each side suffered casualties of 15 percent, and both Wolfe and his French opponent, Montcalm, were killed. Four days later, New France's oldest permanent settlement surrendered to the British. By the time the British reached Montréal, the French army numbered fewer than 3,000 men.

The Treaty of Paris ended the war in 1763. By then, Britain had also seized the French sugar islands in the Caribbean and, after Spain entered the war on the French side, Havana and the Philippines. Pitt would have continued to fight, but the British public was unwilling to pay more to increase the size of the empire. The French, exhausted by war, surrendered all of Canada except for two small fishing islands in return for the right to hold on to the most valuable sugar islands, the most important part

Painted Caribou Skin Coat Innu, ca. 1783–1805. Québec-Labrador Peninsula. Courtesy Innu Nation and The Rooms Corporation of Newfoundland and Labrador, Provincial Museum Division. Photo: Shane Kelly.

of their American empire. France even gave New Orleans and all of its territory west of the Mississippi to Spain as compensation for losing Florida, which the British claimed (see Map 6–3). (Britain let Spain keep Havana and the Philippines.) Britain staked its

Map 6-3 The North American Colonies Before and After the French and Indian War In the Treaty of Paris in 1763, more American territory was transferred than at any time before or since. *Helen Hornbeck Tanner, Atlas of Great Lakes Indian History (Norman: University of Oklahoma Press, 1987), p. 54.*

future on the mainland of North America, believing correctly that it would ultimately be more valuable than the sugar islands of the Caribbean.

Enforcing the Empire

Even before the French and Indian War, some in the British government urged tighter control over the American colonies. Colonists smuggled and even traded with the enemy throughout the war, and colonial assemblies sometimes impeded the war effort. Pitt had increased Britain's debt to pay for the war, rather than waiting for the colonial assemblies. Now, with the war over, Britain faced a staggering debt of £122,603,336. Moreover, there was a huge new territory to govern, one coveted by speculators and settlers and inhabited by Indian tribes determined to resist encroachment.

The American Revolution grew out of Britain's attempts to draw its American colonies more closely into the imperial system. Although various master plans for reorganizing the empire had been circulated, there had never been an overarching design or a clear set of guidelines. By 1763, there was a new resolve to enforce a vision of the empire and the role of colonies in it. In 1760 a new king, the 22-year-old George III, ascended to the throne upon the death of his grandfather. Reasonably well educated, the young king was determined to play a role in government. He changed ministers so frequently that chaos ensued. It is not clear, however, that more enlightened leadership would have prevented the war, for George's ministers pursued a fairly consistent policy toward the colonies. In resisting that policy, the American colonists developed a new and different idea of the purpose of government, one that propelled them to revolution.

Pontiac's Rebellion and Its Aftermath

Because the British had defeated the French and had entered into alliances with the Iroquois and the Ohio valley Indians, peace in the West should have come easily. The British, however, soon made the same mistake that the French had made when they discontinued presents to their Indian allies 15 years earlier. Thinking they could impose their will on the Indians, the British instead found themselves embroiled in another war.

At the end of the French and Indian War, the western Algonquian tribes hoped the British would follow the practices of the middle ground by mediating their disputes, trading with them at good prices, and giving them presents. Lord Jeffrey Amherst, commanding British forces in North America, cut off the presents, believing them too expensive. He thought that threats of an Indian revolt were exaggerated and was willing to take the risk of war.

The war of 1763 is commonly known as Pontiac's Rebellion, named after the Ottawa chieftain who played a prominent role. It was the first battle in a long, and ultimately unsuccessful, attempt by Indians to keep the region between the Mississippi River and the Alleghenies free of European settlers. The Indians seized every fort except for

> What had little Boys and Girls done; what could Children of a Year old, Babes at the Breast, what could they do, that they too must be shot and hatcheted?—Horrid to relate!—and in their Parents Arms! This is done by no civilized Nation in Europe. Do we come to America to learn and practise the Manners of Barbarians? But this, Barbarians as they are, they practise against their Enemies only, not against their Friends.
>
> BENJAMIN FRANKLIN,
> condemning the Paxton Boys

Pitt, Niagara, and Detroit, and Detroit was under siege for six months (see Map 6–4). Casualties were high: about 2,000 civilians, 400 soldiers, and an unknown number of Indians. Tortures by both sides were horrific, and American colonists took out their aggressions on peaceful or defenseless Indians. In December 1763, a party of 50 armed men from the Pennsylvania village of Paxton descended on a tiny community of Christian Indians living at Conestoga Manor, eight miles west of Lancaster. They killed and scalped the six people they found—two men, three women, and a child—and burned their houses. Two weeks later, another group of these "Paxton Boys" broke into the county workhouse, where the remainder of the small tribe had been put for their own protection, and killed them, too.

Although colonial leaders decried acts of violence, they did little to prevent or punish them. British officials saw the failure of the colonists to maintain order on the frontier and protect innocent Indians as further proof of the incompetence of colonial governments. Even before Pontiac's Rebellion ended in a draw, the British had decided that peace with the western Indians could be preserved only by keeping colonial settlers and speculators away. The Proclamation of 1763 attempted to confine the colonists to the east of an imaginary line running down the spine of the Alleghenies. George Washington called the proclamation "a temporary expedient to quiet the minds of the Indians" and ignored it. Other Virginia speculators sought to take the territory by force. A pretext came in 1774 when several settlers killed several Indians, and John Logan, a Mingo Indian, sought vengeance for his slain relatives. Rather than resolving this conflict in the ways of the middle ground, Virginia's royal governor sent

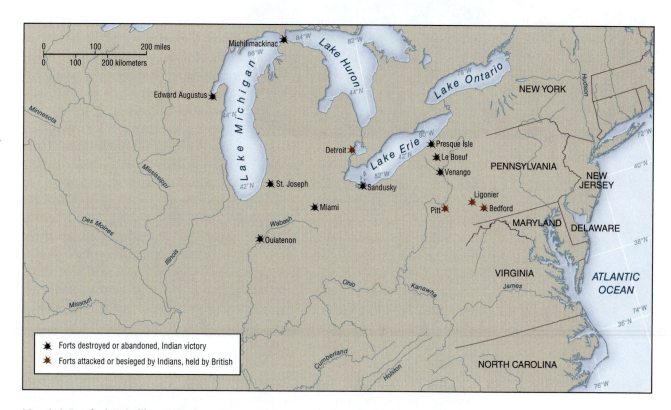

Map 6–4 Pontiac's Rebellion, 1763 The war began when the British abandoned the policy of the middle ground and cut off presents to the western Indians. In their uprising, the Indians destroyed nine British forts and attacked another four before the war ended in a draw. *Tanner,* Atlas of Great Lakes Indian History, *p. 49.*

Negotiating the Conclusion of Pontiac's Rebellion Colonel Henry Bouquet in council with Shawnee, Seneca, and Delaware Indians on the banks of the Muskingum River in October 1764.

a force of 2,000 to vanquish the Indians. Although the Virginians' success in Lord Dunmore's War ended Indian claims to Kentucky, Britain was still not ready to permit speculators or settlers to claim the land.

Paying for the Empire: Sugar and Stamps

On the edge of the British Empire, the colonies were important, but not nearly as important as Britain's domestic concerns. One of George III's highest priorities was to maintain the size of the army. During the French and Indian War, it had doubled, and it was filled with officers loyal to the king. Parliament in 1763 agreed to maintain a huge peacetime army, part of which would be posted in the colonies and West Indies. Colonists feared that the army would enforce customs regulations rather than police the Indians.

This large army, of course, would strain a budget already burdened by a huge war debt. George Grenville, the new prime minister, believed that the colonists should pay a portion of the £225,000 a year that the standing army would cost.

Under Grenville's leadership, Parliament passed four pieces of legislation to force the colonies to contribute to their own upkeep. The Molasses Act of 1733 had established a duty of six cents per gallon, but smugglers paid off customs officials at the rate of one and a half cents a gallon. At Grenville's urging, Parliament passed the Sugar Act (1764), which dropped the duty to three cents but established procedures to make certain it was collected. To discourage smuggling, shippers were required to file elaborate papers each time an item was loaded onto a ship. In addition, accused violators were to be tried in admiralty courts in Nova Scotia, where the burden of proof would be on the defendant and the judgment would be rendered by judges rather than a jury.

To regulate colonial economies in the interest of British creditors, the Currency Act (1764) forbade the issuing of any colonial currency. British merchants had complained that colonists were discharging their debts in depreciated paper money. Moreover, the Sugar Act and the Stamp Act (passed the following year) required that duties

AMERICA AND THE WORLD

>> Paying for War

For most of human history, the costs of war have worked as a check on war making: a country could not spend any more on warfare than it could pay for. Some countries plundered their neighbors. Others taxed their own people, but there are always absolute limits to how much money can be extracted in this way. Other countries borrowed from foreigners, which put them at the mercy of foreign creditors.

In the seventeenth century, the Dutch figured out a new method of financing government: borrowing money from its own citizens by selling them interest-paying bonds. The government then taxed its people to pay off the bonds and the interest, which enabled it to spread out the costs of war over a long period. The result was higher taxes in peacetime—but no excessive burden during times of war. Those who bought government bonds were literally making an investment in their nation and profiting from its success.

This was the method that Britain used to pay for its rise to power beginning in the eighteenth century. It raised astronomical sums of money: £31 million for King William's War, £51 million for Queen Anne's War, £73 million for the Seven Years' War. And with each war, the government borrowed an increasing portion of the costs.

As Britain's war debt increased—it was up to £122,603,336 at the end of the Seven Years' War—the country had to raise taxes to pay for it. The English were paying higher taxes than any other nation in the world except for the Dutch. In fact, at the time of the French Revolution—caused in part by unacceptably high taxes—the British were taxed at a higher rate than the French. Yet the political mechanisms of taxation were so efficient that the government was able to collect tax revenues with relatively little resistance.

This achievement is remarkable when one considers the relative unfairness of the English tax system. The burden fell on the middle classes, whereas both the poor and the affluent were relatively lightly taxed. There was widespread agreement that the wages and necessities of the poor should be taxed lightly or not at all. Instead, the burden should fall, in theory, on the wealthy. Indeed, in 1690, 47 percent of England's revenues came from taxes on land and other property of the rich, but the powerful landowners refused to pay higher rates. As the need for revenue increased, the proportion of taxes paid by the wealthy fell. By 1763, it was down to 23 percent.

In search of revenue, the English government levied excise and stamp taxes, which fell most heavily on the middle classes. By the end of the Seven Years' War, the public had come close to reaching its limit. Already unhappy with the tax on beer, it objected to one on cider to help finance the last year of war.

Parliament worried that it could not increase taxes on its own people any further, and so it looked for other sources of revenue in other parts of its empire. At just the time that Parliament tried to tax the American colonies

Continued

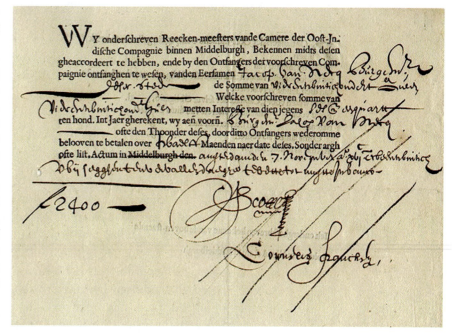

A Dutch bond, issued in 1623.

to pay for the troops stationed there, it was also stationing more forces in Ireland—and trying, unsuccessfully, to get the Irish parliament to pay for them. When the East India Company conquered the huge Indian state of Bengal, King George III imagined that India's wealth was "the only safe method of extracting this country out of its . . . load of debt." In return for letting the East India Company govern Bengal, the government extracted a fee of £400,000 a year, which the Company demanded from the Bengalis. This crushing tax burden, which coincided with a serious drought, plunged Bengal into a famine that killed 10 million people, a third of the population. With strong traditions of local government, the American colonists and the Irish were better able to resist England's attempts to tax them.

---

and taxes both be paid in specie (silver and gold). The colonists complained that there was not anywhere near as much specie in the colonies as they needed.

The third and most important piece of imperial legislation was the Stamp Act (1765). The first direct tax on the American people, the Stamp Act sought to raise revenue by taxing documents used in court proceedings; papers used in clearing ships from harbors; college diplomas; appointments to public office; bonds, grants, and deeds for mortgages; indentures, leases, contracts, and bills of sale; liquor licenses; playing cards and dice; and pamphlets, newspapers (and the ads in them), and almanacs.

The final piece of legislation, the Quartering Act (1765), required the colonies to house troops in public buildings and provide them with firewood, candles, and drink.

Although the colonists objected to all of these pieces of legislation, the Stamp Act was the most troubling. By taxing newspapers and pamphlets, it foolishly angered printers and editors at a time when newspapers were taking the lead in criticizing the government and were perhaps the most significant public institution in the colonies. The Stamp Act also angered lawyers, for every time a lawyer performed the simplest task of his trade, he would have to buy a stamp. These laws fell hardest on the most affluent and politically active colonists, the merchants, lawyers, and printers. All of these pieces of legislation were an attempt to tie the colonies into a modern, centralized state. As the colonists framed their response to the new laws, they struggled with a question central to American history: Could the people share in the benefits of the modern state—in particular a trade protected by its navy and with borders secured by its army—without the state itself?

The British Empire in Crisis

Colonial resistance to the imperial legislation of 1763 to 1765 was swift and forceful. A coalition of elite leaders and common people, primarily in the cities, worked to overturn the most objectionable aspects of the new regulations. In 1765, there was almost no thought of revolution, nor would there be for almost 10 years. Instead, the colonists rested their case on the British Constitution: all they wanted were the rights of Englishmen. Although in theory the colonists, as British subjects, were entitled to all of those rights, precisely how the British Constitution applied to colonists had never been clarified. The first phase of opposition, then, was a debate about the British Constitution, with the colonists insisting on their rights and the British government focusing on the colonists' obligations.

An Argument About Rights and Obligations

All along, Britain had maintained its right to regulate the colonies. Precisely what this meant became a matter of dispute after 1763. Did it mean regulation of trade? Taxation? Legislation? When Parliament passed these pieces of legislation, it acknowledged that the empire was a whole, that the parts existed for the benefit of the whole, and that Parliament had the authority to govern for the whole.

Britons were justifiably proud of their Parliament, one of the premier institutions of self-government in the world at the time. In principle Parliament represented all the elements in society: the king, the aristocrats (in the House of Lords), and the common people (in the House of Commons). It mixed and balanced these three elements of society, which also represented the three possible forms of government—monarchy, rule by the king; aristocracy, rule by hereditary aristocrats; and democracy, rule by the people—thus preventing both tyranny and anarchy and preserving liberty.

The British believed, and American colonists agreed, that their superb government was the product of centuries of struggle. First the aristocrats struggled with the king for more freedom, gaining it in the Magna Carta of 1215, and then the people struggled and won liberty, most recently in the Glorious Revolution of 1688. In this view, liberty was a collective right held by the people against the rulers and a limitation on the power of the monarch. A chief example of public or civil liberty was the right to be taxed only by one's own representatives. Taxes were a free gift of the people that no monarch could demand.

These ideas about the British government can be described as *constitutionalism*. Constitutionalism comprised two elements: the rule of law and the principle of consent, that one could not be subjected to laws or taxation except by duly elected representatives. Both were rights that had been won through struggle with the monarch. In the decade between 1765 and the outbreak of the American Revolution, the colonists worked out their own theory of the place of the colonies in the empire. A consensus formed on the importance of the rule of law and the principle of consent. Those colonists who became revolutionaries never wavered on these two points. In the decade between the Stamp Act and the beginning of the American Revolution, what colonists debated was whether particular pieces of legislation violated these principles and how far colonists should go in resisting those that did.

British officials never denied that the colonists should enjoy the rights of Englishmen. They merely asserted that the colonists were as well represented in Parliament as the majority of Britons. In fact, only 1 out of 10 British men could vote, compared with about 70 percent of American white men. Yet British officials said that all Britons were represented in Parliament, if not "actually," by choosing their own representatives, then by virtual representation, because each member of Parliament was supposed to act on behalf of the entire empire. In Britons' minds, Parliament was supreme, and it had full authority over the colonists. In the decade between the Stamp Act and the beginning of the American Revolution, the controversy turned on only two questions: How forcefully would the British government insist on the supremacy of Parliament? And could colonial radicals put together a broad enough coalition to resist Britain's force when it came?

The Imperial Crisis in Local Context

While newspapers and pamphlets were filled with denunciations of the new imperial legislation, Americans were taking their protests to the streets and to the colonial legislatures. Everywhere, a remarkable cross-class alliance of prosperous merchants and

TECHNOLOGY AND IDEAS

>> The Role of Newspapers in the Imperial Crisis

Colonial newspapers played a crucial role in the imperial crisis of 1765–1774. Following passage of the Stamp Act in 1765, newspapers in the colonies became more politicized than ever. By spreading vital information among the colonies and providing a forum for debating the Stamp Act and subsequent legislation, newspapers helped forge an intercolonial cross-class alliance and a belief in a common American cause. The rise of imperial tensions changed the social role of newspapers and made them an important force in the politics of the British Empire.

Newspaper printing developed along with the rise of Europe in the world economy. News sheets first emerged in seventeenth-century Europe as the need for international communication about trade increased. As conduits for political and economic information between London and the North American colonies, colonial newspapers were, from the very beginning, an essential feature of the British Atlantic world. In early modern England, printers were known as "mechanicks"—skilled craft workers whose trade was controlled and protected by the government. Printers used a rolling press—usually a single, hand-crafted piece of typeface—to press ink onto paper made of pounded rags. For most of the eighteenth century, printing technology remained essentially the same as it had been in Gutenberg's day. North American newspapers were part of a broader "reading revolu-

Front Page of the *Pennsylvania Journal*, October 31, 1765.

tion" between 1689 and 1815, when more people of different social classes sought more information than ever before. The steady expansion of the reading public in the colonies helped create the new sense of common political identity during the Stamp Act crisis.

In the eighteenth century, printers moved out of London and into the major cities of the British Empire, copying material from the *London Gazette*. For most, finding the resources to set up shop was hard enough. Finding the money, materials (ink, paper, typeface, presses), and apprentice labor to keep the enterprise going was even harder. Benjamin Harris published the first colonial newspaper, *Publick Occurrences*, in Boston in 1690. The Bradford family dominated newspaper publishing in Philadelphia and New York in the early eighteenth century (until a young Benjamin Franklin elbowed his way into their business), and Robert Wells dominated the southern colonies. Colonial newspapers saw a slight increase in politicization and readership in the 1740s with the rise of a partisan press in Britain, the War of Jenkins's Ear, and the Great Awakening. By then most adopted a format of four ad-filled pages that would remain the same for the next century. By 1750 there were newspapers in each of the more populous colonies, with most clustered in New York, Pennsylvania, and Massachusetts.

Until the Stamp Act, colonial newspapers were not truly partisan. The fifty or so printing houses that existed in 1765 simply reported basic political and economic information from London. With the imperial controversy of 1765–1776, however, newspapers became increasingly politicized. In fact, patriot newspapers played a critical role in turning public opinion against Great Britain. Between 1760 and the outbreak of the Revolutionary War, the number of newspapers in the colonies more than doubled. Newspapers became a forum for debating and eventually contesting the new British taxes and the authority of Parliament. Meanwhile, papers increasingly supplemented reports from London with news from other colonies and accounts of the Continental Congress, giving shape, however haltingly, to a sense of a common American cause. As reports of other European nations' reactions to the crisis trickled into the colonies, many Americans gained a new sense of their place in the world of "civilized" nations.

Questions

1. To what extent did the imperial crisis influence newspapers, and to what extent did newspapers influence the imperial crisis?

2. What was it about newspapers that gave them a unique role in the creation of an "American" identity?

planters and poor people joined to protect what they perceived as their rights from encroachment by British officials.

By the day that the Stamp Act was to go into effect, November 1, 1765, every colony except Georgia had taken steps to ensure that the tax could not be collected. In Virginia, the House of Burgesses took the lead. A young and barely literate lawyer, Patrick Henry, played a key role in the debate on the Virginia Resolves, the four resolutions protesting the Stamp Act that were passed by the burgesses. They asserted that the inhabitants of Virginia brought with them the rights of Englishmen, that Virginia's royal charters confirmed these rights, that taxation by one's own representatives was the only constitutional policy, and that the people of Virginia had never relinquished these rights. In Boston, too, the protest united the elite with poorer colonists. Massachusetts was still reeling from the loss of life and extraordinary expense of the French and Indian War. Imperialists such as Lieutenant Governor Thomas Hutchinson wanted to tie Massachusetts more tightly to the empire. He advocated a consolidation of power, a diminution of popular government (e.g., by reducing the power of the town meeting), making offices that were elective appointive instead, and limiting the freedom of the press.

Boston's public, with its history of radicalism, was ready for a much stronger response to the Stamp Act than the Massachusetts House of Representatives seemed prepared to make. The *Boston Gazette* criticized the House's resolution as a "tame, pusillanimous, daubed, insipid thing." Once word of the more radical Virginia Resolves arrived, the *Gazette* rebuked the weak political leadership again. A group of artisans and printers who called themselves the Sons of Liberty began organizing the opposition, probably in concert with more prominent men who would emerge as leaders of the revolutionary movement, such as James Otis, John Adams, and his cousin Samuel Adams, the Harvard-educated son of a brewer.

In a carefully orchestrated series of mob actions, Bostonians made certain that the Stamp Act would not be enforced. When the militia refused to protect royal officials, including the collector of the stamp tax, the officials took refuge in Castle William in the harbor. Over several days, the mob systematically vandalized the homes of several wealthy government loyalists, including Hutchinson. Although the mob consisted mostly of artisans and poor people, it had the support of Boston's merchant elite, for no one was ever punished. The protest succeeded, and the Stamp Act was never enforced.

Not only did each colony protest against the Stamp Act, but a majority were now ready to act together. In October 1765, delegates from nine colonies met in New York in the Stamp Act Congress to ratify a series of 14 resolutions protesting the Stamp Act on constitutional grounds. At the same time, activists shut down colonial courts so that no stamps could be used, and merchants agreed not to import any British goods until the act was repealed. With 37 percent of British exports then going to the colonies, this was no idle threat (see Figure 6–3).

Facing this opposition, the British partly backed down. George Grenville was replaced by the 35-year-old Marquess of Rockingham, who preferred racehorses to politics. Parliament repealed the Stamp Act but was not prepared to concede the constitutional point, asserting in the Declaratory Act of 1766 that Parliament "had, hath, and of right ought to have, full power and authority to make laws and statutes . . . to bind the colonies and people of America, subjects of the Crown of Great Britain, in all cases whatsoever."

Contesting the Townshend Duties

Britain gave up on trying to tax the colonies directly, for even some prominent Britons such as William Pitt sided with the colonists on that point. But between 1767 and 1774, those in power still tried to force their vision of empire on the colonies. In response, radical activists and thinkers formed a national opposition and took constitutionalism in

Tarring and Feathering the Customs Officer, 1774 Two Bostonians dress British customs officer John Malcolm in tar and feathers and force him to drink tea, turning him into a "macarony," an effete man who affected the latest fashion.

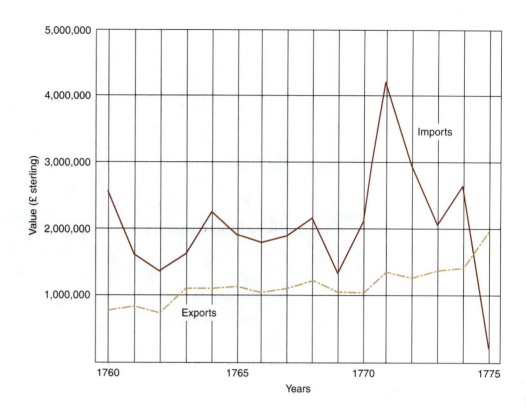

Figure 6-3 Trade Between England and the Colonies In the years between 1760 and 1775, colonial exports to England grew slowly but steadily, dropping off only after the beginning of the Revolution. On the other hand, imports from England—which always exceeded exports—rose and fell in response to political conditions. Colonial nonimportation agreements forced drops in imports after the imposition of the Stamp Act and Townshend Duties. But in both cases, imports increased after repeal, and the growth of imports after repeal of the Townshend Duties was dramatic and unprecedented.

new directions. By the time of the American Revolution, they had turned it into a new theory of government.

After a brief return to power by William Pitt, Charles Townshend, a brilliant but erratic man nicknamed "Champagne Charlie," became the third prime minister in as many years. His first act was to punish New York's assembly, which intentionally violated the Quartering Act. The assembly, denied the right to pass any legislation until it complied with the Quartering Act, quickly backed down.

The colonies refused, however, to comply with the next piece of legislation, the Townshend Revenue Act of 1767, which levied import duties on lead, paint, glass, paper, and tea. Townshend believed that the colonists objected only to taxes within the colonies, "internal taxes," but that they would accept an "external tax," such as an import duty. The revenue would be used to support colonial officials, making them independent of the colonial assemblies that had paid their salaries.

Resistance to the Townshend Act built slowly, as it was hard for colonists to make a case against all duties. Merchants were now complying with the new Revenue Act of 1766, which reduced the duty on molasses. Those colonists most troubled by the first round of imperial legislation, however, were convinced that the Townshend Duties were part of a design for tyranny.

A body of thought known as *republicanism* helped the colonists make sense of British actions. Republicanism was a set of doctrines rooted in the Renaissance that held that power is always dangerous, because "it is natural for Power to be striving to enlarge itself, and to be encroaching upon those that have none." Republicanism supplied constitutionalism with a motive. It explained how a balanced constitution could be transformed into tyranny. Would-be tyrants had access to a variety of tools, including a standing army, whose ultimate purpose was not the protection of the

Repeal of the Stamp Act, 1766 This cartoon shows the repeal of the Stamp Act, with George Grenville and other British officials carrying a coffin containing the act. In the background, languishing on the dock, is cargo that could not be shipped to America during the colonial boycott.

people but their subjection. Tyrants also engaged in corruption, in particular by dispensing patronage positions. So inexorable was the course of power that it took extraordinary virtue for an individual to resist its corruption. Consequently, republican citizens, it was thought, had to be economically independent; the poor were dangerous because they could easily be bought off by would-be tyrants. A secular theory with connections to Puritanism, republicanism asserted that people were naturally weak and that exceptional human effort was required to protect liberty and virtue.

Not only did people have to keep a close eye on power-hungry tyrants, but they also had to look inside themselves. According to republican thought, history demonstrated that republics fell from within when their citizens lost their virtue. The greatest threat to virtue was luxury, an excessive attachment to the fruits of the consumer revolution. When colonists worried that they saw luxury and corruption everywhere, they were criticizing the world that the consumer revolution had created. Although it is understandable why poor people embraced republicanism, it might seem perplexing that wealthy merchants and planters would also strongly denounce "malice, covetousness, and other lusts of man." Yet the legacy of Puritanism was powerful, and even those profiting most from the new order felt ambivalent about its effects on their society. Joining with poorer people in criticizing British officials and accusing them of attempting to undermine colonial liberties helped forge a cross-class alliance.

The colonial legislatures slowly began to protest the duties. Massachusetts's House of Representatives, led by Sam Adams, asked each of the other lower houses in the colonies to join in resisting "infringements of their natural & constitutional Rights because they are not represented in the British Parliament. . . ." When Lord Hillsborough, a hardline secretary of state for the colonies, saw the request, he instructed the colonial governors to dissolve any colonial assembly that received the petition from Massachusetts. Massachusetts refused to rescind it, so Governor Francis Bernard dissolved the legislature. With representative government threatened, those colonial legislatures that had not already ap-

> A Subscription Paper was handed about, enumerating a great Variety of Articles not to be imported from England, which they supposed would muster the Manufacturers in England into a national Mob to support their Interests. Among the various prohibited Articles, were Silks, Velvets, Clocks, Watches, Coaches & Chariots; & it was highly diverting, to see the names & marks, to the Subscription, of Porters & Washing Women.
>
> PETER OLIVER,
> a Boston conservative, ridiculing the nonimportation movement
> and the kinds of people who participated in it

proved the Massachusetts petition did so now—and were then dissolved. In response, many legislatures met on their own, as extralegal bodies.

Not only did legislators assert their own authority, but ordinary people did so as well. In each colony, the radicals who called themselves Sons of Liberty organized a nonimportation movement using both coercion and patriotic appeal. Women were actively recruited into the movement, both to encourage household manufacture (an economic activity redefined as a political one) and to refuse British imports. In 1769 women in little Middletown, Massachusetts, wove 20,522 yards of cloth, and throughout the colonies women signed the nonimportation agreements. This politicization of ordinary people horrified conservative British observers. Although there were pockets of defiance, the movement succeeded in cutting imports dramatically. By the time that the Townshend Duties were repealed in 1770, Britain had collected only £21,000 and lost £786,000 in trade.

A Revolution in the Empire

The resistance to the Townshend Duties established a pattern that would be repeated again and again in the years before the Revolution. Each attempt to enforce the empire met with organized colonial opposition, to which the British government responded with a punitive measure. Ostensibly economic regulations such as the Sugar Act, the Townshend Duties, and the subsequent Tea Act, when rejected by the colonies, led to clearly political responses from Britain. Economics and politics became inseparable, as two visions of the empire came into conflict. Britain saw the colonies as a small but integral part of a large empire held together by an increasingly centralized and powerful government. The goal of the empire was to enhance its collective wealth and power, albeit under a system of constitutional government. Although they did not reject the notion of a larger empire outright, the colonists increasingly equated representative government with prosperity, not just for the empire as a whole but for its citizens in the colonies as well. Each round of colonial protest mobilized a larger segment of the population.

"Massacre" in Boston

Years of conflict with royal officials, combined with a growing population of poor and underemployed, had made Boston the most radical and united spot in the colonies. The political leadership had learned how to win popular favor in their ongoing strife with the governor and those who were loyal to him. The repeated attempts of the British government to enforce its legislation increased pressure on Boston and led finally to revolution.

In an attempt to tighten up the collection of customs duties, the British government, now led by Lord North, decided to make an example of John Hancock, Boston's wealthiest merchant and not yet a confirmed radical. In June 1768, customs commissioners seized Hancock's sloop, the *Liberty*, on a technical violation of the Sugar Act and threatened fines totaling £54,000 (most of which would go to the governor and the informer). All charges were dropped, however, after a riot of 2,000 "sturdy boys and men" sent the customs officials once again fleeing to Castle William for protection. Now Hancock was a radical.

After the *Liberty* riot, Governor Bernard called for troops to support the customs commissioners. Rather than restoring order, the arrival of the troops led to further conflict and a year and a half of tension. The Boston Massacre grew out of these tensions.

What angry colonists called a "massacre" was the culmination of months of scuffling between young men and adolescents and soldiers, perhaps inevitable in a town with so many men competing for work. On March 5, 1770, a fracas between a young apprentice and an army officer escalated as a crowd surrounded the officer, insulting him and pelting him with snowballs. Someone shouted, "Fire!" and the crowd grew. Seven soldiers came to rescue their terrified colleague, and they too were hit

British Landing, 1768 This engraving by Paul Revere depicts the landing of British troops at Boston, on October 1, 1768.

AMERICAN LANDSCAPE

>> Occupied Boston

For a year and a half, Boston was an occupied city. British troops began arriving in October 1768. They were supposed to maintain order and enforce customs regulations in a town thought dangerously out of control.

Republicanism, however, warned that tyrants used standing armies to deprive the people of their liberties. Hence the appearance of British warships and the disembarking of 1,700 soldiers in full "battle array" only increased Bostonians' anxiety. It was, however, the daily interactions between soldiers and locals that demonstrated why occupying armies so often antagonize just the people they are supposed to calm.

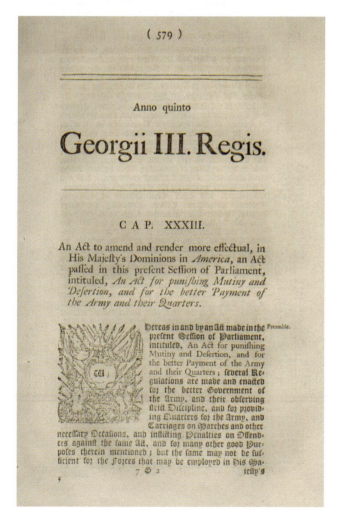

The immediate problem was where to lodge the troops. The Quartering Act required the town to provide housing, but Bostonians refused. Governor Bernard sent the soldiers to an old manufactory that housed the poor. The inhabitants refused to move. The army began renting lodgings wherever it could throughout the city. With the troops scattered, it was impossible for their officers to control them. Within two weeks, 70 soldiers had deserted. Policing civilians, especially your own countrymen and countrywomen, was not an attractive assignment. In order to prevent further desertions, an armed sentry was posted at the only land connection between Boston and the mainland, making Bostonians feel as if they were prisoners in their own city. The army executed one young deserter in full public view. Such harsh punishment shocked the Bostonians.

In a city as small as Boston, filled with so many young soldiers, conflict between citizens and soldiers was almost inevitable. Liquor was cheap, and off-duty soldiers regularly became drunk and offensive. Prostitution increased, and inebriated soldiers assaulted local women. Because sentries could not distinguish between civilians and deserters in civilian clothing, all citizens had to be prepared to stop and identify themselves at the point of a bayonet. Moonlighting soldiers were also willing to work cheaper than Bostonians.

Some officers tried to keep soldiers under control, but there was no political mechanism for containing conflict. Patriots controlled the local justice system and used it to harass misbehaving soldiers. Any sentry who provoked a civilian could find himself before a patriotic magistrate, who made him post a huge bond, no matter how flimsy the charges. Yet even when the charges were truly serious, the attorney general—loyal to the Crown—would not prosecute. Without effective justice, gangs began to take the law into their own hands.

One of the confrontations was caused by John Mein, the publisher of a Boston newspaper. He printed the names of local merchants, some of them Sons of Liberty, who were violating the nonimportation agreements. Cynically, he wanted to demonstrate "that their Patriotism was founded on Self Interest and Malice." When patriots beat up two men who had the misfortune of resembling him, Mein appealed to Acting Governor

Continued

Thomas Hutchinson for protection. Hutchinson said there was nothing he could do until a crime had actually been committed. Mein began carrying a pistol.

On October 28, 1769, a band of patriots fell upon Mein and his partner, throwing bricks at him and shouting, "Knock him down! Kill him!" The two men took refuge with soldiers in a small guardhouse that was soon surrounded by a mob of 200. When the partner's gun went off accidentally, the patriots assumed that Mein had taken the shot. Sam Adams got a friendly magistrate to issue a warrant for Mein's arrest for firing at citizens who were "lawfully and peacefully assembled together."

Certain he would be killed if taken into custody, Mein sent a desperate appeal to Hutchinson. By now the mob had grown to more than 1,000. Hutchinson knew, however, that if he used the army to rescue Mein, it would only "have set the whole province in a flame, and maybe spread farther." So Mein stayed in the guardhouse until he could be smuggled onto a ship leaving Boston.

The army that had come to Boston to maintain order learned that it, like many an army of occupation, was almost powerless in the face of a population that resisted its rule.

with snowballs and taunts of "Kill them." When one was knocked down, he screamed, "Damn you, fire!" and the soldiers fired on the crowd. Eleven men were wounded, and five were killed. One victim was Crispus Attucks, a 47-year-old free black sailor. The soldiers were later tried, but the only two convicted were later pardoned. The British withdrew their troops from Boston.

As long as the British were willing to back down, more serious conflicts could be avoided. The Boston Massacre was followed by a three-year period of peace. The Townshend Duties had been repealed—except the one on tea, which the colonists could not manufacture themselves—and the nonimportation movement had collapsed. Colonial trade resumed its previous pace, and in 1772, imports from England and Scotland doubled. Colonists were not prepared to deny themselves consumer goods for long. The Quartering Act had expired, and the Currency Act was repealed. As long as Britain allowed the colonists to trade relatively unimpeded, permitted them to govern themselves, and kept the army out of their cities, all could be, if not forgotten, at least silenced.

The Empire Comes Apart

Although the British government was controlled by conservatives who believed the colonists would eventually need to acknowledge Parliament's supremacy, the move that led to revolution was more accidental than calculated. The North American colonies were only part of Britain's empire. There were powerful British interests in India, where the British East India Company was on the verge of bankruptcy. Parliament decided to bail out the company, both to rescue its empire in India and to help out influential stockholders. The duty for importing tea into Britain—but not America—was canceled, and Parliament allowed the company to sell directly to Americans through a small number of agents. As a result, the price of tea would drop below that of smuggled Dutch tea. Also, only five men in Massachusetts would be allowed to sell British tea—relatives and friends of the despised Governor Hutchinson. Agents in the other colonies were also well-connected loyalists.

Radicals faced a real challenge, for they realized that once the cheap tea was available, colonists would be unable to resist it. In each port city, activists warned that the

Tea Act (1773) was a trick to con colonists into accepting the principle of taxation without representation. In Philadelphia, a mass meeting pronounced anyone who imported the tea "an enemy to his country."

As might be expected, the most spirited resistance came in Boston, where Hutchinson decided the tea would be unloaded and sold—and the duty paid. Sam Adams led extralegal town meetings attended by 5,000 people each (almost one-third of the population of Boston) to pressure Hutchinson to turn the ships away. When Hutchinson refused, Adams reported back to the town meeting, on December 16, 1773: "This meeting can do nothing more to save the country!" Almost as if it were a prearranged signal, the crowd let out a whoop and poured out of the meetinghouse for the wharf. There, about 50 men, their faces darkened and their bodies draped in Indian blankets, boarded three tea-bearing ships, escorted the customs officials ashore, and opened and dumped 340 chests of tea into Boston Harbor: 90,000 pounds, worth £9,000. Perhaps as many as 8,000 Bostonians observed the "tea party." John Adams, never much for riots, was in awe. "There is," he said, "a Dignity, a Majesty, a Sublimity in this last Effort of the Patriots that I greatly admire."

The British government saw only defiance of the law and wanton destruction of property. Parliament passed five bills in the spring of 1774 to punish Boston and Massachusetts. First, the Boston Port Bill closed the port to all trade until the East India Company was repaid for the dumped tea. Second, the Massachusetts Government Act changed the Charter of 1691. The Council (upper house) would now be appointed by the king, rather than elected by the House; town meetings were forbidden without

Boston Tea Party Here colonists dressed as Mohawk Indians dump crates of tea into Boston Harbor.

approval of the governor; the governor would appoint all the provincial judges and sheriffs; and the sheriffs would select juries, who had until then been elected by the voters. Third, the Administration of Justice Act empowered the governor to send to Britain or another colony for trial any official or soldier accused of a capital crime who appeared unlikely to get a fair trial in Massachusetts. Fourth, a new Quartering Act permitted the quartering of troops in private homes. Fifth was the Quebec Act. It assigned to Québec the Ohio River region, which the colonists coveted. In Québec, there was to be no representative government, civil cases would be tried without juries, and the Roman Catholic religion would be tolerated. Together, these acts were known in Britain as the Coercive Acts and in the colonies as the Intolerable Acts (see Table 6–1).

At the same time, General Thomas Gage was appointed governor of Massachusetts and authorized to bring as many troops to Boston as he needed. Boston soon became an armed camp. The Port Act was easily enforced as Gage deployed troops to close the ports of Boston and Charlestown. The Government Act was another matter. Citizens summoned by the sheriff simply refused to serve on juries, and some judges even refused to preside. When Gage called for an election to the legislature, only some towns elected delegates, and a shadow "Massachusetts Provincial Congress" met in Concord in October 1774. The citizens of Massachusetts had taken government into their own hands.

The British had thought that Massachusetts could be isolated, but they underestimated the colonists' attachment to their liberties. The threat to representative government presented by the Intolerable Acts was so clear that the other colonies soon rallied around Massachusetts. In June 1774, the Virginia Burgesses sent out a letter suggesting a meeting of all the colonies. At about the same time, Massachusetts had issued a similar call for a meeting in Philadelphia. These two most radical colonies spurred the others to meet in early September.

The First Continental Congress

Every colony except Georgia sent delegates to the First Continental Congress, which convened on September 5, 1774. Only a few of the delegates had ever met any of their counterparts from the other colonies, so provincial were the colonies. For seven weeks these strangers met in formal sessions and social occasions. Together they laid the foundation for the first national government.

With Massachusetts and Virginia almost ready to take up arms, and the middle colonies favoring conciliation, the greatest challenge was how to achieve unity. Since Massachusetts needed the support of the other colonies, it was ready to abandon any discussion of offensive measures against the British. In return, the Congress ratified the Suffolk Resolves, a set of Massachusetts resolutions that recommended passive resistance to the Intolerable Acts.

The delegates could now consider national action. Hoping to exert economic pressure on Britain, Congress issued a call for a boycott of all imports and exports between the colonies, Britain, and the West Indies. Then the delegates adopted a Declaration of Rights that for the first time expressed as the collective determination of every colony (except Georgia) what had become standard constitutional arguments. The colonists were entitled to all the "rights, liberties, and immunities of free and natural-born subjects" of England. Parliament could regulate trade for the colonies only by the "consent" of the colonies. Parliament could neither tax nor legislate for the colonies. Again

Table 6-1 Major Events Leading to the Revolutionary War, 1763–1774

1763	Proclamation of 1763	Confines colonists to the east of an imaginary line running down the spine of the Allegheny Mountains.
1764	Sugar Act	Drops duty on molasses to 3 cents/gallon, but institutes procedures to make sure it is collected, such as trial at Admiralty Court (closest is in Nova Scotia), where burden of proof is on defendant and verdict is rendered by judge rather than jury.
1764	Currency Act	Forbids issuing of any colonial currency.
1765	Stamp Act	Places a tax on 15 classes of documents, including newspapers and legal documents; clear objective is to raise revenue.
1765	Quartering Act	Requires colonies to provide housing in public buildings and certain provisions for troops.
1766	Declaratory Act	Repeals Stamp Act, but insists that Parliament retains the right to legislate for the colonies "in all cases whatsoever."
1767	Townshend Revenue Act	Places import duty on lead, paint, glass, paper, and tea; objective is to raise money from the colonies.
1770	Boston Massacre	Several citizens killed by British soldiers whom they had pelted with snowballs; grew out of tensions caused by quartering of four army regiments in Boston to enforce customs regulations.
1773	Tea Act	After Townshend Duties on all items other than tea are removed, British East India Company is given a monopoly on the sale of tea, enabling it to drop price—and cut out middlemen.
1773	Boston Tea Party	To protest Tea Act, Bostonians dump 90,000 pounds of tea into Boston Harbor.
1774	Intolerable Acts	To punish Massachusetts in general and Boston in particular for the "Tea Party":
		1. Port of Boston closed until East India Company repaid for dumped tea.
		2. King to appoint Massachusetts's Council; town meetings to require written permission of governor; governor will appoint judges and sheriffs, and sheriffs will now select juries.
		3. Governor can send officials and soldiers accused of capital crimes out of Massachusetts for their trials.
		4. Troops may be quartered in private homes.
1774	Quebec Act	Gives Ohio River valley to Québec; Britain allows Québec to be governed by French tradition and tolerates Catholic religion there.
1774	First Continental Congress	Representatives of 12 colonies meet in Philadelphia and call for a boycott of trade with Britain, adopt a Declaration of Rights, and agree to meet again in a year.

and again, the Declaration reiterated the twin principles on which resistance to imperial legislation had been based: consent and the rule of law.

Finally, Congress agreed to reconvene in half a year, on March 10, 1775, unless the Intolerable Acts were repealed. The delegates had achieved consensus on the principles that would shortly form the basis for a new and independent national government.

Conclusion

Within a decade, the British Empire had come apart on its westernmost edge. The stage had been set decades earlier when Britain unintentionally allowed the colonies to develop more self-government and personal freedom than in Britain itself, without requiring them to pay a proportionate share of the costs of empire. As a result, the colonies created their own vision, one that linked democratic government and prosperity. Once Britain decided to knit the colonies more tightly into the empire and impose on them the controls of the centralized state, conflict was inevitable. At the same time, both Britons and Americans revered the same constitution, whose values and protections Americans invoked in their protests. That those protests would end in revolution was by no means a foregone conclusion. Revolution would require two key elements: Britain's unwillingness to compromise on issues of governance, and the ability of colonial radicals to convince moderates that there was no other way. By the end of 1774 that point had almost been reached.

Who, What

Sam Adams   206

Thomas Hutchinson   203

Memeskia   185

William Pitt   193

George Washington   187

Albany Plan of Union   187

Constitutionalism   201

Pontiac's Rebellion   196

Proclamation of 1763   197

Republicanism   205

>> TIME LINE

▼1715–1716
Yamasee War

▼1717
French build Fort Toulouse

▼1718
French build New Orleans

▼1720
French build Louisbourg and Fort Niagara

▼1731
French build Fort St. Frédéric

▼1733
Molasses Act

▼1739–1744
War of Jenkins's Ear

▼1741
Attack upon Cartagena fails

▼1744–1748
King George's War

▼1748
Village of Pickawillany established by Memeskia and his band of Miamis

▼1749
French military expedition fails to win back dissident Indians in Ohio Valley

▼1752
Tanacharison cedes huge chunk of Ohio Valley to Virginia

▼1753
French build small forts near forks of Ohio River

▼1754
Albany Plan of Union

▼1754–1763
French and Indian War

▼1755
Braddock's forces defeated

▼1757
British defeated at Fort William Henry, survivors massacred
William Pitt accedes to power in Britain

Review Questions

1. What were the reasons for the conflicts among the British, French, Spanish, and the various Indian tribes on the North American continent?

2. How and why did Britain attempt to reorganize its North American colonial empire?

3. Why did the colonies resist Britain's attempts to reorganize its North American colonial empire?

Critical-Thinking Questions

1. For much of the eighteenth century, Britain and France were at war, involving the American colonies. How did this warfare affect the colonies and their people?

2. What was the series of events that brought Britain and the colonies to the brink of war by 1774? To what extent were they the product of poor leadership? Differing theories of government? Different social experiences?

3. At what point did the American Revolution become unavoidable? Until that point, how might it have been avoided?

For further review materials and resource information, please visit www.oup.com/us/ofthepeople

▼**1758**
Treaty of Easton secures neutrality of Ohio Valley tribes in return for territory west of Alleghenies

▼**1759**
British seize Québec

▼**1763**
Treaty of Paris, ending French and Indian War, signed
Pontiac's Rebellion
Proclamation of 1763
Parliament increases size of peacetime army to 20 regiments

▼**1764**
Sugar Act
Currency Act

▼**1765**
Stamp Act
Quartering Act
Stamp Act Congress

▼**1766**
Declaratory Act

▼**1767**
Townshend Revenue Act

▼**1768**
Lord Hillsborough's circular letter
John Hancock's sloop *Liberty* seized
Treaty of Fort Stanwix

▼**1770**
Boston Massacre

▼**1773**
Tea Act
Boston Tea Party

▼**1774**
Intolerable Acts (known as Coercive Acts in Britain)
Lord Dunmore's War

▼**1775**
First Continental Congress

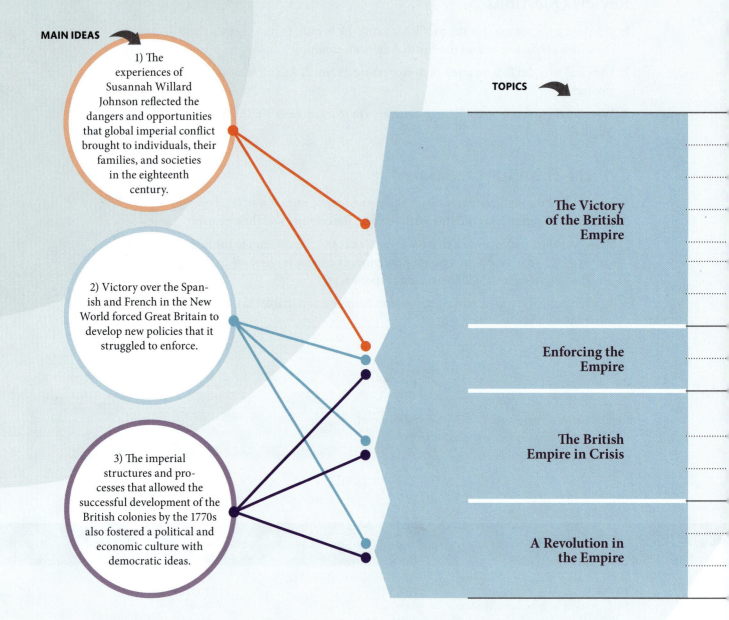

MAIN IDEAS

1) The experiences of Susannah Willard Johnson reflected the dangers and opportunities that global imperial conflict brought to individuals, their families, and societies in the eighteenth century.

2) Victory over the Spanish and French in the New World forced Great Britain to develop new policies that it struggled to enforce.

3) The imperial structures and processes that allowed the successful development of the British colonies by the 1770s also fostered a political and economic culture with democratic ideas.

TOPICS

The Victory of the British Empire

Enforcing the Empire

The British Empire in Crisis

A Revolution in the Empire

CHAPTER 6
CONFLICT IN THE EMPIRE

1713–1774

EVENTS

New War, Old Pattern Another round of inconclusive warfare broke out between England and Spain, followed by inconclusive war between England and France.

The Local Impact of Global War Warfare had a significant economic and political impact in British North America.

The French Empire Crumbles from Within French policy changes caused Indian tribes to seek trade advantages from the British and French both, upsetting the balance of power.

The Virginians Ignite a War A scramble by French and Virginians to defend claims in the Ohio River valley led to war.

From Local to Imperial War The French dominated the early fighting against the British.

Problems with British-Colonial Cooperation Differing expectations about their roles in the war led to poor cooperation among the British and colonials.

The British Gain the Advantage A change in British government led to a renewed war effort and victory over the French.

Pontiac's Rebellion and Its Aftermath British failure to secure Indian alliances led to rebellion and restrictions on colonial expansion.

Paying for the Empire: Sugar and Stamps Parliament enforced one tax and created another to make the colonies help pay for the growing imperial budget.

An Argument About Rights and Obligations Colonists debated whether Parliament had the right to impose new restrictions and taxes within the framework of constitutionalism.

The Imperial Crisis in Local Context Colonists united across social classes to defend their self-perceived rights.

Contesting the Townshend Duties Wary of British tyranny, colonial legislatures protested the Townshend Duties.

"Massacre" in Boston Rising tensions between British troops and Boston colonists resulted in a violent clash.

The Empire Comes Apart After Boston colonists rebelled against the Tea Act, Parliament imposed harsh measures as punishment.

The First Continental Congress Delegates from the colonies met in Philadelphia to consider unified action against the British.

The War Begins

By the end of 1774, conflict between the colonists and Britain seemed unavoidable. The British government, under the leadership of Lord North and King George III, seemed unwilling to make significant concessions. In the colonies, the radical opponents of British rule dominated politics. Despite these signs, no one anticipated eight years of warfare that would make the colonies a single nation under a centralized government.

> Society is in every state a blessing, but government even in its best state is but a necessary evil; in its worst state an intolerable one. . . . Government, like dress, is the badge of lost innocence; the palaces of kings are built on the ruins of the bowers of paradise.
>
> THOMAS PAINE,
> *Common Sense*

The First Battles

Before he became governor of Massachusetts in 1774, General Thomas Gage had a long record of advocating force. He had called for the stationing of troops in Boston in 1768, leading to the Boston Massacre. Even before the Boston Tea Party, he recommended limiting democratic government in Massachusetts. Because he believed that Boston merchants and lawyers were instigating dissent among the poor, he wanted to isolate the colonial Revolutionary elite, by force if necessary.

In the spring of 1775, Gage received orders from England to act decisively against the colonists. He planned to seize the colonists' military supplies, stored at Concord, but alert Bostonians tipped off the patriot leaders once British troops began to march. On the night of April 18, the silversmith Paul Revere and the tanner William Dawes slipped out of Boston on horseback to carry the message that British troops were on the move. Militiamen from several towns began to gather.

The British soldiers arrived at Lexington at daybreak and ordered the militia to surrender, which they refused to do. Exactly what happened next remains unclear. The colonists swore that British soldiers opened fire, saying, "Ye villans [*sic*], ye Rebels, disperse; Damn you, disperse." The British major insisted that the first shot came from behind a tree. British soldiers lost control and fired, and the colonists returned fire. Eight Americans were killed, most while attempting to flee.

At the same time, the Concord militia had assembled and then pulled back about a mile, allowing the British to enter an almost-deserted town. Fighting broke out when a fire the British troops had set to the Concord liberty pole spread to the courthouse. To protect their town, the militia began marching on the British, who fired when the Americans drew near. In the exchange, three British soldiers were killed and several

OUTLINE

The War Begins
The First Battles
Congress Takes the Lead
Military Ardor

DEBATING HISTORY:
   Causes of the American Revolution
Declaring Independence
Creating a National Government
Creating State Governments

Winning the Revolution
Competing Strategies
The British on the Offensive: 1776

AMERICA AND THE WORLD:
   Mercenaries in Global Perspective
A Slow War: 1777–1781
Securing a Place in the World

AMERICAN LANDSCAPE:
   The South Carolina Backcountry

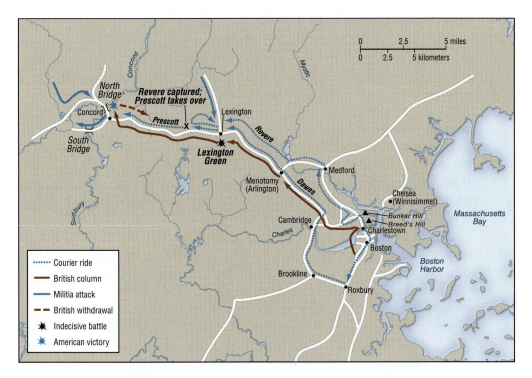

Map 7–1 Battles of Lexington, Concord, and Breed's Hill This map shows the sites of the first battles of the Revolution in and around Boston, along with the routes taken by Paul Revere and William Dawes to warn the colonists of the approach of British troops.

more injured. The British were forced back across the bridge. The entire battle took two or three minutes (see Map 7–1).

Once news of the fighting at Lexington and Concord spread, militias converged on Boston to evict Gage and his troops. More than 20,000 men soon were encamped in Boston. Gage declared that all the inhabitants of Massachusetts who bore arms were rebels and traitors, although he was willing to pardon everyone but John Hancock and Sam Adams, two leaders of the defiant Provincial Congress. Rather than backing down, the colonists fortified Breed's Hill (next to the more famous Bunker Hill) in Charlestown, overlooking Boston. On June 17, Gage sent 2,400 soldiers to take the hill. The cost was enormous: 1,000 soldiers and 92 officers killed or wounded (compared with 370 casualties among the colonists). The British learned not to make frontal assaults against fortified positions.

The Challenge of the Revolution
The Departure of the Loyalists
The Challenge of the Economy
Contesting the New Economy
Can Women Be Citizens?

PRIMARY SOURCE:
   Abigail to John Adams, "Remember the Ladies"
The Challenge of Slavery

A New Policy in the West
The Indians' Revolution
The End of the Middle Ground
Settling the West

Creating a New National Government
A Crippled Congress
Writing a New Constitution
Ratifying the Constitution: Politics
Ratifying the Constitution: Ideas

Conclusion

Other New Englanders were also taking matters into their own hands. A group under Benedict Arnold, an ambitious New Haven merchant, and Ethan Allen, the leader of the Vermont Green Mountain Boys, seized the crumbling fort at Ticonderoga on Lake Champlain and other small posts. In these heady days early in the Revolution, many colonists thought that this would be a quick and painless war.

Congress Takes the Lead

When the Second Continental Congress convened in Philadelphia on May 10, its greatest challenge was to maintain consensus. The most radical leaders, such as Sam and John Adams from Massachusetts and Richard Henry Lee from Virginia, were ready for war. However, many leaders, especially in the middle colonies, still hoped that war could be avoided.

Because Congress was an extralegal body, the elected colonial assemblies might easily have rejected its authority. But one after another, they transferred their allegiance from the British government to Congress. Although some moderates hoped for a negotiated settlement with Britain, they were caught between two sides that both anticipated war. The British refused even to acknowledge the petition sent by the First Continental Congress. That refusal, combined with Gage's attack on Breed's Hill, convinced the moderates that military preparations were necessary. Congress voted to create a Continental army and put it under the leadership of Virginia's George Washington. Not only was Washington experienced in military matters and widely respected, but his selection also helped solidify the alliance between New England and the South. Congress decided to attack Canada in the hope that a significant defeat would force the British to accede to American demands. To justify all of these actions, Congress also adopted the Declaration of the Causes and Necessity of Taking Up Arms, a rousing indictment of British "despotism," "perfidy," and "cruel aggression" drafted by Virginia's Thomas Jefferson.

At the same time, to preserve unity with the moderates, the radicals agreed to petition the king one more time. Without making any concessions, the Olive Branch Petition appealed to George's "magnanimity and benevolence." Nevertheless, on August 23, 1775, the king declared the colonists to be in "an open and avowed Rebellion." Although Congress had neither declared war nor asserted independence, the American Revolution had begun.

Military Ardor

Military ardor in the colonies reached its high point between the fall of 1775 and the spring of 1776. Colonists expected war, and they thought it would be quick and glorious. As a consequence, the first enlistments were for a term of only a year. Even if the war was not over by then, Revolutionaries were fearful of creating a permanent standing army.

In the summer of 1775, the Continental army marched on Canada. Victory would have either forced the British to the bargaining table or at least protected New York and New England from assault from the north. The contingent under General Benedict Arnold's command sailed from Newburyport, Massachusetts, to Maine and then marched 350 miles to Québec. In November, after a grueling march, Arnold's forces prepared to assault Québec, joined by troops under General Richard Montgomery, who had just seized Montréal. The battle was a disaster. Half of the 900 Continental soldiers were killed, captured, or wounded, including Montgomery. By the time the

DEBATING HISTORY
....

>> Causes of the American Revolution

In the wake of Anglo-French imperial wars in 1763, Britain attempted to integrate its colonies more closely into the colonial system through a series of parliamentary acts. The colonists reacted to these developments by putting forth their own ideas about the role of government. Each new effort by Britain to enforce the new order—most notoriously, the Stamp Act of 1765—met concerted resistance from the colonists. As the constitutional crisis unfolded, two visions of the empire emerged, and by 1776, the colonies moved to declare their independence. Historians have disagreed about the primary causes of the American Revolution. Bernard Bailyn sees the roots of the Revolution primarily in the worldview of the American colonists, whereas Woody Holton sees material interests and class tensions as paramount in the coming of the imperial crisis.

BERNARD BAILYN, *The Ideological Origins of the American Revolution* (Cambridge, MA: Belknap Press of Harvard University Press, 1967), pp. 94–95, 22–23.

The intellectual history of the years of crisis from 1763 to 1776 is the story of the clarification and consolidation under the pressure of events of a view of the world and of America's place in it only partially seen before. Elements of this picture had long been present in the colonies—some dated from as far back as the settlements themselves—but they had existed in balance, as it were, with other, conflicting views. Expressed mainly on occasions of controversy, they had appeared most often as partisan arguments, without unique appeal, status, or claim to legitimacy. Then, in the intense political heat of the decade after 1763, these long popular, though hitherto inconclusive ideas about the world and American's place in it were fused into a comprehensive view, unique in its moral and intellectual appeal. It is the development of this view to the point of overwhelming persuasiveness to the majority of American leaders and the meaning this view gave to the events of the time, and not simply an accumulation of grievances, that explains the origins of the American Revolution. For this peculiar configuration of ideas constituted in effect an intellectual switchboard wired so that certain combinations of events would activate a distinct set of signals—danger signals, indicating hidden impulses and the likely trajectory of events impelled by them. Well before 1776 the signals registered in this switchboard led to a single, unmistakable conclusion—a conclusion that had long been feared and to which there could be only one rational response.

WOODY HOLTON, *Forced Founders: Indians, Debtors, Slaves and the Making of the American Revolution in Virginia* (Chapel Hill: University of North Carolina Press, 1999), pp. xvii–xviii, xxi.

Continued

From 1763 to 1776, Indians, merchants, slaves, and debtors helped propel free Virginians into the Independence movement in three distinct ways. First, the free Virginians' efforts to influence imperial policy were contested by Native Americans, British merchants, and enslaved Virginians. The elimination of the government as an instrument or ally of merchants, Indians, and slaves was one reason for white Virginians to rebel against Britain. Second, free Virginians were attracted to the most important resistance strategy of the prewar period—the commercial boycott against Britain—because it seemed likely not only to impel Parliament to repeal laws considered oppressive by white Americans but also to reduce the Virginians' debts to British merchants. Third, the thoroughgoing boycott adopted by the First Continental Congress in October 1774 transformed Virginia's society and economy in unexpected ways. It presented opportunities to enslaved Virginians and put extraordinary pressure upon the colony's small farmers. In responding to those opportunities and pressures, slaves and farmers challenged the authority of the provincial gentry. Those challenges indirectly helped induce gentlemen to turn the protests of 1774 into the Independence movement of 1776. . . . [In this way,] nonelites powerfully influenced Revolutionary politics.

Questions

1. Which of these two interpretations do you find more convincing? Why?

2. Are these two interpretations incompatible? If not, how might they be reconciled?

expedition retreated to New York in the spring, 5,000 men had been lost. The suffering was extraordinary, but it only increased American resolve.

Declaring Independence

By the beginning of 1776, moderates in Congress who still hoped for a peaceful settlement found themselves squeezed from both directions. The king and Parliament were unyielding, and popular opinion increasingly favored independence. Word arrived from Britain that all American commerce was to be cut off and that the British navy would seize American ships and their cargoes. Britain also began hiring German mercenaries known as Hessians, and Virginia's Governor Dunmore shelled Norfolk from warships. He had already offered freedom to any slaves who would fight for the British. Every prediction the radicals had made seemed to be coming true.

Public opinion also pushed Congress toward a declaration of independence. In January 1776, Thomas Paine, an expatriate English radical in Philadelphia, electrified the public with his pamphlet *Common Sense*, which sold 75,000 copies in a short time. In it, Paine liberated Americans from their ties to the British past so that they could start their government fresh. The idea of a balanced constitution that combined king, nobles, and common people in one government was "farcical," and monarchy was "exceedingly ridiculous." Paine had a message for Congress, too: "The period of debate is closed."

Most members of Congress either desired a declaration of independence or thought it inevitable. Most delegates also agreed that unanimity was more important than speed, so they waited through the spring of 1776 as, one by one, the state delegations received instructions in favor of independence. Then, under instructions from his colony, on June 7, 1776, Virginia's Richard Henry Lee asked Congress to vote on the resolution that "these United Colonies are, and of right ought to be, free and independent States." A committee of five, including Thomas Jefferson, Benjamin Franklin, and John Adams, was appointed to draft a declaration of independence. Adams asked Jefferson, a 33-year-old Virginia radical who could write stirring prose, to create the first draft. For four days, the delegates debated the draft and took preliminary votes. A clause that accused King George of forcing African slaves on the colonies was deleted. On July 2, the delegates voted unanimously to declare independence.

Many years later Jefferson insisted that there was nothing original about the Declaration of Independence, and he was not entirely wrong. The long list of accusations against King George, which formed the bulk of the Declaration, contained little that was new, and even some of the stirring words in the preamble had been used by the radicals time and again. Moreover, the Revolutionaries borrowed ideas from a number of British and European sources, including constitutionalism, republicanism, Enlightenment thought (see Chapter 6), and millennial Christian thought. The millennial strain in evangelical Protestantism suggested that the 1,000-year reign of Christ might begin soon in America if Americans would repent their sins, seek a spiritual rebirth, and defend their liberties.

However, in a different sense the Declaration of Independence was truly original. Jefferson's achievement was to reformulate familiar principles in a way that made them simple, clear, and applicable to the American situation.

The most important of these principles was human equality, that all people were born with certain fundamental rights. Second, and closely related, was the belief in a universal, common human nature. If all people were the same and had the same

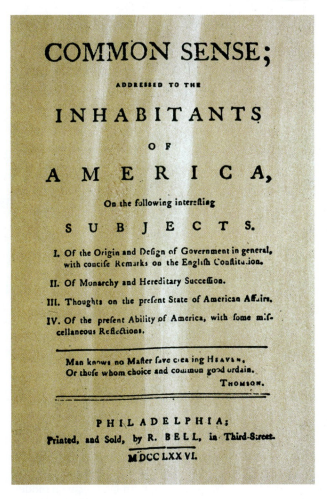

Cover of *Common Sense* Thomas Paine's *Common Sense* sold more than 75,000 copies in just a few weeks.

rights, then the purpose of government was to protect those rights. Just as people created government to protect their rights, they could abolish any government that became despotic. Third, government should represent the people.

It was many years, however, before the radical implications of the Declaration became fully evident to the American people. At the moment, more attention was focused on immediate political struggles. The Revolution succeeded because moderates and radicals were able to create effective alliances, reversing the pre-Revolutionary trend toward class and political conflict. To remain leaders of the opposition to Britain, elite Revolutionaries such as John Hancock continually appealed to poorer, more radical people and looked out for these people's interests, as well as their own. The result was a more moderate revolution than it might otherwise have been and a revolution that succeeded. Just as military fervor reached its high point in the spring of 1776, so did political unity, even if there were ongoing struggles over the meaning of the Revolution.

Creating a National Government

Although treated as if it were a legitimate national government, Congress actually had no more authority over the states than the states were willing to give it, and it had none whatsoever over the people. At the same time that Richard Henry Lee presented

Destruction of Statue of King George. Here, a small crowd in New York City pulls down the statue of King George on July 9, 1776, a few days after independence had been declared.

Congress with his proposal for independence, he also suggested that Congress create a permanent national government, a confederation of the states with a written constitution. John Dickinson, a moderate, was assigned to draft the Articles of Confederation. He sketched out a weak central government with the authority to make treaties, carry out military and foreign affairs, request the states to pay its expenses, and very little else. There was no chief executive, only a Congress in which each state would have one vote. Term limits were imposed on representatives. Any act of Congress would require 9 votes (of 13), and the Articles would not go into effect until all 13 states had approved them.

With state jealousies strong, it took Congress more than a year to revise and accept a watered-down version of the Articles of Confederation. Not until March 1781, near the end of the war, did the final state ratify the Articles of Confederation, putting them into effect. By then, the weaknesses in a national government with no means of enforcing its regulations were becoming evident.

Creating State Governments

In 1776, all attention was focused on state governments, where the new ideas about liberty, equality, and government were put into practice. Americans were exhilarated by the prospect of creating their own governments. Between 1775 and 1780, each of the 13 states adopted a new written constitution.

Because the Revolutionaries feared concentrations of power, the powers of governors in the new states were sharply limited. In Pennsylvania and Georgia, the position of governor was abolished and replaced with a council. Governors were given term limits or required to run for reelection every year. Because royal governors had appointed cronies to powerful positions, the new governors also were stripped of their power of appointment.

The new state constitutions made the legislatures more democratic. The number of representatives was doubled in South Carolina and New Hampshire and more than tripled in Massachusetts. Many constitutions also imposed either term limits or frequent elections for representatives. As the property qualifications for holding office were lowered, poorer men sat in legislatures alongside richer ones. The admission of more ordinary men into government was one of the greatest changes brought about by the Revolution. Now the elite had to learn to share power and to win the votes of men they had once scorned.

Winning the Revolution

The British entered the war with clear advantages in population, wealth, and power, but with a flawed premise about how to win the war. Britain, arguably the world's most powerful nation, had the mistaken idea that the colonists could be defeated by a swift and effective use of force. It also assumed that Americans loyal to the Crown would support British troops, but they alienated Americans with their actions. Probably no more than one-fifth of the population remained loyal to Britain, but many more shifted loyalties depending on local circumstances. The war ultimately became a struggle for the support of this unpoliticized population.

> We are being left like sheep among wolves, were obliged to give up to them our Arms and take purtection. But no sooner we had yielded to them but [they] set to Rob us taking all our livings, horses, Cows, Sheep, Clothing, of all Sorts, money, pewter, tins, knives, in fine Everything that sooted them. Untill we were Stript Naked.
>
> GEORGE PARK,
> a resident of the South Carolina upcountry, complaining about the depredations of the British army

Competing Strategies

British political objectives shifted during the war. The first goal, based on the belief that resistance was being led by a handful of radical New Englanders, was to punish and isolate Boston. This was the strategy of 1774 and 1775, with the Intolerable Acts and the battles of Lexington, Concord, and Breed's Hill. It failed miserably, due to the faulty assumption that well-trained British regulars were necessarily superior to untrained colonial rustics. However, if the British had a misplaced faith in their invincibility, the Americans had a misplaced faith in their moral superiority; but neither faith could guarantee victory. The result was a long war, as both sides tried to avoid decisive engagements that might prove fatal.

For seven years, the two armies chased each other across the Eastern Seaboard. Neither side had huge armies. Moreover, with no consensus in Britain about the strategic or economic value of the colonies, there was always opposition to the war and a limit to the investment that the British were prepared to make in it. Consequently, every battle presented a significant risk that troops who were lost could not be replaced.

Manpower was also a serious problem for the Americans. It was difficult to recruit enough soldiers into the Continental army. After a defeat in battle or near the end of the year when terms of enlistment were up, men left the army to return home. Any defeat demoralized the public, depressing enlistments. Hence there was limited incentive for the army to risk all in battle.

Early in the war, however, both sides hoped for a decisive victory. After the Americans failed in Québec, the British pursued them back to Ticonderoga on Lake

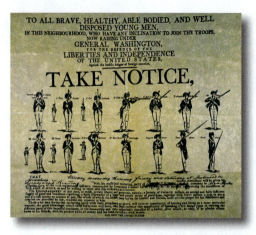

Champlain, where Benedict Arnold's leadership stopped the rout. The war then shifted to southern New York and the middle colonies. Having given up hopes of crushing New England directly, the British planned to isolate the region and defeat the Continental army under George Washington's leadership.

The British also sought to seize all the major American cities, and they did capture Boston, Newport, New York, Philadelphia, Charleston, and Savannah. The capture of these cities, however, did not bring about an American surrender. With 90 percent of Americans living in the countryside, the seizure of a major city did not strike the hoped-for psychological or economic blow.

The British on the Offensive: 1776

Preparing for an offensive in 1776, the new British commander, General William Howe, assembled a huge force on Staten Island: 32,000 soldiers and 13,000 seamen. Some of these soldiers were actually German mercenaries, the Hessians. Anticipating battle and hoping to protect New York, Washington moved his army south to New York (see Map 7–2). He had about 19,000 soldiers, too few for a pitched battle. Half his troops were in Manhattan while the other half, in Brooklyn Heights, dug in to protect Long Island. The British sneaked up behind the Americans in Brooklyn, inflicting heavy casualties, and on August 27, 1776, Washington pulled his remaining forces back into Manhattan. Had the British pursued rapidly, they probably could have crushed Washington's army, but Howe may have been more concerned with winning a peace than a war. After Washington retreated, Howe invited members of the Continental Congress to meet with him privately on Staten Island. He was unable to recognize American independence, which was what the representatives insisted on, so his peace strategy failed.

Still hoping for peace, Howe began pushing Washington back out of Manhattan. Simultaneously, he offered peace to any colonists in the region who would declare their loyalty, and thousands accepted. On November 16, the British forced the Americans out of Manhattan and pursued them to White Plains and then through New Jersey to New Brunswick. The British almost caught Washington twice in New Jersey, but on December 8 the Americans crossed the Delaware at Trenton, taking every boat with them to prevent pursuit. By Christmas Eve, Washington had only 3,000 soldiers, and General Charles Lee, the commander of the other half of the Continental army, had been captured. As Thomas Paine wrote, "These are the times that try men's souls."

Howe had captured New York and New Jersey and was poised to seize Philadelphia (which fell in September 1777). At the end of 1776, the British were close to achieving their objective. Then, on Christmas night, with morale in his army dangerously low, Washington took it across the ice-clogged Delaware and surprised the British garrison at Trenton at dawn, capturing 1,000 Hessian soldiers. About a week later, Washington evaded a British trap and sneaked behind the lines to capture an outpost at Princeton.

These American successes brought another 1,000 troops into the army. More significant, the British decided to concentrate their troops near New Brunswick, fearing the loss of any more garrisons, which were needed to defend the Loyalists. This strategic decision revealed the weakness in the British position and demonstrated

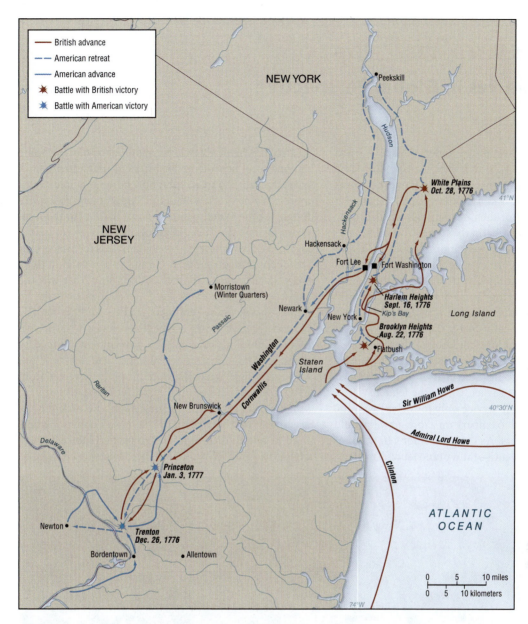

Map 7-2 New York and New Jersey Campaigns, 1776–1777 In the second half of 1776, British troops chased Washington out of New York and across New Jersey. As he would for the remainder of the war, Washington took care never to let the British capture him and his troops, leaving him free to attack at Trenton and Princeton.

why, when victory seemed closest, it was very far away. Without enough troops to overcome the Americans' home advantage, the British needed to ensure that civilians did not aid the Revolutionary War effort. To assure the allegiance of Loyalists, the British had to offer them protection from American reprisals. However, the British were seizing the Americans' goods and property for the war effort. Then, once the garrisons were withdrawn, Loyalists were left alone and vulnerable to the reprisals of the patriots.

The British could control the American countryside only by maintaining troops there, but once the troops were withdrawn, civil warfare would break out. Thus, even

AMERICA AND THE WORLD

>> Mercenaries in Global Perspective

In 1776, the Declaration of Independence warned that King George "is, at this time, transporting large armies of foreign mercenaries to complete the works of death, desolation, and tyranny, already begun." It charged that the use of such mercenaries was "scarcely parallelled in the most barbarous ages, and totally unworthy the head of a civilized nation." In fact, the use of mercenaries was the norm, rather than the exception, in eighteenth-century Europe, with some countries renting and others supplying them. Between one-fifth and two-thirds of the British, French, and Prussian armies were foreigners, typically Swiss, Dutch, and various Germans. Wealthy nations could buy other countries' soldiers, thereby protecting their own citizens' freedom.

The practice of using mercenaries had developed several hundred years earlier. Under the feudal system, a lord could command service only for defensive wars. Any lord who wanted to embark on a foreign war would have to pay for soldiers. As the pace of foreign wars increased in the seventeenth century (and feudalism died),

so also did the practice of hiring foreign soldiers. Some nations soon became major hirers of mercenaries, and others became sources. John Smith, for example, was a mercenary before he joined the Virginia expedition. He fought for the Dutch against Spain and later for the Austrians against the Turks in Hungary.

Unlike these professional soldiers, less fortunate men were conscripted into their country's service only to be shipped off to fight another nation's war. This was the standard practice in the little German principality of Hesse-Cassel, whose renting of soldiers to other nations generated half of the government's revenues in the middle of the eighteenth century. The government claimed to conscript only "masterless servants and loafers," but as Hesse-Cassel grew dependent on the revenue from its mercenaries, it began to reach into peasant families, seizing their servants and younger sons. Because the law exempted from service men who owned homes, parents tried to give all their sons enough property to keep them out of the army. When inheritance laws were changed to

keep parents from dividing their estates, parents began giving their daughters' dowries directly to their sons, sacrificing the girls' prospects for a good match to keep the boys out of the army. In this way, relations between the great nations reached deep into the lives of families.

American colonists rejected the use of mercenaries as "totally unworthy" of a "civilized nation." By the end of the eighteenth century, Enlightenment philosophers had begun to condemn the trade in soldiers—for that is what it was. Under new doctrines of nationalism, men were supposed to fight for patriotism, not for pay, and a nation that hired mercenaries began to seem less than "civilized."

though Washington's victories at Trenton and Princeton were small, they exposed the incapacity of the British to defeat the Revolutionaries unless they settled an army of occupation on the Americans, something they were not prepared to do.

A Slow War: 1777–1781

Washington settled in and enlisted soldiers for a long war. Lacking enough soldiers to confront the British head-on, he mostly led the British on chases across the countryside. Maintaining such an army year after year was expensive, but the Americans were unwilling to be taxed at high rates. Continental soldiers who were from the bottom tier of society suffered grievously; at Jockey Hollow, New Jersey, in the winter of 1779–1780, men roasted their own shoes to eat and even devoured their pet dogs.

In 1777, the British political objective was still the same: to isolate New England by seizing the middle colonies. American troops had the advantage in upstate New York by three to one, however, and they defeated the British under General John Burgoyne at Saratoga, stopping the British advance (see Map 7–3).

The victory at Saratoga convinced the French to enter into a formal alliance, negotiated by Benjamin Franklin, the American envoy. Winning French support was perhaps the major accomplishment of the middle phase of the war: the entry of the French tied down the British in other parts of the world and also brought America more than $8 million in aid.

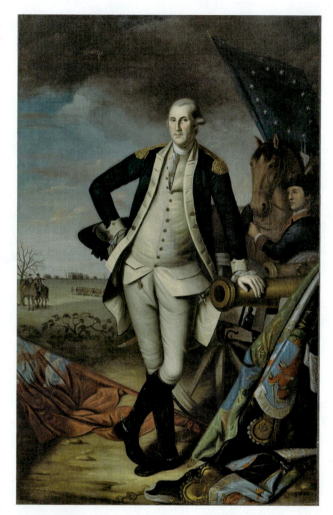

George Washington Washington as he appeared at the Battle of Princeton, in a painting by Charles Willson Peale.

The British had failed to isolate New England, and it proved impossible to pacify the middle colonies. As a result, the focus shifted from the least loyal section of America, New England, to the most loyal area, the South. British war aims shifted, too, in response to political realities at home. Now the war was needed to protect Loyalists from vengeful patriots.

Seeking to capitalize on internal conflicts and to rally southern Loyalists, the British invaded Georgia in 1778 and South Carolina in 1780. After seizing Charleston

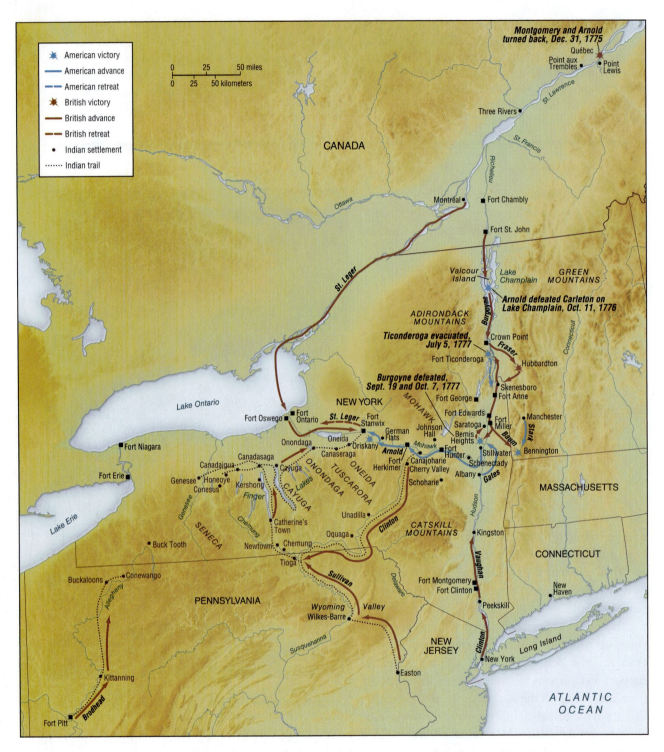

Map 7–3 The Battles for New York The war for New York was waged on two fronts. North of the Hudson River, the Americans failed in their attempt in 1775 to seize Québec, were forced to abandon Fort Ticonderoga in July 1777, but defeated the British at Saratoga that fall. In 1778 and in 1779, west of the Hudson, General Sullivan and his troops succeeded in their goal of destroying the Iroquois and bringing devastation to their land.

and trapping the American commander and thousands of troops, the British ranged out into the countryside, trying to rally the Loyalists and live off the land—the same strategy that had failed in New Jersey.

In the meantime, the Continental army and the militia worked together to wear down the British. The Continental army in the lower South was never large enough for a major battle and was defeated at Camden, South Carolina, in August 1780.

However, as the British marched through South Carolina and North Carolina, they were harassed by bands of irregulars and militia. Each hit depleted the British forces, and each small victory brought more men into the American ranks. This, in fact, became the American strategy as the Continental forces, now commanded in the South by Nathanael Greene, drew the British, led by Lord Cornwallis, on a wild chase, scoring victories at Cowpens and Kings Mountain (see Map 7–4).

Finally, Greene met the British at Guilford Court House in North Carolina in March 1781, inflicting heavy losses on the exhausted enemy. The battle was a draw, but Cornwallis, his forces depleted, retreated to Virginia. Greene's army retook almost all of the Deep South.

The cost to South Carolina, however, was enormous. As each side took control, neighbors attacked each other, plundered each other's farms, and carried away each other's slaves. During the Revolution, one-fourth of South Carolina's slaves simply disappeared. Some ran away, some died of disease, some were stolen by whites, and some followed the British, who in June 1780 promised freedom to all rebel-owned slaves who agreed to fight on their side for the rest of the war. Some were actually shipped off to slavery in the West Indies, but many fought with the British. This use of slaves as soldiers, of course, outraged white patriots, but it hardly pleased the Loyalists either. Loyalist slaveholders did not want their way of life undermined. Had the British been willing to wage a war of liberation, freeing all the southern slaves and using them as soldiers, they might have come closer to winning the war. But the British were fighting to preserve social and political order, not to overturn it. The British nonetheless disrupted the slave system significantly, and this disruption was another aspect to the civil war that beset the region for most of the Revolutionary period.

The British southern strategy had failed, but the Americans were not yet ready to win the war. Cornwallis moved on to Virginia in 1781, capturing Richmond, the new capital, and Charlottesville, coming within a few minutes of capturing Thomas Jefferson. Yet the British had been seriously weakened by the war of attrition. George Washington, working closely with the French—who sent a huge fleet into the Chesapeake near Cornwallis's quarters at Yorktown—led most of his forces, accompanied by French troops, to Virginia and laid siege. Trapped, Cornwallis surrendered on October 19, 1781. Although the Treaty of Paris ending the war would not be signed for two more years, the war was effectively over.

Securing a Place in the World

The United States revolted to escape from the British Empire and to turn its back on European power politics. However, to win the war, the new nation had to strike bargains with those same European powers. These alliances and treaties set the stage for America's struggle for a place in the world order.

Early in the war the United States called on Britain's enemies—France, Spain, and Holland—for support, and it played these new allies off against Britain with the cunning of an Old World diplomat. Benjamin Franklin, Congress's envoy to France, now

AMERICAN LANDSCAPE

>> The South Carolina Backcountry

When William Brown settled his family and their slaves at Matthews Bluff on the Savannah River in the South Carolina backcountry in 1769, the land was a fertile swamp teeming with wild animals. These animals had to be subdued before the family could plant a little corn and raise the livestock that provided their living. There was hardly a road worth the name. Until they could erect a log cabin, the family lived in a tent made out of bark. Only six years later, Brown's oldest sons, Bartlett (20) and Tarleton (18) were drafted into the militia. By the time they returned home at the end of the war, the conflict had destroyed everything they had. Like much of the Carolina backcountry, their home had been laid waste as neighbor fought neighbor, Revolutionary against Loyalist.

Once, when campaigning in Georgia, Tarleton Brown was able to return to his home for the night. Around midnight, he heard the dogs barking and then "a loud rap at the door." "Who's there?" he asked. "Several voices together replied 'Friends.'" They said they were on their way home from the militia and wanted a place to spend the night. Suspicious, Brown turned them away, but when they asked for a torch to light their way, he reconsidered; perhaps they really were fellow patriots. So he opened the door a crack, gave them a light, but shut the door quickly. They knocked again, this time asking for water, but Brown had looked through a crack in the logs and seen that they were Tories. He secured the door and told them to leave, but instead "they denounced me, father, and all the family, threatening to visit vengeance upon the whole household, and with fiendish fury and united strength endeavored to burst the door from its hinges." Failing, they fired their guns through the cracks in the logs, killing Brown's six-year-old brother.

The next time Brown returned home, he knew that his status as a patriot put his family at risk. He and a patriot neighbor thus agreed that if either home were attacked, the other man's family would come to its aid. One night, hearing gunfire, Brown rushed to the neighbor's house, only to find him dead and everything there laid waste. His own family had scattered to the woods.

By this time, Charleston had fallen, and the British army had fanned out, to subdue the rest of the South. Tarleton and his brother Bartlett fled to safety in Virginia. On their way, they passed by the Waxhaw region where British colonel Banastre Tarleton's cavalry had defeated a Revolutionary detachment, massacring the survivors, burning homes, and destroying the local community.

Meanwhile, a band of Loyalists, freed slaves, and allied Indians led by Daniel McGirt moved through Brown's neighborhood, "killing every man he met who had not sworn allegiance to the King." The band killed Brown's father and burned his father's house to the ground. Brown's mother and sisters escaped into the woods.

This was guerilla war, its object to spread terror. Vengeance begat vengeance. When Brown heard what had happened to his family, "my blood boiled within my veins, and my soul thirsted for vengeance." Back in South Carolina, Brown's detachment encountered a Tory. They "gave him his due, and left his body at the disposal of the birds and wild beasts."

Late in the war, Brown contracted smallpox. He returned to his neighbor-

The Brown Cowshed Using archeological evidence, an artist has imagined the cowpen of Catherine Brown, Tarleton Brown's aunt. The cowshed was probably burned down by the Loyalists during the Revolution.

hood to recover, sleeping outdoors, so as not to infect his family. The woman who nursed him turned out to be a Tory "and informed her clan where I was." He had to hide in the woods.

By the time the war was over, much of the backcountry was devastated. Towns were in ruins, farms laid waste, livestock driven off, and many settlers forced to live in the woods. Tarleton Brown had lost almost everything. His mother died soon after, only 47, exhausted by the war. Like much of South Carolina, Brown would have to start all over again.

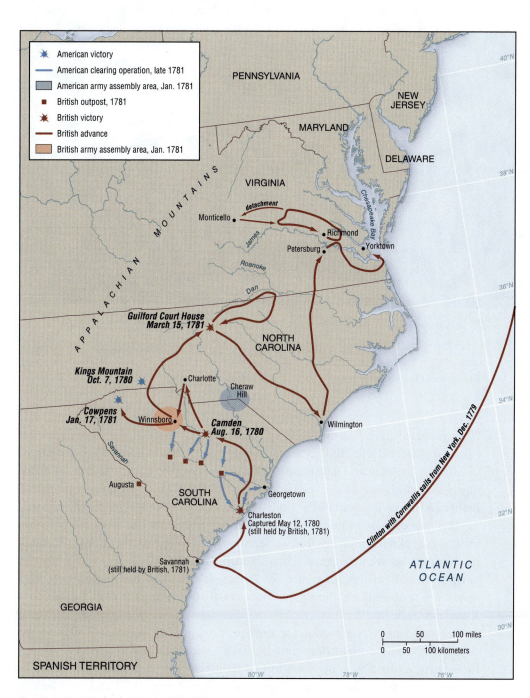

Map 7-4 The War in the South, 1779–1781 In 1779, the theater of action shifted to the South. Washington's objective was to wear the British down, avoiding decisive battles in which his outmanned troops might be defeated. With the help of the French, his strategy succeeded, leading to the British surrender at Yorktown in October 1781.

Surrender of British Army Here Cornwallis surrenders to Washington.

70, arrived at court in 1776 dressed like a country rustic instead of wearing the expected silks and powdered wig. His appearance was a ruse, intended to make the French think that he was innocent and uncalculating. France entered the war in the hope of breaking up the British Empire and reestablishing itself as the world's most powerful nation. France and Spain both wanted the United States to be independent but small and weak.

The United States wanted to secure its independence, first and foremost, but it had no intention of remaining small or feeble. Americans sought a large chunk of Canada, the territory between the Appalachians and the Mississippi River, and the right to navigate the Mississippi. In return for French and Spanish assistance, the United States at first offered only the right to trade, vastly overrating the value in Europe of American trade.

Because America wanted France and Spain to fight for expanded American territory, whereas those countries wanted instead to keep the new nation small, it took three years, until 1778, to negotiate formal treaties. Franklin prodded the French by holding secret truce discussions with a British agent late in 1777 and then leaking reports to well-placed French friends. Although the alliance was an impressive accomplishment, it involved concessions. The Americans promised not to negotiate separately with Britain and to remain France's ally "forever."

The United States broke both promises, the first within a few years and the second in the 1790s. In April 1782, after Cornwallis's surrender at Yorktown but before France and Spain had gained their military objectives, Franklin began peace negotiations with the British. By November, a draft of the treaty had been completed, although Franklin assured the French that nothing would be signed without their consent. The agreement primarily served British and American interests, however. In the Treaty of Paris, signed in 1783, Britain recognized American independence, and the United States acquired the territory between the Appalachians and the Mississippi River and south of the Great Lakes (see Map 7–5).

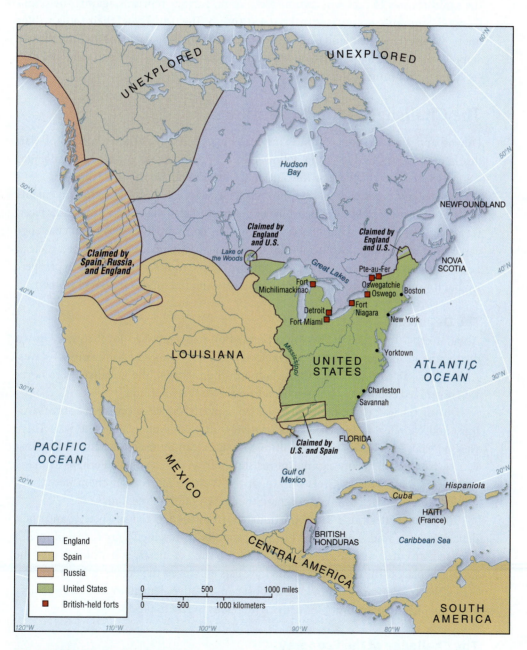

Map 7-5 The Treaty of Paris The Treaty of Paris confirmed the boundaries of the new United States, north to the Great Lakes, south to Spanish Florida, and west to the Mississippi. But it left the British in several forts west of the Appalachians, which they did not abandon until 1797. *Walter LaFeber*, The American Age, *2nd ed. (New York: W. W. Norton, 1994), p. 29.*

In the long run Britain probably struck the shrewder bargain. The land it ceded was of little use. The Americans failed to press for commercial concessions, and by the mid-1780s, the British had forbidden Americans to trade directly with Britain or the West Indies. These restrictions seriously damaged the new nation's economy.

Neither France nor Spain gained much from the war. Although Spain won Florida, neither country achieved its other territorial objectives, and France was left with a large debt.

If America's allies were relative losers, so also were Britain's allies, the American Loyalists and Indian tribes that fought with them. The best the British could do for the Loyalists was to secure a commitment of no further reprisals against them and Congress's promise to consider making restitution. The British sold their Indian allies out by transferring their land (the territory between the Appalachians and the Mississippi) to the United States. Although a stunning achievement, the Treaty of Paris also set the stage for future conflicts.

The Challenge of the Revolution

During and after the Revolution, Americans experienced all the upheavals of war: death, profiteering, and inflation, followed by economic depression. Other challenges were also presented by the new Revolutionary ideas about liberty and equality.

Radicals and moderates had compromised for victory, yet significant disagreements resurfaced once the fighting ended. One of the greatest challenges that Americans faced was designing political structures to contain these conflicts. The other great challenge came from the philosophy of revolution itself. Equality implied a transformed society. Followed to its natural conclusion, not only would the transformation lead to prosperity, but it would also necessarily challenge slavery and the subordination of women.

The Departure of the Loyalists

About 15 to 20 percent of the white population had remained loyal to the Crown during the Revolution, along with a majority of the Indians and a minority of slaves. Although sizable in number (almost half a million whites), the Loyalists were never well organized enough to threaten the success of the Revolution.

During the war, partisan fighting was fierce in contested regions such as the Carolinas and New Jersey, but there was relatively little retribution after the war. There were no trials for treason, mass executions, or significant mob actions directed against whites. Nor was there any significant resistance from the Loyalists. Perhaps as many as 80,000 left for Canada, Great Britain, or the West Indies. Among them were thousands of former slaves who had accepted the British offer of freedom.

The white exiles came disproportionately from the top tier of society, and their departure left a void. Confiscated Loyalist property represented a great deal of wealth to be redistributed, and people just below the top rung of society scrambled to take the Loyalists' places. The departure of the Loyalists enhanced the democratizing tendencies of the Revolution by removing the most conservative element in American society and creating an opportunity for many Americans to rise to power.

The Challenge of the Economy

Wars disrupt the economy in two ways. First, they interfere with production and exchange, hurting some people and creating opportunity for others. Second, because wars are expensive, they require some combination of increased taxation and deficit spending.

Those who suffered the greatest economic hardships and enjoyed the greatest opportunities from the Revolution were those most deeply involved in the market. During the war, trade with Britain and the British West Indies was cut off, and the British navy seized American ships and destroyed the New England fishing industry. After the war, Britain still excluded American ships from the West Indies. Congress, under the Articles of Confederation, was too weak to negotiate a better trade relationship, and merchants trading with Britain and the West Indies were ruined.

At the same time, other opportunities opened up. Merchants willing to risk seizure of their ships continued the trade with Europe and sold the goods they imported at astronomical prices. Privateering made other merchants rich, as did provisioning the Continental army. In 1779 alone, the army spent $109 million on provisions, fueling a wartime economic boom. The army's demand for supplies drove prices up. Prices for grain increased 200 to 600 percent and, in Maryland, 5,000 percent (see Figure 7–1).

Enterprising Americans with a little capital to invest could rise quickly. Not everyone could take advantage of the Revolutionary economy. In fact, although the Revolution eliminated some of the ruling elite, it did not level social classes. Those who could not profit from the war had to work harder and struggle with rising prices. To meet the army's demand for cloth, women increased the pace of home production. Because there were set prices for cloth, women were unable to reap exorbitant profits.

Skyrocketing prices were hardest on those with limited incomes. While Congress debated price controls and some cities set them, aggrieved citizens sometimes took matters into their own hands. In Boston, a mob of at least a hundred women seized a hogshead of coffee from the merchant Thomas Boylston, who was hoarding it. Such

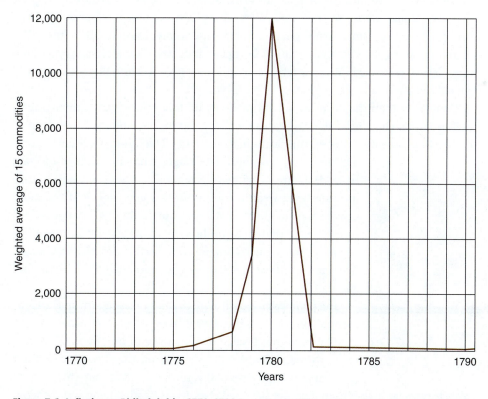

Figure 7–1 Inflation at Philadelphia, 1770–1790 Beginning in 1776, wartime shortages caused prices for basic commodities—beef, chocolate, coffee, corn, flour, molasses, pepper, pork, rum, sugar, tea, wheat, iron, and tar—to skyrocket. By 1781, prices were 12,000 percent higher than a decade earlier. They began to fall the next year, finally reaching prewar levels by late in the decade.

conflicts pitted the community against the entrepreneur and raised serious questions about the purpose of the Revolution: Was it to create opportunities for the individual or to protect the well-being of the community?

After the war, opportunities for profit and prosperity for some increased, whereas a postwar deflation pushed others to misery. Speculation in land and currency offered the fastest ways to become rich. Entrepreneurs bought up paper currency and land patents at a fraction of their worth, counting on the day when they would be redeemed at their face value.

Even before the war ended, there was a clamor for land. Between 1776 and 1790, America's population grew by almost 70 percent, from 2.3 million to 3.9 million, almost all from natural increase. Colonists had long been pushing against the Indians to the west, and by 1783, the Wilderness Road had taken thousands into Kentucky; seven years later, 100,000 people were living in Kentucky and Tennessee.

With the demand for land so great, speculators who could corner huge tracts stood to reap extraordinary profits. Before the Revolution, seven men had secured a patent to 29,350 acres in upstate New York. By the end of the Revolution, three of them were dead; one—a Loyalist—had left the country; and the others were broke or close to it, all victims of the dislocations of war. William Cooper, a small-scale merchant and speculator, bought the patent in a possibly rigged auction for the bargain-basement price of £2,700. Yet his investment was worthless unless Cooper could get others to buy portions of the huge patent from him. After a few months, Cooper sold off thousands of acres not to poor farmers but to speculators who in turn sold farm-sized plots to their own townsmen, turning a profit by increasing the price.

All along the western frontier, farmers rushed to take the new lands, reversing the pre-Revolutionary trend to the cities. With the opening of new regions to the west, America would remain a farming nation for decades more, rather than industrializing rapidly along the rigid class lines of European industrial economies. At the same time, slavery expanded into new territories in the South, ensuring the persistence of inequalities based on race.

Even more than the dislocations of the Revolutionary economy, the financing of the Revolution challenged the American economy. Taxing the population was out of the question, not only because Americans had begun the Revolution precisely to avoid

high taxes but also because Congress had no authority to tax. Instead, it simply printed more money. There was no increase in underlying wealth to back up this currency, and the more Congress printed, the less it was worth. By 1780, Congress had printed more than $241 million. In addition, Congress paid for supplies and soldiers' wages with certificates that circulated like money. These certificates put another $95 million into circulation.

The plan was for each state to raise taxes to buy up the Continental currency and remove it from circulation. However, the states were either unable or unwilling to buy up enough currency to maintain its value. Moreover, the states issued their own paper money. Eventually, the states had to tax their inhabitants at rates far higher than had ever been seen before. Collecting taxes was difficult: people could not pay in hard money, and the Continental currency depreciated so rapidly that it was almost worthless (see Figure 7–2).

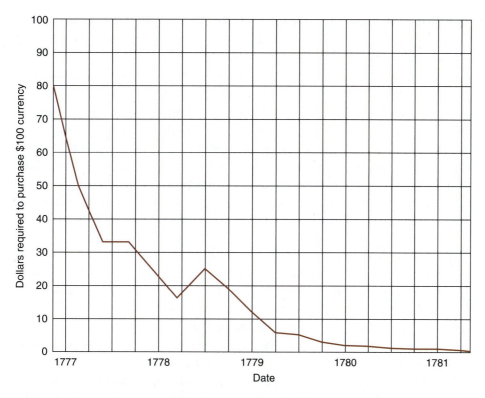

Figure 7-2 Depreciation of Continental Currency, January 1770–April 1781 At the same time that prices were rising, the value of Continental currency was falling dramatically. Between 1777 and 1781, it lost almost all of its value, becoming close to worthless.

By April 1777, Continental currency was worth only half its face value, and by April 1781, only half a percent. By the end of the war, some creditors were refusing to accept paper money for debts owed to them, insisting on hard money instead. When trade with Britain resumed, imports increased sharply (because of pent-up demand for consumer goods), while exports fell (because restrictions kept American goods out of British markets). The result was severe deflation and a flood of cheap imports.

The weak central government was almost powerless to address these economic upheavals. In 1780 it stopped paying the army, which almost led to a mutiny at New-burgh, New York. Congress looked to each state to decide what to do about its debt and which element of its population to serve. Many states showed mercy to debtors. To help pay off debts, some states sold confiscated Loyalist property, whereas others tried to seize Indian lands in the west. Wherever states increased taxes to pay off state debts (as the postwar depression hit), hard-pressed debtors clamored for tax relief. In western Massachusetts, farmers led by Revolutionary War captain Daniel Shays shut down the courts to prevent them from collecting debts. This episode is known as Shays's Rebellion.

Contesting the New Economy

Economic upheaval and popular uprisings against state governments led many Americans to question whether democratic government could survive. The process of rebellion that started in 1765 seemed to be starting again, this time directed against the new republican state governments. Americans now faced the same issue that had led to conflict with Britain: Were they willing to pay for a huge war? Could they avoid the perils of tyranny, on the one hand, and anarchy, on the other? Could they, in short, maintain democratic forms of government?

Shays's Rebellion was simply an extreme form of the protest that occurred in many states. It was an attempt by debtors to force the government to alleviate their economic distress, primarily by shutting down the courts so that their debts could not be collected, but also by passing legislation for the relief of debtors. By 1786, many western Massachusetts farmers had become used to the absence of government, and local courts had been shut down since 1774. Those who put down Shays's Rebellion did so in republican terms, faulting the Shaysites for inadequate virtue.

Such popular uprisings raised serious questions about whether the democratic governments created after the Revolution could contain anarchy. States that faced such uprisings learned that peace could best be preserved by going easy on the rebels. After Shays's Rebellion was put down, John Hancock was elected governor with the support of the Shaysites on a platform of amnesty for the rebels and relief for debtors. As a rule, popular uprisings by economically independent men (as distinguished from those by dependent laborers or slaves) have been punished very lightly in America, which may be a source of American political stability.

The relatively light punishments given to debtor insurgents and the generally inflationary policies of state governments quelled popular unrest, but the postwar depression and the inability of Congress to reopen trade with Britain devastated commerce. The huge national debt went unpaid, leaving numerous creditors holding worthless pieces of paper. Popular unrest had helped debtors but hurt those to whom they owed money. The nationalists, a group of commercial-minded political leaders centered in Congress and including James Madison, Gouverneur Morris, Robert Morris, and Alexander Hamilton, began to make a case for a strong national government that would actively advance commerce and protect private property. These nationalists were, in general, the moderates of the Revolutionary era. Radicals envisioned a weaker central government, a more localized democracy, and a hands-off approach to the economy. Whether these two visions of America could be reconciled was one of the greatest challenges of the Revolution.

Can Women Be Citizens?

The American Revolution raised questions that threatened and in some cases changed the social order. A revolution based on beliefs in human equality and a common human nature brought into question all social relations, including the role of women.

Many women were drawn into the Revolution as consumers. They had eagerly participated in the boycotts of the 1760s and 1770s and had increased home production. Many women identified with the goals of the Revolution and often led riots against merchants suspected of unfair dealings. Women could challenge the Revolutionary governments, as well, when they perceived interference with their rights as consumers and duties as homemakers.

If women were able to extend their traditional economic roles as producers and consumers to support the war effort, there was no consensus on expanding their political roles. Some women pointed out that the right to be taxed only by one's own representatives should apply to them, too. Under the principle of coverture, married women were generally denied the right to own property, but what was the basis for denying the vote to unmarried women who owned property? In 1776, New Jersey extended the vote to unmarried women who met the property qualification (although this right was rescinded in 1807). Although American Revolutionaries were not prepared to let women vote, except in New Jersey, they began to broaden their views of women's intellectual and political capabilities. The state laws that confiscated Loyalists' property, for example, often presumed that married women were capable of making their own political choices. This notion broke with the past, when married women were thought to have no political will separate from that of their husbands.

The Revolution challenged the idea that women lacked independent minds and could not think for themselves. The Enlightenment belief that all human beings had the capacity to reason led to significant improvements in women's education after the war. Reformers, many of them women, argued that if women appeared ignorant or incapable, it was only because of their inferior education.

Enlightenment ideas about women's intellectual abilities meshed neatly with republican ideas about the need for virtue and liberal ideas about the necessity of consent. If the nation's fate depended on the character of its citizens, both men and women should be able to choose intelligent, upright, patriotic partners. The Revolution also accelerated a trend for people to choose their own marriage partners and marry for love rather than for material interest. If women were to make such choices wisely, they must be educated well.

Yet once again the Revolutionary impulse had its limits. Discussions about women's citizenship and capacities implicitly applied only to prosperous white women.

Liberty Displaying Arts and Sciences So powerful was the Revolutionary idea of human equality that many came to believe in the liberating potential of education for both women and blacks.

>> Abigail to John Adams, "Remember the Ladies"

The American Revolution had a profound impact on the lives of women. Whether they were directly affected by military or guerilla fighting, or struggling to hold down the home front in the absence of their sons, fathers, husbands, and brothers, women played a vital role in the war years. Abigail Adams's letters to her husband John when he was away in Philadelphia at the Continental Congress and, later, serving as a diplomat in France and the Netherlands, captured both the ties of affection and the practical concerns felt by many American women. In addition, Abigail Adams was an early advocate of women's rights. Note that the formal rules for spelling were not laid down until early in the next century.

Abigail Adams, "Letter to John Adams, Braintree, March 31st, 1776," in *The Broadview Anthology of Literature of the Revolutionary Period, 1770–1832*, ed. D. L. Macdonald and Anne McWhir (Ontario, Canada: Broadview Press, 2010), pp. 61–62.

Abigail Adams

Braintree March 31, 1776

I wish you would ever write me a Letter half as long as I write you; and tell me if you may where your Fleet are gone? What sort of Defence Virginia can make against our common Enemy? Whether it is so situated as to make an able Defence? Are not the Gentery Lords and the common people vassals, are they not like the uncivilized Natives Brittain represents us to be? I hope their Riffel Men who have shewen themselves very savage and even Blood thirsty; are not a specimen of the Generality of the people.

I [illegible] am willing to allow the Colony great merrit for having produced a Washington but they have been shamefully duped by a Dunmore.

I have sometimes been ready to think that the passion for Liberty cannot be Eaquelly Strong in the Breasts of those who have been accustomed to deprive their fellow Creatures of theirs. Of this I am certain that it is not founded upon that generous and christian principal of doing to others as we would that others should do unto us. Do not you want to see Boston; I am fearfull of the small pox, or I should have been in before this time. I got Mr. Crane to go to our House and see what state it was in. I find it has been occupied by one of the Doctors of a Regiment, very dirty, but no other damage has been done to it. The few things which were left in it are all gone. Cranch has the key which he never deliverd up. I have wrote to him for it and am determined to get it cleand as soon as possible and shut it up. I look upon it a new acquisition of property, a property which one month ago I did not value at a single Shilling, and could with pleasure have seen it in flames. . . .

Tho we felicitate ourselves, we sympathize with those who are trembling least the Lot of Boston should be theirs. But they cannot be in similar circumstances unless pusilanimity and cowardise should take possession of them. They have time and warning given them to see the Evil and shun it.—I long to hear that you have declared an independency—and by the way in the new Code of Laws which I suppose it will be necessary for you to make I desire you would Remember the Ladies, and be more generous and favourable to them than your ancestors. Do not put such unlimited power into the hands of the Husbands. Remember all Men would be tyrants if they could. If perticuliar care and attention is not paid to the Laidies we are determined to foment a Rebelion, and will not hold ourselves bound by any Laws in which we have no voice, or Representation.

That your Sex are Naturally Tyrannical is a Truth so thoroughly established as to admit of no dispute, but such of you as wish to be happy willingly give up the harsh title of Master for the more tender and endearing one of Friend. Why then, not put it out of the power of the vicious and the Lawless to use us with cruelty and indignity with impunity. Men of Sense in all Ages abhor those customs which treat us only as the vassals of your Sex. Regard us then as Beings placed by providence under your protection and in immitation of the Supreem Being make use of that power only for our happiness.

Questions

1. What is Abigail attempting to communicate to her husband in this letter?

2. What arguments does she make in her letter, particularly as regards women's rights? Do you agree with Abigail's arguments? Why or why not?

3. What impression of the relationship between Abigail and John did you obtain from your reading of this letter?

Moreover, almost no one advocated professional education or even knowledge for its own sake for women. Overly intellectual women were ridiculed as "women of masculine minds." Women's education was supposed to make them better wives and mothers and enable them to perform their domestic roles better. Because the family was still the bedrock of the nation, no one was willing to answer a question posed by Abigail Smith Adams in a letter to her husband, John Adams: What recourse was open to women who found that they were treated with "cruelty and indignity" at home?

The ideas of the Revolution presented a powerful challenge to the subordination of women, one that the Revolutionary generation was only partially prepared to meet. Women were recognized as intelligent beings who could make important choices in the market, about their families, and even about their political loyalties. They were partial citizens, and this revealed the limits of Revolutionary doctrines of equality.

The Challenge of Slavery

No institution in America received a greater challenge from the egalitarian ideals of the Revolution than slavery. Although slaves always resisted their enslavement, the world's first organized antislavery movement began before the Revolution with the Pennsylvania Quaker John Woolman, who in 1754 condemned slavery in humanitarian and religious terms. Within a few years, radicals in both the North and the South recognized that the institution was inconsistent with their ideals of freedom.

African American slaves saw immediately that the Revolution offered opportunities for freedom. The rise of egalitarian ideas and wartime disruption enabled thousands of slaves to claim their freedom. Some used a mix of Christian and Revolutionary principles of liberty to petition for "the natural rights and privileges of freeborn men." Others fought for their liberty by joining the Revolutionary forces; by the end of the war, three-fourths of the Rhode Island regiment and perhaps one-fourth of Washington's troops were black. Many more accepted British offers of freedom to slaves who deserted their masters. Tens of thousands of slaves ran away. This combination of Revolutionary ideals of freedom and African American activism presented a significant challenge to white Americans, and they met it in part. Every state north of Delaware eliminated slavery, either in their constitutions or through gradual emancipation laws. In addition, the Northwest Ordinance of 1787 prohibited slavery in the Northwest Territory (the future states of Ohio, Indiana, Illinois, Michigan, and Wisconsin). In the states of the upper South (Virginia, Maryland, and Delaware) legislatures passed laws making it easier to emancipate slaves.

If slavery was eliminated—sometimes slowly—in the North and questioned in the upper South, it still survived in every state south of New Jersey. Revolutionary ideals made slaveholders uncomfortable. Unwilling to eliminate it, they offered excuses, protesting that abolishing slavery was too difficult or inconvenient. Historians still debate whether the inroads made against slavery were one of the Revolution's greatest successes—or whether the inability to curtail it was its greatest failure.

A New Policy in the West

The new nation faced a major challenge in the West. It had to devise a policy consistent with its interests, rejecting the old colonial models of Britain, France, and Spain. But how would the United States organize the new territory acquired through the war? There was no useful model for new territories and their citizens to become equal members of an expanding, democratic nation.

The Indians' Revolution

At the beginning of the American Revolution, most Indians regarded it as a fight among Englishmen that did not concern them. At the end of the war, all Indians were losers, as land-hungry Americans poured into the region beyond the Appalachians.

By 1776, both the British and the Americans were recruiting Indians. Within a few years, Indians on the frontier were drawn into the struggle, usually on the British side. They feared American moves onto their land; also, only the British could provide the customary "presents" that cemented alliances. Indians struck at American communities all along the frontier (see Map 7–6).

In retaliation, Washington ordered "the total destruction and devastation" of Iroquois settlements in New York and western Pennsylvania and the capture of "as many prisoners of every age and sex as possible." In 1778, an expedition under General John Sullivan systematically burned 40 Iroquois towns. One chief said that the Americans "put to death all the Women and Children, excepting some of the young Women, whom they carried away for the use of their Soldiers & were afterwards put to death

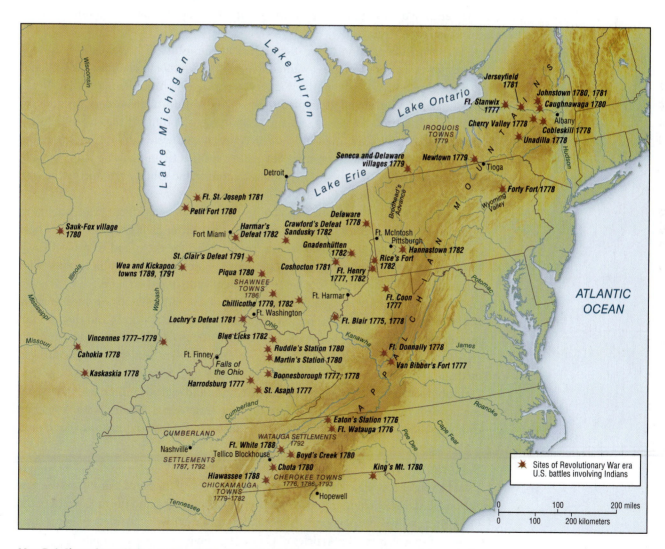

Map 7–6 Sites of Revolutionary War Battles Involving Indians Indians were active participants in the Revolution, fighting on both sides and making the West a significant site of conflict. *Wilcomb Washburn, Handbook of North American Indians (Washington, DC: Smithsonian, 1988), p. 115.*

> It is also your Business Brothers to exert yourselves in the Defense of this Road by which the King, our Father, so fully supplied our Wants. If this is once stopt we must be a miserable People, and be left exposed to the Resentment of the Rebels, who notwithstanding their fair Speeches, wish for nothing more than to extirpate us from the Earth, that they may possess our Lands, the Desire of attaining which we are convinced is the Cause of the present War between the King and his disobedient Children.
>
> SAYENQUERAGHTA,
> a Seneca war chief, addressing an Indian council at Niagara, 1779

in a more shameful manner." Such brutality undermined American efforts to keep Indian allies.

The End of the Middle Ground

The end of the Revolution brought neither peace nor order. The Indians who had won victories on the frontier were amazed when they learned the British had surrendered and given all of the Indians' land to the Americans. Needing land for settlers more than it needed diplomatic allies, the United States soon abandoned the middle ground (see Chapter 2). No longer able to play one group of Europeans against another, Indian tribes had little leverage.

Western Indians soon found themselves in the midst of a competition among whites for their land. Congress wanted to establish a national claim to Indian lands so it could sell them to pay off the war debt, whereas New York, Pennsylvania, North Carolina, and Virginia all attempted to seize land within their borders. Speculators moved in, knowing they could sell land at an immense profit. At the end of the Revolution, one-third of the men in western Pennsylvania were landless, and they believed that the Revolution's promise of equality entitled them to cheap land. Some of the poorest crossed the Appalachians into Kentucky and Ohio, even during the war, squatting on Indian-owned lands.

Those already on the frontier who both suffered from and inflicted violence maintained a visceral hatred of Indians, sometimes advocating their extermination. These settlers expected government to secure frontier land for them and to protect them from the Indians. Congress and the states moved quickly to force Indians, some with no authority to speak for their tribes, to sign treaties ceding their land.

Such treaties (15 were signed between 1784 and 1796) were almost meaningless. Native Americans refused to honor agreements made under duress and that did not include the customary exchange of gifts, and the states would not recognize another state's claims or those of the national government. Indian leaders were encouraged by the British and the Spanish. The Mohawk leader Joseph Brant took his followers to Ontario. Alexander McGillivray united the Creeks and secured military support from the Spanish in Florida. Not until well into the nineteenth century were American claims to Indian land east of the Mississippi secured and Indian resistance put down.

Settling the West

Establishing effective government in the West was one of the biggest problems the new nation faced. Many frontier regions (in particular Kentucky and the area north of the Ohio River, as well as portions of Vermont and Maine) were claimed by competing groups of speculators. The Articles of Confederation gave Congress limited powers of government in the West, but a national policy was necessary. Just after the Revolution, dissident settlers in New York, Pennsylvania, Kentucky (then part of Virginia), and

Tennessee (then part of North Carolina) all hatched plans to create their own states.

Both state governments and nationalists in Congress believed that the Union was in peril. Yet it was difficult to reach a compromise among the competing interests. States wanted Congress to recognize their western claims, whereas states without any claims wanted all of the western lands to be turned over to Congress. Also at issue was which speculators' claims would be upheld, as speculators with dubious claims to the land were selling them to settlers at bargain prices.

The Northwest Ordinance, ratified by Congress on July 13, 1787, was a compromise among these competing interests. Finally realizing that they could not manage vast areas of territory, the large states yielded their claims to Congress (see Map 7–7). Because Congress validated the claims only of respectable speculators, it made losers not only out of unscrupulous ones but also out of anyone who had bought land from them at cheap prices.

The Northwest Ordinance set out a model of government for the western territories that reflected the liberal political philosophy of nationalists in Congress and established a process for the admission of new states into the nation. Rejecting Britain's colonial model

Joseph Brant After the Revolution, the Mohawk leader Joseph Brant took his followers into exile in Canada.

of expansion, it declared that territories would be eligible to apply for statehood once they had 60,000 free inhabitants. There were other important breaks with the past. Slavery was forbidden north of the Ohio River, the first time that a line was drawn barring slaves from a particular region. Trial by jury and habeas corpus were guaranteed, as well as the right to bail and freedom of religion. Cruel and unusual punishments were barred. These were important principles that, except for the provision excluding slavery, would all appear again in the Constitution and Bill of Rights.

The Northwest Ordinance was designed to create an orderly world of middle-class farmers who obeyed the law, paid their debts, worshiped as they pleased, and were protected from despotic government and the unruly poor. The ordinance represented the triumph of the moderate Revolutionaries' vision of government.

Creating a New National Government

At the beginning of the Revolution, radicals and moderates had worked together to accomplish common goals. The years of war, however, slowly pulled radicals and moderates apart. Many moderates, particularly those who served in Congress or as officers in the Continental army, became nationalists. They worked with men from other states on national projects and came to think of the states as a threat to the success of the Revolution. Many of the radicals, meanwhile, retained a local, republican perspective.

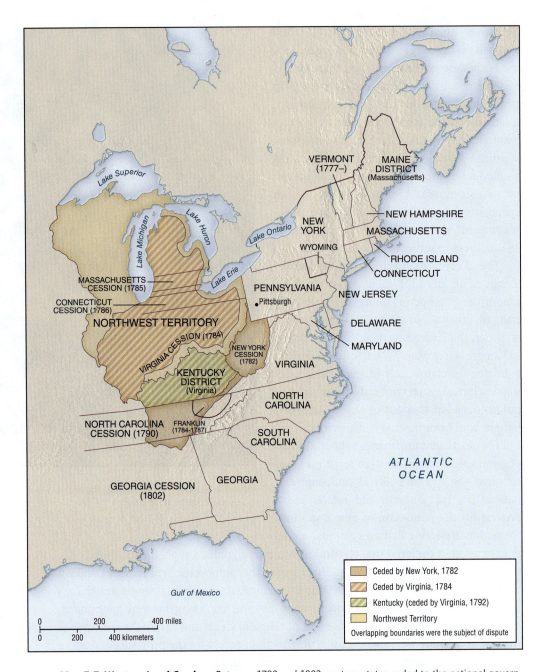

Map 7-7 Western Land Cessions Between 1782 and 1802, eastern states ceded to the national government the territory they claimed in the West. Under the principle established by the Northwest Ordinance, new states were carved out of this territory. Never before had a nation developed such a procedure for bringing in new regions not as colonies but as fully equal states.

They dreaded a centralized government and feared that the Continental army would become a standing army that might take away their liberties.

This split between moderate nationalists and radical localists culminated in the battle over the Constitution, written by the nationalists to create a stronger central government and resisted by the localists, afraid it would subvert liberty. Almost all the problems that led the nationalists to wish for a stronger national government concerned the economy: paying the war debt, paying the soldiers, and improving commerce. The nationalists were deeply involved in the market economy as merchants, financiers, farmers, and planters. The localists, as a rule, were much less involved in the market and suspicious of those who were. As long as taxes were low and their creditors did not harass them, they were satisfied. The Articles of Confederation provided them all the national government and economy they needed.

A Crippled Congress

Nationalists in Congress soon realized that the national government was powerless to address the most pressing economic questions. By 1779, after printing $200 million in paper money that was dropping in value by the day, Congress had shut down its printing presses. It then gave the states the responsibility to provision the army. As legislatures dithered, the unclothed, unfed, and unpaid army threatened mutiny. Congress gave up trying to pay its war debt and passed that back to the states as well. Some states refused. States such as Massachusetts that raised taxes to pay off their portion courted armed upheavals such as Shays's Rebellion.

> If money be the vitals of Congress, is it not precious for those individuals from whom it is to be taken? Must I give my soul, my lungs, to Congress? Congress must have our souls. . . . I tell you, they shall not have the soul of Virginia.
>
> PATRICK HENRY,
> speaking against the ratification of the Constitution

Congress was powerless to alleviate the economic distress. At the end of the war, British goods flooded in again to meet a consumer demand that seemed insatiable. However, there was no comparable British demand for American exports; in fact, Britain closed its ports to American trade. America could not close its ports to British ships, because the Articles of Confederation denied Congress the authority to regulate commerce. Additional foreign loans were out of the question. Congress could not pay back those it had already taken out. Even western policy, Congress's greatest triumph, presented problems. Once the states had ceded western territory to Congress (leading to the Northwest Ordinance), Congress discovered that it takes an army and a great deal of money to police a territory inhabited by Indians and coveted by land-hungry settlers. Congress lacked that money and could not pay the army it had.

Nationalist attempts to strengthen Congress failed, however, lacking the approval of the states. By the middle of the 1780s, several nationalists abandoned that reform in favor of a new and stronger form of government. James Madison and other nationalists began talking about calling a constitutional convention. But the challenge they faced was how to effect changes that the states did not seem to want.

The road to the Constitutional Convention in Philadelphia in 1787 ran through two earlier meetings. First, in 1785, at Madison's suggestion, commissioners from Virginia and Maryland met at George Washington's home, Mount Vernon, to resolve disputes about navigating the Potomac River. Madison suggested a further meeting of representatives from all the states in Annapolis, Maryland, to build on the accomplishments from Mount Vernon. When only 12 men from five states arrived, they called for another meeting, in Philadelphia, nine months later. In those nine months, Shays's Rebellion and the stalemate in Congress persuaded nationalists to consider strengthening the government. Over the summer of 1787, 55 men from twelve states met in Philadelphia to write one of the most influential documents in the history of the world.

Writing a New Constitution

The men assembled in Philadelphia were primarily moderate nationalists. Committed to the goals of the Revolution, they sought, in Madison's words, "republican remedies" for the problems of republican government. The 55 delegates met for almost four months during the summer of 1787, finally ratifying the Constitution on September 17. They deliberated in secret, in order to talk freely and achieve compromises.

Although there were sharp differences of opinion, there were also wide areas of agreement. Most of the delegates had considerable experience in state and national government. George Washington, a member of Virginia's delegation, was the most widely respected man in the nation. He was elected the presiding officer of the convention.

The delegates were young, with most in their 30s and 40s. No one was more important to the convention than James Madison, just 36. He came with a design for the new government already worked out. Known as the Virginia Plan, it became the outline for the Constitution.

The Virginia Plan was a blueprint for substantial change: a strong central government divided into three branches, executive, legislative (itself with two branches), and judicial, that would check and balance one another; a system of federalism that guaranteed every state a republican government; and proposals for admitting new states and amending the Constitution. The only alternative, the New Jersey Plan, was offered on June 15 and quickly rejected. It proposed a single-house legislature, with all states having an equal vote, and a plural executive, chosen by the legislature (see Table 7–1).

The delegates agreed that the new national government would have to be much stronger: Congress would now have the power to collect taxes and duties, to pay the country's debts, to regulate foreign commerce, and to raise armies and pay for them. Once the delegates compromised on a method for choosing the president (by electors chosen in each state) and the length of his term (four years, eligible for reelection), they readily agreed to grant him considerable power to propose legislation, veto bills of Congress (subject to congressional override), conduct diplomacy, and command the armed forces.

The delegates vested judicial authority in the Supreme Court and inferior federal courts and granted them authority over the state constitutions as well. Although the delegates could agree rather easily on the structure and powers of the new govern-

Table 7–1 Key Provisions of the Articles of Confederation, the Virginia Plan, the New Jersey Plan, and the Constitution

	Articles of Confederation	Virginia Plan	New Jersey Plan	Constitution
Executive	None	Chosen by Congress	Plural; chosen by Congress	President chosen by Electoral College
Congress	One house; one vote per state	Two houses	One house	Two houses
Judiciary	None	Yes	Yes	Yes
Federalism	Limited; each state retains full sovereignty	Yes; Congress can veto state laws	Yes; acts of Congress the "supreme law of the states"	Yes; Constitution the "supreme law of the land"; states guaranteed a republican form of government; Supreme Court to adjudicate disputes between states
Powers of Congress	Conduct diplomacy and wage war; cannot levy taxes or raise army	All powers of Articles of Confederation, plus power to make laws for nation	All powers of Articles of Confederation, plus power to regulate commerce and make states pay taxes	Numerous powers, such as levy taxes, declare war, raise army, regulate commerce, and "make all laws which shall be necessary and proper" for carrying out those powers

ment, they argued bitterly anytime the interests of their states seemed in jeopardy. The most difficult issues related to representation: Would the numbers of senators and representatives be based on population or wealth, or would each state have equal numbers? If based on population or wealth, would slaves be counted? Large states generally wanted representation to be based on either population or wealth (they had more of both), whereas northern states did not want slaves to be counted, either as population or as wealth. The conflict between the large and small states was resolved by Roger Sherman's Connecticut (or Great) Compromise: Each state would have an equal number of senators, satisfying the small states. The number of representatives would be based on either population or wealth, satisfying the large states.

The Connecticut Compromise solved the conflict between small and large states, but only by creating another between slave and free states. The South Carolinians were adamant: whether slavery was called population or wealth, the institution must be protected. The argument was fierce, with several delegates threatening to walk out. Finally, the convention compromised. Representation in the House would be based on the entire free population (including women and children, but not Indians) plus three-fifths of the slaves, thus increasing the South's representation. The delegates recognized that the Three-Fifths Compromise was fundamentally illogical, but its acceptance was needed to make the Connecticut Compromise possible.

The Three-Fifths Compromise, or Clause, became the most notorious provision in the Constitution. Although the delegates were careful not to use the word "slave" (instead using bland phrases such as "other persons"), clearly they were establishing a racial line. The convention made two other concessions to slavery. First, it agreed, over Madison's vehement protest, that Congress could not ban the slave trade until 1808 at the earliest. In addition, the Constitution included a fugitive slave clause, which required states to return runaway slaves. The reopening of the slave trade did more to strengthen slavery than the other compromises on slavery. Madison predicted accurately that "twenty years will produce all the mischief that can be apprehended from the liberty to import slaves." Between 1788 and 1808, thousands and thousands of Africans were sold into slavery in the United States.

The nationalists were determined not to leave Philadelphia without a constitution, and they were willing to make whatever compromises seemed necessary. Those compromises were eventually achieved, and the convention adjourned on September 17. The delegates' work was not over, however. Now the Constitution had to be ratified.

Ratifying the Constitution: Politics

There was nothing inevitable about the nation, the Constitution, or the particular form either took. The Constitution was the creation of a small group of men who thought nationally, the Federalists. They then had the difficult task of getting the Constitution ratified by a nation that still thought about government in almost wholly local terms. That the Constitution would be ratified was by no means a given.

The Philadelphia Convention decided that the Constitution would go into effect once nine states had ratified it. They could not bind any states that had not ratified, but the nine signatories could go ahead. Small states were the first to ratify, because they most needed the union. For example, Georgia, the fourth state to ratify, was still in many ways a frontier region, vulnerable to Indian assault, its capital at Augusta an armed camp. The most serious opposition came from the large, powerful states of Massachusetts, New York, and Virginia.

The convention had concluded on September 17, and by December 7, Delaware had already ratified the Constitution. By January 9, 1788, New Jersey, Georgia, and Connecticut followed, with barely any dispute. The Federalists in Pennsylvania forced ratification by using strong-arm tactics. The Federalists in other states learned from this mistake and more willingly made concessions to the Antifederalists (as the opponents of the Constitution were called).

In Massachusetts, as in Pennsylvania, considerable opposition came from the western part of the state among those sympathetic to Shays's Rebellion. In an inspired move that would be used also in Virginia, the Federalists made certain that the Constitution was debated section by section, enabling them to win point by point. And in another key strategic decision, the Federalists agreed that the convention in Massachusetts should propose amendments, not as a condition for ratification but as part of a package that recommended ratification. This concession, which made the Constitution both stronger and more democratic, was critical in winning ratification.

Only three more states were necessary for the Constitution to go into effect. The Federalists postponed or stalled the debate until the states most favorable to the Constitution had ratified it, as it would go into effect once nine states had ratified it. The Virginia ratifying convention was one of the most dramatic and divided. Patrick Henry, who had refused to attend the Philadelphia Convention, saying that he "smelt a rat," spoke in opposition. His impassioned speeches were rebutted by James Madison's careful and knowledgeable remarks. Having worn down the Antifederalists with logic, the Federalists carried the day, and the Constitution was ratified. The Antifederalists agreed to abide by the result, even though there had been threats of armed rebellion. The decision of Antifederalists to accept the Constitution and to participate in the government it created was one of the most important choices made in this era.

In New York, the Federalists stalled debate until news of Virginia's ratification arrived. Then they posed the inevitable question: Ten states had now voted in favor and the Constitution had been ratified; would New York join in or not? New York did, and eventually the Constitution was ratified by all the states. As a condition for ratification, several states had insisted that the first Congress consider a number of amendments. These amendments became the Bill of Rights.

Ratifying the Constitution: Ideas

The Constitution was the product of many compromises, and it did not precisely fit anyone's previous ideas. As the Federalists explained the benefits of the Constitution to skeptical Americans, and as the Antifederalists tried to explain what they thought was wrong with it, a new understanding of what American government should be evolved. Despite significant disagreements, this new understanding, which incorporated the Bill of Rights, was sufficiently broad that Antifederalists could join the new government.

Nonetheless, the differences between the Federalists and Antifederalists were profound. As a rule, the Antifederalists were more rural and less involved in the market, came from the western or backwoods regions, and were more likely to be veterans of the militia than of the Continental army. The Antifederalists were, above all, old-line republicans who warned of the dangers to liberty of corruption, tyranny, and enslavement, although now they spoke against the Federalists, not the British.

The Antifederalists believed passionately in the local community. They asserted that republics could survive only in homogeneous communities, where all people had the same interests and values. They believed that too much diversity, whether economic, cultural, ethnic, or religious, destroyed a republic. One Massachusetts Antifederalist criticized the Constitution because it would not allow states to stop immigration so as "to keep their blood pure." Although Antifederalists, like Federalists, generally supported freedom of religion, they also favored the spread of Protestantism as a means of ensuring morality.

At the same time, the Antifederalists were committed to individual rights, and it is to them that the nation is indebted for the Bill of Rights. They retained the republican fear of power, and they did not trust the person they could not see. If government were remote, then it would become oppressive, it would deprive the people of their liberties, and it would tax them. One of the most consistent complaints of the Antifederalists was not so much that taxation would be enacted without representation as that it would be enacted at all. If the national government needed money, let it ask the states for it (a system that failed under the Articles of Confederation). The Antifederalists displayed the same fear of centralized government and hatred of taxation that had led to their revolt against Britain. The Antifederalist contribution to American political thought was a continuing critique of government itself.

Federalists shared many of the beliefs of the Antifederalists, such as individual rights. Hence they readily accepted the Antifederalist proposal to list and protect those rights as amendments to the Constitution. They were also suspicious of government, most agreeing with Thomas Paine that "government even in its best state is but a necessary evil." The separation of powers and elaborate series of checks and balances that the Constitution created, as well as the system of federalism itself, reflects this fear. The Federalists divided power; unlike the Antifederalists, they did not deny it.

Their experience in the market economy, as officers in the Continental army and as members of the national government, provided the Federalists with a different perspective on political economy. They had come to believe that all people were motivated by self-interest. Unlike the Antifederalists, the Federalists were willing to accept self-interest and build a government around it.

The Federalists were convinced that no government could rest entirely on the virtue of its people. The challenge was to build a government out of imperfect human materials that would preserve liberty instead of destroying it. In *The Federalist* No. 10 (one of a series of 85 essays known as the *Federalist Papers*, written by Madison, Hamilton, and John Jay and published anonymously to influence the ratification debate), Madison explained that the causes of conflict "are sown into the nature of man." The only way of eliminating them would be either by "giving to every citizen the same opinions, the same passions, and the same interests" (the Antifederalist solution) or by destroying liberty itself. But "as long as the reason of man continues fallible, and he is at liberty to exercise it, different opinions will be formed." Toleration was the price of liberty and the necessary result of human imperfection.

In the Philadelphia Convention, the Federalists had been so intent on working out compromises and reconciling competing interests that they did not develop a philosophy to explain the profound changes they were proposing. That philosophy emerged from the ratification debates, in which it was met by the alternative philosophy of the Antifederalists. Both these bodies of thought, sometimes in harmony, sometimes in disagreement, constitute the legacy of the Revolution. This dialogue has continued to frame American government from their day until ours.

Conclusion

In rejecting the increasingly centralized British state, the Revolutionaries were clear about what they did not want. Over the course of the Revolution, they began to envision the kind of society and nation that they hoped to create. It would ensure individual liberty and economic opportunity. But this was a vague vision for the future. As the first modern nation created by revolution, the United States was entering uncharted territory. Winning independence from the world's most powerful nation, ratifying the federal Constitution, and planning for the admission of new territories into the federal union were all extraordinary accomplishments, unique in world history.

Yet there were many problems left unresolved. Not only was Britain still occupying forts in the Northwest Territory, but also the European nations were skeptical that the new nation would survive. Although the United States had more than doubled its size, much of the new territory could not be settled because it was inhabited by Indians who refused to recognize America's sovereignty. There were also disagreements among Americans themselves, particularly about the meaning of democracy. How could a nation founded on the principle of liberty practice slavery? How would individual rights be reconciled with the general welfare? Whose economic interests would be served? The American people had begun a great experiment whose outcome was far from assured.

Who, What

Thomas Jefferson   222

Richard Henry Lee   222

Antifederalists   254

Common Sense   224

Coverture   242

Federalists   253

Loyalists   228

Northwest Ordinance   246

Shays's Rebellion   241

>> TIME LINE

▼1774
Intolerable Acts

▼1775
Battles of Lexington and Concord
Fort Ticonderoga seized
Battle of Breed's Hill
Second Continental Congress convenes
Continental army created, with George Washington in charge
Congress adopts "Declaration of the Causes and Necessity of Taking Up Arms"
George III declares colonists in rebellion

Governor Dunmore offers freedom to Virginia slaves who fight for the British
Continental army attacks Canada

▼1776
Thomas Paine writes *Common Sense*
Declaration of Independence
Articles of Confederation drafted
British capture Manhattan
Washington captures Trenton and Princeton
New Jersey Constitution allows unmarried, property-owning women to vote
Washington captures Princeton

▼1777
British capture Philadelphia
American victory at Saratoga

▼1778
French enter into treaty with United States
British conquer Georgia
Sullivan expedition into New York and Pennsylvania

▼1779
Continental troops winter at Jockey Hollow

▼1780
British conquer South Carolina

Review Questions

1. What was Revolutionary ardor, and why was it highest at the beginning of the war?

2. What were American and British strategies for winning the war? What were the chief challenges the Americans faced in mounting the war, and how did they affect military strategy? What were the constraints on the British in waging a war on American soil?

3. Which Americans believed a stronger central government was needed, and why? What were the compromises they made in writing the Constitution?

4. Describe the political philosophies of the Federalists and Antifederalists.

Critical-Thinking Questions

1. Which group was more democratic, the Federalists or Antifederalists? Or were they democratic (or undemocratic) in different ways?

2. How did Americans respond to the challenges to the social order presented by their doctrine of equality?

3. Assess the relative importance of ideals and economic interests in shaping the history of the period 1775–1787.

For further review materials and resource information, please visit www.oup.com/us/ofthepeople

▼1781
Articles of Confederation ratified
Battle of Guilford Court House
Cornwallis surrenders

▼1782
Franklin begins peace discussions with British

▼1783
Newburgh Conspiracy
Treaty of Paris

▼1785
Land Ordinance of 1785
Virginia and Maryland commissioners meet at Mount Vernon

▼1786–1787
Shays's Rebellion
Meeting at Annapolis

▼1787
Northwest Ordinance
Constitutional Convention

▼1787–1788
Federalist Papers published
Constitution ratified

▼1789
George Washington inaugurated

▼1791
Bill of Rights ratified

The Ninth PILLAR erected !
"The Ratification of the Conventions of nine States, shall be sufficient for the establishment of this Constitution, between the States so ratifying the same." Art. vii.
INCIPIENT MAGNI PROCEDERE MENSES.

MAIN IDEAS

1) A variety of ideas and influences shaped the leaders of the American Revolution and how they articulated the democratic ideal on which they based their arguments and actions.

2) Conflict and compromises during and after the American Revolution laid the basis for a stronger government after 1787.

3) The social, cultural, political, and economic landscapes of the former British colonies underwent massive change in the years between 1775 and 1788. Those changed landscapes particularly affected how women, Native Americans, and enslaved persons would experience democracy in the new United States.

TOPICS

The War Begins

Winning the Revolution

The Challenge of the Revolution

A New Policy in the West

Creating a New National Government

CREATING A NEW NATION

EVENTS

The First Battles Colonists and British soldiers clashed in Massachusetts.

Congress Takes the Lead Congress established an army under George Washington.

Military Ardor Eager for war, the Continental army marched on Canada and met defeat.

Declaring Independence Congress declared independence from Britain.

Creating a National Government Congress created a national government, a confederation of the states, and wrote a constitution, the Articles of Confederation.

Creating State Governments States created new governments with much more democratic constitutions.

Competing Strategies The two armies chased each other across the Eastern Seaboard, with Britain seizing the major cities.

The British on the Offensive: 1776 Howe, the new British commander, seized New York, New Jersey, and Philadelphia, but could not control the countryside.

A Slow War: 1777–1781 The Continental army and militia worked together to wear down the British army and achieve victory.

Securing a Place in the World America secured the support of France and Spain, and a treaty with Britain that recognized independence and sold out the Indians.

The Departure of the Loyalists A large number of Loyalists left America after the war, forfeiting a vast amount of property.

The Challenge of the Economy The weak central government was unable to address economic upheavals during and after the war.

Contesting the New Economy Economic distress led to popular uprisings that raised the question of whether democratic governments could contain anarchy.

Can Women Be Citizens? A revolution based on human equality brought into question all social relations, including the role of women in both society and government.

The Challenge of Slavery Slaves were inspired by egalitarian ideas, and northern states began abolishing slavery.

The Indians' Revolution Indians were drawn into the Revolution, mostly on the British side, and suffered American reprisals.

The End of the Middle Ground The American victory brought to an end the Indians' ability to play one nation off against another.

Settling the West Congress settled competing states' claims on western territories and established a path to statehood for the territories.

A Crippled Congress The national government was powerless to address the most pressing economic issues.

Writing a New Constitution Leaders formed a new national government and Constitution in Philadelphia.

Ratifying the Constitution: Politics After contentious debate, the states ratified the new constitution.

Ratifying the Constitution: Ideas The Constitutional debate created competing sides with different views about American democracy.

CHAPTER

8

COMMON THREADS

>> What were the continuing disagree-
ments about the power of a central
government?

>> What were the conflicting values and
ideas of citizenship?

>> How did the new nation negotiate
with the European powers?

>> What was the status of slavery in the
early republic?

AMERICAN PORTRAIT

>> **Ona Judge Finds Her Freedom**

Ona Judge was only 16 when George and Martha Washington brought her to Philadelphia in 1790. She was Martha Washington's slave, the daughter of Betty, an African American seamstress, and Andrew Judge, a white indentured servant who worked as a tailor at Mt. Vernon. According to the law of slavery, because her mother was enslaved, so too was Ona. When Ona was 10, she was brought to live in Mt. Vernon itself, as a playmate for Martha Washington's granddaughter. She was trained as a seamstress and body servant, and in Philadelphia, at the president's house, she worked as Martha Washington's chambermaid. Her older brother, Austin, was a waiter.

When Washington's term was ending, the slaves were told that they would all soon return to Virginia. Martha Washington planned to give Ona Judge to another granddaughter as a wedding present. Judge decided to liberate herself. "Whilst they were packing up to go to Virginia," she later explained, "I was packing to go, I didn't know where; for I knew that if I went back to Virginia, I should never get my liberty. I had friends among the colored people of Philadelphia, had my things carried there beforehand, and left Washington's house while they were eating dinner."

Judge's friends in the free black community hid her until they could find a way to smuggle her out of the city. The Fugitive Slave Act that Washington had signed in 1793 had made it a crime to help a slave escape bondage. Judge snuck out of Philadelphia aboard a boat bound for Portsmouth, New Hampshire, where, however, it was her bad luck to run into the daughter of the Washingtons' good friend, Senator John Langdon. "Oney!" she called out. "Where in the world have you come from?" The young woman could not understand why anyone would run away "from such an excellent place." "Yes—I know," Judge replied. "But I wanted to be free, misses; wanted to learn to read and write."

Told his slave was in Portsmouth—where slavery was still legal, although unpopular—Washington asked a government official to send Judge back, and to keep it quiet. Neither Washington nor his wife could comprehend why their slave might have left. Washington believed the escape had "been planned by someone who knew what he was about and had the means to defray the expense of it and to entice her off." But when the official met with Judge, she convinced him that she had not been "decoyed away" and that her "only motive for absconding" had been "a thirst for complete freedom." She would "rather suffer death than return to slavery and [be] liable to be sold or given to any other persons."

Washington told the official he was wrong. He was certain that Ona Judge had been seduced, and then abandoned, by a Frenchman and was probably pregnant. He insisted that the official send her back, but the official explained that he did not see how he could do it "without exciting a riot or mob." He even warned the president that increasing numbers of slaves would seek "asylum" in New England and that, "for the good of Society," southerners should consider "the abolition of this species of servitude."

Continued

>> **AMERICAN PORTRAIT**
Continued

Not even the president could persuade the New Englander to return an escaped slave against her will, so Judge remained in New Hampshire. She married a free black sailor, John Staines, and bore three children. She learned to read and converted to Christianity. Several years later, however, one of Martha Washington's nephews turned up at Judge's house, when her husband was at sea. She told him, "I am free now and choose to remain so." When the nephew told Senator Langdon that he planned to seize Judge by force, the senator passed word to Judge so that she could go into hiding.

As the gospel of liberty spread through the new nation, slaves such as Ona Judge seized their own freedom, and along the way they had help from free blacks and whites both, redefining the meaning of American democracy.

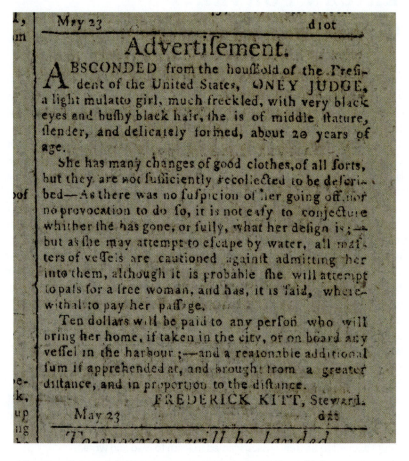

Advertisement by George Washington's steward offering a reward for the return of runaway slave Ona Judge.

OUTLINE

The Struggle to Form a Government
Creating a National Government
The States and the Bill of Rights
Debating the Economy

A Society in Transition
A People on the Move

AMERICAN LANDSCAPE:
   Philadelphia
The First Emancipation Movements
Conflicting Visions of Republican Society

PRIMARY SOURCE:
   Petition from the Pennsylvania Society for Promoting the Abolition of Slavery
The Culture of the Republic

The Struggle to Form a Government

At his presidential inauguration, George Washington confessed that "among all the vicissitudes incident to life, no event could have filled me with greater anxieties" than the news of his election. He was right to worry. Not only was the new nation embarking on an almost unprecedented experiment in democratic government, but the country faced enormous challenges, none greater than proving that a government of the people, by the people, and for the people could work.

Creating a National Government

Although Washington did not take the oath of office until April 30, his term began on March 4, 1789. When he was inaugurated, Congress was already in session. It was not a promising start: only 13 members of the House of Representatives and 8 senators were on hand when the first Congress convened. Yet the new government faced the unprecedented challenge not only of making the new structure work, but also of earning the allegiance of the people. Almost every challenge of the 1790s, from economic policy to controlling the borderlands and managing foreign affairs, was, at base, about creating a government strong enough to gain the loyalty of its citizens, but not so strong that, like the British government against which they had rebelled, it alienated them instead.

Among Congress's first tasks was deciding what the president should be called. Believing that the president needed an impressive title to demonstrate that the new nation was "civilized," a Senate committee recommended "His Highness the President of the United States of America, and Protector of the Liberties." But the House argued that the suggestion smacked of aristocratic pretension and in the end insisted simply on "the President of the United States."

Meanwhile, Congress approved official advisors to the president (the cabinet). Washington's first administration reflected both his own close circle of friends and the political clout of the large states. The president was from Virginia, the most populous state, as were his secretary of state, Thomas Jefferson, and his attorney general, Edmund Randolph. For his secretary of the treasury he chose former aide-de-camp Alexander Hamilton of New York. Washington's vice president (John Adams), his secretary of war (Henry Knox), and his postmaster general (Samuel Osgood) were from Massachusetts. The Constitution had specified the existence of a third branch of government, a federal judiciary, but had not offered much of a blueprint for its structure. Congress might have created a federal system that dominated state

Securing the Nation
  Borders and Boundaries
  Controlling the Borderlands
  The Whiskey Rebellion
  Other Revolutions
  Between France and England

AMERICA AND THE WORLD:
  Citizenship in an Age of Revolution

To the Brink of War
  The Administration of John Adams
  Tensions at Home

DEBATING HISTORY:
  The Politics of the 1790s and Democracy

Conclusion

courts. Recalling the high-handedness of British courts, however, with the Judiciary Act of 1789 Congress created a federal court system with limited power. Under its first chief justice, John Jay, the Supreme Court remained a minor branch of government.

The States and the Bill of Rights

The Federalists had agreed to let the state ratifying conventions propose amendments to the Constitution, possibly to be added as a bill of rights. Two hundred of these had been suggested. Some Federalists originally opposed the idea of a bill of rights: if the Constitution did not protect liberty and property, no appended list of rights would help. But they agreed to allow Congress to make amendments to the Constitution when several states made it a condition for ratification (see Chapter 7).

Within a month of Washington's inauguration, James Madison, recently elected to the House, set about making good on the promise. Madison never expected to incorporate all 200 of the state proposals in a bill of rights, and he never imagined that he could placate all of the groups critical of the Constitution. But he did believe that adding a bill of rights could secure the Antifederalists' support for the Constitution without harming "the structure & stamina of the Government." This belief guided Madison's selection of proposed amendments. He ignored those that would alter the structure of the central government or strengthen the powers of the states at the expense of the federal government, and he dismissed outright one that would have limited the power of Congress to levy taxes. Instead, he focused on amendments that affirmed human rights within the structure already ratified (although the reference to a "well-regulated Militia" in the Second Amendment and the Third Amendment's restrictions on the quartering of soldiers reflected Americans' profound mistrust of standing national armies). The First Amendment protected citizens against congressional interference with freedom of religion, speech, the press, the right of assembly, and the right of petition. The Fourth Amendment protected the rights of citizens "against unreasonable [government] searches and seizures." The Fifth, Sixth, Seventh, and Eighth Amendments laid down the rights of citizens accused of crimes and established protection from "cruel and unusual punishments." The Ninth affirmed that the Constitution's silence on a specific right of the people "shall not be construed" as a denial of that right, and the Tenth ambiguously reserved all rights not delegated to the new government "to the States respectively, or to the people."

Congress eventually sent twelve amendments to the states for ratification. Two were rejected: one on congressional compensation (adopted in 1992 as the Twenty-seventh Amendment) and one covering representation. The remaining ten amendments were declared in force on December 15, 1791.

Debating the Economy

As Congress deliberated the structure of government, Secretary of the Treasury Alexander Hamilton turned to the problem of financial solvency, the problem that had plagued the Confederation (see Chapter 7). His proposals to strengthen the nation by strengthening the economy soon brought to the fore underlying disagreements about the future of the nation.

The first challenge was to raise money for current expenses. Hamilton proposed that Congress place a tariff on imported goods and the foreign ships carrying them. The Tariff Act of 1789 passed easily. In the coming years the federal government would depend on tariffs for the vast majority of its funds (see Table 8–1).

The next challenge was how to pay off the debt left over from the Revolution, a total of $79 million that included not only the amounts the government had borrowed from foreign countries and promised to soldiers and suppliers, but also the debts owed by state governments. In a plan known as "funding and assumption," Hamilton proposed that the government assume all of the debt and pay it off at full value, even the parts that were in badly depreciated paper money. But rather than paying off the national debt immediately, the government would give creditors new federal bonds that paid interest (which in turn would be paid for by a new federal excise tax on whiskey and other luxuries). In this way, Hamilton thought he could turn the national debt into a "blessing" by making sure that people with money had a literal investment in the success of the nation.

Madison and Jefferson were alarmed, however. Not only had most southern states paid their debts by 1790, but many soldiers and ordinary people had sold off their paper money to speculators at far less than its face value—sometimes as little as 10 percent. The speculators would now reap huge profits. Why should they benefit? At the same time, southerners were also unhappy about the possibility that the nation's capital (temporarily located in New York) might be moved permanently to Philadelphia. They preferred a site in Virginia, closer to the center of the country. At last, representatives struck a compromise: Hamilton got his debt plan, and southerners got the nation's capital.

Table 8-1 Sources of Federal Revenue, 1790–1799

	Tariffs	Internal Taxes	Other (inc. sale of public lands)
1790–1791	$4,399,000		$ 10,000
1792	3,443,000	$209,000	17,000
1793	4,255,000	338,000	59,000
1794	4,801,000	274,000	356,000
1795	5,588,000	338,000	188,000
1796	6,568,000	475,000	1,334,000
1797	7,550,000	575,000	563,000
1798	7,106,000	644,000	150,000
1799	6,610,000	779,000	157,000

Source: Curtis P. Nettels, The Emergence of a National Economy, 1775–1815 (New York: Holt, Rinehart and Winston, 1962), p. 221.

Hamilton next recommended the creation of a national bank that would ensure a stable currency and enable the government to mobilize capital for development, two activities he considered essential to an expanding commercial economy. The bank would be chartered by Congress to collect, hold, and pay out government receipts; hold the new federal bonds and oversee their payment; and issue currency; and it would be backed up by government bonds.

The bank proposal passed Congress against the opposition of Madison, Jefferson, and other Virginians, who viewed the bank as an extralegal structure to support the interests of merchants and financiers against "the republican interest." Jefferson advised the president to veto the bill on the grounds that the Constitution gave the federal government no expressed authority to create such an institution, a position known as *strict constructionism*. Hamilton countered that every specified power in the Constitution implied "a right to employ all the means requisite . . . to the attainment" of that power. In granting the federal government the responsibility to coin and regulate money, pass and collect taxes, pay debts, and "make all laws which shall be necessary and proper" to these ends, the Constitution implied the power to create a bank. Washington accepted Hamilton's position and signed the bank bill.

Hamilton's final major recommendation to Congress was that the federal government subsidize domestic manufacturing. Jefferson and Madison were now convinced that the republic was being sold out to speculators and financiers. Hamilton had been using a Philadelphia newspaper, John Fenno's *Gazette of the United States*, to promote his views. In October 1791, Jefferson and Madison prevailed on their friend Philip Freneau to come to Philadelphia to establish a newspaper favorable to their position, and Madison began to use Freneau's *National Gazette* to publish essays in which he framed the rationale for the permanent necessity of political parties in a republic. There would always be schemers who placed self-interest above the good of the whole. Parties, according to Madison, arose in a struggle of the true "republican interest" against such dangerous conspirators, a struggle of "good" against "evil." He identified the two groups as "Republicans" and "Anti-Republicans."

Hamilton's efforts to create a strong government based on a commercial economy alienated those such as Madison and Jefferson who believed Hamilton's policies were "subverting step by step the principles of the Constitution." This theme was taken up by the Democratic Republican Societies, groups that had come together in late 1792 and early 1793 to support the French Revolution. They became the nucleus of the first political party, the Democratic Republicans. They believed that the new government was becoming too strong and thus a threat to "liberty

> One of the advantages of manufacturing is "the employment of persons who would otherwise be idle (and in many cases a burthen on the community), either from the byass of temper, habit, infirmity of body, or some other cause, indisposing, or disqualifying them for the toils of the Country. It is worthy of particular remark, that, in general, women and Children are rendered more useful and the latter more early useful by manufacturing establishments, than they would otherwise be. Of the number of persons employed in the Cotton Manufactories of Great Britain, it is computed that 4/7 [four out of seven] nearly are women and children; of whom the greatest proportion are children and many of them of a very tender age."
>
> ALEXANDER HAMILTON,
> Report on Manufactures, 1791

and equality." The societies included some common people, but most members were from middling and even prosperous families. Washington blamed the societies for spreading "suspicions, jealousies, and accusations of the whole government."

At the same time, the supporters of Hamilton's policies became known as the Federalists, to suggest their commitment to the new government. At first, most candidates resisted formal party alignment, however, and congressional voting patterns showed little sense of "party" discipline. There were several reasons for this, including the tendency of most citizens (including many partisans themselves) to associate political parties with corruption and a loss of independence. By 1796, the opposing groups coalesced into Democratic Republicans and Federalists, and congressional voting patterns revealed a distinct tendency to vote on one side or the other.

A Society in Transition

The new political parties reflected growing divisions in society itself. The end of the Revolution ushered in a period of explosive growth—in the economy, in population, and in territory. As one American observed, "Population is encreasing, new houses building, new lands clearing, new settlements forming, and new manufacture establishing with a rapidity beyond conception." So much change offered opportunity and danger both. Americans responded with both optimism and fear.

A People on the Move

A quarter century of political unrest, compounded by the depression of the 1780s, had stalled the development of the American economy, but once peace was restored, the patterns of growth and development of the mid-eighteenth century resumed. Even with the disruptions of the Revolution, the American population grew at the greatest rate in its entire history in the 1780s, and it continued to double every 20 years, primarily from natural increase. In the 1790s, the United States added 1.4 million people, only 100,000 of whom were immigrants. Many of those immigrants were political refugees, fleeing revolutions in France and Saint-Domingue and political repression in Britain and Ireland. For most of the growing population, native-born or refugees, democracy meant opportunity and political freedom. Thirty thousand, however, were enslaved Africans, purchased to enhance their owners' opportunity at the denial of their own.

The United States was overwhelmingly a rural nation and would remain so until well into the nineteenth century. (Ninety-seven percent of its almost 4 million people enumerated in the first census lived in the countryside, most of them on family farms of 50–100 acres.) As the population grew, thousands of families looked for fertile, inexpensive land so that they could continue as farmers. They found it in the hinterlands of established states and in the territories that would become states over the next several decades. Seeking quick revenue, the government sold large tracts of land to speculators and large proprietors, some of whom were federal officials. Alexander Hamilton and Secretary of War Henry Knox were both silent partners in the huge Macomb Purchase in New York. Speculators also bought up land abandoned by Loyalists. William Cooper, for example, purchased—for a suspiciously low price—the huge Otsego, New York, tract that had been owned by William Franklin.

In regions such as frontier Maine, squatters simply occupied the land that such "great proprietors" hoped to sell for a huge profit. Squatters built small cabins, cleared the land, and planted crops, resisting when the legal owners tried to oust them. Such disputes were typically resolved when the squatters purchased the land—but for far less than the speculators had wanted. The population of Kentucky and Tennessee tripled in the 1790s. By 1800, 220,000 people lived in Kentucky, and not a single adult (excluding Native Americans) had been born in the state. At the same time, settlers were trickling into what would become Indiana, Alabama, and Mississippi, and almost 50,000 moved into Ohio. Because land in these territories was still held by Native Americans, conflict was almost inevitable as settlers pressed the new government to secure the land for them.

American cities grew rapidly, too. Philadelphia and New York grew by almost 50 percent between 1789 and 1800. St. Louis, Detroit, Pittsburgh, Cincinnati, Lexington, Cleveland, Nashville, and Louisville all became important regional centers, serving the surrounding populations. As in the farming regions, the rapid influx of population and its youthfulness—two-thirds of the white population was 25 or younger—made it hard to control. Philadelphia had a particularly large number of young people who were on their own. The result was a boisterous culture, particularly among the lower classes. Men and women of all classes took advantage of a more liberal sexual environment. Rates of adultery and divorce increased, and the proportion of children born outside of marriage doubled. Houses of prostitution flourished, as did taverns such as the one owned by the free African American John York, where "all the loose and idle characters of the city, whether whites, blacks, or mulattoes . . . indulge in riotous mirth and dancing til dawn."

The Quilting Frolic What appears to be a cozy domestic scene actually reveals the complexity of urban life in Philadelphia at the time: We see women putting away their work as fashionably dressed guests arrive. The many consumer objects, from the well-stocked cupboard to the plates on the table and the tea set on the tray held by the African American girl, show that the family is prosperous. So too does the presence of African American servants, both with the exaggerated features that were beginning to become racist stereotypes.

AMERICAN LANDSCAPE

>> Philadelphia

Serving as the nation's capital in the 1790s, Philadelphia was the city where the new doctrines of freedom were given shape, in the new Congress Hall just west of Independence Hall, in humble homes, and in the president's mansion.

Philadelphia was America's biggest city and growing bigger by the day. Between 1780 and 1790, the population grew by more than 50 percent, to 42,520. After the Revolution, European immigrants began to arrive again, and people from the countryside flocked to the city. This rapid growth led to overcrowding, especially for the laboring class. Poor people were renters, living in rooming houses or back alleys, typically in overcrowded wooden buildings. Martin Summers, a laborer, and Henry Birkey, a shoemaker, and their families shared a home—and the annual rent of £18. Tailor William Smith and his wife shared their tiny home—550 square feet—with their three children and two boarders. Mrs. Smith cooked their meals in her fireplace.

Philadelphia was just coming out of the postwar depression. During the depression, even skilled workers had trouble making ends meet, and some, such as shoemaker John Dougherty and his wife Esther and their three children, had to seek poor relief. Other laboring families cut back on their expenses, for example eating more grains and less meat and vegetables and using less firewood. Such economies, of course, weakened them and made them more vulnerable to disease.

As the population increased and land in the center of the city became more valuable, poor people were forced to move to the outskirts of Philadelphia. Wealthier people bought lots in the choicest locations and erected three-story brick houses, 18 feet wide but two or three times as deep, and with separate washhouses, stables, and kitchens.

One of the most splendid homes of the day was the one on Market Street owned by the financier Robert Morris. George Washington had stayed with the Morrises when he attended the Constitutional Convention and liked it so much that when he became president, he rented the house from Morris. By the standards of the day, it was a mansion, two-thirds the size of the White House, which would be built several years later. Even with at least six bedrooms and four servants' rooms, a detached two-story kitchen, an icehouse, a bathhouse, *Continued*

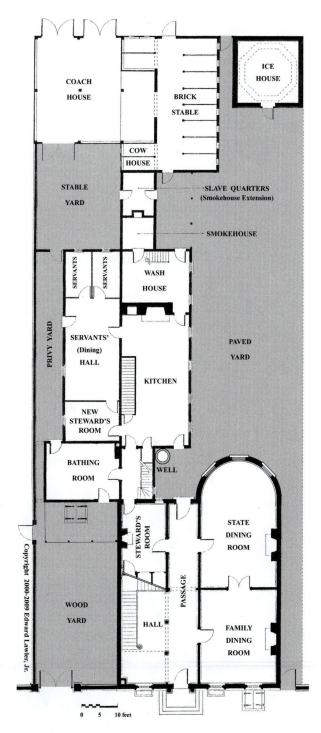

Floor Plan of the President's House in Philadelphia This is how historians think the first floor of George Washington's house might have looked. The servants' hall and the slave quarters were added by Washington in 1790.

and a stable for 12 horses, it was not large enough for Washington's household. Washington added a two-story bow and rooms for his servants. When the Washingtons took up residence in November, they had with them about 30 people, not only the president and his wife Martha but also her grandchildren, his secretary and the secretary's wife, 3 more male secretaries, 8 African slaves, and about 15 white servants. The president's staff lived and worked in the home. Their office was on the third floor, and people who had business with the president had to walk up two flights of stairs and pass by the private chambers to get to it.

Philadelphia was also home to about 1,600 African Americans, two-thirds of whom were free and who created the nation's first significant free black community.

James Oronoko Dexter, one of the leaders of that community, lived only a few blocks from Independence Hall, on the north side of Fifth Street, between Arch and Race, then on the edge of the city. This was a densely populated neighborhood filled with frame-and-brick homes and workshops of artisans, laborers, and merchants. Dexter's two-story house, which he shared with his wife and family, was described in 1791 as "very plain." Dexter's wife Sarah worked as a washerwoman. The center of this community was only two blocks from the president's house.

Philadelphia in the 1790s was a bustling city where people lived and worked in the same buildings, rich and poor living in the same neighborhoods and even the same houses.

In later decades this growing population would provide the workforce for the industrial revolution, but in the first decades of the new nation, most people worked as farmers.

In spite of their hostility to the growing merchant "monied interest," most farmers sought international as well as local markets for their crops. The principal exports were all farm or plantation products—grains, tobacco, and rice. But without the protection of Britain (which banned Americans from trading with British colonies), Americans struggled to secure old markets and establish new ones, at the same time that the British were dumping manufactured goods into the American market at low prices that undercut American manufacturers. As farm families struggled, much of the burden fell on women, who were required to increase production of cloth, butter, and other marketable goods. Their earnings provided the cash that enabled families to make ends meet or, for the more successful, to expand further into the market.

The depression of the 1780s had hit American merchants especially badly. Some had gone bankrupt, while others had made loans to western farmers who could not repay them. By 1790, the remaining trade was concentrated in fewer hands. These merchants sought new markets, for example in Asia. Americans took pride in these early ventures. As the *Massachusetts* prepared to sail for Canton in 1790, "parties of people of every rank of society frequently came on board to gratify their curiosity and express their admiration." The voyage, however, was a disaster. The ship was made of rotten wood, and the crew, which lacked proper instruments and expertise both, guessed at latitude and longitude. It took several years

American Hong in China Each Western nation built its own trading house, or "hong," in Canton. This early-nineteenth century porcelain bowl shows the American hong with the American flag flying above it.

for American merchants to establish an international trade, but over the decade they did, and by 1815, they were reexporting (to Europe and the Caribbean) $23 million in goods a year, including such Asian products as pepper, tea, and Chinese porcelain and fabrics. The profits from this trade financed the establishment of American factories several decades later.

In so diverse a country, its population rapidly growing, spreading across hundreds of thousands of square miles and even trading halfway across the world, how were the people to be attached to the nation?

The First Emancipation Movements

Although slavery had existed in America for over 150 years by the time of ratification of the Constitution, its continued existence in the new republic was not a foregone conclusion. By 1789, many European nations were beginning to reconsider their involvement in the slave trade. Even England, which led all other nations in slave trafficking by the late eighteenth century, outlawed slavery within its borders and by 1783 had begun what would become a 50-year-long drive to abolish both the English slave trade and the ownership of slaves by English subjects abroad (including in the British colonies). Although Napoleon would later resurrect slavery in the French colonies, in 1794 revolutionary France abolished slavery in the nation and all of its colonies.

Could slavery have been abolished in the United States as well? The numbers alone presented a formidable challenge. Roughly 18 percent of the total population of 3.9 million was enslaved, and slavery was a national institution (see Table 8–2). In large areas of Virginia and South Carolina, slaves made up at least half of the population, while in 1789 northerners still owned more than 30,000 slaves (see Map 8–1). New York City had the second-highest number of enslaved people of any city, after Charleston, South Carolina. Northern merchants were active in the overseas slave trade, and countless shippers, merchants, and artisans in the North relied on business ties to the South. Moreover, the Constitution implicitly recognized slavery as a part of the republic in the Three-Fifths Compromise and explicitly protected the slave trade for at least 20 years.

On the other hand, although few were prepared to embrace a racially mixed society, many white

I was about four years old. My mother had several children, and they were sold upon master's death to separate purchasers. She was sold . . . to a Georgia trader. . . . After [my new master] had purchased me . . . he took me before him on his horse, and started home; but my poor mother, when she saw me leaving her for the last time, ran after me, took me down from the horse, clasped me in her arms, and wept loudly and bitterly over me. My master seemed to pity her, and endeavored to soothe her distress by telling her that he would be a good master to me, and that I should not want anything. She then . . . besought my master to buy her and the rest of her children, and not permit them to be carried away by the negro buyers; but whilst thus entreating him to save her and her family, the slave-driver, who had [already] bought her came running in pursuit of her with a raw-hide in his hand. When he overtook us, he told her he was her master now, and ordered her to give that little negro to its owner. . . . [H]e gave her two or three heavy blows on the shoulders . . . , snatched me from her arms, handed me to my master . . . and dragged her back towards the place of sale. My master then quickened the pace of his horse; and . . . the cries of my poor parent became more and more indistinct—at length they died away in the distance, and I never again heard the voice of my poor mother.

Charles Ball,

describing the last time he saw his mother

Table 8-2 Americans in 1790

Population: 3,929,000					
Northeast		**Northcentral**		**South**	
Whites	1,901,000	Whites	50,000	Whites	1,271,000
African Americans	67,000	African Americans	1,000	African Americans	690,000
Urban	160,000	Urban	0	Urban	42,000
Rural	1,807,000	Rural	51,000	Rural	1,919,000
Free African Americans	58,000				
African American slaves	700,000				

Americans considered slavery immoral and contrary to the principles on which their new government had been founded. Almost no one was prepared to make a positive, public defense of the institution. When Ona Judge ran away, George Washington tried to get her back—but out of the public eye.

Many Christian denominations (notably including Quakers, Baptists, and Methodists) spoke out against slavery. None of the first state constitutions specifically recognized slavery, and many central and northern states took steps to outlaw it, either directly in their new state constitutions or in subsequent state supreme court decisions interpreting those constitutions. Vermont, Massachusetts, and New Hampshire enacted state constitutions with broad declarations of rights, although it took a series of court decisions in Massachusetts to apply that declaration to slavery. Pennsylvania had been home to an active abolition movement since at least 1775, when Anthony Benezet organized the Society for the Relief of Free Negroes Unlawfully Held in Bondage. African Americans were important abolitionist voices. In his 1786 Address to the Negroes of the State of New York, Jupiter Hammon, a slave on Long Island and the first published African American author, called on slaves to obey their masters, refrain from stealing, and cultivate humility. But he also noted that slaves would be welcomed in heaven (where "we shall find nobody to reproach us for being black, or for being slaves") and advocated gradual emancipation. As Phillis Wheatley (1753–1784), an African American poet, wrote in "On Being Brought from Africa to America," the subject of salvation spoke to the subject of slavery: "Some view our sable race with scornful eye, / 'Their colour is a diabolic die.' / Remember, Christians, Negros, black as Cain, / May be refin'd, and join th' angelic train."

Although the process of emancipation in the North was sometimes slow and often contested, the first steps toward the elimination of slavery had

Map 8-1 Distribution of Black Population, 1775 At the founding of the nation, the overwhelming majority of African Americans lived in the South and were enslaved. In parts of the South Atlantic states, African Americans had long outnumbered whites. (Future states here are identified in parentheses.) *Lester J. Cappon et al., eds., Atlas of Early American History: The Revolutionary Era, 1760–1790 (Princeton, NJ: Princeton University Press, 1976).*

been taken. By 1804, every state north of Delaware had placed slavery on the road to extinction. In the North, free blacks collected in the port cities, where they found employment, the men most often in the maritime trades and the women as domestic servants. The free black population of New York almost doubled in the 1790s, while that of Philadelphia tripled. Once they were able to choose freely where to live, African Americans began establishing their own neighborhoods (such as the one where Ona Judge sought refuge), their own schools, churches, burial grounds, and organizations. Free property-owning African American males enjoyed the right to vote in many northern and even some southern states in the first years of the republic, although few black men had sufficient property to exercise that right.

Even in the South there were signs of a growing opposition to slavery. Virginia, Delaware, and Maryland all passed laws permitting the private manumission of slaves. As a result, the number of free blacks in the upper South tripled between 1790 and 1810. Although the emancipation movement never took hold in the lower South, even there, slave owners were put on the defensive. In the 1790s, many Americans hoped, and even believed, that slavery would gradually be eliminated.

Conflicting Visions of Republican Society

Agreeing on a structure for the new republic had not been easy. It had taken free Americans thirteen years to frame their government: a year to propose the Articles of Confederation, four years to pass them, seven more to fight over them and devise an alternative (the federal Constitution), and two years to ratify it. Even then, many Americans still opposed ratification, and two states (North Carolina and Rhode Island) had not yet ratified the Constitution when George Washington was sworn into office. Moreover, supporters of the Constitution did not necessarily agree on its meanings or on the principles of a republican society.

Still, there was a common ground of beliefs for many white inhabitants of the new republic. Most free Americans thought the success of the republic depended on the character of its citizens, by which they meant the traits that would enable citizens to protect themselves against either would-be tyrants or lawless mobs. For many, these traits included industriousness, independence, and an ability to put self-interest aside for the larger good. Very often, these qualities were associated with certain types of economic life. When people grew too wealthy and used to luxury, many believed, they grew lazy and were willing to support corrupt governments for their own selfish purposes. Poverty, on the other hand, led to desperation, riots, and anarchy.

This consensus obscured real disagreements about the nature of a republic and about who really embodied its key virtues. In 1790, 97 percent of free Americans lived in nuclear households (parents and children) on farms or in rural villages, where they produced much of their own food, clothes, tools, and furnishings. For this great mass of the people, republican virtue was rooted in the land, and particularly in the working freehold farm. In *Letters from an American Farmer* (1782), J. Hector St. John de Crevecoeur had identified the new nation as "a people of cultivators scattered over an immense territory . . . animated with the spirit of an industry that is unfettered and unrestrained, because each person works for himself." Thomas Jefferson echoed this view in his *Notes on the State of Virginia* (1785). He thought that only the independent farmer could achieve true self-reliance, warning that "dependence begets subservience and venality, [and] suffocates the germ of virtue."

>> Petition from the Pennsylvania Society for Promoting the Abolition of Slavery

Founded just before the American Revolution, the Pennsylvania Society for Promoting the Abolition of Slavery was the oldest abolitionist organization in the western world when it petitioned Congress in 1790 to end the slave trade and emancipate all those held in slavery. Pro-slavery Congressmen denounced the petition, which was signed by the society's president Benjamin Franklin, and took no action on it, holding that the Constitution barred them from curtailing the slave trade until 1808.

That from a regard for the happiness of Mankind an Association was formed several years since in this State by a number of her Citizens of various religious denominations for promoting the *Abolition of Slavery* & for the relief of those unlawfully held in bondage. A just & accurate Conception of the true Principles of liberty, as it spread through the land, produced accessions to their numbers, many friends to their Cause, & a legislative Co-operation with their views, which, by the blessing of Divine Providence, have been successfully directed to the *relieving from bondage a large number of their fellow Creatures of the African Race*. They have also the Satisfaction to observe, that in consequence of that Spirit of Philanthropy & genuine liberty which is generally diffusing its beneficial Influence, similar Institutions are gradually forming at home & abroad.

The seal of The Pennsylvania Society for Promoting the Abolition of Slavery, and for the Relief of Free Negroes Unlawfully Held in Bondage, and for Improving the Condition of the African Race.

That mankind are all formed by the same Almighty being, alike objects of his Care & equally designed for the Enjoyment of Happiness the Christian Religion teaches us to believe & the Political Creed of America fully coincides with the Position. Your Memorialists, particularly engaged in attending to the Distresses arising from Slavery, believe it their indispensable Duty to present this Subject to your notice. They have observed with great Satisfaction that many important & salutary Powers are vested in you for "promoting the Welfare & *securing the blessings of liberty to the People of the United States.*" And as they conceive, that these blessings ought rightfully to be administered, without distinction of Colour, to all descriptions of People, so they indulge themselves in the pleasing expectation, that nothing, which can be done for the relief of the unhappy objects of their care, will be either omitted or delayed.

From a persuasion that equal liberty was originally the Portion, & is still the Birthright of all men, & influenced by the strong ties of Humanity & the Principles of their Institution, your Memorialists conceive themselves *bound to use all justifiable endeavours to loosen the bounds of Slavery* and promote a general Enjoyment of the blessings of Freedom. Under these Impressions they earnestly entreat your serious attention to the Subject of Slavery, that you will be pleased to countenance the *Restoration of liberty* to those unhappy Men, who alone, in this land of Freedom, are degraded into perpetual Bondage, and who, amidst the general Joy of surrounding Freemen, are groaning in Servile Subjection, that you will devise means for removing this *Inconsistency from the Character of the American People*, that you will promote mercy and Justice towards this distressed Race, & that you will Step to the very verge of the Powers vested in you for discouraging every Species of Traffick in the Persons of our fellow men.

Benjamin Franklin, president, Pennsylvania Society for Promoting the Abolition of Slavery, "Petition to Congress," in Gary B. Nash, *Race and Revolution* (Madison, WI: Madison House, 1990), pp. 144–145.

Questions

1. The petitioners say that both the Christian religion and the "political creed of America" support the end to slavery. How do they connect these principles?

2. The petitioners say that slavery represents an "inconsistency" in the "character of the American people." What do they mean?

3. Why do you think the petitioners would have asked Congress to end the slave trade knowing that Congress could not ban it until 1808?

This emphasis on labor and the private ownership of land did not mean that rural Americans opposed manufacturing and trade. Farms were tied to villages that were tied to larger markets in the port cities and overseas. Even Jefferson considered overseas trade essential to rural virtue, because it gave Americans access to manufactured goods without the blight of industrialization. As trade with Britain improved and the demand for American agricultural products grew both in Europe and in the plantation slave colonies of the West Indies, rural Americans agreed that a successful new nation required a booming free international trade.

The profits made by large merchants and landowners were another matter. Farmers, small shopkeepers, landless settlers, and craft workers saw the wealth of large merchant families and families with great landed estates as the moral equivalent of theft. "[N]o person can possess property without laboring," farmer and tavern keeper William Manning emphasized, "unless he get it by force or craft, fraud or fortune, out of the earnings of others." Manning viewed this distinction as "the great dividing line" of society.

Unsurprisingly, merchants and landed proprietors saw matters differently. They agreed that republican virtue resided in labor, but they included commercial labor, which opened markets and expanded trade, nurtured invention, taught discipline, and contributed new wealth to society. Alexander Hamilton, the first secretary of the Treasury, was a chief proponent of this view. Hamilton, who was born in the West Indies, was left on his own at the age of 13 when his mother, a shopkeeper, died. His father, who had never married his mother, had abandoned the family earlier. Hamilton then entered the merchant firm of Beekman and Cruger as a clerk, becoming so valuable that Cruger paid for his college education. These experiences taught Hamilton that the merchant class (traders, investors, and financiers who took risks to generate new wealth, new markets, and new ideas) best embodied the qualities needed in republican citizens.

Just as farmers viewed merchants and financiers with distrust, so wealthy merchants and proprietors often regarded Americans of the middling and laboring ranks as their inferiors. Most people were undisciplined and gullible, Hamilton believed. Easily deceived by fanatics and demagogues, they required proper leadership. City elites dismissed their backcountry compatriots as "yahoos" and "clodpoles." To the rich, the rude huts of homesteaders, their barefoot children, and their diets of beans, potatoes, and coarse bread all signaled not the hardships of settlement but rather the laziness of the settlers. The merchants and proprietors especially disliked the casualness with which country people treated debt. Rural people conducted trade in a combination of barter, cash, and promissory notes, with records kept casually and payments constantly renegotiated. Large-scale merchants and proprietors needed timely payment, preferably in hard currency, to pay off their own debts or to make new deals and investments.

Most white Americans denied that hard work produced republican character in slaves. They argued that because slaves could not own the property they produced, slaves' labor could never lead to self-reliance or the stake in the public order essential to citizenship. This view was rife with contradictions. As Thomas Jefferson, himself a slave owner, pointed out in *Notes on the State of Virginia*, slavery undermined the ambition of slave owners. "[I]n a warm climate, no man will labor for himself who can make another labor for him," Jefferson wrote. If slaves were of bad character, simply because of their status as slaves, then surely the institution of slavery was itself unrepublican.

Nevertheless, the unrepublicanism seemed to attach itself to slaves themselves, rather than to the institution. Even as northern states moved to abolish slavery, many expressed concern about the ability of former slaves to adjust to freedom and democracy and suggested that freed slaves should be resettled in the territories or Africa. In the northern states, although some working-class whites socialized freely with African Americans, other Americans refused to work with them. White passengers refused to ride in stagecoaches alongside them, and landlords refused to rent them any but the worst housing. Meanwhile, the Naturalization Act of 1790 restricted naturalized citizenship to "free white persons" (who had resided in the country for two years).

Although free white women were citizens of the nation, women labored under severe legal disabilities and restrictive social prejudices. Under the English common-law principle of coverture, a married woman subsumed her separate legal identity under that of her husband. While some individual women (usually wealthy women with access to special legal measures) did own property in their own names, as a category married women could not own property or wages, could not enter into contracts, and were not the legal guardians of their own children. Most women lost control of their property when they married and took little property other than their own clothing in divorce.

Social prejudice also made it difficult for most women to earn an independent living. Wives and unmarried women continued to ply their skills as midwives, seamstresses, hucksters, grocers, and milliners and in a variety of other trades. But the more lucrative male crafts and professions were closed to them, and most working women struggled to make ends meet.

A growing bias against the idea of female autonomy marked the final years of the eighteenth century. The earlier years of the century were by no means a golden age of female independence, yet age, wealth, and family appear to have mattered as much as gender in delineating individual status. And for a time it seemed that women (especially wealthy white women) might be among the beneficiaries of the Revolutionary spirit. Indeed, New Jersey granted single, property-owning women the right to vote in 1776 (but rescinded it in 1807), and women participated actively in the discussions both of their own new republic and of the French Revolution. In France and in England, women spoke out publicly against restraints on the natural rights of women.

In the wake of the creation of the new republic, however, attitudes toward women grew more conservative. As the *Apollo Magazine* put it in 1795, the exemplary woman married and asked no more than that "Her good man [was] happy and her Infants clean." Ironically, these hardening attitudes may in some ways have resulted from the experiment in democracy itself. In the face of social and political disorder, controlling the conduct of females may have seemed reassuring to some Americans.

The Culture of the Republic

Americans discussed these views, both the agreements and the disagreements, through a variety of practices—written and simply enacted.

Perhaps most important was the circulation of information through newspapers. Although fewer than 20 newspapers were being published in all the British North American colonies in 1760, by 1790 the new republic claimed 106 newspapers, and by 1800 more than 200. Most stories were strictly local, but editors also published official government documents and reprinted articles from other cities, states, and even countries.

The 1790s also saw the beginnings of an American fictional literature. In 1789, William Hill Brown published *The Power of Sympathy*, often considered the first genuinely American novel because some of its content was based on events in Boston. Other novelists also tried to develop distinctly American stories and themes. Actress and author Susanna Rowson wrote the historical novel *Rachel and Reuben* (1798), which imagined the lives of the fictional heirs of Columbus, and Charles Brockden Brown chose the countryside near Philadelphia as the setting for *Wieland* (1798), a tale of religious zealotry and the fallibility of human reason. In Connecticut, a group of poets known as the Hartford Wits produced a series of political satires celebrating New England as the model for national order and self-discipline.

News was easiest to come by in the cities, but a variety of information sources linked city to backcountry and region to region. Copies of periodicals and books found their way into the countryside, and comparatively high literacy rates produced a reading audience that went beyond urban elites. In shops, taverns, and homes, those who could not read listened as stories were read aloud. Where papers did not reach, travelers, peddlers, and preachers brought information and opinion.

In cities, prosperous Americans established salons (where local luminaries, male and female, gathered to discuss politics and culture), museums, libraries, and specialized societies of learning. Many of these reflected Americans' keen sense of themselves as involved in an important historical undertaking. The Philadelphia subscription library, founded in 1731 by Benjamin Franklin and others, became the de facto library of the government until 1800, when the capital moved to Washington, and the Library of Congress was founded.

For every occasion that drew American citizens together, however, there seemed to be another that divided them. Strong attachments to place and great disparities of condition often transformed seemingly shared values and ideas into fodder for sharp conflicts. Many, if not most, Americans felt stronger attachments to the neighborhoods or states where they lived, rather than to the nation as a whole. If anything, the process of ratification had underscored just how many differences remained among Americans. Advocates had won approval only by putting together a different coalition of interests in each state, not by drawing on a uniform set of interests across all the states. Even so, a bare nine states had ratified the document, and virtually all of these had made qualifications.

The localism of American society in 1789 was evident in daily life, as well as in formal politics. Never traveling far from home, ordinary Americans knew little about other parts of the country and tended to view them as quite different, becoming more exotic—and frightening—the greater the distance. Writing from Massachusetts to Philadelphia in 1776, Abigail Adams had asked John whether it was true that in Virginia the "gentery" were "Lords" and "the common people vassals." Travelers often described other parts of the nation as if they were foreign countries. The hard economic times of the era also nursed a suspicion of strangers. Describing these differences as an East-West contrast was also common in the early years of the nation. Rural revolts in the Carolinas in the 1760s and Shays's Rebellion in western Massachusetts in 1786–1787 had underscored the differences between backcountry farmers and eastern commercial elites, differences that settlers experienced as conflicts between "the people" and eastern governments. This sense of division and distrust persisted in the 1790s.

These disagreements ran deep and were not confined to formal politics or to polite discussion and debate. Newspapers often revealed sharp local bias in vituperative debates over the proper direction of republican politics. They were accompanied into the public arena by vitriolic political tracts and single-page "broadsides" that attacked individual politicians. Among these was William Manning's 1798 "Key of Liberty," condemning the predations of the "Few" upon the "Many."

Not all of the arguments took place in print. Wealthy city people met in parlors and salons to discuss the concerns of the day, and common Americans held their arguments outside courthouses and churches, on post office porches, at liveries and craft shops, and in taverns like the one run by William Manning. Travelers, peddlers, and preachers were sources of information and opinion.

The early republic was also an era of school building—primarily academies to prepare sons for professions or university training and daughters to participate in the discussions (if not the formal electoral politics) of republican society. More than 350 academies for females opened between 1790 and 1830. The first incorporated publicly was the Young Ladies' Academy of Philadelphia (1787). Intended for daughters of prosperous families, to educate them in "Reading, Writing, Arithmetic, English, Grammar, Composition, and Geography," its curriculum implicitly argued that women could flourish in a challenging academic environment.

Citizens also formed societies intended to provide relief to the needy. A group of prosperous Philadelphians established an almshouse to care for and house the poor (and to teach them the values of industry) and a penitentiary to reform criminals by isolating them from one another. Jewish organizations founded in New York in the late eighteenth century provided aid for the city's small Jewish community.

In a variety of occupational and manufacturing societies, masters and journeymen furthered their common interests, sometimes against what they perceived as the haughtiness of the merchants. Many of the trades of Philadelphia participated in the Federal Procession of 1789, for example—a sign to the elites that craft workers had their own expectations of the new republic. Promoting a different vision, Alexander Hamilton and his assistant secretary, Tench Coxe, formed the Society for Establishing Useful Manufactures in 1791, a joint-stock corporation meant to demonstrate the economic virtues of cooperation between the private sector and the government.

Sailmaker's Shop A reconstruction of the interior of a sailmaker's shop.

Securing the Nation

The internal turbulence the United States faced in these years was matched by conflict on the western borders of the nation and in the larger Atlantic community of which the new nation was inextricably a part. Moreover, those conflicts and disagreements about how to resolve them became the major sources of political conflict in the new nation.

Borders and Boundaries

The United States of America had come into formal existence as a republic with the Articles of Confederation in 1781, and its existence had been recognized in the Paris Peace Treaty with Britain in 1783 and again in the ratification of the federal Constitution. Still, much remained unclear, unfinished, and highly contested when George Washington took office in 1789.

On the simplest level, the new republic lacked even clear external borders. Although the Treaty of Paris seemed to describe a very specific territory being ceded from Britain to the United States, things were much less clear on the ground. For example, the treaty set a boundary beginning "from the northwest angle of Nova Scotia, viz., that angle which is formed by a line drawn due north from the source of the St. Croix River to the highlands; along the said highlands which divide those rivers that empty themselves into the river St. Lawrence, from those which fall into the Atlantic Ocean, to the northwesternmost head of Connecticut River; thence down along the middle of that river to the forty-fifth degree of north latitude . . ." across the Great Lakes, down the Mississippi River, and across the border of New Spain to the Atlantic. But what exact spot marked "the source of the St. Croix River"? Where was the "middle" of the Connecticut River? These were not abstract problems: Britain and the United States would argue for years over present-day Maine, and Spain claimed a sizable chunk of present-day Mississippi and Alabama.

A related problem was that much of the territory America claimed was literally unmapped. When his nation sent him to England to resolve trade and boundary disputes (resulting in Jay's Treaty; see "To the Brink of War"), John Jay was handicapped by a lack of basic geographical knowledge about North America. How could he argue for favorable terms when it was unknown how far north "the Mississippi River extends"?

European empires were not the only ones challenging the territorial integrity of the new nation. There were also a hundred thousand or so Native Americans who lived within the boundaries of the republic, many of them crisscrossing large expanses of hunting and growing grounds in seasonal migrations. The United States had acknowledged the sovereignty of Indian nations in eight treaties before the ratification of the Constitution and again in Article I of the Constitution, granting Congress the power "to regulate commerce with . . . the Indian tribes." But the Native Americans rejected both European American ideas of fixed borders and the specific borders delineated in the Treaty of Paris. Most of the "United States of America" was still Indian land to them—the land of the Shawnee, for example, or of the people of the longhouses, or of the turtle people. Settlers kept moving into these lands, however (see Map 8–2).

Even the states of the new nation disagreed on the division of lands within its borders. Many of the original boundary conflicts had been settled in the 1780s, but Virginia, Georgia, and North Carolina still claimed lands running to the Mississippi River (although North Carolina wanted to cede the land to the United States). Massachusetts,

New Hampshire, and New York still fought over present-day Maine. Finally, the attachment of many western settlers to the new nation was so weak that, well into the nineteenth century, some flirted with detaching portions of the West and turning them over to the Spanish or creating another independent nation.

Controlling the Borderlands

For all of its symbolic importance as a source of republican order, the backcountry had so far been marked by constant conflict among owners and settlers and between Indians and Americans. Americans fought with each other over land prices and rights of ownership. In spite of these conflicts, squatters, proprietors, and governments shared the assumption that the land was theirs to fight over. The Treaty of Paris did not acknowledge Indian claims, and treaties promising Indians peace in exchange for land proved illusory (see Chapter 7). By the time Washington took office in 1789, the backcountry was in an uproar. Undisciplined federal troops and state militias roamed western lands in search of a fight, often attacking neutral or sympathetic Indian villages. Betrayed and angry, Indians banded together in loose confederations, retaliating against settlers and striking alliances with the British and Spanish.

By 1789, the Eastern Woodland and Great Lakes nations had been deeply altered by the westward pressure of white settlement. In the North, a group of battered Iroquoian villages traded large

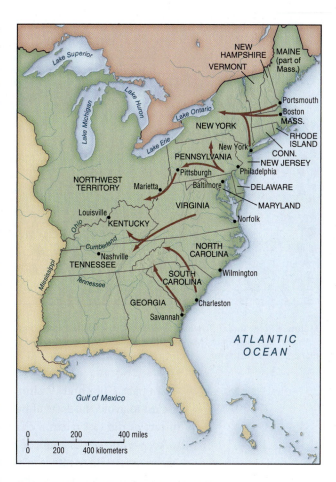

Map 8-2 Western Expansion, 1785–1805 Between the Treaty of Paris (1783) and the Louisiana Purchase (1803), Americans flooded into the territories that lay between the Appalachians and the Mississippi River. Then (as later) migration often followed rivers and valleys into the interior of the continent. *Data from Gregory Evans Dowd*, A Spirited Resistance: The North American Indian Struggle for Unity, 1745–1815 *(Baltimore: Johns Hopkins University Press, 1991), p. 92.*

tracts of land for promises of security and called on tribes of the Northwest Territory to do the same. However, these peoples refused and effectively shut down settlement north of the Ohio River valley. In the South, the Creeks, trapped between white settlements and the Native American nations of the Mississippi River valley, allied with militant Cherokees to keep the Georgia, Tennessee, and Kentucky frontiers ablaze with war parties.

Washington had more reasons to worry about the western territories. By 1789, Spain was actively luring United States settlers into New Spain at the foot of the Mississippi River in order to weaken the loyalty of the West to the new United States government. In the Great Lakes region, Britain hung on to the string of forts it had promised to give up in the Treaty of Paris. Many Americans believed that Britain was biding its time to regain control of the lands south of the Great Lakes.

This turmoil took its toll in the East. The inability of the national government to control Native Americans angered states, would-be settlers, and small-business owners. Landowners complained that their property rights were not being protected, and small settlers complained of favoritism in land distribution. Understanding that

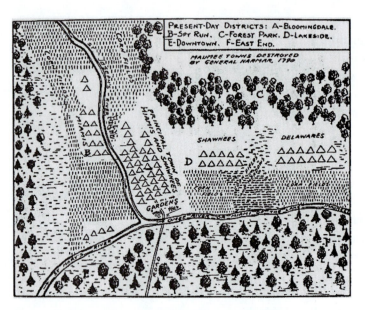

PRESENT-DAY DISTRICTS: A-BLOOMINGDALE. B-SPY RUN. C-FOREST PARK. D-LAKESIDE. E-DOWNTOWN. F-EAST END.

MAUMEE TOWNS DESTROYED BY GENERAL HARMAR, 1790

Maumee River Indian Towns This 1790 drawing suggests the complex economic arrangement of the Maumee River Indian towns and the diverse groups that occupied the towns.

both external relations and the domestic authority of the federal government were at stake, Washington turned immediately to the problem of the backcountry. Working with Secretary of War Henry Knox, Washington sought a more fair and consistent Indian policy, with a preference for "civilizing" Native Americans in order to avoid future conflict. He also used the territories to demonstrate the power of the federal government.

Less than a month after assuming office, Washington submitted to Congress a report by Knox on Indian affairs. Knox argued that the United States should acknowledge a residual Indian "right in the soil" not affected by a treaty between Britain and the United States. That right could be extinguished, he insisted, only by separate dealing with the Indians; he recommended that the United States purchase Indian claims to disputed lands.

In part, Knox and Washington shifted policy in the name of justice, but they also sought to avoid the costs of having to take the Northwest Territory by war. A change in tactics did not mean a change in ultimate goals, however. Although Knox tried to keep white settlers outside treaty boundaries, his policy did not recognize Native Americans' right to refuse to negotiate. Seeking to bolster the authority of the national government, Knox argued that Indian bands were not communities within state borders but rather foreign entities, on the level of nations. Indian relations were therefore properly the business of the federal government. Knox in effect declared Indians aliens on their own lands, using federal policy to define Indians as the ultimate outsiders.

By 1790, continuing troubles in the Northwest Territory convinced Washington to send troops there (see Map 8–3). His first two efforts were dismal failures. In 1790 a combined Native American force led by the Miami war leader Little Turtle routed the United States Army, led by General Josiah Harmar. The next year a much smaller party crushed the troops of territorial governor general Arthur St. Clair. In 1792, Congress authorized a "strong coercive force" (bigger, better paid, and better trained) and Washington turned to a seasoned infantry officer, Pennsylvanian major general Anthony Wayne. By the time Wayne found the Indians in 1794 at Fallen Timbers, near Lake Erie, his army was more than 3,000 strong. Facing a force of only 400 warriors, Wayne claimed a decisive victory.

According to the Treaty of Greenville, signed August 3, 1795, Indians ceded two-thirds of the later state of Ohio and a piece of present-day Indiana. In return, they received annual federal payments ranging from $1,000 to $500 per band. The annuities bought the United States influence within Indian communities and rendered the Indians more economically dependent. The treaty also tried to impose white ideas of work and economy by offering Indians annuities in the form of farm equipment, cows, and pigs.

Indian efforts at confederacy proved less successful in the South, where deep fractures existed within the Cherokee and Creek nations. Older leaders, wearied by con-

Map 8-3 Major Indian Villages and Indian-US Battle Sites, 1789–1800 During its first decade of existence, the new federal government struggled to assert control over the trans-Appalachian territories, claimed by Native Americans as their homelands and coveted by United States settlers and land speculators.

stant warfare, and mixed-heritage populations familiar with white economic and social ways sometimes favored accommodation and entered into agreements they lacked the authority to make. At the Treaty of New York in 1790, Alexander McGillivray and other Creek leaders agreed to exchange lands belonging to the entire Creek nation for annual payments from the federal government and promises of US protection for their remaining lands. A faction of the Cherokee nation signed a similar pact in 1791.

These internal disputes weakened Indian military efforts. When the government proved unable to stop settlers flowing into the future state of Tennessee, younger Creeks, Chickamaugas, Cherokees, and Shawnees repudiated the treaties and attacked the Americans at Buchanan's Station, near Nashville, Tennessee, planning to move on

Nashville itself. Fearing reprisals, older Cherokee leaders betrayed the plan, and the assault was thrown back. US Indian commissioners used military victories to coerce new land cessions and to insinuate white customs more deeply into Indian cultures, especially that of the Cherokees.

Resistance continued, in the North and the South, but dreams of a pan-Indian confederation were temporarily stymied. They would be resurrected at the turn of the century by two Shawnees. One, Tenskwatawa, would become an important prophet. The other, his half-brother, was named Tecumseh.

The Whiskey Rebellion

Another threat to the federal government came from western settlers themselves. By 1791, western settlers were disenchanted with the seeming inability of the government to protect their interests and had begun disregarding federal policy. They trespassed on Indian lands, sent unorganized militias to enforce their claims, and traded illegally with Indians. In 1791, western Pennsylvanians rejected federal authority explicitly, setting the stage for a direct confrontation.

The trouble began with the passage of Hamilton's excise tax. Living in a gateway to the Northwest Territory, residents of western Pennsylvania anticipated an economic bonanza from westward migration but were frustrated with the failure of the government to secure safe passage into the Ohio River valley. Hamilton's tax on spirits fueled their simmering anger over the question of republican fairness. Many Americans regarded excise taxes (internal taxes on specific goods) as unfair in principle. This particular tax seemed targeted specifically at western farmers, who found it cheaper to transport their grain in liquid than in bushel form.

Popular protests intensified at each new report of the army's failure in the Northwest Territory (efforts the tax was supposed to fund). Western Pennsylvanians vowed that they would not pay the tax and urged citizens to treat tax collectors with "contempt." Washington took the challenge seriously, and in August 1794 he sent 13,000 troops into western Pennsylvania. Against this show of force, the Whiskey Rebellion fizzled, but the government drove its point (and power) home. Remaining protestors were rounded up; twenty were sent to Philadelphia to face treason charges, and two were sentenced to death. Washington pardoned them both, but he had proven the authority of federal law.

Western Pennsylvanians were not without sympathizers, however. The congressional elections of 1792 were contests between the policies of Alexander Hamilton, on the one hand, and the beliefs of the self-named "republican interest," on the other, over what it meant to be a republican nation and society.

Other Revolutions

Just as the United States was launching its federal republic, France entered the throes of revolution. After years of fiscal mismanagement by the crown, high unemployment, and widespread malnutrition and starvation, the French bourgeoisie began a reform of the monarchy that soon led to wholesale grassroots revolution. In July 1789, just eight weeks after Washington took the oath of office, the people of Paris stormed the Bastille prison in symbolic rejection of the power of the monarchy. The next month the new National Constituent Assembly abolished feudalism and promulgated the

Declaration of the Rights of Man and of the Citizen, modeled on the American Declaration of Independence.

Initially, most Americans, including many Federalists, supported the French Revolution. As a part of its long eighteenth-century conflict with Great Britain, France had aided the Americans in their own revolution and had recognized the nation and its diplomats after the war. Americans now saw the efforts of the French people to overthrow monarchy as a reflection of their own struggle against Britain, and they read events in France as a confirmation that the United States would lead the world into a new era of democracy.

By 1793, however, as the Parisian mob grew more violent and moderate politicians lost power, many Americans lost their enthusiasm for the French republic. Although many, Jefferson and Madison among them, remained avid French partisans, others grew convinced that France was spiraling into chaos—which would spread to the United States.

Part of their alarm may have derived from events on the French island colony of Saint-Domingue (present-day Haiti) in the West Indies. In 1791, its free people of color led an insurgency against the white planter class but soon lost control in the face of a full-scale revolution by the island's tens of thousands of slaves. Eventually, under the leadership of former slave François-Dominique Toussaint-Louverture, Saint-Domingue would become the first black republic in the Americas.

Washington's response to the revolution in Saint-Domingue was complicated. He did not support the revolutionaries, especially after the movement for equality for free blacks turned into a slave rebellion. Like other slave owners, Washington feared that supporting the Saint-Dominguans would encourage slave rebellion in the southern United States. Still, he did not want to enter into an alliance with France (which sent soldiers to put down the rebellion), as that might seem hostile to the British. His compromise was to order supplies and ammunition sent directly to the island's white-planter ruling class.

Between France and England

Washington would later summarize his foreign policy goals: "The great rule of conduct for us, in regard to foreign nations, is, in extending our commercial relations, to have with them as little political connexion as possible." The United States wanted to trade freely with every nation, but other nations used trade barriers to protect not only their economic but their political interests as well. Washington and his successors thus found that it was one thing to announce a policy and another to achieve it, particularly when Americans too had loyalties to France or England, two nations that were almost continuously at war from 1793 to 1815.

Haitian Revolution The 1791 slave revolt against plantation owners and their families in the then French colony of Saint-Domingue (Haiti). This engraving is from a contemporary German report on the uprising.

AMERICA AND THE WORLD

>> Citizenship in an Age of Revolution

In the heady first days of the French Revolution, many Americans and French people felt a strong bond of kinship, thinking that they were all citizens of the world, engaged in a common revolutionary movement. When Gouverneur Morris arrived in Paris in early 1789, the veteran of the Constitutional Convention was exhilarated to find "on this side of the Atlantic a strong resemblance to what I left on the other—a Nation which exists in Hopes, Prospects, and Expectations. The reverence for ancient Establishments gone, existing Forms shaken to the very Foundation, and a new Order of Things about to take Place." Bowing to popular pressure, the king had agreed to convene the Estates General, the representative body that had not met since 1614. As it renamed itself the National Assembly, issued the Declaration of the Rights of Man, and began to write a constitution, French political leadership looked to Americans for advice and the United States for a model. One of the assembly's leaders was the Marquis de Lafayette, a Revolutionary-minded young nobleman who had paid his own way to America to fight at Washington's side in the American Revolution. He shared a draft of the Declaration of the Rights of Man with Thomas Jefferson, then the US minister to France, and Jefferson passed it on to James Madison, noting, "You will see that it contains the essential principles of ours accommodated as much as could be to the actual state of things here." The first two articles of the final draft declared, "Men are born and remain free and equal in rights. Social distinctions may be founded only upon the general good," and "The aim of all political association is the preservation of the natural and imprescriptible rights of man. These rights are liberty, property, security, and resistance to oppression."

Morris made suggestions for the new French Constitution, while Thomas Paine, who had moved from England to Pennsylvania to play an important role in the American Revolution, came to France and was elected to the National Convention, which succeeded the National Assembly after the monarchy was overthrown.

Declaration of the Rights of Man The Declaration of the Rights of Man and the Citizen, adopted by the French Assembly in 1789, was modeled after the American Declaration of Independence. The first article begins, "Men are born and remain free and equal in rights."

As the Revolution took increasingly radical turns, becoming ever more violent, American opinion began to diverge. Gouverneur Morris soured on the Revolution within a few months, just after seeing a mob drag the severed head and naked body of one man through the streets to his son's home, where they killed the son, cut his body to pieces, and carried about "the mangled Fragments with a Savage Joy." Late in the Revolution, Paine, too, reached a turning point. Calling himself a "citizen of both countries," he argued against the execution of the king. He was thrown in jail (with 15,000 other Parisians) and marked for execution. Paine appealed to Morris, now the American ambassador. Morris's advice: be quiet and hope that they forget about you. How could Morris claim as an American citizen this native-born Briton, who had accepted not only French citizenship but a position in the Revolutionary government? Paine learned the hard way that a citizen of the world had very few protections. He escaped with his life, but barely.

Jefferson, however, thought that the ends justified the means. "My own affections have been deeply wounded by some of the martyrs to this cause," he acknowledged, "but rather than it should have failed, I would have seen half the earth desolated. Were there but an Adam and Eve left in every country, left free, it would be better than as it now is."

By the time the French Revolution was over, and the old order overthrown, tens of thousands had been executed in the Terror, and even more killed by civil war. The leaders fell to violence too, no one safe from the accusation of treason. Was the new order, as Jefferson claimed, worth the cost? Could one be a citizen of the Revolutionary world, dedicated to universal liberty, or did each nation have its own destiny?

These were the questions that gripped not only the French but the Americans too in the age of democratic revolution.

Washington's efforts to avoid the appearance of pro-French partiality were soon tested. On February 1, 1793, France and Spain declared war on Great Britain and Holland. American sentiments were divided. Many Democratic Republicans (among them Jefferson and Madison) viewed with horror the possibility that America might join with its former colonial master against a fellow republic. Hamiltonians, meanwhile, believed that friendly relations with Britain best served American interests. Searching for a middle ground, President Washington endorsed neutrality.

Then, on May 16, Edmond-Charles Genêt, citizen of France, arrived in Philadelphia, the temporary capital. France had several hopes for the Genêt mission. Genêt was supposed to incite the European colonies in the Americas to revolution. He was also to press the United States for a new treaty allowing French naval forces and privateers to resupply in American ports. France's hopes were not entirely fanciful. The impoverished Washington administration had lent money to the new French government and recognized the Republic as the legitimate government of France.

But the French overestimated American support. Giving preferential treatment to French ships could only strain relations between America and England. Barely able to muster a force to the Northwest, Washington was not about to risk a foreign war or to inflame tensions on western borders. Washington considered Genêt's proposals reckless.

Genêt, however, did not believe that Washington's views represented the sentiments of Americans generally. In Philadelphia, he authorized the refitting of a captured English ship as a French privateer, and he encouraged American settlers in Kentucky to attack the Spanish.

Washington was furious. "Is the Minister of the French Republic to set the Acts of this Government at defiance, with impunity?" he fumed. Issuing a formal Proclamation of Neutrality, Washington disavowed Genêt and demanded that he be recalled. Disappointed by Washington's growing support of Federalist policies, Jefferson resigned as secretary of state.

To the Brink of War

Even without Genêt's provocations, by 1794 tensions with Britain were high. There were already issues left over from the Revolution—debts owed to British creditors, compensation due to southerners whose slaves had been seized, and forts the British still occupied in the Northwest. To these were added new irritants: the British navy was confiscating US merchant ships trading with (and for) the French in the Caribbean and impressing their sailors into the British navy. The Americans wanted compensation. Still, Washington sought to avoid confrontation. Even though the British kept the Americans out of West Indian and Canadian ports, US shipping had been steadily expanding, making it hard to argue that British policies were injurious enough to risk a war. Washington dispatched Chief Justice of the Supreme Court John Jay to England to resolve outstanding issues.

Already at war with France, Britain was ready to reduce tensions with the United States. Although Britain was unwilling to let the United States trade with France, Britain agreed to open West Indies ports to smaller US ships. Both countries agreed that (with some exceptions) their ships would receive equal treatment. They agreed as well to establish arbitration boards to determine compensation for prewar debts and the seized ships, as well as to set the boundary between Canada and the United States. Britain also promised to evacuate its forts in the Northwest by June 1, 1796. Jay, an opponent of slavery, did not try very hard to get compensation for the slaves.

Most Americans knew nothing about Jay's Treaty until after it was approved, for the Senate debated it in secret. When Democratic Republicans learned of its contents and its ratification, they were outraged. They protested the closed deliberations and the failure to gain "neutral rights," the right to trade with Britain's enemies. They feared being drawn closer to Britain, their old enemy, and being pulled from France, the nation's first ally. But positive developments in the West helped the fury to subside. First came news of Anthony Wayne's victory against the Great Lakes tribes at Fallen Timbers. Word followed that Thomas Pinckney had also concluded a treaty with Spain, opening the Mississippi River to US navigation and permitting Americans to use the port at New Orleans. (Pinckney's Treaty also set the boundary between the United States and Florida.) Once the United States made peace with Britain, a weak Spain feared a formal alliance would come next and accepted an American presence in the West as a price for peace.

Wayne's victory and Jay's and Pinckney's negotiations seemed at last to open the territories to settlement (see Map 8–4). Western land prices soared, and the US export trade boomed. By the time opponents in the House of Representatives tried to scuttle Jay's Treaty by denying necessary funds, popular sentiment had shifted to strong support for the treaty as a key to prosperity.

The Administration of John Adams

George Washington, reluctant to serve a second term, had been convinced to do so when Jefferson and Hamilton argued that no one else could bring the republic's fractious politics together. But Washington refused to run for a third term, and in 1796 the nation faced its first contested presidential election.

In his farewell address, published on September 19, 1796, Washington made clear his Federalist concern with social order and personal discipline. Having acknowledged the right of the people to alter their Constitution, he stressed the "duty of every

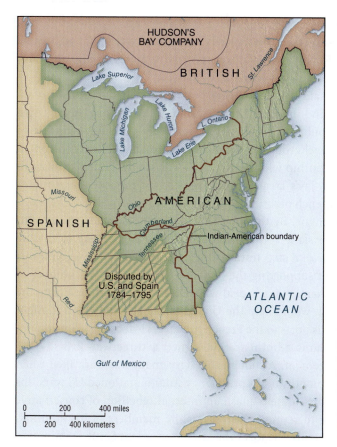

Map 8–4 Extension of US National Territories, 1783, and Extension of US National Territories, 1795
The Treaty of Paris with Great Britain (1783) left the United States' borders with Spain (much of the western and southern boundaries) ambiguous. Those borders were clarified in the Pinckney Treaty with Spain (1795).

individual to obey the established Government" until it was changed "by an explicit and authentic act of the whole people." Sounding themes that would echo through the first half-century of the republic, he warned against unlawful "combinations and associations" with designs on the rightful "power of the people," an image that, 30 years later, would drive the emergence of Jacksonian democracy.

With Hamilton too controversial to be an effective candidate, Federalists selected Vice President John Adams as their choice. Adams had served in the Continental Congress, been a part of the committee to draft the Declaration of Independence, served as representative to France, helped negotiate the peace treaty, and served two terms as vice president. Thomas Pinckney of South Carolina was their vice-presidential choice. For president, Democratic Republicans supported former secretary of state Thomas Jefferson, along with Madison, the most visible opponent of Hamilton. New Yorker Aaron Burr was intended as vice president.

Although contested, the election of 1796 was not decided by popular majority. State legislatures chose two-fifths of the members of the Electoral College. Moreover, procedures in the Electoral College did not distinguish between votes for the offices of president and vice president. The person who received the most electoral votes became president. The person who received the second-highest number of electoral votes became vice president.

This procedure proved dangerously unpredictable in a new age of political parties. Although the Federalist Adams received a majority of electoral votes (71) and became president, the Democratic Republican Jefferson received the second-highest count (68 to Pinckney's 59) and became vice president.

Benjamin Franklin once said that John Adams was "always an honest man, often a wise one, but sometimes, and in some things, absolutely out of his senses." Also cranky, defensive, and self-doubting, he was not the man to negotiate growing party rifts successfully. Against a background of partisan resentment, Adams confronted an increasingly hostile relationship with France. Unsurprisingly, Franco-American relations had been harmed by Jay's Treaty—which seemed to France to ally America with England—and by the French practice of plundering American ships. There was also the issue of Saint-Domingue. By the time John Adams took office, the revolutionaries (now led by former slave Toussaint-Louverture) were seeking to resume trade with the United States as a step toward full independence. The abolitionist Adams had no qualms about supporting the revolutionaries and saw a number of advantages in allying with them. A trade deal with Haiti would further isolate the island from French control, it would help the United States economy, and it might prompt Louverture to close his ports to the French privateers attacking US merchant ships. In June 1799, the Adams administration signed a three-way British–US–Saint-Dominguan trade agreement. Although that agreement was unratified when Adams left office, in the last months of his presidency Adams stationed US warships outside Saint-Dominguan ports to help quash an internal rebellion of conservative free people of color wishing to reimpose slavery, while members of his administration discussed with Louverture the form that an independent Saint-Dominguan republican government might assume. None of this pleased France, particularly not after the rise of Napoleon and the resurgence of French imperial ambitions in the late 1790s.

Even before his inauguration on March 4, 1797, Adams thought about sending a special envoy to France to resolve these issues. When Adams's cabinet objected, the president temporarily abandoned the plan. At the end of March, he learned that new American ambassador Charles Pinckney had been kicked out of France because the French government would "no longer recognize or receive" an ambassador from the United States. Adams decided to send a mission to France, appointing Elbridge Gerry, John Marshall, and Pinckney.

When the American mission arrived, French foreign minister Talleyrand made clear that he expected a bribe for his willingness to talk. Such arrangements were not uncommon in European politics, but to the starched and wary Adams, the idea was abhorrent. He turned over all documentation of the affair to Congress, identifying Talleyrand's agents by letters: X, Y, and Z.

The so-called XYZ Affair prompted a largely Federalist Congress to suspend commercial ties to France, empower American ships to seize armed French vessels, and expand the nation's military. In what became known as the "Quasi-War" (neither nation formally declared war), between 1798 and 1800 the United States and France skirmished on the seas, with the United States capturing more than 80 French ships. In the Convention of 1800, France and the United States agreed to end these hostilities. France agreed to return captured American ships; the United States assumed Americans' claims against the French for damages in shipping; and the earlier Franco-American Alliance was replaced by mutual most-favored-nation status.

Tensions at Home

The military expansion necessary for this conflict soon created tensions at home. Adams and Congress needed $2 million for it, which they found by imposing a tax on houses, land, and slaves. Each state had a specified portion of the cost to pay. The levy on houses, assessed according to the size of the house, fell especially hard on residents of states with few or no slaves or huge plantation estates and was particularly odious to German immigrants, whom it reminded of harsh taxes exacted by the kings of Germany. When the assessors reached eastern Pennsylvania, settled predominately by German immigrants, unrest became civil

A Brawl in Congress The politics of the early republic were often rough. Here two congressmen (one of them later convicted under the Sedition Act) come to blows on the floor of the House of Representatives.

disobedience. Led by John Fries, men of the area raised a small army to chase collectors away, while women poured hot water on the assessors. When the governor tried to have the resisters arrested, Fries's supporters freed them. Adams sent a militia of 1,000 men to capture the leaders. Fries and most of the other leaders were arrested, tried for treason, and sentenced to hang. In the face of strong public sentiment, Adams pardoned the rebels. (This was the second uprising in less than a decade, and in both cases, the rebels were pardoned.)

The Federalists had also used the XYZ Affair and hostilities with France for domestic political purposes. Insisting that pro-French influence endangered the nation, in 1798 Congress passed the Alien and Sedition Acts, aimed at gagging the Democratic Republican opposition and preventing it from using the war issue to win the 1800 election. The acts required a 14-year naturalization period, the highest at any period in American history, and targeted immigrants, whom the Federalists presumed to be Democratic Republicans. The acts also empowered the president to deport any "suspicious" aliens and established a broad definition of sedition, intended to stop all Democratic Republican criticism of the administration's policies.

The Alien and Sedition Acts backfired against the Federalists. Twenty-five prosecutions were eventually brought under the Sedition Act (all against Democratic Republicans), and 10 men were convicted. The acts were so transparently partisan that individuals convicted under them became martyrs to the Democratic Republican cause. A Vermont congressman who published criticisms of administration policies was reelected even as he served out his four-month jail term. But by targeting those believed to be "radical," especially

> There goes the President and they are firing at his arse. . . . I do not care if they fire thro' his arse!
>
> LUTHER BALDWIN,
> Newark, New Jersey, July 1798, as President John Adams passed by. These words would get him tried and convicted of violating the Sedition Act.

DEBATING HISTORY

>> The Politics of the 1790s and Democracy

The politics of the late 1790s have been a puzzle for historians. Were the Alien and Sedition Acts the last gasp of an out-of-touch Federalist party trying in vain to hold back the tide of rising democracy? Or did they indicate a darker, more enduring antiradical, antiforeigner streak in American politics? Gordon S. Wood argues that the Federalists represented a reactionary, monarchical trend that ran counter to main currents of American political belief. Seth Cotlar sees a more complex process, one in which the Federalists may have lost the battle—the Alien and Sedition Acts are now considered both a political and ideological mistake—but won the war. By associating their Jeffersonian opponents with French "Jacobinical" radicalism, they pulled the Jeffersonians to the right. Although the Jeffersonians prevailed, their party—and the subsequent course of American democracy—became more moderate than it might otherwise have been.

A DEMOCRAT.

Democrat This 1791 satirical cartoon connects democracy to the excesses of the French Revolution: "A Democrat," with a crazy look on his face, wears the French colors, has copies of the "Rights of Man" and "Paine" sticking out of his pocket, and stands in front of pole with a head at the top and a noose suspended from it for further executions.

GORDON S. WOOD, *Empire of Liberty: A History of the Early Republic, 1789–1815* (New York: Oxford University Press, 2009), p. 276.

Born in reaction to the popular excesses of the Revolution, the Federalist world could not endure. The Federalists of the 1790s stood in the way of popular democracy as it was emerging in the United Sates, and thus they became heretics opposed to the developing democratic faith. . . . "They have attempted," as Noah Webster observed, "to resist the force of public opinion, instead of falling into the current with a view to correct it. . . ." Indeed, they were so out of touch with the developing popular realities of American life, and their monarchical program was so counter to the libertarian impulses of America's republican ideology, that they provoked a second revolutionary movement that threatened to tear the Republic apart. . . . Only the electoral victory of the Republicans in 1800 ended this threat and brought, in the eyes of many Americans, the entire revolutionary venture of two and a half decades to successful completion.

SETH COTLAR, *Tom Paine's America: The Rise and Fall of Transatlantic Radicalism in the Early Republic* (Charlottesville: University of Virginia Press, 2011), pp. 213–214.

[By the end of the 1790s], the term "Jacobinism" quickly became a repository for a range of political ideas that had once comfortably existed under the banner of "democracy." Cosmopolitan conceptions of citizenship, visions of a government which would take actions to ensure a rough measure of economic equality, and plans to create a more inclusive, participatory, and politically efficacious public sphere became increasingly marginal in American public political discourse, and were [tarred] as foreign principles, manifestations of an un-American ideology that could prove the undoing of the nation. . . . To frame their election as the realization of the democratic strivings of the previous years, Jeffersonians had to position their critics on the left as part of an alien political tradition. . . . Together, leading Jeffersonians and Federalists sheared the word "democracy" of its previously revolutionary, deistical, and even leveling implications. Such ideas were transformed into perversions of democracy; they became "Jacobinical."

Questions

1. Gordon S. Wood and Seth Cotlar both identify political struggles in the 1790s. For Wood, the battle was between backward-looking Federalists and forward-looking Jeffersonians, while for Cotlar, the battle instead was over the meaning of democracy itself. How does each of these historians define and analyze the struggle?

2. Which party was more successful in shaping American democracy, the Federalists or the Democratic Republicans?

---

newspaper editors, and warning immigrants away, the acts silenced the most outspoken opponents of the government.

Although Democratic Republicans insisted that the acts were unconstitutional, they hesitated to challenge them in the Supreme Court, both because the Court was dominated by Federalists and because Democratic Republicans did not want to set a precedent for giving the Supreme Court the power to rule on constitutionality. Instead, Madison and Jefferson encouraged the states to pass resolutions denouncing the Alien and Sedition Acts. Madison, now retired from Congress, authored a set of resolutions in Virginia affirming the rights of states to judge the constitutionality of federal laws. Jefferson, vice president of the United States, framed a more militant set of resolutions for the Kentucky legislature, saying that states might declare federal laws they deemed unconstitutional to be "without force" within their state boundaries.

Jefferson and Madison expected that other states would support the Virginia and Kentucky resolutions, but they did not. Rather, voters simply returned the Democratic Republicans to power in the election of 1800, and the acts expired in 1801.

Before retiring, the Federalist Congress got off one more shot at the Democratic Republicans. Just as the session expired, Congress passed the Judiciary Act of 1801, which gave John Adams the power to expand the federal judiciary by appointing new judges, justices of the peace, attorneys, clerks, and marshals. He promptly filled these positions with good Federalists and then left office.

Conclusion

After a tumultuous first decade, it was not clear that the United States' experiment in government of, by, and for the people could survive. As the nation grew in size and population, the government struggled to maintain not simply order but, even more, the allegiance of its peoples. Americans had fallen into two rival political parties, with rival visions for the future and rival international attachments. Yet, in the midst of all this turmoil, Americans such as Ona Judge maintained a deep commitment to the principle and, even more, realization of freedom. Out of these conflicts and aspirations, a new nation was being born.

Who, What

Abigail Adams   278

John Adams   263

J. Hector St. John de
    Crevecoeur   273

Alexander Hamilton   263

Thomas Jefferson   263

James Madison   264

William Manning   276

George Washington   263

Strict construction of the
    Constitution   266

>> TIME LINE

▼1781
Articles of Confederation ratified

▼1787–1788
Constitution ratified

▼1789
George Washington inaugurated
Judiciary Act of 1789
Tariff Act of 1789
John Fenno founds *Gazette of the United States*
William Hill Brown publishes *The Power of Sympathy*

▼1790
Alexander Hamilton's *Report on the Public Credit*
Assumption Act
Naturalization Act

▼1791
Excise tax (including tax on whiskey) passes
First Bank of the United States
Philip Freneau establishes *National Gazette*
Bill of Rights ratified

▼1792–1794
Whiskey Rebellion

Review Questions

1. What were the key elements of Hamilton's fiscal and economic policies?

2. Why did political parties emerge during Washington's administration? How did the two parties differ, and why was the conflict between them so intense?

3. What was the Whiskey Rebellion? How did it reflect larger tensions in the early republic?

Critical-Thinking Questions

1. Why were foreign and domestic affairs so intertwined in the 1790s?

2. How fragile do you think the new nation was? What were the reasons for that fragility?

3. Could slavery have been eliminated in the 1790s?

For further review materials and resource information, please visit www.oup.com/us/ofthepeople

▼**1793**
Fugitive Slave Act
Edmond Genêt arrives in the United States

▼**1794**
Battle of Fallen Timbers

▼**1795**
Jay's Treaty
Treaty of Greenville
Pinckney's Treaty

▼**1796**
John Adams elected president

▼**1798**
Alien and Sedition Acts

▼**1798–1799**
Virginia and Kentucky resolves

▼**1798–1800**
XYZ Affair and Quasi-War

▼**1800**
Jefferson elected president

▼**1801**
Judiciary Act of 1801

1) The ideas of the American Revolution and their ability to shape a new country and its democratic government were tested in the early years of the republic.

2) The perceived and actual relationships among labor, virtue, and worth presented a particular irony for women and enslaved persons in the new American nation, one that highlighted both the fragility of a young democracy and the tensions within it.

3) Conflicts at home and abroad reflected different views of not only democracy but also the ways that men and women would earn their living and the role of the federal government in assisting them.

The Struggle to Form a Government

A Society in Transition

Securing the Nation

EVENTS

Creating a National Government Washington and Congress began to form a new government.

The States and the Bill of Rights Madison led Congress in crafting the Bill of Rights.

Debating the Economy Alexander Hamilton's plans to strengthen the national economy elicited a strong opposition.

A People on the Move The American population grew at a record rate, began to spread out across the continent, and traded with foreign nations.

The First Emancipation Movements The northern states slowly began to emancipate slaves, while abolitionist organizations started to form.

Conflicting Visions of Republican Society Despite some consensus, real disagreements emerged regarding the nature of the republic and which groups embodied its key virtues.

The Culture of the Republic A national culture began to emerge although local attachments remained strong.

Borders and Boundaries Lacking clear external and internal borders, the new nation faced challenges to its territorial integrity by Europeans, Native Americans, and even some of the states.

Controlling the Borderlands The national government's inability to control Native Americans and European powers angered the states and would-be settlers.

The Whiskey Rebellion Western settlers' refusal to pay the federal excise tax led to armed conflict.

Other Revolutions Americans were divided in their reaction to the increasingly violent French Revolution.

Between France and England As tensions between France and England increased, Washington tried to maintain American neutrality.

To the Brink of War Washington secured a treaty with England to reduce tensions and clarify long-standing disputes.

The Administration of John Adams John Adams was elected president, and as diplomatic relations with France broke down, the two countries came close to war.

Tensions at Home The Federalists' attempt to raise money for war and stifle political opposition backfired, making the opposition more powerful.

COMMON THREADS

>> Why was overseas trade so important to the new nation?

>> How did the way average Americans lived change over the first quarter century of the republic?

>> How were the political debates of ratification and of the 1790s still playing out during Jefferson's and Madison's administrations?

>> What important changes in context and content occurred in US Indian policy over the period of the first four administrations? What was the relationship between the defeat of Native Americans and the expansion of slavery?

>> What roles did organized religion play in shaping the society of the early republic?

A Republic in Transition
1800–1819

>> **Andrew Jackson's America**

Andrew Jackson came of age with the new nation. Already fatherless by the age of one, he later lost "everything that was dear" to him—his mother, his two brothers, and his South Carolina home, too—while he "embarked in the struggle for our liberties" during the Revolution. Jackson's hatred of the British, as well as any form of aristocracy, was deep and enduring. By the age of 21, Jackson had tried out a few trades, settling on that of lawyer; bought his first slave; fought his first duel; and made his way to Tennessee, which had been opened up to settlement by the Americans' victory in the Revolution. In this region, a smart and aggressive young man like Jackson could succeed, but he would need land and slaves. Political connections helped individuals secure land, some of which they would then sell to settlers at a higher price, using the profits to buy slaves to grow cotton. Profits from cotton, in turn, would go toward more land and slaves. Jackson quickly began moving up the social and economic ladder in this frontier region, as a lawyer, politician, land speculator, and slave-owning planter. He was aided by his marriage to a well-connected young woman, Rachel Donelson Robards, who, unfortunately, happened also to be married to another man.

Jackson rose quickly in Tennessee, in short order occupying the offices of representative, senator, and judge. He built, lost, and rebuilt a fortune as a land speculator and planter. (The frontier economy was unstable, and after his first reversal, Jackson developed a strong hatred of banks.) More than anything, though, he longed for a military career, both for the glory and for the opportunity to fight those who blocked his countrymen's occupation of fertile southern lands: the British (who had not yet vacated the West), the Spanish (who held Florida), and the Indian tribes who claimed the land. Jackson offered to round up a "thousand brave Tennesseeans" to help William Henry Harrison defeat Tecumseh: "That banditti ought to be swept from the face of the earth."

At the outbreak of the War of 1812, Jackson received a US commission to lead Tennessee volunteers to Louisiana. Then, in 1813, came orders to avenge a horrific attack by the Red Stick faction of the Creek Indians on a group of white settlers and their Creek allies at Fort Mims, near Mobile, Alabama. The influx of settlers onto Indian lands and the political contests among the Spanish, British, and Americans had destabilized the Indian tribes, encouraging the most violent elements in the tribes to fight more moderate members for supremacy. Even before receiving orders, Jackson rallied his volunteers. "Your frontier is threatened with invasion by the savage foe! Already do they advance towards your frontier with their scalping knifes unsheathed, to butcher your wives, your children, and your helpless babes."

Jackson's forces defeated the Red Sticks in a series of battles known as the Creek War. More Indian combatants died in the final battle at Horseshoe Bend than in any other American-Indian battle in US history. To assure an accurate body count, the Tennessee soldiers cut off the tips of the dead Indians' noses—557 of them. With the victory in the Creek War, Jackson secured his reputation, an appointment in the regular US army, and a treaty that ceded 23 million acres to

Continued

>> **AMERICAN PORTRAIT**
Continued

the United States. It covered not only land that had been occupied by the rebellious Red Sticks but also land occupied by the more moderate Creeks, including those who had actually fought *with* Jackson against their tribesmen.

Further triumphs—and controversy—lay ahead. General Jackson and his troops defeated the British in New Orleans in 1815, at the end of the War of 1812. He then assumed command of the US army in the southern territory to defend against Indians and the Spanish. Jackson secured tens of millions more acres by treaties. He also moved against the Spanish and the Seminoles in Florida, perhaps exceeding his orders; secured Florida for the United States; and executed two British agents in the process. Jackson's aggressive measures gained him powerful critics in Washington but made him a hero to other Americans. What cannot be denied is his role in the expansion of the United States and the southern slave-based economy.

Jackson's advance helped people like him: poor whites looking for opportunity. And the most important factors for advancement in the South remained land and slaves. In this way, opportunity for whites came directly at the expense of Native Americans and enslaved African Americans.

A Politics of Transition

In his inaugural address in 1801, Jefferson strove to put the partisan bitterness of the previous decade behind American politics. He asked Americans to come together "in common efforts for the common good" and assured Federalists that he was committed to the rights of the minority. "Let us, then, fellow-citizens, unite with one heart and one mind," he encouraged. In some ways, Jefferson got his wish: over time many of the policies of the Democratic Republicans would so come to resemble the policies of the Federalists that it would seem as if the two parties had grown closer. In the daily battle of national politics, however, the Democratic Republicans and the Federalists seemed not to share any common ground at all.

> This day I have witnessed one of the most affecting scenes of my life. . . . [Vice President Burr spoke] with so much tenderness, knowledge, and concern that it wrought upon the sympathy of the Senators in a very uncommon manner. . . . [T]he firmness and resolution of many of the Senators gave way, and they burst into tears. There was a solemn and silent weeping for perhaps ten minutes. . . . My colleague, General Smith, stout and manly as he is, wept as profusely as I did. He laid his head upon his table and did not recover from the emotion for a quarter hour or more.
>
> SENATOR SAMUEL MITCHILL,
> telling his wife about Aaron Burr's farewell speech to the Senate

OUTLINE

A Politics of Transition
A Contested Election, an Anxious Nation
Democratic Republicans in Office
The Louisiana Purchase
Embargo

The War of 1812
Madison and the War
Federalist Response

An Economy in Transition
International Markets

AMERICA AND THE WORLD:
   The United States in China
Crossing the Appalachian Mountains
Invention and Exploration

TECHNOLOGY AND IDEAS:
   The Steamboat

A Contested Election, an Anxious Nation

As a fractured country approached its second contested presidential election, in 1800, it was not clear that the nation could survive. Virginia had just thwarted a revolt led by a 24-year-old slave named Gabriel. Recruited from taverns and religious meetings around Richmond, as many as 500 or 600 slaves were prepared to assemble outside of Richmond, take the city, and then spread through the countryside, freeing slaves. Inspired by the American, French, and Haitian revolutions, the conspirators hoped to rally "the poor white people" to their cause of liberty. Gabriel planned to spare those who were "friendly to liberty" and the "poor white women who had no slaves." The conspiracy was discovered, however, and 27 African Americans, including Gabriel, were executed. According to white witnesses, all went to their deaths with "a sense of their rights and a contempt of danger." It was a determination, Congressman John Randolph later cautioned, "which, if it becomes general, must deluge the Southern country in blood."

Would bloodshed among whites follow? Deeply unpopular, John Adams nonetheless ran for a second term. Thomas Jefferson came out of retirement to oppose him. Each side predicted disaster if the opposition won. The election's uncertain outcome only compounded the sense of danger. The Constitution required the presidency to go to the man with the highest number of electoral votes, but both Jefferson and his running mate Aaron Burr received 73 votes. The choice was thrown into the House of Representatives, where Federalists threatened to block Jefferson by supporting Burr. Only after 34 ballots was Jefferson elected, once the Federalists had secured Jefferson's promise to keep Hamilton's financial system.

Democratic Republicans in Office

The peaceful transition of power in 1800 proved that the government could contain intense political conflict. Immediately on gaining office, Democratic Republicans closed the loophole in the Constitution that had led to the electoral stalemate. They quickly passed the legislation that became the Twelfth Amendment (1804), providing for party tickets in national elections. The Democratic Republicans also attempted to reduce the Federalist presence on the Supreme Court by impeaching Associate Supreme Court Justice Samuel Chase. Chase was notorious for his open partisanship during the Sedition Act prosecutions, but it was unclear whether his behavior met the constitutional standard of "Treason, Bribery, and high Crimes and Misdemeanors." In the final vote, Chase was acquitted, and the Supreme Court remained Federalist, five to one. Jefferson's desire for a Democratic Republican Court had to wait.

Early Industrial Society in New England
The Rule of Law and Lawyers

Ways of Life in Flux
Indian Resistance to American Expansion

PRIMARY SOURCE:
  ***Gibbons v. Ogden*: Freedom of Interstate Commerce**

Winners and Losers in the New Economy
Religion

AMERICAN LANDSCAPE:
  Religion in the Backcountry: Cane Ridge, Kentucky
The Problem of Trust in a Changing Society
The Panic of 1819

Conclusion

Before leaving office, the Federalists had tried to pack the courts with Federalists. The Judiciary Act of 1801, passed by the lame-duck Federalist Congress, increased the number of federal judgeships. Adams promptly appointed—and Congress confirmed—loyal Federalists. He also issued commissions for 41 justices of the peace, but they had not yet been acted on when he left office, and Jefferson ordered their appointments withheld. One of those "midnight" appointees, William Marbury, went directly to the Supreme Court, asking it for a "writ of mandamus," a court order compelling the executive to issue the commission. In a landmark decision, Chief Justice John Marshall, speaking for the Federalist-dominated Court, refused—but in a ruling that actually enhanced the Court's power. The provision in the Judiciary Act of 1789 that gave the Supreme Court the power to issue writs of mandamus was unconstitutional. The Constitution had set out the powers of the Supreme Court, and no act of legislation could change them. Marbury was out of luck, but the principle of judicial review (itself nowhere mentioned in the Constitution) had been established. Henceforth, the Supreme Court would decide whether acts of legislation were constitutional or not. Jefferson had won the battle but lost a very big constitutional war.

Jefferson also set out to reduce the size of the federal government. Working with Secretary of the Treasury Albert Gallatin, he slashed the army budget by half and the navy budget by more than two-thirds. He also supported congressional efforts to reduce the $80 million national debt and to repeal internal taxes, including the hated one on whiskey. By 1807 the national debt had been cut in half.

These efforts at thrift were soon derailed by the politics of overseas commerce. The monarchs of the North African nations of Tunis, Algeria, Morocco, and Tripoli had long sought to dominate shipping on the Mediterranean, seizing the ships and enslaving the crews of those nations that refused to pay tribute. In 1794 Congress appropriated a million dollars to ransom captives and another million to build a navy to protect American shipping. By the end of the decade, tribute and ransoms absorbed 20 percent of the US budget. The conflict was about trade and money, not religion. The 1796 Treaty of Tripoli reassured the Arab nations that "the Government of the United States of America is not, in any sense, founded on the Christian religion" and "has in itself no character of enmity against the laws, religion, or tranquility, of Mussulmen [Muslims]."

Jefferson had long opposed paying tribute. When he became president, he was still convinced that it would be "more economical and more honorable" to go to war than continue paying tribute. He asked Congress for an appropriation for warships and gunboats "to protect our commerce and chastise their insolence—by sinking, burning or destroying their ships and vessels wherever you shall find them."

Results were mixed. Democratic Republicans managed to avoid new internal taxes, and they cut the national debt substantially. They were not, however, able to dismantle Hamilton's economic system, which provided the revenue to finance the country's defense. America's military intervention in the Mediterranean was not particularly successful. The United States signed a second treaty with Tripoli in 1805—and paid $60,000 to ransom prisoners. Payments to the other North African states continued until 1815.

The Louisiana Purchase

Many citizens, including Jefferson himself, had long presumed that white Americans would eventually settle west of the Mississippi River, but Pinckney's Treaty of 1795 (which improved American access to the Mississippi) had removed any need for immediate action.

Napoleon Bonaparte changed all that. By the turn of the century, American-French relations had chilled. Ambitious to establish his own empire in the Americas and determined to prevent further United States expansion, in 1800 Napoleon acquired Louisiana from Spain. Jefferson worried that France would eventually send troops to occupy New Orleans. Hoping to thwart Napoleon, Jefferson secretly sent help to the rebels in Saint-Domingue, pushed Native Americans across the Mississippi, and raised an army. He then dispatched Robert Livingston and James Monroe to France to purchase New Orleans and West Florida, too.

Louisiana Purchase Treaty The P. F. stands for "Peuple Français," or "the French People."

By then, Napoleon had lost 30,000 troops in a failed effort to put down the rebellion in Saint-Domingue. Defeated by the island's former slaves and by infectious disease, Napoleon was ready to unload his American territory. He stunned the American agents by offering to sell not only New Orleans but also the entire Louisiana Territory—883,000 square miles. (The Americans claimed that the purchase included West Florida, but Spain denied selling the territory to France. This issue was not resolved until 1819; see Chapter 10.) On April 12, 1803, the deal was struck. The United States purchased the entire Louisiana Territory for $15 million, or roughly 3.5 cents an acre (see Map 9–1).

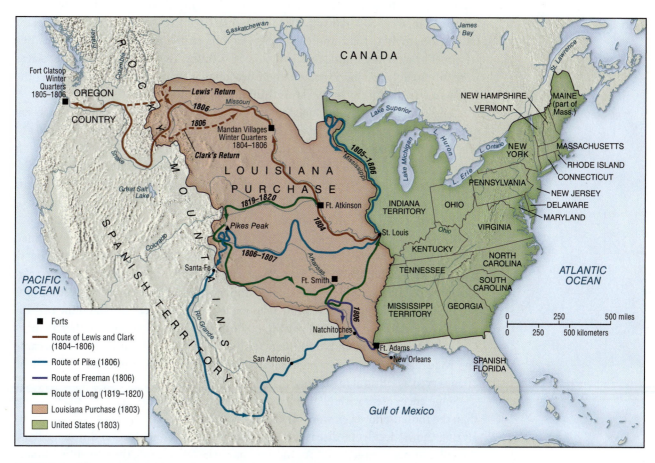

Map 9–1 Louisiana Purchase Although Lewis and Clark made the first exploration of the Louisiana Purchase, other explorers quickly followed. Among the most important were Zebulon Pike, who explored the Arkansas and Red Rivers, and Steven Long, who explored the Arkansas and Platte Rivers. Long described the plains as the "Great American Desert."

Selling the deal to Congress was another matter. Many Democratic Republicans, including Jefferson himself, questioned whether the territory could be acquired and made part of the United States without a constitutional amendment. Federalists worried about whether the United States could govern so vast a territory or make citizens out of its multiracial, largely foreign populace. Reversing the position they had held when the Federalists were in power, Jeffersonians decided that the "necessary and proper" and "general welfare" clauses of the Constitution provided adequate authority. Using the precedent of the Northwest Ordinance (see Chapter 7), Congress set out a path to statehood, granted citizenship to French and Spanish inhabitants of the territory, and ignored the status of Indians living there. Congress also established a government for Louisiana, which soon passed laws to make Louisiana's practices more American: a Black Code defined slaves as property and instructed free people of color never "to conceive of themselves as equal to whites."

Congress also banned the foreign slave trade in Louisiana, fearing that slaves imported from Saint-Domingue would spread revolution. Louisiana had long been a cauldron of slave unrest. This was probably buttressed by events in revolutionary France and Saint-Domingue and by the arrival in New Orleans in 1810 and 1811 of perhaps 10,000 refugees from the revolution in Saint-Domingue—whites, free people of color, and slaves. Some of them joined the 1811 uprising on the German Coast of the Mississippi led by a Louisiana-born slave of mixed racial background, Charles Deslondes. As many as 300 well-organized slaves marched on New Orleans, burning plantations, destroying crops, and gathering weapons on the way. West of the city, they were met by a planter militia and United States troops. Deslondes and 15 other slaves were captured, tried, and executed, their decapitated heads raised on pikes along the road as a warning to any other slaves thinking of rebellion.

Long before Louisiana belonged to the United States, Jefferson began to plan its exploration. Jefferson appointed his trusted secretary, Captain Meriwether Lewis, and another officer, William Clark, to lead the expedition. Lewis was an ambitious soldier with some experience in the Old Northwest. Clark, who had commanded troops on the Mississippi, was a skilled surveyor and mapmaker. Their mission was to follow the Missouri River, chart the territory as far as the Pacific, and scout opportunities for commerce with the Indians of the northern Missouri River, who traded chiefly with the British.

The expedition left St. Louis on May 14, 1804, on three boats containing 45 men and a dog, firearms, medicines, scientific instruments, tools, flour, and salt. The party traveled first up the Missouri River, closely observed by the Mandans, the Minnetarees, and the Hidatsas, who visited their camps and sent ahead stories of these curious people. In early November, the white men made their winter camp. When the expedition broke camp the following spring, a Shoshone woman, Sacagawea, her French-Canadian trapper husband, and their newly born child left with them. She became an invaluable guide and interpreter. Native women such as Sacagawea and Malinche often served as cultural mediators.

Some encounters with Native Americans were less friendly. Far more dangerous than the Indians, however, were waterfalls and rapids, freezing temperatures and paralyzing snows, accidents, diseases (especially dysentery), and dead-end trails. After a difficult portage across the Rocky Mountains in the fall of 1805, the expedition finally reached the Pacific Ocean on November 7, 1805.

Throughout their journey, Lewis and Clark had represented themselves as the envoys of a great nation with whom the Native Americans should now trade. But they also kept an eye out for future settlements. After their return, in 1806, parts of their journals and letters, including detailed maps and drawings, slowly found their way into print, advertising what Jefferson called America's new "empire for liberty."

Other Americans had other plans for the territory west of the Mississippi. In 1805, former vice president Aaron Burr, who had recently killed Alexander Hamilton in a duel, went to New Orleans, looking for a fresh start. He immediately fell in love with it, and saw, too—or so he later claimed—that the United States might extend its sovereignty to include some of Spanish Mexico, where settlers were unhappy with high taxes and little government attention. By 1806 Burr had raised a force of several thousand men. Convinced that Burr intended treason, and wanting to avoid trouble with Spain, Jefferson ordered his arrest. Burr was brought back to Richmond to stand trial before John Marshall, who happened to be presiding over the federal circuit. Marshall interpreted treason in the narrowest sense possible. "Conspiracy is not treason," he instructed the jury. Burr was acquitted, but he was also disgraced. The incident indicated the government's weakness, when a former vice president could raise his own army for his own purposes, whether treasonous or not.

Embargo

In the fall of 1804, Jefferson's popularity was soaring. Internal taxes had been abolished; the national debt was falling; the United States had (seemingly) stood up to international coercion; and, most amazingly, it had acquired a huge western empire. Jefferson won reelection handily, and the Democratic Republicans took control of both houses of Congress. Faced with the prospect of federal surpluses, Jefferson began to contemplate a future role for the federal government encouraging "the great objects of public education, roads, rivers, canals, and such other objects of public improvement as may be thought proper." But Jefferson's second term had barely begun when his attention was riveted to developments in Europe.

In his first inaugural address, Jefferson had counseled "peace, commerce, and honest friendship with all nations, entangling alliances with none." He remained committed to American neutrality, but by 1805 Napoleon's growing power in France and his expansionistic designs on Europe had complicated this policy. On the one hand, Jefferson knew he might need Napoleon's help to settle the unresolved question of West Florida, still claimed by Spain. On the other hand, France's increasing indifference toward American shipping rights raised the possibility that the United States might need Britain as an ally. Napoleon's victory over Austria in 1805 made France the undisputed master of western Europe. At the same time, English victories over the fleets of France and Spain had made

A Philosophic Cock This 1804 cartoon caricatured Jefferson as a "philosophic cock" courting his slave Sally Hemings. Jefferson's Federalist opponents tried to tarnish his reputation by publicizing his relationship with his slave, but the voters reelected Jefferson by a decisive margin.

England the undisputed master of the seas. The stalemate had dire consequences for American shipping.

Jefferson's hopes that Britain might respect the neutrality of American ships were dashed in 1805 when Britain again began seizing ships traveling between enemy ports, taking more than 200 American ships in that year alone. Then Napoleon declared a blockade of England and also began confiscating American ships. In June 1807 the British ship *Leopard* stopped the American frigate *Chesapeake* as it left Norfolk, Virginia. The captain of the *Leopard* demanded the right to search the American ship, insisting that it had recruited British deserters for its crew. When he was denied, he fired on the ship, boarded it, and took four men prisoner, leaving the *Chesapeake* to limp home.

Jefferson immediately ordered all British ships out of American waters and demanded reparation for the *Chesapeake*. In secret sessions, Congress passed an act that permitted only those American ships with the president's express approval to sail into foreign ports and prohibiting foreign ships from the American export trade. In effect, the United States had embargoed itself.

It was the most disastrous policy of Jefferson's career. Because enforcement was impossible, wealthy merchants enjoyed the large profits of smuggling. At the same time, small merchants, sailors, and shopkeepers who depended on steady maritime trade were thrown into crisis, and farmers in the South and West had trouble finding overseas trading outlets. As the economy settled into depression in 1808, the remaining Federalists charged that the embargo was helping Napoleon. Adding to American frustration, Napoleon then slyly claimed the right to attack US ships in any continental port because, by Jefferson's own order, they could not be legal carriers.

The ironies of the embargo did not end there. As violations mounted, ever more repressive versions of the embargo were enacted. The final, fifth Embargo Act (signed January 9, 1809) swept away protections against self-incrimination and the right to due process and trampled on the right to trial by jury. By comparison, even the Alien and Sedition Acts looked tame.

As he himself acknowledged, the Embargo Acts represented the failure of Jefferson's agrarian political economy. His dream of a republic of farmers was dead, the victim of the principles of territorial expansion and free trade on which he had based it. Meeting America's need for manufactured goods solely by "this exuberant commerce," as Jefferson admitted in 1809, "brings us into collision with other powers in every sea, and will force us into every war of the European powers. The converting of this great agricultural country into a . . . mere headquarters for carrying on the commerce of all nations, is too absurd."

The anguish caused by the Embargo Acts exposed long-simmering dissension within Democratic Republican ranks. The most serious rupture came after the Louisiana Purchase. Although Jefferson insisted that West Florida was a part of the Louisiana Purchase, Spain denied ever ceding it to France. Napoleon hedged, but his ministers let it be known that the right price might convince them to lobby the American cause with Spain. Jefferson asked Congress for the money. To Jefferson's most radical critics, this was the Louisiana Purchase all over again—the government exercising powers unauthorized by the Constitution. These critics, led by the Virginian John Randolph, took the name Tertium Quids (the "third something"), neither Federalists nor Democratic Republicans. By 1808, the Quids were threatening open rebellion. To avoid the risk of public brawling, in 1808 party loyalists met in closed caucus to select Jefferson's successor. They chose James Madison. In the election, Madison captured 122 electoral votes to Federalist Charles C. Pinckney's 47. The Democratic Republicans again won both houses of Congress.

From 1801 until 1829, the federal government would remain under the control of a single party. By itself, that did not challenge Democratic Republican principles. Neither Madison nor Jefferson considered a two-party system necessary to American political life. Both, however, warned against the day when a small cadre of like-minded men would meet in secret to choose the nation's ruler. Democratic Republican ascendancy itself had now come to rest on just such a closed institution. Meanwhile, with American hopes for international prestige now a joke, and with commerce and agriculture in trouble, on March 1, 1809, Jefferson signed a bill repealing the Embargo Act. Three days later, Jefferson left the office he now described as a "splendid misery."

The War of 1812

Facing ruptures in his party serious enough to compel him to accept nomination by the kind of closed and antirepublican institution he himself had once condemned, James Madison took office on March 4, 1809. Madison had stood side by side with Thomas Jefferson on virtually every important political and ideological issue since the founding of the nation. Now he inherited his friend's presidential woes.

Madison and the War

In 1809, with Madison's approval, Congress replaced the embargo with the Non-Intercourse Act, reopening trade with all of Europe except England and France but authorizing the president to resume commerce with whichever of these countries dropped its restrictions and attacks on American shipping. The act set off a series of diplomatic feints by England and France, both pretending to change policies without making actual concessions.

France eventually won the game. In the summer of 1810, Napoleon's ministers officially told Madison that, as of November of that year, France would stop seizing American ships if Britain would do likewise. Probably correctly, Britain did not believe France would follow through on this policy. But Madison accepted the French declarations, and he altered American Non-Intercourse Act policy to apply to Britain alone.

Still, war might have been averted. A quarter of a century of European wars and Napoleon's continental policy—which closed continental markets to English goods—had taken its toll on Britain's economy. Although far more powerful militarily than the United States, Britain would have been happy to avoid the cost of an additional war. On June 1, 1812, in light of continuing British attacks on American shipping, Madison requested that Congress declare war on Great Britain. He listed several other reasons, including that the British were "impressing" American seamen into service and instigating Indian attacks in the Northwest. On June 4, the House voted to pass a war bill. On June 18, the Senate concurred. Ironically, unaware of events in the United States, England announced that it was revoking its maritime policy against US ships.

The war vote in Congress went largely along party and regional lines. Proponents, led by Henry Clay of Kentucky and John C. Calhoun of South Carolina, mostly hailed from the West and South. Known as the War Hawks, they were fiercely national-istic and expansionist young men who had come of age since the Revolution. They predicted an easy conquest of Canada—"a mere matter of marching," in Jefferson's words—where they fantasized the people would rise up against British rule. Farmers and planters in the West and South wanted to open up the seas, while western migrants were convinced that Creek and Shawnee resistance was the work of the British, with their forts still along the Great Lakes. New Englanders, however, were adamantly opposed. Shipping was just beginning to recover and their region's prosperity depended on trade with Britain. Even moderate Democratic Republicans were hesitant. They dreaded the cost of the war and doubted that the nation could gear up to take on such a formidable foe.

> The distinction of Federalists and Republicans will cease; . . . the inquiry will be, are you for your country or against it?
>
> TENNESSEE CONGRESSMAN AND WAR HAWK FELIX GRUNDY

All of these tensions were reflected in the election of 1812. Maverick Democratic Republican De Witt Clinton rallied Federalist support and ran against Madison. He lost, with 89 electoral votes (to Madison's 128), but with a higher proportion than the Federalists had enjoyed since the election of 1800.

Doubts about America's war readiness were soon justified. An ill-planned attempt to invade Canada in the summer of 1812 failed. Two thousand American troops surrendered at Detroit, and two advances failed when state militiamen insisted they were not required to leave the country to fight. Commodore Oliver Hazard Perry's dramatic victory on Lake Erie, however, led to another attempt on Canada and a victory at the Battle of the Thames, where the Shawnee leader Tecumseh was killed. Demoralized by his death, the Britons' Indian allies withdrew from the war.

A comparable victory eluded Americans in the Atlantic. After initial successes, the tiny American navy was easily overwhelmed by superior British sea power. Americans turned to private schooners and sloops and by the war's end managed to capture more than 1,300 British vessels. Nevertheless, by 1813 the British navy had succeeded in blockading the American coast from the Chesapeake Bay to New Orleans; in the following year, the blockade extended to New England. The British fleet pummeled coastal cities and villages. On August 24, 1814, British troops invaded Washington, burned the Capitol, the White House, the Treasury Building, and the Naval Yard, and terrorized civilians. The entire cabinet, including President James Madison, had already evacuated.

While Washington smoldered, the British turned to Baltimore. Through the night of September 13, its ships fired on Fort McHenry, the island citadel guarding Baltimore's harbor. Among the anguished observers was a Washington lawyer by the name of Francis Scott Key. Elated that the United States flag still flew over the fort at dawn, Key quickly scribbled the words that would in 1931 become the lyrics of the national anthem, "The Star-Spangled Banner."

In the Old Southwest, Andrew Jackson used the war to suppress Indian resistance to US settlement. In March 1814, he defeated the Red Stick faction of the Creeks at Horseshoe Bend, forcing them to sign a treaty ceding two-thirds of remaining Creek lands to the United States.

Federalist Response

For a time the war worked in favor of the Federalists. In 1812, they doubled their numbers in Congress. New Englanders actively impeded the war effort. Governors refused to call out their militias, and trade with the enemy was rampant. Then, in October 1814, emboldened Massachusetts Federalists called for a convention of the New England states "to lay the foundation for a radical reform in the National compact." They planned to meet on December 15 in Hartford, Connecticut.

A VIEW of the BOMBARDMENT of Fort McHenry, near Baltimore, by the British fleet, taken from the Observatory, under the Command of Admirals Cochrane & Cockburn, on the morning of the 13th of Sept. 1814 which lasted 24 hours, & thrown from 1500 to 1800 shells, in the Night attempted to land by forcing a passage up the ferry branch but were repulsed with great loss.

Fort McHenry Fort McHenry is best known for its role in the War of 1812, when it successfully defended Baltimore Harbor from an attack by the British navy in Chesapeake Bay. It was this bombardment that inspired Francis Scott Key to write "The Star-Spangled Banner."

The Federalists meeting in Hartford were divided. Extreme Federalists, arguing that the Union could not be saved, lobbied for a separate New England confederacy that could immediately seek an end to the war. More moderate voices prevailed, and in the end, the convention sought amendments to the Constitution. The Federalists demanded restrictions on the power of Congress to declare war, an end to the Three-Fifths Compromise allowing slaves to be counted for purposes of representation, exclusion of naturalized citizens from elective federal office, and restrictions on the admission of new states. They also sought to limit the number of terms a president could serve and the frequency with which the presidential candidate could be chosen from a given state.

Federalists misjudged their strength and mistimed their efforts. By 1814, a weary Britain was ready to end the war. Emerging as the dominant power in Europe, Britain had little incentive to offer Americans more than simple peace. Signed in Ghent, Belgium, on December 24, 1814, the treaty that ended the War of 1812 was silent on the issues of free trade and impressment that had triggered the war. The Treaty of Ghent also sidestepped boundary disputes between Canada and the United States. British negotiators did agree to remove British troops from the Old Northwest, in effect acknowledging the failure of Indian resistance to white settlement.

Only Andrew Jackson's victory at New Orleans saved Americans from outright humiliation in the war. After the victory at Horseshoe Bend, his troops moved on to New Orleans, where a British fleet prepared to take control of the mouth of the Mississippi River. Unaware that two weeks earlier, on January 8, 1815, a peace treaty had been signed in Ghent, 7,500 British regulars stormed Jackson's position. In 30 minutes the battle was over, and, miraculously, the Americans had won and Jackson had become a national hero (see Map 9–2).

Map 9–2 Battles and Campaigns of the War of 1812 The War of 1812 was largely a naval war, fought along the Atlantic coast, in the Gulf of Mexico, and on the Great Lakes. Several land campaigns proved important, however: the British ground attack that ended in the looting and burning of the capital, and Jackson's trek overland to New Orleans.

In 1815, the chief political importance of Jackson's victory was the lift it gave to American nationalism and the light it cast on the Federalist Hartford Convention, still meeting in Connecticut. Threatening secession was one thing in a failing war, but quite another in a moment of national triumph. Suddenly, the proceedings at Hartford seemed downright traitorous.

An Economy in Transition

The end of the war ushered in a half century of fundamental economic change and growth. These changes, sometimes called "the market revolution," were reflected in every aspect of society, from religion and politics to family life and everyday values. Paternalistic employment arrangements (apprenticeship, indenturing) gave way to labor contracts and wage labor, and informal transactions to formal contracts. Self-sufficiency declined, while longer-distance market exchange increased. All of these changes were enhanced by improvements in technology and transportation as well as laws to encourage commerce.

International Markets

The economic transformation of the late eighteenth and early nineteenth centuries had many sources. One of the most significant was the gradual revival of overseas commerce at the end of the eighteenth century, much of this supported by conflicts in Europe. As Napoleon tried to spread the French Revolution (and his own power) throughout Europe, Europe remained at war—disrupting agriculture on the Continent and impeding European overseas trade. America shippers happily filled the gap.

This American shipping was of three kinds: export/import (exporting American wheat, rice, indigo, tobacco, and especially cotton to Europe and importing European manufactured goods to growing United States markets); reexport (carrying goods between two foreign ports with an intermediate stop in the United States, often to avoid French and English embargoes on each other's Caribbean colonies); and the simple carrying trade between two foreign ports (as US ships became the main carriers between warring England and France). In addition to farm products and manufactured goods, American ships also carried people: political refugees from France and from Ireland's ill-fated rebellion seeking safety in the new republic and—before 1808, when the slave trade was officially ended—captives from Africa sold into slavery in the Caribbean and the United States.

American shipping tonnage tripled between 1780 and 1810, reaching almost 11 million tons annually. The American share of the traffic between England and the United States grew from 50 percent in 1790 to 95 percent by 1800. The value of the reexport carrying trade also increased from about $500,000 a year in the 1790s to about $60 million a year in 1807. By the first decade of the nineteenth century, American ships were in the harbors of India, the East Indies, China, the Philippines, Japan, and Hawaii and on the Pacific coast of North America and the eastern coast of South America.

The return of overseas trade fed an already rampant inflation (the result of a shortage of gold and silver and a surfeit of local- and state-issued currencies of doubtful values). But it also created many jobs and helped alter the way Americans understood the terms of labor.

Merchants contracted for vessels (built at an astonishing rate), captains hired crews, and teamsters hurried goods to port. Some merchants also invested in port-city manufacturing. They gathered tailors, for example, into large central shops to turn

AMERICA AND THE WORLD

>> The United States in China

Although much of the history of the early republic unfolded in the Atlantic world, the Pacific Ocean was also an important stage for American political and commercial ambitions.

American traders had sent ships to China as early as 1784, when Robert Morris hired the *Empress of China* to sail out from New York to Macao, China. After the Revolutionary War, wealthy Americans were keen to purchase Chinese consumer goods—tea (boycotted during the war), porcelain, silk, and spices—and American merchants (barred from British colonial ports) sought new markets. When the *Empress* returned a year later to realize a $30,000 profit, other American merchants jumped into the China trade.

From the beginning, however, Americans faced problems. First, although the Chinese were willing to trade with foreigners, they did not want foreigners in the country. Traders were forced to stay in designated areas, called *hongs*, where Chinese traders came to them to discuss possible deals. Fearing the settlement of foreign families, the Chinese insisted that any women on board trading vessels (not uncommon at the time) wait on the Portuguese island outpost of Macao.

The second problem was Chinese lack of interest in most products the United States had to offer. The ginseng market was quickly saturated, so American traders shifted to fur pelts obtained in trade with the Indians of the Pacific Northwest. From there they sailed across the Pacific, often stopping in the Sandwich Islands (now Hawaii) to pick up sandalwood for the Chinese market.

Among the American merchants who eventually realized a fortune from this trade was John Jacob Astor, who migrated from Germany to America just after the Revolutionary War and, with his wife Sarah (a smart businesswoman and an expert in furs), set up shop in New York City, dealing mostly in furs from the Canadian Great Lakes region. But after Astor made $50,000 from his first venture in China—a staggering sum for the time—he envisioned a route that would carry New England manufac-

tured goods to the Northwest Indians for furs to be traded with China. He established a trading post in present-day Oregon for that purpose in 1811.

In the meantime, the most successful commodity Americans could sell in China was silver, which the Chinese were willing to take in payment. But the United States had no silver mines, so obtaining the metal required either trading for silver with the Spanish South American colonies or acquiring it in European ports before heading off to China.

As early as the late eighteenth century, Americans found another trading medium: opium. Opium had long been chewed in South and Southeast Asia as a general analgesic, but the far more addictive practice of smoking opium became common only with the introduction of tobacco and contact with foreign merchants and sailors. Britain's trade monopoly in India encouraged English efforts to sell opium in China, but by the first decade of the nineteenth century Americans got in on the action. American ships were being specially designed to carry opium from India to Canton, and some of the early republic's greatest merchants—including Stephen Girard of Philadelphia and James and Thomas Perkins of Boston—amassed fortunes in part on the profits of drug trafficking in Southeast Asia.

out cheap clothing for sailors or to sell to planters for their slaves—even though the new merchant-manufacturers seldom recognized the traditional obligations of shop master to worker: food, housing, and training. Rather, they tended to hire unattached workers, apprentices, or jobless young men and put them to work at some single, specialized aspect of the craft. Some traditional shop masters became merchants, taking investments in ships to carry their goods to southern and Caribbean markets.

The growth of overseas shipping also spurred the development of business services in the early republic, particularly in port cities. The National Bank of the United States would be reauthorized in 1816. In the meantime, citizens formed insurance companies against the risks of loss in trading and local institutions for pooling capital for investment. By 1810 there were more than 100 banks in the nation. Many of these banks, corporations, and insurance companies operated under special state charters that allowed them to function as legal entities. As the businesses mushroomed, so did new jobs for clerks and lawyers.

In the countryside, farming families shifted from a relatively self-sufficient model of agriculture to more commercially oriented enterprises. Farmers were willing to travel longer distances to sell their goods. Whenever possible, they expanded the size of their holdings. In Delaware, for example, families used the profit from women's dairying activities to finance new land to grow wheat for sale in the cities or in Europe. Farmers, like merchants and shop masters, tried to hedge their bets by reducing their costs and liabilities. They ceased using indentured servants, to whom they would have owed year-round room and board and a freedom bonus at the end of their term, in favor of hiring seasonal wage workers, to whom they had no responsibilities in the off-season.

The most significant boost to American commercial agriculture arose from the late eighteenth-century mechanization of the English textile mills and the resulting increased demand for cotton. The colonies had not been an important source of raw cotton, because the only variety that grew well in most of North America was extremely laborious and time-consuming to clean. Spurred by the new English markets, in 1793 Eli Whitney invented a mechanism that increased the amount of this short-staple cotton that could be cleaned in a day from 1 pound to 50 pounds. Almost at a stroke, Whitney's gin made cotton a viable cash crop for much of the South.

The invention occurred at a critical moment. American indigo was losing market share to indigo from the East Indies. The tobacco trade was in decline. The market for rice was still strong, but rice cultivation required such large investments of land and labor as to exclude most farmers from production. Cotton gave the South a new commodity crop, and one that, unlike rice, could be grown on small farms without significant investment. Between 1790 and 1810, American cotton production increased from 3,000 bales to 178,000 bales a year. Increasingly after 1800, cotton was the largest single US export commodity, making the development of the nation, not merely that of the South, dependent on cotton and its labor system, slavery.

At the same time, the United States banned another kind of international trade: that of enslaved Africans. The Constitution forbade a national ban until 1808, but by 1806 every state except South Carolina, which imported almost 40,000 slaves between 1803 and 1807, had ended the trade. In early 1807 Congress banned the international slave trade as of January 1, 1808, but only after debating one troubling issue: What was to be done with the slaves confiscated from ships that defied the ban? Slavery's opponents thought the slaves should be freed, while the institution's defenders feared the introduction of more free blacks. A compromise left it up to the individual states to decide, which meant that Africans confiscated in the South could be sold into slavery there. Americans could agree that no more Africans should be brought into the United States, but not what to do with those who were already there. The ending of the international slave trade was a significant achievement, but the debate gave signs of trouble to come.

Crossing the Appalachian Mountains

After the Treaty of Greenville opened the Ohio River valley, the expansion of overseas markets fed a pent-up desire for new lands in Tennessee, Kentucky, and the soon-to-be state of Ohio (1803). The Land Ordinance of 1785 had provided for sales to private individuals who could afford sections of 640 acres or more at $1 an acre, but that was far beyond the reach of ordinary citizens. Sales were effectively restricted to speculators. Hoping to find a source of revenue, in 1796 Congress made matters worse by raising the price to $2 an acre.

Finally, in 1800, settlers got some relief. The Land Act of 1800 reduced the size of the minimum parcel from 640 acres to 320 acres. For the first time, buyers were permitted to spread their payments over time. In 1804, the minimum size was decreased to 160 acres and the price reduced from $2.00 to $1.64 an acre. Even though the cost of the land and the journey were still prohibitive for many Americans and easy credit sometimes led to unmanageable debt, lower prices per acre, lower minimums, and the promise of credit opened the West to tens of thousands of settlers.

The unprecedented migration set off by the Treaty of Ghent quickly swelled the population of the trans-Appalachian region. Kentucky grew from 220,955 in 1800 to 564,317 in 1820; Tennessee from 105,602 to 422,823; and Ohio from 42,159 to 581,434. Equally important, settlement led to the organization of new states. After Ohio in 1803, nine years passed before the next new state, Louisiana, entered in 1812. But then the admissions came rapid-fire. Indiana became a state in 1816, Mississippi in 1817, Illinois in 1818, and Alabama in 1819. By then both Missouri and Maine were also eager to join the Union.

The westward migration was a remarkably diverse parade. The earliest arrivals were usually hunters, fur traders, explorers, and surveyors. Wealthy speculators (European and American) sometimes traveled to the backcountry just long enough to buy up the best parcels of land, then scurried home to sell them to investors or migrants. Single men (displaced mechanics, sons of poor farmers, husbands sent ahead to purchase land) trekked along dusty roads, sometimes on horseback, often on foot. Andrew Jackson was one of their number. Families soon followed. Some traveled in wagons, packing food and seed, a few household items, and perhaps a gun, herding a cow or a few pigs alongside. But equally common was the sight of a "man, wife, and five children, with all their household goods thrown in a wheelbarrow . . . walking to Ohio."

The backcountry roiled in "anxiety and confusion," one observer noted, as newcomers raced to claim their share of territorial lands. There were cotton lands in the South and huge expanses for grain in the Old Northwest Territory—and favorable possibilities for transportation. Speculators were eager for huge returns on land investment, and migrants were eager to escape debt and taxes, oppressive jobs, and overworked soil.

Invention and Exploration

Western lands offered the potential for vastly enlarged markets within the United States. Settlers wanted to get their tobacco, wheat, corn, hemp, and cotton to coastal and European customers, and merchants and manufacturers were impatient to get their buttons, shoes, pots, pans, and farm tools to rural stores. Making that connection was still a backbreaking task, and the challenge of figuring out how to connect people to land and products to markets spurred some of the century's most important inventions.

The first improvements in transportation came from locally sponsored toll roads. Although states generally granted a special charter of incorporation for such projects, most of the capital came from local investors expecting to benefit from tolls. New York communities increased their road mileage from 1,000 miles in 1810 to more than 4,000 miles in 1820. To bolster the trade from cities such as Cincinnati, Pennsylvania extended an older highway that ran from Philadelphia to Pittsburgh. But the toll roads proved a poor investment. Only one (a short turnpike in Connecticut) paid profits, whereas many made no money at all.

The most important effect of road building in the post–War of 1812 era was the spur it gave to bridge building. The new bridges (such as one constructed over the Hudson River at Newburgh, New York) dramatically improved the time and cost of transport. They were heavily used and usually turned a good profit.

But it was the application of the steam engine to transportation that made the most dramatic difference. By the end of the War of 1812, the steam engine had begun to attract investors. There were some steam-powered overland rail carriers, but they remained fragmentary until the 1850s and conveyed only passengers, not cargo. The use of steam engines to power boats proved more successful. The technology came together in August 1807 when Robert Fulton and his patron Robert Livingston (Jefferson's minister to France during the Louisiana negotiations) announced the Hudson River trial run of the *North River Steamboat of Clermont*, a 140-foot-long vessel with two steam-driven paddle wheels. Fulton wryly described the trip, 150 miles from New York City to Albany, as "rather more favorable than I had calculated." "I ran it up in thirty-two hours, and down in thirty," he boasted.

Although he had not invented the steamboat, Fulton had demonstrated its practical value for transporting people and goods. By 1817 steamboats were common in the coastal waters of the East and across the Great Lakes, but their most telling impact occurred on the western rivers: the Ohio, the Wabash, the Monongahela, the Cumberland, and especially the Mississippi. In 1809 Livingston and Fulton hired Nicholas Roosevelt to survey the river waters from Pittsburgh to New Orleans, and in 1811 they sent the steamboat *New Orleans* downriver from Pittsburgh. After carrying troops and supplies on the river during the War of 1812, in 1815 steamboats began regular private routes upriver on the Mississippi.

The steamboat powered the market development of the Mississippi River valley. Able to travel upstream as well as down, it knit northern and southern regions together in an integrated economic system, with eastern manufactured goods and passengers flowing upriver into the Ohio River valley and northern grain, livestock, and manufactured goods flowing to downstream markets and out through the Gulf of Mexico, joined in Kentucky, Tennessee, and Mississippi by a swelling cargo of cotton. In 1811 the Mississippi River valley produced some 5 million pounds of cotton. Within two decades it produced 40 times that much, virtually all of it carried downstream to market on steamboats. In 1817 the overland route from Cincinnati to Philadelphia or New York took nearly two months. Freight sent downriver from Cincinnati through New Orleans on steamboats and then by packet boat to Philadelphia took about half the time.

The steamboat soon became a conspicuous and controversial symbol of American economic promise. Not only were steamboats fast and exciting, but they were also relatively inexpensive to own and operate, within the reach of small investors eager to have a chance at making their fortunes. Citing the importance of orderly and reliable service, however, state lawmakers often encouraged large enterprises, awarding monopoly rights to specific prime routes. In 1798, Robert Livingston had gained exclusive rights for 20 years over the waters of the state of New York by vessels propelled by steam, a monopoly he revived and expanded to include Robert Fulton in 1803. Fulton and Livingston failed to obtain sole rights to the Mississippi, but in 1811 they succeeded temporarily in gaining a monopoly on steamboat transportation at the mouth of the river. Their success provoked a storm of protest from competitors, who saw government favoring wealth at the expense of the small entrepreneur. In 1819 the monopoly was withdrawn, but many small operators remained convinced of the state's favoritism toward the wealthy. In fact, few got rich running steamboats on the Mississippi. The twists and hidden snags of the shallow river saw to that. Only in the East, where rivers were deeper and where steamboats became fashionable transportation for wealthy travelers, did investors realize large profits.

Even steamboats were limited by the existing waterways. Since the turn of the century, investors and inventors had sought to enlarge those water routes by linking them artificially with canals, but the early history of canals did not portend great success. By the end of the War of 1812, only about 100 miles of canals existed in the United States (the longest ran 27 miles between the Merrimack River and Boston Harbor). None earned much money.

Thus, when at the end of the war New York City mayor De Witt Clinton proposed building a canal to connect Albany and Buffalo (see Map 9–3), he was thought to have taken leave of his senses. The canal would run 364 miles, making it the longest canal in the world. It would require an elaborate system of aqueducts and locks to negotiate a 571-foot rise in elevation and would cost $7 million, the largest investment of the sort in the nation's history. Clinton argued that the canal would "create the greatest inland trade ever witnessed" and would tie the "most fertile and extensive regions of America" to the city of New York, making that city "the granary of the world, the emporium of commerce, the seat of manufactures, the focus of great moneyed operation." In 1817 he convinced the state legislature not only to authorize the project but also to pay for it entirely in state funds, a gamble that amounted to a $5-per-capita levy for the entire population of New York.

Begun on July 4, 1817, the Erie Canal was completed in 1823 and officially opened two years later. At 10:30 on the morning of Wednesday, November 2, 1825, the first boats cleared the final locks and made their way into the Albany basin. Bells pealed, bands played, a huge crowd cheered, and 24 cannons fired successively in a national salute.

Clinton's gamble paid off spectacularly. Passenger boats and transport barges produced revenues high enough for the state to pay for later stages of construction with the profits of early ones. Transportation costs from Buffalo to New York City fell from $100 a ton to about $10 a ton when the canal opened and dropped even lower later on.

TECHNOLOGY AND IDEAS

>> The Steamboat

Although the steam engine and steamboat technologies came from Britain and France, the United States readily adopted the steamboat, and, in the process, transformed the nation. With a vast and expanding interior desperate for effective transportation of goods and people to and from the coast, the early years of the new nation were fraught with frustration. Roads were often no more than dirt paths, impassable in rain and snow, frequently blocked by debris, and disastrous for wheels, axles, and passengers alike. The best way to travel, therefore, was by water. Unfortunately, using the wind to power waterborne craft was unreliable. Animal-drawn barges suffered from the same problems as land traffic. The solution on the nation's navigable rivers and coastline came in the form of the paddle-wheel steamboat.

The inventor and entrepreneur Robert Fulton (1765–1815) had been to England and France and seen those nations' versions of steam engine-driven vessels. He believed not only that he could do better, but also that the owners and operators of steamboats could make substantial fortunes in the United States. After many fits and starts, he launched the first commercial steamboat in the United States in 1807. This vessel was the *North River Steamboat of Clermont*, which made the run on the Hudson River between New York City and Albany in the then-impressive time of 32 hours. He was able to fund this venture in a partnership with his uncle-in-law, Robert Livingston, whose own wealth and political connections were vital in securing the privileges and licenses necessary to conduct this business.

From this small beginning, steamboats became the most significant carrier of people and goods in the whole of the nineteenth century. Even after trains surpassed them in the second half of the nineteenth century, steamboats remained the workhorses of transatlantic travel. Their ability to carry significant amounts of both cargo and passengers led to the wider drive for economic development, settlement, and linkages with the West that had eluded the nation in its early years. The cotton kingdom, the development of New Orleans as a major port, the rise of Cincinnati as a hog-packing center and St. Louis as the gateway to the West, and the knitting together of the Ohio River valley to the Mississippi River valley and beyond forged what Alexander Saxton has called "The White Man's Republic." In addition, the development of steamboat travel forged one of the country's first multimillion-dollar fortunes with "Commodore" Cornelius Vanderbilt's sharp business practices.

Literature and culture also flowed from these wonders of modern technology that hosted sumptuous meals, accommodations, and on-board entertainment for at least their first-class passengers. For example, Samuel Clemens, who wrote under the steamboat-inspired name of Mark Twain, received much of his education working on these cross sections of American life. With sensational boiler explosions, wrecks, and beachings, steamboat

Continued

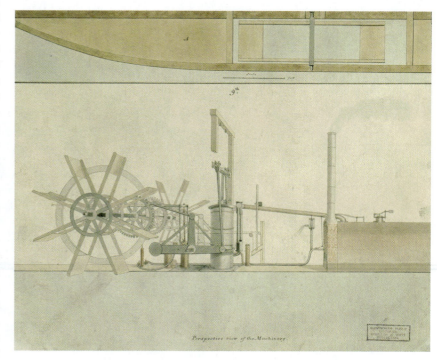

Fulton Steamboat Paddle Wheel The original patent drawing, a perspective view of the machinery drawn for Robert Fulton, 1809.

>> **TECHNOLOGY AND IDEAS** *Continued*

travel provided Americans with their first major experience of the marvels and dangers of technology. Fulton, however, did not live to see the age he had helped usher in. He died of consumption after diving into the icy waters of the Hudson to save a friend from drowning. He was 49 years old.

Questions

1. The steamboat industry in the early nineteenth century faced many and varied problems. Some were technical (such as explosions, wrecks, and beachings), while others were economic (the business was expensive, and price wars could spring up). Do these problems substantially resemble those of any relatively new industry today, such as air travel? How are they similar and different?

2. Was America's embrace of the steamboat more of a cause or a consequence of territorial expansion? Explain your answer.

The Erie Canal set off an explosion of canal building that lasted up to the Civil War, but few later canals duplicated its success.

Early Industrial Society in New England

New Englanders had been experimenting with the idea of water-powered textile mills since the 1780s, when prominent Massachusetts merchants tried to convince the state legislature to support the creation of textile machinery in the United States. In 1790, émigré mechanic Samuel Slater had replicated the English water-powered carding and spinning machines in his mill in Pawtucket, Rhode Island. But Slater lacked the power loom necessary to turn yarn into finished cloth. It took Eli Whitney's invention of the

Erie Canal Opening, 1825 New York governor De Witt Clinton pouring water from Lake Erie into the Atlantic Ocean at the Grand Erie Canal Celebration in New York Harbor on November 4, 1825.

Map 9-3 The Development of Regions and of Roads and Canals By 1830 internal development had fostered a growing transportation infrastructure throughout the United States. That development was regional in character, however. In the southern states, where natural waterways ran from deep in the interior to the coast, citizens saw little need to build additional linkages. In the North, where natural waterways seldom ran directly to coastal outlets, investors were far more willing to spend money on internal development, especially canals.

cotton gin in 1793, some industrial sabotage, and the devastating trade losses during the embargo and the War of 1812 to finally propel Americans to devise a power loom and invest seriously in a domestic textile industry. Boston merchant Francis Cabot Lowell pioneered the shift.

A graduate of Harvard with a knack for machine design, Lowell traveled to England to see the loom for himself and surreptitiously to memorize its plan. Back home,

This daguerreotype of a woman working at a power loom dates from 1850.

working with mechanic Paul Moody, he duplicated the English model in 1814. With a special charter from the Massachusetts legislature, Lowell and his Boston associates (organized as the Boston Manufacturing Company) opened the United States' first fully mechanized textile mill in Waltham, Massachusetts. Within three years the mill had expanded and was paying a whopping 20 percent dividend.

Lowell died in 1817, but under Nathan Appleton's leadership the company (now the Merrimack Manufacturing Corporation) raised more than $8 million to finance a second group of mills in East Chelmsford, Massachusetts. The new mills turned out their first finished cloth in 1823. A sleepy rural village of 200 in 1820, by 1826 East Chelmsford had grown to 2,600 and had incorporated as the city of Lowell, America's first industrial town. The mills relied entirely on the South for their raw cotton. Northern domestic purchase of raw southern cotton grew from 8 million pounds in 1800 to 31.5 million by the end of the war in 1815.

The Waltham system, as Lowell's approach was called, differed from earlier American manufacturing enterprises in several ways. The Waltham mill was the largest industrial undertaking attempted in America up to that time. It housed the full production process, from fiber to finished cloth. It relied on a new organization plan in which a professional managerial rank (separate from the owners) oversaw daily operations. Finally, to cultivate an appearance of benevolence (in contrast to the plight of workers in the English mills), the Waltham system required that employees live on-site in subsidized and supervised housing.

For their workforce, the owners turned to the young rural women from Vermont, New Hampshire, and western Massachusetts. Textiles were traditionally women's work, and power-driven textile machinery was not necessarily identified with either sex. Moreover, female workers were cheaper than men, the result of their long exclusion from customary craft protections and their loss of the right to make contracts if they were married.

In the early years, parents and daughters both saw benefits in mill work for unmarried young women. Presumably, a daughter would leave her family anyway when she married. Having her work in the mills before marriage reduced the number of mouths to be fed at home. The residential system allayed fears that a young woman was compromising her respectability. Matrons supervised company-owned boardinghouses, where operatives lived together in single-sex settings. Strict rules of behavior guided leisure time, and factory bells regulated the workday.

The success of the mills underscored the paradoxes of American slavery and American freedom in the early nineteenth century. In the early years, at least, the women operatives enjoyed a financial and social independence virtually unknown under the parental roof. They lived together under the guidance of a female head of household. They returned home for vacation largely at their own discretion. Many of the young women kept all or most of their pay, enjoying (perhaps for the only time in their lives) a separate disposable income. They developed pride in their work and in their community and began to see themselves as part of a long Yankee history of hard work and independence. All of this was made possible by the fact of slavery in the American South.

The final irony of this contradiction would play out only in the later years of the mills, after employers had cut pay and intensified production. In 1834 and again in 1836, the operatives turned out in defiant strikes—condemning the mill owners for reducing them, "the daughters of freemen," to the condition of slaves.

> Whereas we the undersigned residents of Lowell, moved by a love of honest industry and the expectation of a fair and liberal recompence, have left our homes, our relatives and youthful associates and come hither, and subjected ourselves to all of the danger and inconvenience, which necessarily attend young and unprotected females, when among strangers, and in a strange land . . . we firmly and fearlessly (though we trust with a modesty becoming our sex) claim for ourselves, that love of moral and intellectual culture, that admiration of, and desire to attain and preserve pure, elevated, and refined characters, a true reverence for the divine principle which bids us to render to every one his due; a due appreciation of those great and cardinal principles of our government, of justice and humanity, which enjoins us "to live and let live" . . .
>
> CONSTITUTION OF THE LOWELL FACTORY GIRLS ASSOCIATION, 1834

The Rule of Law and Lawyers

Americans had long emphasized the importance of the written law to the preservation of the republic, but the law became important in new ways in the growing commercial economy. Overseas trade, internal expansion, the buying and selling of land, new inventions—all required complex legal documents and lawyers to draw them up and execute them. The revival of commerce and the work of government converged to make the legal profession attractive. By 1815, lawyers made up about half the members of Congress.

The growing importance of lawyers reflected the growing importance of courts and of the judiciary. Again and again, judicial interpretation reinforced and set the course for market development. When tradition clashed with economic development, judges tended to side with the entrepreneurs. For example, as businesses experimented with the use of water power in manufacturing, they sought to erect dams and millraces that altered the flow of streams. English common law protected the use of waterways undisturbed by alterations upstream. But in 1805, in *Palmer v. Mulligan*, a New York court ruled in favor of the right of development, against customary common-law rights.

On the federal level, the power of the Democratic Republicans (and, later, the Jacksonian Democrats) in the executive and legislative branches was countered by the power of Federalist John Marshall, who was chief justice of the Supreme Court from 1801 until 1835. Between 1805 and 1824, the Marshall Court issued three decisions that brought the Constitution to bear in support of the new market-based economy.

The first, *Dartmouth v. Woodward* (1819), explicitly reinforced the rights of contract. The case concerned an attempt by the New Hampshire legislature to alter the original charter of Dartmouth College, given to the college by King George III in 1769 when the nation was still a set of British colonies. New Hampshire argued that the original charter was not binding on the current state government, but Dartmouth insisted that the charter was in fact a contract, protected under Article VI of the US Constitution, which protected debts and engagements entered into before the Revolution. Acting to ensure the stability of contract in the broadest sense, the Court ruled in Dartmouth's favor.

The case of *McCulloch v. Maryland*, also decided in 1819, upheld the constitutionality of the Second Bank of the United States. The creation of the bank had been one of the successes of the new Democratic Republicans, who had managed to overpower their party's objections to national banks by attracting Federalist votes. The Second Bank had created a number of branches, one of which was in Baltimore. Viewing the presence of the bank within its borders as a threat to its sovereignty, Maryland attempted to assert its authority over the Baltimore branch by taxing it. James W. McCulloch, chief clerk of the branch, refused. Maryland appealed to the Supreme Court, arguing that because the federal government was a creation of the states, its branch institutions could be taxed in the states in which they existed. Marshall's Court unanimously rejected this position. The federal government was superior to the states, the Supreme Court concluded. Because "the power to tax involves the power to destroy," the states could not tax the creations of the federal government, whatever their location. The ruling was a victory for federal power and the Bank both.

Gibbons v. Ogden (1824), the last in Marshall's long line of landmark decisions, concerned a disputed ferryboat monopoly in New York. Having exclusive rights to operate steamboats in the state's waters, Robert Fulton and Robert Livingston had, in turn, "contracted" a part of this right out to Aaron Ogden, giving him a ferry monopoly across the Hudson River from New York to New Jersey. At the same time, however, Thomas Gibbons had obtained a federal license to operate a boat line along a coastal route that came into conflict with Ogden's line. Who controlled these waters and therefore had the right to grant licenses, New York or the federal government? Consistent with its national view of power and development, the Marshall Court found in favor of the federal power. The decision noted that the Constitution had given to Congress (Article I, Section 8) the right "to regulate Commerce with foreign nations, and among the several States." Because the waterways under dispute did not fall clearly within the boundaries of a single state, state power was in this case in conflict with federal power. In such cases, the Marshall Court found, federal power took precedence.

Ways of Life in Flux

Americans at the turn of the century played active roles in the political, social, and economic changes affecting their communities. Those changes grew out of choices some Americans made—to invest in an overseas venture, for example, or to buy new lands in the West to grow wheat or cotton. Their choices affected their own lives and the lives of others and slowly added up to a far more market-driven way of life.

Indian Resistance to American Expansion

Although he expressed benevolence toward Indians, President Jefferson believed that they must give way to American settlement. Not only did the territories represent the supply of land necessary to nurture republican virtues and stabilize republican in-

>> *Gibbons v. Ogden*: Freedom of Interstate Commerce

In the competition for steamboat traffic on the Hudson River in New York, Aaron Ogden, under a license from inventor Robert Fulton, obtained an injunction from New York courts barring the rival company that Thomas Gibbons ran. Daniel Webster argued the case for Gibbons that the state of New York was not allowed to do this. In Gibbons v. Ogden (1824) a unanimous US Supreme Court, for which Chief Justice John Marshall wrote, struck down a New York State regulation of navigation on the Hudson River as a violation of the Commerce Clause of the federal Constitution. In so doing, Marshall claimed exclusive jurisdiction over navigable waters for the federal government and simultaneously promoted the development of steamboat traffic on those waters. The steamboat would become the first of many technological improvements to passenger and cargo transportation, together with the railroads creating a national market across vast spaces of the new nation.

Marshall, C.J.: The subject to be regulated is commerce, and our Constitution being, as was aptly said at the bar, one of enumeration, and not of definition, to ascertain the extent of the power, it becomes necessary to settle the meaning of the word. The counsel for the appellee would limit it to traffic, to buying and selling, or the interchange of commodities, and do not admit that it comprehends navigation. This would restrict a general term, applicable to many objects, to one of its significations. Commerce, undoubtedly, is traffic, but it is something more: it is intercourse. It describes the commercial intercourse between nations, and parts of nations, in all its branches, and is regulated by prescribing rules for carrying on that intercourse. The mind can scarcely conceive a system for regulating commerce between nations which shall exclude all laws concerning navigation, which shall be silent on the admission of the vessels of the one nation into the ports of the other, and be confined to prescribing rules for the conduct of individuals in the actual employment of buying and selling or of barter.

Continued

If commerce does not include navigation, the government of the Union has no direct power over that subject, and can make no law prescribing what shall constitute American vessels or requiring that they shall be navigated by American seamen. Yet this power has been exercised from the commencement of the government, has been exercised with the consent of all, and has been understood by all to be a commercial regulation. All America understands, and has uniformly understood, the word "commerce" to comprehend navigation. It was so understood, and must have been so understood, when the Constitution was framed. The power over commerce, including navigation, was one of the primary objects for which the people of America adopted their government, and must have been contemplated in forming it. The convention must have used the word in that sense, because all have understood it in that sense, and the attempt to restrict it comes too late. . . .

It is the power to regulate, that is, to prescribe the rule by which commerce is to be governed. This power, like all others vested in Congress, is complete in itself, may be exercised to its utmost extent, and acknowledges no limitations other than are prescribed in the Constitution. These are expressed in plain terms, and do not affect the questions which arise in this case, or which have been discussed at the bar. If, as has always been understood, the sovereignty of Congress, though limited to specified objects, is plenary as to those objects, the power over commerce with foreign nations, and among the several States, is vested in Congress as absolutely as it would be in a single government, having in its Constitution the same restrictions on the exercise of the power as are found in the Constitution of the United States.

Chief Justice John Marshall, "Majority Opinion Gibbons v. Ogden, 1824," in *The Constitutional Decisions of John Marshall,* Volume II, ed. Joseph P. Cotton (New York: G. P. Putnam's Sons, 1905), pp. 41–43, 49.

Questions

1. From what provisions of the United States Constitution does Chief Justice Marshall base his decision?

2. Is this a decision in support of economic liberty? Why or why not?

3. Considering what you have learned about Marshall in this chapter, how does his decision in *Gibbons* relate to his general ideas of what the Constitution does?

stitutions, but they also provided a western buffer against Britain, France, and Spain. Preferring peaceful American expansion westward, Jefferson fostered a growing Indian dependency on American agents that would, he hoped, lead them to sell off their lands.

Nevertheless, by the turn of the century, that westward migration was devastating native life and culture. As settlers occupied new lands, Indians lost their villages and fields. Thrown back on the fur trade, they overhunted dwindling grounds. By 1800 many of the pelts and skins brought to traders in the Northwest Territory had actually been hunted west of the Mississippi River, and the deer were all but gone in the Southeast. Protestant missionaries urged the Indians to adopt European American religious and social practices, including male-headed households and private ownership of property. Unscrupulous agents bullied Indian nations into signing away their land. When the Indians resisted, the agents made deals with leaders they knew to be of doubtful legitimacy, promising bounties and annuities for territory.

> To promote [the Indians'] disposition to exchange lands, which they have to spare and we want, for necessaries, which we have to spare and they want, we shall push our trad[e] . . . and be glad to see the good and influential individuals among them run in debt, because we observe that when these debts get beyond what the individuals can pay, they become willing to lop them off by a cession of lands.
>
> THOMAS JEFFERSON, 1803

Native Americans resisted these assaults on their autonomy. Seneca communities accepted some missionary aid but refused to abandon their holdings, gender division of labor, and matrilineal households. The southern nations declined Jefferson's promise of new lands in the West and focused on constructing internal institutions Americans might recognize as "civilized." For example, the Cherokees adopted a series of laws that functioned as a constitution, established a congress, and executed individual land titles. Meanwhile, resistance to European American culture also took the form of a broad movement for spiritual revitalization. Ganioda'yo (Handsome Lake), who rose to influence among the Senecas after 1799, preached revival through a synthesis of traditional beliefs and Christianity, but for other groups revitalization meant cleansing themselves of European American practices. Cherokees revived the Green Corn Ceremony, celebrating personal bonds and repudiating material wealth.

This crisis of survival virtually ensured armed confrontation. As early as 1807, William Henry Harrison, governor of the Indiana Territory, heard rumors of "a general combination of the Indians for a war against the United States." Two Shawnee leaders, Tecumseh and his half-brother, Tenskwatawa (known as the Prophet), coalesced the diffuse anger into organized resistance. Tecumseh's struggles against whites in the Old Northwest and in the South helped him build a pan-Indian alliance. After 1805 Tenskwatawa became the leader of a movement that rejected white culture. About 1808, Tecumseh and Tenskwatawa founded a village in present-day Indiana on the banks of the Tippecanoe River. The Prophet remained there while Tecumseh traveled widely, encouraging organized resistance to white settlement (see Map 9–4).

By 1811, Tecumseh's success alarmed Harrison. That fall, Harrison marched an army toward Tecumseh's village on the Tippecanoe River. Although cautioned by Tecumseh not to be drawn into battle in his absence, on November 7, 1811, the Prophet engaged Harrison's troops and was defeated. The Prophet was discredited, but when

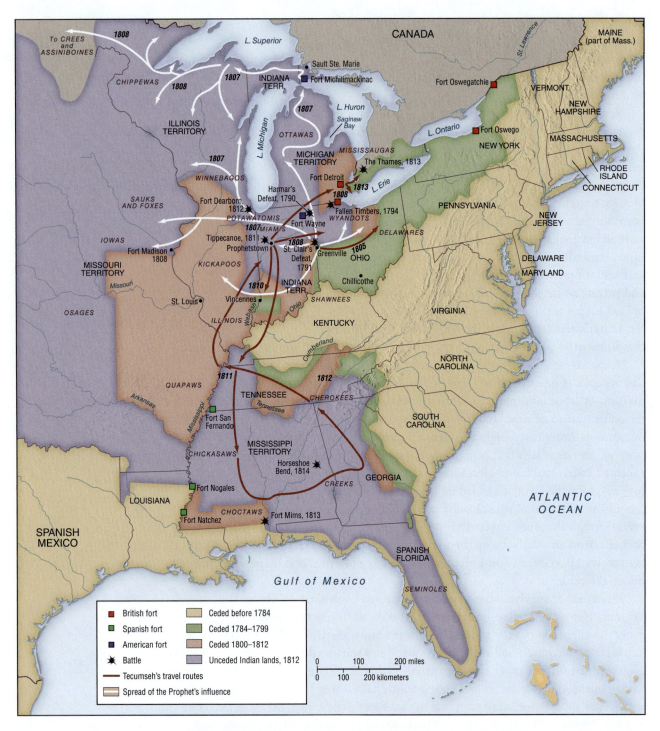

Map 9-4 Mounting Land Pressure, 1784–1812, and the Rise of Tecumseh's Confederation The pan-Indian movement led by Tecumseh and the Prophet was the culmination of years of US incursions into Indian lands and pressure, official and unofficial, on Indians to cede territories to the United States. As this map suggests, the influence of Tecumseh and the Prophet was greatest in the regions most recently ceded or where ongoing pressure was greatest in 1800–1810.

war broke out between Britain and the United States the following year, Tecumseh was still able to amass a huge force for the British. He played a decisive role in the British victory at Detroit but was killed in the Battle of the Thames in 1813. Tecumseh's death marked the end of organized Indian resistance east of the Mississippi.

Winners and Losers in the New Economy

For many Americans, the more cash- and contract-based society at the turn of the century offered both new freedom and new wealth. Large merchants who were able to absorb the risks of war might realize enormous profits in transatlantic shipping. Owners of shipbuilding and related enterprises benefited from the prolonged boom in American shipping. Farmers able to expand their holdings and take advantage of trade networks thrived in the increasingly commercial environment.

The blessings of these new liberties were mixed. New, unskilled workers took jobs away from journeymen, but they were as quickly fired as hired. Wages fell. Near poverty, journeymen in Philadelphia, New York, and Baltimore began to form mutual aid societies, helping each other and laying the foundations for trade associations. But when they tried to

Tenkswatawa (known as the Prophet) The Shawnee Prophet was about 60 in 1830 when George Catlin painted him holding his "medicine fire" in one hand and sacred beads in the other. Catlin said he "has been a very shrewd and influential man, but circumstances have destroyed him . . . and he now lives respected, but silent and melancholy in his tribe."

organize for higher wages, they discovered that in the eyes of the law, these assertions of liberty amounted to a conspiracy against the rights of trade. When Philadelphia journeyman shoemakers demanded a bill of higher wages in 1805–1806 (in the first strike in United States history), they were arrested and required to pay stiff fines.

But craft masters paid, too. New opportunities in manufacturing lured entrepreneurs and merchants who organized bigger shops, hired cheap workers, and offered cutthroat competition. Initially, the traditional craft masters refused to associate with these new entrepreneurs. By the early 1800s, however, their solidarity eroded. Wanting to take advantage of economic opportunities or to cut costs, shop masters began to hire runaway servants with no questions asked or unskilled workers to whom they had fewer lasting obligations.

Americans described these changing relations of labor and society in the language of the Revolution. Elites fretted that the masses were unfit for republican self-government, whereas workers condemned the older structures of authority as repugnant to a free people. However, local conditions were also sources of new social instability. Apprentices ran away not to express allegiance to Jeffersonianism but to escape cruel masters or to seek higher wages. Masters did not hire untrained workers to affirm republican freedom but to protect profits by cutting costs.

Religion

These were years of ongoing religious upheaval, some of it evidence of a new freedom of belief and some of it expressing a sense of profound personal dislocation.

The new demands for personal liberty focused on religion, as well as work and family, as Americans increasingly objected to paying taxes to support state churches. Anglicanism had been disestablished in the South in the 1780s, replaced by the Protestant Episcopal Church. The Congregational Church was disestablished in New England in 1834, and new denominations began thriving in all regions.

Southerners were drawn especially to new evangelical Christian faiths, principally Methodism and various forms of Baptist practice. In contrast to the more staid and ritual-based Episcopal Church, these sects stressed the personal, emotional nature of religion and the ability of individuals to struggle actively for their own redemption. Methodists rejected what they deemed artificial differences among Christians, pronouncing "[o]ne condition, and only one" required for salvation: "a real desire." Their system of itinerant preaching (preachers traveled among congregations, rather than associating with a single church) enabled the clergy to reach out to the dispersed and the displaced. Emphasizing inner truth, a plain style, and congregational independence, evangelical denominations offered a relatively egalitarian vision of the community of believers that was especially attractive to the poor, to enslaved and free African Americans, and to white women. Some congregations questioned the morality of slaveholding itself.

Even before Congregationalism was fully disestablished, it was plagued by breakaway movements from within and by competition from the evangelical sects. The most important splinter groups were the Unitarian and Universalist movements, which held generally positive views of human nature, embraced universal salvation, and offered an alternative to strict Calvinism. Everywhere, the far greater threat to established religion came from the Methodists and Baptists, who found converts among country folks and city workers.

This widespread religious turmoil was expressed in a series of highly emotional revivals at the turn of the century, sometimes called the Second Great Awakening. These began in Virginia and western New England and spread quickly into newly settled areas of Kentucky and Tennessee. The most famous of these revivals occurred in August 1801, in the tiny rural community of Cane Ridge, Kentucky, where thousands of men, women, and children, black and white, free and enslaved, came to watch and experience mass conversions. Eventually, the awakening spread to all parts of the country and to virtually all faiths. Yet many members of older denominations were displeased that revivals were led by unschooled preachers and encouraged unconventional beliefs and extravagant emotionalism. In 1803 to 1805 these misgivings led to schism, as the "Old Light" members of the Kentucky Synod purged "New Light" revivalists. Where Congregationalists and Presbyterians saw confusion in the revivals, Methodists and Baptists saw converts. In the first years of the nineteenth century, the number of Baptist congregations grew from about 400 to about 2,700, and membership in Methodist churches more than doubled, from 87,000 to 196,000. Eager for new members, Methodists founded the national Sunday School Union and the first denominational publishing house in the United States.

Federalists often viewed this religious upheaval as a sign of the deterioration of both politics and morality, but the linkages were seldom so simple. Neither Jefferson nor Madison, the founding lights of the Democratic Republican Party, embraced evangelical faiths. Moreover, far from signaling a drift toward irreligion, this contentious fragmentation of belief at the turn of the century had the effect of securing the language of

AMERICAN LANDSCAPE

>> Religion in the Backcountry: Cane Ridge, Kentucky

Barton W. Stone was a Presbyterian minister, but one with a number of reservations about his church. In particular, Stone doubted the key Presbyterian doctrine of original sin, which directed that all humans were born sinful and were unable to act for their own salvation; salvation, orthodox Presbyterians believed, came completely through the grace of God. To Stone, as to a growing number of dissenting Presbyterian ministers, God had given humans a capacity to yearn toward salvation and required fervent belief and longing as a condition for grace. Religion without that longing seemed to Stone lifeless and cold.

Pastor of the Presbyterian Church of Cane Ridge, Kentucky, Stone worried especially about the deadness to God's grace in the people around him in the backcountry. The year was 1801, and many of Stone's congregants and neighbors were transplants from Virginia and Maryland busy settling new farms, slaves newly forced from their families in the East, and drifters fleeing family and community. Most had few church ties and, in Stone's view, little interest in religion.

But by 1801 something was stirring in the backcountry. Prayer meetings scattered throughout Kentucky were drawing thousands of participants: 4,000 at Concord, for example, and 6,000 at Lexington. Stone went to investigate one in Logan for himself—and was amazed at what he found: "Many, very many fell down . . . in an apparently breathless and motionless state," Stone recorded in his journal, their trances broken only "by a deep groan, or piercing shriek, or by a prayer for mercy most fervently uttered." Then they rose up "shouting deliverance . . . men, women and children declaring the wonderful works of God."

Back in Cane Ridge, Stone began organizing a sacramental Communion service to be held in August, sending out invitations by word of mouth across the region. Participants began to arrive on August 6. As one observer noted: "On the first Sabbath of August, was the Sacrament of Kainridge, the congregation of Mr. Stone.—This was the largest meeting of any that I have ever seen: It continued from Friday till Wednesday. About 12,000 persons, 125 waggons, 8 carriages, 900

communicants. . . ." The prayer meetings continued day after day and deep into the night. News of events at Cane Ridge spread "like fire in dry stubble driven by a strong wind." Soon, the roads were jammed "with wagons, carriages, horsemen, and footmen," as "between twenty and thirty thousand" people (women, men, and children, whites and blacks, Methodists, Baptists, Presbyterians, the churched and the unchurched, anguished sinners, and the merely curious) hastened to the scene. Cane Ridge was the climactic event of the western revivals of 1800–1801, but it fed waves of revivals that moved

METHODIST CAMP MEETING.

into upstate New York (later dubbed "the burned-over district," for the intensity of its meetings). In the first decades of the nineteenth century, religious enthusiasm flamed brightly in the republic. In one sense, there is no surprise in this. Religion had always played an important role in American history. But why this particular outpouring of fervor, and why just at the turn of the century? And why the Kentucky frontier?

Some of the answers lay in the broader rejection of old Calvinist orthodoxies and hierarchical religious styles. The revival ministers preached a theology of self-striving surely welcome to people gambling everything they owned on their ability to make a better life for themselves in the West. And they preached that message with a directness, intimacy, and spontaneous passion that could not have been in starker contrast to the intimidating formality of most Presbyterian and Congregational churches. Ultimately, the Baptists and Methodists were

Continued

the chief beneficiaries of this shift. Although Stone was a Presbyterian, he was dismissed from the Kentucky Synod for his nonconformist beliefs shortly after Cane Ridge and went on to help found the nondenominational Christian Restoration Movement, which had no formal creed.

Why these revivals caught fire on the Kentucky frontier can be answered by the circumstances of frontier life in 1800 and 1801. The new sects were more willing than the Presbyterians and Congregationalists to send itinerant ministers into the field, wherever people lived. Those preachers often found people newly dislocated from family and friends, excited about their new lives but also isolated and homesick. Christian churches had often supplied sites of solace and community for Americans.

The anxieties of the frontier extended beyond the loss of the familiar. These settlers were part of a torrent of expansion across the Appalachians, advancing into territories still claimed by indigenous people and facing constant resistance from Cherokees, Chickasaws, Shawnees, and others. For European Americans, Christianity had long been a boundary of distinction between themselves and Native Americans and a marker of superiority. And it served that purpose again as migrants grappled with the consequences to others of their new opportunities.

religion, especially Protestant Christianity, as an idiom of both identity and exclusion in the new nation. Even as they fought over the correct form of Christian practice, many Americans formulated their visions of the ideal political community in the language of Protestant Christianity and suspected those who disagreed with them not only of bad politics but also of bad faith.

The Problem of Trust in a Changing Society

As old friends headed west for new lands, as young people slipped away from parents or masters, as newcomers swelled the port cities, many Americans began to wonder whom or what they could trust.

Particularly distressing to middling and wealthy Americans were signs that workers and children were forgetting their proper place. The customary discipline of the craft shop seemed to be crumbling. Apprentices demanded better treatment, refused drudgery work, or just ran away. In the larger port cities, unemployed young men gathered on the streets shouting obscenities, frightening children, hassling shopkeepers, and sometimes attacking strangers. Journeymen in Philadelphia and New York demanded better pay and threatened to take their skills elsewhere.

Household society seemed to be falling apart, too. Domestic workers told masters and mistresses that they should now be called "help" instead of "servants." Indentured workers balked at having their lives closely scrutinized. Even children seemed to have found a new "republican" determination to make their own decisions about whom to marry, where to live, and what work to pursue.

To their parents and masters and mistresses, it seemed that the youth and laboring classes were out of control. Indeed, in 1820, half the nation's population was under the age of 16 (compared with 24 percent under 18 in 2010). Parents threatened and cajoled. Masters offered rewards for runaway apprentices. Ministers warned against libertinism (especially young women's fashions, cut too daringly, they thought). Meanwhile, local authorities responded with laws intended to control apprentices and regulate public behavior.

For several reasons, these efforts were largely doomed. The Revolution and its aftermath had changed society. Young people coming of age at the turn of the century had been nurtured on the rhetoric of independence. The market revolution offered them numerous alternatives to older structures of authority. Why should a young person remain on the family farm when there were jobs in nearby towns? Why not just leave the controls of indentures or an apprenticeship? Why languish in Temple, Maine, when New York beckoned?

Rumor and deception thrived everywhere in this landscape. On the brink of war in 1812, one Charles Redheffer told the Philadelphia city government that he had invented a perpetual motion machine. When the city commissioners discovered that Redheffer was actually powering his machine through a hidden cranking device, rather than simply crying foul, they responded with a hoax of their own. They had a local engineer build a similar but even more cleverly deceptive machine. Redheffer fled Philadelphia for New York City, where he was exposed by Robert Fulton (who had his own interest in debunking the machine).

Meanwhile, the New England countryside was filled with treasure hunters who had heard countless rumors of long-buried riches. Some of these seekers were amateur scientists and historians. Some were charlatans, trying to make a quick buck off gullible visitors. Some were just the down-and-outers of New England's changing economy who still believed in miracles that might turn their fortunes around.

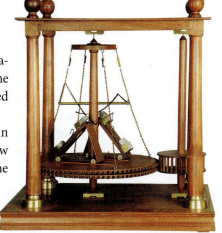

Redheffer's Perpetual Motion Machine

One of these was the treasure seeker Joseph Smith. Smith was born in 1805 to a family of poor farmers in Vermont and grew up in western New York surrounded by economic and religious uncertainty. Although the family moved constantly in a region bursting with development, economic security eluded the Smiths. Perhaps in search of some sense of constancy, Smith was drawn to the religious revivalism that scorched upstate New York, and he believed in direct spiritual revelation. Occasionally Smith and his father used what they claimed were supernatural powers to hire out as guides in what an observer described as "the money digging business." In 1819, however, Joseph Smith's powers of divination took a different turn: he experienced the first of a series of revelations in which he claimed that God had instructed him to found a new church that would teach the true lessons of Jesus Christ. In a second vision a few years later, an angel gave him the location of golden tablets, buried near his home, which described God's intentions for the "latter days" of creation, now approaching. In 1830 Smith published his translation of the ancient writings on the tablets as the Book of Mormon. He formally founded the church now known as the Church of Jesus Christ of Latter-day Saints (or the Mormon Church).

The Panic of 1819

In 1819 Americans learned that the market revolution could produce dream-shattering plunges, as well as exhilarating rises. After he signed the bill chartering the Second Bank of the United States in 1816, James Madison appointed an old political ally, Captain William Jones, as its director. Jones was a poor choice, speculating in bank stock and willing to accept bribes to overlook reckless local practices. By the time he was replaced, bank stock was at an all-time low, and the state banks had glutted the economy with unsecured paper money.

Jones's successor, Langdon Cheves, moved quickly to cut the supply of paper money (too quickly, given that Great Britain was taking the same measures). Cheves began to call in loans and to redeem the bank's holdings of currency issued by the various state banks. Dangerously overextended, the state banks were forced to respond with their own programs of retrenchment. As credit dried up and the value of paper money plummeted, the nation was thrown into depression. Without credit or sufficient circulating money, commodity prices crashed throughout the Atlantic community. The market in cotton, basic to the growing American economy, fell by almost two-thirds. Their mortgages unpaid, farms and businesses failed. And tens of thousands of workers lost their jobs. For three long years, the economy stalled. Visitors to America warned potential immigrants not to come.

Because the branches of the Second Bank of the United States reached far beyond the East Coast, so did the distress of the panic. When the branch in Cincinnati, Ohio, suddenly cashed in the paper money it held from local banks, for example, Cincinnati's booming economy felt the blow, as local banks scurried to collect enough debts to make good on the face value of their paper. Similar shock waves rolled through Kentucky and Tennessee and into the lower South.

Cheves had saved the monetary system of the United States but did not make many friends for the Second Bank. State legislators, who saw the national bank (not runaway local speculation or wildcat state banks) as the villain, scrambled to reduce its power. Fourteen states passed laws preventing the bank from collecting its debts, Kentucky abolished imprisonment for debt, and six states levied heavy taxes on bank branches (a practice soon banned by the Supreme Court in *McCulloch v. Maryland*, discussed earlier). After opening 18 branches in 1817, the Second Bank opened no additional new branches until 1826.

Conclusion

In 1819, Andrew Jackson returned home physically exhausted. He had gone to Washington, where Congress was debating censuring him for his actions in the Seminole War. Henry Clay charged that Jackson's "inhumanity, and cruelty, and ambition" made him no better than the despots of Europe. Jackson's supporters replied, however, that "when at war with a nation which observes no rules . . . the attempt may be made of bringing them to the laws of humanity." Congress could not agree. Nor could the American people. Although crowds cheered Jackson in Baltimore, an important question lingered: After more than a half century of conflict, the United States was finally at peace with both Britain and France, and it had acquired a vast new territory, rapidly filling with an ever-expanding population. As Jackson regained his strength, he and his fellow Americans asked themselves once again what kind of nation they were to be.

>> TIME LINE

▼1800
Thomas Jefferson elected president

▼1801
Judiciary Act of 1801
Cane Ridge (Kentucky) Revival
Barbary War

▼1803
Louisiana Purchase
Marbury v. Madison

▼1804
Jefferson reelected
Lewis and Clark begin exploration of
  Louisiana

▼1805
Palmer v. Mulligan (New York)
Essex Decision (British Admiralty Court)

▼1806
Conspiracy trial of Philadelphia
  journeyman shoemakers

▼1807
First Embargo Act
Hudson River trial
  of Fulton's *North
  River Steamboat
  of Clermont*

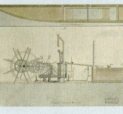

▼1808
External slave trade
  becomes illegal
Madison elected president

▼1809
Non-Intercourse Act

Who, What

De Witt Clinton   308

Robert Fulton   315

Gabriel   301

Thomas Jefferson   325

James Madison   307

John Marshall   302

Tecumseh   308

Market revolution   311

Revivals   328

Review Questions

1. What were the primary challenges facing the Jefferson administration? How well did the administration handle those challenges?

2. What was the market revolution?

3. How did changes in religion help Americans adjust to their rapidly changing world?

Critical-Thinking Questions

1. The War of 1812 was hardly an American victory, yet at its conclusion, the United States was stronger than it had ever been. Why was this so?

2. What challenges did the addition of vast new territories create for the United States, and how did it address them? Why didn't it make colonies out of the new territories?

3. This period saw the development of both cotton plantations in the South and factories in the North. Though seemingly quite different, both were expressions of the market revolution. How so?

For further review materials and resource information, please visit www.oup.com/us/ofthepeople

▼**1810**
American cotton production reaches 178,000 bales

▼**1811**
Tecumseh at peak of influence
Battle of Tippecanoe River

▼**1812**
War of 1812 begins
James Madison reelected

▼**1814**
Federalist Hartford Convention
Treaty of Ghent ends War of 1812

Fully steam-powered textile mills established in Waltham, Massachusetts

▼**1815**
Battle of New Orleans

▼**1817**
Work on Erie Canal begun
Steamboats common on Mississippi River

▼**1819**
Panic of 1819
Dartmouth v. Woodward

McCulloch v. Maryland
Irving publishes "Rip Van Winkle"

▼**1824**
Gibbons v. Ogden

▼**1825**
Erie Canal completed

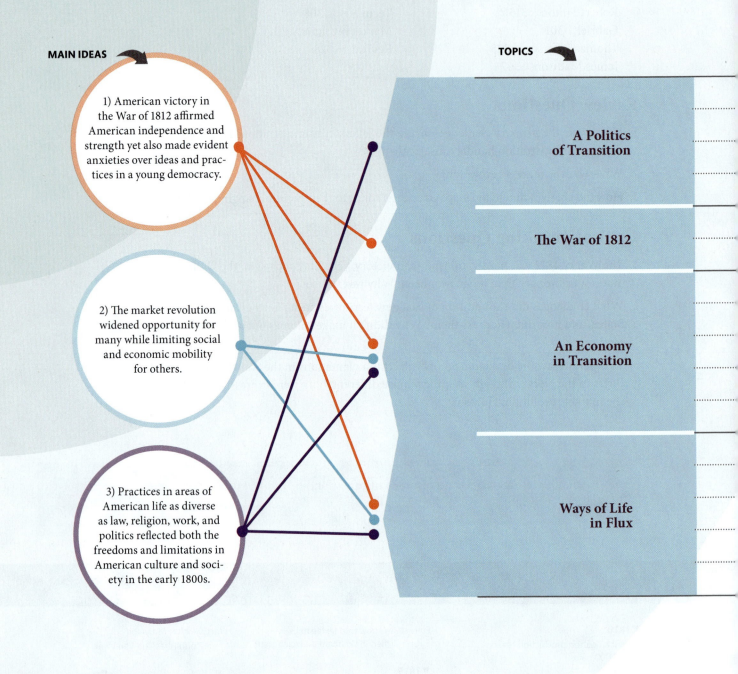

MAIN IDEAS

1) American victory in the War of 1812 affirmed American independence and strength yet also made evident anxieties over ideas and practices in a young democracy.

2) The market revolution widened opportunity for many while limiting social and economic mobility for others.

3) Practices in areas of American life as diverse as law, religion, work, and politics reflected both the freedoms and limitations in American culture and society in the early 1800s.

TOPICS

A Politics of Transition

The War of 1812

An Economy in Transition

Ways of Life in Flux

A REPUBLIC IN TRANSITION

1800–1819

EVENTS

A Contested Election, an Anxious Nation While the country was deeply divided, Jefferson won a contested election.

Democratic Republicans in Office Jefferson's administration worked to reduce the size of the federal government while the Supreme Court established judicial review.

The Louisiana Purchase The United States purchased from France a large parcel of land west of the Mississippi.

Embargo Tensions with England and France led Jefferson to impose a trade embargo, with disastrous consequences for the American economy.

Madison and the War The United States and England waged a war without a clear conclusion.

Federalist Response The Federalists criticized the war, but then suffered politically when peace was declared.

International Markets The growth of overseas shipping spurred American economic development.

Crossing the Appalachian Mountains Unprecedented western migration swelled the population of the trans-Appalachian region.

Invention and Exploration Westward expansion led to new inventions and improvements in transportation.

Early Industrial Society in New England The first fully mechanized textile mill opened, leading to a revolution in American manufacturing.

The Rule of Law and Lawyers Overseas trade and internal expansion required increased sophistication of the courts and judiciary.

Indian Resistance to American Expansion Westward migration devastated native life and culture.

Winners and Losers in the New Economy The new economy altered the nature and relations of labor and society.

Religion Widespread religious awakening was expressed in a series of highly emotional revivals.

The Problem of Trust in a Changing Society Changing social structures and attitudes created growing anxiety and distrust.

The Panic of 1819 An economic panic and subsequent depression underscored the volatility of the emerging market economy.

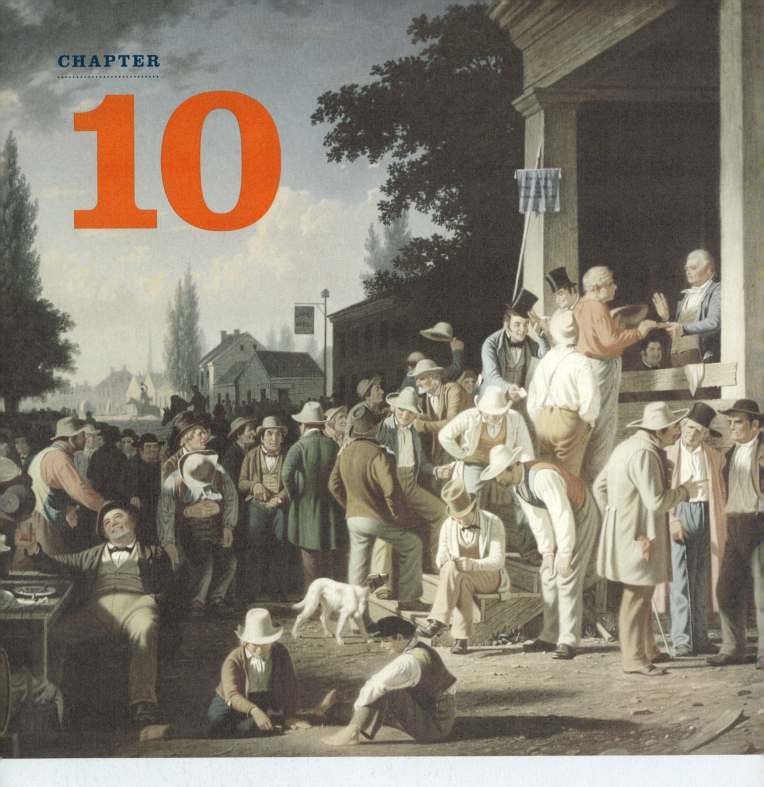

COMMON THREADS

>> Why was the Bank of the United States so controversial in the early republic?

>> How did the market revolution affect wage labor?

>> What actions and policies of the Democratic Republican presidents, 1800–1824, laid the groundwork for Jackson's breakaway movement?

>> Did the territorial expansion of the republic require the removal of Native Americans?

Jacksonian Democracy
1820–1840

AMERICAN PORTRAIT

>> Harriet Noble

By 1824, the New York backcountry was abuzz with talk of Michigan Territory and the opportunities there for families willing to make the trip. The economy was at last bouncing back from the Panic of 1819. Markets for agriculture, in the East or down the Mississippi River, were reviving. Land prices had declined slightly, and families could buy in for smaller parcels.

"My husband," Harriet Noble later wrote, "was seized with the mania," and by September, the Noble family—Harriet, 21, her husband, 23, and their two young daughters—had joined the growing migration of Americans moving west. "Could we have known what it was to be pioneers in a new country, we should never have had the courage to come," Harriet recalled.

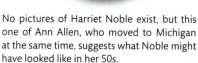

Harriet's husband had already made the journey once that year, with his brother, to scout out land for their families. Now the two families set out. First came a rough trip by wagon over bad roads to Buffalo. Next, after a four-day wait in Buffalo for a steamship that never showed up, a seven-day trip on a schooner across Lake Erie "entirely prostrated with seasickness," Noble recalled. And then, after days of trekking through the Michigan wilderness until "my feet were so swollen I could walk no further," they arrived at Ann Arbor: "some six or seven log huts occupied by as many inmates as could be crowded into them." The Nobles jammed in with the others, so packed that they could not move in the night without stepping on someone's hand or foot. So they survived for a month and a half, until the men managed to put up separate cabins. But that winter most of the community fell mysteriously ill. Deciding they had chosen an unhealthful place, the following spring the Nobles moved again, this time to Dexter, 10 miles west. They were fortunate enough to be able to take over a shell of a log cabin abandoned by discouraged settlers before them. That summer and fall, Harriet and her husband worked together to put a roof over their heads and haul stones to set a fireplace. By the second winter, they had a roof, a floor, a fireplace, and a door. Provisions were always scarce. Waiting 15 days for her husband to return from Detroit with supplies, Harriet ran out of flour. "After being without bread three or four days, my little boy, two years old, looked me in the face and said, 'Ma, why don't you make bread; don't you like it? I do.'"

No pictures of Harriet Noble exist, but this one of Ann Allen, who moved to Michigan at the same time, suggests what Noble might have looked like in her 50s.

The difficulties continued into the next year: First Harriet and her husband were recurrently ill with fever and barely able to work. As they seemed to be recovering, her husband had his hand "blown to pieces" in a gun accident, permanently disabling him and forcing Harriet to do all the field work, the tending of the animals, and the laying by of wood. Not until the following spring, three years after their arrival, did prospects look up, when Harriet's husband was at last able to travel back east to get a nephew to help with the work.

Harriet Noble and her husband were the kind of Americans Andrew Jackson considered the heart of the democracy—ordinary citizens of modest means willing to risk their resources, even their lives, to gain new opportunities and forge new freedoms. They were the people for whom he and his generation had fought the Revolutionary War. Especially after he lost his first bid for

Continued

AMERICAN PORTRAIT
Continued

the presidency in what he considered "a corrupt bargain" among the eastern and western elites, Jackson resolved that these Americans must be protected. Of course, settlers were not the only struggling common Americans by 1824. The port cities were awash with wage laborers trying to support themselves and their families on smaller and smaller paychecks. But Jackson was a man of the pre–market revolution era. He distrusted paper money and wages and banks. His was still a world of settlers to be protected against the rich and well connected. Convinced that he alone could provide that protection, he would do this even if it meant forcibly dispossessing tens of thousands of indigenous people, ignoring the decisions of the Supreme Court, threatening to send federal militia against state authorities, and, all in all, claiming for the executive branch of government an expanse of powers so unprecedented that his critics would label him "the tyrant."

A New National Politics

The conclusion of the War of 1812 brought a new confidence to the American government, a bolder foreign policy, and, for a moment, less contentious national politics. By 1816, the party of Jefferson itself was changing. Both Jefferson and party cofounder James Madison had flexed the muscles of the central government before and during the War of 1812. They had both loathed Hamilton's bank, and Madison had happily allowed its charter to expire in 1811. But that was before the war taught him the importance of a central bank for financing war. In 1816 Madison signed the bill to recharter the bank—on the same terms as the first!

Changes in the Democratic Republican Party

In the early nineteenth century the Democratic Republican Party fell under the influence of a new generation of politicians who came of age during the troubled years of the Confederation Congress. Having witnessed the effects of poor transportation and a weak federal military in the War of 1812, they believed that a strong, activist national government might well be the nation's best protection against localism and fragmentation. By the election of 1824, they would identify themselves as National Republicans.

This new brand of Republicanism was epitomized by four men: Henry Clay of Kentucky, John C. Calhoun of South Carolina, and Daniel Webster and John Quincy Adams of Massachusetts. Clay (1777–1852) entered national politics as the champion of the large planters and merchants of Kentucky, who had turned to the federal government for support for projects (especially transportation) they could not win at home. Calhoun (1782–1850) was first a representative and then senator and vice president.

OUTLINE

A New National Politics
  Changes in the Democratic Republican Party
  James Monroe and National Republicanism
  The Missouri Compromise

AMERICA AND THE WORLD:
  The Monroe Doctrine
  The Election of 1824 and the "Corrupt Bargain"
  The Adams Presidency and the Gathering Forces of
    Democracy

The Social and Political Bases of Jacksonian
  Democracy
  Settlers
  Free Labor
  Suffrage Reform
  Opposition to Special Privilege and Secret Societies

Jacksonian Democracy in Action
  The Election of 1828
  The Bank War

Although both Calhoun and South Carolina later became symbols of states' rights sentiment, in the postwar years South Carolinians believed that their international export economy was best served by a strong federal government.

Adams and Webster, both New Englanders, illustrated the compatibility of National Republicanism with the old Federalist views. Webster promoted the interests of New England's banking classes. He was a strong supporter of protective tariffs after the War of 1812, as Massachusetts merchants shifted from importing to manufacturing. Born in 1767, John Quincy Adams was influenced by his father's Federalist views and was first elected to the Senate in 1800 by the Federalist Massachusetts legislature. Adams broke rank with his party when it opposed the Louisiana Purchase.

Led by Clay, the new nationalists fashioned a vision of a Republican political economy based on individual entrepreneurial and market development (including domestic manufacturing), guided by an active federal government. Not surprisingly, their platform, loosely called the American System, was devised to appeal to local interests and identities. In the West and South, that meant promoting a national subsidy to improve transportation, whereas in the Northeast, it meant a protective tariff for domestic industries. To protect federal credit and stabilize currency and internal credit, they supported a national bank.

The various elements of the American System came before Congress as separate bills after the War of 1812, each with its own supporters. The bills to create the Second Bank of the United States and to increase the national tariffs passed easily and were signed

Henry Clay Henry Clay was 44 when Charles Bird King painted this portrait in 1821, but he looks much younger. He had the power to charm women and men both. Margaret Bayard Smith said that he had a "power of captivation, which no one who was its object could resist."

Dismembering the Bank

PRIMARY SOURCE:
  President Jackson's Bank Veto Message
  The Specie Act

A Policy of Removing Indigenous People
  Jackson and Native Peoples
  The Removal Act
  History, Destiny, and the Remaking of Indian
    Societies

AMERICAN LANDSCAPE:
  Liberty and the Land: Cherokee Removal

The Growth of Sectional Tension
  The Sources of Southern Discontent
  South Carolina's Protest
  The Nullification Crisis

DEBATING HISTORY:
  The Nature of Jacksonian Democracy

Conclusion

by President Madison. Authorized in 1816, the Second Bank of the United States was chartered for 20 years and located in Philadelphia, with the federal government providing one-fifth of its capital and appointing one-fifth of its directors. The tariff bill was less protective than some nationalists wished.

Transportation subsidies fared less well. Madison was skeptical about the constitutionality of this form of federal intervention. In his annual messages of 1815 and 1816, he urged Congress to initiate a constitutional amendment to clarify federal power in this area. A torn Congress eventually passed a bill creating a federal fund for internal improvements. On his last day in office, Madison vetoed it. In 1818, the federal government opened a section of the National Road, a highway that connected Baltimore to Wheeling, Virginia (later West Virginia). Otherwise, federal transportation initiatives fell victim to questions of constitutionality and regional jealousies.

James Monroe and National Republicanism

In 1816, Republican James Monroe ran for the presidency against Rufus King, the last Federalist to vie for that office. In the flush of postwar victory and prosperity and in the aftermath of the Hartford Convention, the returns were lopsided in Monroe's favor: 183 electoral votes to King's 34. He was the third Virginian in a row to hold the office.

Monroe's inaugural address sounded many familiar Republican themes: he praised the virtue of the American people and warned against corruption, greed, and the usurpation of power by foes of the republic. But in explaining the "principles" that would guide him in office, Monroe seemed almost to sound Federalist themes. He suggested the need for a more vigorous national defense and a more aggressive foreign policy toward Europe generally. He also recommended federally subsidized internal improvements as necessary for a prosperous, cohesive nation.

In office, Monroe governed with the nationalist bent suggested in his inaugural address. He asked former Federalist John Quincy Adams to be secretary of state (the presumed stepping-stone to the presidency). Together Monroe and Adams moved toward a more assertive foreign policy.

First, the administration arrived at agreements with Britain limiting British and American forces on the Great Lakes and along the 49th parallel to the Rocky Mountains. Then, in 1819, the United States forced Spain to fix definite borders to the Louisiana Purchase. After the purchase, Jefferson had attempted unsuccessfully to buy Florida from Spain. His successor, Madison, had simply declared that West Florida had been a part of the Louisiana Purchase all along. Taking the Florida peninsula had been left for James Monroe, who sent Andrew Jackson to lead a raid into Florida, ostensibly to frighten the Seminoles. When Jackson appeared to exceed his intentionally vague orders, he faced investigation by Congress (see Chapter 9), but he demonstrated that Spain was too weak, both politically and militarily, to hold onto Florida.

Capitulating to American forcefulness, in the Transcontinental Treaty of 1819, Spain ceded all of Florida to the United States in return for the US government's agreement to assume private American claims against Spain of about $5 million. The Transcontinental Treaty also clarified the border between the United States and Spanish Mexico. The United States gave up claims not only to California (which few considered part of the original purchase) but also to Texas (which many did). The boundary gained in return ran in a series of ascending steps from Louisiana to the Pacific, defining the United States as a nation that spanned the continent.

In the 1820s, under Monroe, the United States began to view itself as American, not quasi-European, and as protector of the Americas against Europe. By 1815 a number of former Spanish colonies, including Argentina, Chile, and Venezuela, had revolted, and an independence movement was under way in Mexico. As these new republics won their independence, they turned to the United States for recognition and support, while the absolute monarchies in Europe sought to preserve and extend their territorial empires. France offered to help Spain regain its colonies in South America. Russia reasserted and strengthened its long-standing claims in the Pacific Northwest.

Disavowing any future new territorial ambitions for itself in the Americas, Great Britain offered to make a joint declaration with the United States warning other nations against intruding in the internal affairs of Western Hemisphere countries. An alliance with Britain would have enhanced US diplomatic credibility, but many Americans suspected that Britain would use its position to squeeze the United States out of South American markets.

Secretary of State John Quincy Adams convinced Monroe to refuse the British offer and, instead, to act independently and issue a unilateral statement of support for the new republics. Adams hoped that being identified with this policy would help him shed the pro-British tag that was associated with many New Englanders.

In his annual message to Congress in 1823, Monroe enunciated the policy that has since become known as the Monroe Doctrine. Monroe asserted a special United States relationship with all parts of North and South America, with which, he insisted, "we are of necessity more immediately connected." "We . . . declare," he added, "that we should consider any attempt on their part to extend their system to any portion of this hemisphere as dangerous to our peace and safety." The Monroe Doctrine marked an important milestone in the development of American nationalism and internationalism. The United States asserted not only a new relation (as peer) to the European nations but also a new relation to the Americas. Surveillance over the nations of North and South America would be the domestic right of the United States.

The Missouri Compromise

Yet just as a more assertive nation flexed its muscles, internal divisions threatened to pull it apart. Since the first compromises on slavery at the Constitutional Convention in 1787 (see Chapter 7), it was clear that slavery had the potential to create fierce conflict. For decades, no one was willing to call the institution a positive good, and northerners and southerners both seemed to agree publicly that slavery was unfortunate and in due course it would just fade away. Nonetheless, each time slavery entered national politics—the debate over Louisiana, setting the terms for ending the slave trade (see Chapter 9)— southerners did all they could to protect the institution. Then, as slavery spread to newly acquired territories, northern opponents of the institution saw clearly that, rather than disappearing, as it seemed to be doing in the North, the institution was becoming stronger elsewhere. In the decade after 1810, the number of slaves in the United States increased 30 percent.

In 1819, when Missouri applied for permission to organize as a state, antislavery politicians made their move. In the House debate, New York representative James

AMERICA AND THE WORLD

>> The Monroe Doctrine

In his annual address to Congress in 1823 (the fore-runner of the modern State of the Union address), President James Monroe declared that "the American continents, by the free and independent condition which they have assumed and maintain, are henceforth not to be considered as subjects for future colonization by any European powers." Seemingly an affirmation of the United States' support for indigenous democratic movements among its neighbors and a reassertion of the young nation's role as the beacon of democratic hope everywhere, the Monroe Doctrine was actually not about democracy at all. It echoed an equally persistent, but quite different, strain of American foreign policy: the desire to avoid entanglement in European wars.

Just as important, the Monroe Doctrine represented the United States' willingness to isolate itself from democratic movements stirring within Europe. In 1820 angry unpaid Spanish soldiers (needed to fight the breakaway American republics) rebelled against their monarchy. The insurgence soon spread to Naples, Italy. After years of domination by the Ottoman Empire, in 1821 Greek revolutionaries launched a conspiracy against the state that ended in civil war. By 1823 the bourgeoisie and commoners of France were growing angry with the assaults of the restored Bourbon monarchy on the franchise and the freedom of the press. Insurgences also occurred among the Poles, the Hungarians, the Czechs, and others. In Great Britain, the fall of Napoleon provoked agitation for parliamentary reform and the broadening of the franchise.

In his 1823 statement, Monroe acknowledged and broadly supported these democratic movements but declared that the situation in Europe was "eminently and conspicuously different" from that in the Americas: "Our policy in regard to Europe," he said, was "not to interfere in the internal concerns of any of its powers; to consider the government de facto as the legitimate government for us."

Even within the Western Hemisphere, the area Monroe specified, the doctrine was ambiguous. The Monroe Doctrine applied to the Americas—but only to Central and South America, and then only to new republics formed by mixed European-American populations. It did not apply to Canada: the United States would not support revolts against the British government there in the 1830s. And the doctrine did not apply to the black republic of Haiti. Moreover, even as Monroe informed Europe that the United States would be the guarantor of the new American republics, some Americans were already coveting northern Mexico.

The abstract principle of democracy did not make the new American republics of special interest to the United States, nor did the specific examples of democracy they represented. They could as well have been insurgent monarchies, as far as Monroe's doctrine was concerned. The "interests" they activated in the United States were a coincidence of politics and geography. European efforts to recapture their broken-away colonies might again bring war to the Americas and to the United States.

The Birth of the Monroe Doctrine Here, President James Monroe and his cabinet discuss foreign policy, crafting what will later be known as the "Monroe Doctrine." Left to right: John Quincy Adams, William Harris Crawford, William Wirt, Monroe, John C. Calhoun, Daniel D. Tompkins, and John McLean.

Tallmadge proposed that Missouri be admitted under two conditions. First, no more slaves were to be brought into the state, and, second, slavery was to be gradually abolished after the state was admitted to the Union. Southerners unanimously opposed the amendment, whereas northerners voted unanimously for it. The more populous North carried the vote. Slavery's defenders warned that such an attack on private property was unconstitutional and would incite "servile war." But slavery's opponents insisted that the institution was both immoral and antirepublican. "You boast of the freedom of your Constitution," Tallmadge told them, "and yet you have slaves in your country."

But when the House bill reached the Senate committee charged with its consideration, the vote was reversed. The Tallmadge amendment died in committee, to be reintroduced in the next session.

By the time Congress reconvened, positions on both sides had hardened. All notions of an antislavery South were now dead. A northern congressman said, "I awoke as from a trance." The struggle over Missouri foreshadowed later congressional debates over slavery and made southerners wary of a strong federal government. As North Carolina senator Nathaniel Macon explained, "If Congress can make canals, they can with more propriety emancipate."

The firestorm over Missouri was finally resolved when Maine applied for statehood as a free state. At that time there were 22 states in the Union, 11 free and 11 slave. Under Speaker of the House Henry Clay's guidance, the bills admitting both states were linked, preserving the balance in the Senate. The compromise also provided that slavery would be permitted in Arkansas Territory but excluded from the rest of the Louisiana Purchase. The compromise passed narrowly in March of 1820.

Almost immediately, another problem arose when Missouri submitted a state constitution that barred free black people and free persons of mixed heritage from the state. This was a clear violation of Article IV of the Constitution, which provided that citizens of one state should enjoy the rights of citizens in all states. Here was another sign of an emerging sectional division over the issue of black citizenship. In 1821, during the second round of the Missouri crisis, that division was just beginning to show itself, as Henry Clay struggled to engineer a second compromise. Congress allowed Missouri to enter under the proposed constitution, but it demanded that the new state legislature promise never to interpret the clause to mean what it so obviously meant, that Missouri reserved the right to deny free African Americans their constitutional rights. The Missouri territorial legislature made the promise but withheld any power to bind the people of the state to what it said. Finally, in August 1821, President James Monroe greeted Missouri as the 24th state of the Union.

> This momentous question, like a fire bell in the night, awakened and filled me with terror. I considered it at once the knell of the union. It is hushed, indeed, for the moment. But this is a reprieve only, not a final sentence. . . . I regret that I am now to die in the belief, that the useless sacrifice of themselves by the generation of 1776, to acquire self-government and happiness to their own country, is to be thrown away by the unwise and unworthy passions of their sons, and that my only consolation is to be, that I live not to weep over it.
>
> THOMAS JEFFERSON,
> commenting on the Missouri Crisis, April 22, 1820

The Election of 1824 and the "Corrupt Bargain"

In the usual order of custom in the young republic, Secretary of State John Quincy Adams would have been Monroe's presumed successor. But by 1824 the Republican Party housed experienced men who considered themselves next in line. In addition to Adams, there were John C. Calhoun (secretary of war), Henry Clay (Speaker of the House), and William H. Crawford of Georgia (secretary of the Treasury, who had suffered a massive stroke in 1823). This group, which called itself the National Republicans, contained some of the nation's most experienced and respected leaders.

And then there was the outlier, Andrew Jackson. In spite of his fame as a war hero, when the Tennessee legislature nominated Jackson for the presidency in 1822, few politicians took the candidacy seriously, given his competition. But by 1824 voting Americans were beginning to pull back from the new expansive Republican vision. As a political unknown, without a legislative record, Jackson was free to run on his image, as a forceful leader and an outsider. An early indication of the storminess of the election came with the Republican nomination. Because James Monroe had not designated a successor, the selection was thrown to the Republican congressional caucus and was expected to benefit Crawford. But this time, the other candidates disowned the caucus as a corrupt and irregular institution so effectively that only 66 of a possible 216 Republican members of Congress even attended. Crawford did get the nod, but its value had been diminished.

In the election, no candidate claimed a majority either of the popular vote or of the Electoral College. The underdog Andrew Jackson came closest, with 43 percent of the popular vote and 99 electoral votes. Next was Adams, with 31 percent of the popular vote and 84 electoral votes. Crawford managed only 41 electoral votes, and Clay came in last with 37. (Calhoun had withdrawn.) See Map 10–1.

The election was thus thrown to the House of Representatives, where members had to select from among the three candidates with the highest electoral count. As the highest vote getter, Jackson was confident at first, but by late December he began to hear rumors "that deep intrigue is on foot." Those rumors were correct. Although Adams did not receive a single popular vote in Kentucky, and although the Kentucky legislature had directed its delegation to vote for Jackson, Clay overrode those instructions and also marshaled support for Adams in other states. Adams received the votes of 13 of the 24 state delegations. Jackson received 7 and Crawford received 4.

Jackson later charged that Adams had bought Clay's support with the promise of the post of secretary of state. Adams did give Clay that job, but Clay had had good reasons for allying himself with Adams. They shared similar political philosophies. In addition, Jackson and Clay vied for the same regional vote. Clay's support for him in 1824 would have helped Jackson build a stronger western base for 1828.

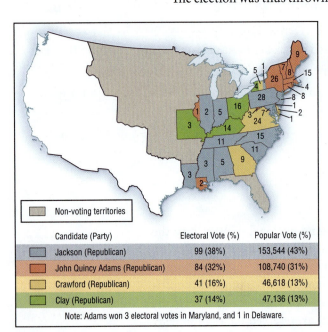

Candidate (Party)	Electoral Vote (%)	Popular Vote (%)
Jackson (Republican)	99 (38%)	153,544 (43%)
John Quincy Adams (Republican)	84 (32%)	108,740 (31%)
Crawford (Republican)	41 (16%)	46,618 (13%)
Clay (Republican)	37 (14%)	47,136 (13%)

Note: Adams won 3 electoral votes in Maryland, and 1 in Delaware.

Non-voting territories

Map 10–1 The Election of 1824 Almost all of Adams's electoral votes came from the Northeast, while Jackson's were spread through the South, the Midwest, and the Mid-Atlantic.

Jackson was furious. His supporters charged that the election had been stolen in a "corrupt bargain" brokered by insiders who debased the virtue of the republic and disregarded the clear will of the electorate.

The Adams Presidency and the Gathering Forces of Democracy

In many respects, Adams's choice of Clay made perfect sense. Since the postwar period both men had shared a commitment to the "American System": the preservation of a national bank, the levying of a national tariff, and the improvement of infrastructure.

Adams continued to support these policies in office, even using his first annual message to Congress in 1825 to lay out a grand vision for federal involvement in the political economy. He called not only for economic projects, such as transportation improvements, but also for the creation of a national university, a national observatory, a naval academy, and an elaborate system of roads and canals supported by federal expenditures. He urged Congress not to be "palsied by the will of our constituents." His opponents railed that this was clear evidence of his intention to benefit the wealthy at the expense of the common people and that this branch of the Republican Party (increasingly identifying itself as the National Republicans) seemed more Federalist than Jeffersonian.

John Quincy Adams was a wise and principled statesman, but he was never able to set an independent agenda for his presidency. He was shadowed by the political battle that began with his election and by his unpopular identification with banking and mercantile interests. Defensive and prickly in public, he did not build strong political alliances, and he misread the gulf developing within the American electorate.

And Jackson's supporters worked hard to discredit Adams, especially on the issue of the tariff. Early on, the federal government had depended on the tariff and on land sales for most of its revenue. By the end of the War of 1812, the importance of the tariff for generating funding had declined, but its role in addressing the growing regional economic differences had increased. The 1816 tariff was protectionist, but only very mildly so, working to give some recognition to the importance of domestic manufactures. But the Panic of 1819, brought on in part by the United States' reliance on world markets, reenergized protectionists: a bill to raise tariffs on the entire list of imported products by 5 percent (even higher for cotton, wool, iron, and glass) failed passage by only one vote. It was broadly supported in the western and middle states and opposed in the South (where it was seen as favoring high-priced New England products), whereas New England split on the issue. But by 1824 New England was committed enough to industrial growth to become solidly pro-tariff. That year, when Congress proposed a tariff that included levies of 35 percent on imported cotton, wool, hemp, and iron, passage was a forgone conclusion.

Passage of the 1824 tariff was ominous for several reasons. First, of course, it was vehemently opposed by the South. Second, neither the North nor the federal government really needed it. In 1824 the federal government reported a surplus of funds, a year when New England manufactures were doing well enough not to need the help. The tariff had become the language of sectionalism, but the underlying conflict was over the power of the federal government. This was not a simple question of nationalism versus localism. Jackson, a nationalist willing to support some level of protective tariff, had even conceded, "It is time we became a little more Americanized." The difference between Adams and Jackson was the question of federal legitimacy. In what actions could the federal government claim the authority of the American people? And in what actions did it overstep that authority? That conflict was now infused with the energy of a rising democratic spirit.

The Social and Political Bases of Jacksonian Democracy

Jacksonian democracy captured the hopes and fears of a rapidly changing country. As settlers such as Harriet Noble and her family looked for opportunity in the West, city dwellers struggled to make a living in the new urban landscape. Anyone who wanted to enter the market—to purchase land or establish a business—needed credit, but in a volatile economy, risk accompanied opportunity. When things went wrong, Americans looked for someone to blame—and for bold politicians to advocate their causes.

Settlers

The migration into the backcountry, set off by the Treaty of Ghent in 1815, continued throughout the 1820s. After Maine in 1820 and Missouri in 1821, no new states entered the Union until Arkansas in 1835. But in the meantime the populations of the new states grew steadily, in some cases doubling and tripling in a single decade: Mississippi grew from 75,448 in 1820 to 136,621 in 1830, Illinois from 55,211 to 157,445, and Indiana from 147,178 to 343,031.

North or South, migrants wanted land. They also wanted easy credit and low prices—but they weren't always convinced that government was their friend in getting these. To be sure, the price of land per acre and the size of the minimum-permitted individual purchase had fallen steadily during the early nineteenth century. The Land Act of 1820 reduced the price to $1.25 per acre for a minimum purchase of 80 acres. In lowering the minimal outlay to $100, however, Congress also eliminated the 1800 provision that had permitted settlers to buy on credit from the government and added the requirement that land that wasn't promptly paid for would go back up for sale. This made small buyers even more dependent on easy credit from local or state banks. There were plenty of these institutions, but state and local bankers were often more interested in putting together big deals with land speculators than in making smaller loans to risky individual settlers. In 1819, when local banks had tried to foreclose on mortgages in arrears, other settlers had formed vigilante committees to intimidate potential buyers and convince the banks that foreclosure was not in their financial interest.

The obstacles to land purchase for ordinary citizens had kept alive the practice of squatting, of claiming land simply by occupying it, demanding that a person's labor on it over time be recognized as a legal claim. As they had in the late eighteenth century, squatters harassed surveyors and ran off sheriff's deputies. Even when a small settler had a legal claim, if the land was good, or the area promising, the settler was likely to have to fight off high-powered lawyers and their clients. Backwoodsmen, squatters, and settlers did not always share the same interests, but probably all would have agreed with William Manning that "no person can possess property without laboring, unless he get it by force or craft," and that "those that labor for a living and those who

Emigrants Crossing the Appalachians This early 19th-century engraving depicts emigrants crossing the Appalachians on their way to Pittsburgh, Pennsylvania. Harriet Noble and her family would have traveled in a similar wagon.

get one without laboring—or, as they are generally termed, the Few and the Many"—was "the great dividing line" of society.

Free Labor

Settlers were not alone in feeling abandoned to the wiles of the wealthy. Although farm labor would dominate the workforce for decades to come, by the second decade of the nineteenth century nonfarming wage labor was becoming more common. Especially in the cities of the coasts, growing numbers of people worked for wages in increasingly precarious circumstances. They had been hard hit by the war, and even improved prosperity afterward left many wage workers with barely enough money to meet their own and their families' needs. Like the frustrated settlers, wage workers worried that the new economy was keeping common working people dependent on the rich. Workers had stuck with Jefferson and Madison through the embargo and the War of 1812, but their patience grew thin.

The Panic of 1819 strengthened that skepticism and gave rise to the beginnings of organized protest in the 1820s. Workers turned out in huge numbers to hear critics denounce the growing inequities of American life. Scotswoman Frances Wright, one of the most popular of these speakers, charged that the clergy conspired to keep workers shackled to superstition, inveighed against slavery, and advocated for women's rights.

In addition, workers began to form unions and go out on strike. Printers, weavers, carpenters, tailors, cabinetmakers, masons, stevedores, and workers in other crafts turned out on strike throughout major cities, protesting poor pay and long hours. Strikers argued that the shorter day was essential if they were to have time to refresh themselves, to be with their families, and to obtain the education necessary for newly enfranchised voters. Over time, these separate strikes merged into citywide and regional labor organizations. The first, the Mechanics' Union, was established in Philadelphia in 1827. Pledged to the 10-hour day, the union protested the exhaustion associated with industrialization and the "evils which . . . arise from a depreciation of the intrinsic value of human labor."

Suffrage Reform

At the founding of the nation, suffrage was restricted not just by gender and race but even more on the basis of property ownership and tax payment. Urban craft workers, who often owned little more than their tools and clothing, demanded the vote as the emblem of liberty. "Suffrage," as one editor insisted, "is the first right of a free people."

Territorial expansion also raised the question of suffrage. Settlers who owned little more than the mortgages on their land saw themselves as the chief embodiment of the democratic spirit.

The new, less settled states led in expanding white male suffrage. Vermont entered the Union in 1791 (the first new state after the original 13) with virtually universal white manhood suffrage. The next year, New Hampshire dropped its last qualification, and Kentucky entered the Union without restrictions on adult white males. Tennessee, which became a state in 1796, required that voters own property but did not set a minimum value. Ohio became a state in 1803 without property requirements for voting, and all the six states admitted between 1812 and 1821 entered with universal white male suffrage (see Map 10–2).

In 1817 Connecticut became the first of the older states to abolish all property qualifications for white men. In 1824, when Jackson made his first run for the presidency, only Virginia, Louisiana, and Rhode Island retained any significant restrictions on white male suffrage, and only 6 of the 24 states retained indirect selection of the delegates to the Electoral College.

The struggle for an expanded male suffrage was fought openly on the landscape of race. As suffrage was extended to all white males, it was withdrawn from African American men in New York, Maryland, Pennsylvania, Connecticut, and New Jersey (where single, propertied women also lost the right to vote). In addition, every new state admitted after 1819 specifically excluded African Americans from the vote. Through suffrage reform, white Americans refashioned the vote as the domain of white citizenship. "The people of this state are for . . . a political community of white persons," one Pennsylvanian asserted bluntly.

The partial exception to this pattern was Rhode Island, where elites blocked universal white male suffrage throughout the 1830s. When, in 1841, white working men called a People's Convention to demand universal white male suffrage, they rejected pleas to include African American men in their demands. Spurned by white working men, African Americans supported the conservative opposition. When state conser-

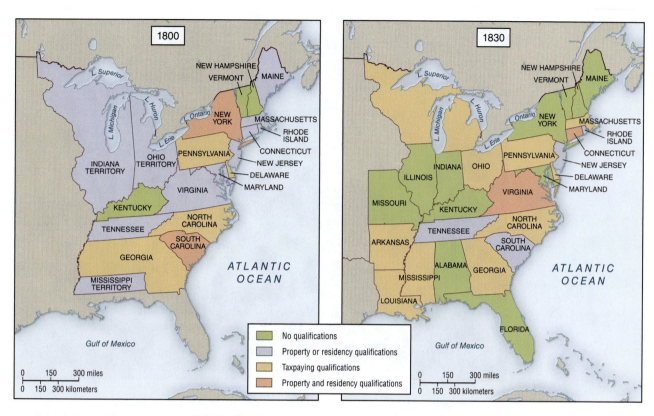

Map 10-2 Toward Universal White Male Suffrage As the western territories organized and entered the Union, they formed a band of states in which there were no property qualifications on white male suffrage, and often minimal taxpaying qualifications. By 1830, Virginia and Connecticut were unusual in the nation for restricting white male suffrage based on both property and tax payment. At the same time, free black males and women lost the vote where they had enjoyed it.

vatives later broadened the franchise, they repaid African American men for their earlier support by including them.

Opposition to Special Privilege and Secret Societies

Since the nation's founding, one strain of American political rhetoric had focused on corrupt insiders who enjoyed opportunities not available to other citizens. In the early nineteenth century, politics became a symbolic battle of the virtuous "many" against the corrupt "few."

Early in the century, specially chartered corporations became visible symbols of affluence and the target of these suspicions. Created by special acts of state legislatures, these corporations were, theoretically, open to all Americans. However, the charters were granted on a personal basis to people of wealth, power, and reputation who were known to individual legislators. The movement to use charters to promote development accelerated after the War of 1812. States chartered companies to build roads, provide transportation, and establish banks. Local

. . . our fathers have purchased for us political rights and an equality of privileges which we have not yet had the intelligence to appreciate, nor the courage to protect, nor the wisdom to enjoy. For although it cannot be denied that in this country there can be no advantages, powers, or privileges which everyone has not an equal right to enjoy, yet do we not see everywhere around us, privileges, advantages, monopolies enjoyed by the few which are denied to the many . . . ?

FREDERICK ROBINSON,
Fourth of July speech, Boston, 1834

The County Election This famous painting by George Caleb Bingham shows voting as a joyous—and manly—activity. Notice the African American man on the left pouring liquor for a white man who is already tipsy, and notice, too, that men of all classes have come together to vote and enjoy the day.

reactions to chartered projects were mixed. Many shared journalist William Leggett's bitterness that "[n]ot a road can be opened, not a bridge can be built, not a canal can be dug, but a charter of exclusive privileges must be granted for the purpose." Some of the specially chartered initiatives, especially banks, provided easy credit to local farmers and workers. When the Panic of 1819 ended that bubble of easy credit, shopkeepers, farmers, and urban workers were devastated. They focused their anger on eastern bankers, especially the Second Bank of the United States, and grew suspicious that the new Republican leadership would increase preferential rules. By 1820 John C. Calhoun noticed the appearance, in "every part of the Union," of "a general mass of disaffection to the Government . . . looking out anywhere for a leader."

Corporations were not the only focus of hard feelings. The old Republican fears of special privilege extended to secret societies that might give their members special access to money and success. In western New York, where the opening of the Erie Canal had ushered in an economic boom and widespread social instability, tensions exploded in a virulent fear of Masons in the late 1820s.

The Masonic movement had originated to counter aristocratic power and protect craft masons, but in the eighteenth century a new Order of Freemasons emerged, made up of urban businessmen, professionals, and politicians who pledged to support one another. By the 1820s the Masons seemed to many working people to embody a dangerous antidemocratic spirit. This distrust was galvanized into popular opposition in 1826 by the mysterious disappearance (and presumed murder) of New Yorker William Morgan, who had written an exposé of the order's purported secret designs on public power. The story spread that Morgan had been abducted to Niagara Falls and then drowned. The outcry against this subversion of justice was magnified by the fact that public officials, including Andrew Jackson and Henry Clay, were also Masons. By 1827 New Yorkers had organized a separate political party to oppose the Masons. The Antimason Party spread from New York into other states, winning local elections in Massachusetts, Pennsylvania, and Vermont. In 1831 Antimasons held the first open presidential nominating convention, choosing William Wirt of Maryland as their candidate. Wirt carried only one state, and the party remained a minor player in national politics. Nevertheless, the battle against cabals illustrated the belief that American party politics was a struggle of common people against the monied aristocracy. This would become a staple of Jacksonian rhetoric.

Jacksonian Democracy in Action

The Democratic campaign of 1828 ushered in a new era of national politics, one that mobilized the public in support of a popular president. To make the point that they were a new breed, Jacksonians began to refer to themselves as "Jacksonian Democrats" (or just "the Democrats").

The Election of 1828

The campaign was personal and vicious. Adams's supporters tarred Jackson as an undisciplined liar and blasphemer. They accused him of having married Rachel Robards before her own divorce was final. Jackson supporters retorted that Adams was a Sabbath breaker, a closet Federalist, and an unprincipled hypocrite who disdained popular government.

Earlier campaigns had been fought primarily on the local level and among a far smaller group of potential voters, but in 1828 New York senator Martin Van Buren coordinated a Democratic national campaign designed to appeal to a mass electorate. Van Buren oversaw the creation of a highly controlled party hierarchy of local and state societies linked to the national organization. He pioneered the use of carefully choreographed demonstrations and converted nonpartisan occasions (such as Fourth of July celebrations) into Democratic rallies. Van Buren also used political imagery to evoke campaign themes. Trading on Jackson's nickname, "Old Hickory" (for the hardest wood in the United States), campaign workers handed out hickory canes at political events. Supporters also used editorials and campaign tracts to describe Jackson as the embodiment of the common man.

When the votes were counted in 1828, Jackson had won a clear majority (see Map 10–3): 56 percent of the popular vote and 178 electoral

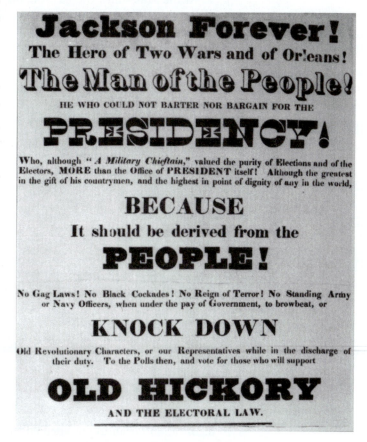

This poster, from the 1828 election, sets out the case for Jackson as a man of the people.

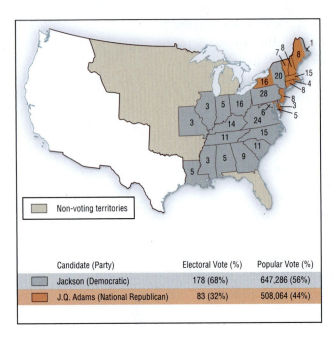

Candidate (Party)	Electoral Vote (%)	Popular Vote (%)
Jackson (Democratic)	178 (68%)	647,286 (56%)
J.Q. Adams (National Republican)	83 (32%)	508,064 (44%)

Non-voting territories

Map 10-3 The Election of 1828 In 1828, Jackson solidified his hold on the South and Midwest and even made inroads in the Northeast.

votes to Adams's 83 electoral votes. Although Adams had retained New England, New Jersey, Delaware, and northern Maryland, Jackson had solidly taken the South and the West, as well as Pennsylvania, most of New York, and even northern Maine.

Jackson was elected by a cross section of voters who identified with his stance as an outsider to, and victim of, eastern elites. Van Buren had put together a coalition of "planters of the South and plain Republicans of the North," actively suppressing the divisive issue of slavery and instead appealing to those who believed that special privilege was denying them their chance of prosperity. He was the candidate of westerners, migrants, settlers, and landowners who opposed eastern banks and congressional land policies, but he also drew support from urban professionals, shopkeepers, laborers, and craftsmen. Jackson claimed the mantle of Jefferson, who also had favored the individual common American and warned against concentrations of economic and political power.

At the same time, the Jacksonians were vague about exactly where the heart of their new democratic movement resided. Structurally, they believed that it evolved from the states, which restrained federal power. At the same time, however, Jackson's strong conviction that he was the people and that his will was indistinguishable from theirs confused matters. The ironic result was a shift of power from the states to the executive during the presidency of the man elected to protect the common man.

> **Thousands and thousands of people, without distinction of rank, collected in an immense mass round the Capitol, silent, orderly, and tranquil, with their eyes fixed on the front of the edifice, waiting the appearance of the President in the portico. The door from the Rotunda opens. . . . [The] old man with his grey locks, that crown of glory, advances, bows to the people, who greet him with a shout that rends the air, the Cannons, from the heights around, from Alexandra and Fort Warburton proclaim the oath he has taken and all the hills reverberate the sound. It was grand—it was sublime!**
>
> MARGARET BAYARD SMITH,
> describing Andrew Jackson's inauguration

The tendency to personalize political struggle characterized Jackson's presidency. He never forgave the National Republicans for publicly questioning the legitimacy of his marriage. Later, he viewed his battle against the Second Bank of the United States in the same highly personal terms: "The Bank," he informed Van Buren, "is trying to kill me, but I will kill it."

If Jackson understood himself as the embodiment of the people's will, he understood the new Democratic Party as its direct instrument. After personal loyalty to Jackson, party loyalty became the avenue to appointment and the justification for an unprecedented turnover in appointees. The overall results were mixed. Jackson expanded the powers of the presidency, but his conviction that he alone embodied the true virtue of the republic also led to personal pettiness, widespread patronage, and turmoil within his cabinet. His efforts to abolish the Second

Bank of the United States created serious hardship for average Americans, and his hostility to Native Americans resulted in widespread death and impoverishment.

The Bank War

The message of the new presidency was clear: reform. Jackson turned his eye on the special privileges and unfair advantages of the rich and well connected. Jackson had long associated this obstacle with Henry Clay, John Quincy Adams, John Calhoun, and the Republican caucus. By 1828 Jackson focused his anger on the Second Bank of the United States.

Jackson hated the bank for all the reasons southerners and westerners did: it was powerful and privileged, and wealthy easterners and foreign investors controlled its private stock. Also, as much as they liked easy credit, most Americans were suspicious of banknotes of all kinds. They had been stung too often by counterfeiters and deadbeats.

But Jackson also had very personal reasons for his opposition. Soon after his first election, Jackson heard rumors that the bank had used its power to buy votes for Adams in 1828. Declaring that the bank threatened "the purity of the right of suffrage," Jackson vowed to oppose it.

Nicholas Biddle, the bank's president, rebuffed Jackson's criticisms. Confident the bank enjoyed broad support, Biddle decided to force the issue before the next presidential election. Although the bank's authorization ran until 1836, on January 6, 1832, Biddle asked Congress to take up renewal early. Jackson may have felt Biddle's behavior to be a personal challenge, because he vetoed it in 1832. "The rich and powerful," he thundered, "too often bend the acts of government to their selfish purposes. . . . [W]hen the laws undertake . . . to make the rich richer, . . . the humble members of society . . . have a right to complain of the injustice of their Government."

> It has all the fury of a chained panther, biting the bars of his cage. It is really a manifesto of anarchy, such as Marat or Robespierre might have issued to the mob of the Faubourg St. Antoine.
>
> NICHOLAS BIDDLE,
> reacting to Jackson's veto message. He thought, incorrectly, that Jackson had overreached.

The Democrats carried the bank veto proudly into the 1832 election as a contest of "the Democracy and the people, against a corrupt and abandoned aristocracy." The Republicans responded that Jackson's veto showed his tendency toward despotism. The Supreme Court had ruled the national bank constitutional, and Congress had voted to recharter it. Jackson had trammeled the authority of the other branches of government, assuming the sole right to determine the future of the bank.

Dismembering the Bank

Jackson won reelection in 1832, although by a smaller majority than in 1828. By 1833 he was ready to disassemble the Second Bank of the United States. He asked Secretary of the Treasury Louis McLane to select other banks into which the federal government could move its deposits. McLane balked, worried that the selection would be compromised by politics and that the state banks would lose all fiscal restraint. Impatient, Jackson replaced McLane with William J. Duane, and then replaced Duane with Attorney General Roger Taney. On October 1, 1833, the federal government began to distribute its deposits to 22 state banks. By the close of the year, the government deposits had been largely removed.

The deposits had been used to make loans to individuals and corporations around the country. To make the funds available, the Second Bank began furiously calling in

>> Jackson's Bank Veto Message

In 1832, shortly before the end of President Andrew Jackson's first term, Congress proposed rechartering the Bank of the United States. Jackson vetoed the bill, and he and the Democrats used the veto as an issue in the reelection campaign. As much as any other address to the American people, Jackson's veto message, a brief excerpt of which follows, sets out his vision for the role of government in advancing economic equality and preventing undemocratic concentrations of political and economic power.

GENERAL JACKSON SLAYING THE MANY HEADED MONSTER.

President Andrew Jackson Destroying the Bank of the United States Here the Bank of the United States is depicted as the many-headed mythological beast, the hydra, whom the hero—in this case, Andrew Jackson—must defeat by lopping off all of its heads.

WASHINGTON, July 10, 1832.

To the Senate.

A bank of the United States is in many respects convenient for the Government and useful to the people. Entertaining this opinion, and deeply impressed with the belief that some of the powers and privileges possessed by the existing bank are unauthorized by the Constitution, subversive of the rights of the States, and dangerous to the liberties of the people, I felt it my duty at an early period of my Administration to call the attention of Congress to the practicability of organizing an institution combining all its advantages and obviating these objections. I sincerely regret that in the act before me I can perceive none of those modifications of the bank charter which are necessary, in my opinion, to make it compatible with justice, with sound policy, or with the Constitution of our country.

The present corporate body enjoys an exclusive privilege of banking under the authority of the General Government, a monopoly of its favor and support, and, as a necessary consequence, almost a monopoly of the foreign and domestic exchange. The powers, privileges, and favors bestowed upon it in the original charter, by increasing the value of the stock far above its par value, operated as a gratuity of many millions to the stockholders.

The act before me proposes another gratuity to the holders of the same stock, and in many cases to the same men. . . .

Every monopoly and all exclusive privileges are granted at the expense of the public, which ought to receive a fair equivalent. The many millions which this act proposes to bestow on the stockholders of the existing bank must come directly or indirectly out of the earnings of the American people. It is due to them, therefore. . . .

It is not conceivable how the present stockholders can have any claim to the special favor of the Government. . . .

It is to be regretted that the rich and powerful too often bend the acts of government to their selfish purposes. Distinctions in society will always exist under every just government. Equality of talents, of education, or of wealth can not be produced by human institutions. In the full enjoyment of the gifts of Heaven and the fruits of superior industry, economy, and virtue, every man is equally entitled to protection by law; but when the laws undertake to add to these natural and just advantages artificial distinctions, to grant titles, gratuities, and exclusive privileges, to make the rich richer and the potent more powerful, the humble members of society—the farmers, mechanics, and laborers—who have neither the time nor the means of securing like favors to themselves, have a right to complain of the injustice of their Government. There are no necessary evils in government. Its evils exist only in its abuses. If it would confine itself to equal protection, and, as Heaven does its rains, shower its favors alike on the high and the low, the rich and the poor, it would be an unqualified blessing. In the act before me there seems to be a wide and unnecessary departure from these just principles.

Continued

Experience should teach us wisdom. Most of the difficulties our Government now encounters and most of the dangers which impend over our Union have sprung from an abandonment of the legitimate objects of Government by our national legislation, and the adoption of such principles as are embodied in this act. Many of our rich men have not been content with equal protection and equal benefits, but have besought us to make them richer by act of Congress. By attempting to gratify their desires we have in the results of our legislation arrayed section against section, interest against interest, and man against man, in a fearful commotion which threatens to shake the foundations of our Union. It is time to pause in our career to review our principles, and if possible revive that devoted patriotism and spirit of compromise which distinguished the sages of the Revolution and the fathers of our Union. If we can not at once, in justice to interests vested under improvident legislation, make our Government what it ought to be, we can at least take a stand against all new grants of monopolies and exclusive privileges, against any prostitution of our Government to the advancement of the few at the expense of the many, and in favor of compromise and gradual reform in our code of laws and system of political economy.

ANDREW JACKSON

Andrew Jackson, "Bank Veto, July 10, 1832," in *The Addresses and Messages of the Presidents of the United States, from 1789 to 1839: Together with the Declaration of Independence and Constitution of the United States* (New York: MacLean and Taylor, 1839), pp. 398–399, 409–410.

Questions

1. How does Andrew Jackson understand equality? What does he think the government's role should be in promoting or protecting it?

2. What problem is Jackson trying to address by refusing to recharter the Bank of the United States?

3. Jackson says it is time for the American people to "review our principles." What does he believe were the principles on which the nation was founded, and how does he think they were distorted?

loans and foreclosing on debts. In effect, Biddle was repeating the process that triggered the Panic of 1819. In six months he took more than $15 million worth of credit out of the economy.

As recession gripped the nation, the Senate passed an unprecedented resolution censuring Jackson for assuming "authority and power not conferred by the constitution and laws." Jackson's response underscored the new "democratic" politics of the times: "The President," he maintained (and no other branch of government), "is the direct representative of the American people." The expansion of white male suffrage (and the spreading practice of electing members of the Electoral College directly) made Jackson the first president who could claim to be elected directly by the voters. Congress, on the other hand, would soon become the power base of elites.

The first recession passed quickly as state banks tapped their federal deposits to churn out loans, and new wildcat banks took advantage of the glut of paper money. Much of the borrowing went for land sales.

The Specie Act

Correctly, Jackson believed that the excess of paper money in circulation had caused the recession. As soon as conditions improved, he implemented a hard-money policy. In 1833 he had announced that the federal government would no longer accept drafts on the Second Bank in payment of taxes, a move that reduced the value of the bank's notes. In 1834 Jackson declared that the "deposit" banks receiving federal monies could not issue paper drafts for amounts under $5 (later raised to $20), an action that reduced the small-denomination paper in circulation. In July 1836 he had the Treasury Department issue the Specie Circular, which directed land offices to accept only coins or precious metals in payment for western lands. This shut out actual settlers, who could not get together enough gold or silver for their purchases. Meanwhile, the Deposit Act, passed in 1836, expanded the number of "pet banks" to nearly 100 and distributed a federal surplus of more than $5 million to the states, on top of

the more than $22 million already deposited in the state banks from the Second Bank of the United States. Underregulated and under local pressure, the state banks could not absorb these funds. They issued loans and printed money that vastly exceeded their assets. When the bubble burst in 1837, the nation faced the worst financial disaster of its young history.

A Policy of Removing Indigenous People

When Jackson looked west, he saw a different sort of problem. For Andrew Jackson, the quintessential "common man" was the western settler, struggling to bring new lands under cultivation and new institutions to life. Pioneers confronted many obstacles in their trek west, but none loomed larger than the resistance of Indian peoples.

Jackson and Native Peoples

The War of 1812 had ended intertribal resistance east of the Mississippi River. By 1828, most of the Great Lakes nations had been pushed out of Ohio, southern Indiana, and Illinois, but the Ojibwa, Winnebago, Sauk, Mesquakie, Kickapoo, and Menominee tribes retained sizable homelands in the region. In the South, in spite of repeated forced cessions, the Chickasaws, Choctaws, Creeks, Cherokees, and Seminoles—the Five "Civilized" Tribes that had adopted American ways—retained ancestral territories.

Jackson's views concerning Native Americans had been settled in the crucible of the Indian wars of the 1790s. "Does not experience teach us that treaties answer no other Purpose than opening an Easy door for the Indians to pass [through to] Butcher our citizens?" he wrote in 1794. Congress should "Punish the Barbarians."

In these views Jackson was no different from many American settlers—some of whom had directly experienced the violence of white incursions into Indian Country, but many of whom formed their ideas long before they ever saw an Indian, basing their preconceptions on inflamed newspaper accounts in the new mass-produced "penny press." Most American settlers saw Indians only in passing. Some of these encounters were surely unnerving, but they were usually of no harm to the settlers. The harm that Indians represented was more basic: they occupied lands recognized as belonging to them in treaties with the federal government. Despite recurrent wars and land cessions, western settlers were no happier with federal initiatives in the 1820s than they had been in the 1790s.

Tension ran especially high in Georgia. There officials complained that the federal government had not kept its promise to remove all Indians from the state, a condition of Georgia's 1802 agreement to cede its western land claims to the federal government. A few Creeks and most of the Cherokee nation remained. In 1826 the federal government pressured the Creeks to give up all but a small strip of their remaining lands in Georgia, but white Georgians were not satisfied. Georgia governor George Michael Troup sent surveyors onto that last piece of Creek land. When President Adams objected to this encroachment on federal treaty powers, Troup threatened to call up the state militia.

The election of Andrew Jackson emboldened Georgians to go after Cherokee land. They invalidated the constitution of the Cherokee nation within Georgia and proclaimed that the Cherokees were subject to the authority of the state of Georgia. When discoveries of gold sent white prospectors surging onto Cherokee land, Georgia refused to stop the trespassers or to protect the Indians. To the contrary, the state passed laws that stripped Cherokees of their rights and their land. Jackson quickly notified the Cherokees that it was his duty, as president, to "sustain the States in the exercise of their rights."

In fact, the states were not exercising their rights. In 1830 the Cherokee nation took the state of Georgia to the Supreme Court, arguing that the Cherokee nation was a "foreign nation in the sense of our constitution and law" and that, as a state, Georgia had no right to pass laws over the inhabitants of a foreign nation. Chief Justice John Marshall agreed that the Cherokees were a distinct political society, but he demurred that they were not a foreign state "in the sense of the constitution, and cannot maintain an action in the courts of the United States." But the following year, *Worcester v. Georgia*, which was not brought by the Cherokee nation, gave Marshall the opportunity to say more. He identified the Cherokee nation as "a distinct community, occupying its own territory, with boundaries accurately described in which the laws of Georgia can have no force, and which the citizens of Georgia have no right to enter but with the assent of the Cherokees themselves or in conformity with treaties and with the acts of Congress." Marshall concluded, "The whole intercourse between the United States and this nation is, by our Constitution and laws, vested in the government of the United States." Georgia had acted unconstitutionally.

Jackson refused to enforce this decision. He had long believed that the best policy would be to remove the Indians entirely from lands sought by settlers. The place he had in mind was across the Mississippi River. Because full-scale removal of the Indians involved shifting populations across state lines and into federal territories, however, it required congressional consent.

The proposed policy was not unopposed. "[I]f, in pursuance of a narrow and selfish policy, we should . . . drive away these remnants of tribes, in such a manner, and under such auspices, as to insure their destruction . . . ," Jeremiah Evarts, secretary of the American Board of Commissioners for Foreign Missions, warned, "then the sentence of an indignant world would be uttered in thunders." In Congress the Native Americans found unexpected allies. To the old Adams men, now led by Henry Clay, "removal" was the policy of states, forced on the federal government. For Congress to pass an act authorizing the policy would mean encouraging states to trample on federal powers.

Van Buren responded by forming a counterlobby, the Board for the Emigration, Preservation, and Improvement of the Aborigines of America, which argued that Indians were ill equipped for contact with white civilization and that removing them was humane. Among the proponents of removal was former president John Quincy Adams. In the end, the bill passed by only five votes and only after four months of debate.

The Removal Act

In 1830 Congress passed and President Jackson signed an act "to provide for an exchange of lands with the Indians residing in any of the states or territories, and for their removal west of the river Mississippi" (see Map 10–4). In one sense, the act only made official and accelerated a policy that Americans had pursued since the founding of the nation. In his State of the Union address that year, Jackson praised the Removal Act as an act of "Philanthropy." He reminded Congress that for generations European Americans had been "leav[ing] the land of their birth to seek new homes in distant regions" and that new lands meant opportunity and liberty. "Doubtless it will be painful to leave the graves of their fathers," he acknowledged of the eastern Indians, "but what do they more than our ancestors did or than our children are now doing?" In fact, leaving "the land of their birth" was for Native Americans not an act of opportunity but rather an eviction from their very identity as a people.

In 1830 the Choctaws were forced from their lands in Mississippi to present-day Oklahoma. The Chickasaws and the Creeks followed in 1832. Then, in 1836, six years after passage of the Removal Act and four years after they had exhausted their judicial options, a small splinter group of the Cherokees (claiming to speak for the whole nation) at last agreed to removal. The Treaty of New Echota provided that within two years the Cherokees would leave the mountains for Indian Territory, in return for safe passage, $5 million, and food, shelter, equipment, and medicine for a year after their arrival. The Senate ratified the treaty in the spring of 1836. The protreaty Cherokees began to leave almost immediately. The overwhelming majority of Cherokees, who considered the treaty fraudulent, remained in the East.

Three years later, after their unsuccessful appeals to the Supreme Court and after several years of resistance, the Cherokees were removed from their eastern lands. In a forced march that became known as the Trail of Tears, they were driven off their homelands to Indian Territory in what is now eastern Oklahoma. Most people had delayed leaving until the last moment and had made few preparations for the journey. Many died of disease, malnutrition, dehydration, and exhaustion along the way.

Indians did not accept removal willingly. In 1831, the Sauk and Fox people (descended from Native Americans who had earlier been pushed across the Great Lakes region) were forced to relocate once again. In their new lands, however, they began to hear rumors of whites desecrating their former burying grounds. When Indians

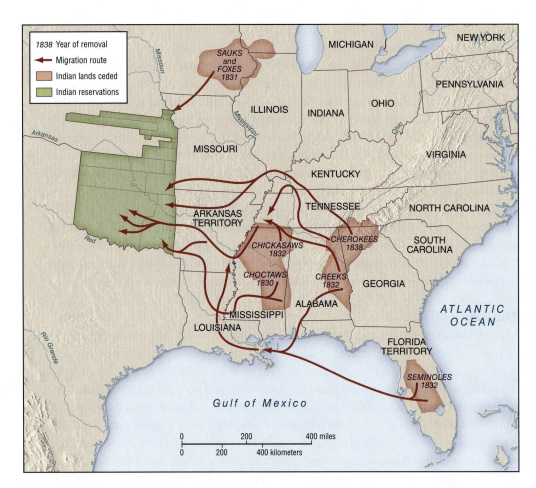

Map 10-4 Indian Removals Jackson's policy of Indian removal required Native American peoples to leave their homelands east of the Mississippi River for government-designated lands west of the Mississippi. Some Indian groups signed treaties ceding their lands, but these groups often lacked authority to do so. Some groups (like the Cherokees) fought removal in court. Others (like the Seminoles, Sauks, and Foxes) fought the policy in open combat.

recrossed the Mississippi to rebury their dead and harvest produce from their old fields, white farmers and the Illinois militia attacked them. The Sauk and Fox Indians turned to a revered old fighter, Black Hawk, who raised a band of 500 warriors. Attacked by state militiamen, they spent the summer fighting a series of skirmishes called Black Hawk's War. Finally, on August 2, 1832, the exhausted remnants of Black Hawk's band were cornered and massacred by the army.

More successful were the Florida Seminoles, also a diverse community including militant Creek warriors, known as Red Sticks, and runaway slaves. When federal troops arrived to remove the Seminoles in 1832, the Indians resisted with skill and determination. Unfamiliar with the terrain and vulnerable to malaria, the American troops were picked off by both disease and snipers. The war dragged on for seven years. Not until 1842 could President John Tyler proclaim victory.

History, Destiny, and the Remaking of Indian Societies

Beginning with Washington, federal policy had encouraged Indians to adopt American ways of life—a private-property-based agrarian economy in which men worked in the fields and women in the home. At the same time, another strand in American thought held that Native Americans were incapable of change and Native American dispossession was inevitable, not only because white Americans were perfectly matched to the land but also because Indians were not. Americans who wanted to seize Indian lands claimed to have tried again and again to help Native Americans survive but considered them incapable of taking full advantage of the land. Ignoring the example of the Five Civilized Tribes, Jackson reflected this view in his 1833 address to Congress. Native Americans, he declared, had "neither the intelligence, the industry, the moral habits, nor the desire of improvement which are essential" to realizing the potential of the land.

This understanding of manifest destiny as entailing the inevitable disappearance of Native Americans made its way into American literature in the 1820s, just as white Americans were considering Indian removal as an official government policy. Its venue was the historical novel. The depiction of Native Americans in antebellum historical novels represented a departure from earlier Indian captivity narratives, which often described Indians as almost incapable of human feeling and bent on the violent destruction of European American civilization. Although the historical novels of the

The Grand National Caravan Moving East In this satirical cartoon, Jackson and Van Buren are on the left, followed by the devil, an army officer, and a group of caged Indians, who represent Indian removal. On the ground, a drunken Jacksonian proclaims, "Hail! Columbia, happy land."

AMERICAN LANDSCAPE

>> Liberty and the Land: Cherokee Removal

More than any other Indian nation, the Cherokees had adapted to American culture. By 1815, with deer in the Southeast depleted, the Cherokees had started herding cattle and hogs. Within a decade, the most successful of them had become cotton planters. They purchased slaves so that the Cherokee women could leave the fields and tend to their homes, like white women. The Cherokee planter elite, many of whom were of mixed Cherokee-white ancestry, converted to Protestantism and adopted the middle-class American values of thrift, hard work, and private property. The Cherokees Americanized their laws and form of government, too, in the process diminishing the traditional role of matrilineal clans and female ownership of property. The Cherokee constitution explicitly banned women from voting and office holding.

The Cherokees also learned to read and write. In 1821 Sequoyah invented the Cherokee syllabary (a system of written symbols representing the sounds of the spoken Cherokee language). It was so easy to learn that by the mid-1820s perhaps half of the Cherokee nation had become literate in their own language, a literacy rate similar to that of southern whites. Members of the elite learned English as well. Cherokee leader John Ridge took

pride in the "march of civilization" among his people. "There is not to my knowledge a solitary Cherokee to be found that depends upon the chase for subsistence and every head of a family has his house & farm."

Underneath the rapid "civilization" of the Cherokees were tensions that came to the fore once the United States announced the removal plan. Not all the Cherokees embraced Americanization as eagerly as the planter elite, and they preserved many traditional values and practices alongside American ones. The elite concluded that removal was inevitable and sought the best terms possible in the Treaty of New Echota (1836). The majority, led by John Ross, resisted. Women, resuming their traditional political role, petitioned Congress. Two thousand followers of the Treaty Party left for the West in 1836. Two years later, federal troops forced the remaining 16,000 Cherokees off their lands.

Cherokees were rounded up, often at the point of a bayonet. Many years later one Cherokee woman remembered: "When the soldier came to our house my father wanted to fight, but my mother told him that the soldiers would kill him if he did, and we surrendered without a fight. They drove us out of our house to join other prisoners in a stockade. After they took us away, my mother begged them to let her go back and get some bedding. So they let her go back and she brought what bedding and a few cooking utensils she could carry and had to leave behind all of our other household possessions." Corrupt land dealers took advantage of the circumstances to buy Cherokee lands cheap, and thieves stripped houses of furniture and equipment.

Gathered at three points (two in Tennessee, one in Alabama) for embarkation, the Cherokees went west in two

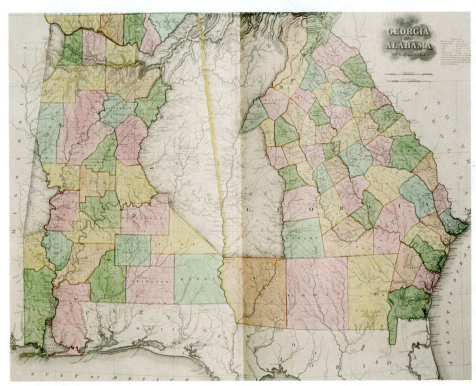

A Map of Georgia and Alabama in 1823 This map shows the two states prior to the Indian Removal Act of 1838.

waves. Under the supervision of the army, three groups totaling nearly 3,000 Cherokees started almost immediately, in the hottest part of the summer. According to a missionary eyewitness, the agent shipped the Cherokees "by multitudes," "[n]ine hundred in one detachment, and seven hundred in another . . . driven onto boats" to carry them up the Tennessee and Ohio Rivers to the Mississippi. "It will be a miracle of mercy if one-fourth escape the exposure to that sickly climate." Hundreds did not.

With the death count mounting, the Cherokees requested authority to manage their own removals and to delay them until the end of summer. After getting this permission, they did everything possible to survive the journey. Those permitted to return to their homes before leaving salvaged what remained. Some of the contingents included hundreds of wagons and thousands of horses, but others were far less well supplied. The wagons carried whoever could not walk, usually the sick and the aged. Others who could still walk bundled their goods in blankets on their backs.

Escorted by soldiers, the contingents sometimes looked like "the march of an army, regiment after regiment, the wagons in the center, the officers along the line and the horsemen on the flanks and at the rear."

At least for the removals they organized, however, the Cherokees established their own internal police. To the meager stocks of salt pork and often moldy corn and wheat flour provided by military suppliers, the Cherokees added whatever they could hunt or forage along the way: turkeys, small game, occasionally deer, and berries. The later removals avoided the diseases of summer but faced the cold winds and ice storms of winter. Many migrants had only thin clothing and few blankets, and the cold was especially hard on elders, children, and the sick.

Removal did not annihilate the Cherokees, but it deeply wounded their society. The entire process claimed at least 4,000 (perhaps as many as 8,000) of the roughly 17,000 Cherokees who were initially rounded up. The United States government had promised to support the migrants during their first year in the West, but government subcontractors lined their own pockets by supplying insufficient and substandard goods. As deaths mounted and poverty, illness, and alcoholism increased, the hatred between proremoval and antiremoval parties within the Cherokee nation ignited into civil war. In the meantime, their ancestral lands had been cleared for white settlers and their African American slaves.

1820s did not romanticize all Native Americans, they did identify among the Indians individuals of high character—of integrity, intelligence, and great sensitivity—but who, significantly, were always doomed to extinction.

Although dispossession was a devastating experience for Native Americans, native societies adapted. The Comanches agreed to make room for removed Indians who would trade with them. Soon the displaced tribes, which had reestablished their agricultural way of life, were trading their crops and government-issued guns and ammunition to the Comanches for their new neighbors' chief commodities, horses and slaves. When they were forced to migrate, the southeastern Indians had brought 5,000 black slaves with them, a workforce they replenished with the enslaved Indians, Mexicans, and Anglo-Americans sold by the Comanches. Ironically, the Indians who were displaced because they supposedly could not adapt took American values and practices with them: representative government, Christianity, and racial slavery. Drawing from their experience, they became middlemen, facilitating the trade between the Comanches to the west and Americans to the east.

As American weapons made their way to the western edge of the Comanche empire, the Spanish became alarmed. They now found that thousands of dollars' worth of gifts no longer purchased the loyalty of the Comanches, who increasingly wanted trade with the wealthier Americans.

Western Comanche in War Dress Comanche culture rewarded risk taking and prowess in war. Warriors made headdresses out of the hair of their captives and the hair of their own wives.

As Spanish influence in the West waned after Mexico achieved independence in 1821, American traders began moving into the region, at first destabilizing it. By 1840, however, the Comanche Empire had established commercial dominance in the southern plains. Josiah Gregg, an American trader, observed that the Comanches "acknowledge no boundaries, but call themselves the lords of the entire prairies."

The Growth of Sectional Tension

The growing fiscal strains in Jacksonian America were matched by brewing sectional conflict. Americans had not always viewed the differences between the political economies of the North and South as bad. Those regional differences had powered northern industrialization during the War of 1812 and had laid the foundation for the National Republican vision of robust nationalism after the war. But economic expansion brought old differences into open conflict. The immediate catalyst was the tariff, but by 1832 the tariff question had ignited a broader debate over the institution of slavery.

The Sources of Southern Discontent

Despite an apparent victory in the Missouri controversy, many white southerners had felt betrayed by northern criticisms of slavery. Economic and political frustrations in the 1820s nurtured that sense of mistreatment, leading the planter class, which had so far dominated the presidency, to see itself as the victim of the federal government.

White southerners read signs of shifting public attitudes toward slavery. Proslavery advocates in Illinois (where many African Americans were already held in indentures comparable to slavery) were unable to elect a proslavery congressman in 1820. In 1824 Ohio asked Congress to consider a plan for the gradual abolition of slavery throughout the United States. On July 4, 1827, New York completed its long process of gradual emancipation, an occasion celebrated by free African Americans as far south as Virginia. And news from England had it that abolitionist William Wilberforce was likely to get slavery outlawed in the British West Indies.

Most important, though, was the economy. By 1828 cotton prices were only about one-third of their 1815 levels. Many planters and farmers tried to compensate for falling profits by planting more acres, but worn-out fields kept production low. Large eastern planters often sold off slaves, lands, and city houses. Many smaller farmers, dependent on cotton as their cash crop to pay off debts, were forced to sell out. Although the Panic of 1819 hurt northern farms and businesses, most of the Northeast bounced back faster than the South, which focused planter attention on the 1816 protective tariff as a sign of government favoritism. They complained that the tariff was unnaturally driving up the prices of European imports, forcing strapped southerners to purchase expensive northern-made products and driving down southern export sales. "We have no objection to the North being enriched by our riches," one Charleston *Mercury* reporter wrote sarcastically in 1827, "but not from our poverty."

Of the slaveholding states, South Carolina was particularly insecure. Its white residents faced a growing African American majority (the result of white migration west) that heightened fears of slave insurrection.

South Carolina's Protest

Passage of the Tariff of 1828, the "tariff of abominations," led to nullification talk in South Carolina and created a new leader, John C. Calhoun. Like other South Carolinians, Calhoun had been disenchanted by the experiences of the 1820s and was a far less enthusiastic nationalist than he had once been. Yet he retained enough faith in the Democratic Party to believe that Democrats would lower the tariff once in office and would see the injury to southern states from such national laws. To encourage both results, in 1828 Calhoun wrote the *South Carolina Exposition and Protest*, a justification for the theory of nullification, under which states might declare particular federal laws null and void within their borders. Although Calhoun published the pamphlet anonymously (still aspiring to the presidency, he was reluctant to associate himself too openly with the extreme position), he let his authorship be widely known, hoping for the support of radicals in his home state. In the *Exposition*, Calhoun argued that the federal government was the creation of the states. In agreeing to create a federal government, the states had ceded some of their powers, but only conditionally, and always reserving the right to do whatever was necessary to ensure their survival as "distinct political communities." A state had the right to assert its sovereignty in defiance of federal policies that might threaten its distinctive character. It was at such a juncture, Calhoun argued, that the states of the South had arrived in 1828. They had become the "minority" culture, their interests and institutions endangered by "the unrestrained will of a majority." The tariff would gradually drain away the money and the independence of the South, subjecting it to northern tyranny.

Much in America's history supported Calhoun's view. The states had existed before the federal Constitution. Representation at the Constitutional Convention and ratification of the Constitution had been by state, and representation in the federal government continued to be on the basis of states. Moreover, defenders of the theory included Thomas Jefferson and James Madison, in their resolutions opposing the Alien and Sedition Acts.

On the other hand, the Constitution's status as the supreme law of the land rested on the fact that it had been ratified by the *people*, acting through special conventions, not by the state governments, and subsequent suffrage reform had enlarged the popular participation of white men. Moreover, after the debacle of the Hartford Convention, states' rights arguments had the whiff of treason. And Calhoun went further than that convention had: he argued explicitly what the Federalists had dared only hint, that if all else failed, states retained the right to withdraw from the compact.

Among those who viewed the federal government as properly the creation of "the people," not of the states, and who regarded threats to withdraw from the Union as unforgivable, was President Jackson.

The Nullification Crisis

Other southern states, less economically pressed than South Carolina and more optimistic that regional political differences could yet be reconciled, did not rush to endorse the *Exposition*. But two events increased political tensions: a seemingly innocuous Senate debate over western land sales that sharpened the rhetoric over sectional differences, and a slave rebellion in Virginia that came closer than any other to succeeding.

Eager to attract population, westerners had long lobbied for a reduction in the price of federal lands. Southern representatives offered to support the measure if the western states would join in opposing the tariff. When, in December 1829, Senator Samuel A. Foot of Connecticut advocated limiting land sales in the West, South Carolina Senator Robert Y. Hayne accused him of conspiring to keep labor prices low in the East and insinuated that the government was keeping land prices artificially high to build a slush fund "for corruption—fatal to the sovereignty and independence of the states."

Rising to defend his region, Senator Daniel Webster of Massachusetts countered that it was South Carolina, not the Northeast, that was a hotbed of disloyalty, pointing for evidence to the *Exposition*. The Revolution had been fought by *the American people*, Webster thundered, and *the American people* had created the federal government. Uncannily foreshadowing, Webster evoked the image of "a once glorious union" "rent with civil feuds, or drenched, it may be, in fraternal blood!" Signaling an acceptance of slavery in "the Union as it is," Webster also insisted that "every true American heart" must recommit itself to the founding spirit of the nation: "Liberty and Union, now and forever, one and inseparable."

Although he supported the federal Union, President Jackson did sympathize with southern complaints about the fairness of tariff levels, and he advocated tariff reform. The Tariff of 1832 lowered duties on many goods to 1816 levels, but not on textiles and iron. In this continued protection for the largest northern industries, South Carolinians saw a defiant reaffirmation of a special relationship between northern interests and the federal government.

By then, the South had been the scene of another slave insurrection. In the summer of 1831 an African American driver and preacher by the name of Nat Turner launched a rebellion in Virginia. The rebellion was put down, and Turner and other conspirators were executed, but unlike earlier plots, this revolt had actually taken place. Inspired by a millennialist fervor, for two days Turner and his followers had effectively controlled parts of southern Virginia, recruiting new allies, executing whites, and freeing slaves. Although the number of active insurrectionists probably never exceeded 70, 57 whites died in the uprising, more than in any previous slave rebellion. Southern whites took their revenge in a monthlong reign of vigilante terror, but the insurrection had left its mark. Southern whites lived in a state of constant fear, convinced that northerners and southern slaves were in league against them. In an 1832 convention, South Carolina radicals voted 136 to 26 to nullify the tariffs of 1828 and 1832 in the state. The acts forbade the collection of the tariffs within South Carolina.

For Jackson, the act of nullification transformed the crisis from a question of regional interests to one of national union. "The laws of the United States must be executed," he declared. "I have no discretionary power on the subject; my duty is emphatically pronounced in the Constitution." He asked Congress for a law specifically affirming his responsibility to compel the collection of the tax in South Carolina, by force of arms if necessary.

Congress rushed to find a compromise. In early 1833 it passed a tariff that gradually reduced duties over the next decade but also passed the law Jackson had requested, known as the Force Bill. Jackson signed both the new tariff law and the Force Bill, a signal to South Carolina that nullification and secession would not be tolerated.

In 1832, with South Carolina virtually alone even among southern states, supporters of nullification had no choice but to withdraw their ordinance. At the same time, they voted to nullify the Force Bill within the boundaries of South Carolina. Jackson let the gesture pass, and at least for the time being, the constitutional crisis was over.

> I consider then the power to annul the law of the United States, assumed by one State, *incompatible with the existence of the Union*, contradicted expressly by the letter of the Constitution, unauthorized by its spirit, inconsistent with every principle on which it was founded, and destructive of the great object for which it was formed.
>
> ANDREW JACKSON,
> Proclamation, December 10, 1832

DEBATING HISTORY

>> The Nature of Jacksonian Democracy

In the run-up to the presidential election of 1828, war hero Andrew Jackson ran against the National Republican program of internal improvements. Jackson portrayed himself as the common man's candidate, the one figure who could defend the interests of the sovereign people against the "aristocratic" minority of corrupt politicians and bankers. He and his followers saw the executive branch as the most democratic branch of government because it directly represented the people's will. In his first term as president, Jackson used the power of his office to push forward a policy of Indian removal (1830), veto the Second National Bank (1832), and intimidate South Carolina into rescinding its Nullification Act (1833). The Whig opposition that emerged in the mid-1830s decried what they saw as the presumptuous power of Jackson, whom they dubbed "King Andrew." Historians have disagreed about the nature of Jackson's presidency. Daniel Walker Howe argues that Jackson's idea of a powerful presidency derived from his sense of self-importance. Sean Wilentz argues that Jackson represented a broader "Jacksonian" idea of the relationship between government and the people, who were the ultimate source of power.

DANIEL WALKER HOWE, *What Hath God Wrought: The Transformation of America, 1815–1848* (New York: Oxford University Press, 2007), pp. 367, 330.

[Jackson] believed in the sovereignty of the American people and in himself as the embodiment of that sovereignty. . . . It was his personal authority, rather than that of the federal government or even the presidential office, which Jackson zealously maintained. . . . Jackson's combination of authoritarianism with a democratic ideology, his identification of his own will with the voice of the people, worked well for him politically. He defined himself as defender of the people against special interests and advocated—unsuccessfully—a constitutional amendment to abolish the electoral college and choose the president by direct popular vote. The populist rhetoric of Jackson and his political associates combined ceaseless condemnation of elite corruption with the antigovernment political ideology that had taken over from Randolph, Taylor, and the Old Republicans. A large segment of the American electorate shared Jackson's belief in the legitimacy of private violence and the assertion of male honor, his trust in natural rather than acquired abilities, and his impatience with limitations on one's will. . . .

Continued

BORN TO COMMAND.

OF VETO MEMORY.

HAD I BEEN CONSULTED.

KING ANDREW THE FIRST.

King Andrew Although Jackson's supporters saw him as a man of the people, his opponents depicted him as a tyrant. In this cartoon he literally tramples the Constitution.

>> **DEBATING HISTORY** *Continued*

SEAN WILENTZ, *Rise of American Democracy: Jefferson to Lincoln* (New York: Norton, 2005), pp. 513–4.

[T]he key to Jacksonian politics [was] a belief that relatively small groups of self-interested men were out to destroy majority rule and, with it, the Constitution. . . . Political abuses formed the matrix of oppression. Accordingly, the cure was political—above all, promulgating the central Jacksonian principle that the majority is to govern. The Jacksonians hardly invented [the idea that power lay with the people and not their representatives], nor did they initiate the expansion of democratic rights and power for ordinary white men that posterity too often associates purely with Andrew Jackson. But they greatly encouraged as well as benefited from that expansion, giving the politics forged earlier by . . . the Jeffersonian Republicans an unprecedented presence and power in national affairs. The Jacksonians' chief institutional innovation . . . was to vaunt the power of the executive—selected, as never before, by the ballots of ordinary voters and not . . . by state legislators—as the only branch of the national government chosen by the people at large. Jackson used that authority to the fullest extent granted him by the Constitution, turning a democratized version of Hamiltonian doctrines about an energetic executive toward goals that would have shocked Alexander Hamilton.

Questions

1. In his account of Jackson's presidency, Howe tends to focus on Jackson himself, while Wilentz's account focuses on the "Jacksonians" in general. How does this difference affect their arguments?

2. Both historians stress Jackson's conviction that he alone embodied the will of the people, but differ as to the motivations behind that belief. What role does Jackson's belief that he represented the people play in each historian's statement, and how does it affect their respective interpretations of Jacksonian democracy?

Conclusion

The Jacksonian consensus was forged from belief in the efficacy of the individual, a distrust of unfair privilege, a commitment to geographic expansionism, and an insistence that slavery be kept out of national politics. Few of these elements were new to Americans, but their meanings had shifted since 1776. The republic was becoming a democracy. But the harmony that seemed to be expressed in the Jacksonian celebration of democracy was misleading. Consensus was always partial, and conflict always present and growing.

>> TIME LINE

▼**1819**
Missouri applies for statehood

▼**1820**
Missouri Compromise
Maine becomes a state

▼**1821**
Missouri becomes a state

▼**1824**
John Quincy Adams elected president (the "corrupt bargain")

▼**1827**
Antimason Party organized

▼**1828**
Andrew Jackson elected president
Virtually universal white male suffrage

Philadelphia workers organize the Philadelphia Working Men's Party
Protective Tariff of 1828 passes
Calhoun writes *South Carolina Exposition and Protest*

▼**1830**
Removal Act passes

African Americans and Native Americans were excluded altogether; workers and women were included only contingently. Within 25 years of Jackson's election, workers were in the streets, hundreds of thousands of Americans were petitioning to end slavery, political parties were in chaos, and the nation stood on the brink of civil war.

Who, What

Black Hawk   360

Nat Turner   366

Antimason Party   351

The "corrupt bargain"   344

The Monroe Doctrine   341

National Republicanism   339

Nullification   365

The Second Bank of the United States   339

Special privilege   349

Review Questions

1. How did the United States show its self-confidence at the end of the War of 1812?

2. What was the Missouri Compromise?

3. Why did Jackson oppose the *South Carolina Exposition and Protest*? Why didn't other southern states support South Carolina in the nullification crisis?

Critical-Thinking Questions

1. How could the Jacksonians create a coalition between two such different interests as southern planters and northern workers?

2. The Cherokees and the other "civilized" tribes were removed from the Southeast even though they had adopted American customs and forms of government. Why?

3. The Second Bank of the United States and Indian removal were simultaneously symbolic and substantial issues. How was this the case?

For further review materials and resource information, please visit www.oup.com/us/ofthepeople

▼1831
Antimason Party holds first open presidential nominating convention

Cherokee Nation v. Georgia

Nat Turner leads rebellion in Virginia

THE LAST OF THE MOHICANS.

JAMES FENIMORE COOPER.

NEW YORK:
D. APPLETON AND COMPANY, PUBLISHERS.

▼1832
Worcester v. Georgia

Black Hawk's War

Jackson vetoes act rechartering Second Bank of the United States

Jackson reelected

Tariff of 1832

South Carolina passes Nullification Resolution

▼1833
Congress passes Force Bill

▼1836
Deposit Act expands number of Jackson's "pet banks" and provides for distribution of federal surplus

1) Access to land and capital in Jackson's America transformed the lives of people in radically different ways.

2) Sectional tensions that played out in American politics in the 1820s and 1830s foreshadowed deeper rifts over race, the economy, and power that would emerge in decades to come.

3) The democratic ideals articulated by the politics and implemented by the policies of Andrew Jackson made evident the limits of those very ideals.

A New National Politics

The Social and Political Bases of Jacksonian Democracy

Jacksonian Democracy in Action

A Policy of Removing Indigenous People

The Growth of Sectional Tension

JACKSONIAN DEMOCRACY

1820–1840

EVENTS

Changes in the Democratic Republican Party A new generation of Democratic Republican party leaders (National Republicans) favored an activist central government.

James Monroe and National Republicanism President James Monroe governed with a nationalist bent and a more assertive foreign policy.

The Missouri Compromise Missouri's admission to the Union caused a confrontation on the issue of slavery in new states.

The Election of 1824 and the "Corrupt Bargain" John Quincy Adams won a closely contested and controversial presidential election.

The Adams Presidency and the Gathering Forces of Democracy Despite an ambitious program, Adams failed to set an independent agenda for his presidency.

Settlers Continued migration into the backcountry increased easy credit and low land prices.

Free Labor As nonfarming wage labor increased, workers began to form unions for better wages.

Suffrage Reform White male suffrage expanded along with disenfranchisement of women and African American men.

Opposition to Special Privilege and Secret Societies Ordinary people perceived corporations and secret organizations as undemocratic.

The Election of 1828 A coalition of voters who resented the eastern "elite" elected Andrew Jackson president over Adams.

The Bank War The Jackson administration vetoed the recharter of the Second Bank of the United States, considering it an engine of privilege.

Dismembering the Bank Jackson moved federal deposits to other banks, triggering a national recession.

The Specie Act Jackson implemented a hard-money policy, which aggravated the recession.

Jackson and Native Peoples Jackson refused to enforce a Supreme Court decision that would have protected Cherokee Indians in the Southeast.

The Removal Act Congress made Indian removal an official American policy.

History, Destiny, and the Remaking of Indian Societies Despite dispossession, Native American societies adapted to a new environment.

The Sources of Southern Discontent White southerners grew increasingly frustrated by the economic downturn and northern criticism of slavery.

South Carolina's Protest Led by Calhoun, South Carolinians questioned the right of the federal government to impose a tariff.

The Nullification Crisis Jackson insisted that "the laws of the United States must be executed."

COMMON THREADS

>> How did the market revolution shape the Benevolent Empire?

>> How did the conditions of paid labor change between 1789 and 1835?

>> Why did many reform movements emerge in the early nineteenth century?

Reform and Conflict
1820–1848

>> Charles Grandison Finney

Charles Grandison Finney had originally trained in the law, but in 1821 he experienced a calling to the ministry. Although Finney's rejection of the Presbyterian belief in original sin worried his teachers, he developed into a charismatic preacher, and after ordination in 1824 he moved to upstate New York to begin his work. The New York Evangelical Missionary Society of Young Men raised money to send missionaries to new settlements of western Pennsylvania, upstate New York, and Georgia. No one was more successful or controversial than Finney, who became an influential advocate for a dynamic Protestantism based on personal responsibility.

By the 1820s, construction of the Erie Canal was drawing even the most remote farmers closer to East Coast markets and enmeshing them in relations of cash and commerce. Inhabitants of towns and small cities were at the center of the rapidly developing market economy. Some people were troubled by the swirl of development around them. Others were attracted to the way the new economy appeared to reward industry, hard work, and personal ambition.

To this latter audience, Finney preached of the power of human spiritual striving. Instead of the stern God of Calvinism, he offered a God of justice, who spoke to a humankind "just as free as a jury" to accept salvation or not. This theology gave great latitude to human effort, but it also placed a new burden on the sinner. If "a man that was praying week after week for the Holy Spirit . . . could get no answer," Finney insisted, it must be that the man "was praying from false motives," not that God had abandoned him.

Finney enjoyed immediate success in the Genesee Valley of New York. Drawn to his preaching were those most benefiting from the economic boom: the families of merchants and bankers and of grain dealers and mill owners, as well as young, ambitious employees in such businesses. Finneyite Presbyterianism gave individual ambition a new role in the process of salvation, a sign of the human potential for good. For America, Finney claimed a new and optimistic religion based on the power of the individual.

Finney's preaching alarmed the Presbyterian establishment in the East, which feared the emotionalism and unorthodoxy of the revivals and Finney's influence in the new western areas. Among the eastern leaders was Lyman Beecher, pastor of the prestigious Hanover Street Presbyterian Church in Boston. Like many New Englanders of his era, Beecher was convinced that America's future greatness lay in transferring New England culture and its orthodoxy westward. Finney represented a dangerous threat to that orthodoxy. In 1832, Beecher moved his family to the new boomtown of the West, Cincinnati, where he wrote *A Plea for the West*, in which he predicted that the final battle of the Christ and the Antichrist would take place in the American West.

Despite their differences, both Beecher and Finney helped democratize American Christianity as champions of the Second Great Awakening. By emphasizing individual free will and

Continued

>> **AMERICAN PORTRAIT**
Continued

the possibility of salvation through good works, Finney's religious teachings held much broader social and political implications. He railed against the evils of alcohol and tobacco. Women played a large role in his revivals, not only as organizers but also as public speakers—a controversial practice. He was also a fierce opponent of slavery. The revivals of the Second Great Awakening helped lay the groundwork for the reform movements that would characterize much of the early and mid-nineteenth century. In this regard, Charles Finney was emblematic of his day. He went on to become president of Oberlin College, a religious institution that also stood as a bastion of women's rights and antislavery ideals. Many of the listeners Finney inspired would go on to become giants of social and political reform, some of whom were more concerned with the explosive issues of the times than with saving their souls.

Perfectionism and the Theology of Human Striving

There was nothing about the depth of Charles Grandison Finney's faith, or its centrality to his life and identity, to set him apart from many others in early nineteenth-century America. The profound revivals of the turn of the century were continuing into the 1830s and set the terms in which many people understood themselves and their world. Some Americans looked at the changes of the preceding decades and saw a nation on the verge of losing its moral compass. Convinced that the day of final reckoning grew near, they preached doom and withdrew from society into covenanted communities to prepare themselves for the end of time. Others remained hopeful that the nation could yet be redeemed. These reformers believed that it was the responsibility of each individual to work actively to perfect American society. Both reformers and separatists, however, shared the conviction that social life should be modeled on the principles of Protestant Christianity (see Map 11–1).

Millennialism and Communitarians

Separatist communities were not new to the American spiritual landscape in these years, and they never accounted for more than a minority of the American people. Nevertheless, they enjoyed renewed success in the 1820s. As a group, these religious communitarians sought to create more perfect societies on earth by withdrawing from daily contact with their neighbors and instituting tightly controlled spiritual, social, and economic regimens.

One of the earliest of these religious communities was the United Society of Believers in Christ's Second Appearing, a radical branch of Quakerism. This group was dubbed "Shakers" by its critics, for the "[d]ancing, singing, leaping, clapping . . . , groans and sighs" that characterized its services. Shakerism was rooted in the experiences of Ann Lee, a late eighteenth-century English factory worker and lay preacher who

OUTLINE

Perfectionism and the Theology of Human Striving
  Millennialism and Communitarians
  The Benevolent Empire

AMERICA AND THE WORLD:
  The American Board of Commissioners for Foreign Missions

Reform and the Urban Classes
  Wage Dependency and Labor Protest

PRIMARY SOURCE:
  Charles Dickens Describes Five Points, NYC
  A New Urban Middle Class

TECHNOLOGY AND IDEAS:
  Textile Mills

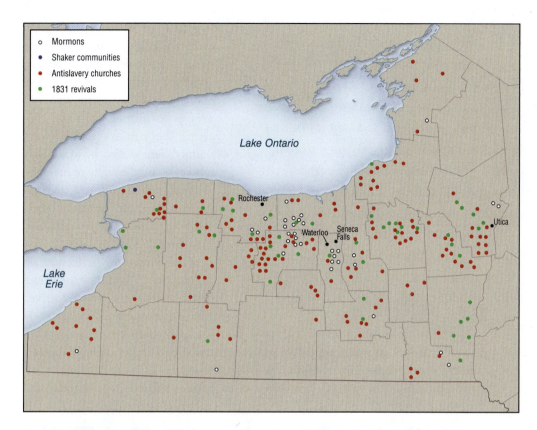

Map 11-1 Revival and Reform Social and economic transformation, religious revival, and social reform movements went hand in hand in the antebellum North. The so-called burned-over district of New York (the region directly served by the Erie Canal) nurtured numerous millennial sects (including Mormons and Shakers), Antimasonry, Finneyite revivals, and antislavery activism, as well as the Seneca Falls Woman's Rights Convention.

believed that she was the second, female embodiment of the Messiah. Lee preached that believers should return to the simplicity and purity of the early Christian church, pooling their worldly resources, withdrawing from the vanities of society, and observing celibacy. The Shakers migrated to North America in 1774 and established their first community near Watervliet, New York. "Mother" Ann died in 1784, but by the turn of the century the Shakers had established a dozen communities in New England. Moving west, they established four settlements in Ohio and Kentucky. By the 1830s, membership approached 4,000.

Shaker beliefs required a community based on a "union of faith, of motives, and of interest" of all members. To ensure this perfect unity, Shakers organized themselves into

AMERICAN LANDSCAPE:
  Freedom and Wage Labor
  Immigration and Nativism
  Internal Migration

Self-Reform and Social Regulation
  A Culture of Self-Improvement
  Temperance

The Common School Movement and Democracy
Penal Reform
Electoral Politics and Moral Reform

Women's Rights
  Women and Reform Movements
  The Seneca Falls Convention

Conclusion

> Almost all the religion in the world has been produced by revivals. God has found it necessary to take advantage of the excitability there is in mankind, to produce powerful excitements among them, before he can lead them to obey. Men are so sluggish, there are so many things to lead their minds off from religions, and to oppose the influence of the gospel, that it is necessary to raise an excitement among them, till the tide rises so high as to sweep away the opposing obstacles. They must be so excited that they will break over these counteracting influences, before they will obey God.
>
> CHARLES GRANDISON FINNEY,
> Lectures on Revivals of Religion, 1835

"families" of 30 to 100 members, each of which was supervised by a panel of eight people (two women and two men to oversee spiritual matters, and two men and two women to oversee temporal concerns). The "families" within a community were guided by a ministry (also composed equally of men and women), and the individual communities submitted to the authority of a head ministry at New Lebanon, New York.

Their search for perfection led the Shakers to repudiate the values of the increasingly market-driven American economy. Although Shakers sold goods to outsiders, they rejected materialism and competitive individualism, allocating individual labor according to the needs of the community. This alternative political and economic arrangement resulted in prosperity and innovation. Shaker gardeners developed the first

Shakers Outsiders labeled members of the United Society of Believers in Christ's Second Appearing "Shakers" after the active twirling and shaking movements that accompanied their services.

American seed industry, and Shaker farmers produced bumper crops of grain and bred large and healthy herds of dairy cattle.

Women appear to have been especially drawn to Shakerism, probably because of the Shaker belief in the spiritual equality of women and men. This was reflected in the organization of the communities, with "sisters" and "female elders" supervising the women's lives and "brothers" and "male elders" supervising the men's. The Shaker practice of celibacy afforded women freedom from the dangers of childbirth.

Like the Shakers, the followers of German farmer George Rapp rejected the private ownership of property and practiced celibacy. Believing that "the kingdom of Jesus Christ is approaching near," they considered it the responsibility of the truly devout to amass great material wealth to put at the disposal of Jesus Christ on his return to earth.

Rapp and several hundred followers arrived in North America in 1803 and migrated to western Pennsylvania, where they established the town of Harmony. They moved in 1815 to the banks of the Wabash River in Indiana Territory, where by 1824 their membership numbered 800. There they grew fruit, grain, and cotton; grazed sheep; and erected a cotton and woolen mill and a distillery. Unfortunately, the climate that made the Wabash hospitable to agriculture also made it hospitable to malaria. After years of malaria scourges, in 1824 the Rappites sold New Harmony to the English social reformer Robert Owen and returned to western Pennsylvania.

The largest and most long-lived of the millennial communities of the early nineteenth century was the Church of Jesus Christ of Latter-day Saints, also known as the Mormons, founded by Joseph Smith Jr. in 1830 (see Chapter 9). In addition to traditional Christian doctrine, the Mormon Articles of Faith included a belief "in the literal gathering of Israel and in the restoration of the Ten Tribes; that Zion (the New Jerusalem) will be built upon the American continent; that Christ will reign personally upon the earth; and, that the earth will be renewed and receive its paradisiacal glory."

Smith's preaching attracted rural followers, most of them displaced by the changing antebellum North. To them, Smith preached that it was God's will that they go forth into the wilderness to found the city of Zion, where they would reign over the coming millennium.

The opposition of their neighbors, who considered Mormon beliefs blasphemous, forced the Mormons to leave New York. Smith first moved his followers to Ohio, and then to Missouri. In 1839 a large group moved on to Illinois, founding the city of Nauvoo. By the early 1840s, Smith had begun to preach the doctrine of plural marriage. The Mormon community split, and anti-Mormon outrage flared anew. Smith was arrested and thrown in jail in Carthage, Illinois, where, on June 27, 1844, he was murdered by a mob (allegedly helped by a jail guard supported by leading citizens). In 1847, following Brigham Young, the Mormons left again, reaching the Great Salt Lake in the West. By 1850, hard work, irrigation, and careful cultivation had turned the desert into a garden paradise inhabited by more than 11,000 people.

The Benevolent Empire

Separatist millennialists were a relatively minor stream in the floods of religious organizing during the 1820s and 1830s. Far more numerous were the Americans who sought to perfect society by carrying the spirit of reform into their own communities. This massive evangelizing of America took many forms. Itinerant Methodists and

Salt Lake City The establishment of a Mormon settlement at Salt Lake City quickly became an important stop for westbound migrants, a place where they could rest and resupply their wagons before completing the journey.

Baptists continued to minister to newly settled churches in the backcountry. By the 1820s, however, even such great metropolises as Boston, Philadelphia, and New York became hothouses of evangelism.

The career of Presbyterian minister Ezra Stiles Ely reflects this shift in mainstream religious life. From 1811 to 1813, Ely was a chaplain for the Society for Supporting the Gospel, working with people who lived in public shelters. He led religious services, distributed Bibles, and prayed at the bedsides of the sick and dying, observing first-hand the growing poverty of American cities. After the War of 1812, he worked the shanties and tenements of New York's poor neighborhoods. He increasingly understood his mission to be not merely providing solace but also converting souls. Ely and other city missionaries believed they could only save people who were chosen by God, but they believed the elect were also among the poor.

"Every truly converted man turns from selfishness to benevolence," Charles Finney said, "and benevolence surely leads him to do all he can to save the souls of his fellow man." The new evangelical emphasis on personal agency soon fostered a

AMERICA AND THE WORLD

>> The American Board of Commissioners for Foreign Missions

The soldiers of the Benevolent Empire did not confine their attention to the United States. In 1810, in the earliest awakenings of the antebellum reform spirit, the General Assembly of Massachusetts (the governing body of the Massachusetts Congregational Church) created the American Board of Commissioners for Foreign Missions, an umbrella organization intended to promote Christian evangelizing in "heathen" lands around the world. The action came at the urging of a group of young Williams College students, who had pledged their lives to the project of "send[ing] the Gospel to the Pagans of Asia, and to the disciples of Mohammed."

Modeled on the London Missionary Society, the ABCFM sent out its first missionaries to Calcutta, India, in 1812, but other groups soon followed—to Hawaii, Turkey, and Palestine in 1819, to China in 1830, and to Africa in 1833. (By then, other Christian denominations in the United States had founded their own foreign missionary branches.) But "foreign" referred to the non-Christianized condition of the target communities, rather than literally to their residence in another country. From very early on the ABCFM sought "to extend the blessing of civilization and Christianity, in all their variety, to the Indian tribes within the limits of the United States." The most famous of these interventions was among the eastern Cherokees, where ABCFM influence encouraged acculturation and, later, voluntary removal.

As with other benevolent enterprises, the efforts of the ABCFM were funded through the donations of a vast network of local societies across the United States (particularly New England). Local supporters sponsored speakers, solicited donations, and produced a stream of pamphlets and letters to the editor on the importance of carrying Christianity to the "ignorant" people of other lands. By mid-century, the foreign missionary movement may

well have been the largest of the undertakings of the Benevolent Empire.

The ABCFM, like other Christian missionary enterprises, consistently linked Christianity with United States culture, and its evangelizing focused as much on teaching the mores of western European society as on the Christian gospel. Making the Christian Bible accessible to non–English speakers involved ABCFM agents in educational and translation projects and sometimes in the creation of a written language for a nonliterate culture. ABCFM schools taught American standards of conduct and dress, as well as the English language. Mission hospitals introduced American medicine. The practice of sending married couples meant that missionary communities replicated American norms of domesticity. In 1817 the Board founded its own school, the Foreign Mission School in Cornwall, Connecticut, for educating converts to return to their own lands as missionaries of Christianity and United States civilization.

Continued

Even as it intervened in the cultures of other societies, discouraging traditional customs and replacing them with the social and religious norms of the United States, the ABCFM shaped Americans' views of other parts of the world. Missionaries constantly wrote letters home. In 1821 the ABCFM founded the magazine *Missionary Herald*, which featured the reports of missionaries. The Board also subsidized the publication of missionaries' recollections of their sojourns abroad. These pages came alive with strange and dangerous customs in exotic places, where ignorant people "jabber[ed] in their horrid jargon," worshiped "idol gods," and lived at "the lowest depths of sin and depravity."

American missionaries in Asia sometimes wrote criticisms of other imperial nations, especially Great Britain for its role in creating the Chinese opium trade (although rarely noted was the American participation in that commerce). Occasionally missionaries reflected critically on their own society. Encountering systems of bondage in other cultures, for example, a few ABCFM agents lamented the survival of slavery in the United States.

But the effect of the American mission movement was to portray the non-European world as a lost paradise, awaiting the arrival of its American rescuers. As one missionary to Hawaii wrote, in the non-Christian world even "the fruits and vegetables . . . taste of heathenism."

---

broad impulse for social reform, expressed in religious terms and organized through a network of charities and associations, often referred to as the Benevolent Empire.

The Benevolent Empire reflected Americans' love of organizing, a tendency observed by Frenchman Alexis de Tocqueville when he visited the United States in 1831–1832. Americans, Tocqueville wrote, "combine to . . . found seminaries, build churches, distribute books, and send missionaries to the antipodes. . . . [I]f they want to proclaim a truth or propagate some feeling by the encouragement of a great example, they form an association."

Local societies linked up into national umbrella groups. Among the largest of these were the American Bible Society (which distributed Bibles in cities and new settlements), the Female Moral Reform Society (devoted to reclaiming women from prostitution), and the American Board of Commissioners for Foreign Missions (which promoted missions in the West). Every major city fostered Bible groups, asylums to help the poor, houses of industry, orphanages, and humane societies, among other charitable organizations. By 1830, evangelicals had also created a Sunday school movement and a movement to prohibit the delivery of mail on the Christian Sabbath.

Benevolent societies combined emotional and rational approaches to reform. The method of the Benevolent Empire was moral suasion. Reformers believed that social change came about not from external rules but rather through the gradual internal awakening of individual moral purpose through personal contact, testimony, and (where needed) exhortation. Yet the Benevolent Empire soon resembled a bureaucratic corporation.

Founded in 1816 in New York by wealthy Christian men, the American Bible Society illustrates this paradox. The society consisted initially of a volunteer board of managers who hired out the printing of Bibles. By 1832, the society was run by a professional staff in its own building in Manhattan. However, the society still depended on idealistic young ministers as its traveling agents and local volunteer organizations as its community contacts.

As they pursued their good deeds—distributing Bibles or religious tracts, praying with the sick—evangelicals came into intimate contact with the poor and ministered to their material needs. They arranged fuel deliveries and medical care, helped homeless families find lodging, and organized soup kitchens. Both men and women were engaged in the charitable associations of the early nineteenth century, but voluntary reform offered special opportunities for women. Women had already been active in organizing maternal societies to improve their parenting habits and Bible societies to discuss their moral failings. By the second decade of the nineteenth century, women were becoming active in the Sunday school movement and founding orphan asylums, homes for wayward girls, and asylums for "respectable" homeless adults. By the 1830s, women were the acknowledged volunteer backbone of the Benevolent Empire.

Reform and the Urban Classes

As well as addressing purely spiritual concerns, the religious organizing of the early nineteenth century also reflected worries about secular life. These concerns focused largely on the cities, where the market revolution and immigration opened huge rifts between the haves and the have-nots.

Wage Dependency and Labor Protest

By 1830, in response to growing markets, master craftsmen had subdivided the production process into smaller, discrete tasks, sending part production (of shoes, hats, or shirts) to outworkers who worked from home and were paid by the number of pieces they completed rather than the hours they worked. In house, employers relied more and more on apprentices or poorly trained helpers, who worked more cheaply than journeymen. As work was subdivided, workers became more interchangeable, and their wages dropped.

The Panic of 1819 had thrown thousands of people out of work, driving wages down and prices up. The reviving economy of the 1820s did not reverse those trends, which were deepened by depressions in 1829 and 1837. In an 1833 appeal, workers in Manayunk, Pennsylvania, protested 14½-hour days in "overheated" rooms "thick with the dust and small particles of cotton, which we are constantly inhaling to the destruction of our health, our appetite, and strength." "Our wages," they declared, "are barely sufficient to supply us with the necessaries of life."

The lives of outwork seamstresses, of whom there were tens of thousands in the eastern cities, were even more harrowing. Philadelphia philanthropist Mathew Carey estimated the wages of Philadelphia seamstresses at $1.25 a week, but a committee of seamstresses revealed that they were lucky to earn $1.12 a week. After rent, they were left with a little more than a nickel a day for food, clothing, heat, and anything else they needed.

By 1830 the urban Northeast was witnessing the damages of wage dependency and the subdivision of labor. In the largest cities, neighborhoods had become stratified by class. The New York neighborhood of Five Points, once a thriving community of master craftsmen and trade shops, by 1829 was home to prostitutes, beggars, public drunks, thieves, and confidence men. High rents crowded whole working families into single unventilated rooms. Many went homeless or threw up shanties.

The organizing begun in the 1820s exploded in the 1830s, both among craft workers and in occupations long excluded from craft recognition. When the Philadelphia Mechanics' Union dissolved, leadership passed to the New England Association of Farmers, Mechanics, and Other Workingmen, founded in 1831 by, among others, Seth Luther. The association used its newspaper, the *New England Artisan*, for worker self-education and organizing.

>> Charles Dickens Describes Five Points, NYC

Charles Dickens, the English writer and speaker, visited New York City in 1842 and made the following notes on his impression of Broadway and the Five Points district. He published them as American Notes. *Dickens had already gained fame and fortune as a novelist with such works as* David Copperfield, Oliver Twist, *and* Great Expectations. *This travelogue was part of a long tradition of writers making observations about the great American experiment.*

This is the place: these narrow ways, diverging to the right and left, and reeking everywhere with dirt and filth. Such lives as are led here, bear the same fruits here as elsewhere. The coarse and bloated faces at the doors, have counterparts at home, and all the wide world over. Debauchery has made the very houses prematurely old. See how the rotten beams are tumbling down, and how the patched and broken windows seem to scowl dimly, like eyes that have been hurt in drunken frays. Many of those pigs live here. Do they ever wonder why their masters walk upright in lieu of going on all-fours? and why they talk instead of grunting?

So far, nearly every house is a low tavern; and on the bar-room walls, are coloured prints of Washington, and Queen Victoria of England, and the American Eagle. Among the pigeon-holes that hold the bottles, are pieces of plate-glass and coloured paper, for there is, in some sort, a taste for decoration, even here. And as seamen frequent these haunts, there are maritime pictures by the dozen: of partings between sailors and their lady-loves, portraits of William, of the ballad, and his Black-Eyed Susan; of Will Watch, the Bold Smuggler; of Paul Jones the Pirate, and the like: on which the painted eyes of Queen Victoria, and of Washington to boot, rest in as strange companionship, as on most of the scenes that are enacted in their wondering presence.

What place is this, to which the squalid street conducts us? A kind of square of leprous houses, some

Five Points, in New York City Once the site of a thriving community of craft shops and smaller retailers, Five Points had become one of New York City's poorest neighborhoods and, as this drawing suggests, a symbol of urban poverty, immorality, and crime.

of which are attainable only by crazy wooden stairs without. What lies beyond this tottering flight of steps, that creak beneath our tread? . . . Ascend these pitch-dark stairs, heedful of a false footing on the trembling boards, and grope your way with me into this wolfish den, where neither ray of light nor breath of air, appears to come. . . .

Here too are lanes and alleys, paved with mud knee-deep, underground chambers, where they dance and game; the walls bedecked with rough designs of ships, and forts, and flags, and American eagles out of number: ruined houses, open to the street, whence, through wide gaps in the walls, other ruins loom upon the eye, as though the world of vice and misery had nothing else to show: hideous tenements which take their name from robbery and murder: all that is loathsome, drooping, and decayed is here. . . .

What is this intolerable tolling of great bells, and crashing of wheels, and shouting in the distance? A fire. And what that deep red light in the opposite direction? Another fire. And what these charred and blackened walls we stand before? A dwelling where a fire has been. It was more than hinted, in an official report, not long ago, that some of these conflagrations were not wholly accidental, and that speculation and enterprise found a field of exertion, even in flames: but be this as it may, there was a fire last night, there are two to-night, and you may lay an even wager there will be at least one, to-morrow. So, carrying that with us for our comfort, let us say, Good night, and climb up-stairs to bed.

Charles Dickens, *American Notes for General Circulation* (Paris: Baudry's European Library, 1842) pp. 109–111, 113.

Questions

1. What is Dickens's overall impression of Five Points—which was, at the time, one of America's worst slums?

2. Among the ills Dickens describes, which, if any, do you think were unique to the United States?

3. Do you think Dickens's observations are accurate, or do his writings reflect a prejudice? Why do you think so?

In February 1831, protest erupted in an unexpected quarter. With wages in sharp decline, over 1,800 tailoresses (women who worked in specific aspects of the tailoring craft) struck the New York garment industry. The tailoresses had been advised not to strike to avoid harsh public censure and to wait for times to improve. Sarah Monroe, the secretary of the union, resisted the advice: "Long have the poor tailoresses of this city borne their oppression in silence, until patience is no longer a virtue—and in my opinion to be silent longer would be a crime." The women drew up a constitution, elected officers, and stayed out on strike for five months.

Deteriorating labor conditions led to protest even in that industrial paradise, Lowell (see Chapter 9). After a decade of rapid expansion, the market stalled in 1834. When prices fell and owners cut wages by 12.5 percent, 800 female operatives walked off their jobs. The protest failed, but two years later, when owners tried to increase the price of company housing, 2,000 operatives went out on strike, forcing owners to rescind the increases. The 1836 victory was fleeting, however. Business was booming, and the owners had a vested interest in keeping the mills open. When business was slow or inventories high, workers would have far less power.

Workers tried to strengthen their position by forming regional and national associations. The most successful national association was the National Trades' Union (NTU), formed in 1834. The NTU survived for a number of years but was unable to effect statewide coordinated actions. In the end, much of its energy went into lobbying for currency reform, worker access to education and free land, and the 10-hour day.

A New Urban Middle Class

Seth Luther framed his criticisms of American industrial society as a struggle between the "producing classes" and the "rich." However, this was not an accurate description. The concept of the "producing classes" was ambiguous, encompassing Americans of many different standards of living and levels of wealth. For Luther, the term meant primarily urban households dependent on wage labor. Luther sometimes distinguished among the "poor," the "rich," and the "middling classes." Americans were proud of their great "middling" ranks of solid farmers and artisans. But the composition of the category had changed by the 1830s, as had its relation to the group Luther now called the "working classes."

These new middling classes were difficult to define exactly. Like the new working classes, the middling classes were primarily urban based. Middle-class households tended to receive their income as fees and salaries, rather than wages, and their paid workers held jobs that required mental, rather than physical, labor. These included doctors, lawyers, ministers, middle managers, agents, supervisors, tellers, clerks, shopkeepers, editors, writers, and schoolteachers.

The relationship of these urban households of moderate means to the new industrial economy was complicated. On the one hand, they were not immune to catastrophic economic reversal, whether sudden unemployment, business failure, or bad speculation. At the same time, the new middle class was created by and benefited from the industrial transformation. The paid occupations on which middle-class families depended had expanded enormously. These jobs brought annual salaries ranging roughly from $1,000 to $1,500, compared with the $300 to $400 an average working man might earn. Middle-class families also tended to have access to other resources through family, friends, and business connections.

The middle class celebrated the new political economy, the expansion of democracy, and the growth of individual opportunity even as it deplored the special privilege

TECHNOLOGY AND IDEAS

>> Textile Mills

Samuel Slater (1768–1835) was a pioneer in American textile mill design. Indeed, he not only introduced the machinery of textile production, but he also created an entirely new kind of "mill town" to provide labor for the industry. Without Slater's contribution, American clothing manufacturing would have developed far more slowly, leaving the country's customers dependent on imported English fabrics and clothing. Southern cotton producers would have had to send the raw cotton abroad. Because of Slater and those who followed his lead in America, the textile industry became the first great success story of industrialization in the North and provided a much closer and more profitable destination for southern cotton. The result was the beginning of a national market, with raw materials flowing to the northern mills and finished clothing going back to southern customers. Ironically, the larger plantation owners clothed their slaves in shirts, pants, and dresses manufactured in northern factories.

Born in Derbyshire, England, Slater was apprenticed as a youth to the Stutt cotton textiles mill where Richard Arkwright's newly designed machine frames were installed. The shuttles, driven by water power (water coursing over giant wheels connected to the machines by a sequence of gears), could weave raw cotton fiber into strands and combine them into fabrics that could next be assembled into finished pieces of clothing. English law forbade the export of the plans for these machines, but Slater memorized the plans and migrated to New England in 1789. Fast-running streams for water power and a surplus of labor (young people whose family farms were no longer productive) provided the basics for manufacturing there. In Pawtucket, Rhode Island, Slater found patrons William Almy and Smith Brown, and together they built America's first textile mill in 1793.

The Pawtucket works depended not only on the Arkwright machinery that Slater designed, but also on a new kind of workforce. Young people, often children, could carry the bobbins of thread and help in other ways. Women were employed at the mechanical spinning wheels. Men supervised the production on the factory "floor." The size and scale of the factory made it profitable. To ensure sufficient cheap labor, Slater created a veritable village around the mill. This "Rhode Island system" and later adaptations would be adopted in "mill towns" throughout the North, and, after the Civil War, throughout the southeast.

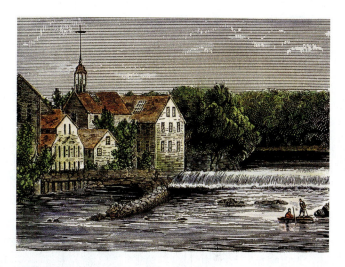

Slater's Textile Mill at Pawtucket, Rhode Island

In the 1830s and 1840s mill towns like that in Lowell, Massachusetts, used an outgrowth of Slater's "Rhode Island system," the "Waltham system." All stages of production took place under one roof, and the employees were young girls who lived away from their families in company housing. Lowell and similar towns outpaced even the Pawtucket works in terms of sheer output. This so-called first industrial revolution transformed the nature of work in manufacturing. After the mill girls began to organize and protest for better wages and conditions, the manufacturers in Lowell and other mill towns replaced them with immigrant workers. America's management-labor conflict had begun. Eventually, American manufacturing would not only equal its British competition, but exceed it in many areas. Samuel Slater's textile mill was part of that development.

Questions

1. Why did England try to prevent the spread of textile manufacturing technology?

2. What elements of late eighteenth-century American society and economy allowed Slater and his mill to succeed? How did changes in the mills in the nineteenth century mirror changes in the surrounding society?

AMERICAN LANDSCAPE

>> Freedom and Wage Labor

In the summer of 1832, only months before Andrew Jackson was elected for his second term as president, former Rhode Island carpenter Seth Luther traveled across New England denouncing the political economy of Jacksonian America. Journeying through Maine, New Hampshire, and Massachusetts, Luther condemned the "tyranny," "avarice," and "exclusive privilege" that drove "AMERICAN MANUFACTURE" and gave his sympathetic audiences a chilling picture of the havoc wrought in the lives of the "producing classes." He spoke of the 15-hour days and "the well-seasoned strap" of the boss—all for a mere 75 cents a day. He described adults exhausted and brutalized and children made "pale, sickly, haggard . . . from the worse than slavish confinement of the cotton mill." He told of one 11-year-old girl whose leg was shattered by an impatient supervisor wielding a stick of wood, and another child who had a board split over her head by "a heartless monster in the shape of an overseer of a cotton mill 'paradise.'" The mills were turning out vast quantities of cottons and woolens. But here, in the lives of workers, was the true product of "the AMERICAN SYSTEM," he jeered. It created a social order in which "manufactures must be sustained by injustice, cruelty, ignorance, vice, and misery," a system in which "the poor must work or starve" while "the rich . . . take care of themselves."

In some respects, Luther's harangue was simply the labor counterpart of a standard Jacksonian political speech. It rang with denunciations of wealth and special privilege, praised the worth and dignity of common people, demanded reform, and flamed with images of the impending Armageddon. However, Luther was speaking in 1832, not 1828, when the common man had presumably reigned triumphant for four years. Luther's exhortation that workers were free men in name only and must now rededicate their lives

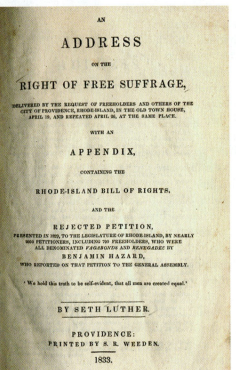

to "LIVE FREEMEN and DIE FREEMEN" hinted at deep failures in Jacksonian democracy.

In some respects, Luther's indictment seems unaccountable. Jackson's landslide 1828 election had brought together a remarkably diverse coalition, including southern planters and northern manufacturers, wage workers and entrepreneurs, and political pragmatists and at least some social and religious perfectionists. These groups represented very different interests, but in 1824 and 1828 they had found enough common ground to produce a clear majority behind the Jacksonian Democrats. By 1832, moreover, Jackson had done much to satisfy the voters. He had removed National Republican appointees. He had supported white claims to Indian lands in the West, opening hundreds of thousands of acres to new settlement. He was preparing to take on the Second Bank of the United States. In national presidential politics, the consensus held. Jackson was reelected in 1832, and his vice president succeeded him to the presidency in 1836.

But Jackson's first term had also revealed disturbing, unreconciled tensions within the new democratic political economy. These tensions arose in part from the very strengths of democracy and economic growth. The expansion of personal liberties created a society in which inequities were all the more obvious. Of all groups, white working men had experienced the most dramatic expansion of their political rights (and, in some respects, their economic independence) in the early nineteenth century. Yet, as Luther made clear, by 1832 many American workers (female, as well as male) felt threatened by the new industrial order. By the early 1830s, worker protests had become common, and working men's parties had begun to assume a more clearly oppositional stance. "The dignity of common labor" had become the rallying cry of protest.

Rather than taking to the streets, Americans of more middling means responded to the volatility of industrial society by attempting to withdraw from it. Although this new middle class continued to insist on the dignity of labor, it grew less certain that the laboring classes could claim this dignity. If workers were poor, perhaps they lacked ambition, were negligent, drank too much, or were irreligious. Criticisms soon focused especially on Irish immigrants, whose growing numbers revealed the virulent anti-Catholicism of many native-born Americans, middle class and working class alike.

of the wealthy. Deeply religious and committed to the doctrines of personal agency, middle-class citizens were churchgoers who both donated to and participated in the causes of the Benevolent Empire.

Individuals who aspired to urban middle-class status took far greater pains to distinguish themselves from the urban poor than from the rich. This was especially evident in their understanding of personal responsibility and material success. In sermons and tracts, children's books, and novels, members of the new middle class described the industrial economy as a test of personal character. Success demonstrated superior individual industriousness and self-discipline; failure signified the opposite. These beliefs took their toll on middle-class families that failed, bringing on social and psychological censure. Nevertheless, middle-class writers continued to hone the idiom of the "common man" into the more class-based language of the "self-made man" of business. From this point of view, the middle class was the repository of moderation in a changing world, the heir of Jefferson's idealized "husbandmen."

Meanwhile, middle-class families struggled to distinguish themselves from the working class. Middle-class parents recoiled from manual labor and urged their sons to become "a rich merchant, or a popular lawyer, or a broker." They expressed a new value for education, even for their daughters. Whereas workers crowded into smaller and smaller homes, the emerging middle class expressed itself in increasingly elaborate residential spaces. The ideal middle-class home, the "cottage," offered a private sitting room for the family and a separate "public" parlor for guests. The parlor was a stage on which the family could proclaim its success through a display of costly furnishings and decorations.

To emphasize their distance from the industrial world, members of the new urban middle class insisted on a "natural" division of temperament and capability between men and women. Although men were required to confront the degradations of labor, women were intended by nature to remain at home to restore the sensibilities of husbands and raise children protected from the ravages of industrialization.

This view of women as the primary influence on children represented a dramatic change in attitude. It was, however, largely inaccurate, as many middle-class women pursued paid labor. They took in boarders, did fancy sewing, opened schools, and worked in family-owned businesses. They all worked unpaid at the daily labor of cooking, cleaning, washing, ironing, preserving food, sewing, and caring for children. Domestic womanhood became the primary symbol of middle-class respectability and a bulwark against the contradictions of the new industrial society.

Immigration and Nativism

Facing enormous changes, even economically secure Americans were alert for sources of potential danger. Many labor leaders and utopians felt that industrialists were posing that danger. More common, however, was the tendency to focus anxieties on the poor, deemed incapable of achieving republican virtue. Immigrants became natural targets, and especially the Catholic Irish.

In spite of the difficulties facing wage workers, the robust economy drew increasing numbers of immigrants from Europe, 90 percent of whom came from England, Germany, or Ireland. The largest group by far was Irish. Plagued by chronic poverty and harsh British rule, almost 60,000 Irish immigrants arrived in the 1820s, 235,000 in the 1830s, and 845,000 during the potato famines of the 1840s. Through most of the period, the Irish accounted for more than one-third of all immigrants.

Their customs and their poverty made Irish immigrants conspicuous. Unable to afford land, they remained crowded in the seaports where they arrived. Desperate, they often had to accept jobs and conditions that native-born workers scorned. With no other place to go, one boss observed, the Irish could "be relied on at the mill all year round."

Not all of the Irish went into mills. Many built roadways, dredged river bottoms, and built canals. Irish women cooked and did laundry for the camps or hired out as domestic workers in middle-class households.

Most of all, the Irish were distinguished by their Catholic religion. By 1830, immigration had virtually doubled the number of Catholics in the country. Not all Catholics were Irish, but many were, making the Irish visible targets of long-standing anti-Catholic prejudices. Anti-Irish stereotypes represented Catholics as given to superstition and unthinking obedience. Funded by the new middle class and supported by Protestant ministers, anti-Catholic newspapers charged the Catholic hierarchy with "tyrannical and unchristian" acts "repugnant to our republican institutions."

By the early 1830s, anti-Catholicism spilled over into street violence. Organizations such as the New York Protestant Association sponsored "public discussions" on the immorality of monks, the greed of priests, and the pope's alleged designs on the American West. The debates would deteriorate into small riots. Anti-Catholicism was especially strong in Massachusetts. In 1834, the associated Congregational Clergy of Massachusetts issued a frantic challenge to Protestants to rescue the republic from "the degrading influence of Popery." Sermons and editorials whipped up a frenzy of anti-Catholic fear. The hysteria was aimed at a convent in Charlestown, Massachusetts, in which, purportedly, nuns were brainwashing innocent Protestant students. On the night of August 11, 1834, a cheering mob burned the convent to the ground. Anti-Catholicism was beginning to serve as a bond among Americans who otherwise had little in common with one another.

> It is a fact, that Popery is opposed in its very nature to Democratic Republicanism; and it is, therefore, as a political system, as well as religious, opposed to civil and religious liberty, and consequently to our form of government. . . .
>
> SAMUEL F. B. MORSE,
> 1835

Internal Migration

The constant stream of internal migrants also heightened the sense of turmoil in antebellum American society. Strong internal migration signaled growth and opportunity, but it also produced a steady flow of individuals who seemed to have no settled stake in American society.

Many of these were westward settlers, but many were marginalized rural folks seeking employment in the cities. There was both a push and a pull to this movement. Children were pushed out from farming families whose land could no longer support them. They were pulled to the cities by the same conditions that destroyed the artisan tradition: the breakdown of the apprentice system and the subdivision of skills.

In the cities, these young people often lived in rented rooms without adult guidance. Young men joined neighborhood fire companies that served as gathering places for fun and sport. Young women navigated the city unescorted. Young people used their earnings to buy the things unavailable in the countryside: new shoes, clothing of the latest cut, hats, and canes. Migrants usually traveled fairly short distances to the nearest large towns and cities and swelled the populations of the midsized cities in which most American manufacturing took place. Reading, Pennsylvania, was a hub for regional manufacturing, transportation, and trading. In the 1840s, Reading's population doubled to 15,000 people. Nearly half of its unskilled laborers had come from within 25 miles, from areas with poor land and big families.

The constant migration of Americans westward provoked alarm among the eastern, urban middle class. Moralistic observers worried that this migration was draining ambitious, upright citizens from the East Coast, leaving the dregs of society behind. Observers also worried about the influence of the West on future American citizens. The West lacked the institutions that easterners associated with civilization and civic responsibility. There were few schools and churches and too many unattached young men, saloons, and brothels. Moreover, westward migration stood for the materialism and greed that easterners were beginning to worry about. The desire for money drove some families on an almost endless migration. One family, the Shelbys, had made four moves west by 1850, when they ended up in Oregon.

Into this troubling land were being born more and more of the nation's young. Once families had begun to pour in, fertility rates in the newly settled areas became far higher than they were in the older, coastal regions. Easterners were alarmed by the specter of a generation of children growing up in the wilderness without proper social constraints. The values of self-reliance, industry, and civic virtue, which only a decade before had seemed to capture the essence of American nationalism, appeared in danger of disappearing. By the 1820s, these fears were being focused on the growing waves of European immigrants.

Self-Reform and Social Regulation

In his address to working men in 1832, Seth Luther explained that he would uncover "principles and practices which will, if not immediately eradicated and forsaken, destroy all the rights, benefits, and privileges intended for our enjoyment, as a free people." Earlier reformers had been far more optimistic. Faced with deep divisions and seemingly impossible obstacles to an ideal industrial society, reformers began to turn away from broad programs of social perfection to endeavors that centered on self-control and external restraint.

A Culture of Self-Improvement

Answering criticisms from fellow senators that only the rich and well-connected enjoyed the benefits of the new American industrial order, in 1832 Henry Clay rose to defend the entrepreneurial class. "In Kentucky," he asserted, "almost every manufactory known to me is in the hands of enterprising and self-made men, who have acquired whatever wealth they possess by patient and diligent labor." Clay's emphasis on personal enterprise captured a perspective increasingly shared by ambitious Americans by the 1830s. Success or failure was less a matter of external injustice and constraint than of individual striving. Those who truly worked hard—who were industrious and clever and frugal—would succeed.

> We must neither feel nor act as if all progress was ended, and man had attained all the perfection of which he is capable. . . . Everywhere one part of our fellow beings are wasting away in luxury, indolence, listlessness, and dissipation; and another part pining in wants and neglect, devoured by discontent and envy; and when we see this can call it neither good nor necessary. We ask that it may be cured, and we turn to the future with full faith that it will be.
>
> ORESTES BROWNSON,
> 1835

The culture of self-improvement was particularly popular among members of the new middle class. The emphasis on self-creation helped to resolve their ambivalence about industrial society: middle-class families had escaped the worst ravages of wage labor not because they were lucky or had some special advantage but because they worked harder.

The culture of self-improvement embraced the body as well. From the 1820s to the 1840s, health reform became a national obsession, as Americans experimented with new diets, clothing, exercise programs, abstinence, and hydropathy, the cleansing of the body through frequent bathing and drinking of water.

Middle-class men and women crowded lectures and devoured writings that espoused the philosophy of self-culture. By 1831 the lyceum movement claimed several thousand local organizations under a national association and sponsored such speakers as the writer Ralph Waldo Emerson, Daniel Webster, and later Abraham Lincoln. Meanwhile, middle-class readers supported a publishing bonanza in novels, periodicals, and tracts devoted to self-improvement.

Lyceum Movement Americans' enormous interest in self-improvement in the antebellum years was reflected in their enthusiasm for public lectures, known as the lyceum movement. This cartoon gently spoofed a lecture by James Pollard Espy, a meteorologist. As the drawing suggests, women were prominent in lyceum audiences.

These publications promoted a variety of images of the self-made American. In his *Leatherstocking Tales*, James Fenimore Cooper celebrated the pioneer. Novels like Catharine Sedgwick's *The Poor Rich Man, and the Rich Poor Man* romanticized urban poverty and suggested that hard work put "true wealth" (virtue) within the reach of even the most humble family.

Although in most cases the myth of the self-made American was decidedly male, it also had important implications for women. On the one hand, it highlighted the importance of childrearing. Periodicals such as the *Ladies Magazine* and *Godey's Lady's Book* and advice books such as Lydia Maria Child's *The Mother at Home* and William Alcott's *The Young Mother* instructed women on the development of the proper mental and moral habits in the young. On the other hand, a generation of female novelists appropriated the themes of self-culture to emphasize female self-reliance. In her 1827 novel *A New-England Tale*, Sedgwick told the story of a young orphan left penniless by an improvident wealthy father and a pampered mother. Jane, the protagonist, learns that hard work builds both economic independence and strength of character and is appropriately rewarded with a prosperous husband, children, and a safe middle-class home.

Lydia Maria Child The author of many books, including *The Frugal Housewife*, Lydia Maria Child fought against slavery and for the rights of Native Americans.

Some writers mounted a determined assault on the new American political and economic order. Transcendentalists such as Ralph Waldo Emerson, Margaret Fuller, and William Ellery Channing believed in the power of the independent mind not only to understand the material environment but also to achieve a spiritual wholeness with the world. They saw that, in contemporary America, self-improvement was often cultivated only for immediate material gain. In his essay "Self-Reliance" (1841), Emerson tried to distinguish true independence of mind from slavish rushing after privilege and celebrity. Although Emerson was a professional man, not a laborer, in many respects his critiques echoed the themes of Seth Luther.

Temperance

Of the many movements for regulating the body, the largest by far—and the longest lived—was the temperance movement. By the 1840s hundreds of thousands of Americans had taken the pledge to swear off demon rum.

Prior to the nineteenth century, liquor played a central role in the lives of Americans. The Puritans (even ministers) had insisted on having their supply of wine, beer, and hard cider, and in craft shops, workers took rum breaks from their labor.

Some religious groups, especially the Quakers and the Methodists, had opposed the drinking of hard liquor in the eighteenth century, but it was only in 1808, in Saratoga, New York, that the first temperance society was formed. Within the next five years, at least four more temperance societies were established in New England.

In the 1820s, the temperance movement was taken over by evangelicals who saw demon rum as the enemy not just of piety but of the self-control essential to the perfection of society. Evangelists began to depict drinking as a sign of social disorder. In a series of six sermons preached in 1825, Lyman Beecher effectively changed the debate over alcohol. He did not call for absolute abstinence, and he urged his followers

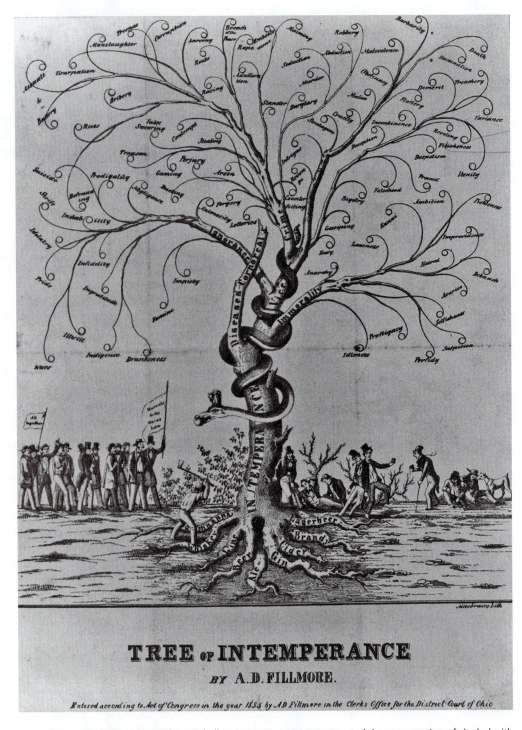

Temperance Movement This antebellum temperance cartoon equated the consumption of alcohol with any number of physical and moral disorders. Even some of those who sympathized with the movement thought it was too moralistic.

to form voluntary associations to drive the demon rum from American society. The following February saw the formation of the American Society for the Promotion of Temperance (ASPT). The ASPT quickly set about organizing local chapters across the country. By 1834 there were at least 5,000 state and local temperance societies.

The Common School Movement and Democracy

By the 1830s, workers, members of the new middle class, and elite philanthropists all identified education as a critical arena for reform. As in other reform movements, however, the motives of different groups varied widely.

Since the founding of the nation, educational opportunities for the sons and daughters of prosperous parents had steadily increased. Children from wealthy urban families had private tutors, followed (for boys) by training in private seminaries and academies. By the 1820s, young women from prosperous northern families could choose from a growing number of seminaries. Meanwhile, subscription schools offered basic education to rural children.

These schools were out of reach for working-class children. Labor reformers linked this lack of schooling directly to the larger process of industrial oppression. In their 1831 constitution, the Working Men's Association of New York placed the demand for "a system of equal, republican education" above every other goal, because education "secures and perpetuates every political right we possess." Seth Luther blasted industrialization for preventing workers "from a participation in the fountains of knowledge." Reformers had founded charity schools in many eastern cities, but workers saw these as inferior. Only free public education, workers argued, could defy "the siege of aristocracy."

Many middle-class parents were also unable to afford private academies. In 1830, fathers in Utica, New York, called for a public school system that would permit children to "keep pace with the age in its improvements" and "calculate their own profits in the world."

Middle-class parents were anxious about daughters, as well as sons. They worried that traditional housewifery skills would be of little use to daughters who faced an increasingly complex market culture and new domestic technologies. Most of all, they worried that their daughters might not marry or might marry into families that would face financial ruin. Concerned that expanded suffrage would introduce volatility into the American electoral process, reformers often supported expanded public education as "the great bulwark of republican government," in the words of New York governor De Witt Clinton. If white working men and their sons were to vote, it was important that they first be educated.

This convergence of interests led to a growing demand for more common schools. Nevertheless, broad segments of the public resisted the idea. In Cincinnati, wealthy property owners opposed paying taxes to send poor children to school. Other skeptics considered the whole idea an invasion of their rights as free citizens. States were often left to passing simple enabling legislation such as Pennsylvania's 1834 act that made public schools a local option.

In 1837 the Massachusetts legislature went further, creating a state board of education and appointing educational reformer Horace Mann as its first secretary. Mann addressed the anxieties of more prosperous Americans. On the one hand, he reassured middle-class parents that relying on an extrafamilial institution was both right and natural, given the changing society. On the other hand, he assured them that nothing else need change about the industrial society on which they depended. Poverty, he wrote, was not decreed by God nor required by American society. Only the lack of education barred the poor from prosperity, and benevolence and education would "disarm the poor of their hostility toward the rich."

Whites were less concerned about the potential hostility of the small free African American community. Until the 1850s, free African American children were excluded from public common schools, and tax monies were not used to establish schools for them. Education for free black children came almost entirely from the work of the free African American community. In the North, the efforts bore fruit, but in the South, opposition to the education of slaves hardened. In fact, many enslaved and free African American southerners did learn to read and write, but usually surreptitiously.

Penal Reform

In the first years of the republic, with memories of British injustice still fresh, Americans tended to think of crime as a problem of bad laws, not flawed people. Fair laws would nurture good republican character, and good republican citizens would respect laws they had had a hand in passing.

Yet by the 1820s eastern cities were incarcerating thousands of citizens—some for debt but many for robbery, larceny, fraud, vagrancy, and disorderly conduct. To many Americans—especially members of the middle class—it seemed that good laws were not sufficient to create a good citizenry. Like salvation, law-abiding behavior was a function of individual effort. Where individuals failed to obey the law, the community must devise some mechanism for its own protection.

The most popular solution from the 1820s on was the establishment of state prison systems, where deviant individuals could be kept apart from the community but could also be rehabilitated. State and city prisons soon began to replace older charity institutions. The two primary models, devised by New York and Pennsylvania, were variants on a single principle: the first step in making prisons places of real reform was to prevent inmates from influencing one another.

The New York version became most widely associated with the penitentiary at Ossining, New York, known as Sing Sing. There, prisoners worked side by side all day but were prevented from talking or even looking at one another. They slept in separate cells. The Pennsylvania model called for absolute isolation of the prisoners.

Visitors often toured these prisons and frequently applauded them, but they also noted the exaggerated hopes that Americans seemed to invest in them. The French visitor Alexis de Tocqueville observed of American reformers: "They have caught the monomanie of the penitentiary system, which to them seems to remedy for all the evils of society."

Electoral Politics and Moral Reform

Frustrated with the seeming resistance of social problems to moral suasion, reformers turned increasingly to electoral politics for solutions. The effect was to fragment and weaken party organization rather than to consolidate it. The political landscape became littered with specialized and often largely local parties, demonstrating the inability of the major parties to address basic social conflicts.

Nowhere was possession of the vote more important than among newly enfranchised white male workers. During the struggles of the 1820s and 1830s, laboring people believed that many of their problems would be remedied only through electoral action. As long as the economic power of employers was backed by laws that oppressed workers (debt laws that imprisoned them, bankruptcy laws that took their property, conspiracy laws that made union organizing illegal), strikes and petitions would never be enough.

By the late 1820s workers had begun to mobilize politically. In 1827 a group of workers in Philadelphia formed the Mechanics' Union of Trade Associations. Within a year that group became the Philadelphia Working Men's Party, a new political party dedicated to "the interests and enlightenment of the working classes." Over the next five years, under various names, the movement spread through most of the nation, becoming strongest in northern cities.

Workers were at a political crossroads. On the one hand, the formation of the Working Men's Party implied that workers were still optimistic that change was possible and that working men thought of themselves as citizens with the right and power to affect the makeup of the republic in such issues as public education, broadened incorporation laws, an end to imprisonment for debt, and banking reform. On the other hand, the organization of a separate political party indicated that workers remained deeply skeptical of the responsiveness of existing parties. Workers were moving toward a distinct identity within the new political economy.

In the winter of 1835–1836 anger at the legal system came to a head. With inflation and unemployment running high, New York City journeymen tailors went out on strike. The leaders of the union were arrested, tried, convicted on conspiracy charges, and fined. The labor press denounced the courts as "the tool of the aristocracy, against the people!" Nearly 30,000 people (the largest crowd in American history to that date) protested the convictions. The protestors resolved to meet the following fall in Utica, New York, to organize a "separate and distinct" political party to represent workers' interests. The 93 "workers, farmers, and mechanics" who met in Utica six months later voted to form the Equal Rights Party.

Labor movements in other states also began to focus on legislative reform. The 10-hour day, a long-standing demand, reemerged in the late 1840s as a central point of labor organizing. Workers in New England supported candidates friendly to the 10-hour day, petitioned legislatures for laws setting work hours, and testified before legislative committees. Female workers testified as well, using their life stories to create sympathy for the cause. It was male workers, however, who had the power to vote representatives out of office.

Other reform movements also began to focus on electoral strategies. The Female Moral Reform Society, which had long worked to redeem prostitutes from their sins, shifted strategies and began working for the passage of rent laws and property protections for women. This growing emphasis on legal reform grew out of an enhanced sense of connection between the reformer and the recipient of her aid.

Throughout the 1840s, temperance workers turned increasingly toward the passing of state laws. Among some temperance advocates (especially females), the shift was motivated by concern for legal protections for the wives and families of alcoholic men. But the use of legal strategies also expressed a growing belief on the part of middle-class, native-born reformers that alcoholism was a problem of the unruly immigrant working classes. As they identified drinkers as fundamentally different from themselves, temperance workers grew less interested in aiding drinkers directly and more willing to take recourse to legal controls.

Women's Rights

Many of the antebellum reform movements generated widespread controversy and passionate disagreement. But no others touched the central nerve of society like the organized abolition movement after 1830 (see Chapter 12) and the women's rights movement. Race and gender, it seemed to many Americans, were defining their nation and society.

Women and Reform Movements

Women from all classes and ranks in antebellum society were beginning to chafe under cultural and legal restrictions on their full autonomy as Americans. The young women workers who marched at Lowell called themselves "daughters of freemen" and edged closer to claiming an independent status as citizens, as did the tailoresses, who were tired of waiting for chivalry to improve their lot. Educated women and women who worked as authors, editors, and educators participated actively in the public discourse and profoundly influenced public opinion. Were they to be regarded as mere subordinates to fathers and husbands?

For many women, the growing importance of suffrage and electoral tactics to reform movements created a new consciousness of their precarious status. Reform work permitted women to participate in shaping the new democratic order and to perfect skills useful in civic culture. They ran meetings, kept track of money and records, and honed their skills at public speaking. Elite women involved in charities also learned to make use of the new institutions of the market revolution. Because married women could not hold property or make contracts in their own names, most women would have had trouble accumulating the money to fund asylums and schools. But these married women, wives and daughters of wealthy and influential men, could use their social position to obtain donations, endorsements, and even special charters (comparable to those granted to male entrepreneurs) that permitted a group of married women to function legally as males.

Reform women soon learned that there were limits to their authority. Even women who were involved in the mildest of reform activities (e.g., as members of the American Bible Society) were rebuked for "acting out of their appropriate sphere." Women engaged in more controversial activities such as labor reform or abolition work were heckled and hounded by mobs.

In 1837, in her *Essay on Slavery and Abolitionism*, Catharine Beecher attacked female abolitionists for violating the bounds of "rectitude and propriety" and for being motivated by unwomanly "ambition." The same year, the Massachusetts clergy criticized Sarah and Angelina Grimké (members of the southern planter class who were touring the North in the abolitionist cause) for daring to take "the place and tone of man as public reformer."

By the late 1830s women involved in abolition work were subjected to growing criticism from within. Although William Lloyd Garrison remained a staunch ally, other leaders, such as Arthur and Lewis Tappan, believed that outspoken, assertive women were embarrassing the movement. For women who had given years of their labor and had endangered their lives in the cause of abolition, these attacks were galling. Disappointing, too, was the willingness of such men to abandon the old moral-reform strategies, which embraced gender equality. The turn toward electoral reform reduced women to second-class status in the movement. They could still raise money, lobby, and speak, but they could not perform the new essential act of reform, voting.

The Seneca Falls Convention

After the 1840 division of the American Anti-Slavery Society over women's participation, abolitionist women spearheaded a drive for an organized women's rights movement. In Seneca Falls, New York, on July 14, 1848, five women (including the seasoned Quaker abolitionist Lucretia Mott and the much younger Elizabeth Cady Stanton) placed an advertisement in the Seneca County Courier stating, "A convention to discuss the social, civil and religious condition and rights of woman will be held in the Wesleyan Chapel, Seneca Falls, New York, on Wednesday and Thursday, the 19th and 20th of July current, commencing at 10 a.m."

The response was overwhelming. On July 19, 300 people (including perhaps 40 men, among them the famous abolitionist Frederick Douglass) showed up. The group debated, voted on, and passed a Declaration of Sentiments (modeled after the Declaration of Independence) and a list of resolutions. They demanded specific social and legal changes for women, including a role in lawmaking, improved property rights, equity in divorce, and access to education and the professions. All of the resolutions passed unanimously but one: a demand for the vote. Even as reform became ever more tied to electoral strategies, some reformers considered suffrage too radical for women.

Seneca Falls Convention Commemorative Stamp The Seneca Falls Convention is regarded by many as the beginning of the women's rights movement. In recognition of the convention's place in American history, the United States Postal Service issued this stamp commemorating its centennial along with three of the movement's most prominent leaders.

We hold these truths to be self-evident: that all men and women are created equal; that they are endowed by their Creator with certain inalienable rights; that among these are life, liberty, and the pursuit of happiness. . . .

This history of mankind is a history of repeated injuries and usurpations on the part of man toward woman, having in direct object the establishment of an absolute tyranny over her. To prove this, let facts be submitted to a candid world.

He has never permitted her to exercise her inalienable right to the elective franchise.

He has compelled her to submit to laws, in the formation of which she had no voice.

He has withheld from her rights which are given to the most ignorant and degraded men—both native and foreigner.

Having deprived her of this first right of a citizen, the elective franchise, thereby leaving her without representation in the halls of legislation, he has oppressed her on all sides.

He has made her, if married, in the eye of the law, civilly dead.

He has taken from her all right in property, even to wages she earns.

He has made her, morally, an irresponsible being. . . .

He has endeavored, in every way he could, to destroy her confidence in her own powers, to lessen her self-respect and to make her willing to lead a dependent and abject life.

"Declaration of Sentiments,"
Seneca Falls Woman's Rights Convention, 1848

Conclusion

When Andrew Jackson took office in 1828, he declared his mission to be "reform." Jackson, of course, meant reform of America's political society and, specifically, personal revenge on the politicians who had earlier denied him the presidency. By the time Jackson left office in 1836, and in the years after, Americans had taken the cause of reform into their own hands. For some, it was a purifying mission, returning the nation to its founding promises of justice and equality. For others, it was an impossible task, tearing apart the fabric of the democracy. In the nation's short history, the West had always functioned as the republic's social and cultural release. Soon that symbol of reconciliation and prosperity would become the site of America's insoluble conflicts.

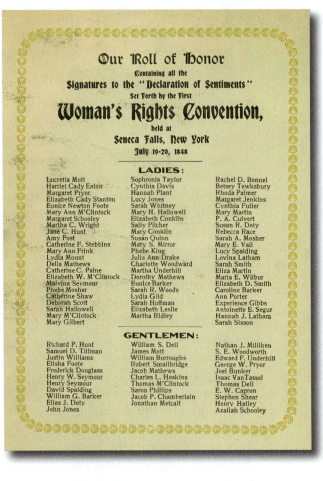

Who, What

Finneyite   373

Lucretia Mott   397

Benevolent Empire   377

Lyceum movement   390

Moral suasion   380

Perfectionism   374

Revivals   374

>> TIME LINE

▼1824

Rappites sell New Harmony to Robert Owen and return to Pennsylvania, establishing third community, Economy

Charles Grandison Finney begins preaching in upstate New York

▼1825

Owen establishes New Harmony labor reform community

▼1826

American Society for the Promotion of Temperance formed

▼1830

Shakers support 60 communities

Joseph Smith organizes the Church of Jesus Christ of Latter-day Saints

▼1831

New England Association of Farmers, Mechanics, and Other Workingmen founded

New York Protestant Association founded

Lyceum movement begins

▼1831–1832

Alexis de Tocqueville visits United States

▼1832

Maria Stewart lectures in Boston

Review Questions

1. What conditions gave rise to labor protest in the 1820s and 1830s? What forms did that protest take?

2. What conditions gave rise to the development of religious communities such as the Shakers?

3. Why did some reformers abandon the tactic of "moral suasion" over time?

Critical-Thinking Questions

1. Antebellum reformers created large organizations to pursue their various goals but also placed a strong emphasis on personal agency and helped shape the image of the "self-made man." How were these two seemingly contradictory ideas able to exist side by side?

2. Did the rise of perfectionism and the Benevolent Empire reflect a new democratic impulse or a desire for social control?

3. Which of the reform movements of this period do you think was most successful? Explain your answer.

For further review materials and resource information, please visit www.oup.com/us/ofthepeople

▼**1834**
Anti-Catholic mob burns Ursuline Convent in Charleston, Massachusetts
Lowell operatives go on strike
National Trades' Union formed
Female Moral Reform Society formed

▼**1835**
Lyman Beecher publishes A Plea for the West

▼**1837**
Bread riots in New York City
Massachusetts creates first state board of education; Horace Mann appointed secretary

▼**1848**
Independent woman's rights movement begins at Seneca Falls, New York

1) The market revolution gave rise to a distinct working-class identity that would eventually push for legislative reform.

2) Inspired by a new religious emphasis on personal responsibility and good works, evangelists carried a spirit of reform into American towns and cities.

3) Realizing the limitations of moral suasion, reformers increasingly turned to electoral politics and the democratic system to pursue their goals.

4) While some organizations were more supportive of gender equality than others, the reform impulse provided the women's movement with momentum that would culminate in the Seneca Falls Convention, marking a major step toward women's equality.

Perfectionism and the Theology of Human Striving

Reform and the Urban Classes

Self-Reform and Social Regulation

Women's Rights

CHAPTER 11
REFORM AND CONFLICT
1820–1848

EVENTS

Millennialism and Communitarians Religious groups withdrew from daily contact with society to form separate utopian communities.

The Benevolent Empire Mass evangelizing across America led to the creation of numerous benevolent reform societies.

Wage Dependency and Labor Protest The market revolution caused the subdivision of labor and reduced wages, prompting workers to organize unions and protest.

A New Urban Middle Class A new "middling class" of workers developed, largely in urban areas, and tried to distinguish itself from the working class.

Immigration and Nativism Economic and social changes led native-born Americans to focus their anxieties on the increasing number of immigrants seeking work, especially the Irish.

Internal Migration A constant stream of internal migration to cities and the West signaled growth and opportunity but also brought a heightened sense of social turmoil.

A Culture of Self-Improvement An emphasis on self-improvement and individual striving helped resolve middle-class ambivalence about industrial society.

Temperance The crusade against alcohol became the largest and longest-lived self-regulation movement in America.

The Common School Movement and Democracy As anxiety over industrialization grew, many working- and middle-class Americans argued for a public school system.

Penal Reform State and city prison systems began to replace older charity institutions and stressed rehabilitation and reform through isolation.

Electoral Politics and Moral Reform Reformers turned increasingly to electoral politics for solutions. Disenchanted with national parties, they created specialized parties to address local issues.

Women and Reform Movements Women participated actively in reform movements, but female activists faced widespread hostility from inside and outside these movements.

The Seneca Falls Convention Marginalized within reform movements, women gathered in upstate New York to declare their rights.

CHAPTER

12

COMMON THREADS

>> What was the impact of the cotton gin on American overseas trade?

>> How did the economic development of the South affect the economic development of the nation?

>> How did the social and cultural development of the South after 1800 affect the daily lives of northerners?

Slavery and the Nation
1790–1860

>> Joseph Cinqué and the *Amistad* Rebellion

He was born Senge Pieh, of the Mende people of West Africa, sometime around 1814, but by the time his case reached the United States Supreme Court he was known as Joseph Cinqué. In 1839 he was captured in his homeland and sent on a Portuguese ship to Cuba. He was sold, along with 110 others, to two Spaniards named José Ruiz and Pedro Montez. Once in Havana, Cinqué and 56 fellow Africans were put on board another ship, *La Amistad*, to be transported to Puerto Principe (Port-au-Prince), where they would be put to work as slaves on Cuban sugar plantations. But the *Amistad* never reached Puerto Principe.

On July 2, 1839, Cinqué led a slave revolt onboard the ship. Seizing control of the vessel, Cinqué ordered the navigator, don Pedro Montez, to sail the rebels back to West Africa. But Montez deceived his captors, sailing eastward toward Africa during the day but turning the ship in a northwesterly direction by night. Instead of landing on the west coast of Africa, the *Amistad* ended up on the north shore of Long Island. There US officials captured the ship and took it to New Haven, Connecticut, where they charged the Africans with mutiny. In both the district and the circuit courts, the Africans were acquitted of the charge of mutiny and ordered to be freed. But the Spaniards, with the support of the US government, appealed the decision to the Supreme Court, which heard the case in March 1840.

By then the *Amistad* rebellion had become national and international news. Abolitionists took up the cause and hired some of the best lawyers in the country to defend the Africans. But President Martin Van Buren, anxious to please his southern constituents, was determined to convict the rebels and return them to slavery in Cuba.

The fate of Joseph Cinqué and his fellow Africans hinged on a seemingly arcane question: Which body of law applied to them? Ruiz and Montez claimed that the Africans were legally their slaves because they had rebelled in Cuban coastal waters, aboard a Cuban ship, and that slavery was legal in Cuba. If Cuban law applied, the Africans would be returned to slavery.

By contrast, if Ruiz and Montez were slave traders, their activities were illegal under Spanish law. Spain had signed treaties with Great Britain outlawing the Atlantic slave trade. Under Spanish law, Cinqué and the other Africans had been illegally enslaved.

The abolitionists hoped to establish a much broader legal point. They believed that slavery was a violation of natural law and that all men were by nature entitled to their freedom. Slavery could exist only in those places where "positive" law—which generally meant slave codes—actually created slavery. A slave who escaped or was transported beyond the boundaries of the territory where slavery had been legally created was automatically presumed to be free. Thus once the *Amistad* rebels were in control of the ship, in international waters, the Cuban laws of slavery no longer applied. Indeed, no laws of slavery applied.

To argue the Africans' case before the Supreme Court the abolitionists hired former president John Quincy Adams. In an extraordinary oral argument that lasted two full days, Adams

Continued

>> **AMERICAN PORTRAIT**
Continued

summarized abolitionist legal doctrine. International law did not recognize slavery, Adams argued, but was based instead on the natural law principle of universal freedom. In rebelling against their captors the Africans had emancipated themselves, Adams explained. Legally, they had restored themselves to their "natural" condition of freedom.

The Supreme Court ruled that Joseph Cinqué and the Africans were free under Spanish law, which outlawed the Atlantic slave trade. The justices were unwilling to accept the radical implications of abolitionist legal doctrine. So although the Cuban slaveholders lost their case, and although the Africans were freed, the Court's decision was not a complete victory for the abolitionists.

In 1842 Joseph Cinqué and the other rebels returned to West Africa, to Sierra Leone. Despite plenty of rumors about his later life, nothing certain is known about his personal fate. But we do know that the antislavery principles his lawyers spelled out in the *Amistad* case would eventually triumph.

Southern Slavery

Southern slavery took many forms in the antebellum years. Some enslaved laborers worked as hired-out field workers or house servants, some worked in mines and mills, and some belonged to small farmers. But most slaves were agricultural laborers, and the great symbol of southern slavery was the plantation that produced staple crops for sale on national and international markets. Over the many centuries of its existence the southern plantation employed workers in a variety of different ways. At the beginning planters used indentured servants and redemptioners, formally free laborers who signed contracts for five, six, or seven years. After the Civil War, planters hired sharecroppers, tenants, or wage laborers to work the land. But from the late seventeenth to the mid-nineteenth century, the southern plantation was synonymous with slave labor. Between the Revolution and the Civil War, slave plantations spread across the southern frontier, creating one of the largest slave societies in history, stretching from Delaware to Texas.

"Property in Man"

By 1860 southern slaves worked in a variety of different circumstances—in cities, in factories, as skilled artisans, cooks, housekeepers, nurses, and most often as field hands. But what made all of them "slaves," no matter what they did or where they lived, was the fact that they were defined as property, treated as property, and defended as property. On the antebellum plantation, free women and children were subordinated to husbands and fathers through the patriarchal laws of marriage and the family. Overseers were employed as wage laborers. But slaves were property of the master.

OUTLINE

Southern Slavery
  "Property in Man"
  The Domestic Slave Trade

TECHNOLOGY AND IDEAS:
  The Cotton Gin
  Plantation Slavery

AMERICAN LANDSCAPE:
  Gowrie: The Story of Profit and Loss on an American Plantation
  Other Varieties of Slavery
  Resistance and Creation Among Southern Slaves

PRIMARY SOURCE:
  John Pendleton Kennedy's *Swallow Barn*: A Traveler's Account of Antebellum Virginia

Unlike land and houses, slaves were movable property, yet colonial slaveholders sometimes tried to protect their slaves from creditors by defining them as real estate. But after 1732 British imperial regulations dictated that land and houses were subject to confiscation for debts, and by the end of the century southern slaveholders in most states simply transferred slaves from the category of "real" property to the much more flexible category of "personal" property. In the nineteenth century, only Kentucky continued to define slaves as a special category of real property. Louisiana devised a similar exception within its distinctive civil law tradition. But the effect was the same: in the nineteenth-century South, what made a slave a slave was his or her condition as the personal property of the master.

By defining slaves as personal property, the slaveholders gave themselves the freedom to buy and sell their slaves virtually without restraint. To be sure, Congress banned the foreign slave trade in the United States as of 1808 (the earliest date permitted by the Constitution). In anticipation of this action, between 1800 and 1808 slave traffickers delivered and southern planters purchased at least 40,000 Africans into American slavery. But by then a domestic trade in slaves was beginning to flourish, becoming a mainstay of southern slavery until the Civil War.

Slavery had already begun to expand westward when Eli Whitney built the first cotton gin in 1793. Nevertheless, his invention stimulated a boom in cotton production and with it the aggressive expansion of the South into the new cotton lands in the West. In response, eastern slave owners began to enhance their profits by trading in slaves—selling their own excess labor farther south and west to newer farms in Mississippi, Alabama, and western Tennessee and Kentucky. There is little evidence that slaveholders consciously "bred" slaves to increase profits. But there is abundant evidence that slaveholders were aware of the additional profits to be garnered from slave women who bore many children, and many went out of their way to encourage slave reproduction.

The Domestic Slave Trade

Wherever there was slavery, there were slave markets. Before 1808 most enslaved people who were forced to migrate south and west did so as a part of planter migrations. But by the 1820s, as many as one-third of all migrating slaves (about 15,000 people a year) went west as the property of traders. The internal slave trade was often a highly organized business, with firms employing 10 or 20 employees (bosses, clerks, guards, agents) in fine offices in Charleston, Richmond, and Baltimore. More than the plantation, the slave market reflected the defining feature of slavery as "property in man."

Slavery and National Development
  Slavery and Industrialization in the Northeast

AMERICA AND THE WORLD:
  The Demand for Raw Cotton
  Slavery and the Laws of the Nation
  Free Black People in a Republic of Slavery

The Politics of Slavery

The Antislavery Movement
Black Abolitionists
Immediatism
Antiabolition Violence
The Emergence of Political Abolitionism
Freedom National, Slavery Local

Conclusion

TECHNOLOGY AND IDEAS

>> The Cotton Gin

In tradition, the old South is seen as an agricultural region, a landscape of plantation and farm, village and forest. In fact, the antebellum South was a highly efficient, capital-rich part of the national and international economy. The reason was the profitability of raw cotton grown and marketed in the South. The easily de-seeded long-staple cotton was limited to the coast of South Carolina and Georgia, hence its nickname "sea island

THE COTTON GIN.

cotton." Only the short-staple cotton plant could grow inland. Before the invention of the cotton gin, which vastly simplified the removal of the tough seeds from small-boll cotton, the entire enterprise would have been unsuccessful. With the use of the cotton gin, southern cotton production exceeded 1.65 billion pounds in 1860.

Eli Whitney was not the only inventor of the cotton gin, but his version, with its adoption of interchangeable parts and relatively low cost, was the one that most southern planters adopted. It was perhaps ironic that Whitney was a New Englander who visited the South only because his prospects in New England seemed dim. A 1793 trip to South Carolina and Georgia changed his life. A craftsman, schoolteacher, and entrepreneur, Whitney quickly grasped the problem with the upland cotton crops. Unfortunately, he lacked the genius of other inventors like Samuel Morse (the telegraph) and

Thomas Alva Edison (electrical devices), as well as their business acumen. His attempts to patent this invention were delayed until 1807, and his plan to establish factories to gin cotton throughout the South failed. It was simply too easy to infringe the patent, with his imitators then selling their wares directly to the planters (though some towns did have large-scale ginning facilities).

The Whitney cotton gin was a very simple machine, a wooden drum to which a crank was attached, with metal hooks that pulled the cotton bolls through a mesh filter. Because the mesh was too fine for the seeds to go through, the fiber emerged seed-free on the other side of the mesh. It did not take much skill to construct the gin (short for engine) and even less to work it. Every cotton grower could afford at least one gin, allowing the smaller farmers to plant and harvest cotton. Cotton became the "king" of southern agricultural production not because it was the most sown and harvested crop (that would be corn), but because just about everyone could grow it.

A gin could clean about 55 pounds of cotton during the workday, and most plantations operated six days a week. (Slaves received and family farmers took the Sabbath off.) Cotton prices varied according to distant market conditions over which the planter had little control, but by the eve of the Civil War, cotton was the number one export of the United States and helped fuel the first industrial revolution in the North (see "Technology and Ideas: Textile Mills," Chapter 11).

Questions

1. Why do you think cotton, and the textiles produced from it, was in such great demand that it became the nation's number-one export and exerted such a huge force on the United States?

2. Is it appropriate to hold Eli Whitney responsible for the impact of the cotton gin on US history (e.g., the expansion of slavery)? Why or why not?

The slave market was a ghastly collision of worlds: for potential buyers, sellers, and onlookers, it was a lively gathering place (like a club or tavern) for white men, whose easy camaraderie stood in stark contrast to the terror of the black people about to be offered for sale. Indeed, the amiability of the market helped potential buyers more easily to see themselves as rational, well-motivated businessmen, rather than purveyors of misery. And yet the truth of the transaction permeated the place—in the audible sobs of mothers and children, in the harsh calculations and coarse comments of attendees, and in the absence of white females, a powerful silent admission that what was occurring at the slave market was so nakedly brutal as to taint the purity of white women.

Some slaves were shipped south on a boat, but they were often driven overland. It was a "singular spectacle," one English visitor to Tennessee remembered. "In the early gray of the morning, [I came upon] a camp of negro slave drivers, just packing up to start. They had about three hundred slaves with them, who had bivouacked the preceding night in chains in the woods." Leading the convoy was "a caravan of nine waggons and single horse carriages, for the purpose of conducting the white people."

Former slave Frederick Douglass, born in Maryland, later described the terror that the threat of being "sold South" struck in the hearts of enslaved African Americans. After his owner died when Douglass was eight or nine years old, the enslaved workers were hustled together to be appraised and allotted—some to be retained by family members, some to be "sold at once to the Georgia traders." "I have no language to express the high excitement and deep anxiety which were felt among us poor slaves

American Slave Market A 19th-century painting of a slave auction, the meeting point for internal slave trade within the southern states.

Charlottesville, Oct. 8, 1852

Dear Husband

I write you a letter to let you know my distress my master has sold albert to a trader on Monday court day and myself and other child is for sale also and I want you to let [me] hear from you very soon before next cort if you can I don't know when I don't want you to wait till Christmas I want you to tell dr. Hamelton and your master if either will buy me they can attend to it know and then I can go afterwards. I don't want a trader to get me they asked me if I had go any person to buy me and I told them no they took me to the court houste too they never put me up a man buy the name of brady bought albert and is gone I don't know where they say he lives in Scottesville my things is in Staunton and if I should be sold I don't know what will become of them I don't expect to meet with the luck to get that way till I am quite heartsick nothing more I am and ever will be your kind wife.

Maria Perkins
To Richard Perkins

during this time," Douglass wrote. "Our fate for life was now to be decided. We had no more voice in that decision than the brutes among whom we were ranked. A single word from the white men was enough—against all our wishes, prayers, and entreaties—to sunder forever the dearest friends, dearest kindred, and strongest ties known to human beings." One in three enslaved children under 14 was separated from at least one parent as a result of westward migration. One in three slave marriages in the upper South was destroyed.

The journeys of 20-year-old Elizabeth Ramsey and her infant daughter, Louisa, were illustrative. Elizabeth and Louisa were sold from South Carolina to a Georgia cotton planter by the name of Cook. When Cook landed in bankruptcy, he fled to Mobile, Alabama, where he hired out both Elizabeth and Louisa as domestic servants. He later sold Elizabeth to a new owner in Texas and her daughter to a man in New Orleans.

Plantation Slavery

The symbol of the nineteenth-century South was the cotton plantation, a large commercial farm owned and operated by a single white family and worked by a large number of enslaved laborers, toiling up and down plowed rows planting the seed in the spring, hoeing the young plants in the hot summer sun, and picking the sticky cotton balls in the autumn. For good reason did this image seem to capture life in the slave South. Although slavery existed in America long before the cotton boom of the late 1790s, that boom vastly increased the demand for slaves. Cotton was a crop highly suitable to slave economies. It could be grown on large plantations tended by gangs of coerced workers who (thanks to the relatively short height of the cotton plant) could be kept under supervision at all times. Of the nearly 4 million enslaved inhabitants of the South in 1860, probably three-quarters lived on plantations with 10 or more slaves.

The number of slaves on a plantation varied widely. Sugar plantations averaged 30 or more workers. Rice plantations were smaller, but still larger on average than cotton and tobacco farms. The wealthiest families of the South owned hundreds of slaves on several different plantations, often hundreds of miles apart. Owning large tracts of land and large numbers of enslaved workers was the highest symbol of status in the South. Cotton plantations proliferated in the new western lands. Meanwhile, tobacco plantations in Virginia and North Carolina, rice plantations in South Carolina and Georgia, and sugar plantations in Louisiana continued to flourish.

SCENE ON A COTTON PLANTATION. GATHERING COTTON.

Cotton Plantation Overseers and slaves on a cotton plantation in the American South: colored engraving, 19th century.

The conditions of slave life varied with the crop. For a slave, there was nothing worse than the harsh life on the sugar plantation. Masters there drove workers hardest, producing the highest rates of sickness and death in the South. The crop cycle for sugar was 13 months or more, which meant that the planting of a new crop overlapped with the harvesting of the old one—producing weeks of almost unbearably intense labor. Because sugar, unlike cotton or tobacco, had to be processed immediately on harvesting, sugar plantations had to have the boiling and pressing machinery to rush the cane immediately into production. For these reasons sugar planters preferred to buy strong adult men. Fewer women meant fewer slave families on sugar plantations. To top it off, this intense exploitation took place in the hottest, swampiest parts of the South. Higher rates of sickness and death combined with lower rates of reproduction meant that sugar planters had to restock their slave labor force frequently with newly purchased slaves. The cost of the sugar presses, plus the cost of buying large numbers of the most expensive slaves—strong young men—meant that only the wealthiest owners could afford to set up sugar plantations. The needs of the sugar parishes of southern Louisiana sustained the Old South's largest slave market, in New Orleans.

Rice cultivation was not quite as lethal, but it was also centered in the sickliest low-country regions of the South—the coastal tidewater regions of South Carolina and Georgia, where rice workers stood ankle deep in mud under the blazing sun in

AMERICAN LANDSCAPE

>> Gowrie: The Story of Profit and Loss on an American Plantation

"Gowrie" was a plantation, 265 acres of fertile rice fields spread across a large island in the middle of the Savannah River, upstream from Augusta, Georgia, and over the border from South Carolina.

In 1833, Gowrie's land and enslaved labor force of 50 people became the property of Charles Manigault. Manigault had lost half of his paternal inheritance in the volatile markets of the early 1820s. By the end of the decade he was eager not simply to restore his wealth but also to establish his family among the ruling dynasties of the South.

For Manigault, Gowrie was the means to that end—an investment and a profit center, but never his "home." He never lived full time at Gowrie and never built a family seat there, preferring instead the elaborate mansion at Marshlands, his plantation seven miles from Charleston. Manigault ran Gowrie from afar, directing affairs through periodic visits and regular letters of instruction to his resident overseer, while he traveled abroad and enjoyed more cosmopolitan living.

For the enslaved workers who lived there, Gowrie held different meanings. It was, above all, a place of hard, forced labor. Rice cultivation began in the winter months, when slaves burned off the old stubble in 15 fields and leveled and plowed the land. Women seeded the rice between mid-March and early June. Then, "trunkminders" (aided by the tides of the Savannah River) opened the elaborate irrigation systems to flood the fields. As the seeds grew into young plants, the slaves periodically drained the fields (to allow for weeding and hoeing) and then reflooded them, until the final flooding in mid-July.

The flooding and draining reduced (but did not eliminate) the work of cultivation. However, it created the additional labor of building, repairing, and cleaning ditches, canals, traps, and drains. Men built the systems, while women hauled in the mud to construct earthworks and hauled away the muck that clogged ditches and canals.

But for its laborers Gowrie was also home and it offered slaves a few advantages, however meager, over life on other types of farms. Because of the economics of scale, rice plantations were among the largest in the South and had unusually large slave populations—119 at Gowrie in 1849. The large workforce created a community of kin and friends unknown to slaves on smaller holdings. Moreover, the complexity of the work led some overseers to retain the task system—which provided slaves with a degree of autonomy in their labor. The breaks in the rhythms of cultivation allowed slaves time to plant their own gardens, yielding produce to improve their diets and perhaps some to sell. The slaves were all but forced to do this. Rice planters such as Manigault underfed their workers in the expectation that the slaves themselves would make up for it in their spare time by fishing, raising chickens, tending vegetable gardens, and exchanging their produce among themselves.

Gowrie was a harsh home. Tending muddy or flooded fields was dangerous and exhausting labor, and accidents were common. Constantly wading in the waters, rice workers were particularly subject to snakebites and to malaria. Being forced out in the unpredictably high tides, hurricanes, and floods to mend dikes and clear canals was part of the dangerous everyday labor on rice plantations. Manigault evidently did little to reduce these dangers. Health decisions were often left up to the overseer (who virtually never called in a doctor) and to a single elderly slave woman (who was hard pressed to care for such a large community).

While Manigault grew spectacularly wealthy, enslaved workers paid the price of a staggeringly high mortality rate, especially among children. None of the six infants who lived at Gowrie when Manigault purchased the estate lived to see adulthood. By January 1835, only half of the original labor force remained alive.

snake-infested, swampland fields. Skilled rice cultivators sometimes operated under a "task" system, in which workers were assigned a specific task for the day and were able to exercise some autonomy over their labor. Over time, however, rice planters shifted to a "gang" labor system more familiar to cotton plantations.

Sugar and rice were restricted by geography to relatively contained coastal regions of the South. The vast majority of slaves worked cultivating cotton and, to a lesser extent, tobacco on farms and plantations in the drier inland regions. Growing seasons for these crops were shorter, and the plantations were more self-sufficient in food-stuffs. As a result, cotton and tobacco slaves were relatively healthy. On large cotton plantations, slaves were more likely to be organized in "gangs," set at repetitive tasks under close supervision. Cotton workers dragged their harvest to the gins that pulled the sticky cotton fibers from their bolls, continuing by the light of torches long after sunset. Tobacco workers were busier in the spring, carefully transplanting young plants and pruning off extra shoots.

Not all plantation slaves were field workers. On tobacco farms, slaves tended the drying leaf. On sugarcane plantations, workshops were needed to wash, chop, and squash the stalks and reduce their juices to sugar. On big cotton and tobacco plantations, as much as one-quarter of the workforce was assigned to domestic service or to crafts intended to make the plantation more self-sufficient. Although white observers tended to view house-hold servants as fortunate, their lot was not necessarily better than that of field workers. Constantly on call, their workday could last even longer than that of field workers. They were also more vulnerable to the whims and moody outbursts of owners.

More independent than the house slaves were the 5 to 8 percent of the workforce trained for craft work. Men became carpenters, ironworkers, and boatmen. A smaller number of women became spinners, weavers, seamstresses, and dairymaids. Because they worked in separate shops, craft workers often enjoyed a degree of autonomy rare for most slaves.

Some plantations were complex economic concerns, with many barns and outbuildings, batteries of craft workers, a village of slave cabins, and an elegantly furnished "big house." Planters such as George Washington and Thomas Jefferson devoted years to creating homes of luxury and ease—in Jefferson's case, in settings artfully arranged to conceal the slaves whose work created the luxury. But many plantation houses were less noble. Northerner Emily Burke described the big house of a Georgia plantation as a husk of a building with unplastered walls, an old plank floor, and a roof like a sieve.

Other Varieties of Slavery

Although most enslaved African Americans were held on fairly sizable plantations, some slaves worked in other settings. On large plantations that

African American Scrubwoman This early 19th-century drawing of an African American scrubwoman is interesting both because it individualizes the subject and because the subject, a worker, is presented in a style of almost classic reflection.

Slave Badge Slaves hired out for wages were often forced to wear badges like this one, identifying them as slaves and indicating their occupation and the place where they worked.

did not always require the work of all the slaves, and on older plantations where the soil was exhausted, planters made part of their income by renting out slaves to other plantations or to small farmers. Other enslaved people were hired out to nonagricultural work. By one estimate, a quarter of all Appalachian slaves were hired out, most to nonagricultural jobs. Other slaves hired themselves out to work in stores, hotels, blacksmitheries, and cotton gin works. Frederick Douglass hired himself out as a skilled caulker on the Baltimore docks.

A smaller number of slaves worked in extractive industries or mills in the South. In Kentucky, Virginia, and West Virginia, for example, slaves toiled in saltworks. White people held virtually all of the supervisory positions, but slaves tended and stirred the boiling kettles of brine and prepared the salt for drying and packing. As the industry grew, it supported an expanding economy in lumber, coal mining, boatbuilding, and shipping (down the Ohio and Mississippi Rivers). Some of these related jobs (cutting lumber, operating boats and ferries, coal mining) were also done by slaves, and some by free workers whose employment depended on a slave-based industry. In the southern Appalachians, the early 1820s saw the beginnings of a gold rush that peaked in the 1830s. By 1833 some 5,000 slaves (men and women) worked in gold mines in one North Carolina county—enough to raise concerns among local white people about the possibilities of rebellion. Slaves also worked as copper and coal miners and in copper smelters and iron forges.

Neither slave owning nor plantation farming typified the experiences of southern whites, most of whom lived on small holdings of several hundred acres or less. In 1860, three out of four southern households had no slaves. Some of these "yeoman" farmers hired slaves from nearby planters, a stepping-stone into the slaveholding class for the most successful. They often relied on nearby planters to gin their cotton, sell their crops, or rent them a slave for a brief period of time. But most yeoman families lived in rough and isolated homes on cheaper lands beyond the plantation districts. They produced as much of their own food as they could, and planted small amounts of cash crops to buy the salt or the guns that they could not produce on their own. Beneath these households, economically and socially, was a white underclass of tenant farmers and day laborers and a precarious free black population.

Although most white people did not own slaves, the institution of slavery influenced their material lives and personal values. Slaveholders could afford to buy the best lands near rivers that provided them with ready access to markets. A workforce of millions of unpaid laborers meant that there were fewer stores and businesses in the slave states than in the North. A large number of rivers flowing from inland regions to coastal ports reduced the need for expensive railroads and canals. All of this meant that the southern economy remained less developed than the North's, and this had important consequences for the southern whites who owned no slaves. For subsistence farmers, the relatively underdeveloped slave economy offered some measure of protection. For more ambitious farmers, slavery restricted economic opportunity to the accumulation of land and slaves. Small farmers could hire field slaves from larger planters more cheaply than they could hire free labor, and planters could put a slave to craft work for less than it would cost to hire a free artisan.

Because southern slavery was overwhelmingly agricultural, the South had fewer and smaller cities than the North. Even in the older seacoast states, less than 3 percent of southerners lived in cities. This number included planters taking refuge during the malaria season, slaves in domestic service for the urban professional class, and the free African American population. Traditionally, southern planters looked to Philadelphia and New York for services and luxury goods. When planters sought alternatives to this pattern of external dependence, they looked not to local villages or towns but to their own plantations, reassigning field workers to produce the butter, cheese, and tools they might otherwise have purchased locally. With a few exceptions, the economies of southern cities were based narrowly on the commerce of slaves and cotton.

Most white southerners lived in rural settings, continuing the patterns of domestic patriarchy that had emerged in the eighteenth century. They had long since accepted the modern notion that freedom and fulfillment were to be found in the private sphere of life, in families and private property. In this view, the good citizen was the patriarchal father who protected his family, stewarded his human and nonhuman resources, and was generous to his neighbors. Whether the farmer was engaged in producing cash crops or concerned primarily with self-sufficiency, his manhood was tied to the economic independence that came with ownership of land.

The slaves were thus another part of the master's property and were fiercely defended as such. But because the accumulation of slaves was a source of wealth in its own right, the economic interests of the master often dovetailed with the benign treatment of his human property. The most consistent calls for reform of the slave system came from efficiency experts who argued that the most profitable plantations were those on which the slaves were well fed, adequately housed, and decently clothed. That was the ideal, of course, but all too many masters were tempted to provide slaves with as little as possible. A rational system of incentives could motivate slave labor, but the whip was often easier. In any case, the proper maintenance of slave property only highlighted the fact that slaves were, after all, property.

Resistance and Creation Among Southern Slaves

For enslaved people, slavery was not merely a system of enforced and often harsh labor. It was also a system of daily survival, practically and emotionally. It was a struggle against arbitrary authority, a monotonous diet, the constant threat of brutal treatment, and the breakup of families and communities. Slavery gave masters so much power over their slaves that the treatment of slaves necessarily varied widely from one owner to another. The slaves themselves spoke of "good masters" and "mean" ones. On any given plantation the impulses of a brutal or a paternalistic master could be offset by an overseer who might be competent or cruel, or by a mistress who might be kindly or mean-spirited. Particular slaves might be singled out as favorites, others for especially harsh treatment.

Yet most masters and slaves came to an accommodation that allowed the system to function on a day-to-day basis. Plantation routine created norms and expectations. Slaves worked "from sunup to sundown" and ate their predictable meals at predictable hours. Diligent masters set clear expectations for the amount of labor their slaves were to perform and equally clear guidelines for the food, clothing, and shelter provided them, as well as the punishments meted out for infractions of the rules. Slaves in turn came to expect certain "privileges" such as free time—generally Saturday afternoon and Sunday,

>> John Pendleton Kennedy's *Swallow Barn*: A Traveler's Account of Antebellum Virginia

From John Pendleton Kennedy, Swallow Barn, Or, A Sojourn in the Old Dominion (1832), we receive the romantic, or "moonlight and magnolias," version of slavery. Slaves rarely appear in the account, and when they do, they are objects of affection . . . or are they? The relationships between slaves and their owners were complicated. See if you can separate the voice of the narrator, who is sympathetic to slavery, from the truth in what he relates.

The gentlemen of Virginia live apart from each other. They are surrounded by their bondsmen and by their dependents; and the customary intercourse of society familiarizes their minds to the relation of high and low degree. They are scattered about like the chiefs of separate clans, and propagate opinions in seclusion, that have the tincture of baronial independence. They frequently meet in the interchange of a large and thriftless hospitality, in which the forms of society are foregone for its comforts, and the business of life thrown aside for the enjoyment of its pleasures. Their halls are large, and their boards ample; and surrounding the great family hearth, with its immense burthen of blazing wood casting a broad and merry glare over the congregated household and the numerous retainers, a social winter party in Virginia affords a tolerable picture of feudal munificence.

Frank Meriwether is a good specimen of the class I have described. He professes to value the sober and hearty virtues of the

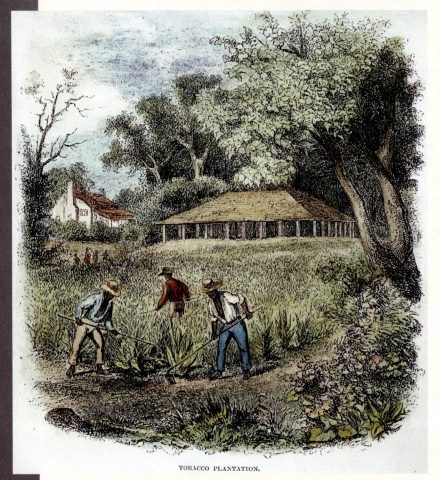

TOBACCO PLANTATION.

country. He has a natural liking for that plain, unadorned character that grows up at home. He seeks companionship with men of ability, and is a zealous disseminator of the personal fame of individuals who have won any portion of renown in the state.

Meriwether is a great breeder of blooded horses; and, ever since the celebrated race between Eclipse and Henry, he has taken to this occupation with a renewed zeal, as a matter affecting the reputation of the state. . . . He has some fine colts in training, that are committed to the care of a pragmatical old negro, named Carey, who, in his reverence for the occupation, is the perfect shadow of his master.

He and Frank hold grave and momentous consultations upon the affairs of the stable, in such a sagacious strain of equal debate, that it would puzzle a spectator to tell which was the leading member in the council. Carey thinks he knows a great deal more upon the subject than his master, and their frequent intercourse has begot a familiarity in the old negro that is almost fatal to Meriwether's supremacy. The old man feels himself authorized to maintain his positions according to the freest parliamentary form, and sometimes with a violence of asseveration that compels his master to abandon his ground, purely out of faint-heartedness. Meriwether gets a little nettled by Carey's doggedness, but generally turns it off in a laugh. I was in the stable with him, a few mornings after my arrival, when he ventured to expostulate with the venerable groom upon a professional point, but the controversy terminated in its customary way. "Who sot you up, Master Frank, to tell me how to fodder that 'ere cretur, when I as good as nursed you on my knee?" "Well, tie up your tongue, you old mastiff," replied Frank, as he walked out of the stable, "and cease growling, since you will have it your own way;"—and then, as we left the old man's presence, he added, with an affectionate chuckle—"a faithful old cur, too, that licks my hand out of pure honesty; he has not many years left, and it does no harm to humour him!"

John Pendleton Kennedy, *Swallow Barn: Or, A Sojourn in the Old Dominion* (New York: G. P. Putnam's Sons, 1906), pp. 71–72, 36–37.

Questions

1. How would you describe the relationship between Frank Meriwether and his slave, Carey? What does the exchange between Meriwether and Carey indicate about the power Meriwether holds over Carey through slavery?

2. With his last remark, what do you think Meriwether was attempting to convince Kennedy of? To what extent was this remark made just for Kennedy's sake?

3. Does this passage support or call into question a benevolent reading of the master-slave relationship? Why do you think so?

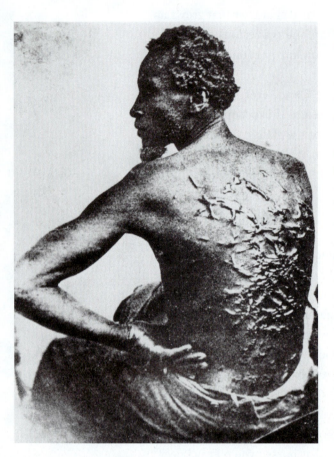

Slave with Scars Slave owners used a variety of methods to maintain worker discipline. Some masters enticed their slaves with small privileges in exchange for hard work and cooperation. Many others relied instead on the cruelty of the lash.

as well as a yearly holiday at Christmas—and passes to leave the plantation to visit spouses and children on neighboring farms. Arbitrary punishments, cruel overseers, or the withdrawal of privileges could disrupt the smooth operation of the plantation and undermine its profitability.

At the same time, slavery vested so much arbitrary power in the master that the system could be defined less by what was routine than by what it allowed. Wanton murder of a slave was illegal, but killing a slave who resisted the master's authority was not. Slaves were maimed and branded often enough that inventors devised special instruments for them, and owners included descriptions of signs of torture in their advertisements for runaway slaves. In 1802 Virginian John Stevens let friends and neighbors know that his runaway slave Toney "has scars on his back [not for his good behavior] and one very noted scar on his breast as large as a man's finger and as long, like unto a gristle; he has been branded on both jaws, he being very crafty, and has laid poison oak on them, and has removed the brand and is now become a scar on each jaw."

Few slaves escaped the familiar casual humiliations of the system. The early life of Elizabeth Keckley (who later purchased her freedom and founded the Contraband Relief Organization to support freed slaves during the Civil War) illustrated common patterns of dislocation. Born in 1818, Keckley scarcely knew her father, who belonged to a different Virginia planter. When she was 18, Keckley was hired out to a man in North Carolina, by whom, cut off from the protection of family and friends, she conceived a child. She later returned to Virginia to live with her mother, but was then forcibly taken to St. Louis. There, faced with the threat of having her aging mother hired out for service, Keckley worked for wages as a seamstress, keeping "bread in the mouths of seventeen persons."

It was not unusual for enslaved women to bear children whose fathers were free and white. Undoubtedly, some intimate relations between enslaved women and free men were consensual, but most were not. In her memoir *Incidents in the Life of a Slave Girl*, Harriet Jacobs described the limited choices available to female slaves. Jacobs's master began making sexual advances when she was only 15: "[S]hudder[ing] to think of being the mother of children who should be owned by my old tyrant," and hoping to make him so mad that he would sell her, Jacobs entered a sexual relationship with another white man, with whom she eventually bore two children.

Among southern whites, nothing was so fearful as the prospect of outright slave rebellion. Historically, slave rebellions are quite rare and almost never successful. But after the successful revolution in Saint-Domingue (Haiti) in 1791, southern masters never fully let down their guard, if only because the slaves themselves periodically reminded whites of the threat. Virginia had been shaken by the Gabriel rebellion in 1800 (Chapter 9). A decade later, the so-called German Coast uprising sent shockwaves through Louisiana (Chapter 9). In the 1820s, South Carolina was traumatized by an alleged slave conspiracy said to have been organized by Denmark Vesey. But the largest and most destructive slave rebellion took place in Southampton County, Virginia, in 1831, led by Nat Turner (Chapter 10). For several days, Turner and his band of rebels scoured the countryside, eventually killing some 60 whites. Whites reacted in kind, suppressing the Turner rebellion with a murderous vengeance that left more than 100 blacks dead. So traumatic was the Turner rebellion that the Virginia legislature debated, but ultimately rejected, a proposal for the gradual abolition of slavery in the state.

Slave resistance usually took forms other than outright or attempted rebellion. Although masters and mistresses were ready enough to punish slaves without cause, individual slaves also set boundaries on that punishment. In his later *Narrative of the Life of Frederick Douglass, An American Slave*, Douglass recalled the day he reached his limit. Douglass had been rented out to Edward Covey, a poor farmer with a reputation for "breaking young slaves." Covey whipped Douglass regularly for six months. And then Douglass was done with it. He fought back, brawling with Covey for two hours until, exhausted and bleeding, the white man gave up. He never tried to whip Douglass again.

Most forms of resistance were less dramatic than Douglass's act of defiance. Feigned illness or ignorance, carelessness, a slow pace of work—all of these diminished the power of the master or mistress or driver, forcing him or her to adjust to the distinctive tempo or personality of the laborer. Field workers carved out implicit understandings with their masters about at least some of the terms of their labor. Task groups finishing early expected to be rewarded with free time. Individuals with particular expertise expected deference from drivers, overseers, and even

THE ESCAPED SLAVE.—Photographed by T. B. Bishop.—[See Page 422.]

"The Escaped Slave" An engraving from a photograph published in *Harper's Weekly,* July 2, 1864. This engraving is from the collection of The Library of Virginia.

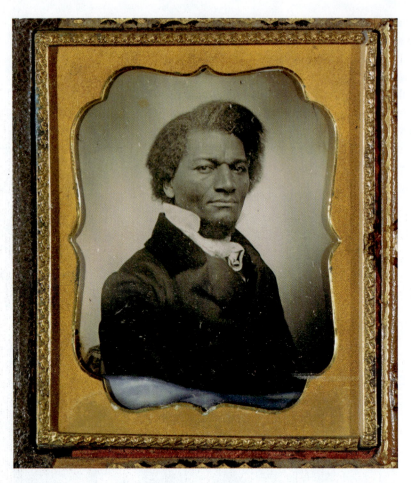

Frederick Douglass

owners. Throughout the South, a two-hour lunch break in the hottest part of the summer day was customary, and slaves had Sunday for their own work and families.

Slaves were also able to accumulate a certain status, based on age or expertise or their place in the slave community, which owners could not ignore altogether. Such a person was Harriet Jacobs's grandmother. In *Incidents in the Life of a Slave Girl*, Jacobs recalled that her grandmother delivered "scorching rebukes" to her master, for which he dared not punish her.

To focus solely on their acts of resistance, however, is to see unfree African Americans only in relation to the institution of slavery. Albeit with one eye always on survival, enslaved African Americans also established familial and community bonds and cultural traditions. Parenthood often came to slaves unchosen or, if chosen, still under circumstances choreographed by owners (who often tried to arrange partners). Certainly, some slaves—like some free people—were unable to navigate the responsibilities of parenthood successfully. Separated from spouses and children, many slaves never had the chance to try. All these conditions make the record of slave parenting all the more impressive. Parents taught their children to fish and hunt and cook. They praised their children. They told them stories about their grandparents and great-grandparents. White owners felt they were the masters of all their chattel, but African American parents made certain their children understood that, as Jacobs remembered her father's words, "You are my child, and when I call you, you should come immediately, if you have to pass through fire and water."

Enslaved Americans also created communities of custom, both formally and informally. Market women carried produce and handicrafts to county seats and gossiped while they traded with local whites. Men fished and trapped small game. Men and women perfected skills at cooking and storytelling, quilt making and wrestling, and gained reputation and status among their friends. Whites denied legal recognition to slave marriages, but slaves sanctioned their own relationships, combining African ceremonies with European wedding rituals.

As slaves built the economy of the South, they also left a lasting imprint on the culture of southern whites and blacks. Enslaved African Americans began converting to Christianity in the late eighteenth century, and many embraced the religious revivals of the early nineteenth century. Yet as they accepted Christianity, they made it their own. Slave preachers made selective use of Christian themes, emphasizing the story of Moses and the escape from bondage over homilies on the importance of absolute obedience. Newly arrived Africans provided a constant infusion of African religious forms, such as dancing, spiritual singing, chanting, and clapping, as well as distinctly African and Afro-Caribbean religions, such as voodoo. Slave religious practice became both the embodiment and the instrument of self-assertion. The call to "cross over Jordan" in the refrain of many slave songs symbolized the harshness of slave life but perhaps also the singer's intention to escape.

Slavery and National Development

By 1827, when New York finally concluded its long abolition process, few slaves resided in the North and Northwest. But in the North, as in the South, dependency on slavery was not a simple matter of owning or not owning slaves. A free American worker might never see a slave and yet be dependent on the shipping business that carried slave-produced goods or the manufacturing or farming enterprises that supplied planters' needs. An American proud of the country's growth might cherish elaborate shirts and petticoats without ever wondering where the cotton came from. A white American might never have seen a slave and yet believe that there was some natural association of African Americans with servility.

Slavery and Industrialization in the Northeast

Commerce bestows its profits in blind disregard for the social systems that link buyers and sellers. As capitalism developed in northwestern Europe and the northern United States, it generated an explosion of commerce that reached across the globe. But instead of spreading freedom, the profits of commerce intensified the various forms of social organization it touched. Commerce made serfdom profitable in eastern Europe; it made patrimonial slavery more profitable in sub-Saharan Africa; it made plantation slavery more profitable in the Americas; and it made factory labor more profitable in England and the northern United States. Here was the paradox that would one day bring civil war to the United States: commerce tied two incompatible societies together, one in the South based on slave labor, the other in the North based on free labor.

The seagoing economy of the central and northern coast had long benefited from commercial ties to southern slavery. Yankee ships and crews carried food to the slave islands of the Caribbean and slave-produced commodities to European markets. By the late eighteenth century, American merchants were second only to British merchants in the slave traffic itself. But in the early nineteenth century the northern economy began to develop robustly on its own, whereas the slave economy continued to depend on the northern and European markets for the sale of its cash crops.

In the North, cities such as Philadelphia, New York, and, later, Chicago began to stretch their economic tentacles deep into the surrounding countryside and its farms to feed a growing army of city factory workers and other wage laborers. Meanwhile, southern cities such as Charleston and New Orleans remained chiefly commercial ports with few signs of the economic development beginning to emancipate northern cities from their long-standing commercial dependence on the southern slave economy.

AMERICA AND THE WORLD

>> The Demand for Raw Cotton

The economic and territorial expansion of the United States in the early nineteenth century was propelled by the cotton boom. And the American cotton boom was propelled by the growing European (primarily English) demand for raw cotton.

Americans were not the only suppliers to British mills. Britain also imported large amounts of raw cotton from its colonies in India (and then returned the finished cloth to colonial markets for sale). But the voyage from India to England was long and difficult, and India production alone was unable to satisfy the voracious English demand. Moreover, American short-staple cotton proved both more durable than India cotton and cheaper because it was produced by slave labor. By 1800, American planters were producing over 36 million bales of cotton (compared to 1.5 million in 1790, three years before Whitney's invention of the cotton gin). By 1830, that volume had grown to nearly 366 million. By then, cotton accounted for roughly half of all American exports, a proportion that kept growing.

As the annual production of cotton increased, so did the number of slaves and the extent of slave territory. In 1790 there were approximately 700,000 enslaved people in the United States. By 1830 that number had nearly tripled, to 2 million. (It would double again in the next 30 years, to almost 4 million.) As the number of slaves increased, so did the price of each person—from an average of about $250 for a field hand in 1790 to $1,500 in 1825—a difference that remained fairly closely correlated with the volume of cotton production. In 1790

most slaves in the United States were held in Virginia, with North and South Carolina and Maryland ranking next in slave populations. By 1830, the number of slaves in Maryland was in decline, but slavery had expanded in Kentucky, Tennessee, Georgia, and Alabama, following the availability of the rich cotton lands in those regions.

Former slave Charles Ball later recalled that the greater British demand for American cotton not only bolstered the internal slave trade but also shaped the qualities that planters looked for in the slaves they purchased. In 1805 Ball overheard another white man advising Ball's master to take his slaves to Columbia or Augusta, where "purchasers were numerous and prices good; prime hands were in high demand, for the purpose of clearing the land in the new country—that the boys and girls, under twenty, would bring almost any price at present . . . and young niggers, who would soon learn to pick cotton, were prime articles in the market."

The international cotton market was not stable during these years. Any number of factors far beyond the control of American producers—the War of 1812, the collapse of credit in 1819, the volatility of world markets—could and did catalyze dramatic shifts in cotton prices. Between October and the end of December in 1818, for example, the value of cotton in American seaports dropped by 26 percent. As the steady growth of cotton cultivation indicates, however, planters' response to declining prices was not to cut back on cultivating cotton but to plant even more.

Boosters of the southern slave economy missed the signs of the North's slowly emerging economic independence because their own cotton economy was thriving. The slaveholders were shipping ever-larger volumes of cash crops to the North—evidence, they thought, of increasing northern commercial dependence on southern slave society. In many ways the slaveholders were right. In the first half of the nineteenth century, merchants in New York and Philadelphia began to specialize in consolidating shiploads of consigned cotton and sending it to England, where agents arranged for sales to English textile manufacturers. Those agents then put together shipments of consumer goods for sale in the United States, often to southern planters. The importance of this commerce to the economy of the North cannot be measured in voyages alone. Every voyage required a ship and a crew. The ships were made in Boston, Salem, Essex, and other New England towns, where local residents were employed in logging or as carpenters, caulkers, or sailmakers and on the rope walks. The crews were mostly New England bred but also came from around the world and included African Americans and Native Americans. Overseas trade also developed the business services of seaport cities. Insurance companies and banks in mid-Atlantic and New England ports catered to southern planters, providing agents for their sales, protecting their goods against the risks of oceanic trade, and holding their debts.

Northerners also benefited from southern consumers. Planters' annual shopping trips to Philadelphia or New York prompted merchants to import expensive English furniture and Chinese porcelain and encouraged tailors, seamstresses, milliners, and glove makers to keep up with the latest European fashions. Peddlers carried household goods into the southern countryside, and northern bookbinders sold religious tracts and prescriptive manuals to southern households. The symbiotic relationship of northern industry and the slave South is nowhere clearer than in the textile mills of early nineteenth-century New England that powered the Industrial Revolution in the North. The desire for such mills was an old story in the republic, but it took slave-produced southern cotton to make that aspiration viable.

The cotton boom (see Figure 12–1) proved that commerce can intensify the differences between buyers and sellers. During and after the War of 1812, as the cotton economy was exploding, Francis Cabot Lowell and his associates made large investments in northern textile mills that employed free wage laborers. The profits of the cotton trade also paid for large tracts of land with rivers and falls and eventually supported industrial towns, with all their ancillary commerce, across Rhode Island and

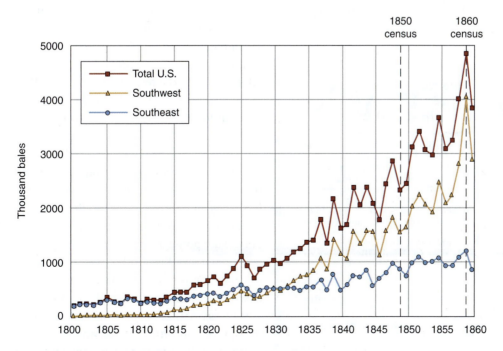

Figure 12-1 Cotton Production by Region, 1800-1 through 1860-1 *Source: James Lawrence Watkins, King Cotton: A Historical and Statistical Review 1790 to 1908 (Santa Barbara, CA: Greenwood Press, 1970).*

Massachusetts. As the textile factories flourished, their commercial ties to the South flourished. In a sense, this was mutual dependency. Northern factory workers needed the cotton slaves produced, and the slaveholders needed northern factories as customers for their cotton. But the cotton trade forged a potentially explosive connection, for it enhanced rather than diminished the differences between northern capitalism and southern slavery.

The many linkages between northern and southern economies led some slaveholders to predict defiantly that the Yankees would never wage war on slavery because they were too dependent on the South. But this was an illusion. What the northerners wanted was cotton, whether it came from Egypt or Alabama, whether it was produced by wage laborers or by slaves. The statistics showing the importance of cotton to America's overseas trade impressed slaveholders. But what those statistics did not show was the far greater volume of trade and commerce within the northern states themselves that was dependent on the development of cities and industry at home rather than oceanic commerce. The textile mills needed the cotton produced by southern slaves, but the mill owners and shoe manufacturers of New England needed even more the northern workers and western farmers who were steadily becoming each other's best customers. By 1860 the South was more dependent on the North than ever, but the North was not nearly as dependent on the South as it had once been.

Slavery and the Laws of the Nation

The men who wrote the Constitution had compromised on the issue of slavery, and it is the nature of compromises to produce ambiguities. After the Constitution was ratified, for example, both New York and New Jersey abolished slavery in their states—completing the process of emancipation in the North. Congress reenacted the Ordinance of 1787, prohibiting the importation of slaves into the Old Northwest and into the federal territories of the Old Southwest. And in 1807, the earliest possible date allowed by the Constitution, Congress prohibited the importation of any more slaves from the Atlantic slave trade. Under the Constitution, the states were now free to abolish slavery on their own, and the federal government assumed the power to regulate and even prohibit slavery in the territories. The Founders' sensibilities were reflected in their deliberate decision to refer to slaves as "persons" rather than property throughout the Constitution.

At the same time, however, the Constitution recognized and even protected slavery from federal interference in the states where it already existed. The Three-Fifths Clause, for example, gave white southerners disproportionate power in the House of Representatives and the Electoral College (in which the number of electors for each state was based on the number of senators and representatives). Article IV gave masters the right to capture and return slaves who ran away: "No person held to service or labour in one

$150 REWARD

RANAWAY from the subscriber, on the night of the 2d instant, a negro man, who calls himself *Henry May*, about 22 years old, 5 feet 6 or 8 inches high, ordinary color, rather chunky built, bushy head, and has it divided mostly on one side, and keeps it very nicely combed; has been raised in the house, and is a first rate dining-room servant, and was in a tavern in Louisville for 18 months. I expect he is now in Louisville trying to make his escape to a free state, (in all probability to Cincinnati, Ohio.) Perhaps he may try to get employment on a steamboat. He is a good cook, and is handy in any capacity as a house servant. Had on when he left, a dark cassinett coatee, and dark striped cassinett pantaloons, new---he had other clothing. I will give $50 reward if taken in Louisvill; 100 dollars if taken one hundred miles from Louisville in this State, and 150 dollars if taken out of this State, and delivered to me, or secured in any jail so that I can get him again.   WILLIAM BURKE.
Bardstown, Ky., September 3d, 1838.

state, under the laws thereof, escaping into another, shall, in consequence of any law or regulation therein, be discharged from such service or labour, but shall be delivered up on claim of the party to whom such service or labour may be due." The article avoided the word "slave," but everybody referred to it as the "fugitive slave clause" of the Constitution.

Legal experts and lawmakers agreed that the Constitution prohibited the federal government from interfering with slavery in the states where it existed. But this left several questions unanswered. Did Congress have the power to interfere with slavery in the territories? Could Congress regulate the interstate slave trade? Was the federal government constitutionally obliged to protect the interests of slaveholders on the high seas? And who was responsible for enforcing the fugitive slave clause, the federal government or individual states? In 1793, for example, Congress enacted a fugitive slave law that made it a federal crime to aid an escaping slave. But it left enforcement of the law to the states, and in the North accused runaways were often guaranteed the due process rights of free citizens, much to the dismay of the slaveholders. The slaveholders objected because slaves were, by definition, not citizens. But northerners resented the Three-Fifths Clause for precisely the same reason. In principle, only citizens were supposed to be counted for purposes of representation. By counting as citizens three-fifths of the slave population, the Constitution rewarded southern states with enough extra representatives and Electoral College votes to help ensure the election of a string of presidents from the South. Their support for a limited federal government helped protect slavery from federal interference.

Local and state laws concerning slavery affected the lives of people in all the states. Northern states, for example, passed personal-liberty laws designed to protect free blacks from being kidnapped into slavery by bounty hunters in search of fugitive slaves. These personal-liberty laws made it much harder for masters to enforce the fugitive slave clause of the Constitution. Southern masters deeply resented what they saw as northern-state interference with their rights of property. Conversely, when Charlestonians, fearful of the influence of free black sailors over South Carolina slaves, empowered sheriffs in southern ports to lock up free black sailors, they affected the lives and the employment of men from Boston and Nantucket and New York. The South Carolina Negro Seamen Act of 1822 not only specified the imprisonment of black sailors but also required a bond from their captains to cover the costs of incarceration. Under pressure from a planters' organization, the sheriff of Charleston imprisoned free Jamaican sailor Harry Elkinson. In court, lawyers argued that any treaty that interfered with the power of the state to guard against internal revolution must be unconstitutional. The court rejected this position, but South Carolina continued to enforce the act. By this time, black sailors made up roughly a fifth of northern seamen—a proportion far higher than their presence in the free population. Sailing was an important occupation for them and their families. The act in effect made hiring them a handicap to any captain using South Carolina's ports and jeopardized the sailors' employment. The South Carolina act was later copied by Louisiana, North Carolina, Alabama, Georgia, Florida, and Texas.

Free Black People in a Republic of Slavery

By 1815, some 200,000 African Americans lived as free inhabitants of the United States, most of them in urban areas. Whether they were more than inhabitants— whether they were citizens—varied from state to state and from North to South.

Free blacks faced formidable discrimination in all parts of the country. In the slave South, their very existence was a threat to the system, both in the possibilities of freedom they represented and in the avenues of communication they offered enslaved people. Southern and border states responded by tightening laws permitting individual emancipation, by increasing surveillance of slaves, and by regulating the movement and occupations of free black people. Southern courts increasingly argued that the "taint" of color followed African Americans out of slavery, assuming that free blacks lacked the privileges and immunities of citizens. Free blacks in the South were barred from militias, from the ownership of weapons, and from occupations that might bring them into contact with slaves, such as operating groceries or taverns. What's more, they lived in daily danger of being enslaved, especially as the demand for slaves in the new southern territories increased. It was worth a free black person's life to cultivate ties with the white community, should he or she need authority to ward off the greed of traders. Some border states—including Maryland, New Jersey, and Ohio—barred free blacks from settling within their borders.

Free blacks in the North suffered from similar discriminations, but their conditions varied from state to state. In New England, blacks could vote and send their children to public schools alongside white children. In other states, such as New York, free black men could vote only if they met a property qualification not required of white men. Elsewhere, blacks were barred from voting altogether. Most northern courts assumed that blacks were citizens entitled to own property, to make contracts, to move about freely, and, if accused of crimes, to have a jury trial. But some northern states, particularly along the borders of the South, prohibited free blacks from moving into the state, thus denying them one of the traditional "privileges and immunities" of citizenship. And, as in the South, blacks were often segregated from whites in schools, churches, theaters, cemeteries, hotels, streetcars, ferries, and railways.

In the North and the South, however, the laws were not always a reliable measure of social practice. Often, free blacks and whites interacted every day in ways that defied state statutes. They did business with one another, at-

---

Detroit, March 23, 1844
Wm. Gatewood
Bedford, Kentucky

Dear Sir:

I am happy to inform you that you are not mistaken in the man whom you sold as property, and received pay for such. But I thank God that I am not property now, but am regarded as a man like yourself, and although I live far north, I am enjoying a comfortable living by my own industry. If you should ever chance to be traveling this way, and will call on me, I will use you better than you did me while you held me as a slave. . . .

I think it is very probable that I should have been a toiling slave on your property today, if you had treated me differently.

To be compelled to stand by and see you whip and slash my wife without mercy, when I could afford her no protection, not even by offering myself to suffer the lash in her place, was more than I felt it to be the duty of a husband to endure, while the way was open to Canada. My infant child was also frequently flogged by Mrs. Gatewood, for crying, until its skin was literally purple. This kind of treatment was what drove me from home and family, to seek a better home for them. But I am willing to forget the past. I should be pleased to hear from you again, on the reception of this, and should also be very happy to correspond with you often, if it should be agreeable to yourself. I subscribe myself a friend to the oppressed, and Liberty forever.

Henry Bibb

tended the same churches, and helped one another in times of need. In some southern states the laws restricted free blacks from owning land and houses, but free blacks did so anyway. Periodically, states and localities would require free blacks to be licensed for certain jobs or to carry freedom papers with them at all times, but the laws were only erratically enforced. The threat of enforcement, however, was a constant source of pressure on free black communities across the South.

Within this complicated mosaic of formal and informal discriminations, free African Americans found ways to survive, to earn a living, and, once in a while, to flourish. By the 1820s, the self-help movement founded at the beginning of the republic had yielded many African American mutual-aid and benevolent associations. Organizing was most lively in Philadelphia, where free blacks established more than 40 new societies between 1820 and 1835, but the self-help impulse extended south to Baltimore and Charleston and north to New York and Boston. Although some societies were clearly limited in membership to relatively prosperous free blacks, self-help organizing crossed economic lines: coachmen, porters, barbers, brick makers, sailors, cooks, and washerwomen all formed associations.

Although the vast majority of free blacks lived in cities, a few lived in the countryside. Some of those owned their own land, but most worked as farm laborers or as sharecroppers (dividing their produce with the white landowner on a preagreed basis, usually not advantageous to the sharecropping family). Free black farm laborers often did not live on the farms they worked, but rather resided in nearby small towns, where they might find at least a few other free black men and women like themselves and where they were freer from white landowners.

The growth of white racial prejudice in the nineteenth century was reflected not simply in the spread of laws discriminating against blacks but also in renewed calls for the abolition of slavery. In 1816, a group including prominent national politicians, northerners, and slave owners formed the American Colonization Society (ACS). Styling itself as a benevolent organization, the Society (whose founders included Andrew Jackson, Francis Scott Key, Daniel Webster, and Henry Clay) determined that because of "unconquerable prejudice resulting from their color," African Americans could succeed only in Africa, which was declared their home (although by 1816 almost all United States slaves had been born in the republic). Made up of wealthy, influential white men, the ACS lobbied Congress for funds. It received $100,000 in 1819 and sent out its first emigrant ship in 1820. Dedicated to removing free African Americans from their native land to Liberia, in Africa, the ACS signaled waning white support for a racially integrated republic.

Even the federal government restricted African Americans from certain occupations. As early as 1798 the secretaries of war and the navy had each tried to bar African Americans from the military. In 1810, the federal government excluded African Americans from delivering the mail.

The Politics of Slavery

In 1817 a Boston reporter, observing the absence of the invidious politics that had plagued the first three decades of nationhood, declared that America had at last achieved "an era of good feeling." That sentiment seemed true three years later when President James Monroe was reelected with all but one electoral vote.

But all was not right with the new republic. Among the festering problems, becoming more apparent even in a time of seeming prosperity, was slavery, its existence ever more controversial. In 1820, Congress defined the slave trade as piracy. Five years later, a US patrol seized the slave ship *Antelope*, sailing under a Venezuelan flag with a cargo of 281 Africans. Declaring the slave trade contrary to natural law, the US Supreme Court freed most of the slaves. Because the United States had no jurisdiction over the laws of other nations and because slavery was legal in Spain and Venezuela, the Court returned the ship and the 39 captives held to be owned by Spaniards.

Free blacks and a significant number of whites continued to attack slavery as immoral and proposed to abolish it. A larger group of white people, though far from committed abolitionists, felt uncomfortable supporting the institution. Northern churchgoers were uneasy with their denominations' acquiescence to slavery, for example, and northern mill owners and merchants, so tied to the institution, nevertheless shied away from acknowledging that linkage publicly. And many northerners who thought very little about slavery at all were aware that the Three-Fifths Clause had helped ensure southern victories in seven of the first eight presidential contests. Had it not been for that clause, they believed, that single northerner, John Adams, would have been reelected president over Thomas Jefferson in 1800.

The Antislavery Movement

The Missouri Compromise (see Map 12-1) was a devastating defeat for the opponents of slavery. For decades they had struggled to hold back the expansion of slavery and the growing power of the slaveholders in national politics. Disgusted by the increasing belligerence of proslavery politicians, antislavery northerners had campaigned to stop slavery once and for all, they hoped, by keeping it out of Missouri. But they had failed, and the consequences of their failure were soon apparent. Slavery's defenders had always used racial politics to try to stop antislavery politics, but their successes were limited and local until the 1820s. Impressed by the strength of antislavery sentiment during the Missouri crisis, southerners joined an emerging political coalition that came to be known as the Democratic Party. This coalition started from the premise that slavery would henceforth be excluded from national politics. It worked. By the late 1820s national antislavery politics was effectively dead.

Black Abolitionists

With the collapse of antislavery politics, leadership of the movement passed to a small group of articulate abolitionists. Free black leaders in the North led the way. They began to wonder whether the American Colonization Society had become a cover for slaveholders who wanted to forestall abolition by insisting that blacks were unfit for self-government. Colonization, which began as a conservative means of supporting abolition, looked more and more like an effort by slaveholders to rid themselves of the troubling presence of free blacks. The transformation of the ACS was further evidence of the collapse of antislavery politics.

There was another, bigger, problem with colonization. By the 1820s almost all African Americans in the United States were American born. Although some later thought about migration to Haiti or to Canada, most claimed the United States as their own. They strongly rebuffed the ACS's attempt to recruit them for relocation efforts. Many earlier black efforts had focused understandably on self-help and community building. The emphasis on self-help grew in the wake of the Missouri debates, the organization of the ACS,

Map 12-1 Westward Expansion and Slavery, 1820 As treaties signed with Great Britain and Spain in 1817, 1818, and 1819 began to outline a United States that would stretch from the Atlantic Ocean to the Pacific, Americans worried about the division of that territory into areas open to slavery and areas closed to slavery. Although in 1820 more acres were closed to slavery than not, the Missouri Compromise permitted slavery in territories where it had not existed before, reinforcing northerners' fears that planter interests dominated in national policy.

and the racism of the early nineteenth century. It was a constant refrain from black abolitionists: "Too long have others spoken for us," John Russwurm and Samuel E. Cornish declared in the first issue of the first independent black newspaper, *Freedom's Journal.*

In the 1820s, free blacks began to form their own all-black antislavery groups, beginning in 1826 with the General Colored Association of Massachusetts. Their protest was not timid. In 1829 David Walker, an early member of the association, published a pamphlet titled *An Appeal to the Colored Citizens of the World,* calling on blacks to take resistance to slavery into their own hands by armed insurrection, if necessary. Walker's protest, like those of other black antislavery writers in this period, targeted the hypocrisies of white people. In his first article, he noted that a South Carolina newspaper article had labeled Turks "the most barbarous people in the world" who "treat the

FREEDOM'S JOURNAL.

"RIGHTEOUSNESS EXALTETH A NATION."

CORNISH & RUSSWURM,
Editors and Proprietors.

NEW-YORK, FRIDAY, JUNE 22, 1827.

VOL. I. NO. 15.

Greeks more like brutes than human beings." In the same paper, however, Walker had also found an advertisement for the sale of "Eight well-built Virginia and Maryland Negro fellows and four wenches [to] positively be sold this day to the highest bidder!" "And what astonished me still more," Walker added, "was, to see in this same humane paper!! the cuts of three men, with clubs and budgets on their backs, and an advertisement offering a considerable sum of money for their apprehension and delivery." Many whites were furious, and southerners put a $3,000 bounty on Walker's head. Walker was undeterred: "Somebody must die in this cause," he added. "I may be doomed to the stake and the fire, or to the scaffold tree, but it is not in me to falter if I can promote the work of emancipation."

Black organizing continued to grow more assertive over the 1830s. Most black abolitionists did not counsel armed insurrection, but a growing number wrote and lectured on slavery and the condition of African Americans in the republic. The year 1829 had also seen the publication of Robert Alexander Young's *The Ethiopian Manifesto: Issued in Defense of the Black Man's Rights in the Scale of Universal Freedom*, and David Walker's *Appeal to the Colored Citizens of the World*, both of which argued for a common, transnational black identity. In 1832 Maria Stewart, a free black woman in Boston, urged African Americans to take their destinies into their own hands. "If they kill us," she said of white opponents, "we shall but die."

These entreaties found responsive audiences. From 1830 until 1835 (and less regularly thereafter), free African Americans met in annual conventions to coordinate antislavery efforts and to secure free African American men "a voice in the disposition of those public resources which we ourselves have helped to earn." This National Negro Convention movement consistently framed its goals in the idiom of "manhood," calling for "the speedy elevation of ourselves and brethren to the scale and standing of men." Nevertheless, African American women worked to raise funds for the antislavery press and to raise awareness by inviting antislavery speakers to address their societies. In 1832 African American women formed female antislavery societies in Salem, Massachusetts, and Rochester, New York.

By the 1840s militant abolitionism had grown common in African American communities. In 1841 escaped slave Frederick Douglass delivered his first public abolitionist speech in Nantucket, Massachusetts; four years later he would publish his blunt autobiography of the brutalities of slavery, *Narrative of the Life of Frederick Douglass, An American Slave, Written by Himself*. In 1843 former slave and itinerant preacher Isabella Baumfree changed her name to Sojourner Truth and became a powerful and popular antislavery speaker throughout New England. Also in 1843, Henry Highland Garnet delivered "An Address to the Slaves of the United States of America," in which he called 4 million American slaves to open rebellion: "[A]rise, arise!" he cried. "Strike for your lives and liberties. Now is the day and the hour. . . . Rather die freemen than live to be slaves."

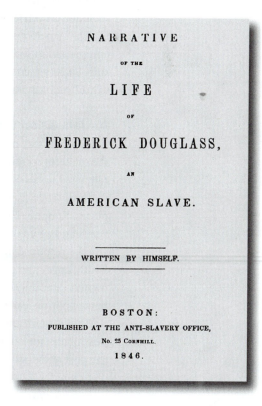

Immediatism

Although many whites in the North disliked the institution of slavery, most were reluctant to confront an issue with such power to ignite violence and division. The most dramatic break came in the person of William Lloyd Garrison, who founded his own abolitionist newspaper, *The Liberator*, in Boston in 1831. In the first issue Garrison announced his absolute rejection of any compromise with slavery: "I will not equivocate—I will not excuse—I will not retreat a single inch—and I will be heard." Garrison's approach was known as immediatism—by which abolitionists meant not the immediate abolition of slavery but the immediate

William Lloyd Garrison

beginning of the process that would lead to slavery's ultimate extinction. In 1831, under Garrison's leadership, the immediatists formed the New England Anti-Slavery Society.

Increasingly inspired by the philosophy of "perfectionism," Garrison and his followers eventually rejected all forms of compromise with slavery, public or personal. They became fierce critics of American religion and even ended up repudiating the Constitution. Few abolitionists went that far. Most were willing to risk contact with the imperfect world. One of these was Theodore Dwight Weld, an early supporter of the Colonization Society. After his conversion in the Finneyite revivals of 1825 and 1826, however, he began to doubt that the Society would ever risk alienating its southern constituency. By the 1830s Weld was a committed abolitionist, and in 1834 he became a full-time antislavery organizer.

There were quick converts to the new, energized antislavery movement, especially in urban areas of the Northeast, upstate New York, Pennsylvania, and in western states heavily settled by New Englanders, especially Ohio. Quakers and liberal Congregationalists were particularly active. Local antislavery societies formed throughout New England in 1832. By the end of 1833, local and state organizations had grown strong enough to support a national society, the American Anti-Slavery Society, which included six African Americans on its original board.

The American Anti-Slavery Society dedicated itself to abolishing slavery without compensation for owners and to the admission of African Americans to full citizenship. Society members pledged to pursue their goals through nonviolent moral suasion, exhorting individuals to undertake voluntary self-reform and the reform of society.

Antiabolition Violence

Although it was nonviolent, moral suasion did not exclude confrontation. In 1835, in the wake of Virginia's unwillingness to take any action against slavery, the Society ratcheted up its challenge to American society, especially the South. The Society dramatically increased its publication of antislavery pamphlets from 100,000 to 1 million pieces. Roughly 20,000 tracts, fliers, and periodicals were mailed to southern destinations, and agents and lecturers spread out across the North.

The response, in the North as well as the South, was immediate and fierce. In the South, anger and panic turned violent. With the memory of Nat Turner still fresh, slave owners denounced the campaign. Southern communities offered rewards for prominent abolition leaders, dead or alive. Vigilante committees were appointed to police free African American neighborhoods, to patrol waters for runaway slaves, and to search post offices for offending materials. In Charleston, South Carolina, a mob broke into the post office, stole abolitionist literature, and burned it publicly.

Even before the 1835 campaign, northerners had begun to express their disapproval of abolitionists. In 1833, whites had boycotted a Connecticut school for young women when its principal, Prudence Crandall, admitted two African American scholars. When Crandall admitted an entirely African American student body, white citizens lobbied for laws to bar black students from the state, threatened Crandall, and burned the school to the ground.

The postal campaign unleashed a new fury in the North. Anti–African American and antiabolitionist riots tore through St. Louis, Pittsburgh, Cincinnati, and Philadelphia, and abolitionist meetings were regularly broken up by mobs.

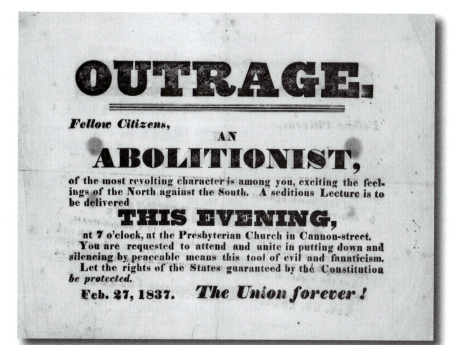

In Boston in 1835, a crowd captured William Lloyd Garrison and dragged him through the streets on a rope.

Antiabolitionist mobs also targeted newspapers. Rioters in Alton, Illinois, destroyed abolitionist newspaper editor Elijah Lovejoy's press four times in 1837. In the last attack, they murdered Lovejoy himself.

Many white northerners who opposed slavery were distressed by the violence. A few northern state legislatures admonished radical abolitionists, although none passed laws restricting abolitionist activity. Many antislavery activists chastised what they saw as the extreme fringe of their own movement, worried that the abolitionists would "inflame the passions of the multitude, including the women and children," in the words of the *Boston Courier*.

Abolitionists were undeterred and even began to find more converts. Antiabolition violence suggested to some moderates that proslavery forces would stop at nothing— the flagrant violation of civil rights, the destruction of property, or murder. They were alarmed when, in his annual address to Congress in 1835, President Jackson asked for measures curtailing antislavery organizing, including closing the mails to abolitionist literature. Congress refused, but northerners were shocked by the idea that the president would go so far to protect southern interests.

Congress's refusal to interfere with the mails was followed by other, less encouraging decisions. Opponents of slavery had long petitioned Congress to end slavery in the nation's capital. Seeking to mollify southerners, in June 1836 the House of Representatives resolved that antislavery petitions to Congress be automatically tabled. The resolution, known as the "gag rule," was renewed by succeeding Congresses until 1844.

The American Anti-Slavery Society was quick to capitalize on the passage of the gag rule. In July the society published *An Appeal to the People of the United States*, charging that the gag rule violated the right of petition. That summer, female antislavery leaders organized a systematic drive to obtain signatures on antislavery petitions.

They traveled across the North, speaking in private parlors and in public halls, and within two years collected some 2 million signatures, more than two-thirds of which were women's.

The petition campaign called attention to the gag rule, to congressional support of slavery, and to the ability of proslavery forces to abridge the rights of all Americans. It also provided moderate northerners with a nonconfrontational avenue of protest. Thanks to a growing awareness of slavery, the American Anti-Slavery Society grew from 225 local auxiliaries in 1835 to more than 1,500 by the end of the decade.

The Emergence of Political Abolitionism

Fearful that the slavery issue would destroy the Union, politicians north and south determined to build a political coalition that would prevent a reoccurrence of the kind of crisis that had erupted over the admission of Missouri. The result was a new party system that began with the emergence of the Democrats, led by Andrew Jackson, and later an anti-Jackson coalition eventually known as the Whigs. Democrats and Whigs were both national parties: each had strong northern and southern wings, meaning that both parties were committed to keeping the slavery issue out of national politics.

At first the focus of antislavery politics shifted to the states. By the mid-1820s, popular clamor had prompted a few northern states to pass laws divorcing them from the national Fugitive Slave Act and making it more difficult for masters to recapture runaway slaves. An 1820 state law made it illegal for Ohio officials to enforce the federal 1793 Fugitive Slave Act and made kidnapping free people of color in Ohio punishable by fines of up to $2,000 and "seven to twenty-one years' imprisonment at hard labor." When proslavery forces tried to scuttle the act in 1826, antislavery workers—black and white—combined to pass another bill that essentially restated the first.

But the emergence of radical abolitionism, and the backlash it provoked, made it seem as though slavery was a threat not simply to the freedom of southern blacks but to the civil rights of northern whites. In defense of slavery, northern speakers were being hounded from their lecterns; northern editors were being dragged through the streets and murdered. The government was even proposing to interrupt the flow of the US mail. The threat slavery posed to northern freedom was the wedge issue that began to push slavery back into national politics.

The lack of support for the petition campaign in Congress led abolitionists to the conclusion that they would have to elect more antislavery men. At first they tried interviewing candidates to sound them out and endorsing only those who expressed satisfactory antislavery views. But it quickly became clear that campaign promises were an unreliable predictor of support for antislavery issues by elected officials. By late 1839 and early 1840 a small group of abolitionists, most of them in New York, decided to launch a political party of their own.

The new interest in electoral politics divided abolitionism. Garrison's growing commitment to perfectionism led him and his followers to object to all forms of government coercion; therefore, they reacted with increasing vehemence against the move into politics. And even among "political abolitionists" there was no clear agreement on the desirability of establishing a third party, what the party should stand for, and whether it should focus on the single issue of slavery or try to broaden its appeal by adopting positions on additional issues. Most abolitionists also flinched at the increasingly aggressive tactics of Garrison's movement and at the visible participation of women and African Americans.

These tensions were palpable in 1840 at the American Anti-Slavery Society's national convention. Participants quickly divided over whether women should participate in deliberations and whether the organization should work to elect abolitionist candidates to office. The Garrisonian branch stacked the convention. When Abby Kelley was elected to a previously all-male committee, anti-Garrisonians walked out. The exodus freed the majority of abolitionists to launch an abolitionist political party. The Liberty Party fielded its first presidential candidate, James Gillespie Birney, in 1840 and again in 1844. Birney had no chance of being elected president, and Liberty Party organizers understood that. Their hope was to gain enough strength in different localities to give antislavery men leverage in swing districts. Though Liberty Party candidates themselves won few elections, they were more successful in many northern localities than Birney's meager presidential votes might otherwise indicate. But the most enduring achievement of the Liberty Party was in its formulation of an antislavery constitutional doctrine and a political platform that went on to become the basis of later electoral success.

Freedom National, Slavery Local

The first premise of the Liberty Party was that freedom was national and slavery merely local. This meant that slavery had no reach beyond the borders of the states where it existed. Everywhere outside those borders—in the western territories, on the high seas, in Washington, DC, and in the free states of the North—the Constitution obliged the federal government to promote freedom and oppose slavery. The Constitution did not allow the federal government to abolish slavery in the states where it already existed, but that did not mean that there could be no national antislavery politics. On the contrary, the federal government could exclude slavery from the western territories, refuse to admit any new slave states, regulate the interstate slave trade, abolish slavery in the nation's capital, and join Great Britain in the suppression of the Atlantic slave trade.

Because political abolitionists had alerted northerners to the disproportionate influence of a "Slave Power" on national politics, they paved the way for a much more successful foray into politics in 1848. By then the War with Mexico had dramatically increased the size of the western territories and many northerners had come to suspect that this was a way of creating more new slave states, increasing the influence of the Slave Power on federal policy. Armed with the same basic principle of "Freedom National, Slavery Local," most of the Liberty Party men joined in a much more successful Free-Soil Party in 1848. This time their candidate, former president Martin Van Buren, garnered a respectable 225,000 votes. The ideological continuity of antislavery politics was provided by Salmon P. Chase, who drafted both the Liberty Party platform of 1844 and the Free-Soil platform of 1848.

Chase did not expect the Free-Soil Party to displace either of the two major parties. Instead, he placed his hopes on a "fusion" with either the Whigs or the Democrats. Over the next four years, successful fusion movements got Chase elected to the Senate from Ohio and Charles Sumner from Massachusetts. But after 1850 both major parties committed themselves more firmly than ever to suppressing all discussion of slavery in national politics. However successful it was in some localities, "fusion" could not be the basis of a successful antislavery political movement.

But neither could the two major parties withstand the pressure of the slavery issue. Over the next several years, the Whig Party collapsed and the Democratic Party split into hostile northern and southern wings. Once that happened, the path was clear for the establishment of a new antislavery party, the Republicans, committed to the same basic principle of "Freedom National, Slavery Local" that had animated political abolitionists for nearly 20 years.

Conclusion

One of the reasons the Founders had compromised with slavery when they produced the Constitution of 1787 was that they thought it was a dying institution. By then most northern states had abolished slavery, increasingly strong antislavery movements were making headway in the two northern states in which it remained, slavery's expansion into the northwestern frontier had been restricted, and the slave economy in the tobacco states seemed to be foundering. But the Founders underestimated slavery's strength in the deep South and could not have predicted that a new machine—the cotton gin—would soon revive southern slavery, making it stronger and more aggressive than ever. The result was a lethal paradox: as slavery became stronger, it also became strictly sectional. As northerners stepped up their fight against slavery's expansion, slaveholders stepped up their defense of slavery. By 1820 it appeared that the experiment in republican government would collapse over the issue of slavery. But a compromise, followed by a determined effort to keep the slavery issue out of national politics, established an uneasy truce that kept the Union intact for another generation. With slavery shoved to the sidelines, American voters turned to the contentious but less threatening issues of economic development and political democracy.

Who, What

Frederick Douglass   407
William Lloyd Garrison   429
American Colonization Society   425

South Carolina Negro Seamen
    Act   423

▼**1791**
Haitian Revolution

▼**1793**
Eli Whitney invents cotton gin

▼**1808**
External slave
    trade illegal

▼**1822**
South Carolina Negro
    Seamen Act
Denmark Vesey
    conspiracy

▼**1826**
General Colored
    Association of
    Massachusetts
    formed

FREEDOM'S JOURNAL.

▼**1827**
Russwurm and Cornish found
Freedom's Journal

▼**1829**
David Walker publishes *An Appeal
to the Colored Citizens of the World*

▼**1830**
National Negro Convention
    movement begins

Review Questions

1. How was slavery generally practiced in the United States?

2. Describe the relationship between southern slavery and northern capitalism.

3. How did the 1808 abolition of the foreign slave trade affect slavery in the United States?

4. What does the phrase "Freedom National, Slavery Local" refer to?

Critical-Thinking Questions

1. In your opinion, did slavery pose more of a benefit or a threat to northern wage laborers? Explain your answer.

2. How did something as dehumanizing as slavery also help foster a rich and distinct African American cultural identity?

3. Compare and contrast the tactics that different abolitionists used to further their cause (for example, speeches, mailings, working within the political system). What are the strengths and weaknesses of each? Which seems to have been most effective?

4. Compare and contrast how slavery brought the North and South closer together and how it drove the two societies apart. How did the cotton trade enhance rather than diminish the differences between northern capitalism and southern slavery?

For further review materials and resource information, please visit www.oup.com/us/ofthepeople

▼**1831**
William Lloyd Garrison begins publication of *The Liberator*
New England Anti-Slavery Society founded
Nat Turner leads rebellion in Virginia

▼**1833**
American Anti-Slavery Society founded

▼**1834**
Anti–African American riots in major cities

▼**1835**
American Anti-Slavery Society begins postal campaign

▼**1836**
Congress passes "gag rule"

▼**1837**
Abolitionist editor Elija Lovejoy murdered in Alton, Illinois

▼**1840**
James Gillespie Birney runs for president as first Liberty Party candidate

▼**1841**
Supreme Court hears *Amistad* case

▼**1848**
Martin Van Buren runs for president on Free Soil Party ticket

NARRATIVE
OF THE
LIFE
OF
FREDERICK DOUGLASS,
AN
AMERICAN SLAVE.

WRITTEN BY HIMSELF.

BOSTON:
PUBLISHED AT THE ANTI-SLAVERY OFFICE,
No. 25 Cornhill.
1846.

1) The expansion of plantation slavery created commercial ties between the North and South but also drove the two societies apart.

2) Many free blacks met discrimination head-on by forming all-black anti-slavery groups and helping to spearhead the abolitionist movement.

3) The centrality of slavery to southern life prompted a violent reaction against abolitionism, which in turn helped the antislavery movement grow even stronger.

4) A lack of legal clarity on the slavery issue allowed both proslavery and antislavery forces to argue that the Constitution was on their side.

Southern Slavery

Slavery and National Development

The Politics of Slavery

CHAPTER 12
SLAVERY AND THE NATION
1790–1860

EVENTS

"Property in Man" Southern slaves were legally defined as personal property, which gave slaveholders the freedom to buy and sell slaves almost without restraint.

The Domestic Slave Trade A highly organized internal slave trade forced many enslaved peoples to migrate south and west and tore slave families apart.

Plantation Slavery The majority of American slaves labored on plantations: large, family-owned farms that specialized in a single crop.

Other Varieties of Slavery Some slaves worked in settings other than plantations, such as stores, hotels, and blacksmith shops.

Resistance and Creation Among Southern Slaves Slave resistance came in a variety of forms, but slaves also established strong community bonds and rich cultures.

Slavery and Industrialization in the Northeast Despite the absence of slavery in the North, the northern economy was linked to and benefited from southern slavery.

Slavery and the Laws of the Nation Although the Constitution protected slavery in the states where it existed, ambiguities in the document left many legal questions unanswered.

Free Black People in a Republic of Slavery The legal status of free blacks and the level of discrimination they encountered varied from state to state.

The Antislavery Movement By the late 1820s national antislavery politics was effectively dead.

Black Abolitionists With the collapse of antislavery politics, leadership of the movement fell to a small group of abolitionists, many of them free northern blacks.

Immediatism William Lloyd Garrison and other radical abolitionists rejected all forms of compromise with slavery and pushed for the immediate beginning of the process that would lead to its extinction.

Antiabolition Violence More direct confrontations, including mob violence, began to occur between abolitionists and defenders of slavery.

The Emergence of Political Abolitionism Despite divisions within abolitionism, a new antislavery political party, the Liberty Party, emerged.

Freedom National, Slavery Local Antislavery political coalitions argued that the Constitution obliged the federal government to oppose slavery in places where it did not already exist.

CHAPTER

13

COMMON THREADS

>> How did the expansion of slavery in the 1820s and 1830s affect US foreign policy in the 1840s?

>> How did settlers' preconceptions of other cultures affect their attitudes toward expansion?

>> How did the Democratic Party change between 1828 and 1848?

>> Was "manifest destiny" consistent with the Monroe Doctrine of 1823 or a repudiation of it?

>> How important were the politics of slavery in the 1840s compared with the previous decade and the decade following?

Manifest Destiny
1836–1848

AMERICAN PORTRAIT

>> Mah-i-ti-wo-nee-ni Remembers Life on the Great Plains

Mah-i-ti-wo-nee-ni was born in the mid-1830s in the Black Hills. Her father was Cheyenne, and her mother was Lakota (or Sioux). Her homelands had been a part of Jefferson's 1803 Louisiana Purchase and would later become the states of South Dakota and Wyoming. In the 1830s, however, the Great Plains were Indian Country.

By the time Mah-i-ti-wo-nee-ni was born, contact with whites had been reshaping the life of Great Plains Indians for more than two centuries. The Cheyennes had once been a semiagricultural people who "planted corn every year . . . then went hunting all summer," returning in the fall to gather the crops. The reintroduction of the horse by the Spanish in the sixteenth century had enabled Plains Indians to become more efficient hunters and more effective raiders. Over time, the Cheyennes had given up farming and had organized their economic life around the hunt, foraging other food as they went, as whole villages migrated to seasonal hunting grounds. Competing for game, they sent out raiding parties to steal horses or take captives for exchange. Mah-i-ti-wo-nee-ni recalled a time in her childhood (probably in 1840) when the Cheyennes and the Arapahoes traveled south to meet in a great peace council with their traditional enemies, the Kiowas, Comanches, and Apaches.

By the 1830s, the proximity of white Americans was beginning to affect the Cheyennes. At the time of the great southern peace council, massive overland migration to the Pacific was already under way. In the West, many Americans believed, the nation renewed its virtues and purified the republican model of government. In the mid-1840s, Americans coined a phrase for this linking of land to liberty. Taking the continent was their "manifest destiny."

American settlement of the West implied a different destiny for Mah-i-ti-wo-nee-ni and her people, however. First came missionaries, exhorting Indians to convert to Christianity. The settlers followed, trampling Indian crops, destroying villages, spreading disease, and decimating the buffalo. At first the US agents among the Cheyennes wished merely to trade gifts of kettles, coffeepots, knives, and blankets for promises to permit settlers to cross Cheyenne lands. Soon, the US government wanted the land itself. Although the nomadic Cheyennes long resisted removal, by 1877, after years of struggle and compromise, Mah-i-ti-wo-nee-ni and her people were forcibly displaced south into Indian Territory.

Because much of the land Americans sought to settle lay within the boundaries of the nation of Mexico, the manifest destiny of white Americans also implied a distinct destiny for Mexicans. Claiming mistreatment by the Mexican government, white American settlers in the Mexican province of Coahuila y Tejas formed the Republic of Texas and sought entry into the United States. In 1846 the United States provoked a war with Mexico to claim large portions of that nation's northern territories.

Continued

>> **AMERICAN PORTRAIT**
Continued

That war gained the United States secure access to the Pacific Ocean. But Americans also paid the costs of the manifest destiny. Each stage of expansion reignited controversies over the institution of slavery. Whereas many white southerners claimed a basic constitutional right to own slaves and felt betrayed by northern opposition, northern reformers inveighed against the immorality of the institution. They flooded the mails with abolitionist tracts and Congress with antislavery petitions. This collision of interests and ideals flared within a national political system ill equipped to respond to it effectively. American politicians continued to seek compromises between slave-owning and non-slave-owning interests, but the party structure was in disarray, with no strong leader to hold it together. By 1848, some Americans were prepared to give up on their government altogether.

The Decline of Jacksonianism

Andrew Jackson had governed on a philosophy of federalism, in which a strong presidency had been necessary to combat, rather than support, the growth of a powerful central government. He had backed territorial expansion, the powers of individual states, and the claims of settlers and had opposed federal control of those processes. By 1836, people in new territories sought admission to the Union, settlers were launching the largest westward migration in the history of the nation, and Jackson's Democratic Party seemed to have reduced the old Republican dynasty (now regrouped as Whigs) to whining observers. But there were costs to Jackson's successes: his hatred of strong central government had thrown the nation's banking system into chaos, his zeal for territorial expansion had helped nurture a strong abolition movement in the North, and his own Democratic Party had grown too diverse to remain stable. Jackson would be succeeded in 1837 by a Democrat known for his political acumen, Martin Van Buren—but the "Little Magician" would lose reelection by a landslide in 1840 and fail again when he ran on a third-party ticket in 1848.

Political Parties in Crisis

The expansion of white male suffrage and the translation of moral-reform agendas into electoral politics energized American politics in the 1830s and 1840s. In 1840, 66 percent of the electorate voted in Massachusetts, 75 percent in Connecticut, and 77 percent in Pennsylvania. Yet the capacity of major political parties to accommodate a wide range of conflicting interests and beliefs was limited.

Increasingly fractured since the election of 1824, the Republican Party had struggled to reorganize in opposition to Andrew Jackson. Jackson's war on the national bank had offered the immediate occasion. Although unable to save the bank, Henry

OUTLINE

The Decline of Jacksonianism
    Political Parties in Crisis
    Van Buren and the Legacy of Jackson

The Political Economy of the Trans-Mississippi West
    Manifest Destiny in Antebellum Culture

PRIMARY SOURCE:
    John O'Sullivan Proclaims a "Nation of Futurity"
    Texas

AMERICAN LANDSCAPE:
    Culture and Politics in Manifest Destiny: Tejanos in Texas

Clay and the anti-Jacksonians narrowly passed a Senate resolution in 1834 censuring Jackson for assuming "authority and power not conferred by the Constitution and the laws." (Jackson had refused to turn over a paper on the bank that he had read to his cabinet.) In the debate before the censure, Clay identified his own anti-Jackson position as "Whiggish" (meant to evoke memories of the English "Whigs" who opposed royal tyranny in the eighteenth century). That label stuck as the name of the new political party.

Former National Republicans in the urban Northeast and upper West made up the bulk of the new Whig Party. Some of these were beginning to doubt the wisdom of uncontrolled territorial expansion, which seemed to promote political corruption, economic disorder, sectional conflict, and the extension of slavery. They feared the disruptive power of wildcat settlers, wage workers, the urban poor, and immigrants. Whigs supported market expansion guided closely by a strong, interventionist central government. They continued to embrace the elements of the earlier "American System": a new national bank, a strong protective tariff, and government-sponsored internal improvements.

By 1834, some former Democrats were also disenchanted with the party of Jackson. Prosperous shopkeepers and middling merchants began to see their own interests as distinct from those of the urban laboring classes and were attracted by the Whig emphasis on discipline and order. Some southerners were still angry over the tariff and the nullification crisis. Some small farmers and shopkeepers wiped out by the depression of 1837 blamed Jackson for their hard times. Workers, who had little trust for the merchant classes at the core of the new Whig Party, tended to form splinter parties or to stay with the Democrats.

Through the 1830s the Whigs were a loose and disorganized opposition. Unable to decide on a single candidate, in 1836 they ran four regional challengers, hoping to deny Van Buren a majority in the Electoral College. The Whig field included William Henry Harrison (governor of Indiana Territory and victor at the Battle of Tippecanoe, nominated by Pennsylvania Antimasons), Senator Hugh Lawson White (Jackson's disenchanted replacement in the Senate, nominated by unhappy Democrats in Tennessee), Senator Daniel Webster (former National Republican and famous orator, nominated by the Massachusetts legislature), and Willie P. Mangum (a protest candidate of the South Carolina Nullifiers).

Jackson's vice president, Martin Van Buren, seemed well positioned for the race. Van Buren was instrumental in creating a successful Democratic coalition, so he was surely the one to hold it together. Van Buren had been constantly at Jackson's side, as secretary of state and as vice president. Few politicians seemed better situated to

Pacific Bound
Nations of the Trans-Mississippi West

Slavery and the Political Economy of Expansion
Log Cabins and Hard Cider: The Election of 1840
And Tyler, Too
Occupy Oregon, Annex Texas

DEBATING HISTORY:
    Manifest Destiny and Race
War with Mexico

AMERICA AND THE WORLD:
    Lt. Rankin Dilworth in the War with Mexico

Conclusion

Martin Van Buren One of the most powerful politicians of his time, Martin Van Buren extolled the virtues of party competition. He was also among the first presidents ever to be photographed.

inherit Jackson's popularity. What was more, Van Buren seemed perhaps uniquely positioned to bridge the growing gulf between northern antislavery and southern proslavery Democrats: his popularity in New York appeared strong enough for him to risk alienating some of the antislavery vote in the effort to gain southern support, a risk he took by publicly declaring himself "the inflexible and uncompromising opponent of any attempt on the part of Congress to abolish slavery in the District of Columbia" or to interfere with slavery "in the states where it exists."

The election was close. Van Buren won part of New England (but not Massachusetts or Vermont). He took his home state of New York, Pennsylvania, Virginia, and North Carolina. And he took Far West states, most of them slave states: Michigan, Illinois (technically free but popularly proslavery, especially in the south), Missouri, Arkansas, Louisiana, Mississippi, and Alabama. He won 58 percent of the electoral vote (after the weighting of the Three-Fifths Compromise in the South) and a bare majority (51 percent) of the popular vote. A shift of fewer than 2,000 votes in Pennsylvania would have denied Van Buren an Electoral College majority and thrown the election to the House of Representatives.

Van Buren and the Legacy of Jackson

In his 1837 inaugural address, Van Buren announced that the nation had arrived at a "singularly happy!" condition. Less optimistic, Missourian Thomas Hart Benton observed that in Van Buren's victory "the rising was eclipsed by the setting sun." Benton was closer to the truth. Van Buren's struggle to unite Jackson's party enough to get elected was only the first of the challenges he inherited.

The signs of the Panic of 1837 were already visible when Van Buren was inaugurated that March. Jackson's pet banks had ensured that western land speculation would be built on easy credit. His hard-money measures that had effectively drained the nation of specie did not end the bubble of credit. It simply diverted its source to European financiers, who got higher interest in the United States than in their home countries. When European banks responded to specie shortages in their own countries by increasing interest on deposits and tightening credit, the Europeans called in their American loans. The sudden collapse of credit was exacerbated by crop failures in 1835 and 1837, which put farmers at greater risk for defaulting on their loans and reduced American exports.

As credit evaporated, interest rates rose, paper money depreciated, and debt mounted. The credit-dependent cotton market began to collapse, taking with it several large import-export firms in New York and New Orleans. After years of high inflation, the failures ignited a run on the overextended banks, as depositors tried to hoard their savings before the hard currency was paid out for mercantile debts. "[E]ven during the Embargo, & war that followed," merchant John Perkins Cushing reported in May of 1837, " . . . there was nothing like the complete prostration of commercial credit & confidence that has taken place within the last two months."

A strong federal hand might have stemmed the damage, but Van Buren shared Jackson's view that the federal government should not manage currency. Van Buren's announcement on May 4 that he intended to maintain the Specie Circular in force ensured continued pressure on banks. On May 10, 1837, frightened depositors drained $650,000 from their reserves, and New York City banks closed. Only a show of military force prevented a riot.

Coinciding with large waves of German and Irish immigration, the

> The inauguration of Martin Van Buren, as President of the United States, took place at the Capitol, in Washington, on Saturday last, at noon. . . . Mr. Van Buren delivered an Inaugural Address on the occasion, which . . . professes to be an avowal of the principles by which the new President intends to be guided in his administration of the government; but with the single exception of the principle of opposition to the abolition of slavery in the District of Columbia, which it expresses with most uncalled for and unbecoming haste and positiveness, he might, with as much propriety, have sung **Yankee Doodle** or **Hail Columbia**, and called it "an avowal of his principles." . . .
>
> Mr. Van Buren's indecent haste to avow his predeterminations on the subject of slavery has not even the merit of boldness. It is made in a cringing spirit of propitiation to the south, and in the certainty that a majority at the north accord with his views.
>
> WILLIAM LEGGETT,
> March 11, 1837

depression hit the East Coast hard. Wages declined faster than prices. Unemployment was widespread, and losses touched even the prosperous middle classes. Troubled times remained until 1843. While Democrats scrambled to avoid political responsibility, the new Whig Party began to look ahead optimistically to 1840.

Although an additional infusion of federal funds to state banks in 1837 might only have fed the frenzy, Van Buren's decision to delay the scheduled distribution added a new confusion. In an effort to return stability to the nation's monetary system, Van Buren proposed that the Treasury Department establish its own financial institutions to receive, hold, and pay out government funds. The institutions would exist solely to manage government accounts and would not issue paper currency or make loans to business.

The proposal for an independent treasury met with substantial opposition. Predictably, Whigs objected that removing government holdings from circulation would reduce capital investment. But many Democrats also thought the new system would retard growth. The independent treasury did not pass until 1840, enacted as an entirely separate, specie-based system, able neither to receive nor to pay out paper currency.

Van Buren's challenges spilled over from domestic to international crises. Twice, the fears and frustrations of Americans along the Canadian border almost brought the United States and Canada/Great Britain to blows. Americans and Canadians had long argued over who owned the rich timber reserves in the Aroostook Valley on the border of Maine and New Brunswick. When Americans heard rumors in

Panic of 1837 "The modern Balaam and his ass." An American cartoon placing the blame for the panic of 1837 and the perilous state of the banking system on outgoing president Andrew Jackson, shown riding a donkey in its cartoon debut as the symbol of the Democratic Party.

1838 that Canadian lumberjacks were infiltrating the region and taking trees at will, the Democratic governor of Maine declared that Maine was under invasion and demanded federal protection. Van Buren sent in the army under General Winfield Scott. Aware that the economy could not support a war, he also instructed Scott to offer terms for a truce. If Canada would acknowledge Maine's predominant interest in the valley, the United States would respect existing Canadian settlements pending final disposition of the area.

Meanwhile, Americans along the northern New York border were picking sides in an internal Canadian rebellion against Great Britain (1837–1838). Although the United States was technically neutral, disgruntled unemployed American workers saw the rebels embodying the spirit of the American Revolution and were drawn to support them against wealthy Canadians and the British government. Recruited by the rebels, sympathetic New Yorkers raised funds and offered ships to transport men and arms to Canada. On December 29, 1837, Canadian pro-British troops crossed the river into Schlosser, New York, captured the *Caroline* (owned by American William Wells), towed it out into the middle of the river, and set it afire. A few months later, Americans retaliated by sinking a British ship. The United States and Britain exchanged diplomatic demands until 1840, when Alexander McLeod, a Canadian deputy sheriff, got drunk in a New York tavern and began bragging that he had killed an American during the *Caroline* incident. New York authorities immediately arrested him and local mobs clamored for blood, while Britain protested that McLeod's status was an international matter, beyond New York's jurisdiction, and threatened to break diplomatic relations. Van Buren, fighting for reelection as the anti-big-government Democratic candidate, was not ready to intervene. Only with the election of a Whig president and Congress in 1840 was McLeod released.

The Political Economy of the Trans-Mississippi West

Jackson had embodied the restless energy and assumed right of white Americans to settle ever deeper in the North American continent. Manifest destiny, the belief that white Americans had a providential right to as much of North America as they wanted, had been a core belief and policy since the founding of the republic. It was implicit in the Northwest Ordinance, in scores of Indian treaties, in the Louisiana Purchase, in the Transcontinental Treaty, in the 1824 Monroe Doctrine, and in the Removal Act of 1830. But only in 1845 did the phrase enter the American vocabulary, when journalist John O'Sullivan proclaimed that it is "[o]ur manifest destiny . . . to overspread the continent allotted by Providence for the free development of our yearly multiplying millions." As the United States' treatment of Native Americans had long made clear, the manifest destiny of the nation was for many Americans racial, as well as territorial and political.

Manifest Destiny in Antebellum Culture

On the simplest level, manifest destiny was a political slogan and a crass claim for property, a way of asserting that Americans wanted and would have the continent all the way to the Pacific. But most Americans resisted such a naked statement of their ambitions and framed—and deeply understood—their aspirations in the language of democracy and freedom. This land was intended by Providence as the physical home of a unique national greatness. In antebellum culture, this understanding of the singularity of North America was often articulated through a linked pair of evocative images: first, the image of the awesome power and natural majesty of the American wilderness, and second, the image of the wilderness giving way to an even nobler state of cultivation on the arrival of American settlers.

Both images were evident in antebellum landscape painting, particularly in the work of a group of artists known as the Hudson River school. Like most Americans of the era, the Hudson River painters were influenced by the Romantic movement sweeping Europe, which emphasized the power and beauty of untamed nature. For example, the canvases of Thomas Cole, the leader of the Hudson River school, depicted wilderness bluffs surrounded by ageless forests presumedly untouched by American settlers. Ancient trees spiked toward the heavens and wild waterfalls cascaded over crags far above the ground in Cole's *Falls of the Kaaterskill* (1826), with a massive gathering storm that underscores the unchecked power of the American wilderness. In these landscapes, the only human figures are usually Native Americans, additional emblems of the primitive beauty of the scene.

Cole and other Hudson River painters often combined these visual celebrations of the American landscape with images of American settlement. In these latter paintings, the arrival of the European Americans seemed to bring to fruition the innate grandeur of nature. Cole's *Landscape* (1825) suggested this harmonious blending of destinies, as did *West Rock, New Haven* (1849), by Connecticut native Frederick Church. The Hudson River paintings sometimes suggested bittersweet sadness at the passing of the wilderness, even as they celebrated the coming of ordered fields and farm towns.

>> John O'Sullivan Proclaims a "Nation of Futurity"

John O'Sullivan was a Democratic Party publicist, and his essay "The Great Nation of Futurity" was the origin of the manifest destiny doctrine of the party. Note what he omits as well as what he includes. This essay is part of a wider conversation about the nature of the United States as well as what its foreign policy should be.

The American people having derived their origin from many other nations, and the Declaration of National Independence being entirely based on the great principle of human equality, these facts demonstrate at once our disconnected position as regards any other nation; that we have, in reality, but little connection with the past history of any of them, and still less with all antiquity, its glories, or its crimes. On the contrary, our national birth was the beginning of a new history, the formation and progress of an untried political system, which separates us from the past and connects us with the future only; and so far as regards the entire development of the natural rights of man, in moral, political, and national life, we may confidently assume that our country is destined to be the great nation of futurity.

It is so destined, because the principle upon which a nation is organized fixes its destiny, and that of equality is perfect, is universal. It presides in all the operations of the physical world, and it is also the conscious law of the soul—the self-evident dictates of morality, which accurately defines the duty of man to man, and consequently man's rights as man. Besides, the truthful annals of any nation furnish abundant evidence, that its happiness, its greatness, its duration, were always proportionate to the democratic equality in its system of government. . . .

What friend of human liberty, civilization, and refinement, can cast his view over the past history of the monarchies and aristocracies of antiquity, and not deplore that they ever existed? What philanthropist

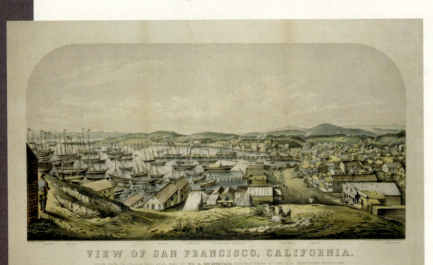

VIEW OF SAN FRANCISCO, CALIFORNIA.

San Francisco in the 1850s

can contemplate the oppressions, the cruelties, and injustice inflicted by them on the masses of mankind, and not turn with moral horror from the retrospect?

America is destined for better deeds. It is our unparalleled glory that we have no reminiscences of battle fields, but in defence of humanity, of the oppressed of all nations, of the rights of conscience, the rights of personal enfranchisement. Our annals describe no scenes of horrid carnage, where men were led on by hundreds of thousands to slay one another, dupes and victims to emperors, kings, nobles, demons in the human form called heroes. We have had patriots to defend our homes, our liberties, but no aspirants to crowns or thrones; nor have the American people ever suffered themselves to be led on by wicked ambition to depopulate the land, to spread desolation far and wide, that a human being might be placed on a seat of supremacy. . . .

Yes, we are the nation of progress, of individual freedom, of universal enfranchisement. Equality of rights is the cynosure of our union of States, the grand exemplar of the correlative equality of individuals; and while truth sheds its effulgence, we cannot retrograde, without dissolving the one and subverting the other. We must onward to the fulfilment of our mission—to the entire development of the principle of our organization—freedom of conscience, freedom of person, freedom of trade and business pursuits, universality of freedom and equality. This is our high destiny, and in nature's eternal, inevitable decree of cause and effect we must accomplish it. All this will be our future history, to establish on earth the moral dignity and salvation of man—the immutable truth and beneficence of God. For this blessed mission to the nations of the world, which are shut out from the life-giving light of truth, has America been chosen; and her high example shall smite unto death the tyranny of kings, hierarchs, and oligarchs, and carry the glad tidings of peace and good will where myriads now endure an existence scarcely more enviable than that of beasts of the field. Who, then, can doubt that our country is destined to be *the great nation* of futurity?

John L. O'Sullivan, "The Great Nation of Futurity," *The United States Democratic Review,* Volume 6, Issue 23, pp. 426–430.

Questions

1. According to O'Sullivan, what is the nature of the United States? What is the mission of the United States, and how is this mission distinct from that of other nations?

2. To what extent does O'Sullivan's version of US history match what you have learned thus far from *Of the People*? In what ways does it differ?

3. What do the differences between O'Sullivan's version of US history and this text's version indicate?

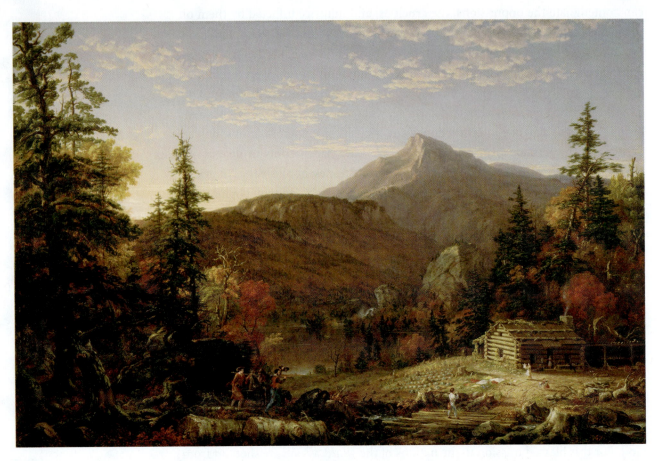

Thomas Cole's *The Hunter's Return* One of the foremost landscape artists of his time, Thomas Cole romanticized nature and the simple life of the independent farmer.

Antebellum poets and novelists took up the theme of the land as well, also often envisioning it as a shifting scenery in which the majesty of the wilderness seemed merely to await transformation at the hands of American pioneers. James Fenimore Cooper's *Leatherstocking Tales* narrated European American settlement of the New York backcountry as a grand myth of manifest destiny, in which settlement tamed the land even as the land itself became the agent through which the newcomers were forged into a new, ennobled society. In *The Last of the Mohicans,* Cooper described the New York backcountry of 1757 as "an impervious boundary of forests" torn by dangerous rapids and rugged passes. By 1793, the fictional time of *The Pioneers,* that same landscape had become "a succession of hills" and "narrow, rich cultivated dales" dotted by "beautiful and thriving villages" and "neat and comfortable farms." In the same spirit, poet William Cullen Bryant visited the Illinois plains in the 1830s and saw not an austere landscape but a vision of "gardens" and "fields, boundless and beautiful." The uniting of the national culture and the land was the "manifest destiny" not only of American citizens but also of the land itself.

Jefferson had imagined this relationship of the people to the land chiefly in terms of the yeoman farmer, with the craftsman a secondary "handmaid." In the wake of innovations in travel and machinery design in the early nineteenth century, however, images of trade and manufacturing began to make their way into ideas about the abundance of the land. Americans would unleash the richness of the continent not only through farming but also through commerce. De Witt Clinton's prediction that the Erie Canal would help make New York City the emporium of the world captured this new vision in the politics of trade. Commerce, Clinton insisted in 1819, would not only collapse regional differences but also "increas[e] the stock of human happiness—by establishing the perpetuity of free government—and by extending the empire of improvement, of knowledge, of refinement and of religion. . . ." The American wilderness, first cultivated into a homestead, would become a huge highway for the transportation of goods and culture.

To this image of North America as a transportation network, Americans added the image of North American power harnessed into manufacturing output. The proof of America's greatness lay not only in the riches coaxed from the land but

> There are several factories in different parts of North-Adams, along the banks of a stream, a wild highland rivulet, which, however, does vast work of a civilized nature. It is strange to see such a rough and untamed stream as it looks to be, so tamed down to the purposes of man, and making cottons, woolens &c.—sawing boards, marbles, and giving employment to so many men and girls; and there is a sort of picturesqueness in finding these factories, supremely artificial establishments, in the midst of such wild scenery. For now the stream will be flowing through a rude forest, with the trees erect and dark, as when the Indians fished there. . . . And taking a turn in the road, behold the factories and their range of boarding-houses, with the girls looking out of the window as aforesaid. And perhaps the wild scenery is all around the very site of the factory, and mingles its impression strangely with those opposite ones.
>
> NATHANIEL HAWTHORNE,
> 1838

also in the seemingly endless array of manufactured goods. Reviewing an exhibit of goods manufactured in Massachusetts in 1839, one magazine correspondent argued that manufacturing "blended harmoniously together" the interests of all Americans. The enjoyments of abundant market goods did not extend to all people, however, and the politics of the marketplace too often became fetid with the stench of greed.

Texas

By the terms of the 1819 Transcontinental Treaty, the United States had given up claims to Spanish lands south of the 42nd parallel. Nevertheless, within a few years Americans began to enter the region.

Many of these immigrants were specifically invited; some were not. The Spanish saw their northern region as a buffer zone against the Lipan Apaches and Comanche Indians and between New Spain and the United States. After independence, the Mexican government expanded those policies by offering land grants to Americans in return for the promise to bring settlers to bolster the sparse population. The first American to accept the invitation was Stephen F. Austin, who began settling a colony on the banks of the Brazos and Colorado Rivers in 1821. By 1830 there were more than 20,000 Americans (including 1,000 slaves) living in the northeastern province of Mexico, bordering Louisiana.

Conflict between immigrant Americans and residents of Texas—known as Tejanos—was inevitable. Tejanos resented the influx of Americans, who were often awarded lands that already belonged to Tejanos or that included Tejano communities. Tejanos

AMERICAN LANDSCAPE

>> Culture and Politics in Manifest Destiny: Tejanos in Texas

When white Americans rebelled against Mexico in 1836, they cited among their justifications not only specific policies of the Mexican government but also what they viewed as the inferiority of the culture of the Mexicans among whom they lived. They called Tejanos immoral, lazy, and "unmanly" largely because Tejanos were not interested in the aggressive forms of development favored by the immigrants. By 1836, there were three major regions of Tejano settlement in northern Mexico: the northernmost Nacogdoches region (inland and closest to Louisiana) and the Bexar-Goliad and Rio Grande regions farther south and closer to the coast of the Gulf of Mexico. The three bore some differences, but they shared a heritage that melded Spanish, Mexican, and native influences to suit the land and the circumstances of survival in a hard and isolated region.

Settlement had come slowly. Although the earliest Spanish foray was in 1716, Spanish authorities (and most Mexican officials, after the national revolution) valued the region as a *frontera*—a boundary land where priests could missionize "heathen" Indians and where soldiers in armed garrisons (*presidios*) could keep out Lipan Apache and Comanche raiding parties. Semiarid, largely void of vegetation, and removed from the comforts of established society, the land offered colonists few rewards. Mortal-ity rates ran high, especially among males (who were required to serve as *ciudadanos armadas*, a sort of armed civilian reserve, in exchange for land) and children. As late as 1821, when Mexico achieved independence, the region held fewer than 2,500 settlers.

As was the case among the settlers, land ownership was central to Tejano culture. By the beginning of the nineteenth century some families and groups of families had left the towns to establish ranches along the rivers that flowed to the Gulf of Mexico, and a class system, based on the private ownership of property, began to take shape. At one extreme were a few wealthy families, settled on large ranches in elaborate houses and employing numerous servants and workers. At the other extreme were the mission Indians, technically free but often held in conditions of semibondage.

Most of the Tejanos came originally from the northern Coahuila Province, where intermarriage among native people, Mexicans, and Spaniards had long been common. Although the Spanish authorities had frowned on it, over time the soldiers in the *presidios* had also intermarried with the colonists and with local Indians. The result was a community in which most people claimed racially mixed heritages.

Most alarming to the white American settlers, locals opposed slavery and repeatedly petitioned their government to stop allowing white Americans to establish the institution in Texas. There had been African American slaves in the region for at least 300 years, but in such small numbers that the institution had little social or economic importance before the early nineteenth century. The number of slaves increased after 1800, when slave traders began to use Texas as an entry to the US market. Especially after Mexico gained its independence, Tejanos condemned the trade as anti-republican. The clash of white Americans and Tejanos spoke to both the past and the future of republicanism in the United States.

complained that the *empresarios* (American landholders) were "nothing more than money-changing speculators" who had no respect for existing claims and did not control their settlers or squatters who used the American colonies to hide stolen livestock.

Although they were happy to take advantage of the cheap prices Mexico offered, many Americans had never fully acknowledged the right of Mexico to these lands. Viewing the region as the natural next frontier for American plantation agriculture, southerners had denounced the 1819 treaty and lobbied John Quincy Adams and Andrew Jackson to purchase the tract free and clear. By 1839 some Americans were convinced that Texas was destined to become the "land of refuge for the American slaveholders."

The immigrants themselves criticized the Mexican government in the language of republicanism. They objected to high taxes, but then so did everybody. They objected to being required to convert to Catholicism in order to intermarry with Mexicans and control their Mexican wives' property, but those laws were not really enforced. They objected to having to adopt the Spanish language. But beneath these objections were more fundamental issues, including a deep discontent—which many Mexicans shared—with the autocratic Mexican government.

Southerners who moved to Texas had a particular complaint—the Mexican government's inconsistent policies on slavery. Like the young United States, the new and unstable Mexican government took an erratic course, at one point banning slavery altogether, at another point allowing slaves to enter the nation but mandating gradual abolition.

By the mid-1820s, however, the immigrants had developed a cotton economy dependent on slave labor that they were determined to preserve. They regarded Mexican inconsistency and resistance as evidence of betrayal. In 1824 Stephen Austin, never a devoted supporter of slavery, devised regulations for his colony with harsh provisions for slaves who tried to escape or free people who abetted runaways. By 1830 Austin had concluded that "Texas must be a slave country. Circumstances and unavoidable necessity compels it. It is the wish of the people there. . . ." In Austin's view, "the people" included only white US immigrants and others who agreed with their goals.

But slavery was not the major reason for the increasing tension between Texas and the Mexican government. After 1830 the government took steps to stem immigration and put troops on the United States–Mexican border. Immigrants saw these measures as obstructions to their rightful claims. The rise of General Antonio López de Santa Anna provided the occasion for registering their complaints. But when Santa Anna dissolved the Mexican Congress and made himself dictator in 1834, Texans—both Anglo and Tejano—sharpened their criticisms. Casting themselves as the quintessential republicans, they and residents of several other Mexican states joined in the rebellion. Hoping to secure US statehood, Texas declared itself a sovereign republic on March 2, 1836.

Four days later the huge Mexican army, led by Santa Anna, attacked and wiped out 187 Texas patriots barricaded in a mission called the Alamo. It was a costly and fleeting victory. Santa Anna's army suffered 1,544 casualties and created martyrs for the rebels' cause. Led by Sam Houston, the rebels retreated east, gathering recruits as they went. On April 21 they surprised Mexican troops on the San Jacinto River and scored a huge victory, capturing Santa Anna himself. Bargaining for his life and freedom, Santa Anna declared Texas a free nation (see Map 13–1). Ecstatic Texans drew up a constitution, made Sam Houston their first president, and called for annexation to the United States.

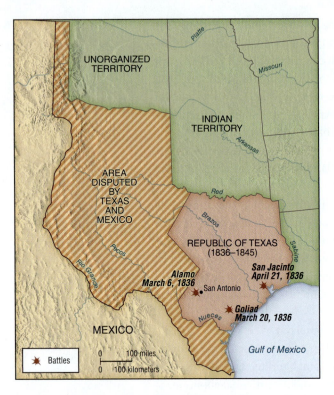

Map 13-1 Republic of Texas After the decisive American victory at San Jacinto that resulted in the independence of Texas, the border dispute between Texas and Mexico continued until it was resolved by the Mexican War a decade later.

With the nation in economic crisis and his own party bickering over who was responsible, the last thing Van Buren wanted as president was a bitter battle over Texas and slavery. He doubted that the Constitution permitted annexation, which he feared would be construed as meddling in Mexico's internal affairs. Anticipating Texas's application for admission, abolitionists had made opposition to annexation a central issue in their massive petition campaign of 1837–1838, expanding the controversy widely in the North. John Quincy Adams had delivered a stirring speech against annexation in the House, and some senators were publicly denouncing slavery in general and especially in Texas. Southerners had responded with their own states' rights petitions. In the end, Van Buren did not submit Texas's request for statehood to Congress.

Pacific Bound

For most white Americans, however, Texas was not the fulfillment of America's manifest destiny. That goal lay in the rich lands beyond the plains. By the time Van Buren left office, the Mississippi River had become the staging ground for a massive migration west.

The migration began as a trickle of missionaries in the 1830s. In 1831 rumors reached the East of four young Indians who had appeared in St. Louis, exhausted and sick, imploring that religious teachers be sent to their people. Two years later, the Methodist *Christian Advocate and Herald* published a letter from a Wyandot Indian who claimed that western tribes hungered for instruction in Christianity. True or not, such stories enabled missionaries to claim they had been invited into Indian communities. In 1834 the Methodist Missionary Society sent the Reverend Jason Lee west to found a mission in the Willamette Valley of Oregon Territory. Two years later, the American Board of Commissioners for Foreign Missions sent six people (including two women) to settle permanent missions in Oregon.

For their first mission, the board selected Marcus and Narcissa Prentiss Whitman, a doctor and a Sunday school teacher. In 1836, the Whitmans established their mission among the Cayuse Indians near Fort Walla Walla on the Columbia River. Their fellow missionaries Henry and Eliza Hart Spalding founded a mission 125 miles away among the Nez Percés.

At first, the Whitmans seemed to thrive. Marcus Whitman preached and doctored among the Cayuses and taught the men agriculture, and Narcissa taught school and oversaw the operation of the large mission. Over the following decade, however, as white immigration swelled, the Cayuses came to view the missionaries as the cause of the influx of white people and new diseases. In 1847, after a deadly measles epidemic, a Cayuse band attacked the mission, killing Marcus and Narcissa Prentiss Whitman and a number of other white people.

By then, migrants to the West Coast were so numerous that the roads of Iowa "were literally lined with long blue wagons . . . slowly wending their way over the broad prairies," leaving deep, rutted tracks. In the years of heaviest migration, watering holes were so overused and sanitary conditions so poor that the road west became a breeding ground for typhoid, malaria, dysentery, and cholera.

Most of the migrants were farming families of moderate means, pushed out of the Midwest by the hard times of 1837. Men often made the decision to leave with little warning to their families. Sarah Cummins remembered returning home from school one day in Illinois to discover that her father had sold the farm and that "as soon as school closes we are to move." Yet even spur-of-the-moment decisions rarely meant immediate departure for the West. Preparations for the trip took up to half a year, and families could expect to spend another half a year on the trail.

Travelers funneled through St. Louis, crossed Missouri to rendezvous with wagon trains near St. Joseph or Independence, Missouri, and then followed one of two main routes west (see Map 13–2). The northern route, known as the Oregon Trail, zigzagged northwest roughly parallel to the Rocky Mountains. The Santa Fe Trail headed southwest out of Independence along the Arkansas River through the future state of Kansas before reaching Mexican lands. At Santa Fe, the trail divided, feeding immigrants west along the Old Spanish Trail or south to Chihuahua, Mexico.

Most overland migrants traveled in families, in groups of families, and occasionally in entire communities. If they lacked team animals, families pulled their possessions in two-wheeled handcarts. For the most part, wagons carried supplies, not people. Most migrants walked west. Moreover, wagons broke down, were washed away in river crossings, or had to be emptied to ease the burden on the animals.

Past the plains, wagon trains sometimes went days without finding water or game. Women and men drove the wagons and herded the cattle, collected firewood, and caught small animals for food. When broken equipment or sickness slowed families, the trains were often forced to leave them behind, lest the others not clear the Rocky Mountains before winter. The harrowing dangers of that possibility were immortalized in the

Westward Migration The overland journey across the plains was slow and difficult at best, but it quickly entered into American legend and became the subject of romanticized images such as this one.

Map 13-2 Major Overland Trails The overland trails to the west started at the Missouri River. The Santa Fe Trail was a conduit for traders and goods to Mexico. The Oregon Trail passed through Wyoming and branched off to California and Oregon.

story of the ill-fated Donner Party, caught in the Sierra Nevadas by an early winter. For four months the group was trapped by snow, slowly starving. When relief finally arrived in mid-February 1847, "the dead were lying about on the snow, some even unburied, since the living had not strength to bury their dead," according to one survivor. Of the 87 persons snowed in, 42 died. It was not a risk worth taking, even if it meant leaving people behind on the plains.

For migrants who reached the West, the rewards were not always immediately apparent. "My most vivid recollection of that first winter in Oregon," one woman recalled, "is of the weeping skies and of Mother and me also weeping." As soon as they were settled, though, many newcomers proclaimed Oregon "this best country in the world." The climate was hospitable to crops of wheat, flax, and corn and to apple and pear orchards. Lumber was plentiful, and the streams were full of fish. Farther south was California, where, after 1848, rumors of "inexhaustible" gold strikes began to filter north and east.

Nations of the Trans-Mississippi West

American settlers felt they were journeying through national territories. Indigenous communities, such as Mah-i-ti-wo-nee-ni's friends and family, viewed the settlers as trespassers in Indian Country.

Most wagon trains departed from Missouri, which meant that settlers first crossed Indian Territory, where Native Americans had been guaranteed refuge from white intrusion (see Map 13–3). Between Independence, Missouri, and the Rocky Mountains lay the Indian nations of the prairies and Great Plains: the Blackfoot and Crow to the northwest; the Sioux, Pawnee, Arapaho, and the two great nations from which Mah-i-ti-wo-nee-ni claimed heritage, the Shoshone and the Cheyenne, through the northern and central plains; and the Kiowa, Apache, Comanche, and Navajo in the Southwest. Along the Pacific were the Yakima, Chinook, Cayuse, and Nez Percé Indians, and to the south, in California, Pomo, Chumash, Yuma, and many other tribes.

Because most of this vast territory was part of Mexico, and because Great Britain laid claim to Oregon, crossing to utopia meant transgressing the boundaries of those nations, as well.

Penny novelists would depict this contact as a violent confrontation in which warlike Indians massacred well-meaning migrants. In fact, of the more than 250,000 settlers who crossed the plains between 1840 and 1860, fewer than 400 were killed by Native Americans. About the same number of deaths was inflicted by white migrants on the Indians.

Prior to massive migration in the 1840s, official US policy toward the Indians had been one of removal, by force or by pressured sale of lands and physical relocation. Even in the 1830s observers saw no evidence that Americans recognized a boundary short of the Pacific Ocean. Alexis de Tocqueville noted that "when it promises these unlucky people a permanent asylum in the West," the US government "is well aware of its inability to guarantee this." By the late 1830s, as the last of the eastern "removals" were completed, federal policy toward Indians began to shift. Removal and resettlement continued to be the primary stated goal, and many western tribes were confined to reservations or moved to Indian Territory. But later removal policies aimed more overtly at individual rather than tribal ownership of reservation lands. Disrupting the land customs of Indians was, of course, what many Americans had long sought, bringing Native Americans into the "civilized" political economy of the United States through individual ownership of property. Allotment became the official policy toward all Indians by the end of the century.

By the mid-1830s, when white Americans started crossing the Mississippi River in huge numbers, most of these nations had already tasted the effects of expansionism. The Comanches (the largest of the southwestern nations) and the Apaches had been at war with European Americans for several centuries, having fought the Spanish, the Mexicans, and, since the 1820s, both the Mexicans and the US settlers in Texas. All of the Plains Indians, especially the Sioux, the Kiowas, and the Comanches, had felt the impact of eastern Indians displaced or officially relocated west. The Sioux had been at war for decades with the Indians of the Old Northwest Territory, who were being pushed across the Mississippi River.

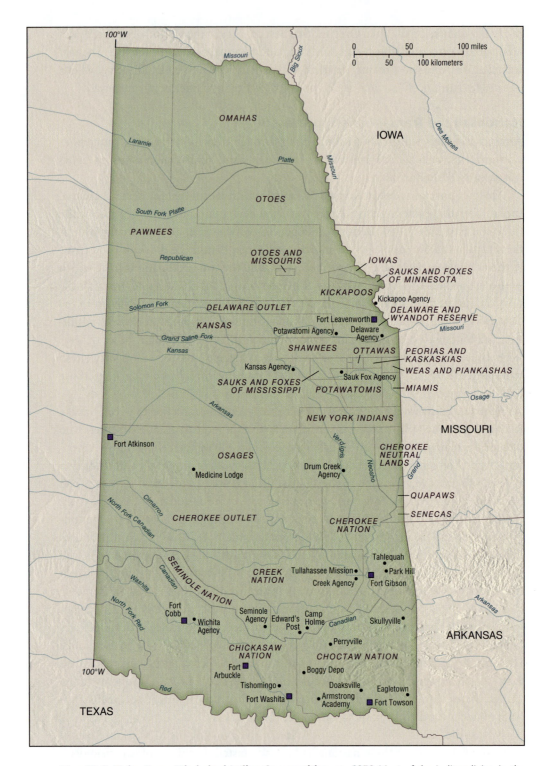

Map 13-3 Major Trans-Mississippi Indian Communities, ca. 1850 Most of the Indians living in the Indian Territories in the 1830s and 1840s had been "removed" from areas east of the Mississippi River. The territories were located west of Arkansas, Missouri, and Iowa. The section to the south (now Oklahoma) was home to Cherokees, Choctaws, Creeks, and Seminoles from the Old Southwest. The northern part (now Kansas and Nebraska) was inhabited by Indians from the Old Northwest.

For the western Indians, the effects of the migration of the 1840s were social, cultural, and economic. Although the number of deaths from warfare was low, deaths from disease were far higher and took especially high tolls on the children and the old, wiping out both the elders who carried a community's history and collective wisdom and the young people who represented its future. Contact gradually altered the Indians' social organization and gender division of labor. As it became harder to claim and protect planting grounds, tribes shifted to more nomadic ways of life. The relative importance of women's foraging and planting diminished, and the relative importance of men's skills as hunters and warriors increased.

By 1840, the northern grasslands and southern plains supported a complex economy of hunting and foraging. Indians consumed corn, melons, berries, wild sweet potatoes, turnips, and fowl and small game, harvested in a seminomadic way of life and traded through networks. At the center of this economy stood the bison, supplying food and material for clothing, shelter, and trade.

This way of life was threatened as the number of bison declined. Settlers' need for food had only a minor impact on the buffalo. More deadly was their fascination with hunting and killing such a huge creature, regardless of whether they needed its meat and hides. Recreational hunting parties, as well as hunters intent on wiping out the Indians' means of support, took their toll. As early as 1842, the Teton Sioux had complained to federal agents that the heavy migrations were harming their hunting grounds. By 1846 the Sioux were demanding that the US government stem the migrations and prevent the migrants from killing animals indiscriminately. When the government ignored the complaints, the Sioux prevented wagon trains from passing until migrants had paid a toll in money, tobacco, or supplies.

Buffalo Hunt The Plains Indians were extremely adept at hunting buffalo, which served as an integral part of their economic systems. Over the course of the nineteenth century, white encroachments rapidly decimated the buffalo herds and brought the species to the brink of extinction.

In the mid-1840s the energies of the federal government were primarily engaged in Texas, where American nationalists were demanding action against Mexico. In the northern plains, the government constructed a chain of forts intended as quarters for armed rifle units called dragoons, who would, theoretically, protect overland migrants from the Indians. The strategy was not very effective, as Indians continued to exert control over white migration through northern Indian Country.

Slavery and the Political Economy of Expansion

As Americans poured west, expansion became a source of national political controversy. The problem was not the principle of manifest destiny, which few questioned. By the late 1830s, expansion was linked in the public debate with the extension of slavery and raised other problems. Southerners viewed northerners as unfaithful to a 50-year-old compromise ratified in the Constitution. Northerners looked at the spread of slavery into the new Southwest (Louisiana, Mississippi, Alabama, and Arkansas) and worried about the political leverage of a new slave state the size of Texas.

> What then ought we to do? Ought we not to move immediately for the admission of Texas into the Union as a slave holding State? Should not the South **demand** it, as indispensable to their security: In my opinion, we have no alternative. To admit Texas as a non-slaveholding State, or to permit her to remain an independent and sovereign non-slave holding state, will be fatal to the Union, and ruinous to the whole country. . . . To the South, it is a question of **safety**; to the North it is one of interest. . . . Would it not be well to break the subject to the people of the South through the public prints? Both parties may unite in that, for it is a **Southern** question, and not one of whiggism and democracy.
>
> ABEL UPSHUR TO JOHN C. CALHOUN,
> August 14, 1843

Log Cabins and Hard Cider: The Election of 1840

Approaching the election of 1840, the major parties were in a balancing act. Both hoped to exploit regional differences but without raising the divisive issues associated with slavery. Whigs considered Van Buren vulnerable, both because of the continuing effects of the depression of 1837 and because he was a northerner who seemed to be blocking the annexation of Texas. Henry Clay, leader of the Whigs, also opposed the annexation, but he calculated that southern Democrats would choose a Kentuckian over a New Yorker. Aware of Van Buren's liabilities in the South, Democrats sought to keep slavery out of the debates, although Van Buren was willing to have northerners see him as the alternative to a southern president. A number of northern Whigs were suspicious of Clay's ties to the South.

Van Buren received the Democratic nomination, but in an effort to skirt the explosive sectional issues, the Whigs turned to William Henry Harrison, the hero of the battle of Tippecanoe and an outspoken advocate of cheap western land. Harrison had run strongest against Van Buren in 1836. To bolster the appeal of their slate, for their vice presidential candidate the Whigs chose a former Democrat, John Tyler of Virginia, a strong advocate of states' rights and (at the time) a Clay supporter.

Harrison was a "sentimental" candidate who the Whigs hoped would evoke feelings of military glory and westward expansion. Avoiding tough issues, they crafted a Jackson-like campaign for "Tippecanoe and Tyler, too." When Harrison was derided as a country bumpkin content with sitting on his porch drinking cider, the Whigs took up the image with gusto. In the "Log Cabin and Hard Cider Campaign," the Whigs celebrated Harrison as a simple man of the people (like Jackson). In fact, Harrison was from a wealthy old Virginia family, but he could be linked to the West, and, as Daniel Webster observed, Harrison's main appeal was the vague "hope of a better time."

The turnout was large, and the popular results were close, but the Electoral College was a different story. Harrison, who had taken every large state but Virginia, triumphed with 234 electoral votes to Van Buren's 60. The Democrats held New Hampshire, Illinois, Missouri, Arkansas, Alabama, Virginia, and South Carolina.

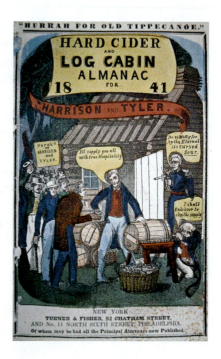

And Tyler, Too

Whig jubilation at their presidential victory was short-lived. Harrison fell ill shortly after his inauguration and died on April 4, 1841, the first president to die in office. Harrison was followed in office by his vice president, John Tyler, whom most observers assumed would serve as a caretaker president until the next general election. He soon proved them wrong, succeeding to the full stature and authority of the presidency.

Tyler's ascendancy threw the Whig Party into chaos, for once in office he reverted to his Democratic roots. Much about Tyler was reminiscent of Jackson. He opposed the American System and favored slavery and the annexation of Texas, and he was willing to use the full power of the executive to enforce those views. Unlike Jackson, Tyler strongly advocated extreme southern states' rights positions.

Tyler's attention was first drawn to diplomatic troubles with Britain. In 1841 the slave crew of the US ship *Creole*, en route from Virginia to New Orleans, had seized control of the vessel and forced it into the port of Nassau, where, by British law, the crew was freed. To no avail, white southerners demanded the return of the crew. Meanwhile, northern anti-British feeling flared over the question of the Oregon Territory, a vaguely defined expanse between northern California and Alaska that Britain and the United States had agreed in 1818 to occupy jointly. By 1842, reports of the North American Pacific Coast as a "storehouse of wealth in all its forests, furs, and fisheries" had stirred both immigration and the American desire to claim the Oregon Territory.

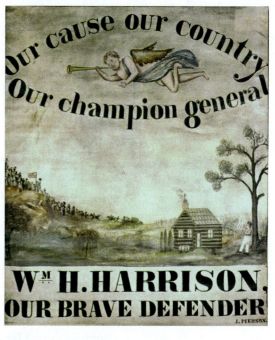

In 1842 US secretary of state Webster and British emissary Ashburton concluded the Webster-Ashburton Treaty, which drew a boundary between the United States and Canada from Maine to the Rocky Mountains (Oregon was left undivided), established terms of extradition between the two nations, and created a joint effort to restrict the international slave trade. Great Britain also agreed not to interfere with foreign vessels.

Tyler's success in foreign relations was overshadowed by his 1841 break with his own party. Led by Henry Clay, Whigs in Congress passed legislation that embodied their platform, including tariff bills, a national bank bill, and a bill to distribute federal surpluses to states. Tyler vetoed almost every initiative. He denounced federal distribution as inappropriate when the federal government was in deficit. At last, in 1842, congressional Whigs offered lower tariff increases and detached the tariff from the question of distribution. Needing federal funds, Tyler signed the bill. Tyler supported the repeal of the independent treasury, a Whig goal, but this, too, proved a bitter victory for the Whigs, because Tyler vetoed the national bank with which the Whigs wanted to replace the independent treasury.

Tyler was soon a president without a party. As early as January 1843, there were calls in the House of Representatives for his impeachment. That year, when Tyler vetoed the bill rechartering the national bank, his entire cabinet resigned, except Webster.

"His Accidency," as opponents dubbed Tyler, proved resilient. Tyler interpreted Democratic gains in the 1842 elections as support for his positions, particularly on the national bank. Urged on by extreme states' rights advocates in Virginia and South Carolina, Tyler took up the cause of the annexation of Texas. After Daniel Webster resigned from the cabinet, Tyler fell almost entirely under the influence of southerners committed to Texas.

Texas did all it could to press for annexation. It allowed Great Britain to serve as an intermediary in Texas's efforts to win official recognition from Mexico and hinted that, as an independent republic, Texas might abolish slavery. The idea of an alliance between Texas and Great Britain reawakened old anti-British sentiments, and the prospect of a non–slave republic so nearby filled southerners with dread.

Seeking to capitalize on these anxieties, in 1843 President Tyler secretly opened negotiations with Texas for admission to the Union, expecting to justify the treaty as necessary protection against British influence. In 1844, Tyler submitted a treaty of annexation to Congress. He hoped that potential opposition would be countered by expansionist interests. He was wrong. Even before the treaty was submitted, John Quincy Adams and 12 other Whigs denounced it as constitutionally unauthorized and warned that it would bring the nation to "dissolution." Abolitionists labeled the move a naked power grab by slave owners. Even moderate northerners worried that annexing Texas would cause war with Mexico, without yielding the North any tangible gains. Some southerners worried that Texas would compete with the depleted cotton and sugar lands of the South.

By then, other election-year dramas were afoot. John Calhoun still longed for the presidency and felt he had a good chance against Tyler, another southerner, if he could deny Van Buren the Democratic nomination. To that end, Calhoun wrote a note to the British minister that the US goal in Texas was to protect slavery against British abolitionists. As Calhoun hoped, the note became public. The explicit association of Texas and slavery drove Van Buren away from endorsing the treaty, weakening his position in the South. An overwhelmingly sectional vote defeated the treaty in Congress, but Calhoun believed a Democratic victory in 1844 would revive it.

Occupy Oregon, Annex Texas

By the fall of 1844 the American political party system was in disarray. Harrison's impressive victory in 1840 had not signaled a broad endorsement of Clay or the American System, any more than Van Buren's victory in 1836 had signaled a strong hard-money, antibank sentiment. To the contrary, between 1836 and 1844 the party system seemed most successful at polarizing American interests, which were already diverging economically (see Table 13–1).

Table 13-1 Personal Income Per Capita by Region: Percentages of United States Average

	1840	1860	1880
United States	100	100	100
Northeast	135	139	141
North Central	68	68	98
South	76	72	51
West	—	—	190

Source: Richard A. Easterlin, "Regional Income Trends, 1840–1950," in American Economic History ed. Seymour E. Harris (New York: McGraw-Hill, 1961), p. 528.

Nowhere was that state of affairs more evident than in the 1844 Democratic convention in Baltimore. Van Buren's supporters believed the party owed him the nomination, yet his liabilities were legion. In the South, proslavery, proannexation Democrats led by Calhoun were vowing to have "a slaveholder for President next time regardless of the man." Andrew Jackson was disappointed with Van Buren's refusal to endorse annexation and encouraged former Tennessee governor James K. Polk to run. In the North, workers and entrepreneurs hard hit by years of deflation were disenchanted with Van Buren. His supporters were unable to block a convention rule requiring a candidate to receive a two-thirds vote to secure the nomination. Van Buren could not marshal that level of support, but neither could Tyler, Calhoun, or Lewis Cass, a compromise candidate. Finally, on the eighth ballot the convention fell back on Jackson's choice, James Polk. Tyler accepted renomination by a renegade group of supporters who styled themselves Democratic Republicans.

The 1844 Democratic Party ran on the platform of manifest destiny, calling for "the reoccupation of Oregon and the reannexation of Texas." It was an odd formulation, given that the United States had several times officially denied possession of Texas and had yet to occupy Oregon fully. The platform went even further on Oregon. Although the US claim to Oregon had never extended beyond the 49th parallel, the Democrats now declared their willingness to go to war to gain the entire region ("Fifty-four forty or fight!"). Their strategy incorporated war fears over Texas into a broader assertion of national destiny.

Meanwhile, in 1844 Henry Clay secured the Whig nomination. Clay was certain that opposition to the extension of slavery was strong enough to block a Texas-Oregon compromise and that Americans would not support a war with Mexico. Clay ran primarily as a supporter of the American System as the necessary means for stabilizing economic growth.

The election results suggested a nation teetering on the edge of political division. Polk, annexation, and manifest destiny won, but by only 38,000 of more than 2.5 million votes cast. More striking, James G. Birney of Ohio, the candidate of the new, explicitly antislavery Liberty Party, drew 62,000 votes, most of them taken from Clay. Had Birney not run, the election might have been a dead heat (see Table 13–2).

Both Tyler and Congress read the election as a referendum on the Democratic platform and specifically on Texas. Early in 1845, with Tyler still in office, a bill approving annexation passed the House. To move it through the Whig-dominated Senate, Senator Robert Walker of Mississippi suggested that the Senate version include the option of negotiating a whole new treaty. Only days away from the presidency, Polk was said to favor this approach, and Whigs thought a revised treaty might get them out

DEBATING HISTORY

>> Manifest Destiny and Race

For most white Americans in the 1830s and 1840s, westward expansion appeared to be their manifest destiny. But expansion also brought conflict in the late 1830s, as it became linked to the extension of slavery. In 1836, Texan independence from Mexico raised the question of whether the United States should annex Texas, which stirred northern fears that a massive new slave state might soon join the Union. In 1844, the Democratic Party nominated James K. Polk on a platform of manifest destiny. As president, Polk oversaw a war with Mexico that greatly increased the territory of the United States and produced a corresponding surge in sectional tensions over slavery. As these tensions grew, the antislavery and proslavery wings of Democratic Party came into clearer focus. Historians disagree about the relationship of the Democratic Party to slavery in this period. Alexander Saxton sees the Democratic Party united around an ideology of white supremacy that legitimized slavery, whereas Jonathan Earle sees antislavery "free-soil" Democrats as legitimately opposed to slavery on moral as well as political and economic grounds.

ALEXANDER SAXTON, *The Rise and Fall of the White Republic: Class Politics and Mass Culture in Nineteenth-Century America* (New York: Verso, 1990), pp. 142, 153–154.

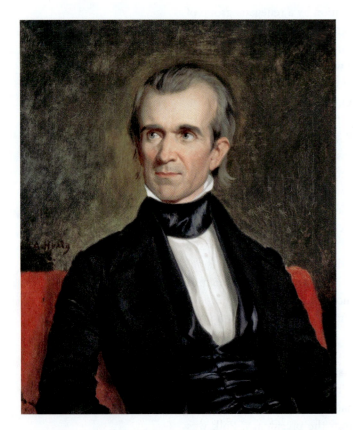

James K. Polk

Jacksonian Democrats asserted the political, civil, and moral equality of white male citizens. . . . Farmers, frontiersmen, urban workers and the middle class had readily accepted the racist legitimization of slavery; and they accepted also the argument that plantation slavery provided the only sure means for quarantining Africans in America. What these acceptances led to, however, was a conclusion that the entry of Africans, slave or free, into the promised land of the West had to be prevented. "I plead the rights of white labor," David Wilmot, a Democrat from Pennsylvania, explained as he introduced the proviso that triggered the crises of the 1850s. "I would preserve to free white labor a fair country, a rich inheritance, where the sons of toil of my own race and color can live without the disgrace which association with negro slavery brings upon free labor."

JONATHAN EARLE, *Jacksonian Antislavery and the Politics of Free Soil, 1824–1854* (Chapel Hill: University of North Carolina Press, 2004), pp. 5, 14–15.

. . . Democratic veterans of the antibank and antimonopoly battles of the 1830s fashioned their own arguments against slavery and its extension. . . . Free-soil Democrats went beyond simple hostility to the Slave Power and its pretenses, linking their antislavery opposition to a land reform agenda that pressed for free land for poor settlers, in addition to land free of slavery. . . . While it is beyond dispute that many Free Soilers were racists (a trait they shared with most white Americans in the nineteenth century), it is inaccurate to view the party and ideology as unprincipled and cynical retreats from the far preferable goal of racial equality. Even Free Soilers such as David Wilmot . . . made it clear that [they] opposed slavery in any form, and in the South as well as the West. Restricting slavery was, for many northern Democrats, the first step toward its eradication. . . . While far from enlightened regarding racial matters from a twenty-first-century perspective, a great majority of Free Soilers opposed the perpetuation of slavery wherever it existed, rejected racist arguments justifying bondage, and insisted on the basic humanity of African-Americans.

Questions

1. How does each historian characterize the role that racism played in the Democratic Party of the 1840s?

2. Both historians stress that the idea of slavery restriction became significant to a growing number of northern Jacksonians in the 1840s. However, each historian offers a different reason for the growing importance of slavery restriction. In what ways do their interpretations of slavery restriction differ?

Table 13–2 The Liberty Party Swings an Election

Candidate	Party	Actual Vote in New York	National Electoral Vote	If Liberty Voters Had Voted Whig	Projected Electoral Vote
Polk	Democratic	237,588	170	237,588	134
Clay	Whig	232,482	105	248,294	141
Birney	Liberty	15,812	0	—	—

of a politically costly position. The Senate approved the amended treaty. The Whigs expected Tyler to concede the decision to the incoming president, but in the last hours of his presidency he sent notice to Texas that (contingent on its own agreement) the republic was annexed to the United States of America. Mexico immediately severed relations with the United States.

War with Mexico

The annexation of Texas was the ostensible cause of the outbreak of war with Mexico in April 1846, but not the only cause. In Polk's eyes, the annexation of Texas was a piece of a larger acquisition: not only Oregon but also present-day New Mexico, Arizona, and California. Polk would have been happy to make these acquisitions peacefully, but he was willing to go to war.

Polk took a two-track approach to foreign relations. In December 1845 he announced his decision to withdraw from negotiations over Oregon, and he called on Congress to terminate the United States–Great Britain Convention of Joint Occupancy. Compromise would be an abandonment of American "territorial rights . . . and the national honour," he insisted, and would be unthinkable. Beyond the combative rhetoric, Polk informed his advisers that he was prepared to hear a compromise offer from England. When one came, proposing a boundary at the 49th parallel, Polk submitted it to Congress. By June 1846 the deal had been struck.

In Oregon, Polk threatened war but quickly accepted peace. However, what Polk really wanted in the Mexican borderlands, Thomas Hart Benton claimed, was "a little war," big enough to justify grabbing the Southwest but not so big as to break the budget. Texas provided the excuse.

As a condition of his surrender and release, the Mexican general Santa Anna had agreed to the Rio Grande as the boundary between Texas and Mexico, a boundary that would have run northward to include present-day New Mexico as well as western Texas. The Mexican government had instead drawn the border at the Nueces River, recognizing only about half the territory claimed by Texans. Polk intended to set the boundary at the Rio Grande, and he may have intended to secure not only the disputed Texas territory but also large portions of northern Mexico.

Polk once again played a double game. As late as September, he appealed for a peaceful resolution. That month, he dispatched former Louisiana congressman John Slidell to Mexico to offer to purchase New Mexico and Texas for $30 million. The Mexican government refused to receive Slidell.

Meanwhile, Polk prepared for war. In the spring of 1845 he had sent 1,500 soldiers, under the command of General Zachary Taylor, allegedly to protect Texas against a possible invasion by Mexico. When Texas approved union with the United States, Polk reinforced Taylor's troops and ordered them to approach the Rio Grande, while also sending an army under Stephen Kearny into the northern part of the disputed territory. In August 1846, Kearny occupied Santa Fe. At the same time, Polk ordered the US squadron in the Pacific closer to the California coast and directed the US consul in California, Thomas Larkin, to encourage local disaffection with the Mexican government. When American settlers in the Sonoma Valley staged a rebellion in June and July, the representatives of the United States claimed California. Kearny later crossed into California to solidify the claim.

By then, Polk's brinkmanship on the Rio Grande had produced results. Mexican troops had crossed the river to drive out Taylor's force, and American soldiers had been killed and wounded. In May 1846, Congress declared that "a state of war exists" between the two nations.

The United States entered the war unprepared. Although 100,000 volunteers signed up, at the outbreak of hostilities the United States Army had only 7,500 troops. Perhaps Polk shared the expansionist view of Mexico as a "miserable, inefficient" nation. Mexico (and New Spain before it) had always been less interested in its northern provinces than in other parts of the nation. Moreover, after a coup, the Mexican government was unstable. With California guarded by John C. Frémont and the naval squadron, the United States could bring its military power to bear on Mexico City.

Finding the right leader proved tricky. Taylor, the obvious choice, was a popular Whig. Polk finally settled on Winfield Scott, who also harbored Whig ambitions. In the late winter of 1847, a squadron of 200 ships conveyed Scott's army of 10,000 soldiers to Veracruz, which surrendered in April. Scott's troops fought their way to the outskirts of Mexico City, which fell after six days on September 14 (see Map 13–4).

For all the success of the American campaign, support for the war steadily eroded. From the beginning, the war raised the question of slavery. Northern Democrats saw the war as a transparent ploy to extend slavery. Antislavery activists spoke out against the war, and opposition grew as stories of US military atrocities filtered back east.

In spite of the unpopularity of the war, a defeated Mexico was so weak that Polk thought of extracting greater concessions. His minister in Mexico, Nicholas P. Trist, opposed this proposal, however. In 1848 Trist negotiated the Treaty of Guadalupe Hidalgo, recognizing the Rio Grande as the border of Texas and granting the United States the territory encompassed in the present states of New Mexico, Arizona, Colorado,

AMERICA AND THE WORLD

>> Lt. Rankin Dilworth in the War with Mexico

Rankin Dilworth was only 18 years old when he entered the United States Military Academy at West Point. By the time he applied to the academy, his mother had been widowed twice, and Dilworth may well have seen the army as his one opportunity to get ahead in life. He was apparently an average cadet, graduating in the middle of his class in 1844, one year behind Ulysses S. Grant, future general of the Union army and president of the United States. But in 1844 neither Grant nor Dilworth was contemplating duty in a civil war. If Dilworth had his sights fixed on anything, it was surely the West, where American territorial ambitions were creating countless opportunities for military advancement.

By the spring of 1846, those opportunities were near at hand. Barracked outside of St. Louis, Dilworth's company was ordered to southern Texas, where hostilities had already broken out between United States troops and the Mexican army. They traveled by boat down the Mississippi and across the Gulf of Mexico to Matamoros, Mexico. From there, they marched up the Rio Grande to Carmargo, Texas, where Dilworth's unit joined with American forces under General Zachary Taylor. From Carmargo, the combined unit proceeded to Monterrey. From April 28 to September 19, 1846, Dilworth kept an almost daily record of that journey.

The diary suggests that, officer or not, Dilworth was shadowed by nostalgia for home. Viewing a beautiful church in Reynosa made him wonder "if I will ever go to church again where I hear the English language spoken." That night, he dreamed he was in church at home "without a thought of camps or bivouacs, with smiling happy faces around me." Awakened by the call to guard duty, "in an instant," he wrote, "I found myself

on the hot sandy plaza of Reynosa, many, many miles from those I love."

Still, Dilworth found much to occupy his attention in the journey south. He took a keen interest in Mexico. Waxing romantic, he compared Mexico to "a magnificent flower garden" dotted with plots of "limes, oranges, lemons, [and] pomegranates." He admired young Mexican women, one of whom he declared "the handsomest female that I have seen since I parted with E. M. M." (his sweetheart back home). Dilworth's descriptions sometimes betrayed the flippant cultural superiority so much a part of American expansionism of the 1840s. "The inhabitants present all shades from pure Indian to the white person," he wrote on one occasion. "Their intelligence is in the same scale."

Dilworth's diary also recorded the daily, and sometimes needless, hardships that would eventually make the campaign infamous in army annals. Swollen with untrained volunteers and newly trained officers (like Dilworth himself), the Mexican campaign was a tutorial in bad luck and bad judgment. Dilworth wrote about tents that collapsed in violent rainstorms, marches through mud so thick that it added 10 pounds to the weight of each boot, and temperatures so hot that soldiers died of heat prostration. He wrote of arrogant and inept officers who could not even march their troops in the right direction. On September 19 near Monterrey, Dilworth encountered an old friend in a different unit. The friend asked Dilworth if he had "heard the 'Elephant' groan," an expression used by the troops to express bitterness and disappointment. Dilworth did not record his reply. Nor did he add any further entries in the diary. On September 21, General Taylor ordered an assault on Monterrey, dividing his

Continued

small band into two groups to attack the city from opposite sides. The western troops won with relative ease, but the eastern forces lost their way in thick cane fields before being caught in deadly Mexican crossfire. Along the city's narrow streets, they were easy targets for sharpshooters. Remarkably, inch by inch, house by house, Taylor's troops carried the day. On September 24, 1846, Mexican general Pedro de Ampudia offered surrender.

None of this mattered to Rankin Dilworth. During the first day's assault a "twelve-pounder cannon ball" had torn off one of his legs. On September 27, at 24 years of age, he died. His family was unable to pay the costs of having his body returned to Ohio. Lieutenant Rankin Dilworth was buried in Monterrey, Mexico.

Utah, and Wyoming, as well as California. In return, the United States paid Mexico $15 million and assumed war claims of American citizens against Mexico. The Senate approved the treaty on March 10, 1848. The following May 25, Mexico concurred.

Although Polk's presidency was dominated by the war with Mexico, the tariff and the independent treasury haunted domestic politics. In each case, Polk was victorious. Like Jackson, Polk opposed protective tariffs, which he saw as benefiting industrialists

Nebel, *Storming of Chapultepec—Quitman's Attack.*

Chapultepec Carl Nebel's depiction of the American attack on the Chapultepec fort, near Mexico City, during the Mexican-American War, September 13, 1847.

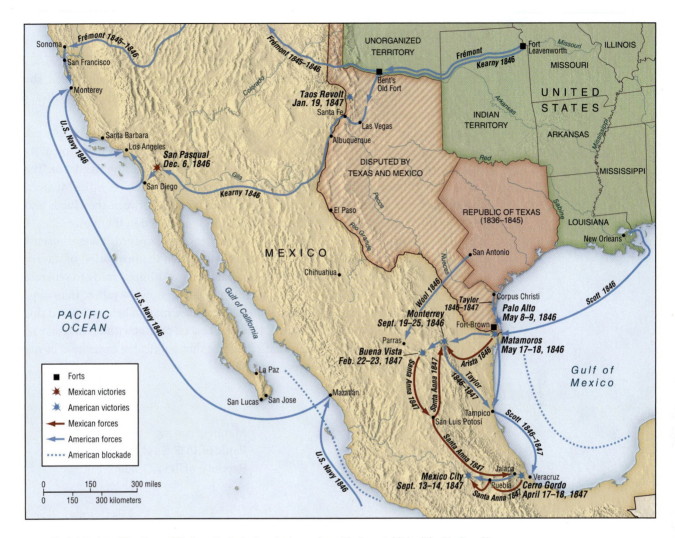

Map 13–4 Mexican War General Zachary Taylor's victories in northern Mexico established the Rio Grande as the boundary between Texas and Mexico. Stephen Kearny's expedition secured control of New Mexico. General Winfield Scott's invasion by sea at Veracruz and his occupation of Mexico ended the war.

at the expense of farmers and republican values. Although Whigs in Congress pushed for higher tariffs to support domestic manufacturing, the 1846 tariff eliminated flat duties and reduced overall levels. Also like Jackson, Polk opposed the national bank. In 1846 he persuaded Congress to reinstate Van Buren's independent treasury to handle the federal government's financial transactions. Meanwhile, he vetoed Whig attempts to enact legislation supporting internal improvements.

Jackson and Polk shared a broad understanding of politics and the use of political machinery. Like Jackson, Polk framed policy battles as battles between good and evil, between individual opportunity and elite finance and capital. At the same time, also like Jackson, Polk exercised executive power as the tool of the people's will. He was convinced that the president, not the legislature (Whig controlled, by his final years in office), represented the people's will. Before he left office, virtually every important item on his political agenda had been accomplished. Lost in that flush of victory was the steady erosion of popular support for the Democratic Party.

Conclusion

In 1820, Fanny Wright noted that many observers worried about the differences between the American North and South, but Wright was optimistic. If all else failed, she declared, the western states, settled by migrants from North and South, would always be "powerful cementers of the Union."

By the end of the 1840s, it was clear that Wright's confidence had been misplaced. The war with Mexico revealed just how far apart the North and South had grown. By 1848, the northern states were deeply committed to a society based on free labor. The southern states, meanwhile, had grown ever more committed to slavery. The Mexican War signaled the beginning of an era in which differences between the North and South would seem undeniable and intractable—and symbolized in the West.

In 1848, Henry David Thoreau spoke to an audience in Concord, Massachusetts, about his refusal to pay poll taxes, which he said supported the institution of slavery and its expansion in the war with Mexico. Thoreau declared himself ready to separate from his government—indeed, to see the Union itself destroyed—rather than support the United States in the West. "How does it become a man to behave toward this American government today?" he asked. "I answer, that he cannot without disgrace be associated with it. I cannot for an instant recognize that political organization as my government which is the slave's government also."

Who, What

Henry Clay   458
Mah-i-ti-wo-nee-ni   439
Tejanos   449
John Tyler   458

Manifest destiny   445
Panic of 1837   442
Republic of Texas   439

>> TIME LINE

▼**1834**
First missionaries arrive in Oregon Territory

▼**1836**
Martin Van Buren elected president
Equal Rights Party formed
Whig Party runs candidates for president
Texas declares independence

▼**1838**
"Aroostook" War
Anti-Slavery Petition campaign at height

▼**1839**
Amistad mutiny

▼**1840**
Independent Treasury Bill
Anti-Slavery Society splits
Liberty Party nominates James Birney for the presidency

Large-scale overland migration to West Coast begins
Whig candidate William Henry Harrison elected president

▼**1841**
John Tyler succeeds Harrison in office
Creole Mutiny

Review Questions

1. What was the depression of 1837 and what were its origins?

2. Why were Whigs cautious about westward migration?

3. Why was the annexation of Texas so controversial?

Critical-Thinking Questions

1. Support for American expansion was often expressed in the language of freedom and civilization. But was there also a racial component to "manifest destiny"? Explain your answer.

2. Did the territorial additions of the 1840s represent a departure (in method or intent) from earlier acquisitions?

3. How and why did the Democratic Party change between 1828 and 1848?

For further review materials and resource information, please visit www.oup.com/us/ofthepeople

▼**1842**
Webster-Ashburton Treaty

▼**1844**
James Polk is elected president

▼**1845**
The United States annexes Texas

▼**1846**
The United States declares war on Mexico

▼**1848**
Independent women's rights movement begins at Seneca Falls, New York
Treaty of Guadalupe Hidalgo
Teton Sioux tax white settlers passing through their lands

1) The celebration of "manifest destiny" and the harsh realities of the Panic of 1837 prompted many families to make the journey west.

2) The philosophy of "manifest destiny" directly contributed to diplomatic tensions with Great Britain over Oregon, outright war with Mexico, and the continued decimation of Indian nations.

3) As American democracy expanded, the Democratic Party had trouble accommodating a growing range of issues and crises, allowing the Whig Party to win the presidency for the first time.

4) Polk's presidency drew heavily from Jackson's legacy. He framed policy battles as battles between good and evil, expanded the power of the executive, and pushed strongly for American expansion.

The Decline of Jacksonianism

The Political Economy of the Trans-Mississippi West

Slavery and the Political Economy of Expansion

EVENTS

Political Parties in Crisis As democracy expanded, the major political parties had difficulty accommodating a wide range of conflicting interests and beliefs.

Van Buren and the Legacy of Jackson President Martin Van Buren struggled with the Panic of 1837 and international crises.

Manifest Destiny in Antebellum Culture America's desire to possess the continent to the Pacific Ocean was celebrated in art and literature, and framed in the language of democracy and freedom.

Texas Americans immigrated to northern Mexico, battled the Mexican army over slavery and property claims, and won independence. The new Republic of Texas petitioned the United States for annexation, but political concerns delayed the process.

Pacific Bound Scores of migrant families traveled west along overland routes to Oregon and California.

Nations of the Trans-Mississippi West American expansion impacted western Indian nations on social, cultural, and economic levels.

Log Cabins and Hard Cider: The Election of 1840 William Henry Harrison, running as a Whig, defeated Martin Van Buren's effort at reelection.

And Tyler, Too John Tyler ascended to the presidency after Harrison's death, reverted to his Democratic roots, and threw the Whig Party into chaos.

Occupy Oregon, Annex Texas James K. Polk ran on a platform of manifest destiny and won a close presidential election, but the narrow margin of his victory suggested a nation teetering on the edge of political division.

War with Mexico Polk's expansionist agenda and the annexation of Texas sparked a war with Mexico. American victory led to the acquisition of present-day New Mexico, Arizona, and California.

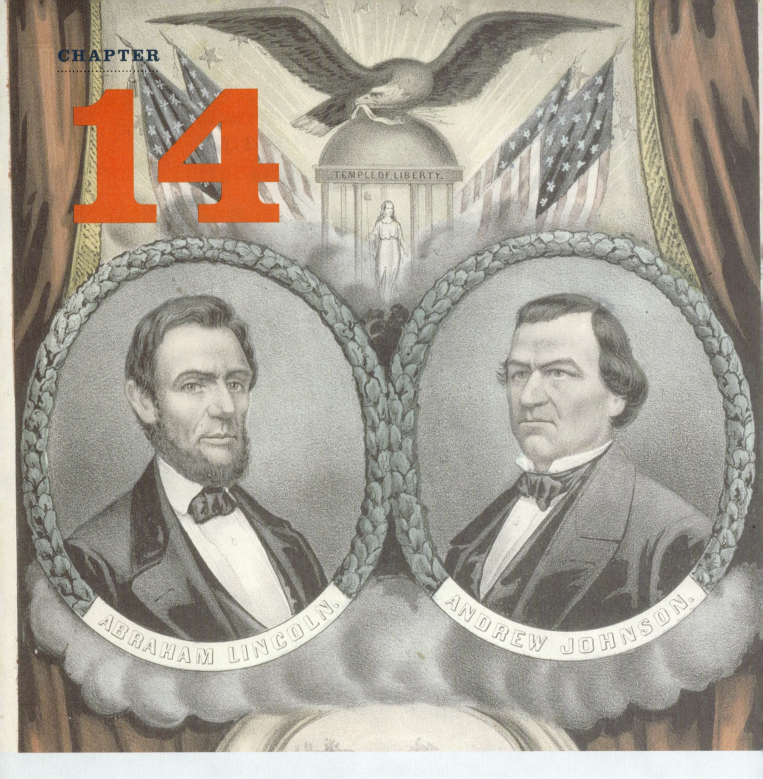

COMMON THREADS

>> In previous chapters you read about the development of the American economy and the expansion of slavery. In what ways did these developments become sources of tension between the North and South during the 1850s?

>> The conflict between Whigs and Democrats during the 1830s and 1840s is sometimes called "the first party system." How did this change in the 1850s?

>> Do you think that by 1860 the Civil War was "irrepressible"?

The Politics of Slavery
1848–1860

>> Frederick Douglass

Frederick Douglass denounced the war with Mexico as "disgraceful, cruel, and iniquitous." Northern support for what he saw as a slaveholders' war reinforced Douglass's conviction that the US Constitution had created an unholy union of liberty and slavery. The only solution was for New England to secede. "The Union must be dissolved," Douglass wrote, "or New England is lost and swallowed up by the slave-power of the country."

Douglass had been urging disunion for several years, ever since he became the most compelling antislavery voice in America. His authority derived from his extraordinary intelligence, his exceptional skill as a public speaker, and above all from his personal experience. Frederick Douglass was not simply an abolitionist; he was also the most famous runaway slave in America.

He was born Frederick Augustus Washington Bailey in Talbot County, Maryland, in 1818. At the age of seven he was sent to Baltimore, where he became a skilled caulker in the shipyards. There he hired out his labor, paying his master three dollars each week and keeping the rest himself. He grew to resent the arrangement, and for the rest of his life he would associate freedom with the right to earn a living. When his master ended their arrangement and demanded that the slave hand over all his earnings, Frederick planned his escape.

On May 3, 1838, he dressed as a sailor and boarded a northbound train using borrowed papers. By September he was calling himself Frederick Douglass and was living and working in New Bedford, Massachusetts. He began attending antislavery meetings. He subscribed to William Lloyd Garrison's fiery abolitionist newspaper, *The Liberator*. In 1841 he was invited to speak during an abolitionist convention and stunned his listeners with an eloquent recital of his experience as a slave. Garrison was in the audience, and he invited Douglass to speak for the American Anti-Slavery Society. For the next several years Douglass was a leading spokesman for the Garrisonian wing of the abolitionist movement.

The Garrisonians felt that the Constitution was hopelessly corrupted by its compromises with slavery. They saw no point in pursuing political reforms, advocating instead the separation of the North from the South. The Garrisonians rejected all violent efforts to overthrow slavery, including slave rebellion, in favor of moral persuasion of their opponents. Frederick Douglass initially believed all of these things.

The Mexican War was a turning point for Douglass. By the late 1840s, he saw growing numbers of northerners join the Free-Soil Party, fighting the expansion of slavery, and wondered why this could not become a political coalition against slavery itself. During the 1850s Douglass moved further from the Garrisonians: he openly supported slave rebellion, realized that political action was necessary to eliminate slavery, and came to doubt the wisdom of dismissing the Constitution as a proslavery document.

Douglass moved closer to mainstream northern politics because antislavery sentiment had reentered the mainstream. Since the 1820s, the major parties had studiously avoided the

Continued

>> AMERICAN PORTRAIT *Continued*

topic of slavery. But the annexation of Texas in 1845 spurred some abolitionists to push slavery back into national politics, first by flooding the South with antislavery literature and Congress with antislavery petitions and then by organizing a Liberty Party dedicated to halting slavery's expansion—a position known as "free soil." By 1848 a Free-Soil Party was attracting hundreds of thousands of votes.

Even as Garrison and his followers were withdrawing from the mainstream of the antislavery movement, other abolitionists were successfully shoving antislavery back into the political mainstream. By the middle of the 1850s the Whig Party collapsed in the North and was replaced by the new Republican Party, openly hostile to slavery and sworn to restricting its expansion. Soon after, the Democratic Party split into northern and southern wings. For the first time in American history a major political party could accommodate a radical abolitionist like Frederick Douglass. By 1861 he was urging the president to uphold the Constitution by suppressing the South's attempt to secede.

The Political Economy of Freedom and Slavery

The politics of slavery reemerged at a moment of tremendous economic growth. As the depression of the 1840s lifted, the American zeal for internal improvements revived. The canals built between 1800 and 1830 were widened during the 1840s and 1850s to accommodate the new steamboats. Railroad construction, which had collapsed during the 1840s, came back stronger than ever in the 1850s. On the eve of the Civil War, the United States boasted more miles of railroad track than the rest of the world combined. No less spectacular was the rapid adoption of the telegraph. Invented by Samuel F. B. Morse in 1844, the telegraph made virtually instantaneous communication possible across oceans and continents. By 1860, there were 50,000 miles of telegraph wire in America. The first transcontinental line was completed in 1861.

These developments might have inhibited the growth of sectionalism. An efficient transportation and communication network helped integrate the United States into a single national market. But market integration only tied together two different societies based on two very different systems of labor. By the 1850s the differences between North and South overwhelmed the connections that bound them together.

A Changing Economy in the North

The 1850s were booming years for northern farmers, now connected firmly to the national market. It took less than a week to ship meat and grains from midwestern cities to the East Coast. Because of the dramatic reduction in transportation costs, northern

OUTLINE

The Political Economy of Freedom and Slavery
A Changing Economy in the North

TECHNOLOGY AND IDEAS:
  The Telegraph
The Slave Economy
The Importance of the West

Slavery Becomes a Political Issue
Wilmot Introduces His Proviso

A Compromise Without Compromises
The Fugitive Slave Act Provokes a Crisis
The Election of 1852 and the Decline of the Whig
  Party

Nativism and the Origins of the Republican Party
  The Nativist Attack on Immigration
  The Kansas-Nebraska Act Revives the Slavery Issue
  Kansas Begins to Bleed

farmers could devote more time and effort to producing crops for sale rather than for subsistence at home. Thanks also to inventions like the steel plow, seed drills, and the McCormick reaper, northern farmers increased production of goods for market, quadrupling productivity between 1820 and 1860.

Farmers could grow more crops for sale because more Americans were living in cities and working for wages, producing little of their own food, clothing, or shelter. Yet so productive was American agriculture that a shrinking proportion of farmers could feed a growing proportion of city dwellers and factory workers. In 1820, 75 percent of the labor force was devoted to agriculture. By 1860 the figure was 57 percent. Wage labor in the North grew so rapidly that native-born workers could not fill the demand. In the mid-1840s the number of Europeans coming to the United States jumped sharply, and 3 million arrived in the decade between 1845 and 1854. More than two-thirds were Irish or German, many of them Roman Catholic. By 1855 a larger proportion of Americans was foreign born than at any other time in the nation's history.

Many immigrants, especially the Irish, came to America impoverished and congregated in the growing cities and factory towns of the North. By 1860, immigrants made up more than one-third of the residents in northern cities with populations of at least 10,000. These newcomers became wage laborers in numbers that far outstripped their proportions in the population. Men worked in unskilled jobs on the docks, at construction sites, on railroads and canals, or in the coal mines and iron foundries of Pennsylvania. Women worked as seamstresses, laundresses, or domestic servants. In the textile mills and shoe factories of New England, Irish families worked together.

Industrialization was not the only reason for the growth of wage labor. By the 1850s a growing white-collar middle class also lived off their wages. As industrial production increased, businesses opened large downtown stores to sell their goods. Between 1859 and 1862, for example, A. T. Stewart built a huge dry goods store covering a full square block in lower Manhattan. The financial needs of these enterprises were met by an expanding number of banks, insurance companies, and accounting firms that employed armies of white-collar workers.

> Without firing a gun, without drawing a sword, when they [Northerners] make war upon us [Southerners] we can bring the whole world to our feet. . . . What would happen if no cotton was furnished for three years? . . . England would topple headlong and carry the whole civilized world with her. No, sir, you dare not make war on cotton. No power on earth dares make war upon it. Cotton is king.
>
> SENATOR JAMES HENRY HAMMOND,
> South Carolina, 1858

AMERICA AND THE WORLD:
  Slavery as a Foreign Policy

AMERICAN LANDSCAPE:
  Lawrence, Kansas

A New Political Party Takes Shape

PRIMARY SOURCE:
  Sumner's "Crime Against Kansas" Speech
The First Sectional Election

The Labor Problem and the Politics of Slavery
The Dred Scott Decision
The Lecompton Constitution Splits the Democratic
  Party
The "Irrepressible" Conflict

The Retreat from Union
John Brown's War Against Slavery
Northerners Elect a President

Conclusion

TECHNOLOGY AND IDEAS

>> The Telegraph

Samuel F. B. Morse (1791–1872) was the most un-likely of inventors. Indeed, his early life was full of contradictions. A scion of Calvinist Massachusetts preachers, trained to the ministry at Yale, he instead chose to become a painter and studied art in England. Though he stayed in England during the War of 1812, he opposed the war. When he returned, he spurned his ancestral religion and became a Unitarian. Perhaps even more shameful in the eyes of the rest of the family, he rejected conservative Federalism in favor of Jeffersonian democracy. At the same time, he sought commissions to paint portraits of the wealthy and powerful. He returned to Europe in the 1830s, again seeking to make a living by his art.

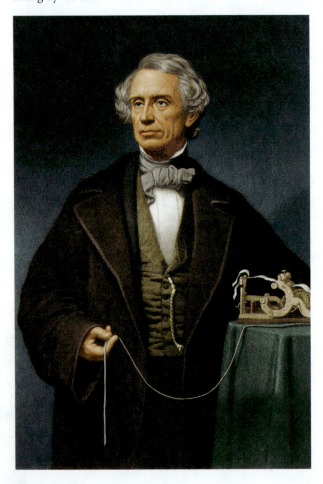

Samuel Morse and His Telegraph

Morse knew about the emerging science of electro-magnetism, by which a current could be sent through a wire to close a distant switch. In the 1820s, Joseph Henry, an American scientist, had experimented with sending electromagnetic signals through wires to receivers miles away. In 1837, Morse showed that telegraph messages could be sent and deciphered many miles away. Throughout the 1830s and 1840s, Morse refined his telegraph, introducing the "relay" to amplify the signal, allowing communication over even longer distances. He also invented a system of long and short impulses, each group representing a letter of the alphabet, to transmit messages in words. But Morse was as busy fending off competitors as he was trying to get sponsors for his own telegraph system. He found that acquiring patents in 1840 and 1846 for his single-wire/relay system did not prevent competitors in the United States, England, Scotland, and continental Europe from trying to sell their own versions of the telegraph. One lawsuit over the patent rights went all the way to the US Supreme Court, in the end vindicating Morse's claim of having invented the telegraphic system. In 1845, he formed the Magnetic Telegraph Company (which became Western Union) to protect his investment. It was the ancestor of the American Telegraph and Telephone Company (AT&T).

By the end of the 1840s, moreover, Morse had found the perfect complement to the telegraph—the railroads. By stringing his single-wire telegraph on poles along railroad rights-of-way, he could make rail travel far safer and more efficient. This, along with some able lobbying, gained him support in the US Congress. The telegraph linked city to city and by the 1850s stretched across the country. News, political information, and business items, as well as personal communications, soon flowed with the speed of electromagnetism, a foretaste of today's Internet. The Associated Press (AP) followed, as did the consolidation of the nation's markets.

International projects soon led to the laying of a transatlantic cable, a transpacific cable, and the spread of telegraphy to the far corners of the earth. When Morse died on April 2, 1872, less than a month shy of his eighty-first birthday, he had received honors from many nations and left an estate worth $500,000, the equivalent of over $9 million today. But the impact of his credited invention was far greater.

Questions

1. What advantage did securing a patent for the telegraph give Morse?

2. The telegraph was one of the first inventions that greatly increased the speed at which Americans were able to communicate. Are there any disadvantages to the relatively instantaneous transmission of information?

Economic growth in the North during the 1850s rested on important social changes. A rural society became more urban. Industry was replacing agriculture as the driving economic force. Wage laborers were replacing small farmers and craftsmen. A Protestant nation saw its first great wave of Catholic immigrants. Machines made it possible for one person to cultivate more acres than ever before. A political economy based on new sources of wealth and new forms of work was being born.

The Slave Economy

It made sense for the wealthy South Carolina planter James Henry Hammond to declare in 1858, "Cotton is king." It had been a prosperous decade for southern slaveholders. Recovering from the doldrums of the 1840s, the price of cotton remained steady, and the price of slaves rose sharply. Southern states threw themselves into railroad construction, building a substantial network. Steamboats plied the South's rivers. Telegraph wires sped news of cotton prices from New York to New Orleans and deep into the plantation belt. Southerners boasted of their commitment to progress and prosperity. Slavery was thriving. So why shouldn't Hammond confidently defy slavery's critics?

The South had changed in many ways during the previous century. It had expanded across half the continent (see Map 14–1). Cotton had become its most profitable crop. The Atlantic slave trade was over, and a native-born, largely Christian slave population had grown up. There were important signs of social change, especially in the upper South. The immigrant workers Frederick Douglass met on the Baltimore docks faced the same process of economic development as the dockworkers of New England. The steady sale of slaves from the upper to the lower South reduced the political influence of slaveholders in such states as Maryland, Kentucky, and Delaware. Indeed, among whites across the South the proportion of slaveholding families had been declining for decades, from one in three in 1830 to one in four by 1860.

As slavery expanded, however, it brought commerce and prosperity but not economic development. The slave economy had always been intensely commercial, more so than northern capitalism, but its profits were concentrated among slaveholders who were, by 1860, among the richest group of Americans. That wealth enabled slaveholders to monopolize the best lands to the detriment of small farmers. Moreover, slaveholders reinvested their profits not in machinery that increased productivity but in more slaves. As a result, slaveless farmers in the South were much poorer than their northern counterparts, and the southern economy was far less developed than the northern.

The Importance of the West

Both the North and the South coveted western lands. By 1850 many northerners believed that slavery, if allowed to expand into the West, would deprive free laborers of an important source of prosperity and independence. But slaveholders had come to

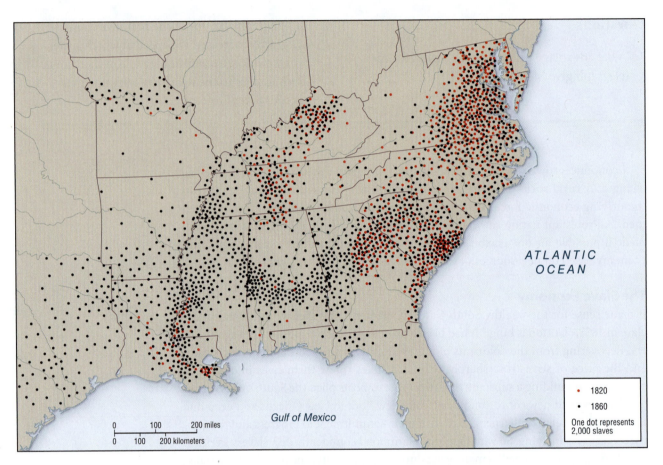

Map 14-1 Slavery's Expansion The westward expansion of the slave economy created political turmoil from 1820 until the Civil War. Sustained by an extensive internal slave trade that sold thousands of humans each year, slavery's expansion required one of the greatest forced migrations in history.

believe that their prosperity depended on the spread of the slave economy into the West. The disposition of the land acquired in the war with Mexico forced Americans into a sustained public debate over the future of slavery.

Slavery had expanded more than halfway across the continent of North America in about half a century, and white southerners viewed territorial expansion as a sign of progress. The westward movement of the southern frontier demonstrated the continued strength of the slave economy. Halting that movement would undermine southern prosperity. It was an insult to the moral decency of white southerners, an obstacle to their economic vitality. But above all else it was an infringement on the slaveholders' inalienable rights of property, which included the constitutional right to carry their property with them wherever they saw fit. So argued slavery's defenders with increasing vehemence in the 1850s. But the economic growth of the North created equally strong ties between the East and the West. Mountains and rivers generally ran north and south, but turnpikes, canals, and especially railroads tended to run east and west, linking northeastern cities to the western frontier. Of the approximately 20,000 miles of railroads built in the 1850s, few crossed the Mason-Dixon line to link the northern and southern economies (see Map 14–2).

For northerners, the West was essential to prosperity. The public lands of the West "are the great regulator of the relations of Labor and Capital," Horace Greeley explained,

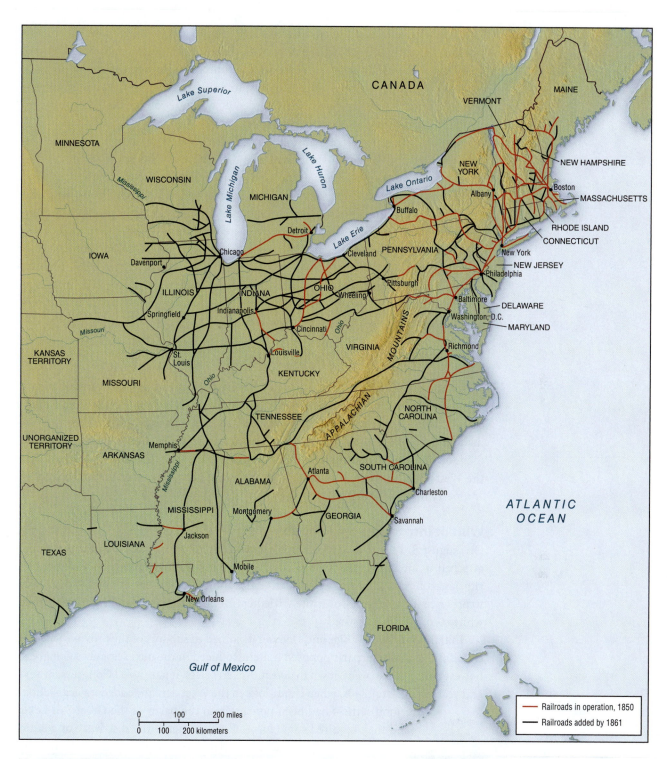

Map 14–2 Railroad Expansion This map shows that there were two distinct patterns of railroad development in the United States. In the North, rail lines connected the western states to the eastern seaboard. In the South, railroads tied the inland plantation districts to the coastal ports. Few lines connected the North to the South.

"the safety valve of our industrial and social engine." This safety-valve theory was repeated regularly in the North, even though there was not much truth in it. To move west, buy land, and establish a farm required resources far beyond the means of many, perhaps most, wage laborers. Nevertheless, to many northerners, westward expansion was critical to their entire social order. It was no wonder that the westward expansion of slavery caused so much anxiety in the North.

Northern and southern expansion were incompatible. The slaveholders were "settlers with means," bringing their wealth and their slave laborers with them. They easily bought up the best lands, usually river bottoms with the most productive soil and the readiest access to markets. Slaves provided a reliable source of labor, making it easier for slaveholding pioneers to clear land, build homes, and start producing profitable crops. Slaveless farmers could not compete with this. Without slaves, labor was scarce on the frontier, and farm families could rely only on their own labor and any help neighbors could offer. Because the size of free farms was restricted by the amount of labor a family could perform, the best lands were more widely dispersed among settlers wherever slavery was excluded. Free farmers quickly saw the expansion of slavery as a threat to their own prospects in the West.

Slavery Becomes a Political Issue

Westward expansion forced the issue of slavery back into the political mainstream in the late 1840s. During the heyday of the "second party system," Whigs and Democrats had tacitly agreed to suppress open debates over slavery, but the Mexican War made it hard to maintain that silence. For nearly 15 years, national politics would focus on one crucial question: Should Congress restrict the movement of slavery into the West? Behind that question lay a larger moral issue, the wrong and the right of "property in man."

Wilmot Introduces His Proviso

On August 8, 1846, David Wilmot, a Democratic congressman from Pennsylvania, attached to an appropriations bill an amendment banning slavery from all the territories acquired in the war with Mexico. The aim of the famous Wilmot Proviso was to preserve western lands for white settlement. "I plead the cause and rights of the free white man," Wilmot insisted.

Initially, northern Whigs and Democrats joined in support of the proviso, whereas their southern counterparts opposed it. Reintroduced in the next session of Congress, however, the proviso went down to defeat. Nevertheless, it paralyzed Congress for several years in the late 1840s, when conditions in the West demanded federal legislation. Mormon settlers had been pouring into the basin of the Great Salt Lake, and they required some form of government. The discovery of gold in California brought a rush of settlers and much disorder to the mining camps of the Sierra foothills and the boomtown of San Francisco. Territorial governments required congressional action, but Congress was frozen by sectional differences.

By 1850, four positions had hardened. At one extreme were antislavery northerners favoring a Wilmot-like solution to ban slavery in all the territories. At the other extreme were the southern followers of John C. Calhoun, who argued that Congress had no right

Prospectors Following the discovery of gold in California, prospectors from around the world headed for the mining camps that sprang up along the foothills of the Sierra Nevada mountains.

to interfere with the property rights of slaveholders in the territories. In between were two compromise positions. Some wanted to extend the Missouri Compromise line and push the North-South division all the way to the Pacific Ocean. Finally, there was popular sovereignty, which gave settlers the right to decide for themselves whether they would have slavery in their territory.

The four positions disrupted the major parties. In the presidential election of 1848, antislavery men bolted both the Democrats and the Whigs for the Free-Soil Party. With the Wilmot Proviso as their platform, Free-Soilers won 14 percent of the northern vote. Meanwhile, proslavery fire-eaters threatened to walk out of the Democratic convention. The Whigs survived to elect President Zachary Taylor, a hero of the war with Mexico. The triumph was short-lived, however. In 1849 President Taylor urged New Mexico and California to apply directly for admission to the Union, bypassing the usual territorial stage. California's application for statehood came with a constitution that prohibited slavery, provoking a fight over whether new slave states should be admitted to the Union. The House of Representatives, with a strong northern majority, reaffirmed the Wilmot Proviso, condemned the slave trade in Washington, DC, and almost abolished slavery in the District of Columbia. The Senate, with a strong southern wing, blocked all such measures.

This was no ordinary stalemate. Fistfights broke out in the halls of Congress. Representatives challenged each other to duels. Threatening secession, proslavery partisans called for a southern-rights convention to meet at Nashville in June 1850. The stage was set for one of the most dramatic debates in congressional history.

A Compromise Without Compromises

Into this stalemate marched the "great triumvirate" of distinguished old senators, Henry Clay of Kentucky, Daniel Webster of Massachusetts, and John C. Calhoun of South Carolina. Clay, instrumental in securing the Missouri Compromise of 1820, tried one last time to save the Union. He devised a series of eight resolutions designed to balance the conflicting interests of North and South. Under one pair of measures California would be admitted as a free state, but the rest of the Mexican territories would have no conditions regarding slavery attached to their applications for statehood. The second pair of resolutions limited the number of slave states that could be carved out of Texas Territory but in return required the federal government to assume Texas's debt. The third pair abolished the slave trade in Washington, DC, but protected slavery itself from federal interference. The final two provisions favored the South: a formal promise not to interfere in the interstate slave trade and a new fugitive slave law.

Clay gathered all eight provisions into a single package, derided by critics as the Omnibus Bill. His goal was simple: to gain enough support from centrists in each party to override both southern fire-eaters and northern Free-Soilers.

The congressional debate over Clay's package in the spring and summer of 1850 in-cluded a series of extraordinary speeches. Appealing for sectional harmony, Daniel Webster eloquently supported the compromise measures. Calhoun, by contrast, spoke very much as a southern man. He warned that the bonds of unity had been snapped by the North's continued agitation of the slavery question. If the right of property in slaves was not enforced, the Union would be severed. In response, New York's William H. Seward argued that the Constitution gave Congress every right to restrict slavery in the territories.

The sectional hostilities exposed in the debate suggest why Clay's Omnibus Bill was doomed. Antislavery senators voted against the bill for its provisions protecting slavery. Proslavery senators opposed it for its restrictions on slavery. On July 31, after months of wrangling, the Senate killed the package. Exhausted and angry, Clay gave up and left Washington. The old generation had failed to resolve the crisis.

From then on national politics would be domi-nated by a new generation of congressional leaders. Seward of New York was one of them. Another was Senator Stephen A. Douglas, the "Little Giant" from Illinois who used his adroit parliamentary skills to rescue the compromise. He broke the omnibus package up into five separate bills, each designed to win different majorities. Antislavery and moderate congressmen joined to admit California as a free state. Proslavery congressmen voted with moder-

Senator Stephen A. Douglas The "Little Giant" from Illinois became the leading advocate of "popular sovereignty" as a solution to the crisis over slavery in the 1850s.

ates to pass a fugitive slave law. By similar means, Congress settled the Texas border, determined that New Mexico and Utah would apply for statehood under the principle of popular sovereignty, and abolished the slave trade in the District of Columbia. Although proslavery and antislavery forces never compromised on a single issue, the five bills that Douglas and his allies steered through Congress came to be known as the Compromise of 1850.

Douglas's efforts were aided by the untimely death of the president. Zachary Taylor's replacement, Millard Fillmore, was more sympathetic to sectional reconciliation and called the Compromise of 1850 the "final settlement" of the slavery question. For the next few years moderate politicians avoided all discussion of slavery. In the short run, the compromise apparently worked. A southern-rights convention at Nashville fizzled, and the radical edge of the southern-rights movement was blunted. But fire-eaters in the South and Free-Soilers in the North insisted that the day of reckoning had only been postponed. And in the North, opposition to one feature of the compromise, the fugitive slave law, came with unanticipated intensity.

The Fugitive Slave Act Provokes a Crisis

The Fugitive Slave Act was one of the least debated features of the 1850 Compromise. The Constitution had a fugitive slave clause, and a law enforcing the clause had existed since 1793. Why, then, did the new Fugitive Slave Act provoke such an uproar? Many northern states had passed laws to restrain fugitive slave catchers by guaranteeing the rights of due process to accused runaways. The 1850 statute took jurisdiction over fugitive slave cases away from northern courts and gave it to federal commissioners, thus violating the fundamental premise of all antislavery politics—that slavery was merely local, whereas freedom was national.

The Fugitive Slave Act sent terror through northern African American communities. Slaves who had run away decades earlier now risked being captured and sent back to the South. Even free-born blacks feared being kidnapped into slavery, unable to prove their freedom in a court of law. In the North, vulnerable African Americans moved to the far West, the upper North, or Canada. A convention of blacks denounced the Fugitive Slave

Poster Warning of Fugitive Slave Act The Fugitive Slave Act met strong resistance in many parts of the North. This Boston poster captures the atmosphere of fear and civil disobedience that gripped the city following the Compromise of 1850. It warns all blacks, free or fugitive, to be on the lookout for slave catchers.

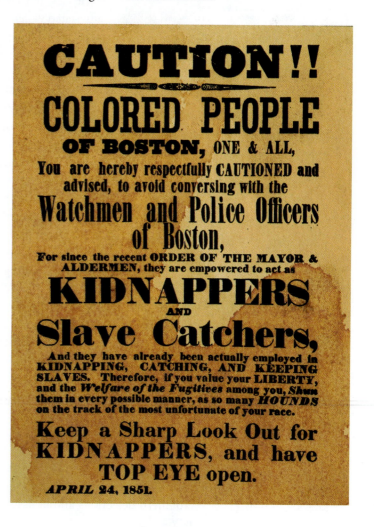

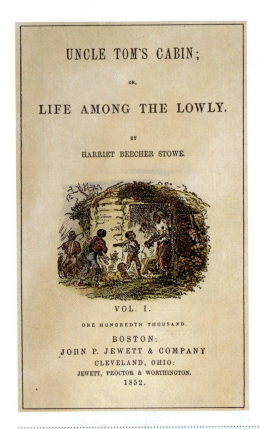

UNCLE TOM'S CABIN;

OR,

LIFE AMONG THE LOWLY.

BY

HARRIET BEECHER STOWE.

VOL. I.

ONE HUNDREDTH THOUSAND.

BOSTON:
JOHN P. JEWETT & COMPANY
CLEVELAND, OHIO:
JEWETT, PROCTOR & WORTHINGTON.
1852.

Uncle Tom's Cabin The tremendous popularity of Stowe's book reflected the surprisingly intense northern concern about the Fugitive Slave Act of 1850.

Act as "the most cruel, unconstitutional, and scandalous outrage of modern times."

White abolitionists were no less vehement. Even white northerners who cared little about the fate of blacks were upset. The South seemed to be imposing its laws and institutions on the North, making slavery national. Appalled by the act, Harriet Beecher Stowe published the great antislavery novel *Uncle Tom's Cabin* in 1852. The astonishing success of Stowe's novel was a measure of northern anxiety. In vivid prose, Stowe drew a sentimental portrait of a slave mother and her infant child as they fled from a master who had contracted to sell them apart. Few readers missed the point. Anyone who helped Eliza save her child violated the Fugitive Slave Act of 1850.

Many northerners did tolerate violations of the Fugitive Slave Act. Fillmore vowed to enforce the law with federal marshals if necessary, but Frederick Douglass, far from his earlier pacifism, advocated violent resistance. "A half dozen or more dead kidnappers carried down South," he suggested, "would cool the ardor of Southern gentlemen."

> The Fugitive Slave Law. . . . is a degradation and a scandalous outrage on religious liberty. . . . This vile, infernal law does not interfere with singing of psalms, or anything of that kind, but with the weightier matters of the law, judgment, mercy, and faith. It makes it criminal for you, sir, to carry out the principles of Christianity. It forbids you the right to do right—forbids you to show mercy—forbids you to follow the example of the good Samaritan.
>
> FREDERICK DOUGLASS,
> August 11, 1852

The Election of 1852 and the Decline of the Whig Party

White southerners were outraged by the North's unwillingness to obey the Fugitive Slave Act. The Democratic Party made enforcement of the Compromise of 1850 its rallying cry in 1852. The Democrats, torn by sectional divisions, nominated Franklin Pierce, a northerner felt to be sympathetic to southern interests. The Democratic platform pledged to silence discussion of slavery by strict federal enforcement of the Compromise of 1850, "the act for reclaiming fugitives included."

The Whigs found no such unifying principle. White southerners abandoned the party because of its antislavery advocates, and northern voters punished the Whigs who supported the Compromise of 1850 (see Figure 14–1). Henry Clay wrote the Fugitive Slave Act. Daniel Webster backed it. Millard Fillmore signed and aggressively enforced it. All were Whigs. The Whig Party convention in Baltimore nominated Winfield Scott of Virginia after 52 ballots and despite nearly unanimous southern opposition. Southern delegates secured a platform that reaffirmed the party's commitment to the Compromise of 1850, forcing the Whigs to run a candidate who was objectionable in the South on a platform that was objectionable in the North.

Southern defections all but assured a major Whig defeat in the election. Pierce won 254 electoral votes to Scott's 42. The Democratic candidate won 27 out of 31

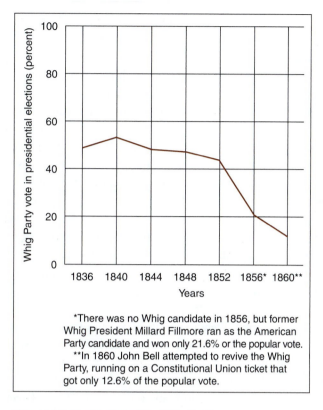

Figure 14-1 The Decline of the Whig Party

states. Severely weakened by these results, the Whigs were unable to meet a political challenge that erupted in the early 1850s: hostility to immigrants, also known as nativism.

Nativism and the Origins of the Republican Party

The politics of nativism destroyed a Whig Party already weakened by sectionalism. From 1852 through 1854 the nativist American Party gained surprising strength. Hostility to immigrants, however, was not enough to rally northerners concerned about slavery. What, then, would replace the Whig Party in the North? A new political force, the Republican Party, was dedicated to making freedom national.

The Nativist Attack on Immigration

For a while the arrival of large numbers of Catholic immigrants stirred nearly as much animosity among Yankee Protestants as did slavery. In the early 1850s the Catholic Church was known for its conservatism. The pope expressed contempt for "progress," and the Vatican condemned the liberal revolutions sweeping Europe in 1848 that were widely supported by Americans.

Anti-Catholicism had about it a strong odor of middle-class condescension. Nativism appealed to shopkeepers, independent craftsmen, and clerks, people for whom the Protestant ethic of steadiness and sobriety was a scriptural injunction. They disdained a working class of Irish and German immigrants who drank heavily, lived in squalor, and lacked economic independence. But it was immigrant voting, particularly among Irish Catholics, that most troubled nativists: the Irish voted Democratic.

The Democrats' appeal to Irish Catholics was double-edged. On the one hand, the party's populist rhetoric attracted immigrants stung by the snobbery of Yankee Whigs. At the same time, as Democrats stepped up their racist invective, Irish Americans heaped contempt on African Americans with whom they competed for jobs and housing. Democrats cultivated this sentiment, using racism to welcome Irish voters into politics at a time when many were working to keep immigrants out. The consequences for sectional politics were significant. The Democrats argued that abolition would force white workers into economic competition with an inferior race. Supported by the Irish voting bloc, the Democratic Party sponsored new restrictions on the civil rights of free African Americans in many northern states.

In the elections of 1854, those who believed that immigration was the greatest threat to their way of life voted for the American Party. (They were often called "Know-Nothings" because of their origins in a secret organization whose members insisted they "knew nothing" about it.) Voters caring more about the threat of slavery voted for the Free-Soil Party. American Party candidates won 25 percent of the vote in New York and 40 percent in Pennsylvania; in Massachusetts, they took control of the state legislature.

In 1854 nativism seemed likely to eclipse slavery as the great issue of American politics. But slavery and nativism were never entirely separate issues. Middle-class Yankees often viewed the struggle against Catholicism as inseparable from the struggle against slavery. Both were said to represent authoritarianism, ignorance, and a rejection of the "modern" values of individualism and progress. Given the close ties between nativism and antislavery sentiment, it was unclear which issue would prevail. In the end, the slavery issue tore the American party apart, just as it was tearing the nation apart. The driving wedge was the expansion of slavery into the western territories.

The Kansas-Nebraska Act Revives the Slavery Issue

In 1853, the House of Representatives passed a bill banning slavery in Nebraska Territory on the grounds that it fell north of the Missouri Compromise line. Southerners killed the Nebraska Bill in the Senate. The next year Stephen Douglas reintroduced it, this time organizing the territory on the principle of popular sovereignty.

No one was satisfied with Douglas's proposal. Northerners were outraged that the 1850 agreement to extend the Missouri Compromise line was so quickly scuttled. Militant southerners, suspicious of attempts to regulate slavery in the territories, demanded that the Missouri Com-

"Know Nothing" Party Cartoon, 1854 This cartoon supporting the nativist American (Know-Nothing) party shows an Irish immigrant wearing a barrel with a sign saying "Irish Whiskey" about to club a German immigrant wearing a barrel and a sign saying "Lager Bier." They are running away carrying a ballot box to illustrate that the Irish and other immigrants are stealing the election.

promise be repealed. Douglas withdrew the bill and reintroduced it in 1854 with a new twist. He split Nebraska Territory in two, Kansas to the west of the slave state of Missouri and Nebraska to the north of Kansas. Both were to be organized on the principle of popular sovereignty, suggesting that Kansas might become a slave state and Nebraska a free state. To win southern congressional support, the final version of Douglas's bill repealed the Missouri Compromise of 1820 (see Map 14–3).

Debate over the bill was ferocious: Southerners denied that Congress had the right to regulate slavery in the territories. They claimed that slavery was protected wherever the Constitution was sovereign, as it was in the territories. Northerners noted that the federal government had been regulating slavery in the territories since the 1780s. They believed that freedom was national and that slavery was protected only in the states where it was legal. The territories, they believed, should be the preserve of freedom.

In the end, the Kansas-Nebraska Act became law. Yet, as with other southern victories, it increased support for northern antislavery politicians. It persuaded many northerners that popular sovereignty was a proslavery swindle, even though Douglas believed it would produce mostly free states. For that very reason southerners came to mistrust popular sovereignty as well. Douglas had paid a heavy price for his victory. In the 1854

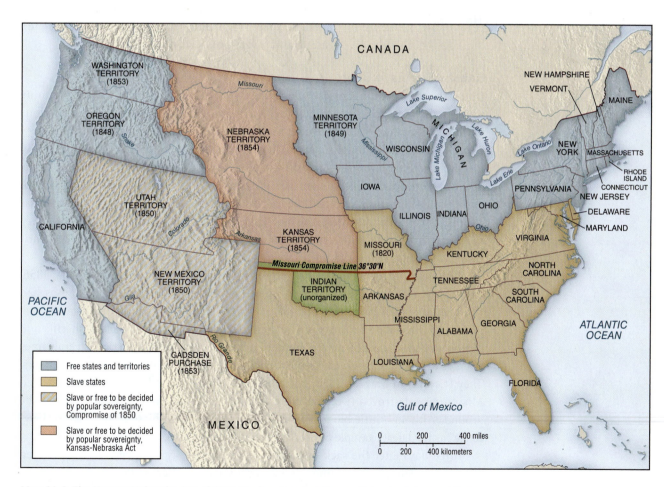

Map 14-3 The Kansas-Nebraska Act of 1854 Stephen Douglas's Kansas-Nebraska Act carved Kansas Territory out of the larger Nebraska Territory. Because Missouri was already a slave state, the map indicates that slaveholders could move west and settle in Kansas. But because Kansas lay north of the 1820 Missouri Compromise line, many northerners wanted slavery restricted from the territory.

elections the number of northern Democrats in Congress fell from 91 to 25. The fallout from the Kansas-Nebraska Act would split the Democratic Party in two, destroy the credibility of popular sovereignty, and damage expansionism as a political program.

One of the most important results of the struggle over the Kansas-Nebraska Act was the emergence of Abraham Lincoln. Douglas was widely denounced in his home state of Illinois for having helped open Kansas to slavery, facing hostile voters and the sharp criticism of Lincoln, his longtime political rival. Lincoln had largely left public life, but the Kansas-Nebraska Act brought him out of semiretirement. He followed Douglas around the state, demanding the restoration of the Missouri Compromise. In Peoria, on October 16, 1854, Lincoln gave a speech summing up his arguments against slavery and had it published. He pronounced slavery "a great moral wrong," insisted on the humanity of blacks, and denounced the dehumanization of slaves. He said slavery was founded on greed, selfishness, and unrestrained self-interest. Blacks were human beings, not property, Lincoln argued, and like all human beings freedom was their natural condition. With this remarkable speech, Lincoln reemerged as one of the state's leading antislavery politicians.

> Near eighty years ago we began by declaring that all men are created equal; but now from that beginning we have run down to the other declaration, that for some men to enslave others is a "sacred right of self-government." These principles can not stand together. They are as opposite as God and mammon.
>
> ABRAHAM LINCOLN,
> Peoria, Illinois, October 16, 1854

Kansas Begins to Bleed

Under the terms of the Kansas-Nebraska Act, the people in Kansas would determine whether their territory would enter the Union as a slave state or a free state. Elections for the territorial legislature were set for March 1855. Hoping to secure an antislavery victory, the New England Emigrant Aid Company sent settlers opposed to slavery. By Election Day, proslavery settlers still would have won a fair fight. But when the polls opened, proslavery partisans from Missouri crossed the border and cast thousands of phony ballots. This undermined the legitimacy of the newly elected proslavery legislature. To make matters worse, the new legislature made it a crime to question slavery in Kansas, made it a capital crime to protect fugitive slaves, and expelled the few antislavery members who had been elected.

Free-state settlers repudiated the proslavery government and, in January 1856, elected a governor and legislature of their own. By the spring of 1856, Kansas had two competing governments, a proslavery one in Lecompton and an antislavery one in Topeka. Free-state settlers were by then in the majority. Nevertheless, sheriffs and federal marshals, backed up by "border ruffians" from Missouri, tried several times to enter the town of Lawrence (see American Landscape, p. 490) to arrest free-staters. They tried again May 21, 1856, but most of the free-staters had fled. The frustrated Missourians destroyed two printing presses and burned the Free State Hotel to the ground. Although little blood was shed, the eastern press blasted the "sack of Lawrence" as the latest example of proslavery violence. Kansas, they said, was bleeding.

Three days after the sack of Lawrence, Kansas really did begin to bleed, when John Brown launched his famous raid on proslavery settlers at Pottawatomie Creek. Brown was an awesome and in many ways a frightening man, a religious zealot convinced it was his personal mission to cleanse the nation of the sin of slavery. The

AMERICA AND THE WORLD

>> Slavery as a Foreign Policy

The Franklin Pierce administration's disastrous support for the Kansas-Nebraska Act undermined its ability to pursue the expansionist policies of its Democratic predecessors. To be sure, Pierce blustered about America's right to more Mexican territory and to parts of the Caribbean, particularly Cuba. But all of Pierce's expansionist efforts were southward, promising the expansion of slavery. This was hardly an accident. Southerners dominated Pierce's cabinet, and he appointed slaveholders to crucial diplomatic posts.

Pierce sent a South Carolinian, James Gadsden, to Mexico with instructions to spend up to $50 million to acquire a large portion of northern Mexico. Mexico's leader resisted the extravagant offer. Gadsden returned with a treaty giving the United States just enough territory for a transcontinental railroad across the southern tier of the nation. But even this was too much for most northern senators. For the first time in American history, Congress rejected land ceded to the United States. The Gadsden Purchase ended up with only a small piece of land for $10 million on the southern border of the United States.

The expansionist Pierce fared even worse in Cuba. He appointed Pierre Soulé, a Louisianan, as minister to Spain. Soulé was instructed to negotiate the purchase of Cuba, with the understanding that if Spain refused to sell he should encourage the Cubans to rebel. To Soulé the Spanish government offered an extraordinary response. It proposed to free millions of Cuban slaves and arm them for the defense of the island against a possible American invasion.

The United States responded with the Ostend Manifesto, which declared that Cuba was "naturally" a part of the United States and urged Spain to accept an offer of $120 million for the island. If Spain refused, the United States would "wrest" the island by force.

The Ostend Manifesto was issued in 1854 at the height of northern reaction against the Kansas-Nebraska Act and was denounced as another example of slavery's insatiable hunger for expansion. Southerners were not merely making slavery national, they were making it international. Expansionism was now hopelessly tainted by its association with slavery. As Pierce's secretary of state, William L. Marcy, admitted, "the Nebraska question" had shattered the Democratic Party in the North "and deprived it of that strength which was needed and could have been more profitably used for the acquisition of Cuba."

AMERICAN LANDSCAPE

>> Lawrence, Kansas

Eli Thayer was more interested in making money than in spreading freedom when he secured a charter for the Massachusetts Emigrant Aid Society in April 1854. But one month later, Congress passed the Kansas-Nebraska Act, and Thayer's organization became the focus of an effort to fill Kansas with northern settlers who opposed the spread of slavery. Thayer's organization soon had a new name, the New England Emigrant Aid Company, and a treasurer with deep pockets and an even deeper desire to halt the spread of slavery. He was Amos Lawrence, and when the settlers reached the prairie, they named their settlement after him. Within a year everybody was talking about Lawrence, Kansas.

Lawrence quickly became the center of the "free-state" movement in Kansas, and settlers established two anti-slavery newspapers, the *Kansas Free State* and the *Herald of Freedom*. If the goal of the New England Emigrant Aid Company was to overwhelm Kansas with free-state settlers who could outvote the proslavery forces, their campaign failed. When elections for the territorial legislature were held on March 30, 1855, a flood of "border ruffians"

crossed into Kansas from Missouri, casting thousands of ballots for candidates who favored slavery. "There are eleven hundred coming over from Platte County to vote," boasted Senator David Rice Atchison, the unofficial leader of the proslavery forces, "and if that ain't enough we can send five thousand—enough to kill every God-damned abolitionist in the territory."

The free-state settlers and their supporters quickly declared the elections and the new legislature fraudulent and set up a "government" of their own. Charles Robinson, the "governor" of the free state and the Emigrant Aid agent in Lawrence, wrote stormy letters of protest. He also asked for arms and ammunition. "We want 200 of Sharp's rifles & two cannon for Lawrence people," Robinson wrote. From New York, the pastor of Brooklyn's Plymouth Church, the Reverend Henry Ward Beecher, obliged by organizing a campaign to send the rifles ("Beecher's Bibles") to the frontier. Over the next year, the free-state settlers armed themselves in preparation for battle. Meanwhile, the proslavery state government grew increasingly impatient with the growing abolitionist stronghold at Lawrence. In April 1856, Sheriff Samuel Jones was shot in the back while in Lawrence, and proslavery forces sprang into action. Several free-state leaders were indicted for "treason." Robinson was arrested. A grand jury recommended that the town's Free State Hotel be demolished and anti-slavery newspapers be shut down. The US marshal for Kansas urged all "law abiding" settlers to converge on Lawrence so that he could serve warrants on the free-state leaders.

Sheriff Jones led a posse of 750 men bent on destroying the "hotbed of abolitionism" under a flag emblazoned with the words "Southern Rights." They invaded the offices of both newspapers and tossed the presses into the river. They ransacked the Free State Hotel, fired their cannon at it, then set it on fire. The mob pillaged several houses and burned down Robinson's house. Only one person was killed, but the town was largely demolished. Newspapers around the country dubbed the attack the "sack of Lawrence."

At stake in the battle over Lawrence were competing conceptions of democracy. Southerners had built an aggressive slaveholders' democracy in which white men were as proud of their freedom as they were jealous of their property rights in slaves. For the free-state settlers, slavery and democracy were fundamentally incompatible. The territories were the common property of the nation, and freedom was national. Thus the war on the Kansas prairie was a prelude to the civil war that would erupt nationwide a few years later.

The sack of Lawrence did not discourage the free-state settlers who lived there. They rebuilt their town, attracted ever more settlers to their cause, and within a few years were in the majority. For proslavery partisans, Lawrence survived as a symbol of the abolitionism they so despised. During the Civil War they attacked Lawrence again, and again the town survived.

wrath of God, not moral persuasion or political organization, was Brown's solution to the problem of slavery.

The day after he learned of the sack of Lawrence, Brown organized a band of seven men, among them four of his sons and a son-in-law, to take revenge. Armed with swords, Brown's troops went into battle late on May 24. They shot James Doyle in the head, split open the skulls of two of Doyle's sons, and then hacked up the bodies. They committed similar atrocities at two other settlers' cabins. None of the victims were wealthy slaveholders, but all had expressed proslavery sentiments. Then Brown and his men went back to their camp, having stolen several horses along the way.

As blood flowed in the western territories, another battle erupted on the floor of Congress. Prompted by the sack of Lawrence, abolitionist senator Charles Sumner of Massachusetts delivered a two-day harangue exposing the "Crime Against Kansas." Two years earlier, Sumner had delivered a very different kind of speech, "Freedom National, Slavery Regional," in which he specified a number of federal antislavery policies and the principles underlying them. By contrast, the "Crime Against Kansas" was a deliberately provocative speech, overflowing with invective and littered with vulgar sexual metaphors. Proslavery forces, Sumner said, had set out to "rape" the virgin territory of Kansas. He accused Senator Andrew Butler of South Carolina of consorting with a "polluted . . . harlot, Slavery." Two days later, Congressman Preston S. Brooks, a nephew of Butler's, brutally attacked Sumner with his cane, beating him senseless and forcing him to absent himself from the Senate for the next few years.

Across the South, Brooks was hailed as a hero. Southern congressmen prevented his expulsion from the House. Northerners, shocked by the South's reaction to the Sumner-Brooks affair, responded by voting for a new Republican Party dedicated to halting the expansion of the "slave power."

A New Political Party Takes Shape

The election of 1856 presented Americans with a clear choice. A candidate's position on the Kansas-Nebraska Act betrayed a widening circle of convictions—about slavery's expansion, about the relative value of wage labor and slave labor, and about the morality of human property itself. At stake was the fundamental conflict over whether freedom, or slavery, was to be the "national" policy of the United States. In the past the Whigs and Democrats had avoided sectional issues by running candidates who appealed to both the North and the South. In 1856 a new major party, the Republicans, appealed exclusively to northern voters.

>> Sumner's "Crime Against Kansas" Speech

For several hours standing at his desk on the floor of the US Senate on May 19 and 20, 1856, Senator Charles Sumner, a Republican from Massachusetts, gave a formal oration about the troubles afflicting the territory of Kansas. He entitled this speech "The Crime Against Kansas" and recited it largely from memory. In it, he laid out what he believed to be a conspiracy by proslavery interests against the rest of the United States. Two days later, on May 22, Representative Preston S. Brooks, a Democrat from South Carolina, caned Sumner while the senator was seated at that same desk. See if you can tell from these excerpts why Brooks might have taken offense at what Sumner had said.

SOUTHERN CHIVALRY — ARGUMENT versus CLUB'S.

But the wickedness which I now begin to expose is immeasurably aggravated by the motive which prompted it. Not in any common lust for power did this uncommon tragedy have its origin. It is the rape of a virgin Territory, compelling it to the hateful embrace of Slavery; and it may be clearly traced to a depraved longing for a new slave State, the hideous offspring of such a crime, in the hope of adding to the power of slavery in the National Government. Yes, sir, when the whole world, alike Christian and Turk, is rising up to condemn this wrong, and to make it a hissing to the nations, here in our Republic, *force*—aye, Sir, FORCE,—has been openly employed in compelling Kansas to this pollution, and all for the sake of political power. There is the simple fact, which you will vainly attempt to deny, but which in itself presents an essential wickedness that makes other public crimes seem like public virtues. . . .

But, before entering upon the argument, I must say something of a general character, particularly in response to what has fallen from senators who have raised themselves to eminence on this floor in championship of human wrongs. I mean the senator from South Carolina, [Mr. BUTLER], and the senator from Illinois, [Mr. DOUGLAS], who, though unlike as Don Quixote and Sancho Panza, yet, like this couple, sally forth together in the same adventure. I regret much to miss the elder senator from his seat; but the cause, against which he has run a tilt with such activity of animosity, demands that the opportunity of exposing him should not be lost; and it is for the cause that I speak. The senator from South Carolina has read many books of chivalry, and believes himself a chivalrous knight with sentiments of honor and courage. Of course he has chosen a mistress to whom he has made his vows, and who, though ugly to others, is always lovely to him; though polluted in the sight of the world, is chaste in his sight—I mean the harlot, slavery. . . .

With regret, I come again upon the senator from South Carolina, [Mr. Butler,] who, omnipresent in this debate, overflowed with rage at the simple suggestion that Kansas had applied for admission as a State; and, with incoherent phrases discharged the loose expectoration of his speech, now upon her representative, and then upon her people. There was no extravagance of the ancient Parliamentary debate which he did not repeat; nor was there any possible deviation from truth which he did not make, with so much of passion, I am glad to add, as to save him from the suspicion of intentional aberration. But the senator touches nothing which he does not disfigure—with error, sometimes of principles, sometimes of fact. He shows an incapacity of accuracy, whether in stating the Constitution or in stating the law, whether in the details of statistics or the diversions of scholarship. He cannot open his mouth, but out there flies a blunder. . . .

But it is against the people of Kansas that the sensibilities of the senator are particularly aroused. Coming, as he announces, "from a State"—ay, sir, from South Carolina—he turns with lordly disgust from this newly-formed community, which he will not recognize even as "a body politic." Pray, sir, by what title does he indulge in this egotism? Has he read the history of "the State" which he represents? He cannot surely have forgotten its shameful imbecility from slavery, confessed throughout the revolution, followed by its most shameful assumptions for slavery since. He cannot have forgotten its wretched persistence in the slave trade as the very apple of its eye, and the condition of its participation in the Union. He cannot have forgotten its constitution, which is republican only in name, confirming power in the hands of the few, and founding the qualifications of its legislature on a "settled freehold estate and ten negroes." And yet the senator, to whom that "State" has in part committed the guardianship of its good name, instead of moving, with backward treading steps, to cover its nakedness, rushes forward, in the very ecstasy of madness, to expose it by provoking a comparison with Kansas.

Charles Sumner, "The Crime Against Kansas, May 19th–20th 1856," in *The Crime Against Kansas: The Apologies for the Crime; The True Remedy* (Boston: John P. Jewett & Company, 1856), pp. 5–6, 9, 86–87.

Questions

1. What was Sumner's evaluation of Senator Butler's character, and, given that Butler was Brooks's father's cousin, why might this evaluation have angered Congressman Brooks?

2. Consider the timing of this speech. What possible reasons might Sumner have had for making such a provocative speech at this time?

3. What is the value, if any, in this type of rhetoric?

The First Sectional Election

In 1856 antislavery brought together the Democratic Party's opponents in the North in the new Republican Party. Its first presidential candidate was John C. Frémont.

The Republican Party platform called for a prohibition on the expansion of slavery into any western territories, and on this nearly all Republicans were agreed. But a party of former Whigs and Democrats had trouble unifying on anything else, and decades of partisan rivalry left a lingering mistrust. Former Whigs wanted the federal government to sponsor a transcontinental railroad and to set high tariffs to protect industries. They proposed a homestead act to encourage small farmers to settle the West and supported the creation of land-grant colleges to foster innovation in agriculture. But Republicans who had once been Democrats were suspicious of such "whiggish" plans for big government. They believed that the "money power" they had long opposed as Jacksonian Democrats had been transformed into a "slave power" that now threatened the freedom of northern whites. Opposition to slavery's expansion in the western territories, on the principle of Freedom National, was what held Republicans together.

The Democrats faced an even more daunting challenge: to find a candidate acceptable to both the northern and southern wings of the party. They turned to James Buchanan of Pennsylvania, "a northern man with southern principles." Where the Republicans promised to interfere with slavery in the territories, the Democrats pledged "non-interference by Congress with slavery," thereby keeping the principle of popular sovereignty alive without actually endorsing it. Northern and southern Democrats could thus unite around a candidate committed, above all else, to ending public discussion of slavery. After decades of silencing discussion of slavery, in large part by emphasizing white supremacy, by the 1850s the Democrats' resort to racist appeals became desperate. Antislavery politics was back in the mainstream, and the Democrats were splitting apart along sectional lines. A newly intensified racism was all that held the Democratic Party together.

Nevertheless, by 1856 Buchanan and the Democrats could claim to be the only ones who could prevent the breakup of the Union. Southern leaders repeatedly warned that if Frémont and the Republicans won, the South would secede. The Democrats played on widespread fears of disunion. The "grand and appalling issue" of the campaign, Buchanan wrote, is "Union or Disunion."

For the first time, Americans were asked to decide in a presidential election whether the Union was worth preserving. Would the Union be based on a society whose wealth came from the labor of slaves or from the progress of free labor?

The Labor Problem and the Politics of Slavery

Northern Democrats warned that a Republican victory would flood the North with emancipated slaves, "side by side in competition with white men." The interest of northern workers therefore required the preservation of southern slavery within the Union. The most articulate spokesman for this view was Stephen Douglas. Douglas did not repudiate the promise of equality in the Declaration of Independence. Instead, he argued that it was never intended for an "inferior race" of blacks.

Republicans insisted that slavery degraded all labor, black and white. Unpaid slave labor suppressed the wages of free workers, Republicans argued. The expansion of slavery therefore threatened the well-being of free labor in the North. Republicans held that slavery destroyed the work ethic by withholding from slaves any incentive to diligence and industry and by encouraging a disdain for hard work and self-discipline among the masters. By stifling the economic progress of the South, slavery was said to deny opportunities to poor whites as well. An inefficient workforce and an aristocratic ruling class would doom the South to economic backwardness. In contrast, Republicans depicted the North as a society in which labor was free and hard work was rewarded. The Protestant virtues of thrift, sobriety, and diligence were cultivated, opportunities for upward mobility were many, and progress was manifest. Republicans supported protective tariffs for the same reason they opposed slavery—they believed that high wages would ensure the upward mobility of free workers.

Southern spokesmen insisted that blacks did not respond to the incentives of free labor the way whites did and that whites, in turn, could not work efficiently in hot climates such as the South. Slavery solved this dual problem. It was the only way to get blacks to work productively in an otherwise unproductive climate. The proof, the slaveholders argued, was the booming, expanding slave economy. The southern labor system provided a poor white man with the opportunity to rise up the social ladder by acquiring land and slaves "as soon as his savings will admit." Southern Democrats hailed slavery for preserving the economic independence of free whites in terms reminiscent of the Republican defense of wage labor as a stepping stone to self-employment. Slave property was, in this view, a reward for the same virtues of thrift and industry that Yankees thought they alone embraced.

But for many northerners, the only possible explanation for the South's apparent prosperity was the existence of a "slave power" that kept slavery artificially alive by opening the door to its continual expansion. Most Republicans believed that "property in man" was not only immoral but that the Constitution did not protect slaves as a right of property. Other Republicans were attracted to the "slave power" theory because it allowed whites to feel threatened by slavery without having to sympathize with the plight of the slaves. The greater evil was not the oppression of the slave but the power of the slaveholder.

The Republicans did not succeed in the short run. In 1856, Buchanan won five northern states and all but one of the slave states, securing 45 percent of the popular vote and 174 electoral votes. Frémont swept the upper North and Ohio, winning 114 electoral votes (see Map 14–4). The surprise was not that Frémont lost, but that he did so well. All the Republicans needed to win four years later was Pennsylvania and either Illinois or Indiana. Never before had a sectional party done so well in a presidential election. The slavery issue would not disappear until slavery itself did.

> Slave labor, in each individual case, and for each small measure of time, is more slow and inefficient than the labor of a free man. . . . Suppose it is admitted that the labor of slaves, for each hour or day, will amount to but two-thirds of what hired free laborers would perform in the same time. But the slave labor is continuous, and every day at least it returns to the employers and to the community, this two-thirds of full labor. . . . [T]he subjection of people of the same race with their masters—of equals to equals . . . would be slavery of the most objectionable kind. It would involve most injustice and hardship to the enslaved—would render it more difficult for the masters to command and enforce obedience—and would make the bonds of servitude more galling to the slaves, because of their being equal to their masters (and, in many individual cases, greatly superior) in natural endowments of mind.
>
> EDMUND RUFFIN,
> *The Political Economy of Slavery* (1853)

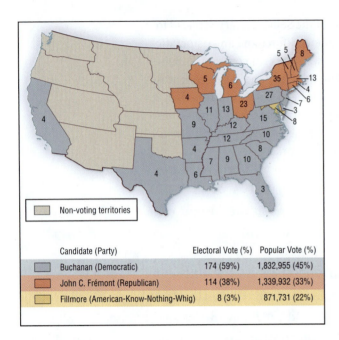

Candidate (Party)	Electoral Vote (%)	Popular Vote (%)
Buchanan (Democratic)	174 (59%)	1,832,955 (45%)
John C. Frémont (Republican)	114 (38%)	1,339,932 (33%)
Fillmore (American-Know-Nothing-Whig)	8 (3%)	871,731 (22%)

Non-voting territories

Map 14-4 The Election of 1856 The presidential electoral map of 1856 reveals the growing sectional division. Although he lost the election, the Republican Frémont won a string of victories across the upper North and lost narrowly in Pennsylvania, Indiana, and Illinois. By winning those states four years later, the openly antislavery Abraham Lincoln could be elected president simply by winning the North.

The Dred Scott Decision

In 1857, Democrat James Buchanan was inaugurated as president. His efforts to silence the slavery issue proved a disastrous failure. By the end of 1858 the nation's most prominent Republican, William Seward, had declared the sectional conflict between North and South "irrepressible." When Buchanan left office in 1861, his party was in disarray, a Republican had been elected his successor, and the Union had collapsed.

Within days of the inauguration, the Supreme Court, dominated by southern Democrats, issued one of the most controversial decisions in American history. The case stretched back to 1833, when John Emerson, an army surgeon from Missouri, was assigned to Fort Armstrong, Illinois, and took a slave named Dred Scott with him. Emerson spent two years in Illinois and two more years at Fort Snelling in Wisconsin Territory (now Minnesota). Slavery was illegal in Illinois and Wisconsin Territory. Back in Missouri in 1846, Scott sued his owners, claiming that several years of residence on free soil made him legally free. After losing his suit in 1854, Scott appealed to the US Supreme Court. By then two questions stood out: First, was Dred Scott a citizen, such that his suit had standing in a court of law? Second, did the laws of the free state of Illinois or the free territory of Wisconsin prevail over the master's property right?

The justices could have upheld the lower court's decision against Scott. But instead the majority decided, with some inappropriate coaxing from Buchanan, to render a sweeping decision covering some of the most explosive issues of the day.

The majority decision against Scott did not create the uproar. The problem was Chief Justice Roger Taney's provocative and partisan opinion. Taney argued, first, that Dred Scott was not a citizen because he was black. Since before the republic, he reasoned, African Americans had "been regarded as . . . so far inferior that they had no rights which the white man was bound to respect." Because their ancestors had been slaves in 1776, Taney reasoned, blacks could not be citizens in 1857. The problem was that Taney was wrong about 1857 and 1776: free blacks were discriminated against throughout America but northern courts consistently recognized blacks as citizens. Blacks held property, entered into contracts, brought suits in court, and exercised the rights of speech, press, and assembly.

Second, Taney ruled that slaves were property, like any other property, and the Constitution "expressly affirms" the right of property in slaves. Dred Scott's residence in Wisconsin Territory could not make him a free man, because the Missouri Compromise, which excluded slavery from the territory, was an unconstitutional infringement on the right of property. Nor could his residence in Illinois make Scott free, because the right of property included the right of "sojourn."

Taney's decision made the southern defense of slavery into the law of the land. It effectively made slavery national and freedom merely local. Neither Congress nor western settlers could legally exclude slavery from the territories, because any such exclusion would trample on the slaveholders' sacred rights of property. The only human beings who fell into the category of "property" were black slaves. In a thoroughly political ruling, Taney had declared unconstitutional both the northern Democrats' policy of popular sovereignty and the northern Republican policy of free soil. The one political position left standing by the Court was that of the southern slaveholders. Owning slaves was a right of property, and only blacks could be slaves.

The Lecompton Constitution Splits the Democratic Party

When the Court undermined popular sovereignty as a viable political position, it contributed to the sectional division of the Democratic Party. But the cause of the final Democratic rupture was again Kansas. In 1858 Congress had to choose between two different constitutions accompanying the territory's petition for admission to the Union. The so-called Lecompton Constitution was drawn up by proslavery partisans, representing a minority of Kansas residents. Free-staters, knowing they were in the majority, submitted their constitution to a popular referendum, whereas supporters of the Lecompton Constitution sent their document directly to Congress. Buchanan supported the proslavery minority. But the leading northern Democrat in the Senate, Stephen Douglas of Illinois, rejected the Lecompton Constitution because it violated his principle of popular sovereignty.

Douglas was in a difficult position. Southern Democrats assailed popular sovereignty as an affront to their rights of property in slaves. Northern critics pointed out that the Dred Scott decision had rendered popular sovereignty meaningless. In their famous 1858 debates, Lincoln shrewdly forced Douglas to confront the issue at Freeport, Illinois. Given the Dred Scott decision, Lincoln asked, can the people of a territory legally exclude slavery? In what became known as the Freeport Doctrine, Douglas argued that the people of a territory could exclude slavery simply by refusing to pass the laws necessary to protect it. That way no master would dare go there with his human property. Douglas's logic infuriated southern Democrats and split the party into northern and southern wings in 1860.

The "Irrepressible" Conflict

By the late 1850s the conflict between the North and the South began to seem irrepressible to more and more Americans. Northern Democrats, led by Douglas, tried desperately to preserve a middle ground that would prevent the Union from breaking apart. Similarly, the Whigs in the border states struggled to devise yet another compromise to save the Union. But the middle ground was giving way to the irreconcilable positions of the Republican Party in the North and the Democratic Party in the South.

More than ever, the Democratic Party in the South was the voice of the slaveholding class, its sole purpose the defense of the inalienable right of property in slaves. On most matters, southern Democrats were staunch advocates of states' rights as a defense of slavery against a strong central government. They opposed protective tariffs and federal support for internal improvements (railroads, canals, turnpikes), and they were suspicious of efforts to reestablish a national bank. Property was the creation of the states and if a state created "property in man" the federal government was obliged to protect it, like any other form of property. In response to Douglas's "Freeport Doctrine," Mississippi senator Jefferson Davis proposed a federal slave code that would be imposed on any western territory that refused to protect slave property.

Meanwhile, northern Republicans were moving in the opposite direction, questioning not only the constitutional right of property in slaves but also the sanctity of property

Lincoln-Douglas Debate Painting In 1858 a little-known Illinois Republican, Abraham Lincoln, ran against Stephen A. Douglas for the US Senate. Their seven campaign debates, one of them pictured above, brilliantly spelled out the differences between Democrats and Republicans over slavery. Though Lincoln lost the election, he did so well in the debates that his party nominated him for the presidency two years later.

rights themselves. Whigs once revered the rule of law and the authority of the courts. But their Republican descendants, disgusted by the proslavery bias of the Supreme Court, began denouncing the "superstitious reverence" for judges. Republicans also questioned the primacy of property rights. The most powerful Republican in the 1850s, New York senator William Seward, declared that "property . . . has always a bias toward oppression." And in 1859 Abraham Lincoln praised Thomas Jefferson for elevating human rights over property rights. He repeatedly denounced the Dred Scott decision and argued that there was no such thing as a constitutional right of property in slaves. The Constitution, Republicans argued, recognized slaves not as property but as "persons."

As the 1860 elections approached, the business of Congress was again stalled by the bitter division over slavery. So deep were the divisions that the House of Representatives was unable to elect a speaker. After several northern congressmen endorsed an inflammatory antislavery book published by Hinton Rowan Helper, infuriated southern legislators tied Congress up in knots.

For years the conflict between the North and the South over slavery was said to be "irreconcilable." Frederick Douglass often said that Liberty and Slavery were at war with one another and that there could be no peace until one or the other was vanquished, until either slavery or freedom was the law everywhere in the land. George Fitzhugh, the most extreme proslavery theorist, had long argued the same thing. By the late 1850s, such talk had drifted into the mainstream. Southern politicians began to claim that the slave states were no longer safe within the Union. In Illinois, Abraham Lincoln opened his 1858 race for the US Senate with a speech declaring that "a house divided against itself cannot stand." The most famous expression of this sentiment came in a speech by William Seward in 1858. The division over slavery, he said, "is an irrepressible conflict between opposing and enduring forces, and it means that the United States must and will, sooner or later, become either entirely a slaveholding nation, or entirely a free-labor nation."

By the time of Seward's speech, emotions were running so high, North and South, that it was easy to miss the substance of the disagreement. In truth, slaveholders had little choice but to take the position they did. Their economy, society, and political power rested on their property rights in slaves. And despite the overheated rhetoric, the principles on which the slaveholders stood were in their own way reasonable and logical. Slaves were property, and property rights were supposed to be sacred. At the same time, it made perfect sense for northerners to defend the superiority of free labor. Their own way of life, and the prosperity of their economy, rested on the principle of free labor—that no human being could rightfully own another. The aggressive expansion of slavery and the disproportionate power of the slaveholders in national politics seemed to threaten freedom everywhere. The northerners no less than the southerners had to defend themselves.

But if the conflict between the North and South was irrepressible, that did not mean that civil war was inevitable. The slide from dissension to armed conflict began in late 1859.

The Retreat from Union

Between 1859 and 1860 both the North and the South rejected the sanctity of the Union. In the South, the retreat from unionism was a reaction to John Brown's raid on Harpers Ferry. Brown's death was greeted as a martyr's execution in much of the North, leading many southerners to conclude that a union of the North and the South was no longer viable. In 1860, with the election of Abraham Lincoln, the North ceased compromising with slavery for the sake of maintaining the Union.

John Brown's War Against Slavery

In the fall of 1858, the mysterious John Brown reemerged to launch another battle in his private war against slavery. By the late 1850s, Brown had concocted a plan to invade Virginia and free the slaves. Friends told Brown his plan was unworkable. Frederick Douglass advised him to give it up. But Brown found financial support from a group of well-connected Bostonians dazzled by his appeal to action rather than words. Brown rented a farm in Maryland, near the town of Harpers Ferry in western Virginia, where a small federal arsenal was located. He apparently planned to capture the arsenal and distribute the guns to local slaves, inciting a rebellion. On the evening of October 16, 1859, Brown and 18 followers crossed the Potomac River with a wagonload of guns and seized the armory. Brown ordered his men to scour the countryside to liberate slaves and take slaveholders prisoner. They found Colonel Lewis Washington, a member of the first president's family, and took him back to Harpers Ferry as a hostage. Mission accomplished, Brown sat back and waited for the slaves to rise.

The slaves did not rise, but the military did. Marines were sent from Washington, DC, led by Lieutenant Colonel Robert E. Lee and his assistant, Lieutenant J. E. B. Stuart, later to become leading Confederate generals. On the morning after Brown seized Harpers Ferry, the militia surrounded the arsenal. The next day Stuart ordered Brown to surrender, and when Brown refused, 12 marines charged in with bayonets. Two of Brown's men and one marine were killed, and Brown was wounded. The rebellion was over in less than two days.

The entire raid was "absurd," Abraham Lincoln later said. "It was not a slave insurrection," he added. "It was an attempt by white men to get up a revolt among slaves, in which the slaves refused to participate." The condemnation of Brown by northerners and the embarrassment of Brown's supporters initially calmed southern outrage. Over the next weeks, however, northern opinion changed from contempt to admiration. Brown's eloquent

> I John Brown am now quite **certain** that the crimes of this **guilty, land: will** never be purged **away**; but with Blood. I had **as now I think: vainly** flattered myself that without **verry much** bloodshed; it might be done.

JOHN BROWN'S LAST WORDS,
December 2, 1859

John Brown Artist John Curry's painting of John Brown brilliantly captures Brown's larger-than-life personality. The biblical imagery is reminiscent of Moses and suggests Brown's sense of himself as an agent of the Lord sent by God to lead his nation out of bondage.

statements and dignified behavior in prison, at his trial, and on the gallows moved many northerners to extraordinary demonstrations of sympathy. On December 2, the day Brown was hanged, northern churches tolled their bells. Militia companies fired salutes. Public buildings across the North were draped in black. Although mainstream politicians disavowed Brown and his raid, white southerners were shocked to see John Brown become a hero to many northerners. The *Baltimore Sun* said the South could not "live under a government, the majority of whose subjects or citizens regard John Brown as a martyr and a Christian hero, rather than a murderer and robber." In the end, though, it was not John Brown's raid that led the South to secede from the Union. It was the election of Abraham Lincoln.

Northerners Elect a President

In February 1860, as the nation's focus shifted from John Brown to the coming presidential election, Abraham Lincoln traveled to New York to speak to influential eastern Republicans sizing up possible candidates. Speaking in the newly opened Cooper Institute—later known as Cooper Union—Lincoln extended the argument he had made during his debates with Stephen Douglas. When southerners defended their right of property in slaves, Lincoln argued, they were presuming a constitutional right that did not exist. Instead, the Constitution protected slavery in narrow ways and only in the states where it already existed. Moreover, if the slave states seceded from the Union, they would forfeit whatever constitutional protection slavery did have. By making a radical claim—that there was no constitutional right of property in slaves—and by tying it to a threat to interfere with slavery if the South seceded, Lincoln established his antislavery credentials among leaders of the Republican Party. The Cooper Union Address helped Lincoln win his party's nomination, but it also proved to southern Democrats that his election would be a direct threat to slavery.

Lincoln could not hope to win any votes in the South, and he was attacked as a "sectional" candidate. But by 1860 no major party candidate could appeal to both the North and the South. There were, in effect, two different presidential elections that year. In the slave states a southern Democrat ran against a Constitutional Unionist. In the free states a northern Democrat ran against a Republican. But no one doubted that slavery was the issue, or that the fate of the Union and the future of slavery had become inextricably linked to one another.

The Democratic Party met in April in Charleston, South Carolina, the center of extreme secessionist sentiment. Southern fire-eaters demanded federal recognition of slavery in all the territories as part of the Democratic platform. But Stephen Douglas, the leading candidate for the nomination, insisted on a reaffirmation of popular sovereignty. Douglas had a bare majority of the delegate supporters, enough to push his platform through, but not enough to win the party's nomination. When Douglas's plank was passed, 49 delegates from eight southern states walked out. The convention was deadlocked. After 57 ballots, the Democrats adjourned, agreeing to reconvene in Baltimore a month and a half later.

The delay only made matters worse. In Baltimore, 110 southerners nominated their own candidate, giving the Democrats two presidential aspirants in 1860. Stephen Douglas ran in the North advocating popular sovereignty and insisting that the Union itself hung in the balance of the election. John Breckinridge, the southern candidate, ran on a platform calling for federal recognition of slavery in all the territories. Another candidate, John Bell of Tennessee, tried to revive the Whig Party by running on a Constitutional Unionist ticket. No candidate had much chance of winning.

The Republicans were far more united. Sensing victory, tens of thousands of Republicans poured into Chicago. The leading candidate for the nomination was William H. Seward of New York. But his strength was limited to the uppermost states in the North. In the border states, such as Pennsylvania, Indiana, and Illinois, Seward's antislavery politics were seen as too radical, and he faced opposition even in his home state of New York. The party needed a candidate with impeccable antislavery credentials but seemingly moderate enough to carry the critical states of the lower North. That candidate was Abraham Lincoln.

GRAND, NATIONAL UNION BANNER FOR 1864.
LIBERTY, UNION AND VICTORY.

Lincoln made clear his view that slavery was immoral, that owning slaves was not a constitutionally protected property right and that the entire slave system should be placed "in the course of ultimate extinction." Prohibiting the expansion of slavery into all the western territories was the Republican Party's line in the sand— the one issue on which it would not compromise. But "ultimate extinction" required a much broader antislavery agenda. Republicans would surround the slave states with a "cordon of freedom," surrounding them with free states, free territories, and free oceans. They would oppose the admission of any new slave states to the Union, return enforcement of the fugitive slave clause to the states, and withdraw federal protection from slavery on the high seas. They would make freedom national, even international, and slavery merely local. By these means the Republicans hoped to make slavery so dangerous and unprofitable that the slave states themselves would gradually abolish it on their own. No major party had ever run a candidate dedicated to such a program.

Horrified by the Republican agenda, leading southerners threatened to withdraw from the Union if Lincoln was elected. Yet throughout the campaign, the Republicans scoffed at secessionist threats from the South, as did Breckinridge the Democrat and Bell the Constitutional Unionist. But Douglas was so convinced that the election of Lincoln would result in secession and war that he actively campaigned as the only candidate who could hold the Union together. When Lincoln's victory became clear, Douglas made a series of speeches in the slave states—"not to ask for your votes for the Presidency," he told his audiences, "but to make an appeal to you on behalf of the Union."

Lincoln won every free state except New Jersey. Douglas got the second-largest number of votes but took only one state, Missouri. Breckenridge took 11 slave states, although his support was concentrated in districts with the lowest proportions of slaves. The slaveholders continued to vote their traditional Whig sympathies, supporting John Bell's Constitutional Unionist candidacy.

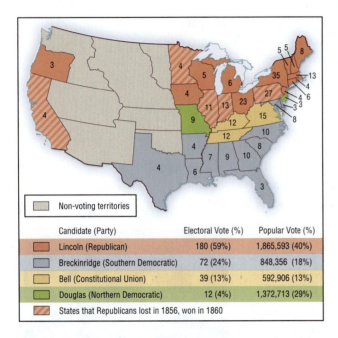

Candidate (Party)	Electoral Vote (%)	Popular Vote (%)
Lincoln (Republican)	180 (59%)	1,865,593 (40%)
Breckinridge (Southern Democratic)	72 (24%)	848,356 (18%)
Bell (Constitutional Union)	39 (13%)	592,906 (13%)
Douglas (Northern Democratic)	12 (4%)	1,372,713 (29%)

Non-voting territories

States that Republicans lost in 1856, won in 1860

Map 14–5 The Election of 1860 By 1860, no presidential candidate could appeal to voters in both the North and the South. By then, the northern population had grown so rapidly that a united North could elect Lincoln to the presidency without any southern support.

Lincoln did not campaign in the South; his name was not even on the ballot in most of the slave states. He won by appealing exclusively to voters in the North (see Map 14–5), which is why Lincoln could run on a platform dedicated to slavery's "ultimate extinction." Antislavery forces in the North were doubly vindicated: not only did the Republican victory show wide appeal for an antislavery platform, but it also suggested that a dynamic economy based on free labor was bound to grow faster than a slave society. In their own way, white southerners agreed. They concluded that no matter what assurances Lincoln gave them, the future of slavery in the Union was doomed.

Conclusion

Frederick Douglass had misgivings about Lincoln but sincerely hoped that the Republicans would win the 1860 elections. "Slavery is the issue—the single bone of contention between all parties and sections," he insisted. Slavery and freedom had guided the nation along two diverging pathways. The North was developing an urban, industrial economy based on the productive energy of wage labor. In the South, a prosperous slave economy depended on a system of commercialized agriculture in which laborers were commodities as much as the cash crops they produced. The political tensions arising from these differences finally pushed the nation into civil war. And as the war progressed, the same fundamental differences would shape the destiny of the Union and Confederate forces.

Who, What

John Brown   488
Stephen Douglas   486

Frederick Douglass   473
John C. Frémont   494

>> TIME LINE

▼1838
Frederick Douglass escapes from slavery

▼1844
Samuel F. B. Morse invents the telegraph

▼1846
David Wilmot introduces his "proviso"

▼1847
Treaty of Guadalupe Hidalgo

▼1848
Zachary Taylor elected president

▼1850
Taylor dies; Millard Fillmore becomes president
Compromise of 1850

▼1852
Uncle Tom's Cabin published in book form
Franklin Pierce elected president

Abraham Lincoln   488
Charles Sumner   491
Roger Taney   496
"Bleeding Kansas"   488
Compromise of 1850   483
Dred Scott decision   496

Fugitive Slave Act   483
Harpers Ferry   499
Know-Nothing   486
Ostend Manifesto   489
Popular sovereignty   481
Wilmot Proviso   480

Review Questions

1. What were the major differences between the northern and southern economies by the 1850s?

2. How did the war with Mexico provoke a conflict over slavery?

3. What did the Republican Party stand for?

4. What was the Kansas-Nebraska Act, and why was it so important?

5. What were the major issues in the Lincoln-Douglas debates?

Critical-Thinking Questions

1. Was the slavery battle primarily a conflict between two different economic systems, or was it more of a moral issue?

2. Which congressional action in this period did the most to push the nation toward civil war (the Wilmot Proviso, the Compromise of 1850, the Kansas-Nebraska Act, the debate over the Lecompton Constitution)? Explain your answer.

3. How did developments that first appeared to be victories for the South end up benefiting the antislavery cause in the long run?

4. Violence played a role in the debate over slavery even before the first shots of the Civil War. In your opinion, was John Brown's violent crusade justified? Why or why not?

For further review materials and resource information, please visit www.oup.com/us/ofthepeople

▼**1854**
Gadsden Purchase ratified
Kansas-Nebraska Act
Ostend Manifesto

▼**1856**
"Bleeding Kansas"
Sumner-Brooks affair
James Buchanan elected president

▼**1857**
Dred Scott decision

▼**1858**
Lincoln-Douglas debates

▼**1859**
John Brown's raid on Harpers Ferry

▼**1860**
Abraham Lincoln elected first Republican president

▼**1861**
South secedes from Union, Civil War begins

1) Debates over the future of slavery in the western territories plagued the American political system for more than a decade and led to civil war.

2) A poorly constructed compromise on the slavery issue quickly fell apart once the status of the Kansas and Nebraska territories came into question.

3) Developments in Kansas allowed various groups to unite around a single antislavery party and simultaneously tore the pro-slavery party apart.

4) Even before the first shots of the Civil War, the emotional charge of the slavery issue prompted figures on both sides to abandon political discourse for violence and vigilantism.

The Political Economy of Freedom and Slavery

Slavery Becomes a Political Issue

Nativism and the Origins aof the Republican Party

A New Political Party Takes Shape

The Retreat from Union

EVENTS

A Changing Economy in the North Industry began to replace agriculture as the driving force of the northern economy, and a rural society became more urban.

The Slave Economy The South stretched across half the continent, with cotton its most profitable crop, yet while the expansion of slavery brought commerce to the region, it did not bring economic development.

The Importance of the West The North and South disagreed over the future of slavery in the new western territories.

Wilmot Introduces His Proviso Congressman David Wilmot's bill to ban slavery from all the territories acquired in the Mexican War hardened positions and set the stage for a fierce congressional debate.

A Compromise Without Compromises Senator Stephen Douglas steered the Compromise of 1850 through Congress, but neither proslavery nor antislavery forces actually relented on a single issue.

The Fugitive Slave Act Provokes a Crisis Many northerners were outraged over the Fugitive Slave Act, perceiving it as the imposition of southern laws and institutions on the North.

The Election of 1852 and the Decline of the Whig Party Southerners abandoned the Whig Party in droves, all but assuring the election of Democrat Franklin Pierce to the presidency.

The Nativist Attack on Immigration Nativism grew with the increased arrival of Catholic immigrants and found a political voice in the "Know-Nothing" Party.

The Kansas-Nebraska Act Revives the Slavery Issue The issue of slavery in Kansas and Nebraska led to the repeal of the Missouri Compromise and hardened both proslavery and antislavery attitudes.

Kansas Begins to Bleed Elections concerning the future of slavery in Kansas led to electoral fraud and violence.

The First Sectional Election Northern opponents of slavery created the Republican Party in 1856 and ran John C. Frémont for president.

The Labor Problem and the Politics of Slavery The North and South debated slavery's impact on economic progress and efficiency.

The Dred Scott Decision A controversial Supreme Court ruling made the southern defense of slavery the law of the land.

The Lecompton Constitution Splits the Democratic Party Congressional debate over the Lecompton Constitution in Kansas split the Democratic Party along sectional lines.

The "Irrepressible" Conflict Attempts at compromise on the slavery issue eventually gave way to the irreconcilable positions of the North and the South.

John Brown's War Against Slavery Hoping to incite a rebellion, Brown captured the armory at Harpers Ferry, but was quickly arrested and executed.

Northerners Elect a President With the southern vote split, a more unified North elected Republican Abraham Lincoln as president.

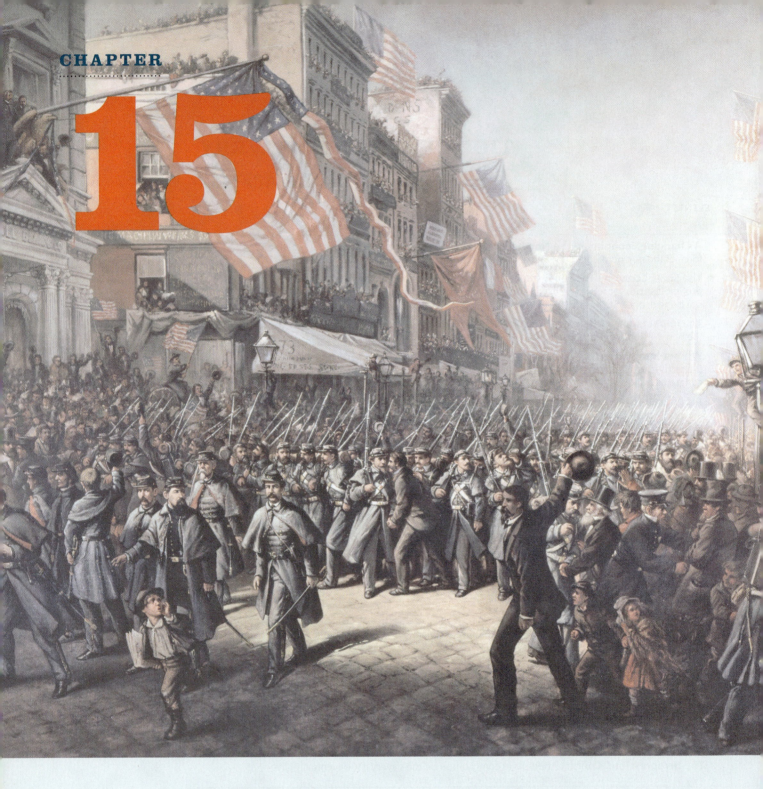

CHAPTER

15

COMMON THREADS

>> What made the South secede from the Union?

>> In what ways did the military strategies of the North and South reflect the differences between the two regions?

>> What was the relationship between emancipation and war?

>> Why did the South lose the Civil War? Why did the North win?

>> What happened to the slaves who were freed by the war?

A War for Union and Emancipation 1861-1865

>> Edmund Ruffin

Edmund Ruffin was born in 1794 into one of the wealthiest planter families in eastern Virginia. By the age of 20 he was the master of a substantial plantation on the James River. Yet from his youth Edmund Ruffin was discontented and angry. He coveted a political career, but his contempt for democracy made that impractical. In 1823 he was elected to the Virginia state senate, but he was unwilling to forge the alliances and make the compromises that would bring him political influence. Before his term expired, Ruffin resigned his seat, "tired and disgusted with being a servant of the people." He never held public office again.

During the 1830s and 1840s Ruffin retreated to his plantations, publishing the results of his experiments in crop rotation, drainage, and new fertilizers. His work paid off in improved productivity, higher profits, and public esteem. But Ruffin, more interested in politics than farming, used his fame as an agricultural reformer to spread his proslavery message. By 1850 Ruffin was urging Virginians to secede from the Union to preserve slavery.

Ruffin moved from reformer to secessionist through the logic of political economy. A more productive slave economy, he reasoned, would protect the South from the growing power of the industrializing North. Inspired by other proslavery authors, Ruffin set all the world's peoples on a sliding scale from the most savage to the most civilized. The only way for barbaric peoples to rise above savagery, Ruffin claimed, was for the powerful and industrious to force these shiftless people to work, usually by enslaving them. Slavery thus spurred both civilization and prosperity.

But Ruffin's defense of slavery left several important questions unanswered: Who, for example, should be enslaved? It was both morally objectionable and socially disruptive for equals to enslave equals. Southern slavery escaped this problem, Ruffin believed, because whites enslaved only racially inferior blacks. And what of the abolitionist claim that slavery was less efficient than wage labor? Ruffin agreed that in principle slaves lacked the motive of self-interest that made wage laborers more efficient, but he pointed to exceptional conditions in the United States. As long as western lands could absorb the surplus labor of the North, free laborers would work on their own farms at their own pace. But slaves were compelled to labor on precious cash crops grown in climates where, Ruffin believed, only African Americans could work. As long as these exceptional conditions prevailed, slavery would be as efficient as free labor.

Once the West filled up, Ruffin argued, free men and women would be forced to sell their labor at miserably low wages. Eventually, the misery of free laborers would give rise to socialism and anarchy. Thus, northerners would pay the price of perpetual social unrest for their wealth and prosperity. Southern whites, by contrast, had struck the perfect balance between material well-being and social peace. By enslaving an "inferior" race, they could raise the general level of civilization without the disruptions associated with wage labor.

Continued

>> **AMERICAN PORTRAIT**
Continued

Edmund Ruffin had always believed that slavery was the issue dividing the North from the South. As war approached, a growing number of northerners reached the same conclusion. For many southerners, the only way to protect slavery was to leave the Union. For northerners, the only way to preserve the Union was to destroy slavery. Edmund Ruffin was not surprised that the northern crusade to preserve the Union was inseparable from the crusade to abolish slavery.

Liberty and Union

Southerners made it clear that they were going to war to preserve their rights of property in slaves. In 1861 Confederate president Jefferson Davis justified secession on the grounds that northern Republican rule would make "property in slaves so insecure as to be comparatively worthless." Southerners talked in general about defending "states' rights" or "property rights," but they were referring specifically to the right of the states to maintain slavery and to the right of individuals to hold property in slaves. These were among the cherished principles that white southerners had inherited from the Founding Fathers of the nation. Slavery had been legal in every one of the thirteen colonies represented in the Declaration of Independence. In declaring their own independence, white southerners believed they were affirming rather than rejecting the legacy of the American Revolution. Their rights and prosperity were no longer safe in the Union the Founders had created. So they made a confederacy of their own in which slavery could survive unharmed, forever.

> We affirm that these ends for which this Government was instituted have been defeated, and the Government itself has been destructive of them by the action of the non-slaveholding States. Those States have assumed the right of deciding upon the propriety of our domestic institutions; and have denied the rights of property established in fifteen of the States and recognized by the Constitution; they have denounced as sinful the institution of Slavery; they have permitted the open establishment among them of a society, whose avowed object is to disturb the peace and eloin the property of the citizens of other States. They have encouraged and assisted thousands of our slaves to leave their homes; and those who remain, have been incited, by emissaries, books and pictures, to servile insurrection.
>
> "DECLARATION OF THE CAUSES WHICH INDUCED THE SECESSION OF SOUTH CAROLINA,"
> December 1860

OUTLINE

Liberty and Union
  The South Secedes
  Civilians Demand a Total War
  Slaves Take Advantage of the War
  Military Strategy and the Shift in War Aims

  PRIMARY SOURCE:
  "The Battle Hymn of the Republic" and "Dixie"

  Mobilizing for War

The Confederate States of America
Union Naval Supremacy
Southern Military Advantages
The Slave Economy in Wartime
What Were Soldiers Fighting For?

The Civil War as Social Revolution
Union Victories in the West
Southern Military Strength in the East
Universal Emancipation

But the Union was a sacred thing for most northerners, a beacon of liberty in a world of tyranny. To break the Union apart would be treason, but it would also prove that democratic republics could not hold themselves together. If the Union collapsed, "the last best hope" of the oppressed peoples of the world would go down with it. Republicans declared that slavery was the cause of the war, and by the time the fighting started they openly endorsed emancipation as a legitimate means of suppressing the rebellion. Northern Democrats, by contrast, rarely cared enough about the plight of African Americans to support a war for their freedom, but most were ready to fight in defense of the Union. Most northerners could thus rally around the cause of "Union," even if Republicans and Democrats disagreed over emancipation. In his inaugural address of March 1861, Lincoln reasserted the commonplace assumption, shared by most abolitionists, that the federal government could not constitutionally abolish slavery in a state where it already existed. But he also denied that there was a constitutional right to property in slaves and warned that, by seceding, the South risked losing whatever federal protection slavery did enjoy. Like most northerners, Lincoln would fight to restore the Union; like most Republicans, he was prepared to use emancipation as a weapon.

The South Secedes

As the news of Lincoln's election flashed across telegraph wires, the South Carolina state legislature called a secession convention. On December 20, 1860, the state withdrew from the Union on the grounds that northerners had elected a president who denied the existence of a right of property in slaves. "They have encouraged and assisted thousands of slaves to leave their homes," South Carolina declared, "and those who remain have been incited . . . to servile insurrection." Within weeks, Mississippi, Florida, Alabama, Georgia, Louisiana, and Texas followed suit (see Map 15–1). Then, as quickly as it had begun, the secession movement came to a halt. The slave states of the upper South refused to leave the Union simply because Lincoln was elected. Ardent secessionists began to suspect that the South was not unified in its opposition to the North.

The upper South was dominated by cooperationists rather than secessionists. Cooperationists were committed to remaining in the Union provided that the Lincoln administration "cooperated" with the South. Thus, even after Lincoln's inauguration, Virginia, Arkansas, and Missouri would not

AMERICA AND THE WORLD:
   The Diplomacy of Emancipation
   Emancipation in Practice

AMERICAN LANDSCAPE:
   Freedman's Village, Arlington, Virginia

The War at Home
   The Care of Casualties

TECHNOLOGY AND IDEAS:
   The Repeating Rifle

Northern Reverses and Antiwar Sentiment
Gettysburg and the Justification of the War
Discontent in the Confederacy

The War Comes to a Bloody End
   Grant Takes Command
   The Theory and Practice of Hard War
   Sherman Marches and Lee Surrenders
   From Emancipation to Abolition
   The Meaning of the Civil War

Conclusion

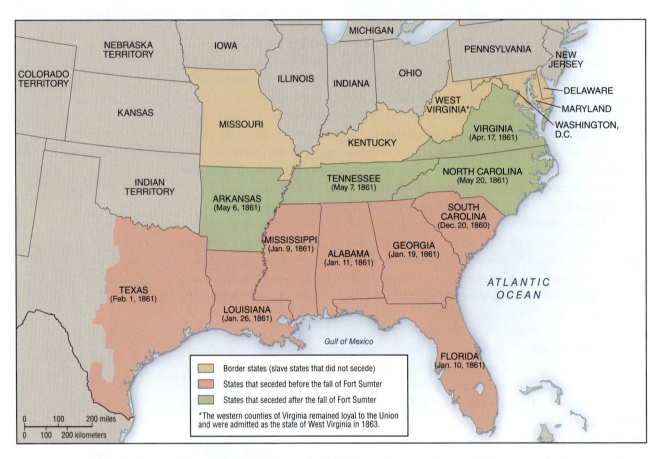

Map 15-1 The Secession of the Southern States The South seceded in two stages. During the "secession winter" of 1860–1861, the lower South states seceded in reaction to the election of Abraham Lincoln. The following spring, the upper South seceded in response to Lincoln's attempt to resupply Fort Sumter. The border slave states of Maryland, Delaware, Kentucky, and Missouri never left the Union.

secede. The state legislatures of Kentucky and Delaware refused to authorize secession conventions, and in Tennessee and North Carolina the voters refused. Lincoln and many Republicans hoped that if they moved cautiously they could keep the upper South in the Union and thereby derail the secession movement. But cooperationism turned out to be a weak foundation for a rebuilt Union. Cooperationist loyalty required the federal government to meet certain demands for the protection of slavery.

Cooperationist demands were the basis of several proslavery attempts at sectional compromise. The most famous was a series of constitutional amendments proposed by Senator John J. Crittenden of Kentucky. The Crittenden Compromise would have restored the Missouri Compromise line and guaranteed federal protection of slavery south of that line in all territories currently held or later acquired by the United States. It would have prohibited Congress from abolishing slavery in Washington, DC, and from regulating the interstate slave trade. Finally, it called for the compensation of masters unable to recover fugitive slaves from the North.

Each of these concessions was unacceptable to the Republicans, especially the one issue on which they steadfastly refused to compromise—the expansion of slavery into the territories. But taken together, the six constitutional amendments and three congressional resolutions that made up the Crittenden Compromise represented a wholesale repudiation of everything the Republican Party stood for. The "compromise" would make slavery rather than freedom national. And once the lower South seceded, the Republicans concluded that any compromise amounted to surrender to southern blackmail.

The conflict over slavery had become irreconcilable. By the spring of 1861, most southerners agreed with Edmund Ruffin that there should be no more compromise with the North. Even "cooperationists" insisted that the southern states had a right to secede and should do so if Lincoln committed any act of overt "coercion." It was also clear that the confrontation would come at one of the two Union forts still in the seceded states—Fort Pickens in Pensacola, Florida, or Fort Sumter in Charleston Harbor. Realizing that Pickens was indefensible, Jefferson Davis sent the flamboyant P. G. T. Beauregard to Charleston Harbor to prepare defenses against the impending Union invasion. Out of respect for his long years of service to the cause, Ruffin was invited to South Carolina and given the privilege of firing one of the first shots of the Civil War. At 4:30 in the morning on April 12, 1861, Ruffin aimed a rifle at Fort Sumter and began shooting. For 33 hours Confederates bombarded the fort, located on an island in Charleston Harbor, to block its resupply by the US government. With no alternative, the Union commander raised the white flag of surrender. Fort Sumter fell to the Confederates, and the Civil War began.

Though he hoped for peace, Lincoln had long since concluded that a war was inevitable. He probably understood that his attempt to resupply Fort Sumter would provoke an armed assault. But by announcing in advance that he was sending only nonmilitary provisions, Lincoln had maneuvered the South into firing the first shot. For southerners who had declared their independence months earlier, any federal attempt to supply Sumter, with food or with weapons, amounted to a declaration of war. And so the war came. The day Fort Sumter surrendered, Lincoln issued a call to the states for 75,000 militiamen to report for duty within 90 days. The governors of Tennessee, Virginia, North Carolina, Arkansas, Kentucky, and Missouri refused to comply with Lincoln's request. Two days later Virginia seceded, and within a month Arkansas, Tennessee, and North Carolina did the same. Northern hopes of holding on to the upper South had vanished.

But the South remained divided. Four slave states (Kentucky, Maryland, Delaware, and Missouri) never joined the Confederacy. In the mountains of western North Carolina and eastern Tennessee, unionist sentiment remained strong during the war years. Virginia was literally torn apart. The western third of the state voted overwhelmingly against secession, and when the eastern slaveholders decided to leave the Union, western counties formed their own state government. (In 1863 the state of West Virginia was admitted to the Union.) Where slavery was weak, support for secession was weak also. Where slavery thrived, so did the sentiment for secession. Yet despite these internal divisions, support for secession was remarkably widespread in the South, and over the next four years white southerners would put up a long, hard fight to sustain the independence of the Confederacy.

Civilians Demand a Total War

Some Americans expected the war to last only a few months, and Lincoln's first call for troops asking volunteers to enlist for 90 days suggested that he agreed. But within days he called for a much larger number of three-year enlistments. Confederate soldiers initially signed up for 12 months but were later required to serve "for the duration" of the war. Although both sides began with relatively limited military and political goals, the conflict descended into a "hard" war that produced shocking numbers of military casualties, horrifying massacres of black prisoners, and the deliberate destruction of the homes and farms of southern whites. In the end, hard war would also mean the unconditional surrender of Confederate armies and the end of southern slavery.

In the weeks following Fort Sumter, enthusiasm for war overflowed in the Union and the Confederacy. Military victory was not enough. In the spring of 1861, one southern woman prayed that "God may be with us to give us strength to conquer them, to exterminate them, to lay waste to every Northern city, town and village, to destroy them utterly." In 1862 southern troops burned the town of Chambersburg, Pennsylvania, to the ground, and in 1864 Jefferson Davis sent Confederate agents to New York City, where they set fire to 10 hotels, hoping to send the city up in flames.

Northerners felt no differently toward southerners. Even before fighting began, Ohio senator Benjamin Wade talked of "making the south a desert." After Fort Sumter, one northern judge argued that the North should "restore New Orleans to its native marshes, then march across the country, burn Montgomery to ashes, and serve Charleston in the same way. . . . We must starve, drown, burn, shoot the traitors."

The military was more hesitant, and neither side was prepared for battle nor sought it. For several months, Union and Confederate commanders concentrated on building up their armies. The entire US Army had only 16,000 troops scattered across the conti-

Thomas Nast's *Seventh Regiment Departing for the War from New York City, April 1861* The enthusiasm on display was typical of popular sentiment in both the North and the South at the very beginning of the war. Neither side was prepared for the long and bloody war that followed.

nent. Under the direction of aged war hero General Winfield Scott, Union strategy was initially designed to use the North's naval superiority to blockade the entire South, but there was almost no navy, either. Yet, as spring became summer, civilians in the North and the South demanded more. "Forward to Richmond!" cried Horace Greeley, echoing northern sentiment for a swift capture of the new Confederate capital.

Slaves Take Advantage of the War

In the South, the enthusiasm for battle was compounded by fantasies of a race war between African Americans and whites. The lower South seceded while still in the grip of the insurrection panics that followed John Brown's raid on Harpers Ferry. Few slaves actually joined with Brown, but that did little to calm the fears of southern whites. Such fears were usually exaggerated, but by 1861 they were not.

As the war began, slaves struggled to collect war news. House servants reported conversations at the masters' residences to field hands in the slave quarters. Every neighborhood had one or two literate slaves who got hold of a newspaper. News of the war spread along what the slaves called the "grapevine telegraph."

Shortly after Lincoln was inaugurated, several slaves in Florida escaped to Fort Pickens, claiming their freedom. In Virginia, scarcely a month after Fort Sumter, Union commander Benjamin F. Butler refused to return three runaway slaves on the grounds that they would have been put to work on Confederate military fortifications. Butler considered the runaways "contrabands" of war, and the label stuck. As the number of contrabands mounted, Butler demanded that his superiors clarify Union policy. "As a military question it would seem to be a measure of necessity to deprive their masters of their services," he wrote on May 27, 1861. Immediately realizing the importance of Butler's idea, Lincoln called his cabinet together to discuss the matter on May 30. After the meeting, Secretary of War Simon Cameron telegraphed Butler that his proposal to retain "contraband" slaves "is approved." The Fugitive Slave Act was effectively nullified.

But universal emancipation was still a long way off. For every runaway who made it to Union lines, hundreds were still trapped in slavery on southern farms and plantations, and most would remain trapped until the war was over. War disrupted slave life, but if slavery survived the war, the plantations would recover. It had happened many times before in the long history of human slavery; it had even happened in America. Southern slave society had weathered the upheaval of the American Revolution, and slaveholders vowed that slavery would outlast the Civil War as well. The slaves were determined to win their freedom, but their masters had the guns. To succeed, the slaves would need allies—the US government and the Union army.

Military Strategy and the Shift in War Aims

No single military strategy defined either the Confederate or Union war efforts, as there was wide disagreement among leaders on both sides about the best way to win the war. But in general the South pursued a defensive strategy. If Confederate armies could hold off Union attacks, using interior lines to move men to different theaters of war, they might be able to wear down the North until it gave up the fight. Throughout the war, Confederate commanders moved their armies like chess pieces across the southern playing field to engage larger Union armies: from the Shenandoah Valley to Manassas, from New Orleans to Shiloh, from northern Virginia to Tennessee. It was a mostly successful strategy. But the Confederates also pursued a more aggressive if less

>> "Battle Hymn of the Republic" and "Dixie"

Music played an important part for both sides in the Civil War, on the home front and for the combatants. Martial music had long been a part of warfare serving to inspire, console, build camaraderie, and keep combat units in step with one another. Two songs gained widespread popularity, one for each side: "The Battle Hymn of the Republic" for the Union, and "Dixie" for the Confederacy. "The Battle Hymn of the Republic" comes from two sources: a poem by Julia Ward Howe published in the Atlantic Monthly magazine in 1862 and the music reputedly by William Steffe. "Dixie," the unofficial anthem of the Confederacy and the South after the war, has a much more tangled history. Usually attributed to minstrel-show songwriter and Ohioan Daniel Decatur Emmett, its words are meant to represent a slave singing longingly of his lost plantation home. Interestingly enough, the song was so popular after its original performance in 1859 that Abraham Lincoln adopted it as one of his campaign songs for the presidential race in 1860.

"The Battle Hymn of the Republic"

Mine eyes have seen the glory
Of the coming of the Lord;
He is trampling out the vintage
Where the grapes of wrath are
  stored;
He hath loosed the fateful lightning
Of His terrible swift sword;
His truth is marching on.

Chorus
Glory! Glory! Hallelujah!
Glory! Glory! Hallelujah!
Glory! Glory! Hallelujah!
His truth is marching on.

I have seen Him in the watchfires
Of a hundred circling camps
They have builded Him an altar
In the evening dews and damps;
I can read His righteous sentence
By the dim and flaring lamps;
His day is marching on.

Chorus
I have read a fiery gospel writ
In burnished rows of steel:
"As ye deal with My contemners,
So with you My grace shall deal":

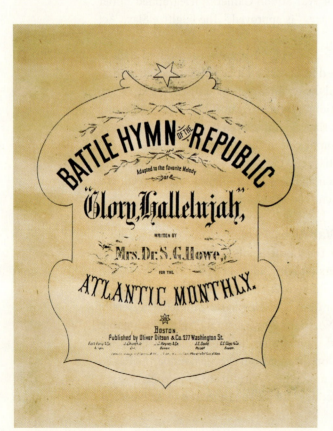

Let the Hero born of woman
Crush the serpent with His heel,
Since God is marching on.

Chorus
He has sounded forth the trumpet
That shall never call retreat;
He is sifting out the hearts of men
Before His judgment seat;
Oh, be swift, my soul, to answer Him;
Be jubilant, my feet;
Our God is marching on.

Chorus
In the beauty of the lilies
Christ was born across the sea,
With a glory in His bosom
That transfigures you and me;
As He died to make men holy,
Let us die to make men free;
While God is marching on.

Chorus

"Dixie"

I wish I was in the land of cotton,
    old times there are not forgotten,
Look away, look away, look away,
    Dixie Land.
In Dixie Land where I was born in,
    early on a frosty mornin',
Look away, look away, look away,
    Dixie Land.

Then I wish I was in Dixie, hooray!
    hooray!
In Dixie Land I'll take my stand to
    live and die in Dixie,
Away, away, away down South in
    Dixie,
Away, away, away down South in
    Dixie.

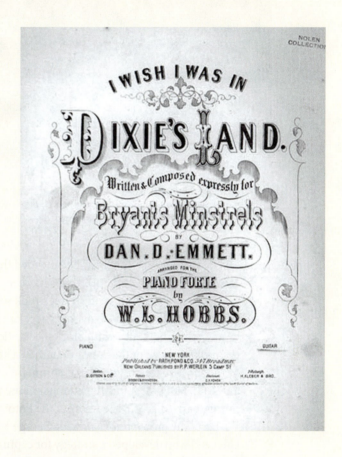

Julia Ward Howe, "Battle Hymn of the Republic/John Brown's Body," and Daniel Decatur Emmet, "Dixie," in *America: Readings in Themes and Eras*, ed. Mary S. Sheridan (Lanham, MD: University Press of America, 1992), pp. 131–132, 132–133.

Questions

1. How would you characterize the tone of each of these songs? How are the songs similar to each other? How are they different?

2. During the Civil War, how might different audiences have reacted differently to these songs?

3. How might our interpretations of these songs today differ from the interpretations of people who lived during the Civil War?

Escaping Slaves Designated "contrabands" of war, these Virginia slaves are escaping to Union lines in August 1862. The Lincoln administration took office with a promise not to interfere with southern slavery, but runaways like those pictured here helped push the Union toward a policy of emancipation.

successful strategy. Robert E. Lee invaded the North twice, for example, in September 1862 and July 1863, and both times his armies were defeated.

A more aggressive Union strategy took some time to develop. At the outset, General Winfield Scott proposed a gigantic siege of the entire South, choking the Confederacy by an increasingly successful blockade. Critics derided this as "the anaconda plan." But the naval squeeze of the South remained a key element of northern strategy, and some of the most successful northern commanders were admirals, such as David Farragut and Andrew Foote. Lincoln had much more trouble with his generals than with his admirals, particularly in the Army of the Potomac that fought most of the major battles in the East. The problems began with George McClellan, who replaced Scott as general in chief and who developed a strategy for capturing the Confederate capital of Richmond, Virginia. Eventually Lincoln realized that capturing territory was no replacement for defeating armies, and until the last year of the war he struggled with a succession of eastern generals who could not see their goal to be the destruction of the Confederate armies. It was not enough to drive Robert E. Lee's army out of Maryland or Pennsylvania, Lincoln insisted; the army itself had to be destroyed. The capture of Richmond, too, was a strategic fantasy so long as Lee's armies were waiting somewhere nearby. Not until 1863, with Grant's capture of the Confederate armies trapped in Vicksburg, did Lincoln feel he had a general who shared his strategic commitment to the unconditional surrender of Confederate armed forces. By then, Lincoln had also embraced a final strategy, "hard war," aimed at undermining the morale of southern civilians.

The first test of Union and Confederate military strength came on July 21, 1861, near a creek called Bull Run at the town of Manassas Junction, Virginia, 25 miles from Washington (see Map 15–2). Everyone knew the battle was coming. Spectators with picnic baskets followed the Union army out of Washington to watch from the surrounding hillsides. Among the southerners who came to watch was Edmund Ruffin.

The Confederates stretched a defensive line eight miles along Bull Run and waited for the attack. Along their interior lines, the Confederates made the first strategic use of the railroad to shift reinforcements quickly from the Shenandoah Valley to the Manassas battlefield. The battle itself, fought by poorly trained and untested troops, resembled a brutal struggle between two armed mobs more than a well-executed set of maneuvers. Still, the arrival of Confederate reinforcements proved crucial. And the first battle of Bull Run did establish at least one new military reputation. A southern officer named Thomas J. Jackson, perched on his horse "like a stone wall," inspired his men to drive back the Union advance. The green Union troops retreated. Heading east toward Washington, frightened spectators clogged the road in panic, and the retreat turned into a rout. It would not be the last time "Stonewall" Jackson would give the Union army grief.

Most southerners were ecstatic, even overconfident, after their victory. By contrast, the chaos in the Union ranks shocked the North into realizing that this would be no 90-day war. To discipline the Union troops, Lincoln put George B. McClellan in command of the Army of the Potomac.

Map 15-2 The Virginia Campaigns of 1861–1862 Between the first and second battles of Bull Run, the Confederate armies in Virginia consistently frustrated northern attempts to capture Richmond, the capital of the Confederate States of America. Superior southern generalship was largely responsible for the northern defeats.

Bull Run also coincided with the enactment of the Union's earliest emancipation policy. The day before the battle Senate Republicans had endorsed an amendment to a confiscation bill that would emancipate the slaves of all rebels coming into Union lines. The First Confiscation Act, passed by Congress on August 5 and signed by Lincoln the next day, declared that masters would permanently "forfeit" the labor of any slaves used in support of the rebellion. Two days later the War Department instructions for implementing the new law declared that the forfeited slaves were "discharged from service," that is, emancipated. These earliest emancipations applied to slaves who voluntarily entered Union lines from seceded states. Union soldiers were, however, prohibited from "enticing" slaves away from their owners.

The August 8 War Department instructions were repeatedly given to Union commanders as they occupied new positions along the South Atlantic coast. By December President Lincoln noted in his first annual message to Congress that numerous slaves were escaping to Union lines and under the terms of the First Confiscation Act were "thus liberated." This was "military emancipation," applied to areas in rebellion against the Union. But in the same message to Congress Lincoln also urged lawmakers to pass legislation encouraging the four border states still in the Union to sell their slaves to the federal government, which would then "liberate" them gradually. This was gradual abolition, the second antislavery policy pursued by Republicans, and it applied to loyal rather than disloyal areas of the South. Both policies were justified in the name of suppressing the rebellion.

Also among the North's war aims was its determination to keep England and France from recognizing the Confederate government, which in turn hoped to keep Europeans from respecting the Union blockade of southern ports. A diplomatic crisis loomed in late 1861 when a Union navy captain intercepted a British ship, the *Trent*, in Havana and forced two Confederate commissioners to disembark before allowing the *Trent* to sail on. The commissioners had slipped through the blockade and were headed for Europe, hoping to secure diplomatic recognition of the Confederacy. When the British protested, the administration wisely released them. "One war at a time," Lincoln supposedly said.

Mobilizing for War

By the end of the first summer, both sides realized that the conflict would last for more than a few months and would demand every resource the North and South could command. But in 1860 neither side had many military resources to command. By the end of the war, approximately 2.1 million men had served in the Union armed forces and another 900,000 in the Confederacy. To raise and sustain such numbers was an immense political and social problem. To feed, clothe, and arm them was an equally immense technological problem. To pay for such armed forces was an immense economic problem. The Civil War became a test of the competing economies of the North and the South (see Figure 15–1).

The Confederate States of America

By the spring of 1861, secessionists had persuaded 11 states to leave the Union. In a constitutional convention in Montgomery, Alabama, they drafted a basic charter for their new government, the Confederate States of America, with its capital at Rich-

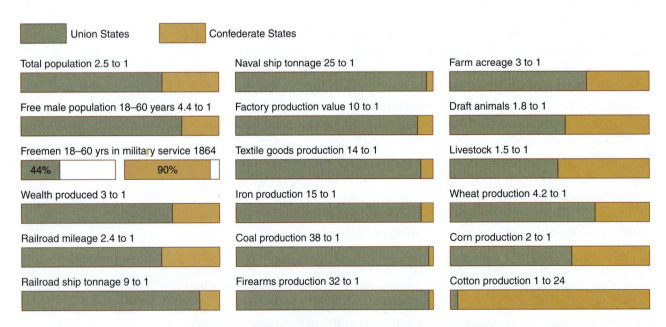

Figure 15-1 The Productive Capacities of the Union and Confederacy Not only did the northern economy dwarf the South's industrial capacity, it also outpaced southern agricultural production in everything but cotton.

mond, Virginia. They selected as president an experienced politician and Mississippi planter, Jefferson Davis.

The Confederate constitution varied in interesting ways from the US Constitution. The Confederate chief executive served a single, six-year term and had a line-item veto, for example. But the most important differences had to do with slavery. The slaveholders preferred their markets the same way they preferred their power over the slaves—without restraints. The free market in slaves captured this dual preference perfectly. So it made sense that the Confederate constitution defined slaves as property and protected slavery as an inviolable right of property. The Confederate constitution similarly included an ironclad fugitive slave clause that could not be undermined by any state, ensured the right of masters to "sojourn" with their slaves, and protected slavery in all territories acquired by the southern nation.

There were also several political differences between the United States of America and the Confederate States of America. The most striking was the absence of a two-party system in the South. The Whig Party had collapsed in the North during the early 1850s, and the Republican Party took its place. Throughout the war, the northern Democrats represented a strong but loyal opposition to the Lincoln administration. In the South, by contrast, the Democratic Party ruled without opposition after the Whigs collapsed.

> The prevailing ideas entertained by [Thomas Jefferson] and most of the leading statesmen at the time of the formation of the old Constitution were, that the enslavement of the African was in violation of the laws of nature; that it was wrong in principle, socially, morally and politically. . . . Our new Government is founded upon exactly the opposite ideas; its foundations are laid, its cornerstone rests, upon the great truth that the negro is not equal to the white man; that slavery, subordination to the superior race, is his natural and moral condition.
>
> ALEXANDER STEPHENS,
> vice president of the Confederate States of America

A consistent source of tension was the South's commitment to states' rights, which often conflicted with the need to mount a concerted defense of the new nation. This led to conflicts between Jefferson Davis and several state governors, in particular Joseph E. Brown of Georgia and Zebulon Vance of North Carolina. Brown and Vance were loyal Confederates, but in their zeal to protect their states, they frequently locked horns with the Confederate president.

It is not clear how any of these political and constitutional differences affected the outcome of the war. Southerners realized soon enough that their devotion to the free market would lose them the war. In the end, the Confederacy would sustain itself with a command economy the likes of which the United States has never seen, before or since. Abraham Lincoln was certainly more personable than his Confederate counterpart and better able than the prickly Davis to slough off his critics. But Lincoln's critics were, if anything, more threatening than Davis's. Northern opponents of the war were sometimes violent, though more often they expressed their opposition through the Democratic Party. Like Davis, Lincoln had to deal with obstreperous states, and at least a few northern governors seemed determined to undermine the Union war effort. Both presidents suspended habeas corpus and jailed dissidents to counteract the threat of internal subversion. And whatever its weaknesses, the Confederate government managed to survive for four years against a massive Union invasion. In the end, the Confederacy failed because its armies, not its politics, were weaker than the Union's.

Union Naval Supremacy

The conviction that commerce ruled the world came naturally to the leaders of southern slave society. At the start of the war, Confederate strategists believed they could bring their enemies to heel by starving them of cotton. By withholding their most valuable cash crop from the market, they would cripple northern industry and force England to recognize Confederate independence.

The Yankees knew better. From the outset, northern strategists hoped to use their superior naval forces to prevent the Confederacy from selling its cotton abroad. By the closing months of 1861, the Union navy controlled vast stretches of the Atlantic and Gulf coasts. By early 1862, Union forces were in a position to enforce their blockade, except for a magnificent new weapon designed to thwart Union naval supremacy.

The South refitted an old Union ship, the *Merrimac*, with thick iron plates that rendered it all but impervious to conventional weapons. Rechristened the *Virginia*, the ironclad ship sailed into Union-controlled waters at Hampton Roads, Virginia, on March 8, 1862, and wrought havoc on helpless northern ships. But that night the Union's own ironclad, the *Monitor*, arrived from New York. For most of the next day the "battle of the ironclads" raged on, with neither vessel dominating. The standoff left the Union navy in control of the coast and better able to enforce its blockade. After the battle, the *Virginia* slipped up the James River to assist in the defense of Richmond, but in May the Confederates destroyed the ironclad rather than allowing it to be captured by Union forces.

Beyond the blockade, the greatest achievements of the Union navy came in those rare but crucial occasions when it launched joint operations with the army. This was not easy, with no Pentagon and no Joint Chiefs of Staff to coordinate the two branches of the military. Any joint army-navy ventures would depend on the commanders involved or on the direct participation of President Lincoln—the only person who could issue orders to both branches of the armed services. There were successful joint operations early in the war—at Port Royal in November 1861, the capture of New Orleans in early 1862, and the collaboration between U. S. Grant and Andrew Foote in the capture of Forts Henry and Donelson a few months later. But just as often, communication broke down and the results—in the unsuccessful effort to capture Charleston and in the Red River campaign of 1864—were disastrous. Still, by the end of the war, the Union had built one of the largest and most modern navies in the world, not to be matched in American history until World War II.

Southern Military Advantages

The Union dominated the naval war, but on land the Confederates had several advantages. More southerners had gone to military academies than had northerners, and early on they brought skill and discipline to the Confederate army that the Union could not match. The South's greatest advantage, however, was that it was defending its own territory. It did not have to invade the North, destroy the Union army, or wipe out the North's industrial capacity. Closer to their sources of supply, southern armies operated in the midst of a friendly civilian population, except for the slaves.

By contrast, the North had to fight an offensive war. It had to invade the South, destroy the Confederate armies, capture and retain a huge territory, and wipe out the

South's capacity to fight. Northern soldiers fought on unfamiliar ground surrounded by a hostile civilian population, not counting the slaves.

The Union required longer lines of supply and much larger provisions. An invading northern army of 100,000 men had to carry with it 2,500 wagons and 35,000 animals. It consumed 600 tons of supplies a day. The farther it penetrated southern territory, the more men were needed to maintain increasingly tenuous supply lines. The more territory Union troops conquered, the more they were shifted from battle duty to occupation forces. As a result, many major battles were fought by roughly even numbers of Union and Confederate troops.

In tactical terms—that is, in individual battles—the defensive posture of the Confederate army was an advantage. Forts and cities on high ground (such as Vicksburg and Fredericksburg) could defend against large numbers of invading troops. But strategically, a purely defensive posture threatened to thin out southern armies as they stretched themselves along a border that was hundreds of miles long. Confederate general Robert E. Lee combined elements of both approaches in an "offensive-defensive" strategy. He was aggressive in his approach to battle and in his willingness to invade the North, yet he always tried to maneuver his armies into a defensive position that allowed him to hold off much larger Union forces.

Besides his commitment to destroying enemy armies rather than capturing territory, Lincoln developed a second basic strategy for overcoming the South's advantage in operating from interior lines. To take advantage of the North's superior numbers, Lincoln wanted his generals to launch coordinated attacks on different southern armies at different times. This strategy had worked in New Orleans. Once Farragut's naval forces had breached Confederate defenses on the lower Mississippi River, the army was able to capture New Orleans without a fight in part because the southern troops had been pulled from the city to meet Grant's army at Shiloh. But Lincoln found that launching coordinated attacks was easier on paper than it was in practice. Until the end of the war, the commander in chief was frustrated by Union generals who did not press their armies forward in time, allowing Confederates to continue shifting their own forces to meet Union assaults that came one after another rather than all at once.

The Slave Economy in Wartime

Secessionists argued that slavery gave the South several clear military assets. Because they were agricultural workers, the slaves could be shifted easily from cash crops to foodstuffs. Unlike the urban and industrial sectors of the North, the rural slave economy of the South could retreat from staple crops into subsistence agriculture for the duration of the war. With this single stroke, the Confederacy could feed its civilians, supply its armies, and cripple the enemy by starving the industrial world's mills of desperately needed cotton. With slaves at home doing the work, a very high proportion of white men were able to serve in the southern military. Within the Confederate armies, slaves and free blacks were impressed into nonmilitary service as construction workers, teamsters, nurses, and cooks, freeing up more white soldiers to fight. In all of these ways slavery reduced the North's advantage in the number of military-age men.

The relative backwardness of the slave economy had certain military advantages. Because of slavery, the South had remained a largely rural society. Southern country boys could shoot guns and ride horses better than shopkeepers and factory workers in the Yankee armies. In the first years of the war, the southern cavalry was far superior to its northern counterpart, and many white southerners assumed that one average Confederate could easily whip two Yankees.

But the southerners assumed incorrectly. They overestimated England's dependence on American cotton and underestimated the strength of Britain's economic ties to the North. The English refused to break the blockade of the South or grant diplomatic recognition to the Confederacy. King Cotton diplomacy failed, and so did the slave economy. If slavery freed 60 percent of southern men for military service, it kept from military service the 40 percent of the population that was enslaved. With masters and their sons off to war, farm productivity collapsed, and in the end the rural South had trouble feeding itself. It also became harder to control the slaves left behind and, when Union armies approached, harder still to keep slaves from running off. Even the superiority of the southern cavalry gave way as the growing use of rifles made traditional cavalry charges deadly.

Above all, slavery diminished the South's industrial strength. Ninety percent of the nation's factories were in the North. Furthermore, the bulk of the Confederacy's industrial capacity was located in the upper South, which was overrun by Union forces early in the war. Even if its arms and supplies were severely restricted, the South did manage to produce enough rifles, gunpowder, and ammunition. Generally well armed, the Confederate soldier was not well fed or well clothed and often fought in rags and barefoot.

Slavery also crippled the South's ability to finance its war. The cotton crop was systematically embargoed. Because slaves earned no income, they could not be taxed as northern workers were, and white southerners remained true to the Jacksonian tradition of resistance to taxation. To finance its military campaign, the South began to print money in huge quantities. By 1865, a Confederate dollar had the purchasing power that one Confederate cent had had in 1861.

Tredegar Iron Works in Richmond, Virginia, 1865 This was the South's largest industrial plant. Because the South lagged so far behind the North in industrial capacity, protecting the Tredegar works was essential to the Confederate war effort.

In the North, prospering farms and growing factories generated substantial taxable income. In addition to the $600 million raised from taxes on incomes and personal property, the government eventually sold $1.5 billion worth of Union bonds and also floated war bonds. The North also supplemented its tax revenues by printing money, the famous "greenbacks," which became legally acceptable as currency everywhere in the country. To ease the flow of so many dollars, the Republicans passed the National Bank Act in 1863. This law rationalized the monetary system, making the federal government what it remains today, the only printer of money and the arbiter of the rules governing the nation's banks.

On balance, the southern slave economy did remarkably well. The Confederacy staggered through the war with ragged soldiers, starving civilians, makeshift factories, and inflated currency. But as long as it could sustain its armies in the field, the Confederacy survived. Johnny Reb and Billy Yank had the ammunition they needed to fight. The question was, did they have the will to fight on and the commanders they needed to win the war?

What Were Soldiers Fighting For?

Political, military, and economic differences are the tangible reasons that armies win or lose wars, but there are also important psychological reasons. Southern soldiers fought from a variety of motives, but above all, they fought to protect their homes and their families from Yankee invasion. Most Confederate soldiers took for granted that they were fighting to preserve slavery, and they saw the threat to slavery in personal terms, even when they themselves owned no slaves. Small farmers were no less devoted to the rights of property than large planters. In the southern economy, slavery was the only real avenue of advancement. To own a slave was a symbol of mastery, but more than that, it was the source of prosperity.

The defense of homes and slaves gave southern patriotism a concrete and individualistic flavor. The "spirit of 1776" loomed large in the letters and diaries of Confederate soldiers, who saw themselves fighting to preserve the rights and liberties that their forefathers had won from Great Britain. But the right they fought for was the right to own slaves, and the liberty they defended was freedom from government interference with slavery.

Nevertheless, class distinctions affected the levels of patriotism in the Confederate army. Slaveholders and their sons were far more likely to express patriotic sentiments than were soldiers from yeoman families. Troops from states in which slavery was relatively unimportant, such as North Carolina, were less enthusiastic about the war than were troops from states such as South Carolina in which slavery was strong.

Class divisions were less severe in the Union army. Impoverished immigrants sometimes joined the military to secure a steady income or a substantial bounty. But Catholic immigrants were less likely to fight than native-born Protestants. The most common motivation among northern soldiers was also patriotism. They, too, thought of themselves as the proud protectors of America's revolutionary heritage, but their patriotism was more abstract. Unlike the Confederates, Yankee troops were not fighting to protect their homes and families. Rather, they were fighting in defense of northern society in general, for an idealized notion of what America meant. The Union as a "beacon of liberty" throughout the world was a common theme in the letters and diaries of northern soldiers.

Most northern soldiers believed that slavery had caused the war, but only a few were motivated by antislavery principles, and many denied that they were risking their lives to free slaves. As civilian soldiers, they reflected shifts in northern public opinion against slavery. Antislavery views became more common beginning in late 1861, and soldiers' views changed with the tides of war. There were racist backlashes among Yankee troops, but there was also growing support for the abolition of slavery. By the end of the conflict, most northern soldiers believed that to restore the Union and destroy the Confederacy they would have to abolish slavery as well.

The Civil War as Social Revolution

By 1862 the North and the South had built up powerful military machines. At the same time, the North's war aims were shifting to include universal emancipation and the destruction of the southern social system. In the earliest months of the war Republicans in Congress and the Lincoln administration adopted the view that emancipation was a military necessity, but they restricted emancipation to slaves coming voluntarily into Union lines. Within a year they would shift to a policy of universal emancipation as part of an emerging policy of "hard war." Throughout the South, a civil war erupted within the Civil War. As the Union army swept through the South gathering up thousands of slaves fleeing for freedom, the South unleashed a campaign of violence and intimidation aimed at thwarting the unfolding process of emancipation. The outcome of this civil war on the ground depended on the fate of the Union and Confederate armies on the field of battle.

Union Victories in the West

In early February 1862, the Union army and navy joined in an aggressive strike deep into Confederate Tennessee. Assisted by the naval bombardment under the direction of Andrew Foote, Ulysses S. Grant's Union forces captured Fort Henry on the Tennessee River and, shortly thereafter, Fort Donelson on the Cumberland River (see Map 15–3). To the shock of Confederate officers at Fort Donelson, Grant insisted on "unconditional and immediate surrender."

The war's growing ferocity became clear eight weeks later, at the battle of Shiloh. General P. G. T. Beauregard, the hero of Fort Sumter and Manassas, caught Grant's troops off guard at a peach orchard at Shiloh Church in southern Tennessee. The Confederate's surprise attack on April 6 forced the Union

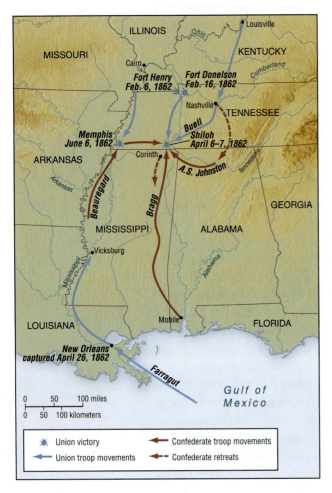

Map 15–3 The War in the West in 1862 As Union armies floundered in the East, northern troops in the West won a decisive series of battles. Here the nature of the war changed. First, General Ulysses S. Grant demanded "unconditional surrender" of the southern troops at Forts Henry and Donelson. Then a bloody battle at Shiloh foreshadowed the increasing brutality of the war. Finally, the western theater produced two of the Union's most effective generals, Grant and William Tecumseh Sherman, and its greatest naval victory, David Farragut's stunning capture of New Orleans.

lines steadily backward, although the line did not break. Beauregard telegraphed Richmond with news of his victory. But on the morning of April 7, Confederate troops were stunned by a Union counterattack that pushed Beauregard's army back over the ground it had taken the day before. When the Confederates finally retreated, the two armies had suffered an astounding 23,741 casualties, dwarfing all previous losses but foreshadowing things to come. The Civil War was quickly becoming a fight for the total destruction of the enemy.

With Confederate forces busy at Shiloh, New Orleans had few defenses beyond two forts on the Mississippi River 75 miles south of the city. But they were impressive forts. It took six days of Yankee bombardment before Union commander David Farragut attempted to break through. In the middle of the night of April 24, his fleet pushed upriver through a blaze of burning rafts and Confederate gunfire that lit up the sky. Within a few days the Confederates evacuated both forts, and New Orleans fell to Union forces.

Union victories in the West gave rise to northern optimism that war would be over by summer. Republicans seized the mood to enact a bold legislative agenda. During the first half of 1862, Congress and President Lincoln substantially reorganized the structure of national government in the North. Lincoln appointed Edwin M. Stanton as secretary of war and named Henry Wager Halleck as general in chief of the Union forces. Stanton was not much of a military strategist, and Halleck, who was said to be, was paralyzed when it came to giving orders to commanders in the field. But both were effective bureaucrats, and, with the help of Quartermaster General Montgomery Meigs and a brilliant railroad engineer named Henry Haupt, they built a powerful war-making machine that kept the huge, far-flung Union armies well supplied.

Congress was also active. For years, Democratic majorities had blocked passage of laws that Republicans considered essential. Now the Republicans had the votes and the popular support to push their agenda through Congress. They began with a critical financial reform. To sustain the integrity of the currency, the Republicans passed a Legal Tender Act protecting northern greenbacks from inflationary pressure. To maintain military manpower, they instituted the first draft in United States history. In addition, in 1862 they established a system of land-grant colleges designed to promote agricultural development and passed a Homestead Act offering land at low prices to settlers in the West. Finally, the Republicans financed the construction of the nation's first transcontinental railroad. Together these laws reflected the Republican Party's commitment to the active use of the government to preserve the Union and promote capitalist development.

The Confederate government also reformed its bureaucracy to sustain its military struggle. Southern leaders realized that it was a mistake to withhold the region's cotton from the world market. A year into the war, the Confederate economy was showing signs of the weakness that would lead it to the brink of complete financial collapse. As a remedy, the Confederate Congress passed a comprehensive tax code, but with disappointing results. In April 1862 the Confederacy established a national military draft. By centralizing taxation and conscription, however, Jefferson Davis's government created powerful resistance from advocates of states' rights. Thus, whereas victories in the West allowed northern Republicans to enact an expansive legislative agenda, the Confederate government had trouble winning popular support for its own centralizing measures, despite the success of its troops in the Peninsula campaign of 1862.

Southern Military Strength in the East

In the Peninsula campaign, the Union army sought to capture the Confederate capital, Richmond, as Lincoln expected George B. McClellan to do as commander of the Army of the Potomac. McClellan's great strength was his ability to administer and train a huge army, instilling discipline and restoring troop morale after the defeat of Bull Run. But McClellan was reluctant to fight, exaggerating the size of his opponents' forces and demanding more troops before he would take the offensive. Throughout the fall and winter of 1861 and 1862, McClellan stubbornly resisted Lincoln's suggestions to attack. Vain and arrogant, McClellan held all politicians in contempt, and none more than the president.

Under intense pressure, and with his own reputation at stake, McClellan did devise an elaborate strategy to capture Richmond. He very slowly moved his huge army of 112,000 men up the peninsula between the York and James Rivers. Instead of directly attacking Richmond, however, McClellan dug in at Yorktown, overestimating the size of his enemy. The Confederates quickly learned to manipulate McClellan's weaknesses. They moved small numbers of soldiers back and forth to make him think there were more enemy troops than there really were and planted fake cannons along their lines. Then, during the night of May 4, 1862, the outnumbered Confederates withdrew toward Richmond. When McClellan discovered their escape, he declared it a Union victory.

The Army of the Potomac inched its way toward Richmond, but it never took the offensive. Instead, it was the Confederates, initially led by General Joseph E. Johnston, who forced Union troops into battle. The southerners attacked the divided Union forces at Seven Pines on May 31, and both sides took heavy losses. Far more serious were the brutal battles of the Seven Days beginning in late June. During this campaign, Johnston was wounded and replaced by Robert E. Lee, who repulsed but did not destroy McClellan's larger army. Still, Lee had saved Richmond and sent the Union army back to new fortifications at Harrison's Landing, where McClellan sat until he was finally ordered to bring his big army back to Washington, DC. There McClellan did for his troops what he did best: he revived their sagging morale and whipped them back into shape. But he still would not do the fighting. Defying the desperate orders of Lincoln and Halleck, McClellan let Union general John Pope take the offensive alone. Hampered by generals loyal to McClellan, Pope led his troops to a disastrous defeat at the second battle of Bull Run (August 29–30), while McClellan's huge army stood by.

By the fall of 1862, the Union and Confederate forces had reached a military stalemate. The North had scored tremendous victories in the West. In the East, however, Robert E. Lee turned out to be one of the most skillful and daring commanders of the war. Stonewall Jackson, Lee's "right arm," had also proven himself brilliantly aggressive.

Having turned back the Union invasion on the peninsula and defeated the Union army in a second battle at Bull Run, Lee decided to invade the North. He hoped the Confederacy could win the war in the East before losing it in the West. Lee marched his confident troops across the Potomac into Maryland, where he was met by McClellan's army at Sharpsburg, beside Antietam Creek, on September 17 (see Map 15–4).

McClellan nearly lost Antietam. He had Lee's plans in advance, but he took his time and squandered the advantage. Once engaged, McClellan launched his troops in consecutive assaults rather than a single simultaneous maneuver, allowing the Confederates to shift their men around the battlefield as fighting moved to different locations. He held back his reinforcements, missing a chance to break the center of the vulnerable Confederate line. The delay gave Confederate reinforcements time to arrive and turn back an attack on Lee's right. But the Union troops fought with astonishing determination, and Lee's men suffered staggering casualties. His invasion blocked, Lee quickly retreated back into Virginia. It might have been even worse for the South, but despite intense pressure from Washington, McClellan refused to send his fresh reserves after the disoriented southerners as they fell back across the Potomac. When McClellan boasted that his army had forced the Confederates off "our soil," Lincoln fumed, "It's all 'our soil.'" The point was not to send Lee's army back to Virginia but to defeat it. The president had run out of patience and after the fall elections fired McClellan. A total of 4,800 soldiers died and 18,000 more were wounded at Antietam, the single bloodiest day of the war. Nevertheless, Antietam was a Union victory, and Lincoln used it to release a preliminary Emancipation Proclamation, implementing the policy of universal emancipation called for by Congress earlier in the year.

Universal Emancipation

In the first half of 1862, Republicans passed a raft of antislavery laws. These laws were designed to do two different but related things: First, they would undermine the Confederacy by undermining slavery. Second, they would put intense pressure on the loyal slave states to abolish slavery on their own. If the two policies—military emancipation and gradual state abolition—worked, slavery would not survive the war.

Republicans were confident that under the laws of war they could emancipate slaves of all rebels in the seceded states. But what about four slave states that had remained loyal to the Union? Union commanders in the border states adopted a hands-off policy, declaring that their soldiers should be neither "slave catchers nor slave thieves." But the policy was easier to state in principle than to implement in practice. In search of their freedom, slaves in the border states were drawn to Union camps where northern soldiers often welcomed them, sometimes in defiance of orders. Different commanders issued different orders. In September Lincoln ordered General John C. Frémont to implement the First Confiscation Act in Missouri, a loyal slave state. By the end of 1861 emancipation policy in the border states was hopelessly confused. To clarify the situation, in March 1862 Congress prohibited the use of Union troops to return fugitives to the South. The effect of the law, and probably the point, was to put tremendous pressure on the border states to abolish slavery on their own.

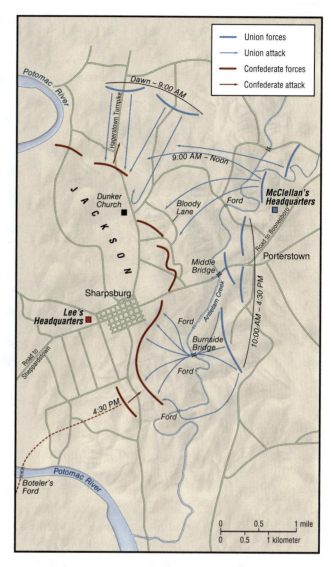

Map 15-4 The Battle of Antietam In September 1862, southern general Robert E. Lee led the Confederacy's first invasion of the North. He was stopped at Sharpsburg, Maryland, by Union troops under the command of George B. McClellan. Antietam was the bloodiest single day of the war, but it was an important turning point for the North. It gave Lincoln the victory he was waiting for to announce the preliminary Emancipation Proclamation.

The Battle of Antietam The victory of the Union army at Antietam Creek, Maryland, enabled Lincoln to take his first public steps toward emancipation.

In April 1862 Congress moved further by abolishing slavery in Washington, DC. For the first time, the federal government actually abolished slavery in a place where it already existed. It had emancipated slaves as individuals, but never abolished slavery. In June Congress prohibited slavery in the western territories. Meanwhile, the Lincoln administration began aggressively prosecuting slave traders at home, even as Secretary of State William Seward negotiated a treaty with Great Britain that led, within a few short years, to the nearly complete suppression of the centuries-old Atlantic slave trade. By the summer of 1862 Republicans had taken advantage of the war to construct a "cordon of freedom" around the slave South.

In July Congress passed a Second Confiscation Act, immediately emancipating all slaves in Union-occupied areas of the Confederacy and authorizing the president to issue a proclamation emancipating the slaves in all unoccupied areas in rebellion. Congress also passed a militia act removing the word "white" from the requirements for enlistment in the Union army. Thereafter, all "able-bodied male citizens" were eligible for military service.

A few days after he signed the Second Confiscation Act into law, Lincoln arrived at a cabinet meeting on July 22, 1862, with an Emancipation Proclamation. But Secretary of State William Seward warned the president that recent military losses in Virginia would make such a proclamation seem like an act of desperation to the rest of the world. Lincoln agreed. He would wait for a battlefield victory to make his proclamation public. Antietam was that victory. On September 22, five days after Lee was turned back, Lincoln issued a preliminary proclamation threatening to free the slaves in areas still in rebellion 100 days later. One month later he proposed a plan of gradual emancipation in all areas under Union control. Nobody expected any of the seceded states to return to the Union, and on January 1, 1863, Lincoln issued his Emancipation Proclamation.

Reactions were swift and predictable. Jefferson Davis, the president of the Confederate States of America, denounced Lincoln's proclamation as the most despicable act "in the history of guilty man." Abolitionists and free blacks rejoiced and celebrated Proclamation Day at gatherings across the North. Other northerners, particularly Democrats, were enraged by the idea that the war was being fought to free the slaves, and some northern soldiers were embittered. "I came out to fight for the restoration of the Union . . . ," one northern soldier wrote, "not to free the niggers." But most Union troops already knew that for the war to end, the South had to be destroyed, and with it the institution of slavery.

The Proclamation and African Americans On January 1, 1863, African Americans celebrated their freedom all across the country, even in those parts of the South that were technically unaffected by the proclamation. By assuming their freedom in this way, the former slaves gave a far broader meaning to the proclamation than it technically allowed.

By the time Lincoln issued the Emancipation Proclamation on January 1, 1863, the Union had been freeing slaves for more than a year. But the proclamation changed federal policy in two crucial ways. First, it lifted the ban on "enticement" of slaves that had been in place ever since the War Department had approved General Butler's contraband policy on May 30, 1861. With the Proclamation, Union soldiers were now explicitly authorized to go onto southern farms and plantations to entice slaves away from their owners. Second, Union recruiters were especially encouraged to entice black men to leave their owners and secure their freedom by enlisting in the Union army. Hundreds of Union recruitment agents followed the northern armies as they penetrated deeper into the plantation districts of the Confederate states. The proclamation also increased the pace of emancipation in the South. Where contraband slaves had previously come into Union lines by the dozens or maybe hundreds, northern armies were now ferrying thousands of fugitives to Union-occupied areas. It made no difference whether a master had been kind or cruel; the slaves left anyway. "We were all laboring under a delusion," one South Carolina planter confessed. "I believed that these people were content, happy, and attached to their masters."

> [T]he conduct of the Negro in the late crisis of our affairs has convinced me that we were all laboring under a delusion. . . . Born and raised amid the institution, like a greate many others, I believed it was necessary to our welfare, if not to our very existence. I believed that these people were content, happy, and attached to their masters. But events and reflection have caused me to change these opinions. . . . If they were content, happy, and attached to their masters why did they desert him in the moment of his need and flock to the enemy whom they did not know; and thus left their, perhaps, really good masters whom they had known from infancy?
>
> LOUIS MANIGAULT,
> South Carolina planter, June 10, 1865

AMERICA AND THE WORLD

>> The Diplomacy of Emancipation

"The Emancipation Proclamation," Henry Adams wrote from London, "has done more for us here than all our former victories and all our diplomacy. It is creating an almost convulsive reaction in our favor." Adams was part of the American legation that had been struggling since the war began to prevent England and other European nations from formally recognizing the Confederate States of America. It was unlikely that England would do so, and unlikely that France would do it if England did not. But there were powerful elements in Britain who openly hoped for Union defeat and called for diplomatic recognition of the Confederacy. With every northern military reversal, the South's supporters grew more vocal. The Emancipation Proclamation tilted the diplomatic balance irreversibly in favor of the North. Huge pro-Union rallies across England declared their support for Union and freedom. At Exeter Hall in London, one of the largest such rallies "has had a powerful effect," Richard Cobden declared. "It has closed the mouths of those who have been advocating the side of the South. Recognition of the South, by England, whilst it bases itself on slavery, is an impossibility."

There was a similar reaction across Europe. As soon as Lincoln proclaimed the universal emancipation of rebel slaves, nearly all diplomatic support for the Confederacy was silenced. After January 1, 1863, only the complete military victory of the South over the North could have won substantial diplomatic recognition for the Confederacy. Whatever the Emancipation Proclamation meant for slavery in the South, it signaled the diplomatic triumph of the North.

Sketch of Queen from *Punch*

Emancipation in Practice

As the number of escaping slaves grew, Union commanders began constructing massive contraband camps across the South. Yet the Union was unprepared for the huge numbers pouring into the makeshift camps. Diseases, especially smallpox, raged through the camps. Food and shelter were in short supply. For some slaves the filth and disorder of the camps were so terrible that they went back to their farms and plantations. Over time, however, the army and northern volunteers learned to organize the camps more efficiently. Just across the Potomac River from Washington, DC, on the Arlington estate that had been owned by Robert E. Lee's family, the government built a model contraband camp known as "Freedman's Village." It had a school, a hospital, and a cemetery that was the nucleus for what would later become Arlington National Cemetery.

But most contraband camps were temporary, set up quickly as Union troops moved through an area and just as quickly taken down. The camps were transfer points—the first place slaves went before the army shipped them off to permanent camps or to cities outside the war zones. The camps were a major development in the history of

AMERICAN LANDSCAPE
....
>> Freedman's Village, Arlington, Virginia

When Mary Lee's father died in 1857, her husband, Robert E. Lee, became executor of the family's plantation at Arlington, Virginia, across the Potomac River from Washington, DC. The will stipulated that the slaves at Arlington were to be freed, but because the estate was burdened with debts, Lee had the will revoked and took charge of the plantation himself. He began selling off slaves, and within a few years he had broken up all but one of the slave families on the plantation. Expecting to be freed, the slaves were instead worked harder than ever. Lee, they complained, was a "hard taskmaster" and "the worst man I ever saw." They began running away.

When the Civil War broke out, the areas surrounding Washington, DC—including Arlington—came under the control of the Union army almost immediately. When Congress abolished slavery in the nation's capital on April 12, 1862, large numbers of contraband slaves began escaping into the city from nearby Virginia and Maryland. After Lincoln issued his Emancipation Proclamation on January 1, 1863, the contraband camps in Washington were soon overcrowded and overwhelmed. In May, Union officials decided to move the contrabands to a new location, Freedman's Village, to be constructed on the Lee estate at Arlington. Freedman's Village would serve two distinct purposes. First, it would remove the freed people from the crowded, unhealthy camps in the city, where diseases spread rapidly. Second, Freedman's Village was also designed as a model for the dozens of contraband camps springing up across the South as more and more slaves came into Union lines and were freed.

By 1864 Freedman's Village had 50 homes and as many as 2,000 residents. There was a hospital, a laundry, a kitchen, a home for elderly slaves, and a schoolhouse. The buildings were neatly arranged around the pond, and the Village became a destination for dignitaries and journalists. But there were complaints from the freed people about the rigid rules they were expected to follow. To pay for the camp, the residents were expected to work in adjoining fields. They earned $10 per month but had to pay back half for the camp's upkeep. That was hardly enough, they complained, to set them on the road to economic independence. Yet despite attempts by

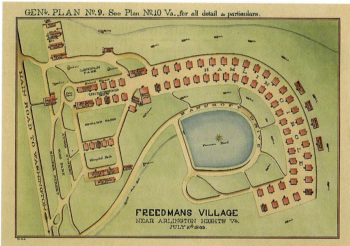

the government to close Freedman's Village down, the freed people resisted, and the camp remained open until the end of the century.

By then, however, Arlington had been transformed yet again. On June 15, 1864, the quartermaster general of the Union armies, Montgomery Meigs, wrote to the secretary of war, Edwin M. Stanton, suggesting that "the land surrounding the Arlington Mansion, now understood to be the property of the United States, be appropriated as a National Military Cemetery." Stanton approved the proposal, and within weeks the bodies of Union soldiers were being laid to rest at Arlington. Meigs saw to it that the graves were laid out "encircling" the mansion house, and, in the garden once cultivated by Lee's mother-in-law, Meigs placed a mass grave of unknown soldiers who had died at Manassas. By June 1864 there were 2,600 Union soldiers buried at Arlington National Cemetery.

No one missed the symbolism. By 1863 Robert E. Lee was the Confederacy's most daunting military commander. To northerners, he was a symbol of treason as well. What could be more appropriate than to turn his family's plantation first into a model village for former slaves and then into a national grave for fallen Union soldiers? The cemetery would survive, but Freedman's Village would disappear, and with it the hope for the future it once represented.

emancipation. For the first time, the slaves—particularly women, children, and the elderly—had somewhere to go once they escaped from their masters.

The filth and danger of the contraband camps reinforced the Republican Party's commitment to establishing a system of free labor on the farms and plantations of the Union-occupied South. The policy had begun to take shape in the earliest weeks of the war, when General Butler proposed putting "contraband" slaves to work for the Union rather than return them to labor for the Confederacy. In early 1862 the Union occupation of the Sea Islands off the coast of South Carolina and Georgia prompted the first important wartime "experiment" in free labor. By the end of that year "contract" labor systems were being established on the plantations of Union-occupied Louisiana and the lower Mississippi Valley. By the time universal emancipation was implemented in 1863, Union generals and Republican policymakers looked at the restoration of the plantations on the basis of free labor as the only practical solution to the humanitarian crisis posed by the military emancipation of hundreds of thousands of slaves.

For young black men, however, there was a new alternative to plantation labor: enlistment in the Union army. Although they had fought in the American Revolution and the War of 1812, blacks had never been allowed in the regular army. The Militia Act of July 17, 1862, finally allowed black troops. Shortly after Lincoln signed the law, his administration began selectively authorizing the creation of black units. But the July statute still restricted enlistment to "citizens." In November the attorney general ruled that, contrary to what the Supreme Court had ruled in the 1857 Dred

Company E, 4th United States Colored Infantry, at Fort Lincoln, Washington, DC, 1865 African Americans serving in the Union army symbolized the revolutionary turn the Civil War took with emancipation as the policy of the North. Despite overwhelming loss of life by the African American troops, their bravery impressed many northerners and helped change white attitudes about the goals of the Civil War.

Scott decision, free or emancipated blacks were indeed citizens of the United States. The ruling removed the last legal obstacle to full-scale black enlistment. Lincoln, having earlier expressed misgivings about black troops, authorized full-scale enlistment in the Emancipation Proclamation. He was soon a zealous convert to the importance of black troops. "The bare sight of 50,000 armed and drilled black soldiers upon the banks of the Mississippi," he said in March 1863, "would end the rebellion at once." Before the war was over, 186,000 blacks had joined, 134,111 of them recruited in the South.

For African Americans, especially for former slaves, the experience of fighting a war for emancipation was exhilarating. In a society with increasingly sharp distinctions between men and women, slaves who became soldiers often felt as though they were becoming men. "Now we sogers are men," one black sergeant explained, "men the first time in our lives."

Black Union troops were an astonishing spectacle for those still enslaved, but to white southerners, this was the "world turned upside down." As African American troops marched through the streets of southern cities, whites shrieked in horror and could barely control their rage and indignation. But southern whites were not alone in their opposition to the revolutionary turn the Civil War had taken.

Although they made up nearly 10 percent of the Union army, black soldiers were never treated as the equals of white soldiers. On the assumption that black troops would be used primarily in noncombat roles, they were initially paid at lower rates than white soldiers. Even after their pay was equalized, few African Americans were commissioned as officers. They were often held back from combat for fear that Confederates would kill them if captured. But blacks performed respectably in combat and changed the minds of many northern whites. Black soldiers were among the most aggressive in spreading emancipation still further across the Confederacy. Moreover, their numbers tipped the balance of northern and southern forces decisively in favor of the Union army, thereby contributing critically to the defeat of the Confederacy.

> If we hadn't become sojers, all might have gone back as it was before; our freedom might have slipped through de two houses of Congress and President Linkums' four years might have passed by and notin' been done for us. But now tings can neber go back, because we have showed our energy and our courage and our naturally manhood.
>
> THOMAS LONG,
> former slave, 1st South Carolina Volunteers

The War at Home

African American troops could not end the rebellion "at once," as Lincoln hoped. The war persisted for two more years, and as body counts rose and hardships mounted, civilians in the North and the South began to register their discontent.

The Care of Casualties

At Shiloh, 24,000 men had fallen in two days of fighting. Almost as many fell during a single day of fighting at Antietam. The following year 50,000 men would die or suffer wounds at Gettysburg. At the battles of Chickamauga and Franklin, Tennessee, Confederate troops would suffer appalling losses. And in Grant's struggle against Lee in the spring of 1864, both sides would lose 100,000 men in seven weeks. Casualties, partly due to inept leadership and inadequately prepared troops, were mostly the result of military technology outpacing battlefield tactics. Generals ordered traditional charges on enemy

TECHNOLOGY AND IDEAS

>> The Repeating Rifle

The standard infantry weapon during the Civil War on both sides was the rifled musket. Only a little more sophisticated in its design (principally the firing mechanism) than the weapons of the Mexican-American War, the Springfields and Enfields had a range of 300 yards but were accurate for only a small part of that distance. They were loaded through the muzzle of the gun, and in skilled hands they could be discharged about 3 times a minute. That said, they still inflicted over 80 percent of the battlefield wounds.

Continental inventors and gunsmiths had already made progress on breach-loading rifles—rifles that were loaded from the back of the barrel, or breach of the weapon—rather than through the muzzle of the barrel. The German needlegun and the French Cassepot were single-shot breach loaders that could be reloaded and discharged over 10 times a minute. Process in machine tool design for manufacturing firearms, metallurgy for making bullets, and large-scale factory production enabled American inventors to invent repeating breach-loading weapons in the years immediately prior to the Civil War, rifles that could be fired accurately over 25 times a minute.

The two leading repeating rifles that found their way into the Civil War were the Henry and the Spencer. Both were invented in the late 1850s, the former by Benjamin Tyler Henry, a New Haven, Connecticut, gunsmith employed by Oliver Winchester's firearms business, and the latter by Christopher Spencer, an employee of Samuel Colt's arms company. Both weapons featured a breach-loading, lever-action operation. Spent rounds' casings were ejected, and additional rounds, stored in the stock, were loaded into the breach by operating a lever behind the trigger guard. The Henry, an infantry rifle, fired a .44-caliber bullet. The Spencer, most often adopted by cavalry units, fired a .52-caliber bullet. While only a few hundred of the two weapons were produced early in the war, by war's end thousands were in federal army and navy hands. Units armed with these repeaters scored spectacular successes over Confederate troops in the later years of the war.

The key invention that allowed rapid fire was the introduction of the rimfire bullet in the 1850s. First designed for repeating handguns, the rimfire was perfect for the Henry and the Spencer rifles. Instead of a paper cartridge atop which sat the lead projectile, the rimfire cartridge contained the primer, the propellant, and the bullet in a copper or brass jacket. The rifle's firing pin struck the metal rim (a thin circular plate) at the back of the cartridge and ignited the primer, which fired the gunpowder and propelled the bullet out of the barrel. The rimfire was far more expensive to produce than paper cartridges, and it required reserves of copper unavailable to the Confederacy.

It was the shortage of ammunition rather than the complexity or unreliability of the Henry or the Spencer that limited the adoption of repeating rifles during the conflict. Union procurement officers were reluctant to order production of the repeaters because of the cost of bullets, fearing that troops untrained in the use of repeating rifles would quickly exhaust ammunition supplies. While Confederate soldiers greatly admired the repeating rifles, when found on the battlefield the weapons were useless to the Confederates without the rimfire ammunition.

Questions

1. The repeating rifle originated in the North. How does the story of its development and spread illuminate larger differences between North and South?

2. Does an increase in the rapidity of fire necessarily lead to victory on the battlefield? Why or why not?

lines even though newly developed rifles and repeating carbines made such assaults almost suicidal.

If new military technology multiplied the casualties, primitive medical practices did even more damage. Of the approximately 750,000 soldiers who died, two out of three were felled by disease. Thousands of soldiers were killed by contaminated water, spoiled food, inadequate clothing and shelter, mosquitoes, and vermin. Crowded military camps bred dysentery, diarrhea, malaria, and typhoid fever. Nobody knew what "germs" were or that sterilization made any difference. No one knew what caused typhoid fever or malaria. There were no antibiotics, and liquor was often the only anesthesia. The only cure for gangrene was amputation, so field hospitals were littered with piles of sawed-off arms and legs.

In one area, nursing, the Civil War advanced the practice of medicine. The Civil War overturned long-standing prejudices against the presence of women in military hospitals. Hundreds of southern women volunteered their services to Confederate forces. In the North the thousands of women who volunteered their services to the Union army had to overcome barriers against them. In mid-1861, however, northern reformers persuaded Lincoln to recognize the services of the United States Sanitary Commission. A private

> I went unrestrained, into all the largest hospitals. In the first of these an amputation was being performed, and at the door lay a little heap of human fingers, feet, legs, and arms. . . . Soldiers sat by the severely wounded, laving their sores with water. In many wounds the balls still remained and the discolored flesh was swollen unnaturally. There were some who had been shot in the bowels, and now and then they were frightfully convulsed, breaking into shrieks and shouts. Some of them iterated a single word, as, "doctor," or "help," or "God," or "oh!" commencing with a loud spasmodic cry, and continuing the same word until it died away in cadence. The act of calling seemed to lull the pain.

GEORGE TOWNSEND,
journalist, visiting a field hospital during the Peninsula campaign

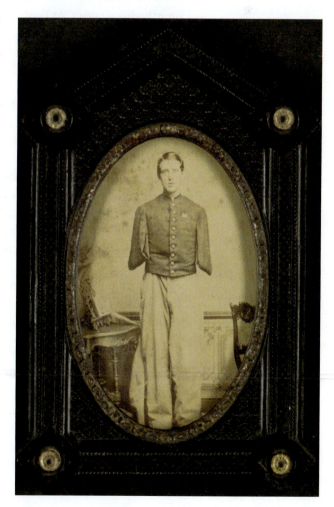

Civil War Amputee Tens of thousands of Civil War soldiers like Private Alfred Stratton lost at least one limb to the conflict.

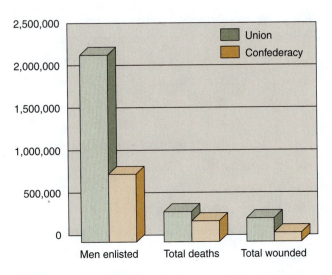

Figure 15-2 Casualties of War

organization led by men but staffed by thousands of women, the "Sanitary" helped reform the Army Medical Bureau. It established the first ambulance corps for the swift removal of wounded soldiers from the battlefield, pioneered the use of ships and railroad cars as mobile hospital units, and made nursing a respectable profession for women after the war ended.

But these heroic efforts could not undo the fact that the Civil War had caused unprecedented bloodshed (see Figure 15–2). As the war dragged on, and as the aims of the war shifted, Americans voiced their opposition to the policies of the Lincoln and Davis administrations.

Northern Reverses and Antiwar Sentiment

Lincoln struggled for years to find a commander who could stand up to great southern generals such as Robert E. Lee and Stonewall Jackson. For failing to crush Lee's army after Antietam, Lincoln fired McClellan and gave command of the Army of the Potomac to a reluctant Ambrose Burnside. But Burnside could not match Lee's brilliant, unorthodox strategy. At Fredericksburg, Virginia, on December 13, 1862, Lee's army defeated Burnside's men in a calamitous slaughter. Lincoln quickly replaced Burnside with "Fighting Joe" Hooker, a braggart who was scarcely better at fighting than Burnside had been. At Chancellorsville, Virginia, in May 1863, Lee overwhelmed Hooker's forces in one of the bloodiest Union defeats of the war.

Northern military reverses fueled a wave of opposition to emancipation. Northern Democrats had always favored compromise with the South on slavery and continued to argue that the restoration of the Union was the only legitimate aim of the war. In the elections of 1862, Peace Democrats (known as Copperheads) took control of the legislatures in Illinois and Indiana and threatened to withhold troops. In southern Illinois, troops deserted in droves in early 1863, after the Emancipation Proclamation was issued. Democrats were scandalized when the War Department authorized the formation of African American regiments in early 1863.

The beginning of military conscription in March 1863 further outraged northern Democrats. Because northern draftees could escape conscription by paying a $300 commutation fee, many working-class men, especially Irish immigrants, complained that the rich could buy their way out of combat. But although the Irish were underrepresented in the Union army and there were ways for working men to pay the commutation fee, the taint of inequity was so strong that Congress abolished commutation.

Drafting white men to fight for black emancipation provoked anger among some northerners. Dissent became sufficiently widespread that Lincoln claimed the constitutional authority to suspend habeas corpus. The Peace Democrats' leading spokesman, Clement L. Vallandigham, attacked the president's "despotic" measures. If forced to choose between loss of freedom for whites and continued enslavement of African Americans, he said, "I shall not hesitate one moment to choose the latter alternative."

In 1862, whites protesting the drift toward emancipation rioted in several northern cities. In New York City, Irish Democrats rioted in the streets at the opening of a draft office. Working-class immigrants had suffered most from wartime inflation and were most susceptible to competition from African Americans. Their frustration exploded into the New York City draft riots, which began on July 13, 1863, and lasted several days.

Rioters assaulted well-dressed men on the streets and attacked the homes of leading Republicans, but they mostly targeted blacks. White mobs lynched a dozen African Americans and set fire to the Colored Orphan Asylum. More than 100 people died, most of them rioters. Violent northern opposition to the war later subsided, partly because the draft riots had discredited the Copperheads but also because of the improving military fortunes of the Union army.

Gettysburg and the Justification of the War

As criticism of the Lincoln administration swelled in the summer of 1863, Lee sensed an opportunity to launch a second invasion of the North. On July 1, the opposing armies converged on the small town of Gettysburg, Pennsylvania (see Map 15–5). For three days they fought the most decisive battle of the war. On the first day, it looked as though the South was on its way to another victory. Confederate troops pushed the Union enemy backward through the town streets and onto the hills to the south. Now in command of the heights, Union general George Gordon Meade secured a two-mile line of high ground during the night. On the second day, Lee ordered two flanking attacks and a third assault on the Union center, but the Union line held. On the third day, against the advice of his trusted general James Longstreet, Lee ordered a direct attack by George Pickett's troops on the fortified Union center. Pickett's charge was a devastating loss for the southern troops. On July 4, the Confederates began the retreat back toward the Potomac River, where rising waters trapped them for more than a week. Lincoln furiously urged Meade to go after Lee's trapped army and finish the job. But by the time Meade launched an attack, the river had subsided, and Lee's army escaped. Again, Lincoln was mortified by the insufficiently aggressive instincts of his generals.

As northerners celebrated Lee's defeat, news came of another Union victory in the West. For months the Mississippi River town of Vicksburg, Mississippi, had proved invincible, frustrating General Grant. After a series of failed maneuvers, Grant laid siege to the town (see Map 15–6). He cut Vicksburg off from all supplies and waited until its soldiers and civilians were starved into submission. For six weeks the people of Vicksburg lived in caves, bombarded by sharpshooters during the day and by

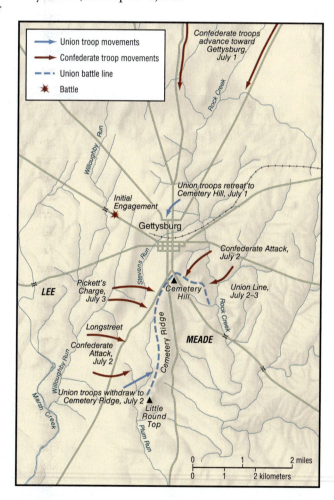

Map 15–5 The Battle of Gettysburg, July 1–3, 1863 In three extraordinary days in Gettysburg, Pennsylvania, the Union army turned back Lee's second invasion of the North. The Union victory, combined with equally important successes in the West at the same time, turned the tide of the war in the North's favor. At the dedication of a military cemetery at Gettysburg a few months later, Lincoln articulated his most profound justification for waging war against the South.

Gettysburg—The Aftermath The bodies of dead soldiers litter the battlefield at Gettysburg. Shortly thereafter, workers rushed to bury the corpses in time for the dedication of the battlefield as a military cemetery. Lincoln's powerful address promised "a new birth of freedom—and that government of the people, by the people, for the people, shall not perish from the earth."

Map 15-6 The Siege of Vicksburg, 1862–1863 Following a series of unsuccessful efforts to capture Vicksburg, Mississippi, from the Confederates, Grant settled down for a long siege. After the southern troops surrendered, in July 1863, the Union quickly gained complete control of the Mississippi River and, in so doing, split the Confederacy in two. With the fall of Vicksburg, the Confederacy all but lost the war in the West.

cannon fire at night. They subsisted on mules and rats. On June 28, Confederate soldiers inside the city threatened mutiny, and less than a week later, Vicksburg surrendered. His experience with McClellan had led Lincoln to distrust sieges, and at first he was dubious about Grant's plans. But when Vicksburg surrendered, so did a large Confederate army holed up inside it. Lincoln joyfully pronounced Grant's Vicksburg campaign "brilliant." The Confederate commander at Port Hudson surrendered shortly thereafter. The Mississippi River was now opened to Union navigation, and the Confederacy was split in two. Vicksburg and Gettysburg were the greatest Union victories of the war.

Despite his disappointment with Meade, Lincoln came to realize the significance of the Union victory at Gettysburg. In November, he went to Gettysburg to speak at the dedication of a military cemetery at the battlefield. There he articulated a profound justification of the Union war effort. The Civil War, Lincoln said, had become a great test of democracy and of the principle of human equality. The soldiers who died at Gettysburg had dedicated their lives to those principles, the president noted. It remained only "for us the living" to similarly "resolve that these dead shall not have died in vain—that this nation, under God, shall have a new birth of freedom—and that government of the people, by the people, for the people, shall not perish from the earth."

With the Gettysburg Address, Lincoln took brilliant advantage of the North's improving military fortunes to elevate the meaning of the war beyond the simple restoration of the Union. After 1863, antiwar sentiment in the North diminished substantially. In the South it exploded.

Discontent in the Confederacy

The South was divided over secession from the very beginning. Four slave states—Maryland, Delaware, Kentucky, and Missouri—never even joined the Confederacy. The entire western portion of Virginia "seceded" from the state and rejoined the Union as the new state of West Virginia. Brutal guerilla warfare broke out in the mountains of eastern Tennessee and western North Carolina, where hostility to the Confederacy was widespread.

Most whites in the seceded states remained loyal to the Confederacy, but many attacked the government of Jefferson Davis. Although formed in the name of states' rights, the Confederate government became a huge centralized bureaucracy that taxed white southerners far beyond anything in their prewar experience. The Confederate government burned private stores of cotton and impressed slaves into service, enraging the slaveholders for whom the war was being fought in the first place.

The government in Richmond was forever wrestling with the states for control of military enlistments. The South relied much more heavily on draftees than did the North. A "planter's exemption" designed to thwart emancipation allowed the sons of wealthy slaveholders to purchase replacements, an action that generated tremendous hostility. Ordinary southerners complained of a "rich man's war but a poor man's fight." The most important resistance came from Georgia, where powerful politicians launched a vitriolic assault on the Confederate government. Faced with swelling internal opposition, Davis followed Lincoln's course and suspended habeas corpus in many parts of the Confederacy.

Southerners, military and civilian, suffered proportionally far more casualties than did northerners. Deprivation and physical destruction were common experiences in the Civil War South. Confederate money was becoming worthless, and the army swallowed up much of the food supply. Bread riots erupted in a dozen southern cities in 1863. By 1864, life for millions of southerners had become miserable and desperate. Women wrote desperate letters to their husbands and sons in the Confederate armies, begging them to come home and rescue their families from the threat of starvation.

The War Comes to a Bloody End

In the face of bread riots, war weariness, and disloyal slaves, a crippled Confederacy nonetheless sought desperately to maintain itself. At the same time, northern society seemed stronger than ever. Amidst the most ferocious fighting ever witnessed on North American soil, the commander in chief ran for reelection to the presidency and won.

Grant Takes Command

During the summer of 1863, Union forces under William S. Rosecrans pushed Braxton Bragg's Confederate troops out of central Tennessee. Bragg retreated east to Chattanooga, a critical rail terminal. Prodded by Washington, Rosecrans began moving his army toward Chattanooga in mid-August, later joined by Ambrose Burnside. Outnumbered and almost surrounded, Bragg abandoned Chattanooga and retreated into Georgia. Jefferson Davis sent reinforcements and ordered Bragg to return to the offensive. At the same time, Union general George Thomas reinforced Rosecrans and Burnside. On September 19 the two armies discovered each other at Chickamauga

Creek in eastern Tennessee. In two days, the bloodiest battle of the western theater ended in the Union troops' retreat and almost total rout.

Weeks after their defeat at Chickamauga, Union armies were still stuck in Chattanooga unable to feed themselves. A frustrated President Lincoln swiftly reorganized the command of the western theater, putting General Grant in charge of all Union armies west of the Appalachians. In November 1863, Grant and William Tecumseh Sherman rescued the Union troops trapped at Chattanooga. Together with General Thomas, they dislodged the Confederates from the city. Two days later, Union forces routed the enemy at Lookout Mountain, driving Confederate troops into Georgia. The war in the West was nearly over.

Lincoln at last had a general who would fight. In March 1864 he put Grant in charge of the entire Union army. Grant decided on a simple two-pronged strategy: he would take control of the Army of the Potomac and confront Lee's Army of Northern Virginia while Sherman would hunt down and destroy Joseph E. Johnston's troops in Georgia. In these two engagements, the Civil War reached its destructive heights. "From the summer of 1862, the war became a war of wholesale devastation," John Esten Cooke explained. "From the spring of 1864, it seems to have become nearly a war of extermination."

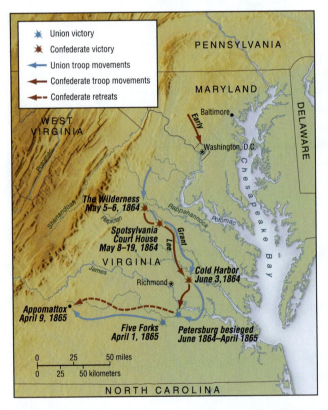

Map 15-7 The Virginia Theater, 1864-1865 In May and June 1864, Grant and Lee confronted each other directly in a bloody series of battles in Virginia. The indecisive outcome was a Vicksburg-like siege by Grant, this time of the city of Petersburg, where Lee dug in with his fortified troops. The shockingly high number of casualties, with no clear winner, nearly cost Lincoln his reelection to the presidency in November.

The Theory and Practice of Hard War

McClellan, Burnside, and Hooker had all withered under Lee's assaults. When Grant got to Virginia in early 1864 to do battle with Lee, he did not wither (see Map 15-7). The two generals hurled their men at one another, often directly into the lines of fire. The result was a series of unspeakably bloody encounters beginning in the spring of 1864. The first battle took place on May 5 and 6, in a largely uninhabited stretch of thick woods. Appropriately called the Wilderness, the terrain made it difficult to see for any distance and impossible for armies to maintain strict lines. Soldiers and commanders alike were confused by the woods and smoke, by the roar of gunfire, and by the wailing of thousands of wounded. Entire brigades got lost. In two days of fighting, the Union army suffered 17,000 casualties, the Confederates 11,000; and there was more to come.

Grant's goal was to break through Lee's defensive line and capture Richmond. With smoke still billowing in the Wilderness, Grant marched his army south hoping to outflank Lee at Spotsylvania Court House. As usual, Lee kept one step ahead, and from May 10 to May 12 the bloodbath was repeated. There were another 18,000 Union and 12,000 Confederate casualties. Still Grant pushed his men farther south. Determined to break through Lee's defenses, Grant waged a series of deadly skirmishes culminating in a frightful assault at Cold Harbor on June 3. Bodies piled on top of bodies until finally Grant had to call a halt. Seven thousand Union men were killed or wounded at Cold Harbor, most of them in the first 60 minutes of fighting. The armies moved south yet again, but when Lee secured the rail link at Petersburg (critical to the defense of Richmond), Grant settled in for a prolonged siege. The brutal Virginia campaign had not ended the war. More than 50,000 Union men were killed or wounded, but Grant had not destroyed Lee's army or taken Richmond. The war was at a standoff, and Lincoln was up for reelection in November.

Three other military achievements saved the election of 1864 for the Republicans. The first, in late August, was the Union capture of Mobile Bay, the last major southern port still controlled by the Confederates. The entire southern coastline was now virtually sealed. Next came General Philip Sheridan's Union cavalry raid through the Shenandoah Valley in September and his defeat of the Confederate cavalry's raid into Maryland. Ordered by Grant to wipe out the source of supplies for Lee's army, Sheridan's men swept through the Shenandoah Valley, burning barns and killing animals. Sheridan's campaign demonstrated that the Union army now had a cavalry that could match and defeat the Confederacy's. Meanwhile, General Sherman took Atlanta, providing Lincoln and the Republicans with a third piece of good news. On September 1, as the election campaign was heating up in the North, Sherman telegraphed Lincoln: "Atlanta is ours, and fairly won."

After Atlanta, Sherman came to believe that the South's civilians had to be subdued along with its armies. He would not attack civilians directly, but he would systematically destroy their homes and farms—even whole towns and cities. The white South, Sherman concluded, would remain rebellious until forced to taste the bitter reality of civil war. "War is cruelty," he told the citizens of Atlanta who petitioned him for mercy, "and the only way the people of Atlanta can hope once more to live in peace and quiet at home, is to stop the war." But Sherman was merely the theorist of this type of warfare. Lincoln was its administrator. It was Lincoln who demanded unconditional surrender. It was he who determined to destroy the southern social order by emancipating all the slaves. He allowed Grant to pursue his relentless military campaigns. And now he was sanctioning the systematic destruction of the homes, the property, and even the food supplies of southern civilians. If this was not "total" war, it was something very close to it.

Northern Democrats were horrified by the destructive turn the war had taken. In 1864 they nominated George McClellan, the general Lincoln had fired, for president on a platform advocating compromise, a swift end to the war, and a negotiated settlement with the South. Lincoln's policy of hard war was the major issue of the campaign. The fact that McClellan won 45 percent of the votes suggested that many in the North disapproved of the administration's policy. But by Election Day, Mobile was in Union hands, Sheridan had laid waste to the Shenandoah Valley, and Sherman had taken Atlanta. The majority of northern voters could smell a Union victory, and Lincoln won convincingly. All Confederate attempts to offer anything less than unconditional surrender were rejected. Lee's hopes were dashed, and the siege of Petersburg continued.

Sherman Marches and Lee Surrenders

A week after Lincoln's reelection, Sherman's men burned half of Atlanta to the ground, turned east, and marched toward the sea (see Map 15–8). Confederate general John Bell Hood tried to distract Sherman by moving west toward Alabama and

Atlanta in Ruins Much of Atlanta lay in ruins after General Sherman captured and burned the city. The northern general had made a conscious decision to make war "hell" by destroying the property of the southern civilians who supported the war.

then up into Tennessee, but Union troops led by George Thomas destroyed Hood's forces in devastating battles at Franklin and Nashville, Tennessee. There was almost nothing left of the Confederate army between the Mississippi River and the Appalachian Mountains.

Meanwhile, Sherman's troops raged through the Georgia countryside. In late December, Sherman telegraphed Lincoln and presented him with Savannah as a Christmas gift. From Savannah, Sherman's men marched northward into South Carolina, the birthplace of secession. There, Union soldiers brought the practice of hard war to its ferocious climax. They torched homes and barns, destroyed crops, and slaughtered livestock. With Charleston in Union hands and the state capital of Columbia in flames, Sherman moved northward. By then, events in Virginia were bringing the war to a conclusion. Lee's army was fatally weakened when Union forces closed off Petersburg's last line of supply. On April 2, 1865, the Army of the Potomac broke through the Confederate defenses and forced Lee to abandon Petersburg. The next day, Confederate leaders abandoned Richmond. Lee moved his tired and hungry troops westward in one last attempt to elude Grant's force, but when he reached Appomattox Court House, Lee surrendered, and the war was over.

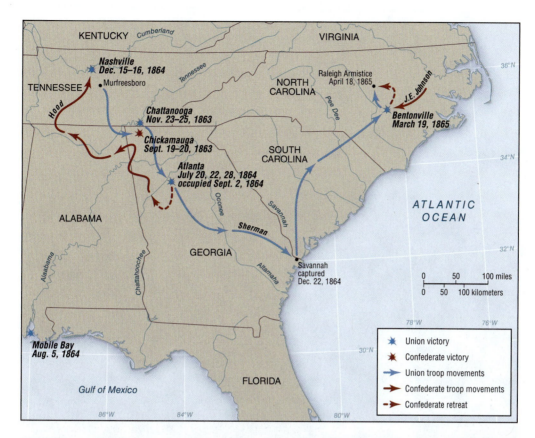

Map 15-8 The Atlanta Campaign and Sherman's March, 1863–1865 Lincoln's reelection was saved in part by Sherman's capture of Atlanta. It was here that Sherman spelled out his theory that war must be made unbearable to southern civilians if the North was to win. From Atlanta he went on to capture Savannah after his famed "march to the sea." Sherman then turned his troops northward to cut an even greater path of destruction through South Carolina.

From Emancipation to Abolition

In the spring of 1864, as Grant was launching his ferocious campaign against Lee's army in Virginia, Republicans in Congress came to the conclusion that neither military emancipation nor gradual state abolition would be enough to destroy slavery. They turned instead to a third policy, a Thirteenth Amendment to the Constitution abolishing slavery everywhere, forever.

By the end of the war, military emancipation had freed approximately half a million of the South's 4 million slaves. Lincoln and the Republicans believed that those slaves "practically" freed by the war could never be re-enslaved, but no one could be certain that those still in slavery when the war ended would be freed once the rationale for "military emancipation" had disappeared. The second route to slavery's destruction—state abolition—likewise proved inadequate. When the war ended, only 6 of the 15 slave states had abolished slavery, and only after intense pressure from Republicans in Washington. That pressure, too, was likely to diminish once the fighting stopped.

Two border states—Kentucky and Delaware—strenuously resisted all Union antislavery policies. In Congress they repeatedly declared that when the Union was restored those freed by the war would be re-enslaved. Indeed, re-enslavement had been the official policy of the Confederate government, and there was no reason to believe

With Lee's surrender to Grant at Appomattox, the Civil War came to an end.

that the seceded states would abandon their commitment to slavery if the Confederacy was defeated. In principle, even those states that had abolished slavery could re-establish it.

By early 1864 Republicans concluded that only a constitutional amendment could fully and permanently destroy slavery. The Senate passed the amendment easily, thanks in part to the vocal support of a few prominent War Democrats. But in the House Democrats closed ranks against it. In June they were able to deprive the amendment of the two-thirds vote needed to send it to the states for ratification. By then the Republicans had renominated Lincoln on a platform endorsing the Thirteenth Amendment, thereby ensuring that the 1864 election would be a referendum on war and abolition.

After his election victory in November, Lincoln and his cabinet scrambled to secure a handful of Democratic votes needed to get the amendment through the House of Representatives. Congress finally passed the amendment and sent it to the states in January 1865. It was not ratified until December, but in the intervening months most of the slaves were in fact emancipated.

When Lee surrendered, many slaves and slaveholders spontaneously concluded that slavery itself was finished and began making new arrangements. Officers of the Freedmen's Bureau, an agency of the US Army, stayed on when the war ended and enforced emancipation on farms and plantations across the South. A month after Lincoln's assassination, the new president, Andrew Johnson, required the defeated southern states to endorse emancipation as a condition for readmission to the Union. In the ensuing months, hundreds of thousands of slaves across the South were offered "contracts" to continue working as free laborers on their old farms and plantations.

In late 1865, Secretary of State Seward made it clear that President Johnson expected the reorganized states to ratify the Thirteenth Amendment before they were restored to the Union. In December 1865, Seward formally announced that the amendment had been ratified. After 250 years, slavery was finally abolished.

The Meaning of the Civil War

Despite the draft riots, Copperheads, wartime inflation, and terrible loss of life, the Civil War years had been good for the North's economy. Mechanization allowed northern farmers to increase wheat production, despite losing one-third of the farm labor force to the army. Huge orders for military rations propelled the growth of the canned-food industry. The railroad boom of the 1850s persisted through the war. By contrast, the slave economy was crushed. Much of the South lay in ruins. Thousands of miles of railroad track had been destroyed. One-third of the livestock had been killed; one-fourth of the young white men were dead. In 1860 the North and the South had identical per capita incomes and nearly identical per capita wealth. By 1870 the North was 50 percent wealthier than the South.

The redistribution of political power was equally dramatic. Until 1860, slaveholders and their allies had controlled the Supreme Court, dominated the presidency, and exercised disproportionate influence in Congress. The Civil War destroyed the slaveholding class and with it the slaveholders' political power. Abolition was finally accomplished.

Some 750,000 men—maybe as many as 850,000—died during the Civil War. If anything justified the slaughter, abolition did. Yet even Lincoln was stunned by the price the nation had paid. He wondered whether the bloodshed was a form of divine retribution for the unpardonable sin of slavery. In his second inaugural address, in March 1865, he prayed that the "mighty scourge of war may speedily pass away." But, Lincoln added, "if God wills that it continue, until all the wealth piled up by the bondman's two hundred and fifty years of unrequited toil shall be sunk, and until every drop of blood drawn with the lash, shall be paid by another drawn with the sword, as was said three thousand years ago, so still it must be said, 'the judgments of the Lord, are true and righteous altogether.'"

Conclusion

The president who had led the nation through the Civil War would not oversee the nation's reconstruction. On the evening of April 14, 1865, a disgruntled southern actor named John Wilkes Booth assassinated Abraham Lincoln at Ford's Theater in Washington, DC. Lincoln had given some thought to the question of how to reincorporate the defeated southern states into the Union, but when he died neither he nor his fellow Republicans in Congress had agreed on any particular plan. Would the Union simply be restored as swiftly as possible? Or would the South be reconstructed, continuing the revolution begun during the Civil War? At the moment Lincoln died, nobody was sure of the answer to these questions. They would emerge over the next several months and years, as the freed people in the South pressed to expand the meaning of their freedom.

Who, What

Jefferson Davis   508
U. S. Grant   520
Robert E. Lee   516
Abraham Lincoln   519
George B. McClellan   517
Edmund Ruffin   507
William T. Sherman   540
Antietam   526
Appomattox   542
Arlington   530
Blockade   513

Bull Run   516
Conscription   525
Contrabands   513
Cooperationism   510
Draft riots   537
Fort Sumter   511
Gettysburg   533
Hard war   512
King Cotton diplomacy   522
Secession   508
Vicksburg   516

Review Questions

1. What reasons did southerners give for seceding?

2. What were the relative military advantages of the North and the South at the beginning of the war?

>> TIME LINE

▼**1860**
South Carolina secedes

▼**1861**
Lower South secedes
Abraham Lincoln inaugurated

First shots fired at Fort Sumter
Upper South secedes
North declares runaway slaves
    "contraband"
First battle of Bull Run
McClellan takes command of Army of the
    Potomac
First Confiscation Act
Trent affair

▼**1862**
Battles of Fort Henry and Fort Donelson
"Battle of the ironclads"
Battle of Shiloh
Union capture of New Orleans

Slavery abolished in Washington, DC
Homestead Act
Confederacy establishes military draft
Peninsula campaign
Slavery prohibited in western territories
Second Confiscation Act,
    Militia Act, and Internal
    Revenue Act all passed
    by northern Congress
Second battle of Bull Run
Battle of Antietam
Preliminary Emancipation
    Proclamation
Battle of Fredericksburg

3. What made emancipation a "military necessity"?

4. How much antiwar sentiment was there in the Union and the Confederacy?

Critical-Thinking Questions

1. What role did the different economic systems of the North and South play in the Civil War?

2. Both the North and South suspended civil liberties during the conflict. In your opinion, did the stakes of the war justify such measures? Explain your answer.

3. What were the military merits of Sherman's "hard war" in Georgia and South Carolina? Did the nature of the conflict warrant such a course of action?

For further review materials and resource information, please visit www.oup.com/us/ofthepeople

▼**1863**
Emancipation Proclamation
Union establishes military draft
Battle of Chancellorsville
Battle of Gettysburg
Vicksburg surrenders
New York City draft riots
Battle of Chickamauga
Gettysburg Address
Battle of Lookout Mountain

▼**1864**
Wilderness campaign
Battle of Cold Harbor

Siege of Petersburg begins
Sherman captures Atlanta
Philip Sheridan raids Shenandoah Valley
Lincoln reelected
Sherman burns Atlanta and marches to
   the sea
Battles of Franklin and Nashville

▼**1864–1865**
Sherman's march through the Carolinas

▼**1865**
House of Representatives approves
   Thirteenth Amendment
Lincoln's second inauguration
Lee surrenders to Grant at Appomattox
Lincoln assassinated

1) Union military victories paved the way for a Republican political agenda of commercial and industrial advances, leaving the North more developed at the end of the war than it had been at the beginning.

2) The realities of "total war" led to the deliberate targeting of civilian homes, property, food supplies, and the wholesale destruction of towns and cities.

3) In the course of only a few years, the status of many southern slaves evolved from chattel, to contraband runaways, and, for some, to Union army soldiers.

4) The war transformed the South from a prosperous slave society to a decimated and war-torn region whose class and economic structure had been completely obliterated.

Liberty and Union

Mobilizing for War

The Civil War as Social Revolution

The War at Home

The War Comes to a Bloody End

A WAR FOR UNION AND EMANCIPATION

1861-1865

EVENTS

The South Secedes After Lincoln's election, 11 states seceded from the Union while 4 "border" slave states chose to remain.

Civilians Demand a Total War Initially, most Americans expected a quick end to the war, but as the conflict dragged on, civilians from both sides pushed for a "hard" war.

Slaves Take Advantage of the War Many slaves fled to northern lines as news of the war spread, prompting the Union to effectively nullify the Fugitive Slave Act.

Military Strategy and the Shift in War Aims An aggressive Union strategy took time to develop, while the Confederates, for the most part, pursued a defensive strategy.

The Confederate States of America The secessionists established a new government and drafted a constitution, but struggled to balance war needs and a commitment to states' rights.

Union Naval Supremacy Naval strategy helped the Union war effort through blockades and occasional joint operations with the army.

Southern Military Advantages The South's war effort was largely aided by the superior training of its military officers and by the fact that it was defending its own territory.

The Slave Economy in Wartime Slavery damaged the southern war effort by diminishing its industrial strength and crippling its ability to finance the war.

What Were Soldiers Fighting For? Southern soldiers fought, above all, to protect their homes and families from Yankee invasion. Northerners battled to restore the Union and, over time, to abolish slavery.

Union Victories in the West Union victories in the West gave rise to northern optimism, and Republicans pursued an active legislative agenda of capitalist development.

Southern Military Strength in the East Confederate forces capitalized on Union mistakes in the East, successfully defended Richmond, and reached a military stalemate with the North.

Universal Emancipation Lincoln issued the Emancipation Proclamation after Antietam, and northern public opinion slowly came to embrace emancipation as a war strategy.

Emancipation in Practice As the number of slave refugees continued to grow, many took shelter in army camps, while others joined the Union army.

The Care of Casualties Primitive medical practices multiplied casualties; two-thirds of all soldiers who died in the war were felled by disease.

Northern Reverses and Antiwar Sentiment Northern antiwar sentiment rose with losses on the battlefield, emancipation, and military conscription.

Gettysburg and the Justification of the War Lincoln took advantage of the North's military victories to elevate the meaning of the war beyond the restoration of the Union.

Discontent in the Confederacy Southerners suffered proportionally far more casualties, deprivation, and physical destruction than did northerners.

Grant Takes Command Lincoln put the aggressive Grant in charge of the entire Union army after the general's victories in the western theater.

The Theory and Practice of Hard War Grant and Lee fought a series of immensely bloody encounters, while Sherman advocated harsher military measures toward the South.

Sherman Marches and Lee Surrenders Sherman's army raged through the Georgia and South Carolina countryside, and Lee surrendered shortly after Grant's successful siege of Richmond.

From Emancipation to Abolition The Thirteenth Amendment to the Constitution permanently abolished slavery in the United States.

The Meaning of the Civil War The Civil War brought immense changes, including a redistribution of political power, a more centralized national government, and the destruction of American slavery.

RADICAL MEMBERS OF THE FIRST LEGISLATURE AFTER THE WAR

COMMON THREADS

>> In what ways did emancipation and wartime Reconstruction overlap?

>> When did Reconstruction begin?

>> Did Reconstruction change the South? If so, how? If not, why not?

>> What brought Reconstruction to an end?

Reconstructing a Nation
1865–1877

>> John Dennett Visits a Freedmen's Bureau Court

John Richard Dennett arrived in Liberty, Virginia, on August 17, 1865, on a tour of the South reporting for the magazine *The Nation*. The editors wanted accurate weekly accounts of conditions in the recently defeated Confederate states, and Dennett was the kind of man they could trust: a Harvard graduate, a firm believer in the sanctity of the Union, and a member of the class of elite Yankees who thought of themselves as the "best men" the country had to offer.

At Liberty, Dennett was accompanied by a Freedmen's Bureau agent. The Freedmen's Bureau was a branch of the US Army established by Congress to assist the freed people. Dennett and the agent went to the courthouse because one of the Freedmen's Bureau's functions was to adjudicate disputes between the freed people and southern whites.

The first case was that of an old white farmer who complained that two blacks who worked on his farm were "roamin' about and refusin' to work." He wanted the agent to help find the men and bring them back. Both men had wives and children living on his farm and eating his corn, the old man complained. "Have you been paying any wages?" the Freedmen's Bureau agent asked. "Well, they get what the other niggers get," the farmer answered. "I a'n't payin' great wages this year." There was not much the agent could do, but one of his soldiers volunteered to go and tell the blacks that "they ought to be at home supporting their wives and children."

A well-to-do planter came in to see if he could fire the blacks who had been working on his plantation since the beginning of the year. The planter complained the workers were unmanageable now that he could no longer punish them. The sergeant warned the planter not to beat his workers as if they were still slaves. In that case, the planter responded, "Will the Government take them off our hands?" The agent suspected that the planter was looking for a way to discharge his laborers at the end of the growing season but before they had been paid. "If they've worked on your crops all the year so far," the agent told the planter, "I guess they've got a claim on you to keep them a while longer."

Next came a "good-looking mulatto man" representing a number of African Americans worried that they would be forced to sign five-year contracts with their employers. "No, it a'n't true," the agent said. They also wanted to know if they could rent or buy land to work for themselves. "Yes, rent or buy," the agent said. But with no horses, mules, or ploughs, the former slaves wanted to know "if the Government would help us out after we get the land." The agent had no help to offer, except for a note from the bureau authorizing them to rent or buy their own farms.

The last case involved a field hand who came to complain that his master was beating him with a stick. The agent told the field hand to go back to work. "Don't be sassy, don't be lazy when you've got work to do; and I guess he won't trouble you." The field hand left but came back a

Continued

>> AMERICAN
PORTRAIT
Continued

minute later and asked for a letter to his master "enjoining him to keep the peace, as he feared the man would shoot him, he having on two or three occasions threatened to do so."

Most of the cases Dennett witnessed centered on labor relations, which often spilled over into other matters, including the family lives of the freed people, their civil rights, and their ability to buy land. The freed people preferred to work their own land but lacked the resources to rent or buy farms. Black workers and white owners who negotiated wage contracts had trouble figuring out each other's rights and responsibilities. The former masters wanted to retain as much of their old authority as possible. Freed men wanted as much autonomy as possible, whereas freed women were forced to seek the patriarchal protection of their husbands.

The Freedmen's Bureau was in the middle of these conflicts. Most agents tried to ensure that freed people were paid for their labor and were not brutalized as they had been as slaves. Southern whites resented this intrusion, and their resentment reached sympathetic politicians in Washington, DC. The Freedmen's Bureau became a lightning rod for the political conflicts of the Reconstruction period.

Conditions in the South raised several questions for lawmakers in Washington. How far should the federal government go to protect the economic well-being and civil rights of the freed people? What should the federal government require of southern states to be readmitted to the Union? Politicians disagreed violently on these questions. At one extreme was Andrew Johnson, who, as president, believed in small government and a speedy readmission of the southern states and looked on the Freedmen's Bureau with suspicion. At the other extreme were radical Republicans, who believed that the federal government should redistribute confiscated land to the former slaves, guarantee their civil rights, and give African American men the vote. They viewed the Freedmen's Bureau as too small and weak to be effective. In between were moderate Republicans who at first tried to work with the president. But as reports of violence and the abusive treatment of the freed people reached Washington, Republicans shifted toward the radical position.

It went back and forth this way: policy makers in Washington responded to events in the South, and events in the South were shaped in turn by policies from Washington. What John Dennett saw in Liberty, Virginia, was a good example of this. The Freedmen's Bureau agent listened to the requests of former masters and slaves, his responses shaped by the policies established in Washington. But those policies were, in turn, shaped by reports on conditions in the South sent back by Freedmen's Bureau agents like him and by journalists like John Dennett. From this interaction the politics of Reconstruction, and with it a "New South," slowly emerged.

OUTLINE

Wartime Reconstruction
Experiments with Free Labor in the Lower Mississippi Valley
Lincoln's Ten Percent Plan Versus the Wade-Davis Bill
The Freed People's Dream of Owning Land

Presidential Reconstruction, 1865–1867
The Political Economy of Contract Labor
Resistance to Presidential Reconstruction
Congress Clashes with the President

PRIMARY SOURCE:
  How Free Is Free? A Sharecropping Contract
  Origins of the Fourteenth Amendment

AMERICAN LANDSCAPE:
  Race Riots in Memphis and New Orleans

Congressional Reconstruction
  Origins of the Black Vote
  Radical Reconstruction in the South
  Achievements and Failures of Radical Government
  The Political Economy of Sharecropping

Wartime Reconstruction

For several years, emancipation overlapped with Reconstruction. Emancipation began early in the war and was not completed until the very end of 1865. Experiments with Reconstruction therefore began during the war, long before emancipation was complete. Indeed, what is known as "presidential Reconstruction" was also the crucial phase in the completion of emancipation. Congress and the president often had very different ideas about how to reconstruct the defeated Confederacy, but on one thing they agreed from the very beginning. Until the Thirteenth Amendment was ratified in December 1865, state emancipation was the most legally secure means of abolishing slavery. Congress and the president therefore agreed that before any southern state could be readmitted to the Union, it had to emancipate its own slaves.

After that, however, came other contentious questions. What system of free labor would replace slavery? What civil and political rights should the freed people receive? During the war Congress and the Lincoln administration responded piecemeal to developments in regions of the South under Union control. A variety of approaches to Reconstruction emerged.

Experiments with Free Labor in the Lower Mississippi Valley

In November 1861, several of the Sea Islands off South Carolina were occupied by Union troops. The slaveholders fled the advancing Union army, leaving behind between 5,000 and 10,000 slaves. In December President Lincoln declared that under the terms of the First Confiscation Act they had been "liberated." So began the first notable "rehearsal for Reconstruction." Within months the abandoned plantations of the Sea Islands were being reorganized. Eventually black families were given small plots of their own to cultivate, and in return for their labor they would receive a "share" of the year's crop. When the masters returned after the war to reclaim their lands, the labor system evolved into what would become known as "sharecropping."

Southern Louisiana also came under Union control early in the war. The sugar and cotton plantations around New Orleans provided another major experiment in the transition from slave to free labor. Unlike in the Sea Islands, however, Louisiana's planters did not abandon their plantations, and tens of thousands of slaves were involved. Union commanders faced a dilemma. The plantation workers were no longer slaves, but their masters were still in place, so the plantations could not be broken up. And sugar plantations could not be effectively organized into small sharecropping units. The unusual labor system that emerged played an important role in the politics of Reconstruction.

The Retreat from Republican Radicalism
    The Impeachment and Trial of Andrew Johnson
    Republicans Become the Party of Moderation

AMERICA AND THE WORLD:
    Reconstructing America's Foreign Policy

Reconstructing the North
    The Fifteenth Amendment and Nationwide African
        American Suffrage
    Women and Suffrage

    The Rise and Fall of the National Labor Union

The End of Reconstruction
    Corruption as a National Problem
    Liberal Republicans Revolt
    A Depression and a Deal "Redeem" the South

DEBATING HISTORY:
    The Nature of Reconstruction

Conclusion

Union general Nathaniel Banks, hoping to stem the flow of black refugees to Union lines and prevent the shocking numbers of deaths among blacks in the contraband camps, issued stringent regulations designed to put the freed people back to work quickly. The Banks Plan required freed people to sign yearlong contracts to work on their former plantations, often for their former owners. Workers would be paid either 5 percent of the proceeds of the crop or three dollars per month. The former masters would provide food and shelter, and African American workers were forbidden to leave the plantations without permission. So harsh were these regulations that to many critics Banks had simply replaced one form of slavery with another. But as harsh as it was, the Banks Plan was not slavery, and most of the freed people returned to work fully aware of the difference. The Banks Plan was implemented throughout the lower Mississippi Valley, especially after the fall of Vicksburg in 1863.

> A few days ago, a gentleman below the city hired a new overseer. . . . He was in the habit of wielding the whip pretty freely, and of using abusive language to the negro women. . . . [A] delegation from the field-hands waited upon the proprietor, and very respectfully stated their objections against the newcomer. . . . He dismissed them with an oath. . . . The delegation at once went to their cabins, packed up their little bundles, and started on the road to Fort Jackson. They knew, that, once there, they could get employment. They had not gone far, however, before the master came to his senses. He was no longer the owner of mere chattels. . . . He called them all back; told them they should have any overseer they wanted: upon which they unpacked their bundles, and went quietly to the field, as if nothing had happened.
>
> GEORGE HEPWORTH,
> surveying the effect of the Banks Plan in Louisiana, 1863

The Banks Plan touched off a political controversy. Established planters had the most to gain from the plan, which preserved much of the prewar labor system. Louisiana Unionists, who had remained loyal to Washington, formed a Free State Association to press for more substantial changes. Lincoln publicly supported the Free State movement and issued a Proclamation of Amnesty and Reconstruction to undermine the Confederacy by cultivating the support of southern Unionists. The Proclamation contained, in outline, the first plan for reconstructing the South.

The most important thing Lincoln's plan did was to require Louisiana to abolish slavery as the price for readmission to the Union. The precedent for such a precondition had been established earlier the same year for West Virginia. Lincoln quickly applied that precedent to the seceded states, beginning with Florida and Louisiana. But the attempt to establish a loyal government in Florida foundered, so Louisiana became the first great experiment in wartime Reconstruction.

Lincoln's Ten Percent Plan Versus the Wade-Davis Bill

Beyond requiring the abolition of slavery, Lincoln's Ten Percent Plan promised full pardons and the restoration of civil rights to all those who swore loyalty to the Union, excluding only a few high-ranking Confederate military and political leaders. When the number of loyal whites in a former Confederate state reached 10 percent of the 1860 voting population, they could organize a new state constitution and government. Abiding by these conditions, Free State whites met in Louisiana in 1864 and produced a new state constitution. It abolished slavery, but it also denied blacks the right to vote.

By the spring of 1864 such denials were no longer acceptable to radical Republicans. Unionists in Louisiana developed strong ties to leading radicals in Congress, such as Thaddeus Stevens of Pennsylvania and Charles Sumner of Massachusetts. Most radicals favored federal guarantees of the civil rights of former slaves, including the right to vote, and were prepared to use the full force of the federal government to enforce congressional policy in the South. Although the radicals never formed a majority in Congress, they gradually won over the moderates to many of their positions. When Congress took control of Reconstruction after the elections in 1866, the process became known as "radical Reconstruction."

The radicals were particularly strong in New Orleans, thanks to the city's large and articulate community of free blacks. In the spring of 1864 they sent a delegation to Washington to meet with President Lincoln and press the case for voting rights. The next day, Lincoln wrote to the acting governor of Louisiana suggesting a limited suffrage for the most intelligent blacks and for those who had served in the Union army. The suggestion was ignored. Free blacks in New Orleans and former slaves then demanded civil and political rights and the abolition of the Banks labor regulations. Radicals complained that Lincoln's Ten Percent Plan was too kind to former Confederates and that the Banks Plan was too harsh on former slaves.

Swayed by events in Louisiana, congressional radicals rejected Lincoln's plan. In July 1864, Congressmen Benjamin F. Wade and Henry Winter Davis proposed a different Reconstruction plan. Under the Wade-Davis Bill, Reconstruction could not begin until a majority, rather than merely 10 percent, of a state's white men swore an oath of allegiance to the Union. In addition, the Wade-Davis Bill guaranteed full legal and civil rights to African Americans, but not the right to vote. Lincoln pocket-vetoed the bill because it required Louisiana to emancipate its slaves as a condition for readmission to the Union. Lincoln believed that only he, as commander in chief, could emancipate slaves as a necessity of war. He included an emancipation provision in his own plan for Louisiana Reconstruction.

The Louisiana experience made several things clear. The radical Republicans were determined to press for more civil and political rights for blacks than moderates initially supported; however, the moderates showed a willingness to move in a radical direction. Equally important, any Reconstruction policy would have to consider the wishes of southern blacks.

The Freed People's Dream of Owning Land

Freedom meant many things to the former slaves. It meant that they could move about their neighborhoods without passes, that they did not have to step aside to let whites pass them on the street. Following emancipation, southern blacks withdrew from white churches and established their own congregations, and during Reconstruction the church emerged as a central institution in the southern black community. Freedom also meant literacy. Even before the war ended, northern teachers poured into the South to set up schools. When the fighting stopped, the

Charlotte Forten Born to a prominent African American family in Philadelphia, Charlotte Forten was one of many northern women who went to the South to become a teacher of the freed slaves. Forten helped found the Penn School on St. Helena's Island in South Carolina.

MARRIAGE OF A COLORED SOLDIER AT VICKSBURG BY CHAPLAIN WARREN OF THE FREEDMEN'S BUREAU.

Freedman Wedding Because slave marriages had no legal standing, many freed people got married as soon as they could. Pictured here is one such wedding, performed at the Freedmen's Bureau.

US Army helped recruit and organize thousands more northern women as teachers. As a result, hundreds of thousands of southern blacks became literate within a few years.

More important, former slaves went out of their way to have their marriages secured by the law. In 1865 marriage became an urgent necessity for many recently freed slaves, particularly women. Under slavery, black women were valued in part for their labor and in part for their ability to reproduce more slaves. With emancipation, black women and their offspring were no longer valuable as property, and some planters, hoping to avoid the expense of caring for them, began expelling women and children from their plantations in late 1865. Desperate women quickly realized that their best hope for survival was the patriarchal protection of their husbands. Once married, their husbands would demand sharecropping contracts that allowed their families to live with them on the plantations. For the first time in their lives, black women across the South became what the law called "domestic dependents." Emancipation moved black women—no longer human property—out of slavery and into patriarchy.

The freed people also wanted land, without which they saw no choice but to work for their old masters. As the war ended, many African Americans had reason to believe that the government would help them become landowners. In early 1865, Union general William Tecumseh Sherman discovered how important land was to the freed people on the Sea Islands off the Carolinas. "The way we can best take care of ourselves is to have land," they declared, "and turn it out and till it by our own labor." Persuaded by their arguments, Sherman issued Special Field Order No. 15 granting captured land to the freed people. By June, 400,000 acres had been distributed to 40,000 former slaves.

Congress seemed to be moving in a similar direction. In March 1865, the Republicans established the Bureau of Refugees, Freedmen and Abandoned Lands, commonly known as the Freedmen's Bureau. The bureau became involved in the politics of land redistribution and controlled the disposition of 850,000 acres of confiscated and abandoned Confederate lands. In July 1865, General Oliver Otis Howard, the head of the bureau, directed his agents to rent the land to the freed people in 40-acre plots that they could eventually purchase. Many agents believed that to reeducate them in the values of thrift and hard work, the freed people should be encouraged to save money and buy land for themselves. From the bureau's perspective, redistributing land was like giving it away to people who had not paid for it.

The former slaves, however, felt they had more than earned a right to the land. "The labor of these people had for two hundred years cleared away the forests and produced crops that brought millions of dollars annually," H. C. Bruce explained. "It does seem to me that a Christian Nation would, at least, have given them one year's support, 40 acres of land and a mule each." Even Abraham Lincoln seemed to agree. But in April 1865 Lincoln was dead, and Andrew Johnson became president of the United States.

Presidential Reconstruction, 1865–1867

When Andrew Johnson took office in April 1865, it was still unclear whether Congress or the president would control Reconstruction policy and whether that policy would be lenient or harsh. As with so many Democrats, Johnson's sympathy for the common man did not extend to African Americans. Yet as wartime governor of Tennessee, Johnson had struggled tirelessly to get slavery abolished in the state, and in his first year as president he demanded that the former slave states abolish slavery as a condition for readmission to the Union. Nevertheless, Johnson grew increasingly determined to reconstruct the South in his own way and blind to the interests of the freed people. In 1866 he drifted away from the Republicans who controlled Congress, becoming bitter and resentful in the process.

The Political Economy of Contract Labor

In the mid-nineteenth century, Congress was normally out of session from March until December. Taking office in April 1865, Johnson hoped to use the recess to complete the Reconstruction process and present it to lawmakers in December. At the end of May the president offered amnesty and the restoration of property to white southerners who swore an oath of loyalty to the Union, excluding only high-ranking Confederate military and political leaders and very rich planters. He named provisional governors to the seceded states and told them to organize constitutional conventions. To be readmitted to the Union, the seceded states were first required to abolish slavery, preferably by ratifying the Thirteenth Amendment. Johnson also required the states to nullify their secession ordinances and repudiate their Confederate war debts. These terms were far more lenient than those Lincoln and the congressional Republicans had contemplated. They did nothing to protect the civil rights of the former slaves.

Johnson's leniency encouraged defiance among white southerners. Secessionists had been barred from participating in the states' constitutional conventions, but they participated openly in the first elections held late in the year after Johnson issued thousands of pardons. Leading Confederates thus assumed public office in the southern states. As required, the former Confederate states began abolishing slavery, and in the fall of 1865 the last great wave of emancipation spread across the South. Right up to the end of the war most slaveholders hoped to retain their slaves, even if they were forced to rejoin the Union. When the last holdouts—and there were many thousands of them—were finally forced to accept emancipation, they were furious and resentful. As the new state governments were coming into existence, a wave of violence spread across the South.

Blacks who had been freed earlier were not immune to the reaction. Back in power, white southerners demanded the restoration of all properties confiscated or abandoned during the war. In September 1865 Johnson ordered the Freedmen's Bureau to return all confiscated and abandoned lands to their former owners, and in late 1865 former slaves were being forcibly evicted from the 40-acre plots they had been given by the Union army or the Freedmen's Bureau.

Alongside their emancipation ordinances, the Johnsonian state governments enacted a series of "Black Codes" that severely restricted the civil rights of freed people. In

New Orleans, La., August 2, 1866

U. S. Grant, General, Washington, D.C.

The more information I obtain about the affair of the 30th, in this city, the more revolting it becomes. It was no riot; it was an absolute massacre by the police. . . . It was a murder which the Mayor and the police of the city perpetrated without the shadow of a necessity; furthermore, I believe it was premeditated, and every indication points to this. I recommend removing this bad man. I believe it would be hailed with the sincerest gratification by two-thirds of the population of the city. There has been a feeling of insecurity on the part of the people here on account of this man, which is now so much increased that the safety of life and property does not rest with the civil authorities, but with the military.

P. H. Sheridan
Major-General Commanding

many states the Black Codes *were* the emancipation statutes. Vagrancy laws, for example, allowed police to arrest and fine virtually any black man. If he could not pay the fine, the "vagrant" was put to work on a farm, often the one operated by his former master. Even more disturbing to the former slaves were apprenticeship clauses that allowed white officials to remove children from their parents' homes and put them to work as "apprentices" on nearby farms.

Presidential Reconstruction left the freed people with no choice but to sign labor contracts with white landlords that restricted their personal, as well as their working, lives. In one case, a South Carolina planter contractually obliged his black workers to "go by his direction the same as in slavery time." Contracts required blacks to work for wages as low as one-tenth of the crop, and cotton prices were falling. It is no wonder that contract labor seemed little different from slavery.

Resistance to Presidential Reconstruction

In September 1865, blacks in Virginia issued a public appeal for assistance. They declared that they lacked the means to make and enforce legal contracts, because the Black Codes denied African Americans the right to testify in court in any case involving a white person. Many planters blocked the development of a free labor market by agreeing among themselves to hire only their former slaves and by fixing wages at a low level. Finally, there were many cases of black workers who had obeyed the terms of their contracts being "met by a contemptuous refusal of the stipulated compensation."

Across the South, whites reported a growing number of freed people unwilling to accept the humiliating conditions of the contract labor system. Some blacks refused to perform specific tasks, whereas others were accused of being "disrespectful" to their employers or to whites in general. Most important, thousands of freedmen declined to sign contracts at the end of the year.

As white backlash and black defiance spread, reports of violence flooded into Washington. A former slave named Henry Adams claimed that "over two thousand colored people" were murdered around Shreveport, Louisiana, in 1865. Near Pine Bluff, Arkansas, in 1866, a black community was burned to the ground by whites. Blacks were assaulted for not speaking to whites with the proper tone of submission, for disputing the terms of labor contracts, or for failing to meet the standards white employers expected. Through relentless intimidation, whites prevented blacks from buying their own land or attending political meetings to press for civil rights.

Northerners read these reports as evidence that whites were resisting emancipation and that "rebel" sentiment was reviving in the South. When Congress returned in

December 1865, moderate Republicans were already suspicious of presidential Reconstruction. Radicals argued that the contract system made a mockery of their party's commitment to free labor, and insisted that the only way to protect the interests of the freed people was to grant them the right to vote.

Congress Clashes with the President

Increasingly distressed by events in the South, Republican moderates in Congress were radicalized. They accepted the need for a more active government in the South and endorsed voting rights for black men. President Johnson, meanwhile, became obsessed with fears of "negro rule" in the South. When he insisted on readmitting southern states clearly controlled by unrepentant Confederates, Congress refused. Instead, the Republicans formed a Joint Committee on Reconstruction to propose the terms for readmission, reflecting Congress's determination to follow its own course.

> The Congress owes it to its own character to set the seal of reprobation upon a doctrine which is becoming too fashionable, and unless rebuked will be the recognized principle of our Government. Governor Perry and other provisional governors and orators proclaim that "this is the white man's Government." The whole copperhead party, pandering to the lowest prejudices of the ignorant, repeat the cuckoo cry, "This is the white man's Government." Demagogues of all parties, even some high in authority, gravely shout, "This is the white man's Government." What is implied by this? That one race of men are to have the exclusive right forever to rule this nation, and to exercise all acts of sovereignty, while all other races and nations and colors are to be their subjects, and have no voice in making the laws and choosing the rulers by whom they are to be governed. Wherein does this differ from slavery except in degree? Does not this contradict all the distinctive principles of the Declaration of Independence?
>
> CONGRESSMAN THADDEUS STEVENS,
> speech on Reconstruction, December 18, 1865

In February 1866, Congress voted to extend the life of the Freedmen's Bureau and empowered the bureau to set up its own courts, which would supersede local jurisdictions wherever civil authorities were not functioning properly. The bureau's record during its first year had been mixed. In the area of labor relations, the bureau often sided with the landowners and against the interests of the freed people. But it also emancipated thousands of slaves, provided immediate relief to thousands of individual freed people, and assisted in the creation of schools. The bureau's effectiveness varied with the commitments of its agents. Some agents sided instinctively with the former masters. The more idealistic agents often acted under difficult circumstances to protect the freed people from racist violence, unfair employers, and biased officials. Thousands of freedmen and freedwomen looked to the bureau as their only hope for justice; for the same reason, thousands of southern whites resented the bureau, and they let Andrew Johnson know it.

To the amazement of moderate Republicans, Johnson vetoed the bill to extend the life of the Freedmen's Bureau, claiming that the legislation would increase the power of the central government at the expense of the states. He invoked the Jacksonian ideal of the free market, insisting that the "laws that regulate supply and demand" were the best way to resolve the labor problem in the South. Republicans fell just short of the two-thirds vote needed to override the veto. Johnson reacted by attacking the

>> How Free Is Free?
A Sharecropping Contract

For Republicans, the essence of "free labor" was the contract, the notion that either a governing figure and his people, or a wealthy man and those who labored for him, both had to subscribe voluntarily to an explicit agreement outlining their mutual responsibilities in order for their relationship to be binding. Unfortunately, after the war, because of the power imbalance between them, southern blacks freed from slavery but without land sometimes had little choice but to sign stringent labor contracts with their landlords. Often these landowners had previously been slave owners. After several years of struggle and negotiations between the former slaves and their former masters, a system emerged that was known as sharecropping. The tenant, or "cropper," would sign an annual contract to work a plot of land in return for a share of the crop. The following is a typical sharecropping contract from 1886, between a landlord named A. T. Mial, of Wake County, North Carolina, and a sharecropper named Fenner Powell.

This contract made and entered into between A. T. Mial of one part and Fenner Powell of the other part both of the County of Wake and state of North Carolina—

Witnesseth—That the Said Fenner Powell hath barga-ned and agreed with the Said Mial to work as a cropper for the year 1886 on Said Mial's land on the land now occupied by Said Powell on the west Side of Poplar Creek and a point on the east Side of Said Creek and both South and North of the Mial road, leading to Raleigh, That the said Fenner Powell agrees to work faithfully and dili-gently without any unnecessary loss of time, to do all manner of work on Said farm as may be directed by Said Mial, And to be respectful in manners and de-portment to Said Mial. And the Said Mial agrees on his part to furnish mule and feed for the same and all plantation tools and Seed to plant the crop free of charge, and to give the said Powell One half of all crops raised and housed by Said Powell

> Here we see Mial's lawyer drawing on the old notion of a contract as being voluntarily entered into on both sides in order for it to be binding.

> As readers, we may wonder if most labor contracts of that era specified good "manners and deportment." It would be necessary to look at a contract made between two white people to learn that this was in fact unusual.

> We might have thought that it would be obvious that the owner would provide tools and seed free of charge. It would be a good idea to look at farm records from the era to see if landowners often charged. Maybe Fenner Powell knew he had to ask for this clause.

Why might Mial's lawyer have wanted to make sure that Powell could not claim ownership of half the seed?

Having seen many legal documents, a historian knows that in the absence of literacy, leaving a print or imprint replaced the use of a signature. But how do you think the system lent itself to abuse?

on Said land except the cotton seed. The Said Mial agrees to advance as provisions to Said Powell fifty pound of bacon and two sacks of meal per month and occasionally some flour to be paid out of his the Said Powell's part of the crop or from any other advance that may be made to Said Powell by Said Mial. As witness our hands and seals this the 16th day of January A.D. 1886.

Why do you think the lawyer wouldn't specify exactly how much flour Mial would give, as opposed to bacon and corn meal?

Contract between Alonzo T. Mial and Fenner Powell, January 1886, in Roger Ransom and Richard Sutch, *One Kind of Freedom: The Economic Consequences of Emancipation*, (New York: Cambridge University Press, 1977), p. 91.

Questions

1. Does the contract seem fair to you?

2. What does the landlord agree to provide to the sharecropper, and what does the sharecropper agree to do in return?

3. In what ways does sharecropping resemble slavery? In what ways is it significantly different?

BUREAU R. F. & A. L.,
10th DISTRICT, LEX., SUB DISTRICT, KENTUCKY.
CONTRACT.
Know All Men by These Presents, That *Abraham Bledsoe* of the County of Mason, State of Kentucky, am held and firmly bound to THE UNITED STATES OF AMERICA, in the sum of FIVE HUNDRED DOLLARS, for the payment of which I bind *my* Heirs, Executors, and Administrators, firmly by these presents, in this contract:—That I am to furnish the person whose name is subjoined (freed laborer,) quarters, fuel, substantial and healthy rations, all necessary medical supplies in case of sickness, and the amount set opposite *His* name, per month; one half to be paid at the expiration of every three months, for the services rendered for each three months preceding, the balance at the expiration of the year *Henry Bledsoe* agrees to work faithfully for the said *Abraham N Bledsoe* obeying all his instructions in good faith, and in case *He* leaves his service before the expiration of this contract (provided not driven off or maltreated,) *He is* to forfeit all wages due at the time of leaving.

NO.	NAMES	AGE	RATES PER MONTH DOLLS.	CENTS.
	Henry Bledsoe	17	6	66⅔
	Or 80$ pr Annum.			

Said Bledsoe farther agrees to increase Henry wages to One Hundred dollars per year if he works well and briskly.

This contract is to commence *January 1st 1866* and close with the year.

Given in triplicate, at Maysville, this *16th* day of *June* 1866.
A Bledsoe

Witness:
H C Campbell. B J Tone Sup't. of 10th District.
Registered at Maysville, Ky., this *16* day of *Jan*. 1866.

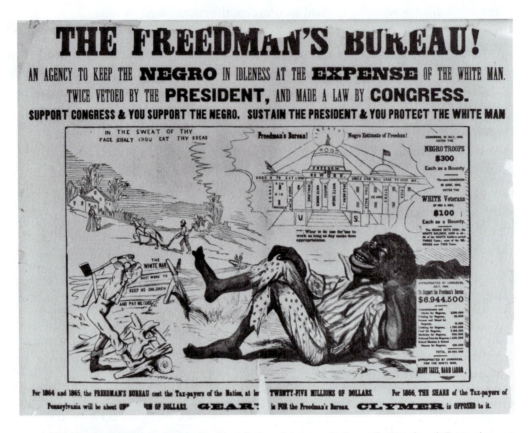

The Freedmen's Bureau Led by President Andrew Johnson, attacks on the Freedmen's Bureau became more and more openly racist in late 1865 and 1866. This Democratic Party broadside was circulated during the 1866 election.

Republicans in Congress and questioning the legitimacy of the Joint Committee on Reconstruction.

Origins of the Fourteenth Amendment

In March 1866 Congress passed a landmark Civil Rights Act. It overturned the Dred Scott decision by granting United States citizenship to Americans regardless of race. This marked the first time that the federal government intervened in the states to guarantee due process and basic civil rights. But Johnson vetoed the Civil Rights Act of 1866. Alongside the usual Jacksonian rhetoric about limited government, Johnson justified his veto on racist grounds. He doubted that blacks "possess the requisite qualifications to entitle them to all the privileges and immunities of citizens of the United States."

Johnson's actions and rhetoric forced moderate Republicans to confront him. The Republican Congress overrode Johnson's veto of the Civil Rights Act and passed another Freedmen's Bureau Bill. Again Johnson vetoed it, but this time Congress overrode his veto.

To ensure the civil rights of the freed people, the Joint Committee on Reconstruction proposed a Fourteenth Amendment to the Constitution. The most powerful and controversial of all the Constitution's amendments, it guaranteed citizenship to all males born in the United States, regardless of color (see Table 16–1). Although the amendment did not guarantee blacks the right to vote, it based representation in Congress on a state's

AMERICAN LANDSCAPE
>> Race Riots in Memphis and New Orleans

A few weeks after Congress passed the Civil Rights Act, white mobs in Memphis rioted for three days. In the year since the war had ended, the city's black population had multiplied four times over as former slaves fled the countryside for better opportunities in the city. But whites in Memphis grew increasingly hostile to the presence of so many blacks. "Would to God they were back in Africa, or some other seaport town," the Memphis *Argus* complained, "anywhere but here." Under President Andrew Johnson's terms for a newly reconstructed government, the old Memphis elite had been displaced by Irish politicians at least as hostile to freed people as the old guard. Conflict between whites and blacks broke out on the streets of Memphis.

In this atmosphere of heightened racial tension, one incident sparked a riot. On May 1, 1866, after two hack drivers—one black, one white—had a traffic accident, police arrested the black man. A group of black veterans tried to prevent the arrest. A white crowd gathered and began rioting in the streets. Over the next three days, white mobs burned hundreds of homes, destroyed churches, and attacked black schools. Five black women were raped, and nearly fifty people, all but two of them black, were killed.

Three months later, white mobs in New Orleans rioted as well. Once again, both the state and city governments were falling into the hands of former Confederates. But the New Orleans massacre had a more explicitly political dimension. Its well-established community of free blacks had, by the middle of 1866, grown disillusioned with the direction Reconstruction was taking in Louisiana and New Orleans. A group of radicals sought to bring the state's 1864 constitutional convention back into session. They proposed giving blacks the vote, stripping "rebels" of the franchise, and establishing an entirely new state government. The convention was scheduled to meet on July 30.

But as the delegates met, white mobs set out to stop them. Led by police and firemen, many of them Confederate veterans, whites first attacked a parade of about 200 blacks marching to the Mechanics' Institute to support the delegates. At the convention hall, the mobs began shooting and killing the delegates trying to escape through the windows, even after they raised the white flag of surrender. When the mob finally dispersed,

34 blacks and 3 white supporters had been killed, and another 100 had been injured.

The Memphis and New Orleans massacres quickly became political issues in the North, thanks in large part to Johnson's reaction. In late August the president undertook an unprecedented campaign tour designed to stir up voters' hostility to Congress, but his trip backfired. He blasted congressional Republicans, blaming them for the riots, and suggested that radical congressman Thaddeus Stevens should be hanged. Republicans charged in turn that Johnson's own policies had revived the rebellious sentiments that led to the massacres.

Continued

The elections of 1866 became a referendum on competing visions of what American democracy should mean. For President Johnson, "democracy" meant government by local majorities, which often meant white supremacy. For African Americans and a growing number of Republicans in Congress, genuine democracy demanded a firm foundation of equal civil and political rights. The results were "overwhelmingly against the President," the *New York Times* noted, "clearly, unmistakably, decisively in favor of Congress and its policy." The Republicans gained a veto-proof hold on Congress, and Republican moderates were further radicalized. Congressional Reconstruction was about to begin.

Table 16-1 Reconstruction Amendments, 1865–1870

Amendment	Main Provisions	Congressional Passage (2/3 majority in each house required)	Ratification Process (3/4 of all states including ex-Confederate states required)
13	Slavery prohibited in United States	January 1865	December 1865 (27 states, including 8 southern states)
14	1. National citizenship for all men and women born in the United States	June 1866	Rejected by 12 southern and border states, February 1867
	2. State representation in Congress reduced proportionally to number of voters disfranchised		Radicals make readmission of southern states hinge on ratification
	3. Former high-ranking Confederates denied right to hold office		Ratified July 1868
	4. Confederate debt repudiated		
15	Denial of franchise because of race, color, or past servitude explicitly prohibited	February 1869	Ratification required for readmission of Virginia, Texas, Mississippi, Georgia. Ratified March 1870.

voting population. This punished southern states by reducing their representation if they did not allow blacks to vote.

By mid-1866, Congress had refused to recognize the state governments established under Johnson's plan, and it had authorized the Freedmen's Bureau to create a military justice system to override the local courts, thereby guaranteeing the former slaves basic rights of due process. Finally, it made ratification of the Fourteenth Amendment by the former Confederate states a requirement for readmission to the Union. Congress and the president were now at war, and Andrew Johnson went on a rampage.

Congressional Reconstruction

Johnson's outrageous behavior during the 1866 campaign, capped by a Republican sweep of the elections, ended presidential Reconstruction. Congressional Reconstruction would be far different. It was an extraordinary series of events, second only to emancipation in its impact on the history of the United States.

Origins of the Black Vote

The Congress that convened in December 1866 was far more radical than the previous one, evidenced clearly by the emerging consensus among moderate Republicans that southern blacks should be allowed to vote. Radical Republicans and black leaders had been calling for such a policy for two years, but moderate Republicans initially resisted the idea. At most, moderates contemplated granting the vote to veterans and to educated blacks who had been free before the war. Not until early 1867 did the majority of Republicans conclude that the only way to avoid a lengthy military occupation of the South was to put political power into the hands of all male freedmen.

Andrew Johnson finally pushed the moderate Republicans over the line. Ignoring the results of the 1866 elections, Johnson urged the southern states to reject the Fourteenth Amendment. Frustrated Republicans finally repudiated presidential Reconstruction. On March 2, 1867, Congress assumed control of the process by passing the First Reconstruction Act. It reduced the southern states to the status of territories and divided the South into five military districts directly controlled by the army (see Map 16–1). Before the southern states could be readmitted to the Union, they had to draw up new "republican" constitutions, ratify the Fourteenth Amendment, and allow black men to vote.

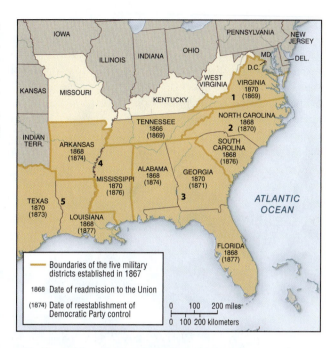

Map 16–1 Reconstruction and Redemption By 1870 Congress readmitted every southern state to the Union. In most cases the Republican Party retained control of the "reconstructed" state governments for only a few years.

The Second Reconstruction Act, passed soon after, established the procedures to enforce black suffrage by placing the military in charge of voter registration. Johnson vetoed both acts, but in both cases Congress immediately overrode him. This was congressional Reconstruction at its most radical, and for this reason it is often referred to as "radical Reconstruction."

Radical Reconstruction in the South

Beginning in 1867 the constitutions of the southern states were rewritten, thousands of African Americans began to vote, and hundreds of them assumed public office. Within six months, 735,000 blacks and 635,000 whites had registered to vote across the South. Blacks formed electoral majorities in South Carolina, Florida, Mississippi, Alabama, and Louisiana. In the fall these new voters elected delegates to conventions that drew up progressive state constitutions that guaranteed suffrage for all men, mandated public education systems, and established progressive tax structures.

The governments elected under congressional authority were based on an unstable political coalition. Northern whites were prominent in the southern Republican Party. Stereotyped as greedy carpetbaggers, they included Union veterans who stayed in the South, idealistic reformers, well-meaning capitalists, and opportunists on the make. More important to the Republican coalition were southern whites, or scalawags. Some of them lived in up-country regions that resisted secession and the Confederacy. Others had been Whigs before the war and were now hoping to regain some former influence. But new black voters were the backbone of the Republican Party in the South. They were a varied lot. Elite black artisans and professionals did not always share the interests of poor black farmers and farm laborers, but most African Americans were united by a shared interest in securing civil rights.

Hiram Revels The first nonwhite US senator, Hiram Revels, represented Mississippi during radical Reconstruction (1870–1871).

Although in the long run class and race divisions weakened the party, in the late 1860s and early 1870s the southern Republicans launched an impressive experiment in interracial democracy in the South. Racist legend paints these years as a dark period of "negro rule" and military domination, but military rule rarely lasted more than a year or two, and only in South Carolina did blacks ever control the legislature. Blacks who held office were largely members of the prewar free African American elite of teachers, ministers, and small businessmen rather than sharecroppers or farm workers. These Reconstruction legislatures were more representative of their constituents than most legislatures in nineteenth-century America (see Figure 16–1).

Achievements and Failures of Radical Government

Once in office, southern Republicans had to cultivate a white constituency and at the same time serve the interests of the blacks who elected them. To strengthen this biracial coalition, Republican politicians emphasized government support for economic development. Republican legislatures granted tax abatements for corporations and spent vast sums to encourage the construction of railroads. They preached a "gospel of prosperity" that promised to benefit ordinary white southerners.

In the long run, the gospel of prosperity did not hold the Republican coalition together. Outside investors were unwilling to risk their capital on a politically unstable region. By the early 1870s, black politicians questioned the diversion of scarce revenues to railroads and tax breaks for corporations. Instead, they demanded public services, especially universal education. But more government services meant higher property taxes at a time of severe hardship. White small farmers had been devastated by the Civil War. Unaccustomed to paying high taxes, and believing strongly in limited government, they grew increasingly receptive to Democratic appeals for restoration of "white man's government." Thus southern Republicans were unable to unite the diverse interests of their constituents.

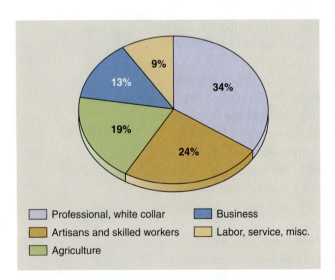

Professional, white collar — 34%
Artisans and skilled workers — 24%
Agriculture — 19%
Business — 13%
Labor, service, misc. — 9%

Figure 16-1 Occupations of African American Officeholders During Reconstruction Although former slaves were underrepresented among black officeholders, the Reconstruction governments were among the most broadly representative legislatures in US history.

Despite powerful opposition at home and lukewarm support from Washington, DC, radical governments in the South boasted several important achievements. They funded the construction of hospitals, insane asylums, prisons, and roads. They introduced homestead exemptions that protected the property of poor farmers. Republican legislatures established public school systems that were a major improvement over their antebellum counterparts. The literacy rate among southern blacks rose steadily. Nevertheless, public schools for southern blacks remained inadequately funded and sharply segregated.

The Political Economy of Sharecropping

Congressional Reconstruction made it easier for the former slaves to negotiate the terms of their labor contracts. Republican state legislatures abolished the Black Codes and passed "lien" laws that gave black workers more control over the crops they grew. Workers with grievances had a better chance of securing justice, as southern Republicans became sheriffs, justices of the peace, and county clerks, and as southern courts allowed blacks to serve as witnesses and sit on juries.

The strongest card in the hands of the freed people was a shortage of agricultural workers in the South. After emancipation, thousands of blacks sought opportunities in towns and cities or in the

"Radical Members" One of the greatest achievements of congressional Reconstruction was the election of a significant number of African Americans to public office. Only in South Carolina, however, did African Americans ever form a legislative majority.

North. And even though most blacks remained in the South as farmers, they reduced their working hours in several ways. Black women still worked the fields, but they spent more time nursing their infants and caring for their children. And the children went to school when they were able. The resulting labor shortage forced white landlords to renegotiate their labor arrangements with the freed people.

The contract labor system that had developed during the war and under presidential Reconstruction was replaced with a variety of regional arrangements. On the Louisiana sugar plantations, the freed people became wage laborers. But in tobacco and cotton regions, where most freed people lived, a new system of labor called sharecropping developed. Under this system, an agricultural worker and his family typically agreed to work for one year on a particular plot of land, with the landowner providing the tools, seed, and work animals. At the end of the year the crop was split, perhaps one-third going to the sharecropper and two-thirds to the owner.

Sharecropping shaped the economy of the postwar South by transforming the production and marketing of cash crops. Landowners broke up their plantations into family-sized plots, worked by sharecroppers in family units with no direct supervision. Each sharecropping family established its own relationship with local merchants to sell crops and buy supplies. Merchants became crucial to the southern credit system, because most southern banks could not meet the banking standards established by Congress during the Civil War. Storekeepers, usually the only people who could extend credit to sharecroppers, provided sharecroppers with food, fertilizer, animal feed, and other provisions during the year until the crop was harvested.

These developments had important consequences for white small farmers. More merchants fanned out into up-country areas inhabited mostly by ordinary whites, areas now served by railroads sponsored by the Reconstruction legislatures. With merchants offering credit and railroads offering transportation, small farmers started to produce cash crops. Thus Reconstruction accelerated the process by which southern yeomen abandoned self-sufficient farming in favor of cash crops.

Sharecropping spread quickly among black farmers in the cotton South. By 1880, 80 percent of cotton farms had fewer than 50 acres, and the majority of those farms were operated by sharecroppers (see Maps 16–2 and 16–3). Sharecropping had several advantages for landlords. It reduced their risk when cotton prices were low and encouraged workers to increase production without costly supervision. Further, if sharecroppers changed jobs before the crop was harvested, they lost a whole year's pay. But there were also advantages for the workers. For freed people with no hope of owning their own farms, sharecropping at least rewarded their hard work. The bigger the crop, the more they earned. It gave them more independence than contract labor.

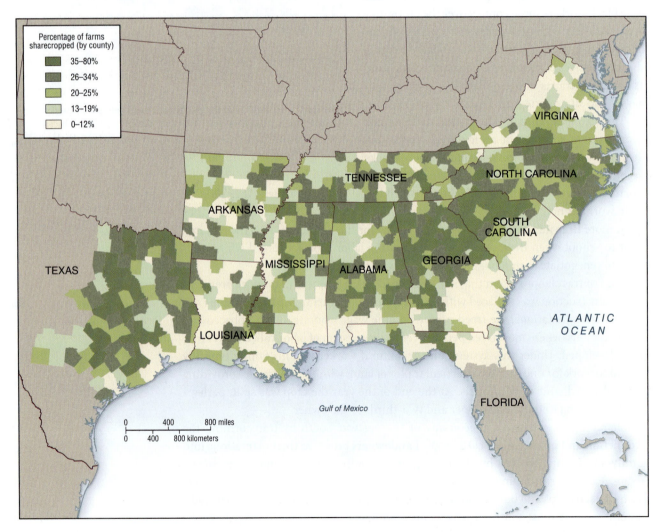

Map 16-2 Sharecropping By 1880 the sharecropping system had spread across the South. It was most common in the inland areas, where primarily cotton and tobacco plantations existed before the Civil War.

Sharecropping also allowed the freed people to work in families rather than in gangs. Freedom alone had rearranged the powers of men, women, and children within the families of former slaves. Parents gained new control over their children. They could send sons and daughters to school, or put them to work. Successful parents could give their children an important head start in life. Similarly, African American husbands gained new powers.

The marriage laws of the mid-nineteenth century that defined the husband as the head of the household were irrelevant to slaves, because their marriages had no legal standing. With emancipation, these patriarchal assumptions of American family law shaped the lives of freed men and women. Once married, women often found that their property belonged to their husbands. The sharecropping system further assumed that as head of the household the husband made the economic decisions for the entire family. Men signed most labor contracts, and most contracts assumed that the husband would take his family to work with him.

Sharecropping shaped the social system of the postwar South. It influenced the balance of power between men and women. It established the balance of power between landowners and sharecroppers. It tied the southern economy to agriculture, in

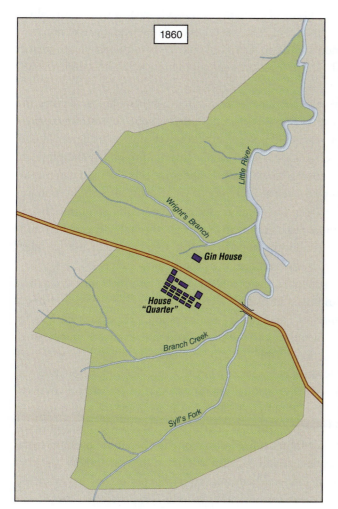
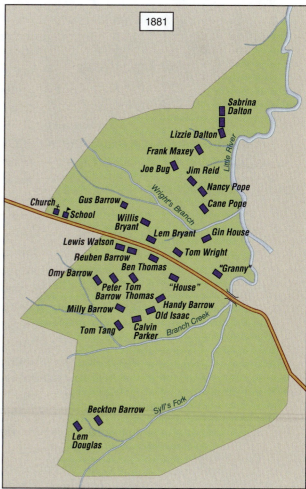

Map 16-3 The Effect of Sharecropping on Southern Plantations: The Barrow Plantation in Oglethorpe County, Georgia Sharecropping cut large estates into small landholdings worked by sharecroppers and tenants, changing the landscape of the South.

particular to cotton production, impeding the region's overall economic development. Yet amid these changes, the Republican Party was retreating from its commitment to the freed people.

The Retreat from Republican Radicalism

By the late 1860s, fractures in the Republican coalition were weakening the party's commitment to radical Reconstruction. By 1868, the Republicans were presenting themselves as the party of moderation. The success of this appeal brought the last major achievements of Reconstruction.

The Impeachment and Trial of Andrew Johnson

Throughout 1866 and much of 1867, President Johnson waged a relentless campaign against Congress and the radicals. Inevitably, this conflict led to a struggle over control of the military in the South. The First Reconstruction Act placed the entire South under direct military power. The Freedmen's Bureau was a branch of the US Army. Judicial authority was vested in the provost marshals. The military also oversaw voter registration. But as the commander in chief of the military, Johnson removed dozens of Freedmen's Bureau officials who enforced the Civil Rights Act of 1866. He replaced Republican provost marshals with men hostile to Congress and contemptuous of the former slaves. In short, Johnson went out of his way to undermine the will of Congress.

Impeachment Ticket Congressmen were besieged with requests for these tickets to the Senate gallery by constituents who wanted to observe the impeachment proceedings.

Radicals called for Johnson's impeachment, but moderates and conservatives resisted. Instead, Congress hoped to restrain the president by refining the Reconstruction Acts and by using the Tenure of Office Act of March 2, 1867. This act prohibited the president from removing officials whose appointments required congressional approval, such as Secretary of War Edwin M. Stanton, who was sympathetic to the Republicans. A related statute required that all presidential orders to the military pass through General Ulysses S. Grant. Republicans hoped that this would prevent the president from removing military officials who enforced the Reconstruction Acts.

Congress's actions only provoked the president. In his veto messages and public pronouncements Johnson indulged in blatant racist pandering. He played on fears of "amalgamation," "miscegenation," and racial "degeneration." He expressed fear for the safety of white women, when the evidence suggested that black women were most in danger. In the off-year elections of 1867, northern Democrats played the race card successfully. Democratic victories erased many of the Republican gains of 1866 and inspired the president to defy congressional restraints. As a deliberate provocation, Johnson asked Secretary of War Stanton to resign on August 5, 1867. Stanton refused, and the president appointed General Grant as interim secretary of war. Stanton would not budge, so in February 1868 Johnson fired him. For this the House of Representatives voted to impeach the president and put him on trial in the Senate.

For all the animosity that Johnson had aroused by his obnoxious behavior, the senators trying him took their job seriously. Many were concerned that the Tenure of Office Act, which Johnson was accused of violating, was in fact unconstitutional. Others wondered whether his technical breach of the law was serious enough to warrant his removal from office. These and other doubts, along with Johnson's promise of good behavior in the future, led the Senate to acquit the president by a single vote.

Republicans Become the Party of Moderation

While Andrew Johnson was on trial in the Senate, voters in Michigan voted overwhelmingly to reject a new state constitution that granted blacks the right to vote. Coming on the heels of Democratic victories in 1867, the Michigan results were read by Republicans as a rejection of radical Reconstruction.

During the 1868 elections, Republicans repudiated the radicals' demand for nationwide black suffrage, arguing that the black vote was a uniquely southern solution to a uniquely southern problem. The northern states should be free to decide this issue for themselves. Congress readmitted six southern states to the Union, demonstrating that Republican policies had restored law and order to the South. By nominating General Ulysses Grant as their presidential candidate, the Republicans confirmed their retreat from radicalism. "Let Us Have Peace" was Grant's campaign slogan.

By contrast, the Democrats nominated Horatio Seymour, who ran a vicious campaign of race-baiting. The Democratic platform denounced the Reconstruction Acts and promised to restore white rule to the South. Seymour suggested that a Democratic president might nullify the governments organized under congressional Reconstruction. Whereas the Republicans promised order and stability, the Democrats seemed to promise continued disruption. Northern fears were confirmed by the election violence that swept the South, incited by southern Democrats to keep black voters from the polls.

> **Question:** Where did you come from?
> **Answer:** I came from Winston County.
> **Question:** What occasioned your coming here?
> **Answer:** I got run by the Ku-Klux. . . .
> **Question:** What did they do to you?
> **Answer:** . . . They surrounded me in the floor and tore my shirt off. They got me out on the floor; some had me by the legs and some by the arms and the neck and anywhere, just like dogs string out a coon, and they took me out to the big road before my gate and whipped me until I couldn't move or holler or do nothing, but just lay there like a log, and every lick they hit me I grunted just like a mule when he is stalled fast and whipped. . . .
> **Question:** Did they tell you they whipped you because you were a radical?
> **Answer:** They told me, "God damn you, when you meet a white man in the road lift your hat; I'll learn you, God damn you, that you are a nigger, and not to be going about like you thought yourself a white man."
>
> CONGRESSIONAL TESTIMONY OF WILLIAM COLEMAN,
> Macon, Mississippi, November 6, 1871

The Ku Klux Klan, which systematically intimidated potential black voters, was one of several secretive organizations dedicated to the violent overthrow of radical Reconstruction and the restoration of white supremacy. They included the Knights of the White Camelia, the Red Shirts, and the Night Riders. In addition to harassing and attacking African Americans, these organizations worked in the main to restore the political power of the Democratic Party in the South. They intimidated white Republicans, burned homes of black families, and lynched African Americans who showed signs of political activism. In 1868 the Ku Klux Klan served as the paramilitary arm of the southern Democratic Party.

AMERICA AND THE WORLD

>> Reconstructing America's Foreign Policy

Before the Civil War, Republicans associated expansionism with slave power and the Democratic Party. But with the triumph of nationalism, the Republicans equated overseas expansion with the spread of liberty. In 1867 Secretary of State William Seward negotiated the purchase of Alaska from Russia. The acquisition ignited expansionist dreams of eventual US control of all of North America, including Canada and Mexico, and "all the West Indian Islands."

The administration was equally adroit in its negotiations with Great Britain over the settlement of the so-called Alabama claims. In 1872 the English accepted responsibility for having helped equip the Confederate navy during the Civil War and agreed to pay over $15 million for damage to American shipping by the *Alabama* and other southern warships built in England.

In 1870, a diverse coalition came together to support the annexation of the island nation of Santo Domingo, now the Dominican Republic. The Grant administration strongly supported the treaty, and Republicans who had once objected to any scheme associated with slavery now endorsed annexation. It would, they claimed, allow "our neighbors to join with us in the blessings of our free institutions." Thus the abolition of slavery in the United States was said to have purified the motives for American expansion. Even Frederick Douglass endorsed the annexation of Santo Domingo as a way to help the island's inhabitants rise out of their grinding poverty. But Grant's aggressive foreign policy was not uncontested. Grant tried to bulldoze the treaty through Congress but was thwarted by Senator Charles Sumner of Massachusetts, the powerful chairman of the Foreign Relations Committee. Sumner took a principled stance against imperial ventures in general, but he was particularly concerned with protecting the independence of the black republic of Haiti, which shared the island with Santo Domingo. A handful of Republicans, including Carl Schurz and Oliver P. Morton, also opposed the treaty, but most of the party sided with Grant. Yet Sumner succeeded in having the treaty rejected, by a 28–28 tie vote, thanks to the opposition of Senate Democrats. They opposed annexation for racist reasons: they objected to incorporating into the United States an island populated by dark-skinned peoples of an inferior race. The prewar alignments on expansionism were reversed by the Civil War. Republicans spearheaded American imperialism, and Democrats largely opposed it.

As a means of restoring white supremacy, the Klan's strategy of violence backfired. During a wave of disgust that swept across the North, the Republicans regained control of the White House, along with 25 of the 33 state legislatures, and quickly seized the opportunity to preserve the achievements of Reconstruction.

The Republicans reinforced their moderate image by attempting to restore law and order in the South. Congressional hearings produced vivid evidence of the Klan's violent efforts to suppress the black vote. Congress responded with a series of Enforcement Acts designed to "enforce" the recently enacted Fifteenth Amendment (see "The Fifteenth Amendment and Nationwide African American Suffrage," following). After some hesitation, the Grant administration used the new laws to prosecute the Klan and diminish political violence throughout the South. As a result, the 1872 presidential elections were relatively free of disruption.

The Ku Klux Klan The Klan was one of a number of racist vigilante groups trying to restore the Democratic Party to power in the postwar South.

Reconstructing the North

Although Reconstruction was aimed primarily at the South, the North was affected as well, especially by the struggle over the black vote. The transformation of the North was an important chapter in the history of Reconstruction.

The Fifteenth Amendment and Nationwide African American Suffrage

Before the Civil War, blacks in the North were segregated in theaters, restaurants, cemeteries, hotels, streetcars, ferries, and schools. Most northern blacks could not vote, either because they were expressly denied the privilege or because of discriminatory property requirements that blacks alone were required to meet. The Civil War galvanized the northern black community to fight racial discrimination, with some success. In 1863 California removed the ban on black testimony in criminal courts. Two years later Illinois did the same. During the war, many northern cities abolished streetcar segregation. But faced with black voting, northern whites retained their racial prejudices. In 1865 voters in three northern states (Connecticut, Wisconsin, and Minnesota) rejected constitutional amendments to enfranchise African American men. In 1867, even as Congress was imposing the black vote on the South, black suffrage was defeated in Ohio, Minnesota, and Kansas.

The shocking electoral violence of 1868 persuaded many northerners that, given the chance, southern whites would quickly strip blacks of the right to vote. In Iowa and Minnesota, voters finally approved black suffrage. In 1869 Republicans passed the Fifteenth Amendment to the Constitution, which prohibited the use of "race, color, or previous condition of servitude" to disqualify voters anywhere in the United States. By outlawing voter discrimination on the basis of race, the Fifteenth Amendment protected the most radical achievement of congressional Reconstruction.

The Fifteenth Amendment brought Reconstruction to the North by overturning state laws that discriminated against black voters. In addition, Congress required ratification of the amendment in those southern states still to be readmitted to the Union. Virginia, Mississippi, and Texas did so and rejoined the Union. On March 30, 1870, the Fifteenth Amendment became part of the Constitution. For the first time, racial criteria for voting were banned everywhere in the United States, North as well as South.

Women and Suffrage

The issue of black voting divided northern radicals, especially feminists and abolitionists, who had long been allies in the struggle for emancipation. Signs of trouble appeared as early as May 1863 at the convention of the Woman's National Loyal League in New York City. The League had been organized to assist in defeating the slave South. One of the convention's resolutions declared that "there never can be a true peace in this Republic until the civil and political rights of all citizens of African descent and all women are practically established." For some delegates, this went too far. They argued that it was inappropriate to inject the issue of women's rights into the struggle to restore the Union.

By the end of the war, radical pressure for black suffrage in addition to emancipation caused a rancorous debate among reformers. Abolitionists argued that, although they supported women's suffrage, the critical issue was the protection of the freed people of the South. This, abolitionist Wendell Phillips argued, was "the Negro's Hour." Some women's rights activists felt betrayed. For 20 years they had pressed their claims for the right to vote. They were loyal allies of the Republicans and were now abandoned by them. It would be better, Elizabeth Cady Stanton argued, to press for "a vote based on intelligence and education for black and white, man and woman." Because voting rights based on "intelligence and education" would have excluded virtually all the freed slaves, as well as the working-class Irish, Germans, and Chinese, Stanton's remarks revealed a strain of elitism that further alienated abolitionists.

Not all feminists agreed with Stanton, and as racist violence erupted in the South, abolitionists argued that black suffrage was more urgent than women's suffrage. "I have always championed women's right to vote," argued Frederick Douglass, "but it will be seen that the present claim for the negro is one of the most urgent necessity."

Stanton was unmoved by such arguments. Supporters of women's suffrage opposed the Fifteenth Amendment on the grounds that it subjected elite, educated women to the rule of base and illiterate males, especially immigrants and blacks. Abolitionists favored universal suffrage, not the "educated" suffrage that Stanton was calling for. The breach between reformers weakened the coalition of radicals pushing to maintain a vigorous Reconstruction policy in the South.

Elizabeth Cady Stanton A leading advocate of women's rights, Stanton was angered when Congress gave African American men the vote without also giving it to women.

The Rise and Fall of the National Labor Union

Inspired by the radicalism of the Civil War and Reconstruction, industrial workers across the North organized dozens of craft unions, Eight-Hour Leagues, and workingmen's associations, all designed to protect northern workers who were overworked and underpaid. They called strikes, initiated consumer boycotts, and formed consumer cooperatives. In 1867 and 1868, workers in New York and Massachusetts campaigned to enact laws restricting the workday to eight hours. Soon, workers began electing their own candidates to state legislatures.

Founded in 1866, the National Labor Union (NLU) was the first significant postwar effort to organize all "working people" into a national union. William Sylvis, an iron molder, founded the NLU and became its president in 1868. He denied any "harmony of interests" between workers and capitalists. On the contrary, every wage earner was at war with every capitalist, whose "profits" robbed working people of the fruits of their labor.

Under Sylvis's direction the NLU advocated a wide range of political reforms, not just bread-and-butter issues. Sylvis believed that through organization American workers could take the "first step toward competence and independence." He argued for a doubling of the average worker's wages. He supported voting rights for blacks and women. Nevertheless, after a miserable showing in the elections of 1872, the NLU fell apart. By then, Reconstruction in the South was also ending.

> Within the last seven years we have passed through the most gigantic war the world ever saw. A rebellion such as no other government could have successfully combated. . . . No man in America rejoiced more than I at the downfall of negro slavery. But when the shackles fell from the limbs of those four millions of blacks, it did not make them **free** men; it simply transferred them from one condition of slavery to another; it placed them upon the platform of the white workingmen, and made all slaves together. I do not mean that freeing the negro enslaved the white; I mean that we were slaves before, always have been, and that that abolition of the right of property in man added four millions of black slaves to the white slaves of the country. We are now all one family of slaves together; and the labor reform movement is a second emancipation proclamation.
>
> SPEECH BY WILLIAM SYLVIS,
> September 16, 1868

The End of Reconstruction

National events had as much to do with the end of Reconstruction as did events in the South. Reacting to a nationwide outbreak of political corruption in the late 1860s and 1870s, influential northern liberals, supporters of Reconstruction, abandoned the Republican Party in disgust in 1872. The end of Reconstruction finally came after electoral violence corrupted the 1876 elections. Republican politicians in Washington, DC, responded with a sordid political bargain that came to symbolize the end of an era.

Corruption as a National Problem

Postwar America witnessed an extraordinary display of public dishonesty. Democrats were as prone to thievery as Republicans. Northern swindlers looted the public treasuries. In the South, both black and white legislators took bribes. Corruption, it seemed, was endemic to postwar American politics.

If corruption was everywhere in the late 1860s and 1870s, it was largely because there were more opportunities for it than ever before. The Civil War and Reconstruction had swollen government budgets. Never before was government so active in collecting taxes and disbursing vast sums for the public good. Under the circumstances, many government officials traded bribes for votes, embezzled public funds, or used insider knowledge to defraud taxpayers.

The federal government set the tone. In the most notorious case, the directors of the Union Pacific Railroad set up a dummy corporation called the Crédit Mobilier, awarded it phony contracts, and protected it from inquiry by bribing influential congressmen. The Grant administration was eventually smeared with scandal as well. Although personally honest, the president surrounded himself with rich nobodies and army buddies rather than respected statesmen. Grant's own private secretary was exposed as a member of the "Whiskey Ring," a cabal of distillers and revenue agents who cheated the government out of millions of tax dollars every year.

State and city governments in the North were no less corrupt. Wealthy businessmen curried favor with politicians whose votes would determine where a railroad would be built and which land would be allocated for rights of way. State officials accepted gifts, received salaries, and sat on the boards of corporations directly affected by their votes. Municipalities awarded lucrative contracts to build schools, parks, libraries, water and sewer systems, and mass-transportation networks, creating temptations for corruption. The Tweed Ring alone bilked New York City out of tens of millions of dollars. By these standards, the corruption of the southern Reconstruction legislatures was relatively small.

But corruption in the South had particular significance for Reconstruction. Southern Republicans of modest means depended heavily on the money they earned as public officials. They were responsible for the collection of unusually high taxes and for economic development projects. For many, the lure of corruption proved overwhelming. The Republican governor of Louisiana grew rich while in office by "exacting tribute" from railroads seeking state favors. Corruption on a vast scale implied petty corruption as well: some legislators sold their votes for as little as $200.

Opponents of Reconstruction often used attacks on corruption to undermine Republican policies. Their strategy helped galvanize opposition, destroying Republican hopes of attracting white voters. Finally, corruption in the South stirred a backlash against active government nationwide, weakening northern support for Reconstruction. The intellectual substance of this backlash was provided by influential liberal Republicans, many of whom had strongly supported radical Reconstruction.

William Marcy Tweed The boss of New York's notoriously corrupt "Tweed Ring" was parodied by the great cartoonist Thomas Nast. His portrayal of the bloated public official became an enduring symbol of governmental corruption.

Liberal Republicans Revolt

The label "liberal Republicans" covered a small but influential group of intellectuals, politicians, publishers, and businessmen from the northern elite who were disgusted by postwar corruption and discouraged by the failure of radical Reconstruction to bring peace to the South.

Liberal philosophy was deeply suspicious of democracy. Liberals argued that any government beholden to the interests of the ignorant masses was doomed to corruption. They believed that public servants should be chosen on the basis of intelligence, as measured by civil service examinations, rather than by patronage appointments through corrupt party machines. To liberals, party politics was the enemy of good government.

Liberals grew increasingly alienated from the Republican Party and from President Grant. Above all, they resented the fact that the Republican Party had changed as its idealistic commitment to free labor waned and its radical vanguard disappeared. To emerging Republican leaders, getting and holding office had become an end in itself.

As Republicans lost their identity as moral crusaders, liberal reformers proposed a new vision of their own. In 1872 they supported Horace Greeley as the Democratic presidential candidate. The liberal plank in the Democratic platform committed the party to universal equality before the law, the integrity of the Union, and support for the Thirteenth, Fourteenth, and Fifteenth Amendments. At the same time, liberals demanded "the immediate and absolute removal of all disabilities" imposed on the South, as well as a "universal amnesty" for ex-Confederates. Finally, the liberals declared their belief that "local self-government" would "guard the rights of all citizens more securely than any centralized power." In effect, the liberals were demanding the end of federal efforts to protect the former slaves.

In the long run, the liberal view would prevail, but not with the voters of 1872. The liberals' biggest liability was their presidential candidate. Horace Greeley's reputation and Republican background were too much, and Democrats refused to vote for him. Grant was easily reelected, but Republicans saw the returns as evidence that Reconstruction was becoming a political liability.

The 1874 elections confirmed the lesson. Democrats made sweeping gains across the North, and an ideological stalemate developed. For a generation, neither party would clearly dominate American politics. The Republicans would take no more risks in support of Reconstruction.

During his second term, Grant did little to protect black voters from violence in the South. Not even the Civil Rights Act of 1875 undid the impression of waning Republican zeal. Ostensibly designed to prohibit racial discrimination in public places, the act lacked enforcement provisions. The bill's most important clause, prohibiting segregated schools, was eliminated from the final version. Southern states ignored even this watered-down statute, and in 1883 the Supreme Court declared the last major piece of Reconstruction lawmaking unconstitutional.

A Depression and a Deal "Redeem" the South

Angered by corruption and high taxes, white voters in the South answered the Democratic Party's appeal for restoration of white supremacy. As the number of white Republicans fell, the number of black Republicans holding office in the South increased, even as the Grant administration backed away from civil rights. But the persistence of black officeholders only reinforced the Democrats' determination to "redeem" their states from Republican rule. Democrats had taken control of Virginia in 1869, North Carolina in 1870, Georgia in 1871, and Texas in 1873. Then panic struck.

In September 1873, America's premier financial institution, Jay Cooke & Company, went bankrupt after overextending itself on investments in the Northern Pacific Railroad. Within weeks, hundreds of banks and thousands of businesses went bankrupt.

The country sank into a depression that lasted five years. Unemployment rose to 14 percent as corporations slashed wages. To protect their incomes, railroad workers tried to organize a nationwide union and attempted to strike several times. The strikes failed.

As the nation turned its attention to labor unrest and economic depression, the Republican Party's commitment to Reconstruction all but disappeared. Democrats regained control of the governments of Alabama and Arkansas in 1874. In the few southern states where black Republicans clung to political power, white "redeemers" used violence to overthrow the last remnants of Reconstruction.

Mississippi established the model in 1875, and it became known as "the Mississippi Plan." Confident that Washington would no longer interfere in the South, Democrats launched an all-out campaign to regain control of the state government. Crude appeals to white supremacy reduced the dwindling number of scalawags. To defeat black Republicans, White Leagues used violence and intimidation to keep blacks from the polls. Republicans were beaten, forced to flee, and in several cases murdered. Washington ignored African American pleas for protection. In the end, enough blacks were kept from the polls and enough scalawags voted their racial prejudices to put the Democrats in power. Mississippi was "redeemed."

The tactics used in Mississippi were repeated elsewhere the following year, with dramatic consequences for the presidential election of 1876. Amidst a serious economic depression, and with an electorate tired of Reconstruction, the Democrats stood a good chance of winning the presidency. The Democratic candidate, Samuel J. Tilden, won 250,000 more votes than the Republican, Rutherford B. Hayes (see Map 16–4). But electoral fraud in South Carolina, Louisiana, Florida, and Oregon threw the results into doubt.

If all of the electoral votes from those states went to Hayes, he would win, but if even a single electoral vote went to Tilden, he would win, the first Democrat to win the presidency in 20 years. The outcome was determined by an electoral commission with a Republican majority, which awarded every disputed electoral vote to the Republican Hayes, casting doubt on the legitimacy of his presidency. What he did shortly after taking office suggested that he had won thanks to a "compromise" with the Democrats to end Reconstruction in the South. There is no proof that such a deal was ever actually made. Nevertheless, Hayes ordered the federal troops guarding the Republican statehouses in South Carolina and Louisiana to leave. This order marked the formal end of military occupation of the South and the symbolic end of Reconstruction. By late 1877, every southern state had been redeemed by the Democrats.

The following year the Supreme Court began to issue rulings that further undid the achievements of Reconstruction. In *Hall v. DeCuir* (1878), the Supreme Court invalidated a Louisiana law prohibiting racial segregation on public transportation. In 1882, the justices declared unconstitutional a federal law protecting southern African Americans against racially motivated murders and assaults. More important, in the Civil Rights Cases of 1883, the Supreme Court

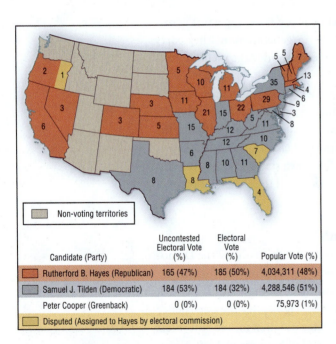

Candidate (Party)	Uncontested Electoral Vote (%)	Electoral Vote (%)	Popular Vote (%)
Rutherford B. Hayes (Republican)	165 (47%)	185 (50%)	4,034,311 (48%)
Samuel J. Tilden (Democratic)	184 (53%)	184 (32%)	4,288,546 (51%)
Peter Cooper (Greenback)	0 (0%)	0 (0%)	75,973 (1%)
Disputed (Assigned to Hayes by electoral commission)			

Map 16–4 The Presidential Election, 1876 In 1876 the Democratic presidential candidate, Samuel Tilden, won the popular vote but was denied the presidency because the Republicans who controlled Congress chose to interpret voting irregularities in Louisiana, South Carolina, Oregon, and Florida in a way that gave their candidate, Rutherford B. Hayes, all of the disputed electoral votes.

DEBATING HISTORY

>> The Nature of Reconstruction

I n 1865, Congress passed the Thirteenth Amendment requiring state abolition as a prerequisite for readmission to the Union. Slaves were no longer property, but beyond that lay difficult questions about freed people's civil and political rights. The leniency of presidential Reconstruction (1865–1867) emboldened uncompromising planters in the South. They rejected equal rights legislation and established an oppressive contract system that bound slaves to the land. Radical Republicans in Congress wrested control of Reconstruction policy, passing the Reconstruction Acts.

A Freedmen's Bureau School

These guaranteed blacks the right to due process and compelled southern states to rewrite their constitutions, among other things. The Fourteenth Amendment (1868) gave blacks citizenship; and the Fifteenth Amendment (1870) ensured the voting rights of black men. In the late 1860s and 1870s, class and race divisions undermined the Republican coalition in the South, while labor unrest in the North and political corruption in the national government sapped support for the radical goal of racial equality under the law. While most historians agree that Reconstruction failed to achieve black civil rights in the short term, they have disagreed over whether it accomplished any lasting social reform. C. Vann Woodward argued that the Republican Party never quite rallied to the cause of black equality, whereas Eric Foner found that Reconstruction achieved important safeguards for black Americans despite the brevity and limitations of the radical program.

C. VANN WOODWARD, "The Seeds of Failure in Radical Race Policy," in *New Frontiers of the American Reconstruction*, ed. Harold Hyman (Urbana: University of Illinois Press, 1966), pp. 130, 147.

[Republicans] were far from agreeing on the status, the rights, the equality, or the future of the Negro. . . . The party that emerged triumphant from the crusade to save the Union and free the slave was not in the best political and moral position to expand the rights and assure the equality of the freedman. There undoubtedly did emerge eventually an organization determined to overthrow Andrew Johnson's states'-rights, white-supremacy policies and to take over the control of the South. But that was a different matter. On the issue of Negro equality the party remained divided, hesitant, and unsure of its purpose. The historic commitment to equality it eventually made was lacking in clarity, ambivalent in purpose, and capable of numerous interpretations. . . . [O]ne is left to wonder how much radical Reconstruction was really concerned with the South and how much with the party needs of the Republicans in the North.

Continued

>> DEBATING HISTORY *Continued*

ERIC FONER, *Reconstruction: America's Unfinished Revolution, 1863–1877* (New York: Harper & Row, 1988), pp. 602–603.

To be sure, the era of emancipation and Republican rule did not lack enduring accomplishments. The tide of change rose and then receded, but it left behind an altered landscape. . . . If blacks failed to achieve the economic independence envisioned in the aftermath of the Civil War, Reconstruction closed off even more oppressive alternatives than the Redeemers' New South. . . . [W]hether measured by the dreams inspired by emancipation or the more limited goals of securing blacks' rights as citizens and free laborers, and establishing an enduring Repub-

lican presence in the South, Reconstruction can only be judged a failure. . . . [Yet p]erhaps the remarkable thing about Reconstruction was not that it failed, but that it was attempted at all and survived as long as it did.

Questions

1. What standards do these historians use to judge Reconstruction, and how do those standards affect their respective arguments?

2. What factors might explain the differences in these two historians' arguments about Reconstruction?

---

declared that the Fourteenth Amendment did not pertain to discriminatory practices by private persons. The Supreme Court thus completed the retreat from Reconstruction.

Conclusion

Inspired by an idealized vision of a society based on equal rights and free labor, Republicans expected emancipation to transform the South. Freed from the shackles of the slave power, the region would soon become a shining example of democracy and prosperity. If the results were less than Republicans expected, the achievements of Reconstruction were still impressive. Across the South, African American men and women carved out a space in which their families could live more freely than before. Black men by the tens of thousands elected to office some of the most democratic state legislatures of the nineteenth century. Thousands more black workers repudiated an objectionable contract-labor system in favor of a new compromise known as sharecropping. Furthermore, Reconstruction added three important amendments to the Constitution that transformed civil rights and electoral laws throughout the nation.

Nevertheless, the Republicans quickly washed their hands of Reconstruction. They left southern blacks unprotected in a hostile world. Sharecropping offered blacks little hope of real economic independence. Democratic redeemers excluded blacks from the

>> TIME LINE

▼1863
Lincoln's Proclamation of Amnesty and Reconstruction

▼1864
Wade-Davis Bill

▼1865
General Sherman's Special Field Order No. 15
Freedmen's Bureau established
Lincoln's second inaugural

Lincoln assassinated; Andrew Johnson becomes president
General Howard's Circular 13
President Johnson orders the Freedmen's Bureau to return confiscated lands to former owners
Joint Committee on Reconstruction established by Congress

▼1866
Congress renews Freedmen's Bureau; Johnson vetoes renewal bill

Civil Rights Act vetoed by Johnson
Congress overrides presidential veto of Civil Rights Act
Congress passes Fourteenth Amendment
Congress passes another Freedmen's Bureau Bill over Johnson's veto
Republicans sweep midterm elections

substance of power. Tired of Reconstruction, Americans turned their attention to the new problems of urban, industrial America.

Who, What

Nathaniel Banks   554

John Dennett   551

U. S. Grant   558

Horace Greeley   577

Oliver Otis Howard   556

Andrew Johnson   557

Elizabeth Cady Stanton   574

William Sylvis   575

Black Codes   557

Fifteenth Amendment   573

Fourteenth Amendment   562

Freedmen's Bureau   556

"Liberal" Republicans   576

National Labor Union   574

Redemption   578

Sharecropping   553

Ten Percent Plan   554

Tenure of Office Act   570

Review Questions

1. What made congressional Reconstruction "radical"?

2. How did conditions for the readmission of states into the Union change over time?

3. How did Reconstruction change the South?

4. How did Reconstruction change the North?

5. What were the major factors that brought Reconstruction to an end?

Critical-Thinking Questions

1. Compare and contrast wartime Reconstruction, presidential Reconstruction, and congressional (radical) Reconstruction. What were the key differences between the three phases?

2. How critical was the failure of land redistribution for blacks? Was sharecropping an acceptable substitute for achieving economic freedom? Why or why not?

3. In what ways did the tactics of white supremacists in this period end up hurting their own cause?

For further review materials and resource information, please visit www.oup.com/us/ofthepeople

▼**1867**
First and Second Reconstruction Acts
Tenure of Office Act

▼**1868**
Johnson fires Secretary of War Stanton
House of Representatives impeaches Johnson
Senate trial of Johnson begins
Acquittal of Johnson
Fourteenth Amendment ratified
Ulysses S. Grant wins presidential election

▼**1869**
Congress passes Fifteenth Amendment

▼**1870**
Fifteenth Amendment ratified

▼**1872**
"Liberal Republicans" leave their party
Grant reelected

▼**1873**
Financial "panic" sets off depression

▼**1875**
"Mississippi Plan" succeeds
Civil Rights Act of 1875 enacted

▼**1876**
Disputed presidential election

▼**1877**
Electoral commission awards presidency to Rutherford B. Hayes

1) Blatantly discriminatory policies such as forced labor contracts and the "Black Codes" led to the radicalization of Republican congressmen and the end of presidential Reconstruction.

2) Freed slaves never received federal land grants, but many ended up as sharecroppers and helped shape the new social and economic systems of the postwar South.

3) Tensions between the executive and legislative branches of the federal government led to the first impeachment of a president in the nation's history.

4) Over the course of Reconstruction, the Republican Party transitioned from a radical platform of racial and social equality to a slow abandonment of those aims in the face of economic depression, labor unrest, and changes in public opinion.

5) Widespread electoral violence toward blacks by southern white supremacists persuaded northern whites to set aside their long-standing resistance to black suffrage and support the Fifteenth Amendment.

Wartime Reconstruction

Presidential Reconstruction, 1865–1867

Congressional Reconstruction

The Retreat from Republican Radicalism

Reconstructing the North

The End of Reconstruction

CHAPTER 16

RECONSTRUCTING A NATION

1865–1877

EVENTS

Experiments with Free Labor in the Lower Mississippi Valley The plantations of the Sea Islands and southern Louisiana served as the earliest "rehearsals" for Reconstruction and sparked political controversy.

Lincoln's Ten Percent Plan Versus the Wade-Davis Bill Lincoln and congressional radicals debated the conditions under which Confederate states would be allowed to return to the Union.

The Freed People's Dream of Owning Land Former slaves carved out new communities and institutions, reunited with family members, and pursued land ownership.

The Political Economy of Contract Labor Free southern blacks were forced to sign labor contracts and adhere to new laws that severely restricted their civil rights.

Resistance to Presidential Reconstruction Blacks resisted the contract labor system and faced violent reprisals from southern whites.

Congress Clashes with the President Republican moderates in Congress grew more radical and challenged President Johnson's Reconstruction agenda.

Origins of the Fourteenth Amendment Congress passed the Civil Rights Act over Johnson's veto and proposed a constitutional amendment granting citizenship to all males born in the United States, regardless of color.

Origins of the Black Vote A more radicalized Congress passed two Reconstruction Acts and secured black suffrage in most of the South, again over Johnson's veto.

Radical Reconstruction in the South Southern Republicans launched an experiment in interracial democracy in the South.

Achievements and Failures of Radical Government Southern Republicans were unable to unite the diverse interests of their constituents but still boasted several important achievements.

The Political Economy of Sharecropping The rapid emergence of sharecropping reshaped the social, economic, and physical landscape of the postwar South.

The Impeachment and Trial of Andrew Johnson Tensions between Congress and the president resulted in impeachment and a trial in which Johnson was acquitted.

Republicans Become the Party of Moderation Facing opposition, Republicans transitioned into a more moderate position and nominated Ulysses S. Grant as their presidential candidate.

The Fifteenth Amendment and Nationwide African American Suffrage The Fifteenth Amendment brought Reconstruction to the North by overturning state laws that discriminated against black male voters.

Women and Suffrage Black suffrage left some women's rights activists feeling betrayed, and created tensions among radicals.

The Rise and Fall of the National Labor Union Postwar workers formed a national union, but it quickly fell apart after a miserable showing in the elections of 1872.

Corruption as a National Problem Corruption at the local, state, and federal levels—although widespread in both parties—allowed opponents of Reconstruction to undermine Republican policies.

Liberal Republicans Revolt A small but influential group of Republicans pushed for an end to federal protection of former slaves.

A Depression and a Deal "Redeem" the South Labor unrest, economic depression, and the end of military occupation severely diminished Republican commitment to Reconstruction and helped Democrats regain control of every southern state.

Appendix A

Historical Documents

The Declaration of Independence

When in the course of human events, it becomes necessary for one people to dissolve the political bands which have connected them with another, and to assume, among the powers of the earth, the separate and equal station to which the Laws of Nature and of Nature's God entitle them, a decent respect to the opinions of mankind requires that they should declare the causes which impel them to the separation.

We hold these truths to be self-evident, that all men are created equal, that they are endowed by their Creator with certain unalienable Rights, that among these are life, liberty and the pursuit of happiness. That to secure these rights, governments are instituted among men, deriving their just powers from the consent of the governed; that whenever any form of government becomes destructive of these ends, it is the right of the people to alter or to abolish it, and to institute new Government, laying its foundation on such principles and organizing its powers in such form, as to them shall seem most likely to effect their safety and happiness. Prudence, indeed, will dictate that Governments long established should not be changed for light and transient causes; and, accordingly, all experience hath shown, that mankind are more disposed to suffer, while evils are sufferable, than to right themselves by abolishing the forms to which they are accustomed. But when a long train of abuses and usurpations, pursuing invariably the same object evinces a design to reduce them under absolute despotism, it is their right, it is their duty, to throw off such government, and to provide new guards for their future security. Such has been the patient sufferance of these colonies; and such is now the necessity which constrains them to alter their former systems of government. The history of the present King of Great Britain is a history of repeated injuries and usurpations, all having in direct object the establishment of an absolute tyranny over these States. To prove this, let facts be submitted to a candid world:

He has refused his assent to laws, the most wholesome and necessary for the public good.

He has forbidden his governors to pass laws of immediate and pressing importance, unless suspended in their operation till his assent should be obtained; and, when so suspended, he has utterly neglected to attend to them.

He has refused to pass other laws for the accommodation of large districts of people, unless those people would relinquish the right of representation in the legislature, a right inestimable to them and formidable to tyrants only.

He has called together legislative bodies at places unusual, uncomfortable, and distant from the depository of their public records, for the sole purpose of fatiguing them into compliance with his measures.

He has dissolved representative houses repeatedly, for opposing with manly firmness his invasions on the rights of the people.

He has refused for a long time, after such dissolutions, to cause others to be elected; whereby the legislative powers, incapable of annihilation, have returned to the People at large for their exercise; the State remaining in the mean time exposed to all the dangers of invasion from without, and convulsions within.

He has endeavored to prevent the population of these States; for that purpose obstructing the laws for naturalization of foreigners; refusing to pass others to encourage their migrations hither, and raising the conditions of new appropriations of lands.

He has obstructed the administration of justice, by refusing his assent to laws for establishing judiciary powers.

He has made judges dependent on his will alone, for the tenure of their offices, and the amount and payment of their salaries.

He has erected a multitude of new offices, and sent hither swarms of officers to harass our people, and eat out their substance.

He has kept among us, in times of peace, standing armies without the consent of our legislatures.

He has affected to render the Military independent of, and superior to, the civil power.

He has combined with others to subject us to a jurisdiction foreign to our constitution and unacknowledged by our laws; giving his assent to their acts of pretended legislation:

For quartering large bodies of armed troops among us;

For protecting them, by a mock trial, from punishment for any murders which they should commit on the inhabitants of these States;

For cutting off our trade with all parts of the world;

For imposing taxes on us without our Consent;

For depriving us, in many cases, of the benefits of Trial by Jury;

For transporting us beyond Seas to be tried for pretended offences;

For abolishing the free System of English Laws in a neighbouring Province, establishing therein an Arbitrary government, and enlarging its Boundaries so as to render it at once an example and fit instrument for introducing the same absolute rule into these colonies;

For taking away our charters, abolishing our most valuable laws, and altering fundamentally the forms of our governments;

For suspending our own legislatures, and declaring themselves invested with power to legislate for us in all cases whatsoever.

He has abdicated government here, by declaring us out of his protection and waging war against us.

He has plundered our seas, ravaged our coasts, burnt our towns, and destroyed the lives of our people.

He is at this time transporting large armies of foreign mercenaries to complete the works of death, desolation and tyranny, already begun with circumstances of cruelty and perfidy scarcely paralleled in the most barbarous ages, and totally unworthy the head of a civilized nation.

He has constrained our fellow citizens taken captive on the high seas to bear arms against their country, to become the executioners of their friends and brethren, or to fall themselves by their hands.

He has excited domestic insurrections amongst us, and has endeavored to bring on the inhabitants of our frontiers, the merciless Indian savages, whose known rule of warfare, is an undistinguished destruction of all ages, sexes and conditions.

In every stage of these oppressions we have petitioned for redress in the most humble terms; our repeated petitions have been answered only by repeated injury. A prince whose character is thus marked by every act which may define a tyrant, is unfit to be the ruler of a free people.

Nor have we been wanting in attentions to our British brethren. We have warned them from time to time of attempts by their legislature to extend an unwarrantable jurisdiction over us. We have reminded them of the circumstances of our emigration and settlement here. We have appealed to their native justice and magnanimity, and we have conjured them by the ties of our common kindred to disavow these usurpations, which, would inevitably interrupt our connections and correspondence. They, too, have been deaf to the voice of justice and of consanguinity. We must, therefore, acquiesce in the necessity, which denounces our separation, and hold them, as we hold the rest of mankind, enemies in war, in peace friends.

We, therefore, the representatives of the United States of America, in general Congress, assembled, appealing to the Supreme Judge of the world for the rectitude of our intentions, do, in the name, and by the authority of the good people of these colonies, solemnly publish and declare, that these united colonies are, and of right ought to be free and independent states; that they are absolved from all allegiance to the British Crown, and that all political connection between them and the state of Great Britain, is and ought to be totally dissolved; and that, as free and independent states, they have full power to levy war, conclude peace, contract alliances, establish commerce, and to do all other acts and things which independent states may of right do. And for the support of this declaration, with a firm reliance on the protection of Divine Providence, we mutually pledge to each other our lives, our fortunes and our sacred honor.

The Constitution of the United States of America

We the People of the United States, in Order to form a more perfect Union, establish Justice, insure domestic Tranquility, provide for the common defence, promote the general Welfare, and secure the Blessings of Liberty to ourselves and our Posterity, do ordain and establish this Constitution for the United States of America.

Article I

Section 1

All legislative Powers herein granted shall be vested in a Congress of the United States, which shall consist of a Senate and House of Representatives.

Section 2

The House of Representatives shall be composed of Members chosen every second Year by the People of the several States, and the Electors in each State shall have the Qualifications requisite for Electors of the most numerous Branch of the State Legislature.

No Person shall be a Representative who shall not have attained to the Age of twenty five Years, and been seven Years a Citizen of the United States, and who shall not, when elected, be an Inhabitant of that State in which he shall be chosen.

Representatives and direct Taxes shall be apportioned among the several States which may be included within this Union, according to their respective Numbers, which shall be determined by adding to the whole Number of free Persons, including those bound to Service for a Term of Years, and excluding Indians not taxed, three fifths of all other Persons. The actual Enumeration shall be made within three Years after the first Meeting of the Congress of the United States, and within every subsequent Term of ten Years, in such Manner as they shall by Law direct. The Number of Representatives shall not exceed one for every thirty Thousand, but each State shall have at Least one Representative; and until such enumeration shall be made, the State of New Hampshire shall be entitled to choose three, Massachusetts eight, Rhode-Island and Providence Plantations one, Connecticut five, New York six, New Jersey four, Pennsylvania eight, Delaware one, Maryland six, Virginia ten, North Carolina five, South Carolina five, and Georgia three.

When vacancies happen in the Representation from any State, the Executive Authority thereof shall issue Writs of Election to fill such Vacancies.

The House of Representatives shall choose their Speaker and other Officers; and shall have the sole Power of Impeachment.

Section 3

The Senate of the United States shall be composed of two Senators from each State, chosen by the Legislature thereof for six Years; and each Senator shall have one Vote.

Immediately after they shall be assembled in Consequence of the first Election, they shall be divided as equally as may be into three Classes. The Seats of the Senators of the first Class shall be vacated at the Expiration of the second Year, of the second Class at the Expiration of the fourth Year, and of the third Class at the Expiration of the sixth Year, so that one third may be chosen every second Year; and if Vacancies happen by Resignation, or otherwise, during the Recess of the Legislature of any State, the Executive thereof may make temporary Appointments until the next Meeting of the Legislature, which shall then fill such Vacancies.

No Person shall be a Senator who shall not have attained to the Age of thirty Years, and been nine Years a Citizen of the United States, and who shall not, when elected, be an Inhabitant of that State for which he shall be chosen.

The Vice President of the United States shall be President of the Senate, but shall have no Vote, unless they be equally divided.

The Senate shall choose their other Officers, and also a President pro tempore, in the Absence of the Vice President, or when he shall exercise the Office of President of the United States.

The Senate shall have the sole Power to try all Impeachments. When sitting for that Purpose, they shall be on Oath or Affirmation. When the President of the United States is tried, the Chief Justice shall preside: And no Person shall be convicted without the Concurrence of two thirds of the Members present.

Judgment in Cases of Impeachment shall not extend further than to removal from Office, and disqualification to hold and enjoy any Office of honor, Trust or Profit under the United States: but the Party convicted shall nevertheless be liable and subject to Indictment, Trial, Judgment and Punishment, according to Law.

Section 4

The Times, Places and Manner of holding Elections for Senators and Representatives, shall be prescribed in each State by the Legislature thereof; but the Congress may at any time by Law make or alter such Regulations, except as to the Places of chusing Senators.

The Congress shall assemble at least once in every Year, and such Meeting shall be on the first Monday in December, unless they shall by Law appoint a different Day.

Section 5

Each House shall be the Judge of the Elections, Returns and Qualifications of its own Members, and a Majority of each shall constitute a Quorum to do Business; but a smaller Number may adjourn from day to day, and may be authorized to compel the Attendance of absent Members, in such Manner, and under such Penalties as each House may provide.

Each House may determine the Rules of its Proceedings, punish its Members for disorderly Behaviour, and, with the Concurrence of two thirds, expel a Member.

Each House shall keep a Journal of its Proceedings, and from time to time publish the same, excepting such Parts as may in their Judgment require Secrecy; and the Yeas and Nays of the Members of either House on any question shall, at the Desire of one fifth of those Present, be entered on the Journal.

Neither House, during the Session of Congress, shall, without the Consent of the other, adjourn for more than three days, nor to any other Place than that in which the two Houses shall be sitting.

Section 6

The Senators and Representatives shall receive a Compensation for their Services, to be ascertained by Law, and paid out of the Treasury of the United States. They shall in all Cases, except Treason, Felony and Breach of the Peace, be privileged from Arrest during their Attendance at the Session of their respective Houses, and in going to and returning from the same; and for any Speech or Debate in either House, they shall not be questioned in any other Place.

No Senator or Representative shall, during the Time for which he was elected, be appointed to any civil Office under the Authority of the United States, which shall have been created, or the Emoluments whereof shall have been increased during such time; and no Person holding any Office under the United States, shall be a Member of either House during his Continuance in Office.

Section 7

All Bills for raising Revenue shall originate in the House of Representatives; but the Senate may propose or concur with Amendments as on other Bills.

Every Bill which shall have passed the House of Representatives and the Senate, shall, before it become a Law, be presented to the President of the United States: If he approve he shall sign it, but if not he shall return it, with his Objections to that House in which it shall have originated, who shall enter the Objections at large on their Journal, and proceed to reconsider it. If after such Reconsideration two thirds of that House shall agree to pass the Bill, it shall be sent, together with the Objections, to the other House, by which it shall likewise be reconsidered, and if approved by two thirds of that House, it shall become a Law. But in all such Cases the Votes of both Houses shall be determined by yeas and Nays, and the Names of the Persons voting for and against the Bill shall be entered on the Journal of each House respectively. If any Bill shall not be returned by the President within ten Days (Sundays excepted) after it shall have been presented to him, the Same shall be a Law, in like Manner as if he had signed it, unless the Congress by their Adjournment prevent its Return, in which Case it shall not be a Law.

Every Order, Resolution, or Vote to which the Concurrence of the Senate and House of Representatives may be necessary (except on a question of Adjournment) shall be presented to the President of the United States; and before the Same shall take Effect, shall be approved by him, or being disapproved by him, shall be repassed by two thirds of the Senate and House of Representatives, according to the Rules and Limitations prescribed in the Case of a Bill.

Section 8

The Congress shall have Power

To lay and collect Taxes, Duties, Imposts and Excises, to pay the Debts and provide for the common Defence and general Welfare of the United States; but all Duties, Imposts and Excises shall be uniform throughout the United States;

To borrow Money on the credit of the United States;

To regulate Commerce with foreign Nations, and among the several States, and with the Indian Tribes;

To establish an uniform Rule of Naturalization, and uniform Laws on the subject of Bankruptcies throughout the United States;

To coin Money, regulate the Value thereof, and of foreign Coin, and fix the Standard of Weights and Measures;

To provide for the Punishment of counterfeiting the Securities and current Coin of the United States;

To establish Post Offices and post Roads;

To promote the Progress of Science and useful Arts, by securing for limited Times to Authors and Inventors the exclusive Right to their respective Writings and Discoveries;

To constitute Tribunals inferior to the supreme Court;

To define and punish Piracies and Felonies committed on the high Seas, and Offences against the Law of Nations;

To declare War, grant Letters of Marque and Reprisal, and make Rules concerning Captures on Land and Water;

To raise and support Armies, but no Appropriation of Money to that Use shall be for a longer Term than two Years;

To provide and maintain a Navy;

To make Rules for the Government and Regulation of the land and naval Forces;

To provide for calling forth the Militia to execute the Laws of the Union, suppress Insurrections and repel Invasions;

To provide for organizing, arming, and disciplining the Militia, and for governing such Part of them as may be employed in the Service of the United States, reserving to the States respectively, the Appointment of the Officers, and the Authority of training the Militia according to the discipline prescribed by Congress;

To exercise exclusive Legislation in all Cases whatsoever, over such District (not exceeding ten Miles square) as may, by Cession of particular States, and the Acceptance of Congress, become the Seat of the Government of the United States, and to exercise like Authority over all Places purchased by the Consent of the Legislature of the State in which the Same shall be, for the Erection of Forts, Magazines, Arsenals, dock-Yards, and other needful Buildings;—And

To make all Laws which shall be necessary and proper for carrying into Execution the foregoing Powers, and all other Powers vested by this Constitution in the Government of the United States, or in any Department or Officer thereof.

Section 9

The Migration or Importation of such Persons as any of the States now existing shall think proper to admit, shall not be prohibited by the Congress prior to the Year one thousand eight hundred and eight, but a Tax or duty may be imposed on such Importation, not exceeding ten dollars for each Person.

The Privilege of the Writ of Habeas Corpus shall not be suspended, unless when in Cases of Rebellion or Invasion the public Safety may require it.

No Bill of Attainder or ex post facto Law shall be passed.

No Capitation, or other direct, Tax shall be laid, unless in Proportion to the Census or enumeration herein before directed to be taken.

No Tax or Duty shall be laid on Articles exported from any State.

No Preference shall be given by any Regulation of Commerce or Revenue to the Ports of one State over those of another; nor shall Vessels bound to, or from, one State, be obliged to enter, clear, or pay Duties in another.

No Money shall be drawn from the Treasury, but in Consequence of Appropriations made by Law; and a regular Statement and Account of the Receipts and Expenditures of all public Money shall be published from time to time.

No Title of Nobility shall be granted by the United States: And no Person holding any Office of Profit or Trust under them, shall, without the Consent of the Congress, accept of any present, Emolument, Office, or Title, of any kind whatever, from any King, Prince, or foreign State.

Section 10

No State shall enter into any Treaty, Alliance, or Confederation; grant Letters of Marque and Reprisal; coin Money; emit Bills of Credit; make any Thing but gold and silver Coin a Tender in Payment of Debts; pass any Bill of Attainder, ex post facto Law, or Law impairing the Obligation of Contracts, or grant any Title of Nobility.

No State shall, without the Consent of the Congress, lay any Imposts or Duties on Imports or Exports, except what may be absolutely necessary for executing it's inspection Laws: and the net Produce of all Duties and Imposts, laid by any State on Imports or Exports, shall be for the Use of the Treasury of the United States; and all such Laws shall be subject to the Revision and Control of the Congress.

No State shall, without the Consent of Congress, lay any Duty of Tonnage, keep Troops, or Ships of War in time of Peace, enter into any Agreement or Compact with another State, or with a foreign Power, or engage in War, unless actually invaded, or in such imminent Danger as will not admit of delay.

Article II

Section 1

The executive Power shall be vested in a President of the United States of America. He shall hold his Office during the Term of four Years, and, together with the Vice President, chosen for the same Term, be elected, as follows:

Each State shall appoint, in such Manner as the Legislature thereof may direct, a Number of Electors, equal to the whole Number of Senators and Representatives to which the State may be entitled in the Congress: but no Senator or Representative, or Person holding an Office of Trust or Profit under the United States, shall be appointed an Elector.

The Electors shall meet in their respective States, and vote by Ballot for two Persons, of whom one at least shall not be an Inhabitant of the same State with themselves. And they shall make a List of all the Persons voted for, and of the Number of Votes for each; which List they shall sign and certify, and transmit sealed to the Seat of the Government of the United States, directed to the President of the Senate. The President of the Senate shall, in the Presence of the Senate and House of Representatives, open all the Certificates, and the Votes shall then be counted. The Person having the greatest Number of Votes shall be the President, if such Number be a Majority of the whole Number of Electors appointed; and if there be more than one who have such Majority, and have an equal Number of Votes, then the House of Representatives shall immediately choose by Ballot one of them for President; and if no Person have a Majority, then from the five highest on the List the said House shall in like Manner choose the President. But in choosing the President, the Votes shall be taken by States, the Representation from each State having one Vote; A quorum for this purpose shall consist of a Member or Members from two thirds of the States, and a Majority of all the States shall be necessary to a Choice. In every Case, after the Choice of the President, the Person having the greatest Number of Votes of the Electors shall be the Vice President. But if there should remain two or more who have equal Votes, the Senate shall choose from them by Ballot the Vice President.

The Congress may determine the Time of choosing the Electors, and the Day on which they shall give their Votes; which Day shall be the same throughout the United States.

No Person except a natural born Citizen, or a Citizen of the United States, at the time of the Adoption of this Constitution, shall be eligible to the Office of President; neither shall any Person be eligible to that Office who shall not have attained to the Age of thirty five Years, and been fourteen Years a Resident within the United States.

In Case of the Removal of the President from Office, or of his Death, Resignation, or Inability to discharge the Powers and Duties of the said Office, the Same shall devolve on the Vice President, and the Congress may by Law provide for the Case of Removal, Death, Resignation or Inability, both of the President and Vice President, declaring what Officer shall then act as President, and such Officer shall act accordingly, until the Disability be removed, or a President shall be elected.

The President shall, at stated Times, receive for his Services, a Compensation, which shall neither be increased nor diminished during the Period for which he shall have been elected, and he shall not receive within that Period any other Emolument from the United States, or any of them.

Before he enter on the Execution of his Office, he shall take the following Oath or Affirmation:—"I do solemnly swear (or affirm) that I will faithfully execute the Office of President of the United States, and will to the best of my Ability, preserve, protect and defend the Constitution of the United States."

Section 2

The President shall be Commander in Chief of the Army and Navy of the United States, and of the Militia of the several States, when called into the actual Service of the United States; he may require the Opinion, in writing, of the principal Officer in each of the executive Departments, upon any Subject relating to the Duties of their respective Offices, and he shall have Power to grant Reprieves and Pardons for Offences against the United States, except in Cases of Impeachment.

He shall have Power, by and with the Advice and Consent of the Senate, to make Treaties, provided two thirds of the Senators present concur; and he shall nominate, and by and with the Advice and Consent of the Senate, shall appoint Ambassadors, other public Ministers and Consuls, Judges of the supreme Court, and all other Officers of the United States, whose Appointments are not herein otherwise provided for, and which shall be established by Law: but the Congress may by Law vest the Appointment of such inferior Officers, as they think proper, in the President alone, in the Courts of Law, or in the Heads of Departments.

The President shall have Power to fill up all Vacancies that may happen during the Recess of the Senate, by granting Commissions which shall expire at the End of their next Session.

Section 3

He shall from time to time give to the Congress Information of the State of the Union, and recommend to their Consideration such Measures as he shall judge necessary and expedient; he may, on extraordinary Occasions, convene both Houses, or either of them, and in Case of Disagreement between them, with Respect to the Time of Adjournment, he may adjourn them to such Time as he shall think proper; he shall receive Ambassadors and other public Ministers; he shall take Care that the Laws be faithfully executed, and shall Commission all the Officers of the United States.

Section 4

The President, Vice President and all civil Officers of the United States, shall be removed from Office on Impeachment for, and Conviction of, Treason, Bribery, or other high Crimes and Misdemeanors.

Article III
Section 1

The judicial Power of the United States shall be vested in one supreme Court, and in such inferior Courts as the Congress may from time to time ordain and establish. The Judges, both of the supreme and inferior Courts, shall hold their Offices during good Behaviour, and shall, at stated Times, receive for their Services a Compensation, which shall not be diminished during their Continuance in Office.

Section 2

The judicial Power shall extend to all Cases, in Law and Equity, arising under this Constitution, the Laws of the United States, and Treaties made, or which shall be made, under their Authority;—to all Cases affecting Ambassadors, other public Ministers and Consuls;—to all Cases of admiralty and maritime Jurisdiction;—to Controversies to which the United States shall be a Party;—to Controversies between two or more States;—between a State and Citizens of another State;—between Citizens of different States;—between Citizens of the same State claiming Lands under Grants of different States, and between a State, or the Citizens thereof, and foreign States, Citizens or Subjects.

In all Cases affecting Ambassadors, other public Ministers and Consuls, and those in which a State shall be Party, the supreme Court shall have original Jurisdiction. In all the other Cases before mentioned, the supreme Court shall have appellate Jurisdiction, both as to Law and Fact, with such Exceptions, and under such Regulations as the Congress shall make.

The Trial of all Crimes, except in Cases of Impeachment, shall be by Jury; and such Trial shall be held in the State where the said Crimes shall have been committed; but when not committed within any State, the Trial shall be at such Place or Places as the Congress may by Law have directed.

Section 3

Treason against the United States, shall consist only in levying War against them, or in adhering to their Enemies, giving them Aid and Comfort. No Person shall be convicted of Treason unless on the Testimony of two Witnesses to the same overt Act, or on Confession in open Court.

The Congress shall have Power to declare the Punishment of Treason, but no Attainder of Treason shall work Corruption of Blood, or Forfeiture except during the Life of the Person attainted.

Article IV

Section 1

Full Faith and Credit shall be given in each State to the public Acts, Records, and judicial Proceedings of every other State. And the Congress may by general Laws prescribe the Manner in which such Acts, Records and Proceedings shall be proved, and the Effect thereof.

Section 2

The Citizens of each State shall be entitled to all Privileges and Immunities of Citizens in the several States.

A Person charged in any State with Treason, Felony, or other Crime, who shall flee from Justice, and be found in another State, shall on Demand of the executive Authority of the State from which he fled, be delivered up, to be removed to the State having Jurisdiction of the Crime.

No Person held to Service or Labour in one State, under the Laws thereof, escaping into another, shall, in Consequence of any Law or Regulation therein, be discharged from such Service or Labour, but shall be delivered up on Claim of the Party to whom such Service or Labour may be due.

Section 3

New States may be admitted by the Congress into this Union; but no new State shall be formed or erected within the Jurisdiction of any other State; nor any State be formed by the Junction of two or more States, or Parts of States, without the Consent of the Legislatures of the States concerned as well as of the Congress.

The Congress shall have Power to dispose of and make all needful Rules and Regulations respecting the Territory or other Property belonging to the United States; and nothing in this Constitution shall be so construed as to Prejudice any Claims of the United States, or of any particular State.

Section 4

The United States shall guarantee to every State in this Union a Republican Form of Government, and shall protect each of them against Invasion; and on Application of the Legislature, or of the Executive (when the Legislature cannot be convened), against domestic Violence.

Article V

The Congress, whenever two thirds of both Houses shall deem it necessary, shall propose Amendments to this Constitution, or, on the Application of the Legislatures of two thirds of the several States, shall call a Convention for proposing Amendments, which, in either Case, shall be valid to all Intents and Purposes, as Part of this Constitution, when ratified by the Legislatures of three fourths of the several States, or by Conventions in three fourths thereof, as the one or the other Mode of Ratification may be proposed by the Congress; Provided that no Amendment which may be made prior to the Year One thousand eight hundred and eight shall in any Manner affect the first and fourth Clauses in the Ninth Section of the first Article; and that no State, without its Consent, shall be deprived of its equal Suffrage in the Senate.

Article VI

All Debts contracted and Engagements entered into, before the Adoption of this Constitution, shall be as valid against the United States under this Constitution, as under the Confederation.

This Constitution, and the Laws of the United States which shall be made in Pursuance thereof; and all Treaties made, or which shall be made, under the Authority of the United States, shall be the supreme Law of the Land; and the Judges in every State shall be bound thereby, any Thing in the Constitution or Laws of any State to the Contrary notwithstanding.

The Senators and Representatives before mentioned, and the Members of the several State Legislatures, and all executive and judicial Officers, both of the United States and of the several States, shall be bound by Oath or Affirmation, to support this Constitution; but no religious Test shall ever be required as a Qualification to any Office or public Trust under the United States.

Article VII

The Ratification of the Conventions of nine States, shall be sufficient for the Establishment of this Constitution between the States so ratifying the Same.

The Word, "the," being interlined between the seventh and eighth Lines of the first Page, the Word "Thirty" being partly written on an Erazure in the fifteenth Line of the first Page, The Words "is tried" being interlined between the thirty second and thirty third Lines of the first Page and the Word "the" being interlined between the forty third and forty fourth Lines of the second Page.

Attest William Jackson Secretary

Done in Convention by the Unanimous Consent of the States present the Seventeenth Day of September in the Year of our Lord one thousand seven hundred and Eighty seven and of the Independence of the United States of America the Twelfth In witness whereof We have hereunto subscribed our Names,

G°. Washington
Presidt and deputy from Virginia

Delaware
Geo: Read
Gunning Bedford jun
John Dickinson
Richard Bassett
Jaco: Broom

Maryland
James McHenry
Dan of St Thos. Jenifer
Danl. Carroll

Virginia
John Blair
James Madison Jr.

North Carolina
Wm. Blount
Richd. Dobbs Spaight
Hu Williamson

South Carolina
J. Rutledge
Charles Cotesworth Pinckney
Charles Pinckney
Pierce Butler

Georgia
William Few
Abr Baldwin

New Hampshire
John Langdon
Nicholas Gilman

Massachusetts
Nathaniel Gorham
Rufus King

Connecticut
Wm. Saml. Johnson
Roger Sherman

New York
Alexander Hamilton

New Jersey
Wil: Livingston
David Brearley
Wm. Paterson
Jona: Dayton

Pennsylvania
B Franklin
Thomas Mifflin
Robt. Morris
Geo. Clymer
Thos. FitzSimons
Jared Ingersoll
James Wilson
Gouv Morris

Articles

In addition to, and Amendment of the Constitution of the United States of America, proposed by Congress, and ratified by the Legislatures of the several States, pursuant to the fifth Article of the original Constitution.

(The first ten amendments to the US Constitution were ratified December 15, 1791, and form what is known as the "Bill of Rights.")

Amendment I

Congress shall make no law respecting an establishment of religion, or prohibiting the free exercise thereof; or abridging the freedom of speech, or of the press; or the right of the people peaceably to assemble, and to petition the Government for a redress of grievances.

Amendment II

A well regulated Militia, being necessary to the security of a free State, the right of the people to keep and bear Arms, shall not be infringed.

Amendment III

No Soldier shall, in time of peace be quartered in any house, without the consent of the Owner, nor in time of war, but in a manner to be prescribed by law.

Amendment IV

The right of the people to be secure in their persons, houses, papers, and effects, against unreasonable searches and seizures, shall not be violated, and no Warrants shall issue, but upon probable cause, supported by Oath or affirmation, and particularly describing the place to be searched, and the persons or things to be seized.

Amendment V

No person shall be held to answer for a capital, or otherwise infamous crime, unless on a presentment or indictment of a Grand Jury, except in cases arising in the land or naval forces, or in the Militia, when in actual service in time of War or public danger; nor shall any person be subject for the same offence to be twice put in jeopardy of life or limb; nor shall be compelled in any criminal case to be a witness against himself, nor be deprived of life, liberty, or property, without due process of law; nor shall private property be taken for public use, without just compensation.

Amendment VI

In all criminal prosecutions, the accused shall enjoy the right to a speedy and public trial, by an impartial jury of the State and district wherein the crime shall have been committed, which district shall have been previously ascertained by law, and to be informed of the nature and cause of the accusation; to be confronted with the witnesses against him; to have compulsory process for obtaining witnesses in his favor, and to have the Assistance of Counsel for his defence.

Amendment VII

In Suits at common law, where the value in controversy shall exceed twenty dollars, the right of trial by jury shall be preserved, and no fact tried by a jury, shall be otherwise re-examined in any Court of the United States, than according to the rules of the common law.

Amendment VIII

Excessive bail shall not be required, nor excessive fines imposed, nor cruel and unusual punishments inflicted.

Amendment IX

The enumeration in the Constitution, of certain rights, shall not be construed to deny or disparage others retained by the people.

Amendment X

The powers not delegated to the United States by the Constitution, nor prohibited by it to the States, are reserved to the States respectively, or to the people.

Amendment XI

Passed by Congress March 4, 1794. Ratified February 7, 1795.

Note: Article III, Section 2, of the Constitution was modified by Amendment XI.

The Judicial power of the United States shall not be construed to extend to any suit in law or equity, commenced or prosecuted against one of the United States by Citizens of another State, or by Citizens or Subjects of any Foreign State.

Amendment XII

Passed by Congress December 9, 1803. Ratified June 15, 1804.

Note: A portion of Article II, Section 1, of the Constitution was superseded by the Twelfth Amendment.

The Electors shall meet in their respective states and vote by ballot for President and Vice-President, one of whom, at least, shall not be an inhabitant of the same state with themselves; they shall name in their ballots the person voted for as President, and in distinct ballots the person voted for as Vice-President, and they shall make distinct lists of all persons voted for as President, and of all persons voted for as Vice-President, and of the number of votes for each, which lists they shall sign and certify, and transmit sealed to the seat of the government of the United States, directed to the President of the Senate;—the President of the Senate shall, in the presence of the Senate and House of Representatives, open all the certificates and the votes shall then be counted;—The person having the greatest number of votes for President, shall be the President, if such number be a majority of the whole number of Electors appointed; and if no person have such majority, then from the persons having the highest numbers not exceeding three on the list of those voted for as President, the House of Representatives shall choose immediately, by ballot, the President. But in choosing the President, the votes shall be taken by states, the representation from each state having one vote; a quorum for this purpose shall consist of a member or members from two-thirds of the states, and a majority of all the states shall be necessary to a choice. [And if the House of Representatives shall not choose a President whenever the right of choice shall devolve upon them, before the fourth day of March next following, then the Vice-President shall act as President, as in case of the death or other constitutional disability of the President.—]* The person having the greatest number of votes as Vice-President, shall be the Vice-President, if such number be a majority of the whole number of Electors appointed, and if no person have a majority, then from the two highest numbers on the list, the Senate shall choose the Vice-President; a quorum for the purpose shall consist of two-thirds of the whole number of Senators, and a majority of the whole number shall be necessary to a choice. But no person constitutionally ineligible to the office of President shall be eligible to that of Vice-President of the United States.

*Superseded by Section 3 of the Twentieth Amendment.

Amendment XIII

Passed by Congress January 31, 1865. Ratified December 6, 1865.

Note: A portion of Article IV, Section 2, of the Constitution was superseded by the Thirteenth Amendment.

Section 1

Neither slavery nor involuntary servitude, except as a punishment for crime whereof the party shall have been duly convicted, shall exist within the United States, or any place subject to their jurisdiction.

Section 2

Congress shall have power to enforce this article by appropriate legislation.

Amendment XIV

Passed by Congress June 13, 1866. Ratified July 9, 1868.

Note: Article I, Section 2, of the Constitution was modified by Section 2 of the Fourteenth Amendment.

Section 1

All persons born or naturalized in the United States, and subject to the jurisdiction thereof, are citizens of the United States and of the State wherein they reside. No State shall make or enforce any law which shall abridge the privileges or immunities of citizens of the United States; nor shall any State deprive any person of life, liberty, or property, without due process of law; nor deny to any person within its jurisdiction the equal protection of the laws.

Section 2

Representatives shall be apportioned among the several States according to their respective numbers, counting the whole number of persons in each State, excluding Indians not taxed. But when the right to vote at any election for the choice of electors for President and Vice-President of the United States, Representatives in Congress, the Executive and Judicial officers of a State, or the members of the Legislature thereof, is denied to any of the male inhabitants of such State, being twenty-one years of age,* and citizens of the United States, or in any way abridged, except for participation in rebellion, or other crime, the basis of representation therein shall be reduced in the proportion which the number of such male citizens shall bear to the whole number of male citizens twenty-one years of age in such State.

Section 3

No person shall be a Senator or Representative in Congress, or elector of President and Vice-President, or hold any office, civil or military, under the United States, or under any State, who, having previously taken an oath, as a member of Congress, or as an officer of the United States, or as a member of any State legislature, or as an executive or judicial officer of any State, to support the Constitution of the United States, shall have engaged in insurrection or rebellion against the same, or given aid or comfort to the enemies thereof. But Congress may by a vote of two-thirds of each House, remove such disability.

Section 4

The validity of the public debt of the United States, authorized by law, including debts incurred for payment of pensions and bounties for services in suppressing insurrection or rebellion, shall not be questioned. But neither the United States nor any State shall assume or pay any debt or obligation incurred in aid of insurrection or rebellion against the United States, or any claim for the loss or emancipation of any slave; but all such debts, obligations and claims shall be held illegal and void.

Section 5

The Congress shall have the power to enforce, by appropriate legislation, the provisions of this article.

*Changed by Section 1 of the Twenty-sixth Amendment.

Amendment XV

Passed by Congress February 26, 1869. Ratified February 3, 1870.

Section 1

The right of citizens of the United States to vote shall not be denied or abridged by the United States or by any State on account of race, color, or previous condition of servitude.

Section 2

The Congress shall have the power to enforce this article by appropriate legislation.

Amendment XVI

Passed by Congress July 2, 1909. Ratified February 3, 1913.

Note: Article I, Section 9, of the Constitution was modified by Amendment XVI.

The Congress shall have power to lay and collect taxes on incomes, from whatever source derived, without apportionment among the several States, and without regard to any census or enumeration.

Amendment XVII

Passed by Congress May 13, 1912. Ratified April 8, 1913.

Note: Article I, Section 3, of the Constitution was modified by the Seventeenth Amendment.

The Senate of the United States shall be composed of two Senators from each State, elected by the people thereof, for six years; and each Senator shall have one vote. The electors in each State shall have the qualifications requisite for electors of the most numerous branch of the State legislatures.

When vacancies happen in the representation of any State in the Senate, the executive authority of such State shall issue writs of election to fill such vacancies: Provided, That the legislature of any State may empower the executive thereof to make temporary appointments until the people fill the vacancies by election as the legislature may direct.

This amendment shall not be so construed as to affect the election or term of any Senator chosen before it becomes valid as part of the Constitution.

Amendment XVIII

Passed by Congress December 18, 1917. Ratified January 16, 1919. Repealed by Amendment XXI.

Section 1

After one year from the ratification of this article the manufacture, sale, or transportation of intoxicating liquors within, the importation thereof into, or the exportation thereof from the United States and all territory subject to the jurisdiction thereof for beverage purposes is hereby prohibited.

Section 2

The Congress and the several States shall have concurrent power to enforce this article by appropriate legislation.

Section 3

This article shall be inoperative unless it shall have been ratified as an amendment to the Constitution by the legislatures of the several States, as provided in the Constitution, within seven years from the date of the submission hereof to the States by the Congress.

Amendment XIX

Passed by Congress June 4, 1919. Ratified August 18, 1920.

The right of citizens of the United States to vote shall not be denied or abridged by the United States or by any State on account of sex.

Congress shall have power to enforce this article by appropriate legislation.

Amendment XX

Passed by Congress March 2, 1932. Ratified January 23, 1933.

Note: Article I, Section 4, of the Constitution was modified by Section 2 of this amendment. In addition, a portion of the Twelfth Amendment was superseded by Section 3.

Section 1

The terms of the President and the Vice President shall end at noon on the 20th day of January, and the terms of Senators and Representatives at noon on the 3d day of January, of the years in which such terms would have ended if this article had not been ratified; and the terms of their successors shall then begin.

Section 2

The Congress shall assemble at least once in every year, and such meeting shall begin at noon on the 3d day of January, unless they shall by law appoint a different day.

Section 3

If, at the time fixed for the beginning of the term of the President, the President elect shall have died, the Vice President elect shall become President. If a President shall not have been chosen before the time fixed for the beginning of his term, or if the President elect shall have failed to qualify, then the Vice President elect shall act as President until a President shall have qualified; and the Congress may by law provide for the case wherein neither a President elect nor a Vice President shall have qualified, declaring who shall then act as President, or the manner in which one who is to act shall be selected, and such person shall act accordingly until a President or Vice President shall have qualified.

Section 4

The Congress may by law provide for the case of the death of any of the persons from whom the House of Representatives may choose a President whenever the right of choice shall have devolved upon them, and for the case of the death of any of the persons from whom the Senate may choose a Vice President whenever the right of choice shall have devolved upon them.

Section 5

Sections 1 and 2 shall take effect on the 15th day of October following the ratification of this article.

Section 6

This article shall be inoperative unless it shall have been ratified as an amendment to the Constitution by the legislatures of three-fourths of the several States within seven years from the date of its submission.

Amendment XXI

Passed by Congress February 20, 1933. Ratified December 5, 1933.

Section 1

The eighteenth article of amendment to the Constitution of the United States is hereby repealed.

Section 2

The transportation or importation into any State, Territory, or Possession of the United States for delivery or use therein of intoxicating liquors, in violation of the laws thereof, is hereby prohibited.

Section 3

This article shall be inoperative unless it shall have been ratified as an amendment to the Constitution by conventions in the several States, as provided in the Constitution, within seven years from the date of the submission hereof to the States by the Congress.

Amendment XXII

Passed by Congress March 21, 1947. Ratified February 27, 1951.

Section 1

No person shall be elected to the office of the President more than twice, and no person who has held the office of President, or acted as President, for more than two years of a term to which some other person was elected President shall be elected to the office of President more than once. But this Article shall not apply to any person holding the office of President when this Article was proposed by Congress, and shall not prevent any person who may be holding the office of President, or acting as President, during the term within which this Article becomes operative from holding the office of President or acting as President during the remainder of such term.

Section 2

This article shall be inoperative unless it shall have been ratified as an amendment to the Constitution by the legislatures of three-fourths of the several States within seven years from the date of its submission to the States by the Congress.

Amendment XXIII

Passed by Congress June 16, 1960. Ratified March 29, 1961.

Section 1

The District constituting the seat of Government of the United States shall appoint in such manner as Congress may direct:

A number of electors of President and Vice President equal to the whole number of Senators and Representatives in Congress to which the District would be entitled if it were a State, but in no event more than the least populous State; they shall be in addition to those appointed by the States, but they shall be considered, for the purposes of the election of President and Vice President, to be electors appointed by a State; and they shall meet in the District and perform such duties as provided by the twelfth article of amendment.

Section 2

The Congress shall have power to enforce this article by appropriate legislation.

Amendment XXIV

Passed by Congress August 27, 1962. Ratified January 23, 1964.

Section 1

The right of citizens of the United States to vote in any primary or other election for President or Vice President, for electors for President or Vice President, or for Senator or Representative in Congress, shall not be denied or abridged by the United States or any State by reason of failure to pay poll tax or other tax.

Section 2

The Congress shall have power to enforce this article by appropriate legislation.

Amendment XXV

Passed by Congress July 6, 1965. Ratified February 10, 1967.

Note: Article II, Section 1, of the Constitution was affected by the Twenty-fifth Amendment.

Section 1

In case of the removal of the President from office or of his death or resignation, the Vice President shall become President.

Section 2

Whenever there is a vacancy in the office of the Vice President, the President shall nominate a Vice President who shall take office upon confirmation by a majority vote of both Houses of Congress.

Section 3

Whenever the President transmits to the President pro tempore of the Senate and the Speaker of the House of Representatives his written declaration that he is unable to discharge the powers and duties of his office, and until he transmits to them a written declaration to the contrary, such powers and duties shall be discharged by the Vice President as Acting President.

Section 4

Whenever the Vice President and a majority of either the principal officers of the executive departments or of such other body as Congress may by law provide, transmit to the President pro tempore of the Senate and the Speaker of the House of Representatives their written declaration that the President is unable to discharge the powers and duties of his office, the Vice President shall immediately assume the powers and duties of the office as Acting President.

Thereafter, when the President transmits to the President pro tempore of the Senate and the Speaker of the House of Representatives his written declaration that no inability exists, he shall resume the powers and duties of his office unless the Vice President and a majority of either the principal officers of the executive department or of such other body as Congress may by law provide, transmit within four days to the President pro tempore of the Senate and the Speaker of the House of Representatives their written declaration that the President is unable to discharge the powers and duties of his office. Thereupon Congress shall decide the issue, assembling within forty-eight hours for that purpose if not in session. If the Congress, within twenty-one days after receipt of the latter written declaration, or, if Congress is not in session, within twenty-one days after Congress is required to assemble, determines by two-thirds vote of both Houses that the President is unable to discharge the powers and duties of his office, the Vice President shall continue to discharge the same as Acting President; otherwise, the President shall resume the powers and duties of his office.

Amendment XXVI

Passed by Congress March 23, 1971. Ratified July 1, 1971.

Note: Amendment XIV, Section 2, of the Constitution was modified by Section 1 of the Twenty-sixth Amendment.

Section 1

The right of citizens of the United States, who are eighteen years of age or older, to vote shall not be denied or abridged by the United States or by any State on account of age.

Section 2

The Congress shall have power to enforce this article by appropriate legislation.

Amendment XXVII

Originally proposed Sept. 25, 1789. Ratified May 7, 1992.

No law, varying the compensation for the services of the Senators and Representatives, shall take effect, until an election of representatives shall have intervened.

Lincoln's Gettysburg Address

Four score and seven years ago our fathers brought forth on this continent, a new nation, conceived in Liberty, and dedicated to the proposition that all men are created equal.

Now we are engaged in a great civil war, testing whether that nation, or any nation so conceived and so dedicated, can long endure. We are met on a great battle-field of that war. We have come to dedicate a portion of that field, as a final resting place for those who here gave their lives that that nation might live. It is altogether fitting and proper that we should do this.

But, in a larger sense, we can not dedicate—we can not consecrate—we can not hallow—this ground. The brave men, living and dead, who struggled here, have consecrated it, far above our poor power to add or detract. The world will little note, nor long remember what we say here, but it can never forget what they did here. It is for us the living, rather, to be dedicated here to the unfinished work which they who fought here have thus far so nobly advanced. It is rather for us to be here dedicated to the great task remaining before us—that from these honored dead we take increased devotion to that cause for which they gave the last full measure of devotion—that we here highly resolve that these dead shall not have died in vain—that this nation, under God, shall have a new birth of freedom—and that government of the people, by the people, for the people, shall not perish from the earth.

Appendix B

Historical Facts and Data

US Presidents and Vice Presidents

Table App B-1 Presidents and Vice Presidents

	President	Vice President	Political Party	Term
1	George Washington	John Adams	No Party Designation	1789–1797
2	John Adams	Thomas Jefferson	Federalist	1797–1801
3	Thomas Jefferson	Aaron Burr George Clinton	Democratic Republican	1801–1809
4	James Madison	George Clinton Elbridge Gerry	Democratic Republican	1809–1817
5	James Monroe	Daniel D. Tompkins	Democratic Republican	1817–1825
6	John Quincy Adams	John C. Calhoun	Democratic Republican	1825–1829
7	Andrew Jackson	John C. Calhoun Martin Van Buren	Democratic	1829–1837
8	Martin Van Buren	Richard M. Johnson	Democratic	1837–1841
9	William Henry Harrison	John Tyler	Whig	1841
10	John Tyler	None	Whig	1841–1845
11	James Knox Polk	George M. Dallas	Democratic	1845–1849
12	Zachary Taylor	Millard Fillmore	Whig	1849–1850
13	Millard Fillmore	None	Whig	1850–1853
14	Franklin Pierce	William R. King	Democratic	1853–1857
15	James Buchanan	John C. Breckinridge	Democratic	1857–1861
16	Abraham Lincoln	Hannibal Hamlin Andrew Johnson	Union	1861–1865
17	Andrew Johnson	None	Union	1865–1869
18	Ulysses Simpson Grant	Schuyler Colfax Henry Wilson	Republican	1869–1877
19	Rutherford Birchard Hayes	William A. Wheeler	Republican	1877–1881
20	James Abram Garfield	Chester Alan Arthur	Republican	1881
21	Chester Alan Arthur	None	Republican	1881–1885
22	Stephen Grover Cleveland	Thomas Hendricks	Democratic	1885–1889
23	Benjamin Harrison	Levi P. Morton	Republican	1889–1893
24	Stephen Grover Cleveland	Adlai E. Stevenson	Democratic	1893–1897
25	William McKinley	Garret A. Hobart Theodore Roosevelt	Republican	1897–1901

Continued

Table App B-1 Presidents and Vice Presidents (*cont*)

	President	Vice President	Political Party	Term
26	Theodore Roosevelt	Charles W. Fairbanks	Republican	1901–1909
27	William Howard Taft	James S. Sherman	Republican	1909–1913
28	Woodrow Wilson	Thomas R. Marshall	Democratic	1913–1921
29	Warren Gamaliel Harding	Calvin Coolidge	Republican	1921–1923
30	Calvin Coolidge	Charles G. Dawes	Republican	1923–1929
31	Herbert Clark Hoover	Charles Curtis	Republican	1929–1933
32	Franklin Delano Roosevelt	John Nance Garner Henry A. Wallace Harry S. Truman	Democratic	1933–1945
33	Harry S. Truman	Alben W. Barkley	Democratic	1945–1953
34	Dwight David Eisenhower	Richard Milhous Nixon	Republican	1953–1961
35	John Fitzgerald Kennedy	Lyndon Baines Johnson	Democratic	1961–1963
36	Lyndon Baines Johnson	Hubert Horatio Humphrey	Democratic	1963–1969
37	Richard Milhous Nixon	Spiro T. Agnew Gerald Rudolph Ford	Republican	1969–1974
38	Gerald Rudolph Ford	Nelson Rockefeller	Republican	1974–1977
39	James Earl Carter Jr.	Walter Mondale	Democratic	1977–1981
40	Ronald Wilson Reagan	George Herbert Walker Bush	Republican	1981–1989
41	George Herbert Walker Bush	J. Danforth Quayle	Republican	1989–1993
42	William Jefferson Clinton	Albert Gore Jr.	Democratic	1993–2001
43	George Walker Bush	Richard Cheney	Republican	2001–2009
44	Barack Hussein Obama	Joseph Biden	Democratic	2009–

Admission of States into the Union

Table App B-2 Admission of States into the Union

	State	Date of Admission		State	Date of Admission
1	Delaware	December 7, 1787	26	Michigan	January 26, 1837
2	Pennsylvania	December 12, 1787	27	Florida	March 3, 1845
3	New Jersey	December 18, 1787	28	Texas	December 29, 1845
4	Georgia	January 2, 1788	29	Iowa	December 28, 1846
5	Connecticut	January 9, 1788	30	Wisconsin	May 29, 1848
6	Massachusetts	February 6, 1788	31	California	September 9, 1850
7	Maryland	April 28, 1788	32	Minnesota	May 11, 1858
8	South Carolina	May 23, 1788	33	Oregon	February 14, 1859
9	New Hampshire	June 21, 1788	34	Kansas	January 29, 1861
10	Virginia	June 25, 1788	35	West Virginia	June 20, 1863
11	New York	July 26, 1788	36	Nevada	October 31, 1864
12	North Carolina	November 21, 1789	37	Nebraska	March 1, 1867
13	Rhode Island	May 29, 1790	38	Colorado	August 1, 1876
14	Vermont	March 4, 1791	39	North Dakota	November 2, 1889
15	Kentucky	June 1, 1792	40	South Dakota	November 2, 1889
16	Tennessee	June 1, 1796	41	Montana	November 8, 1889
17	Ohio	March 1, 1803	42	Washington	November 11, 1889
18	Louisiana	April 30, 1812	43	Idaho	July 3, 1890
19	Indiana	December 11, 1816	44	Wyoming	July 10, 1890
20	Mississippi	December 10, 1817	45	Utah	January 4, 1896
21	Illinois	December 3, 1818	46	Oklahoma	November 16, 1907
22	Alabama	December 14, 1819	47	New Mexico	January 6, 1912
23	Maine	March 15, 1820	48	Arizona	February 14, 1912
24	Missouri	August 10, 1821	49	Alaska	January 3, 1959
25	Arkansas	June 15, 1836	50	Hawaii	August 21, 1959

Glossary

Antinomianism   The belief that moral law was not binding on true Christians. The opposite of Arminianism, antinomianism held that good works would not count in the afterlife. Justification, or entrance to heaven, was by faith alone. *See* Calvinism.

Arminianism   Religious doctrine developed by the Dutch theologian Jacobus Arminius that argued that men and women had free will and suggested that hence they would earn their way into heaven by good works.

Armistice   A cessation of hostilities by agreement among the opposing sides; a cease-fire.

Associationalism   President Herbert Hoover's preferred method of responding to the Depression. Rather than have the government directly involve itself in the economy, Hoover hoped to use the government to encourage associations of businessmen to cooperate voluntarily to meet the crisis.

Autarky   At the height of the world depression, industrial powers sought to isolate their economies within self-contained spheres, generally governed by national (or imperial) economic planning. Japan's Co-Prosperity Sphere, the Soviet Union, and the British Empire each comprised a more or less closed economic unit.

Benevolent Empire   The loosely affiliated network of charitable reform associations that emerged (especially in urban areas) in response to the widespread revivalism of the early nineteenth century.

Berdache   In Indian societies, a man who dressed and adopted the mannerisms of women and had sex only with other men. In Native American culture, the berdache, half man and half woman, symbolized cosmic harmony.

Blockade   A military tactic used in both land and naval warfare by which a location is sealed off to prevent goods or people from entering or leaving.

Budget deficit   The failure of tax revenues to pay for annual federal spending on military, welfare, and other programs. The resulting budget deficits forced Washington to borrow money to cover its costs. The growing budget deficits were controversial, in part because the government's borrowing increased both its long-term debt and the amount of money it had to spend each year to pay for the interest on loans.

Busing   The controversial court-ordered practice of sending children by bus to public schools outside their neighborhoods in order to promote racial integration in the schools.

Calvinism   Religious doctrine developed by the theologian John Calvin that argued that God alone determines who will receive salvation and, hence, men and women cannot earn their own salvation or even be certain about their final destinies.

Carpetbagger   A derogatory term referring to northern whites who moved to the South after the Civil War. Stereotyped as corrupt and unprincipled, "carpetbaggers" were in fact a diverse group motivated by a variety of interests and beliefs.

Charter colony   Settlement established by a trading company or other group of private entrepreneurs who received from the king a grant of land and the right to govern it. The charter colonies included Virginia, Plymouth, Massachusetts Bay, Rhode Island, and Connecticut.

City busting   As late as the 1930s, President Roosevelt and most Americans regarded attacking civilians from the air as an atrocity, but during World War II cities became a primary target for US warplanes. The inaccuracy of bombing, combined with racism and the belief that Japanese and German actions justified retaliation, led American air commanders to follow a policy of systematically destroying urban areas, particularly in Japan.

Communist   Member of the Communist Party or follower of the doctrines of Karl Marx. The term (or accusation) was applied more broadly in the twentieth century to brand labor unionists, progressives, civil rights workers, and other reformers as agents of a foreign ideology.

Communitarians   Individuals who supported and/or took up residence in separate communities created to embody improved plans of social, religious, and/or economic life.

Commutation   The controversial policy of allowing potential draftees to pay for a replacement to serve in the army. The policy was adopted by both the Union and Confederate governments during the Civil War, and in both cases opposition to commutation was so intense that the policy was abandoned.

Consent   One of the key principles of liberalism, which held that people could not be subject to laws to which they had not given their consent. This principle is reflected in both the Declaration of Independence and the preamble to the Constitution, which begins with the famous words "We the people of the United States, in order to form a more perfect union."

Conspiracy theory   A belief that history is shaped intentionally by unseen powers. Conspiracy theory lay behind the McCarthy anti-Communism hearings, which assumed that American society and government had been infiltrated by countless Communist spies.

Constitutionalism   A loose body of thought that developed in Britain and the colonies and was used by the colonists to justify the Revolution by claiming that it was in accord with the principles of the British Constitution. Constitutionalism had two main elements. One was the rule of law, and the other the principle of consent, that one cannot be subject to laws or taxation except by duly elected representatives. Both were rights that had been won through struggle with the monarch. Constitutionalism also refers to the tendency in American politics, particularly in the early nineteenth century, to transpose all political questions into constitutional ones.

Consumer revolution   A slow and steady increase over the course of the eighteenth century in the demand for, and purchase of, consumer goods. The consumer revolution of the eighteenth century was closely related to the Industrial Revolution.

Consumerism   An ideology that defined the purchase of goods and services as both an expression of individual identity and essential to the national economy. Increasingly powerful by the 1920s and dominant by the 1950s, consumerism urged people to find happiness in the pursuit of leisure and pleasure more than in the work ethic.

Containment   The basic US strategy for fighting the cold war. As used by diplomat George Kennan in a 1947 magazine essay, "containment" referred to the combination of diplomatic, economic, and military programs necessary to hold back Soviet expansionism after World War II.

Contraband of war   In its general sense, contraband of war was property seized from an enemy. But early in the Civil War the term was applied to slaves running to Union lines as a way of preventing owners from reclaiming them. The policy effectively nullified the fugitive slave clause of the US Constitution. It was a first critical step in a process that would lead to a federal emancipation policy the following year.

Cooperationists   Those southerners who opposed immediate secession after the election of Abraham Lincoln in 1860. Cooperationists argued instead that secessionists should wait to see if the new president was willing to "cooperate" with the South's demands.

Copperhead   A northerner who sympathized with the South during the Civil War.

Crop lien   The first right to the proceeds of a harvested crop, given by farmers to their creditors. At the beginning of the growing season, farmers paid on credit for seeds, supplies, and food to get them through the year. They repaid these debts when the crop was sold.

Deindustrialization   The reverse of industrialization, as factory shutdowns decreased the size of the manufacturing sector. Plant closings began to plague the American economy in the 1970s, prompting fears that the nation would lose its industrial base.

Democratic Republicans   One of the two parties to make up the first American party system. Following the fiscal and political views of Jefferson and Madison, Democratic Republicans generally advocated a weak federal government and opposed federal intervention in the economy of the nation.

Détente   This French term for the relaxation of tensions was used to describe the central foreign policy innovation of the Nixon administration—a new, less confrontational relationship with Communism. In addition to opening a dialogue with the People's Republic of China, Nixon sought a more stable, less confrontational relationship with the Soviet Union.

Diffusion   The controversial theory that the problem of slavery would be resolved if the slave economy was allowed to expand, or "diffuse," into the western territories. Southerners developed this theory as early as the 1800s in response to northerners who hoped to restrict slavery's expansion.

Disfranchisement   The act of depriving a person or group of voting rights. In the nineteenth century the right to vote was popularly known as the franchise. The Fourteenth Amendment of the Constitution affirmed the right of adult male citizens to vote, but state-imposed restrictions and taxes deprived large numbers of Americans—particularly African Americans—of the vote from the 1890s until the passage of the Voting Rights Act of 1964.

Domestic patriarchy   The practice of defining the family by the husband and father, and wives and children as his domestic dependents. Upon marriage a wife's property became her husband's, and children owed obedience and labor to the family until they reached adulthood. In combination with an exclusive male suffrage, domestic patriarchy described the political as well as the social system that prevailed among free Americans until the twentieth century.

Downsizing   American corporations' layoffs of both blue- and white-collar workers in an attempt to become more efficient and competitive. Downsizing was one of the factors that made Americans uneasy about the economy in the 1990s, despite the impressive surge in the stock market.

Dust Bowl   Across much of the Great Plains, decades of wasteful farming practices combined with several years of drought in the early 1930s to produce a series of massive dust storms that blew the topsoil across hundreds of miles. The area in Texas and Oklahoma affected by these storms became known as the Dust Bowl.

E-commerce   Short for "electronic commerce," this was the term for the Internet-based buying and selling that was one of the key hopes for the computer-driven postindustrial economy. The promise of e-commerce was still unfulfilled by the start of the twenty-first century.

Encomienda   A system of labor developed by the Spanish in the New World in which Spanish settlers (*encomenderos*) compelled groups of Native Americans to work for them. The *encomendero* owned neither the land nor the Indians who worked for him, but had the unlimited right to compel a particular group of Indians to work for him. This system was unique to the New World; nothing precisely like it had existed in Europe or elsewhere.

"Establishment"   The elite of mainly Ivy League–educated, Anglo-Saxon, Protestant, male, liberal northeasterners who supposedly dominated Wall Street and Washington after World War II. The Establishment's support for corporations, activist government, and containment engendered hostility from opposite poles of the political spectrum—from conservatives and Republicans like Richard Nixon at one end and from the New Left and the Movement at the other. Although many of the post–World War II leaders of the United States did tend to share common origins and ideologies, this elite was never as powerful, self-conscious, or unified as its opponents believed.

Eugenics   The practice of attempting to solve social problems through the control of human reproduction. Drawing on the authority of evolutionary biology, eugenists enjoyed considerable influence in the United States, especially on issues of corrections and public health, from the turn of the century through World War II. Applications of this pseudoscience included the identification of "born" criminals by physical characteristics and "better baby" contests at county fairs.

Farmers' Alliance   A group organized in the late nineteenth century to help farmers pool their knowledge and resources. By 1890 it had entered politics, endorsing candidates and building the political connections in the South and West that would lead to the Populist Party.

Federalists   One of the two political parties to make up the first American party system. Following the fiscal and political policies proposed by Alexander Hamilton, Federalists generally advocated the importance of a strong federal government, including federal intervention in the economy of the new nation.

Feminism   An ideology insisting on the fundamental equality of women and men. The feminists of the 1960s differed over how to achieve that equality: while liberal feminists mostly demanded equal rights for women in the workplace and in politics, radical feminists more thoroughly condemned the capitalist system and male oppression and demanded equality in both private and public life.

Feudalism   A social and political system that developed in Europe in the Middle Ages under which powerful lords offered less powerful noblemen protection in return for their loyalty. Feudalism also included the economic system of manorialism, under which dependent serfs worked on the manors controlled by those lords.

Fire-eaters   Militant southerners who pushed for secession in the 1850s.

Flexible response   The defense doctrine of the Kennedy and Johnson administrations. Abandoning the Eisenhower administration's heavy emphasis on nuclear weapons, flexible response stressed the buildup of the nation's conventional and special forces so that the president had a range of military options in response to Communist aggression.

Front   Early twentieth-century mechanized wars were fought along a battle line or "front" separating opposing sides. By World War II, tactical innovations—blitzkrieg, parachute troops, gliders, and amphibious landings—complicated warfare by breaking through, disrupting, or bypassing the front. The front thus became a more fluid boundary than the fortified trench lines of World War I. The term also acquired a political meaning, particularly for labor and the left. A coalition of parties supporting (or opposing) an agreed-upon line could be called a "popular front."

Galveston Plan   A system of municipal government by appointed commissioners, each with responsibility for a utility or service. After a hurricane devastated Galveston, Texas, in 1900, unelected commissioners temporarily took charge to oversee relief and rebuilding efforts.

Gentility   A term without precise meaning that represented all that was polite, civilized, refined, and fashionable. It was everything that vulgarity was not. Because the term had no precise meaning, it was always subject to negotiation, striving, and anxiety as Americans, beginning in the eighteenth century, tried to show others that they were genteel through their manners, their appearance, and their styles of life.

Glass ceiling   The invisible barrier of discrimination that prevented female white-collar workers from rising to top executive positions in corporations.

Globalization   This term first came into use during the 1980s to describe the web of technological, economic, military, political, and cultural developments binding people and nations ever more tightly together. America had been defined by its relationship to the world for centuries, but the coining of the term *globalization* reflected the emergence of closer international ties.

Great Society   President Lyndon Johnson's ambitious legislative program embodying the vision of the activist new liberalism of the 1960s. Enacted from 1965 to 1968, the Great Society sought to wipe out poverty, end segregation, and enhance the quality of life for all Americans.

Greenbackers   Those who advocated currency inflation by keeping the type of money printed during the Civil War, known as "greenbacks," in circulation.

Gridlock The political traffic jam that tied up the federal government in the late 1980s and the 1990s. Gridlock developed from the inability of either major party to control both the presidency and Congress for any extended period of time. More fundamentally, gridlock reflected the inability of any party or president to win a popular mandate for a bold legislative program.

Horizontal integration More commonly known as "monopoly." An industry was "horizontally integrated" when a single company took control of virtually the entire market for a specific product. John D. Rockefeller's Standard Oil came close to doing this.

Humanism A Renaissance intellectual movement that focused on the intellectual and artistic achievements of humankind. Under the patronage of Queen Isabel, Spain became a center of European humanism.

Immediatism The variant antislavery sentiment that demanded immediate (as opposed to gradual) personal and federal action against the institution of slavery. This approach was most closely associated with William Lloyd Garrison and is dated from the publication of Garrison's newspaper, *The Liberator*, in January 1831.

Imperialism A process of extending dominion over territories beyond the national boundaries of a state. In the eighteenth century, Britain extended imperial control over North America through settlement, but in the 1890s, imperial influence was generally exercised through indirect rule. Subject peoples generally retained some local autonomy while the imperial power controlled commerce and defense. Few Americans went to the Philippines as settlers, but many passed through as tourists, missionaries, traders, and soldiers.

Individualism The social and political philosophy celebrating the central importance of the individual human being in society. Insisting on the rights of the individual in relationship to the group, individualism was one of the intellectual bases of capitalism and democracy. The resurgent individualism of the 1920s, with its emphasis on each American's freedom and fulfillment, was a critical element of the decade's emergent consumerism and Republican dominance.

Industrious revolution Beginning in the late seventeenth century in western Europe and extending to the North American colonies in the eighteenth century, a fundamental change in the way people worked, as they worked harder and organized their households to produce goods that could be sold, so they could have money to pay for the new consumer goods they wanted.

Information economy The postindustrial economy, gradually emerging in the mid- to late twentieth century, in which sophisticated communications, computing, biomedical technology, and services took the place of manufacturing.

Initiative, recall, and referendum First proposed by the People's Party's Omaha Platform (1892), along with the direct election of senators and the secret ballot, as measures to subject corporate capitalism to democratic controls. Progressives, chiefly in western and midwestern states, favored them as a check on the power of state officials. The *initiative* allows legislation to be proposed by petition. The *recall* allows voters to remove public officials, and the *referendum* places new laws or constitutional amendments on the ballot for the direct approval of the voters.

Interest group An association whose members organize to exert political pressure on officials or the public. Unlike political parties, whose platforms and slates cover nearly every issue and office, an interest group focuses on a narrower list of concerns reflecting the shared outlook of its members. With the decline of popular politics around the turn of the twentieth century, business, religious, agricultural, women's, professional, neighborhood, and reform associations created a new form of political participation.

Isolationist Between World War I and World War II, the United States refused to join the League of Nations, scaled back its military commitments abroad, and sought to maintain its independence of action in foreign affairs. These policies were called isolationist, although some historians prefer the term "independent internationalist," in recognition of the United States' continuing global influence. In the late 1930s, isolationists favored policies aimed at distancing the United States from European affairs and building a national defense based on air power and hemispheric security.

Jim Crow laws   Statutes discriminating against nonwhite Americans, particularly in the South. The term specifically refers to regulations excluding blacks from public facilities or compelling them to use ones separate from those allotted to whites.

Joint-stock company   A form of business organization that was a forerunner to the modern corporation. The joint-stock company was used to raise both capital and labor for New World ventures. Shareholders contributed either capital or their labor for a period of years.

Judicial nationalism   The use of the judiciary to assert the primacy of the national government over state and local government and the legal principle of contract over principles of local custom.

Keynesian economics   The theory, named after the English economist John Maynard Keynes, that advocated the use of "countercyclical" fiscal policy. This meant that during good times the government should pay down the debt, so that during bad times it could afford to stimulate the economy with deficit spending.

Knights of Labor   The first national federation of trade unions, led by Terence V. Powderly. The Knights grew to its fullest size in the mid-1880s before a steep decline. The federation was based on the premise of a common interest of all producers (for example, farmers and industrial workers), and it supported reform as well as united action by workers.

Liberalism   A body of political thought that traces its origins to John Locke and whose chief principles are consent, freedom of conscience, and property. Liberalism held that people could not be governed except by their own consent and that the purpose of government was to protect people as well as their property.

Linked economic development   A form of economic development that ties together a variety of enterprises so that development in one stimulates development in others, for example, those that provide raw materials, parts, or transportation.

Longhorn cattle   Rangy, tough, resourceful cattle found on the southern Great Plains. They were ideal for long cattle drives like those along the Abilene Trail.

Lyceum movement   A voluntary adult-education movement that swept New England and the Mid-Atlantic states in the early and mid-nineteenth century, credited in large part to the efforts of Josiah Holbrook. Lyceum organizations hosted educational lectures in towns and cities. Lecturers included such prominent speakers as Ralph Waldo Emerson, Mark Twain, and Abraham Lincoln.

Manifest destiny   A term first coined in 1845 by journalist John O'Sullivan to express the belief, widespread among antebellum Americans, that the United States was destined to expand across the North American continent to the Pacific and had an irrefutable right to the lands absorbed in this expansion. This belief was frequently justified on the grounds of claims to political and racial superiority.

Market revolution   The term used to designate the period of the early nineteenth century, roughly 1815–1830, during which internal dependence on cash markets and wages became widespread.

Mass production   A system of efficient, high-volume manufacturing based on division of labor into repetitive tasks, simplification, and standardization of parts, increasing use of specialized machinery, and careful supervision. Emerging since the nineteenth century, mass production reached a critical stage of development with Henry Ford's introduction of the moving assembly line at his Highland Park automobile factory. Mass production drove the prosperity of the 1920s and helped make consumerism possible.

Massive resistance   The rallying cry of southern segregationists who pledged to oppose the integration of the schools ordered by the *Supreme Court in Brown v. Board of Education* in 1954. The tactics of massive resistance included legislation, demonstrations, and violence.

Massive retaliation   The defense doctrine of the Eisenhower administration that promised "instant, massive retaliation" with nuclear weapons in response to Soviet aggression.

McCarthyism   The hunt for Communist subversion in the United States in the first years of the cold war. Democrats, in particular, used the term, a reference to the sometimes disreputable tactics of Republican Senator Joseph R. McCarthy of Wisconsin, in order to question the legitimacy of the conservative anti-Communist crusade.

Mercantilism   An economic theory developed in early-modern Europe to explain and guide the growth of European nation-states. Its goal was to strengthen the state by making the economy serve its interests. According to the theory of mercantilism, the world's wealth, measured in gold and silver, was fixed; that is, it could never be increased. As a result, each nation's chief economic objective must be to secure as much of the world's wealth as possible. One nation's gain was necessarily another's loss. Colonies played an important part in the theory of mercantilism. Their role was to serve as sources of raw materials and as markets for manufactured goods for the mother country alone.

Middle ground   The region between European and Indian settlements in North America that was neither fully European nor fully Indian, but rather a new world created out of two different traditions. The middle ground came into being every time Europeans and Indians met, needed each other, and could not (or would not) achieve what they wanted through use of force.

Millennialism   A strain of Protestant belief that holds that history will end with the thousand-year reign of Christ (the millennium). Some Americans saw the Great Awakening, the French and Indian War, and the Revolution as signs that the millennium was about to begin in America, and this belief infused Revolutionary thought with an element of optimism. Millennialism was also one aspect of a broad drive for social perfection in nineteenth-century America.

Minstrel show   Form of popular entertainment in the nineteenth century, with black performers or white ones pretending to be black. Minstrel shows included music, comedy acts, and drama.

Modern Republicanism   President Dwight Eisenhower's middle-of-the-road legislative program of the 1950s. Reflecting traditional Republican faith in limited government and balanced budgets, Modern Republicanism still left alone such liberal programs as Social Security and farm subsidies.

Modernization   The process by which developing countries in the third world were to become more like the United States—in other words, capitalist, independent, and anti-Communist. Confidence about the prospects for modernization was one of the cornerstones of liberal foreign policy in the 1960s.

Moral suasion   The strategy of using persuasion (as opposed to legal coercion) to convince individuals to alter their behavior. In the antebellum years, moral suasion generally implied an appeal to religious values.

Mugwump   Name applied to liberal reformers in the late nineteenth century. Unattached to either major party, Mugwumps would endorse any candidate supportive of civil service reform, a secret ballot, and honest government.

Mutual aid societies   Organizations through which people of relatively meager means pooled their resources for emergencies. Usually, individuals paid small amounts in dues and were able to borrow large amounts in times of need. In the early nineteenth century, mutual aid societies were especially common among workers in free African American communities.

National Republicans   Over the first 20 years of the nineteenth century, the Republican Party gradually abandoned its Jeffersonian animosity toward an activist federal government and industrial development and became a strong proponent of both of these positions. Embodied in the American system, these new views were fully captured in the party's designation of itself as National Republicans by 1824.

Nativism   A bias against anyone not born in the United States and in favor of native-born Americans. This attitude assumes the superior culture and political virtue of white Americans of Anglo-Saxon descent, or of individuals assumed to have that lineage. During the period 1820–1850, Irish immigrants became the particular targets of nativist attitudes.

Neoconservatism   Form of conservative ideology that advocated the aggressive promotion of democracy abroad by the United States in order to make a better and more secure world.   Emerging in the 1970s and 1980s, neoconservative ideas influenced the foreign policy of President George W. Bush.

New conservatism   The resurgent conservative ideology of the 1950s and 1960s reiterated the old conservatism's faith in individual freedom and liberal government and added an aggressive, anti-Communist defense policy.

New Federalism   Conservative policy of President Richard Nixon intended to limit the federal government by returning revenue and control to state and local government.

New Left   The radical student movement that emerged in opposition to the new liberalism in the 1960s. The New Left condemned the cold war and corporate power and called for the creation of a true "participatory democracy" in the United States. Placing its faith in the radical potential of young, middle-class students, the New Left differed from the "old left" of the late nineteenth and early twentieth centuries, which believed workers would lead the way to socialism.

New Right   The conservative movement that swept Ronald Reagan into power in 1980 and sustained his presidency. The New Right was much like the new conservatism of the 1950s and 1960s, but with greater emphasis on social issues such as abortion.

Nickelodeon   The first venue for motion pictures, a machine that showed a movie (lasting several minutes) for a nickel. Galleries with dozens of such machines, and the first movie theaters, came to be called "nickelodeons" as a result.

Omaha Platform   The Populist Party's program endorsed at the party's national convention in Omaha in 1892. Among its planks were government ownership of railroads and telegraph lines, the direct election of senators, a subtreasury system, and an expansion of the money supply.

Patriotism   Love of country. Ways of declaring and displaying national devotion underwent a change from the nineteenth to the twentieth centuries. Whereas politicians were once unblushingly called patriotic, after World War I the title was appropriated to describe the sacrifices of war veterans. Patriotic spectacle in the form of public oration and electoral rallies gave way to military-style commemorations of Armistice Day and the nation's martial heritage.

Patronage   *See* Spoils system.

Political economy   Traditionally, the study of the connections between economics and politics. In this text, political economy refers to the relationships between the economy, politics, and the daily lives of ordinary people. Use of the term underscores the importance of the economy in shaping American life and the importance of politics in shaping the economy. However, the economy and politics did not simply shape, but were in turn shaped by, the lives and cultural values of ordinary men and women.

Political machine   An organization controlling a party, usually dominated by a "boss" and held together by loyalty and the distribution of rewards to those who had done the organization service.

Political virtue   In the political thought of the early republic, the personal qualities required in citizens if the republic was to survive.

Popular sovereignty   A solution to the slavery controversy espoused by leading northern Democrats in the 1850s. It held that the inhabitants of western territories should be free to decide for themselves whether or not they wanted to have slavery. In principle, popular sovereignty would prevent Congress from either enforcing or restricting slavery's expansion into the western territories.

Populism   The ideology of the People's (Populist) Party in the 1890s, opposing the eastern economic elites and favoring government action to help producers in general and farmers in particular.

Postindustrial economy   The service- and computer-based economy that succeeded the industrial economy, which had been dominated by manufacturing, at the end of the twentieth century.

Principle of judicial review   The principle of law that recognizes in the judiciary the power to review and rule on the constitutionality of laws. First established in *Marbury v. Madison* (1803) under Chief Justice John Marshall.

Producers ideology   The belief that all those who lived by producing goods shared a common political identity in opposition to those who lived off financial speculation, rent, or interest.

Proprietary colony   Colony established by a royal grant to an individual or family. The proprietary colonies included Maryland, New York, New Jersey, Pennsylvania, and the Carolinas.

Public opinion   Not quite democracy or consent, public opinion was a way of understanding the influence of the citizenry on political calculations. It emerged in the eighteenth century, when it was defined as a crucial source of a government's legitimacy. It was associated with the emergence of a press and a literate public free to discuss, and to question, government policy. In the twentieth century, Freudian psychology and the new mass media encouraged a view of the public as both fickle and powerful. Whereas the popular will (a nineteenth-century concept) was steady and rooted in national traditions, public opinion was variable and based on attitudes that could be aroused or manipulated by advertising.

Realism   A major artistic movement of the late nineteenth century that embraced writers, painters, critics, and photographers. Realists strove to avoid sentimentality and to depict life "realistically."

Reconquista   Literally "reconquest." Between the eleventh and the fifteenth centuries, Christian nobles in Spain and Portugal fought to eject Muslim conquerors who had come from North Africa in the seventh and eighth centuries. In 1492, Ferdinand and Isabel defeated the last remaining Muslim ruler.

Reconversion   The economic and social transition from the war effort to peacetime. Americans feared that reconversion might bring a return to the depression conditions of the 1930s.

Reexport trade   Marine trade between two foreign ports, with an intermediate stop in a port of the ship's home nation. United States shippers commonly engaged in the reexport trade during the European wars of the late eighteenth and early nineteenth centuries, when England and France tried to prevent each other from shipping or receiving goods. United States shippers claimed that the intermediate stop in the United States made their cargoes neutral.

Republicanism   A set of doctrines rooted in classical antiquity that held that power is always grasping and dangerous and presents a threat to liberty. Republicanism supplied constitutionalism with a motive by explaining how a balanced constitution could be transformed into a tyranny as grasping men used their power to encroach on the liberty of citizens. In addition, republicanism held that people achieved fulfillment only through participation in public life, as citizens in a republic. Republicanism required the individual to display virtue by sacrificing his (or her) private interest for the good of the republic.

Requerimiento **(the Requirement)**   A document issued by the Spanish Crown in 1513 in order to clarify the legal bases for the enslavement of hostile Indians. Each conquistador was required to read a copy of the *Requerimiento* to each group of Indians he encountered. The *Requerimiento* promised friendship to all Indians who accepted Christianity, but threatened war and enslavement for all those who resisted.

Safety-valve theory   An argument commonly made in the nineteenth century that the abundance of western land spared the United States from the social upheavals common to capitalist societies in Europe. In theory, as long as eastern workers had the option of migrating west and becoming independent farmers, they could not be subject to European levels of exploitation. Thus the West was said to provide a "safety-valve" against the pressures caused by capitalist development.

Scab   Slang term for a worker employed during a strike; a strikebreaker.

Scalawag   A derogatory term referring to southern whites who sympathized with the Republicans during Reconstruction.

Second-wave feminism   The reborn women's movement of the 1960s and 1970s that reinterpreted the first wave of nineteenth- and early twentieth-century feminists' insistence on civil rights and called for full economic, reproductive, and political equality.

Separation of powers   One of the chief innovations of the Constitution and a distinguishing mark of the American form of democracy, in which the executive, legislative, and judicial branches of government are separated so that they can check and balance each other.

Sharecropping   The practice of a tenant farming the landlord's ground for a share of the crop, sold when the harvest came in. This became a common form of employment for former slaves in the post–Civil War South.

Slave power   In the 1850s northern Republicans explained the continued economic and political strength of slavery by claiming that a "slave power" had taken control of the federal government and used its authority to keep slavery alive artificially.

Slave society   A society in which slavery is central to the economy and political structure, in contrast to a *society with slaves*, in which the presence of slaves does not alter the fundamental structures of the society.

Slavery   A system of extreme social inequality distinguished by the definition of a human being as property, or chattel, and thus, in principle, totally subordinated to the slave owner.

Social Darwinism   Darwin's theory of natural selection transferred from biological evolution to human history. Social Darwinists argued that some individuals and groups, particularly racial groups, were better able to survive in the "race of life."

Spoils system   The practice of politicians rewarding their friends with offices and contracts.

Stagflation   The unusual combination of stagnant growth and high inflation that plagued the American economy in the 1970s.

Strict constructionism   The view that the Constitution has a fixed, explicit meaning that can be altered only through formal amendment. Loose constructionism is the view that the Constitution is a broad framework within which various interpretations and applications are possible without formal amendment.

Subtreasury   A government-run bank in which farmers could get low-interest loans using their crops as collateral. The creation of subtreasuries formed a key plank in the Populist platform.

Suburbanization   The spread of suburban housing developments and, more broadly, of the suburban ideal.

Supply-side economics   The controversial theory, associated with economist Arthur Laffer, that drove "Reaganomics," the conservative economic policy of the Reagan administration. In contrast to liberal economic theory, supply-side economics emphasized that producers—the "supply side" of the economic equation—drove economic growth, rather than consumers—the "demand side." To encourage producers to invest more in new production, Laffer and other supply-siders called for massive tax cuts.

Tammany Hall   A fraternal organization in New York City that developed into a Democratic political machine, electing officials, mobilizing voters, and allotting contracts. Its enemies saw it as a symbol of corrupt, selfish, and incompetent government.

Tariff   A tax on goods moving across an international boundary. Because the Constitution allows tariffs only on imports, as a political issue the tariff question has chiefly concerned the protection of domestic manufacturing from foreign competition. Industries producing mainly for American consumers have preferred a higher tariff, while farmers and industries aimed at global markets have typically favored reduced tariffs. Prior to the Civil War, the tariff was a symbol of diverging political economies in North and South. The North advocated high tariffs to protect growing domestic manufacturing ("protective tariffs"), and the South opposed high tariffs on the grounds that they increased the cost of imported manufactured goods.

Taylorism   A method for maximizing industrial efficiency by systematically reducing the time and motion involved in each step of the production process. The "scientific" system was designed by Frederick Taylor and explained in his book *The Principles of Scientific Management* (1911).

Temperance   Moderation, or the use of something with restraint. In the Gilded Age, the temperance movement opposed the use of alcohol.

Trusts   Corporate arrangements to unify action in production and distribution among different firms. Shareholders handed over control of their stock to a board that held the shares in trust and operated the combined concerns.

Universalism   Enlightenment belief that all people are by their nature essentially the same.

Vaudeville   A type of variety show popular in the late 1800s and early 1900s. Vaudeville was family friendly and included songs, band performances, skits, comedy routines, and circus acts.

Vertical integration   The practice of taking control of every aspect of the production, distribution, and sale of a commodity. For example, Andrew Carnegie vertically integrated his steel operations by purchasing the mines that produced the ore, the railroads that carried the ore to the steel mills, the mills themselves, and the distribution system that carried the finished steel to consumers.

Virtual representation   British doctrine that said that all Britons, even those who did not vote, were represented by Parliament, if not "actually," by representatives they had chosen, then "virtually," because each member of Parliament was supposed to act on behalf of the entire realm, not only his constituents or even those who had voted for him.

Voluntarism   A style of political activism that took place largely outside of electoral politics. Voluntarism emerged in the nineteenth century, particularly among those Americans who were not allowed to vote. Thus women formed voluntary associations that pressed for social and political reforms, even though women were excluded from electoral politics.

Waltham system   Named after the system used in early textile mills in Waltham, Massachusetts, the term refers to the practice of bringing all elements of production together in a single factory setting with the application of non-human-powered machinery.

Wampum   Shell beads used by Indians of the Eastern Woodlands to make jewelry and to memorialize political agreements; later used as currency in the trade networks established between Europeans and Indians.

Watergate   The name of the Washington, DC, office and condominium complex where five men with ties to the presidential campaign of Richard Nixon were caught breaking into the headquarters of the Democratic National Committee in June 1972. "Watergate" became the catchall term for the wide range of illegal practices of Nixon and his followers that were uncovered in the aftermath of the break-in.

Whig Party   The political party founded by Henry Clay in the mid-1830s. The name derived from the seventeenth- and eighteenth-century British antimonarchical position and was intended to suggest that the Jacksonian Democrats (and Jackson in particular) sought despotic powers. In many ways the heirs of National Republicans, the Whigs supported economic expansion, but they also believed in a strong federal government to control the dynamism of the market. The Whig Party attracted many moral reformers.

Whitewater   With its echo of Richard Nixon's "Watergate" scandals in the 1970s, "Whitewater" became the catchall term for the scandals that plagued Bill Clinton's presidency in the 1990s. The term came from the name of a real estate development company in Arkansas. Clinton and his wife Hillary supposedly had corrupt dealings with the Whitewater Development Corporation in the 1970s and 1980s that they purportedly attempted to cover up in the 1990s.

Women's rights movement   The antebellum organizing efforts of women on their own behalf, in the attempt to secure a broad range of social, civic, and political rights. This movement is generally dated from the convention of Seneca Falls in 1848. Only after the Civil War would women's rights activism begin to confine its efforts to suffrage.

Photo Credits

Index

A

AAA. *See* Agricultural Adjustment Act
ABC, 932
Abdel-Rahman, Sheikh Omar, 1091
Abenaki Indians, 181–82
ABM (Anti-Ballistic Missile) treaty, 1008
Abolition, 396–97, 426–34, 473–74
  African Americans involved in, 272, 426–29, 430
  colonization solution, 425, 426
  first movements, 271–73
  gradual, state, 517–18, 527, 543
  immediatism, 429–30
  Pennsylvania Society petition, 274–75
  Texas annexation and, 460, 474
  violence against, 430–32
Abortion
  conservative attack on, 1036, 1041, 1042, 1054, 1055, 1087
  legalization of, 1016
  NOW on, 989
  prohibition of, 626, 627
  rates of (1980s), 1056(map)
Abu Ghraib, 1100
Abzug, Bella, 1016(photo)
Acadians, 191
Acid rain, 1045
Acid rock, 988
Acid test, 988
Acoma Pueblo, 134(photo)
Acquired immune deficiency syndrome (AIDS), 1055–57, 1083, 1088
Act of Toleration, 79
ACT UP (AIDS Coalition to Unleash Power), 1056
Action Comics, 817
Adams, Abigail, 244–45, 246, 278
Adams, Brooks, 698, 700
Adams, Charles Frances, 656
Adams, Henry, 530, 558, 681, 710
Adams, John, 204, 211, 244–45, 246, 278, 301, 426
  American Revolution and, 222
  Declaration of Independence and, 224–25
  presidency of, 288–91, 293
  vice presidency of, 263, 289
Adams, John Quincy, 344–46, 353
  Amistad incident and, 403–4
  election of 1828 and, 351–52
  National Republican philosophy and, 338–39
  Native Americans and, 358, 359
  as secretary of state, 340, 341
  Texas annexation and, 451, 452, 460
Adams, Samuel, 201, 204, 206–7, 211, 221, 222
Adams, Samuel Hopkins, 725
Addams, Jane, 716, 729, 734, 762
  Hull-House and, 721, 723–24
  NAACP and, 728
  Roosevelt's (Theodore) nomination and, 742
  World War I entry opposed by, 753, 754, 756

Administration of Justice Act of 1774, 212
Admiral Electrical Appliances, 932
Adventures of Huckleberry Finn (Twain), 640
Advertising, 791, 806, 932–33, 954
Affirmative action, 1018, 1035, 1036, 1054, 1055, 1057, 1058, 1084
Afghanistan
  Soviet invasion of, 1029, 1047–48, 1065, 1091
  terrorist presence in, 1071–72, 1092, 1093
  U.S. occupation of, 1071–72, 1093, 1099, 1100, 1104
AFL. *See* American Federation of Labor
AFL-CIO, 928
Africa
  in the age of discovery, 13(map)
  Arab Spring in, 1104
  cell phone use in, 1073
  cold war and, 895
  Obama administration and, 1104
  origination of humankind in, 4
  Portuguese explorations in, 10–12, 14, 16
  Reagan Doctrine in, 1050–51
  slave trade in, 12, 86, 147–48
  slavery practiced in, 148, 419
African Americans
  affirmative action and, 1013–14, 1057, 1058, 1084
  Atlanta Compromise, 694–95, 728
  Black Power movement, 983, 984–86, 989, 1018
  as Civil War soldiers, 529, 532–33, 536, 634
  colleges and universities for, 636
  distribution of population (1775), 272(map)
  employment discrimination, 425, 693, 761, 851, 911, 985
  Exodusters, 603, 604(photo)
  Great Depression and, 823
  Great Migration, 761–62
  Homer's paintings of, 641
  in industrial America, 660, 662
  labor unions and, 789
  in late 19th century, 691–96
  lynchings of, 537, 571, 694, 695(photo), 727, 732, 761, 762, 802, 805, 839, 861, 911
  in mid-20th century, 940
  minstrel shows and, 620–22, 641
  in modern era, 804–6
  music of, 793, 810, 941–42, 1058
  New Deal programs and, 835–36, 839
  New Negro, 762, 797, 804–6
  populist, 672
  in post-civil rights era, 1083–84
  progressivism and, 727–29, 732
  in Reagan era, 1057–59
  Reconstruction and, 553–74, 577–80, 660
    experiments with free labor, 553–54

Freedmen's Bureau, 544, 551–52, 556, 557, 559, 562(photo), 564, 570
  land ownership dream, 556–57
  in public office, 565, 566, 567(photo), 577
scientific racism on, 638, 694
"separate but equal" doctrine, 694, 952
sharecropping and, 553, 560–61, 567–70, 602–3, 631
Spanish-American War and, 701, 702
in sports, 625
as strikebreakers, 602
Vietnam War and, 982
voting rights, 559, 562–64, 571, 653, 659, 662, 665, 911
  disfranchisement, 682, 695–96, 732, 806, 910
  Fifteenth Amendment, 564(table), 573–74, 577, 579
  free blacks (during slavery), 273, 348–49, 424
  grandfather clause, 695, 729
  origins of, 564–65
  registration drives, 966, 976, 977–78
  Ten Percent Plan, 554–55
World War I and, 761–62, 763
World War II and, 851–52, 861–62, 869, 871–72
See also Civil rights movement; Free black population (during slavery); Jim Crow system; Race riots; Slavery
Afro-American Council, 727
Age of exploration, 9–12
Age of Reform, The (Hofstadter), 675
Aging population, 1079(map)
Agnew, Spiro, 1023, 1025
Agrarian Revolt, 670–72, 675
Agricultural Adjustment Act (AAA), 830, 835, 844
Agricultural Marketing Act of 1929, 825
Agriculture. *See* Farming/agriculture
Agriculture Department, 661, 665, 736, 830
Aguilar, Jerónimo de, 3
Aguinaldo, Emilio, 704, 705
Aid to Families with Dependent Children, 1012
AIDS. *See* Acquired immune deficiency syndrome
AIDS Coalition to Unleash Power (ACT UP), 1056
AIG, 1101
Air Quality Act of 1967, 975
Air traffic controllers' strike, 1045, 1046(photo)
Aircraft
  Lindbergh's flight, 797
  World War II, 863, 864(figure), 867(photo)
  Wright brothers' flight, 787
Aircraft carriers, 860–61
Ajax (CIA operation), 944
Akron, Ohio, 790

Akron Tire, 760
Alabama
  Civil War and, 541–42
  prior to Removal Act, 362(map)
  secession of, 509
  settlement of, 268
  slavery in, 405, 420, 458
  statehood, 314
Alabama (ship), 572
Alamo, Battle of, 451
Alaska, 1028
  purchase of, 572, 663
  statehood, 941
Albany, 49, 51, 123, 160, 193
Albany Movement, 966
Albany Plan of Union, 187
Albert, Dorothy, 892
Albright, Madeleine, 1087
Alcatraz Island, Indian occupation of, 1020
Alcohol
  Crusade against, 655
  Native Americans and, 166
  in New Netherland, 50
  taverns, 162, 268
  taxes on, 284, 302
  See also Prohibition; Temperance movement
Alcorn, Allan, 1005
Alcott, Louisa May, 640
Alcott, William, 391
Alexander VI, Pope, 16
Alfonso VI, king of Castile, 8
Alger, Horatio, 601, 637
Algeria, 302, 866
Algonquian Indians, 40, 49, 60(photo), 127
  Beaver Wars and, 53
  French and Indian War and, 185, 191, 196
  French colonizers and, 43, 47, 48, 130, 182
Ali, Muhammad, 982
Alianza Federal de Mercedes, 1018
Alien and Sedition Acts, 291–93, 301, 306, 365
All in the Family (television program), 1023(photo)
Allegheny River, 186
Allen, Ethan, 222
Allende, Salvador, 1011
Alliance for Progress, 971
Allis-Chalmers, 867
Almshouses, 163, 279
Almy, William, 385
Alonso, 37, 38
Alsop, Joseph, 914
Altgeld, Peter, 670
Aluminum Company of America, 759
Alvarado, Pedro de, 30
Amalgamated Clothing Workers, 837
Amazon.com, 588, 1077
"America" (Ginsberg), 951
America First Committee, 855
America in 1492 (Josephy, ed.), 26–27
America the Beautiful (film), 946
American Anti-Slavery Society, 397, 430, 431–32, 433, 473

American Bible Society, 380–81, 396
American Board of Commissioners
    for Foreign Missions
    (ABCFM), 359, 379–80, 452
"American Century, The" (Luce), 871
American Civil Liberties Union, 874
American Colonization Society
    (ACS), 425, 426, 430
American Defense Society, 754
American Expeditionary Force (AEF),
    764, 770
American Federation of Labor (AFL),
    687, 696–97, 720, 789, 837,
    928
American GI Forum, 941
American Imperialism (May), 706–7
American Indian Movement (AIM),
    1019–20
American Medical Association
    (AMA), 626
American Mercury, 798
American National Exhibition,
    946–47
American Party (Know-Nothings),
    485, 486
American Professional Football
    Association, 792
American Protective Association
    (APA), 657
American Psychiatric Association,
    1021
American Railway Union (ARU),
    687, 697
American Recovery and Reinvestment
    Act of 2009, 1103
American Republic, 261–97, 299–335
    borders and boundaries of, 280–81
    conflicting visions of, 273–77
    controlling the borderlands,
        281–84
    culture of, 277–79
    economy of, 265–67, 311–22, 327
    extension of territories
        (1783/1795), 289(map)
    invention and exploration in,
        315–18
    politics of transition in, 300–307
    problem of trust in, 330–31
    struggle to form a government,
        263–67
    in transition, 267–79
    ways of life in, 322–32
American Revolution, 220–48, 265,
    285, 286, 299, 532
    British offensive in, 228–31
    British surrender, 233, 236(photo),
        237
    causes of, 223–24
    challenges following, 238–46
    competing strategies in, 227–28
    conflicts leading to, 182, 183–84,
        196, 198–213
    first battles of, 220–22
    hardships during, 231
    military ardor during, 222–24
    Native Americans and, 238, 247–48
    Second (Reagan's call for), 1061
    territory negotiations following,
        233–38, 280
American Slavery, American Freedom
    (Morgan), 120–21
American Society for the Promotion
    of Temperance (ASPT), 393
American System, 339–40, 345, 386,
    441, 459
American Telephone and Telegraph
    Company (AT&T), 476,
    1045
American Women (report), 989
America's Cup yacht race, 625
Amherst, Lord Jeffrey, 192, 196
Amish, 145

Amistad incident, 403–4
Ampudia, Pedro de, 466
Amsterdam News, 851
Anaconda copper mine, 611
Anaconda plan, 516
Anarchists, 670
Anasazi Indians, 7
Anatomy of a Kiss, The (film), 794
Anderson, John, 1042
Anderson, Sherwood, 700, 798, 822
Andros, Edmund, 122–23, 124, 125
Angelino, Joseph T., 826
Anglican Church, 79, 124, 125, 172,
    328
Anglo-Powhatan Wars, 74, 78
Angola, 1051
Angola prison, 832–33
Angolite, 833
Antebellum era, 473–505
    manifest destiny in culture of,
        445–49
    political economy in, 474–80
    politics of slavery in, 480–85
    women's rights in, 396–97
Antelope (slave ship), 426
Anti-Ballistic Missile (ABM) treaty,
    1008
Anti-Imperialist League, 704
Anti-Republicans, 266
Anti-Saloon League, 763, 806
Antibiotics, 935
Antietam, Battle of, 526–27, 528, 533,
    536, 1093
Antifederalists, 254–55, 264
Antimason Party, 351, 441
Antin, Mary, 817
Antinomianism, 95
A&P grocers, 592, 787
Apache Indians, 134, 136, 137, 439,
    455, 608
Apartheid, 1050–51
Apollo (moon project), 965
Apollo Magazine, 277
Appalachian Mountains, 236, 237,
    238, 247, 248, 314, 412
*Appeal to the Colored Citizens of the
    World, An* (Walker), 427–28,
    429
*Appeal to the People of the United
    States, An* (American Anti-
    Slavery Society), 431
Apple, R. W., 1060
Apple Computer, 1036, 1038–39,
    1040
Appleton, Nathan, 320
Appomattox Court House, 542,
    544(photo)
Arab Spring, 1104
Arapaho Indians, 136, 439, 455, 605
Arawak Indians. *See* Taino Indians
Arbella (ship), 88
Archaic period, 5
Ardennes Forest, 855, 862, 879
Area Redevelopment Act of 1961, 966
Argentina, 341
    communism in, 971
    Great Depression and, 838
Ariane lauch vehicle, 1076
Arizona, territory acquired by U.S.,
    463, 464
Arizona (battleship), 856
Arkansas
    secession of, 509–10, 511
    slavery in, 458
    statehood, 346
Arkansas River, 123, 453
Arkansas Territory, 343
Arkwright, Richard, 385
Arlington National Cemetery, 530,
    531
Arminianism, 84, 95, 172
Armour, Philip, 590, 597

Arms reduction
    ABM treaty, 1008
    "Atoms for Peace" plan, 945
    INF Treaty, 1065
    Limited Test Ban Treaty, 972
    modern era movement, 809
    Reagan administration and, 1048,
        1065
    SALT I, 1008
    SALT II, 1026, 1029, 1048
    START, 1065
Armstrong, Edward Howard, 772
Armstrong, Louis, 793
Armstrong, Neil, 1012
Army
    McCarthy hearings, 917
    post-revolution era, 241, 250, 251
Army General Order 13, 762
Army of the Potomac, 516, 517, 526,
    536, 540, 542
Arnold, Benedict, 222, 228
Arnold, Matthew, 634, 639
Aroonstook Valley, 443–44
Arrangement—New York (Matulka),
    790(photo)
Arthur, Chester A., 660, 661–62
Articles of Confederation, 226, 239,
    248, 251, 252(table), 255, 273
Asian American Political Alliance
    (AAPA), 1019
Asian Americans
    activism, 1018–19
    population growth, 1083
Asiatic Squadron, 700
Aspirin, 717
Assemblies of God, 1041
Association of Community Chests and
    Councils, 823
Associationalism, 809, 825
Astor, John Jacob, 312
Astor, Sarah, 312
A&T Four, 961, 962
Atari, 1005, 1038
Atchison, David Rice, 490
Atlanta, Sherman's capture of, 541,
    542(photo), 543(map)
Atlanta Compromise, 694–95, 728
Atlantic Charter, 856
Atlantic Monthly, 514, 639, 742
Atlantic Wall, 878
Atomic Age, 914
Atomic bomb, 864, 885, 894, 895
    American fear of, 914
    development of, 883–84
    Japan attacked with, 882–84, 902,
        914
    Rosenberg case, 916, 944
    Soviet, 883, 884, 898, 902, 914
Atomic Energy Act of 1954, 943
"Atoms for Peace" plan, 945
AT&T. *See* American Telephone and
    Telegraph Company
Attucks, Crispus, 210
Atwater, Wilbur, 726
Augusta (cruiser), 856
Auschwitz concentration camp, 874
Austin, Stephen F., 449, 451
Australia
    Iraq War and, 1097
    Ottawa Accords and, 838
Austria
    King George's War and, 183
    Napoleon's victory over, 305
    World War II and, 853, 854
Austria-Hungary, 749, 753, 764, 765
Autarkies, 838–39, 893, 894
*Autobiography of Benjamin Franklin,
    The* (Franklin), 170–71
Automobiles
    bailout of industry, 1102, 1103
    consumer safety concerns, 974
    decline in industry, 1000, 1101

    Japanese, 1002, 1052, 1053
    mass production of, 784–85, 788
    in mid-20th century, 926, 931
    in modern era, 784–87, 792, 798
    suburbanization and, 790
    World War I impact on industry,
        760
    youth culture and, 795
    See also Chevrolet; Chrysler; Ford
        Motor Company; General
        Motors
"Axis of evil," 1097
Ayllón, Lucas Vázquez de, 24
Azores, 16
Aztecs, 3, 6, 17, 18, 24
    smallpox in, 27(photo)
    Spanish conquest of, 20–23

B

B-1 (strategic bomber), 1047
B-2 (Stealth bomber), 1047
B-17 (Flying Fortress), 856, 863
B-24 (Liberator), 863, 866
B-25 (bomber), 857
B-29 (bomber), 880, 884, 902
B-29 (Superfortress), 863
B-47 (Stratojet), 944(photo)
B-52 (bomber), 1008
Babaataa, Afrika, 1058
Babbitt (Lewis), 798
Baby boom generation, 935,
    936(table), 1004, 1039–40,
    1079
Backcountry, 234–35, 281–82, 314,
    346
Bacon, Francis, 167
Bacon, Nathaniel, 116–17
Bacon's Rebellion, 116–17, 122
Bailyn, Bernard, 223
Baker, Ray Stannard, 683, 725
Bakker, Jim, 1060
Balanced Budget and Emergency
    Deficit Control Act of 1985,
    1062
Baldwin, Luther, 291
Balfour, James, 157(photo)
Balfour, Jemima, 157(photo)
Ball, Charles, 271, 420
Ballinger, Richard, 741
Baltic Sea, 9
Baltimore, 154, 160
    free black population of, 425
    War of 1812 and, 308
Baltimore and Ohio Railroad, 586
Baltimore Sun, 500
Bank holidays, 828
Bank of America, 1101
Bank of the United States, First, 313,
    338
    See also National bank
Bank of the United States, Second,
    322, 338
    Jackson and, 352–57, 386, 440–41
    panic of 1819 and, 331–32, 350
    terms of charter, 339–40
Banking Act of 1935, 829
Banks
    in American Republic, 313
    Clinton and, 1081
    depression of 1837 and, 442, 443
    Dodd-Frank Act and, 1103
    Great Depression and, 819, 821,
        825
    in modern era, 787
    New Deal legislation, 828–29, 834
    panic of 1819 and, 331–32
    panic of 1893 and, 587, 681–82
    Wilson and, 743
Banks, Nathaniel, 554
Banks Plan, 554, 555
Baptists, 128, 174, 219, 272, 328,
    329–30, 378, 720

Barbados, 87, 115, 159
Barbed wire, 613, 749
Baring Brothers, 681
Barlowe, Arthur, 54
Barnes, Jonathan, 164
Barnett, Ross, 966
Barrios, 804, 941, 1018
Bartholdt, Richard, 628
Barton, Bruce, 791
Baruch, Bernard, 759, 763
Baseball, 624–25, 792, 911–12
Bastille, storming of, 284
Bataan Peninsula, 857
Batten, Barton, Durstine, and Osborn, 791
"Battle Hymn of the Republic" (song), 514–15
Baum, L. Frank, 673
Bavaria, 773
Bay of Pigs incident, 971
Bay of Santiago de Cuba, 700
Bayard, Blandina Kierstede (deed for land purchase), 109(photo)
Bear Stearns, 1100
Beat movement, 951
Beatles, 987
Beatniks, 951
Beauregard, P. G. T., 524–25
Beaver Wars, 53
Bedford Cut Stone Co. v. Journeymen Stone Cutters' Assn., 788
Bedroom Blunder, A (film), 794
Beecher, Catharine, 396
Beecher, Henry Ward, 490
Beecher, Lyman, 373, 392–93
Beekman and Cruger, 276
Béjarano, José, 1003
Belgium, 749, 753, 855
Belgium Relief, 726, 824
Bell, Alexander Graham, 623
Bell, John, 501
Bellamy, Edward, 668–69
Belleau Wood, Battle of, 770
Benevolent Empire, 377–81, 387
Benezet, Anthony, 272
Benin, 12
Benton, Thomas Hart, 442, 463
Bergerud, Eric M., 991–92
Beringia land bridge, 4
Berkeley, Lord John, 109, 116, 117
Berlin
  airlift, 900–902
  division of, 895
Berlin Wall
  erection of, 971
  fall of, 1065, 1066
Bernard, Francis, 207, 208, 209
Bernstein, Carl, 1024
Berry, Chuck, 942
Bessemer, Henry, 595
Bessemer process, 595
Best Years of Our Lives, The (film), 914
Bethune, Mary McLeod, 839
Beveridge, Albert, 697, 742
Beverley, Robert, 118
Bhopal pesticide plant accident, 1061
Bibb, Henry, 424
Bicycle, 625
Biddle, Nicholas, 353, 357
Bierce, Ambrose, 639, 704
Bierstadt, Albert, 738
Big business
  consolidation of, 597–98
  in modern era, 787
  rehabilitation of (1980s), 1037–41
  rise of, 592–98
  scandals in (1980s), 1060
  See also Corporations
Big stick diplomacy, 737–40
Big Three (allies' leaders), 894–95, 897(photo)
Bill Haley and the Comets, 942
Bill of Rights, 249, 255, 264–65

Billion Dollar Congress, 662
Biltmore Estate, 599(photo)
Bin Laden, Osama, 1093, 1099–1100
  beliefs of, 1091–92
  capture and death of, 1104
Biotechnology, 1077
Bird, Kai, 756
Birkey, Henry, 269
Birmingham
  African American church bombing in, 976
  civil rights activism in, 966–67
  manufacturing in, 790
Birney, James G., 433, 461–63
Birth control. *See* Contraception
Birth control pill, 988
Birth of a Nation (film), 728
Birth rates
  in colonial America, 150–51
  of Hispanic Americans, 1059
  in mid-20th century, 935
  of Native Americans, 25
Bison, 457, 608
Bizerte, 866
Black, Hugo, 874
Black and Decker Company, 760
Black belt, 603
Black Belt (Motley), 762(photo)
Black Codes, 304, 557–58, 567
  See also Slave codes
Black Eagles, 862(photo)
Black Hawk, 360
Black Hawk's War, 360
Black Kettle, 607–8
Black Panthers, 985–86, 989, 1019, 1021–22, 1023
Black Power, 983, 984–86, 989, 1018
Black Star Line, 805
Black Tuesday, 818–19, 1062
Blackfoot Indians, 136, 455
Blacklisting, 915
Blaine, James G., 660, 664
Blair, Ezell, 961, 994
Blair Education Bill, 662
Bland, Alden, 762
Bland-Allison Act of 1878, 660
Bleeding Kansas, 488–91
Bliss, William Dwight Porter, 720
Blitzkrieg, 855
Blue-collar workers, 791, 935
Blue Eagle banner, 833, 835
Board for the Emigration, Preservation, and Improvement of the Aborigines of America, 359
Bob Jones University, 1058
Bodnar, John, 632–33
Boeing, 867
Boesky, Ivan, 1037, 1039, 1060
Bohemian Charitable Association, 823
Boland Amendment, 1050, 1060
Boleyn, Anne, 83
Bolling, Raynal C., 755
Bolshevik Revolution, 764, 765, 769, 893
Bombs
  neutron, 1047
  proximity fuse, 864
  See also Atomic bomb; Hydrogen bomb
Bonaparte, Napoleon, 271, 290, 307, 311, 342
  Louisiana Purchase and, 303
  trade embargo and, 305–6
Bonds, 199, 265, 266, 523, 681
  junk, 1037
  war, 523
Bonus Marchers, 825–26
Book of Mormon, 331
Booth, John Wilkes, 545
Border ruffians, 488, 490
Bosnia-Herzegovina, 1090–91
Bosses, political, 652, 666

Boston
  American Revolution and, 227, 228
  in colonial era, 92
    founding of, 87
    growth of, 160, 162
    immigration to, 145
    newspapers of, 203
    poverty in, 163
    protest and resistance in, 184, 203–4, 207–12
    tax rates (1645-1774), 184(figure)
  free black population of, 425
  port of, 155
  Route 128, 1037
  school busing in, 1014, 1015
  slavery in, 163
Boston Courier, 431
Boston Gazette, 204
Boston Manufacturing Company, 320
Boston Massacre, 207–10, 213(table), 220
Boston News-Letter, 162
Boston Port Bill, 211, 212
Boston Tea Party, 211–12, 213(table), 220, 1104
Bougainville, 880
Bouquet, Henry, 198(photo)
Bowers v. Hardwick, 1056
Boxer movement, 707, 708
Boxing (prizefighting), 622–24, 625
Boycotts
  grape, 1018
  Knights of Labor, 669
  Montgomery bus, 953
  outlawing of, 697, 777
Boylston, Thomas, 239
Bozeman Trail, 607
Braceros, 869, 940
Braddock, Edward, 187–90, 192
Bradford, William, 84–85
Brady, Mathew, 642
Bragg, Braxton, 539
Brains Trust, 827–28, 830
Brandeis, Louis, 727, 735, 742
Brando, Marlon, 950
Brant, Joseph, 248, 249(photo)
Brazil, 56, 159
  Dutch claim to, 50–51
  Great Depression and, 838
  Portuguese claim to, 16, 23, 31
  space program and, 1076
  student protest in, 987
Brazos River, 449
Breckinridge, John, 501
Breckinridge, Sophonisba, 719
Breed's Hill, Battle of, 221(map), 222, 227
Brest-Litovsk, Treaty of, 765
Bretton Woods Conference, 882, 895, 1013
Bridge building, 315, 595, 666
Brief and True Report of the New Found Land of Virginia, A (Hariot), 58–59
British-American Tobacco Company, 699
British East India Company, 159, 200, 210, 211
Broadsides, 279
Bronco Busters and Range Riders Union, 720
Brooklyn Bridge, 666
Brooklyn Dodgers, 911
Brooklyn Heights, 228
Brooks, Preston S., 491, 492
Brotherhood of Sleeping Car Porters, 789, 851, 911
Brown, Charles Brockden, 278
Brown, Helen Gurley, 989
Brown, John, 488–91, 499–500, 513
Brown, Joseph E., 519
Brown, Linda, 952

Brown, Oliver, 952
Brown, Smith, 385
Brown, Sterling, 805
Brown, Tarleton, 234–35
Brown, William Hill, 278
Brown Berets, 1018, 1023
Brown Power, 1017–18
Brown University, 175
Brown v. Board of Education, Topeka, Kansas, 952–53, 954, 962, 1083
Brownlow (slave ship), 150
Brownson, Orestes, 390
Bruce, H. C., 556–57
Bryan, Joseph, 861
Bryan, William Jennings, 741, 742, 750, 753
  "Cross of Gold" speech, 689–90
  imperialism opposed by, 704
  Scopes trial and, 801
  World War I entry opposed by, 754
Bryant, Anita, 1055
Bryant, William Cullen, 448
Buchanan, James, 494, 495, 496, 497
Buchanan, Patrick, 1085
Buchanan's Station, 283–84
Buchenwald concentration camp, 874
Buckley, William F., 963, 964
Buffalo
  destruction of, 608
  hunted by Native Americans, 8, 29, 136
  hunted by whites, 457
Buffalo Soldiers, 702
Bulgaria, 1065
Bulge, Battle of, 879
Bulger, William, 1014
Bull Run, Battles of, 516–17, 526
Bunau-Varilla, Philippe, 739
Bunker Hill, Battle of, 221
Bureau of Foreign Commerce, 686
Bureau of Indian Affairs (BIA), 607, 831, 1019, 1020
Bureau of Refugees, Freedmen and Abandoned Lands. *See* Freedmen's Bureau
Burger, Warren, 1023, 1054
Burgoyne, John, 231
Burke, Edmund, 104
Burke, Emily, 411
Burns, Arthur T., 823
Burnside, Ambrose, 536, 539, 540
Burr, Aaron, 289, 300, 301, 305
Burroughs, William, 951
Burton, Harold, 818
Bush, George H. W., 1042, 1087
  Bosnia crisis and, 1090–91
  election of 1988 and, 1080
  election of 1992 and, 1080
  Persian Gulf War and, 1089
Bush, George W., 1075(photo), 1081, 1087, 1088, 1102
  on home ownership, 1101(photo)
  Iraq War and, 1097–1100
  space program and, 1076
  terrorism threat and, 1092, 1093, 1094
Bush Doctrine, 1097
Business. *See* Big business
Busing, school, 1013, 1014, 1054, 1057
Butler, Andrew, 491
Butler, Benjamin F., 513, 529, 532
Buzzanco, Robert, 991
Byrd, William, II, 164

C

Cable News Network. *See* CNN
Cabot, John, 17, 39
Caciques, 16
Cahokia, 7
Cajuns, 191
Cakchiquel Indians, 28

Calhoun, John C., 344, 350, 353
    National Republican philosophy
        and, 338–39
    nullification crisis and, 364–65
    slavery issue and, 458, 461, 480–81,
        482
    War of 1812 and, 307
California
    acquired by U.S., 463, 464, 466
    gold strikes in, 455, 480,
        481(photo), 606, 611
    migration to, 941
    Proposition 13, 1027
    Proposition 187, 1082
    statehood, 481, 482
    Transcontinental Treaty on, 340
Calley, William, Jr., 1008
Calorie, importance of, 726–27
Calorimeter, 726
Calusas, 19–20
Calvert, Charles, 125
Calvert, Sir George, 79
Calvin, John, 83
Calvinism, 51, 83–84, 105, 106, 143,
        167, 172, 175, 328
Cambodia
    bombing of, 1008–11, 1025
    Khmer Rouge in, 1026
Camden, Battle of, 233
Camera, 642–43
Cameron, Simon, 513
Camp David Accords, 1028–29, 1051
Camp Logan, 763
Canada
    American Revolution and, 222, 236
    annexation refused by, 664
    border dispute with U.S., 443–44
    French and Indian War and,
        194–95
    French surrender of, 195
    Jay's treaty and, 288
    King George's War and, 183
    King William's War and, 126–27
    Monroe Doctrine not applied
        to, 342
    NAFTA and, 1082
    in NATO, 899
    New France, 39, 42–48
    Ottawa Accords and, 838
    rebellion against Great Britain,
        444–45
    role in French empire, 130–31
    space program and, 1076
    War of 1812 and, 307–8, 309
    Webster-Ashburton Treaty and,
        460
Canals, 316, 319(map), 474
    See also Erie Canal; Love Canal;
        Suez Canal
Canary Islands, 12
Cane Ridge revival, 328, 329–30
Canfora, Alan, 1010
Cannons, 10
Canterbury, Robert, 1009
Cape Breton Island, 193
Cape of Good Hope, 12
Capital gains taxes, 1028
Capitalism
    Bellamy's critique of, 668–69
    in colonial America, 151, 155, 160
    communism vs., 893–94, 896
    George's critique of, 667–69
    Puritans and, 90
    Roosevelt (Franklin) and, 834–35
    slavery and, 419–22
    welfare, 788, 789
    See also Industrial capitalism
Caravel, 10
Carey, Mathew, 381
Caribbean, 23, 50, 51, 77, 196
    British seizure of, 195
    French in, 132–33
    origin of name, 15

Reagan Doctrine in, 1049, 1050
    Roosevelt Corollary in, 740, 741
    U.S. presence in, 740(map)
    Wilson administration and, 752–53
Caribbean Basin Initiative, 1050
Caribs, 15
Carlos V, king of Spain, 18
Carmichael, Hoagy, 796
Carmichael, Stokely, 985
Carranza, Venustiano, 751
Carson, Rachel, 975
Carswell, G. Harrold, 1023
Cartels, 598
Carter, Jimmy, 1024, 1035, 1043, 1045,
        1046, 1048, 1050
    background of, 1027
    election of 1976 and, 1027
    election of 1980 and, 1042
    human rights and, 1029, 1047,
        1049
    presidency of, 1027–29
Carter, William H., 587
Carteret, Lord George, 109
Cartier, Jacques, 41–42, 44, 45, 64
Caruso, Enrico, 637
Casablanca, 880
Casey, William, 1061
Cass, Lewis, 461
Cassepot, 534
Cassettari, Rosa, 585–86, 589, 598,
        600, 611, 614, 629
Castle William, 204, 208
Castro, Fidel, 971, 1059, 1098
Catawba Indians, 940
Cather, Willa, 639
Catherine of Aragon, 53, 83
Catherine the Great, empress of
        Russia, 168–69
Catholicism
    in antebellum era immigrants,
        475, 477
    anti-Catholicism, 387, 388, 485–86,
        657, 658, 665
    Democratic Party attacks on, 811
    Dominion of New England and,
        124
    in England, 53, 83, 106
    German Americans and, 145
    in immigrant culture, 628, 630–31
    in Kongo, 165
    in Maryland colony, 79, 125
    in mid-20th century, 935
    Native Americans and, 45, 113, 134
    nativism vs., 485–86
    in the Philippines, 705
    Puritan view of, 83–84
    Quebec Act and, 212
    Queen Anne's War and, 127
    Roosevelt (Franklin)
        administration and, 839
    slaves and, 133
    in Spain, 54
    in Texas, 451
    women's suffrage opposed in, 719
Catt, Carrie Chapman, 719, 762
Cattle, 92, 154
Cattlemen, 610–12
Cayuse Indians, 452, 455
CBS, 932
CCC. See Civilian Conservation Corps
Cellular and mobile telephones, 1073
Centers for Disease Control, 912, 1056
Central America
    Reagan Doctrine in, 1049–50
    Taft administration and, 750

Central Intelligence Agency (CIA)
    Bay of Pigs incident, 971
    Chilean election and, 1011
    cold war activities of, 915, 917,
        944–45
    contra rebels and, 1050
    creation of, 899
    failure to detect 9/11 plot, 1093
    hearings on secret operations of,
        1026
    Nixon's use of, 1023
    terrorism countermeasures and,
        1104
Central Pacific Railroad, 605
Central Park, 666
Central Treaty Organization
        (CENTO), 949
Chaco Canyon, 7
Challenger (space shuttle), 1063–64
Chambers, Whittaker, 916
Champlain, Samuel de, 45–47, 64
Chancellorsville, Battle of, 536
Chaney, James, 976
Channing, William Ellery, 391
Chaplin, Charlie, 783
Charles I, king of England, 79, 87, 105
Charles II, king of England, 105, 106,
        109–11, 122
Charles V, emperor of Spain, 39
Charleston, 113, 115, 166, 172
    American Revolution and, 228,
        231
    Civil War and, 520, 542
    colonial era growth, 160
    free black population of, 425
    French and Indian War and, 193
    port of, 155
    slavery in, 163, 164, 271
Charleston Mercury, 364
Charlottesville, 233
Charter colonies, 79
Charter of Libertyes and Priviledges,
        109
Charter of 1691, 211
Charter of Virginia, 72–73
Charters, corporate, 349–51
Chase, Salmon P., 433
Chase, Samuel, 301
Chattanooga, Battle of, 539–40
Chávez, César, 1018
Chavez, Linda, 1035–36, 1054, 1059
Checks and balances, system of, 252
Cheney, Dick, 1097
Chenoweth, Helen, 1083
Chernobyl nuclear accident, 884, 1061
Cherokee Indians, 183, 281, 282–84,
        330, 379
    internal institutions of, 325
    removal policy and, 358, 359,
        362–63
Cherokee Strip, 683
Chesapeake (frigate), 306
Chesapeake Bay, 49, 79, 308
Chesapeake colonies, 70–83, 164
    economy of, 152, 154
    forces shaping, 79
    gender roles and social order in, 82
    New England compared with,
        82–83, 87
    origins of slavery in, 80–81
Chesapeake Indians, 61
Cheves, Langdon, 331, 332
Chevrolet, 787, 926, 931, 974
Cheyenne Indians, 136, 439, 455, 605,
        607–8
Chicago
    African Americans in, 761, 762,
        985
    Burnham's city plan for, 733(photo)
    business concentration in, 790
    Days of Rage in, 1021
    fire of, 587, 591
    industrial era growth in, 591

    in late 19th century, 682–83
    19th Ward, 715, 721, 729
Chicago Commons, 585
Chicago Inter Ocean, 653
Chicago Mercantile Exchange,
        1102(photo)
Chicago Movement, 985
Chicago Record, 683
Chicago River, 666
Chicago Tribune, 854
Chicano Student Movement of Aztlán
        (MEChA), 1018
Chicanos, 1017–18
    See also Mexican Americans
Chickahominy River, 69
Chickamauga, Battle of, 533, 539–40
Chickamauga Indians, 283
Chickasaw Indians, 114, 330, 358, 359
Child, Lydia Maria, 391
Child labor, 385, 386, 601, 655, 666,
        669, 719, 720–21, 732, 744,
        795, 845
Child mortality rates, 151, 631
Children
    in American Republic, 330
    in colonial era, 82, 93
    of Huron Indians, 46–47
    latchkey, 870
    in mid-20th century, 935
    in slavery, 118, 165, 261, 418
    See also Youth
Chile, 4, 341
    communism in, 971
    Nixon administration and, 1011
    Valparaiso riot, 664
China
    atomic weapons testing, 883
    Boxer movement in, 707, 708
    Columbus's planned voyage to,
        14, 15
    early explorations of, 13–14
    economic power of, 1106
    Eisenhower administration and,
        945
    globalization and, 1073
    Iraq War and, 1097
    Japanese attack on (WWII), 852,
        853, 856, 903
    Japanese war with, 685, 699
    Korean War and, 898, 905
    "loss" of, 903, 905
    missionaries in, 699, 707
    Nixon administration and, 1007,
        1008
    oil demand in, 699, 1101
    Open Door Note, 707–9, 741
    opium trade and, 159, 312, 380
    Reagan administration and, 1049
    revolution in, 898, 902–3
    space program and, 1076
    Taft administration and, 741, 750
    Taiping Rebellion in, 589
    trade with, 8, 10, 312, 1074
    United Nations and, 881
    U.S. attempts to stabilize, 811
    U.S. court in, 740
    Wal-Mart in, 1074, 1075(photo)
    Wilson administration and, 750
Chinchow-Aigun railway, 741
Chinese exclusion acts, 656–57, 670
Chinese immigrants, 589, 656–57,
        1019
Chinook Indians, 455
Chippewa Indians, 187
Chisholm, Shirley, 999, 1013, 1021,
        1030
Chisholm Trail, 610
Chocolate, 29
Chocolate Kiddies revue, 810
Choctaw Indians, 132, 358, 359
Cholera, 453, 591, 738, 776
Christian Advocate and Herald, 452
Christian Broadcast Network, 1042

Christian Restoration movement, 329
Christianity
  fundamentalist, 801
  Native Americans and, 16, 17, 18
  slavery opposed by, 272
  slaves converted to, 174, 418–19
  See also Evangelical Christianity;
    Missionaries; individual
    religions
Chrysler, 1027, 1102, 1103
Chuichi, Nagumo, 861
Chumash Indians, 455
Church, Frederick, 445
Church of England, 83–84, 94, 105
Church of Jesus Christ of Latter-day
  Saints. *See* Mormons
Churchill, Winston
  "Iron Curtain" speech, 896
  at Potsdam Conference, 882,
    897(photo)
  World War II and, 855–56, 864–65,
    871, 880
  at Yalta Conference, 894–95
CIA. *See* Central Intelligence Agency
Cibola, Seven Cities of, 24–25
Cientificos, 751
Cigar Makers' International Union,
  696
Cincinnati Redlegs, 917
Cinncinnati Red Stockings, 624
Cinqué, Joseph, 403–4
CIO. *See* Congress of Industrial
  Organizations
Cities and urbanization
  in American Republic, 268, 278
  in colonial America, 160–63
  culture and (*see* Urban culture)
  government of, 666, 729–32
  industrial, 591–92
  middle class of, 384–87
  migration to, 388–89
  in modern era, 789–90
  percentage of population in (1890-
    1920), 717(figure)
  reform and, 381–89
  in the South, 413, 691–93
  turn-of-the-century, 691–93,
    729–32
Citizenship
  African Americans and, 277, 343,
    496, 532–33, 562, 579
  French Revolution and, 286–87
  women and, 242–46, 277
City Beautiful movement, 624, 732
City busting, 880
Civil Rights Act of 1866, 562, 563, 570
Civil Rights Act of 1875, 577
Civil Rights Act of 1957, 954
Civil Rights Act of 1964, 976, 977,
  978, 989
Civil Rights Cases of 1883, 578–80
Civil rights movement
  COFO, 976, 977
  CORE, 872, 911, 976
  in Eisenhower era, 952–54
  Freedom Riders, 966
  Freedom Summer, 976, 977–78
  grassroots activism for, 962
  Johnson (Lyndon) administration
    and, 976–78
  Kennedy administration and,
    966–70
  Little Rock school desegregation,
    953–54
  post-World War II, 910–12
  SCLC, 953, 966, 967, 976, 978
  sit-ins, 961, 962
  SNCC, 962, 966, 976, 978, 982, 985
Civil service, 577, 656, 659, 660, 915
Civil Service Commission, 656, 660
Civil War, 507–49, 629, 634, 653, 656,
  658, 685, 1093
  antiwar sentiment, 536–37

beginning of, 511
blockade in, 520, 522
Brady's photos of, 642, 643(photo)
care of casualties, 533–36
casualties in, 536(figure), 545
civilian reactions to, 533–39
commutation policy, 536
Confederate discontent, 539
Confederate military advantages,
  520–21
Confederate strength in the East,
  526–27
end of, 542
final battles in, 539–42
hard war strategy, 512, 516, 524,
  540–41, 542
Homer's paintings of, 641
justification of, 537–38
meaning of, 545
military strategy and shift in aims,
  513–18
mobilizing for, 518–24
planter's exemption in, 539
popular support for, 511–12
productive capacities of opponents,
  518(figure)
reasons for fighting in, 523–24
as a social revolution, 524–33
Union naval supremacy, 512, 520
Union reverses in, 536–37
Union victories in the West,
  524–25
Civil Works Administration (CWA),
  829, 839
Civilian Conservation Corps (CCC),
  829, 839
Cixi, dowager empress of China,
  707, 708
Clark, Tom, 915
Clark, William, 304
Clay, Henry, 332, 353, 389–90,
  440–41, 460
  abolition movement and, 425
  as a Mason, 351
  Missouri Compromise and, 343,
    482
  National Republican philosophy
    and, 338–39
  Native Americans and, 359
  presidential candidacies of, 344–
    45, 458, 461, 463
  slavery issue and, 482, 484
  War of 1812 and, 307
Clayton Antitrust Act of 1914, 743
Clean Air Act of 1963, 975
Clean Air Act of 1970, 1026
Clean Waters Restoration Act of
  1966, 975
Cleary, John, 1010
Cleveland, Frances Folsom, 661
Cleveland, Grover, 656, 659, 660–62,
  664, 665, 689
  imperialism opposed by, 697, 704
  Morgan bailout loan and, 681–82,
    688
  Pullman workers' strike and, 687
Cliff dwellings, 7
Clinton, Bill, 1077, 1080–81, 1087
  Bosnia crisis and, 1090–91
  "don't ask, don't tell" policy, 1088
  elections of, 1080, 1081
  impeachment of, 1081
  terrorism threat and, 1092
Clinton, De Witt
  on common school movement, 393
  Erie Canal construction and, 316,
    318(photo), 449
  War of 1812 and, 308
Clothing, colonial era, 157
CNN, 1073, 1089
Coahuila y Tejas, 439
Coal mining, 412, 631, 666, 697,
  735, 908

Coatzacoalcos region, 20
Cobden, Richard, 530
Coca-Cola, 867
Cocaine, 717, 1055
Cocoa, 159
Codices, 29
Cody, Buffalo Bill, 620
Coercive Acts. *See* Intolerable Acts
Coffee, 159, 239, 838
Coffeehouses, 159
Coffin, Howard E., 758
COFO. *See* Council of Federated
  Organizations
Cohan, George M., 637, 871
Coinage Act of 1873, 658
Coit, Stanton, 721
COLAs (cost-of-living adjustments),
  908
Colbert, Jean-Baptiste, 130
Cold Harbor, Battle of, 541, 1093
Cold war, 891–906, 962, 1000
  American life after, 1088–99
  American unfamiliarity with, 893
  Asian alliances, 948(map)
  Carter administration and, 1028
  civil rights movement and, 954
  coining of term, 896
  conformity and, 934
  consumerism and, 926, 946–47
  in Eisenhower era, 942, 944–50
  end of, 1065–66
  ethnicity decline and, 935
  gender roles and, 936
  globalization and, 1072
  ideological competition in, 893–94
  impact on everyday life, 914–20
  Middle East and, 895, 949(map)
  national security and, 895–906
  origins of, 893–95, 897–98
  space program and, 955
  See also Communism; Soviet
    Union
Cole, Thomas, 445
Cole (destroyer), 1092
Coleman, William, 571
Collateralized debt obligations
  (CDOs), 1100, 1101
College of New Jersey, 175
Colleges and universities
  in colonial America, 91, 172, 175
  flaming youth on campus, 796–97
  GI Bill and, 906–7
  Johnson (Lyndon) administration
    and, 974
  modern, 635–36
  progressivism and, 727
  for women, 636, 718
Collier, John, 831
Collier's (magazine), 950
Colombia, 23, 183
  civil war in, 739
  Panama Canal and, 664
Colonial America
  charter colonies, 79
  children in, 82, 93
  consumerism in, 143–44, 151,
    156–60
  east of the Mississippi (1720),
    131(map)
  empires in collision, 130–37
  expansion of settlement (1720-
    1760), 146(map)
  family life in, 152–53
  marriage in, 82, 93, 128, 150–51,
    153, 164
  population explosion in, 144–51
  proprietary colonies, 79, 112
  royal colonies, 79, 125
  transatlantic economy and, 151–60
  varieties of experience in, 160–66
  See also American Revolution;
    Dutch colonies; English
    colonies; French colonies;

New World; Spanish
  colonies
Colonizers, 652
Colorado
  gold strikes in, 611
  territory acquired by U.S., 464
Colorado River, 449, 951
Colored Farmers' Alliance, 672
Colored Orphan Asylum, 537
Colt, Samuel, 534
Columbia (space shuttle), 1076
Columbia College, 175
Columbia River, 452
Columbia University, 823, 942, 951
Columbian Exchange, 28–29
Columbian Exposition, 623, 683
Columbus, Christopher, 5, 8, 12–17,
  18, 29, 30, 38, 39, 56, 167,
  278, 683
  arrival in Spain, 9
  first voyage of, 14–15
  theories of, 12–13
Comanche Indians, 136, 137, 182–83,
  363–64, 439, 449, 450, 455,
  608
Commission on National Goals, 955
Commission plan, 729–30
Committee on Public Information
  (CPI), 759
Committee to Re-Elect the President
  (CREEP), 1024, 1025
Commodore, 1038
Common school movement, 393–94
Common Sense (Paine), 220, 224,
  225(photo)
*Common Sense Book of Baby and
  Child Care* (Spock), 935
Commons, John R., 727
Communications technology, 1072–73
Communism
  capitalism *vs.*, 893–94, 896
  collapse of, 1065–66
  crusades against, 915
  Johnson administration and,
    978–79
  labor unions and, 834, 908, 917
  New Deal programs and, 834
  Nixon administration and, 1006,
    1011
  Reagan administration and, 1036,
    1047–51
  Red Scares, 776–77, 801, 915, 918
  in third world, 945–50, 970–71,
    978–79
  See also Cold war; Soviet Union
Communist Party of the United States
  of America (CPUSA), 834,
  891–92, 915
Communitarians, 374–77
Community Action Programs (CAP),
  974
Commutation, 536
Company E, 4th United States Colored
  Infantry, 532(photo)
Compass, 10
Compromise of 1850, 482–83, 484
Computers, 1036–39, 1040, 1077,
  1078
  emergence of, 926–27
  new economy and, 1036–37
Comstock, Anthony, 619–20, 624, 625,
  639, 641, 643, 646
Comstock Law, 619, 626
Comstock Lode, 611, 612
Concord, Battle of, 220–21, 227
Conestoga Manor, 197
Confederacy
  capital of, 513, 516, 518–19, 520,
    526, 539, 540, 542
  currency of, 522, 539
  discontent in, 539
  government of, 518–20
  military advantages of, 520–21

military strength in the East, 526–27
motives of soldiers in, 523
slave states refusing to join, 511, 527, 539
See also Secession
Conformity, 930, 934
Confucius Plaza, 1019
Congregationalism, 172, 328, 329–30, 430, 599
Congress
in American Republic, 263–64
Billion Dollar, 662
post-revolution problems, 251
Reconstruction and, 559–62
in revolutionary era, 225–26
Congress of Industrial Organizations (CIO), 837, 839, 908, 928
Congress of Racial Equality (CORE), 872, 911, 976
Congressional Government (Wilson), 742
Congressional Reconstruction, 564–70
Conkling, Roscoe, 659, 660
Connecticut, 52
Constitutional ratification and, 254
voting rights in, 348
Connecticut colony, 87, 97, 124, 125
Connecticut Compromise, 253
Connecticut River, 49, 96, 106, 109, 280
Connecticut River valley, 154
Connor, Eugene ("Bull"), 966–67
Conquest
consequences of, 25–30
morality of, 18
Conscientious objectors, 757, 759
Conscription
Civil War, 525, 536–37, 539
Selective Service Act, 899
Vietnam War, 981, 982
World War I, 757–58, 761, 764
World War II, 855
Consent, principle of, 201, 213
Conservation movement, 736–39
Conservatism, 1035–59
abortion issue and, 1036, 1041, 1042, 1054, 1055, 1087
backlash against 1960s, 990, 1021–24, 1054–55
creating a majority, 1036–43
culture wars and, 1085, 1086–87
family values issue, 1085
neo, 1097
new, 963–64, 973
New Deal and, 844–45
in new economic era, 1080–81
setbacks for agenda, 1061
social values of, 1054–59
See also Reagan Revolution
Conservative Manifesto, 844
Conservative Mind, The (Kirk), 963
Consciousness-raising groups, 1014
Conspicuous consumption, 783
Conspiracy theory, 891
Constellation (carrier), 861
Constitution, 219, 249, 250–55, 271, 274, 304, 321–22, 323, 343, 422–23, 433, 473, 483, 496, 500
key provisions of, 252(table)
ratification of, 252, 253–55, 264–65, 273, 278, 280, 365
strict constructionism, 266
writing, 251–53
Constitution, British, 200
Constitution, Confederate, 519
Constitution of the Lowell Factory Girls Association, 321
Constitutional Convention, 251–55, 341, 365
Constitutional Unionist Party, 500, 501

Constitutionalism, 201, 204–5, 225
Constructive engagement, 1051
Consumer Product Safety Commission, 1012
Consumer Protection Agency, 1028
Consumer revolution, 151, 157, 158, 160, 206
Consumerism
in colonial America, 143–44, 151, 156–60
in evangelical Christianity on, 143–44
habit-forming products, 159
mid-20th century, 925–34
challenges to, 950–55
cold war and, 926, 946–47
the good life and, 926–34
in modern era, 790–92, 797
Containment policy, 898–99, 902, 903, 905, 906, 945, 947, 970
Continental Congress, First, 212–13, 213(table), 222
Continental Congress, Second, 222
Continuous flow, 598
Contra rebels, 1050, 1060–61
Contraband camps, 530–33, 554
Contraband Relief Organization, 416
Contrabands, 513, 516(photo), 529
Contraception
birth control pill, 988
changing attitudes toward, 794
legalization of access, 975
restriction of access, 626, 627
Sanger's activism, 719, 794
Contract labor, 557–58, 567, 568
Contract law, 321–22
Convention of 1800, 290
Convict lease system, 832–33
Coode, John, 125
Coode's Rebellion, 79, 125
Cook, Will Marion, 810
Cooke, John Esten, 540
Coolidge, Calvin, 784
presidency of, 808–11, 821
vice presidency of, 807
Cooling-off treaties, 750
Cooper, Anthony Ashley (Earl of Shaftesbury), 112–13, 124
Cooper, James Fenimore, 391, 448
Cooper, William, 240, 267
Cooper Union, 500
Cooperationism, 509–11
Coors brewery, 1059
Copper, 41, 412, 611, 613
Copperheads, 536, 537, 545
Coquette (film), 812
Coquille Indians, 940
Coral Sea, Battle of, 859, 860
CORE. *See* Congress of Racial Equality
Cornell University, 635, 797
Cornish, Samuel E., 427
Cornwallis, Lord, 233, 236(photo), 237
Coronado, Francisco Vásquez de, 25, 133
Corporation for Public Broadcasting, 974
Corporations
chartered, 349–51
consolidation of, 688, 1077
economic decline and (1970s), 1000
large-scale organization, 787
mid-20th century, 928
multinational, 1002–4, 1073
See also Big business
Corregidor, 857
"Corrupt bargain" (election of 1824), 338, 344–45
Corruption
in early 20th century government, 717

Galveston Plan on, 693
in industrial era government, 665
muckraking on, 725
in New Deal programs, 835
in Reconstruction programs, 575–76
Roosevelt's (Theodore) crackdown on, 734
Cortés, Hernando, 3–4, 20–23, 29, 30
Cortés, Martín, 56
Corwin, Jonathan, 128
Cosmopolitan, 722
Cost-plus contracts, 760, 866
Cotlar, Seth, 292, 293
Cottagers, 154
Cotton, 106, 311, 314, 405, 413, 451, 670, 691
in antebellum era, 475, 477
Civil War and, 520, 521, 522, 525, 539
global demand for, 420
market collapse, 442
plantations, 409(photo), 411, 553
price decline, 332, 364, 420, 558, 789
production by region (1800-1860), 421(figure)
sea island, 406
sharecropping and, 567, 568, 603
textile mills and, 313, 320, 385, 420, 421–22
transport of, 315–16
Cotton, John, 94–95
Cotton gin, 313, 319, 405, 406, 420, 434
Cotton States Exposition, 694–95
Coughlin, Charles, 817, 834
Council of Economic Advisors, 912
Council of Federated Organizations (COFO), 976, 977
Council of the Indies, 18
Counterculture, 986–89, 1085
Country music, 941
Couzens, James, 730
Coverture, 242, 277
Covey, Edward, 417
Covenant Chain, 123
Cowboys, 610–12
Cowpens, Battle of, 233
Cox, Archibald, 1024–25
Cox, James M., 807
Coxe, Tench, 279
Coxey, Jacob, 683
Crack, 1055
Crandall, Prudence, 431
Crawford, William H., 344
Crazy Horse, 608
Credit, consumer, 113, 442, 567–68, 791
Credit cards, 929
Credit Mobilier, 576
Credit Reinvestment Act of 1995, 1081
Creek Indians, 136, 183, 248, 281, 282–83
Jackson's campaign against, 299–300, 308
removal policy and, 358, 359, 360
Creel, George, 759, 765
Creole (slave ship), 459
Crevecoeur, J. Hector St. John De, 273
"Crime Against Kansas" speech, 491, 492–93
Crittenden, John J., 510
Crittenden Compromise, 510–11
Croatan (carrier), 861
Croker, Richard (cartoon), 667(photo)
Croly, Herbert, 735, 741
Cromwell, Oliver, 105
Crop liens, 691
Cross of Gold, The (Debreuil), 689(photo)
"Cross of Gold" speech, 689–90
Crow Indians, 455, 605, 608

Crusade, The (against alcohol), 655
Crusades, 9
Crystal Palace, 623
Cuba, 705, 838, 1051
annexation issue, 664, 701
Bay of Pigs incident, 971
independence achieved, 704
missile crisis, 966, 971–72
Ostend Manifesto and, 489
revolution in, 699–704, 971
under Spain, 25, 697
Wilson administration and, 752
Cuban-American Treaty of 1903, 1098
Cuban Americans, 1059
Cugoano, Ottobah, 147
Cullen, Countee, 805
Cultural feminism, 1014–16
Culture
of American Republic, 277–79
of industrial America, 619–49
high, 620, 631, 633–38, 639, 641
immigration and, 628–33
popular, 620, 633, 639, 641
realism, 619, 639–45
manifest destiny in, 445–49
postmodern, 1078
of precontact Americas, 26–27
See also Modern culture; Urban culture
Culture and Anarchy (Arnold), 634
Culture and Natural Areas of Native North America (Kroeber), 26
Culture wars, 1083, 1085, 1086–87
Cumberland River, 315
Cummins, Sarah, 453
Currency
in American Republic, 331–32
in Civil War, 522, 523, 525, 539, 658
in colonial era, 106, 184, 198
Confederate, 522, 539
Continental, depreciation of (1770-1781), 241(figure)
great contraction of, 820
greenbacks, 523, 525, 658–59, 671
"In God We Trust" added to, 935
in industrial era, 658–59, 660, 671
Jackson's policy, 357, 443
in modern economy, 688–91
panic of 1893 and, 681–82
in post-revolution era, 240–41, 251
Van Buren's policy, 442–43
Currency Act of 1764, 198, 210, 213(table)
Cushing, John Perkins, 443
Custer, George Armstrong, 607–8
Cvetic, Matt, 891–92, 924
CWA. *See* Civil Works Administration
Czechoslovakia
communism collapse in, 1065
Soviet invasion of, 987
World War II and, 854
Czolgosz, Leon, 734

D

D-Day, 878
Daguerre, Louis, 642
Daley, Richard, 985, 986, 993
Dallas (television program), 1039
Daly, Marcus, 611
Dams, 321, 830, 868, 904, 951
Danbury Hatters case, 697
Dardanelles, 896
Darrow, Clarence, 801
Dartmouth College, 175, 322
Dartmouth v. Woodward, 321–22
Darwin, Charles, 638
Daughters of Bilitis, 940
Davenport, James, 175
Davenport, John, 96
Davidson, Donald, 798
Davis, Benjamin O., 861
Davis, Henry Winter, 555

Davis, Jefferson, 508, 511, 512, 519, 525
  criticism of, 539
  on Emancipation Proclamation, 529
  federal slave code proposed by, 497
Davis, John W., 808
Dawes, William, 220
Dawes Severalty Act of 1887, 609–10, 661
Day care, 870
Day The Earth Stood Still, The (film), 955
Dayan, Moshe, 861
Days of Rage, 1021
De La Warr, Lord, 74
De Soto, Hernando, 24, 25
Deadly Mantis, The (film), 955
Dean, James, 950
Dean, John, 1024
"Death of Captain Waskow, The" (Pyle), 875–77
Debs, Eugene V., 683, 687–88, 697, 720
  imperialism opposed by, 704
  imprisonment of, 758
  presidential candidacy of, 742
Debtors' prisons, 166, 169, 332
Decade of the Hispanic, 1059
Declaration of Independence, 224–25, 230, 289, 494, 508
Declaration of Rights, 212–13
Declaration of Sentiments, 397
Declaration of the Causes and Necessities of Taking Up Arms, 222
Declaration of the Causes Which Induced the Secession of South Carolina, 508
Declaration of the Rights of Man and of the Citizen, 285, 286
Declaratory Act of 1766, 204, 213(table)
Deephaven (Jewett), 639
Deepwater Port Commission, 692, 693
Defense Department, 1072, 1087
Defense of Marriage Act of 1996, 1088, 1103
Deficit spending, 845, 866, 1103
Deflation, 240, 241, 669, 671
Deganawidah, 8
Deindustrialization, 1004, 1013, 1026, 1036, 1045, 1058
Del Monte Company, 630
Delaware
  in colonial era, 162
  Constitutional ratification and, 254
  emancipation resisted in, 543
  secession resisted by, 510, 511, 539
  slavery in, 246, 273
Delaware Indians, 49, 192
Delaware River, 49, 50, 79, 106
  Washington's crossing of, 228
Dell Computer, 1036, 1037
Delta Democrat-Times, 977, 978
Democracy
  Adams (John Q.) presidency and, 345–46
  common school movement and, 393–94
  Enlightenment ideas on, 169–72
  expert dictatorship *vs.*, 725
  exporting, 905
  Jacksonian (*see* Jacksonian Democracy)
  neoconservatism on, 1097
  participatory, 964
  politics of 1790s and, 292–93
  in post-revolution era, 241–42
  Puritans and, 89, 90
  rise of, 75–76
  Roosevelt (Theodore) on, 734
  women's associations impact on, 719
  World War I fought for, 757

Democratic Party
  African Americans and, 839
  civil rights movement and, 966
  Civil War and, 519, 525, 529, 541
  current stance of, 1105
  election of 1840 and, 458
  election of 1844 and, 461–63
  election of 1848 and, 481
  election of 1852 and, 484–85
  election of 1856 and, 491, 494
  election of 1860 and, 500–501
  election of 1868 and, 571
  election of 1872 and, 577
  election of 1876 and, 578
  election of 1880 and, 659, 660
  election of 1888 and, 662
  election of 1896 and, 689, 690
  election of 1912 and, 742
  election of 1920 and, 807
  election of 1928 and, 811
  election of 1932 and, 826, 827
  election of 1936 and, 839
  election of 1964 and, 973
  election of 1968 and, 993
  erosion of popular support for, 467
  gold standard and, 689
  Hispanic vote and, 1059
  immigrant vote and, 485–86
  in industrial America, 652, 653–54, 658, 659–60, 665, 672
  Jackson and, 352, 440, 441
  Kansas-Nebraska Act and, 488
  labor unions and, 836, 837, 908, 909
  in modern era, 807, 811
  New Deal and, 835, 839, 845
  nullification crisis and, 365
  post-World War II troubles of, 912–13
  racism in, 486, 494, 572
  Reconstruction and, 570, 571, 575, 577–78
  sectional split in, 474, 497
  slavery issue and, 426, 432, 433–34, 462–63, 464, 480, 481, 495, 497–99, 500–501, 509, 536
  Thirteenth Amendment and, 544
  Van Buren and, 443
Democratic Republicans, 287, 300, 304, 322, 328
  Alien and Sedition Acts and, 291–93
  changes in, 338–40
  dominance of, 301–2, 305, 307, 321
  election of 1796 and, 289
  Jay's Treaty and, 288
  trade embargo and, 306
  views of, 266–67
  War of 1812 and, 308
Denmark
  Virgin Island purchase offer, 663–64
  World War II and, 855
Dennett, John, 551–52
Dependents' Pension Law, 662
Deposit Act of 1836, 357
Depressions
  of 1780s, 270
  of 1808, 306
  of 1829, 381
  of 1837, 381, 441, 442–43, 444(photo), 458
  See also Financial crisis of 1890s; Great Depression; Panics
Deregulation, 1027–28, 1045, 1081
Descartes, 49
Deslondes, Charles, 304
Détente, 1006, 1007, 1011, 1026, 1028, 1029, 1047
Detroit
  housing riots in, 869
  as motor city, 790

  race riots in, 871–72, 984
  War of 1812 and, 308, 327
Detroit, Treaty of, 908–9
Dewey, George, 700, 704, 705
Dewey, Thomas E., 882, 913
DeWitt, John L., 872
Dexter, James Oronoko, 270
Dexter, Sarah, 270
Dexter Avenue Baptist Church, 953
Dhahran, 901–2
Díaz, Porfirio, 664, 751
Díaz del Castillo, Bernal, 21
Dickens, Charles, 382–83
Did Monetary Forces Cause the Great Depression? (Temin), 821
Dido, 219
Diem, Ngo Dinh, 949, 972
Dien Bien Phu, 947
Diggers, 988
Dilworth, Rankin, 465–66
Dingley Tariff Act, 690
Dinosaur National Monument, 951
Dior, Christian, 943
Diphtheria, 168, 935
Disease
  AIDS, 1055–57, 1083, 1088
  in Chesapeake colonies, 80
  cholera, 453, 591, 738, 776
  in Civil War soldiers, 535
  diphtheria, 168, 935
  gangrene, 535
  gonorrhea, 763
  hepatitis, 85
  influenza, 27, 775–76
  mad cow, 776
  malaria, 168, 360, 375, 410, 413, 453, 535, 700
  measles, 168, 452
  mill-child's cough, 601
  Native Americans and, 20, 25–28, 85, 137, 168, 192, 304, 360, 452, 457, 610
  plague, 28
  polio, 827, 935
  rickets, 822
  SARS, 776
  smallpox, 22, 25, 27, 167, 168–69, 192, 234–35, 530, 776
  during Spanish-American War, 700–701
  tuberculosis, 715
  typhoid fever, 71, 453, 535, 715, 935
  typhus, 27, 738, 776
  yellow fever, 591
Disfranchisement, 682, 695–96, 732, 806, 910
Disney World, 1004
Disneyland, 928(photo), 941, 1004, 1088
Diversity
  changing composition of, 1083
  of colonial-era cities, 162–63
  in Pennsylvania colony, 109–12
  survival of, 941–42
Divorce rate, 268, 277, 626, 627, 1085
"Dixie" (song), 514, 515
Dixon, John F., 770
Doby, Larry, 912
Doctors Without Borders, 1074
Dodd-Frank Act, 1103
Doeg Indians, 116
Dole, Robert, 1027, 1081
Dole, Sanford, 704
Dole, William P., 609
Dollar-a-year men, 866
Dollar diplomacy, 741, 750
Dominican missionaries, 37
Dominican Republic, 739–40, 811, 979
Dominion of New England, 124
Domino, Fats, 942
Domino theory, 948, 979

Donner Party, 454
Donovan, Raymond, 1060
"Don't ask, don't tell" policy, 1088, 1103
Doolittle, James, 857, 859, 917
Double V campaign, 872
Doughboys, 764, 770
Dougherty, Ester, 269
Dougherty, John, 269
Douglas, Aaron, 805
Douglas, Stephen A., 494
  Kansas-Nebraska Act and, 486–87
  Lecompton Constitution and, 497
  Lincoln debates with, 497, 498(photo), 500
  Omnibus Bill and, 482–83
  presidential candidacy of, 500–501
Douglass, Frederick, 397, 407–8, 412, 417, 418(photo), 429, 477, 498
  on fugitive slave law, 484
  on Harper's Ferry raid, 499
  life and times of, 473–74
  on Lincoln, 502
  on Santo Domingo annexation proposal, 572
  on women's suffrage, 574
Dow Chemical Company, 1003
Dow Jones industrial average, 1078, 1101, 1105(figure)
Doyle, James, 491
Draft. *See* Conscription
Draft riots, 536–37
Drake, Sir Francis, 42, 54, 60, 64
Dreadnought-class warships, 860
Dred Scott decision, 496–97, 498, 532–33, 562
Drug use
  conservative view of, 1054–55
  counterculture, 987
Duane, William J., 353
Dubinsky, David, 837
DuBois, W. E. B., 728, 761, 805, 872
Duho, 15(photo)
Dukakis, Michael, 1080
Duke, James B., 699
Dulles, John Foster, 944, 949
Dumbarton Oaks meeting, 881
Dumont, 932
Dunmore, Lord, 198, 224
Duplex Printing Press Co. v. Deering, 788
Dust Bowl, 823, 830
Dutch colonies, 49–53, 63, 96
  See also New Netherland
Dutch East India Company, 49, 159
Dutch East Indies, 856
Dutch Reformed Church, 51
Dutch West India Company, 49–50, 51
Dyer, Mary, 122
Dylan, Bob, 987
Dynamic obsolescence, 931
Dynasty (television program), 1039

E

E. J. Korvettes, 925–26, 927, 929, 931, 956
Eads Bridge, 595(photo)
Eagleton, Thomas, 1024
Eakins, Thomas, 641, 642
Earle, Jonathan, 462–63
Earth Day, 1012
East Louisiana Railway, 693–94
Eastern Europe
  cold war and, 895, 899
  communism collapse in, 1065
Eastern State Mental Hospital, 172
Eastern Woodlands Indians, 8, 281
Eastman, George, 643
Easton, Treaty, 194
Eaton, Theophilus, 96
EBay, 1077
Echo Park Dam, 951

Echota, Treaty of, 362
Eckert, J. Presper, Jr., 926–27
Eckford, Elizabeth, 954(photo)
Economic Opportunity Act of 1964, 973
Economic Recovery Act of 1981, 1045
Economies of scale, 598
Economy
  in 1970s, 1000–1004
  in 1990s-2000s, 1100–1102, 1104–6
  of American Republic, 265–67, 311–22, 327
  Carter administration and, 1028
  Enlightenment ideas on, 169–72
  global (by 1600), 31(map)
  global (2011), 1074(map)
  of industrial America, 658–65
  information, 1077–78
  mid-20th century, 926–28
  modern, 688–91
  in modern era, 784–90
  new, 1036–37, 1077–83
  Nixon administration and, 1013
  Obama administration and, 1102–3, 1104–5
  personal income per capita (1840-1880), 461(table)
  post-revolution, 238–42
  post-World War II, 906–7
  Reagan administration and, 1044–46, 1061–62
  of slavery, 412–13, 521–23
  transatlantic (colonial era), 151–60
  of Virginia colony, 75–76
  of the West, 610–13
  world (Reagan era), 1052
  World War I and, 759–60
  World War II and, 866–67
  See also Political economy
Edict of Nantes, 44
Edison, Thomas Alva, 406, 591, 622, 637, 786, 793
Education
  in American Republic, 279
  bilingual instruction in, 1018, 1019
  cold war concerns, 955
  in colonial America, 93
  common school movement, 393–94
  experts' takeover of, 725
  for freed slaves, 555–56, 567
  under industrial capitalism, 601
  Johnson (Lyndon) administration and, 974
  parochial schools, 628, 631, 657, 665
  prayer prohibited in public schools, 975
  public, 393–94, 630–31, 666
  segregated, 952–54, 962, 976, 985
  vouchers proposed, 1054
  for women, 243, 246, 279, 393, 636, 718, 796
  See also Colleges and universities
Education Department, 1054
Edwards, Jonathan, 172, 175
Egan, Raymond B., 791
Egypt, 838
  Arab Spring in, 1104
  Camp David Accords and, 1028–29, 1051
  cotton from, 670
  Israeli conflicts with, 1001, 1011
  Suez Canal crisis, 949
Ehrlichman, John, 1024
Eight-Hour Leagues, 574
Eighteenth Amendment, 763
Eighth Amendment, 264
Einstein, Albert, 864, 883
Eisenhower, Dwight D.
  background of, 942
  on Buchenwald, 874
  as NATO commander, 899, 942

presidency of, 942–50, 956, 962, 965, 970, 971
  civil rights and, 954
  cold war and, 942, 944–50
  farewell address, 955
  Vietnam War and, 972, 979
  World War II and, 866, 878, 942
Eisenhower, Mamie, 943, 944
Eisenhower Doctrine, 949
El Dorado, 77
El Salvador, 1050
Electoral College (early procedures), 289–90
  See also Presidential elections
Electricity
  Franklin's experiments with, 167
  industry aided by, 784
  introduction of, 591
  TVA and, 830
Elementary and Secondary School Act of 1965, 974
Elizabeth I, queen of England, 53, 54, 55, 61, 70, 83, 86, 105
Elkins Act of 1910, 735
Elkinson, Harry, 423
Ely, Ezra Stiles, 378
Ely, Richard T., 638, 639, 727
Emancipation, 524, 527–33, 553
  completion of, 543–45
  diplomacy of, 520
  final wave of, 557
  military, 517, 527, 543
  northern opposition to, 272–73, 536–37
  in practice, 530–33
  universal, 527–29
Emancipation Proclamation, 527, 528–29, 530, 531, 533, 536, 967
Embargo Acts, 306, 307
Emergency Banking Act, 828
Emergency Economic Stabilization Act of 2008, 1102
Emergency Relief Appropriations Bill, 835
Emerson, John, 496
Emerson, Ralph Waldo, 390, 391
Emmett, Daniel Decatur, 514
Empire of Liberty (Wood), 292
Employment Act of 1946, 912
Employment discrimination
  African Americans and, 425, 693, 761, 851, 911, 985
  women and, 909–10, 989, 1055, 1087
Empresarios, 451
Empress of China (ship), 312
Encomienda system, 16, 18, 23, 24, 25, 31, 42, 134–35
Endangered Species Act of 1973, 1027
"Enemies from Within" speech, 918–19
Energy crises, 1001, 1002(photo), 1004, 1028
Energy Department, 1028
Enfield rifle, 534
Enforcement Acts, 573
England, 53–55
  African population of, 81
  American Civil War and, 518, 520, 522, 530
  civil war in, 105
  Columbus turned down by, 14
  Dutch conflicts with, 106–9
  French conflicts with, 123, 124, 126–27, 131–32, 182, 285–87, 288, 305
  Glorious Revolution in, 79, 106, 121, 124–26, 201
  Ireland conquered by, 54–55
  King George's War, 183, 184–85
  King William's War, 126–27, 199

land claims in American Republic, 280, 281
  as Native American allies, 248, 281
  Native Americans in, 56–57
  opium trade with China, 159, 312, 380
  political hierarchy in, 164–65, 201
  Puritan movement in, 83
  Queen Anne's War, 114, 126–27, 182, 199
  Samoa claimed by, 664
  slave trade and, 54, 86–87, 117, 149, 271
  slave trade banned in, 403, 433, 528
  slavery abolished in, 271
  Spanish conflicts with, 42, 53–54, 57, 61, 63–64, 70, 133, 183, 287, 305
  tension between American Republic and, 288
  textile mills of, 313, 420
  trade with America
    in colonial era, 205(figure)
    embargo, 305–7
    growth in, 311
    post-revolution policy, 238, 239, 241, 242, 251, 270, 276, 288, 290
  turmoil in 1600s, 104–6
  War of Jenkins's Ear, 183, 203
  women's rights discussed in, 277
  world's fair of, 623
  See also American Revolution; English colonies; English empire; Great Britain; War of 1812
English colonies, 55–61, 69–101, 104–32, 181–217
  1660, 88–89(map)
  impact of global war in, 183–84
  instability in, 104
  new colonies and patterns, 106–15
  New World exploration, 16–17, 39
  resistance to Crown in, 184, 192–93, 196, 198–213
  unrest and repression in, 124–26
  See also Chesapeake colonies; French and Indian War; Jamestown; Maryland colony; New England; Pennsylvania colony; Roanoke; South Carolina colony; Virginia colony
English empire
  attempts at, 53–61
  in crisis, 200–207
  dissent in, 124–27
  enforcing, 196–200
  Native American policy, 123
  plan of, 104–6
  victory of, 182–96
ENICAC (Electronic Numerical Integrator and Computer), 926–27
Enlightenment, 161, 166–72, 175, 176, 225, 243
Enterprise (carrier), 859, 860, 861
Environmental policy
  Bush (George H. W.) administration and, 1080
  Carter administration and, 1027, 1028
  conservation movement, 736–37
  Johnson (Lyndon) administration and, 974–75
  NAFTA and, 1082
  Nixon administration and, 1012–13
  Reagan administration and, 1045, 1061
  rebirth of, 951
Environmental Protection Agency (EPA), 1012, 1045, 1060

Episcopalianism, 328, 599, 1041
Equal Employment Opportunity Commission (EEOC), 976, 989
Equal Pay Act of 1963, 989
Equal rights amendment (proposed)
  1940s, 910
  1970s, 1016–17, 1022, 1055
Equal Rights Party, 395
Erasmus, 49
Erie Canal, 316–18, 350, 373, 449, 585
Ervin, Sam, 1024
Espionage Act of 1917, 758
Essay on Slavery and Abolitionism (Beecher), 396
Esso Gasoline, 932
Estate taxes, 1045
Esteban the Moor, 24–25
Estonia, 1065
Ethiopia, 853
Ethiopian Manifesto, The (Young), 429
Ethnic cleansing, 1091
Ethnic Heritage Studies Act of 1972, 1023
Ethnicity
  in industrial America, 629–30
  in mid-20th century, 935
  white, 1022–23
  See also Diversity
Eugenics, 725, 727
Euro, 1974
Europe
  cold war in, 900(map)
  in pre-Columbian era, 8–13
  witchcraft trials in, 129
  World War II in, 865(map), 878–79
Europe First strategy, 864
European Economic Community, 1074
European Space Agency (ESA), 1076
European Union (EU), 1074
Evangelical Christianity, 225, 328
  consumerism and, 143–44
  growth of, 1036, 1041(map)
  in industrial America, 634
  temperance movement and, 392–93
Evarts, Jeremiah, 359
Evers, Medgar, 911
Everybody's (magazine), 722, 743
"Evil empire," 1047
Evinrude Company, 760
Evolutionary theory
  Scopes trial and, 801
  Social Darwinism and, 638
Excise taxes, 265, 284
Executive branch, establishment of, 252
Executive Order 8802, 851
Executive Order 9066, 1019
Executive Order 9981, 911
Exodusters, 603, 604(photo)
Expansionism
  commercial, foreign policy and, 663–64
  Native American resistance to, 322–27
  political economy of, 458–67
  of settlement (1720-1760), 146(map)
  of slavery, 458, 462–63, 477–80, 510
  See also Land; Manifest Destiny; West
Experts, dictatorship of, 725–27
Explorer 1 (satellite), 955
Export-Import Bank, 854
Exports
  in 1970s, 1002
  in American Republic, 270, 311, 313
  in colonial era, 153, 153(map), 155, 156, 204

Exports (continued)
　Great Depression and, 821
　in industrial era, 664
　in late 19th century, 684
　in post-revolution era, 241
　Reagan administration and, 1062
Exxon Mobil, 688

F

Facebook, 1073, 1077
Fair Deal, 913, 943, 963
Fair Employment Board, 911
Fair Employment Practices
　Committee, 851
Fair Labor Standards Act of 1938, 845
Fairbanks, Douglas, Sr., 783–84, 797
Fairchild Semiconductor, 1040
Fall, Albert B., 808
Fallen Timbers, 282, 288
Falls of the Kaaterskill (Cole), 445
Falwell, Jerry, 1042, 1060
Family Assistance Plan, 1012
Family life
　colonial economy of, 152–53
　current trends in, 1085
　immigrant culture and, 631
　in mid-20th century, 935
　in modern era, 795
　Puritan, 91–93
　sharecropping and, 569
　in slavery, 418
Family values, 1085
Fannie Mae, 1101
Farewell to Manzanar (Wakatsuki),
　874
Farmers' Alliance, 651, 671–72
Farming/agriculture
　in Africa, 12
　Agrarian Revolt, 670–72, 675
　in American Republic, 273–76,
　　313, 327
　in colonial America, 92, 152–53
　the Columbian exchange, 28–29
　decline in (modern era), 789
　emergence of, 5
　Great Depression and, 822–23, 825
　in Great Plains region, 612–13
　in industrial America, 670–72
　in mid-20th century, 935
　Native Americans and, 8
　New Deal measures, 830–31, 845
　Warehouse Act, 744
Farnham, Marynia, 936–40
Farragut, David, 516, 521, 525
"Fat Man" (atomic bomb), 883
Faubus, Orval, 954
Fauset, Jessie, 805
FBI. See Federal Bureau of
　Investigation
Federal-Aid Highway Act of 1956, 929
Federal Alliance of Land Grants, 1018
Federal budget
　in 1970s, 1000
　in American Republic, 265–66
　Bush (George W.) administration
　　and, 1081
　Clinton administration and, 1080
　Eisenhower administration and,
　　943
　in modern era, 808
　Nixon administration and, 1012
　Obama administration and, 1103,
　　1105
　post–World War II, 907
　Reagan administration and,
　　1045–46, 1062
　Roosevelt (Franklin)
　　administration and, 845, 866
Federal Bureau of Investigation (FBI)
　Black Panthers infiltrated by, 1021,
　　1023
　cold war activities of, 891–92, 915
　failure to detect 9/11 plot, 1093

Federal Communications
　Commission (FCC), 933
Federal Deposit Insurance
　Corporation, 829
Federal Emergency Relief
　Administration (FERA), 829
Federal Farm Board, 825
Federal government
　creation of, 225–26, 249–55, 263–64
　Democratic Republicans and,
　　338–39
　expanding (1955–1970), 976(table)
　Great Depression and, 823–24, 825
　in industrial America, 659–65
　Jackson's attempt to limit, 345–46,
　　440
　Jefferson's attempt to limit, 302
　Johnson (Lyndon) era growth
　　of, 975
　Nixon's attempt to limit, 1012–13
　Reagan's attempt to limit, 1044
　Roosevelt (Theodore) era growth
　　of, 735
　Truman era growth of, 912
Federal Highway Act of 1921, 808
Federal Home Loan Mortgage
　Corporation (Freddie Mac),
　　1101
Federal National Mortgage
　Association (Fannie Mae),
　　1101
Federal Procession of 1789, 279
Federal Reserve Act of 1913, 743
Federal Reserve Board, 743–44, 983,
　　1001, 1045, 1101
　Great Depression and, 821
　New Deal legislation and, 829
Federal Trade Commission (FTC),
　　743, 744, 808, 1026
Federalist No. 10, The, 255
Federalist Papers, 255
Federalists, 267, 322, 339
　Alien and Sedition Acts and,
　　291–93
　Bill of Rights and, 264
　Constitutional ratification and,
　　253, 254–55
　election of 1796 and, 289
　election of 1816 and, 340
　French Revolution and, 285
　Jefferson presidency and, 300,
　　301–2, 304
　religious revivalism distrusted
　　by, 328
　states' rights and, 365
　trade embargo and, 306
　War of 1812 and, 308–11
Female Moral Reform Society, 380,
　　395
Feminine Mystique, The (Friedan), 989
Feminism
　conservative condemnation of,
　　1055
　cultural, 1014–16
　lesbian, 1016
　in mid-20th century, 940
　in modern era, 795
　radical, 989–90, 1014, 1022
　See also Women's rights
Feminization of poverty, 1055
Fenno, John, 266
Ferdinand, Archduke, 749
Ferdinand, king of Spain, 9, 14, 39, 53
Ferguson, John H., 694
Ferkauf, Gene, 925–26, 928
Ferkauf, Harry, 925
Ferraro, Geraldine, 1046
Fermi, Enrico, 883
Fertile Crescent, 5, 6, 12
Field, Cyrus, 587
Fields, W. C., 622
Fifteenth Amendment, 564(table),
　　573–74, 577, 579

Fifth Amendment, 264
Filipino immigrants, 1019
Fillmore, Millard, 483, 484
Film noir, 914
Financial crisis of 1890s, 586–87,
　　681–91
Financial Services Modernization Act
　of 1999, 1081
Finland, 765
Finney, Charles Grandison, 373,
　　376, 378
Fire department, 591, 666
Fireside chats, 828, 829(photo)
First Amendment, 264, 1097
First Confiscation Act, 517, 527, 553
First Reconstruction Act, 565, 570
First world, 904, 945
Fish, Hamilton, 664
Fish-ins, 1019
Fisk University, 636, 728
Fithian, Philip Vickers, 151
Fitzgerald, F. Scott, 764, 793, 798,
　　799–800
Fitzhugh, George, 498
Five "Civilized" Tribes, 358, 361
Five Nations (of Iroquois), 43–44, 48,
　　52, 53
Five Points neighborhood, 381,
　　382–83
Flaming youth, 795, 796–97, 798
Flaming Youth (Adams), 795
Flappers, 795
Flexible response, 970–71, 978
Floponik (nickname for first U.S.
　satellite), 955
Florida
　British claim to, 195
　Civil War and, 513
　Jefferson's attempts to obtain, 303,
　　305, 306
　migration to, 941, 1004
　Pinckney's Treaty and, 288
　Reconstruction and, 554
　secession of, 509
　Spain's ceding of, 300, 340–41
　Spanish in, 19–20, 24, 42, 133, 166,
　　238, 248
Foch, Ferdinand, 770
Foner, Eric, 579, 580
Fontana, Marco, 630
Food and Agriculture Organization,
　　727
Food stamp program, 974
Foot, Samuel A., 365
Football, 625, 792
Foote, Andrew, 516, 520, 524
Force Bill, 366
Forced Founders (Holton), 223–24
Ford, Gerald, 1024, 1025–27
Ford, Henry, 784–85, 786, 791, 928
Ford Foundation, 904
Ford Motor Company, 730, 784–86,
　　787–88, 790–91, 1000, 1088
　economic crisis and, 1102
　World War I and, 760
　World War II and, 866
Fordism, 784–85, 791
Fordney-McCumber Tariff of 1922,
　　808
Foreign Mission School, 379
Foreign policy
　Carter's, 1028–29
　commercial expansion and,
　　663–64
　Ford's, 1026
　Nixon's, 1006–8
　Obama's, 1103–4
　Reagan's, 1047–52
　in Reconstruction era, 572
　Republican (modern era), 809–11
　Roosevelt's (Theodore), 737–40
　slavery as, 489
　Taft's, 741

Forests
　clearing of, 90–91
　preservation of, 736–37
Forging the Shaft: A Welding Heat
　(Weir), 668(photo)
Forrestal, James, 901
Fort Beauséjour, 188, 191
Fort Biloxi, 123, 131, 132(photo)
Fort Bull, 191
Fort Cahokia, 123
Fort Carillon, 191, 193
Fort Caroline, 42
Fort Detroit, 197
Fort Donelson, 520, 524
Fort Duquesne, 188, 192, 193
Fort Frontenac, 193
Fort Henry, 520, 524
Fort Kaskaskia, 123
Fort Laramie, 605
Fort Laramie Treaty, 607
Fort Louisbourg, 183, 193
Fort McHenry, 308, 309(photo)
Fort Mims, 299
Fort Niagara, 131, 188, 191, 197
Fort Orange, 49, 51
Fort Oswego, 191
Fort Phil Kearny, 606
Fort Pickens, 511, 513
Fort Pitt, 193, 197
Fort Riley, 775
Fort St. Frédéric, 131, 188
Fort Sumter, 511, 512, 524
Fort Ticonderoga, 191, 193, 222,
　　227–28
Fort Toulouse, 131, 166
Fort Walla Walla, 452
Fort William Henry, 191, 192, 193
Forten, Charlotte, 555(photo)
Fortune (magazine), 822, 854
Forty-Niners' gold rush, 611
Forty-ninth parallel, 340, 461, 463
Forty-second parallel, 449
Four Freedoms, 871
Fourteen Points, 765–69, 771, 773
Fourteenth Amendment, 565, 577,
　　579, 580, 694, 952, 1016
　origins of, 562–64
　provisions of, 564(table)
Fourth Amendment, 264
Fox, Richard Kyle, 624
Fox people, 359–60
France
　American Civil War and, 518, 530
　American Revolution and, 231,
　　233–38, 285, 286
　arms-reduction accord (1920s),
　　809
　Columbus turned down by, 14
　English conflicts with, 123, 124,
　　126–27, 131–32, 182, 285–
　　87, 288, 305
　financial crisis of 1890s and, 681
　Jay's Treaty and, 290
　jazz in, 810
　King George's War, 183, 184–85
　King William's War, 126–27, 199
　Monroe Doctrine and, 342
　Open Door Note and, 707–8
　Panama Canal and, 739
　Quasi-War, 290–91
　Queen Anne's War, 114, 126–27,
　　182, 199
　slavery abolished in, 271
　Spanish colonialism supported
　　by, 341
　Spanish conflicts with, 42, 136,
　　182–83
　student protest in, 987
　Suez Canal crisis, 949
　trade embargo and, 305–7
　United Nations and, 881
　in Vietnam (French Indochina),
　　838, 859, 906, 947

witchcraft trials in, 129
women's rights discussed in, 277
word's fair of, 623
World War I and, 749, 753, 754, 756, 757, 764, 765, 770, 771, 773
World War II and, 852, 853, 854, 855, 859, 863, 864, 878, 879, 894
XYZ Affair, 290, 291
zones of occupation and, 895
See also French colonies; French empire; French Revolution; Louisiana Purchase
Franciscan missionaries, 134, 135
François I, king of France, 41
Frank, Thomas, 1086–87
Franklin, Battle of, 533, 542
Franklin, Benjamin, 143, 167, 172, 203, 274, 278, 290, 588
American Revolution and, 231
autobiography of, 170–71
Declaration of Independence and, 224
French and Indian War and, 187, 193
negotiations with France, 233–37
on Paxton Boys, 196
Franklin, William, 267
Franks, Abe, 891
Franks, Nancy, 891
Fraternal organizations, 629
Freddie Mac, 1101
Fredericksburg, Battle of, 521, 536
Free black population (during slavery), 133, 165, 273, 412, 413, 496
education for, 394
Fugitive Slave Act of 1850 and, 483
Missouri Compromise and, 343
in Philadelphia, 270, 273
restrictions on, 81, 303, 348–49, 423, 424–25, 486
ways of life, 423–25
Free-Soil Party, 433, 462–63, 473, 474, 481, 482, 483, 486
Free Speech Movement (FSM), 986–88
Free State Association, 554
Free State Hotel, 488, 490
Freed, Alan, 942
Freedman's Village, 530, 531
Freedmen's Bureau, 544, 557, 559, 562(photo), 564, 570
court of, 551–52
establishment of, 556
Freedmen's Bureau Bill, 562
"Freedom National, Slavery Regional" speech, 491
Freedom Riders, 966
Freedom Schools, 976, 977
Freedom Summer, 976, 977–78
Freedom Trash Can, 990
Freedom's Journal, 428(photo)
Freehold farms, 273–76
Freeport Doctrine, 497
Freeways, 929
Frémont, John C., 464, 494, 495, 527
French and Indian War, 182, 184–96, 198, 203
causes of, 184–87
conclusion of, 195
from local to imperial, 187–91
North American colonies before and after, 195(map)
problems with British-colonial cooperation, 192–93
second phase of, 194(map)
as Seven Years' War, 187, 199
start of, 187
French colonies, 49, 62, 63, 104, 130–33, 182–83
Beaver Wars and, 53

in Canada, 39, 42–48
coffee cultivation in, 159
exploration and settlement (1603-1616), 45(map)
Louisiana colony, 123, 131–32, 136
New World exploration, 41–42
South Carolina region and, 113
See also French and Indian War
French empire
attempts to establish, 130–33
crumbling of, 184–87
French Revolution, 199, 266, 267, 277, 284–85, 286–87, 311
Freneau, Philip, 266
Frethorne, Richard, 80
Frick, Henry Clay, 687
Friedan, Betty, 989, 1016(photo)
Friedman, Milton, 820–21
Friedman, Thomas L., 1072
Fries, John, 291
FTC. See Federal Trade Commission
Fuchs, Klaus, 883, 916, 917
Fugitive Slave Act of 1793, 261, 423, 432
Fugitive Slave Act of 1850, 482, 483–84, 513
Fugitive slave clause
of Confederate constitution, 519
of Constitution, 253, 423, 483
Fukushima Daiichi nuclear accident, 884
Fulbright, J. William, 982
Fuller, Margaret, 391
Fulton, Robert, 315, 316, 317, 318, 322, 323, 331
Fundamental Constitutions, 112–13, 124
Fundamentalist Christianity, 801
Fundamentals, The (essays), 801
Funding and assumption, 265
Funston, Frederick, 705
Fur trade, 79, 155, 160, 312
in Dutch colonies, 49, 50, 51–52, 62
French-Indian, 39, 42, 45, 47, 48, 62, 63, 130–31
overhunting and, 47, 90, 325
in South Carolina colony, 113

G

Gabriel (slave revolt leader), 301, 417
Gaddis, John Lewis, 897–98
Gadsden, James, 489
Gadsden Purchase, 489
Gage, Thomas, 212, 220, 221, 222
Galaxy, The, 643
Gallatin, Albert, 302
Galveston, Texas hurricane, 692–93, 729, 730
Galveston Plan, 693
Galveston Wharf Company, 692
Gandhi, Mohandas, 727, 838, 872, 961
Gang system in slavery, 411
Gangrene, 535
Gangsta rap, 1058
Ganioda'yo, 325
Garfield, James A., 659, 660
Garland, Hamlin, 639
Garnet, Henry Highland, 429
Garrison, William Lloyd, 396, 429–30, 431, 432–33, 473
Garvey, Marcus, 805–6
Gary, Elbert, 777
"Gas and water" socialism, 720
Gates, Bill, 1036, 1038, 1039, 1078, 1080
GATT (General Agreement on Tariffs and Trade), 1074–75
Gay Liberation Front, 1021
Gays. See Homosexuality
Gaza Strip, 1029, 1051
Gazette of the United States, 266
Gellhorn, Martha, 874

Gender roles
in Chesapeake colonies, 82
in colonial America, 152–53
in mid-20th century, 936–40
in modern era, 794–95
in Native Americans, 137
slave codes and, 118
in Tenochtitlan, 22
Victorian view of, 625–28
See also Women
General Agreement on Tariffs and Trade (GATT), 1074–75
General Colored Association of Massachusetts, 427
General Electric, 867, 1037–39
General Federation of Women's Clubs, 718
General Motors (GM), 787, 837, 908, 928, 931, 974, 1053, 1088, 1102, 1103
Genêt, Edmond-Charles, 287, 288
Genetics, 1077
Geneva Accords, 949
Geneva Convention, 1097, 1098, 1099
Genízaros, 136, 137
Gentility, 158–59, 169
George, Henry, 667–69, 670
George III, king of England, 196, 198, 200, 220, 222, 225, 230, 322
George Kennan (Seidler), 899(photo)
Georgia, 203, 212
American Revolution and, 231
Civil War and, 539, 540, 541–42
Constitutional ratification and, 253, 254
creation of government in, 226
founding of, 160, 166
Native American land in, 281, 358
prior to Removal Act, 362(map)
secession of, 509
slavery in, 165–66, 174, 409, 420
Spanish plan to demolish, 183
territory disputes in, 280
German Coast uprising, 417
German immigrants/Americans
in American Republic, 291
in antebellum era, 475
Catholic Church and, 630
in colonial era, 145, 147
during depression of 1837, 443
in industrial America, 630, 658
nativism and, 388, 485
World War I and, 758–59
Germany
Berlin airlift, 900–902
division of, 895
financial crisis of 1890s and, 681
Great Depression and, 838
Manila Bay occupied by, 704
Nazi-Soviet pact, 854–55
Open Door Note and, 707–8
post–World War II, 895–96
Samoa claimed by, 664
Shandong Peninsula occupied by, 699
Spanish Civil War and, 854
Taft administration and, 741
terrorist bombing in, 1052
Venezuela loan and, 739
witchcraft trials in, 129
World War I and, 726, 749, 753, 756, 757, 764, 765–71, 773, 811, 821
World War II and, 852, 853, 854–57, 859, 863, 864, 866, 878–79, 882, 894
Gernon, Maude, 715
Geronimo, 607(photo)
Gerry, Elbridge, 290
Gerstacker, Carl, 1003
Gestapo, 853
Gettysburg, Battle of, 533, 537–38
Gettysburg Address, 538, 1106

Ghent, Treaty of, 309–10, 314, 346
Ghettos, 761
Ghost Dance movement, 608–9
GI Bill, 906–7
Gibbons, Thomas, 322, 323
Gibbons v. Ogden, 322, 323–24
Gibson, Charles Dana, 759
Gibson Girl, 759
Gideon v. Wainwright, 975
Gilbert, Sir Humphrey, 55
Gilded Age. See Industrial America
Gilman, Daniel Coit, 635
Ginsberg, Allen, 951
Ginseng, 312
Girard, Stephen, 312
Gladden, Washington, 622, 720
Glasnost, 1065
Glass ceiling, 1055
Glass-Steagall Banking Act of 1933, 828–29
Gleeson, William, 729
Glenn, John, 965–66
Glidden, Joseph, 613
Globalization, 1072–76
cold war and, 1072
communications technologies and, 1072–73
contesting, 1082–83
defined, 1072
moving people, 1075
multinationals and NGOs, 1073–74
trade and, 1074–75, 1082–83, 1101
Glorious Revolution, 79, 106, 121, 124–26, 201
God and Man at Yale (Buckley), 963
Godey's Lady's Book, 391
Goebbels, Joseph, 818, 878
Goethals, George W., 739
Golan Heights, 1029
Gold
in Africa, 12
in American Republic economy, 311
in Colombia, 23
in colonial economy, 106, 200
mercantilism and, 48
in Mexico, 21, 71
on Native American land, 358
in New World, 15, 16, 24, 31, 38, 42
percentage of world in U.S. treasuries, 884–85
Gold rush(es), 412, 455, 480, 481(photo), 606, 608, 611, 613, 738
Gold standard, 658–59, 660, 681
battle of the standards, 689–91
end of, 1013
in Great Depression, 825
Golden Gate Park, 666, 988
Golden parachutes, 1037, 1039
Goldwater, Barry, 954, 964, 973, 990, 1043
Gompers, Samuel, 696–97, 704
Gonorrhea, 763
Good, Sarah, 103, 128
Good Housekeeping (excerpt from), 937–39
Good Neighbor policy, 854
Goodman, Andrew, 976
Google, 1077
Gorbachev, Mikhail, 1065–66
Gore, Al, 1081
Gosnold, Bartholomew, 56
Gospel music, 942
Gould, Jay, 669–70
Government. See Federal government; Municipal governments; State governments
Government Bureau (Tooker), 916(photo)
Gowrie (plantation), 410
Grace, Thomas, 1010
Graceland, 951

Gracia Real de Santa Teresa de Mose, 133
Graham, Billy, 935, 943(photo)
Gramm-Leach-Bliley Act, 1081
Gramm-Rudman Act, 1062
Granada, 9, 14
Grand Army of the Republic, 653
Grand Union, 591
Grandfather clause, 695, 729
Grandmaster Flash, 1058
Grange, 671
Grant, Ulysses S., 465
    Civil War and, 516, 520, 521, 524, 533, 537–38, 540–41, 542, 543
    presidency of, 571, 572, 573, 576, 577, 608, 659, 664
    as secretary of war, 570
Grape boycott, 1018
Grateful Dead, 988
Graul, Rita, 1015
Gray, Asa, 638
Great Awakening, 143, 150, 166–67, 172–75, 176, 203
    cultural conflicts and, 174
    effects of, 175
    origins of, 172
    Second, 328, 373–74
Great Britain
    Alabama claims settled by, 572
    arms-reduction accord (1920s), 809
    Berlin airlift and, 902
    Canadian border dispute, 443–44
    Canadian rebellion against, 444–45
    Creole incident, 459
    financial crisis of 1890s and, 681
    Fourteen Points and, 773
    Great Depression and, 838
    Greek civil war and, 896
    India controlled by, 200, 210, 312
    Iraq War and, 1097, 1099
    joint declaration offered by, 341
    limitation of forces on Great Lakes/Rockies, 340
    Manila Bay occupied by, 704
    Monroe Doctrine and, 342
    Open Door Note and, 707–8, 741
    Oregon Territory land claims, 455, 459
    Panama Canal and, 739
    Potsdam Conference and, 895
    Suez Canal crisis, 949
    Texas annexation issue and, 460
    United Nations and, 881
    World War I and, 749, 753, 756, 757, 764, 765, 769–70, 771, 773
    World War II and, 852, 853, 854, 855–56, 858, 864–65, 866, 882
    Yalta Conference and, 894–95
    zones of occupation and, 895
    See also England
Great Compromise, 253
Great Depression, 818–49, 852, 853, 894, 963
    causes of, 819–21
    effects of, 821–24
    global impact of, 838–39
    See also New Deal
Great Gatsby, The (Fitzgerald), 798, 799
Great Lakes Indians, 281, 288, 357
Great Lakes region, 7, 62, 63, 123, 237, 281, 308, 312, 315, 340
Great Migration, 761–62
"Great Nation of Futurity, The" (O'Sullivan), 446–47
Great Pacific Railway, 612
Great Pile Up, 759
Great Society, 972–76, 981–82, 1000, 1012, 1022, 1042, 1044, 1057, 1062

coming apart of, 983–94
    major programs of, 973–75
    personal freedom in, 975–76
    white ethnics and, 1023
Great Upheaval, 670
Great Western Railroad, 586
"Great White Hope," 625
Greater Asia Co-Prosperity Sphere, 838
Greece
    civil war in, 896, 898
    revolution of, 342
Greeley, Horace, 478–80, 577
Green Berets, 970
Green Corn Ceremony, 325
Greenback Labor Party, 658
Greenbackers, 658–59
Greenbacks, 523, 525, 658–59, 671
Greene, Nathanael, 233
Greenglass, David, 916
Greenland, 17
Greenpeace, 1074
Greensboro sit-ins, 961, 962
Greenville, Mississippi, 977–78
Greenville, Treaty of, 282, 314
Greenwich Village, 951
Greer, USS, 856
Gregg, Josiah, 364
Grenada, 1050
Grenville, George, 198, 204
Grenville, Sir Richard, 57
Griffith, D. W., 727–28, 783
Grimké, Angelica, 396
Grimké, Sarah, 396
Griswold v. Connecticut, 975, 988
Gross Clinic, The (Eakins), 641
Gross national product
    Great Depression, 821
    mid-20th century, 926
Groves, Leslie R., 864
Grundy, Felix, 308
Guadalcanal, 862, 871
Guadalupe Hidalgo, Treaty of, 464–66
Guadeloupe, 133
Guam, 697, 701, 857, 880
Guantánamo Bay (Gitmo), 1097, 1098–99, 1103
Guatemala, 28, 30, 838, 944, 971
Guilford Court House, 233
Guiteau, Charles (letter from), 660(photo)
Gullah language, 165
Gunpowder, 10
Gunther, Blair, 892
Gutenberg, Johannes, 10, 202
Guzmán, Jacobo Arbenz, 944
Gypsies, in Nazi Germany, 853

H

Habeas corpus, 249, 519, 536, 539
Hackensack River, 111
Haig, Douglas, 770
Haight-Ashbury, 988
Haiti, 285, 290, 572, 664
    communism in, 971
    Monroe Doctrine not applied to, 342
    Taft administration and, 741
    Wilson administration and, 752
Hakluyt, Richard, 54
Haldeman, H. R., 1024
Haley, Bill, 942
Half-Way Covenant, 122
Hall v. DeCuir, 578
Halleck, Henry Wager, 525, 526
Halve Maen (ship), 49
Hamer, Fannie Lou, 976
Hamilton, Alexander, 242, 255, 289, 301, 302
    Burr's shooting of, 305
    national bank and, 266, 338
    as secretary of treasury, 263, 265–67, 276, 279, 284

Hamilton, Alice, 715–16, 718, 721, 762
Hamilton, Andrew, 162
Hammon, Jupiter, 272
Hammond, James Henry, 475, 477
Hancock, John, 208, 221, 225, 242
Hancock, Winfield, 659
Handlin, Oscar, 632
Handsome Lake, 325
Hanna, Marcus, 690
Hanover Street Presbyterian Church, 373
Hard war strategy, 512, 516, 524, 540–41, 542
Harding, Rebecca, 639
Harding, Warren G., 807–8, 809, 811, 812(photo), 821, 860
Hardwick, Thomas, 776
Hariot, Thomas, 58–59, 60
Harlem, 861, 984
Harlem Renaissance, 805
Harmar, Josiah, 282
Harmony, Pennsylvania, 377
Harper's Ferry raid, 499–500, 513
Harper's Magazine, 634
Harper's Weekly, 641, 742
Harris, Benjamin, 203
Harris, Joel Chandler, 620
Harrison, Benjamin, 662–65, 704
Harrison, Shelby, 722
Harrison, William Henry, 299, 458–59, 461
    death of, 459
    loss to Van Buren, 441
    Native Americans and, 325
Harrison-McKinley Tariff of 1890. *See* McKinley Tariff of 1890
Harrison's Landing, 526
Hartford Convention, 309, 311, 340, 365
Hartford Wits, 278
Harvard Club, 755
Harvard College, 91
Harvard University, 172, 638, 863
Harvey, William ("Coin"), 684
Hate stikes, 872
Hathorne, John, 128
Haupt, Henry, 525
Havana, 195
Haverly, J. H., 621
Hawaii
    annexation of, 664, 704
    statehood, 941
Hawkins, John, 54, 86
Hawley-Smoot Tariff of 1930, 825, 854
Hawthorne, Nathaniel, 449
Hay, John, 690, 697, 707–8, 709
Hayes, Rutherford B., 578, 659–60
Haymarket Square disaster, 670
Hayne, Robert Y., 365–66
Haynsworth, Clement, 1023
Haywood, William D. ("Big Bill"), 720, 758
Hazlitt, William, 833
Head Start, 974
Headright, 73
Health Care and Educational Reconciliation Act of 2010, 1103
Health care crisis, 1078–79
    See also National health insurance
Health reform, 390
Hearst, William Randolph, 700, 833, 854
Hefner, Hugh, 934
Heisenberg, Werner, 883
Heldner, Franz, 1000
Hell Fighters, 810
Helper, Hinton Rowan, 498
Helsinki agreement, 1026
Hemingway, Ernest, 798
Henry, Benjamin Tyler, 534
Henry, Joseph, 476
Henry, O., 639

Henry, Patrick, 203, 251, 254
Henry VII, king of England, 16–17, 53
Henry VIII, king of England, 53, 56, 83
Henry of Navarre, 44
Henry the Navigator, Prince, 10
Hepatitis, 85
Hepburn Act of 1906, 735
Hepworth, George, 554
Herald of Freedom, 490
Heritage USA, 1060
Heroin, 717
Herron, George, 720
Hersey, John, 871
Hesse-Cassel, 230–31
Hessians, 224, 228, 230–31
Hetch Hetchy Canyon (Bierstadt), 738(photo)
Hetch Hetchy Valley acqueduct, 738–39
Hewlett-Packard, 1038, 1040
Hidatsas, 304
Hidden Persuaders, The (Packard), 932, 954
Higginson, Thomas Wentworth, 634, 639
High culture, 620, 631, 633–38, 639, 641
Higher Education Act of 1965, 974, 1016
Highway Safety Act of 1966, 974
Highways, 931(table)
Hill-Burton Act of 1946, 912
Hillman, Sidney, 837
Hillsborough, Lord, 207
Hinckley, John W., 1043
Hip-hop, 1058
Hippies, 988, 989
Hippisley, Alfred, 707
Hirohito, emperor of Japan, 884
Hiroshima, atomic bombing of, 883, 884, 914
Hispanics
    decade of (1980s), 1059
    population decline in mid-19th century, 612
    population growth, 1083, 1084(map)
Hispaniola, 16, 25, 86
Hiss, Alger, 915–16, 917
"History of the Standard Oil Company" (Tabell), 722
Hitler, Adolf, 817–18, 838, 853, 855, 856, 864, 874, 878, 879, 894, 963, 1089
    Roosevelt's cable to, 854
    suicide of, 882
Ho Chi Minh, 861, 947, 972
Hochelaga, 41, 43
Hoffman, Abbie, 1021
Hoffman, Frederick L., 638, 639
Hofstadter, Richard, 675
Hog Island Shipyard, 759, 760(photo)
Hohokam Indians, 7
Holding companies, 598
Holland/Netherlands
    American Revolution and, 233
    bonds introduced in, 199
    English conflicts with, 106–9
    French and Spanish war with, 287
    independence secured by, 49, 69
    Puritans in, 84
    World War II and, 855
    See also Dutch colonies
Holly, Buddy, 942
Hollywood, 792
Hollywood Ten, 915
Holmes, John Clellon, 951
Holmes, Oliver Wendell, 776
Holocaust, 874
Holton, Woody, 223–24
Homeland Security Department, 1093
Homer, Winslow, 641

Homestead Act, 525, 604
Homestead Steel Works, 687, 688
Homesteaders, 612–13, 684
Homogeneity, 934–42
Homosexuality
    AIDS crisis and, 1055–57, 1088
    in cold war era, 914
    expanding rights, 1087–88, 1103
    gay power movement, 1020–21
    in mid-20th century, 940
    in modern era, 794
    in Nazi Germany, 853
    Victorian view of, 626, 628
Honda Accord, 1052
Honduras, 741
    communism in, 971
    Wilson administration and, 752
Hongs, 312
Hood, John Bell, 541–42
Hooker, Fighting Joe, 536, 540
Hooker, Thomas, 96
Hoover, Herbert, 826, 854, 1027
    election of, 811
    Great Depression and, 819, 824–26,
        828, 829, 833, 845, 963
    as secretary of commerce, 809
    World War I charities organized by,
        726, 824
Hoover, J. Edgar, 891–92
Hoovervilles, 824
Hopkins, Harry, 829, 835
Horizontal consolidation, 598
Hornet (carrier), 859, 860, 861
Horses, 23, 29, 136, 439
Horseshoe Bend, Battle of, 299, 308,
    310
Hotline, U.S-Soviet, 972
House, Edward, 753, 757, 775
House I Live In, The (film), 871
House of Commons (Britain), 201
House of Lords (Britain), 201
House of Representatives' Un-
    American Activities
    Committee (HUAC),
    891–92, 915, 916
Housing
    in American Republic, 269–70
    in colonial era, 93, 121
    crisis of 2000s, 1100–1101
    discrimination in, 761, 910, 930,
        985
    in modern era, 792, 798
    Powhatan and English, 76(photo)
    of Tenochtitlan, 22
    veterans' demand for, 907(photo)
    World War II shortage, 869
    See also Mortgages (home);
        Suburbs
Housing and Urban Development
    Department, 974
Houston, Sam, 451
How the Other Half Lives (Riis), 591,
    642, 644–45
Howard, Oliver Otis, 556
Howe, Daniel Walker, 367
Howe, Elias, 685
Howe, Gertrude, 715
Howe, Julia Ward, 514
Howe, William, 228
Howells, William Dean, 639
"Howl" (Ginsberg), 951
HUAC. *See* House of Representatives'
    Un-American Activities
    Committee
Hudson, Henry, 49, 64
Hudson River, 49, 50, 109, 315, 317,
    322, 323
Hudson River school of painting, 445
Huerta, Victoriano, 751
Hughes, Charles Evans, 732, 754–56
Hughes, Langston, 761, 805
Huguenots, 42, 44
Huizinga, Johan, 727

Hull, Cordell, 839, 854, 856
Hull-House, 715, 721, 722(photo), 729
Hull-House Maps and Papers (survey),
    721
Human Be-In, 988
Human rights, 125, 264, 1029, 1047,
    1049
Human sacrifice, 6, 20
Humanitarianism, 172
Humphrey, Hubert, 992–93
Humphrey-Hawkins Bill, 1028
Hungary, 945, 1065
Hunt-ins, 1019
Hunter-gatherers, 4–5, 7, 23, 24
Hunter's Return, The (Cole),
    448(photo)
Huntington, Collis P., 597
Huron Indians, 41, 43–47, 48, 53, 62
Huronia, 46–47
Hurston, Zora Neale, 798, 805
Hussein, Saddam
    capture and execution of, 1100
    Persian Gulf War and, 1089, 1090
    second war with U.S., 1097–1100
Hutcheson, Francis, 169
Hutchinson, Anne, 94–96
Hutchinson, Thomas, 203, 204, 210,
    211
Hydrogen bomb, 883, 898, 906, 914,
    917
Hydropathy, 390

I

I Led Three Lives (film), 892
I Love Lucy (television program), 932
I Was a Communist for the FBI (film),
    891, 892, 915
Iberian Peninsula, 8–9
IBM, 1036, 1038, 1039
Ibn Saud, 901
ICC. *See* Interstate Commerce
    Commission
Ice Age, 4–5
Idaho, 611
*Ideological Origins of the American
    Revolution, The* (Bailyn), 223
Idrisi, al-, 11
Ikebuchi, Kosuke, 1053
*I'll Take My Stand: The South and the
    Agrarian Tradition* (essays),
    798
Illinois
    pro-slavery advocates in, 364
    settlers in, 346
    statehood, 314
Illinois Board of Trade, 828
Illinois Territory, 132
Illustrados, 705
Immediatism, 429–30
Immigration
    Alien and Sedition Acts, 291–93,
        301, 306, 365
    in American Republic, 267
    in antebellum era, 475, 477
    Asian, 1019
    Civil War and, 523
    in cold war era, 892, 914
    in colonial era, 144–47
    culture of immigrants, 630–31
    globalization and, 1075
    illegal, 940–41, 1059, 1082
    immigrant experience, 632–33
    in industrial America, 628–33,
        656–58
    labor market and, 585–86, 589–90
    in modern era, 801–2
    nativism *vs.,* 387–88, 485–86,
        656–57, 801–2
    panic of 1873 and, 587
    Proposition 187, 1082
    World War I and, 753
    See also Migration, internal
Immigration Act of 1921, 802

Immigration Act of 1924, 802
Immigration Act of 1965, 1019
Immigration and Nationality Act of
    1952, 914, 940–41
Immigration Reform and Control Act
    of 1986, 1059
Impeachment
    of Clinton, 1081
    of Johnson (Andrew), 570–71
Imperial Valley Workers Union, 804
Imperialism, 697–709
    debate on reasons for, 706–7
    opposition to, 704
    sea power and, 697–99
    world of, 708–9(map)
Imports
    in 1970s, 1002
    in American Republic, 311
    in colonial era, 156, 161
    Great Depression and, 821
    in post-revolution era, 241
    Reagan administration and, 1062
In re Debs, 697
Incas, 17, 23, 24
Incidents in the Life of a Slave Girl
    (Jacobs), 416, 418
Income tax, 732, 741, 835, 1045
Indentured servants, 76, 77, 144,
    146, 154
    in American Republic, 313, 330
    in Barbados, 115
    importation from Europe to
        America (1580-1775),
        147(map)
    in Pennsylvania colony, 112
    profitability of using, 80–81
    Puritans and, 86–87
    treatment of, 80
India, 904
    atomic weapons testing, 883
    British control of, 200, 210, 312
    coffee cultivation in, 159
    cotton from, 420, 670
    Great Depression and, 838
    oil demand in, 1101
    silver minting ceased in, 681
    space program and, 1076
Indian, John, 103
Indian Patrol, 1019
Indian Reorganization Act of 1934,
    831
Indian Self-Determination Act of
    1975, 1020
Indian Territory, 325, 359, 377, 439, 455
    See also Reservations (Native
        American)
Indiana
    settlement of, 268, 346
    statehood, 314
Indiana Plan, 725
Indiana University, 796, 835
Indigo, 106, 152, 153, 311, 313
Individualism, 783
    in colonial America, 130
    culture of, 797
    Great Awakening and, 175
    politics of, 808–9
Indonesia, 159
Industrial America
    culture of, 619–49
        high, 620, 631, 633–38, 639, 641
        immigration and, 628–33
        popular, 620, 633, 639, 641
        realism, 619, 639–45
        urban (*see* Urban culture)
    politics of, 651–79
        economic issues, 658–65
        government activism and limits,
            665–66
        styles, 652–58
    rival visions of, 741–44
    See also Industrial capitalism;
        Industry

Industrial armies, 683
Industrial capitalism, 585–617, 716,
    784
    big business rise, 592–98
    individualism and, 797
    new social order under, 598–603
    political economy of global,
        586–92
    in the West, 604–10
Industrial Revolution, 160, 385, 421,
    1077–78
Industrial unions, 837
Industrial Workers of the World
    (IWW; Wobblies), 720, 758
Industrious revolution, 151, 153, 175
Industry
    deindustrialization, 1004, 1013,
        1026, 1036, 1045, 1058
    major American (ca. 1890),
        597(map)
    modern era development of,
        784–87
    slavery and, 419–25
    Taylorism and, 686–87, 788, 791
    during World War II, 866–70
    See also Industrial America;
        Industrial capitalism;
        Manufacturing
IndyMac Bank, 1101
INF (Intermediate-Range Nuclear
    Forces) Treaty, 1065
Infant mortality rates, 82, 1018
Inflation, 1079
    in 1960s, 983
    in 1970s, 1000, 1013, 1026, 1028
    in 1980s, 1045
    in American Republic, 311
    at Philadelphia (1770-1790),
        239(figure)
*Influence of Sea Power upon History,
    The* (Mahan), 697
Influenza, 27
    pandemic of 1918, 775–76
Information economy, 1077–78
Initiative, 732
Inoculation. *See* Vaccines/inoculation
Inquiry (secret committee), 757
Inquisition, 129
Installment plan, introduction of, 685
Insurance companies, 313, 1081
Intel, 1040
Interest groups, 718
Interest rates, 983, 1045
Intermediate-Range Nuclear Forces
    Treaty (INF), 1065
Internal Security Act of 1950, 917,
    940
International Council of Nurses, 719
International Ladies' Garment
    Workers, 837
International Monetary Fund, 882,
    1072
International Red Cross, 1073
International Space Station, 1076
Internationalism, 852, 1089
Internet, 588, 1072–73
Interstate Commerce Commission
    (ICC), 661, 665, 734, 808
Intolerable Acts, 212, 213, 227
Invasion of America, The (Jennings),
    62
Invasion of the Saucer Men (film), 955
Invasion Within (Maglio), 1086
Inventions, 784
Iran
    American hostages in, 1029, 1042,
        1043
    in "axis of evil," 1097
    Carter administration and, 1029,
        1042
    cold war era, 895, 944, 949
    Iraq war with, 1052
Iran-Contra affair, 1060–61

Iraq
　Iran war with, 1052
　Persian Gulf War, 1088, 1089–90
　second war with U.S., 1097–1100,
　　1102, 1103
Ireland, 9, 200, 267
　British conquest of, 54–55
　potato famine in, 388, 589
　rebellion in, 311
Irish immigrants/Americans, 590
　in antebellum era, 475
　Catholic Church and, 630
　Civil War and, 536–37
　in colonial era, 115, 145
　during depression of 1837, 443
　in industrial America, 630, 631,
　　657, 658
　nativism and, 388, 485–86, 657
　World War I and, 753
"Iron Curtain" speech, 896
Ironclads, "battle" of, 520
Iroquois Indians, 8, 46, 183, 281
　Beaver Wars and, 53
　Covenant Chain joined by, 123
　devastation of during revolution,
　　247–48
　Dutch colonizers and, 49, 52–53
　French and Indian War and, 186,
　　187, 188, 194, 196
　French colonizers and, 41, 43–44,
　　47, 48
　region of, in mid-17th century,
　　44(map)
Isabel, queen of Spain, 9, 14, 16, 30,
　　39, 53
Isolationism
　Bush's (George H. W.) repudiation
　　of, 1089
　during World War II, 852, 854–55
Israel, 1092, 1097
　atomic weapons testing, 883
　Camp David Accords and, 1028–
　　29, 1051
　Iraq bombing of, 1089
　Six-Day War, 1011
　space program and, 1076
　Suez Canal crisis, 949
　Yom Kippur War, 861, 1001, 1011
Isthmus of Panama, 54
It Came From Beneath the Sea (film),
　955
Italian immigrants, 590, 630, 636,
　657
Italy
　arms-reduction accord (1920s),
　　809
　Great Depression and, 838
　Spanish Civil War and, 854
　World War I and, 753
　World War II and, 853, 856, 878,
　　882, 894
It's a Wonderful Life (film), 914
Ives, Charles, 637–38
Ivy League, 625
IWW. See Industrial Workers of the
　World

J

J. Walter Thompson (ad agency), 791
Jackson, Andrew, 314, 344–46, 348,
　　398, 443, 451, 459, 461
　abolition movement and, 425,
　　431, 432
　background of, 299–300
　Bank of the United States and,
　　352–57, 386, 440–41
　censuring of, 441
　"corrupt bargain" accusation, 338,
　　344–45
　as a Mason, 351
　Native Americans and, 299–300,
　　308, 332, 340, 353, 357–59,
　　361, 367

　nickname of, 351
　nullification crisis and, 365, 366
　Polk compared with, 466–67
　presidency of, 351–59, 365, 366,
　　367–68, 440–42
　War of 1812 and, 299, 300, 308,
　　310–11
　western settlement and, 337–38,
　　445
Jackson, Henry, 1026
Jackson, Jesse, 985, 1058
Jackson, Rachel Donelson Robards,
　　299, 351
Jackson, Thomas J. ("Stonewall"), 517,
　　526, 536
Jackson State College shootings,
　　1008–11
Jackson-Vanik Amendment, 1026
Jacksonian Antislavery and the Politics
　of Free Soil (Earle), 462–63
Jacksonian Democracy, 289, 321,
　　346–57
　in action, 351–57
　decline of, 440–45
　nature of, 367–68
　social and political bases of,
　　346–51
Jacobs, Harriet, 416, 418
Jagerson, Nada, 1054
Jamaica, 25, 57, 159
James, Duke of York, 106, 109
James, Henry, 628, 640, 641
James I, king of England, 61, 70, 72,
　　76, 105
James II, king of England, 106, 124
James River, 71, 77, 526
Jamestown, 38, 61, 69, 70, 71–76, 83,
　　84, 85, 117, 132
　Dutch and, 51
　reason for failure of, 71
　starvation in, 71–74
Japan
　arms-reduction accord (1920s),
　　809
　atomic bombing of, 882–84, 902,
　　914
　China attacked by (WWII), 852,
　　853, 856, 903
　China's war with, 685, 699
　Columbus's planned voyage to, 15
　economic rise of, 1002
　globalization and, 1073
　Great Depression and, 838
　labor unions in, 908
　Open Door Note and, 707–8,
　　709, 741
　Pearl Harbor attack, 853, 856–57,
　　858, 860, 865, 872, 882, 894,
　　1093
　post-World War II, 895–96
　Reagan administration and, 1052
　space program and, 1076
　student protest in, 987
　trade with, 664, 1052
　U.S. companies of, 1053
　World War I and, 769, 773
　World War II and, 852, 853, 854,
　　856–58, 860–61, 863, 864,
　　878, 879–80, 882–84, 894
Japanese Americans
　World War II internment of, 852,
　　872–74, 1019
　World War II military service
　　by, 861
Japanese immigrants, 1019
Jaworski, Leon, 1025
Jay, John, 255, 264, 280, 288
Jay Cooke & Company, 577
Jay's Treaty, 280, 288, 290
Jazz, 619, 792–93, 810, 941, 1058
Jazz Age, 793, 798, 799
Jazz Singer, The (film), 792,
　　793(photo)

Jefferson, Thomas, 273, 289, 315, 328,
　　338, 347, 352, 387, 426, 448,
　　498, 667, 689
　Alien and Sedition Acts and, 293,
　　365
　American Revolution and, 222, 233
　Declaration of Independence and,
　　224–25
　Enlightenment ideas and, 167
　French Revolution and, 285, 286,
　　287
　Louisiana Purchase and, 302–4,
　　306, 339, 439
　Missouri Crisis and, 343
　national bank and, 266
　Native Americans and, 322–25
　presidency of, 300–307
　as secretary of state, 263, 265, 287
　slaves owned by, 276, 411
　vice presidency of, 290, 293
Jefferson Airplane, 988
Jenkins, Robert, 183
Jennings, Francis, 62–63
Jeremiads, 121
Jesuit missionaries, 37, 45
Jewett, Sarah Orne, 639
Jewish Charities, 823
Jews
　in American Republic, 279
　in Barbados, 115
　Democratic Party attacks on, 811
　Ford's anti-Semitism, 786
　immigration of, 589, 631, 657
　in mid-20th century, 935
　in Nazi Germany, 853
　in Netherlands, 49
　in Portugal, 51
　in Roosevelt (Franklin)
　　administration, 839
　in Soviet Union, 1026
　in Spain, 8, 9, 16, 49
Jiang Jieshi, 902–3
Jihad, 1092
Jim Crow system, 695, 953
　death of, 976–78
　inventing, 693–94
　World War I and, 763
Jingoes, 664, 697, 699, 704
Job Corps, 974
Jobs, Steve, 1036, 1038, 1039, 1040
Jockey Hollow, 231
John Deere tractor company, 759
Johns Hopkins University, 635, 742,
　　863
Johnson, Andrew, 544–45
　impeachment and trial of, 570–71
　Reconstruction and, 552, 557,
　　559–64, 565, 570–71
Johnson, Anthony, 81
Johnson, Hiram, 742
Johnson, Jack, 625
Johnson, James, 181, 193
Johnson, Lyndon B., 972–79, 985,
　　1013, 1022, 1062
　background of, 973
　Black Power movement and, 986
　civil rights and, 976–78
　election of 1964 and, 973
　election of 1968 and, 990–92
　mandate of, 973
　Vietnam War and, 978–79, 981–83,
　　990–92, 1011, 1026
　See also Great Society
Johnson, Samuel, 659
Johnson, Susannah Willard, 181–82,
　　184, 193
Johnson, Sylvanus, 184
Johnson, Tom, 730
Johnson, William, 188, 191
Johnston, Joseph E., 526, 540
Joint Chiefs of Staff, 899
Joint-stock companies, 54, 55, 87, 279
Joliet, Louis, 123

Jones, Samuel ("Golden Rule"), 730
Jones, Samuel (sheriff), 490
Jones, William, 331
Jones Mixer, 598
Joplin, Scott, 637
Jordan, Winthrop, 120
Joseph, Chief, 608
Josephy, Alvin, Jr., 26–27
Journal of the American Medical
　　Association, 715
JPMorgan Chase, 1100
Judge, Andrew, 261
Judge, Ona, 261–62, 272, 273
Judicial branch, establishment of, 252
Judiciary Act of 1789, 264, 302
Judiciary Act of 1801, 293, 302
Junk bonds, 1037
"Just Say No" campaign, 1055
Justice Department, 665, 758
Juvenile delinquency, 870, 950, 951

K

Kahler, Dean, 1010
Kahn, Gus, 791
Kaiser Shipyards, 867
Kalakaua, king of Hawaii, 664
Kameny, Frank, 1020
Kansas
　bleeding, 488–91
　sack of Lawrence, 488, 490–91
　See also Kansas-Nebraska Act of
　　1854
Kansas Free State, 490
Kansas-Nebraska Act of 1854, 486–88,
　　489, 490, 491
Kasserine Pass, 866
Kearny, Stephen, 464
Keckley, Elizabeth, 416
Kelley, Abby, 433
Kelley, Florence, 718–19, 721
Kellie, Luna, 651, 676
Kellogg-Briand Pact, 809
Kemp-Roth Bill, 1045
Kennan, George, 896, 898, 899(photo)
Kennebec River, 70
Kennedy, Anthony, 1054
Kennedy, Edward, 1015
Kennedy, John F., 632, 964–72, 978,
　　992, 993, 994, 1012
　assassination of, 972
　Bay of Pigs incident, 971
　civil rights and, 966–70
　Cuban Missile Crisis, 966, 971–72
　Johnson compared with, 973
　Vietnam War and, 972, 979
　women's rights and, 989
Kennedy, John Pendleton, 414–15
Kennedy, Robert F., 992, 993(photo),
　　994
Kent State University shootings, 1008,
　　1009–10
Kentucky
　emancipation resisted in, 543
　Lord Dunmore's War and, 198
　Native Americans in, 281
　secession resisted in, 510, 511, 539
　settlement of, 240, 248, 268, 314
　slavery in, 405, 412, 420
　statehood, 348
　voting rights in, 348
Kenya, U.S. embassy attack in, 1092
Kerensky, Alexander, 765
Kerouac, Jack, 951
Kerry, John, 1081
Kersands, Billy, 621
Kesey, Ken, 988
Key, Francis Scott, 308, 425
"Key of Liberty" (Manning), 279
Keynes, John Maynard (Keynesian
　　economics), 845, 855, 866,
　　1044
Keystone Bridge Company, 595
Khmer Rouge, 1026

Khomeini, Ayatollah Ruholla, 1029
Khrushchev, Nikita, 970
    Berlin Wall and, 971
    Eisenhower's meeting with, 945
    Kitchen Debate, 943, 946–47
Kickapoo Indians, 357
Kierstede, Hans, 111
Kierstede, Sara Roelofs, 111
Kim Il Sung, 903
King, Martin Luther, Jr., 966–70, 985,
        986, 1018, 1057, 1058
    assassination of, 992, 994
    "I have a dream" speech, 970
    last speech of, 983
    Montgomery bus boycott, 953
    Vietnam War condemned by, 982
King, Rodney, 1084
King, Rufus, 340
King Cotton diplomacy, 522
King George's War, 183, 184–85
King Philip's War, 115, 122–23
King William's War, 126–27, 199
King's fifth, 23
Kings Mountain, Battle of, 233
Kinney, Mary Farmer, 1004
Kinsey, Alfred C., 933
Kiowa Indians, 439, 455
Kirk, Russell, 963
Kirkpatrick, Jeane J., 1049, 1055
Kissinger, Henry, 905, 1006, 1007,
        1011, 1025
Kitchen Debate, 943, 946–47
Kitty Hawk (airplane), 787
Klamath Indians, 940
Kneel-ins, 962
Knights of Labor, 669–70, 672, 696
Knights of the White Camelia, 571
Know-Nothings. See American Party
Knox, Henry, 263, 267, 282
Knox, Philander, 734–35
Kodak camera, 643
Kolko, Gabriel, 731, 732
Kongo, 165
Kool Herc, 1058
Korea, 838
    airliner shot down by Soviets,
        1048–49
    Japanese occupation of, 699, 903
    North, 1097
    South, 947
    trade with, 664
Korean War, 898, 903–5, 906, 943,
        945
Korematsu, Fred, 872–74
Korvettes. See E. J. Korvettes
Kosovo, 1091
Krause, Allison, 1009
Kristallnacht, 853
Kroc, Ray, 931
Kroeber, Alfred Louis, 26
Ku Klux Klan, 728, 798, 811, 967
    emergence of, 571–73
    rebirth of, 802–3
Kuwait, 1089
Kwanzaa, 985

L

La Follette, Robert M. ("Fighting
        Bob"), 732–33, 741, 752–53,
        754, 757, 758, 808
La Salle, René-Robert Cavelier, Sieur
        de, 123, 131
Labor Day, 666
Labor force. See Workforce
Labor unions
    Amalgamated Clothing Workers,
        837
    American Federation of Labor,
        687, 696–97, 720, 789, 837,
        928
    American Railway Union, 687, 697
    Bronco Busters and Range Riders
        Union, 720

Brotherhood of Sleeping Car
        Porters, 789, 851, 911
Cigar Makers' International Union,
        696
communism and, 834, 908, 917
Congress of Industrial
        Organizations, 837, 839,
        908, 928
    defeat of (modern era), 788–89
    deindustrialization and, 1004
Imperial Valley Workers Union,
        804
    industrial, 837
    in industrial America, 666
Industrial Workers of the World,
        720, 758
International Ladies' Garment
        Workers, 837
Knights of Labor, 669–70, 672, 696
Mechanics' Union of Trade
        Associations, 348, 381, 395
    mid-20th century, 928
National Labor Union, 575
National Trades' Union, 384
New Deal legislation and, 833,
        836–39
    in new economy, 1079
    outlawing of activities, 777
Pennsylvania Slovak Catholic
        Union, 629
    post-World War II, 908–9
Professional Air Traffic Controllers
        Organization, 1045,
        1046(photo)
    Reagan administration and, 1036,
        1044, 1045
    in Reconstruction era, 574–75
    retreat from politics, 696–97
    revolutionary ideas and, 720
Screen Actors Guild, 1045
Unión de Trabajadores del Valle
        Imperial, 804
Union of Russian Workers, 777
United Automobile Workers, 837,
        869, 908
United Farm Workers of America,
        1018
United Mine Workers, 697, 735,
        837, 908
    women and, 697, 789, 870
World War I and, 758, 763
World War II and, 869, 870
See also Strikes
Ladies Magazine, 391
Lady Chatterley's Lover (film), 933–34
Lafayette, Marquis de, 286
Lafayette Escadrille, 754
Lafeber, Walter, 706
Laffer, Arthur, 1044–45
Lake Erie, 308
Lake Michigan, 715
Lakota Sioux Indians, 608
Land
    in American Republic, 267–68
    in Appalachian region, 314
    colonial era supply of, 152, 154,
        163–64
    conservation movement, 736–37
    English encroachments on Indian,
        78(map)
    freed slaves' dream of owning,
        556–57
    growth of public, 737(map)
    industrial capitalism impact on,
        613
    Native American use patterns, 90
    obstacles to obtaining, 346–47
    post-revolution speculation, 240,
        248–49, 267
    Puritan distribution and use of,
        88–91
    Senate dispute over prices, 365–66
See also Expansionism

Land Act of 1800, 314
Land Act of 1820, 346
Land-grant colleges, 525, 636
Land Ordinance of 1785, 314
Land pressure, 163–64, 326(map)
Land riots, 154
Landon, Alf, 843
Landscape (Cole), 445
Lane, Ralph, 57, 60
Langdon, John, 261, 262
Lanham Act, 870
Lansing, Robert, 753
Larkin, Thomas, 464
Las Casas, Bartolomé de, 18
Lasch, Christopher, 1022
Last of the Mohicans, The (Cooper),
        448
Latchkey children, 870
Lathrop, Julia, 721
Latin America
    cold war and, 895, 903
    in colonial era, 130
    Good Neighbor policy and, 854
    Kennedy and, 971
    Rio Pact, 903
    Roosevelt (Theodore) and,
        737–40
    Wilson and, 752
Latvia, 1065
Lau v. Nichols, 1019
Laud, William, 105
Law of Civilization and Decay, The
        (Adams), 698
Lawrence, Amos, 490
Lawrence, D. H., 933
Lawrence, Kansas, 488, 490–91
Lawrence v. Texas, 1088
Laws of Burgos, 18
Lawson, John, 113(photo)
Lawyers, 321–22
Lead poisoning, 715
League of Five Nations, 8
League of Nations, 726, 727, 765, 773,
        774, 776, 809, 880–81
League of United Latin American
        Citizens (LULAC), 804, 941
Lease, Mary Elizabeth, 673–74
Leatherstocking Tales (Cooper), 391,
        448
Leaves of Grass (Whitman), 640–41
Lebanon, 1060
    Eisenhower Doctrine, 949
    Israeli invasion of, 1051
Lecompton Constitution, 497
LeConte, Joseph, 638
Ledbetter, Huddie ("Leadbelly"),
        832(photo)
Lee, Ann, 374–77
Lee, Charles, 228
Lee, Jason, 452
Lee, Mary, 531
Lee, Richard Henry, 222, 224,
        225–26
Lee, Robert E.
    Arlington estate of, 530, 531
    Civil War and, 516, 521, 526–27,
        528, 533, 536, 537, 540, 543
    Harper's Ferry raid and, 499
    surrender of, 542, 544(photo)
Legal Services Program, 974
Legal Tender Act, 525
Leggett, William, 350, 443
Legislative branch, establishment
        of, 252
Lehman Brothers, 1101
Leisler, Jacob, 125
LeMay, Curtis, 880
Lenape Indians, 111
Lend-Lease bill, 855–56
Lenin, Vladimir, 765, 774, 893
Leopard (ship), 306
Lesbian feminism, 1016
Lesbians, 940, 1087–88

"Letter from Birmingham Jail" (King),
        967, 968–69
Letters from an American Farmer
        (Crevecoeur), 273
Leviathan, USS, 775
Levitt, William J., 928–29, 930
Levittown, 928–29, 930, 931, 934
Lewis, Diocletian, 655
Lewis, Jerry Lee, 942
Lewis, John L., 837, 908
Lewis, Joseph, 1010
Lewis, Meriwether, 304–5
Lewis, Sinclair, 798
Lexington, Battle of, 220–21, 227
Lexington (carrier), 859, 860
Libel laws, 162
Liberalism
    in colonial America, 109
    culture wars and, 1085, 1086–87
    frustrations of, post-WWII,
        912–13
    in industrial America, 656, 660,
        665
    new, 962–63, 972, 973, 975, 978,
        979, 985, 993, 1022
    Roosevelt (Franklin) and, 845
Liberator, The, 429, 473
Liberia, 425
Liberty (sloop), 208
Liberty Baptist College, 1042
Liberty Party, 433, 461, 463(table), 474
Libraries, 172, 278, 636–37
Library Company of Philadelphia, 172
Library of Congress, 278
Libya, 1051–52, 1104
Lichtenstein, Roy, 988
Lien laws, 567
Life (magazine), 871, 896
"Life in the Iron Mills" (Harding), 639
Light bulb, invention of incandescent,
        591
Liliuokalani, queen of Hawaii, 664,
        704
Limited Test Ban Treaty, 972
Limited war, 979–81
Lincoln, Abraham, 390, 514, 609, 652,
        682, 839
    assassination of, 544, 545
    Civil War and, 511, 513, 516, 517,
        519, 520, 521, 524–31, 533,
        535–42, 545
    Cooper Union address, 500
    Douglas debates with, 497,
        498(photo), 500
    elections of, 499, 500–502, 541, 544
    Gettysburg Address, 538, 1106
    Reconstruction and, 553, 554–55,
        557
    secession and, 510, 511
    on slavery, 488, 497, 498, 500, 501,
        502, 509
    Thirteenth Amendment and,
        543, 544
Lindbergh, Charles A., 797, 855
Linked economic development, 155
Lipan Apaches, 449, 450
Lipkind, Ann, 891
Lippmann, Walter, 729, 734, 743, 754,
        756, 773, 775, 777–78
    "cold war" coined by, 896
    League of Nations, 774
    life and times of, 749–50
    as secretary for Inquiry, 757
Lipton, Thomas, 625
Liquor. See Alcohol
Literacy
    in American Republic, 278
    of Cherokees, 362
    of freed slaves, 555–56, 567
    in industrial America, 637
    of Mexican Americans, 1018
    of Puritans, 84
Literacy tests, 718

Literature
  of American Republic, 278
  of antebellum era, 448
  of modern era, 798
  realism in, 639–41
  self-improvement and, 391–92
Lithuania, 1065
Little Bighorn, Battle of, 608
"Little Boxes" (song), 934
"Little Boy" (atomic bomb), 883
Little Rock school desegregation, 953–54
Little Turtle, 282
Living Theater, 988–89
Livingston, Robert, 303, 315, 316, 317, 322
Lloyd, Henry Demarest, 586, 593
Localism, 278, 338, 345
Locke, John, 112–13, 124–25, 167, 169
Lockheed Aircraft, 1000
Lodge, Henry Cabot, 697, 773, 774
Loewe v. Lawlor, 697
"Log Cabin and Hard Cider Campaign," 458–59
Logan, James, 172
Logan, John, 197
Lon Nol, 1008
London Gazette, 203
London Missionary Society, 379
Lonely Crowd, The (Riesman), 934
Long, Huey, 832, 834
Long, Thomas, 533
Long Island, 50, 109, 228
Longhorn cattle, 610
Longhouses, 46
Longstreet, James, 537
Looking Backward (Bellamy), 668–69
Lord Dunmore's War, 198
Los Alamos nuclear research facility, 868, 883, 916
Los Angeles Times, 872
Lost generation, 798–801
Louis XIV, king of France, 123, 124
Louisiana
  Civil War and, 532
  Reconstruction and, 553–55
  secession of, 509
  slave revolts in, 417
  slavery in, 341, 405, 458
  statehood, 314
  voting rights in, 348, 695
Louisiana colony, 123, 131–32, 136, 191
Louisiana Purchase, 306, 339, 343, 439, 445
  borders fixed, 340–41
  details of, 302–4
Louisiana State University, 834
Love Canal, 1028
Lovejoy, Elijah, 431
Lowell, Francis Cabot, 319–20, 421
Lowell, Massachusetts, 320, 384, 385, 396
Loyalists (American Revolution), 228–29, 231, 233, 238, 241, 243, 267
Loyalty oaths, 917
LSD, 944, 988
Luce, Henry, 871
Ludendorff, Erich, 769
Luftwaffe, 855
Luicte, 867
Lundberg, Ferdinand, 940
Lusitania (ship), 753–54, 755
Luther, Seth, 381, 384, 386, 389, 391, 393
Lutherans, 145, 631
Lyceum movement, 390
Lynchings, 537, 571, 657, 694, 695(photo), 727, 732, 761, 805
  laws against urged, 762, 839, 911
  during World War II, 861

Lynd, Helen, 798
Lynd, Staughton, 798

M

M1 rifle, 863
Maastricht Treaty, 1074
MacArthur, Douglas, 825, 857, 880, 905
McCain, Franklin, 961
McCain, John, 1102
McCall's (magazine), 935
McCarran Act of 1950, 892
McCarthy, Eugene, 990, 992
McCarthy, Joseph, 914, 917, 918–19, 944
McCarthyism, 892, 914, 917–20, 1020
McClellan, George B., 516, 517, 526–27, 538, 540
  Lincoln's firing of, 527, 536, 541
  nominated for president, 541
McCloy, John J., 756, 874
McClure's (magazine), 688, 722, 725
McCormick reaper, 475
McCulloch, James W., 322
McCulloch v. Maryland, 322, 332
Macdonald, Dwight, 871
McDonald's, 931, 941, 1074
McFarlane, Robert, 1061
McGillivray, Alexander, 248, 283
McGinty, Joe ("Iron Man"), 624
McGirt, Daniel, 234
McGovern, George, 1024
Machine gun, 749
Machine politics, 652, 729, 733
Macintosh PC, 1038
McKay, Claude, 805
MacKenzie, Donald Scott, 1010
McKinley, William, 662, 664
  assassination of, 734
  China policy, 707, 708
  election of, 690
  imperialism and, 697, 698, 699
  Philippine-American War and, 705
  Spanish-American War and, 700, 701, 704
McKinley Tariff of 1890, 662, 686, 699, 704
Mclain, Rose, 878
McLane, Louis, 353
McLeod, Alexander, 444–45
McNeill, Joseph, 961
Mclain, Rose
Macomb Purchase, 267
Macon, Nathaniel, 343
Mad cow disease, 776
Mad Men (television program), 933
Maddox (destroyer), 979
Madeira, 12, 16
Madero, Francisco, 751
Madison, James, 242, 265, 287, 289, 328
  Alien and Sedition Acts and, 293, 365
  background of, 219
  Bank of the United States and, 266, 331, 338, 340
  Bill of Rights and, 264
  Constitutional Convention and, 251, 252, 253, 254, 255
  French Revolution and, 285, 286
  War of 1812 and, 307–8, 347
Magellan, Ferdinand, 39, 705
Maglio, Domenick, 1086
Magna Carta, 201
Magnavox Odyssey, 1005
Magnetic Telegraph Company, 476
Mah-i-ti-wo-nee-ni, 439–40, 455
Mahan, Alfred Thayer, 697–98, 699, 700, 769
Mahican Indians, 51–52
Mail-order catalog, 588
Maine, 123
  Canadian border issue, 443–44, 460

disputes over ownership, 281
land speculation in, 248
squatters in, 267
statehood, 314, 343, 346
Maine (battleship), 700
Maisonrouge, Jacques, 1003
Malaria, 168, 360, 375, 410, 413, 453, 535, 700
Malaya, 838
Malcolm X, 985
Mali Empire, 12
Malinche (Malintzin; doña Marina), 3–4, 20, 29, 30, 31, 56, 304
Malleus Maleficarum, 129
Malone, Dudley Field, 801
Man Nobody Knows, The (Barton), 791
Manchuria, 699, 838
Mandan Indians, 304
Mandel, Max, 892
Mangum, Willie P., 441
Manhattan
  American Revolution and, 228
  purchase of, 49
  See also New York City
Manhattan Project, 864, 867, 868(map), 882, 883, 944
Manifest destiny, 361, 439–40, 452, 458, 461
  in antebellum culture, 445–49
  defined, 445
  racism and, 462–63
  Tejano culture and, 450
Manigault, Charles, 410
Manigault, Louis, 529
Manigault, Peter, 158(photo)
Manila Bay, Battle of, 700
Mann, Horace, 393–94
Manning, William, 276, 279, 346
Manors, 109
Mansfield, Jayne, 936
Manteo, 55, 56, 61, 64
Manufacturing
  in American Republic, 266
  in antebellum era, 448–49
  in colonial era, 91, 106
  in late 19th century, 684–86
  relative share of world (1880-1913), 684(figure)
  See also Industry
Manumission, 118, 273
Manzanar Relocation Camp, 873–74
Mao Zedong, 902–3, 905
Maps
  early examples of, 11
  first geographically accurate, 17
  King Philip's (Metacom's), 122(photo)
Marbury, William, 302
March Against Death, 1008
March on Washington (1894), 683
March on Washington (1932), 825–26
March on Washington (1962), 967–70
March on Washington (1969), 1008
March on Washington Movement (MOWM), 851, 852
Marco Polo, 10
Marconi, Guglielmo/Guillermo, 772, 793
Marcy, William L., 489
Marianas, 880
Marijuana, 987
Market revolution, 311, 330, 331
Marquette, Jacques, 123
Marriage
  in colonial America, 82, 93, 128, 150–51, 153, 164
  current trends in, 1085
  freed slaves and, 556, 569
  French-Native American, 47
  in Huron Indians, 46
  in industrial America, 626
  inter-ethnic, 935

in modern era, 794
  Mormon, 377
  in Native American culture, 47
  polygamous/polygynous, 37, 47, 137, 377, 626
  in post-revolution era, 243
  same-sex, 1088, 1103
  in slavery, 151, 408, 418
  Spanish-Native American, 30
Marroquín, José, 739
Marshall, George C., 856, 864, 899
Marshall, James, 611
Marshall, John, 290, 302, 305, 321–22, 323, 358
Marshall, Thurgood, 872, 952
Marshall Islands, 880
Marshall Plan, 899, 901, 904
Martin, Thomas, 764
Martinique, 133, 159
Mary I, queen of England, 53, 56, 83
Mary II, queen of England, 106, 125
Maryland, 239
  Civil War and, 526
  free blacks barred from, 424
  secession resisted by, 511, 539
  slavery in, 246, 273, 420
  voting rights in, 348
Maryland (battleship), 856
Maryland colony
  establishment of, 79
  Glorious Revolution and, 124, 125
Mason, John, 97
Masons, 161–62, 350–51
Mass production, 784–85, 788
Massachusetts
  anti-Catholicism in, 388
  in colonial era
    British war efforts supported by, 184
    in Dominion of New England, 124
    immigration to, 145
    King Philip's War, 122
    newspapers of, 203
    protest and resistance in, 203–4, 206–7, 211–12
    as a royal colony, 125
  Constitutional ratification and, 253, 254
  creation of government in, 227
  French and Indian War and, 193, 203
  same-sex marriage in, 1088
  slavery issue, 272
  territory disputes in, 280
Massachusetts (ship), 270
Massachusetts Bay colony, 82–84, 85–87
  See also Puritans
Massachusetts Bay Company, 87
Massachusetts Congregational Church, 379
Massachusetts Emigrant Aid Society, 490
Massachusetts General Court, 88–89, 91–93
Massachusetts Government Act, 211–12
Massachusetts Provincial Congress, 212, 221
Massasoit, 85, 122
Massive retaliation doctrine, 944, 945, 970
Mather, Cotton, 167, 168
Mattachine Society, 940, 1020
Mauchly, John William, 926–27
Maumee River Indian towns, 282(photo)
May, Ernest, 706–7
"May Day" (Fitzgerald), 799–800
May Laws, 589
Mayaguez (ship), 1026
Mayan Indians, 3, 6, 20

Mayflower (ship), 84
Mayflower Compact, 84
Mayors, reform, 730–32
MCI, 1045
Me Decade, 1022, 1024
Meade, George Gordon, 537, 538
Measles, 168, 452
Mechanics' Institute, 563
Mechanics' Union of Trade
    Associations, 348, 381, 395
Medicaid, 974, 990, 1103
Medicare, 974, 975, 1044, 1062, 1103,
    1105, 1106
Medicine Lodge Treaty, 607, 608
Meese, Edwin, III, 1060
Meeting the Communist Threat
    (Paterson), 897
Meigs, Montgomery, 525, 531
Mein, John, 209–10
Memeskia, 185–87
Memphis *Argus,* 563
Memphis race riots, 563–64
Mencken, H. L., 798
Menéndez, Francisco, 133
Menéndez de Avilés, Pedro, 42
Mennonites, 145, 613, 759
Menominee Indians, 357
Mercantilism, 48, 54, 106, 107, 109,
    132, 169
Mercenaries, 230–31
    See also Hessians
Merchants, 155, 270–71, 276, 567–68
Meredith, James, 966
Meredith, William, 860
Mergers, 688, 787, 928, 1037–39, 1077
Merrill Lynch, 1101
Merrimac (ship), 520
Merrimack Manufacturing
    Corporation, 320
Merrimack River, 316
Merry Pranksters, 988
Mesoamerica, 6–7
Mesquakie Indians, 357
Mestizos, 30, 135
Metacom (King Philip), 122, 123
Methodist Missionary Society, 452
Methodists, 143, 174, 272, 328, 329–
    30, 377, 391, 452, 1041
Métis culture, 47
Meuse-Argonne, Battle of, 770–71
Mexica people, 20–23
Mexican Americans, 1059
    activism in (1970s), 1017–18
    conservatism and, 1035–36
    derogatory names used for, 940
    in mid-20th century, 940–41
    in modern era, 803–4
    music of, 942
    World War II and, 861
Mexican immigrants, 803–4, 869,
    940–41, 1059, 1082, 1083,
    1103
Mexican Revolution, 751–52, 802
Mexican War, 433, 439–40, 463–66,
    467(map), 468, 473, 478, 481
    causes of, 463
    terms of surrender, 464–66
Mexico, 25, 71, 305, 1004
    Aztecs in, 17, 20–23
    cold war era, 944
    commercial expansionism in, 664
    Gadsden Purchase and, 489
    independence from Spain, 341,
        364, 450
    lands in trans-Mississippi West,
        455
    NAFTA and, 1082
    pre-Columbian culture of, 6–8
    Reagan administration and, 1052
    Spanish conquest and rule, 20–23,
        24, 130
    Texas independence, 449–52, 457,
        460, 462

    Transcontinental Treaty on, 340
    Wal-Mart in, 1073
    Zimmerman Telegram, 756
    See also Mexican Revolution;
        Mexican War
Mial, A. T., 560–61
Miami Indians, 184–85, 282
Miami River, 185
Michigan, 571
Microsoft, 1036, 1038, 1039, 1078
Middle class
    African American, 1058, 1084
    in antebellum era, 475
    common school movement and,
        393
    culture and, 634
    early 20th century, 717–18
    immigrant, 631
    in industrial America, 667–69
    under industrial capitalism, 591,
        600
    in mid-20th century, 935
    in new economy, 1079
    radicalism in, 667–69
    self-improvement and, 390
    urban, 384–87
Middle East
    Arab Spring in, 1104
    cold war and, 895, 949(map)
    Nixon administration and, 1011
    Obama administration and, 1104
    Reagan administration and,
        1051–52
Middle ground
    abandonment of, 116–17
    creation of, 47–48
    end of, 248
Middle Ground, The (White), 63
Middle passage, 150
Middletown (Lynd and Lynd), 798
Middletown, Massachusetts, 207
Midway, Battle of, 859, 861
Midway Plaisance, 623–24
Migrant workers, 789, 1018
Migration, internal
    in American Republic, 267–71
    to cities, 388–89
    Great, 761–62
    of pre-Columbian peoples, 4–5
    See also Immigration
Military
    Bush (George W.) administration
        and, 1081
    gays in, 1088, 1103
    racial discrimination in, 763,
        861–62, 911
    Reagan administration and, 1047
    women in, 862, 910, 1087
    See also Army; Navy
Military-industrial complex, 955
Militia Act of 1862, 532
Milk, Harvey, 1055–56
Milken, Michael, 1037, 1039, 1060
Mill-child's cough, 601
Millennialism, 225, 374–77
Miller, Jeffrey, 1009
Miller, Thomas, 755
Mills, C. Wright, 954
Milosevic, Slobodan, 1091
Milton Berle Show (television
    program), 932
Mingo Indians, 197
Minimum wage, 763, 845
Mining, 613
    coal, 412, 631, 666, 697, 735, 908
    copper, 412, 611
    gold, 412
Mining camps, 585, 611–12
Minnetarees, 304
Minstrel shows, 620–22, 641
Miranda v. Arizona, 975
Miss America pageant, protest against,
    990

Miss Amelia C. Van Buren (Eakins),
    641
Missionaries
    in China, 699, 707
    to foreign countries, 379–80, 698
    Native Americans and, 45, 133,
        134, 135, 325, 439, 452
    in Philippines, 707
    western migration of, 452
Missionary Herald, 380
Missions, 134, 452
Mississippi
    French settlement in, 131
    secession of, 509
    settlement of, 268, 346
    slavery in, 405, 458
    statehood, 314
    voter-registration drives in, 966,
        976, 977–78
Mississippi Freedom Democratic
    Party (MFDP), 976
Mississippi Plan, 578
Mississippi River, 7, 24, 196, 248, 280,
    281, 303, 325, 358–59, 412,
    452, 455
    bridge built over, 595
    Civil War and, 525, 538
    French explorations of, 123, 131
    great flood of 1927, 824
    Pinckney's Treaty and, 288, 302
    post-revolution negotiations, 236,
        237, 238
    steamboats on, 315–16
    War of 1812 and, 310, 357
    See also Trans-Mississippi West
Mississippi River valley, 132, 183, 281,
    315–16, 317, 553–54
Mississippian Indians, 7–8, 24
Missouri
    Civil War and, 527
    secession resisted by, 509–10,
        511, 539
    statehood, 314, 343, 346
Missouri Compromise, 344, 426, 481,
    482, 486–87, 488, 496
    Crittenden Compromise and, 510
    tenets of, 341–43
    See also Compromise of 1850
Missouri Crisis, 343, 426, 432
Missouri River, 304
MIT, 863
Mitchell, Billy, 770
Mitchell, John, 735, 1025
Mitchell, Samuel, 300
Mittelberger, Gottlieb, 154
Mobile Bay, Union Capture of, 541
Mobilian Indians, 132
Moctezuma II, 3, 20, 21, 22, 23
Model Cities Program, 974
Model T Ford, 785, 786
Modern culture, 790–806
    consumerism in, 790–92
    family and youth in, 795
    gender roles in, 794–95
    individualism in, 797
    limits of, 797–806
    lost generation in, 798–801
    recreation in, 792–94
    religion in, 801
    sexuality in, 794
    social class and prosperity in, 798
Modern era, 783–815
    culture of (*see* Modern culture)
    economy in, 784–90
    politics and government (New
        Era), 806–11
Modern Republicanism, 942, 943, 965
Modern Woman: The Lost Sex
    (Farnham and Lundberg),
    936–40
Modoc Indians, 608
Mogollon Indians, 7
Mohawk Indians, 52, 53, 122–23, 248

Mojados, 940
Molasses Act of 1733, 198
Molotov, V. M., 895
Mondale, Walter, 1046, 1058
*Monetary History of the United States,
    1867-1960, A* (Friedman and
    Schwartz), 820–21
Money power theory, 494
Monitor (ship), 520
Monongahela River, 315
Monopolies, 734
Monroe, James, 344, 425
    New Orleans/Florida purchase
        attempt, 303
    presidency of, 340–41, 342, 343
Monroe, Marilyn, 936
Monroe, Sarah, 384
Monroe Doctrine, 341, 342, 445
Montagnais Indians, 45
Montana, 611
Montcalm, Louis-Joseph de, 192,
    193, 195
Monte Verde site (Chile), 4
Montez, Pedro, 403
Montgomery, Richard, 222
Montgomery bus boycott, 953
Montgomery Ward and Company, 588
Montréal, 195, 222
Moody, Paul, 320
Moon walk, 1012
"Moondog's Rock 'n' Roll Party"
    (radio program), 942
Moore, Amzie, 872
Moors, 8–9
Moral Majority, 1042, 1060
Moral suasion, 380, 394, 430
Moratorium Day, 1008
Morgan, Edmund, 120–21
Morgan, J. Pierpont, 592, 597, 689,
    742, 753, 755
    arranges loan to treasury, 681–82,
        688, 734
    consolidation movement led by,
        688
    gold standard supported by, 690
    Knox's lawsuit against, 734–35
    mail bomb sent to, 776
Morgan, William, 350–51
Morgan v. Virginia, 910, 911
Mormons, 331, 377, 480, 605, 626
Morocco, 302, 866
Morrill Land Grant Act of 1862,
    636
Morris, Gouverneur, 242, 286–87
Morris, Robert, 242, 269, 312
Morrison, John, 600–60I
Morrison, Paul, 891
Morse, Samuel F. B., 388, 406, 474,
    476
Mortality rates
    in Chesapeake colonies, 80
    child, 151, 631
    infant, 82, 1018
    in Jamestown, 74
Mortgages (home), 929
    introduction of, 792
    subprime, 1081, 1100, 1101
Morton, Jelly Roll, 793
Morton, Oliver P., 572
Mose, 165
Moses, Robert, 976
Mosque-Cathedral (Córdoba, Spain),
    10(photo)
Mossadeq, Mohammad, 944
Most-favored-nation policies, 743
Mother at Home, The (Child), 391
Mott, Lucretia, 397
Mount Vernon, 251, 261
Movement, the, 1021–22, 1024
Movies
    cold war era, 914, 915
    introduction of, 622
    modern era, 783–84, 792, 794

Movimiento Estudiantil Chicano de
    Azlán (MEChA), 1018
Moynihan, Daniel Patrick, 1012
Mozambique, 1051
Ms. (magazine), 1016
Muckraking, 725, 763
Mugwumps, 656
Muir, John, 736, 739
Mujahedeen, 1047–48
Mullaney, Craig, 1071–72, 1104
Müller, Friedrich Max, 635
Multinationals, 1002–4, 1073
Municipal governments
    in industrial America, 666
    progressivism and, 729–32
Munsey, Frank, 742
Murrow, Edward R., 874, 932
Museums, 278, 636
Music
    acid rock, 988
    country, 941
    gangsta rap, 1058
    gospel, 942
    hip-hop, 1058
    of industrial America, 619, 636,
        637–38
    jazz, 619, 792–93, 810, 941, 1058
    mid-20th century, 941–42
    of modern era, 792–93, 794
    opera, 636
    orchestral, 636
    popular, 792–93, 794, 941–42
    rap, 1058, 1059
    rhythm and blues, 942
    rock and roll, 942, 950, 987, 1058
Muslims
    in Africa, 12, 14
    Nation of Islam, 985
    in Portugal, 8, 10
    reconquista and, 8–9
    in Spain, 8, 9, 16
Mussolini, Benito, 838, 839, 853
Mutual aid societies, 327, 425, 629
Mutual assured destruction, 1048
MX Peacekeeper, 1047
"My Day" (newspaper column), 843
My Lai massacre, 1008
Mystic Fort, 97
"Myth of Tet, The" (Buzzanco), 991

N

NAACP. *See* National Association for
    the Advancement of Colored
    People
Nader, Ralph, 974
NAFTA (North American Free Trade
    Agreement), 1082
Nagasaki, atomic bombing of, 883,
    884, 914
Namibia, 1051
Narragansett Bay, 94
Narragansett Indians, 85, 96–97
*Narrative of the Life of Frederick
    Douglass, An American Slave*
    (Douglass), 417, 429
Narváez, Pánfilo de, 24
NASA. *See* National Aeronautics and
    Space Administration
Nashville, Battle of, 542
Nashville sound, 941
Nasser, Gamal Abdel, 949
Natchez Indians, 132
Nation, The, 551
Nation building, 904–5
Nation of Islam, 985
National Aeronautics and Space
    Administration (NASA),
    955, 965, 1012, 1076
National American Woman Suffrage
    Association (NAWSA), 654,
    719, 762
National Association for the
    Advancement of Colored

People (NAACP), 718, 762,
    805, 861, 872
    civil rights, 911, 952, 953, 976
    creation of, 728–29
National Association of
    Manufacturers, 686, 697
National bank, 266, 460, 467
    See also Bank of the United States
National Bank Act of 1863, 523
National Broadcasting Company. *See*
    NBC
National Civil Service Reform League,
    656
National Conference of Catholic
    Bishops, 1047
National Consumers League, 719
National Credit Corporation, 825
National Defense Education Act, 955
National Defense Mediation Board
    (NDMB), 869
National Endowment for the Arts, 974
National Endowment for the
    Humanities, 974
National Farmers' Alliance and
    Industrial Union, 651
National Football League, 792
National Gazette, 266
National government. *See* Federal
    government
National health insurance, 912, 1079,
    1103
National Industrial Recovery Act
    (NIRA), 833, 834–35, 837,
    844
National Institute of Mental Health,
    912
National Labor Relations Act. *See*
    Wagner Act
National Labor Relations Board
    (NLRB), 837
National Labor Union (NLU), 575
National Lead Company, 715
National League, 624, 911
National Liberation Front, 972
National Negro Convention, 429
National Organization for Women
    (NOW), 989, 1014
National Origins Act of 1924, 803
National Police Gazette, 624
National Refiners' Association, 598
National Republicanism, 338–41,
    345, 364
    election of 1824 and, 338, 344
    Jackson and, 352, 441
    Monroe and, 340–41
National Review, 963
National Road, 340
National Security Act of 1947, 899
National Security Council (NSC),
    899, 906
National Security League, 754
National Trades' Union (NTU), 384
National Traffic and Motor Vehicle
    Safety Act of 1966, 974
National Union for Social Justice, 834
National War Labor Board, 764
National Woman's Party (NWP),
    719, 762
National Youth Administration Office
    of Negro Affairs, 839
Nationalism
    Bellamy's version, 669
    New, 741–42
Nationalist Clubs, 668–69
Nationalists, 242, 253
Native Americans
    activism in (1970s), 1019–20
    alcohol consumption in, 166
    in the American Republic, 280,
        281–84, 322–27
    American Revolution and, 238,
        247–48
    backcountry land claims, 281–82

Bacon's Rebellion and, 116–17
captives taken by, 181–82, 184,
    185(figure)
Cleveland and, 661
in colonial era
    diverse relationships with
        Europeans, 62–63
    Dutch colonies and, 49, 51–53
    English colonies and, 71, 74–75,
        78–79, 84–85, 90, 96–97,
        131–32
    French colonies and, 41–42,
        43–48, 123, 130, 131–32,
        182–83
    New England and, 121, 122–23
    Pennsylvania colony and, 111
    Pilgrims and, 84–85
    Puritans and, 90, 96–97
    Scotch-Irish and, 145
    South Carolina colony and,
        113–15
    Spanish colonies and, 14–31,
        133–37, 182–83
    Virginia colony and, 116–17
Dawes Severalty Act, 609–10, 661
destruction of subsistence, 608–10
diseases affecting, 20, 25–28, 85,
    137, 168, 192, 304, 360, 452,
    457, 610
enslavement of, 15–16, 18, 20, 31,
    80, 113–15, 118, 122, 132,
    134, 135, 136, 137
in European countries, 56–57
horse impact on culture, 23, 29,
    136–37, 439
Jackson and, 299–300, 308, 332,
    340, 353, 357–59, 361, 367
King Philip's War, 115, 122–23
King William's War, 126–27
Louisiana Purchase and, 303, 304
major villages and battle sites,
    283(map)
manifest destiny and, 361, 439–40,
    445
in mid-20th century, 940
New Deal legislation and, 831
New World explorations, 14–31,
    39–40
Pontiac's Rebellion, 196–98
precontact world of, 4–8, 26–27
progressivism and, 728
Queen Anne's War, 126–27
religious practices, 134, 325, 330,
    608–9
removal policy and, 357–64, 367,
    455
treaties signed by, 79, 85, 248, 280,
    281, 282, 283, 299–300, 359,
    362, 607, 608
War of 1812 and, 308, 327
in the West, 247–48, 281–82, 452,
    455–58, 604–10
    conflicts with whites, 606(map)
    major communities, 456(map)
    See also French and Indian
        War; Indian Territory;
        Reservations (Native
        American); individual tribes
Nativism, 387–88, 485–86, 656–57,
    801–2
NATO. *See* North Atlantic Treaty
    Organization
Natural rights, 125
Natural selection, 638
Naturalization Act of 1790, 277
Nauvoo, 377
Navajo Indians, 134, 455, 608, 861
Navigation Acts, 106, 107–8, 124
Navy
    Civil War and, 512, 520
    creation of, 302
    imperialism and, 697–99
    increased strength of, 686

Korean War and, 905
War of 1812 and, 308
warship tonnage of world's,
    698(figure)
World War I and, 764–65
World War II and, 856, 861
NAWSA. *See* National American
    Woman Suffrage Association
Nazi-Soviet pact, 854–55
Nazism, 838, 853
NBC, 794, 932
Nebraska. *See* Kansas-Nebraska Act
    of 1854
Needlegun, 534
Negro Leagues, 911–12
Nehru, Jawaharlal, 904
Neoconservatism, 1097
Netherlands. *See* Holland/Netherlands
Neurasthenia, 626
Neutrality Acts, 854, 855
Neutron bomb, 1047
Nevada, 611
Nevins, Allan, 661
New Amsterdam, 49, 63, 109, 110–11
New conservatism, 963–64, 973
New Deal, 826–46, 855, 868, 869, 871,
    908, 912, 913, 943, 963, 965,
    1006, 1012, 1044, 1045
    banking system and, 828–29, 834
    coalition of, 839–43
    crisis of, 843–45
    criticism of, 833–35
    employment programs, 829,
        831–33, 835–36
    farm crisis and, 830–31, 845
    federal relief, 831
    first hundred days, 826–33
    Great Society compared with, 973
    origin of term, 826–27
    second, 833–43
    Social Security system, 836, 844, 845
New Echota, Treaty of, 359
New Economic Policy, 1013
New economy
    politics of, 1077–83
    technology role, 1036–37
New Empire, The (Lafeber), 706
New England, 82–97
    in 1640s, 96(map)
    American Revolution and, 222,
        227–28, 231, 239
    under assault, 121–23
    captives taken by Native
        Americans, 184, 185(figure)
    colonial economy of, 152, 154–55
    description of settlements, 92–93
    Dominion of, 124
    early industrial society in, 318–21
    free black population of, 424
    land pressure in, 164
    tariff of 1816 and, 345
    War of 1812 and, 308–9
    See also Puritans; individual states
        and colonies
New England Anti-Slavery Society,
    430
New England Artisan, 381
New England Association of Farmers,
    Mechanics, and Other
    Workingmen, 381
New England Emigrant Aid Company,
    488, 490
New-England Tale, A (Sedgwick), 391
New Era, 797, 806–11
New Federalism, 1012, 1044
New France, 39, 42–48, 85
New Freedom, 742, 743–44
New Frontier, 965–72
    See also Kennedy, John F.
New Guinea, 5, 859, 860
New Hampshire
    creation of government in, 227
    slavery issue, 272

territory disputes in, 281
voting rights in, 348
New Hampshire colony, 87, 124, 125
New Jersey
    American Revolution and, 228–31, 233
    Constitutional ratification and, 254
    in Dominion of New England, 124
    free blacks barred from, 424
    land riots in, 154
    slavery abolished in, 422
    women's suffrage in, 242–43, 277, 348
New Jersey Plan, 252
New Laws of 1542, 18
New Left, 964, 981, 986, 987, 989, 1014, 1023
New liberalism, 962–63, 972, 973, 975, 978, 979, 985, 993, 1022
New Light religious groups, 328
"New Look" strategy, 944
New Mexico
    acquired by U.S., 463, 464
    Spanish conquest and reconquest, 133–36
    statehood, 481, 483
New Nationalism, 741–42, 744
New Negro, 762, 797, 804–6
New Negro for a New Century, A (Washington), 804
New Netherland, 49–53, 62, 95
    becomes New York, 106–9
    private sector role in, 49–50
New Netherland Company, 49
New Orleans, 166, 305
    Civil War and, 520, 521, 525
    France surrenders to Spain, 195
    French settlement in, 123, 131
    jazz in, 793
    Louisiana Purchase and, 303, 304
    Pinckney's Treaty and, 288
    port of, 288
    race riots in, 563–64
    Reconstruction and, 555
    slave market of, 409
    War of 1812 and, 300, 308, 310
New Orleans (steamboat), 315
New Republic, 735, 749, 774
New Right, 1036
New Spain, 39, 280, 281, 449, 464
New Sweden, 50
New Woman, 718–19, 794–95, 797, 804
New World
    consequences of conquest, 25–30
    division of, 16–17
    European objectives in, 38–39
    as a geographical barrier, 39–42
    morality of conquest, 18
    Spain in, 14–31
    voyages of exploration, 41(map)
New World Order, 1088
    components of, 1089
    retreat from, 1090–91
New York
    American Revolution and, 224, 229(map), 232(map)
    British-Indian alliance dominated by, 123
    capital located in, 265
    colonial newspapers of, 203
    Constitution ratification and, 253, 254
    in Dominion of New England, 124
    free black population of, 424
    Glorious Revolution and, 125–26
    land riots in, 154
    land speculation in, 240, 248
    Native Americans in, 247
    penal reform in, 394
    port of, 154, 155
    slavery abolished in, 364, 419, 422
    territory disputes in, 281
    voting rights in, 348

New York, Treaty of, 283
New York Central Railroad, 586
New York City
    American Revolution and, 228
    business concentration in, 790
    Civil War and, 512
    colonial era growth in, 160, 162
    colonial era poverty in, 163
    colonial era society of, 110–11
    draft riots in, 536–37
    free black population of, 425
    industrial era growth in, 591
    library acquired by, 172
    New Netherland becomes, 106–9
    republic era growth in, 268
    slavery in, 110, 163, 271
    See also Manhattan
New York Customs House, 659
New York Evangelical Missionary Society of Young Men, 373
New York Herald, 700, 701
New York Journal, 700
New York Protestant Association, 388
New York Radical Women, 990
New York Society for the Suppression of Vice, 619
New York Stock Exchange, 828, 838
New York Sun, 682, 700
New York Times, 821, 874, 901, 1011, 1039
New York Times v. Sullivan, 975
New York Tribune, 776
New-York Weekly Journal, 162
New York Yankees, 792
Newfoundland, 10, 17, 39, 45, 56, 57
Newlands Reclamation Act of 1902, 736
Newport, 155, 172, 228
Newport, Christopher, 70–71
Newspapers, 806
    abolitionist, 431
    in American Republic, 277, 279
    in colonial America, 162, 202–3
    in industrial America, 652–53
Newton, Huey P., 985–86
Newton, Isaac, 167
Nez Percé Indians, 455, 608
NGOs (nongovernmental organizations), 1073–74
Niagara Movement, 728
Nicaragua, 811
    Reagan administration and, 1050, 1060–61
    Taft administration and, 741
    Wilson administration and, 752
Nicholson, Nancy, 1053
Nickelodeons, 622, 792
Night Riders, 571
Nimitz, Chester W., 858, 859, 860, 861, 880
9/11 Commission Report, The, 1094–96
Nineteenth Amendment, 762
Nintendo, 1005
Ninth Amendment, 264, 1016
NIRA. See National Industrial Recovery Act
Nix v. Williams, 1054
Nixon, Pat, 1007(photo)
Nixon, Richard, 1044
    election of 1960 and, 965
    election of 1968 and, 993
    election of 1972 and, 1021, 1023–24
    Ford's pardon of, 1026
    foreign policy, 1006–8
    Hiss case and, 916
    Kitchen Debate, 943, 946–47
    presidency of, 1006–14, 1022, 1023–25, 1028, 1047
        affirmative action and, 1014
        southern strategy, 1023

    Vietnam War and, 1006, 1008–11
    Watergate scandal, 1024–25
    women's rights and, 1016
    vice presidency of, 943, 946–47
Nixon Doctrine, 1006–7
Noble, Harriet, 337–38, 346
Non-Intercourse Act of 1809, 307
Nongovernmental organizations (NGOs), 1073–74
Noonan, Peggy, 1063
Normandy invasion, 878, 879(photo)
Norris, George, 753
Norsemen, 10
North
    antiabolition violence in, 430–31
    emancipation opposition in, 272–73, 536–37
    free black population of, 424–25
    growing estrangement from South, 497–99
    political economy in antebellum era, 474–77
    Reconstruction impact, 573–75
    slavery in, 271, 419–22
    Union revered in, 509
    West importance to, 478–80
    See also Civil War; individual states and colonies
North, Lord, 208, 220
North, Oliver, 1061
North American Aviation, 869
North American Free Trade Agreement (NAFTA), 1082
North Atlantic Treaty Organization (NATO), 899, 942, 949, 1089, 1091, 1093
North Carolina
    American Revolution and, 233
    Civil War and, 523, 539
    Constitution ratification and, 273
    land speculation in, 248
    secession of, 510, 511
    slavery in, 412, 420
    territory disputes in, 280
North Carolina Agricultural and Technical College, 961
North Korea, 1097
North Pole, 49
North River Steamboat of Clermont, 315, 317
Northeast, slavery and industrialization in, 419–22
Northern Pacific Railroad, 577
Northern Securities, 734–35
Northern Woodlands Indians, 46
Northwest Ordinance of 1787, 246, 249, 251, 304, 445
Northwest Passage, 17, 39, 40, 49
Northwest Territory, 256, 284, 314, 455
    Native American claims, 281–82
    Russian claims, 341
    slavery prohibited in, 246
Northwestern University, 715
Norway, 855
Notes on the State of Virginia (Jefferson), 273, 276
Nova Scotia, 183, 191, 280
NOW. See National Organization for Women
NSC-68, 906
Nuclear power, 884, 943, 1028
Nuclear weapons
    in cold war era, 894, 895, 896, 914, 944, 945
    Kennedy administration and, 970, 971–72
    "New Look" strategy, 944
    Nixon administration and, 1007–8
    Reagan administration and, 1047, 1048–49
    See also Arms reduction; Atomic bomb; Hydrogen bomb

Nueces River, 464
Nullification Act of 1833, 367
Nullification crisis, 364–66, 367, 441
Nuremberg Laws, 853
Nye, Gerald P., 854

O

Oates, William C., 694
Obama, Barack, 1102–5
Oberlin College, 374
Ocala Platform, 672, 690
Occoneechee Indians, 117
Occupational Safety and Health Administration (OSHA), 1012, 1045
Occupy movement, 1106
O'Connell, Thomas, 1015
O'Connor, Sandra Day, 1054, 1055
Office of Economic Opportunity (OEO), 973–74
Office of Price Administration, 869
Office of War Information, 869
Ogden, Aaron, 322, 323
Oglethorpe, James, 166, 169, 183
Ohio
    free blacks barred from, 424
    settlement of, 248, 268, 314
    slavery issue, 364, 430, 432
    statehood, 314, 348
    voting rights in, 348
Ohio Company, 186, 187
Ohio Gang, 807, 808
Ohio River, 7, 212, 248, 315, 412
Ohio River valley, 185–87, 281, 284, 314, 317
Ohio State University, 796
Oil
    ARAMCO and, 901–2
    Carter administration and, 1027
    Chinese market for, 699
    embargo, 1001, 1004, 1011, 1013
    exports to Japan ceased (WWII), 856
    in Iran, 1029
    Mexican exports, 751
    Persian Gulf War and, 1089
    price increase, 1101
    as principle power source, 907
    Reagan administration and, 1045, 1051, 1052
Ojibwa Indians, 357
Okinawa, Battle of, 884
Oklahoma (battleship), 856
Old Light religious groups, 328
Old Spanish Trail, 453
Old Time Gospel Hour (television program), 1042
Olive Branch Petition, 222
Oliver, Peter, 207
Olympics of 1980, 1029
Omaha Platform, 671, 672, 690
Omnibus Bill, 482–83
Omnibus Housing Act, 966
Omnibus Trade and Competitiveness Act of 1988, 1052
"On Being Brought from Africa to America" (Wheatly), 272
On the Origin of Species (Darwin), 638
On the Road (Kerouac), 951
Oñate, Juan de, 133, 134
Onesimus, 167
Ontario, 248
OPEC (Organization of the Petroleum Exporting Countries), 1001
Opechancanough, 78
Open Door Note, 707–9, 741, 765, 852, 853, 854
Open shop, 788, 789
Open Skies proposal, 945
Opera, 636
Operation Breadbasket, 985
Operation Desert Shield, 1089
Operation Desert Storm, 1089

Operation Iraqi Freedom, 1097
Operation Linebacker, 1011
Operation Mongoose, 971
Operation PUSH (People United to
    Save Humanity), 1058
Operation Rolling Thunder, 979
Operation Trinity, 883
Operation Wetback, 941
Opium trade, 159, 312, 380
Oppenheimer, J. Robert, 883, 902, 944
Oratam, Sachem, 111
Orchestral music, 636
Order of Freemasons. See Masons
Ordinance of 1787, 422
Oregon system, 732
Oregon Territory, 454–55, 459–60,
    461, 463
Oregon Trail, 453
Organization Man, The (Whyte), 934
Organization of American States
    (OAS), 903
Organization of the Petroleum
    Exporting Countries
    (OPEC), 1001
Original Dixieland Band, 810
Orinoco, 77
Orista Indians, 42
Orphans, 163
Osborn, Sarah (revival attendee), 174
Osborne, Sarah (witch hunt victim),
    103
Osgood, Samuel, 263
OSHA. See Occupational Safety and
    Health Administration
Ostend Manifesto, 489
O'Sullivan, John, 445, 446–47
Oswald, Lee Harvey, 972
Otis, James, 204
Ottawa Accords, 838, 855
Ottawa Indians, 187
Ottoman Empire, 159
Our Country (Strong), 628
Outsourcing, 1078, 1079
Overland Trail, 604–5
Owen, Robert, 375

P

P-51 Mustang, 863
Pacification, 18, 699
Packard, Vance, 932, 954
Packingtown, 590, 602(photo)
Page, Patti, 941
Pahlavi, Shah Mohammad Reza, 944
Paine, Thomas, 167, 220, 224, 228,
    255, 286, 287
Paint-ins, 962
Painters' Row, 598–99
Painting, 445, 641
Pakistan, 883, 1104
Pale of Settlement, 589
Paleo-Indians, 4
Palestine Liberation Organization
    (PLO), 1051
Palin, Sarah, 1102
Palmer, A. Mitchell, 773, 776
Palmer raids, 777
Palmer v. Mulligan, 321
Pan-American Conference (1889), 664
Pan-American Conference (1933), 854
Panama, 54
    Carter administration and, 1028
    revolution in, 739
    Wilson administration and, 752
Panama Canal, 664, 944
    Carter's agreement on, 1028
    construction of, 737–39
Panics
    of 1819, 331–32, 345, 350, 357,
        364, 381
    of 1873, 577–78, 586–87
    of 1893, 586, 587, 681–82, 699, 729
    See also Depressions; Financial
        crisis of 1890s

Paquiquineo. See Velasco, don Luis de
Paris, Treaty of
    American Revolution, 233, 237–38,
        280, 281
    French and Indian War, 195
    Spanish-American War, 701, 704
Park, George, 227
Parkman, Frances, 656
Parks, 666
Parks, Rosa, 953
Parliament, British, 104–5, 106, 124,
    198, 201, 204, 210, 211,
    212–13
Parochial schools, 628, 631, 657, 665
Parris, Samuel, 103, 104
Participatory democracy, 964
Partisan politics
    decline of, 718
    voluntarism compared with, 654
Patent medicines, 717
Patents, 784
Paterson, Thomas G., 897
Patient Protection and Affordable
    Health Care Act of 2010,
    1103
Patronage system, 577, 656, 659, 660,
    835, 839
Patrons of Husbandry, 671
Patroons, 50
Patton, George S., 825–26, 866, 874,
    878
Patuxet Indians, 85
Paul, Alice, 719, 762
Pawnee Indians, 136, 455
Paxton Boys, 196, 197
Payne-Aldrich Tariff of 1909, 741
Payola, 954
PBSUCCESS (CIA operation), 944
Peace Corps, 971
Peace Democrats. See Copperheads
Peace dividend, 1089
Peace movement, 809
Peaceful coexistence policy, 945, 1008
Pearl Harbor
    acquisition of, 704
    Japanese attack on, 853, 856–57,
        858, 860, 865, 872, 882, 894,
        1093
Peleliu, Battle of, 880
Pendleton Civil Service Act, 660
Penicillin, 864
Penis envy, 940
Penn, William, 109, 111, 112(photo)
Penn Central Railroad, 1000
Pennsylvania
    abolitionism in, 272, 430
    Constitutional ratification and, 254
    creation of government in, 226
    German settlers in, 291
    land speculation in, 248
    Native Americans in, 247
    penal reform in, 394
    voting rights in, 348
    Whiskey Rebellion in, 284
Pennsylvania colony, 106, 154, 185,
    186
    diversity and prosperity in, 109–12
    founding of, 109
    immigration to, 145
    newspapers of, 203
    slavery in, 112, 163
Pennsylvania Hospital, 172
Pennsylvania Journal, 202(photo)
Pennsylvania Railroad, 586, 593–94,
    595, 761
Pennsylvania Slovak Catholic Union,
    629
Pennsylvania Society for Promoting
    the Abolition of Slavery
    (petition), 274–75
Pentagon Papers, 1011, 1025
People's Convention, 348
People's Party. See Populism

Pequot Indians, 86
Pequot War, 96–97
Perestroika, 1065
Perfectionism, 374–81, 430, 432
Perkins, Frances, 836, 843, 844
Perkins, George W., 742
Perkins, James, 312
Perkins, Maria, 408
Perkins, Thomas, 312
Perot, H. Ross, 1080
Perpetual motion machine, 331
Perry, Oliver Hazard, 308
Pershing, John J., 752, 764, 770, 771
Persian Gulf War, 1088, 1089–90
Personal computer (PC), 1036,
    1037(figure), 1038–39
Personal income per capita (1840-
    1880), 461(table)
Personnel management, 687
Peru, 17, 23, 24
Petersburg, siege of, 541, 542
Petition of Right, 105
Phelan, James, 738
Philadelphia, 111, 211
    African Americans in, 761
    American Revolution and, 228
    capital located in, 265, 269, 287
    colonial era growth in, 160
    colonial era newspapers of, 203
    colonial era poverty in, 163
    commerce and culture in ca. 1760,
        161(map)
    free black population of, 273, 425
    French and Indian War and, 193
    industrial era growth in, 591
    inflation at (1770-1790),
        239(figure)
    library acquired by, 172
    port of, 154, 155
    republic era culture of, 269–70
    republic era growth in, 268, 269
Philadelphia and Reading Railroad,
    681
Philadelphia Centennial Exposition,
    641
Philadelphia Negro, The (DuBois), 728
Philadelphia Plan, 1014
Philbrick, Herbert, 892
Philip II, king of Spain, 37, 42, 56
Philippine-American War, 704–7
Philippines, 697
    annexation of, 704
    British seizure of, 195
    Carter administration and, 1029
    Eisenhower administration and,
        947
    Great Depression and, 838
    revolution in, 699, 700, 704
    Taft as governor of, 741
    U.S. rule phased out, 707
    U.S. war with, 704–7
    World War II and, 856, 857, 880
Phillippine Sea, Battle of, 861
Phillips, Wendell, 574
Phips, Sir William, 127
Phonograph, 637, 793
Photography, 642–43
Pickawillany, 185–87
Pickett, George, 537
Pickford, Mary, 783–84, 788, 790, 795,
    797, 810, 811–12
Pierce, Franklin, 484–85, 489
Pierce, Palmer E., 764
PIGS (Poles, Italians, Greeks, and
    Slavs), 1023
Pilgrims, 56, 57, 82, 84–85, 92
Pinchot, Gifford, 736, 738, 741
Pinckney, Charles C., 307
Pinckney, Thomas, 288, 289, 290
Pinckney's Treaty, 288, 302
Pingree, Hazen, 730
Pinochet, Augusto, 1011
Pioneer Hi-Bred Corn Company, 830

Pioneers, The (Cooper), 448
Piracy, 42, 426
    See also Privateering
Pitt, William, 193, 194, 195, 196,
    204, 205
Pittsburgh, 790
Pittsburgh Courier, 872
Pittsburgh Survey, 722
Plague, 28
Plains Indians, 29, 455, 606, 607
    manifest destiny and, 439–40
    warfare among, 136–37
Plains of Abraham, 195
Planned Parenthood v. Casey, 1087
Plantations, 419
    in Barbados, 115
    cotton, 409(photo), 411, 553
    culture of, 164–65
    economic efficiency of, 152
    indentured servants on, 80–81
    rice, 408, 409–11
    slavery system on, 81, 408–11
    sugar, 408, 409, 411, 553, 567
    tobacco, 154, 165, 408, 411
Planter's exemption from
    conscription, 539
Plattsburg training camp, 755–56
Playboy (magazine), 934
Playhouse 90 (television program), 932
Plea for the West, A (Beecher), 373
Pledge of Allegiance, 624
Plessy, Homer, 693–94
Plessy v. Ferguson, 694, 729, 952
Plumbers, White House, 1025
Plutonium, 883
Plymouth Church, 490
Plymouth colony, 70, 82, 84–85, 87,
    92, 122, 124
Pocahontas, 56, 57, 69–70, 74–75, 77
Poindexter, John, 1061
Point Four program, 904
Pokanoket Indians, 85
Poland
    communism collapse in, 1065
    German invasion of, 852, 855
    Iraq War and, 1097
    Russia's loss of, 765
    Soviet Union and, 894, 895
    witchcraft trials in, 129
Police department, 591, 666, 725, 734
Polio, 827
Polio vaccine, 935
Polish immigrants, 631
Political economy
    in antebellum era, 474–80
    of contract labor, 557–58
    of expansion, 458–67
    of global capitalism, 586–92
    of mercantilism, 106
    of New World, 15–16
    of Puritan society, 90–91
    of sharecropping, 567–70
    of slavery, 79–81, 477
    of South Carolina colony, 112–15
    of trans-Mississippi west, 445–58
    See also Economy; Politics
Political parties
    in American Republic, 266–67
    in crisis (Jacksonian era), 440–44
    in industrial America, 652–54
Politics
    of 1790s and democracy, 292–93
    of abolition, 432–33
    of American Republic transition,
        300–307
    of individualism, 808–9
    of industrial America, 651–79
        economic issues, 658–65
        government activism and limits,
            665–66
        styles, 652–58
        late 19th century retreat from,
            691–97

machine, 652, 729, 733
moral reform and, 394–95
new (early 20th century), 716–20
of new economy, 1077–83
New Era in, 797, 806–11
new national (19th century),
    338–46
partisan, 654, 718
popular, 656, 695–96
of slavery, 425–34, 480–85, 494–95
voluntarism in, 652, 654
women in, 1087
See also Political economy
Polk, James K., 461–67
    election of, 461–63
    Mexican War and, 463–66
    national bank and, 467
Polygamy, 137, 377, 626
Polygyny, 37, 47
Pomo Indians, 455
Ponce de León, Juan, 19–20
Pong, 1005
Pontiac's Rebellion, 196–98
*Poor Rich Man and the Rich Poor Man,
    The* (Sedgwick), 391
Poor Richard's Almanack (Franklin),
    588
Pop art, 988
Popé, 135
Pope, John, 526
Popper, Karl, 891
Popular culture, 620, 633, 639, 641
Popular front strategy, 834
Popular politics
    critics of, 656
    decline of, 695–96
Popular sovereignty, 483, 494, 497,
    500–501
    defined, 481
    Kansas-Nebraska Act, 486–88
Population
    in American Republic (1790),
        272(table)
    black, distribution of (1775),
        272(map)
    of British colonies in America
        (1660 and 1710), 118(table)
    English, of Virginia (1607-1640),
        75(table)
    explosion of 18th century, 144–51
    of foreign birth by region (1880),
        629(map)
    growth in American Republic,
        267, 268
    growth in colonial cities, 160
    Hispanic, decline in, 612
    Hispanic, growth in, 1083,
        1084(map)
    of Mesoamerica, 6
    in modern era, 789–90
    Native American, 27, 1020(map)
    of New France, 48
    percentage living in cities (1890-
        1920), 717(figure)
    post-revolution growth, 240
    of pre-Columbian North America,
        6
    proportion living in cities (1790-
        1900), 591(figure)
    slave, 147, 151, 271
    world (1650-2000), 29(figure)
Populism, 651, 665, 732, 834
    differing views of, 675–76
    free silver issue and, 672, 683,
        689, 690
    rise of, 672–76
Populist Vision, The (Postel), 675–76
Port Huron Statement, 964
Port Moresby, 859
Port Royal, 520
Porter, Katherine Anne, 775
Portrait of a Lady (James), 640
Ports, 154, 155, 313

Portugal, 56, 159
    African explorations by, 10–12,
        14, 16
    Columbus turned down by, 14
    Dutch takeover of Brazil, 50–51
    Jews of, 51
    Muslims of, 8, 10
    New World colonization, 16, 23,
        30–31
    slave trade, 12
Postal service, 665, 758
Postel, Charles, 675–76
Postmodern culture, 1078
Potato famine (Irish), 388, 589
Potatoes, 29
Potomac River, 78, 79, 251, 537
Potsdam Conference, 882, 895,
    897(photo)
Pottawatomie Creek slave revolt,
    488–91
Pound, Roscoe, 727
Poverty
    in African Americans, 1058
    in American Republic, 273, 279
    in colonial America, 152, 163
    Johnson (Lyndon) administration
        and, 973–74, 975–76
    Kennedy administration and, 966
    in Mexican Americans, 1017, 1018
    in mid-20th century, 928
    in modern era, 798
    Reagan administration and, 1061
    war on, 973–74, 975–76
    women in, 1055, 1087
    See also Welfare system
Powderly, Terence, 669
Powell, Colin, 1084
Powell, Fenner, 560–61
Power
    crisis of misplaced, 954–57, 961, 962
    new approaches to, 962–65
Power Elite, The (Mills), 954
Power of Sympathy, The (Brown), 278
Powers, Francis Gary, 945, 947(photo)
Powers, John J., 1003
Powers, Johnny, 729
Powhatan (chief), 69–70, 74, 78
Powhatan Indians, 37–38, 61, 69–70,
    71, 79
    destruction of, 78–79
    troubled relations with, 74–75
Predestination, 83, 84, 94, 105, 127
Preparation, doctrine of, 95
Presbyterian Magazine, 801
Presbyterians, 105, 145, 328, 329–30,
    373–74, 599, 1041
Presidential Commission on the Status
    of Women, 989
Presidential elections
    of 1796, 288–90
    of 1800, 301, 689
    of 1804, 305
    of 1808, 306–7
    of 1812, 308
    of 1816, 340
    of 1824, 344–45
    of 1828, 351–52
    of 1832, 353
    of 1836, 441–42, 461
    of 1840, 440, 458–59
    of 1844, 461–62, 463(table)
    of 1848, 433, 440, 481
    of 1852, 484–85
    of 1856, 491–95, 496(map)
    of 1860, 499, 500–502
    of 1864, 541, 544
    of 1868, 571
    of 1872, 573, 575, 577, 659
    of 1876, 578, 659(table)
    of 1880, 659, 660
    of 1884, 659(table)
    of 1888, 659, 662
    of 1892, 672

    of 1896, 689–91, 695, 697,
        719(figure), 806, 807(figure)
    of 1900, 719(figure), 807(figure)
    of 1904, 718, 719(figure),
        807(figure)
    of 1908, 719(figure), 741,
        807(figure)
    of 1912, 719(figure), 720, 741,
        742–43, 807(figure)
    of 1916, 719(figure), 754–56,
        807(figure)
    of 1920, 719(figure), 806, 807–8
    of 1924, 807(figure), 808, 811
    of 1928, 807(figure), 811
    of 1932, 826–28
    of 1936, 839, 843
    of 1940, 855
    of 1944, 882
    of 1948, 913
    of 1952, 943
    of 1956, 943
    of 1960, 964–65
    of 1964, 973, 990
    of 1968, 990–93
    of 1972, 999, 1021, 1023–24
    of 1976, 1026–27
    of 1980, 1036, 1042–43
    of 1984, 1046
    of 1988, 1080
    of 1992, 1080
    of 1996, 1081
    of 2000, 1081
    of 2004, 1081
    of 2008, 1081, 1102
Presidential Reconstruction, 553,
    557–64, 565, 579
Presley, Elvis, 942, 950–51
Press, freedom of, 162, 203, 264, 975
Prince of Wales (cruiser), 856
Princeton, Battle of, 228, 231
Princeton University, 175, 742, 796–97
Printing press, 10, 162(map)
Prisoners from the Front (Homer), 641
Prisons/penetentiaries
    in American Republic, 279
    Angola, 832–33
    reform movements, 394
Privateering, 54, 55, 239
Prizefighting. *See* Boxing
Proclamation Day, 529
Proclamation of 1763, 197, 213(table)
Proclamation of Amnesty and
    Reconstruction, 554
Producers' ideology, 667–68, 669
Producing classes, 384, 386
Professional Air Traffic Controllers
    Organization (PATCO),
    1045, 1046(photo)
Progress and Poverty (George), 667,
    668–69
Progressive Party, 742, 808
Progressivism, 716, 720–33, 777
    current, 1104
    differing views of, 731–32
    experts and, 725–27
    race issues and, 727–29
    Roosevelt (Theodore) and, 734,
        735, 742, 744
    settlement house work, 721–22
    in state and local politics, 729–33
    Wilson and, 742–43, 744
    World War I and, 750, 760
Prohibition, 750, 763, 796, 808, 827
    See also Temperance movement
Propaganda
    cold war, 945
    World War I, 759
Proposition 13, 1027
Proposition 187, 1082
Proprietary colonies, 79, 112
Prostitution, 268, 380, 395, 619, 627,
    750, 763, 794
    in China, 740

    in colonial era, 209
    houses of, 627(map)
Protestantism
    in American Republic, 330
    Antifederalists and, 255
    decline in church membership, 1041
    in England, 53, 54, 83
    in Maryland colony, 125
    in mid-20th century, 935
    nativism and, 657
    reformers and separatists in, 374
    social class and, 599
    temperance movement and, 658
Providence Island, 85–87, 97
Proximity fuse bomb, 864
Prussia, 183
Public Broadcasting Act of 1967, 974
Public education, 393–94, 630–31, 666
Public sphere, 162
Public Works Administration, 833
Publick Occurrences, 203
Pueblo Bonito, 7
Pueblo Indians, 133–36, 137
Puerto Ricans, 940, 1059
Puerto Rico
    under Spain, 25, 697
    Spanish-American War and, 701
Pullman workers' strike, 687–88, 689
Pure Food and Drug Act of 1906, 735
Puritans, 82–97, 105, 109, 121–23,
    124, 127–28, 145, 391
    beliefs of, 83–84
    dissension in the ranks, 93–97
    English origins of movement, 83
    family life in, 91–93
    political economy of, 90–91
    prosperity impact on religion,
        121–22
    social organization of, 87–90
    See also Pilgrims
Putnam, Ann, Jr., 128
Pychon, Thomas, 989
Pyle, Ernie, 866, 875–77

Q

Qaddafi, Muammar, 1052
Qaeda, Al, 1071, 1091–93, 1097, 1099,
    1104
    global reach of, 1092(map)
    in Iraq, 1100
Qingdao port, 699
Quakers, 128, 145, 374, 391
    in England, 111
    in Pennsylvania colony, 109, 111
    persecution of, 122
    slavery opposed by, 272, 430
Quartering of soldiers, 192–93
    Quartering Act of 1765, 200, 205,
        209, 210, 213(table)
    Quartering Act of 1774, 212
    Third Amendment on, 264
Quasi-War, 290–91
Québec, 47, 130, 212
    American Revolution and, 222, 227
    French and Indian War and, 194–95
    King George's War and, 183
    King William's War and, 127
    post established at, 45
Quebec Act of 1774, 212, 213(table)
Queen Anne's War, 114, 126–27,
    182, 199
Quiz show scandal, 954

R

Rabaul, 880
Race riots, 984–85
    in Detroit, 871–72, 984
    in Harlem, 861, 984
    King (Martin Luther) assassination
        and, 992
    King (Rodney) beating and, 1084
    during Reconstruction, 563–64
    in Watts, 984, 1084

Race Traits and Tendencies of the American Negro (Hoffman), 638
Rachel and Reuben (Rowson), 278
Racism
    in the Democratic Party, 486, 494, 572
    manifest destiny and, 462–63
    scientific, 623, 635, 638–39, 694, 721
    slavery justified by, 81, 115, 120–21, 486, 494
Radical feminism, 989–90, 1014, 1022
Radical Reconstruction, 555, 565–67, 570–73
Radical Republicans, 552, 564–65, 570
Radio
    decline of political affiliation, 806
    invention of, 793–94
    superheterodyne receiver, 772
Railroads
    Baltimore and Ohio Railroad, 586
    buffalo kills sponsored by, 608
    Central Pacific Railroad, 605
    Chinchow-Aigun railway (China), 741
    Civil War and, 545
    corruption problem, 576
    deaths among builders of, 610
    East Louisiana Railway, 693–94
    expansion of, 474, 477, 478, 479(map), 603
    first transcontinental, 525, 605
    Great Pacific Railway, 612
    Great Western Railroad, 586
    growth of (1850-1890), 594(map)
    Interstate Commerce Commission and, 661
    labor union for workers, 687, 697
    New York Central Railroad, 586
    Northern Pacific Railroad, 577
    panic of 1873 and, 577–78
    panic of 1893 and, 587
    Penn Central Railroad, 1000
    Pennsylvania Railroad, 586, 593–94, 595, 761
    Philadelphia and Reading Railroad, 681
    racial segregation, 693–94
    Southern Pacific Railroad, 593(photo)
    strikes, 578, 586, 659, 669–70, 908
    telegraph complemented by, 476
    Texas Pacific Railroad, 586
    Union Pacific Railroad, 576, 605
    the West and, 613
    Wisconsin Idea, 732
    World War I nationalization of, 759
Raleigh, Sir Walter, 38, 55, 56, 58, 60–61, 77
Ramsey, Elizabeth, 408
Randolph, A. Philip, 789, 851, 885, 911
Randolph, Edmund, 263
Randolph, John, 301, 306
Rankin, Jeannette, 856
Ransom, John Crowe, 798
Rap music, 1058, 1059
Rape, 16, 25, 29, 135, 136, 705
Rapp, George, 377
Rappahannock River, 56
Rauh, Joseph, 851
Rauschenbusch, Walter, 720
Raza, La, 804
Raza Unida, La, 1018
RCA, 932, 1039
Reading, Pennsylvania, 389
Reading revolution, 202–3
Reagan, Nancy, 1043, 1055
Reagan, Ronald, 993, 1035, 1036, 1042–55, 1060–67, 1076, 1080, 1081, 1090
    African Americans and, 1057, 1058

AIDS crisis and, 1056
assassination attempt on, 1043–44
as California governor, 990
comeback of, 1065–66
domestic policy, 1043–46
elections of, 1036, 1042–43, 1046
foreign policy, 1047–52
Iran-Contra affair, 1060–61
shrinking government, 1044
style of, 1043–44
Reagan Doctrine, 1049–51
Reagan Revolution, 1043–52, 1061, 1062, 1066, 1080
    abroad, 1047–52
    at home, 1043–46
Reaganomics, 1044–46, 1061
Realism, artistic, 619, 639–45
Rebel Without a Cause (film), 950
Recall, 732
Reciprocity, 664
Reconquista, 8–9, 63
Reconstruction, 545, 551–83, 656, 660, 802, 839
    achievements and failures of, 566–67
    congressional, 564–70
    corruption problem in, 575–76
    end of, 575–89
    nature of, 579–80
    the North and, 573–75
    presidential, 553, 557–64, 565, 579
    radical, 555, 565–67, 570–73
    "redemption" from, 565(map), 577–80
    resistance to, 558–59
    Ten Percent Plan, 554–55
    Wade-Davis Bill, 555
Reconstruction: America's Unfinished Revolution (Foner), 580
Reconstruction Acts, 571, 579
Reconstruction Amendments, 564(table)
Reconstruction Finance Corporation (RFC), 825, 828
Reconversion, 906–12
Red Cloud, 606, 607
Red Hat camp, 832, 833
Red Menace, The (film), 915
Red River campaign of 1864, 520
Red Scares, 776–77, 801, 915, 918
Red Shirts, 571
Red Stick faction of Creek Indians, 299–300, 308, 360
Red Thunder, Tropic Lightning (Bergerud), 991–92
Redemption (from Reconstruction), 565(map), 577–80
Redemptioners, 112, 118, 144, 146
Redheffer, Charles, 331
Reed, David A., 839
Reed, James A., 774
Reed, Thomas Brackett, 662
Reese, James, 810
Referendum, 732
Reform, 381–97
    electoral politics and, 394–95
    health, 390
    penal, 394
    progressivism and, 729–33
    religious, 374, 375(map), 377–81
    the urban classes and, 381–89
    women involved in, 396–97
    during World War I, 762–64
Reform mayors, 730–32
Regents of the University of California v. Allan Bakke, 1014
Rehnquist, William, 1054
Reinhardt, Django, 810
Religion
    in American Republic, 328–30
    in England, 53, 54, 83, 105–6
    Enlightenment ideas and, 167, 172
    freedom of, 249, 255, 264, 975

in industrial America, 634
mid-20th century resurgence of, 935, 936(table)
in modern era, 801
Native American practices, 134, 325, 330, 608–9
"old time," 801
perfectionism and, 374–81
prayer prohibited in public schools, 975
scandals in (1980s), 1060
separation of church and state, 94, 219
socialism and, 720
See also Missionaries; Revivalism; individual religions
Religious Right, 1041–42
Religious tolerance
    Dominion of New England and, 124
    Edict of Nantes, 44
    Enlightenment and, 167
    in Maryland colony, 79, 125
    in Netherlands, 49
    in New Netherland, 51, 106
    in Pennsylvania colony, 109, 111, 154
    Puritan view of, 94–96
    in South Carolina colony, 112
Remington Arms, 763
Removal Act of 1830, 359, 445
Removal policy, 357–64, 367, 455
Reno, Janet, 1087
Republic. *See* American Republic
Republic of Texas, 439, 451–52
Republic of the Congo, 971
Republican Party
    African Americans and, 839
    Civil War and, 523, 524, 525, 527, 528, 531, 541
    current stance of, 1104, 1105
    election of 1856 and, 491–95
    election of 1860 and, 500–502
    election of 1864 and, 541
    election of 1868 and, 571
    election of 1872 and, 577
    election of 1876 and, 578
    election of 1880 and, 659, 660
    election of 1888 and, 659, 662
    election of 1896 and, 689, 690, 696
    election of 1912 and, 742
    election of 1916 and, 754, 756
    election of 1920 and, 807–8
    election of 1932 and, 826, 827
    election of 1936 and, 839
    election of 2008 and, 1102
    emancipation and, 517
    gold standard and, 689, 690
    Great Depression and, 819–21
    Hispanic vote and, 1059
    in industrial America, 652, 653–54, 658, 659–60, 665, 672
    Jackson and, 440–41
    labor unions and, 908
    liberal faction, 576–77
    on "loss" of China, 903
    Modern, 942, 943, 965
    in modern era, 806, 807–11
    New Deal and, 844, 845
    as party of moderation, 571–73
    radicals in, 552, 564–65, 570
    Reconstruction and, 552, 554–55, 556, 559–67, 570–73, 575, 576–77, 578, 579–80
    response to activism of '60s and '70s, 1023–24
    secession issue and, 510–11
    slavery issue and, 434, 474, 485, 494–99, 501, 508, 509, 510–11
    Thirteenth Amendment and, 543, 544
Republicanism, 205–6, 209, 225

Republicans (Madison's designation), 266
Requerimiento, 17
Reservations (Native American), 79, 585, 609–10, 940, 1019
    New Deal legislation, 831
    origins of, 605–8
Restore Our Alienated Rights (ROAR), 1014, 1015
Restrictive covenants, 910, 930
Resumptionists, 658
Resurrectionists, 652
Reuther, Walter, 908
Revels, Hiram, 566(photo)
Revenue Act of 1766, 205
Revenue Act of 1935, 835
Revere, Paul, 220
Revivalism, 328–30, 331, 375(map)
    See also Great Awakening
Revolutionary War. *See* American Revolution
Reynolds, Malvina, 934
Rhode Island
    American Revolution and, 246
    Constitution ratification and, 273
    voting rights in, 348–49
Rhode Island colony, 87, 94, 95, 122, 124, 125
Rhode Island system, 385
Rhodes, James, 1009, 1010
Rhythm and blues (R & b), 942
Rice, 115, 152, 153, 270, 311, 313
    plantations, 408, 409–11
    slavery routine, 154, 409–11
Rice, Condoleezza, 1084
Richardson, Elliot, 1025
Richmond
    American Revolution and, 233
    as Confederate capital, 513, 516, 518–19, 520, 526, 539, 540–41, 542
Richmond, David, 961
Richthofen, Oswald Freiherr Von, 697
Rickets, 822
Ridge, John, 362
Riesman, David, 934
Rifle, repeating, 534
Right to Life movement, 1055, 1087
Riis, Jacob, 591, 642, 644–45
Rimfire bullet, 534
Rio Grande, 130, 464
Rio Pact, 903
Rise and Fall of the White Republic, The (Saxton), 462
Rise of American Democracy (Wilentz), 368
Rise of Silas Lapham, The (Howells), 639
Risk Rule, 1087
RJR Nabisco, 1039
RKO, 792
Road building, 315, 319(map)
Roanoke, 55–61, 64, 71
Roanoke Indians, 60, 61
ROAR. *See* Restore Our Alienated Rights
Robber barons, 598, 934
Robertson, Pat, 1042
Robinson, Charles, 490
Robinson, Frederick, 349
Robinson, Jackie, 911–12
Rochefort, Joseph, 859
Rock and roll, 942, 950, 987, 1058
"Rock Around the Clock" (song), 942
Rockefeller, John D., 597, 598, 681, 735, 776, 1078
Rockefeller, Nelson, 1026, 1027
Rockhill, William, 707
Rockingham, Marquess of, 204
Rocky Mountains, 304, 340, 453, 455, 460, 613
Roe v. Wade, 1016, 1055
Roebuck, Alvah, 588

Roger, king of Sicily, 11
Rolfe, John, 74–75, 77, 80
Rolling Stones, 987
Romantic movement, 445, 641
Rommel, Erwin, 866
Roosevelt, Eleanor, 776, 830, 839, 851, 989
    letters to, 840–42
    newspaper column of, 843
Roosevelt, Franklin D., 776, 826–46, 883, 912, 973, 1043
    African Americans and, 839, 851, 861
    background of, 827
    as Cox's running mate, 807
    death of, 882
    elections of, 826–28, 839, 843, 855, 882
    fireside chats of, 828, 829(photo)
    Holocaust dismissed by, 874
    polio of, 827
    World War II and, 852, 853–58, 861, 863–66, 869, 871, 872, 880
    at Yalta Conference, 894–95
    See also New Deal
Roosevelt, Nicholas, 315
Roosevelt, Theodore, 733–42, 743, 744, 827
    big stick diplomacy, 737–40
    conservation movement, 736–37
    imperialism and, 697, 698–99
    on labor strife, 720
    on muckraking, 725
    Philippine-American War and, 707
    professional background of, 698, 733–34
    re-election attempt, 741–42
    Spanish-American War and, 700, 702–3, 734
    on sports, 625
    Square Deal, 735
    trust busting and, 734–35
    World War I and, 754, 755, 756
Roosevelt and the Rough Riders (lithograph), 702(photo)
Roosevelt Corollary, 740, 741
Rosecrans, William S., 539
Rosenberg, Ethel, 916, 944
Rosenberg, Julius, 916, 944
Rosie the Riveter, 869
Ross, John, 362
Rough Riders, 700, 702
Route 128, 1037
Rowley, Massachusetts land distribution, 90(table)
Rowson, Susanna, 278
Royal Africa Company, 106
Royal colonies, 79, 125
Royal Society of London, 172
Rubin, Jerry, 1039
Ruby, Jack, 972
Ruef, Abraham, 717, 738, 739
Ruffin, Edmund, 495, 507–8, 511, 517
Ruiz, José, 403
Rule of law, 201, 213, 321–22
Rumania, 1065
Rumsfeld, Donald, 1097, 1098
Rural regions
    in American Republic, 267
    in colonial America, 163–64
    migration from, 388–89
    in modern era, 790
Russell, James, 1010
Russell Sage Foundation, 722
Russia
    Alaska purchased from, 572, 663
    Bolshevik Revolution in, 764, 765, 769, 893
    claims in Pacific Northwest, 341
    Iraq War and, 1097
    Jews of, 589, 657
    McDonald's in, 1074

Open Door Note and, 707–8, 709, 741
    space program and, 1076
    wheat from, 671
    World War I and, 749, 753, 756, 764, 765, 769
    See also Soviet Union
Russwurm, John, 427
Rustbelt, 1004, 1006(map), 1037
Rutgers University, 175
Ruth, Babe, 792, 797, 812(photo)
Rwanda, 838

S

Sabin polio vaccine, 935
Sacagawea, 304
Sacco, Nicola, 777
Safety-valve theory, 480
Safstrom, David, 1093
Sagamité, 47
Sagebrush Rebellion, 1027
Sailmaker's shop, 279(photo)
Sailmakers' Society Certificate of Membership, 156(photo)
St. Augustine, 24, 42, 55, 133, 134, 165, 166, 183
St. Clair, Arthur, 282
St. Croix River, 280
Saint-Domingue, 133, 267, 285, 290, 303, 304, 416
St. Lawrence River, 39, 41, 42, 43, 45, 47, 127, 194, 280
St. Louis (refugee ship), 874
Saipan, 880
Salazar, Rubén, 1018
Salem witchcraft trials, 103–4, 127–30, 163
Salk polio vaccine, 935
Salons, 278, 279
SALT. See Strategic Arms Limitation Treaty
Salt Lake City, 378(photo), 605
Saltworks, 412
Salvation Army, 718
San Francisco
    beat movement in, 951
    counterculture in, 988
    gold rush in, 480, 613, 738
    same-sex marriage in, 1088
San Francisco sound, 988
San Jacinto River, 451
San Joaquin Valley, 1018
San Juan Hill, Battle of, 701, 702–3
San Salvador, 14
Sand Creek massacre, 606, 608
Sandalwood, 312
Sanders, Mark, 1036
Sandinistas, 1050, 1060
Sandwich Islands, 312
Sanger, Margaret, 719, 794
Santa Anna, Antonio López de, 451, 464
Santa Fe, 133, 135, 464
Santa Fe Trail, 453
Santo Domingo, 86, 133, 572, 663
Saratoga, Battle of, 231
Saratoga (carrier), 860
SARS (severe acute respiratory syndrome), 776
Satellites, 1073, 1076
Saturday Night Massacre, 1025
Satyagraha, 838
Saudi Arabia
    attacks on U.S. soldiers in, 1092
    oil supplies of, 901–2
    Persian Gulf War and, 1089
Sauk Indians, 357, 359–60
Savage, Augusta, 805
Savannah, 166, 172
    American Revolution and, 228
    Civil War and, 542
    colonial era growth, 160
Savannah Indians, 114

Savannah River, 166
Save Our Children, 1055
Savio, Mario, 986
Saxton, Alexander, 462
Saxton, Robert, 317
Sayenqueraghta, 248
Scabs, 602
Scalawags, 565, 578
Scalia, Antonin, 1054
Scalpings, 122, 137, 197, 606
Schechter Poultry Corporation v. United States, 835
Scheuer, Sandra, 1009
Schine, David, 917
Schlafly, Phyllis, 1017
Schlesinger, Arthur M., Jr., 963
School District of Abington Township v. Schempp, 975
Schools. See Colleges and universities; Education
Schroeder, William, 1009
Schurz, Carl, 572
Schwab, Charles M., 759
Schwartz, Anna J., 820–21
Schwarzkopf, Norman, 1089
Schwerner, Michael, 976
Scientific management, 682, 686, 788
Scientific racism, 623, 635, 638–39, 694, 721
SCLC. See Southern Christian Leadership Conference
Scopes, John (trial of), 801
Scotch-Irish, 145, 146
Scotland
    emigration from, 145
    religious revolt in, 105
Scott, Dred, 496–97, 498, 532–33, 562
Scott, Tom, 593, 594
Scott, Winfield, 444, 464, 484, 513, 516
Scottsboro Boys, 834
Screen Actors Guild, 1045
SDI. See Strategic Defense Initiative
SDS. See Students for a Democratic Society
Sea Islands, 165, 532, 553, 556
Seale, Bobby, 985
Seamstresses, 381
Search for Order, The, 1877-1920 (Wiebe), 731–32
Sears, Richard Warren, 588
Sears, Roebuck, 587, 588, 929
SEATO. See Southeast Asia Treaty Organization
Secession, 508, 509–11, 539
Second Amendment, 264
Second Confiscation Act, 528
Second Reconstruction Act, 565
Second world, 904, 945
Securities and Exchange Act of 1934, 829
Securities and Exchange Commission, 829
Sedgwick, Catharine, 391
Sedition Act of 1918, 758
See It Now (television program), 932
"Seeds of Failure in Radical Race Policy, The" (Woodward), 579
Seeger, Alan, 754
Selective Service Act of 1948, 899
Self-improvement, 389–91
"Self-Reliance" (Emerson), 391
Semiconductors, 1036
Seminole Indians, 300, 332, 340, 358, 360
Seneca Falls Convention, 397
Seneca Indians, 325
"Separate but equal" doctrine, 694, 952
Separatists, 84, 85, 94, 374–77
September 11 terrorist attacks, 1071, 1072, 1089, 1092–96, 1100, 1104

casualties in, 1093
    report, 1094–96
Sepulveda, Juan Ginés de, 18
Sequoyah, 362
Serbia, 749
Sesame Street (television program), 974
Settlement houses, 721–22, 843
Seven Cities of Cibola, 24–25
Seven Days, Battles of, 526
700 Club, The (television program), 1042
Seven Years' War, 187, 199
    See also French and Indian War
Seventeenth parallel, 947–48
Seventh Amendment, 264
Seventh Cavalry, 607
Seventh Regiment Departing for the War from New York City, April 1961 (Nast), 512
Severe acute respiratory syndrome (SARS), 776
Seward, William Henry, 482, 496, 498, 501, 528, 664
    Alaska purchase and, 572, 663
    on emancipation, 545
Sewing machine, 601
Sex and the Single Girl (Brown), 989
Sexual Behavior in the Human Female (Kinsey), 933
Sexual Behavior in the Human Male (Kinsey), 933
Sexuality/sexual relations
    in American Republic, 268
    in colonial era, 82, 164
    counterculture, 988
    in mid-20th century, 933–34, 950
    in modern era, 794
    slave-white, 163, 165, 416
    Spanish-Native American, 29–30
    in Victorian era, 625–28
Seymour, Horatio, 571
Shaftesbury, Earl of. See Cooper, Anthony Ashley
Shakers, 374–77
Shakespeare, William, 56, 634–36
Shandong Peninsula, 699
"Share Our Wealth" program, 834
Sharecropping, 425, 585, 631, 823
    contract for, 560–61
    defined, 553
    political economy of, 567–70
    regions employing, 568(map)
    as wage labor, 602–3
Sharia law, 901, 902
Sharon Statement, 964
Shaw, Albert, 688
Shaw, Anna Howard, 719
Shawnee Indians, 280, 283–84, 308, 325, 330
Shays, Daniel, 241
Shays' Rebellion, 241, 242, 251, 254, 278
Sheen, Fulton J., 935
Shelby family, 389
Shelley v. Kraemer, 910
Shenandoah Valley raid, 541
Shenzhou launch vehicle, 1076
Shepard, Alan, 965
Sheridan, Philip, 541, 558
Sherman, Roger, 253
Sherman, William Tecumseh, 540, 541–42, 556, 607
Sherman Anti-Trust Act of 1890, 662, 665, 697, 734–35
Shiloh, Battle of, 521, 524–25, 533
Shipbuilding, 155, 327
Shipping, 327, 412
    in American Republic, 288, 302, 305–7, 308, 311
    in colonial era, 152, 155
    in industrial America, 662
Shirley, William, 188, 191

"Shock and awe" policy, 1099
Shockley Semiconductor Laboratory, 1040
Shoemakers' strike, 327
Shoho (carrier), 859, 860
Shopping malls, 929
Shore, Barbara, 891
Shore, Jack, 891
Shoshone Indians, 455
Shriver, Sargent, 1024
Shuster, Joe, 817–18
Siberia, 769, 773
Sicily, 878
Siegel, Jerry, 817–18
Sierra Club, 718, 739, 951
Sierra Nevada Mountains, 454, 613
Silent majority, 1023, 1024
Silent Spring (Carson), 974–75
Silicon Valley, 1037, 1040
Silk, 838
Silver
    in American Republic economy, 311
    Chinese trade and, 312
    in colonial economy, 106, 200
    Comstock Lode, 611
    free coinage issue, 672, 683, 689–91
    India ceases minting, 681
    in industrial era economy, 658–59, 660, 662, 671, 672
    mercantilism and, 48
    in Mexico, 23, 25
    in New World, 31, 38
    in Peru, 23
Simon and Garfunkel, 987
Simpson-Mazzoli Act, 1059
Sinai Peninsula, 1028–29
Sinatra, Frank, 871, 941
Sinclair, Upton, 717, 721, 725, 735
Sing Sing prison, 394
Singapore, 857
Singer, Isaac Merrit, 685
Singer Sewing Machine Company, 685
Single-parent families, 1058, 1085
Single tax, 668
Sioux Indians, 136, 455, 457, 605
Sirhan, Sirhan, 992
Sissle, Noble, 810
Sit-ins, 961, 962
Sitting Bull, 608–9, 620
Six-Day War, 1011
Sixth Amendment, 264
Sky loom, Pueblo song of, 7
Slater, Samuel, 318, 385
Slave badge, 412(photo)
Slave codes, 115, 117, 118, 119(table), 120, 163, 403, 497
    See also Black Codes
Slave power theory, 491, 494, 495
Slave revolts, 365, 416–17
    in colonial era, 163
    Deslondes', 304
    Gabriel's, 301, 417
    German Coast uprising, 417
    Harper's Ferry, 499–500, 513
    Pottawatomie Creek, 488–91
    in Saint-Domingue, 285, 290, 304, 416
    Stono Rebellion, 165
    Turner's, 366, 417, 430
    Vesey's, 417
Slave trade, 31, 147–50, 165, 460
    Africa and, 12, 86, 147–48
    banning of, 304, 311, 313–14, 405, 422, 528
    Constitution and, 253, 271, 274
    domestic, 405–8
    Dutch and, 50–51, 106
    England and, 54, 86–87, 117, 149, 271
    England's ban on, 403, 433, 528
    number of slaves imported, 147, 148(figure), 313

as piracy, 426
slave ship voyage, 148, 149–50
Slavery, 403–37, 473–505
    in Africa, 148, 419
    in American Republic, 267, 271, 276–77
    American Revolution and, 224, 233, 246
    Amistad incident, 403–4
    birth rate in, 151
    in the Caribbean, 133
    in cities, 163
    Civil War and, 513, 516(photo), 517–18, 521–24, 539
    common elements in, 117–18
    Confederate constitution on, 519
    Constitution and, 253, 271, 422–23, 433, 473, 483, 496, 500
    consumer culture and, 144, 156, 158, 159, 160
    cotton gin and, 313, 405
    Crittenden Compromise, 510–11
    culture of, 164–65
    Declaration of Independence clause (deleted), 225
    economy of, 412–13, 521–23
    education denied in, 394
    expansion of, 458, 462–63, 477–80, 510
    as foreign policy, 489
    freedom national, slavery local position, 433–34, 491, 494, 501
    Freeport Doctrine, 497
    gang system in, 411
    in Georgia, 165–66, 174, 409, 420
    Great Awakening on, 144, 174
    house slaves, 411
    impact on textile mill workers, 320–21
    Jay's Treaty and, 288
    Kansas-Nebraska Act, 486–88, 489, 490, 491
    labor problem and, 494–95
    last-ditch efforts to preserve, 507–11
    in Louisiana colony, 132
    Louisiana Purchase and, 304
    manumission, 118, 273
    Mexican War and, 464, 468, 478, 480
    middle passage, 150
    Missouri Compromise, 341–43, 364, 426, 481, 482, 486–87, 488, 496, 510
    national development and, 419–25
    Native Americans in, 15–16, 18, 20, 31, 80, 113–15, 118, 122, 132, 134, 135, 136, 137
    Native Americans practicing, 363
    nativism and, 486
    in New York City, 110, 163, 271
    in Pennsylvania colony, 112, 163
    political economy of, 79–81, 477
    politics of, 425–34, 480–85, 494–95
    population in, 147, 151, 271
    in post-revolution era, 238, 240, 246
    price per person, 420
    property law on, 496–97, 498, 499
    punishment practices, 416, 417
    Puritans and, 86–87
    regional tensions caused by, 364
    religious practices in, 328, 418–19
    in South Carolina colony, 113–15, 164, 174
    southern system, 404–19
    Spanish and, 23, 133
    task system in, 165, 410, 411, 417
    in Texas, 450, 451–52, 458, 460, 461, 462, 482
    Three-Fifths Compromise, 253, 271, 309, 422, 423, 426, 442

tobacco cultivation and rise of, 77
Tyler on, 459
Van Buren on, 442
varieties of, 411–13
variety of slave reactions, 413–19
in Virginia colony, 80, 81, 117–19, 120–21, 165
Washington's slaves, 261–62, 272, 285, 411
western territory and, 249, 427(map), 477–80, 486, 528
Wilmot Proviso, 480–81
work routine in, 154
    See also Abolition; Emancipation; Slave revolts; Slave trade
Sledge, Eugene B., 859, 880
Slidell, John, 464
Sloan, Alfred P., 819
Smallpox, 22, 25, 27, 167, 168–69, 192, 234–35, 530, 776
Smallpox inoculation, 167, 168–69
Smith, A. W., 726
Smith, Adam, 169
Smith, Al, 811, 839
Smith, John, 56, 69–70, 71, 74, 78, 230
Smith, Joseph, Jr., 331, 377
Smith, Margaret Bayard, 352
Smith, William, 269
Smith Act, 915
Smith and Wesson Company, 763
Smith v. Allwright, 872, 910, 911
SNCC. *See* Student Nonviolent Coordinating Committee
Social class
    in American Republic, 276
    in colonial cities, 160–63
    in Confederacy, 523
    under industrial capitalism, 591, 598–603
    of industrial era immigrants, 631
    in mid-20th century, 934–35
    in modern era, 798
    in new economy, 1079–80
    Puritans and, 89–90
    in South Carolina colony, 112–13
    in Spanish colonies, 135–36
    See also Middle class; Upper class; Wealthy; Working class
Social closure, 755
Social clubs, 718–19
Social Darwinism, 635, 638–39, 657, 668, 684, 698, 710
Social Gospel, 628, 720
Social networking, 1073
Social regulation, 389–95
Social Security, 1106
    Bush (George W.) and, 1081
    increase in beneficiaries, 1079
    introduction of, 836, 844, 845
    Reagan and, 1044, 1062
Social Security Act of 1935, 836
Social Security Reform Act of 1983, 1044
Social workers, 721–22, 725
Socialism, 716, 720
Socialist Party, 720, 758
Society for Christian Socialists, 720
Society for Establishing Useful Manufactures, 279
Society for the Relief of Free Negroes Unlawfully Held in Bondage, 272
Sociology, 727
Solomon Islands, 860, 880
Somalia, 1090
Somervell, Brehon B., 866
Somoza, Anastasio, 1050
Songhay Empire, 12
Sonoma Valley, 464
Sons of Liberty, 204, 207, 209
Sontag, Susan, 989
Soulé, Pierre, 489
Souls of Black Folk, The (DuBois), 728

Sousa, John Philip, 637
South
    African American migration from, 603, 604(photo), 761–62
    American Revolution and, 222, 231–33, 235(map)
    cities of, 413, 691–93
    colonial economy in, 152, 153–54
    free black population of, 273, 423–25
    growing estrangement from North, 497–99
    growing tension in, 364–66
    Native Americans in, 281, 282–84, 357–58
    New Deal and, 835–36, 845
    party politics in, 652
    populism in, 672
    progressivism and, 721, 732
    racial discrimination in, 695–96, 910, 911, 953–54
    railroads in, 477, 603
    religious experience in, 328
    secession in, 508, 509–11, 539
    slavery opposition in, 273
    slavery system in, 404–19
    tariff of 1816 opposed in, 345
    World War II industry in, 868–69
    See also Civil War; Confederacy; Reconstruction; individual states and colonies
South Africa, 903, 1050–51
South Carolina
    American Revolution and, 231–33, 234–35
    backcountry, 234–35
    Civil War and, 523, 542
    creation of government in, 227
    nullification crisis and, 364–66, 367
    Reconstruction and, 566
    secession of, 508, 509
    slave revolts in, 417
    slavery in, 253, 271, 313, 409, 420, 423
South Carolina colony, 106, 124, 133, 147, 164, 166, 174
    the Barbados connection, 115
    economic growth in, 152
    political economy of, 112–15
    Spanish and, 113, 114, 183
South Carolina Exposition and Protest, 365, 366
South Carolina Negro Seamen Act of 1822, 423
South Carolina Nullifiers, 441
South Dakota, 608
South Korea, 947
Southdale shopping mall, 929, 931
Southeast
    European colonization of, 43(map)
    trade routes in, 114(map)
Southeast Asia Treaty Organization (SEATO), 948–49
Southern Baptist Convention, 801, 1041
Southern Christian Leadership Conference (SCLC), 953, 966, 967, 976, 978
Southern Manifesto, 953
Southern Pacific Railroad, 593(photo)
Southern strategy, 1023
Southern Syncopated Orchestra, 810
Soviet Union
    Afghanistan invaded by, 1029, 1047–48, 1065, 1091
    American National Exhibition in, 946–47
    atomic bomb of, 883, 884, 898, 902, 914
    Berlin airlift, 900–902
    Carter administration and, 1028, 1029
    collapse of, 1065–66, 1072

containment and, 898–99, 902, 903, 905, 906, 945, 947, 970
détente and, 1006, 1007, 1011, 1026, 1028, 1029, 1047
Eisenhower adminstration and, 944–47
"evil empire" designation, 1047
Great Depression and, 838
hotline between U.S. and, 972
Kennedy administration and, 970–72
Korean War and, 903–5
League of Nations organized without, 774
massive retaliation doctrine, 944, 945, 970
Nazi-Soviet pact, 854–55
Nixon administration and, 1006–8, 1011
official U.S. recognition of, 894
Open Skies proposal, 945
peaceful coexistence policy, 945, 1008
popular front strategy, 834
post-World War II relations with, 893–99
Potsdam Conference and, 882, 895, 897(photo)
Reagan administration and, 1047–51, 1065–66
space program and, 955, 965, 1012
Spanish Civil War and, 854
spies for, 915–17
student protest in, 987
trade with former republics of, 1074
United Nations and, 881, 898–99
World War II and, 852, 854–55, 856, 857–58, 864, 878, 882, 884
Yalta Conference and, 894–95
See also Cold war; Communism; Russia
Space program
cold war and, 955
globalization and, 1076
Kennedy administration and, 965–66, 1012
Nixon administration and, 1012
Spain
American Revolution and, 233, 236, 237, 238
Canary Islands seized by, 12
English conflicts with, 42, 53–54, 57, 61, 63–64, 70, 133, 183, 287, 305
French and Indian War, 195–96
French conflicts with, 42, 136, 182–83
Jews of, 8, 9, 16, 49
land claims in American Republic, 280, 281
land claims south of 42nd parallel, 449
Louisiana acquired from, 303
Muslims of, 8, 9, 16
Native Americans and, 56, 248, 281, 363–64
Netherlands independence from, 49, 69
in the Philippines, 705
Pinckney's Treaty and, 288
Providence Island destroyed by, 87
slave trade banned in, 403, 404
slavery in, 426
War of Jenkins's Ear, 183
See also Spanish-American War; Spanish colonies; Spanish empire
Spalding, Eliza Hart, 452
Spalding, Henry, 452
Spanish-American War, 685, 699–704, 709, 715, 734, 1098

Spanish Armada, defeat of, 54, 61
Spanish Civil War, 854
Spanish colonies, 104, 130, 133–37, 182–83
exploration routes, 19(map)
New World exploration, 14–31
objectives of, 38–39
outposts, 42, 133
revolts and independence in, 341
South Carolina region and, 113, 114, 183
See also Cuba; Florida; Mexico; New Mexico
Spanish empire
establishment of, 23
remnants of, 697
Spanish influenza, 775–76
Spanish Inquisition, 129
Speakeasies, 763
Special Field Order No. 15, 556
Special Negro Fund, 839
Specie Circular, 357, 443
Spector, Ronald, 880
Speech, freedom of, 264, 975
Speedwell (ship), 84
Spencer, Christopher, 534
Spheres of influence, 895
Spillman, John, 832
Spirit of St. Louis (airplane), 797
Spock, Benjamin, 935
Spoils system, 652
Sport utility vehicles (SUVs), 1078, 1101
Sports
in modern era, 792
professionalization of, 622–25
racial discrimination in, 911–12
women in, 626
Spotsylvania Court House, 540
Spring Valley Water Company, 738
Springfield rifle, 534
Sprint, 1045
Spruance, Raymond, 861
Sputnik (satellite), 955
Squanto, 56, 57, 85, 96
Square Deal, 735
Squatters, 267–68, 346–47
Stagflation, 1000, 1001(table), 1026, 1045
Staines, John, 262
Stalin, Josef, 894–96, 900–902
at Potsdam Conference, 882, 895, 897(photo)
World War II and, 855, 864–65
at Yalta Conference, 894–95
Stamp Act of 1765, 198, 200, 201, 202, 203–4, 204, 206(photo), 213(table), 223
Stamps, Robbie, 1010
Standard Oil, 598, 665, 725, 735, 1078
Stanford University, 635, 824, 1040
Stanton, Edwin M., 525, 531, 570
Stanton, Elizabeth Cady, 397, 574
"Star-Spangled Banner, The" (national anthem), 308, 625
Stark (destroyer), 1052
Starr, Ellen, 721
START (Strategic Arms Reduction Talks Treaty), 1065
State governments
Bill of Rights and, 264–65
Constitutional Convention on, 252–53
creation of, 226–27
in industrial America, 665–66
New Federalism, 1012, 1044
progressivism and, 732–33
State University of New York, 907
Staten Island, 228
States' rights, 339, 365, 459, 460, 497, 508, 519, 525
Steam engine, 315
Steamboat, 315–16, 317–18, 322, 474, 477

Steel industry, 592, 595–97, 598, 688, 790, 926, 1052
Steel mills, 596, 603
Steelworkers' strikes, 687, 688, 776–77
Steffe, William, 514
Steffens, Lincoln, 717, 722, 725, 743, 749
Stein, Gertrude, 798
Steinem, Gloria, 1016
Stephens, Alexander, 519
Sterilization, forced, 725
Stevens, John, 416
Stevens, Robert T., 917
Stevens, Thaddeus, 555, 559, 563
Stevenson, Adlai, 943
Stewart, A. T., 475
Stewart, Maria, 429
Stimson, Henry, 856, 866
Stimulus package, 1103
Stock market
crash of 1929, 817, 818–19, 838, 1102
crash of 1987, 1062, 1065, 1078
crash of 2008, 1101–2
in new economy, 1078, 1080
Stone, Barton W., 329
Stone, I. F., 882
Stonewall Inn riot, 1021
Stono Rebellion, 165
Stop the Draft Week, 982, 983(photo)
Storyville, 619
Stowe, Harriet Beecher, 484, 643
Straight, Willard, 755, 775
Strategic Arms Limitation Treaty (SALT I), 1008
Strategic Arms Limitation Treaty (SALT II), 1026, 1029, 1048
Strategic Arms Reduction Talks (START) Treaty, 1065
Strategic Defense Initiative (SDI; "Star Wars"), 1048, 1090
Stratton, Alfred, 535(photo)
Strauss, Levi, 611
Streetcar suburbs, 717–18
Stretchout, 788
Strict constructionism, 266
Strikes
air traffic controllers, 1045, 1046(photo)
coal miners, 735, 908
criminalization of, 327, 697, 788
decrease in modern era, 789
in Dhahran, 902
during Great Depression, 837
hate, 872
under industrial capitalism, 602
post-World War II, 908–9
Pullman workers, 687–88, 689
railroad workers, 578, 586, 659, 669–70, 908
shoemakers, 327
steelworkers, 687, 688, 776–77
tailoresses, 384
tailors, 395
textile mill, 321, 384
United Automobile Workers, 837, 869, 908
United Farm Workers of America, 1018
Strong, Josiah, 628
Strong mayor system, 729
Stuart, J. E. B., 499
Student Homophile League, 1021
Student Nonviolent Coordinating Committee (SNCC), 962, 966, 976, 978, 982, 985
Student protests, 986–88, 1008–11
Student Volunteer Movement, 699
Students for a Democratic Society (SDS), 964, 981, 1021
Stutt cotton textiles, 385
Stuyvesant, Peter, 50, 51, 111
Submerged Lands Act of 1953, 943

Subprime mortgages, 1081, 1100, 1101
Subscription schools, 393
Subtreasuries, 671, 672
Suburbs, 600
in mid-20th century, 928–29, 930, 940
in modern era, 790
streetcar, 717–18
Sudan, 1092
Suez Canal, 949
Suffolk Resolves, 212
Suffrage. *See* Voting; Women's suffrage
Sugar, 12, 23, 106, 133
in Barbados, 115
Cuban, 699
in Dutch colonies, 51
Hawaiian, 664
increased demand for, 156, 157, 159
plantations, 408, 409, 411, 553, 567
slavery routine, 154
Sugar Act of 1764, 198, 208, 213(table)
Sullivan, John, 247
Summers, Martin, 269
Sumerians, 12
Sumner, Charles, 433, 491, 492–93, 555, 572
Sumner, William Graham, 638
Sumrak, Martin, 892
Sunbelt, 1004, 1006(map), 1037
Sunday, Billy, 763
Sunday School movement, 380, 381
Sunday School Union, 328
Sunrise Demester (television program), 932
Superfund, 1028, 1061
Superheterodyne receiver, 772
Superman, 817–18
Supply-side economics, 1044–45
Supreme Court
on abortion legality, 1016, 1055, 1087
on affirmative action, 1014
in American Republic, 263–64
on antisodomy laws, 1056, 1088
on the Bank of the United States, 322, 332, 353
on bilingual instruction, 1019
on Bush-Gore election, 1081
Civil War impact on influence in, 545
cold war legislation and, 892
creation of, 252
Democratic Republicans and, 293, 301–2, 321
on Guantánamo detainees, 1097, 1099
on Japanese American internment, 874
on labor union activities, 777, 788
"midnight appointees" of, 302
on Native American land rights, 358, 359
New Deal legislation and, 834–35, 837, 843, 844
Nixon appointees, 1023
on Nixon tapes, 1025
Pentagon Papers and, 1011
on personal freedom, 975
on racial discrimination, 577, 578–80, 694, 729, 872, 910, 911, 952–53, 961, 966, 1058
Reagan appointees, 1054
on school busing, 1014
on school segregation, 952–53, 954, 962
on sexual material, 933–34
Sherman Anti-Trust Act and, 665
on slavery issues, 403–4, 426, 496–97, 498
on strikes, 697
support for market economy, 321–22, 323–24

Susquehanna River, 186
Susquehannock Indians, 53, 79, 117
Sutter, John, 611
Sutter's mill, 611
Swaggart, Jimmy, 1060
Swallow Barn (Kennedy), 414–15
Swann v. Charlotte-Mecklenburg Board of Education, 1014
Swansea, 122
Sweat houses, 46
Sweatshops, 601
Swift, Gustavus, 590, 597
Swimming Hole, The (Eakins), 641, 642(photo)
Switzerland, 129
Sylvis, William, 575
Syngman Rhee, 903
Syria, 1001, 1011

T

Taft, Robert, 855, 913
Taft, William H., 741–43, 750, 811
Taft-Hartley Act of 1947, 908, 913
Tailoresses, 384, 396
Tailors, 395
Taino Indians, 15, 16
Taiping Rebellion, 589
Taiwan, 838, 903
    Eisenhower and, 947
    Nixon and, 1007
Takagi, Takeo, 860
Tales of the Jazz Age (Fitzgerald), 799
Taliban, 1071, 1093, 1098, 1100, 1104
Tallmadge, James, 341–43
Tammany Hall, 652, 657, 666, 743
Tanacharison, 186
Taney, Roger, 353, 496–97
Tanzania, U.S. embassy attack in, 1092
Tappan, Arthur, 396
Tappan, Lewis, 396
Tarawa, 880
Tarbell, Ida, 722, 725
Tariff Act of 1789, 265
Tariffs
    of 1816, 339–40, 345, 364
    of 1824, 345–46
    of 1846, 466–67
    of abominations (1828), 364–65, 366
    in American Republic, 265
    Dingley Tariff Act, 690
    Fordney-McCumber, 808
    globalization and, 1074
    Hawley-Smoot, 825, 854
    in industrial America, 660, 661–62, 665, 670
    in late 19th century, 684, 689, 690
    McKinley, 662, 686, 699, 704
    Payne-Aldrich, 741
    Reagan administration and, 1052
    on sewing machines, 685
    Tariff Act of 1789, 265
    Underwood-Simmons, 743
TARP (Troubled Asset Relief Program), 1102
Task Force Hornets (Beall-Smith), 860(photo)
Task system in slavery, 165, 410, 411, 417
Tate, Allen, 798
Taverns, 162, 268
Tax Reform Act of 1986, 1061
Taxes
    in American Republic, 284, 291, 302
    Antifederalists on, 255
    Bush (George H. W.) and, 1080
    Bush (George W.) and, 1081
    capital gains, 1028
    in colonial America, 106, 116, 184, 193, 198–200, 203–7, 210–11
    estate, 1045
    excise, 265, 284

income, 732, 741, 835, 1045
    Reagan and, 1045, 1061, 1062, 1080
    Roosevelt (Franklin) and, 835, 836
    single, 668
    Taft and, 741
Taylor, Frederick Winslow, 686, 788
Taylor, Zachary
    death of, 483
    Mexican War and, 464, 465–66, 481
    presidency of, 481
Taylorism, 686–87, 788, 791
Tea, 312
    colonial era demand for, 156, 157
    European history of consumption, 159
    tax on, 205, 210–11
Tea Act of 1773, 210, 213(table)
Tea Party movement, 1104, 1105, 1106
Teach-ins, 982
Teapot Dome scandal, 808
Technology
    communications, 1072–73
    economic impact of, 1036–37
Tecumseh, 284, 299, 308, 325–27
Teenagers. *See* Youth
Tejanos, 449–51, 1059
Telegraph, 474, 476–77, 587
Telephone, 623
Telephone industry deregulation, 1045
Televangelists, 1042
Television
    consumerism and, 932–33
    Johnson-era measures, 974
    religious programs on, 935, 1042
Telstar, 966, 1073
Temin, Peter, 820, 821
Temperance movement, 391–93, 395, 654–56, 657–58, 719
    See also Prohibition
Ten Percent Plan, 554–55
Tender Is the Night (Fitzgerald), 764
Tenements, 601, 630(photo), 715, 717, 722
Tennent, Gilbert, 173–74
Tennessee
    Civil War and, 524, 539–40, 542
    Native Americans in, 281, 283–84
    secession of, 510, 511
    settlement of, 240, 249, 268, 314
    slavery in, 405, 420
    statehood, 348
    voting rights in, 348
Tennessee Valley Authority (TVA), 830, 831(map), 833, 904
Tenochtitlan, 21, 22–23
Tenskwatawa (the Prophet), 284, 325, 327(photo)
Tenth Amendment, 264
Tenure of Office Act of 1867, 570
Teotihuacan, 6
Terrell, Mary Church, 693(photo)
Terrorism, 1091–97
    attacks on U.S. embassies, 1092
    Obama administration and, 1104
    Reagan administration and, 1051–52
    war on, 1071, 1093–97, 1099, 1104
    World Trade Center bombing (1993), 1091
    See also September 11 terrorist attacks
Tertium Quids, 306
Tet Offensive, 990, 991–92
Teton Sioux Indians, 457
Tex-Mex cuisine, 1059
Texaco, 932
Texas
    American influx, 449–51
    annexation, 451–52, 458, 459, 460, 461, 462, 463–64, 474
    border settlement, 483
    independence issue, 449–52, 457, 460, 462

Republic of, 439, 451–52
    secession of, 509
    slavery in, 450, 451–52, 458, 460, 461, 462, 482
    Slidell's purchase offer, 464
    Transcontinental Treaty on, 340, 449
Texas Pacific Railroad, 586
Textile mills, 318–21, 421–22, 601, 603
    English, 313, 420
    Lowell, 320, 384, 385, 396
    Rhode Island system, 385
    stretchout in, 788
    Waltham system, 320, 385
Thames, Battle of, 308, 327
Thayer, Eli, 490
Third Amendment, 264
Third Winter at Topaz, The (Hibi), 872(photo)
Third world, 903, 904–5
    communism expansion feared, 945–50, 970–71, 978–79
    Reagan Doctrine in, 1049–51
Thirteenth Amendment, 543–45, 553, 557, 564(table), 577, 579
Thirty-eighth parallel, 903, 905
This Side of Paradise (Fitzgerald), 798
Thomas, George, 539, 540, 542
Thompson, J. Edgar, 594, 597
Thoreau, Henry David, 468
Three-Fifths Compromise, 253, 271, 309, 422, 423, 426, 442
Three Mile Island nuclear accident, 884, 1028
Thurmond, Strom, 913
Till, Emmett, 953
Tilden, Samuel J., 578, 659
Tillotson, John, 172, 173
Timbuktu, 12
Time (magazine), 859, 916
Time-on-target technique, 863
Time Warner, 1077
Timucuan Indians, 24(photo)
Tinian, 880
Tippecanoe, Battle of, 441, 458
Tippecanoe River, 325
Tisquantum. *See* Squanto
Title IX, 1016
Title VII, 989
Tituba, 103–4, 127, 128
Tlatelolco, 22
Tlaxcalan people, 21, 22, 29–30
Tlecuiluatzin (doña Luisa), 30
To Secure These Rights (report), 911
Tobacco, 82, 106, 116, 117, 125, 154, 159, 165, 270, 311
    declining market for, 313
    economic importance of, 75–76, 77, 79, 152, 153
    increased demand for, 156, 157
    labor requirements, 77, 80
    plantations, 154, 165, 408, 411
    sharecropping and, 567
Tobacco pipe, 74(photo)
Tocqueville, Alexis de, 380, 394, 455, 634
Todd, Silas, 150
Toledo, 8
Tom Paine's America (Cotlar), 293
Tomatoes, 29
Toney, 416
Tonkin Gulf Resolution, 979
Toomer, Jean, 805
Tordesillas, Treaty of, 16
Torture
    of Abu Ghraib detainees, 1100
    of Guantánamo detainees, 1097, 1098
    Native Americans and, 45
    in Philippine-American War, 705
    in Pontiac's Rebellion, 197
    of slave revolt rebels, 163

on slave ships, 150
    of slaves, 416
Total war, 759, 859
Tourgée, Albion, 694
Tourism, 1075
Toussaint-Louverture, François-Dominique, 285, 290
Townsend, Francis, 834
Townsend, George, 535
Townshend, Charles, 205
Townshend Revenue Act of 1767, 205, 207, 210, 213(table)
Toyota, 1053
Trade
    in addictive substances, 159
    in American Republic, 270–71, 276, 288, 290, 305–7, 311–14
    Bretton Woods Conference on, 882, 895
    in colonial era, 49–53, 90–91, 106, 113–14, 205(figure), 212
    GATT, 1074–75
    globalization and, 1074–75, 1082–83, 1101
    in industrial era, 663–64
    in late 19th century, 684–86
    mercantilism, 48, 54, 106, 107, 109, 132, 169
    most-favored-nations, 743
    NAFTA, 1082
    in New Netherland, 49–53
    North Atlantic routes (end of 16th century), 40(map)
    post-revolution agreements, 238, 239, 241, 242, 251, 270
    in pre-contact Europe, 8, 9–10
    Reagan administration and, 1052, 1062
    reciprocity, 664
    Roosevelt (Franklin) administration and, 854
    Wilson administration and, 743
    world (on the eve of discovery), 9(map)
    World War I and, 753
    See also Exports; Fur trade; Imports; Slave trade; Tariffs
Trade associations, 327
Trail of Tears, 359
Train, George Francis, 612
Tramp laws, 666
Trans-Mississippi West, 445–48
Transcendentalism, 391
Transcontinental Treaty of 1819, 340–41, 445, 449
Transplanted, The (Bodnar), 632–33
Transportation
    in early 19th century, 315–18, 339, 340
    racial segregation on, 578, 693–94
    See also Automobiles; Bridge building; Railroads; Road building; Steamboat
Traps for the Young (Comstock), 619
Treasure hunters, 331
Treaty Party, 362
Tredegar Iron Works, 522(photo)
Trent (ship), 518
Trenton, Battle of, 228, 231
Triangle Shirtwaist Company fire, 717, 718(photo)
Tripoli, 302
Tripoli, Treaty of, 302
Trist, Nicholas P., 464
Triumph of Conservatism, The (Kolko), 732
Troubled Asset Relief Program (TARP), 1102
Troup, George Michael, 358
Truman, Harry S., 979
    atomic bombing of Japan and, 882–84
    Chinese revolution and, 903

civil rights and, 911
cold war and, 891, 894, 895, 896–99, 902, 903, 905, 906, 915, 917, 918, 944, 945
comeback of, 913
Korean War and, 905
on labor unions, 908
liberalism and, 912–13
Point Four program, 904
at Potsdam Conference, 882, 895, 897(photo)
women's rights and, 910
Truman Doctrine, 896–98, 914, 1007
Trusts
Clayton Antitrust Act, 743
motives for forming, 598
NIRA and, 833
Roosevelt (Theodore) and, 734–35
Sherman Anti-Trust Act, 662, 665, 697, 734–35
Taft and, 741
Wilson and, 742, 743
Truth, Sojourner, 429
Truth in Securities Act of 1933, 829
Tuberculosis, 715
Tugwell, Rexford, 830
Tulare Lake, 613
Tule Lake internment camp, 873
Tunis, 302
Tunisia, 866, 1104
Tuolumne River, 738
Turkey
cold war era, 895, 896, 949
World War I and, 753
Turner, Frederick Jackson, 684
Turner, Nat, 366, 417, 430
Turner, Ted, 1073
Turner Broadcasting, 1077
Tuskegee Airmen, 862
Tuskegee Institute, 636, 694, 728
TVA. See Tennessee Valley Authority
Twain, Mark, 317, 621, 639, 640, 704
Tweed, William Marcy, 576(photo)
Tweed Ring, 576
Twelfth Amendment, 301
Twenty-seventh Amendment, 265
Twenty-sixth Amendment, 1022
Twenty Years at Hull-House (Addams), 723–24
Twitter, 1073
Two Treatises of Government (Locke), 124–25
Tyler, John, 360, 458–63
Typhoid fever, 71, 453, 535, 715, 935
Typhus, 27, 738, 776

U
U-2 spy plane, 945
U-boat, 753, 764–65, 856
UAW. See United Automobile Workers
Ukraine, 765
UMW. See United Mine Workers
"Uncle Remus" stories (Harris), 620
Uncle Tom's Cabin (Stowe), 484
Underdevelopment, 904–5
Underwood-Simmons Tariff of 1913, 743
Unemployment
in 1970s, 1000, 1004, 1026
in 1980s, 1045
in 2000s, 1104, 1105
in African Americans, 1084
depression of 1837 and, 443
Great Depression and, 819, 821–22
mid-20th century, 928
in modern era, 784
in new economy, 1078
panic of 1893 and, 683
post-World War II, 906
Unión de Trabajadores del Valle Imperial, La, 804
Union Iron Company, 595
Union of Russian Workers, 777

Union of Soviet Socialist Republics (USSR). See Soviet Union
Union Pacific Railroad, 576, 605
Unions. See Labor unions
Unitarianism, 328
United Artists, 783, 797
United Automobile Workers (UAW), 837, 869, 908
United Farm Workers of America, 1018
United Fruit, 944
United Mine Workers (UMW), 697, 735, 837, 908
United Nations (UN), 945
Food and Agriculture Organization, 727
Iraq inspections and, 1097
Korean War and, 905
Persian Gulf War and, 1089
planning, 881, 894–95
Somalia relief efforts and, 1090
Soviet Union and, 881, 898–99
United Nations Declaration on Human Rights, 910
United Nations Relief and Rehabilitation Administration (UNRRA), 882
United Race, 1018
United Services Organization (USO), 859
United States Information Agency (USIA), 945
United States Sanitary Commission, 535–36
United States v. Leon, 1054
UNIVAC 1 (Universal Automatic Computer), 927
Universal Negro Improvement Association (UNIA), 805–6
Universalism, 161–62, 328
University of Alabama, 967
University of California, 638
University of California at Berkeley, 986–88, 1019
University of California at Davis, 1014
University of Chicago, 635
University of Colorado at Boulder, 1035
University of Illinois, 796
University of Michigan, 715, 973
University of Mississippi, 966
University of Paris, 987
University of Pennsylvania, 926
University of Wisconsin, 684, 725
Unsafe at Any Speed (Nader), 974
Untermenschen, 853
Upper class
mid-20th century decline of, 934
World War I and, 755–56
See also Wealthy
Uprooted, The (Handlin), 632
Upshur, Abel, 458
Urban culture, 619–22
realism in, 639–44
varieties of, 620–22
Urbanization. See Cities and urbanization
Uriburu, José, 838(photo)
Uruguay Round, 1074
U.S. Steel, 688, 777
USA Patriot Act, 1097
Utah
statehood, 483
territory acquired by U.S., 466

V
V-J Day, 885(photo)
Vaccines/inoculation
polio, 935
smallpox, 167, 168–69
Vallandigham, Clement L., 536

Van Buren, Martin, 441–45, 467
Amistad incident and, 403
election of 1828 and, 351–52
election of 1836 and, 441–42, 461
election of 1840 and, 440, 458–59
election of 1844 and, 461
election of 1848 and, 433, 440
Native Americans and, 359
presidency of, 442–45
Texas annexation issue, 452, 460
Vance, Zebulon, 519
Vanderbilt, Cornelius, 317
Vanderbilt University, 635
Vanzetti, Bartolomeo, 777
Vaudeville, 622
Veblen, Thorstein, 727
Velasco, don Luis de (Paquiquineo), 37–38, 56, 64
Venezuela, 341
Columbus's voyage to, 15
Germany's loan to, 739
slavery in, 426
Vermont
land speculation in, 248
slavery issue, 272
statehood, 348
voting rights in, 348
Vermont Green Mountain Boys, 222
Verrazano, Giovanni da, 39, 40
Versailles, Treaty of, 773–74, 852
Vertical integration, 598
Vesey, Denmark, 417
Vespucci, Amerigo, 17
Veterans Administration, 912
Vice, crusade against, 619–20, 763
Vicksburg, siege of, 516, 521, 537–38, 554
Victoria, Queen of England, 626
Victorian era, 625–28
Video games, 1005
Viet Minh, 947
Vietnam
division of, 947–49
France in (French Indochina), 838, 856, 906, 947
trade with, 1074
Vietnam syndrome, 1047, 1050, 1090
Vietnam War, 771, 905, 978–83, 990–93, 1021, 1029, 1047, 1062, 1089
anti-war movement, 981–83, 986, 987, 993, 1008–11, 1022, 1023
casualties in, 1011
ending, 1008–11
escalation (1960-1968), 981(table)
expenditures for, 1000, 1013
Johnson administration and, 978–79, 981–83, 990–92, 1011, 1026
Kennedy administration and, 972, 979
limited war, 979–81
major battles, 980(map)
My Lai massacre, 1008
Nixon administration and, 1006, 1008–11
Operation Linebacker, 1011
Operation Rolling Thunder, 979
pardons for draft resisters, 1027
surrender of South Vietnam, 1026
Tet Offensive, 990, 991–92
Tonkin Gulf Resolution, 979
Vietnamization, 1008
Villa, Francisco ("Pancho"), 751–52
Vincennes (missile cruiser), 1052
Virgin Islands, 662–64
Virginia
American Revolution and, 233
Civil War and, 513, 517(map), 540–41, 542, 543
Constitution ratification and, 253, 254

land speculation in, 248
Reconstruction and, 558
secession of, 509–10, 511
slave revolts in, 365, 417 (see also Slave revolts, Gabriel's; Slave revolts, Harper's Ferry; Slave revolts, Turner's)
slavery in, 246, 271, 273, 412, 414–15, 420
territory disputes in, 280
voting rights in, 348
Virginia (ship), 520
Virginia colony, 61, 69, 70–79, 116–19, 193
Bacon's Rebellion in (See Bacon's Rebellion)
charter of, 72–73
founding of, 70–71
French and Indian War and, 186, 187
Hariot's account of, 58–59
Massachusetts Bay colony compared with, 82
Pontiac's Rebellion and, 197–98
protest and resistance in, 203, 212
slavery in, 80, 81, 117–19, 120–21, 165
social change in, 116
tobacco cultivation in, 75–76, 77, 79, 80, 116, 117
Virginia Company, 56, 58, 69, 70–71, 72, 74, 76, 80, 82, 84, 98
Virginia Plan, 252
Virginia Resolves, 203, 204
VISTA (Volunteers in Service to America), 974
Voice of America, 945
Voluntarism, political, 652, 654
Voluntary Relocation Program, 940
Voodoo, 419
Voting
African Americans and, 559, 562–64, 571, 653, 659, 662, 665, 911
disfranchisement, 682, 695–96, 732, 806, 910
Fifteenth Amendment, 564(table), 573–74, 577, 579
free blacks (during slavery), 273, 348–49, 424
grandfather clause, 695, 729
origins of, 564–65
registration drives, 966, 976, 977–78
Ten Percent Plan, 554–55
in colonial America, 201
in England (colonial era), 201
lowering of age for, 1022
participation (1840-1896), 653(figure)
participation (1896-1920), 719(figure)
participation (1896-1928), 807(figure)
universal white male suffrage, 348, 349(map), 440
women and (see Women's suffrage)
Voting Rights Act of 1965, 978, 1057, 1058

W
Wabash River, 315
Wade, Benjamin, 512, 555
Wade-Davis Bill, 555
Wade-ins, 962
Wage labor
in antebellum era, 475
in colonial America, 155–56
discontent in 19th century, 347–48
freedom and, 386–87
in industrial America, 621(table)
sharecropping as, 602–3
Wagner, John ("Honus"), 624

Wagner, Robert, 837
Wagner Act (National Labor Relations Act), 837, 844
Wakatsuki, Jeanne, 873–74
Wake, 857
Wal-Mart, 1073, 1074, 1075(photo), 1078
Walker, David, 427–29
Walker, Robert, 461
Wall Street bombing, 777(photo)
"Wall Street Owns the Country" (Lease), 673–74
Wall Street Reform and Consumer Protection Act, 1103
Wallace, George, 967, 990, 993, 1023–24
Wallace, Henry, 818, 830, 871, 912, 913
Wallace v. Jaffree, 1054
Waltham system, 320, 385
Wampanoag Indians, 122
Wampum trade, 52(map)
Wanchese, 55, 56–57, 60, 64
Wannamaker's department store, 592
War bonds, 523
War Brides Act of 1945, 914
War Democrats, 544
War Hawks, 307
War Industries Board (WIB), 759–61
War of 1812, 307–11, 315, 316, 319, 327, 338, 339, 345, 357, 364, 420, 421, 476, 532, 733
  battles and campaigns of, 310(map)
  Federalist response, 308–11
  Jackson and, 299, 300, 308, 310–11
  Madison and, 307–8, 347
War of Jenkins's Ear, 183, 203
War on drugs, 1055
War on poverty, 973–74, 975–76
War on terror, 1071, 1093–97, 1099, 1104
War Powers Act of 1973, 1026
Ward, Aaron Montgomery, 588
Warehouse Act, 744
Warhol, Andy, 988
Warner Brothers, 792, 892
Warner Communications, 1077
Warren, Earl, 892, 952, 975, 1023
Warren, Robert Penn, 798
Wars of the Roses, 53
Washington, Booker T., 636, 694–95, 728, 804
Washington, D.C.
  capital moved to, 278
  march on (1894), 683
  march on (1932), 825–26
  march on (1962), 967–70
  march on (1969), 1008
  Randolph's march (cancelled), 851, 852
  slavery abolished in, 481, 482, 483, 510, 528
  War of 1812 and, 308
Washington, George
  American Revolution and, 222, 228, 231, 233, 246, 247
  on Braddock's defeat, 189–90
  Constitutional Convention and, 251, 252
  French and Indian War and, 187, 188–90
  Native Americans and, 247, 360
  Philadelphia home of, 269–70
  Pontiac's Rebellion and, 197
  presidency of, 264, 266, 267, 273, 280, 281, 282, 287
    cabinet, 263
    farewell address, 288–89
    proposed title, 263
    Saint-Dominique rebellion and, 285
    Whiskey Rebellion, 284
  slaves owned by, 261–62, 272, 285, 411

Washington, Jesse, 695(photo)
Washington, Lewis, 499
Washington, Martha, 261, 363, 262
Washington Naval Conference, 809
Washington Naval Treaty of 1922, 860
Washington Post, 730, 860, 1024
Washinton, Martha, 270
Washita Creek, Battle of, 607, 608
Water conservation, 736–37
Water cure (torture method), 705
Water Quality Act of 1965, 975, 1061
Watergate scandal, 1024–25
Watts riots, 984, 1084
Wayne, Anthony, 282, 288
WCTU. *See* Women's Christian Temperance Union
We Now Know (Gaddis), 897–98
Wealth
  in colonial America, 152(figure)
  percentage of controlled by U.S., 885
Wealth of Nations, The (Smith), 169
Wealthy
  under industrial capitalism, 599–600
  in new economy, 1080
  See also Upper class
Weapons
  of mass destruction (WMD), 1097, 1099
  in World War II, 862–64
  See also Nuclear weapons
Weathermen, 1021
Weaver, James B., 672
Webster, Daniel, 323, 390, 459
  abolition movement and, 425
  National Republican philosophy and, 338–39
  nullification crisis and, 366
  presidential candidacy of, 441
  as secretary of state, 460
  slavery issue and, 482, 484
Webster-Ashburton Treaty, 460
Weir, John Ferguson, 641
Welch, Joseph, 917
Weld, Theodore Dwight, 430
Welfare capitalism, 788, 789
Welfare system
  Clinton and, 1080–81
  conservative view of, 1085
  Nixon and, 1012
  Reagan and, 1044
Wells, Robert, 203
Wells, William, 444
Wells-Barnett, Ida B., 694, 727, 728
Wensley, Elizabeth Paddy, 87(photo)
Werowocomoco, 69
Wesleyan University, 726
West
  antigovernment sentiment in, 1027
  Civil War and, 524–25
  clearing for capitalism, 604–10
  conflicts over land distribution in, 281–82
  economic transformation of, 610–13
  Exoduster migration to, 603, 604(photo)
  expansion in (1785-1805), 281(map)
  experience of migrants, 337–38
  final land rush in, 683–84
  frontier closed in, 604, 613
  impact of migration to, 388–89
  land cessions, 250(map)
  major overland trails, 453, 454(map)
  new policy in post-revolution, 246–49
  Senate dispute over land prices, 365–66
  settlement of, 248–49, 314

  slavery issue, 249, 427(map), 477–80, 486, 528
  trans-Mississippi, 445–48
  World War II industry in, 868–69
  See also Northwest Territory; individual states
West, Dorothy, 805
West Bank, 1051
West Indies, 106, 130, 133, 152, 154, 159, 198, 212, 364
  American slaves shipped to, 233
  economic growth in, 155
  trade with, 238, 239, 276, 288
  See also Caribbean; Saint-Domingue
West Rock, New Haven (Church), 445
West Virginia
  secession from Virginia, 511, 539
  slavery in, 412
Western Union, 476
Westinghouse, 867
Westmoreland, William, 981
Westo War, 113–14
What Hath God Wrought (Howe), 368
What's the Matter with Kansas (Frank), 1086–87
Wheat, 153, 154, 311, 313, 545, 612, 613, 671, 690, 789
Wheatley, Phillis, 272
Wheeler, Burton, 855
Wheelwright, John, 96
Whig Party, 443, 461, 463, 464, 467, 486, 497, 498, 519, 565
  attempts to revive, 501
  decline of, 474, 484–85
  election of 1836 and, 441
  election of 1840 and, 458–59
  election of 1844 and, 461
  election of 1848 and, 481
  election of 1852 and, 484–85
  election of 1856 and, 491, 494
  formation of, 440
  political philosophy of, 441
  slavery issue and, 432, 433, 480, 481, 484–85
  Tyler and, 459, 460
Whiskey Rebellion, 284
Whiskey Ring, 576
White, Hugh Lawson, 441
White, John, 60, 61
White, Richard, 62, 63
White, William Allen, 757
White Citizens' Councils, 953
White City, 623–24
White-collar workers, 600, 601, 788, 935
White ethnics, 1022–23
White Leagues, 578
"White Man's Republic," 317
White Over Black (Jordan), 120
White supremacy, 462, 571–73, 577–78, 653, 704, 727
Whitefield, George, 143–44, 160, 172–74
Whiting, Richard A., 791
Whitman, Marcus, 452
Whitman, Narcissa Prentiss, 452
Whitman, Walt, 600, 640–41, 643
Whitney, Eli, 313, 318–19, 405, 406, 420
Why Not the Best? (Carter), 1027
Whyte, William H., Jr., 934
Wichita Indians, 136
Widows, 82, 162, 163
Wiebe, Robert H., 731–32
Wieland (Brown), 278
Wilberforce, William, 364
Wild One, The (film), 950
Wilderness Act of 1964, 975
Wilderness campaign, 540
Wilderness Road, 240
Wilderness Society, 951
Wilentz, Sean, 367, 368
Wilkie, Wendell L., 855

Willamette Valley, 452
Willard, Frances, 654–55
William of Orange, 106, 125
Williams, Bert, 622
Williams, Eunice, 184
Williams, Roger, 94, 95
Williams College, 379
Wilmington, 154
Wilmot, David, 480
Wilmot Proviso, 480–81
Wilson, Charles, 928
Wilson, Woodrow, 735, 742–44, 750–59, 775, 777, 807, 811, 827
  Fourteen Points, 765–69, 773
  League of Nations, 765, 773, 774
  Mexican Revolution and, 751–52
  New Freedom, 742, 743–44
  Paris peace negotiations, 773–74
  stroke suffered by, 774
  World War I and, 750, 753–59, 762–69
WIN (Whip Inflation Now) program, 1026
Winchester, Oliver, 534
Windows computer system, 1039
Winesburg, Ohio (Anderson), 798
Wingfield, Edward Maria, 71
Wingina, 60
Winnebago Indians, 357
Winthrop, John, 87–88, 93, 94, 95, 96
Wirt, William, 351
Wisconsin Idea, 732–33
Wise, John, 172
Witch Hammer, The, 129
Witchcraft trials, 103–4, 127–30, 163
Witte, Edwin, 867
Wolfe, James, 193, 194–95
Wolfe, Tom, 1022
Wolfowitz, Paul, 1097
Woman's National Loyal League, 574
Women
  in the abolition movement, 396–97, 431–33
  African, 81
  African American, 429, 567, 569
  in American Republic, 270, 277, 279
  in Benevolent Empire, 381
  Civil War and, 535–36
  in colonial America, 79, 80, 82, 162, 166, 207
    Puritan, 93, 94
    witchcraft accusations and, 127–30
  as delegates in 1912 election, 742
  education of, 243, 246, 279, 393, 636, 718, 796
  Great Awakening and, 374
  in industrial America, 625–28
  labor unions and, 697, 789, 870
  literary depictions of, 640
  middle-class (19th century), 387
  Native American, 8, 304, 362
  New Woman, 718–19, 794–95, 797, 804
  political voluntarism and, 654
  in post-revolution era, 239, 242–46
  in post-World War II era, 909–10
  in postfeminist era, 1085–87
  property rights denied to, 166, 242, 277, 396
  Roosevelt (Franklin) administration and, 843
  self-improvement and, 391
  in Shakerism, 377
  single mothers, 1058, 1085
  social clubs, 718–19
  in textile mills, 320–21, 385, 396, 601
  in the workforce, 277, 601, 762, 788, 869–70, 871(photo), 909–10, 936, 1004, 1055, 1079, 1085

World War I and, 762–63, 764
World War II and, 862, 869–70
See also Feminism; Gender roles;
    Women's rights; Women's
    suffrage
Women Accepted for Volunteer
    Emergency Service
    (WAVES), 862
Women's Army Corps (WACs), 862,
    910
Women's Christian Temperance
    Union (WCTU), 654–56,
    658, 763
Women's Health Protective
    Committee (WHPC), 693
Women's International League
    for Peace and Freedom,
    809(photo)
Women's liberation movement, 989–
    90, 1014–17
Women's rights
    Adams (Abigail) on, 244–45, 246
    in American Republic, 277
    in antebellum era, 396–97
    conservatives on, 1055
    post-World War II, 910
    rebirth of movement, 989–90
    women's liberation movement,
        989–90, 1014–17
    See also Feminism
Women's Strike for Equality, 1017
Women's suffrage, 396, 397, 652, 655,
    716, 719, 742, 750, 754
    African American suffrage and, 574
    in New Jersey, 242–43, 277, 348
    Nineteenth Amendment, 762
Wonderful Wizard of Oz, The (Baum),
    673
Wood, Gordon S., 292
Wood, Leonard, 702, 755
Wooding, Sam, 810
Woodstock music festival, 1021,
    1022(photo)
Woodward, Bob, 1024
Woodward, C. Vann, 579
Woolman, John, 246
Woolworth stores, 787, 961, 962
Worcester v. Georgia, 358
Workers' compensation, 715, 744, 836
Workforce
    African Americans in, 851–52,
        1058
    in American Republic, 327
    blue-collar workers in, 791, 935
    in colonial era, 80
    contract, political economy of,
        557–58
    deindustrialization and, 1004
    experiments with free labor,
        553–54
    global migration of, 589–90
    in industrial America, 666, 669–76
    makeup of (1938-1947), 870(figure)

mid-20th century, 927–28, 936
minimum wage and, 763, 845
modern era transformation of,
    787–88, 790–91
New Deal programs, 829, 831–33,
    835–36
in new economy, 1078, 1079
outsourcing in, 1078, 1079
political mobilization in, 394–95
post-World War II, 909–10
scientific management and, 682,
    686, 788
Taylorism and, 686–87, 788, 791
wage dependency and protest,
    381–84
white-collar workers in, 600, 601,
    788, 935
Wilson administration and, 744
women in, 277, 601, 762, 788, 869–
    70, 871(photo), 909–10, 936,
    1004, 1055, 1079, 1085
World War I, 761–63
World War II, 869–70
See also Employment
    discrimination; Labor
    unions; Unemployment;
    Wage labor; Working class
Workhouses, 163
Working class
    African American, 1058
    common school movement and,
        393
    immigrant, 631, 633(figure)
    under industrial capitalism, 591,
        600–602
    middle class distinguished from,
        384, 387
    in new economy, 1079
    See also Workforce
Working Men's Association of New
    York, 393
Working Men's Party, 395
Workmen's compensation, 602
Works Progress Administration
    (WPA), 835–36, 839
World Bank, 882, 904, 1072
World Economic Forum, 1073–74
World Health Organization (WHO),
    776
World Series, 624
World Trade Center bombing (1993),
    1091
World Trade Organization (WTO),
    1075, 1083, 1101
World War I, 685–86, 726, 749–50,
    753–74, 786, 809, 811, 821,
    824, 853, 854
    aims in, 756–57
    armistice in, 771
    casualties in, 771
    Congress urged to vote for entry,
        756–58
    conscientious objectors, 757, 759

dissent suppressed, 758–59
economic regimentation during,
    759–60
election campaign of 1916 on,
    754–56
final offensive in, 769–73
last attempts at peace, 756
Lusitania incident, 753–54, 755
neutrality during, 753
Paris peace negotiations, 773–74
preparedness campaign, 754
training of soldiers, 755–56,
    764–65
U.S. entry, 750, 757–58
Western front, 769(map),
    771(photo)
World War II, 771, 845, 851–89, 903,
    942
    atomic bomb deployed, 882–84,
        902, 914
    Axis powers in, 853
    casualties in, 884
    D-Day, 878
    declaration of, 852, 855
    in Europe, 865(map), 878–79
    Europe First strategy, 864
    geopolitical logic of, 881(map)
    Holocaust and, 874
    idealism and fear during, 871–78
    industry during, 866–70
    isolationism during, 852, 854–55
    Nazi-Soviet pact, 854–55
    negotiations following, 893–96
    Normandy invasion, 878,
        879(photo)
    in the Pacific, 858(map), 879–80
    recruitment and training of troops,
        859–62
    second front in, 864–66, 878
    surrender of Germany, 882
    surrender of Japan, 884
    turning the tide in, 857–66
    U.S. entry, 856
    V-J Day, 885(photo)
    weapons technology in, 862–64
World Wide Web, 1073
World's fairs, 623–24
Wosniak, Steve, 1038
Wounded Knee
    Native American demonstration
        at, 1020
    Native Americans massacred at,
        608–9, 688
Wozniak, Steve, 1040
WPA. *See* Works Progress
    Administration
Wrentmore, Douglas, 1010
Wright, Frances, 348, 468
Wright, Orville, 787
Wright, Wilbur, 787
Wrigley gum, 867
WTO. *See* World Trade Organization
Wyandot Indians, 452

Wyman, David, 874
Wyoming
    statehood, 652
    territory acquired by U.S., 466

X

Xicotencatl, 30
XYZ Affair, 290, 291

Y

Yakima Indians, 455
Yale University, 172, 638
Yalta Conference, 894–95
Yamamoto, Isoroku, 858
Yamasee War, 114–15
Yamato race, 853
Yellow-dog contracts, 789
Yellow fever, 591
Yeltsin, Boris, 1065
Yemen, 159
Yeo, John, 125
Yippies (Youth Independent Party),
    1039, 1041
Yom Kippur War, 861, 1001, 1011
York, John, 268
York River, 78–79, 526
Yorktown (carrier), 859, 860, 861
Yorktown surrender, 233, 237
Yoruba people, 12
Yosemite National Park, 738–39
Young, Brigham, 377
Young, Robert Alexander, 429
Young Americans for Freedom, 964
Young and Rubicam, 932
Young Ladies' Academy of
    Philadelphia, 279
Young Mother, The (Alcott), 391
Young Women's Christian Association
    (YWCA), 719
Your Show of Shows (television
    program), 932
Youth
    counterculture, 986–89, 1085
    in mid-20th century, 950–51
    in modern culture, 795
Yucatan Peninsula, 6, 20
Yugoslavia, 1090–91
Yuma Indians, 455
Yuppies, 1039–40
YWCA (Young Women's Christian
    Association), 719

Z

Zapata, Emiliano, 751
Zenger, John Peter, 162
Zimmerman Telegram, 756
Zimmermann, Arthur, 756
Zones of occupation, post-WWII, 895,
    900–902
Zoot suits, 861
Zuni Pueblo, 24–25
Zwillenberg, Joe, 925
Zyklon-B gas, 874

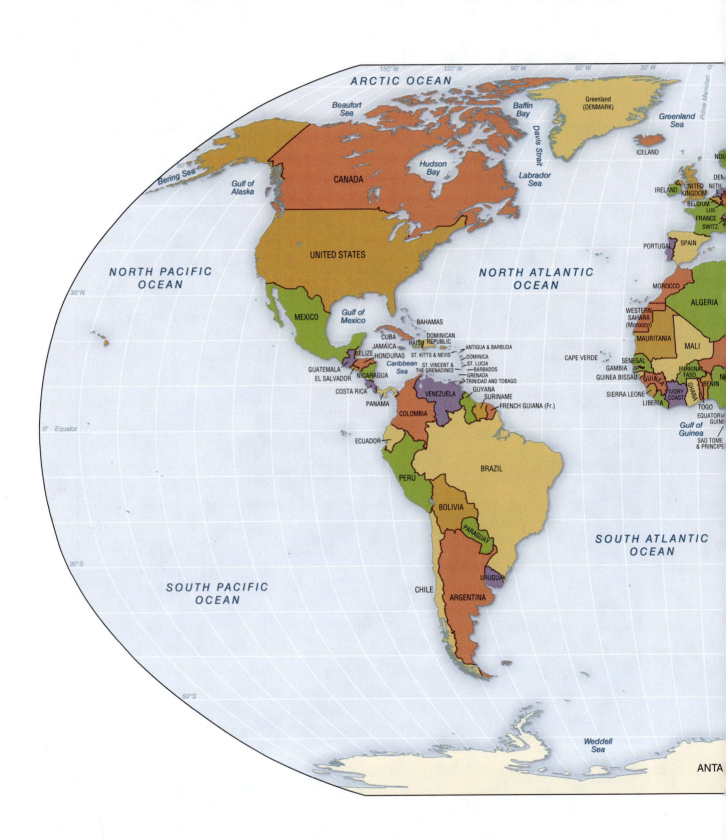

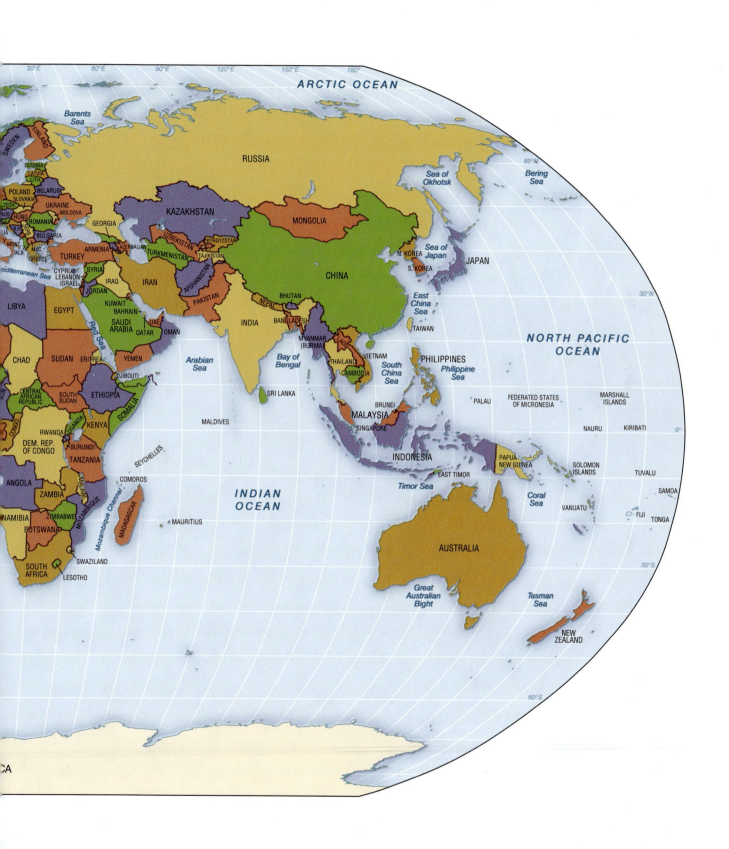